November 25–29, 2019
Miami Beach, FL, USA

I0131889

**Association for
Computing Machinery**

Advancing Computing as a Science & Profession

MSWiM'19

Proceedings of the 22nd International ACM Conference on

Modeling, Analysis and Simulation
of Wireless and Mobile Systems

Sponsored by:

ACM SIGSIM

Association for Computing Machinery

Advancing Computing as a Science & Profession

The Association for Computing Machinery
1601 Broadway, 10th Floor
New York, NY 10019-7434

ISBN: 978-1-4503-6904-6 (Print)

Additional copies may be ordered prepaid from:

ACM Order Department
PO Box 30777
New York, NY 10087-0777, USA

Phone: 1-800-342-6626 (USA and Canada)
+1-212-626-0500 (Global)
Fax: +1-212-944-1318
E-mail: acmhelp@acm.org
Hours of Operation: 8:30 am – 4:30 pm ET

22nd ACM MSWiM 2019 General Chair Welcome

Welcome to the 22nd ACM International Conference on Modelling, Analysis, and Simulation of Wireless and Mobile Systems (MSWiM). This year, MSWiM will be held in the diverse and multi-cultural Miami Beach, USA, a coastal resort city being filled with wonderful landscapes, warm beaches, and eye-catching sites. Over the years, MSWiM has established itself as a leading venue where some of the best research works, trends and directions in the area of modeling and performance evaluation of wireless and mobile systems are presented and discussed. This year is no exception!

The 22nd MSWiM will feature a high-quality scientific program, two distinguished keynotes addressed by the following outstanding experts, Prof. Yuanyuan Yang from Stony Brook University, USA, and Prof. Sundaraja Sitharama Iyengar from the Florida International University, USA, and one invited lecture addressed by the distinguished Prof. Stephan Olariu from Old Dominion University, USA.

The winner of this year's *Reginald G. Fessenden Award* will be announced at the ACM MSWiM 2019 banquet dinner. The *Reginald G. Fessenden Award* has been established five years ago and it is granted to a distinguished researcher to recognize excellence and remarkable contributions in research work in the field of Wireless Communications and Mobile Networking. We take this opportunity to congratulate Prof. Victor C. M. Leung from The University of British Columbia, awarded with the 2018 *Reginald G. Fessenden Award* in recognition of *"his visionary contributions to the convergence of wireless networking and mobile computing technologies".*

Along with the main conference program, four symposia will be held this year: *MobiWac, DIVANet, PE-WASUN and Q2SWinet.* Over the years, these symposia have become successful and quite competitive in their own right, covering new research trends, visionary works and several specializations within mobile and wireless systems.

Putting together a high-quality conference like MSWiM requires a great team effort. We wish to express our gratitude to those who have managed the many practical details of the event. We would like to thank this year's TPC Co-Chairs, Salil Kanhere and Paolo Bellavista, who have managed the entire technical program process, and the volunteer efforts of TPC members and external reviewers. We also would like to thank Rodolfo W. L. Coutinho (Poster Chair), Peng Sun (Demo/Tools Chair), Sharief Oteafy (Workshop Chair), Xi Zhang (Tutorials Chair), Suranga Seneviratne, Moayad Aloqaily and Mirela Notare (Publicity Co-Chairs), and Noura Aljeri (Web Chair). We also express our appreciation to the MSWiM Steering Committee for their guidance and support. Last but not least, we wish to thank our main sponsor, ACM SIGSIM. Finally, many thanks to all of you for your participation.

We are very pleased to welcome you to MSWiM 2019 and fascinating Miami Beach. We are certain that you will find this year's event full of stimulating ideas and discussions.

Antonio A. F. Loureiro
MSWiM'19 General Chair
Federal University of Minas Gerais, Brazil

22nd ACM MSWiM 2019 Program Chairs' Welcome

The technical program of the 22nd ACM International Conference on Modeling, Analysis, and Simulation of Wireless and Mobile Systems (MSWiM), held in Miami, USA in November 2019 continues to build upon the high standards set by the previous editions of the conference. In 2019, the call for papers attracted the relevant number of 100 submissions for review in all areas of mobile and wireless systems. The submitted papers came from all over the world, for a total of 34 countries. This reflects the worldwide visibility and the truly international profile of MSWiM, also shown by the composition of its Technical Program Committee, with members affiliated to universities and industry in 30 countries spread over five continents.

By rapidly analysing the received submissions, the five most commonly listed topics during the submission process of MSWiM'19 were:

- Performance Evaluation and Modeling

- Analytical Models

- Wireless Mesh Networks, Mobile Ad Hoc Networks, Vehicular Networks

- Wireless Network Algorithms and Protocols

- Sensor and Actuator Networks

This clearly shows the centrality and focus of the conference on models and evaluation of the performance of different types of wireless mobile systems, including sensors and actuators in cyber physical systems and Internet of Things, thus following the successful tradition of MSWiM, which works to be the international reference point for the community working on the challenging issues of performance modelling, simulation, and in-the-field measurements of mobile and wireless systems in different application domains, from smart cities/communities to vehicular networks/applications, from geographically distributed Internet of Things to industrial cyber physical systems.

The submissions included a large number of papers of very high quality, making the selection process difficult and competitive. The 81 members of the Technical Program Committee worked efficiently and responsibly under tight time constraints to produce the reviews (at least 3 independent reviews for any paper, with an average of almost 3.5 reviews per paper) for the final paper selection. In the end, after this rigorous review process, we were able to select 31 regular papers, which correspond to an acceptance rate of approximately 31%. An additional small set of 10 short papers were recommended to be included in the technical program owing to their quality and contribution.

In addition, among the full regular papers, the following four were shortlisted as candidates for the best paper award:

- Towards Accurate Clock Drift Modeling in Wireless Sensor Networks Simulation by David Hauweele and Bruno Quoitin (University of Mons, Belgium)

- Joint Link-level and Network-level Reconfiguration for mmWave Backhaul Survivability in Urban Environments by Yuchen Liu, Qiang Hu and Douglas Blough (Georgia Institute of Technology, USA)

- Analysis of Age of Information Threshold Violations by Antonoio Franco, Bjorn Landfeldt and Ulf Korner (Lund University, Sweden)
- SEE: Scheduling Early Exit for Mobile DNN Inference during Service Outage by Zizhao Wang, Wei Bao, Dong Yuan, Liming Ge, Nguyen Tran and Albert Zomaya (The University of Sydney, Australia)

Based also on presentation quality and on the evaluation of a committee working during the MSWiM'19 conference, the winner among these three papers will be announced at the conference banquet and will be reported in the proceedings of the next edition of the conference (MSWiM'20).

At this point, we take the opportunity of this welcome message to congratulate the winners of the best paper award for MSWiM'18:

- FastLink: An Efficient Initial Access Protocol for Millimeter Wave Systems by Irmak Aykin and Marwan Kunzru (University of Arizona, USA)

Finally, we would like to sincerely thank all the Authors who trusted us with their work and who supported the conference with their many and valuable submissions. In addition, the final result of this technically excellent and very interesting technical program would not have been possible without the dedication and hard work of many colleagues: we would like to thank all the members of the Technical Program Committee for their sense of responsibility and responsiveness under very tight deadlines; special thanks go to all the members of the Organizing Committee and, last but certainly not least, to the General Chair Antonio Loureiro and Steering Committee Chair Azzedine Boukerche. Thanks to all this dedicated work, we are now able and happy to welcome you to this promising edition of MSWiM'19, with a vibrant technical program that is expected to attract your interest and to stimulate fruitful discussions and cross-fertilizing interactions during the days of the conference. Enjoy!

With warm regards,

Paolo Bellavista
MSWiM'19 Program Co-Chair
University of Bologna, Italy

Salil Kanhere
MSWiM'19 Program Co-Chair
University of New South Wales, Australia

Table of Contents

Keynote Talks

Session: Mobility Modeling

Session: WiFi

Session: Security

Session: Performance Evaluation

Session: Connected Vehicles

Session: Physical Layer and Medium Access

Session: Mobile Crowdsensing and Edge Computing

MSWiM 2019 Conference Organization

General Chair: Antonio A. F. Loureiro *(Federal University of Minas Gerais, Brazil)*

Program Co-Chairs: Salil Kanhere *(University of New South Wales, Australia)*
Paolo Bellavista *(University of Bologna, Italy)*

Posters Chair: Rodolfo W. L. Coutinho *(University of Ottawa, Canada)*

Demo/Tools Chair: Peng Sun *(University of Ottawa, Canada)*

Tutorial Chair: Xi Zhang *(Texas A&M University, USA)*

Workshop Chair: Sharief Oteafy *(De Paul University, USA)*

Publicity Co-Chairs: Suranga Seneviratne *(University of Sydney, Australia)*
Moayad Aloqaily *(Carleton University, Canada)*
Mirela Notare *(Barddal University, Brazil)*

Local Organization Committee: Peng Sun *(University of Ottawa, Canada)*
Noura Aljeri *(University of Ottawa, Canada)*
Andre Campolina *(University of Ottawa, Canada)*

Web Chair: Noura Aljeri *(University of Ottawa, Canada)*

Program Committee: Agustinus Borgy Waluyo *(Monash University, Australia)*
Andrea Munari *(Aachen University, Germany)*
Andrea Passarella *(IIT-CNR, Italy)*
Andreas Willig *(University of Canterbury, New Zealand)*
Angelos Antonopoulos *(Technological Centre of Catalonia, Spain)*
Antonio A. F. Loureiro *(Federal University of Minas Gerais, Brazil)*
Augusto Casaca *(INESC-ID, Portugal)*
Azzedine Boukerche *(University of Ottawa, Canada)*
Bjorn Landfeldt *(Lund University, Sweden)*
Chun-Ying Huang *(National Chiao Tung University, Taiwan)*
David Eckhoff *(University of Erlangen, Germany)*
Dimitri Papadimitriou *(Nokia Bell Labs)*
Edmundo Monteiro *(University of Coimbra, Portugal)*
Enzo Mingozzi *(University of Pisa, Italy)*
Ergin Dinc *(University of Cambridge, UK)*
Fabrizio Granelli *(University of Trento, Italy)*
Floriano De Rango *(University of Calabria, Italy)*
Francesco Lo Presti *(Universita' di Roma Tor Vergata, Italy)*
Francesco Renna *(Universidade do Porto, Portugal)*
Francesco Restuccia *(Northeastern University, USA)*
Gautam Bhanage *(Cisco Systems)*
Go Hasegawa *(Osaka University, Japan)*

Program Committee (continued): Gregorio Procissi *(University of Pisa, Italy)*
Holger Karl *(University of Paderborn, Germany)*
Hongyi Wu *(Old Dominion University, USA)*
Isabelle Guérin Lassous *(Université Claude Bernard Lyon 1, France)*
Jalel Ben-Othman *(University of Paris 13, France)*
James Gross *(Royal Institute of Technology, Sweden)*
Jose Saldana *(University of Zaragoza, Spain)*
Jussi Kangasharju *(University of Helsinki, Finland)*
Justin Rohrer *(Naval Postgraduate School)*
Kimon Kontovaslis *(NCSR Demokritos, Germany)*
Kiyohide Nakauchi *(National Institute of Information and Communications Technology, Japan)*
Klaus Wehrle *(RWTH Aachen University, Germany)*
Lorenzo Donatiello *(Università di Bologna, Italy)*
Marco Cello *(Rulex)*
Maurizio Naldi *(University of Rome "Tor Vergata", Italy)*
Miki Yamamoto *(Kansai University, Japan)*
Noriaki Kamiyama *(Fukuoka University, Japan)*
Paulo Pinto *(Universidade Nova de Lisboa, Portugal)*
Peng-Yong Kong *(Khalifa University, UAE)*
Periklis Chatzimisios *(Alexander TEI of Thessaloniki and Bounemouth University, Germany)*
Pietro Manzoni *(Universitat Politecnica de Valencia, Spain)*
Raja Jurdak *(CSIRO)*
Raquel Mini *(PUC-Minas, Brazil)*
Ravi Prakash *(University of Texas at Dallas, USA)*
Renato Lo Cigno *(University of Trento, Italy)*
Roberto Rojas-Cessa *(New Jersey Institute of Technology, USA)*
Shingo Ata *(Osaka City University, Japan)*
Sotiris Nikoletseas *(University of Patras & Computer Technology Institute, Greece)*
Tao Han *(University of North Carolina at Charlotte, USA)*
Torsten Braun *(University of Bern)*
Xavier Masip-Bruin *(Universitat Politecnica de Catalunya, Spain)*
Yang Xu *(New York University, USA)*
Yiu-Wing Leung *(Hong Kong Baptist University, Hong Kong)*

Steering Committee: Azzedine Boukerche *(University of Ottawa, Canada (Chair))*
Sajal K. Das *(Missouri University of Science and Technology, USA)*
Lorenzo Donatiello *(Università di Bologna, Bologna, Italy)*
Jason Yi-Bing Lin *(National Chiao-Tung University, Taiwan)*
William C.Y. Lee *(AirTouch Inc.)*
Simon Taylor *(Brunel University, UK)*

MSWiM 2019 Sponsors

A Vision towards Pervasive Edge Computing

Yuanyuan Yang
Stony Brook University, USA
yuanyuan.yang@stonybrook.edu

ABSTRACT

This talk presents an emerging pervasive edge computing paradigm where heterogeneous mobile edge devices (e.g., smartphones, tablets, IoT and vehicles) can collaborate to sense, process data and create many novel applications at network edge. We propose a data centric design where data become self-sufficient entities that are stored, referenced independently from their producers. This enables us to design efficient and robust data discovery, retrieval and caching mechanisms. The future research agenda including scalable data discovery, cache management, autonomous processing, trust, security and privacy, incentives and semantic data naming) will be discussed.

CCS CONCEPTS

• **Human-centered computing** → **Ubiquitous and mobile computing**; • **Networks** → *Cyber-physical networks*; Naming and addressing; In-network processing.

KEYWORDS

Pervasive computing, edge computing, data discovery and delivery

ACM Reference Format:
Yuanyuan Yang. 2019. A Vision towards Pervasive Edge Computing. In *22nd Int'l ACM Conference on Modeling, Analysis and Simulation of Wireless and Mobile Systems (MSWiM '19), November 25–29, 2019, Miami Beach, FL, USA.* ACM, New York, NY, USA, 1 page. https://doi.org/10.1145/3345768.3362038

1 SHORT BIO

Yuanyuan Yang received the BEng and MS degrees in computer science and engineering from Tsinghua University, Beijing, China, and the MSE and PhD degrees in computer science from Johns Hopkins University, Baltimore, Maryland, USA. Dr. Yang is a SUNY Distinguished Professor in the Department of Electrical & Computer Engineering and Department of Computer Science at Stony Brook University, New York, USA. She is currently on leave serving as a Program Director at the US National Science Foundation. She has served as the Associate Dean for Academic Affairs of College of Engineering and Applied Sciences at Stony Brook University and a Division Director of New York State Center of Excellence in Wireless and Information Technology.

Dr. Yang is internationally recognized for her contributions in parallel & distributed computing systems and networking. She was named an IEEE Fellow in 2009 for contributions to the area. Her current research interests include cloud computing, edge computing and mobile computing. Her research group currently develops data center architectures and virtual machine placement algorithms in cloud computing systems, data discovery/retrieval/caching mechanisms in edge computing systems, and wireless energy-charging algorithms and mobile data gathering mechanisms in wireless rechargeable sensor networks.

MSWiM '19, November 25–29, 2019, Miami Beach, FL, USA
© 2019 Copyright held by the owner/author(s).
ACM ISBN 978-1-4503-6904-6/19/11.
https://doi.org/10.1145/3345768.3362038

A Roadmap for the Acceleration of Technology in Computational Science for the next Decade

Sitharama Iyengar
Florida International University, USA
iyengar@cs.fiu.edu

ABSTRACT

This talk covers a detailed direction for developing a Roadmap in the discipline of Computer Science for the next Decade. Over the past two decades, the science of computing has changed drastically both in the context of theory and applications. Dr. Iyengar is going to cover his experiences of four decades in areas of Sensor Fusion, Quantum Computing and theory of Machine Learning and AI for various applications. The duration of the talk is 1 hour and there will be time for discussions after the seminar.

CCS CONCEPTS

• **Social and professional topics** → *Management of computing and information systems*; • **Theory of computation** → *Machine learning theory.*

KEYWORDS

Computer science, theory, applications

ACM Reference Format:
Sitharama Iyengar. 2019. A Roadmap for the Acceleration of Technology in Computational Science for the next Decade. In *22nd Int'l ACM Conference on Modeling, Analysis and Simulation of Wireless and Mobile Systems (MSWiM '19), November 25–29, 2019, Miami Beach, FL, USA.* ACM, New York, NY, USA, 2 pages. https://doi.org/10.1145/3345768.3351528

1 SHORT BIO

Dr. S. S. Iyengar, PhD, D.Sc (h.c.), Distinguished University Professor & Director - SCIS, Florida International University S. S. Iyengar is a Distinguished University Professor, Ryder Professor and Director of the School of Computing and Information Sciences at Florida International University, Miami. Dr. Iyengar is a pioneer in the field of distributed sensor nerworks/sensor fusion, computational aspects of robotics and high performance computing. He has published over 600 research papers and has authored/edited 22 books published by MIT Press. John Wiley & Sons, Prentice Hall, CRC Pres, Springer Verlag, etc. These publications have been used in major universities all over che world. He has many patents and some patentents are featured in the World's Best Technology Forum in Dallas, Texas. His research publications are on the design and analysis of efficient algorithms, parallel computing, sensor networks, and robotics. Daring the last four decades has supervised over 55 Ph.D. students, 100

Master's students, and many undergraduate studenes who are now faculty at Major Universities worldwide or Scientists or Engincers at National Lab/Industries around the woeld. He has also had many undergraduate stadents working on his research projects.

Dr. Iyengar is a member of the European Academy of Sciences, a Life Fellow of IEEE, a Fellow of ACM, a Fellow of AAAS, a Fellow of the National Academy of Inventors NAI and a Fellow of Society of Design and Process Program (SPDS), Fellow of Institution of Engineers (FIE), a Fellow of the American Instituse for Medical and Biological Engineering (AIMBE), was warded a Distinguished Alumnus Award of the Indian Institute of Science, Bangalore, and the IEEE Computer Society Technical Achievement for the contributions to sensor fusion algorithms, and parallel algorithms. He also received the IBM Distinguished Faculkty Award, NASA Fellowship Summer Awards at Oakridge National Lab and the Jet Propulsion Lboratory. He is a Village Fellow of the Academy of Transdisciplinary Learning and Advanced Studies in Austin, Texas, 2010. Dr.

Iyengar was bonored by the Institute of Electrical and Electronics Engineers" (IEEE) Cybermatics Congress in Atlanta, Georgia, where he received the Outstanding Research Award known as the "Test of Time Award" for his work in creating the Brooks-Iyengar Algorithm (2019).

He has also received various national and international awards including the Times Network NRI (Non-Resident Indian) of the Year Award for 2017, a presigious award for Global Indian leaders received out of five thousand nominations; the most distinguished Ramamoorthy Award at the Sociery for Design and Process Science (SDPS 2017): the National Academy of Inventors Fellow Award in 2013: the NRI Mahatma Gandhi Pradvasi Medal at the House of Lords in London in 2013: a Lifetime Achievement Award conferred by International Society of Agile Manufacturing (ISAM) in recognition of his illustrious career in teaching, research and administracion and a lifelong contribution to the fields of Engineering and Computer Science at Indian Institute of Technology (BHU). In 2012, Iyengar and Nulogix were awarded the 2012 Innovation-2-Industry (i2i) Florida Award. Iyengar received a Distinguished Research Award from Xaimen Uiversity, China for his rescarch in Sensor Networks, Computer Vision and Image Processing. Iyengar's landmark contributions with his research group include the development of grid coverage for surveillance and target location in distributed sensor networks and the Beooks Iyengar fusion algorithm. He has also been awarded Honorary and Doctorate of Science and Engineering Degree. He serves on the advisory board of many corporations and universities around the world. He has served on many National Science Boards such as NIH - National Libeary of Medicine in Bioinformatics, National Science Foundation review panel, NASA Space Science, Department of Homeland Security, Office of Naval Security, and many ochers. His contribution to the US Naval Research Laboratory was a centerpiece of a pioneering effort to develop image analysis for science and technology and to expand the goals of the US Naval Research Laboratory.

The impact of his research contributions can be seen in companies and National Labs like Raytheon, Telecordia, Motorola, the United States Navy, DARPA, and other US agencies. His contribution in DARPAS's program demonstration with BBN, Cambridge, Massachussetts, MURI, researchers from PSU/ARL, Duke, University of Wisconsin, UCLA, Cornell university and LSU has been significant He is also the founding Editor of the International Journal of Distributed Sensor Networks. He has been on the editorial board of many journals and is also a PhD Committee Member at various universities, including CMU, Duke University, and many others throughout the world. He is presently the Editor of ACM Computing Surveys and ocher journals. He is also the founding director of the FIU's Discovery Laboratory. His research work has been cited extensively. His fundamental work has been transitioned into unique technologies. All through his four-decade long professional career, Dr. Iyengar has devoted and employed mathematical morphology in a unique way for quantitative understanding of computational processes for many applications.

REFERENCES

[1] M. Hadi Amini, Kianoosh G. Boroojeni, S.S. Iyengar, Panos M. Pardalos, Frede Blaabjerg, and Asad M. Madni. 2018. Sustainable Interdependent Networks: From Theory to Application (Studies in Systems, Decision and Control). (2018).
[2] Bin Shi and S S Iyengar. 2019. Mathematical Theories of Machine Learning: Theory and Application. (2019).

Where Are You Going Next?
A Practical Multi-dimensional Look at Mobility Prediction

Babak Alipour
University of Florida, USA
babak.ap@ufl.edu

Leonardo Tonetto
Technical University of Munich
Germany
tonetto@in.tum.de

Roozbeh Ketabi
University of Florida, USA
roozbeh@ufl.edu

Aaron Yi Ding
Delft University of Technology
The Netherlands
aaron.ding@tudelft.nl

Jörg Ott
Technical University of Munich
Germany
ott@in.tum.de

Ahmed Helmy
University of Florida, USA
helmy@ufl.edu

ABSTRACT

Understanding and predicting mobility are essential for the design and evaluation of future mobile edge caching and networking. Consequently, research on human mobility prediction has drawn significant attention in the last decade. Employing information-theoretic concepts and machine learning methods, earlier research has shown evidence that human behavior can be highly predictable. Whether high predictability manifests itself for different modes of device usage, across spatial and temporal dimensions is still debatable. Despite existing studies, more investigations are needed to capture intrinsic mobility characteristics constraining predictability, to explore more dimensions (e.g. device types) and spatiotemporal granularities, especially with the change in human behavior and technology.

We investigate practical predictability of next location visitation across three different dimensions: device type, spatial granularity and temporal spans using an extensive longitudinal dataset, with fine spatial granularity (AP level) covering 16 months. The study reveals *device type* as an important factor affecting predictability. Ultra-portable devices such as smartphones have "on-the-go" mode of usage (and hence dubbed "*Flutes*"), whereas laptops are "sit-to-use" (dubbed "*Cellos*"). The goal of this study is to investigate practical prediction mechanisms to quantify predictability as an aspect of human mobility modeling, across time, space and *device types*. We apply our systematic analysis to wireless traces from a large university campus. We compare several algorithms using varying degrees of temporal and spatial granularity for the two modes of devices; *Flutes* vs. *Cellos*.

Through our analysis, we quantify how the mobility of *Flutes* is less predictable than the mobility of *Cellos*. In addition, this pattern is consistent across various spatio-temporal granularities, and for different methods (Markov chains, neural networks/deep learning, entropy-based estimators). This work substantiates the importance of predictability as an essential aspect of human mobility, with direct application in predictive caching, user behavior modeling and mobility simulations.

KEYWORDS

mobility, prediction, markov chain, neural networks, wireless networks, device types

ACM Reference Format:
Babak Alipour, Leonardo Tonetto, Roozbeh Ketabi, Aaron Yi Ding, Jörg Ott, and Ahmed Helmy. 2019. Where Are You Going Next? A Practical Multi-dimensional Look at Mobility Prediction. In *22nd Int'l ACM Conference on Modeling, Analysis and Simulation of Wireless and Mobile Systems (MSWiM '19), November 25–29, 2019, Miami Beach, FL, USA*. ACM, New York, NY, USA, 8 pages. https://doi.org/10.1145/3345768.3355923

1 INTRODUCTION & RELATED WORK

In recent years, large-scale research on human mobility has thrived due to the availability of location data collected from portable computing and communication devices, such as laptops, smartphones, smartwatches and fitness trackers [1]. One particular aspect of human mobility that has gained a lot of attention lately is predictability. Prediction techniques constitute fundamental mechanistic building blocks for many mobile protocols and applications, ranging from resource allocation to caching and recommender systems [2, 3]. In addition, potential improvements to next-hop prediction can lead to more accurate bandwidth predictions, which benefits QoE for users of mobile networks [4].

The seminal work by [5], utilizing cellular network data, established an approach towards understanding and measuring the predictability of human mobility patterns, with their equally important contribution with respect to the data-driven analysis of large mobile populations, and their efforts in devising a framework to study the theoretical limits of predictability. The methods introduced in their framework are founded in information theory and have since been extensively applied in the area of mobility modeling and prediction. Later studies that built on [5] addressed either the specifics of the prediction problem (e.g., different formulations [6] of the individual's change of location, analyzed different contexts of mobility) or the shortcomings of the original approach (that relied on coarse spatio-temporal granularity). Authors in [7] used Wireless LAN (WLAN) traces from a university campus network and reported multi-modal entropy distributions which can be partially explained by the demographics of the population (*i.e.*, age, gender, major of studies). Other entropy based studies include vehicular mobility [8–10], online social behavior [11, 12], complex systems [13], cellular network traffic [14] and public transport utilization [15]. In addition, the devices' form factor affects the mode of usage and varied traffic profiles ([16–19]), but these studies either do not consider predictability or do not account for different spatio-temporal resolutions. We have chosen our methods based on the literature to measure and compare both theoretical and practical limits of predictability for "on-the-go" *Flutes* and "sit-to-use" *Cellos*, with varying degrees of spatio-temporal granularity, while also looking at the correlation of prediction accuracy with mobility and network traffic profiles using extensive fine-granularity traces (based on our earlier work in [19]).

The *main* questions addressed in this study are: i. How different are *Flutes* and *Cellos* in terms of predictability? ii. How does the predictability of these device types change with different *spatio-temporal granularity* (5, 15, 30 min, 1 hour and 2 hours; access point and building level)? iii. Does the *choice of method* or predictor (*e.g.* Markov Chain, neural networks such as LSTM, CNN and Transformer [20], BWT or LZ based estimators, which are introduced in Section 2) significantly alter the answers to aforementioned questions?

This study provides the following main contributions: 1. Quantifying the differences of *Flutes* and *Cellos* for prediction analysis, evaluated on a real-world large-scale dataset. 2. Comparison of several well-known algorithms (Markov Chains, Neural Networks) and LZ/BWT-based theoretical bounds across different time and space scales for Flutes and Cellos. 3. Use of prediction accuracy as part of the user profile for modeling, and investigation of its correlation with a combination of network traffic and mobility features.

The paper is structured as follows: First, the main approach and methods are presented in Sec. 2. Then, the details of the dataset and experiment setup are discussed in Sec. 3. The experiment results are presented in Sec. 4. Sections 5 and 6 present the discussion on potentials implications of the findings and conclude the paper.

2 MAIN APPROACH & METHODS

We investigate two methods to measure predictability; a theoretical method based on entropy, and a systems method based on practical predictor algorithms. Following we provide the entropy estimation based definition and discuss the different algorithms studied in this paper, including a reference-point Markov Chains approach, and more sophisticated deep learning approaches.

2.1 Entropy Estimation

Entropy is defined as the level of order (or disorder) of a system, and is founded on information theory. It has been adopted in previous studies to establish bounds on predictability under certain assumptions [5, 6]. We utilize it in our study to gauge the performance of our practical predictors. For a random process, this metric is sensitive to both the relative frequency of events and their inter-dependencies [15]. To estimate a baseline of predictability, we compute the *time-uncorrelated* entropy (S^{unc}) which only takes into account the frequency of the observed events. For the upper-bound of predictability we compute two *time-correlated* estimators based on compression algorithms (S^{lz} and S^{bwt}) which also consider the memory of the system. We define *maximum predictability* as the probability of predicting the most likely state of x_i given a state x_j, which is computed from the entropy S of a given sequence of events based on [5], with the refinements proposed by [6]. For a complete description on *entropy estimation*, we kindly refer the reader to [21, 22].

2.2 Predictors

Markov Chain-based predictor. A Markov chain (MC) with a discrete state space has been applied for user mobility prediction [23, 24]. In an order-k Markov predictor, the state space consists of tuples of k location names (e.g., AP), where the next location prediction depends solely on the most recent preceding k-tuple. We build the model on the data so that observed k-tuples comprise the states. The transition probabilities are learned based on the frequency of appearances of such a transition in observations. The probability for a transition from the current state $S = X_i X_{i+1} ... X_j$ to $X_{i+1} X_{i+2} ... X_j X_{j+1}$ where $j - i = k$ and each X_i is the symbol for each location, is represented as $P X_{j+1} = c \mid S = X_i X_{i+1} ... X_j$ for all c observed in data and is learned based on the reappearance frequency of such a sequence. If the predictor of order k encounters a new sequence that has never seen before, it falls back to the lower, $k - 1$ order recursively. The base case is $O(0)$ which is simply the frequency distribution of all symbols observed so far.

Deep learning. Recent approaches to sequence prediction use deep Recurrent Neural Networks (RNN) or Convolutional Neural Networks (CNN). Recurrent neural networks have loops within their cells, allowing information to persist and thus enabling the neural network to connect previous information to make a reasonable prediction of the future state of the modeled system. Certain types of RNNs are capable of learning long-term dependencies. There are multiple variants of RNNs, including Long short-term memory (LSTM) [25] and Gated Recurrent Unit (GRU) [26]. These networks can learn dynamic temporal patterns and have successfully been applied in speech recognition, text-to-speech engines and predicting next location [27, 28].

CNNs learn convolutional filters to extract latent information across the data (i.e. 1D CNNs learn different temporal locality patterns) and use that information for predicting the next location. CNNs have a local receptive field. The receptive field is the region of the input that affects a specific unit of the network, which can be increased by techniques such as stacking more layers.

The Transformer [20] is a novel neural network architecture that only uses self-attention, without any recurrence or convolution, to learn global dependencies between input and output. These networks can be parallelized better (a major shortcoming of RNNs), and also have a global receptive field (as opposed to the local receptive field of CNNs).

In our study, we use a multi-layer LSTM, 1D CNN and a Transformer to predict movements of users based on similar input tuples used for MC-based predictors, as described in the next section. Neural networks are computationally expensive and tend to require hyper-parameter tuning. Thus the deep model is run only on a sample of users in this study. One goal of this study is to analyze the payoff (and cost) of adding complexity to the predictor (e.g. LSTMs), versus the simpler MC-based predictors, while considering different temporal and spatial bins for Flutes vs Cellos.

3 DATASETS & EXPERIMENTAL SETUP

To study the regularity of human behavior, we performed a data-driven analysis applying our methods to a university campus WiFi traces from the University of Florida (UF). The dataset was collected from networks providing wireless access to a large number of portable devices via access points deployed in non-residential areas, including classrooms, computer laboratories, libraries, offices, administrative premises, cafeterias, and restaurants.

Every trace entry contains a unique user identifier (*uuid*), time-stamp and an access point unique identifier (*apid*). Based on the *apid*'s string we are able to identify the building as well as the room in which an access point (AP) was located. Only the geographical coordinates of buildings are known. Table 2 contains a brief summary of the UF dataset with mean (μ) and standard deviation (*std*), where N_{ap} is number of unique access points observed per device, N_{day} number of unique days with at least one record, N_{rec} number of records during data collection, and *total* number of devices available for at least 7 days and accessed more than 5 APs.[1]

3.1 UF traces

The UF traces were collected for 16 months (September/2011-December/2012) and contain over 1700 wireless access points (APs) deployed in 140 buildings which were used by 300K devices. A sample (sythenic) record is shown in Table 1. Its raw records were captured from associations and sessions timeout in which the unique user id (*uuid*) was the MAC address. These *uuid* although hashed, still contained the

Organizationally Unique Identifier (OUI)[2] allowing us to distinguish *Flutes* and *Cellos*, as detailed in [19]. This dataset was collected before MAC address randomization became widely available. However, in most current implementations, the randomization only happens in case of probe requests for a network, and once connected to some SSID, the device either presents its original MAC or a generated MAC that does not change per association. Besides, many networks require authentication that allows tracking on higher levels in the network stack (e.g. application). This work is concerned with wireless connectivity being provided to users, and it will always come from discrete points (for example, access points), as opposed to continuous movements in an open field. Thus, all collected WiFi traces are processed as discrete time-series, defined next.

3.2 Discrete-time Series

Given a set a of timely ordered events $X = \{x_t : t = 1, \cdots, n\}$, where x_t is the realization of X at time t for $t \in T$, we say that a timeseries is *discrete* if T are measurements taken at successive times spaced at uniform intervals w, also referred to as sampling rate (defining the temporal granularity).

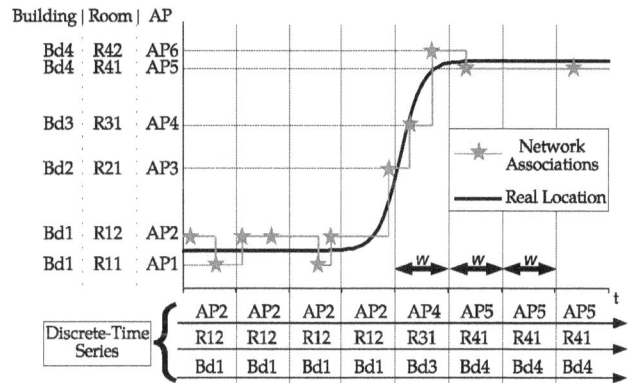

Figure 1: Location of the device is sampled at a constant rate.

Figure 1 depicts an example of how the real location of a device is sensed by the wireless management system through AP associations (red stars) and finally how the discrete-time series is obtained. For a given sampling time window w, our *discrete-time* series may result in different sequences depending on whether we choose an AP or a building as the level of spatial resolution.

From Figure 1, for the first 4 time steps the device switched its associated AP without a real location change. This switch in AP association can be triggered by the mobile device (e.g. stronger wireless signal) or by the network management system (e.g. load balancing).

Note that it is important to define the resolution for *space* and *time*, *i.e.*, how big a location is in space (or point-of-interest) and how often we are going to sample from the input signal. In this example, larger values of w could eliminate this

---

[1]Transient devices are not counted to ensure the analysis is carried out on devices that are mobile and benefit from predictive systems the most, while stationary devices (e.g. plugged-in Cellos) and guests that never return to campus are ignored.

[2]http://standards.ieee.org/faqs/regauth.html#17

Table 1: AP logs sample data columns

User IP	UUID	AP name	AP MAC	Lease begin time	Lease end time
10.130.90.3	00:11:22:00:00:00	b422r143-win-1	00:1d:e5:8f:1b:30	1333238737	1333238741

Table 2: Statistics per device available for at least 7 days & accessed more than 5 APs.

	N_{ap}		N_{day}		N_{rec}		Total Devices
	μ	std	μ	std	μ	std	
UF	127.3	142.3	63.5	59.2	1861	5121	138028

ping-pong effect of switching between APs without actually moving, but also cause loss of information when the user transits from one location to another. On the contrary, very small values of w could over-sample long periods when the user is not moving. Similarly, different values of spatial resolution could mitigate noise but eliminate information from the traces. Choosing these parameters is often influenced by the characteristics of the available dataset as well as the targeted application of the study.

Step Value. A weighing mechanism is used to pick the corresponding location to represent a time step. During a time interval, we weigh every observed location of the device with the duration of time at that location and pick the one with the highest weight to represent that step. We assign a user to a specific location ℓ in the time interval δt between an association at ℓ and the next association at any other location, but only if $\delta t < t_{max}$. After t_{max} the device will be in an *unknown* state [5] until the next network event which will reveal its location for future steps.

3.3 Experiments

The design of our experiments is based on our study's questions: i. How different are *Flutes* and *Cellos* in terms of predictability? ii. How does the predictability of these device types change with different spatio-temporal granularity? iii. Does the choice of method or predictor significantly alter the answers to the aforementioned questions? Thus, we evaluated a matrix, involving *combinations* of the following dimensions:

- Device Types: *Flutes* vs. *Cellos*.
- Temporal Resolutions: 5 min, 15 min, 30 min, 1 hour and 2 hours.
- Spatial Resolutions: Access Points, and Buildings.
- Methods: A. Well-known sequence prediction algorithms from machine learning literature (Markov Chains, Neural Networks) B. Entropy-based Estimations of predictability upper-bounds.

The temporal resolutions are chosen based on the related literature, and the spatial resolutions are determined by the granularity of the dataset. The experiments were implemented in Python, the neural networks were implemented using Tensorflow [3] and Keras. Training is carried out in an *online*

---

[3]TensorFlow: Large-Scale Machine Learning on Heterogeneous Systems. Software available from tensorflow.org.

manner and the evaluation is through providing a sliding window of k observations to the predictor and testing the prediction correctness of the next symbol. The *fraction of correct next symbol predictions*, or success rate, is the prediction accuracy metric.

4 EXPERIMENTAL RESULTS

4.1 Spatio-Temporal Resolutions

To answer the first two questions of this study, particularly "ii. How does the predictability of these device types change with different *spatio-temporal granularity*?", Table 3 summarizes the median accuracy of an LSTM predictor for Flutes and Cellos with different spatial and temporal granularity.

The choice of granularity is application-dependent, for example, to predict foot traffic at buildings and congestion planning based on density, building level analysis is more appropriate. Cellos show more predictable behavior overall, as the fraction of correct next symbol predictions is higher for Cellos across the board. At the AP level, with longer time bins, the accuracy for both Flutes and Cellos decreases. This observation is in line with previous findings [6]. At 15min time intervals, the difference between Flutes and Cellos is at its maximum, then drops and remains stable for longer time intervals. At the building level, the accuracy follows a less regular pattern but both Flutes and Cellos are most predictable at 5min intervals (mainly due to long repeats of the same location in the sequence). Cellos' accuracy drops for 30min bins and goes back up again. On the other hand, Flutes are more predictable in 30min bins than 15min, 1h or 2h bins.

Looking across all temporal bins, Fig 2 presents the empirical cumulative distribution function (ECDF) of prediction accuracy at AP and building spatial granularity. The "sit-to-use" *Cellos* show significantly higher predictability at every percentile; this is reasonable given their lower mobility [19] and mode of usage. In fact, prediction accuracy is highly correlated with other mobility and network traffic features of mobile wireless users, we will take a brief look at these correlations in Section 5 and Fig 4.

4.2 Comparison of Methods

To answer the third question of this study, "iii. Does the choice of method or predictor significantly alter the answers to the aforementioned questions?", here we compare the experiment results for different methods: 1) *MC*: Markov Chain 2) *LSTM*: A type of recurrent neural network 3) *CNN*: 1D convolutional neural network 4) *Transformer*: A type of self-attention neural network 4) *Hr_LZ*: Theoretical predictability based on the Lempel-Ziv (LZ) entropy estimator 5) *Hr_BWT*: Theoretical predictability based on the Burrows-Wheeler transform (BWT) entropy estimator. A summary of

Table 3: Median accuracy percentages of LSTM (sequence len. 40) for *Flutes* vs *Cellos*, 5min-2h temporal and AP/Bldg spatial granularity.

	AP		Building	
	F	C	F	C
5 min	33.22	42.25	44	63.4
15 min	21.42	36.9	34.53	58.06
30 min	21.88	27.39	39.56	50.78
1 hour	19.67	24.33	32.62	52.03
2 hour	17.17	22.5	32.6	59.62

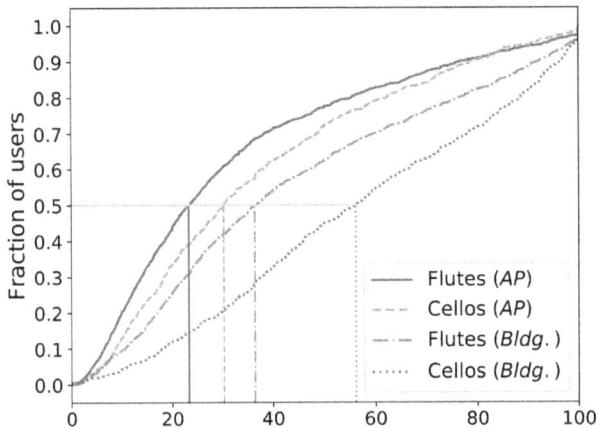

Figure 2: ECDF of LSTM Prediction Accuracy for *Flutes* & *Cellos* at AP and Building spatial levels (all temporal levels combined, vertical lines denote medians, sequence length 40).

comparisons is presented in Table 4, for temporal granularity of 1h and 15min, highlighting the difference of *Cellos - Flutes*.

In all cases *Cellos* are more predictable than *Flutes*, regardless of the choice of method (with a minor exception of LZ predictor at 15 minutes time and building level which might be due to intrinsic instability of LZ based estimator). The difference in median accuracy for *Flutes* vs *Cellos* is up to 25% (Building level, 15 minutes window, sequence length 40, *Flutes* 33.97% vs *Cellos* 59.03%). Other temporal choices result in a similar pattern. Another notable observation is that while the neural networks are more complex, and require vastly more computing power, they only achieve modest increase compared to Markov Chains in *some* scenarios (e.g., *Cellos*, at the building level and sequence length 40, from 48.56% to 52.5%). This is a trade-off that needs to be considered in the design of predictive caching systems. In addition, increasing the sequence length k (i.e. the number of previous time steps available to the predictor) impacts the Markov Chain model more than the neural networks. This is particularly pronounced for 15 minutes time window, in fact, the neural networks do not lose much accuracy from increasing sequence length 5 to 40 in case of the 1 hour time window. Also, the theoretical LZ and BWT based estimators, show higher upper bounds compared with the best of the

algorithms, with sequence length 5 Markov Chains and CNNs being the closest practical algorithms for the 15 minutes case. The predictors are far behind in the 1h case, suggesting room for improvement via tuning for specific time and space granularities. The run time of LSTM is the longest, followed by CNN (not shown for brevity). In addition, in case of the Transformer, at 1 hour temporal resolution, median accuracy is slightly higher compared to LSTM in most cases. However, in the shorter 15 minute resolution, the accuracy is significantly better for Flutes (average accuracy $\approx$14% higher than LSTM), and slightly better for Cellos. This shows the utility of adapting advances in deep learning to mobility prediction.

4.3 Top 2 Locations

In order to improve the obtained success rate in predicting the next location, we evaluated our prediction methods when considering the top 2 possible locations. In other words, we evaluate the accuracy of the predictors when considering not only the best possible location but the two places where the user is most likely to be found in the next time slot. In this case, we are interested in assessing this improvement which could be beneficial for preemptive caching systems.

Overall, we observe an increase of up to 20% in the median accuracy of all predictors evaluated. Figure 3 depicts the differences between the top 1 and top 2 for CNN's in different temporal and spatial levels. Interestingly, more pronounced improvements were observed at higher spatial levels (buildings) where top 1 accuracy was already higher. The upward trend continues when measuring the top 3 accuracy, though it is less dramatic. The change in accuracy, of top 1 to top 3, for LSTMs followed a similar pattern.

These improvements could be explained by the expected uncertainty in choosing where to go next being better described by more than one location. When deciding between these multiple options, a user is likely to use information not available in our mobility traces. Therefore, when asking our predictor for the next step with the highest probability, these top locations would seem random, and allowing even a small number of top choices (> 1) greatly improves its success rate.

To numerically support this conjecture, we look into the average uncertainty in picking a next location given by $U_{\text{next}} = 2^{S_{\text{rate}}}$, where S_{rate} is the entropy rate estimated, for which we used the BWT algorithm (S^{bwt}, see Section 2.1). For a user's sequence of visited locations, this metric summarizes the average uncertainty about the user's next step at every location, therefore the higher this number the more random the next steps seem to be for a given pair of spatial and temporal levels. Table 5 presents the expected U_{next}, for both Flutes (**F**) and Cellos (**C**). Interestingly, these values not only correlate with the obtained values for accuracy but also shows a clear correspondence with the increase in accuracy when using the top 2. For example, at the AP and 1-hour levels we observe a high U_{next} as well as a marginal improvement from top 1 to top 2, while in contrast at building and 15 minutes levels U_{next} are lower and the improvements for our predictor accuracy are more pronounced.

Table 4: Summary of Median Accuracy for *Flutes* vs *Cellos* with different methods (Diff is $Cellos - Flutes$) and sequence lengths for 15min and 1h time windows.

Seq Len	Predictor	AP, 1h			Bldg., 1h			AP, 15min			Bldg., 15min		
		F	C	Diff	F	C	Diff	F	C	Diff	F	C	Diff
5	MC	21.05	25.95	+4.90	38.25	53.50	+15.25	61.72	70.30	+8.58	75.00	87.60	+12.60
	LSTM	21.62	25.00	+3.38	35.03	50.00	+14.97	40.00	44.56	+4.56	52.44	65.56	+13.12
	CNN	16.45	24.27	+7.82	34.94	50.00	+15.06	50.00	59.80	+9.80	64.60	76.94	+12.34
10	MC	17.98	25.6	+7.62	36.72	50.28	+13.56	52.25	61.97	+9.72	68.00	82.25	+14.25
	LSTM	20.83	26.31	+5.48	37.50	50.66	+13.16	31.14	44.62	+13.48	45.38	64.56	+19.18
	CNN	18.06	22.62	+4.56	36.20	52.03	+15.83	49.20	58.80	+9.60	64.56	74.00	+9.44
20	MC	18.1	24.52	+6.42	36.28	49.94	+13.66	38.50	48.22	+9.72	57.30	74.94	+17.64
	LSTM	21.22	24.19	+2.97	36.12	50.78	+14.66	29.17	41.00	+11.83	43.62	61.47	+17.85
	CNN	18.44	23.60	+5.16	35.28	50.00	+14.72	37.84	48.12	+10.28	50.00	65.00	+15.00
40	MC	17.88	23.61	+5.73	35.1	48.56	+13.46	27.97	31,00	+3.03	47.12	65.80	+18.68
	LSTM	19.67	24.33	+4.66	32.62	52.03	+19.41	23.30	39.40	+16.10	33.97	59.03	+25.06
	CNN	18.75	23.97	+5.22	35.25	52.50	+17.25	27.62	44.70	+17.08	41.25	62.10	+20.85
	LZ	46.90	52.60	+5.70	58.78	66.40	+7.62	72.70	76.06	+3.36	79.60	79.10	-0.50
	BWT	66.44	69.44	+3.00	73.70	79.90	+6.20	83.30	88.06	+4.76	88.60	92.20	+3.60

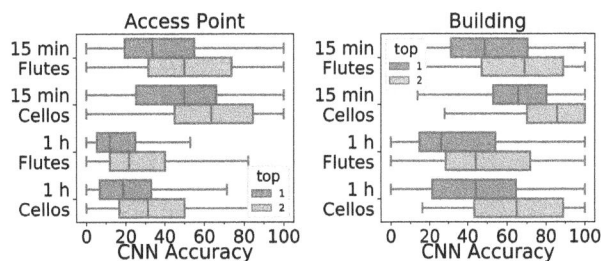

Figure 3: CNN accuracy for top 1 and top 2 locations.

Table 5: User's expected uncertainty μ when choosing next location ($U_{\text{next}} = 2^{S_{\text{rate}}}$). Error given by standard deviation σ.

		AP		Building	
		$\mu \pm \sigma$	95th-%	$\mu \pm \sigma$	95th-%
15 minutes	F	3.10 ± 1.3	5.3	2.17 ± 0.7	3.3
	C	2.05 ± 0.7	3.3	1.56 ± 0.4	2.2
1 hour	F	5.50 ± 2.4	9.7	3.65 ± 1.7	6.5
	C	3.48 ± 1.6	6.37	2.10 ± 0.9	3.7

These findings show one of the trade-offs a predictive caching system would need to consider, that is to find the balance between the number of places to prefetch assets and the desired level of cache hit ratio.

5 DISCUSSION & FUTURE WORK

In this paper, we define our research problem as predicting the next symbol in a discrete-time series for users with two categories of devices. The next symbol either denotes the next access point or building in the visitation sequence. The accuracy is evaluated as the fraction of the next symbols predicted correctly.

While some earlier studies investigated a similar problem setup, our study has notable implications. For example, across device types, predictability can vary significantly, with Cellos showing typically higher predictability. Also, with larger time windows such as 1 hour, it is easy to miss short stays (since one location visit with a duration of 31 minutes would result in other locations in that 1 hour window being ignored). On the other hand, a short time window results in multiple repetitions of the same location in the sequence, potentially achieving high prediction accuracy even when the method is not predicting the *transitions* well. Further, we also note that allowing prediction algorithms to look further back does not help prediction in most cases; this might be an artifact of the users' likelihood to stay in place over limited time spans, which makes predicting a 'stay' straightforward while predicting a location transition remains challenging.

Our results highlight the importance of considering the device type, context, and application in order to choose an appropriate time and space granularity; the best performing method differs across these dimensions. Furthermore, we observe a significant increase in accuracy, of up to 20%, when considering the top 2 possible next locations compared to only measuring top 1 accuracy, highlighting the complexity of these predictions based only in the history of visits from a user. In some cases, such as 1 hour, access point level prediction, the median of the top 2 accuracy of the population is nearly twice as high as the median top 1 accuracy. Many misclassifications occur because the prediction algorithm is simply confused between only two places. For certain applications, such as predictive caching, it can be worthwhile to consider preloading in more than one location to improve the user experience at the expense of increased resource consumption, a trade-off to measure in future studies.

Interesting possible problems yet to be addressed include, taking the distance between possible locations into account when selecting a future stop, as well as cluster users with similar mobility patterns to further improve the prediction accuracy of their movements.

All the findings here are based on the university dataset (Sec. 3), which provides a peek into only a subset of the population, so we emphasize the importance of reproducing these analyses on other datasets in different settings.

Correlations with Mobility and Network Traffic. Figure 4 shows the correlation of prediction accuracy with a sample of features that describe the mobility or network traffic of users. PDT(W/E) and TJ(W/E) are mobility features while AAT(W/E) and AI(W/E) are traffic features. PDTW is the time spent at the user's preferred building (most common) on weekdays (PDTE for weekends). TJW is the total sum of jumps (distance) for the weekdays while TJE describes the same feature for weekends. AATW is the average of active time (as indicated by network usage) of the user for weekdays (AATE for weekends). AIW stands for the average inter-arrival time of flows on weekdays, and AIE for weekends ([19, 29]).

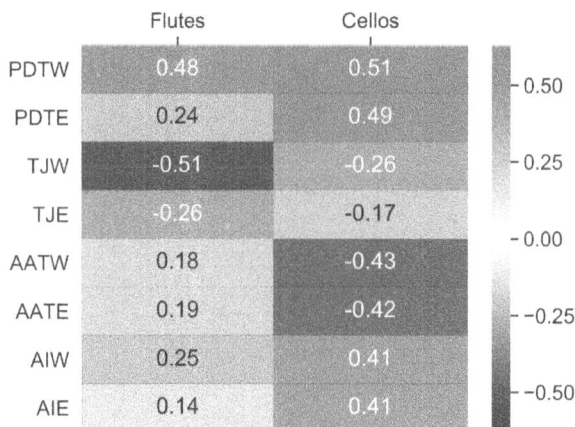

Figure 4: Pearson Correlation of Prediction Accuracy with several Mobility and Network Traffic Features.

The results present significant correlations between the prediction accuracy, with not only the *mobility features*, but also *network traffic features*. These correlations vary across device types (*Flutes* vs *Cellos*), and in time (*Weekdays* vs

Weekends). This is a very important observation for the design of *predictive caching* systems, importantly, it might be possible to improve prediction of *where* the user is going based on network traffic profile while noting the different modes of usage based on device types. We leave the investigation of incorporating this extra information and potential improvements to future work.

Integrated Mobility-Traffic Modeling. Given the observed correlations, we hypothesize that the use of *predictability* as a feature in an integrated mobility-traffic generative model could lead to more realistic synthetic traces. Such a data-driven generative model would be an essential tool for network simulations and capacity planning. Notably, it can also be made *privacy preserving*, since collected traces would be replaced with realistic synthetic data that captures mobility, network traffic, predictability, and their relationships. Further study is beyond the scope of this work and is left for future work.

6 CONCLUSION

In this work, we sought to answer three questions: i. How different are *Flutes* and *Cellos* in terms of predictability? ii. How does the predictability of these device types change with different *spatiotemporal granularity*? iii. Does the *choice of method* or predictor significantly alter the answers to the aforementioned questions? For this purpose, we processed a large-scale dataset from a campus environment, and grouped the devices into two categories; and chose a set of methods for the comparisons including Entropy-based estimators and popular algorithms such as Markov Chains and Neural Networks.

The results of experiments show the movements of *Cellos* ("sit-to-use") are significantly more predictable than *Flutes* (up to 25% difference in accuracy). This pattern is consistent across various temporal granularities (5 min to 2 hours), spatial granularities (Access Point and Building level), and for different methods (Markov Chains, Neural Networks, Entropy-based Estimators). We illustrate that the performance of predictors depends strongly on the span of temporal bins. Markov Chains tend to outperform deep learning models in shorter time-bins while LSTMs and CNNs usually show a higher accuracy in longer time-bins. CNNs have mostly similar accuracy to LSTMs in the latter case but have significantly better run time on a modern GPU. Furthermore, looking at the top 2 locations we observe an increase of up to 20% suggesting that higher accuracy is achievable when considering multiple possible next locations.

We also found significant correlations among prediction accuracy, *mobility features*, and also *network traffic features*, varying across device types, an important observation for the design of predictive caching systems where it might be possible to improve mobility prediction based on network traffic profile. We plan to further investigate the use of *predictability as a feature* in an integrated mobility-traffic generative model, and its application in state-of-the-art predictive caching systems.

ACKNOWLEDGEMENT

This work was partially funded by NSF Award 1320694. We gratefully acknowledge the support of NVIDIA Corp. with the donation of the Titan Xp GPU used for this research.

REFERENCES

[1] K. Jayarajah, R. K. Balan, M. Radhakrishnan, A. Misra, and Y. Lee, "Livelabs: Building in-situ mobile sensing & behavioural experimentation testbeds," in *MobiSys*. ACM, 2016.

[2] V. Siris, X. Vasilakos, and D. Dimopoulos, "Exploiting mobility prediction for mobility, popularity caching and dash adaptation," in *WoWMoM*, 2016.

[3] N. Lathia, "The anatomy of mobile location-based recommender systems," in *Recommender Systems Handbook*. Springer, 2015.

[4] T. Mangla, N. Theera-Ampornpunt, M. Ammar, E. Zegura, and S. Bagchi, "Video through a crystal ball: Effect of bandwidth prediction quality on adaptive streaming in mobile environments," in *MoVid*. ACM, 2016.

[5] C. Song, Z. Qu, N. Blumm, and A.-L. Barabási, "Limits of predictability in human mobility," *Science*, 2010.

[6] G. Smith, R. Wieser, J. Goulding, and D. Barrack, "A refined limit on the predictability of human mobility," *PerCom*, 2014.

[7] P. Cao, G. Li, A. Champion, D. Xuan, S. Romig, and W. Zhao, "On human mobility predictability via WLAN logs," in *Proc. INFOCOM*, Apr. 2017.

[8] Y. Li, D. Jin, P. Hui, Z. Wang, and S. Chen, "Limits of predictability for large-scale urban vehicular mobility," *IEEE T-ITS*, 2014.

[9] J. Wang, Y. Mao, J. Li, Z. Xiong, and W. X. Wang, "Predictability of road traffic and congestion in urban areas," *PLoS ONE*, 2015.

[10] R. Gallotti, A. Bazzani, M. D. Esposti, and S. Rambaldi, "Entropic measures of individual mobility patterns," *JSTAT*, 2013.

[11] T. Takaguchi, M. Nakamura, N. Sato, K. Yano, and N. Masuda, "Predictability of conversation partners," *Physical Review X*, 2011.

[12] R. Sinatra and M. Szell, "Entropy and the predictability of online life," *Entropy*, vol. 16, no. 1, pp. 543–556, 2014.

[13] R. Hanel and S. Thurner, "A comprehensive classification of complex statistical systems and an axiomatic derivation of their entropy and distribution functions," *Epl*, vol. 93, no. 2, 2011.

[14] X. Zhou, Z. Zhao, R. Li, Y. Zhou, and H. Zhang, "The predictability of cellular networks traffic," in *ISCIT 2012*, 2012.

[15] G. Goulet-Langlois, H. N. Koutsopoulos, Z. Zhao, and J. Zhao, "Measuring regularity of individual travel patterns," *IEEE T-ITS*, 2017.

[16] G. Maier, F. Schneider, and A. Feldmann, "A first look at mobile hand-held device traffic," in *PAM*. Springer, 2010.

[17] X. Chen, R. Jin, K. Suh, B. Wang, and W. Wei, "Network performance of smart mobile handhelds in a university campus wifi network," *ACM IMC*, 2012.

[18] U. Kumar, J. Kim, and A. Helmy, "Changing patterns of mobile network (WLAN) usage: Smart-phones vs. laptops," *IWCMC*, 2013.

[19] B. Alipour, L. Tonetto, A. Yi Ding, R. Ketabi, J. Ott, and A. Helmy, "Flutes vs. cellos: Analyzing mobility-traffic correlations in large wlan traces," in *IEEE INFOCOM*, 2018.

[20] A. Vaswani, N. Shazeer, N. Parmar, J. Uszkoreit, L. Jones, A. N. Gomez, Ł. Kaiser, and I. Polosukhin, "Attention is all you need," in *NIPS*, 2017, pp. 5998–6008.

[21] H. Cai, S. R. Kulkarni, and S. Verdú, "Universal entropy estimation via block sorting," pp. 1551–1561, 2004.

[22] Y. Gao, I. Kontoyiannis, and E. Bienenstock, "Estimating the entropy of binary time series: Methodology, some theory and a simulation study," *Entropy*, vol. 10, no. 2, pp. 71–99, 2008.

[23] L. Song, D. Kotz, R. Jain, and X. He, "Evaluating location predictors with extensive Wi-Fi mobility data," in *INFOCOM*, 2004.

[24] X. Lu, E. Wetter, N. Bharti, A. J. Tatem, and L. Bengtsson, "Approaching the limit of predictability in human mobility," *Scientific reports*, vol. 3, 2013.

[25] S. Hochreiter and J. Schmidhuber, "Long short-term memory," *Neural computation*, vol. 9, no. 8, pp. 1735–1780, 1997.

[26] K. Cho, B. Van Merriënboer, C. Gulcehre, D. Bahdanau, F. Bougares, H. Schwenk, and Y. Bengio, "Learning phrase representations using rnn encoder-decoder for statistical machine translation," *arXiv:1406.1078*, 2014.

[27] J. Schmidhuber, "Deep learning in neural networks: An overview," *Neural networks*, vol. 61, pp. 85–117, 2015.

[28] A. Karatzoglou, A. Jablonski, and M. Beigl, "A seq2seq learning approach for modeling semantic trajectories and predicting the next location," in *ACM SIGSPATIAL*, 2018.

[29] B. Alipour, M. Al Qathrady, and A. Helmy, "Learning the relation between mobile encounters and web traffic patterns: A data-driven study," in *ACM MSWIM*, 2018.

Stationarity for the Small World in Motion Mobility Model

Nils Aschenbruck
Institute of Computer Science, University of Osnabrück
aschenbruck@uos.de

Christian Heiden
Institute of Computer Science, University of Osnabrück
cheiden@uos.de

Hanna Döring
Institute of Mathematics, University of Osnabrück
hanna.doering@uos.de

Matthias Schwamborn
Institute of Transportation Systems,
German Aerospace Center (DLR)
matthias.schwamborn@dlr.de

ABSTRACT

Human mobility has been shown to have significant impact on the performance of Opportunistic Networks. For reliable performance evaluation, it is important to make sure the models used are in steady state. The mobility model Small World In Motion (SWIM) incorporates statistical properties of human movements in its results and is, at the same time, easy to configure. However, SWIM is not in steady state. In this paper, we show how a steady state for SWIM can be achieved.

ACM Reference Format:
Nils Aschenbruck, Hanna Döring, Christian Heiden, and Matthias Schwamborn. 2019. Stationarity for the Small World in Motion Mobility Model. In *22nd Int'l ACM Conference on Modeling, Analysis and Simulation of Wireless and Mobile Systems (MSWiM '19), November 25–29, 2019, Miami Beach, FL, USA.* ACM, New York, NY, USA, 5 pages. https://doi.org/10.1145/3345768.3355935

1 INTRODUCTION

Several synthetic mobility models have been proposed during the last two decades (cf. [1]). General models like Random Waypoint (RWP) [6] are easy to use and to analyze, but are known to be unrealistic. Nevertheless, one of the fundamental problems of relevance, especially when models are used in simulations, is non-stationarity. For RWP, this was analyzed and described extensively (cf. [4, 15, 17]). In the last years, there has been significant progress towards more realistic mobility models for human trajectories (cf., e.g., [5, 10]). While these models are far more realistic, stationarity was (to the best of our knowledge) only examined for the Self-similar Least-Action Walk (SLAW) model [10] in [14].

In this paper, we examine the mobility model Small World In Motion (SWIM) [8, 9, 12]. We show that the standard version of SWIM will never reach a deterministic steady state. It fails to satisfy the mixing condition. Thus, we modify SWIM in a way the model reaches a steady state while keeping its basic properties.

The remaining part of this paper is organized as follows: First, we review the related work in Section 2. Then, we provide details on the original SWIM [8, 9, 12] (Section 3). In Section 4, we show how a steady state for SWIM can be reached. Then, we evaluate the impact. Finally, we conclude the paper and point out directions for future research (Section 6).

2 RELATED WORK

2.1 Opportunistic Networks

Mobility models are commonly used to model node movements in mobile networks performance evaluation. In Opportunistic Networks (OppNets), mobile nodes communicate wirelessly with other mobile nodes via a direct one-hop connection. Mobile nodes represent sender, router, and receiver at the same time [13]. Message sending follows a *store-carry-forward* paradigm meaning that if a node A wants to send a message to node C, it may have to send this message to one or more other adjacent nodes B_i which may eventually forward that message to node C. There is typically never an end to end connection between all nodes in the network. To overcome the network partitioning, the movement of the mobile nodes is needed. These mobile nodes *carry* the messages to the next hop. Because of the fact that mobile nodes may occasionally encounter long periods without having other nodes in their communication range, and forwarding protocols have to decide whether or not to take the opportunity to forward a message to another node, these networks are called *opportunistic* networks. Because of the dynamic network structure, the delivery rate of OppNets depends heavily on the movements of its mobile nodes. Thus, a sophisticated selection of a suitable mobility model is crucial for the simulative performance evaluation of OppNets. One important metric is the Inter-Contact Time (ICT). The ICT is a contact-related metric describing the amount of time that lies between two successive contacts of two people. In other words, it describes how long it takes for two individuals to see each other again. Chaintreau *et al.* [3] discovered that the distributions of the ICTs also follows a power-law.

2.2 Steady States

A priori the mobility models begin with any initial distribution. Therefore, it is not clear if a steady state exists and it is likely that the distribution differs from the invariant distribution. Since one is typically interested in the properties of the steady state, one often does not take the first hours of simulations the so-called burn-time into account. But, of course, discarding initial data for some time interval does not guarantee a system in steady state by itself. Therefore, it is important to either start the simulation in the invariant distribution or to study mixing times indicating how long the burn-time should be. For RWP, [17] pointed out this problem. In case of RWP and generalizations of it, the existence of the invariant distribution was proved and explicit formulas are known, where in [11, 15, 16] renewal theory is applied, [2] uses palm calculus, and [4] prove an ergodic theorem. In [14] the authors provide algorithms how to sample steady state locations and pause-times in SLAW by a Chi-Square test.

3 BACKGROUND

The mobility model Small World In Motion (SWIM) [8, 9, 12] is an easily configurable social moblity model for realistic human movements. The model is based on two assumptions: humans tend to visit places that are *popular* and *nearby* their home. These criteria are used to evaluate, equal in size, squared cells C that cover the whole simulation area and contain locations where nodes can move to. Additionally, both criteria can be weighted with a factor $\alpha \in [0, 1]$ by

$$\text{weight}(C) = \alpha \cdot f_{\text{nearby}}(C) + (1 - \alpha) \cdot f_{\text{popular}}(C) \qquad (1)$$

where f_{nearby} is small for large distances between the node's home and C while f_{popular} depends on the amount of people the node has seen in C before. The greater the value for α, the more likely nodes choose to visit locations nearby their homes and the less their decision depends on the popularity of a place.

The simulation area itself is of squared size as well, resulting the same number of row and column cells. The diagonal size of a single cell can be specified with a parameter r that at the same time sets the nodes transmission range. This guarantees that two nodes that are in the same cell are in communication range of each other. However, it is also possible for nodes to communicate with each other even though they are not in the same cell since cells are only used for assigning popularity values to regions on the simulation area. The actual decision on whether two nodes are in communication range of each other is based on a circular area around every individual node with its radius being equal to the specified parameter r.

At the beginning of the simulation, the simulation area is divided into squared cells depending on the transmission range provided by the user. Then, all mobile nodes are placed in a random location on the simulation area, their so-called *home*. Every node has an individual function that contains weights. These weights represent the preference for visiting a particular cell within the simulation area. The weights are calculated with the formula given in Equation (1) where the distance function is calculated by the shortest distance, or *flight distance*, between the home of the node and the cellcenter of the other cell:

$$f_{\text{nearby}}(C) = \frac{1}{m_1} \cdot \frac{1}{\left(1 + \frac{1}{r} \|h_A - C\|\right)^2},$$

where $m_1 = \max \frac{1}{(1+\frac{1}{r}\|h_A - C_j\|)^2}$ is the maximum over all cells C_j in the simulation area. Initially, the popularity function is 0 for every cell.

After initialization and given that the simulation time is not over and a node's waiting time ends, the node selects a target cell with a probability that is proportional to the assigned weight in its popularity function. In this cell, it chooses a random location

to which the node will move in constant time following a straight line. When the node reaches its destination location, it counts the number of nodes that are in communication range and updates the popularity function for that cell accordingly. The distance function stays constant. Finally, it waits for a certain amount of time until it starts to move again choosing the next destination by the new popularity function.

It remains to explain the popularity function. Two nodes are in the communication range of each other, if the Euclidean distance between them is smaller or equal to their transmission range r. Let d be the nodes' density of the network depending on the transmission range r, the number of nodes n and the simulation area A

$$d = \frac{\pi \cdot r^2 \cdot n}{|A|}.$$

Note that in [9] $|A|$ is set to 1 by definition.

Then, we can define the popularity function by

$$f_{\text{popular}}(C) = \frac{1}{m_2}\left(1 + \frac{1}{d}\#\{\text{nodes seen in cell } C \text{ until now}\}\right),$$

with $m_2 = \max\left(1 + \frac{1}{d}\#\{\text{nodes seen in cell } C_j \text{ until now}\}\right)$ being the maximum over all cells C_j in the simulation area.

In Equation (2), $t_w(x)$ represents the waiting time for a node given a uniform random variable $x \in [0, 1]$. The waiting time upper bound can be set with a parameter T_w. The value e_w is another parameter that controls the slope of the power-law. This value is chosen such that the shape of the resulting wait time function matches the wait time distribution of real traces.

$$t_w(x) := \begin{cases} (1 - x)^{\frac{-1}{e_w + 1}} & \text{if} \quad t_w(x) \le T_w, \\ T_w & \text{else} \end{cases} \qquad (2)$$

By drawing x from a uniform distribution, t_w is more likely to render "short" waittimes than "long" ones.

Due to the bounded waiting time function and the fact that nodes move between two locations in constant time, the authors of SWIM prove that the ICT distribution has an exponential cut off, i. e., it follows an exponential distribution after a certain threshold value. Furthermore, they showed in an evaluation of three different scenarios that the ICT distribution follows a power-law before that threshold value.

4 ENSURING STATIONARITY

It is desirable to conduct simulations in a steady state (cf. Section 2.2). For SWIM, to the best of our knowledge, this challenge has not been addressed before.

4.1 Problem Statement

To motivate this challenge, we generate traces of length 360 days based on the parameters for InfoCom05 from [9]. We want to analyze the distance traveled per node for different intervals of time and define the following metric. Let t_0, t_1, t_2 be points in time and l_{t_0, t_1}^k the distance traveled of a node k in interval $[t_0, t_1]$. We define $\text{ldiff}_{t_i}^k$ for a point in time t_i and a node k as the difference between the distances traveled in two successive intervals.

$$\text{ldiff}_{t_i}^k = |l_{t_{i-2}, t_{i-1}}^k - l_{t_{i-1}, t_i}^k| \qquad (3)$$

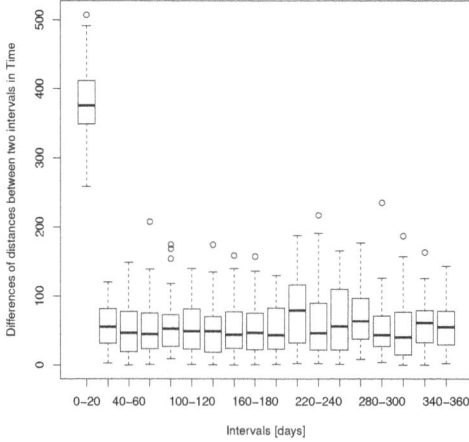

Figure 1: Difference of walking distances between two consecutive intervals of time (InfoCom05, interval length 20 days).

In figure 1, we show the distribution of $\mathrm{ldiff}_{t_i}^k$ over all nodes k (visualized as boxplot). It can be seen that the values in the first interval are much larger than the following ones. This fact is independent of the length of the interval and the parameters of the scenario. There seems to be a decay in the walking distance over time. At least, the figure clearly shows that the model is not in steady state at the beginning. This motivated us to take a closer look on the stationarity of SWIM.

The former SWIM process (cf. Section 3) including all time-dependent popularity functions and the waiting times at each time t is a Markov process, but non-irreducible (e.g., the state where all popularity functions are zero will only appear in the first step) and fails to satisfy the mixing condition: The movement will always depend on the first decisions, where people meet randomly and form a cluster afterwards. Therefore, one can not state a deterministic distribution function for the steady state, as e.g., by the ergodicity of the RWP in [15]. The idea for the rest is to put these random formation of clusters in a pre-computation.

4.2 Approach

We are aiming at a steady state, meaning that the distribution of the walkers does not vary in time any more. As described in Section 3, in SWIM the distribution of the next waypoint depends on two functions: The deterministic function f_{nearby} is constant in time, where f_{popular} depends on the movements of all participants implying that it varies in time. In a steady state, we ask for the convergence of the popularity function to a deterministic function in probability. Therefore, our approach is to study the fluctuations of the popularity function and fix it close to steady state. We study the two variants, where we fix

variant a) one popularity function for each node
variant b) the same averaged popularity function for all nodes.

For $t \geq 0$, we define the process Y_t by the vector of the position of each participant at time t and their waiting times at t. The distribution of the position is stationary due to the fixed popularity function, where the distribution function F_W of the waiting times is given by the bounded Pareto distribution (bounded power law) with parameter β, minimum p_{min} and cutoff c (the maximal waiting time) for $t > 0$. In order to adopt the random beginning of our simulation, we have to define the distribution of the waiting time in zero T_i for node i. Let W be a bounded Pareto distributed random variable independently of all other random variables. Due to renewal theory the distribution function is given by

$$
\begin{aligned}
\mathbb{P}(T_i \leq x) &= \frac{\int_0^x \left(1 - F_W(t)\right) dt}{\mathbb{E}[W] + 1} \\
&= \frac{\int_0^{p_{\mathrm{min}}} 1\, dt + \frac{1}{1-(\frac{p_{\mathrm{min}}}{c})^\beta} \int_{p_{\mathrm{min}}}^x (\frac{p_{\mathrm{min}}}{t})^\beta - (\frac{p_{\mathrm{min}}}{c})^\beta dt}{\frac{p_{\mathrm{min}}^\beta}{1-(\frac{p_{\mathrm{min}}}{c})^\beta} \frac{\beta}{\beta-1} \left(\frac{1}{p_{\mathrm{min}}^{\beta-1}} - \frac{1}{c^{\beta-1}}\right) + 1} \\
&= \frac{\frac{\beta}{\beta-1} p_{\mathrm{min}} - \frac{p_{\mathrm{min}}^\beta}{\beta-1} x^{1-\beta} - (\frac{p_{\mathrm{min}}}{c})^\beta x}{p_{\mathrm{min}}^\beta \frac{\beta}{\beta-1} + 1 - \frac{1}{\beta-1}(\frac{p_{\mathrm{min}}}{c})^\beta (\beta c + \beta - 1)}
\end{aligned} \tag{4}
$$

for $p_{\mathrm{min}} \leq x \leq c$ and $\beta > 1$ as well as

$$
\mathbb{P}(T_i = 0) = \frac{1}{\frac{p_{\mathrm{min}}^\beta}{1-(\frac{p_{\mathrm{min}}}{c})^\beta} \frac{\beta}{\beta-1} \left(\frac{1}{p_{\mathrm{min}}^{\beta-1}} - \frac{1}{c^{\beta-1}}\right) + 1}
$$

for the probability of the event that node i is on its way to a new cell. The summand +1 in the denominator takes into consideration that (at time zero) some nodes might be on their way to the next cell, analogous to [14, p. 328].

Fixing the popularity function (for each participant or one for all participants) the discretized process $(Y_{t+ic})_i$, $i = 1, 2, 3, \ldots$, is per definition a stationary Markov chain for any $t > 0$, meaning that the law of Y_{t+ic} equals the law of $Y_{t+(i+1)c}$ for all i using the constant popularity function(s) and the cutoff time c of the waiting time. So the simulation directly starts in the steady state, meaning that no additional initialization (or burn) is needed.

For the process $(Y_t)_{t \in (0,\infty)}$, the strong mixing coefficient is defined by

$$
\alpha(s) := \sup \Big\{ \big|P(A \cap B) - P(A)P(B)\big| : 0 < t < \infty,
$$
$$
A \in Y_0^t, B \in Y_{t+s}^\infty \Big\}.
$$

Clearly, due to the cutoff time of the waiting times we have $\alpha(s) \to 0$ for $s \to \infty$. Therefore, the stochastic process $(Y_t)_t$ is strong mixing and, in particular, ergodic. Ergodicity implies that the Markov chain time average along sample paths is equal to the ensemble average.

The following calculation holds true for SWIM and our proposed simplified SWIM model. The contact time is the time two nodes stay in contact before one of them moves away. For small α, nodes prefer popular places, such that the typical location to meet will be in the cluster. For bigger α, it will more and more depend on the nodes' homes and two nodes will typically meet in areas close to their homes. Therefore, the distribution of the remaining common waiting time of both walkers is a lower bound for the contact time: Say both walkers meet in the largest cluster, the possibility to move

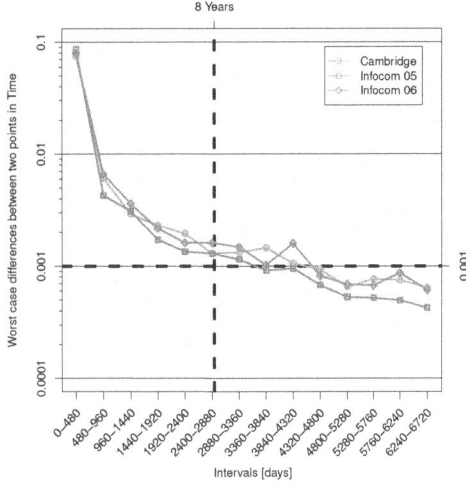

Figure 2: Percentage of Contacts

and remain in contact is positive. This implies that we have a lower bound for T_C if we calculate the remaining waiting time at a random time

$$\mathbb{P}(T_C \leq x) \leq \frac{\int_0^x \left(1 - F_W(t)\right)dt}{\mathbb{E}[W]} = \frac{x}{\mathbb{E}[W]} \text{ for } 0 \leq x < p_{\min}$$

and for $p_{\min} \leq x \leq c$

$$
\begin{aligned}
\mathbb{P}(T_C \leq x) &= \frac{\frac{\beta}{\beta-1}p_{\min} - \frac{p_{\min}^{\beta}}{\beta-1}x^{1-\beta} - (\frac{p_{\min}}{c})^{\beta}x}{p_{\min}^{\beta}\frac{\beta}{\beta-1}\left(\frac{1}{p_{\min}^{\beta-1}} - \frac{1}{c^{\beta-1}}\right)} \\
&= \frac{\beta p_{\min}^{1-\beta} - x^{1-\beta} - \frac{\beta-1}{c^{\beta}}x}{\beta(p_{\min}^{1-\beta} - c^{1-\beta})}
\end{aligned}
\tag{5}
$$

as shown in (4) with the only difference that there is no +1 in the denominator (we know that both nodes meet, i.e. stay at the cell for some time), see [14, eqn. (14)].

For n participants, let $i(t)$ be the location of the ith device at time t, $1 \leq i \leq n$. The typical number n_C of nodes in a cell C is given by $\mathbb{E}[n_C] = \sum_{i=1}^{n} \mathbb{P}(i \text{ chooses cell } C)$. Let the constant popularity function for node i and cell C be $w_i(C)$, then $\mathbb{E}[n_C] = \sum_{i=1}^{n} \frac{w_i(C)}{\sum_{j=1}^{N} w_i(C_j)}$. Note that even for the averaged popularity function the weights are not equal for the different nodes, because they include the distance function.

Let two nodes A and B leave visibility after seeing each other at time 0, such that one node moves into a new cell and leaves visibility. Let $A(t)$ and $B(t)$ be the positions of the nodes A and B at time t, respectively. The ICT is defined by

$$T_I = \inf\{t > 0 : \|A(t) - B(t)\| \leq r\}.$$

The exponential decay dichotomy is not changed by our version, so the tail of the ICT T_I has an exponential decay which can be proved similar to [9, p. 4]. Say node A moves at time 0 to a different cell. Node B has a remaining waiting time T_B distributed as defined in (5).

4.3 Model Extension

As before, the first step of SWIM is to fix the home cells in a precomputation. Now, we calculate the popularity function in a precomputation, too. We let run the original SWIM, which adapts the popularity function after each movement. In order to end the precomputation we need to define a threshold. Let $c_{i,j}^t(n)$ represent the number of contacts in a cell (i, j) the node n encounters until time t, whereas $C^t(n)$ denotes the sum of all contacts node n encounters in all cells until time t. With $y_{i,j}^t(n) = \frac{c_{i,j}^t(n)}{C^t(n)}$ we define the percentage of contacts a node n had in a cell (i, j) with respect to all cells. For determining the threshold of the pre-computation, we want to analyze the amount of change of y because our tests showed that over time the value of y will converge to a certain value. Therefore, we define $d_{i,j}^{t_0, t_1}(n)$ that calculates the amount of change for two points in time:

$$d_{i,j}^{t_0, t_1}(n) = \left| y_{i,j}^{t_1}(n) - y_{i,j}^{t_0}(n) \right|$$

Plotting the results yielded that the amount of change is clearly getting smaller over time. In order to compute the threshold we decided to only use the maximum values of d to get a worst case estimation (also seen in figure 2):

$$d_{max}^{t_0, t_1} = \max_{\forall(i,j)\forall n} \left\{ \left| y_{i,j}^{t_1}(n) - y_{i,j}^{t_0}(n) \right| \right\}, \tag{6}$$

see also the approach in [7] for Kolmogorov-Smirnov testing in multivariate settings.

Figure 2 shows d_{max} on a long time scale of several years. All three models show significant differences during the first year. Here, the pre-computation can stop after 8 years. As the pre-computation only needs to be done once and can be saved/reloaded, there is no negative impact on the simulation performance and/or scalability.

5 EVALUATION

For the evaluation of algorithms and protocols in OppNets typical contact-related metrics like the ICT, CD, and the absolute number of contacts are relevant. The ICT provides an estimate for the communication delay in the network, as it is the time between two consecutive contacts of the same pair of two moving nodes. The CD is the time two mobility nodes are in communication range of each other and gives an impression on the amount of information that can be exchanged between them. The absolute number of contacts is used to show the frequency of contacts of the network, as many contacts represent many opportunities to forward data.

We performed an evaluation similar to the one provided for the original SWIM [9]. We used the same scenarios (Cambridge, InfoCom05, and InfoCom06) and compared the original SWIM with our extended variant. We performed the pre-computation and derived the popularity functions per node. For the evaluation, we considered both variants: (a) with individual popularity functions per node, and (b) with a popularity function averaged over all nodes. The second variant has the advantage that it is easier to parametrize and reproduce, as less pre-computation data needs to be transferred. The disadvantage may be a worse fit to the original SWIM.

The results are shown in figure 3. Due to space limitation, we only show plots for InfoCom05. The Empirical Complementary Cumulative Distribution Functions (ECCDFs) of ICTs and CDs for all

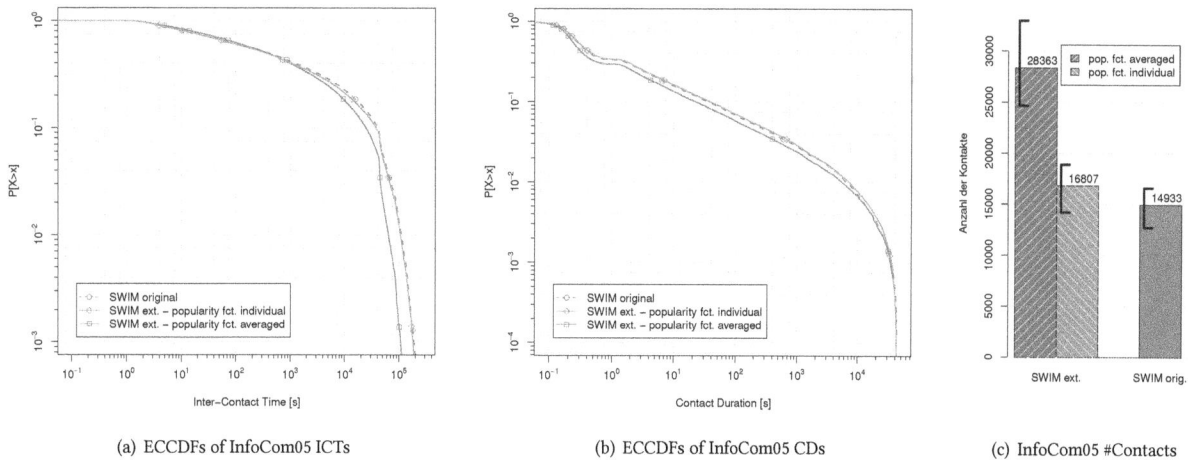

(a) ECCDFs of InfoCom05 ICTs

(b) ECCDFs of InfoCom05 CDs

(c) InfoCom05 #Contacts

Figure 3: Contact metrics (CD, ICT, number of contacts) for InfoCom05

three variants are very similar. The individual popularity functions (variant (a)) show a slightly better fit to original SWIM. However, the differences of the averaged SWIM seem to be neglectable.

The largest difference can be observed for the number of contacts. If the popularity function is averaged, the number of contacts is significantly higher. The reason for this is that popular places are (when averaged) popular for everyone. Thus, there is a higher likelihood to meet there. With individual popularity functions, each nodes has its own popular places. If these are not popular for others as well, there is less likelihood to meet others.

Overall, our extension in the variant with individual popularity functions matches the properties of the original SWIM sufficiently. As it has the big advantage of a stationary distribution and no decay in the number of contacts over time, we recommend to use this variant.

6 CONCLUSION AND FUTURE WORK

The mobility model Small World In Motion (SWIM) incorporates statistical properties of human movements in its results and is, at the same time, easy to configure. However, SWIM is not in steady state. In this paper, we have shown that the standard version of SWIM will never reach a deterministic steady state. It fails to satisfy the mixing condition. We have successfully modified SWIM in such a way that the model reaches a steady state while keeping its basic properties. Our evaluation shows that the extended variant matches the properties of the original SWIM successfully.

In the future, we plan to extend SWIM to include geographic restriction and to add more realistic signal propagation modeling. We also plan to work on alternative approaches from a mathematical perspective.

ACKNOWLEDGMENTS

This work was supported in part by the German Research Foundation (DFG), Project No. AS341/3-2 as well as the "Stifterverband für die Deutsche Wissenschaft" (H170 5701 5020 20951).

REFERENCES

[1] Nils Aschenbruck, Aarti Munjal, and Tracy Camp. 2011. Trace-based Mobility Modeling for Multi-hop Wireless Networks. *Computer Communications* 34, 6 (2011), 704–714.
[2] Jean-Yves Le Boudec. 2007. Understanding the simulation of mobility models with palm calculus. *Performance Evaluation* 64, 2 (2007), 126–146.
[3] Augustin Chaintreau, Pan Hui, Jon Crowcroft, Christophe Diot, Richard Gass, and James Scott. 2007. Impact of Human Mobility on Opportunistic Forwarding Algorithms. *IEEE Transactions on Mobile Computing* 6, 6 (2007), 606–620.
[4] Hanna Döring, Gabriel Faraud, and Wolfgang König. 2016. Connection times in large ad-hoc mobile networks. *Bernoulli* 22, 4 (2016), 2143–2176.
[5] Marta C. González, César A. Hidalgo, and Albert-László Barabási. 2008. Understanding Individual Human Mobility Patterns. *Nature* 453, 7196 (2008), 779–782.
[6] David B Johnson and David A Maltz. 1996. Dynamic source routing in ad hoc wireless networks. In *Mobile Computing*. 153–181.
[7] Ana Justel, Daniel Pe na, and Rubén Zamar. 1997. *Statist. Probab. Lett.* 35, 3 (1997), 251–259.
[8] Sokol Kosta, Alessandro Mei, and Julinda Stefa. 2010. Small World in Motion (SWIM): Modeling Communities in Ad-Hoc Mobile Networking. In *Proc. of the Conference on Sensor, Mesh and Ad Hoc Communications and Networks (SECON)*.
[9] Sokol Kosta, Alessandro Mei, and Julinda Stefa. 2014. Large-Scale Synthetic Social Mobile Networks with SWIM. *IEEE Transactions on Mobile Computing* 13, 1 (2014), 116–129.
[10] Kyunghan Lee, Seongik Hong, Seong Joon Kim, Injong Rhee, and Song Chong. 2012. SLAW: Self-Similar Least-Action Human Walk. *IEEE/ACM Transactions on Networking* 20, 2 (2012), 515–529.
[11] Guolong Lin, Guevara Noubir, and Rajmohan Rajamaran. 2004. Mobility models for ad hoc network simulation. In *Proc. of the Conference on Computer Communications (INFOCOM)*, Vol. 1. 463.
[12] Alessandro Mei and Julinda Stefa. 2009. SWIM: A Simple Model to Generate Small Mobile Worlds. In *Proc. of the Conference on Computer Communications (INFOCOM)*. 2106–2113.
[13] Vinícius F.S. Mota, Felipe D. Cunha, Daniel F. Macedo, José M.S. Nogueira, and Antonio A.F. Loureiro. 2014. Protocols, Mobility Models and Tools in Opportunistic Networks: A Survey. *Elsevier Computer Communications* 48 (2014), 5–19.
[14] Aarti Munjal, William C. Navidi, and Tracy Camp. 2014. Steady-State of The SLAW Mobility Model. *Journal of Communications* 9, 4 (2014), 322–331.
[15] William Navidi and Tracy Camp. 2004. Stationary Distributions for the Random Waypoint Mobility Model. *IEEE Transactions on Mobile Computing* 3, 1 (2004), 99–108.
[16] William Navidi, Tracy Camp, and Nick Bauer. 2004. Improving the Accuracy of Random Waypoint Simulations through Steady-State Initialization. *Proc. of the Conference on Modeling and Simulation* (2004), 319–326.
[17] Jungkeun Yoon, Mingyan Liu, and Brian Noble. 2003. Random Waypoint Considered Harmful. *Proc. of the Conference on Computer Communications (INFOCOM)* (2003), 1312–1321.

Dynamically Tuning IEEE 802.11's Contention Window Using Machine Learning

Yalda Edalat
Department of Computer Science and Engineering,
University of California Santa Cruz, USA
yalda@soe.ucsc.edu

Katia Obraczka
Department of Computer Science and Engineering,
University of California Santa Cruz, USA
katia@soe.ucsc.edu

ABSTRACT

The IEEE 802.11's binary exponential backoff (BEB) algorithm plays a critical role in the throughput performance and fair channel allocation of IEEE 802.11 networks. In particular, one of BEB algorithm's parameters, the *Contention Window* determines how long a node needs to wait before it (re)transmits data. Consequently, choosing adequate values of the *Contention Window* is crucial for IEEE 802.11's performance. In this paper, we introduce a simple, yet effective machine learning approach to adjust the value of IEEE 802.11's *Contention Window* based on present- as well as recent past network contention conditions. Using a wide range of network scenarios and conditions, we show that our approach outperforms both 802.11's BEB as well as an existing contention window adjustment technique that only considers the last two transmissions. Our results indicate that our contention window adaptation algorithm is able to deliver consistently higher average throughput, lower end-to-end delay, as well as improved fairness.

KEYWORDS

machine learning, contention window, IEEE 802.11, backoff, experts, Fixed-share

ACM Reference Format:
Yalda Edalat and Katia Obraczka. 2019. Dynamically Tuning IEEE 802.11's Contention Window Using Machine Learning. In *22nd Int'l ACM Conference on Modeling, Analysis and Simulation of Wireless and Mobile Systems (MSWiM '19), November 25–29, 2019, Miami Beach, FL, USA.* ACM, New York, NY, USA, 8 pages. https://doi.org/10.1145/3345768.3355920

1 INTRODUCTION

The IEEE 802.11 standard, also known as WiFi, specifies two types of MAC protocols, namely the Distributed Coordination Function (DCF) and the Point Coordination Function (PCF). DCF is IEEE 802.11's most widely used medium access mechanism and uses the Carrier Sensing Multiple Access/Collision Avoidance (CSMA/CA) protocol[1]. CSMA/CA arbitrates access to the shared communication

---

[1]DCF provides two modes of operation: the *Base Mode* which uses CSMA and the *Collision Avoidance Mode*, which uses CSMA/CA.

medium using a contention-based, on-demand distributed mechanism. One of the key components of IEEE 802.11's DCF is the Binary Exponential Backoff (BEB) algorithm which was introduced to mitigate channel contention and prevent collisions of packets simultaneously transmitted by multiple stations. It delays the retransmission of a collided packet by a random time, chosen uniformly over n slots ($n > 1$), where n is a parameter called *Contention Window*, or (CW). The BEB algorithm works as follows: CW is initially set based on a pre-specified minimum value, (CW_{min}). If a collision happens, the station chooses an exponentially increased CW until it reaches CW's pre-specified maximum value (CW_{max}). As such, CW can significantly impact IEEE 802.11's performance. Choosing small CW values may result in more collisions and backoffs. On the other hand, choosing large CW may result in unnecessary idle airtime and additional delay. In either case, the channel is not used efficiently. Therefore, the value of CW should be adjusted considering the actual level of contention in the channel.

In this paper, we develop a simple, yet effective machine learning approach based on the *Fixed-Share* technique [8] [9] to adjust the value of CW based on recent past network contention. Unlike the original BEB algorithm which increases or decreases CW based solely on the status of the most recently transmitted packet, our method also accounts for recent network contention conditions in addition to last packet's transmission status. We evaluated our contention window adaptation algorithm using a wide range of scenarios including infrastructure-based as well as multi-hop ad-hoc environments. Our results indicate that our contention window adaptation algorithm is able to deliver consistently higher average throughput, lower end-to-end delay, as well as improved fairness.

The rest of this paper is organized as follows. Section 2 provides a brief overview of IEEE 802.11's Binary Exponential Backoff (BEB) algorithm and presents related work. Our machine learning based approach to dynamically adjust 802.11's contention window is described in Section 3. Section 4 and Section 5 present our experimental methodology and results, respectively. Section 6 concludes the paper and discusses directions for future work.

2 BACKGROUND AND RELATED WORK

IEEE 802.11's Binary Exponential Backoff (BEB) algorithm was introduced in order to decrease the chance of collision of frames simultaneously (re)transmitted by multiple stations. In the original BEB algorithm, if a node wants to transmit a data frame, it first senses the channel for a *DCF Inter frame Space (DIFS) interval* to check whether the channel is idle. If the channel is sensed idle, the node transmits the data packet immediately. Otherwise, i.e., if the channel is busy, the node selects a random backoff time value between 0 and CW (as shown in Equation 1) to re-try and avoid collisions. The backoff time is decremented every slot thereafter when the node senses the medium idle. When the backoff time reaches zero, the node can then initiate transmission.

$$Backoff\ time = random\ [0, CW] \times slot\ time \qquad (1)$$

If the transmission is unsuccessful, CW will be doubled for the next transmission up to a maximum value specified by CW_{max}. In the case of a successful transmission, CW is reset to CW_{min}.

A number of drawbacks with the original BEB algorithm have been identified. Fairness is one of them; for instance, resetting CW to CW_{min} after a successful transmission may cause the node who succeeds in transmitting to dominate the channel for an arbitrarily long period of time. As a result, other nodes may suffer from severe short-term unfairness. Additionally, the current state of the network (e.g., load) should be taken into account in selecting the most appropriate backoff interval.

Motivated by BEB's impact on the performance of 802.11, considerable attention from network researchers and practitioners has focused on optimizing IEEE 802.11's backoff algorithm.

We categorize related work on improving IEEE 802.11's BEB performance in two groups: the first group focuses on how to increase or decrease the size of CW, whereas the second group targets setting the values of CW_{min} and CW_{max}, i.e., CW's upper and lower bounds. Due to space constraints, we only list references to efforts more directly related to our work in each group.

Increasing/decreasing CW

Under this category we highlight the MACAW protocol [3], the History-Based Adaptive Backoff (HBAB) algorithm [1], the Inverse Binary Exponential Backoff (iBEB) approach [2], the Binary Negative-Exponential Backoff (BNEB) [10] protocol, and the New Binary Exponential Back-off (N-BEB) [14].

Setting CW's lower and upper bounds

Another group of papers focuses on optimizing the values of CW_{min} and CW_{max}. Approaches that fall under this category include IEEE 802.11e, [11], and [7].

Using machine learning to improve network protocol performance

Recently, machine learning (ML) techniques have gained significant traction and have been used in a wide range of applications. Specifically in the context on computer networking performance management, in [12], the Fixed-Share algorithm is used to estimate TCP's round-trip time. In our prior work [5], we estimate collision rate using an algorithm called SENSE which employs a combination of Fixed-Share and Exponentially-Weighted Moving Average (EWMA). In [6], SENSE estimates network contention which is then used to enable/disable RTS/CTS in IEEE 802.11 networks.

3 AUTOMATICALLY ADJUSTING IEEE 802.11'S CONGESTION WINDOW

In this section, we introduce the proposed machine learning based contention window adaptation approach. As the complexity and heterogeneity of networks and their applications grow, the use of

ML techniques to adequately manage network in order to meet application requirements becomes increasingly attractive for a number of reasons. For instance, machine learning algorithms can learn and adapt to network and application dynamics autonomically. Some ML techniques do not require a-priori knowledge of the operating environment; they acquire this knowledge as they operate and adjust accordingly without needing complex mathematical models of the system.

To the best of our knowledge, our proposed algorithm is the first to use ML to automatically adjust IEEE 802.11's CW based on packet transmission history. We should point out that one of our main goals was to design an algorithm that achieves significant performance gains, yet is simple, low cost, low overhead, and easy to implement. To this end, we designed a simple, yet effective algorithm based on the *Fixed-Share algorithm* [8] to tune IEEE 802.11's CW. We start with a brief description of the Fixed-Share algorithm.

3.1 Fixed-Share Algorithm

The Fixed-Share algorithm is part of the Multiplicative Weight algorithmic family which has shown to yield performance improvements in a variety of on-line problems [8], [12]. This family of algorithms combines predictions of a set of experts $\{x_1, x_2, ..., x_N\}$ to calculate the overall prediction denoted by $\hat{y}_t$. Each expert has a weight $\{w_1, w_2, ..., w_N\}$ representing the impact of that expert on the overall predictor. Based on the difference between each expert's prediction and the real data represented by y_t, the weight of each expert is updated [5]. Algorithm 1 shows Fixed-Share Experts' pseudo-code. Each expert is initialized with a value within the range of the quantity to be predicted and the weight of all experts is initialized to $\frac{1}{N}$, where N is the number of experts. At every iteration, based on each expert's current weight and value, the prediction for the next trial is calculated as shown in the **Prediction** step of the algorithm. The **Loss Function** step then checks how good the prediction of each expert was using a loss function $L_{i,t}(x_i, y_t)$. The result of the loss function loss for each expert is used in the **Exponential Update** step to adjust the experts' weights by multiplying the current weight of the $i - th$ expert by $e^{-\eta \times L_{i,t}(x_i, y_t)}$. The *learning rate* η is used to determine how fast the updates will take effect, dictating how rapidly the weights of misleading experts will be reduced. Finally, in the **Sharing Weights** step, a fixed fraction of the weights of experts that are performing well is shared among the other experts. The goal of this step is to prevent large differences among experts' weights [9]. The amount of sharing can be adjusted through the *sharing rate* parameter α.

3.2 Proposed Approach

We propose a modified version of the Fixed-Share algorithm to dynamically set IEEE 802.11's CW. More specifically, as illustrated in Algorithm 2, we design loss- and gain functions that account for current network conditions. Our proposed technique works as follows. Similarly to the standard Fixed-Share algorithm (Algorithm 1), in the **Initialization** step in Algorithm 2, the weight of all experts is set to $\frac{1}{N}$, where N is the number of experts. Each expert is assigned a fixed value within the range of $[CW_{min}, CW_{max}]$. In our current implementation, we assign the values of 15, 22, 33, 50,

---

Algorithm 1 Fixed-Share Algorithm

Parameters:
$$\eta > 0, 0 \le \alpha \le 1$$

Initialization:
$$w_{1,1} = ... = w_{N,1} = \tfrac{1}{N}$$

Prediction:
$$\hat{y}_t = \frac{\sum_1^N w_{i,t} \times x_i}{\sum_1^N w_{i,t}}$$

Loss Function:
$$L_{i,t}(x_i, y_t) = \begin{cases} (x_i - y_t)^2 & , x_i \ge y_t \\ 2 \times y_t & , x_i < y_t \end{cases}$$

Exponential Update:
$$\acute{w}_{i,t} = w_{i,t} \times e^{-\eta \times L_{i,t}(x_i, y_t)}$$

Sharing Weights:
$$Pool = \sum_{i=1}^N \alpha \times \acute{w}_{i,t} \qquad w_{i,t+1} = (1-\alpha) \times \acute{w}_{i,t} + \tfrac{1}{N} \times Pool$$

75, 113, 170, 256, 384, 576, 865, and 1023 to 12 experts forming a geometric sequence with ratio of 1.5.

The reason we pick these values is that first of all we wanted to keep CW_{min} and CW_{max} unchanged according to the IEEE 802.11 standard. Furthermore, since BEB's adjustment is considered to be quite aggressive [3], we employ a multiplicative factor of 1.5 which yields less drastic backoff process.

Additionally, we have experimented with different numbers and values of experts and have not seen any significant change in the results. Due to space limitations, we do not include these results.

In the **CW Calculation** step, $\hat{CW}_t$, which is CW's estimate for time t, is calculated based on the current value of the experts and their weights. Clearly, experts with more weight will have more influence on the next CW. In the **Loss/Gain Function** step, the performance of all experts is evaluated based on their value, $\hat{CW}_t$, and whether the previous packet transmission was successful or not.

Loss/Gain Function: The loss and gain functions are designed to adjust CW based on present- as well as recent past network conditions. Our loss/gain function works as follows: if a packet is transmitted successfully, it means that there may be additional bandwidth available in the network. Therefore, we reduce the weight of the experts higher than $\hat{CW}_t$ because they are less aggressive experts. Weight reduction is done proportional to the difference between the value of that expert and CW which means the higher the expert is, the more aggressively its weight will be reduced. We also increase the weight of experts lower than $\hat{CW}_t$ because we want to push for potentially more aggressive CW. This weight increase is done proportional to the value of the expert. Experts with value closer to the current CW will experience higher weight increase. For the experts with value much lower than the current CW, the risk of failure is higher, therefore their weight increase is lower. These weight decrease and increase of experts will result in a lower value for the next CW and, as a result, the next transmission will be scheduled more aggressively.

Analogously, in the case of unsuccessful transmissions, the loss/gain function will increase the weight of experts with values higher than $\hat{CW}_t$ and reduce the weight of experts with values lower than $\hat{CW}_t$.

This will result in higher CW for the next packet transmission and less chance of collision.

Overhead: The overhead incurred by our algorithm is a function of the number of experts used. There is a cost-performance tradeoff between the number of experts and how well the algorithm can capture network dynamics. However, as previously discussed, there is a diminishing returns effect, wherein beyond a certain number of experts, there is minimal performance impact. As far as storage overhead, additional storage is used to keep the experts' values and their weights. As for computation overhead, assuming the contention window is adjusted at every attempted transmission, the **CW Calcultion**, **Loss/Gain Function**, and **Sharing Weights** steps in Algorithm 2 are executed. These involve simple arithmetic operations and are not computationally onerous, which are consistent with one of our main design goals, i.e., developing a simple, light-weight algorithm that can run at line rate. In fact, one of our directions for future work is to implement our algorithm in a real testbed to validate its performance.

Algorithm 2 Proposed Algorithm

Initialization:
$$w_{1,1} = ... = w_{N,1} = \tfrac{1}{N}$$
$$x_1 = CW_1, x_2 = CW_2, ..., x_N = CW_N,$$

CW Calculation:
$$\hat{CW}_t = \lfloor \frac{\sum_1^N w_{i,t} \times x_i}{\sum_1^N w_{i,t}} \rfloor$$

Loss/Gain Function:
- If packet received successfully:
$$w_{i,t+1} = \begin{cases} [1 - \frac{x_i - \hat{CW}_t}{x_i}] \times w_{i,t} & , x_i > \hat{CW}_t \\ [1 + \frac{x_i}{\hat{CW}_t}] \times w_{i,t} & , x_i \le \hat{CW}_t \end{cases}$$
- If packet is not received successfully:
$$w_{i,t+1} = \begin{cases} [1 + \frac{\hat{CW}_t}{x_i}] \times w_{i,t} & , x_i > \hat{CW}_t \\ [1 - \frac{\hat{CW}_t - x_i}{\hat{CW}_t}] \times w_{i,t} & , x_i \le \hat{CW}_t \end{cases}$$

Sharing Weights:
$$Pool = \sum_{i=1}^N \alpha \times \acute{w}_{i,t} \qquad w_{i,t+1} = (1-\alpha) \times \acute{w}_{i,t} + \tfrac{1}{N} \times Pool$$

---

4 EXPERIMENTAL METHODOLOGY

In this section, we describe our experimental setup including the scenarios, traffic loads, as well as performance metrics used when evaluating the proposed approach. We compare the performance of our technique against both the original IEEE 802.11 contention window adjustment technique as well as the History-Based Adaptive Backoff (HBAB) algorithm [1]. As such, we also provide a brief overview of HBAB.

4.1 Experimental Setup

We ran experiments using the *ns-3* [4] network simulator and its implementation of the IEEE 802.11n for both infrastructure-based and ad-hoc network scenarios. In our simulations, we use typologies with 100 nodes randomly placed in a $1000x1000m_2$ area. In order to vary network contention conditions, we vary the number of sender nodes. We explore how dynamically our method is able to adjust the contention window and its effect on network performance. Table 1 summarizes the parameters describing our experimental setup and their values. Note that AODV [13] routing was used only in the multi-hop ad-hoc experiments.

Traffic Load: We used synthetic data traces as well as traces collected in real networks to drive our simulations. Table 2 summarizes the synthetic data parameters and their values. Our real traffic traces ere collected in two different settings, namely: (1) a public hot spot and (2) a company campus network using a wireless sniffer (Table 3). Note that since there are 10 and 5 individual flows in the hot spot and company traces, respectively, we replicate these flows in scenarios with higher number of nodes.

Performance Metrics: We evaluate our contention window adjustment technique by comparing its performance against IEEE 802.11's original mechanism as well as HBAB [1]. As performance metrics, we use average throughput and average end-to-end delay. Average throughput is calculated as the ratio between the number of received packets and the total number of transmitted packets averaged over all nodes. Average end-to-end delay is given by the interval of time between when a packet was received and when it was sent averaged over all received packets. Channel access fairness is an important issue in MAC protocol design. As such, we also evaluate the proposed approach's fairness by comparing its minimum, maximum, and average throughput against those of IEEE 802.11's BEB and HBAB.

Table 1: Simulation setup parameters and their values

Area	1000mx1000m
Number of nodes	100
Traffic	CBR and real traces
IEEE 802.11 Version	802.11n
Number of experts	12
CW_{min}	15
CW_{max}	1023
Routing protocol	AODV

Table 2: Synthetic trace

Simulation time	200s
Traffic type	CBR
Frame size	1024 Bytes
Data rate	54 Mbps

4.2 History-Based Adaptive Backoff

We use HBAB in the performance evaluation of our proposed contention window adjustment mechanism as it represents mechanisms that, similarly to ours, use transmission status history to set CW. History-Based Adaptive Backoff (HBAB) [1] increases or decreases the congestion window CW based on the current- as well as past data transmission trials. HBAB defines two parameters

Table 3: Hot spot and company trace

	Hot spot	Company
Location	Coffee shop	Company campus
Number of flows	10	5
Duration	20 minutes	30 minutes
Frame size	34-2150 byte range	34-11000 byte range
802.11 version	802.11n	802.11n

α and N; α is a multiplicative factor used to update CW and N is the number of past transmission trials considered by the algorithm. The outcome of the previous N transmission trials is stored in $ChannelState$; failed transmissions are represented by 0 while successful ones bt 1. For example, if $N = 2$, $ChannelState = \{0,1\}$ means that the last transmission succeeded but the previous one failed. Larger values of N mean larger windows into the past but require, albeit relatively small, additional memory.

Algorithm 3 shows HBAB's pseudo-code. Note that we follow HBAB's implementation in [1] and use $\alpha = 1.2$ and $N = 2$, i.e., HBAB examines the status of the two previous and consecutive data transmissions, as well as the current one, to make a decision on how to adjust CW. In case the current transmission is successful, but the two previous transmissions failed, i.e., $ChannelState[0] = 0$ and $ChannelState[1] = 0$, the new value of CW is set to the current CW divided by α. Otherwise, CW is set to CW_{min}. In case the current transmission is unsuccessful, CW is multiplied by α.

As illustrated in Algorithm 3, HBAB's original design presented in [1] is described only for $N = 2$. Another reason that we do not use $N > 2$ in our implementation of HBAB is because, as shown in Algorithm 3, HBAB's state space grows with N which means that we would need to define "manually" how to adjust CW for all the possible outcomes of the previous N transmissions.

Algorithm 3 HBAB Algorithm

Initialization:
$$CW = CW_{min}, \alpha > 1$$
$$ChannelState[0] = 1, ChannelState[1] = 1$$

If current transmission succeeds:

$$CW = \begin{cases} \frac{CW}{\alpha} & , ChannelState[0] = 0 \\ & and\ ChannelState[1] = 0 \\ CW_{min} & , otherwise \end{cases}$$

If transmission failed:
$$CW = CW \times \alpha$$

ChannelState update:
$$\begin{cases} ChannelState[0] = ChannelState[1] \\ ChannelState[1] = 0, last\ transmission\ failed \\ ChannelState[1] = 1, last\ transmission\ succeeded \end{cases}$$

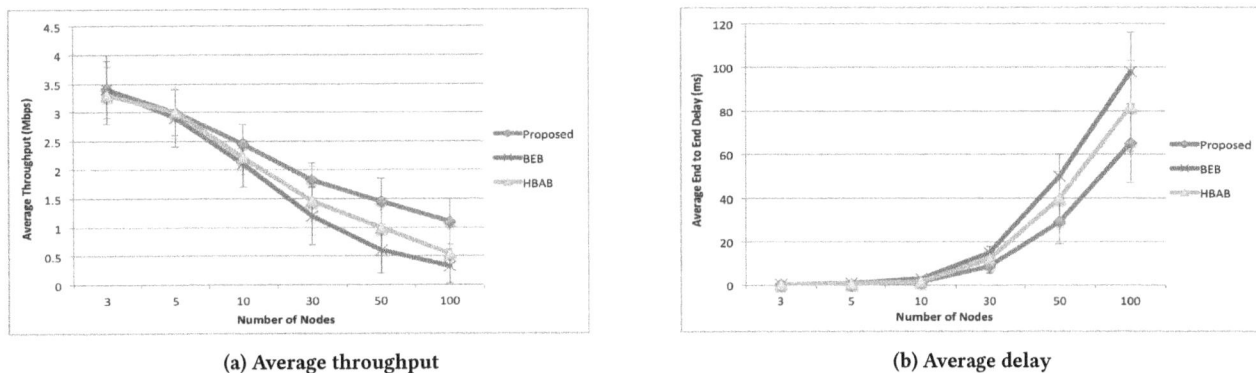

(a) Average throughput

(b) Average delay

Figure 1: Average throughput and delay as a function of number of senders for hot-spot traffic trace in infrastructure-based scenario

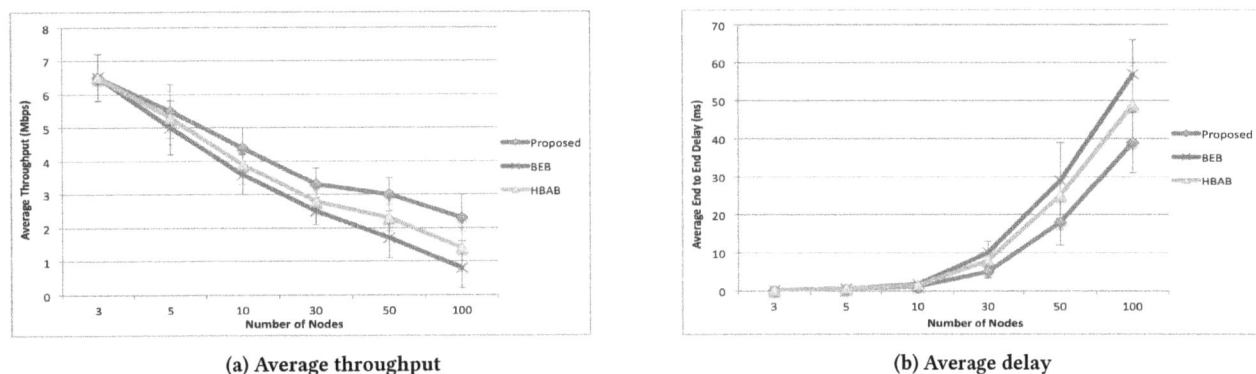

(a) Average throughput

(b) Average delay

Figure 2: Average throughput and delay as a function of the number of senders for company campus traffic trace in infrastructure-based scenario

5 RESULTS

As described in Section 4, we evaluate our approach using two types of scenarios, namely: infrastructure-based and infrastructure-less (or multi-hop ad-hoc) networks. We start by presenting results obtained for the infrastructure-based scenarios followed by the infrastructure-less scenario results. In all graphs, each data point is calculated by averaging over 10 runs that use different random seeds.

5.1 Infrastructure-based Scenarios

In the infrastructure-based experiments, randomly selected nodes send traffic to the Access Point (AP) which is placed in the center of the area being simulated. We drive the experiments using the synthetic and real (i.e., hot spot and company campus) traffic traces described in Section 4 and vary the number of senders as follows: 3, 5, 10, 30, 50, and 100.

Average Throughput and End-to-end Delay: We compare the average throughput and end-to-end delay of our method against IEEE 802.11's BEB and HBAB for different number of nodes and traffic traces, i.e., synthetic, hot-spot, and company campus data traces. We observe in all traces, similar trends for both average

throughput and end-to-end delay. Figures 1, and 2 show the average throughput and end-to-end delay of our method, BEB and HBAB. Note that, due to space limitations, we do not include average throughput and end-to-end delay results for the synthetic dataset. As expected, average throughput decreases and end-to-end delay increases as the number of senders increases. For lower number of senders, e.g., 3 and 5, all three algorithms perform similarly. However, as the number of senders increases resulting in higher network contention, our approach is able to achieve better average throughput and end-to-end delay performance when compared to IEEE 802.11's BEB and HBAB for all three traffic traces.

Table 4 summarizes the throughput and delay improvement achieved by our congestion window adaptation algorithm when compared to BEB's and HBAB's for 100 senders in the infrastructure-based scenario for all traffic traces. We observe that in such more heavily loaded environments, our approach is able to achieve significant gains both in throughput (up to 220% over BEB and 92% over HBAB) as well as in end-to-end delay (up to 33% over BEB and up to 21% over HBAB).

Fairness: In order to evaluate the ability of our contention window adaptation algorithm to provide a fair share of the channel to participating stations, Table 5 shows the minimum, average, and

23

Table 4: Throughput and delay improvement of proposed congestion window adaptation algorithm compared to IEEE 802.11's BEB and HBAB in infrastructure-based scenario with 100 senders for all traffic traces

	BEB Throughput	HBAB Throughput	BEB Delay	HBAB Delay
Synthetic	180%	90%	28%	12%
Hot-spot	220%	92%	33%	20%
Company	170%	64%	31%	21%

Table 5: Minimum, average, and maximum throughput, and standard deviation achieved by our approach, BEB, and HBAB for synthetic data trace in infrastructure-based scenario with 100 senders

	Minimum (Mbps)	Average (Mbps)	Maximum (Mbps)	Standard Deviation
Proposed	0.64	1.2	1.96	0.48
BEB	0	0.51	2.12	0.89
HBAB	0	0.75	1.56	0.62

maximum throughput reported by stations when using our algorithm compared against BEB and HBAB for the synthetic data trace in the infrastructure-based scenario with 100 senders. Both the difference between the maximum and minimum throughput as well as the standard deviation (also reported in Table 5) show that our approach yields superior fairness performance when compared to both BEB and HBAB. As previously discussed, the main reason for BEB's less fair channel allocation is due to the reset of CW to CW_{min} upon a successful transmission, which gives certain nodes higher chance to seize the channel. HBAB shows improvement over BEB's fairness by avoiding immediate reset of CW to CW_{min} after single successful transmission, but still only considers short term packet transmission history which results in less fair channel allocation when compared to our approach. We should point out that BEB is able to yield the highest maximum throughput which is consistent with its resetting of CW to CW_{min} upon a successful transmission.

The graphs in Figure 3 showing CW variation over time for the nodes with minimum and maximum throughput for the synthetic trace in the infrastructure-based scenario with 100 senders reiterate our observations. We notice from Figure 3 that for both BEB and HBAB, CW for the node that reports the minimum throughput stays practically constant at CW_{max} for almost the whole experiment. In the case of the maximum throughput node, its CW varies considerably between CW_{min} and CW_{max}, i.e., 1023, during the whole run under both BEB and HBAB. Under our approach, the maximum throughput node's CW is able to reach steady state quite fast around 400.

CW **Variation:** In Figure 3a which shows the CW variation for the node with maximum throughput, we observe significant CW oscillation between CW_{min} and CW_{max} under BEB and HBAB. In the case of our approach, CW stays fairly constant throughout the

experiment. The reason is that, after each successful transmission, the weight of experts with value higher than the current CW will be reduced and the weight of experts with value lower than CW will be increased. Therefore, for the next transmission, since the CW is calculated as the weighted sum of all experts, its value decreases slowly. Also, in the case of unsuccessful transmission, the weight of experts with values higher than current CW are increased and the weight of experts with values lower than CW are decreased. And again, since the CW is calculated as the weighted sum of all experts, the next CW will be slightly higher for the next transmission. In other words, through the experts and their weights, our approach is able to account for recent past as well as the present.

Figure 3b shows the variation of CW over time for the node with the lowest average throughput in the infrastructure-based scenario with 100 senders using the synthetic traffic trace. As the results in Table 5 indicate, BEB's and HBAB's minimum throughput is 0 which indicates that there are some nodes in the network that suffer from starvation. From Figure 3b, we observe that, relatively early in the experiment, CW of the node with the lowest throughput stabilizes at CW_{max} which considerably decreased the node's chance to acquire the channel, ultimately resulting in "starvation", i.e., zero throughput.

5.2 Infrastructure-less Scenarios

In the ad-hoc experiments, randomly selected senders send data traffic to randomly selected receivers according to the three traffic traces described in Section 4. Similarly to the infrastructure-based experiments, the number of senders vary as follows: 3, 5, 10, 30, 50, and 100.

Average Throughput and End-to-end Delay: We compare the average throughput and end-to-end delay of our method compared with BEB and HBAB for different number of senders and traffic traces in the ad-hoc scenario. Similarly to the trend reported in the infrastructure-based experiments, we observe that, for lower number of senders, all three methods perform similarly. However, when the number of senders increase, which result in higher network contention, our method is able to achieve higher average throughput and lower average end-to-end delay when compared to both BEB and HBAB. Figures 4 and 5 show the average throughput and end-to-end delay of our method compared versus BEB and HBAB. Similarly to the infrastructure-based experiments, we do not include average throughput and end-to-end delay results for the synthetic dataset due to space limitations.

Table 6 summarizes the throughput and delay improvement achieved by our congestion window adaptation algorithm when compared to BEB's and HBAB's for 100 senders in the ad-hoc scenario for all traffic traces. Similarly to what was observed for the infrastructure-based experiment, in high contention networks, our approach yields significant improvement both in average throughput (up to 257% over BEB and 78% over HBAB) and average end-to-end delay (up to 37% over BEB and 23% over HBAB).

Fairness: To evaluate our algorithm's fairness in ad-hoc scenarios, we show the minimum, average, and maximum throughput for the synthetic traffic trace with 100 senders in Table 7. Like the results

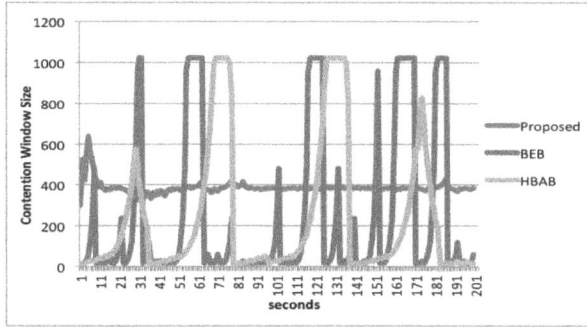

(a) Maximum throughput

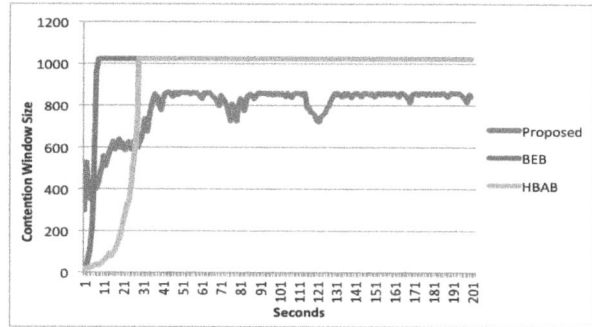

(b) Minimum throughput

Figure 3: Contention window size variation over time for the nodes with minimum and maximum throughput for synthetic trace in infrastructure-based scenario with 100 senders

Table 6: Throughput and delay improvement of proposed congestion window adaptation algorithm compared to IEEE 802.11's BEB and HBAB in ad-hoc scenario with 100 senders for all traffic traces

	BEB Throughput	HBAB Throughput	BEB Delay	HBAB Delay
Synthetic	230%	75%	31%	21%
Hot-spot	240%	78%	37%	23%
Company	257%	63%	35%	17%

Table 7: Minimum, average, and maximum throughput, and standard deviation achieved by our approach, BEB, and HBAB for synthetic data trace in ad-hoc scenario with 100 senders

	Minimum	Average	Maximum	Standard Deviation
Proposed	0.43	1.05	1.6	0.41
BEB	0	0.3	1.8	0.75
HBAB	0	0.6	1.2	0.52

reported for the infrastructure-based experiments, our approach is able to reduce the gap between the minimum and maximum average throughput with a lower standard deviation, an indication of its ability to deliver improved fairness when compared to BEB and HAB.

CW **Variation:** Figure 6 shows *CW* variation over time for both the nodes that yield the maximum and minimum average throughput under our approach as well as under BEB and HBAB in the ad-hoc scenario with 100 senders using the synthetic traffic trace. Like the trend observed in the infrastructure-based experiments, our approach is able to achieve steady state relatively quickly for both the nodes with maximum- and minimum throughput. The graphs in Figure 6 also show that our approach is able to close the gap between the *CW*s of the highest- and lowest throughput nodes which is another indication of improved fairness.

6 CONCLUSION

In this paper, we introduce a simple, yet effective machine learning approach to adjust the value of IEEE 802.11's *Contention Window* based on present- as well as recent past network contention conditions. Using a wide range of network scenarios and conditions, we show that our approach outperforms both 802.11's BEB as well as an existing contention window adjustment technique that only considers the last two transmissions. Our results indicate that our contention window adaptation algorithm is able to deliver consistently higher average throughput, lower end-to-end delay, as well as improved fairness. As future work, we plan to explore alternate loss functions as well as validate our approach in real testbeds.

ACKNOWLEDGMENTS

This research has been partly supported by grant CNS 1321151 from the US National Science Foundation.

REFERENCES

[1] Maali Albalt and Qassim Nasir. 2009. Adaptive backoff algorithm for IEEE 802.11 MAC protocol. *International Journal of Communications, Network and System Sciences* 2, 04 (2009), 300.

[2] Khaled Hatem Almotairi. 2013. Inverse binary exponential backoff: Enhancing short-term fairness for IEEE 802.11 networks. In *ISWCS 2013; The Tenth International Symposium on Wireless Communication Systems*. VDE, 1–5.

[3] Vaduvur Bharghavan, Alan Demers, Scott Shenker, and Lixia Zhang. 1994. MACAW: a media access protocol for wireless LAN's. *ACM SIGCOMM Computer Communication Review* 24, 4 (1994), 212–225.

[4] Gustavo Carneiro. 2010. NS-3: Network simulator 3. In *UTM Lab Meeting April*, Vol. 20. 4–5.

[5] Yalda Edalat, Jong-Suk Ahn, and Katia Obraczka. 2016. Smart experts for network state estimation. *IEEE Transactions on Network and Service Management* 13, 3 (2016), 622–635.

[6] Yalda Edalat, Katia Obraczka, and Bahador Amiri. 2018. A machine learning approach for dynamic control of RTS/CTS in WLANs. In *Proceedings of the 15th EAI International Conference on Mobile and Ubiquitous Systems: Computing, Networking and Services*. ACM, 432–442.

[7] Lassaad Gannoune. 2006. A Non-linear Dynamic Tuning of the Minimum Contention Window (CW min) for Enhanced Service Differentiation in IEEE 802.11 ad-hoc Networks. In *2006 IEEE 63rd Vehicular Technology Conference*, Vol. 3. IEEE, 1266–1271.

[8] David P Helmbold, Darrell DE Long, Tracey L Sconyers, and Bruce Sherrod. 2000. Adaptive disk spin-down for mobile computers. *Mobile Networks and Applications* 5, 4 (2000), 285–297.

[9] Mark Herbster and Manfred K Warmuth. 1998. Tracking the best expert. *Machine learning* 32, 2 (1998), 151–178.

[10] Hyung Joo Ki, Seung-Hyuk Choi, Min Young Chung, and Tae-Jin Lee. 2006. Performance evaluation of binary negative-exponential backoff algorithm in

(a) Average throughput

(b) Average delay

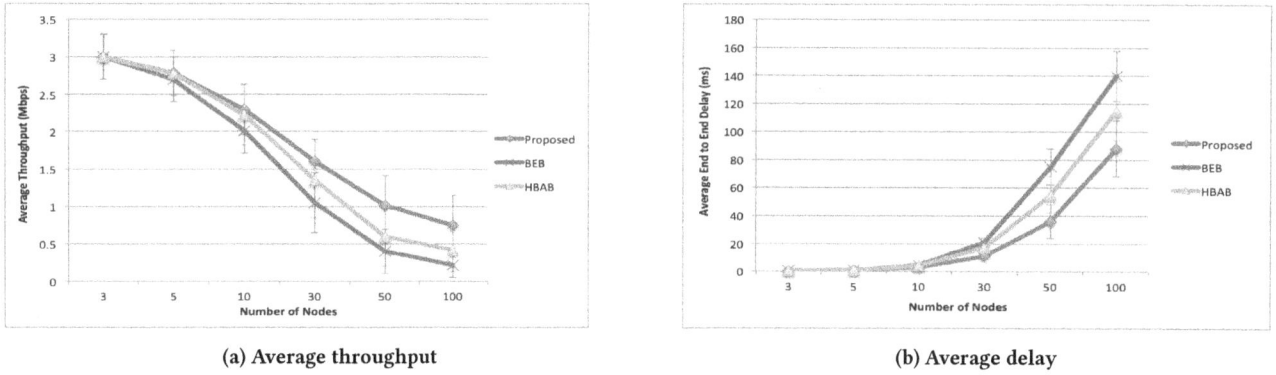

Figure 4: Average throughput and delay as a function of the number of senders for hot-spot data in ad-hoc scenarios

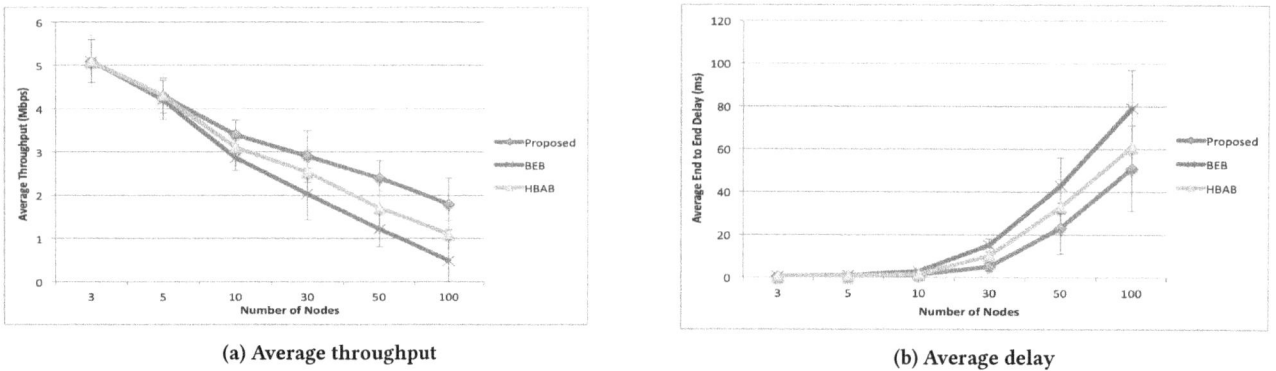

(a) Average throughput

(b) Average delay

Figure 5: Average throughput and delay as a function of the number of nodes for company data in ad-hoc scenarios

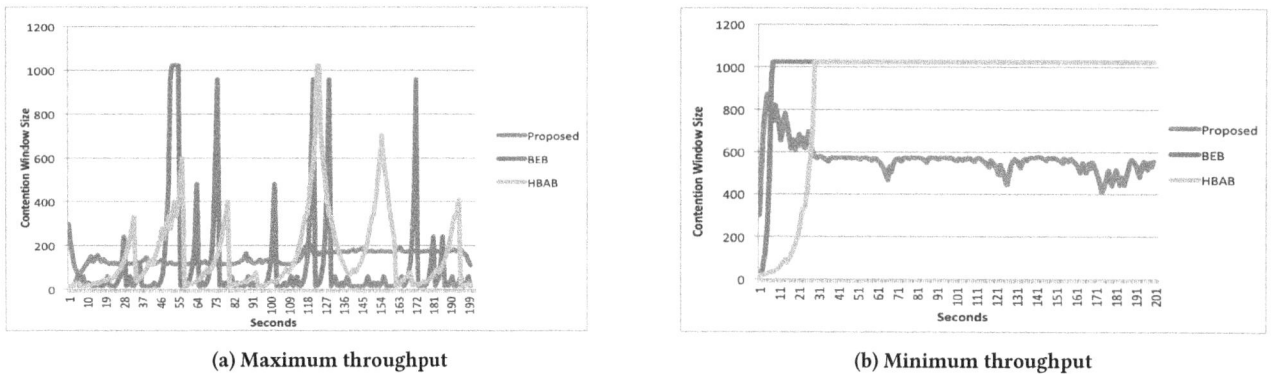

(a) Maximum throughput

(b) Minimum throughput

Figure 6: Contention window size variation over time for the nodes with minimum and maximum throughput for synthetic trace in ad-hoc scenario with 100 senders

IEEE 802.11 WLAN. In *International Conference on Mobile Ad-Hoc and Sensor Networks*. Springer, 294–303.

[11] Adlen Ksentini, Abdelhamid Nafaa, Abdelhak Gueroui, and Mohamed Naimi. 2005. Determinist contention window algorithm for IEEE 802.11. In *2005 IEEE 16th International Symposium on Personal, Indoor and Mobile Radio Communications*, Vol. 4. IEEE, 2712–2716.

[12] Bruno Astuto Arouche Nunes, Kerry Veenstra, William Ballenthin, Stephanie Lukin, and Katia Obraczka. 2014. A machine learning framework for TCP round-trip time estimation. *EURASIP Journal on Wireless Communications and Networking* 2014, 1 (2014), 47.

[13] Charles Perkins, Elizabeth Belding-Royer, and Samir Das. 2003. *Ad hoc on-demand distance vector (AODV) routing*. Technical Report.

[14] Mohammad Shurman, Bilal Al-Shua'b, Mohammad Alsaedeen, Mamoun F Al-Mistarihi, and Khalid A Darabkh. 2014. N-BEB: New backoff algorithm for IEEE 802.11 MAC protocol. In *2014 37th International Convention on Information and Communication Technology, Electronics and Microelectronics (MIPRO)*. IEEE, 540–544.

Simulation and Performance Evaluation of the Intel Rate Adaptation Algorithm

Rémy Grünblatt
remy@grunblatt.org
Univ Lyon, EnsL, UCBL, CNRS, Inria, LIP & CITI, France

Isabelle Guérin-Lassous
isabelle.guerin-lassous@ens-lyon.fr
Univ Lyon, EnsL, UCBL, CNRS, Inria, LIP, France

Olivier Simonin
olivier.simonin@insa-lyon.fr
Univ Lyon, INSA Lyon, Inria, CITI, France

ABSTRACT

With the rise of the complexity of the IEEE 802.11 standard, rate adaptation algorithms have to deal with a large set of values for all the different parameters which impact the network throughput. Simple trial-and-error algorithms can no longer explore solution space in reasonable time and smart solutions are required. Most of the WiFi controllers rely on proprietary code and the used rate adaptation algorithms in these controllers are unknown. Very few WiFi controllers provide their rate adaptation algorithms when they do not rely on the Minstrel-HT algorithm, which is implemented in the Linux kernel. Intel WiFi controllers come with their own rate adaptation algorithms that are implemented in the Intel IwlWifi Linux Driver which is open-source.

In this paper, we have reverse-engineered the Intel rate adaptation mechanism from the source code of the IwlWifi Linux driver, and we give, in a comprehensive form, the underlying rate adaptation algorithm named Iwl-Mvm-Rs. We describe the different mechanisms used to seek the best throughput adapted to the network conditions. We have also implemented the Iwl-Mvm-Rs algorithm in the ns-3 simulator. Thanks to this implementation, we can evaluate the performance of Iwl-Mvm-Rs in different scenarios (static and with mobility, with and without fast fading). We also compare the performances of Iwl-Mvm-Rs with the ones of Minstrel-HT and IdealWifi, also implemented in the ns-3 simulator.

ACM Reference Format:
Rémy Grünblatt, Isabelle Guérin-Lassous, and Olivier Simonin. 2019. Simulation and Performance Evaluation of the Intel Rate Adaptation Algorithm. In *22nd Int'l ACM Conference on Modeling, Analysis and Simulation of Wireless and Mobile Systems (MSWiM '19), November 25–29, 2019, Miami Beach, FL, USA.* ACM, New York, NY, USA, 8 pages. https://doi.org/10.1145/3345768.3355921

1 INTRODUCTION

One of the requirements of the IEEE 802.11 standard (also known as the *WiFi* technology) is the ability to handle portable and mobile stations, required in applications such as mobile robot fleets. For this purpose, the IEEE 802.11 physical layer (*PHY*) defines many transmission features that can be chosen and combined in order to ensure the good receipt of data, notwithstanding changes in the transmission channel caused by mobility or propagation effects. Examples of such transmission features are the transmission modulation and coding scheme, the use of space-time block coding, the guard interval length, the channel width or the number of spatial streams. The IEEE 802.11 standard defines which combinations of transmission features are allowed and forbidden, but it does not enforce any behaviour regarding how these features should be chosen, letting each station (*STA*) in charge of deciding its own transmission features. The combination of these different transmission parameters corresponds to a transmission rate. The algorithms automatically choosing these parameters, called **rate adaptation algorithms** (*RAAs*), may optimize transmissions with regards to different metrics such as robustness, throughput [13] or energy consumption [14]. With the rise of the complexity of the physical layer of the IEEE 802.11 standard, the size of the search space of the different transmission parameters has increased by two orders of magnitude, making the design of efficient rate adaptation algorithms an active field of research. Indeed, simple trial-and-error algorithms can no longer explore solution space in reasonable time.

A large number of rate adaptation algorithms have been proposed in the literature. It is difficult to know which solutions are effectively used in real WiFi products as a large part of the code of WiFi drivers is proprietary and not accessible. Some WiFi Linux drivers, like the Soft-MAC drivers, have the advantage of using the Media Access Control management entity implemented inside the Linux kernel in the mac80211 component, allowing an open-source implementation to drive multiple pieces of hardware. Currently, two rate adaptation algorithms are implemented in mac80211, namely Minstrel [4] and Minstrel HT [6]. Only a handful of Soft-MAC drivers use their own rate control algorithms and not the ones implemented inside the mac80211 component. This is for instance the case of the Intel wireless main driver, named *IwlWiFi*, that uses its own rate adaptation algorithms Iwl-Agn-Rs and Iwl-Mvm-Rs.

As far as we know, no study in the literature describes the rate adaptation algorithms used by Intel and their performance. This absence of study is surprising for several reasons. Rate adaptation plays an important part in 802.11 performances, such as throughput or delay and these performances have an impact on the communication quality. Intel WiFi controllers are common, as they are used in many laptops, but also in more exotic devices, such as the Intel Aero Ready-to-Fly UAVs (Unmanned Aerial Vehicle). The mobility capabilities of these devices lead to greater dynamics in radio conditions, and therefore introduce a need for a suitable and efficient rate adaptation algorithm.

In this paper, we study a rate adaptation algorithm used in real WiFi products. Our main contributions are the following:

- We present the RAA used in recent Intel hardware wireless network interface controllers (WNIC), Iwl-Mvm-Rs, which has been reversed-engineered from the Intel IwlWiFi Linux driver source code. This is the first study that gives and explains the rate adaptation algorithm used by Intel in a comprehensive form.
- We compare and analyze the performances of the Iwl-Mvm-Rs, IdealWifi and Minstrel-Ht RAAs with regard to the mobility of stations using simulation. In particular, we show that Iwl-Mvm-Rs is better at dealing with mobility, in the tested scenarios, than the two other algorithms. We use the network simulator ns-3 because this is the most up-to-date simulator concerning the WiFi technology and because several RAAs are already implemented in NS-3.
- We provide an open source implementation of the Iwl-Mvm-Rs algorithm in the network simulator NS-3.

The paper is organized as follows. Section 2 gives the main new features that have been introduced in the IEEE 802.11n and 802.11ac versions and that are used in the rate adaptation algorithms under study in this paper. A brief state-of-the-art on RAAs for WiFi networks is also provided. In Section 3 we describe the rate adaptation algorithm Iwl-Mvm-Rs we have reverse-engineered from the Intel IwlWiFi Linux Driver source code. We give a short description on the implementation of this algorithm in the ns-3 simulator. Then, in Section 4, we compare, by simulation the performance of Iwl-Mvm-Rs with two other algorithms. Finally, we conclude in Section 5.

2 BACKGROUND AND RELATED WORK

2.1 WiFi Networks

Most of the current WiFi products use the IEEE 802.11n and 802.11ac standards[1]. Several new approaches have been introduced to improve performances compared to the first IEEE 802.11 modes. At the physical layer, stations can be equipped with multiple antennas and MIMO (Multiple-Input Multiple-Output) is used to increase transmission rates and reliability by transmitting multiple spatial streams simultaneously and by exploiting the spatial diversity. The maximum coding rate is increased from 3/4 to 5/6 and a short guard interval of 400 ns is introduced to improve spectral efficiency. In addition, it is possible to aggregate several channels in order to transmit on larger channel width. 802.11n offers the possibility to transmit on 40MHz channels, while the use of 80MHz or 160MHz channels is possible with 802.11ac.

The combination of the modulation type and the coding rate is represented by a Modulation and Coding Scheme index (MCS)[1]. Coupled to the channel width, the number of spatial streams and the guard interval length, these parameters define a physical transmission rates.

At the MAC layer, the frame aggregation mechanism aggregates multiple data frames before transmission. Two aggregation mechanisms have been proposed: A-MSDU (Aggregate MAC Service Data Unit) aggregates several MSDUs, carried within a single data MAC protocol data unit (MPDU), and A-MPDU (Aggregate MAC Protocol

Data Unit) aggregates several MPDUs carried within a single physical layer convergence procedure service data unit (PSDU). While not changing the physical transmission rate, these schemes allow for less overhead and therefore higher throughputs.

2.2 Rate Adaptation Algorithms

Wifi offers a large range of transmission parameters. Taking into account guard interval duration, channel bandwidth, MCS index and the number of spatial streams, 802.11ac supports 312 different transmission combinations resulting in 122 different rates, while 802.11n supports 130 combinations and 70 transmissions rates.

The problem of rate adaptation for WiFi networks has been studied for two decades, since the IEEE 802.11a/b amendments that introduce multiple transmission rates. For 802.11n/ac standards, various solutions have been proposed in the literature[3, 5, 9–11]. Among the recent works on the subject, one can note the works in [8, 12]. The solution described in [8] is one of the first solutions to consider the mobility and its impact on the transmission rate adaptation. The solution is based on an adaptive learning mechanism. Even if this solution shows promising results, it is not yet implemented in WiFi interfaces.

3 THE INTEL RATE ADAPTATION ALGORITHM

Intel wireless chips use the IwlWiFi driver. It comes with its own rate adaptation algorithms: Iwl-Agn-Rs and Iwl-Mvm-Rs, the former being un-maintained, and limited to 802.11n hardware, while the latter is being used with 802.11ac compatible Mvm hardware. Therefore, we focus our study on the algorithm Iwl-Mvm-Rs. As far as we know, there is no study that describes this algorithm and its performances. Only the code is open. To come with a comprehensive algorithm, we have reverse-engineered the code provided by Intel [2]. The IwlWiFi driver has approximately 72.000 source lines of code, 40% of which are used by the Mvm hardware. The RAA is located in the rs.c file which has approximately 3200 source lines of code. In the following subsection, we provide a description of the Iwl-Mvm-Rs algorithm.

3.1 Algorithm Description

Iwl-Mvm-Rs takes care of managing the Modulation and Coding Scheme (MCS) index, but also whether to transmit in a legacy mode (802.11a or 802.11g) or in a non-legacy mode (802.11n or 802.11ac) in a SISO or MIMO way. It chooses which antenna or subset of antennas to transmit with, and whether a Short Guard Interval (Sgi) or a Long Guard Interval (Lgi) is used. It also decides when to enable frame aggregation, and can do transmission power control under certain conditions, but this has not been studied in this paper.

Iwl-Mvm-Rs has two main components: MCS Scaling[2] and Column Scaling. MCS Scaling tries to maximize the throughput by only changing the MCS, while Column Scaling tries to find a better *column*, which is a combination of *mode* (legacy, SISO, MIMO), *guard interval*, and *antenna configuration* parameters. The algorithm starts with the lowest transmission rate, which has the best reliability, and interleaves MCS Scaling phases and Column Scaling phases,

---

[1]For 802.11n, the MCS index is used to encode the number of spatial streams, but we use it here as defined by the 802.11ac standard.

[2]Even if the MCS concept does not exist until 802.11n, this term is used as a handy shortcut to refer to both MCS and data rates.

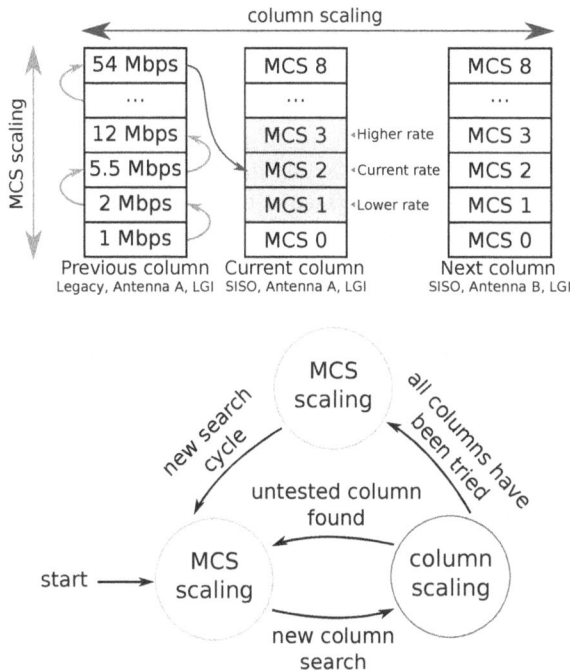

Figure 1: (Top) Example of sequence of decisions made by the RAA Iwl-Mvm-Rs; (Bottom) Flowchart of the different states of the RAA Iwl-Mvm-Rs.

forming a "search cycle". Column Scaling starts when the MCS Scaling phase chooses not to change MCS. The alternation of MCS Scaling and Column Scaling continues until all the columns have been tried, which means the end of the search cycle and the MCS scaling phase runs until the beginning of a new search cycle. Figure 1 sums up the different steps of the algorithm, steps described in more details hereafter.

MCS Scaling. The MCS scaling algorithm can take one of the following decisions: lowering the MCS index, raising the MCS index, or keep using the current MCS index. The decision is made in a deterministic manner, according to the maximum theoretical throughput and the measured throughput of adjacent MCS indexes as well as the measured throughput of the current MCS. It therefore prevents from switching to a MCS implying a theoretical throughput lower than the current measured throughput, or to a MCS whose measured throughput is worse than the current one, for example.

The theoretical throughput is hardcoded into tables for each mode (legacy, SISO, MIMO), each MCS index, and for the four possible guard interval and aggregation parameters (Sgi, Lgi, Sgi+Agg, Lgi+Agg). The measured throughput for each MCS index is computed by multiplying the success ratio of up to the last 62 frame transmissions at this MCS with the theoretical throughput when using this MCS. At least 8 successful transmissions or 3 failed transmissions are required to compute the success ratio: no decisions are taken until these thresholds are met. The decisions are the following:

(1) if the success ratio is too small ($< 15\%$) or the measured throughput is zero, **decrease** the MCS index;
(2) else:
    (a) if the measured throughputs with the lower and higher adjacent MCS indexes are unknown;
    (b) or the measured throughput with the lower adjacent MCS index is worse and the measured throughput with the higher adjacent MCS index is unknown;
    (c) or the measured throughput with the higher adjacent MCS index is better;
    increase the MCS index;
(3) else, if the measured throughputs with the lower and higher adjacent MCS indexes are worse, **maintain** the MCS index;
(4) else, if the success ratio is lower than 85% and the lower adjacent MCS index throughput can theoretically beat the current measured throughput, and:
    (a) if the measured throughput with the lower adjacent MCS index is better;
    (b) or the measured throughput with the lower adjacent MCS index is unknown;
    decrease the MCS index;
(5) else, **maintain** the MCS index.

Column Scaling. Each column has a set of "next columns" that the driver will try if they can theoretically beat the current measured throughput (by looking at the maximum theoretical throughput of the columns), and if they have not been already tested during the search cycle. When trying a new column, if the measured throughput in this column is better than the throughput in the previous one, the RAA keeps using it. Otherwise the column is marked and the RAA reverts back to the old column, into the MCS scaling phase.

The initial starting MCS index in the new column is chosen according to the success ratio: if it is high enough (more than 85%), the smaller MCS index whose theoretical throughput is higher than the current theoretical throughput is chosen. Otherwise, the smaller MCS index whose theoretical throughput is higher than the current measured throughput is chosen. After a column switch, the measured throughput of the previous column are dropped.

New Search Cycle. After the end of a search cycle, the algorithm does MCS Scaling until the start of a new search cycle. This start is triggered when:

(1) too many frames have failed (160 in legacy, 400 otherwise) since the beginning of the previous cycle;
(2) too many frames have succeeded (400 in legacy, 4500 otherwise) since the beginning of the previous cycle;
(3) too much time has been spent after the end of the previous search cycle. The maximum time between two consecutive cycles is set to 5 seconds.

Aggregation. A-MSDU is disabled in non-legacy mode when the MCS index is smaller than 5 (corresponding to a modulation type of 16-QAM, QPSK or BPSK), or when the MCS index is decreased. A-MPDU is enabled on a per-hardware queue basis, depending on the traffic identifier of the data.

Retry Chain. Frames are re-transmitted up to 15 times. The first re-transmission uses the same transmissions parameters, the next

4 re-transmissions use the lower two MCS indexes in the same column, and the ones after change the used column and use decreasing MCS indexes and alternating antennas.

Bandwidth. The RAA uses the maximum bandwidth supported by the standard it uses and by the STA it communicates with. For legacy rates, it therefore uses 20Mhz, but it may use 40Mhz, 80Mhz or 160Mhz for non-legacy rates.

3.2 Simulation and Validation

In order to study the Iwl-Mvm-Rs algorithm and evaluate its performance in various scenarios, we have implemented it in the ns-3 simulator. The source code is available in [7].

ns-3 code. The algorithm has been implemented as a *VHT* (Very High Throughput) low-latency WifiManager in ns-3 . As the language used to implement the manager algorithms in ns-3 is C++, one could have blindly translated the rate adaptation algorithm of the driver code from C to C++ and simulate the behaviour of Iwl-Mvm-Rs. Still, many parts of the driver code have only housekeeping functions for the underlying hardware, such as catching unexpected bugs or re-synchronizing the state of the rate adaptation algorithm (that runs in the CPU) with the state of the hardware (the WNIC). As these behaviours should not happen in a simulator, the RAA in the simulator has been re-implemented using the skeleton of the RAA in the Intel driver, but is not a one-to-one correspondence. The number of source lines of code of the simulated RAA is thus cut by two-thirds with regards to the driver code.

The simulation covers most of the algorithm but ignores some part of the original RAA for the sake of simplicity. First, it blindly enables A-MPDU aggregation when possible, as we assume no real-time traffic will be sent. Then, the retry chain does not use decreasing transmission rates but instead uses the current transmission rate. As re-transmissions of lost MPDUs in a A-MPDU frame are not made using this retry chain because missing MPDUs are resent as a part of the next A-MPDU, and as the first re-transmission rate used in the retry chain is the original transmission rate, we believe this simplification introduces no major changes in the results of our simulations.

Validation. In order to validate the behaviour of the simulated code, we have compared the decisions of the rate adaptation algorithm with the decisions of a real piece of hardware, the Intel Corporation Wireless 8260 WNIC, in different situations. To get an easy access to the decisions made by the RAA on a Linux system, one can load the IwlWifi Linux kernel module with the option 'debug=0x00100000', which enables debug messages about the rate adaptation process inside the kernel log (accessible using the 'dmesg' command). Multiple patterns observed over-the-air are correctly reproduced in the simulator, but these results are not presented here due to space constraints.

4 PERFORMANCE EVALUATION AND MOBILITY

We use the network simulator ns-3 (version 3.29) to evaluate and compare the performances of Iwl-Mvm-Rs with the Minstrel-Ht and IdealWifi algorithms. We choose Minstrel-Ht because it is implemented in the mac80211 kernel component. Minstrel-Ht and

IdealWifi algorithms are also the only algorithms implemented in the simulator supporting VHT, that is to say 802.11ac. There exists a third rate adaptation algorithm in ns-3 supporting VHT, ConstantRate, which is of limited interest as it uses static transmission parameters and therefore does not perform any rate *adaptation*. The ns-3 IdealWifi manager transmits the signal-to-noise (SNR) ratio of each frame using a perfect out-of-band mechanism, to the emitter. The latter then chooses transmission parameters maximizing throughput and maintaining the bit error rate (BER) below 10^{-5}. To measure the adaptability and the responsiveness of these algorithms, we design two simulation scenarios involving node mobility or sudden changes in the communication channel characteristics, as well as a scenario where the transmission conditions do not change, acting as a baseline simulation. All of the devices use 2 antennas supporting 2 spatial streams in transmission and reception (so-called "2x2:2" devices) using a 20Mhz bandwidth and the channel 42 (5210MHz).

Simulations #1 and #2 involve two stations (STA), both running the same RAA, one acting as UDP traffic generator and the other one acting as a sink, and the simulation #3 introduces a relay STA. At $t = 1s$, the traffic generator sends UDP datagrams of size 1420 bytes to the sink, until the end of the simulation, either at the specified data rate, either in saturation.

4.1 Scenario #1 - Fixed distance

In this scenario, the two STAs are static and are separated by a fixed distance. Simulations last 30 seconds and each result is the mean of 5 simulations. The distance is increased with a step of 1m. The simulation uses the log-distance path loss model, described in Equation (1), which models the path loss *Pl* as a function of the distance d and of γ, an environment-dependent constant called the loss exponent, and the power Pl_0 at distance $d = d_0$.

$$Pl(d) = Pl_0 + 10\gamma \log_{10}(\frac{d}{d_0}) \qquad (1)$$

We optionally add a Nakagami-*m* fast fading loss model to account for the changes in power due to the presence of multiple paths. The expression of the added loss, denoted *Pn*, at distance d and when incoming power is equal to P is given in Equation. (2).

$$Pn(d, P) = X(m, P/m) \qquad (2)$$

with X a realization of the X Erlang random variable whose density function is:

$$f(x; k, \mu) = \frac{x^{k-1}e^{-\frac{x}{\mu}}}{\mu^k (k-1)!} \quad \text{for } x, \mu \geq 0$$

The parameter m is chosen to be 1.5 for distances smaller than 80m and 0.75 for distances bigger than 80m, which are the default parameters used in the ns-3 model.

The mean throughput (measured at the application level of the sink) with regards to distance is depicted on Figure 2, without fast-fading (on top) and with fast-fading (bottom). Without fast-fading, as no time-varying fading is present, the reception power of the frames remains constant during each simulation. While Minstrel-Ht and Iwl-Mvm-Rs have overall comparable performances, IdealWifi performs significantly worse at distance larger than 15 meters

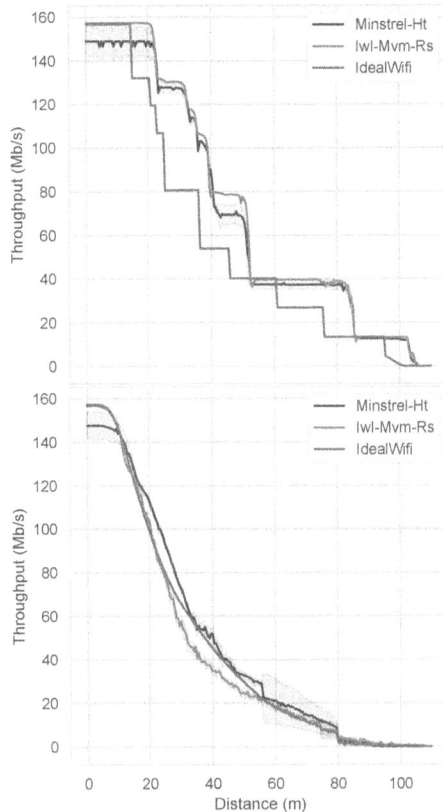

Figure 2: Scenario 1. Throughput as a function of the distance between the source and the sink in the first scenario, without fast-fading (top) and with fast-fading (bottom). Shaded regions represent the standard deviation.

because it does not use transmission rates that would result in a BER bigger than 10^{-5}. By doing so, it does not use transmission parameters that would result in a better throughput. With Nakagami-m fading, overall, MINSTREL-HT performs best, and IWL-MVM-RS performs worst. For example, at distance $d = 45$m, throughput is divided by a factor 2.2 for IWL-MVM-RS compared to the case without fast-fading, while it is only divided by a a factor 1.7 for MINSTREL-HT and a factor 1.1 for IDEALWIFI.

We now comment on the reasons behind the loss of throughput for the IWL-MVM-RS algorithm. The Nakagami-m fading is a time varying fading. It means that the reception power for each frame may vary a lot while the position or the mobility of the STAs remains the same, with periods of destructive fading and constructive fading. Looking at the transmission rates used by IWL-MVM-RS, we can observe that overall, the average transmission rate of IWL-MVM-RS is lower than the ones of MINSTREL-HT and IDEALWIFI. The reasons behind this behaviour are present in the two phases of the IWL-MVM-RS algorithm, the MCS scaling phase and the Column scaling phase. First, in the MCS scaling phase, the algorithm will make its decisions based on at least 3 failed transmissions or 8 successful transmissions. The randomness introduced by the fading may result, locally, in bad performances when these

decisions are made, leading the algorithm to stop its exploration and choose a smaller transmission rate instead of climbing the MCS ladder and finding a transmission rate that would result in a better throughput over the long term. At the heart of this behaviour is the asymmetry between the number of failed transmissions and the number of successful transmissions needed to take a decision, as well as the low number of frames required to take a decision. A bigger test window would result in more robust estimations of the potential throughput associated with a given MCS. Then, in the column scaling phase, only a single MCS (corresponding to the smaller MCS index whose theoretical throughput is higher than the current theoretical throughput or the current measured throughput, depending on the success ratio) is tested to decide whether a more in-depth exploration (*i.e.* a MCS scaling phase) should be done in the tested column. As previously, this single test can be very short and coincide with a period of destructive fading, resulting in the whole column being wrongly marked as unsuitable.

Figure 3 confirms the results from Figure 2. It represents, for each manager, the distribution on the transmission rates used by the source to send its frames when the distance between the source and the destination is 45m. Without fading, IDEALWIFI use a lower transmission rate for a large number of frames compared to IWL-MVM-RS and MINSTREL-HT. These latter two mainly use the same transmission rate, but IWL-MVM-RS sends more frames and sometimes use a higher transmission rate. Table 1 gives the associated mean transmission rate and the success ratio. It shows that without fading IWL-MVM-RS achieves a good trade-off between the mean transmission rate and the success ratio, leading to the highest throughput with this distance. Conversely, Figure 3 shows that, with fading, IWL-MVM-RS mainly uses smaller transmission rates than the other solutions. MINSTREL-HT uses the higher transmission rates for most of the sent frames and thus has the higher mean transmission rate. Table 1 shows that the transmission rates used by MINSTREL HT also lead to frames losses since its achieved success ratio is around 71%. However the trade-off achieved by this manager is good enough to transmit data with the highest throughput.

Table 1: Scenario 1. Mean transmission rate and success ratio for a distance of 45m.

Solution	Without fading		With fading	
	Mean transmission rate (Mb/s)	Success ratio	Mean transmission rate (Mb/s)	Success ratio
IWL-MVM-RS	86.1	97.5%	38.3	88.5%
MINSTREL-HT	80.7	98.1%	74.0	71.5%
IDEALWIFI	57.0	99.9%	56.4	83.2%

4.2 Scenario #2 - Circular Alternating Walls Shadowing

In this scenario, the source moves in circle around the static sink, at constant speed. The overall distance $d_s = 30m$ between the two STAs does not change during the simulation, but walls are present at distance $d_w = 15m$ for angles θ ranging in $[\pi/4; \pi/2]$,

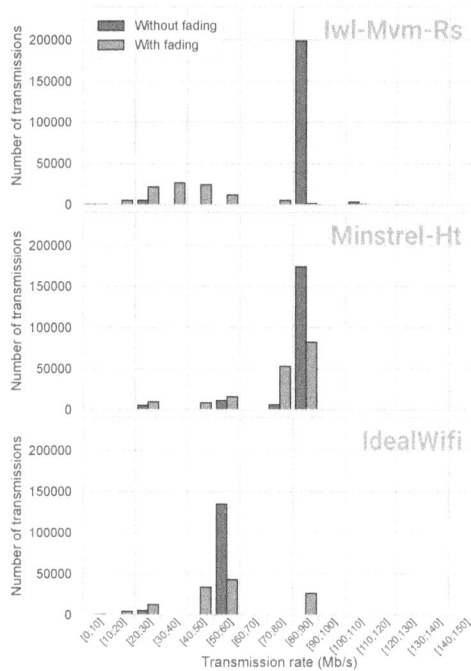

Figure 3: Scenario 1. Distribution of the used transmission rates for the frame sent by the source, without or with fading and for a distance of 45m. Top to bottom: IwL-Mvm-Rs, Minstrel-Ht, IdealWifi.

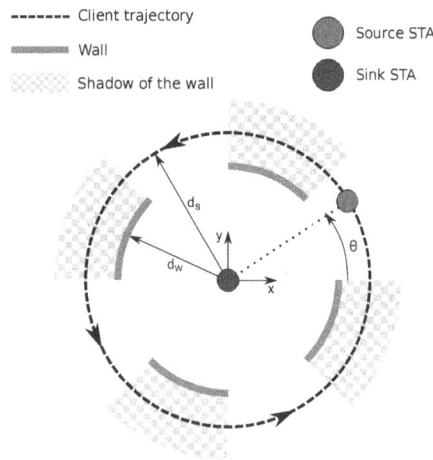

Figure 4: Scenario 2. Top view of the "Circular Alternating Walls" simulation. Walls create shadows leading to sudden changes in the channel between the source and the sink.

$[3\pi/4; \pi]$, $[-3\pi/4; -\pi/2]$ and $[-\pi/4; 0]$, as shown on Figure 4. In the "shadows" of the walls, a fixed loss of 5 dBm is added to account for the presence of an obstacle. A log-distance path loss model is used, as well as an optional fast Nakagami-m fading. Each simulation lasts five laps and each result is the mean of 5 simulations.

A perfect rate adaptation algorithm would detect the presence of a wall between the source and the sink without having to send

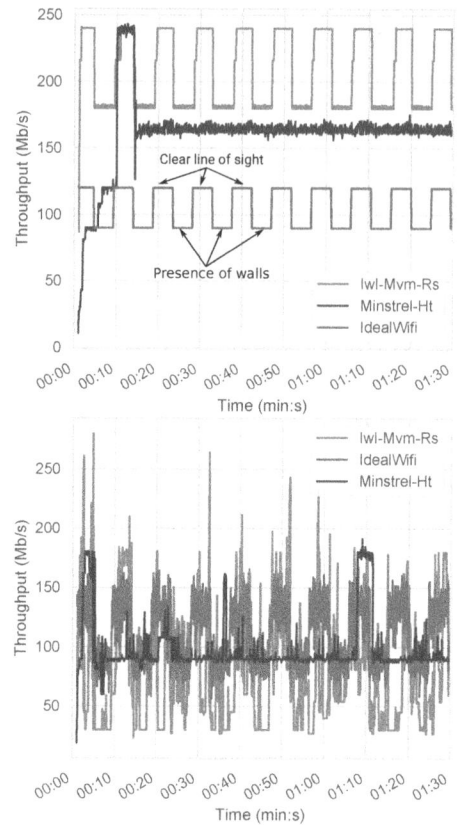

Figure 5: Scenario 2. Evolution of the throughput in the Alternating Wall Scenario for a source throughput of 125 Mb/s and a speed of 5 m/s. Throughput are averaged over periods of 50 ms. Top is without fading, bottom is with fading.

a frame and would change its transmission parameters as soon as needed to counteract the loss induced by shadowing. A slightly less perfect RAA can detect the presence of a wall by detecting changes in its inputs, for example the RSSI, and acts upon these changes to use the best transmission parameters. This is the approach used by IdealWifi, based on the SNR computed at the destination, but this approach is not used in practice for two main reasons. First, it's not realistic to have a perfect out-of-band mechanism for the receiver to send the SNR to the transmitter. Second, it's not always useful to react upon every change in the channel. Indeed, if we consider an hypothetical channel that perfectly transmits one frame out of two and attenuates the other one, then a simple reactive algorithm such as IdealWifi will fail to achieve good performances. As the channel alternates between good and bad transmission conditions and as the RAA uses the previous state of the channel (i.e. an history of 1 frame) to decide which transmission parameters it will use for the next frame, frames with a high transmission rate will be transmitted when the channel is bad, resulting in losses, and frames with low transmission rates will be transmitted when the channel is good, leading to a successful delivery but a loss in throughput. To avoid these pitfalls, real-world RAAs use an history of frame transmission successes and losses and average over this history,

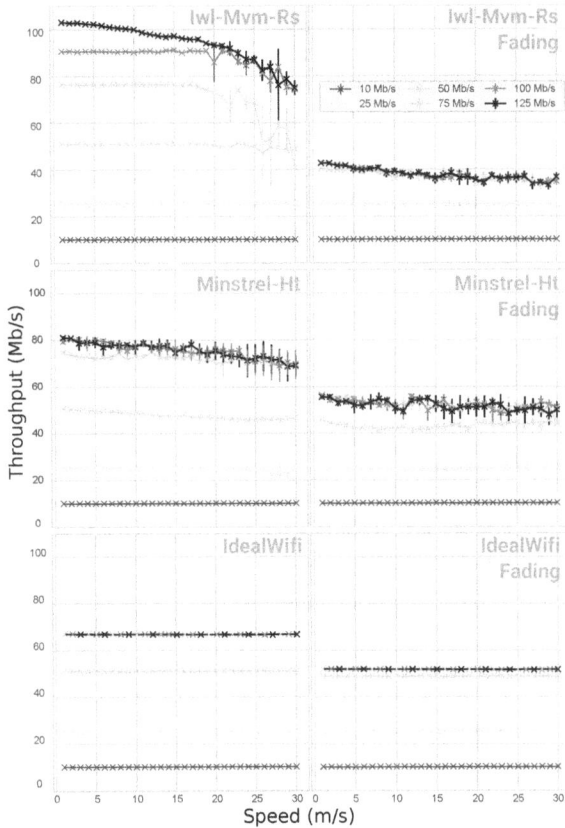

Figure 6: Scenario 2. Evolution of the throughput with regards to the speed and the throughput of the source. Left: without fading, Right: with Nakagami-*m* fading. The vertical bars represent the standard deviation.

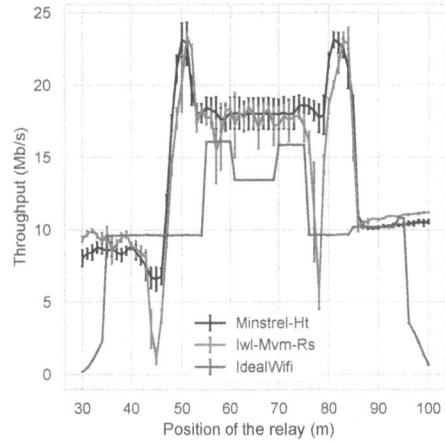

Figure 7: Scenario 3. Evolution of the end-to-end throughput with regards to the relay position. The source is located at d=0m and the sink is located at d=130m.

using methods like the exponentially weighted moving average of Minstrel or Minstrel-Ht, or a simple average for Iwl-Mvm-Rs. These averages act as low-pass filters and create inertia, which in turns may create unresponsiveness in the decisions of the RAAs.

The goal of the *Circular Alternating Walls* scenario is to test the responsiveness of the RAAs. By making sudden changes in the channel, we can illustrate how well a RAA can react to the presence of a wall or a building, which is important in an urban context. The quicker the RAAs adapt, the best, as they can use the full capacity of the channel. Figure 5 presents the evolution of the throughput in this scenario, for a source throughput of 125 Mb/s and a speed of 5 m/s. Without fading, one can observes that the Minstrel-Ht algorithm is not switching rate when walls are present while Iwl-Mvm-Rs and IdealWifi react to the presence of walls, which illustrates the fact that a RAA might not adapt at all to the presence of walls.

Figure 6 shows the evolution of the throughput with regard to speed for the three managers, with and without fading. One observes that above a certain source throughput, the sink throughput measured at the application level decreases as the speed of the moving source increases for both Minstrel-Ht and Iwl-Mvm-Rs. For source throughput of 10Mb/s and 20Mb/s, the impact of the source

speed is limited as the same transmission rate is used whether the source is in the shadows or not, because it can accommodate the needs in throughput. At higher source throughput, such as 75Mb/s and above, a small but steady decrease of the throughput with the speed of the source can be observed for Minstrel-Ht. The big differences in performances between Minstrel-Ht and Iwl-Mvm-Rs are explained by the fact the former does not do any adaptation (as shown on Fig. 5) while the latter does.

4.3 Scenario #3 - Two-hop Flow with Relay

In this scenario, one considers three static STAs communicating in a two-hop fashion. The source sends packets to the sink, packets which are forwarded by the relay. The source is positioned at $x = 0$m and the sink is positioned at $x = 130$m, while the relay position changes depending on the scenario. As in the *Fixed distance* scenario (Scenario 1), the source saturates its communication link with UDP datagrams at $t = 1$s until the end of the simulation that lasts 30s. The results in terms of throughput (measured at the application level of the sink) depending on the position of the relay are displayed on Figure 7. We observe a central symmetry in the throughput results, centered on $x = 65$m, which is expected due to the topology of the simulation. When the relay is far from one of the endpoint (source or sink), then the obtained throughput is low since one of the links is of bad quality. As a result, the sink throughput is capped by the throughput of the low quality link.

With all three RAAs, we get the best performance when the relay is not equidistant from the source and the sink. This is explained by threshold effects, as the quality of the channel does not change linearly with the distance, leading to a higher mean channel quality between the source, the relay and the sink at distance 72m than at 65m. The fact that the IdealWifi manager exhibits this behaviour, while solely basing its decisions on SNR, is another argument for this explanation. In Table 2, one compares the mean transmission rate and the success ratio for the source-relay and the relay-sink links. for the two links, when the relay is located at 65m and 82m from the source.

Table 2: Scenario 3. Mean transmission rate and success ratio.

Solution	$d = 65$		$d = 82$	
	Mean transmission rate (Mb/s)	Success ratio	Mean transmission rate (Mb/s)	Success ratio
Iwl-Mvm-Rs				
source - relay	42.6	94.5%	42.7	94.5%
relay - sink	43	99.5%	64.3	97.5%
Minstrel-HT				
source - relay	43.7	92.1%	41.5	91.9%
relay - sink	38.9	92.1%	85.6	98.6%

One observes that when the distance between the source and the relay is 82m, the transmission rate and the success ratio are similar to the ones obtained when the distance is 65m. However, the second link has a better quality which results in higher transmission rates. This increase of transmission rate has also an impact on the medium occupancy. Indeed, even if the number of sent frames on the second link is higher with a distance of 82m than with 65m, the radio medium is less used by the relay when $d = 82$. This results in more radio accesses for the source that can send more frames when $d = 82$ compared to $d = 65$ although the radio conditions are similar on the first link. For instance, the source with Iwl-Mvm-Rs sends 61900 frames when $d = 82$ whereas it sends 53535 frames when $d = 65$. As a result, the end-to-end throughput at the sink is higher when $d = 82$m.

5 CONCLUSION

In this paper, we have described the rate adaptation algorithm Iwl-Mvm-Rs used by Intel WiFi interfaces. To obtain this algorithm, we have retro-engineered the code of the IwlWiFi driver. We have shown that the Iwl-Mvm-Rs algorithm consists of cycles that include two main parts: the MCS scaling algorithm that seeks to maximize the throughput by changing the MCS and the Column scaling that seeks to find a better parameter combination including the mode (legacy, SISO, MIMO), the guard interval and the antenna configuration. We have implemented the Iwl-Mvm-Rs algorithm in the ns-3 simulator. Thanks to this implementation, we have compared the Iwl-Mvm-Rs algorithm with the Minstrel-HT and IdealWifi algorithms provided in NS-3. Minstrel-HT is also used by real WiFi interfaces. The obtained results on the tested scenarios show that:

- Without fading and node mobility, Minstrel-HT and Iwl-Mvm-Rs perform similarly, as the asymmetry in the number of lost frames or frames in success taken into account in the test window are not adapted to high variable radio conditions. even if the rate adaptation mechanisms are different and do not lead to the same used transmission rates and success ratio. IdealWifi obtains limited performance due to its conservative and rigid behavior.
- Without fading and with mobility, Iwl-Mvm-Rs shows good results, compared to Minstrel-HT and IdealWifi, specifically when the throughput of the source is high. Iwl-Mvm-Rs is able to quickly adapt its transmission rate to the change

of radio conditions due to the presence of walls contrary to Minstrel-HT and IdealWifi.
- With fading and whatever the mobility, the use of Iwl-Mvm-Rs gives lower performance than with Minstrel-HT and IdealWifi. The algorithm has difficulties to deal with the randomness introduced by the fading, due in parts to the small test windows on which it bases its decisions, as well as the asymmetry in the number of lost frames or successful frames needed to makes its decisions.

ACKNOWLEDGMENTS

The authors would like to thanks the Direction Générale de l'Armement (DGA) and the Fédération Informatique de Lyon (FIL) for their financial support.

REFERENCES

[1] 2016. IEEE Standard for Information technology - Telecommunications and information exchange between systems Local and metropolitan area networks - Specific requirements - Part 11: Wireless LAN Medium Access Control (MAC) and Physical Layer (PHY) Specifications. *IEEE Std 802.11-2016 (Revision of IEEE Std 802.11-2012)* (Dec 2016), 1–3534. https://doi.org/10.1109/IEEESTD.2016.7786995

[2] Linux Kernel Contributors. [n.d.]. Intel IwlWiFi Driver ; Linux Kernel Source Tree. https://github.com/torvalds/linux/tree/master/drivers/net/wireless/intel/iwlwifi.

[3] Lara B. Deek, Eduard Garcia Villegas, Elizabeth M. Belding, Sung-Ju Lee, and Kevin C. Almeroth. 2014. Intelligent Channel Bonding in 802.11n WLANs. *IEEE Trans. Mob. Comput.* 13, 6 (2014), 1242–1255. https://doi.org/10.1109/TMC.2013.73

[4] S. Derek. [n.d.]. Minstrel. http://madwifi-project.org/browser/madwifi/trunk/ath_rate/minstrel/minstrel.txt.

[5] Kai-Ten Feng, Po-Tai Lin, and Wen-Jiunn Liu. 2010. Frame-Aggregated Link Adaptation Protocol for Next Generation Wireless Local Area Networks. *EURASIP J. Wireless Comm. and Networking* 2010 (2010). https://doi.org/10.1155/2010/164651

[6] F. Fietkau. [n.d.]. Minstrel HT: New rate control module for 802.11n. https://lwn.net/Articles/376765/.

[7] R. Grünblatt, I. Guérin-Lassous, and O. Simonin. [n.d.]. Source Code of the Iwl-Mvm-Rs implementation in the NS-3 simulator. https://github.com/rgrunbla/ns-3-iwl-mvm-rs.

[8] Raja Karmakar, Samiran Chattopadhyay, and Sandip Chakraborty. 2017. IEEE 802.11ac Link Adaptation Under Mobility. In *42nd IEEE Conference on Local Computer Networks, LCN 2017, Singapore, October 9-12, 2017.* 392–400. https://doi.org/10.1109/LCN.2017.90

[9] Lito Kriara and Mahesh K. Marina. 2015. SampleLite: A Hybrid Approach to 802.11n Link Adaptation. *Computer Communication Review* 45, 2 (2015), 4–13. https://doi.org/10.1145/2766330.2766332

[10] Duy Nguyen and J. J. Garcia-Luna-Aceves. 2011. A practical approach to rate adaptation for multi-antenna systems. In *Proceedings of the 19th annual IEEE International Conference on Network Protocols, ICNP 2011, Vancouver, BC, Canada, October 17-20, 2011.* 331–340. https://doi.org/10.1109/ICNP.2011.6089072

[11] Ioannis Pefkianakis, Yun Hu, Starsky H. Y. Wong, Hao Yang, and Songwu Lu. 2010. MIMO rate adaptation in 802.11n wireless networks. In *Proceedings of the 16th Annual International Conference on Mobile Computing and Networking, MOBICOM 2010, Chicago, Illinois, USA, September 20-24, 2010.* 257–268. https://doi.org/10.1145/1859995.1860025

[12] Sanjib Sur, Ioannis Pefkianakis, Xinyu Zhang, and Kyu-Han Kim. 2016. Practical MU-MIMO user selection on 802.11ac commodity networks. In *Proceedings of the 22nd Annual International Conference on Mobile Computing and Networking, MobiCom 2016, New York City, NY, USA, October 3-7, 2016.* 122–134. https://doi.org/10.1145/2973750.2973758

[13] Sanjib Sur, Ioannis Pefkianakis, Xinyu Zhang, and Kyu-Han Kim. 2016. Practical MU-MIMO User Selection on 802.11Ac Commodity Networks. In *Proceedings of the 22Nd Annual International Conference on Mobile Computing and Networking (MobiCom '16).* ACM, New York, NY, USA, 122–134. https://doi.org/10.1145/2973750.2973758

[14] Iñaki Ucar, Carlos Donato, Pablo Serrano, Andres Garcia-Saavedra, Arturo Azcorra, and Albert Banchs. 2016. Revisiting 802.11 Rate Adaptation from Energy Consumption's Perspective. In *Proceedings of the 19th ACM International Conference on Modeling, Analysis and Simulation of Wireless and Mobile Systems (MSWiM '16).* ACM, New York, NY, USA, 27–34. https://doi.org/10.1145/2988287.2989149

Optimal Access Point Placement for Multi-AP mmWave WLANs

Yuchen Liu, Yubing Jian, Raghupathy Sivakumar and Douglas M. Blough

Georgia Institute of Technology, Atlanta, GA, 30332

ABSTRACT

mmWave communication in 60GHz band has been recognized as an emerging technology to support various bandwidth-hungry applications in indoor scenarios. To maintain ultra-high throughputs while addressing potential blockage problems for mmWave signals, maintaining line-of-sight (LoS) communications between client devices and access points (APs) is critical. To maximize LoS communications, one approach is to deploy multiple APs in the same room. In this paper, we investigate the optimal placement of multiple APs using both analytical methods and simulations. Considering the uncertainty of obstacles and clients, we focus on two typical indoor settings: random-obstacle-random-client (RORC) scenarios and fixed-obstacle-random-client (FORC) scenarios. In the first case, we analytically derive the optimal positions of APs by solving a thinnest covering problem. This analytical result is used to show that deploying up to 5 APs in a specific room brings substantial performance gains. For the FORC scenario, we propose the shadowing-elimination search (SES) algorithm based on an analytic model to efficiently determine the placement of APs. We show, through simulations, that with only a few APs, the network can achieve blockage-free operation in the presence of multiple obstacles and also demonstrate that the algorithm produces near-optimal deployments. Finally, we perform ns-3 simulations based on the IEEE 802.11ad protocol at mmWave frequency to validate our analytical results. The ns-3 results show that proposed multi-AP deployments produce significantly higher aggregate performance as compared to other common AP placements in indoor scenarios.

CCS CONCEPTS

• **Networks** → **Wireless local area networks; Network performance analysis;** • **Mathematics of computing** → **Mathematical optimization.**

KEYWORDS

Millimeter wave; multi-AP; optimal placement; blockage

ACM Reference Format:

Yuchen Liu, Yubing Jian, Raghupathy Sivakumar and Douglas M. Blough. 2019. Optimal Access Point Placement for Multi-AP mmWave WLANs. In *22nd Int'l ACM Conference on Modeling, Analysis and Simulation of Wireless and Mobile Systems (MSWiM '19), November 25–29, 2019, Miami Beach, FL, USA*. ACM, New York, NY, USA, 10 pages. https://doi.org/10.1145/3345768.3355914

1 INTRODUCTION

With the increase in data demand and bandwidth-intensive applications, both academia and industry are pursuing new wireless technologies beyond WiFi and LTE. Millimeter wave (mmWave) communication has the potential to provide multi-gigabit per second data rates due to the large available unlicensed bandwidth [1, 2], and several standardization efforts such as IEEE 802.11ad and WiGig operating on 60GHz mmWave frequency band have already achieved per-link data rates of 7 Gbps in indoor WLANs [3, 4].

However, mmWave signals suffer more severe path loss and penetration loss compared to lower-frequency signals. Even though the use of high-gain directional antennas can help compensate for poor propagation, it is still challenging for mmWave communication to overcome blockage effects [5]. Therefore, line-of-sight (LOS) connectivity between access points (APs) and clients becomes critical to boost link performance, and when mmWave links are blocked by obstacles such as humans and furniture, signal strength is degraded by about 30dB for non-LOS paths [6], which results in lower throughput. Since the transmission ranges are very limited in a typical indoor setting, any link with LoS connectivity between an AP and the client is likely to have a high data rate, and maximizing the number of LOS links will also maximize network throughput.

To overcome blockages and maintain LOS paths in mmWave WLANs, three approaches are: 1) the use of reflected signals, 2) the use of relay nodes, and 3) infrastructure diversity, i.e., multiple APs. Several previous works [7, 8] use reflections to steer around obstacles and provide some blockage resilience, such as in [9], which proposed a solution where 60 GHz signals can bounce off data center ceilings. However, these indirect LOS transmissions suffer severe attenuation due to the absorption of the reflecting surface [10]. Some other works [11–13] use relay nodes to maintain connectivity, and presented different relay selection algorithms. A concern with relays is the end-to-end latency increase due to the additional processing time at each hop and the relatively long-distance transmission, which may interrupt upper layer protocols. With the trend for dense AP deployments, we consider the use of multiple APs as a promising approach to address the blockage problem.

Some related works have focused on protocol design or scheduling strategy for multi-AP indoor mmWave WLANs to maintain LOS communication [14–16]. However, these works do not consider the placement problem with multiple APs, which could provide great benefits for their protocols. Intuitively, severe blockage effects can be mitigated with a good deployment strategy of APs in indoor environments, which will significantly improve the LOS performance of mmWave communication. To our knowledge, there are a few works that have considered the multi-AP deployment issue in mmWave WLANs [17, 18]. In [17], the authors proposed a heuristic algorithm that determines the locations of AP and relays to maximize the coverage by sensing reflection profile. In [18], the impact of base station deployment on LOS probability in 5G indoor scenarios was studied based on simulations, but only five special deployment cases were considered, where the devices followed a linear arrangement, i.e., deployed along the center line of a room.

In this paper, we study the coverage and placement of multiple APs in an indoor scenario such as Fig. 1. Due to the uncertainty of obstacles (e.g. furniture or humans) and client devices, we consider two indoor scenarios: random-obstacle random-client (RORC) scenario and fixed-obstacle random-client (FORC) scenario. In the first case without any obstacle information, the problem becomes how to deploy multiple APs to achieve optimal LOS performance in a bare room. By solving a thinnest covering problem, we derive the optimal positions of multiple APs for arbitrary-sized rectangular rooms. In FORC scenarios where obstacles are fixed and their locations/dimensions are known, e.g. the furniture has been placed in the room, we propose a shadowing-elimination search (SES) algorithm that determines multi-AP locations based on geometric analysis, and the placement of APs achieving full coverage (blockage-free) is also investigated. To evaluate the performance of multi-AP deployments in RORC scenarios, we use the ns-3 simulator based on IEEE 802.11ad protocol at mmWave frequency of 60 GHz. Through simulation results, the proposed optimal placement of APs outperforms other common AP deployment methods in both LOS probability and user throughput.

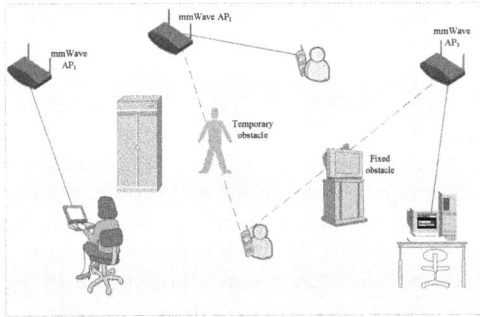

Figure 1: Multi-AP mmWave indoor wireless networks.

2 BLOCKAGE MODEL AND MOTIVATION

In this section, we use a stochastic geometric method to analyze blockage effects in indoor environments and evaluate the LOS performance theoretically.

From the 2-dimensional perspective, obstacles such as stationary furniture or temporarily stopped humans are assumed to form a Boolean scheme of rectangles [19]. The centers C_o of these rectangles fall within the room and form a homogeneous Poisson point process (PPP) of density λ, where the obstacle density is defined as the expected number of obstacles in unit area. The widths W_o and lengths L_o are assumed to be i.i.d. distributed and follow the normal distribution as $N(\mu_w, \sigma_w^2)$ and $N(\mu_l, \sigma_l^2)$, respectively. The orientation θ_o of every obstacle is assumed to be uniformly distributed in $(0, 2\pi]$. In this way, each obstacle $B_o(w, l, \theta)$ is completely characterized by the quadruple $\{C_o, W_o, L_o, \Theta_o\}$.

Based on the Boolean scheme for obstacles in 2D blockage model [20], we obtain the blockage area between client i and AP j as:

$$S_b(w, l, \theta, r) = d_{i,j} \cdot (|\cos\theta| \cdot w + |\sin\theta| \cdot l) + w \cdot l \quad (1)$$

where $d_{i,j}$ is the horizontal distance between AP and its served client, w, l, θ are the obstacle's width, length and orientation, respectively. Then, the expectation of the total number of obstacles K blocking the link between client i and AP j is derived as:

$$E[K] = \int_{W_o} \int_{L_o} \int_{\Theta_o} \frac{1}{2\pi} S_b(w, l, \theta, d) f_{W_o}(w) f_{L_o}(l) dw dl d\theta$$
$$= \frac{2d_{i,j} \cdot (\mu_w + \mu_l)}{\pi} + \mu_w \cdot \mu_l \quad (2)$$

Now we introduce the height effects of obstacles and extend the blockage model to 3 dimensions. It is known that an obstacle intersecting the link between client and AP with a horizontal length of d blocks the LOS path if and only if its height $h_o > h_x$, where $h_x = H_A + \frac{x}{d} \cdot (h_c - H_A)$, and H_A and h_c are the heights of AP and client ($H_A > h_c$), respectively.

Since the heights of obstacles are usually different in reality, we assume that the obstacle's height h_o follows the uniform distribution $H_o \sim U(a_o, b_o)$ in following parts of this paper, thus in this 3-dimensional model, each obstacle $B_o(w, l, h, \theta)$ is extended to be characterized by the quintuple $\{C_o, W_o, L_o, H_o, \Theta_o\}$. We then use B to denote the event that the LOS path between the AP and the client is blocked. Assuming that the height of client h_c also follows the uniform distributions $U(a_c, b_c)$, the conditional probability that an obstacle blocks the LOS path is:

$$\varepsilon = \int_{-\infty}^{+\infty} P(B|h_c) \cdot f_H(h_c) dh_c$$
$$= \int_{a_c}^{b_c} [1 - \int_0^1 \int_0^{y \cdot h_c + (1-y)H_A} f_H(h_o) dh dy] \cdot f_H(h_c) dh_c \quad (3)$$
$$= 1 - \frac{2H_A - b_o - a_o}{2 \cdot (b_c - a_c)} \cdot \ln(\frac{H_A - a_c}{H_A - b_c}).$$

Note that ε is independent of K when the intersections with obstacles form a PPP on the LOS path between AP and client. Therefore, incorporating the heights of obstacles only introduces a constant scaling factor ε to results that ignore the height. According to the PPP thinning property, $E[K]'$ in 3D blockage model is $\varepsilon E[K]$ for incorporating the height effect of obstacles. Finally, we arrive at the LOS probability between client i and AP j:

$$P_{LOS_{i,j}} = \exp\{-\lambda \cdot [\frac{2d_{i,j}(\mu_w + \mu_l)}{\pi} - \frac{d_{i,j}(\mu_w + \mu_l)(2H_A - b_o - a_o)}{\pi(b_c - a_c)} \cdot$$
$$\ln(\frac{H_A - a_c}{H_A - b_c}) - \frac{\mu_w \mu_l(2H_A - b_o - a_o)}{2 \cdot (b_c - a_c)}) \cdot \ln(\frac{H_A - a_c}{H_A - b_c}) + \mu_w \cdot \mu_l]\}. \quad (4)$$

With this analytical result, we investigate how the AP's height H_A affects the LOS probability. According to Eq. (4), we find that P_{LOS} increases monotonically with increasing H_A, **which proves that the largest AP height provides the maximum LOS probability**. Therefore, APs should be mounted on the ceiling of the room to achieve the best LOS performance. In what follows, we focus on 2D deployment of ceiling-mounted APs in different indoor scenarios, and the 3D coordinates of APs can be easily obtained by adding the APs' height (i.e., the room's height).

3 MULTI-AP PLACEMENT IN RORC SCENARIOS

In these scenarios, all obstacles and clients are randomly distributed, and the problem of maximizing LOS probability is equivalent to deploying APs so as to maximize the coverage of a given room.

3.1 Horizontal distance minimization

In a specific room, we assume that clients are randomly located and will find the closest APs for connection. Thus our objective is to deploy N APs in order to maximize the minimum LOS probability between each AP and its served users, and the problem can be formulated as:

$$\max_{Pos} \min_{i \in U} \{ \max_{j \in AP} P_{LOS_{i,j}} \}, \forall Pos \in Rm. \tag{5}$$

where Pos are positions of APs and should not beyond the range of room. To simplify Eq. (5), we give the specific room sizes and obstacle distributions in Eq. (4), and it is observed that $P_{LOS_{i,j}}$ is inversely proportional to the horizontal distance $d_{i,j}$ between the client and AP. Therefore, we can reformulate the problem in Eq. (5) as finding APs' positions that minimize the maximum horizontal distance between the random client and its served AP, which can be described as:

$$\arg \min_{Pos} \max \{ \min_{i \in U} \|u_i - Pos_j\|_2 \}, \forall u, Pos \in Rm. \tag{6}$$

Of particular note, with several specific (known) clients u in the room, the RORC scenario is transformed to a random-obstacle-fixed-client (ROFC) scenario, and we can find the optimal locations of APs by solving Eq. (6).

However, it is not easy to find the optimal positions of multiple APs without known users in the RORC scenario, since it will take an impractically long time to obtain the optimal solution by solving Eq. (6) when the number of APs is larger than 2.

For rectangular rooms, we can transform this multi-AP deployment (MD) problem into the *Thinnest covering (TC) problem* [21], which is a classical mathematical problem that aims to find n congruent discs (circles) with the smallest radius r_n that cover a specific rectangle. As Fig. 2 shows, the goal of the *Thinnest covering problem* is equivalent to our objective function in Eq. (6), which is trying to find optimal placement of n APs that minimizes the maximum horizontal distance (referred to as the achievable distance d_{ac}) between a random client and its serving AP. Here r_n in the TC problem is equal to d_{ac} in the MD problem, and the center point of each circle in TC problem is the optimal position of each AP. In what follows, we derive the optimal placement for different numbers of APs in RORC scenarios.

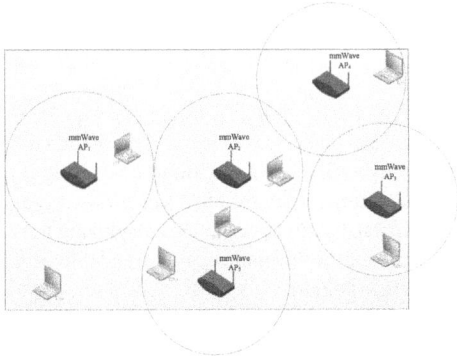

Figure 2: An example of covering a room with multiple APs.

3.2 Multi-AP deployment cases

In this part, we use both analytic methods and the simulated annealing approach in [21, 22] to solve this *Thinnest covering problem*, and derive the optimal locations of single or multiple APs in arbitrary-sized rectangular rooms.

First, we start with the simplest case when n is 1, i.e., deploying a single AP to achieve maximum LOS probability. Since ceiling-mounted APs are utilized, here we just focus on 2D placement of AP in RORC indoor settings. In a specific room with the length r_l and width r_w ($r_l \geq r_w$), the thinnest covering of a rectangle with one circle is shown in Fig. 3 (a), and **the optimal position for single AP is** $(\frac{r_l}{2}, \frac{r_w}{2})$. The achievable distance d_{ac}, i.e., the smallest radius of the circle r_1, is $\frac{1}{2}\sqrt{r_l^2 + r_w^2}$. This result shows that deploying the single AP in the center of the room provides the best LOS performance for randomly located clients.

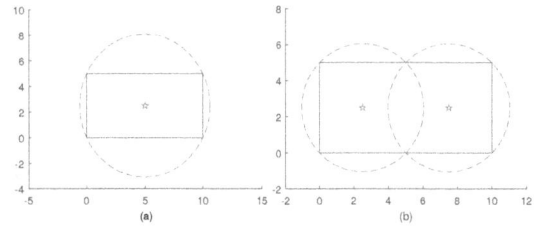

Figure 3: Optimal positions of 1-2 APs ($r_l = 10$m, $r_w = 5$m).

In the 2-AP deployment case, the unique thinnest covering with two circles is shown in Fig. 3 (b), thus **the optimal positions for two APs are** $(\frac{r_l}{4}, \frac{r_w}{2})$ and $(\frac{3r_l}{4}, \frac{r_w}{2})$, and $d_{ac} = \frac{1}{4}\sqrt{r_l^2 + 4r_w^2}$.

Considering the 3-AP deployment, there are two types of thinnest covering in terms of room sizes (shown in Fig. 4). With different length-width ratios of the room, we derive **the optimal positions for three APs as:**

$$(x_i^*, y_i^*) = \begin{cases} (\frac{r_l}{6}, \frac{r_w}{2}), (\frac{2r_l}{3}, \frac{r_w}{4}), (\frac{2r_l}{3}, \frac{3r_w}{4}), & \text{if } \frac{r_l}{r_w} \leq \frac{3}{2}; \\ (\frac{r_l}{6}, \frac{r_w}{2}), (\frac{r_l}{2}, \frac{r_w}{2}), (\frac{5r_l}{6}, \frac{r_w}{2}), & \text{if } \frac{r_l}{r_w} > \frac{3}{2}. \end{cases} \tag{7}$$

The corresponding d_{ac} are $\frac{\sqrt{16r_l^4 + 40r_l^2 r_w^2 + 9r_w^4}}{16r_l}$ and $\frac{\sqrt{r_l^2 + 9r_w^2}}{6}$, respectively.

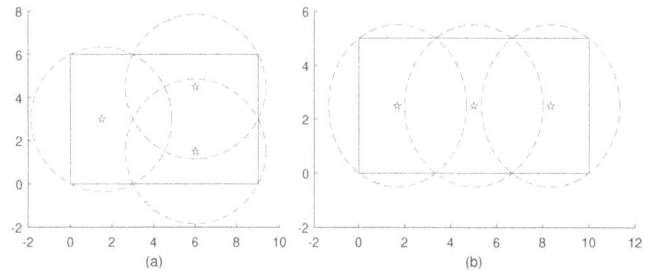

Figure 4: Optimal positions of 3 APs ((a) $r_l = 9$m, $r_w = 6$m; (b) $r_l = 10$m, $r_w = 5$m).

In the same way, **the optimal positions** (x_i^*, y_i^*) **for 4-AP case are** derived as follow:

$$\begin{cases} (\frac{r_l}{4}, \frac{r_w}{4}), (\frac{r_l}{4}, \frac{3r_w}{4}), (\frac{3r_l}{4}, \frac{r_w}{4}), (\frac{3r_l}{4}, \frac{3r_w}{4}) \ if \ \frac{r_l}{r_w} \le \sqrt{\frac{5+16\sqrt{10}}{15}}; \\ (K_{x1}, \frac{r_w}{2}), (\frac{r_l}{2}, 0), (\frac{r_l}{2}, r_w), (r_l - K_{x1}, \frac{r_l}{2}) \ if \ \sqrt{\frac{5+16\sqrt{10}}{15}} < \frac{r_l}{r_w} < \frac{4}{\sqrt{3}}; \\ (\frac{r_l}{8}, \frac{r_w}{2}), (\frac{3r_l}{8}, \frac{r_w}{2}), (\frac{5r_l}{8}, \frac{r_w}{2}), (\frac{7r_l}{8}, \frac{r_w}{2}) \quad if \ \frac{r_l}{r_w} \ge \frac{4}{\sqrt{3}}, \end{cases}$$

$$(8)$$

where $K_{x1} = \sqrt{\frac{r_w^2}{36}(2\sqrt{\frac{r_l^2}{r_w^2}+3} - \frac{r_l}{r_w})^2 - \frac{r_w^2}{4}}$. The corresponding d_{ac} are $\frac{\sqrt{r_l^2+r_w^2}}{4}$, $\frac{2\sqrt{r_l^2+3r_w^2}-r_l}{6}$ and $\frac{\sqrt{r_l^2+16r_w^2}}{8}$, respectively. As Fig. 5 shows, there are 3 optimal deployment types for 4-AP case with respect to different length-width ratios of the room.

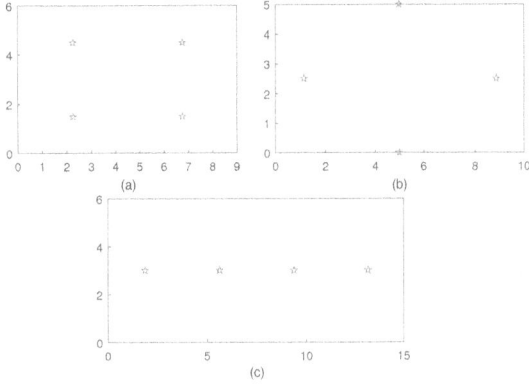

Figure 5: Optimal positions of 4 APs ((a) $r_l = 9$m, $r_w = 6$m; (b) $r_l = 10$m, $r_w = 5$; (c) $r_l = 15$m, $r_w = 6$m).

Considering the 5-AP deployment, the situation becomes more complicated since there are four types of thinnest covering in terms of different length-width ratios of room (shown in Fig. 6), where **the optimal positions (x_i^*, y_i^*) of these 5 APs are derived as:**

$$\begin{cases} Type \ I: \ (\frac{r_l}{6}, K_{y1}), (\frac{r_l}{2}, K_{y1}), (\frac{5r_l}{6}, K_{y1}), (\frac{r_l}{4}, K_{y2}), (\frac{3r_l}{4}, K_{y2}), \\ \qquad\qquad if \ \frac{r_l}{r_w} \le 2.02; \\ Type \ II: \ (K_{x2}, \frac{r_w}{4}), (K_{x2}, \frac{3r_w}{4}), (\frac{r_l}{2}, \frac{r_w}{2}), (r_l - K_{x2}, \frac{r_w}{4}), \\ \qquad\qquad (r_l - K_{x2}, \frac{3r_w}{4}), \qquad if \ 2.02 < \frac{r_l}{r_w} \le 2.35; \\ Type \ III: \ (K_{x3}, \frac{r_w}{2}), (K_{x4}, 0), (K_{x4}, r_w), (K_{x5}, \frac{r_w}{2}), \\ \qquad\qquad (r_l - K_{x3}, \frac{r_w}{2}), \qquad if \ 2.35 < \frac{r_l}{r_w} \le \frac{5}{\sqrt{3}}; \\ Type \ IV: \ (\frac{r_l}{10}, \frac{r_w}{2}), (\frac{3r_l}{10}, \frac{r_w}{2}), (\frac{r_l}{2}, \frac{r_w}{2}), (\frac{7r_l}{10}, \frac{r_w}{2}), (\frac{9r_l}{10}, \frac{r_w}{2}), \\ \qquad\qquad if \ \frac{r_l}{r_w} > \frac{5}{\sqrt{3}}. \end{cases}$$

$$(9)$$

where

$$\begin{cases} K_{y1} = \sqrt{D_5(1)^2 - \frac{r_l^2}{36}}, \ K_{y2} = r_w - \sqrt{D_5(1)^2 - \frac{r_l^2}{16}}, \\ K_{x2} = \sqrt{D_5(2)^2 - \frac{r_w^2}{16}}, K_{x4} = 2\sqrt{D_5(3)^2 - \frac{r_w^2}{4}} + D_5(3), \\ K_{x3} = \sqrt{D_5(3)^2 - \frac{r_w^2}{4}}, \ K_{x5} = 3\sqrt{D_5(3)^2 - \frac{r_w^2}{4}} + 2D_5(3), \end{cases}$$

$$(10)$$

where $D_5(i)$ ($1 \le i \le 4$) is the achievable distance d_{ac} of *Type i*, and $D_5(1)$ is the smallest positive real root of the equation in Theorem 5 of [21], $D_5(2) = \frac{1}{6}\sqrt{5r_l^2 - 2r_l\sqrt{4r_l^2 - 9r_w^2}}$, $D_5(3) = \frac{1}{16}(3\sqrt{r_l^2 + 8r_w^2} - r_l)$, and $D_5(4) = \frac{1}{10}\sqrt{r_l^2 + 25r_w^2}$.

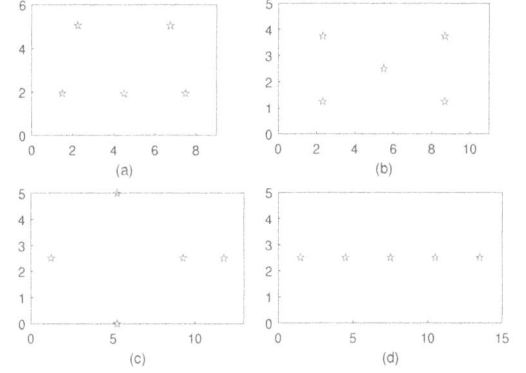

Figure 6: Optimal positions of 5 APs ((a) $r_l = 9$m, $r_w = 6$m; (b) $r_l = 11$m, $r_w = 5$; (c) $r_l = 13$m, $r_w = 5$m; (d) $r_l = 15$m, $r_w = 5$m).

In the 6-AP deployment case, we also have four different types which are shown in Fig. 7, and **the optimal positions of these 6 APs are derived as follows:**

$$\begin{cases} Type \ I: \ (\frac{r_l}{6}, \frac{r_w}{4}), (\frac{r_l}{6}, \frac{3r_w}{4}), (\frac{r_l}{2}, \frac{r_w}{4}), (\frac{r_l}{2}, \frac{3r_w}{4}), \\ \qquad\quad (\frac{5r_l}{6}, \frac{r_w}{4}), (\frac{5r_l}{6}, \frac{3r_w}{4}), \ \ if \ \frac{r_l}{r_w} \le 2.92; \\ Type \ II: \ (K_{x6}, \frac{r_w}{4}), (K_{x6}, \frac{3r_w}{4}), (K_{x7}, \frac{r_w}{2}), (K_{x8}, 0), \\ \qquad\quad (K_{x8}, r_w), (K_{x9}, \frac{r_w}{2}), \ \ if \ 2.92 < \frac{r_l}{r_w} \le 2 + \frac{\sqrt{5}}{2}; \\ Type \ III: \ (K_{x10}, \frac{r_w}{2}), (K_{x11}, \frac{r_w}{2}), (\frac{r_l}{2}, 0), (\frac{r_l}{2}, r_w), \\ \qquad\quad (r_l - K_{x11}, \frac{r_w}{2}), (r_l - K_{x10}, \frac{r_w}{2}), if \ 2 + \frac{\sqrt{5}}{2} < \frac{r_l}{r_w} \le \frac{6}{\sqrt{3}}; \\ Type \ IV: \ (\frac{r_l}{12}, \frac{r_w}{2}), (\frac{r_l}{4}, \frac{r_w}{2}), (\frac{5r_l}{12}, \frac{r_w}{2}), (\frac{7r_l}{12}, \frac{r_w}{2}), \\ \qquad\quad (\frac{3r_l}{4}, \frac{r_w}{2}), (\frac{11r_l}{12}, \frac{r_w}{2}), \ \ if \ \frac{r_l}{r_w} > \frac{6}{\sqrt{3}}. \end{cases}$$

$$(11)$$

where

$$\begin{cases} K_{x6} = \sqrt{D_6(2)^2 - \frac{r_w^2}{16}}, K_{x7} = 2\sqrt{D_6(2)^2 - \frac{r_w^2}{16}} + \sqrt{D_6(2)^2 - \frac{r_w^2}{4}}, \\ K_{x8} = D_6(2) + 2\sqrt{D_6(2)^2 - \frac{r_w^2}{16}} + 2\sqrt{D_6(2)^2 - \frac{r_w^2}{4}}, \\ K_{x9} = r_l - \sqrt{D_6(2)^2 - \frac{r_w^2}{4}}, \ K_{x10} = \sqrt{D_6(3)^2 - \frac{r_w^2}{4}}, \\ K_{x11} = 3\sqrt{D_6(3)^2 - \frac{r_w^2}{4}}. \end{cases}$$

$$(12)$$

Here the achievable distance of *Type I* $D_6(1) = \frac{1}{12}\sqrt{4r_l^2 + 9r_w^2}$, $D_6(2)$ of *Type II* is the smallest positive root of following equation:

$$2\sqrt{4D_6(2)^2 - r_w^2} + 2D_6(2) + \sqrt{4D_6(2)^2 - 1/4r_w^2} - r_l = 0, \quad (13)$$

and $D_6(3) = \frac{1}{30} \cdot (4\sqrt{r_l^2 + 15r_w^2} - r_l)$, $D_6(4) = \frac{1}{12}\sqrt{r_l^2 + 36r_w^2}$.

For other optimal placement cases with more than 6 APs, we can use the same way to first solve the thinnest covering problem, and then derive the optimal positions of APs in different types. Actually, for all cases reported on in later sections, deploying 6 APs provides more than sufficient performance gains and deploying additional APs provides little benefit.

In particular, from the optimal placement results of 1~6 APs, it is observed that there always exists one special deployment type that linearly arranges APs when the room is longer (i.e., r_l/r_w is large), such as the results shown in Fig. 4 (b), Fig. 5 (c), Fig. 6 (d) and Fig.7 (d), thus we make an important conclusion:

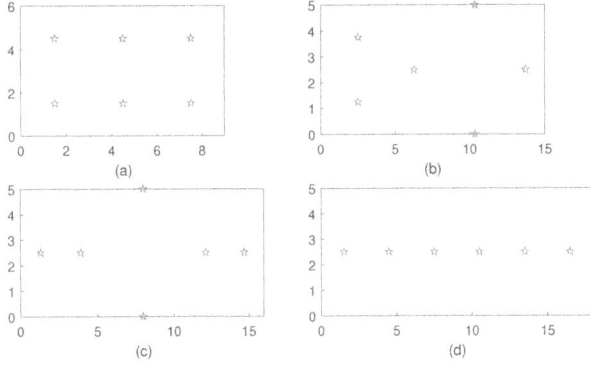

Figure 7: Optimal positions of 6 APs ((a) $r_l = 9$m, $r_w = 6$m; (b) $r_l = 15$m, $r_w = 5$; (c) $r_l = 16$m, $r_w = 5$m; (d) $r_l = 18$m, $r_w = 5$m).

Theorem 1 *(Linear arrangement condition) In a specific room* $(r_l \times r_w \times r_h)$ *with N APs, if* $r_l/r_w > N/\sqrt{3}$, *the optimal deployment method is to linearly arrange APs on the ceiling and along the center line of the shorter edge of room, where the optimal position of* i^{th} *AP is* $(\frac{(2i-1)r_l}{2N}, \frac{r_w}{2}, r_h)$.

PROOF. According to the geometric analysis for thinnest covering of a longer rectangle, we can find the smallest radius of circles $r_n = d_{ac} \geq \frac{1}{2}\sqrt{(\frac{r_l}{N \cdot r_w})^2 + 1}$, and the linear covering like in Fig. 4 (b) is the only arrangement that attains the lower bound of r_n if $r_l/r_w > N/\sqrt{3}$. Then we can derive the y-axis coordinate of each AP must be in the middle of short edge of the room, and x-axis coordinate for i^{th} AP along the longer edge of room is $[(2i-1)r_l]/2N$. Since we adopt the ceiling-based APs to achieve better LOS performance (see Sec. 2), the z-axis of each AP is obtained as r_h. □

3.3 Analysis of multi-AP degree

Based on the preceding theoretical analysis of multi-AP deployment in RORC scenarios, here we investigate the performance benefits of different numbers of APs.

First, we derive the expected LOS probability (ELP) as a metric for subsequent evaluation. Since a randomly-located client can be viewed as a random point distributed in a circle with a radius of D_n (i.e., achievable distance d_{ac}), ELP of a random client and its connected AP is derived as:

$$ELP = \int_0^{D_n} P_{LOS_{i,j}}(x) \cdot \frac{2x}{D_n^2} dx$$
$$= \frac{2e^{-C_2}}{C_1^2 \cdot D_n^2} \cdot (1 - e^{-C_1 \cdot D_n} - C_1 \cdot D_n \cdot e^{-C_1 \cdot D_n}) \qquad (14)$$

where $C_1 = \frac{2\varepsilon \cdot \lambda \cdot (\mu_l + \mu_w)}{\pi}$, $C_2 = \varepsilon \cdot \lambda \cdot \mu_l \cdot \mu_w$, $P_{LOS_{i,j}}$ has been derived in Eq. (4), and D_n is the maximum horizontal distance which can be obtained in Sec. 3.2 in terms of the number of APs n.

We evaluate the expected LOS probability with respect to the degree of APs and obstacle density. Fig.8 (a) shows the results in a 9m × 6m room, and we find that deploying an odd number of APs brings smaller performance improvement than deploying an even number of APs, e.g., deploying 3 APs brings little performance

increase compared with deploying 2 APs, but there is a relatively larger improvement with 4 APs instead of 3 APs. Besides, the performance gains become much smaller with higher numbers of APs, and this result is more obvious in Fig.8 (b) with a "longer" room (18m × 5m), especially when the number of APs is larger than 5, the sixth AP only brings a performance increase of less than 1%.

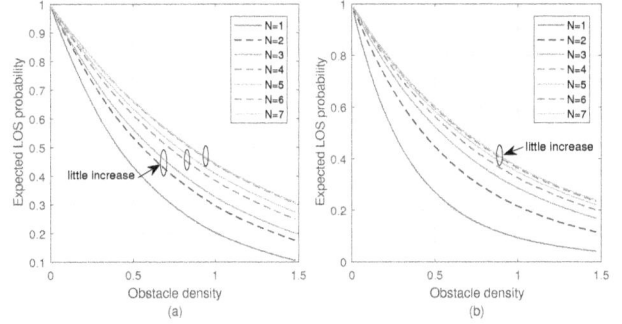

Figure 8: Excepted LOS probability vs. degree of AP and obstacle density.

In addition, we also investigate how room sizes affect the LOS performance. In Fig.9, with the specific obstacle density ($\lambda = 0.4$) and room's length-width ratio ($r_l/r_w = 2.5$), it shows that the ELP decreases as the room size increases with different numbers of APs, and this is because the maximal horizontal distance (D_n) increases with a larger room, which results in a higher probability of experiencing blockage between an AP and its clients. On the other hand, as the number of APs increases with a specific room area, the performance improvement brought by higher numbers of APs is marginal, where the average performance increases over different room areas from 2nd AP to 7th AP are 40.21%, 10.56%, 4.43%, 2.17%, 1.43% and 1.06%, respectively. Considering the cost of commercial mmWave AP devices, such as TP-Link Talon AD7200 Multi-Band Wi-Fi Router at $350 [23], the second "$350" brings 40.21% potential performance increase, but the sixth or seventh "$350" only brings around 1% improvement, which also accords with *the law of diminishing marginal utility*. Therefore, we demonstrate that **a number of APs of up to 5 offer higher relative performance gains**, while improvements brought by higher degrees are marginal.

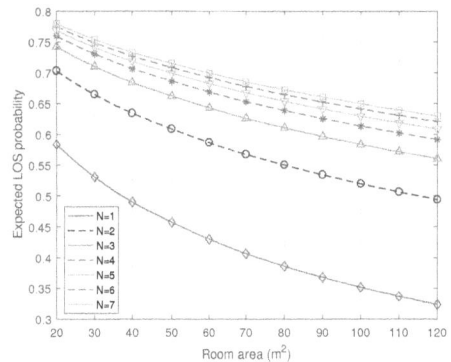

Figure 9: Excepted LOS probability vs. room size with different number of APs.

4 MULTI-AP PLACEMENT IN FORC SCENARIOS

In this section, we consider another more realistic scenario, where the furniture such as tables, bookshelf or other objects with "obvious" heights [1] has been placed in the room, which forms a FORC scenario. With these fixed and known obstacles in indoor settings, we investigate how to deploy the single or multiple APs that provides better LOS communications for random-located clients.

4.1 Shadowing area minimization

In the FORC scenario, to achieve better LOS performance with multiple APs, the problem becomes finding locations of ceiling-mounted APs that can provide maximum effective LOS region for clients in the presence of known obstacles. In other words, the objective is to deploy APs so as to minimize the shadowing region (SR) caused by obstacles, so the formulated problem is described as:

$$\arg\min_{Pos} \bigcup_{i \in Obs} SA_i, \forall Pos \in Rm \qquad (15)$$

where SA_i is the area of SR caused by the obstacle i, and Pos are the positions of APs.

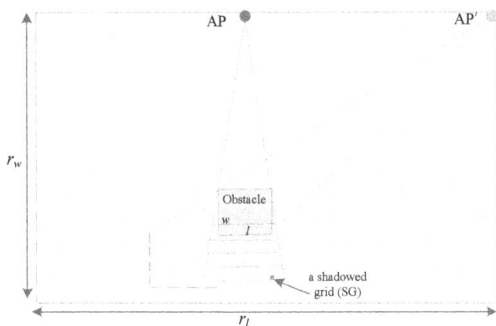

Figure 10: Top view of the SR caused by a single obstacle.

Fig. 10 shows an example of SR caused by a fixed obstacle, and the shape or size of SR is determined by several factors, such as the size of obstacle and the relative positions between AP and the obstacle. Here we make the assumption that obstacles in the room have only two orientations: $0°$ and $90°$, which means that the edges of obstacle will be parallel with the walls. This assumption is reasonable in practice since we typically deploy furniture in the same direction as one of the walls in the room.

To solve Eq. (15) and find the placement of APs, we introduce a *grid-based shadowing search* (GSS) method to calculate the shadowing area (SA), where the main idea is to first divide the rectangle (see Fig. 10) into a large number of small grids with side length[2] l_g. Then, we find all shadowed grids (SG) whose center points fall in the shadowing region. After traversing all grid elements, SA is found as the cumulative area of shadowed grids. According to a geometric analysis, we determine that a grid element is shadowed if its center point exists in a shadowing polygon formed by an AP

---

[1]Here the object with the height larger than general height of client is considered as the obvious obstacle, since objects with very small heights will have no effect on LOS paths between ceiling-mounted APs and clients.
[2]A smaller l_g provides more accurate results but has higher computational cost.

and known obstacles. Due to space limitations, a detailed geometric analysis of this point-existent problem is not presented but can be found in our companion technical report [24].

4.2 Single-AP single-obstacle case

In this part, we start from a simple case where there are a single AP and one obstacle in the room. By using the GSS method to obtain SA in terms of different AP's positions, we can find the optimal AP's position which has minimum shadowing area SA_{min}. Assuming the clients are randomly distributed in the room, the LOS probability can be derived as $SA_{min}/(r_w \cdot r_l)$.

Fig. 11 shows an example with one fixed obstacle in a specific room (12m*8m*3m), and we observe that the optimal position of AP will be on one edge of the room (the red region shown in Fig. 11 (a)), and the corresponding LOS probabilities with different AP's positions are shown in Fig. 11 (b).

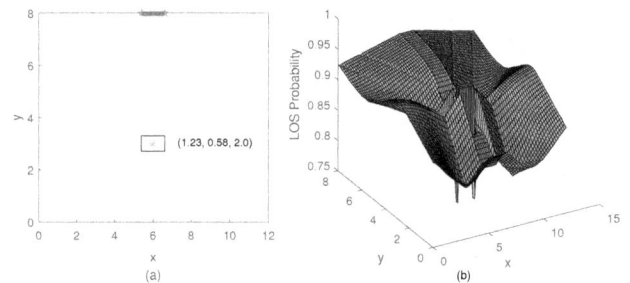

Figure 11: Optimal position of AP in a single-obstacle case (obstacle's height $h_o = 2.0$m).

When we consider a similar case but the obstacle has a lower height ($h_o = 1.2$m), it is observed that the optimal position of AP is now above the obstacle (shown in Fig. 12). Therefore, we conclude that the obstacle's height has a significant impact on the optimal position of an AP, and **deploying the AP on one edge of the room or directly above the obstacle achieves the best LOS performance in single-obstacle cases.**

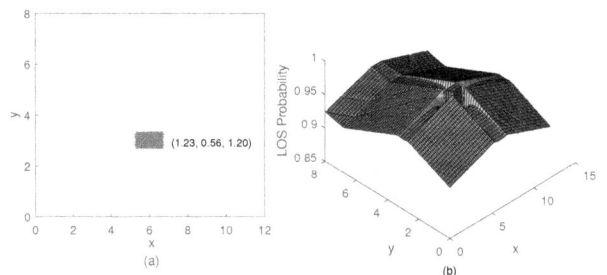

Figure 12: Optimal position of AP in a single-obstacle case (obstacle's height $h_o = 1.2$m).

4.3 Single-AP multi-obstacle case

Considering multi-obstacle cases with a single AP, one important step is to first find the union of SRs (i.e., without overlapping area) caused by different obstacles, and then the optimal placement of AP can be obtained by solving Eq. (15). Here, Algorithm 1 shows the method of calculating shadowing area with multiple obstacles for each AP's position. For every obstacle i, GSS method is conducted to get shadowed-grid set SG_i, which includes all grids shadowed by this obstacle (Line 3). Then, we start to check whether the grid in SG_i has already been put in SG_{new} (Lines 4-5), and if not, this new shadowed grid will be added in SG_{new} (Lines 5-6). This step is used to eliminate the overlapping shadowing area caused by different obstacles. After traversing all known obstacles, the union of SRs is obtained (Line 10), and finally we find the optimal position of AP by solving Eq. (15).

Algorithm 1 Finding the union of SR in multi-obstacle case

Input: Obs (obstacles' positions), pos (AP's position), G (grid set), l_g (grid length), $params$ (includes r_w, r_l, H_A, size of each obstacle)
Output: SA_u
1: SG_{new}=[]; // init the shadowed-grid set
2: **for** each obstacle $i \in Obs$ **do**
3:     $[SA_i, SG_i]$ = GSSFunction($Obs(i)$, pos, G, $params$);
4:     **for** each grid $j \in SG_i$ **do**
5:         **if** ($j \notin SG_{new}$) **then**
6:             SG.add($G(j)$);
7:         **end if**
8:     **end for**
9: **end for**
10: SA_u=size(SG_{new}) · l_g^2;
11: **return** SA_u, SG_{new};

Fig. 13 shows two multi-obstacle cases with the optimal AP placement. In Fig. 13 (a), because four obstacles have the same sizes and are symmetrically located, there exist four equivalent positions (red stars) to optimally deploy the AP with minimum SR, but if all the heights of these obstacles are changed to 2.0m, we have only one optimal position of AP (blue star), which also implies that the heights of obstacles have a significant impact on optimal AP deployment. For another case shown in Fig. 13 (b), where multiple obstacles with different sizes are randomly distributed, only one optimal position of AP is found to achieve best LOS performance. From the results of these cases, we observe that the AP deployment in FORC scenarios is obviously different from that in RORC scenarios (placing AP in the center of the room), which means that **the optimal AP placement is closely related to whether the information of obstacles is known or not.**

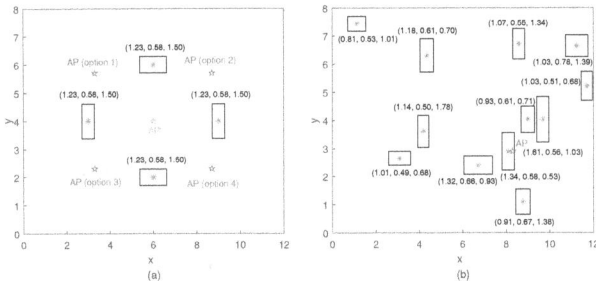

Figure 13: Optimal position of AP in multi-obstacle cases.

4.4 Multi-AP multi-obstacle case

In this part, we consider the multi-AP placement in FORC scenarios. Actually the optimal positions of multiple APs can be found by using the same method as in single-AP cases, but it is hard to solve Eq. (15) within a reasonable time when the number of APs is larger. Therefore, we propose a shadowing-elimination search (SES) algorithm to heuristically solve this multi-AP deployment problem.

Algorithm 2 summarizes the steps of the SES algorithm. First, considering all grids within the room, Algorithm 1 is conducted to get the union of shadowing area for each possible AP's position (Lines 3-5). Then, the optimal position of the first AP is found which has the minimum SR (Lines 6-7). Before starting to find the next AP's position, the grid set G is updated as the shadowed-grid set of first AP (Line 8), which means that the following AP will be placed at the position that eliminates the most remaining SRs of the first AP. With this process, we can find all positions of N APs with the minimum remaining SR of the first AP and achieve maximum coverage.

Algorithm 2 Shadowing-elimination search

Input: Obs, l_g, $params$, N
Output: P_{ap}
1: G=[all grids $\in Rm$]; // first consider all grids
2: **for** each AP i from 1 to N **do**
3:     **for** each pos of AP i **do**
4:         $[SA_{u_i}, SG_i]$=FindUnionSR(Obs, pos, G, l_g, $params$);
5:     **end for**
6:     AP_i=arg min$\{SA_{u_i}\}$;
7:     P_{ap}.add(AP_i);
8:     G=[grids in SG_i]; // update G
9: **end for**
10: **return** P_{ap};

By running the SES algorithm, Fig 14 shows the placement of multiple APs in the same scenarios with Fig 13. By deploying 3 APs in each case, their remaining shadowing areas are 0.11m^2 and 0.56m^2, respectively.

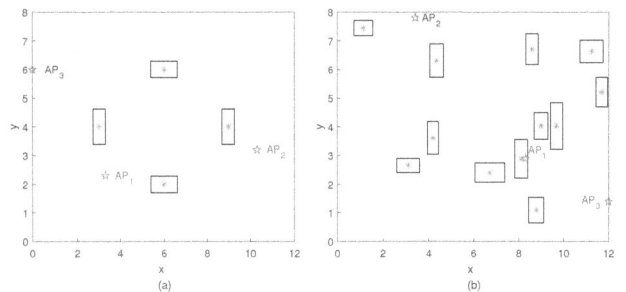

Figure 14: Multi-AP deployment in multi-obstacle cases.

4.5 Blockage-free multi-AP mmWave WLANs

As the density of AP increases, the remaining shadowing area will be entirely eliminated to achieve full coverage, i.e., the mmWave network scenario becomes blockage-free and randomly-located clients can always have LOS connections. In this part, we investigate how to place multiple APs to make the environment become blockage-free (shown in Algorithm 3). Based on the SES algorithm, we find the optimal position of the first AP (Lines 4-8), and then the grid set G is updated for following shadowing elimination process (Line 9). Next, we compute the LOS probability P_{LOS} which is related to the remaining shadowing area, and once all SR is eliminated such that P_{LOS} becomes 1, the whole process is terminated (Lines 10-13). Finally, the required number of APs and their respective positions are obtained (Line 16).

Algorithm 3 Finding multi-AP deployment to achieve the blockage-free condition

---

Input: $Obs, l_g, params$
Output: $P_{ap}; NumAP$
1: Gd=[all grids $\in Rm$]; // first consider all grids
2: $i = 1$;
3: **while** $i > 0$ **do**
4:    **for** each pos of AP i **do**
5:       $[SA_{u_i}, SG_i]$=FindUnionSR($Obs, pos, G, l_g, params$);
6:    **end for**
7:    AP_i=arg min$\{SA_{u_i}\}$;
8:    P_{ap}.add(AP_i);
9:    G=[grids in SG_i]; // update G
10:   $P_{LOS} = 1 - \frac{SA_{u_i}}{r_l \cdot r_w}$;
11:   **if** $P_{LOS} = 1$ **then**
12:      **break**; // stop finding the next AP
13:   **end if**
14:   $i = i + 1$;
15: **end while**
16: **return** $P_{ap}, NumAP = i$;

By running Algorithm 3, Fig. 15 shows two examples of placing multiple APs to achieve the blockage-free condition. It is observed that 3 and 4 APs are required in Fig. 15 (a) and (b), respectively, and with following multi-AP deployments in both cases, every client will have LOS communication because of the full coverage.

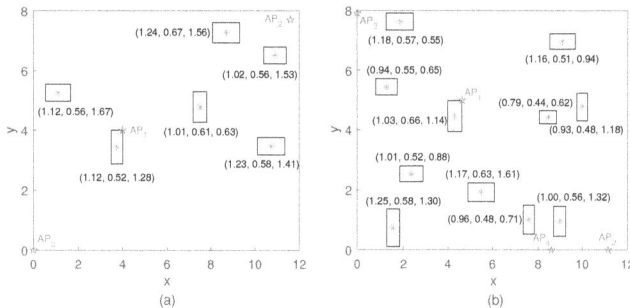

Figure 15: The deployment of multiple APs in blockage-free cases.

5 PERFORMANCE STUDY

In this section, we do the simulation-based analysis in multi-AP mmWave WLANs. First, the simulation platform based on ns-3 mmWave model is introduced. Then, we evaluate the network performance with proposed AP deployments in different scenarios.

5.1 ns-3 mmWave indoor network model

To incorporate the features of indoor configurations, we modified the ns-3 simulator based on IEEE 802.11ad protocol [25].

First, we implement the indoor scenario with an obstacle model that has following features: 1) obstacles are modeled as cuboids and placed on the floor; 2) the center of the obstacle follows a Poisson point process with a specific density; 3) the width and length of obstacle follow truncated normal distributions as W~ $\mathcal{TN}$(0.56, 0.08, 0.25, 1.25) and L~ $\mathcal{TN}$(1.08, 0.18, 0.5, 1.75); 4) the obstacle's height and orientation follows uniform distribution as H~ $\mathcal{U}$(0.5, 2) and $\Theta \sim \mathcal{U}(0, \pi)$. Besides, random-located client (i.e. wireless device) is viewed as a random point, and its height follows a uniform distribution as $\mathcal{U}$(0.3, 1.5). These parameters are derived by using a real-life lab environment as a guiding example.

Second, to build an accurate channel model for indoor mmWave communication, we collect 5 sets of experimental estimations of path loss model (including the path loss exponent and distribution of fast fading), where all experiments are performed with LOS connections in the lab environment [26].

5.2 Performance in RORC scenarios

In this part, we evaluate network performance with optimal multi-AP placement in RORC scenarios, and all simulation parameters of mmWave system are adopted from Sec. 5.1. Here LOS probability and aggregate throughput are considered as main metrics for evaluation. First, considering a specific room where $r_l = 12$m, $r_w = 8$m, we compare the network performance of proposed multi-AP deployment (see Sec. 3.2) against that of three common deployment methods, which are 1) random deployment, 2) linear arrangement where APs are deployed according to Theorem 1, and 3) edged deployment where AP are randomly placed on the edges of room. With a specific obstacle density λ=0.3, Fig. 16 (a) and (b) shows the LOS probability and throughput performance over 1~6 APs, respectively. It is observed that proposed optimal deployment outperforms other three deployment methods. Compared with the linear deployment method, the optimal placement provides the obvious improvement on LOS probability and throughput when the number of APs increases. The random deployment shows worse performance when deploying fewer number of APs, and the edged deployment always provides worst performance due to its limited coverage.

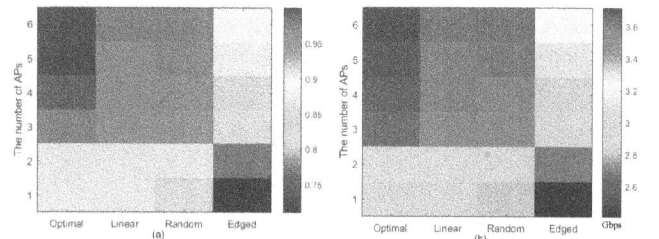

Figure 16: Deployment methods comparisons.

Second, with optimal placement of single AP or multiple APs in the room, we evaluate the network performance with different obstacle densities. In Fig. 17 (a), we observe that the LOS probability decreases when the obstacle density becomes higher due to server potential blockage effects, and with higher degree of deployed APs, both LOS and throughput performance (shown in Fig. 17 (b)) will be improved but the increase becomes marginal (less than 1%) when deploying 6 APs, and this result confirms our theoretical analysis in Sec. 3.3. On the other hand, we can see that the throughput is always consistent with LOS performance, which confirms that LOS is a critical requirement for indoor mmWave communication. Thus, in what follows, we focus solely on LOS performance.

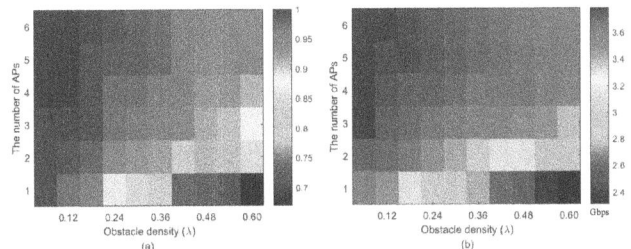

Figure 17: Network performance vs. obstacle density.

5.3 Performance in FORC scenarios

In this part, we evaluate the all-client LOS rate (ALR) in an indoor scenario shown in Fig. 15 (b), where 11 fixed obstacles are deployed. With randomly located clients, we conduct hundreds of simulations, and ALR is 1 if all clients have LOS connections in each case, otherwise it is 0. By using the SES algorithm to determine multi-AP placement in this scenario, Fig.18 shows the ALR performance with different numbers of APs and random clients. First, we can see that ALR achieves over 90% when deploying 3 APs even with 15 randomly located clients, which is a huge improvement compared to the single AP case. Second, we know that full coverage will be achieved with deployment of 4 APs (shown in Fig. 15 (b)), and here Fig. 18 indeed shows ALR is over 99.99% with 4 APs deployed, which validates our SES algorithm since all shadowing areas are almost eliminated with generated AP placement.

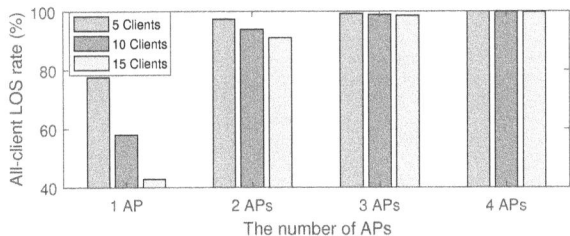

Figure 18: All-client LOS rate vs. number of APs.

In addition, we compare the LOS performance between the optimal multi-AP placement (by solving Eq. (15) in a brute-force method) and the placement generated by the SES algorithm (referred to as SES deployment). To achieve a blockage-free condition, Fig. 19 shows the optimal result and SES result. Through the ALR comparison (shown in Fig. 20), the performance of SES deployment is very close to that of optimal deployment with same number of APs, and even though one more AP is required by SES algorithm to entirely eliminate shadowing region, but actually after deploying the third AP shown in Fig 19 (b), ALR is above 98.5% without the 4th

AP, and the remaining shadowing area is only 0.73 m² (shown in Tab. 1), which is very close to full coverage. Therefore, the proposed SES algorithm provides near-optimal multi-AP deployment in the evaluated scenarios. In addition, the SES algorithm has obviously lower time cost to generate results as shown in Tab. 1 for this case.

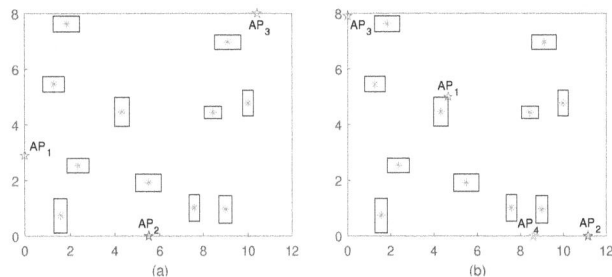

Figure 19: Multi-AP placements for blockage-free case. ((a) Optimal solution, (b) Solution from SES algorithm)

Table 1: The remaining shadowing area (RSA) and time cost with SES algorithm and optimal (brute-force) solution.

No. AP	1	2	3	4	Time cost (hr)
Opt's RSA (m²)	16.13	1.43	0	N/A	~85
SES's RSA (m²)	16.13	3.56	0.73	0	0.75

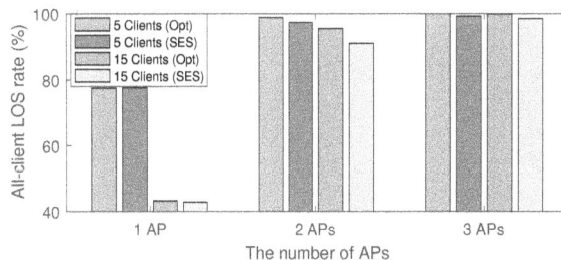

Figure 20: ALR comparison between optimal and SES results.

Considering the computation efficiency of proposed algorithm, we also compare the time costs (TC) of brute-force (BF) method and SES algorithm in terms of different number of fixed obstacles. As shown in Tab. 2, the time cost of generating optimal solution with BF method has a nearly exponential increase when there exists over 4 obstacle in FORC scenarios, but the time cost of SES algorithm has only a gently increase as the number of obstacles increase, which shows an absolute advantage in computation efficiency with multiple fixed obstacles.

Table 2: The time cost comparisons with SES algorithm and optimal (brute-force) method.

No. of Obstacles	2	4	6	8	10
BF's TC (hr)	0.23	2.57	13.21	36.32	82.35
SES's TC (hr)	0.18	0.26	0.48	0.59	0.68

Finally, we compare the number of required APs to achieve blockage-free conditions with the SES algorithm and the optimal solution. Since it is too time consuming to get optimal results with a large number of obstacles, here we considered cases with a few obstacles, and then evaluated the average number of APs to achieve full coverage. Fig. 21 shows that the number of required APs with SES algorithm is close to optimal, and as the obstacle scale increases, the gap between SES and optimal becomes smaller, which validates the performance of the SES algorithm.

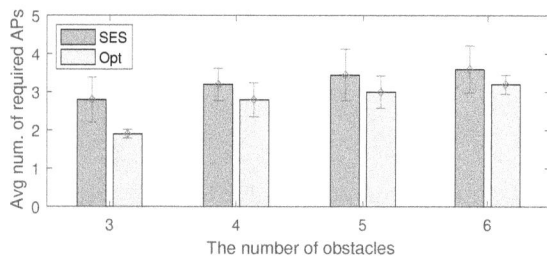

Figure 21: Avg. no. of required APs vs. no. of obstacles.

6 DISCUSSION

Our results can be directly used in practice for network deployment in several ways. If APs are pre-deployed before a room is furnished, or if it is expected that furniture will be moved frequently and moving AP locations is difficult, then APs should be deployed according to the optimal locations derived from the thinnest covering problem solution in the RORC scenario. However, if APs can be positioned after furniture locations are known, then they should be deployed at the locations provided by the SES algorithm for the multi-AP, multi-obstacle FORC scenario.

In addition, the proposed analytical model and algorithms in this paper can also generate AP placements for non-rectangular rooms, if those rooms are combinations of several rectangular rooms. For example, considering an "L-shaped" room, we can divide it into two rectangular rooms, and generate the optimal (near-optimal) positions of APs for each of them separately.

On the other hand, considering the cost of multiple mmWave AP devices used in indoor scenarios, an alternative is to deploy a single AP and multiple low-cost relays to extend the AP's coverage. In this case, the only additional step is to select an appropriate position for the unique AP among all generated optimal locations. One strategy would be to place the AP at the position with best coverage. For example, in RORC scenarios, we choose the optimal location that has the smallest achievable distance d_{ac}, while in FORC scenarios, the AP could be deployed at the position that is the first one generated by the SES algorithm.

7 CONCLUSION

In this paper, we considered coverage and deployment issues in multi-AP mmWave WLANs. Based on our analytic model, the optimal locations of multiple APs were derived in RORC scenarios, and we showed that deploying up to 5 APs provides the highest performance gains. In the FORC scenario, the shadowing-elimination search algorithm was proposed to determine the placement of APs, and full coverage is achieved with enough APs. Through ns-3 IEEE

802.11ad simulations at 60GHz, the network performance of proposed AP deployments is shown to be always superior to that of other common placement methods. Besides, we also validate that the proposed SES algorithm can generate near-optimal placement of APs, which provides desirable network performance for clients.

ACKNOWLEDGMENTS

This research was supported in part by the National Science Foundation through Award CNS–1813242.

REFERENCES

[1] Xiong Wang, Linghe Kong, Fanxin Kong, Fudong Qiu, Mingyu Xia, Shlomi Arnon, and Guihai Chen. Millimeter wave communication: A comprehensive survey. *IEEE Communications Surveys & Tutorials*, 20(3):1616–1653, 2018.
[2] Theodore S Rappaport et al. Millimeter wave mobile communications for 5g cellular: It will work! *IEEE access*, 1, 2013.
[3] Ieee std 802.11ad-2012, 2012. URL: https://ieeexplore.ieee.org/stamp/stamp.jsp?arnumber=6392842.
[4] Thomas Nitsche et al. Ieee 802.11 ad: directional 60 ghz communication for multi-gigabit-per-second wi-fi. *IEEE Communications Magazine*, 2014.
[5] Yuchen Liu and Douglas M Blough. Analysis of blockage effects on roadside relay-assisted mmwave backhaul networks. In *2019 IEEE International Conference on Communications (ICC)*, pages 1–7. IEEE, 2019.
[6] Sumit Singh et al. Blockage and directivity in 60 ghz wireless personal area networks: From cross-layer model to multihop mac design. *Journal on Selected Areas in Communications*, 27(8):1400–1413, 2009.
[7] Minyoung Park and Helen K Pan. A spatial diversity technique for ieee 802.11 ad wlan in 60 ghz band. *IEEE communications letters*, 16(8):1260–1262, 2012.
[8] Zulkuf Genc et al. Robust 60 ghz indoor connectivity: Is it possible with reflections? In *2010 IEEE 71st vehicular technology conference*. IEEE, 2010.
[9] Xia Zhou et al. Mirror mirror on the ceiling: Flexible wireless links for data centers. *ACM SIGCOMM Computer Communication Review*, 42(4):443–454, 2012.
[10] Mathew K Samimi et al. Characterization of the 28 ghz millimeter-wave dense urban channel for future 5g mobile cellular. *NYU Wireless TR*, 1, 2014.
[11] Yong Niu et al. Blockage robust and efficient scheduling for directional mmwave wpans. *IEEE Transactions on Vehicular Technology*, 64(2):728–742, 2015.
[12] Kan Song et al. A fast relay selection algorithm over 60ghz mm-wave systems. In *2013 15th IEEE International Conference on Communication Technology*, 2013.
[13] Yuchen Liu et al. Blockage avoidance in relay paths for roadside mmwave backhaul networks. In *2018 IEEE 29th Annual International Symposium on Personal, Indoor and Mobile Radio Communications (PIMRC)*, pages 1–7. IEEE, 2018.
[14] Fan Zhou et al. Making the right connections: Multi-ap association and flow control in 60ghz band. In *IEEE INFOCOM 2018-IEEE Conference on Computer Communications*, pages 1214–1222. IEEE, 2018.
[15] Xiaoqi Qin et al. On ap assignment and transmission scheduling for multi-ap 60 ghz wlan. In *2017 IEEE 14th International Conference on Mobile Ad Hoc and Sensor Systems (MASS)*, pages 189–197. IEEE, 2017.
[16] Sanjib Sur et al. Towards scalable and ubiquitous millimeter-wave wireless networks. In *Proceedings of the 24th Annual International Conference on Mobile Computing and Networking*, pages 257–271. ACM, 2018.
[17] Zhicheng Yang et al. Sense and deploy: Blockage-aware deployment of reliable 60 ghz mmwave wlans. In *2018 IEEE 15th International Conference on Mobile Ad Hoc and Sensor Systems (MASS)*, pages 397–405. IEEE, 2018.
[18] Wei Li et al. Analysis of base station deployment impact on los probability model for 5g indoor scenario. In *2017 IEEE/CIC International Conference on Communications in China (ICCC)*, pages 1–5. IEEE, 2017.
[19] Richard Cowan. Objects arranged randomly in space: an accessible theory. *Advances in Applied Probability*, 21(3):543–569, 1989.
[20] Tianyang Bai et al. Analysis of blockage effects on urban cellular networks. *IEEE Transactions on Wireless Communications*, 13(9):5070–5083, 2014.
[21] Aladár Heppes and Hans Melissen. Covering a rectangle with equal circles. *Periodica Mathematica Hungarica*, 34(1-2):65–81, 1997.
[22] Johannes Bernardus Marinus Melissen et al. Covering a rectangle with six and seven circles. *Discrete Applied Mathematics*, 99(1-3):149–156, 2000.
[23] Tp-link talon ad7200 multi-band wi-fi router, 2016. URL: https://www.pcmag.com/review/347405/tp-link-talon-ad7200-multi-band-wi-fi-router.
[24] Yuchen Liu and Douglas M Blough. Technical report for grid-based shadowing search method. (available to reviewers at: http://blough.ece.gatech.edu/TR-Multi-AP-indoor.pdf).
[25] Hany Assasa and Joerg Widmer. Implementation and evaluation of a wlan ieee 802.11 ad model in ns-3. In *Proceedings of the Workshop on ns-3*. ACM, 2016.
[26] Peter FM Smulders. Statistical characterization of 60-ghz indoor radio channels. *IEEE Transactions on Antennas and Propagation*, 57(10):2820–2829, 2009.

802.11ac Frame Aggregation is Bottlenecked: Revisiting the Block ACK

Muhammad Inamullah and Bhaskaran Raman

Indian Institute of Technology Bombay, Mumbai, Maharashtra, India

{inamullah,br}@cse.iitb.ac.in

ABSTRACT

Frame aggregation improves performance of 802.11 networks by eliminating many overheads the single-frame transmissions incur. An originator builds and sends an aggregate (A-MPDU) of packets (MPDUs or subframes) from a window of 64 sequence numbers, and a block ACK then acknowledges the same window. The mechanism works fine till there are no packet losses. With the advent of packet losses (and their subsequent reporting by the block ACK), holes appear in the originator's aggregation window. An A-MPDU constructed immediately after by the originator then becomes smaller in size due to these holes. We discuss the effect of such inadvertent shortening of transmitted A-MPDUs on the performance of WLAN. We propose modifications to the block ACK and aggregation mechanisms, and show through our ns-3 simulations that the change improves the network throughput by up to 20% in hidden node scenario in simple basic service sets (BSSs) consisting of 32 to 48 STAs. Our analysis shows that improvement in the worst case throughput can be as high as 400% for the highest VHT MCS indexes with our proposed modifications.

CCS CONCEPTS

• **Networks → Network protocols; Wireless local area networks.**

KEYWORDS

802.11ac, block ACK, A-MPDU, frame aggregation, WLAN

ACM Reference Format:
Muhammad Inamullah and Bhaskaran Raman. 2019. 802.11ac Frame Aggregation is Bottlenecked: Revisiting the Block ACK. In *22nd Int'l ACM Conf. on Modeling, Analysis and Simulation of Wireless and Mobile Systems (MSWiM'19), Nov. 25–29, 2019, Miami Beach, FL, USA.* ACM, New York, NY, USA, ?? pages. https://doi.org/10.1145/3345768.3355936

1 INTRODUCTION

Frame aggregation introduced in 802.11n (11n) enables a STA (originator) send a block (aggregate) of frames with a single channel access attempt. The recipient then acknowledges the block through a block ACK (BA). Thus the mechanism prevents overheads like multiple DCF interframe spacing (DIFS), backoff intervals, and short

interframe spacing (SIFS), and hence saves channel time and gives higher throughput.

The strength of frame aggregation thus comes from the ability to aggregate many subframes, up to a maximum of 64. But in our simulation of 11n WLANs, which we describe now, we observe Aggregate MAC Protocol Data Units (A-MPDUs) attaining smaller sizes than what the current PHY rate allows for.

In the simulation, a UDP application running on AP sends 1472-byte packets to a station (STA) at high enough rate so that the AP queue always has packets to aggregate. Every second, the AP-STA distance is changed by 1 m and is fixed for 1 s. The horizontal blue lines in Figure 1 show that A-MPDUs correctly attain maximum sizes corresponding to the PHY rates the rate adaptation algorithm selects (shown as horizontal green lines) based on SNR values. What is intriguing is the gamut of all sizes the A-MPDUs take between the distances 22 and 29 m, shown as blue dots, which poses the question as to why many transmitted A-MPDUs are shorter in size than the maximum allowed under the corresponding PHY rate.

A STA transmits an A-MPDU smaller than the maximum allowed whenever the transmission queue has retry frames with non-consecutive sequence numbers (§ 2). We study this problem and its effect on the performance of WLAN in the presence of hidden node related collisions. In the following section, we explain the problem, and propose the solution in the form of increased size of the aggregation window and the bitmap of the compressed BA.

Our results, with hidden nodes that increase subframe losses, show up to 20% improvement with our modified aggregation window and BA in overall network throughput for UDP traffic, and up to 50% reduction in file upload time over TCP.

Now a little background to understand why our approach is significant. An originator appends a MAC header to each of the upper layer packets before aggregating them into an A-MPDU,

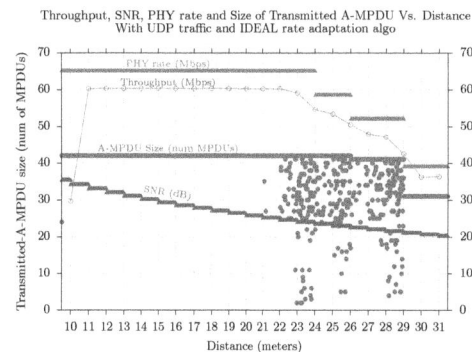

Figure 1: A-MPDU size variation with SNR. Other quantities, labels showing units, are plotted with the same scale

which enables individual subframe recovery, which is not possible with the other form of aggregation–Aggregate MAC Service Data Unit (A-MSDU) [16]. 802.11ac (11ac) increases the number of bytes an A-MPDU can carry from 64 KB of 11n to 1 MB. We refer to this limit as "A-MPDU length", and reserve "A-MPDU size" for the number of frames in an A-MPDU. 11ac also mandates every data transmission, even a single subframe, to be an A-MPDU.

Any solution that uses A-MSDU to solve the problem of A-MPDU shortening will at least be inefficient because an A-MSDU incurs a much larger cost when lost, and since A-MSDUs have a limit on their size (11,454 bytes), an A-MPDU built even with the largest A-MSDUs cannot encompass the available 1 MB 11ac byte length.

Compressed BA consisting of 64-bit bitmap was first proposed in [12] and is adopted by 11n. Modification to the structure of the BA in the context of MU-MIMO to prevent padding bits is proposed in [4]. In contrast, our work considers the large PHY rates of 802.11ac and proposes a modification of the compressed BA to ensure the maximum possible 64-subframe A-MPDU size even when there are retry frames.

In [11], authors report low frame aggregation levels in their trace-based experiments, and argue that small sizes of *received* A-MPDUs are due to the loss of MPDUs between receiver-side hardware and the driver. Our work, however, investigates the shortening of A-MPDU at the *transmitter*-side.

There are various works on improving the aggregation efficiency. An enhanced two-level frame aggregation where throughput is maximized by adjusting the aggregation level and length of A-MSDU frame through linear programming optimization is presented in [9]. A centrally controlled enabling and disabling of frame aggregation based on the traffic demand and the presence of real-time (VoIP) flows is given in [15]. In [10] optimization of aggregation for multi-rate WLANs is done by aggregating the packets in MAC queue for all links that have the same rate, and broadcasting the aggregate frame at that rate. Mutually optimal values of the A-MPDU frame size and the number of spatial streams are found in [17] to better utilize the VHT features of aggregation and spatial multiplexing. The work in [7] proposes a hybrid two-level aggregation to prevent dummy delimiters needed to maintain Minimum MPDU Start Spacing. In summary, these works propose algorithms either to decide on which aggregation mechanism to use and when to use it, or to decide the optimum aggregation sizes for the underlying PHY rates so that the wireless channel is efficiently utilized. They neither address the underutilization of aggregation capacity available in 11ac, nor consider the effect of BA and retry frames on aggregation sizes, both of which we take into account.

Throughput reduction due to mobility when long A-MPDUs are used is addressed in [3]. The authors propose adaptation of TXOP based on mobility that they quantify from frame error rate. Our approach is, on the other hand, to keep most of the 802.11ac parameters like TXOP unchanged while examining the efficiency of current A-MPDU aggregation mechanism.

While discussing limitations of hybrid frame aggregation in 802.11ad networks, the authors conclude in [2] that A-MPDU aggregation is better with moderate frame sizes. We also use the 1500 byte frame sizes for 802.11ac for our analysis, and propose that A-MPDU aggregation can be better if we have longer BA bitmaps.

Differentiating the cause of loss due to noise, collisions, and hidden nodes by observing differences in loss patterns within A-MPDUs is done in [1]. Our work identifies the need to devise an RA algorithm that works better with the VHT rates and frame aggregation. The work inn [1] can be used with our work to design such an RA algorithm.

None of the above works though considers the problem of shortening of transmitted A-MPDU due to previous subframe losses. [14] indicates that at very high data rates, the window of 64 limits the efficiency, whereas [13] explains that BA window (i.e., the aggregation window) cannot move forward beyond the first retry frame, making the next A-MPDU smaller in size. These works do not analyze the problem further.

Our contributions are 1) the thorough analysis to establish the relationship between the gaps in aggregation window, due to prior subframe losses, and the size of an outgoing A-MPDU, 2) the evaluation of the effect of such shortening of A-MPDUs on network throughput, and 3) our modification to the BA mechanism.

In the rest of the paper, we formulate the problem of outgoing A-MPDUs in § 2, provide modification to the BA in § 3, present ns-3 simulations and results in § 4, and conclude in § 5.

2 PACKET LOSSES, THE BA, AND THE A-MPDU SIZE

In this section we explain how the presence of retry frames affects the size of a transmitted A-MPDU.

An originator builds an A-MPDU as large as possible picking frames from, and not exceeding beyond, a window of 64 consecutive sequence numbers (as long as total length ≤ the byte length and TXOP ≤ 5.484 ms) because the BA bitmap can acknowledge only 64 consecutive sequence numbers starting from the first unsent frame.

As per Figure 2(a), if the BA reports a loss of R frames, $1 \leq R \leq a + 64 - x$, the number of subframes in the next A-MPDU, $R + x - a$, will be less than 64 whenever $R < a + 64 - x$. In the worst-case, an A-MPDU with *only* the first subframe lost renders the next A-MPDU to single-subframe. See [6] for details.

As an example, a STA sends an A-MPDU with sequence numbers 31 to 94 at time t_1. At t_2 the BA announces the loss of frames 55, 62 and 63. At t_3, the next A-MPDU includes the retry frames numbered 55, 62, and 63 (3 frames) then frames 95 through 118 (24 frames). The aggregation window is of 64 sequence numbers but the transmitted A-MPDU has only 27 subframes.

On the other hand, if only the frame 31 is lost, the next window at t_3 will be from 31 to 94, but the next A-MPDU will only consist of single subframe: the one with sequence number 31.

We next propose our modifications to keep the A-MPDU size at the maximum.

2.1 Maximizing the A-MPDU Size

For an originator to be able to always transmit A-MPDUs of maximum allowed size, we need to modify the existing update procedure of the aggregation window so as to consider both the number of retry packets and the maximum allowed size.

To modify it, we let the window grow by $MaxSize - R$ sequence numbers after every BA, as shown in Figure 2(b). Due to the existing

(a) Existing

(b) Modified

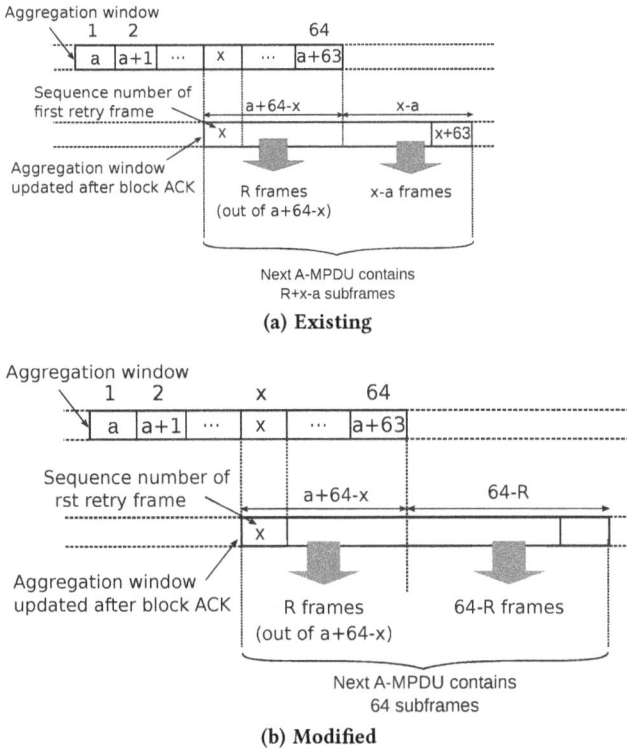

Figure 2: Updating the aggregation window.

02.11 BA bitmap size of 64, *MaxSize* is currently 64, which we maintain in this work.

In the worst case, the above update procedure makes the window grow by *MaxSize* − 1 whenever only the first subframe is retransmitted. We have shown in [6] that, thanks to the 802.11 retry limit, the aggregation window will stop after reaching a size of 505 for the current *MaxSize* of 64.

Note that this change does not affect the receiver's buffer, as the existing implementations have large buffer for the sake of efficiency. For example, ns-3 has a buffer-size of 1024 frames, which enables receivers to transfer bulk of frames to the upper layers at a time. The latency, which depends on the number of retries a packet is allowed to make, is also unchanged.

Since the BA acknowledges the entire aggregation window, the BA-bitmap size needs to be equal to the maximum possible size of the aggregation window, which we present in § 3

The next section presents the throughput gains our changes can bring.

2.2 Possible Throughput Gain

We have seen in the last section that the worst case occurs when only the 1st subframe is repeatedly lost. We have shown in [6] that the throughput in the worst case is given as: $Throughput_{wc} = (bits\_in\_A\text{-}MPDU)/(T_{wc} + 8 * T_{ca})$, where $T_{wc} = T_{64} + 7 * T_1$ is the worst-case transmission time of an A-MPDU, and T_{64} and T_1

are, respectively, transmission times of 64-subframe and single-subframe A-MPDUs, each including the BA time, and T_{ca} is the channel access time for a frame.

With 67.5 μs average backoff time, 34 μs DIFS, and UDP datagrams with 1472 bytes payload, the worst case throughput gains with our aggregation and BA can reach up to 300% and 400% for 80 and 160 MHZ channels respectively for the highest MIMO and MCS indexes [6]. We omit the details here in the interest of space.

3 IMPLEMENTATION OF MODIFIED BA

In this section, we give details of the modification to the BA to preserve the A-MPDU size in the presence of subframe losses.

Existing bitmap size of the BA is 64 bits. (We decide to modify it because 11ac has obsoleted the basic BA). For an aggregation window of 505 bits, discussed in § 2.1, we increase the BA bitmap size from 64 to 512 bits, the next power of 2. This change requires 448 extra bits per BA, adding typically an additional 20 μs for successful transfer of 64-subframe A-MPDU at 175.5 Mbps [6]. This overhead is negligible compared to the 5.484 ms TXOP.

Ns-3 [1] still only implements the 11n length of 64 KB for A-MPDUs. This limits the maximum number of subframes (of length 1536 bytes) in an A-MPDU to 42. We modify ns-3 to increase the byte length from 64 KB to 1 MB, conforming to 11ac.

Thus we take 512-bit BA bitmap size and 64-subframe A-MPDUs while evaluating performance gain with our modifications. In the following section we report our simulations and results.

4 SIMULATION SETUP AND RESULTS

We simulate a WLAN with hidden nodes and evaluate the network performance when a small number of nodes send high rate uplink traffic and rest of the STAs send low rate uplink traffic (for example VoIP traffic). We present here results of two simulations: one UDP CBR uplink traffic and the other a TCP file upload both interfered by the VoIP uplink traffic from hidden nodes.

We simulate three different WLAN sizes consisting of 32, 40 and 48 nodes randomly placed on a planar disc of radius 30 m with AP at the center. Each node uses the ns-3's default propagation loss model: a log distance model with a reference loss of 46.6777 dB at a reference distance of 1 m. To create the hidden nodes we set transmit power of nodes such that it drops below CCA_threshold value beyond 30 m, so that the farthest nodes on the disc can communicate with the AP, but STAs separated by more than 30 m cannot hear each other. We present results for multiple independent runs for each simulation scenario.

We first selected MinstrelHT, but since it performs poorly in the presence of hidden node related losses, we simulate with ideal RA of ns-3 that selects the rate based on the actual SNR values that the receiver sends out-of-band to the transmitter. Note that this explicit feedback is only possible in a simulator. In real world the transmitter has no direct knowledge of receiver's SNR, and thus bases its rate adjustment on packet losses.

Now let us describe our traffic model. For UDP traffic, ns-3's UDP On-Off applications on one or more STAs in each scenario send a high rate UDP CBR traffic (so that the STAs' queues are always full) to a packet sink on the AP. We use identical settings for the

---

[1]We use version 28 of ns-3.

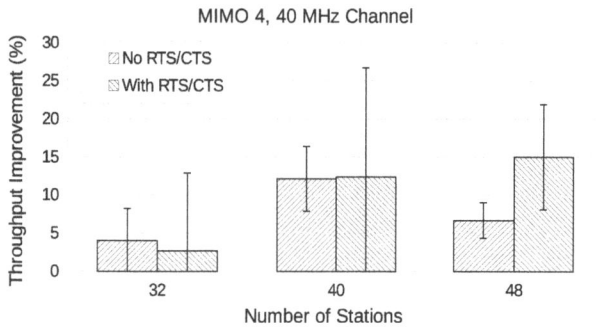

Figure 3: Throughput improvement for UDP traffic with hidden nodes. (Error bars show standard deviation for 7 runs).

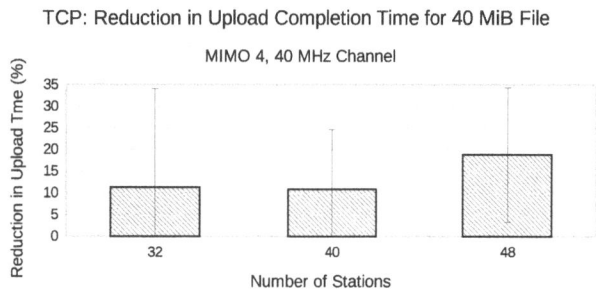

Figure 4: Reduction in median file upload time with hidden nodes. (Error bars show standard deviation for 5 runs).

random number seeds for start times of the applications and for the on/off intervals of the applications. Other STAs send a VoIP traffic. As described in [8], a VoIP sender generates PCM-encoded data at a rate 64 Kbps, which it gathers every 20 ms, that is 160 bytes chunks. If we assume that RTP as the transport protocol, 12 bytes are further added [8]. Packets of size 172 bytes (160B + 12B RTP header) sent every 20 ms give 68800 bps traffic rate. Furthermore, classical conversational model is given as 0.352 s of talkspurt and 0.65 s of silence [5]. We simulate such a VoIP conversational traffic in ns-3 setting an On-Off application with a data rate of 68800 bps and having random on and off times with an exponential distribution with means of 0.352 s and 0.65 s, respectively. The simulation runs for 20 s.

We simulate TCP traffic with ns-3 BulkSendApplication on one or more STAs. The application sends on a TCP connection a 40 MB file to the AP as quickly as possible and stops. The other STAs send the same VoIP traffic as above.

We compare the results for two implementations: one, with our modified BA of 512 bit bitmap and A-MPDU of 64 subframes for 1ac, and the other with the existing implementation of ns-3 (64 bit BA bitmap and 64-subframe A-MPDUs) with the A-MPDU byte limit changed from 64 KB of HT to 1 MB of VHT.

We find up to 20% improvement in network throughput when a single node sends the high rate uplink CBR traffic, and up to 50% reduction in upload time of a 40 MB file from a single node.

Real scenarios often have more than one nodes uploading heavy traffic. To understand the overall network performance in such scenarios, we make 20% of nodes in each network send uplink CBR traffic (100 Mbps each) to the AP and experience collisions from hidden nodes transmitting the low rate CBR VoIP traffic. We see 10 to 15% improvement in overall network throughput (Figure 3). Figure shows results for both with and without RTS/CTS handshake.

Similarly, to understand the effect on TCP performance when multiple nodes upload files, we setup 4 STAs in every scenario to upload 40 MB file each, with hidden nodes as above. Figure 4 shows up to 20% average reduction in median file upload time from the 4 STAs.

4.1 Analysis and Explanation of Results

We observe improvement in both the UDP and TCP performance when we maintain the A-MPDU size at 64 subframes.

We simulated both with and without RTS/CTS handshake, and as shown in Figure 3 our approach improves network performance in both the cases, and hence is complimentary to the RTS/CTS mechanism. Since RTS/CTS frames are transmitted at low rates, their overhead sometimes surpasses their benefit in reducing hidden node related losses. For example, we find network throughput drop from 181 Mbps to 176 Mbps when RTS/CTS is enabled, in an unmodified BA simulation for 48-node WLAN. Our approach nevertheless shows improvement in both the cases because it reduces interframe overheads, and not the packet losses, by guaranteeing maximum sizes for outgoing A-MPDUs.

To see how much effective our modification is, we plot the CDF of sizes of all transmitted A-MPDUs, counting only those A-MPDUs as short whose sizes reduced due to the presence of retry frames in the queue, and count all A-MPDUs that are small-sized due to insufficient TxQ as âĂIJfull-sizedâĂİ.

According to CDFs for the simulations of Figure 3, less than 50% A-MPDUs have 32 or less subframes (i.e., are half the maximum size), while 10% of the A-MPDUs have 8 or less subframes in most of the cases.

For example, Figure 5 gives CDFs of A-MPDU sizes for a typical run with UDP traffic in a 40-node WLAN. The BA 64 curve shows 30% A-MPDUs having a size less than or equal to 32. Whereas, for BA 512 (i.e., our modification), all A-MPDUs have sizes 64 (shown by a vertical line at size 64). Our modification thus makes all A-MPDUs transmit with maximum size (giving a throughput gain of 10% in this run).

Our calculated worst case throughput improvement is 80% for HT MCS 31 (which is equivalent to VHT MCS 7, MIMO 4) [6], but our simulations could achieve up to 20%. This is because not all transmissions are worst case, as described below.

Our modification is more effective if subframes lost from the previous A-MPDU are more towards its beginning, and will have no effect if tail end of the A-MPDU is lost, in which case the next AMPDU will be built in full size starting from the position of the first retry frame, or if the entire A-MPDU is lost, it will be retransmitted entirely. In our simulation, we find 15-20% A-MPDUs being lost

CDF of Transmitted A-MPDU Sizes

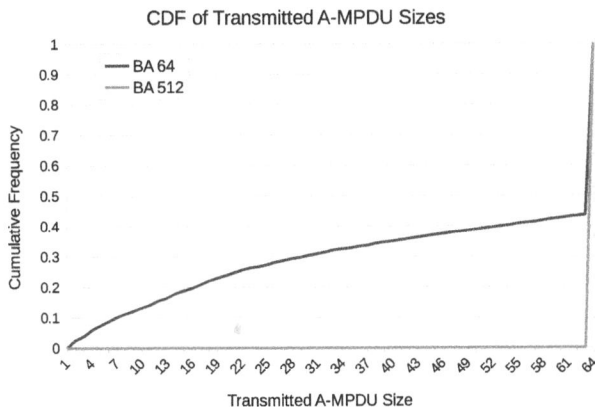

Figure 5: CDFs of sizes of transmitted A-MPDUs for the existing BA (BA 64) and the modified BA (BA 512).

fully. In fact, the 48-node bar of Figure 3 for the no-RTS/CTS case shows lesser average improvement than that of 40-node bar because average number of small-sized AMPDUs reduce from above 40% in 40-node scenario to below 30% in 48-node WLAN, whereas complete A-MPDU losses remain nearly the same.

Hence our simulations demonstrate that maximum A-MPDU size, needed to fully utilize the high data rates available with 802.11ac, is maintained when the subframe losses and the size of transmitted A-MPDU are decoupled with the help of modified aggregation window and BA.

Another interesting fact is that even ensuring a 64-subframe size for A-MPDUs is an underkill for 11ac PHY rates. The maximum number of 1536-byte subframes that can fit a 1 MB A-MPDU, for VHT MCS-MIMO 4-7 (PHY rate = 540 Mbps) is 514 subframes, with a ceiling of 682 subframe for MCS-MIMO values 8-5 and higher. This means that even a BA of 512 bits bitmap is not sufficient to acknowledge such large A-MPDUs. We need to think in a different way to acknowledge larger A-MPDUs so as to tap the full potential of 11ac. One such mechanism is using the basic BA (see Section 3); though ac has announced its end-of-life.

Also note that our work is relevant in the high density networks targeted in 802.11ax. In these WLANs, not only that intra-BSS hidden nodes affect uplink transfers, but also inter-BSS hidden nodes cause collisions with downlink transmissions. Thus, for example, for soliciting BA for a DL multicast aggregate frame, 11ax defines GCR MU BAR. In response to MU BAR, every STA sends BA simultaneously in UL MU transmission. Now, if even a single STA could not receive some subframes, the aggregation window of the AP can not slide forward. Our proposed larger aggregation window, along with our modified BA, can accommodate sufficient number of subframes so that the next A-MPDU attains its maximum size. More work is needed to fully address the problem in the context of MU OFDMA and multicast in 11ax.

5 CONCLUSION

In this work we learn that for 802.11ac the limit of 64 subframes for A-MPDUs is unnecessarily short and inhibits performance. Loss of

subframes further drops the size of A-MPDUs. Our investigation finds that the root cause is the size of BA bitmap that decides the aggregation window size and, if holes emerge in the window due to retries, originator builds a smaller A-MPDU. We propose that the BA bitmap should be elongated to 512 bits to accommodate more sequence numbers in the aggregation window so as to maintain the A-MPDU size at least at 64. Our simulations show that in the presence of subframe losses, our modified BA and aggregation mechanisms give improvement of 15-20% in overall throughput.

Moreover, within one TXOP an A-MPDU can have as many as 682 subframes of 1536 bytes each at the very high data rates of 802.11ac. Since A-MPDU aggregation is mandatory in the 11ac standard, such large A-MPDUs supported by a correspondingly modified BA scheme need to be adopted to fully tap the potential of very high data rates.

REFERENCES

[1] R. Anwar, K. Nishat, M. Ali, Z. Akhtar, H. Niaz, and I. A. Qazi. 2014. Loss differentiation: Moving onto high-speed wireless LANs. In *IEEE INFOCOM 2014 - IEEE Conference on Computer Communications*. 2463–2471.
[2] H. Assasa, S. Kumar Saha, A. Loch, D. Koutsonikolas, and J. Widmer. 2018. Medium Access and Transport Protocol Aspects in Practical 802.11 ad Networks. In *2018 IEEE 19th International Symposium on "A World of Wireless, Mobile and Multimedia Networks" (WoWMoM)*. 1–11.
[3] Seongho Byeon, Kangjin Yoon, Okhwan Lee, Sunghyun Choi, Woonsun Cho, and Seungseok Oh. 2014. MoFA: Mobility-aware Frame Aggregation in Wi-Fi. In *Proceedings of the 10th ACM International on Conference on Emerging Networking Experiments and Technologies (CoNEXT '14)*. ACM, New York, NY, USA, 41–52.
[4] C. Chung, T. Chung, B. Kang, and J. Kim. 2013. A-MPDU using fragmented MPDUs for IEEE 802.11ac MU-MIMO WLANs. In *2013 IEEE International Conference of IEEE Region 10 (TENCON 2013)*. 1–4.
[5] H. Hassan, J. M. Garcia, and C. Bockstal. 2006. Aggregate Traffic Models for VoIP Applications. In *Int. Conf. on Digital Telecom. (ICDT'06)*. 70–70.
[6] Muhammad Inamullah and Bhaskaran Raman. 2018. Poster: Frame Aggregation in 802.11ac: Need for Modified Block ACK. In *The 24th Annual International Conference on Mobile Computing and Networking, October 29-November 2, 2018, New Delhi, India (MobiCom '18)*. ACM, 3. https://doi.org/10.1145/3241539.3267736
[7] Y. Kim, E. Monroy, Okhwan Lee, Kyung-Joon Park, and Sunghyun Choi. 2012. Adaptive two-level frame aggregation in IEEE 802.11n WLAN. In *2012 18th Asia-Pacific Conference on Communications (APCC)*. 658–663.
[8] James F. Kurose and Keith W. Ross. 2012. *Computer Networking: A Top-Down Approach* (6th ed.). Pearson.
[9] J. Liu, M. Yao, and Z. Qiu. 2015. Enhanced Two-Level Frame Aggregation with Optimized Aggregation Level for IEEE 802.11n WLANs. *IEEE Communications Letters* 19, 12 (Dec 2015), 2254–2257.
[10] A. Majeed and N. B. Abu-Ghazaleh. 2012. Packet aggregation in multi-rate wireless LANs. In *2012 9th Annual IEEE Communications Society Conference on Sensor, Mesh and Ad Hoc Communications and Networks (SECON)*. 452–460.
[11] N. Mishra, A. Chaurasia, A. Kallavi, B. Raman, and P. Kulkarni. 2015. Usage of 802.11n in practice: A measurement study. In *2015 7th International Conference on Communication Systems and Networks (COMSNETS)*. 1–8.
[12] T. Nakajima, Y. Utsunomiya, Y. Nishibayashi, T. Tandai, T. Adachi, and M. Takagi. 2005. Compressed Block Ack, an efficient selective repeat mechanism for IEEE802.11n. In *2005 IEEE 16th International Symposium on Personal, Indoor and Mobile Radio Communications*, Vol. 3. 1479–1483.
[13] Ioannis Pefkianakis, Yun Hu, Starsky H.Y. Wong, Hao Yang, and Songwu Lu. 2010. MIMO Rate Adaptation in 802.11N Wireless Networks. In *Proceedings of the Sixteenth Annual International Conference on Mobile Computing and Networking (MobiCom '10)*. ACM, New York, NY, USA, 257–268.
[14] Eldad Perahia and Robert Stacey. 2013. *Next Generation Wireless LANs: 802.11N and 802.11Ac* (2nd ed.). Cambridge University Press, New York, NY, USA.
[15] J. Saldana, J. Ruiz-Mas, and J. AlmodÁşvar. 2017. Frame Aggregation in Central Controlled 802.11 WLANs: The Latency Versus Throughput Tradeoff. *IEEE Communications Letters* 21, 11 (Nov 2017), 2500–2503.
[16] D. Skordoulis, Q Ni, H Chen, A. P. Stephens, Changwen Liu, and A. Jamalipour. 2008. IEEE 802.11N MAC Frame Aggregation Mechanisms for Next-generation High-throughput WLANs. *Wireless Comm.* 15, 1 (Feb. 2008), 40–47.
[17] M. Yazid and A. Ksentini. 2018. Modeling and Performance Analysis of the Main MAC and PHY Features of the 802.11ac Standard: A-MPDU Aggregation vs Spatial Multiplexing. *IEEE Trans. on Veh. Tech.* 67, 11 (Nov 2018), 10243–10257.

A Transparent and Multimodal Malware Detection Method for Android Apps

Dali Zhu
Institute of Information Engineering,
Chinese Academy of Science
School of Cyber Security, University
of Chinese Academy of Sciences
Beijing, China
zhudali@iie.ac.cn

Tong Xi
Institute of Information Engineering,
Chinese Academy of Science
School of Cyber Security, University
of Chinese Academy of Sciences
Beijing, China
xitong@iie.ac.cn

Pengfei Jing
Institute of Information Engineering,
Chinese Academy of Science
Beijing, China
jingpengfei@iie.ac.cn

Di Wu
Institute of Information Engineering,
Chinese Academy of Science
Beijing, China
wudi@iie.ac.cn

Qing Xia
Institute of Software, Chinese
Academy of Science
Beijing, China
xiaqing2018@iscas.ac.cn

Yiming Zhang
Institute of Information Engineering,
Chinese Academy of Science
School of Cyber Security, University
of Chinese Academy of Sciences
Beijing, China
zhangyiming@iie.ac.cn

ABSTRACT

While recent works have shown that deep learning method can improve the malware classification accuracy, the lack of the transparency has restricted its application in anti-virus scan engines. Existing researches have attempted to provide solutions to give high-fidelity explanations of the model's decision. However, current methods are not optimized for application security task, leading to a poor performance in Android malware detection. In this paper, we propose a backtracking method to infer suspicious features of the apps to explain the reason of classification. Besides, we also propose a malware detection model based on the fusion convolutional neural network using different types of features (e.g., permission, API, URL, etc.). For maximizing the benefits of encompassing multiple feature types, our framework trains the sub-models for each type of features separately and merges them at the end of the system to obtain a comprehensive classification result. The experimental results show that the backtracking method has a significant improvement in fidelity level compared with existing methods. Furthermore, we evaluate the performance of the proposed framework with other existing works. Leveraging the backtracking method, our framework has better performance in classification and significantly reduces detection time by 69% compared with prior approaches.

CCS CONCEPTS

• **Security and privacy → Malware and its mitigation.**

MSWiM '19, November 25–29, 2019, Miami Beach, FL, USA
© 2019 Association for Computing Machinery.
ACM ISBN 978-1-4503-6904-6/19/11...$15.00
https://doi.org/10.1145/3345768.3355915

KEYWORDS

Android malware detection; transparency; backtracking; convolutional neural network

ACM Reference Format:
Dali Zhu, Tong Xi, Pengfei Jing, Di Wu, Qing Xia, and Yiming Zhang. 2019. A Transparent and Multimodal Malware Detection Method for Android Apps. In *22nd Int'l ACM Conference on Modeling, Analysis and Simulation of Wireless and Mobile Systems (MSWiM '19), November 25–29, 2019, Miami Beach, FL, USA.* Miami Beach, USA, 10 pages. https://doi.org/10.1145/3345768.3355915

1 INTRODUCTION

Up to the final quarter of 2018, exceeding 30 million Android malware samples were identified around the world [25]. Users are suffering from various security incidents as well as financial losses caused by malicious apps. Due to the significance of the Android system which is accessible worldwide, there have been a large amount of research works for Android malware detection [2, 9, 10, 12, 17, 18, 22, 29, 35, 39, 41, 43].

Challenge 1: The previous works have proved that the detection approaches based on deep learning model perform better than the traditional methods and it helps to achieve high classification accuracy by using various features [9]. However, using one model to train multiple types of features increases the complexity of the model and causes confusion for the detection system due to mutual interference between different kinds of features [29]. Therefore, it is challenging to design a classification model that could be trained well to fit different features and learned the relationship between various features. To address this problem, [18] first proposed a detection method using several independent sub-models to train different kinds of features. The sub-models they chose are deep neural networks made up of fully-connected layers which consists of two hidden layers. However, the designed sub-models don't have strong capability of feature extraction and a lot of useful information is lost during the training step. Besides, the model is made up of multi-layer perceptron which has so many parameters that it costs much time on training and testing processes. Previous works have found that the convolutional neural network (CNN) can play a significant role in malware detection due to its strong ability in feature extraction [16, 26]. However, these methods don't propose a solution on the interference between different features.

Challenge 2: So far, current works have successfully applied deep learning technique to malware detection and achieved exceptionally high accuracy [18, 22, 29, 32]. However, the deep neural network is a complex model with multiple layers so that it troubles the developers to track significant data from thousands of parameters. Therefore, researchers can only obtain a certain decision from the neural nets but don't know what caused it [6]. The lack of transparency reduces developer's trust in models and restricts their application in anti-virus scan engines. There are several previous works to improve the transparency of neural networks [13, 24, 30]. However, they focus on image analysis, natural language processing or PC malware and can't be applied to Android malware detection directly. These existing methods assume the classification boundary is linear. Whereas, in Android malware detection, the boundary of malware and benign applications is usually non-linear. It leads to a serious misunderstanding or interpretation errors.

In this paper, we propose a multimodal detection method based on fusion convolutional network to address different types of features. The proposed deep learning method has strong feature extraction ability of analyzing the internal relationship among features to achieve higher classification accuracy. Besides, we also propose a backtracking method to identify a set of features that play a key role in classification to improve the transparency of the detection model. It's too complex to explain the proposed fusion convolutional model directly. Thus, we rebuild a small model to approximated the proposed complex model using knowledge distillate technique. Then, we propose a decision process for the small model to identify the most influential features that make key contributions to the classification. More important, it improves the performance of Android malware detection using only these key features instead of the complete ones. Leveraging the proposed backtracking method, the detection framework has a significant improvement in reducing the detection time while maintaining a high classification accuracy.

This paper makes the following major contributions:

- **A backtracking method to improve the transparency of the deep learning model.** We propose a backtracking method to solve the limitation of poor interpretability of the malware detection based on neural network. The method generates high-fidelity explanation results for our proposed classification model.
- **A multimodal malware detection method.** We propose a multimodal malware detection method based on convolutional neural network. It trains sub-models to using different types of features separately and merges them at the end of the framework for an overall forecast result.
- **Comprehensive Evaluation.** We completed experiments on the data set of 19,600 samples (11,000 benign and 8,600 malicious apps). The experimental results show that the proposed backtracking method successfully locates the key features of the application. It provides high-fidelity explanation

of the classification model and improves the performance of the detection method. We compare the proposed method with other advanced works. Leveraging the backtracking method, our framework significantly reduce detection time by 68%, while maintaining an f1-score of 95.89%.

Paper Organization. The rest of the paper is organized as follows: §2 introduces the background. §3 explains the overall architecture of our proposed framework. §4 describes the proposed backtracking method. §5 presents the implementation of the detection method. And the dataset and evaluation results are shown in §6. Finally, §7 discusses the related work, and §8 concludes.

2 BACKGROUND

In this section, we introduce some background that is necessary for understanding the rest of this paper including the features used in our proposed method and the concept of knowledge distillation which is performed in the backtracking method.

2.1 The Definition of Features

Existing malware detection methods based on the deep neural network achieves high classification accuracy and some advanced systems have the ability to classify the samples into their families. [19, 33, 34, 40, 42]. They analyze at least one features extracted from the application for classification. These features includes dangerous permissions, sensitive APIs, URLs and etc.

2.1.1 Dangerous Permissions. To complete malicious behaviors, the developer have to apply for some dangerous permissions in *Manifest* file. Thus, according to the type and quantity of system permissions that the application applies, the possibility that the app is malware can be obtained to some extent. For example, [22] selected 22 dangerous ones from 135 system permissions as the malware detection features using the Decision Tree (DT) classification algorithm, which improved the detection efficiency of the detection system significantly without affecting the classification performance. This method defaults to the premise that applications which only apply the remaining 113 permissions don't have malicious behavior, but it's against reality obviously. And the experimental result also proved that it led a high rate of FP [22].

2.1.2 Sensitive APIs. The functions in Android program consist of several third-party API calls and system calls which is an essential step that must be carried out by malware developers to achieve malicious behavior. Therefore, most of the current malicious application detection systems take the API called by the application as the classification feature. Similar to [22], [28] selects sensitive APIs from all system APIs through selection algorithms, but this also misleads the system to ignore the hidden maliciousness in other APIs. More importantly, unlike the permissions, different APIs can be combined to perform a particular function. The suspiciousness of the same API will be significantly different with different combinations. [43] proposed a context-based API call graph method that can characterize sensitive APIs based on contextual relationships.

2.1.3 Malicious URLs. Malicious URL injection is one of the techniques used in malware. Illegal developers add a URL-loaded code segment to a benign app and the code segment doesn't have malicious behavior. So it is more effective to avoid detection by the

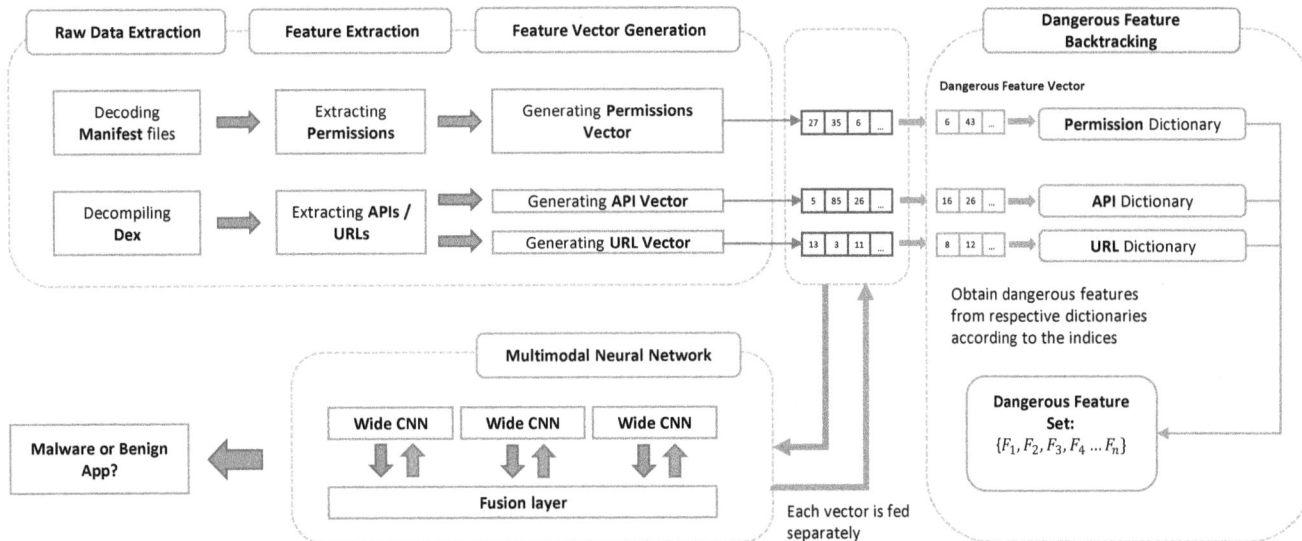

Figure 1: The architecture of the proposed framework. The blue arrow points to the direction of data flow in the detection system, and the red arrow points to the backtracking process.

system. After the user install the application, the program runs and downloads malicious codes from the URL's address. There are so many different URLs used in the network and the length of URL dictionary is close to infinity. So, it's necessary to simplify the raw URLs before building the URL dictionary, After an investigation, we find that different URLs can be recognized effectively according to the host address. So, we ignore the server path, query field, parameters, fragments and other information in the URL, and only retain the host address as the detection feature. For example, an application contains the following URL https://dl.acm.org/results.cfm?query=android, and https://dl.acm.org/ indicates the URL after refining. After the simplification, the size of URL dictionary is significantly reduced, making it possible to be analyzed in the malware detection.

2.2 Knowledge Distillation

Hinton et al. [14] first propose the concept of knowledge distillation in 2015. Generally speaking, the performance of classification and generalization is positively correlated with the complexity of models. The most powerful models are made up of large-scale neural networks or multiple sub-models. However, the complexity of these models is too high to deploy them in reality. Therefore, the authors propose to transfer the knowledge of these powerful models to a smaller one, which is called knowledge distillation. Generally, the performance of the small model acquired by knowledge distillation is significantly better than that of the small model which learns the knowledge from beginning. With the help of this concept, this paper propose an effective backtracking method in Section §4.

3 PROPOSED FRAMEWORK

3.1 Overview

We propose a framework that uses various types of features (e.g. permissions, APIs, URLs and etc.) for Android malware detection.

We depict the architecture of the proposed framework in Figure 1. First, the preprocessing module extracts classification features (*permission, API, URL*) from raw APK files, and assigns a unique index to each specific feature according to feature dictionaries. The output of this step is three feature vectors indicating the three types of the features. After the preprocessing module, our framework feeds the feature vectors to the sub-models separately. Then, it merges the sub-models in a fusion network and obtains the final classification result.

In addition to assigns a label to the application, our framework combines the backtracking method introduced in §2, identifying a set of features that make important contributions to the classification, and accelerating the detection process. We test several neural network based classification models for comparison and find that the proposed model outperforms with baselines (refer to §6 for detailed performance evaluation).

3.2 Preprocessing Module

The preprocessing module is conducted to convert raw data into recognizable vectors for neural networks. To explain clearly, we divide the module into three specific sub-modules (*Raw Data Extraction, Feature Extraction, and Feature Vector Generation*). Each of them is independent of others to complete a specific function. These sub-modules are revealed in the next subsection.

3.2.1 Raw Data Extraction. The target of the raw data extraction process is to make Android APK (Android Package Kit) files interpretable. An APK file is unzipped by UnZip [36], and a manifest file, a *dex* file, and shared library files are extracted first. Then the manifest file and *dex* file are decoded or decompiled using Apktool [38] that converts executable code to smali code. After that, .smali files are generated that contain the complete system calls and context of different API calls.

3.2.2 Feature Extraction. The feature extraction process is performed to obtain the required feature data from the raw data. The essential feature types are explained in §2.

First, the permission features are extracted from the manifest XML file. Permissions applied by the application are surrounded by the XML tree tag *<android-permission>* which can be extracted using regular expressions.

API features are located in *.smali* files which are the decompiled results of a *.dex* file. Smali code is a disassembler implementation for Dalvik (Android Virtual Machine), and API called in the program usually be after the keyword *invoke*. By scanning Dalvik byte codes, the API methods extracted from the smali file. Also, during the byte code scanning, it's necessary to retain the calling order of APIs in the program.

In the case of URL features, URLs are merely collected from the whole *smali* uncompiled files without considering the location of them. As §2 mentioned, the raw URLs are simplified by removing useless fields.

3.2.3 Feature Vector Generation. The feature vector generation process is conducted to compose feature vectors using extracted features in the previous procedure. Three kinds of the feature vector are generated from extracted features. The input of the neural network must be vectors rather than string format. As a result, it's an essential method of replacing strings with the corresponding indices. We refer to the file that holds the mapping as a dictionary. According to three kinds of features used in the detection system, three dictionaries are constructed. The dictionaries store permission features, API features and URL features extracted from the training set samples and assign each feature a unique identifier (index). An embedding layer is constructed after the input layer of the neural network proposed. After learning, each element in the input vector is mapped into a word vector. As a result, the index in the dictionary only needs to distinguish each feature without other semantic information. For simplicity, we assign a natural number index to each feature from 1 onwards, and the length of the dictionary is the size of the feature set extracted from the training set samples. To enhance the robustness of the detection system, it's necessary to consider the new features contained in the test set. These features are not present in the training set, and we use index 0 to represent them. Feature vectors constructed with feature indices are fed to the neural network which is introduced in the next section.

3.3 Neural Net Learning Module

Neural Net Learning Module is the core module of the malware detection system. The main goal of this module is to decide whether the Android application is malware or not according to analyze the three types of feature vectors. Figure 2 shows the architecture of fusion convolutional neural network for malware detection.

Three types of feature vectors are fed to the corresponding sub-models separately. All of sub-models have the same structure except the hyper-parameters. Each one consists of an embedding layer, a convolution layer, a max-pooling layer, and a fully connected layer. The sub-models are independent of each other, and they connect to the merging layer that is the first layer of the fusion network. The fusion network is a multi-layer perceptron network. Notice

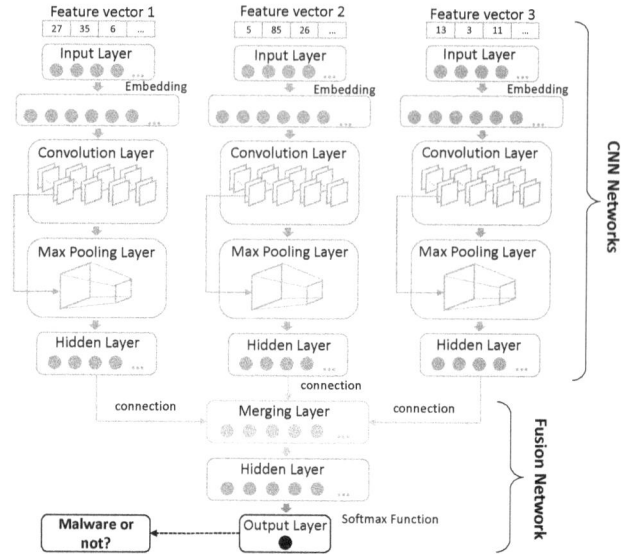

Figure 2: Fusion convolutional neural network

that there is an embedding layer [4] before the convolution layer. The embedding layer converts a positive integer into a vector of fixed size. It helps the model to find the semantic similarity between different features.

In addition, the activation function used in the CNN networks is the rectified linear units (ReLU) activation function [27]. ReLU's gradient is constant in most cases, helping to solve the convergence problem of deep networks. Another advantage of ReLU is its biological rationality, which is more in line with the characteristics of biological neurons than *sigmoid* function and *tanh* function.

The classification result is obtained from the last layer of the fusion network. It labels the sample where '1' represents malware and '0' indicates benign apps. The parameters of fusion convolutional neural network are summarized in Table 1.

3.3.1 Learning Strategy. In practice, the number of features which are extracted from the feature extraction module has a large range of variation no matter the application is malware or benign. However, the neural network requires input vectors to keep the same length for different applications. Thus, it's reasonable to build the multimodal deep learning model by padding zeros to feature vectors when the features can't be achieved. And we truncate the feature sequence whose length exceeds the threshold.

In the training process, the network adopts the gradient descent method to update the parameters of the model continuously. To solve the problem of partially extracted features, when we trained the fusion convolutional network, each sub-model based on CNN corresponding to a specific feature type is pretrained first. And we fine tune the whole network after that. This learning strategy dramatically improves the training efficiency of the model as well as obtaining high classification accuracy of the detection system.

3.3.2 Avoid Overfitting. Overfitting is a relatively common problem in neural networks. It means that the classifier has higher accuracy on the training set and unsatisfactory performance on

Table 1: The parameters used in each layer in the fusion convolutional neural network

Feature	Layer	Neurons	Parameters	Filter	Activation Function
PERMISSION	Embedding Layer	-	100×500	-	-
	Convolution Layer	98×200	3×500×200	number:200 size:3×500 stride:1 (padding)	ReLU
	Max Pooling Layer	-	-	size:5×1 stride:2 (padding)	-
	Fully Connected Layer	1,024	48×200×1,024	-	ReLU
API	Embedding Layer	-	2,000×500	-	-
	Convolution Layer	998×200	5×500×200	nubmer:200 size:5×500 stride:2 (padding)	ReLU
	Max Pooling Layer	-	-	size:5×1 stride:2 (padding)	-
	Fully Connected Layer	1,024	498×200×1,024	-	ReLU
URL	Embedding Layer	-	100×500	-	-
	Convolution Layer	98×200	3×500×200	number:200 size:3×500 stride:1 (padding)	ReLU
	Max Pooling Layer	-	-	size:2×1 stride:2 (padding)	-
	Fully Connected Layer	1,024	49×200×1,024	-	ReLU
ALL	Merging Layer	3×1,024	-	-	-
	Fully Connected Layer	1,024	3×1,024×1,024	-	ReLU
	Output Layer	1	1,024×1	-	Softmax

the test set. In other words, the model can't be used effectively in reality. To avoid overfitting problems, dropout regularization [37] is adopted in our model. Dropout can be used as a trick to train the deep neural network. In each training batch, the overfitting phenomenon can be significantly reduced by ignoring half of the feature detector (making half of the hidden layer node value zero). In our model, the CNNs are trained with a dropout rate of 0.2. This rate is generally used in typical neural networks. We select 20% percent of the samples in training set as validation set randomly and use the cross-validation method to optimize the hyper-parameters of the model. We optimize the hyper-parameters of the model for a best performance on the verification set.

3.3.3 Exception Catch. To enhance the robustness of the detection, the framework considers the legality of the input feature vector and the exception handling in the detection phase. The generated feature vector is checked before it is fed to the neural network. If the feature vector length is less than the threshold, it will be padded with value zero. On the other hand, if the element in the vector is outside the dictionary range, the framework treats it as unregistered words and revalues it. Besides that, an exception handling code block is added to the detection system. If an error occurs during the detection process, the program will write the error information to the log file and continue to complete the detection without crashing. These measures mainly ensure that the detection model can finish the detection completely and improve the robustness of the detection.

3.4 Backtracking Module

The backtracking module is designed to provide interpretable explanation for our proposed fusion convolutional network. The goal of this module is to identify the features that play a key role in classification. These key features is a part of the total features which have much contributions to the detector classification. It's difficult to select the key features directly from the complex model, considering the vanishing gradient problem happened in deep neural network. Thus, leveraging the knowledge distillation technique,

we transfer the knowledge of the fusion convolutional model to a student model with simple construction first. Then, we propose a decision process to identify the most significant features in detector decision through the student model. It is worth noting that the backtracking algorithm obtains is the indices of the significant features, so it is also necessary to transfer the indices to specific feature according to the dictionaries. The detailed description of backtracking method is presented in §4.

4 BACKTRACKING METHOD

The existing malware detection methods based on neural network [18, 22, 29] often have trouble in getting enough information for classification. In this section, we motivate our work by demonstrating these issues. This paper not only implements the detection of Android malicious applications driven by data through depth model but also proposes a simple and effective method to mine the part of the input that has an important impact on the classification.

Because the calculation process of a deep neural network is mostly located in the implicit semantic space, and it is difficult to directly explain the reasoning process. Therefore, this paper doesn't attempt to directly explain the features from the perspective of hidden layer visualization, but through training a simple network similar to the performance of the model. Then, "scoring" the input parts of the simple network leading to the decision-making of the classification layer, calculating the areas with the highest scores as the most influential areas for decision-making.

This process is called backtracking. Backtracking is divided into two steps. Firstly, a small model, named SNet, that fits the output probability distribution of the original complex large model, is trained by knowledge distillation. Then, malicious regions are calculated by backtracking the decision of the SNet.

4.1 Knowledge Distillation

If a simple network is trained directly, its performance often differs greatly from that of the large model. It's easy to leads to a large deviation between he simple network and the complex decision-making model. Therefore, in order to reduce the performance gap between simple networks and large models, knowledge distillation is used to transfer and compress knowledge from large models (teacher model) into small models (student model). So that, the probability distribution of the output of small model approximates that of the large models. It works when we have trained a deep detection model with excellent generalization performance. We modify some parameters of the decision network for the knowledge distillation process. The traditional form of softmax function is replaced by the temperature-dependent softmax function shown in (1).

$$Softmax_{temp} = \frac{exp(w_i/T)}{\sum_j exp(w_j/T)} \qquad (1)$$

It is the traditional softmax function when T equals to 1. Adjust the temperature value T until the output probability distribution of softmax shows a significant 'softening', which is called 'distillation'. The model used for distillation is generally a large-scale neural network or a large-scale integrated model with excellent performance called teacher model. Each sample in the training set is re-inferred from the teacher model with a temperature value of T, resulting in a 'soft label' for each sample. The simple model to be trained for backtracking is called the student model, and it is jointly trained according to the original hard tags labeled in the training set and the soft tags generated by the teacher model. Therefore, the loss function is obtained by the original cross entropy L_{CE} corresponding to the hard tag and the cross entropy L_{KD} formed by the soft tag. As shown in (2).

$$L = \partial L_{KD} + (1 - \partial)L_{CE} \qquad (2)$$

Where ∂ is the proportion of knowledge distillation loss, generally between 0.5 and 1.0. After knowledge distillation, the knowledge of the teacher model can be transferred to the student model used to calculate malicious areas. Since the student model is responsible for visualization, it is necessary to have a unique mapping path for each input area to the label. Therefore, this paper designs a student model consists a single-layer convolutional with a convolution kernel of size one. Of course, after some post-processing tricks, the size of the convolution kernel can be extended to more than one, and even multiple sets of sizes can be used at the same time. However, for the convenience of algorithm description, the most simple convolution layer is taken as an example for introduction. We define the this shallow neural network, student model, as SNet. The structure diagram of the SNet is shown in Figure 3. As shown in the Figure 3,

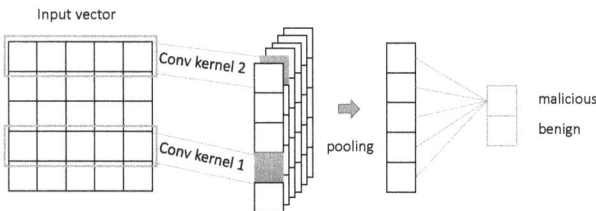

Figure 3: The structure of SNet.

each token embedding of the input text is convolved by convolution kernels of size one to obtain corresponding matching scores, and then the classification layer is connected to the global pooling layer.

After that, if the embedding can be retained through the pooling layer, it will be multiplied by the weight of the classification layer, and the result is its contribution to the classification layer decision.

4.2 Decision Process

According to the processes introduced in previous subsection, it is easy to get the calculation path of the final decision for each token of the input. As a result, the method uses the following steps to get the final top k features that are the most critical to classification decision. Based on the above considerations, the following algorithm is proposed to backtrack the key features.

Step1: For an unknown sample, running the complete inference path until the final classification logits is obtained. In this process, all of the convolutional feature maps and the corresponding convolution kernel ids are marked down.

Step2: For each calculation graph, it's easy to find the maximum value and the index of its position. Then, we multiply the maximum value by the weight of the convolution kernel from the classification layer to obtain a weighted matching score.

Step3: In this step, we resort and deduplicate all the weighted matching results obtained in step 2. After that, taking a maximum value from several weighted matching scores which have the same position index. Thereby, we obtain a unique score for each of the selected features.

Step4: The scores of the different features obtained in step 3 are sorted again. And the top k features that make the most important contribution to the classification decision are selected.

5 IMPLEMENTATION

We implemented a transparent, multimodal Android malware detection method. The code of the framework is written in python and runs across platforms. In neural net learning module, we utilize some great python libraries like TensorFlow [1], pickle and numpy to complete the construction of neural networks, storage of intermediate files, and numerical calculations. The code of different modules has been packaged, and the system can complete the detection automatically after storing new APK samples in the specified path.

6 EVALUATION

6.1 Dataset

Considering the different distribution of malicious applications at home and abroad, we have chosen a centralized solution that the samples collected from diverse sources to train and test our proposed detection system. A detailed description of its composition is shown in Table 2. The dataset used to evaluate the method contains malicious apps collected from well-known anti-virus software vendors (e.g. 360 [20] and Kaspersky [21]), and popular malware datasets such as Virus-share [31] and Drebin [3]. Besides, we crawl benign apps from Google Play and Wandoujia app store. After that, we leverage the Virus Total for label verification. When all of the virus detector in VirusTotal consider the sample as benign, the app is labeled as a benign application. The dataset contains a total of 19,600 samples, including 8,652 malicious applications and 10,948 benign apps. Then, we messed up the crawled samples randomly and divided the data set into a training set and test set in a ratio

Table 2: Summary of the dataset used for evaluation. The domestic samples are clawed from 360 Security Company and Wandoujia App Store, while the foreign samples are collected from Drebin, Kaspersky and Google Play.

Source	Malicious	Benign	Total
Domestic	4,990	6,294	**11,284**
Foreign	3,662	4,654	**8,316**
Total	**8,652**	**10,948**	**19,600**

Table 3: The structure and parameters of MDLN.

Networks	Layer	Parameter setting	
Initial DNNs	Input	5,000 neurons	ReLU
	Hidden	2,500 neurons	ReLU
	Hidden	1,000 neurons	ReLU
Final DNNs	Merging	500 neurons	ReLU
	Hidden	100 neurons	ReLU
	Hidden	10 neurons	ReLU
	Output	1 neuron	Sigmoid

of 8:2. The training and validation processes are completed on the training set, and the evaluation experiments are computed in the test set.

6.2 Comparison with Prior Work

In this subsection, we introduce four baselines for comparison. The first two baselines are used to verify the validity and high-fidelity of the proposed backtracking method. And the remaining two baselines are applied to compare the performance of our detection method.

6.2.1 With LIME. LIME [30] is a state-of-the-art method used to explain Natural Language Processing (NLP) models and image applications. The authors propose an advanced method to help developers understand the reasons behind predictions. First, It learns an interpretable model locally around the prediction. Then, they proposed a method to select a set of key instances via sub-modular optimization to improve the transparency of the deep learning model. This method is widely used in image processing and NLP task.

6.2.2 With Random Feature Selection Method. Random feature selection method is the simplest way to sample from a large set of data. It selects features randomly as the explanation for the detection result.

6.2.3 With Multimodal Deep Learning Networks. [18] proposed a detection framework with multiple deep learning networks. The authors didn't name the system which is mentioned in the paper. For the sake of simplicity, it is referred to as Multimodal Deep Learning Networks (MDLN). MDLN implemented a fusion network to detect malicious applications for the first time. The system fits multiple features with sub-models, avoiding the performance degradation mentioned in §1 using single deep learning model. MDLN used several deep networks to pre-train each feature individually, then connected the trained networks' output layers and inputted them into a decision maker to get the final prediction result. Table 3 shows the structure and parameters of MDLN which is quoted from [18]. Compared with the detection model proposed in this paper (see Table 1 for details), the MDLN has the following two shortcomings. First, the initial DNNs applied in MDLN are the same size for different types of features. The simple type of feature such as permission is fed into a sophisticated model which lead the model to overfitting. Second, the fully connected network is a standard classification network. However, This network has a weak ability to extract feature, and the number of parameters is exponentially

increased. As a result, the sub-models they used are inefficient and it has a space for improvement.

6.2.4 With HinDroid. HinDroid [15] is an advanced malicious application detection system using API features. It analyzes the relationship between APIs and proposes a multi-kernel learning method to map API features to high dimensional space. Then, the boundary of malware and benign apps is drawn by the classifier. HinDroid can generate an inspection report that shows dangerous APIs called by the sample. Certainly, HinDroid also has its limitations. The system only analyzes the API features which affects the accuracy of the decision, and the detection can be evaded easily using techniques such as code obfuscation. Then, it's not an end-to-end solution method. The feature extraction module is relatively independent of the classification module, and the internal links between features are easily lost, resulting in performance degradation.

6.3 Effectiveness

The first goal of detection system is to improve classification accuracy as much as possible. To make the detection system can be applied in a real environment, we collect domestic and foreign applications to build the dataset for training and evaluating the proposed model. It is necessary to mix samples which are crawled from local and foreign sources for to improve the generalization of the detection system. After statistics, we found that although the types of malicious applications are the same at home and abroad, the distribution of them is quite different. The domestic malicious applications focus on advertising and privacy theft. In comparison, malicious apps from foreign pay more attention to paid SMS and financial fraud. The distribution of the samples is shown in Figure 4.

6.3.1 BackTracking Results. To evaluate the correctness of the explanation, we adopt the three fidelity tests designed by [13].
Feature Deduction Test: Constructing a sample $t(x)_1$ by nullifying the key features from the instance x, and examining the positive classification rate (PCR).
Feature Augmentation Test: First, we select one random instance r from the opposite class. Then, constructing $t(x)_2$ by replacing the feature values of instance r with those of key features and examining the PCR.
Synthetic Test: Constructing $t(x)_3$ as a synthetic instance and preserving the feature values of the key features while randomly assigning values for the remaining features. The we examine the PCR of the classification.

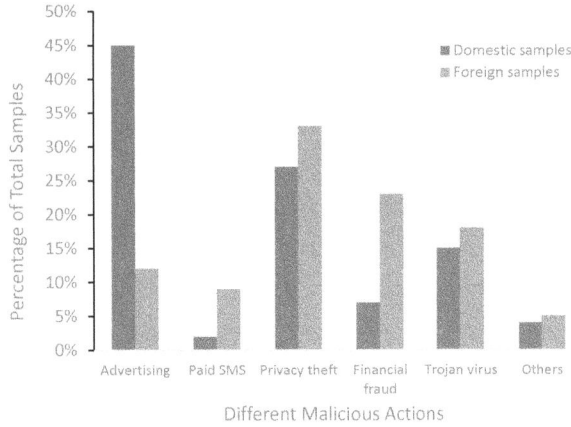

Figure 4: The distribution of the samples. Large differences in sample distribution from different sources

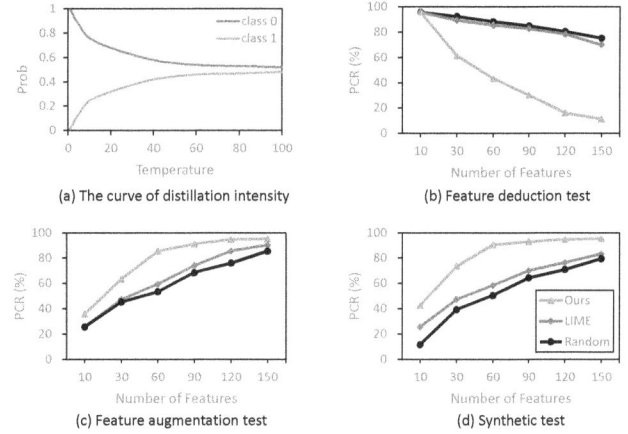

Figure 5: The results of different fidelity tests

Figure 5(a) shows the curve of decision probability of the two categories (class 0 and class 1 represent neutral benign samples and malicious samples respectively) with temperature T. The probability distribution of this sample without knowledge distillation is [0.9986, 0.0014], and as the T increases, the entropy of the distribution also increases.

Figure 5(b) shows the results from feature deduction test. A lower PCR represent that produced features are more significant to the classification decision. By only removing the top 150 features selected by the backtracking method, the malware detector drops the PCR to 20% or lower. That is the top 150 features play an important role in decision and count only 30% of the total features.

Figure 5(c) shows the results of feature augmentation test. A higher PCR represents the selected features are more significant to the test samples. More than 60% of the testing samples reverse their labels by replacing the top 60 features.

Figure 5(d) shows a similar trend for the synthetic test. With the increase of the number of the key features, the malware detector achieves a higher classification accuracy. The synthetic samples have nearly 90% of the chance to make a right decision using only 90 features.

Across all of these tests, our proposed backtracking method outperforms baselines by a big margin. Our method is more suitable for Android malware detection considering the high-fidelity of the explanation. In addition to improve the transparency of the deep learning model, the backtracking method also helps to make the detection method more efficient. The results have shown that a few key features could help the detector make a right decision. Thus, we only use these key features for our detection method instead of the total 3,000 features. It sizable reduces the time cost of the detection while maintaining a satisfactory performance in classification.

6.3.2 Classification Performance. We evaluate the performance of malware detection systems using the measures shown in Table 4. These indices are typical indicators for assessing the performance of the detection system. For malware detection system, FP rate is an essential evaluation reference. If the rate of FP is too high, the

Table 4: Performance indices of Android malware detection.

Indices	Description
True Positive (TP)	# of apps correctly classified as malware
True Negative (TN)	# of apps correctly classified as benign
False Negative (FN)	# of apps mistakenly classified as malware
False Positive (FP)	# of apps mistakenly classified as benign
Accuracy	(TP+TN)/(TP+TN+FP+FN)
Precision	TP/(TP+FP)
Recall	TP/(TP+FN)
F1-Score	2×Precision×Recall/(Precision+Recall)

Table 5: The classification performance using the backtracking method

	Original	After Backtracking
Feature Numbers	3,000	150
Accuracy(%)	97.21	96.54
Precision(%)	96.34	95.48
F1-score(%)	96.78	95.89
Recall(%)	96.34	95.75
FP Rating(%)	1.17	1.23
Time(s)	15	7

detection system mistakes more malware to benign ones, which causes enormous damage to the ecosystem of Android. F1-score is determined by precision rate and recall rate so that it can judge the performance of the system comprehensively.

Table 5 shows the classification performance using the backtracking method. The backtracking method not only provide interpretable explanations for our detection model, but also reduce the detection time significantly, while maintaining a satisfactory performance in classification.

The accuracy, precision, f1-score, recall and false positive rating for each experiment are shown in Table 6. We can see that most of the test metrics of the method perform well and it's in line with expectations. The proposed method can maintain a low false

Table 6: Comparison of our framework (using backtracking method), MDLN [18] and HinDroid [15] in accuracy, precision, f1-score, recall, and false positive rating. The cases where the method outperforms others are in bold. The data used in the experiment is test set which is not used in the training process.

Samples	Accuracy(%)			Precision(%)			F1-score(%)			Recall(%)			FP Rating		
	Ours	MD	Hin	Ours	MD	Hin	Ours	MD	Hin	Ours	MD	Hin	Ours	MD	Hin
Malware	**97.52**	95.12	92.34	**96.44**	95.74	93.22	**96.73**	95.54	93.07	**97.34**	95.34	92.92	**0.92**	1.23	1.43
Benign	**94.52**	90.18	91.26	**94.63**	92.52	92.16	**94.85**	92.38	91.47	**92.58**	92.24	90.79	**1.45**	1.75	2.54
Malware & Benign	**96.54**	92.74	91.83	**95.48**	93.48	92.55	**95.89**	93.61	92.20	**95.75**	93.75	91.85	**1.23**	1.56	2.03

positive rate of 1.23% and a higher accuracy rate of 95.54% in the test set which has complex sample distribution. Compared with HinDroid, MDLN performs better on most experimental results, which shows the necessity of using various kinds of features in malware detection.

Table 7: The time cost in training and testing processes using different detection systems. The testing time in the table refers to the average value obtained on the test set.

System	Training Time (h)	Testing Time (s)
MDLN	7.2	23
HinDroid	0.2	31
Ours(total features)	4.3	15
Ours	4.3	7

6.3.3 Time Consumption. In addition to classification accuracy, the time cost of the detection system is also an important indicator. Table 7 shows the time consumed by different detection systems to detect the same test samples. The testing time reflects the system's response speed in general. The proposed method has fewer parameters than MDLN so that it can complete the model training process in less time. HinDroid uses statistical learning methods instead of deep learning model that cost a few time in the training module. However, it takes longer to predict new samples due to the loose connection of different modules. Therefore, the detection system proposed consumes the least amount of time to predict a new sample, which is especially important in large-scale sample discrimination tasks. Compared to MDLN that has a similar framework, our method (without using backtracking method) reduces the detection time from 23s to 15s, a drop of more than 34%. Besides, we only use the selected features for our detection method instead of the total 3,000 features. It further reduces the time cost from 15s to 7s, just one-third of the time spent on MDLN.

6.4 Experiment Platform

We performed the evaluation experiments on a server with 64 Intel Xeon e5-2609 CPU, GeForce GTX TITAN X GPU running at 256GB of physical memory. The iterative parameter calculation of the model was completed on the GPU which is specified by TensorFlow and other instruction codes are executed on CPU. The time spent on model training is shown in Table 7. Besides that, we installed a 10TB hard disk for the server to store enough training samples on it.

7 RELATED WORK

Android Malware Detection. There has been many proposed researches on Android malware detection that rely on static [2, 3, 11, 12, 17, 18, 35, 39] or dynamic [5, 7, 8, 23] analysis. SigPID [22] used significant permissions to identify the application is malware or not and achieved high classification accuracy through the feature selection method. Besides, PFESG [39] provided a method for refining features. It selected 51 permission features from all 832 features as classification features, which reduced the feature dimension significantly and improved the classification efficiency. HinDroid [15] considered the various relationships between APIs and found the intrinsic correlations among APIs through multi-kernel transformation. RevealDroid [12] analyzed the relationship between permissions and APIs and proposed a lightweight, obfuscation-resilient detection system.

Systems Based on Neural Network. Researchers are more and more focus on detection system based on the neural network since 2015. The neural network is an end-to-end model which feeds feature vectors into the net directly, and the network outputs the classification results. This method integrates the feature extraction process and classification process, and the accuracy of classification is improved contrast with traditional methods. R2-d2 [16] converted the binary program of the APK into an image, translating the malware detection issue to the image classification problem. Then the authors designed a CNN-based classification system. Kim et. [18] proposed a multimodal deep learning method using various features. They used up to five features and got the state of art performance in malware detection. Though the classification accuracy has sizable improvement, the weak interpretability of its internal parameters leads the difficulties to understand the basis of judgment for malicious samples.

8 CONCLUSION

In this paper, we propose a classification model based on multiple convolutional neural networks to further improve the feature extraction and classification capabilities of the system. Besides that, we propose a backtracking method to provide high-fidelity explanation of the deep learning detection method. The backtracking method selected the most important features that make a key contribution to the classification decision. Leveraging the backtracking method, we design a transparent, multimodal CNN-based Android malware detection framework, and complete an extensive evaluation. The experimental results show that our method has significant improvement in time cost over existing approaches, while maintaining an advanced performance in classification.

ACKNOWLEDGMENTS

This work was supported by the National Key Research and Development Program of China (No. 2016YFB0801001, No. 2016YFB0801004, No. 2017YFB0801900), the National Natural Science Foundation of China (No. 61701494), and the Youth Star project of the Institute of Information Engineering, CAS (No. Y8YS016104).

REFERENCES

[1] Martín Abadi, Paul Barham, Jianmin Chen, Zhifeng Chen, Andy Davis, Jeffrey Dean, Matthieu Devin, Sanjay Ghemawat, Geoffrey Irving, Michael Isard, et al. 2016. Tensorflow: A system for large-scale machine learning. In *12th USENIX Symposium on Operating Systems Design and Implementation (OSDI)*. 265–283.

[2] Joey Allen, Matthew Landen, Sanya Chaba, Yang Ji, Simon Pak Ho Chung, and Wenke Lee. 2018. Improving Accuracy of Android Malware Detection with Lightweight Contextual Awareness. In *Proceedings of the 34th Annual Computer Security Applications Conference (ACSAC)*. ACM, 210–221.

[3] Daniel Arp, Michael Spreitzenbarth, Malte Hubner, Hugo Gascon, Konrad Rieck, and CERT Siemens. 2014. Drebin: Effective and explainable detection of android malware in your pocket.. In *Proceedings of the 2017 Annual Network and Distributed System Security Symposium (NDSS)*. 23–26.

[4] Yoshua Bengio, Réjean Ducharme, Pascal Vincent, and Christian Jauvin. 2003. A neural probabilistic language model. *Journal of machine learning research* 3, 2 (2003), 1137–1155.

[5] Iker Burguera, Urko Zurutuza, and Simin Nadjm-Tehrani. 2011. Crowdroid: behavior-based malware detection system for android. In *Proceedings of the 1st ACM workshop on Security and privacy in smartphones and mobile devices*. ACM, 15–26.

[6] Davide Castelvecchi. 2016. Can we open the black box of AI? https://www.nature.com/news/can-we-open-the-black-box-of-ai-1.20731

[7] Sen Chen, Minhui Xue, Zhushou Tang, Lihua Xu, and Haojin Zhu. 2016. Stormdroid: A streaminglized machine learning-based system for detecting android malware. In *Proceedings of the 11th ACM on Asia Conference on Computer and Communications Security (AsiaCCS)*. ACM, 377–388.

[8] Santanu Kumar Dash, Guillermo Suarez-Tangil, Salahuddin Khan, Kimberly Tam, Mansour Ahmadi, Johannes Kinder, and Lorenzo Cavallaro. 2016. Droidscribe: Classifying android malware based on runtime behavior. In *2016 IEEE Security and Privacy Workshops (SPW)*. IEEE, 252–261.

[9] Ming Fan, Jun Liu, Xiapu Luo, Kai Chen, Zhenzhou Tian, Qinghua Zheng, and Ting Liu. 2018. Android malware familial classification and representative sample selection via frequent subgraph analysis. *IEEE Transactions on Information Forensics and Security (TIFS)* 13, 8 (2018), 1890–1905.

[10] Ali Feizollah, Nor Badrul Anuar, Rosli Salleh, Guillermo Suarez-Tangil, and Steven Furnell. 2017. Androdialysis: Analysis of android intent effectiveness in malware detection. *computers & security* 65 (2017), 121–134.

[11] Yu Feng, Osbert Bastani, Ruben Martins, Isil Dillig, and Saswat Anand. 2017. Automatically learning android malware signatures from few samples. In *Proceedings of the 2017 Annual Network and Distributed System Security Symposium (NDSS)*.

[12] Joshua Garcia, Mahmoud Hammad, and Sam Malek. 2018. Lightweight, obfuscation-resilient detection and family identification of Android malware. *ACM Transactions on Software Engineering and Methodology (TOSEM)* 26, 3 (2018), 11.

[13] Wenbo Guo, Dongliang Mu, Jun Xu, Purui Su, Gang Wang, and Xinyu Xing. 2018. Lemna: Explaining deep learning based security applications. In *Proceedings of the 2018 ACM SIGSAC Conference on Computer and Communications Security (CCS)*. ACM, 364–379.

[14] Geoffrey Hinton, Oriol Vinyals, and Jeff Dean. 2015. Distilling the knowledge in a neural network. *arXiv preprint arXiv:1503.02531* (2015).

[15] Shifu Hou, Yanfang Ye, Yangqiu Song, and Melih Abdulhayoglu. 2017. Hindroid: An intelligent android malware detection system based on structured heterogeneous information network. In *Proceedings of the 23rd ACM SIGKDD International Conference on Knowledge Discovery and Data Mining (KDD)*. ACM, 1507–1515.

[16] TonTon Hsien-De Huang and Hung-Yu Kao. 2018. R2-d2: Color-inspired convolutional neural network cnn-based android malware detections. In *2018 IEEE International Conference on Big Data (Big Data)*. IEEE, 2633–2642.

[17] Roberto Jordaney, Kumar Sharad, Santanu K Dash, Zhi Wang, Davide Papini, Ilia Nouretdinov, and Lorenzo Cavallaro. 2017. Transcend: Detecting concept drift in malware classification models. In *26th USENIX Security Symposium (USENIX Security 17)*. 625–642.

[18] TaeGuen Kim, BooJoong Kang, Mina Rho, Sakir Sezer, and Eul Gyu Im. 2019. A Multimodal Deep Learning Method for Android Malware Detection Using Various Features. *IEEE Transactions on Information Forensics and Security (TIFS)* 14, 3 (2019), 773–788.

[19] Bojan Kolosnjaji, Ghadir Eraisha, George Webster, Apostolis Zarras, and Claudia Eckert. 2017. Empowering convolutional networks for malware classification and analysis. In *2017 International Joint Conference on Neural Networks (IJCNN)*. IEEE, 3838–3845.

[20] 360 Security Lab. 2018. 360 Security Guards. https://www.360.cn/

[21] Kaspersky Lab. 2018. Kaspersky Lab. https://www.kaspersky.com.cn/

[22] Jin Li, Lichao Sun, Qiben Yan, Zhiqiang Li, Witawas Srisa-an, and Heng Ye. 2018. Significant permission identification for machine-learning-based android malware detection. *IEEE Transactions on Industrial Informatics* 14, 7 (2018), 3216–3225.

[23] Martina Lindorfer, Matthias Neugschwandtner, and Christian Platzer. 2015. Marvin: Efficient and comprehensive mobile app classification through static and dynamic analysis. In *2015 IEEE 39th Annual Computer Software and Applications Conference (ACSAC)*. IEEE, 422–433.

[24] Scott M Lundberg and Su-In Lee. 2017. A unified approach to interpreting model predictions. In *Advances in Neural Information Processing Systems*. ACM, 4765–4774.

[25] McAfee. 2019. McAfee Mobile Threat Report. https://www.mcafee.com/enterprise/en-us/assets/reports/rp-mobile-threat-report-2019.pdf

[26] Niall McLaughlin, Jesus Martinez del Rincon, BooJoong Kang, Suleiman Yerima, Paul Miller, Sakir Sezer, Yeganeh Safaei, Erik Trickel, Ziming Zhao, Adam Doupe, et al. 2017. Deep android malware detection. In *Proceedings of the Seventh ACM on Conference on Data and Application Security and Privacy (CDASP)*. ACM, 301–308.

[27] Vinod Nair and Geoffrey E Hinton. 2010. Rectified linear units improve restricted boltzmann machines. In *Proceedings of the 27th international conference on machine learning (ICML)*. ICMLPO, 807–814.

[28] Vinod P Nair, Harshit Jain, Yashwant K Golecha, Manoj Singh Gaur, and Vijay Laxmi. 2010. Medusa: Metamorphic malware dynamic analysis usingsignature from api. In *Proceedings of the 3rd International Conference on Security of Information and Networks (ICSIN)*. ACM, 263–269.

[29] Xiaorui Pan, Xueqiang Wang, Yue Duan, XiaoFeng Wang, and Heng Yin. 2017. Dark Hazard: Learning-based, Large-Scale Discovery of Hidden Sensitive Operations in Android Apps.. In *Proceedings of the 2017 Annual Network and Distributed System Security Symposium (NDSS)*.

[30] Marco Tulio Ribeiro, Sameer Singh, and Carlos Guestrin. 2016. Why should i trust you?: Explaining the predictions of any classifier. In *Proceedings of the 22nd ACM SIGKDD international conference on knowledge discovery and data mining*. ACM, 1135–1144.

[31] J-Michael Roberts. 2011. Virus Share.(2011). *URL https://virusshare. com* (2011).

[32] Sankardas Roy, Jordan DeLoach, Yuping Li, Nic Herndon, Doina Caragea, Xinming Ou, Venkatesh Prasad Ranganath, Hongmin Li, and Nicolais Guevara. 2015. Experimental study with real-world data for android app security analysis using machine learning. In *Proceedings of the 31st Annual Computer Security Applications Conference (ACSAC)*. ACM, 81–90.

[33] Joshua Saxe and Konstantin Berlin. 2015. Deep neural network based malware detection using two dimensional binary program features. In *2015 10th International Conference on Malicious and Unwanted Software (MALWARE)*. IEEE, 11–20.

[34] Joshua Saxe and Konstantin Berlin. 2017. eXpose: A character-level convolutional neural network with embeddings for detecting malicious URLs, file paths and registry keys. *arXiv preprint arXiv:1702.08568* (2017).

[35] Yuru Shao, Xiapu Luo, Chenxiong Qian, Pengfei Zhu, and Lei Zhang. 2014. Towards a scalable resource-driven approach for detecting repackaged Android applications. In *Proceedings of the 30th Annual Computer Security Applications Conference (ACSAC)*. ACM, 56–65.

[36] Christian Spieler. 2009. UnZip. http://infozip.sourceforge.net/UnZip.html

[37] Nitish Srivastava, Geoffrey Hinton, Alex Krizhevsky, Ilya Sutskever, and Ruslan Salakhutdinov. 2014. Dropout: a simple way to prevent neural networks from overfitting. *The Journal of Machine Learning Research (JMLR)* 15, 1 (2014), 1929–1958.

[38] Connor Tumbleson and Ryszard Wiśniewski. 2019. APKTOOL. https://ibotpeaches.github.io/Apktool/

[39] Chengcheng Wang and Yuqing Lan. 2017. PFESG: Permission-based Android Malware Feature Extraction Algorithm. In *Proceedings of the 2017 VI International Conference on Network, Communication and Computing (CNCC)*. ACM, 106–109.

[40] Wei Wang, Mengxue Zhao, and Jigang Wang. 2018. Effective android malware detection with a hybrid model based on deep autoencoder and convolutional neural network. *Journal of Ambient Intelligence and Humanized Computing (JAIHC)* (2018), 1–9.

[41] Zhenlong Yuan, Yongqiang Lu, Zhaoguo Wang, and Yibo Xue. 2014. Droidsec: deep learning in android malware detection. In *ACM SIGCOMM Computer Communication Review (CCR)*. ACM, 371–372.

[42] Jixin Zhang, Kehuan Zhang, Zheng Qin, Hui Yin, and Qixin Wu. 2018. Sensitive system calls based packed malware variants detection using principal component initialized MultiLayers neural networks. *Cybersecurity* 1, 1 (2018), 10.

[43] Mu Zhang, Yue Duan, Heng Yin, and Zhiruo Zhao. 2014. Semantics-aware android malware classification using weighted contextual api dependency graphs. In *Proceedings of the 2014 ACM SIGSAC conference on computer and communications security (CCS)*. ACM, 1105–1116.

A Comprehensive Empirical Analysis of TLS Handshake and Record Layer on IoT Platforms

Ramzi A. Nofal
Santa Clara University
Internet of Things Research Lab
Department of Computer Science and
Engineering
Santa Clara, CA, USA
rnofal@scu.edu

Nam Tran
Santa Clara University
Internet of Things Research Lab
Department of Computer Science and
Engineering
Santa Clara, CA, USA
nvtran@scu.edu

Carlos Garcia
Santa Clara University
Internet of Things Research Lab
Department of Computer Science and
Engineering
Santa Clara, CA, USA
cdgarcia@scu.edu

Yuhong Liu
Santa Clara University
Internet of Things Research Lab
Department of Computer Science and
Engineering
Santa Clara, CA, USA
yliu@scu.edu

Behnam Dezfouli
Santa Clara University
Internet of Things Research Lab
Department of Computer Science and
Engineering
Santa Clara, CA, USA
bdezfouli@scu.edu

ABSTRACT

The Transport Layer Security (TLS) protocol has been considered as a promising approach to secure Internet of Things (IoT) applications. The different cipher suites offered by the TLS protocol play an essential role in determining communication security level. Each cipher suite encompasses a set of cryptographic algorithms, which can vary in terms of their resource consumption and significantly influence the lifetime of IoT devices. Based on these considerations, in this paper, we present a comprehensive study of the widely used cryptographic algorithms by annotating their source codes and running empirical measurements on two state-of-the-art, low-power wireless IoT platforms. Specifically, we present fine-grained resource consumption of the building blocks of the handshake and record layer algorithms and formulate tree structures that present various possible combinations of ciphers as well as individual functions. Depending on the parameters, a path is selected and traversed to calculate the corresponding resource impact. Our studies enable IoT developers to change cipher suite parameters and immediately observe the resource costs. Besides, these findings offer guidelines for choosing the most appropriate cipher suites for different application scenarios.

KEYWORDS

energy, encryption, wireless, elliptic curve, key exchange

ACM Reference Format:
Ramzi A. Nofal, Nam Tran, Carlos Garcia, Yuhong Liu, and Behnam Dezfouli. 2019. A Comprehensive Empirical Analysis of TLS Handshake and Record Layer on IoT Platforms. In *22nd Int'l ACM Conference on Modeling, Analysis and Simulation of Wireless and Mobile Systems (MSWiM '19), November 25–29, 2019, Miami Beach, FL, USA.* ACM, New York, NY, USA, 10 pages. https://doi.org/10.1145/3345768.3355924

1 INTRODUCTION

The Internet of Things (IoT) is a system of interrelated computing/smart devices, such as smart homes, health-care devices as well as autonomous driving systems, that are provided with unique identifiers and the ability to transfer data over a network without requiring human-to-human or human-to-computer interactions [1]. Due to its wide application, some studies predict that by the end of 2020, nearly 50 billion smart, connected objects will exist [2]. It is projected in a white paper by Arm that a trillion new IoT devices will be produced between now and 2035 [3]. However, the lack of security has been recognized as one of the major issues that hinders the rapid adoption of IoT systems [4].

The Transport Layer Security (TLS) protocol, which provides authentication, data integrity, and encryption between two communication parties has been widely adopted for securing communications. Therefore, extensive studies have been recently proposed to apply TLS in IoT applications. Unfortunately, the high security of TLS comes at the cost of high computational and energy demands, due to the complexity of the cryptographic algorithms adopted by TLS. More importantly, due to the limited resources available to the IoT edge devices, achieving a certain security level while minimizing the resource consumption of TLS remains one of the foremost challenges of using TLS in IoT applications [5]. The need to strike a balance between security and resource consumption in IoT applications forms the basis of this work.

In this paper, we mainly focus on the two major layers of TLS: the *handshake protocol layer* and the *record layer*, as shown in Figure 1. The handshake protocol layer, which adopts *Public Key*

TLS Handshake Protocol	TLS Alert Protocol	Application Protocol
TLS Record Layer		
Transport Layer (TCP or UDP)		

Figure 1: TLS Layers

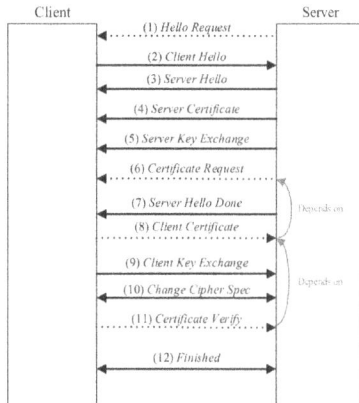

Figure 2: A visualization of the entire TLS handshake with dotted lines representing optional messages

Cryptography (PKC), allows the server and the client to authenticate each other and negotiate a set of cryptographic keys before the application layer transmits or receives its first byte of data. The record layer, which adopts *symmetric cryptography*, handles data fragmentation, encryption and decryption as well as sending and receiving TLS messages to and from the transport layer (TCP or UDP).

TLS has several advantages over other protocols. As mentioned, it is widely adopted, highly secure, and easily implementable. An observation by Google demonstrates that more than 25% of connections to its server use TLS [6]. Another report carried out by Mozilla reveals more than 50% of observed connections use TLS [7]. Also, using TLS extensions may help reduce the number of messages exchanged between client and server. On the other hand, the adoption of TLS presents some challenges. From the IoT point of view, the computing requirements of TLS may be too demanding considering resource-constrained IoT devices. One can argue that this problem can be partially overcome by substituting DTLS.However, IoT protocols such as MQTT, which implement information-centric networking, rely on connection-oriented protocols such as TCP and TLS to establish communication paths between publishers and subscribers.

Although much research has been conducted to measure the energy consumption of PKC and symmetric cryptography algorithms on IoT boards [5, 8], very few investigate the energy consumption of TLS protocol. Furthermore, the existing studies on TLS [9] (i) often lack generality by focusing on obsolete devices or a limited number of cipher suites, and (ii) are not sufficiently deep into each individual function, thereby severely limiting the capability to evaluate diverse cipher suites based on various application requirements.

This paper addresses the aforementioned concerns by evaluating the performance of cipher suites using two state-of-the-art and resource-constrained IoT edge devices. To accomplish this, we examine and annotate the source code of the cipher suites to enable these IoT boards to interface with our energy measurement platform. By analyzing the data collected from our testing platforms, this work brings an update to the field's understanding of the real world resource consumption impact from varying the parameters of TLS handshake and record layers. Consequently, our main contribution is a set of guidelines, embodied by a set of tree representations, to show all the possible configurations of a cipher suite. Depending on the usage parameters, different paths are traversed on the tree edges. This allows the IoT developer to modify the parameters relevant to the cipher suite as well as the certificate and immediately find the resource consumption impact. Moreover, these guidelines provide directions for selecting the most appropriate cipher suites according to different application scenarios.

The rest of this paper is organized as follows. Section 2 specifies the TLS handshake's messages, presents the algorithms associated with each message, and provides a brief overview of the record layer. In Section 3, the set of algorithms in a cipher suite are analyzed. The testing platforms, experimental procedure and design choices are presented in Section 4. Section 5 discusses experimental results and proposes guidelines for the most suitable cipher suite family depending on usage scenarios. Related works are discussed in Section 6. Finally, Section 7 concludes the paper and proposes future research directions.

2 TLS'S HANDSHAKE AND RECORD LAYERS

As discussed earlier, the TLS protocol is designed to establish a secure channel between a client and a server to provide information authenticity, confidentiality, and integrity. Specifically, its handshake layer adopts different PKC algorithms for identity authentication and allows the negotiation of a cipher suite, which consists of a set of cryptographic algorithms. This enables data confidentiality and integrity later in the record layer. Since the detailed understanding of the handshake procedure is essential for analysing resource consumption, we first summarize the phases of this procedure as follows. The entire process is presented in Figure 2.

(1) *Hello Request*: This message may be sent by the server at any time as a notification that the client should begin a new negotiation. The client may ignore this message or send *Client Hello* when convenient.

(2) *Client Hello*: This message is sent when the client first connects to the server or in response to a *Hello Request*. The record of this message contains the following fields: (i) TLS version, (ii) a random number, (iii) an optional Session ID to quickly resume a previous TLS connection and skip some steps of the TLS handshake, (iv) a list of cipher suites (specifies the key exchange algorithm, bulk encryption algorithm, MAC, and a Pseudo-Random Function (PRF)), (v) the compression method, which is often *null* to avoid CRIME attacks [10].

(3) *Server Hello*: This message is sent by the server in response to *Client Hello*. A Server Hello message includes: (i) TLS version, (ii) a random number, (iii) session ID: in case *Client Hello*'s session ID is not empty, the server looks into its session cache for a match, and (iv) the cipher suite selection chosen from the

client list, which should be the strongest suite supported by both sides.

(4) *Server Certificate*: The server must send a certificate message immediately after *Server Hello*. The certificate type must be appropriate for the selected cipher suite key exchange algorithm.

(5) *Server Key Exchange*: This message is sent immediately after the *Server Certificate* message. Only for Ephemeral Diffie-Hellman (DHE), Diffie-Hellman (DH), and RSA key exchange the server uses this message to specify the cryptographic parameters. In the case of Ephemeral Elliptic Curve Diffie-Hellman (ECDHE) the key exchange parameters reside in the *Server Certificate* message. If the key exchange is based on EC, the server specifies the curve name only. Both the server and the client can derive the curve parameters, such as prime p and generator G, based on the NIST standard [11]. The server also chooses a random private key a, computes $a * G$ as the public key, and saves it in `server_params`. In addition to this, the server also signs the data with its private key.

(6) *Certificate Request*: A server can optionally request a certificate from the client. This message, if sent, will immediately follow *Server Key Exchange* message. The message *Certificate Request* specifies the certificate types that the client may offer and a list of supported hashing/signature algorithms pairs that the server is able to verify, according to [12].

(7) *Server Hello Done*: This message is sent by the server to indicate the end of the *Server Hello* message.

(8) *Client Certificate*: This message is sent only if the server requests a certificate, which must be appropriate for the negotiated cipher suite's key exchange algorithm. The client signs the certificate. In this paper, we use either RSA or ECDSA as the signing algorithms.

(9) *Client Key Exchange*: This message is sent after receiving *Server Hello Done*. This message contains the client's DH public key, due to our choice of using ECDH or ECDHE as PKC. If the cipher does not indicate ephemeral key like ECDH, the message will be empty.

(10) *Change Cipher Spec*: This message is sent by both the client and server, as the final non-encrypted message, in order to notify the other party that subsequent messages are protected under the most recently negotiated cipher suite.

(11) *Certificate Verify*: This message is sent by the client only when *Client Certificate* is sent, in order to provide explicit verification for its own certificate. This message contains all the messages sent or received starting at the message *Client Hello* and up to but not including this message. This requires the client to buffer the messages or compute or buffer the hash of the previous messages.

(12) *Finished*: This message is sent immediately after *Change Cipher spec*, in order to verify that the key exchange and authentication processes have been successful. The *Finished* message is the first protected packet with the most recently negotiated algorithms, keys, and secrets. Before transmitting any encrypted data, both the client and the server generate several keys including the encryption keys, MAC keys and IV (nonce) using the master_secret as the seed for the PRF.

After the handshake phase is completed, the data transmitted between the client and server at the record layer will be secured by applying the symmetric cryptographic algorithms negotiated above in the listed steps. In the next section, we will investigate the algorithms and their individual functions, that construct a cipher suite, in detail.

3 CIPHER SUITE'S SET OF ALGORITHMS

A cipher suite is a set of cryptographic algorithms used for handshake and record layer, consisting of the following tasks: key exchange, signature for authentication, bulk encryption, and message integrity. For example, consider the following cipher suite: ECDHE_RSA_WITH_AES_128_GCM_SHA256.

This means that this cipher suite uses the following algorithms: Ephemeral Elliptic Curve Diffie-Hellman for key exchange, RSA for signature (verifying and signing), AES in GCM mode with 128-bit keys for bulk encryption/integrity, and SHA256 for key derivation (in the case of CBC, SHA256 is used as the hash function for HMAC). For IoT applications, in particular, ECC provides the same level of security using smaller key size compared to RSA. Therefore, we select an optimized version of ECC, called micro-ECC [13], to measure the resource consumption of ECDSA and ECDHE. In this section, we analyze the computations of each algorithm.

It should be noted that the negotiated hash function is used to implement HMAC - for non-AE (Authenticated Encryption) ciphers - and/or to implement PRF (via P_hash) to expand the secret keys [12]. The computations below occur on the client side:

(1) Key exchange: The computation used by EC requires inputs from the certificate, including the curve name, containing $[a, b]$ (public curve parameters), p (prime modulus specifying the size of the finite field), N (number of points on the curve), G (a generator), the order n and the co-factor h of the subgroup. Therefore the computations by ECDHE include the generation of a random number r chosen from $\{1, 2, ..., n - 1\}$ (the private key) as well as the calculation of the public key $r * G$ and the shared key $r * s$, where s is the server's public key.

(2) Digital signature: The client certificate is signed based on the cryptographic parameters sent by the server in message *Client Certificate*. For RSA signing: the computation is $s = t^d \mod N$, where t is the hash value of the certificate content, d is the client's private key and N is the RSA modulus. For ECDSA signing, a random number k is generated from $\{1, 2, ..., n - 1\}$, where n is the subgroup order. Then, the following steps occur: find the point $R = k * G$, find the value $r = R_x \mod n$ (where R_x is the x-coordinate of R) and calculate $s = k^{-1} * (t + r * d) \mod n$ (where d is the client private key and k^{-1} is the multiplicative inverse of k modulo n). The pair (r, s) is the signature.

(3) Signature verification: The signature verification is executed only on the hash value of the certificate content, regardless of algorithm. For RSA signature verification, the signature is represented by the value z. The computation is $s = t^{p_k} \mod N$, where t is the hash value and p_k is the CA's public key, and N is the RSA modulus. The last computation of this algorithm (negligible operation) is to compare if $s == z$. For ECDSA, the signature is represented by two values (r, s). In order to verify the signature, the CA's public key C_{pk} is

Table 1: The utilized IoT edge devices and their features

Device	BCM4343W (BCM)	CYW43907 (CYW)
MCU	ARM Cortex M4	ARM Cortex R4
Word Size	32-bit	32-bit
SRAM	128 KB	2 MB
Clock Frequency	100 MHz	320 MHz
WiFi Standards	802.11b/g/n	802.11b/g/n
On-chip Crypto Core	Not Available	Available

needed, which is hard-coded in our implementation. Let t be the hash value of the certificate content. The client then calculates $u_1 = s^{-1} * t \mod n$ and $u_2 = s^{-1} * r \mod n$, where s^{-1} is the multiplicative inverse of s modulo n. Then, the computation becomes $R = u_1 * G + u_2 * C_{pk}$. The last step is to validate if $r == R_x \mod n$, where R_x is the x coordinate of R.

(4) Message authentication: this is calculated for data integrity only on non-AE ciphers.

To achieve a comprehensive understanding of the resource consumption of the TLS protocol's cryptographic algorithms, in this work, we evaluate each computation discussed above. In the next section, we will discuss the evaluation methodology in detail.

4 METHODOLOGY

In this section, we present an overview of the testbed's components and the testing procedure. We also highlight the main performance measurement parameters.

4.1 IoT Edge Devices

The features of the two IoT edge devices employed in this work are summarized in Table 1. Our first testing platform, CYW43907 (CYW) [14], is an embedded wireless system-on-a-chip (SoC) manufactured by Cypress Semiconductor. Boasting the powerful ARM Cortex-R4 processor and an on-chip cryptography core, the CYW board is optimized for IoT computation-heavy applications and supports hardware-accelerated AES. The second platform, BCM4343W (BCM) [15], is an SoC built by Avnet. The BCM board provides less processing power from its ARM Cortex-M4 processor, lacking cryptographic hardware acceleration. It should be noted that the CYW board is more expensive than the BCM board, which justifies its superior specifications. The CYW board is better suited for computation-heavy tasks, thanks to its abundant computational power. In contrast, the more economical BCM platform is better for large-scale deployments. This contrast between devices allows us to generalize our experimental results of cipher suite performance and guidelines across both computation-heavy as well as scalable IoT scenarios.

4.2 Energy Measurement Tool

In this work, we adopt a powerful evaluation platform, EMPIOT, which is a fully software-controlled tool for the energy measurement of IoT devices [16]. EMPIOT is a shield board that is installed on top of a Raspberry Pi. The start-stop mechanism of EMPIOT energy measurements can be carefully controlled by utilizing the GPIO pins of the Raspberry Pi. The energy measurement accuracy

Figure 3: Components of the testbed used for performance evaluation

of EMPIOT is 0.4 μW. When measuring data from IoT devices using 802.15.4 and 802.11 wireless standards, the EMPIOT's energy measurement errors are less than 3%. When using 12-bit sampling resolution, this tool can stream 1000 samples per second. All energy and time measurements in this study have been carried out using this platform.

Figure 3 depicts the EMPIOT's components and connections with the IoT boards. The output signals from the IoT device under test to the GPIO pins of EMPIOT act as triggers to the measurement sequence. Once triggered by a positive edge signal, the EMPIOT measures the values of current (with precision of 100 μA) and voltage (with precision of 4 mV). Data measured using the EMPIOT is stored into a text file within the Raspberry Pi's on-board memory.

4.3 Cryptographic Algorithms

Cypress Semiconductor's WICED Studio version 6.1.0, the standard SDK for our testing platforms, includes a library of cryptographic algorithms [17]. To provide RSA, SHA256 and SHA384 functionalities, the WICED security library uses the *mbed TLS* free, open-source library[1]. For ECDSA, we again make use of a sample test program from the mbed TLS library that has been provided within WICED Studio. For the more optimized uECC-version ECDSA and uECC-version ECDHE, we use the implementations from the micro-ECC (μECC) library, also available in WICED Studio. Resistant to known side-channel attacks, the lightweight uECC implementations of ECDSA and ECDHE are more optimized and efficient than the standard implementations. Both uECC-version ECDSA and uECC-version ECDHE support five standard curves – secp160r1, secp192r1, secp224r1, secp256r1, and secp256k1, as well as 8, 32 and 64-bit architectures. Last but not least, we use AES-CBC and AES-GCM from the same open-source library within this software development kit. For all these implementations, we have modified

---

[1]https://tls.mbed.org/

and annotated the source codes to integrate fully with our energy measurement platform for resource consumption measurement.

4.4 Evaluation Process

In a single-thread configuration, we evaluate both the energy consumption and time duration for each individual algorithm (RSA, ECDSA, uECC-version ECDSA, uECC-version ECDHE, AES-CBC and AES-GCM) in our cipher suites. The evaluation follows three steps:

4.4.1 Initialization. In order to initialize an RSA experiment, the desired key size is set. Using the two common key sizes, 1024 and 2048 bits, we test RSA's hashing, encryption, decryption, signing and verification functions. Before each ECDSA experiment, the desired curve is set. Using three common curves, secp192r1, secp224r1 and secp256r1, we test ECDSA's hashing, random number generation, signing and verification operations. Similarly, the same setup for ECDSA is followed in the testing of uECC-version ECDSA. Lastly, for each uECC-version ECDHE experiment, using previously mentioned three common curves, we test uECC-version ECDHE's random number generation, public key generation, and secret calculation operations. To initialize SHA256 and SHA384 experiments, the input buffer length is set to 128 bytes. Last but not least, we test AES-CBC and AES-GCM across two buffer sizes (128 bytes and 512 bytes) as well as three key sizes (128 bits, 192 bits and 256 bits).

4.4.2 Starting Energy and Time Measurement. The first GPIO positive-edge trigger is enacted at time T_s, signaling EMPIOT to commence energy measurement. Depending on the specific combination of a particular experiment's parameters such as key size and curve size, the function being tested is repeated for N times using a `for` loop. Although the overhead of the `for` loop structure and the `if` statement is included, we find that the time and energy consumed by these operations are negligible.

4.4.3 Completing Energy and Time Measurement. Following the conclusion of the Nth encryption at time T_e, a second positive-edge GPIO pin is enacted, signaling EMPIOT to conclude energy measurement. Over an interval $[T_s, T_e]$, EMPIOT gathers 1000 samples per second of instantaneous current and voltage values. Each sample is also captured with a timestamp on it. Representing the total number of samples taken over the interval as M, the following equation is used to obtain total energy consumption E_{total} (J) over the interval: $E_{total} = \sum_{i=1}^{M} \frac{(I_i V_i + I_{i-1} V_{i-1})}{2}(t_i - t_{i-1})$ where I and V stand for current and voltage, respectively. The total energy is calculated using the trapezoidal rule. The sum of $I_i V_i$ and $I_{i-1} V_{i-1}$ represents the sum of the two bases of a trapezoid. The term $t_i - t_{i-1}$ stands for the height of the mentioned trapezoid. The area of the trapezoid represents the total energy consumed. For each specific combination of a particular experiment's parameters, the number of repetitions is denoted by N. We are only interested in the energy consumption per repetition, and so the average energy consumption per repetition with unit as joules (J) is calculated as follows: $\bar{E} = \frac{E_{total}}{N}$, where N is the number of repetitions. To acquire the total amount of time, the first sample's timestamp in seconds (s) is subtracted from the last sample's timestamp, as follows: $T_{total} = T_e - T_s$, where T_s is the time the first positive-edge

Table 2: Mean energy consumption (joule) per repetition

Platform	BCM			CYW		
Curve Type	192	224	256	192	224	256
ECDSA						
Signing	0.0405	0.0545	0.0817	0.0388	0.0515	0.0748
Verification	0.0788	0.1068	0.3831	0.0743	0.0992	0.1458
uECC-version ECDSA						
Signing	0.0197	0.0253	0.0451	0.0083	0.0111	0.0192
Verification	0.0206	0.0276	0.0502	0.0089	0.0120	0.0207

Table 3: Mean duration (second) per repetition

Platform	BCM			CYW		
Curve Type	192	224	256	192	224	256
ECDSA						
Signing	0.2080	0.2781	0.4193	0.0458	0.0610	0.0883
Verification	0.4037	0.5435	0.8257	0.0891	0.1187	0.1743
uECC-version ECDSA						
Signing	0.0343	0.0445	0.0813	0.0070	0.0098	0.0175
Verification	0.0361	0.0486	0.0900	0.0076	0.0106	0.0190

trigger is called and T_e is the time the second positive-edge trigger is called, concluding data sampling. To acquire the average duration per repetition, we follow the same principle as in the previous energy consumption calculation: $\bar{T} = \frac{T_{total}}{N}$, where N is the number of repetitions.

The entire evaluation process above is repeated for all the tests outlined in the initialization step.

5 EXPERIMENTAL RESULTS

First, we discuss the performance difference between regular ECDSA and uECC-implemented ECDSA to support our decision to use the uECC implementations of ECDSA and ECDHE for all the measurements. As mentioned in Section 4, we test both standard ECDSA and uECC-implemented ECDSA. Tables 2 and 3 show the mean energy consumption and duration per repetition in joules (J) and seconds (s), respectively, for both ECDSA and uECC-implemented ECDSA's individual functions on the BCM and CYW boards. We notice that, on average, regular ECDSA's signing and verification operations consume approximately 2x to 8x more energy than uECC-implemented ECDSA's signing and verification operations. Hence, we decide to use uECC-implemented ECDSA and uECC-implemented ECDHE for the evaluations.

For the rest of this section, we present and evaluate performance results for the following four cipher suite families:

(1) ECDHE_RSA_WITH_AES*[2]_SHA*[3]
(2) ECDHE_ECDSA_WITH_AES*_SHA*
(3) RSA_WITH_NULL_SHA*
(4) ECDHE_anon_WITH_AES*_SHA*

Each family represents a set of cipher suites. As mentioned, each cipher suite consists of the following tasks: key exchange and authentication, with bulk encryption and message integrity. Cipher suites with anon authentication means the client does not need to

[2]AES* stands for AES_128(256)_CBC(GCM)
[3]SHA* stands for SHA256(384)

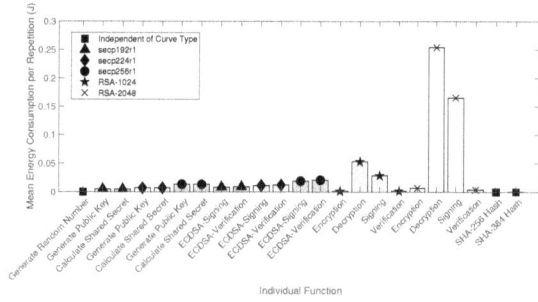

(a) Energy - CYW

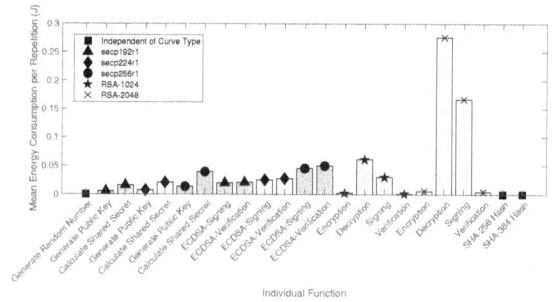

(b) Energy - BCM

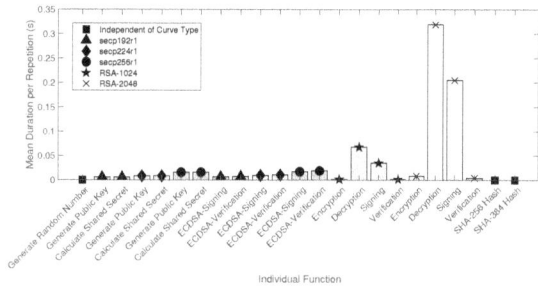

(c) Duration - CYW

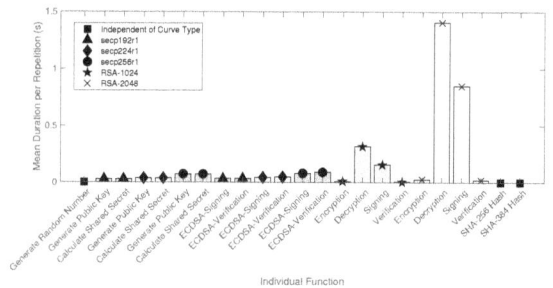

(d) Duration - BCM

Figure 4: Mean energy consumption and duration of the elementary individual functions that construct any cipher suite from the four families, using three elliptic curves as well as RSA-1024 and RSA-2048 as parameters across two IoT platforms. We notice that as an individual function's curve size increases, that function's energy consumption also increases. Similarly, as RSA key size increases, RSA's individual functions demand more energy.

authenticate the servers. Cipher suites with NULL encryption means no encryption is required, yet message integrity is still needed. In particular, in Subsection 5.1, we present the energy consumption and duration of all the fine-grained building blocks that make up the four families above. Based on these building blocks, in Subsection 5.2, we select seven widely-used cipher suites from the four families as examples and discuss their energy consumption and duration in detail. In addition, we present two tree-like diagrams to illustrate all possible cipher suites within the four families. Finally, in Subsection 5.3, we provide a set of guidelines on selecting the most appropriate cipher suites for different application scenarios.

5.1 Resource Consumption of Individual Building Blocks

Figure 4 presents both energy consumption (J) and time duration (s) for all the building blocks of the cipher suites from the four listed families. Measurement parameters include three elliptic curves secp192r1, secp224r1 and secp256r1 as well as RSA-1024 and RSA-2048. Each subplot contains groups of bars, distinguished by the legend markers, representing the characteristics of each cipher suite's elementary individual functions. For instance, the markers show which elliptic curve a function belongs to, or if the function is a part of RSA-1024 or RSA-2048. These results show that in cipher suites using RSA, the signing is always more computationally

expensive in terms of energy consumption (about 21x-46x) and duration (about 21x-45x) than verification for the same key size. We also notice that for cipher suites using ECDSA, the signing and the verification's energy consumption is closely matched for the same key size. A similar trend is noticed for execution duration.

Cipher suites using RSA and ECDSA can be compared with each other by referring to Table 4. This table lists comparable key sizes for symmetric and asymmetric-key cryptosystems, with both theoretical and industrial ECC key sizes, based on the most popular algorithms for attacking them [18]. For example, using industrial ECC 160-bit key size provides the same level of security as using RSA-1024. We actually use curve secp192r1 for ECDSA, which employs a 192-bit key size. With this comparison on the BCM platform testing RSA-1024 and ECDSA using curve secp192r1, the verification for ECDSA consumes almost 20x more energy than RSA's. In terms of duration, the verification for RSA is almost 6.5x quicker than ECDSA's. On the other hand, RSA's signing demands approximately 1.5x more energy compared to ECDSA's signing. Duration-wise, RSA's signing takes approximately 4.5x more compared to ECDSA's signing. Similarly, considering Table 4, we can compare RSA-2048 and ECDSA using curve secp224r1, which employs a 224-bit key size. For this case, the verification for ECDSA consumes about 6.4x more energy than RSA's verification while ECDSA's signing demands approximately 6.6x more energy than RSA's signing. In terms of execution time, the verification for ECDSA lasts about

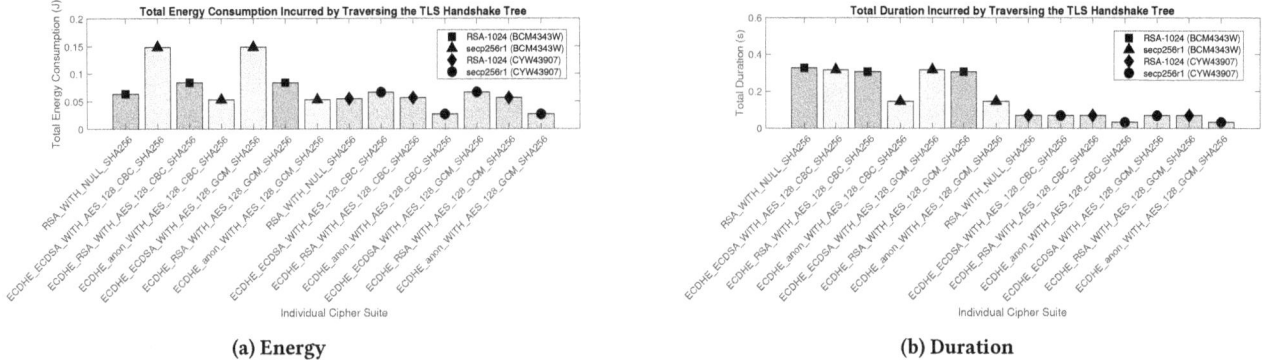

(a) Energy

(b) Duration

Figure 5: Total energy and duration of seven widely used cipher suites from the four families across the BCM and CYW platforms.

2.2x longer than RSA's verification while RSA's signing lasts approximately 19x longer than ECDSA's signing. Furthermore, from the same figures, we notice that RSA's decryption is more costly energy-wise and duration-wise than encryption across two keys.

Table 4: Comparable Key Sizes (in bits)

Symmetric	Theoretical ECC	Industrial ECC	DH/DSA/RSA
80	163	160	1024
112	233	224	2048
128	283	256	3072
192	409	384	7680
256	571	512	15360

For shared or premaster key generation using ECDHE, we notice that the larger the curve size, the greater the energy consumption of the function belonging to that curve. The same trend in energy consumption translates to duration. For shared or premaster key generation using ECDHE, we notice on the same figures that the larger the curve size is, the greater the execution duration of the function belonging to that curve. Random number generation's energy consumption and execution duration are constant, as it is not associated with any curve. Since generating the public key and computing the shared secret depend on the curve size, certainly, increased security comes with a higher demand for energy and higher cost for duration. The behaviors described above for energy consumption and duration are detected on both of our IoT testing platforms.

5.2 Resource Consumption of Prevalent Cipher Suites

Based on the above analysis of the fine-grained individual functions, this subsection further explores the resource consumption of all possible cipher suites from the four families.

Since each cipher suite consists of several functions, to find the full energy consumption or duration of a cipher suite, we simply need to sum up all the functions' energy consumption or duration data values. Figure 5 shows the aggregate energy and duration of seven widely-used cipher suites from the four families. Each bar represents the total energy consumption (a) or duration (b) of the entire set of algorithms that forms the cipher suite. Once again, it is obvious that the CYW platform outperforms the BCM board for both energy consumption and duration, thanks to the CYW's on-chip cryptography core.

To provide in-depth guidelines on how each family should be selected, we present two tree-like diagrams to show every single function that constructs a TLS cipher suite. Figures 6 and 7 depict all possible sequences of functions in the handshake and the record layer, respectively, with different parameters such as key size, curve type and data size. It should be noted that in Figure 7, GCM, which is AEAD[4], combines encryption and integrity (the GMAC component of the GCM algorithm) together. In contrast, for CBC, the integrity is split from encryption/decryption.

In order to illustrate the impact of different sequences on resource consumption, two possible paths, shown by green and red lines in Figure 6, are compared. The red path does not include authentication and uses only RSA 1024-bit key exchange. The green path utilizes RSA-1024 authentication and uses ECDHE key exchange with the secp256r1 curve. Nevertheless, the green path is a more secure solution. Upon analysis, when using the CYW board,

---

[4]Authenticated Encryption with Associated Data

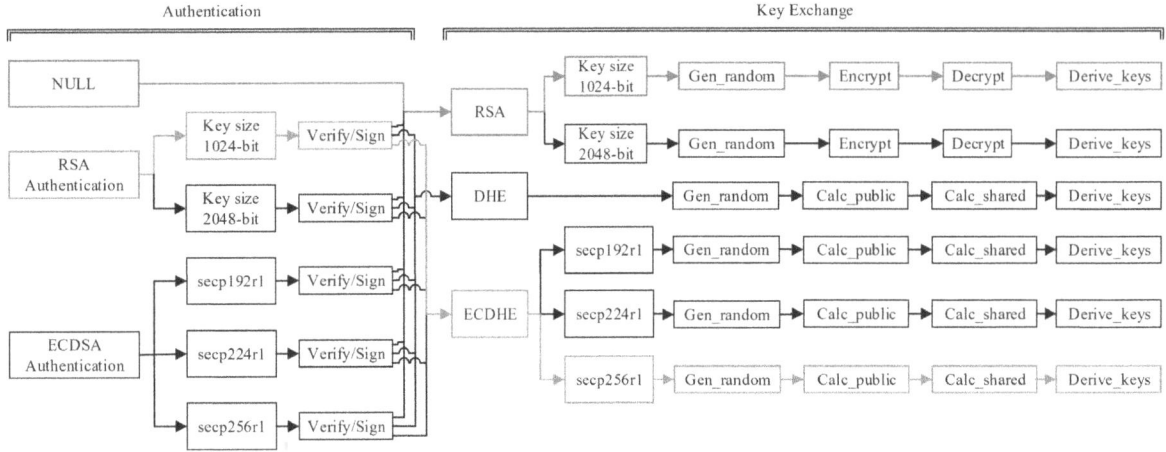

Figure 6: TLS Handshake Tree

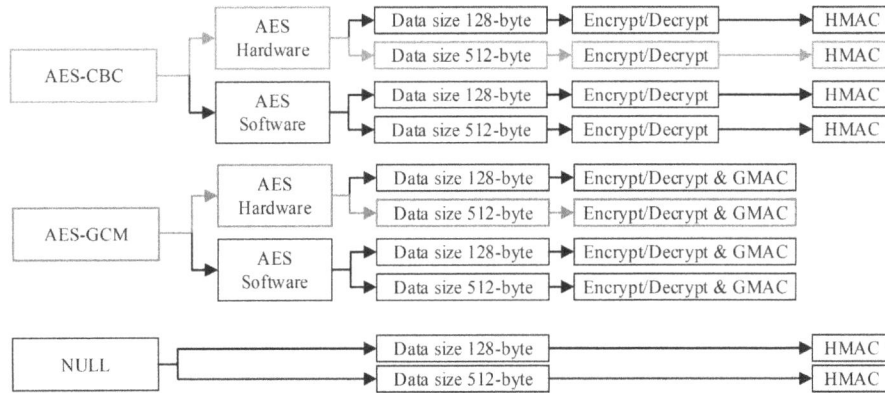

Figure 7: TLS Record Layer Tree

we notice that the red path uses 1.07x more energy and takes the same amount of time as the green path. In the case of the BCM platform, the energy consumption of red path is 0.43x of that of the green path, while the time taken by both paths are equal.

Now, to show resource consumption differences within the record layer, as shown in Figure 7, an example is provided. Representing two possible sequences, the green and red paths correspond to bulk ciphers AES-CBC and AES-GCM, respectively. Since it is known that symmetric key cryptography is way faster than asymmetric key cryptography, we may select any two arbitrary paths as examples. In Figure 7, using the CYW board, both paths use the hardware implementation of AES with a 128-bit key size and a 512-byte data size. Based on the data, the red path uses 1.36x more energy and takes 1.28x longer the green path. The same paths cannot be modeled on the BCM platform, as it does not support hardware acceleration for AES. Still, using the software implementation on the BCM to model these paths, we also see that AES-GCM has higher resource consumption than AES-CBC as it uses 1.79x more energy and takes 1.80x longer.

These comparisons provide an overview of the resource consumption incurred by different cipher suites for both handshake and record layer. This enables us to transition to providing specific guidelines on cipher suite selection in the next section.

5.3 Guidelines for Cipher Suite Selections

Based on our experimental results, we propose the following guidelines for selecting appropriate families depending on usage requirements.

Scenario 1: This scenario arises in applications requiring authenticity, confidentiality, and integrity. Such applications include healthcare (e.g., body area sensors) and smart homes (e.g., smart door locks, security systems), where confidentiality and privacy play a critical role. Family 1 and family 2 are most suitable for this scenario. Depending on application requirements, a longer (or shorter) key can be adopted to achieve higher (or lower) security. Assuming same key and signature size, family 2 consumes about 1.5x more energy and takes the same amount of time as family 1. Therefore, family 2 is recommended when both cipher suite families are available, while family 1 may be chosen in the absence of family 2.

Scenario 2: This scenario arises in applications requiring authenticity and integrity, but not necessarily confidentiality. Applications for this scenario may include smart city sensors that transmit non-confidential data but still require authenticity and integrity. Family 3 is most suitable for this scenario. If we add confidentiality to this family, for data size 512-byte, we may increase the energy consumption by approximately 1.001x. Though insignificant, if the data increases to 50KB, the energy consumption will increase by approximately 1.5x. Adding confidentiality may significantly increase energy consumption in the long run.

Scenario 3: This scenario arises in applications requiring confidentiality and integrity, but not necessarily authenticity. Family 4 is most suitable for this scenario. Even though this family is vulnerable to man-in-the-middle (MITM) attacks, it can still be used for closed-environment applications such as sensors on a military jet or in machine actuators in a factory's local network. Adding authenticity to this scenario (e.g., using RSA verification) will increase the energy consumption on the client side by only 1.05x. However, the overhead of managing and transmitting certificates increases dramatically.

This leads us to the culmination of this work. Based on energy and duration measurements, the right cipher suite family can be chosen to fulfill user requirements while achieving a desired balance between security and efficiency. Specifically, as future work, we recommend dynamic cipher suite adjustments to balance IoT devices' security and resource consumption, based on real-time network condition changes, such as changes to transmitted data type, traffic volume and wireless signal quality. When a change occurs, a new cipher suite negotiation may be launched accordingly.

6 RELATED WORK

There are many papers that analyze the power consumption of security protocols on resource-constrained platforms like IoT devices. Some works are conducted to analyze the impact of symmetric cryptography on the resource consumption of IoT devices [19–21]. In the study by Munoz et al. [19], the authors measure the duration and energy consumption of AES-CBC on both the CYW and BCM platforms. In [21], the authors compare hardware and software AES implementations on an FPGA. In [20], the authors test the impact of increasing AES key size on energy consumption.

In addition, many studies explore the resource consumption of PKC [22–25]. Potlapally et al. [5] study the Secure Sockets Layer (SSL) and the underlying PKC algorithms. The authors in [26] evaluate PKC's influence on four IoT devices mainly using the RSA and ECC families, but not Diffie-Hellman, which is the most widely used PKC family on IoT devices. These studies, however, ignore cipher suites that use ephemeral keys, a popular approach that provides higher security while requiring extra computations. Furthermore, although using customized EC library dedicated for resource-constrained devices is highly recommended, the existing studies often provide no information on their implementations for EC.

The following papers focus on the resource consumption of TLS. In [8], the authors provide a novel model of energy demand for end-to-end data communication. Their approach is to represent

the energy consumption of each node in the network as a function. However, the specific information of the energy measurement process, particularly the data collection process and the types of tested IoT platforms, is absent. The authors in [27] evaluate the performance costs of TLS by using the same cipher suites that are used in our paper. Nevertheless, their study is not carried out using resource-constrained devices. In addition, for both [8] and [27], the authors do not analyze the fine-grained functions within the cipher suites, severely limiting their capability to evaluate diverse cipher suites based on various application requirements. While Gerez et al. investigate the energy and time consumption of TLS, they only focus on the handshake and ignore the record layer [28]. Moreover, their experiments are only carried out using three specific cipher suites on one IoT board, which greatly limits the generality of their results.

Our paper improves on these existing studies by (1) considering both the handshake and record layer of TLS, (2) measuring the resource consumption of each individual function, and (3) improving the results' generality by adopting two state-of-the-art resource-constrained IoT boards and evaluating various widely-used cipher suites. We also provided comprehensive tree diagrams to reflect all the possible paths of processes in the handshake and record layers. These representations not only facilitate flexible calculation of the resource consumption of different cipher combinations, but also provide guidelines for selecting the most appropriate cipher suite according to different application demands.

7 CONCLUSION

Due to the ever increasing number of IoT platforms that need to establish secure connections, we consider the three most important factors of IoT security: authenticity, confidentiality and integrity. Given the resource constraints and long term communication patterns of IoT devices, it is crucial to, depending on the application at hand, choose a proper cipher suite that minimizes resource consumption while ensuring the required security level.

In this paper, we presented a comprehensive study of the most widely-used cryptographic algorithms by annotating their source codes and running empirical measurements on two state-of-the-art IoT platforms (i.e. CYW and BCM). Also, we formulated the tree structures that cover various possible cipher combinations. We showed that by carefully choosing the right cipher suite family based on application requirements, energy consumption can be significantly reduced. For example, in use cases such as smart home and healthcare where high-level security is demanded, selecting ECDHE_RSA_WITH_AES*_SHA* can reduce energy consumption by 3x. Another example can be seen in smart city applications, where using RSA_WITH_NULL_SHA* results in savings up to 1.6x in the long run.

In this work, we did not consider the impact of real-time network condition variations such as the changes to transmitted data type, traffic volume and wireless signal quality, on the resource consumption. Although we focused on TLS 1.2, TLS 1.3 is already available, providing some changes with respect to TLS 1.2 [29]. Nevertheless, the migration towards TLS 1.3 will take a long time and hence, our analysis remains relevant for all current devices using TLS up to 1.2. The energy-duration study of TLS 1.3 is left as a future work.

ACKNOWLEDGMENT

This work has been partially supported by research grant CYP001 from Cypress Semiconductor Corporation.

REFERENCES

[1] Behnam Dezfouli, Marjan Radi, and Octav Chipara. REWIMO: A real-time and reliable low-power wireless mobile network. *ACM Transactions on Sensor Networks (TOSN)*, 13(3):17, 2017.

[2] Habib Ur Rehman, Muhammad Asif, and Mudassar Ahmad. Future applications and research challenges of iot. In *International Conference on Information and Communication Technologies (ICICT)*, pages 68–74. IEEE, 2017.

[3] One trillion new iot devices will be produced by 2035. URL https://learn.arm.com/route-to-trillion-devices.html.

[4] Jorge Granjal, Edmundo Monteiro, and Jorge Sá Silva. Security for the internet of things: a survey of existing protocols and open research issues. *IEEE Communications Surveys and Tutorials*, 17(3):1294–1312, 2015.

[5] Nachiketh R Potlapally, Srivaths Ravi, Anand Raghunathan, and Niraj K Jha. A study of the energy consumption characteristics of cryptographic algorithms and security protocols. *IEEE Transactions on mobile computing*, 5(2):128–143, 2006.

[6] URL https://transparencyreport.google.com/https/overview.

[7] Klint Finley. Half the web is now encrypted. that makes everyone safer, Jun 2017. URL https://www.wired.com/2017/01/half-web-now-encrypted-makes-everyone-safer/.

[8] Arcangelo Castiglione, Alfredo De Santis, Aniello Castiglione, Francesco Palmieri, and Ugo Fiore. An energy-aware framework for reliable and secure end-to-end ubiquitous data communications. In *5th International Conference on Intelligent Networking and Collaborative Systems (INCoS)*, pages 157–165. IEEE, 2013.

[9] Tim Dierks and Eric Rescorla. The transport layer security (tls) protocol version 1.2. 2008.

[10] Fitzgerald Shawn Sarkar, Pratik Guha. Attacks on ssl a comprehensive study of beast, crime, time, breach, lucky 13 and rc4 biases. *iSecPartners*, pages 1–23, 2013.

[11] Lily Chen and Dustin Moody. Elliptic Curve Cryptography, 2017. URL https://csrc.nist.gov/Projects/Elliptic-Curve-Cryptography.

[12] E. Rescorla T. Dierks. The transport layer security (tls) protocol version 1.2. https://tools.ietf.org/html/rfc5246, Aug 2008.

[13] Zhe Liu, Xinyi Huang, Zhi Hu, Muhammad Khurram Khan, Hwajeong Seo, and Lu Zhou. On emerging family of elliptic curves to secure internet of things: Ecc comes of age. *IEEE Transactions on Dependable and Secure Computing*, 14(3): 237–248, 2017.

[14] Cypress Semiconductor. CYW943907AEVAL1F Evaluation Kit, 2018. URL http://www.cypress.com/documentation/development-kitsboards/cyw943907aeval1f-evaluation-kit.

[15] Avnet Inc. Avnet BCM4343W IoT Starter Kit, 2018. URL http://cloudconnectkits.org/product/avnet-bcm4343w-iot-starter-kit.

[16] Behnam Dezfouli, Immanuel Amirtharaj, and Chia-Chi Chelsey Li. EMPIOT: An energy measurement platform for wireless IoT devices. *Journal of Network and Computer Applications*, 121:135–148, 2018.

[17] Cypress Semiconductor. WICED Studio, Mar 2018. URL http://www.cypress.com/products/wiced-software.

[18] S. Blake-Wilson, N. Bolyard, V. Gupta, C. Hawk, and B. Moeller. Elliptic Curve Cryptography (ECC) Cipher Suites for Transport Layer Security (TLS). https://tools.ietf.org/html/rfc4492, May 2006.

[19] Pedro Sanchez Munoz, Nam Tran, Brandon Craig, Behnam Dezfouli, and Yuhong Liu. Analyzing the resource utilization of aes encryption on iot devices. In *Asia-Pacific Signal and Information Processing Association Annual Summit and Conference (APSIPA)*, pages 1–8, 2018.

[20] Diaa Salama Abd Elminaam, Hatem Mohamed Abdual-Kader, and Mohiy Mohamed Hadhoud. Evaluating the performance of symmetric encryption algorithms. *IJ Network Security*, 10(3):216–222, 2010.

[21] Anton Biasizzo, Marko Mali, and Frank Novak. Hardware implementation of aes algorithm. *Journal of Electrical Engineering*, 56(9-10):265–269, 2005.

[22] William Freeman and Ethan Miller. An experimental analysis of cryptographic overhead in performance-critical systems. In *7th International Symposium on Modeling, Analysis and Simulation of Computer and Telecommunication Systems*, pages 348–357. IEEE, 1999.

[23] Neil Daswani and Dan Boneh. Experimenting with electronic commerce on the palmpilot. In *International Conference on Financial Cryptography*, pages 1–16. Springer, 1999.

[24] Abdullah Almuhaideb, Mohammed Alhabeeb, Phu Dung Le, and Bala Srinivasan. Beyond fixed key size: Classifications toward a balance between security and performance. In *24th IEEE International Conference on Advanced Information Networking and Applications (AINA)*, pages 1047–1053, 2010.

[25] George Apostolopoulos, Vinod Peris, Prashant Pradhan, and Debanjan Saha. Securing electronic commerce: reducing the ssl overhead. *IEEE Network*, 14(4): 8–16, 2000.

[26] Krzysztof Piotrowski, Peter Langendoerfer, and Steffen Peter. How public key cryptography influences wireless sensor node lifetime. In *Proceedings of the fourth ACM workshop on Security of ad hoc and sensor networks*, pages 169–176, 2006.

[27] Lin-Shung Huang, Shrikant Adhikarla, Dan Boneh, and Collin Jackson. An experimental study of tls forward secrecy deployments. *IEEE Internet Computing*, 18(6):43–51, 2014.

[28] Alejandro Hernandez Gerez, Kavin Kamaraj, Ramzi Nofal, Yuhong Liu, and Behnam Dezfouli. Energy and processing demand analysis of tls protocol in internet of things applications. In *2018 IEEE International Workshop on Signal Processing Systems (SiPS)*, pages 312–317, 2018.

[29] E. Rescorla. The transport layer security (tls) protocol version 1.3. https://tools.ietf.org/html/rfc8446, Aug 2018.

Secrecy in Dual-Hop Relaying Network Using the Independent Randomize-and-Forward Strategy

Feiwen Li
Yongming Wang*
Institute of Information Engineering, Chinese Academy of Sciences, Beijing, China
School of Cyber Security, University of Chinese Academy of Sciences, Beijing, China
{lifeiwen,wangyongming}@iie.ac.cn

ABSTRACT

In this paper, we investigate secure communication for a dual-hop relay channel in the presence of an eavesdropper. A novel independent randomize-and-forward (IRF) strategy is proposed to enhance the secrecy performance, where the relay maps the decoded message to an independent message set then encodes the message by random-coding argument. For the discrete model, we establish the achievable rate-equivocation for the IRF strategy. For the Gaussian model, we derive the perfect secrecy rate of IRF strategy and compare it with decode-and-forward (DF), amplify-and-forward (AF) and noise-forwarding (NF) strategies. Theoretical analysis indicates that the relay's engagement of independent secure coding enhances the security of transmission. Numerical results also show the proposed IRF strategy can significantly improve the secrecy performance of the dual-hop relay channel in some cases.

CCS CONCEPTS

• **Security and privacy → Information-theoretic techniques**; *Mobile and wireless security*;

KEYWORDS

relaying network, eavesdropper, rate-equivocation region, secrecy rate, independent randomize-and-forward(IRF)

ACM Reference Format:
Feiwen Li and Yongming Wang. 2019. Secrecy in Dual-Hop Relaying Network Using the Independent Randomize-and-Forward Strategy. In *22nd Int'l ACM Conference on Modeling, Analysis and Simulation of Wireless and Mobile Systems (MSWiM '19), November 25–29, 2019, Miami Beach, FL, USA.* ACM, New York, NY, USA, 8 pages. https://doi.org/10.1145/3345768.3355928

1 INTRODUCTION

Based on Shannon's seminal work [9] which quantified secrecy in communication systems, Wyner introduced the wire-tap channel [13] and developed the notion of secrecy capacity which characterizes the fundamental limit of secure communication over noisy

*Corresponding author

channels. Then Csiszár and Körner [1] extended it to the broadcast channel with confidential messages and indicated the wire-tap channel is a special case of the general broadcast channel.

Recent years, secrecy in the multi-hop network has been investigated extensively. The application of relay increases achievable rates and robustness compared to direct communication. Meanwhile, the utility of relay cooperation can improve the security of wireless communication. In [5], Lai introduced the four-terminal relay-eavesdropper channel as shown in Fig. 1, devised several cooperation strategies which facilitated the secure communications and characterized the corresponding achievable rate-equivocation region. Subsequently, the combinatory cooperation schemes were exploited to achieve a new rate-equivocation region for the relay-eavesdropper channel [10]. In [6], Marina et al. generalized the coding scheme proposed by Csiszár [1] and derived a larger achievable rate-equivocation region than Lai's result [5]. Xu et al. proposed a new achievable scheme which combines noisy network coding and the interference assisted strategy to improve the achievable secrecy rate for the relay-eavesdropper channel [8]. However, the present works simply view the relay-eavesdropper channel as a generalization of the wire-tap channel. Accordingly, the secure coding schemes for the relay-eavesdropper channel only consider introducing the randomness by stochastic encoding at the source to confuse the eavesdropper. In particular, a novel multi-hop forwarding scheme called randomize-and-forward (RF) where randomization is added in every hop to ensure maximal ambiguity at the eavesdropper(s) was proposed in [4]. Recently, Jameel et al. [3] provided a comprehensive survey on the cooperative relaying and jamming strategy. From this, we know that decode-and-forward (DF), compress-and-forward (CF) and amplify-and-forward (AF) are typical relaying schemes in the one-way relaying system with single antenna. Noise-forwarding (NF) is more like a jamming scheme than a relaying scheme. The classic relay cooperative strategies are summarized as follows:

- DF: the relay first decodes codewords and then re-encode the message to cooperate with the source. Different from that in the classic relaying, each massage in DF is associated with many codewords in order to confuse the eavesdropper.
- AF: the relay transmits a weighted version of the noisy signal received from the source. This scheme allows beamforming between the source and the relay without requiring the relay to fully decode.
- CF: In addition to the independent codewords to confuse the eavesdropper, the relay also sends a quantized version of its noisy observations helping the destination in decoding the source's message.

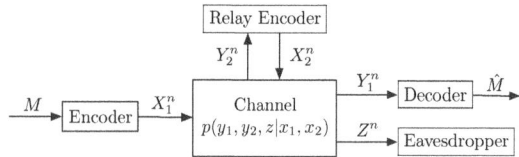

Figure 1: The dual-hop relay channel in the presence of an eavesdropper (The relay-eavesdropper channel)

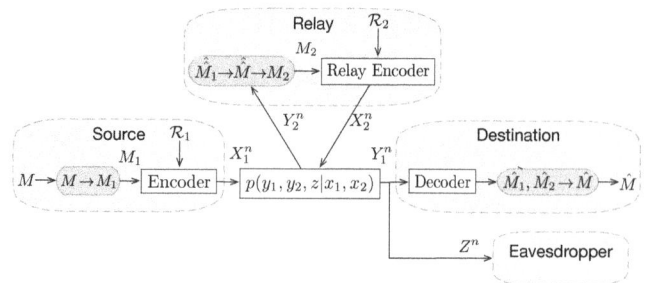

Figure 2: An illustration of the independent randomize-and-forward strategy for the relay-eavesdropper channel

- NF: the relay transmits codewords independent of the source message to confuse the eavesdropper. The secrecy capacity can be improved though the relay fails to offer performance gains. It can be viewed as a special case of the interference assisted strategy for wiretap channel with a helping interferer [11].

Mo et al.[7] analyzed the secure connection in cooperative wireless communication with DF and RF strategies and showed RF always outperforms DF. Cooperative relaying such as DF, CF and AF is able to increase the achievable rate of the legitimate channel, but this advantage can also be provided to the wiretap channel. Although forwarding noise can weaken the eavesdropper's channel, it does not benefit the legitimate channel.

In this paper, we study the secrecy in the dual-hop relay channel in the presence of an eavesdropper. Our work here is motivated by the fact that the relay can improve the capacity of the legitimate channel by forwarding messages. Meanwhile, the forwarded messages cannot be utilized by the eavesdropper to get more source messages, but become interference to weaken the eavesdropping channel. Therefore, we propose a novel independent randomize-and-forward (IRF) strategy which is illustrated in Fig. 2. At this point, we wish to differentiate our strategy from the earlier relevant works. We define one primary message set and two independent subordinate message sets in this paper. The source maps the primary message to one subordinate message set. The relay decodes the message transmitted by the source and recovers the primary message, then maps it to the other subordinate message set. Hence unlike the RF, the messages encoded by the source and the relay are two independent ones rather than an identical one. Moreover, the stochastic coding is implemented twice at the source and the relay, respectively. Intuitively, the additional randomness may increase the eavesdropper's uncertainty about confidential information. We establish the achievable rate-equivocation region and the perfect secrecy rate of the relay-eavesdropper channel for the IRF strategy. We also show the numerical results of simulation and compare the achievable perfect secret rate of IRF strategy with those of DF, AF and NF.

The organization of this paper is as follows. Section 2 introduces the system model and preliminary definition. Section 3 characterizes the achievable rate-equivocation region and the achievable perfect secrecy rate for IRF strategy. The analytical results of the paper are validated by numerical simulation in Section 4. Section 5 concludes the paper.

2 SYSTEM MODEL AND PRELIMINARY DEFINITION

We study the dual-hop relay channel in the presence of an eavesdropper (also called the relay-eavesdropper channel) given in Fig.1, which consists of a source (S) who wishes to communicate to a destination (D) with the help of a relay (R) while keeping the message confidential from an eavesdropper (E). Assume the four terminals know the channel statistics ahead of time. We also assume that the relay can always decode the source messages without any error. The channel is discrete memoryless and denoted by

$$(\mathcal{X}_1 \times \mathcal{X}_2, p(y_1, y_2, z|x_1, x_2), \mathcal{Y}_1 \times \mathcal{Y}_2 \times \mathcal{Z})$$

where $\mathcal{X}_1$ and $\mathcal{X}_2$ are finite input alphabets at the soure and the relay, $\mathcal{Y}_1$, $\mathcal{Y}_2$ and $\mathcal{Z}$ are finite output alphabets at the destination, the relay and the eavesdropper, respectively. $p(y_1, y_2, z|x_1, x_2)$ is the channel transition probability, where $x_i \in \mathcal{X}_i$, $y_i \in \mathcal{Y}_i$ ($i = 1, 2$) and $z \in \mathcal{Z}$.

Definition 2.1. $(2^{nR}, 2^{nR_1}, 2^{nR_2}, n)$ codes $C_{1,n}$ and $C_{2,n}$ for the relay-eavesdropper Channel consist of:

- a primary message set $\mathcal{M} = [1, 2^{nR}]$ and two subordinate message sets $\mathcal{M}_i = [1, 2^{nR_i}]$, $i = 1, 2$;
- two sources of local randomness $\mathcal{R}_i$, $i = 1, 2$;
- a mapping function at the source $h_1 : \mathcal{M} \to \mathcal{M}_1$, which maps the elements from the set $\mathcal{M}$ to $\mathcal{M}_1$, it may not be a full mapping or one-to-one mapping;
- a stochastic encoding function at the source $f_1 : \mathcal{M}_1 \times \mathcal{R}_1 \to \mathcal{X}_1^n$, which maps the message $\mathcal{M}_1$ and a realization of the local randomness $r_1 \in \mathcal{R}_1$ to a codeword $x_1 \in \mathcal{X}_1$;
- a decoding function at the relay $g_1 : \mathcal{Y}_2^n \to \mathcal{M}_1^n \cup \{?\}$, which maps its channel observation $\mathcal{Y}_2^n$ to a message $\hat{m}_1 \in \mathcal{M}$ or an error message ?, then recovers $\mathcal{M}$ through $\mathcal{M}_1$;
- a mapping function at the relay $h_2 : \mathcal{M} \to \mathcal{M}_2$, which maps the elements from the set $\mathcal{M}$ to $\mathcal{M}_2$;
- a stochastic encoding function at the relay $f_2 : \mathcal{M}_2 \times \mathcal{R}_2 \to \mathcal{X}_2^n$, which maps the message $\mathcal{M}_2$ and a realization of the local randomness $r_2 \in \mathcal{R}_2$ to a codeword $x_2 \in \mathcal{X}_2$;
- a decoding function at the destination $g_2 : \mathcal{Y}_1^n \to \mathcal{M}_1^n \mathcal{M}_2^n \cup \{?\}$, which maps channel observations $\mathcal{Y}_1^n$ from direct and forwarding links to messages $\hat{m}_1 \in \mathcal{M}_1$ and $\hat{m}_2 \in \mathcal{M}_2$ respectively or an error message ?, and then recovers $\mathcal{M}$ through $\mathcal{M}_1$ and $\mathcal{M}_2$.

Remark 1. The above definition gives an overview of the IRF strategy. Actually, the information that we want to transmit is $M \in \mathcal{M} = \{1, 2^{nR}\}$, it is first mapped to $M_1 \in \mathcal{M}_1 = \{1, 2^{nR_1}\}$ at the source and then mapped to $M_2 \in \mathcal{M}_2 = \{1, 2^{nR_2}\}$ at the relay, where M_1 and M_2 are independent. We assume M, M_1 and M_2 are chosen uniformly at random. In this case, the destination can decode both M_1 and M_2, then choose the better one (which has a larger codeword rate) to recover M.

Remark 2. A superposition codebook for the relay-eavesdropper channel consisted of two independent codebooks partitioned into "bins" (sub-codebooks). Hence, we say that a relay-eavesdropper code possesses two independent stochastic codes $C_{1,n}$ and $C_{2,n}$ at the source and the relay respectively.

The reliability performance of $C_{i,n}$ ($i = 1, 2$) is measured in terms of its average error probability

$$P_e(C_{1,n}) \triangleq \mathbb{P}[\hat{\hat{M}}_1 \neq M_1 \text{ and } \hat{M}_1 \neq M_1 | C_{1,n}] \tag{1}$$

$$P_e(C_{2,n}) \triangleq \mathbb{P}[\hat{M}_2 \neq M_2 | C_{2,n}] \tag{2}$$

$$P_e(C_n) \triangleq \mathbb{P}[\hat{M} \neq M | C_{1,n} \text{ and } C_{2,n}] \tag{3}$$

where $\hat{\hat{M}}_1$ is the relay's estimation of the source message M_1, $\hat{M}_1$ and $\hat{M}_2$ are the destination's estimations of the source message M_1 and the relay message M_2, respectively. $\hat{M}$ denote the destination's estimation of M.

The secrecy performance is measured in terms of the equivocation at the eavesdropper

$$Re \triangleq \frac{1}{n} H(M|Z^n) \tag{4}$$

$$Re_1 \triangleq \frac{1}{n} H(M_1|Z^n, X_2) \tag{5}$$

$$Re_2 \triangleq \frac{1}{n} H(M_2|Z^n, X_1) \tag{6}$$

where Z^n is the observation at the eavesdropper.

Remark 3. This secrecy criterion guarantees that the rate of information leaked to the eavesdropper from one user is limited even if the other user's transmitted message is compromised[12].

Definition 2.2. A rate tuple (R, Re) is said to be achievable if for any $\epsilon_n > 0$, $\tau_n > 0$, there exists $(2^{nR}, 2^{nR_1}, 2^{nR_2}, n)$ codes $C_{1,n}$ and $C_{2,n}$ such that for n is large enough, the following holds:

$$R_i = \frac{1}{n} \log_2 M_i, i = 1, 2 \tag{7}$$

$$R \leq \min\{R_1, R_2\} \tag{8}$$

$$P_e(C_{i,n}) \leq \epsilon_n, i = 1, 2 \tag{9}$$

$$\frac{1}{n} H(M_1|Z^n, X_2^n) \geq Re_1 - \tau_n \tag{10}$$

$$\frac{1}{n} H(M_2|Z^n, X_1^n) \geq Re_2 - \tau_n \tag{11}$$

$$Re \leq \min\{Re_1, Re_2\} \tag{12}$$

Remark 4. The IRF strategy can improve the achievable secrecy rate when the link between the source and the destination (S-D) is noisier than the relaying link (S-R-D). Otherwise, the relay does not need to work, and this model is equivalent to Wyner's wire-tap channel. Therefore, definition 2.2 is based on the fact that link S-R-D is better than link S-D. In this case, the destination chooses the message from the link S-R-D to recover the primary message.

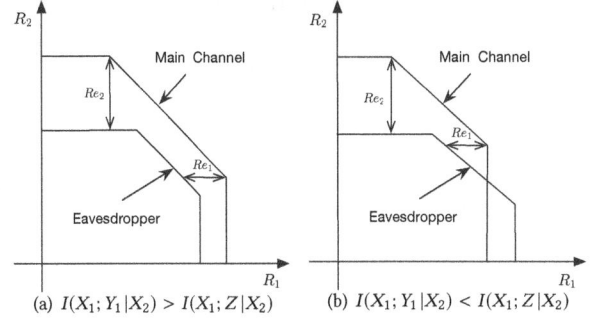

(a) $I(X_1; Y_1|X_2) > I(X_1; Z|X_2)$ (b) $I(X_1; Y_1|X_2) < I(X_1; Z|X_2)$

Figure 3: The rate region of the compound MACs of the relay-eavesdropper channel for a fixed input distribution $p(x_1)p(x_2)$

3 MAIN RESULTS

In this section, we present the achievable rate-equivocation region and the secrecy rate of the relay-eavesdropper channel for the IRF strategy. In addition, we give one example to illustrate the results.

3.1 Discrete memoryless channel: achievable rate-equivocation region

We characterize the achievable rate-equivocation region of the IRF strategy in this part. To make this easier to follow, we first consider the dual-hop relay channel without the direct transmission in the presence of an eavesdropper, then generalize it to the relay-eavesdropper channel. We assume that the direct link between the source and the destination is not available due to the bad condition.

THEOREM 3.1. *In the dual-hop relay channel without direct transmission in the presence of an eavesdropper, the rate pairs in the closure of the convex hull of all (R, R_e) satisfying*

$$R < \min\{I(V_1; Y_2|V_2), I(V_2; Y_1)\}$$
$$R_e < R$$
$$R_e < [\min\{I(V_1; Y_2|V_2) - I(V_1; Z|V_2), \tag{13}$$
$$I(V_2; Y_1) - I(V_2; Z|V_1)\}]^+$$

for some distribution $p(v_1, v_2, x_1, x_2, y_1, y_2, z) = p(v_1)p(v_2)p(x_1|v_1)$ $p(x_2|v_2)p(y_1, y_2, z|x_1, x_2)$, are achievable using the independent randomize-and-forward (IRF) strategy.

Hence, for the IRF strategy, the following perfect secrecy rate of no direct transmission (NDT) is achievable

$$R_s^{(\text{IRF-NDT})} = \sup_{p(v_1)p(v_2)p(x_1|v_1)p(x_2|v_2)} [\min\{I(V_1; Y_2|V_2) - I(V_1; Z|V_2),$$
$$I(V_2; Y_1) - I(V_2; Z|V_1)\}]^+ \tag{14}$$

PROOF. Please refer to the Appendix.   □

To achieve the perfect secrecy rate given in Theorem 3.1, we provide a novel forwarding scheme that involves two independent message sets and two independent codebooks at the source and the relay respectively. A key idea of the proposed IRF is that the relay with transceiver capability can also implement stochastic encoding.

Consider a more general scenario, the direct transmission between the source and the destination is available.

The destination receives messages from two links, the first one is the direct transmission (S-D) and the second one is the dual-hop relaying link (S-R-D). Then the destination decodes the messages and chooses the better one (which has larger equivocation rate) to recover the primary message. The source and the relay to the destination can be viewed as a multiple access channel (MAC). Similarly, the source and the relay to the eavesdropper can be viewed as the other MAC, so the relay-eavesdropper channel can be considered as a compound MAC. Fig. 3 shows the rate region of the both MACs for a fixed input distribution $p(x_1)p(x_2)$. In the figure, R_1 is the codeword rate of the source, and R_2 is the codeword rate of the relay.

We can observe from Fig. 3(a) that the perfect secrecy rate is positive without the relay, the destination decodes the messages transmitted from the relay and then recovers the confidential messages due to $R_{e2} > R_{e1}$. In Fig. 3(b), the perfect secrecy rate is zero for this independent distribution in the absence of the relay. If the relay forwards the messages by IRF strategy, the perfect secrecy rate is improved significantly. On the one hand, the destination may achieve a larger codeword rate. On the other hand, relay plays the role of an interferer for the eavesdropper, since the eavesdropper cannot get any useful information about the source message via decoding the relay message.

The next result establishes the optimal achievable rate-equivocation region of the relay-eavesdropper channel for the IRF strategy.

THEOREM 3.2. *In the relay-eavesdropper channel, the rate pairs in the closure of the convex hull of all (R, R_e) satisfying*

$$R < \max\{I(V_1; Y_1),$$
$$\min\{I(V_1; Y_2|V_2), I(V_2; Y_1|V_1)\}\}$$
$$R_e < R$$
$$R_e < [\max\{I(V_1; Y_1) - I(V_1; Z),$$
$$\min\{I(V_1; Y_2|V_2) - I(V_1; Z|V_2),$$
$$I(V_2; Y_1|V_1) - I(V_2; Z|V_1)\}\}]^+ \quad (15)$$

for some distribution $p(v_1, v_2, x_1, x_2, y_1, y_2, z) = p(v_1)p(v_2)p(x_1|v_1) p(x_2|v_2)p(y_1, y_2, z|x_1, x_2)$, are achievable using the randomize and forward (IRF) strategy.

Hence, for the IRF strategy, the following perfect secrecy rate is achievable

$$R_s^{(IRF)} = \sup_{p(v_1)p(v_2)p(x_1|v_1)p(x_2|v_2)} [\max\{I(V_1; Y_1) - I(V_1; Z),$$
$$\min\{I(V_1; Y_2|V_2) - I(V_1; Z|V_2),$$
$$I(V_2; Y_1|V_1) - I(V_2; Z|V_1)\}\}]^+ \quad (16)$$

PROOF. See the Appendix. □

Note that if the link S-D is noisier than the relaying link S-R-D, the destination chooses the relay message to recover the primary message. Conversely, if the link S-D is better than the link S-R-D, the relay does not need to transmit message. The relay node determines the message whether or not to transmit according to the channel state. Therefore, Theorem 3.2 is the optimal result of direct transmission (DT) and IRF strategy.

3.2 Gaussian channel: achievable perfect secrecy rate

Now, we consider the Gaussian relay-eavesdropper channel, where the signals received at the relay, the destination and the eavesdropper are given by

$$y_{2,k} = h_{sr}x_{1,k} + n_{2,k}$$
$$y_{1,k} = h_{sd}x_{1,k} + h_{rd}x_{2,k} + n_{1,k} \quad (17)$$
$$z_k = h_{se}x_{1,k} + h_{re}x_{2,k} + n_k$$

where $h_{sd}, h_{sr}, h_{se}, h_{rd}$ and h_{re} are the fading gain coefficients associated with S-D, S-R, S-E, R-D and R-E links. n_1, n_2 and n are the i.i.d. Gaussian noise with unit variance at the destination, the relay and the eavesdropper, respectively. The source and relay inputs X_1 and X_2 satisfy average block power constraints, i.e., $\sum_{k=1}^m E[X_{1,k}^2] \le mP_1$ and $\sum_{k=1}^m E[X_{2,k}^2] \le mP_2$.

For IRF, we let $X_1 \sim \mathcal{N}(0, P_1)$, $X_2 \sim \mathcal{N}(0, P_2)$. Here X_1 and X_2 are independent, straightforward calculations of (16) result in

$$R_s^{(IRF)} = [\max\{\frac{1}{2}\log_2(\frac{1 + |h_{sd}|^2P_1}{1 + |h_{se}|^2P_1}), \quad (18)$$
$$\min\{\frac{1}{2}\log_2(\frac{1 + |h_{sr}|^2P_1}{1 + |h_{se}|^2P_1}), \frac{1}{2}\log_2(\frac{1 + |h_{rd}|^2P_2}{1 + |h_{re}|^2P_2})\}\}]^+.$$

Lai derived the achievable secrecy rate of DF, NF and AF cooperation strategies, now we review the results of [5].

For DF, the achievable secrecy rate is given by

$$R_s^{(DF)} = \max_{c,P}[\min\{\frac{1}{2}\log_2(\frac{1 + |h_{sr}|^2P}{1 + |h_{se}c + h_{re}|^2P_2 + |h_s|^2P}),$$
$$\frac{1}{2}\log_2(\frac{1 + |h_{sd}c + h_{rd}|^2P_2 + |h_s|^2P|^2P}{1 + |h_{sd}c + h_{rd}|^2P_2 + |h_s|^2P})\}]^+ \quad (19a)$$
$$s.t. \quad |c|^2P_2 + P \le P_1 \quad (19b)$$

For NF, X_1 and X_2 are independent, the achievable secrecy rate is given by

$$R_s^{(NF)} = [\min\{\frac{1}{2}\log_2(1 + |h_{sd}|^2P_1),$$
$$\frac{1}{2}\log_2(\frac{1 + |h_{sd}|^2P_1 + |h_{rd}|^2P_2}{1 + |h_{se}|^2P_1 + |h_{re}|^2P_2}),$$
$$\frac{1}{2}\log_2(\frac{(1 + |h_{re}|^2P_2)(1 + |h_{se}|^2P_1)}{1 + |h_{se}|^2P_1 + |h_{re}|^2P_2})\}]^+ \quad (20)$$

For AF, the achievable secrecy rate is given by

$$R_s^{(AF)} = \max_{\alpha,\beta,\gamma,P}[\frac{1}{4}\log_2(\frac{\det\{P H_1 H_1^H + A\}\det B}{\det\{P H_2 H_2^H + B\}\det A})]^+ \quad (21a)$$
$$s.t. \begin{cases} (1 + |\alpha|^2 + |\beta|^2)P \le 2P_1 \\ |\gamma|^2(|h_{sr}|^2P + 1) \le 2P_2 \end{cases} \quad (21b)$$

where

$$H_1 = \begin{bmatrix} h_{sd} & 0 \\ \beta h_{sd} + \gamma h_{sr}h_{rd} & \alpha h_{sd} \end{bmatrix}$$

$$H_2 = \begin{bmatrix} h_{se} & 0 \\ \beta h_{se} + \gamma h_{sr}h_{re} & \alpha h_{se} \end{bmatrix}$$

$$A = \begin{bmatrix} 1 & 0 \\ 0 & 1 + |\gamma h_{rd}|^2 \end{bmatrix} \quad B = \begin{bmatrix} 1 & 0 \\ 0 & 1 + |\gamma h_{re}|^2 \end{bmatrix}.$$

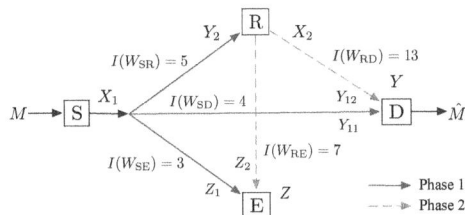

Figure 4: An example of the physically degraded relay channel with physically degraded eavesdropper

Here, α, β and γ are chosen to satisfy the average power constraints of the source and the relays.

3.3 An example

The theorem proposed above can be seen from the following simple example. We assume the relay works in half-duplex mode. For simplicity, we consider the physically degraded relay channel with an degraded eavesdropper, which can be express as

$$p(y_{11}, y_{12}, y_2, z_1, z_2 | x_1, x_2) \tag{22}$$
$$= p(y_2|x_1)p(y_{11}|y_2)p(z_1|y_{11})p(y_{12}|x_2)p(z_2|y_{12})$$

We adopt the same system model [2]. The communication system as shown in Fig.4 works in two phases (i.e.,time division half-duplex mode):

- Phase 1: S broadcasts the length-n encoded signal vector X_1 into the channel. The corresponding signal vectors received at D, R and E are denoted by Y_{11}, Y_2 and Z_1, respectively.
- Phase 2: Upon receiving Y_2 in the first phase, R decodes the message and regenerates a length-n signal vector X_2, which is broadcasted into the channel. The corresponding signal vectors received by D and E are denoted by Y_{12} and Z_2, respectively.

Note that D and E receive signal vectors from S and R on orthogonal channels since two phases of transmission.

In this example, we assume that all channel links are symmetric and discrete memoryless with binary inputs. For convenience, $W_{i,j}$ denotes the channel link between node $i \in \{S, R\}$ and node $j \in \{R, D, E\}$. $I(W_{i,j})$ (unit: bit/transmission) denotes the symmetric capacity of the channel $W_{i,j}$. As shown in Fig.4, for the phase 1, the link capacities to R, D and E are given by $I(W_{SR}) = 5$, $I(W_{SD}) = 4$ and $I(W_{SE}) = 3$, respectively. Similarly, for the phase 2, the link capacities to D and E are given by $I(W_{RD}) = 13$ and $I(W_{RE}) = 7$.

For the half-duplex degraded relay-eavesdropper channel defined in (22), the maximum achievable perfect secrecy rate of DF strategy given by Duo [2] is

$$R_s^{(DF)} = \min\{I(W_{SD}) + I(W_{RD}), I(W_{SR})\} - I(W_{RE}) - I(W_{SE}) \tag{23}$$

Accordingly, the maximum achievable perfect secrecy rate of this example is

$$R_s^{(DF)} = [\min\{(13 + 4), 5\} - 3 - 7]^+ = 0 \tag{24}$$

Therefore, secure transmission is not possible.

However, according to the theorem provided in this paper we can obtain

$$R_s^{(IRF)} = \max\{I(W_{SD}) - I(W_{SE}), \min\{I(W_{SR}) - I(W_{SE}),$$
$$I(I(W_{RD}) - I(W_{RE}))\}\}$$
$$= \max\{(4 - 3), \min\{(5 - 3), (13 - 7)\}\} = 2 \tag{25}$$

Hence, 2 bits of information can be transmitted securely over the relay-eavesdropper channel.

Remark 4: The eavesdropper can overhear the message transmitted by the source and the relay. However, it does not mean that the information obtained from the relay can affect eavesdropper's understanding and judgment of the information transmitted by the source. As shown in the above example, if R-D channel is superior to R-E channel, the relay implements random-coding to hide the confidential messages, so that the eavesdropper cannot get any useful information about the source message from the relay.

4 NUMERICAL RESULTS AND OBSERVATIONS

In this section, we investigate the performance of the proposed IRF strategy numerically. For simplicity, we consider a simple two-dimensional system model, in which the source is located at $(0, 0)$, the destination is located at $(1, 0)$, the relay is located at $(x, 0)$, and the eavesdropper is located at $(0, 1)$. To hight the effects of distances, channels between any two nodes are modeled by a simple line-of-sight channel including the path loss effect. For example, $h_{i,j} = d_{i,j}^{-\gamma}$ $(i \neq j)$, where $d_{i,j}$ is the distance between node $i \in \{s, r\}$ and $j \in \{r, d, e\}$, $\gamma > 1$ is the path-loss coefficient. The transmit power constraint is fixed at $P_1 = 1$, $P_2 = 8$.

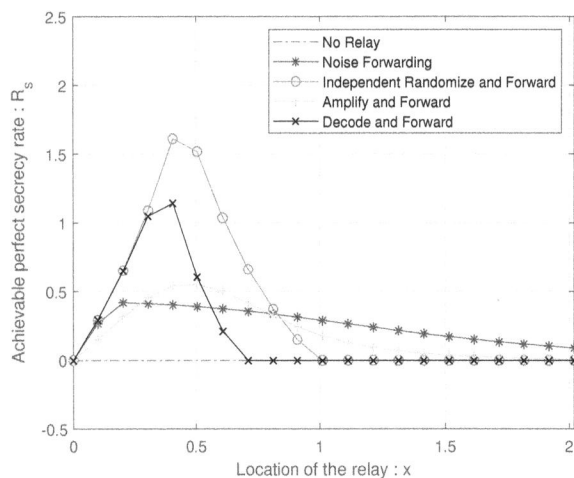

Figure 5: Comparison of the achievable perfect secrecy rates of the proposed IRF scheme and existing forwarding schemes

In Fig. 5, the theoretical curves for the perfect secrecy rate of four schemes were plotted using equations (18), (19), (20), and (21), respectively. We assume the path-loss coefficient is 2. We can see

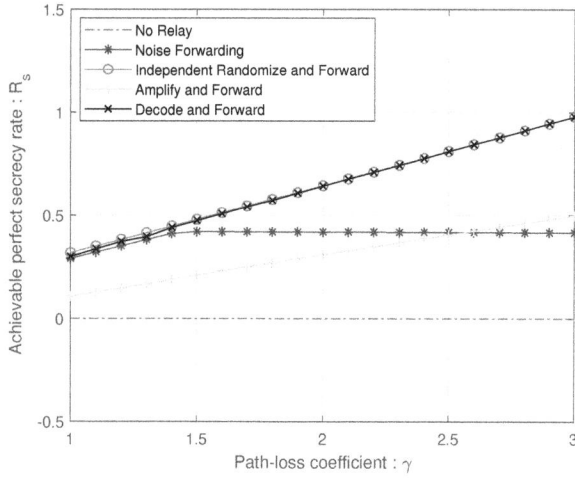

Figure 6: Achievable perfect secrecy rates versus path-loss coefficient, with $d_{sr} = 0.2$

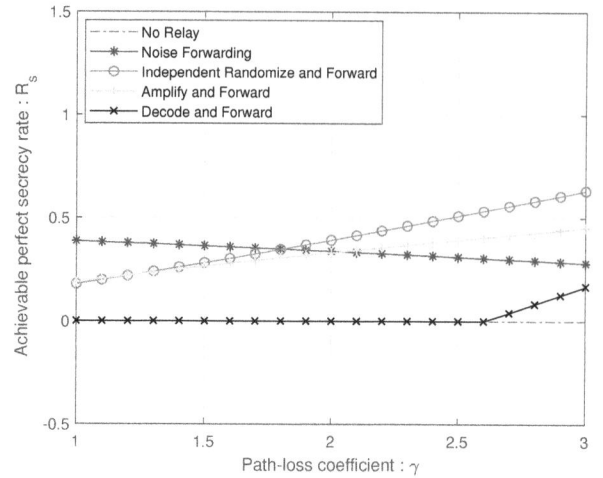

Figure 8: Achievable perfect secrecy rates versus path-loss coefficient, with $d_{sr} = 0.8$

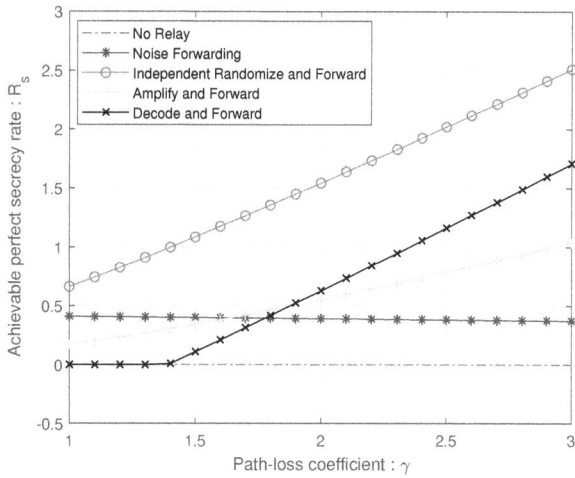

Figure 7: Achievable perfect secrecy rates versus path-loss coefficient, with $d_{sr} = 0.5$

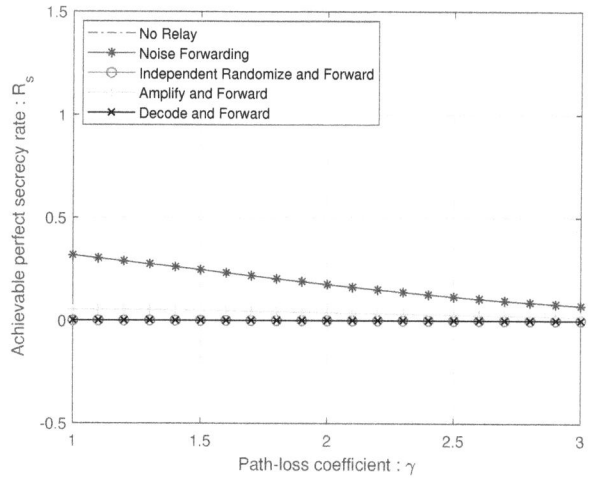

Figure 9: Achievable perfect secrecy rates versus path-loss coefficient, with $d_{sr} = 1.5$

that, when the relay is close to the source, the perfect secrecy rate of the IRF is almost the same as the DF. As the relay moves away from the source, IRF performs better than the DF. We can find the optimal relay position to achieve the highest perfect secrecy rate. When the relay is far away from the source NF performs better than the others.

The impact of the achievable secrecy rates of four schemes against the variation of path-loss coefficient is shown in Fig. 6, when the relay is closed to the source. Interestingly, one can see that the performance of the proposed IRF scheme is almost the same as DF scheme and outperforms the other two schemes.

Fig. 7 plots the achievable secrecy rates of four schemes when the relay is located at the middle of the source and the destination.

It can be seen that the proposed IRF scheme provides the best performance as compared to the others.

Fig. 8 shows the effect of path-loss coefficient on achievable secrecy rates when the relay is close to the destination. The curves indicate that the proposed IRF strategy is worse than the NF strategy for $\gamma \leq 1.8$, and outperforms it when $\gamma > 1.8$. Fig. 9 indicates when the relay is far away from the source, only the NF strategy can achieve the positive secrecy rate.

5 CONCLUSION

In this paper, we propose a novel independent randomize-and-forward (IRF) scheme to improve the achievable secrecy rate of the relay-eavesdropper channel. The message we actually want to transmit is mapped to two independent message sets at the source and the relay respectively. Then the relay assumed with transceiver capability is able to generate an independent codebook and use the random-coding scheme based on its channel state. Furthermore, the corresponding achievable rate-equivocation region and perfect secrecy rate for the proposed scheme are derived. Analytic and numerical results are provided and show that the proposed IRF strategy can offer larger secrecy rates than the present works in some cases. Future work includes extending the scheme developed in this paper to multi-hop relaying network. In addition, effective mapping functions which map the original message to two independent subordinate message sets are worthy of in-depth study.

REFERENCES

[1] I. Csiszar and J. Korner. 1978. Broadcast channels with confidential messages. *IEEE Trans.Inf. Theory* IT-24, 3 (May 1978), 339–348.
[2] Bin Duo, Wang Peng, Yonghui Li, and Branka Vucetic. 2014. Secure transmission for relay-eavesdropper channels using polar coding. *IEEE International Conference on Communications* (2014), 2197–2202.
[3] Georges Kaddoum Furqan Jameel, Shurjeel Wyne and Trung Q. Duong. 2018. A Comprehensive Survey on Cooperative Relaying and Jamming Strategies for Physical Layer Security. *IEEE Communications Surveys and Tutorials* (2018).
[4] O. Ozan Koyluoglu, C. Emre Koksal, and Hesham El Gamal. 2010. On Secrecy Capacity Scaling in Wireless Networks. *IEEE Transactions on Information Theory* 58, 5 (2010), 3000–3015.
[5] Lifeng Lai and Hesham El Gamal. 2008. The Relay-Eavesdropper Channel: Cooperation for Secrecy. *IEEE Trans.Inf. Theory* 54, 9 (September 2008), 4005–4019.
[6] Ninoslav Marina, Hideki Yagi, and H. Vincent Poor. 2011. Improved Rate-Equivocation Regions for Secure Cooperative Communication. *IEEE Int. Symposium on Information Theory* (2011).
[7] Jianhua Mo, Meixia Tao, and Yuan Liu. 2012. Relay Placement for Physical Layer Security: A Secure Connection Perspective. *IEEE Communications Letters* 16, 6 (2012), 878–881.
[8] Xu Peng, Zhiguo Ding, Xuchu Dai, and Kin K. Leung. 2013. An improved achievable secrecy rate for the relay-eavesdropper channel. In *Wireless Communications and Networking Conference*. 2440–2445.
[9] C. E. Shannon. 1949. Communication theory of secrecy systems. *Bell Syst.tech.j* 28, 4 (October 1949), 656–715.
[10] Amir Sonee and Somayeh Salimi. 2010. A new achievable rate-equivocation region for the relay-eavesdropper channel. In *Electrical Engineering*.
[11] Xiaojun Tang, Ruoheng Liu, P Spasojevic, and H. V Poor. 2009. Interference-assisted secret communication. *IEEE Information Theory Workshop* (2009).
[12] Ender Tekin and Aylin Yener. 2008. The Gaussian Multiple Access Wire-Tap Channel. *IEEE Transactions on Information Theory* 54, 12 (2008), 5747–5755.
[13] Wyner and D A. 1975. The wire-tap channel. *Bell Syst.tech.j* 54, 8 (1975), 1355–1387.

A PROOF OF THEOREM 3.2

As Theorem 3.1 is a special case of Theorem 3.2, the proof of Theorem 3.1 is similar to Theorem 3.2 and we omit it here.

Here we prove the achievable rate-equivocation region of the general relay-eavesdropper channel given in Theorem 3.2. The first term of (16) is the secrecy capacity of Wyner's wiretap channel which has been proved in [13]. So we only provide the proof of the second term and the theorem we need to prove simplifies to

$$R_s^{(\mathrm{IRF})} = \sup_{p(v_1)p(v_2)p(x_1|v_1)p(x_2|v_2)} [\min\{I(V_1;Y_2|V_2) - I(V_1;Z|V_2),$$
$$I(V_2;Y_1|V_1) - I(V_2;Z|V_1)\}]^+$$

We first replace V_1, V_2 in the above equation with X_1, X_2 by prefixing a memoryless channel with input V_1, V_2 and transmission probability $p(x_1|v_1)p(x_2|v_2)$ as reasoned in [1]. The hypothetical channel introduces randomness which might be useful to improve the equivocation rate. We refer to the secure coding scheme of the relay-eavesdropper channel studied by Lai [5], the difference is

that the relay channel is not viewed as a "whole" in this paper. The relay stochastic encoder is separated from the source's which is equivalent to having two independent "sources" for the destination and the eavesdropper.

We define the following

$$\mathcal{W}_1 = \{1, \cdots, 2^{n[R_1 - I(X_1;Z|X_2)]}\}$$
$$\mathcal{L}_1 = \{1, \cdots, 2^{nI(X_1;Z|X_2)}\}$$
$$\mathcal{J}_1 = \{1, \cdots, 2^{n(\tilde{R}_1 - [R_1 - I(X_1;Z|X_2)])}\}$$
$$\mathcal{W}_2 = \{1, \cdots, 2^{n[R_2 - I(X_2;Z|X_1)]}\}$$
$$\mathcal{L}_2 = \{1, \cdots, 2^{nI(X_2;Z|X_1)}\}$$
$$\mathcal{J}_2 = \{1, \cdots, 2^{n(\tilde{R}_2 - [R_2 - I(X_2;Z|X_1)])}\}$$

where $\tilde{R}_1 = I(V_1; Y_2|V_2) - \epsilon_1$, $\tilde{R}_2 = I(V_2; Y_1|V_1) - \epsilon_2$, $R_1 = I(X_1; Y_2|X_2) - \epsilon_1'$ and $R_2 = I(X_2; Y_1|X_1) - \epsilon_2'$.

Furthermore, we let h_i be the partition that divide $\mathcal{L}_i$ into $|\mathcal{J}_i|, (i = 1, 2)$ equal size subsets. Moreover, we assume that $R' = \min\{R_1 - I(X_1; Z|X_2), R_2 - I(X_2; Z|X_1)\} - \epsilon' > 0$, if this is not the case, we set $\mathcal{W}_1 = \mathcal{W}_2 = \{1\}$, $\mathcal{L}_1 = \{1, \cdots, 2^{nR_1}\}$ and $\mathcal{L}_2 = \{1, \cdots, 2^{nR_2}\}$.

(1) Codebook Generation

Randomly generate 2^{nR_1} independent and identically distributed (i.i.d.) n-sequence at the source with probability $p(\mathbf{x}_1) = \prod_{i=1}^{n} p(x_{1,i})$, index them as $\mathbf{x}_1(\mathbf{a})$, $\mathbf{a} = (a_{w1}, a_{j1})$ and $\mathbf{a} \in [1, 2^{nR_1}]$. We also generate 2^{nR_2} i.i.d. n-sequence $\mathbf{x}_2(\mathbf{b})$, $\mathbf{b} = (b_{w2}, b_{j2})$ and $\mathbf{b} \in [1, 2^{nR_2}]$ at the relay randomly according to $p(\mathbf{x}_2) = \prod_{i=1}^{n} p(x_{2,i})$. The codebooks are assumed known by all the terminals.

(2) Encoding

For a given rate pair (R, R_e) with $R \leq R'$ and $R_e \leq R$, we give the following coding strategy. Let the message to be transmitted at block i be $m(i) \in \mathcal{M} = [1, \cdots, 2^{nR}]$.

Assume the transmitter is to send the message at block i be $m_1(i) \in \mathcal{M}_1 = [1, \cdots, 2^{nR_1}]$ which is mapped from the message set $\mathcal{M}$. The stochastic encoder at transmitter firstly form the following mappings.

- If $\tilde{R}_1 > R_1 - I(X_1; Z|X_2)$, let $\mathcal{M}_1 = \mathcal{W}_1 \times \mathcal{J}_1$. The stochastic encoder at transmitter chooses a mapping for each message $m_1(i) = (w_1(i), j_1(i)) \rightarrow (w_1(i), l_1(i))$, where $l_1(i)$ is chosen randomly from the set $h_1^{-1}(j_1(i)) \subset \mathcal{L}_1$ with uniform distribution.
- If $\tilde{R}_1 \leq R_1 - I(X_1; Z|X_2)$, the stochastic encoder chooses a mapping $m_1(i) = (m_1(i), l_1(i))$, where $l_1(i)$ is chosen uniformly from the set $\mathcal{L}_1$.

Assume the relay is to transmit the message at block i be $m_2(i) \in \mathcal{M}_2 = [1, \cdots, 2^{n\tilde{R}_2}]$. Then the stochastic encoder at the relay node form the following mapping.

- If $\tilde{R}_2 > R_2 - I(X_2; Z|X_1)$, let $\mathcal{M}_2 = \mathcal{W}_2 \times \mathcal{J}_2$. The stochastic relay encoder maps each message $m_2(i) = (w_2(i), j_2(i))$ to $(w_2(i), l_2(i))$, where $l_2(i)$ is chosen randomly from the set $h_2^{-1}(j_2(i)) \subset \mathcal{L}_2$ with uniform distribution.
- If $\tilde{R}_2 \leq R_2 - I(X_2; Z|X_1)$, the stochastic encoder chooses a mapping $m_2(i) = (m_2(i), l_2(i))$, where $l_2(i)$ is chosen uniformly from the set $\mathcal{L}_2$.

The message $m_1(i)$ intended to send at block i is associated with $(w_1(i), l_1(i))$. We let $a(i) = (w_1(i), l_1(i))$, the transmitter sends $\mathbf{x}_1(a(i))$. At the end of block $i-1$, the relay has an estimation $\hat{a}(i-1)$ which can further calculate $\hat{w}_1(i-1)$ and recover $\hat{w}(i-1)$. Then the relay maps $\hat{w}(i-1)$ to $w_2(i)$. Assume that the relay intends to send the message $m_2(i)$ at block i is associated with $(w_2(i), l_2(i))$ and let $b(i) = (w_2(i), l_2(i))$. Thus the relay sends the corresponding codeword $\mathbf{x}_2(b(i))$. Obviously, the relay has a block delay for the source.

At block 1, the source sends $\mathbf{x}_1(w_1(1), l_1(1))$, the relay sends $\mathbf{x}_2(1)$. At block B, the source sends $\mathbf{x}_1(1)$, the relay sends $\mathbf{x}_2(w_2(B), l_2(B))$.

(3) *Decoding*

At the end of block i, the relay declares that it receives $\hat{a}(i)$ if this is the only one such that $(\mathbf{x}_1(\hat{a}(i)), \mathbf{y}_2(i))$ is jointly typical. It is obviously that if $R_1 \leq I(X_1; Y_2|X_2) - \epsilon_1$, based on the asymptotic equipartition property (AEP), one has $\hat{a}(i) = a(i)$ with probability goes to 1. Having $\hat{a}(i)$, the relay can get the estimation of the message $m_1(i)$ by letting:

- $\hat{m}_1(i) = (\hat{w}_1(i), \hat{j}_1(i)) = (\hat{w}_1(i), g_1(\hat{l}_1(i)))$, if $\tilde{R}_1 > R_1 - I(X_1; Z|X_2)$;
- $\hat{m}_1(i) = \hat{w}_1(i)$, if $\tilde{R}_1 \leq R_1 - I(X_1; Z|X_2)$.

Similarly, suppose that at the end of block i, the destination implements separate decoding[11] and declares that $\hat{b}(i)$ is received, if $(\mathbf{x}_2(\hat{b}(i)), \mathbf{y}_1(i))$ are jointly typical. It is easy to see that if $R_2 \leq I(X_2; Y_1|X_1) - \epsilon$, we have $\hat{b}(i) = b(i)$ with probability goes to 1, as n increases. The destination can get the estimation of the message $m_1(i)$ in the same way. In addition, the destination can also implement joint decoding[11], declares that $\hat{a}(i)$ and $\hat{b}(i)$ are received, if $(\mathbf{x}_1(\hat{a}), \mathbf{x}_2(\hat{b}))$ is the only pair such that $(\mathbf{x}_1(\hat{a}), \mathbf{x}_2(\hat{b}), \mathbf{z})$ is jointly typical. Then the destination chooses the better of $\hat{m}_1(i)$ and $\hat{m}_2(i)$ to recover $m(i)$.

(4) *Equivocation computation*

Now we consider the equivocation rate at the eavesdropper, which can be viewed as discrete memoryless multiple access channel. After receiving z, the eavesdropper declares that $\acute{m}_1 \in M_1$ is received if

i) separate decoding: $\mathbf{x}_1(\acute{a})$ is the only codeword such that $(\mathbf{x}_1(\acute{a}), \mathbf{z})$ is jointly typical;
or
ii) joint decoding: $(\mathbf{x}_1(\acute{a}), \mathbf{x}_2(\acute{b}))$ is the only pair such that $(\mathbf{x}_1(\acute{a}), \mathbf{x}_2(\acute{b}), \mathbf{z})$ is jointly typical.

The eavesdropper makes an error if neither i) nor ii) occurs, or if $\acute{m}_1 \neq M_1$.

$$
\begin{aligned}
H(M_1|Z, X_2) &= H(M_1, Z|X_2) - H(Z|X_2) \\
&= H(M_1, Z, X_1|X_2) - H(X_1|M_1, Z, X_2) \\
&\quad - H(Z|X_2) \\
&= H(X_1|X_2) + H(M_1, Z_1|X_1, X_2) \\
&\quad - H(X_1|M_1, Z, X_2) - H(Z|X_2) \\
&\geq H(X_1) + H(Z|X_1, X_2) \\
&\quad - H(X_1|M_1, Z, X_2) - H(Z|X_2)
\end{aligned}
\tag{26}
$$

Firstly, let us calculate $H(X_1|M_1, Z_1, X_2)$. The eavesdropper can do separate decoding. At the end of block i, given M_1, the eavesdropper knows $w_1(i)$, hence it will decode $l_1(i)$ by letting $l_1(i) = \acute{l}_1(i)$, if

$\acute{l}_1(i)$ is the only one such that $(\mathbf{x}_1(w_1(i), \acute{l}_1(i)), \mathbf{z})$ are jointly typical. Since $l_1 \in [1, 2^{nI(X_1; Z|X_2, U)}]$, we have

$$
Pr\{\mathbf{x}_1(w_1(i), \acute{l}_1(i)) \neq \mathbf{x}_1(a_1(i))\} \leq \epsilon_1 \tag{27}
$$

Then based on Fano's inequality, we have

$$
\frac{1}{n} H(X_1|M_1 = m_1, Z_1, U) \leq \frac{1}{n} + \epsilon_1 I(X_1; Z_1|U) \tag{28}
$$

Hence, we have

$$
\begin{aligned}
&\frac{1}{n} H(X_1|M_1, Z, X_2) \\
&= \frac{1}{n} \sum_{m_1 \in M_1} p(M_1 = m_1) H(X_1|M_1 = m_1, Z, X_2) \leq \epsilon_2
\end{aligned}
\tag{29}
$$

when n is sufficiently large.

Since the channel is memoryless, we have

$$
H(Z|X_2) - H(Z|X_1, X_2) \leq nI(X_1; Z|X_2) + n\delta_n \tag{30}
$$

where $\delta_n \to 0$, as $n \to \infty$.

Now from the code construction, we have

- $H(X_1) = nR_1$, if $\tilde{R}_1 > R_1 - I(X_1; Z|X_2)$. In this case, we get

$$
nRe_1 = H(M_1|Z) \geq n[R_1 - I(X_1; Z|X_2) - \epsilon_3]
$$

- $H(X_1) = n[\tilde{R}_1 + I(X_1; Z|X_2)]$, if $\tilde{R}_1 \leq R_1 - I(X_1; Z|X_2)$. Hence,

$$
\begin{aligned}
nRe_1 &\geq n[\tilde{R}_1 + I(X_1; Z|X_2)] - nI(X_1; Z|X_2) - \epsilon_3 \\
&= n(\tilde{R}_1 - \epsilon_3)
\end{aligned}
$$

we get the perfect secrecy in this case.

Next, we discuss the equivocation rate in the second phase.

$$
\begin{aligned}
H(M_2|Z, X_1) &\geq H(X_2) + H(Z|X_1, X_2) \\
&\quad - H(X_2|M_2, Z, X_1) - H(Z|X_1)
\end{aligned}
\tag{31}
$$

which follows from the same derivation as the inequation (26).

In a similar way, we have

- $H(X_2) = nR_2$, if $\tilde{R}_2 > R_2 - I(X_2; Z|X_1)$. In this case, we get

$$
nRe_2 = H(M_2|Z, X_1) \geq n[R_2 - I(X_2; Z|X_1) - \epsilon_3]
$$

- $H(X_1, X_2|U) = n[\tilde{R}_2 + I(X_2; Z|X_1)]$, if $\tilde{R}_2 \leq R_2 - I(X_2; Z|X_1)$. Accordingly,

$$
\begin{aligned}
nRe_2 &\geq n[\tilde{R}_2 + I(X_2; Z|X_1)] - nI(X_2; Z|X_1) - \epsilon_3 \\
&= n(\tilde{R}_2 - \epsilon_3)
\end{aligned}
$$

we get the perfect secrecy in this case.

Theorem 3.2 has been proved up to now.

Three-Dimensional Matching based Resource Provisioning for the Design of Low-Latency Heterogeneous IoT Networks

Ajay Pratap

ajaypratapf@mst.edu

Department of Computer Science
Missouri University of Science and Technology
Rolla, MO, USA.

Venkata Sriram Siddhardh Nadendla

nadendla@mst.edu

Department of Computer Science
Missouri University of Science and Technology
Rolla, MO, USA.

Federico Concone

federico.concone@unipa.it

Department of Computer Engineering
University of Palermo,
Viale delle Scienze, Palermo, Italy.

Sajal K. Das

sdas@mst.edu

Department of Computer Science
Missouri University of Science and Technology
Rolla, MO, USA.

ABSTRACT

Internet-of-Things (IoT) is a networking architecture where promising, intelligent services are designed via leveraging information from multiple heterogeneous sources of data within the network. However, the availability of such information in a timely manner requires processing and communication of raw data collected from these sources. Therefore, the economic feasibility of IoT-enabled networks relies on the efficient allocation of both computational and communication resources within the network. Since fog computing and 5G cellular networks approach this problem independently, there is a need for joint resource-provisioning of both communication and computational resources in the networks. As the solution to this problem, we propose a novel three-dimensional matching based resource provisioning algorithm that minimizes average service latency in the presence of various resource constraints, task deadlines and non-identical preferences at IoT devices, fog access points (FAPs) and small-cell access points (SAPs) in 5G networks. We prove the stability and termination of the proposed algorithm and also demonstrate that our proposed algorithm outperforms other state-of-the-art algorithms through both, simulation and real-world experiments on the laboratory test-bed.

CCS CONCEPTS

• **Mathematics of computing → Matchings and factors**; • **Networks → Network algorithms**; **Network resources allocation**.

MSWiM '19, November 25–29, 2019, Miami Beach, FL, USA
© 2019 Association for Computing Machinery.
ACM ISBN 978-1-4503-6904-6/19/11...$15.00
https://doi.org/10.1145/3345768.3355906

KEYWORDS

Resource Provisioning; PRB; 5G; IoT; Fog; SAP; Matching

ACM Reference Format:

Ajay Pratap, Federico Concone, Venkata Sriram Siddhardh Nadendla, and Sajal K. Das. 2019. Three-Dimensional Matching based Resource Provisioning for the Design of Low-Latency Heterogeneous IoT Networks. In *22nd Int'l ACM Conference on Modeling, Analysis and Simulation of Wireless and Mobile Systems (MSWiM '19), November 25–29, 2019, Miami Beach, FL, USA.* ACM, New York, NY, USA, 8 pages. https://doi.org/10.1145/3345768.3355906

1 INTRODUCTION

Internet of Things (IoT) is a networking paradigm where ubiquitous smart-devices share information among each other to improve services in diverse applications such as smart grid, smart health, smart city, smart transportation and so on [17, 26]. However, the ever-increasing deployment of low-cost IoT devices with limited computing capabilities introduces many computational challenges in the provisioning of services. In order to alleviate this problem, CISCO Systems, Inc. has developed a novel solution called fog computing, which offloads the computational load from the cloud to one/more *fog access points* (FAPs) that are closer to IoT devices [3, 23, 24] within the network hierarchy. Consequently, there is an escalating growth in the demand for radio resources (e.g spectrum) to support communication between the ever-increasing number of IoT devices and FAPs. 5G cellular architecture is currently being developed to support the spectrum demand in IoT networks through dense deployment of *small-cell access points* (SAPs) (e.g. femtocell access point, picocell access points, microcell access points), along with Macro Base Station (MBS) within the cellular architecture [4, 12, 14, 19–22]. This paper addresses the problem of resource provisioning in a novel IoT network architecture where fog computing and 5G cellular technologies are integrated together to simultaneously address limitations in both communication and computation.

The main challenge in designing intelligent services for IoT networks is to allocate resources across multiple heterogeneous entites in order to perform various kinds of tasks[1], each having non-identical, heterogeneous resource demands and stringent performance constraints (e.g. in terms of latency and/or quality of service) as shown in Table 1. For example, a driving aid service that leverages augmented reality technology relies on heterogeneous tasks such as object classification, tracking and recommender systems. However, such services demand significant computational capabilities which are not typically available at IoT devices. Although centralized architectures have necessary computational resources at the cloud/MBS, it is not always feasible to meet the stringent latency requirements, especially when the packets traverse through long queues and routes over the network. For example, even supremely advanced, geographically diverse gaming cloud server networks have difficulties guaranteeing application latency under 80 ms [6]. In order to overcome this limitation, we propose a fog-based architecture where tasks are off-loaded to nearby FAPs via availing necessary communication resources at SAPs, and delivered back accordingly to the respective IoT devices.

Motivating Appplication. Consider the problem of designing a smart health system where human activities are recognized based on information collected from various IoT devices (e.g. accelerometers and gyroscopes in mobile devices). For example, elderly people living in a retirement communities collapse frequently due to loss of balance. Therefore, a fall detection system helps mitigate latency by allowing appropriate healthcare personnel to attend their injuries on time. Similarly, sleep monitoring is another human activity recognition system needed to monitor and diagnose patients in a hospital. The raw data collected from the IoT devices and/or sensors have to be processed to extract relevant features for classification purposes. Since IoT devices have low computational capabilities and limited battery power, this data processing task needs to be performed by FAPs which provide real-time computational services on an on-demand basis. However, communication resources are needed to transfer information back and forth between IoT devices and FAPs, which are controlled by SAPs. In this paper, we design a novel architecture based on three-dimensional matching to accomodate the three types of agents, a.k.a. IoT devices, FAPs and SAPs, to address this resource allocation problem. For validation purposes, we consider a human activity recognition task in a smart health system to test the performance of our architecture.

Our Contributions. In this work, our goal is to minimize the average service latency at the IoT devices, via designing appropriate resource allocation strategies at FAPs and SAPs, in the presence of

---

[1]We refer to *task* as a basic unit of effort which cannot be further divided into sub-tasks.

Applications	Latency
Home automation, video surveillance	10 seconds
Web search, sensor readings	1 second
Interactive web site, smart building, analytic	100 milliseconds
Virtual reality, smart transportation	10 milliseconds
Haptics, robotics, real-time manufacturing	1 millisecond

Table 1: Applications and allowable latency.

non-identical preferences at IoT devices, FAPs and SAPs. However, this introduces a contention with maximally allocating resources to increase the number of tasks served. Therefore, in order to serve this ill-posed problem, we propose a three-dimensional matching based algorithm to solve the above problem. We have also proved that our proposed algorithm converges to the stable matching solution in a fixed number of iterations. We have validated our proposed algorithm on data collected from real prototypes implemented in our laboratory.

The remaining of paper is organized as follows. Section 2 explains existing works. Section 3 includes system model. Section 4 describes three-dimensional matching algorithm for IoT-enable networks. Section 5 presents theoretical analysis. Section 6 presents a performance analysis based on both simulation and prototype based experiments. Section 7 concludes this work.

2 RELATED WORK

In [1], authors discussed a resource allocation problem in IoT-enabled network. The proposed solution was applicable in assigning services to heterogeneous IoT demand model in the multiple network interfaces. The main drawback of this approach was slow convergence rate due to which this method is not suitable for densely deployed IoT networks [8]. In [29], a joint resource allocation and stable performance based model was studied. Authors, applied Stackelberg game and a many-to-many matching game model to maximize the utility of users, cloud and fog nodes. In [27], a joint radio and computational resource allocation problem is discussed in view of energy and latency requirements; and further a distributive method to solve the formulated optimization problem was proposed. The main drawback of this approach is to consider one centralized cloud service provider. The central point dependency may be obstacle in the case of expansion and elaboration of exiting infrastructure. In [16], authors proposed a three-dimensional matching based resource allocation technique for sensor and actuator model. The main drawback of this approach is stable matching convergence. The proposed scheme may not always guaranty a stable matching outcome in a large number of heterogeneous IoT devices.

In [15], a cost efficient resource allocation problem is formulated as an optimization problem and further double matching based algorithm proposed based on deferred acceptance algorithm from two-side matching to three-side matching. Convergence and computational complexity are major outfits of this approach. In [5], authors applied many-to-one version of deferred acceptance algorithm [11, 25] in-order to minimize the maximum gap between required and achieved latency for task execution in fog enabled networks. Authors did not talk anything about the radio resources availability and its allocation procedure which actually play a major part in task offloading to FAP. In [13], authors formulated joint radio and computational resource with respect to cost performance per user as an optimization problem. Further, a many-to-one matching based algorithmic model proposed to offload the task to FAP with help of cloud service provider. However, this approach is not suitable for critical deadline applications. Moreover, authors have assumed that all the users will share the radio and computational

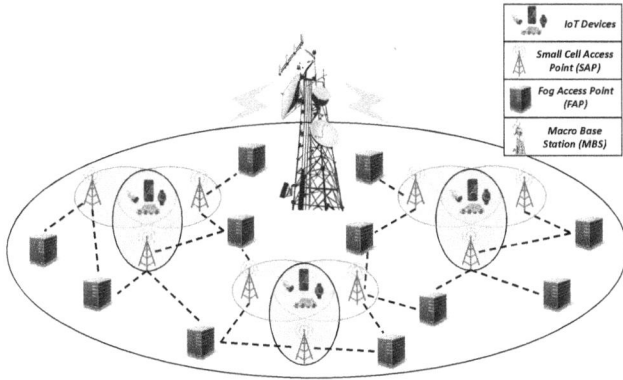

Figure 1: Heterogeneous IoT Networks

resources, equally regardless of data size and their deadline. So, equal distribution of resources do not justify the importance of different heterogeneous tasks and respective deadlines.

The existing approaches are not applicable in the three agents model where IoT, FAP and SAP will work altogether to achieve the heterogeneous task's deadline in limited available radio and computational resource of network. As each IoT device works independently regardless of others co-exiting tasks, it becomes very important to model these three agents altogether keeping deadline and limited availability of resources into consideration, and minimize the average service latency of task execution. Considering all these inhibitions of heterogeneous networks, in the following, we propose our system model followed by problem formulation.

3 SYSTEM MODEL

Consider a heterogeneous IoT network as shown in Fig. 1 which comprises of three types of agents: (i) IoT devices (which generate tasks), (ii) Small Cell Access Points, or SAPs (which control the communication resources), (iii) Fog Access Points, or FAPs (which control the computational resources), and (iv) a Macro Base Station or MBS (which moderates all the other agents in the network). Let $\mathbb{I} = \{I_1, \ldots, I_K\}$, $\mathbb{F} = \{F_1, \ldots, F_R\}$ and $\mathbb{L} = \{L_1, \ldots, L_S\}$ denote the sets of K IoT devices, R FAPs and S SAPs respectively. In this paper, we assume that FAP, F_r, is equipped with M_r processors running with a cycle rate of c_r so that the total FAP's computational power is given by $(M_r \cdot c_r)$ processor cycles. Similarly, we assume that each SAP controls N_s atomic resources for communication purposes called Physical Resource Blocks (PRBs) [10, 30], which comprises of $W = 180kHz$ bandwidth and 0.5 ms time within a standard Orthogonal Frequency Division Multiple Access model [9].

When an IoT device generates a task, it will attempt to find the computational and communication resources needed to execute the task successfully. This search is driven by the IoT device's goal to *minimize the service latency*. The service latency $\Gamma_{k,r}^s$, due to the triplet (I_k, F_r, L_s), mainly comprises of three components, as shown below:

$$\Gamma_{k,r}^s = T_{trans}(k,r,s) + T_{comp}(k,r,s) + T_{recv}(k,r,s), \quad (1)$$

where $T_{trans}(k,r,s)$ is the transmit time from IoT device I_k to FAP F_k on the PRBs assigned by L_s, $T_{comp}(k,r,s)$ represents the computation time of the task generated by I_k at FAP F_r, and $T_{recv}(k,r,s)$ represents the receive time from FAP F_k to IoT device I_k on the PRBs assigned by L_s.

Let $x_{k,r}^s$ be a binary variable defined as follows:

$$x_{k,r}^s = \begin{cases} 1 & \text{if } L_s \text{ allocates a PRB to } (I_k, F_r), \\ 0 & \text{otherwise.} \end{cases} \quad (2)$$

Since the availability of PRBs is limited at any given SAP, we have the following allocation constraint at L_s:

$$\sum_{k=1}^{K} x_{k,r}^s \leq N_s, \quad (3)$$

for all $s = 1, \cdots, S$.

Assuming that the data size is D_k, the transmit time $T_{trans}(k,r,s)$ in Equation (1) can be calculated as

$$T_{trans}(k,r,s) = \frac{D_k}{\Upsilon_{k,r}^s}, \quad (4)$$

where

$$\Upsilon_{k,r}^s = W \cdot N_s \cdot x_{k,r}^s \cdot \log_2\left(1 + SINR_{k,r}^s\right) \quad (5)$$

is the maximum achievable data rate between IoT I_k and FAP F_r. Here, N_s is the total number of available PRBs at SAP L_s, and $SINR_{k,r}^s$ is the signal-to-interference-plus-noise ratio[2] between IoT I_k and F_r by using available PRBs at SAP L_s.

At FAP F_r, the compute time $T_{comp}(k,r,s)$ depends on the data size D_k, and the computational power of F_r, and can be calculated as follows:

$$T_{comp}(k,r,s) = \frac{D_k}{y_{k,r}^s \cdot M_r \cdot c_r}, \quad (6)$$

where $y_{k,r}^s$ denotes the computational resource allocation to the pair (I_k, L_s) as defined below:

$$y_{k,r}^s = \begin{cases} 1, & \text{if } F_k \text{ allocates CPU to } (I_k, L_s) \\ 0, & \text{otherwise.} \end{cases} \quad (7)$$

Finally, we assume that the size of the task's outcome is significantly smaller[3] than the original data size D_k. As a result, we neglect the contribution of receive time $T_{recv}(k,r,s)$ in the estimation of service latency $\Gamma_{k,r}^s$, and model $T_{recv}(k,r,s)$ as a random negligible time.

In this paper, our goal is to address the contention between minimizing the overall service latency

$$U = \frac{1}{K} \cdot \sum_{s=1}^{S} \sum_{r=1}^{R} \sum_{k=1}^{K} x_{k,r}^s \cdot y_{k,r}^s \cdot \Gamma_{k,r}^s, \quad (8)$$

---

[2]For the sake of simplicity, we assume that the channel exhibits flat fading. However, this can be easily extended to frequency-selective fading channels as well.
[3]For example, in the case of binary classification of images, the outcome is a binary variable, whereas the input size D_k is the size of the image itself.

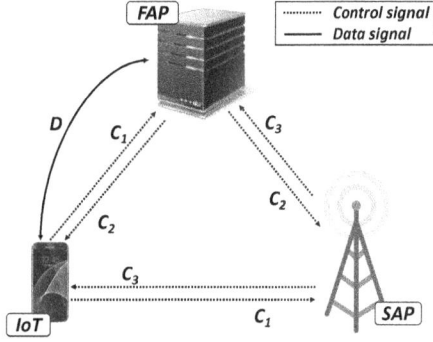

Figure 2: Network Interactions

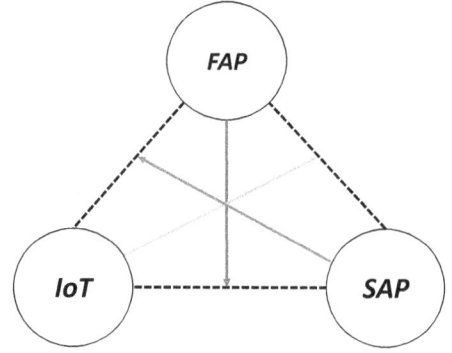

Figure 3: Preference model

and maximally allocating resources at both FAPs and SAPs, which is given by

$$V = \frac{1}{K} \cdot \sum_{s=1}^{S} \sum_{r=1}^{R} \sum_{k=1}^{K} x_{k,r}^{s} \cdot y_{k,r}^{s}. \qquad (9)$$

Due to the ill-posed nature of the problem, we model this interaction between different players (namely IoT devices, FAPs and SAPs) using matching, where appropriate triplets $(I_k, F_r, L_s) \in \mathbb{I} \times \mathbb{F} \times \mathbb{L}$ for all $I_k \in \mathbb{I}, F_r \in \mathbb{F}$ and $L_s \in \mathbb{L}$ are assigned to achieve the above stated goal. However, since each agent results in a specific preference ordering over two agents, this problem can not be solved using traditional two-sided matching approaches [2]. Since three-dimensional matching is an NP-complete problem [18], we propose a novel three-dimensional pairwise matching in order to minimize the average service latency in the network.

4 THREE-DIMENSIONAL MATCHING

In this section, we propose the resource allocation algorithm based on three-dimensional matching of a triplet $\zeta = (I_k, F_r, L_s)$, where these three agents cooperate with each other to minimize service latency. We assume that the IoT devices, FAPs and SAPs are selfish in nature, and need to communicate with each other in order to reveal their preferences. In order to facilitate this interaction, we design the following communication protocol between the agents.

4.1 Communications Protocol

In this section, we present a communication protocol that supports necessary interaction between agents in forming a matching triplet (I_k, F_r, L_s). As shown in Figure 2, whenever a task is generated at the IoT device I_k, it sends a control signal C_1 to FAP F_r and SAP L_s, and requests necessary resources to complete the task. Upon receiving the control signal C_1, F_r sends back another control signal C_2 to I_k and L_s. At the same time, L_s replies back to IoT and FAP using control signal C_3. Once this handshaking process is completed among the agents, the respective SAP allocates the required number of PRBs to the link IoT-FAP. Finally, respective IoT device receives the final result after the task at FAP is executed.

4.2 Construction of Preference Orders

One of the main phases of the proposed algorithm is the construction of preference orders at each agent. Once a task is generated at the IoT device I_k, then it has a choice to team with any FAP-SAP pair. However, since IoT devices are concerned about minimizing service latency, it constructs a preference order over the set of all FAP-SAP pair based on the following relation:

$$(F_r, L_s) >_k (F_{r'}, L_{s'}) \Leftrightarrow \Gamma_{k,r}^{s} < \Gamma_{k,r'}^{s'}. \qquad (10)$$

Similarly, FAP constructs the preference order over the set of all IoT-SAP pairs based on the computational time required to complete the task. In other words, FAP follows these two rules while selecting the appropriate pairs. More specifically, the FAP F_k can minimize the computational time of successful task allocations by (i) picking tasks in the order of decreasing computational load, and (ii) identifying those tasks that have a greater chance of PRB allocations. Therefore, FAP prepares a preference list based on the following relation:

$$(I_k, L_s) >_r (I_{k'}, L_{s'}) \Leftrightarrow T_{comp}(k, r, s) < T_{comp}(k', r, s'), \qquad (11)$$

which means FAP prefers the IoT-SAP pair to which computational latency for successful completion of task is less.

Similarly, SAP prepares the preference ordering of IoT and FAP based on transmission latency. In other words, SAP selects the IoT-FAP link, which has higher achievable data rate and consequently it will result in lower transmission latency. The preference ordering of IoT-FAP link is prepared as per following expression:

$$(I_k, F_r) >_s (I_{k'}, F_{r'}) \Leftrightarrow T_{trans}(k, r, s) < T_{trans}(k', r', s). \qquad (12)$$

4.3 Desired Properties of a Match

Let μ denotes the match, which comprises of the set of all approved triplets at any given iteration. Furthermore, let $\zeta_B = (I_k, F_r, L_s) \in \mu$ be one of any approved triplets at the start of some intermediate iteration within the algorithm. If the IoT device I_j ($j \neq k$) reveals its proposal to (F_r, L_s) to include the triplet $\bar{\zeta}_B = (I_j, F_r, L_s)$ in μ, contention arises between the current match μ and a potential match $\mu - \zeta_B \cup \bar{\zeta}_B$. This contention can be resolved based on the following *blocking triplet* concept:

DEFINITION 1. *For any $j = 1, \cdots, K$ and $k = 1, \cdots, K$, a triplet $\bar{\zeta}_B = (I_j, F_r, L_s)$ blocks the triplet $\zeta_B = (I_k, F_r, L_s)$ from being included in μ if*

  (i) $U(\mu - \zeta_B \cup \bar{\zeta}_B) < U(\mu)$, and

  (ii) $(I_j, F_r) >_s (I_k, F_r)$ and $(I_j, L_s) >_r (I_k, L_s)$.

This definition implies that if the IoT device I_j results in lower average service latency than I_k (Equation 8), by forming a triple with (F_r, L_s), then (I_j, F_r, L_s) forms a blocking triple and will replace (I_k, F_r, L_s) in μ [18].

In this paper, we define stability of a three-dimensional match based on the blocking triplet concept.

DEFINITION 2. *A matching μ is stable if there exist no blocking triplet for μ.*

In the following section, our objective is to find the stable matching among IoTs, SAPs and FAPs in the networks.

4.4 Proposed Algorithm

The proposed three-dimensional matching algorithm found in Algorithm 1 takes the sets of IoT devices, FAPs with respective computational power, SAPs with respective available PRBs as input, and delivers a three-dimensional stable matching μ as an output. Broadly, the algorithm can be divided into two phases: (i) Preference List Estimation, and (ii) Matching.

In the *Preference List Estimation* phase, service latency $\Gamma_{k,r}^s$ is estimated for every possible triplet $(I_k, F_r, L_s) \in \mathbb{I} \times \mathbb{F} \times \mathbb{L}$, as shown in Line 1. Note that the estimation of $\Gamma_{k,r}^s$ depends on the computation of both T_{comp} and T_{trans}, which are needed to evaluate preference orders at both FAPs and SAPs respectively. Then, each agent prepares a preference list over the pair of other two agents, as shown in Equations (10-12), and reveals them to MBS, as stated in lines 3-5.

In the *Matching* phase, each unmatched IoT device I_k sends a proposal to FAP-SAP pair (F_r, L_s) on the top of its respective preference list in Line 8. As stated in Line 9, if MBS finds the pairs (I_k, L_s) and (I_k, F_r) in $\mathbb{F}_{PrefList}$ and $\mathbb{L}_{PrefList}$ (which are updated to include those pairs that were never evaluated in the past) respectively, then the triplet (I_k, F_r, L_s) is included in the match μ. However, if FAP F_r or SAP L_s or both are not listed in $\mathbb{F}_{PrefList}$ and $\mathbb{L}_{PrefList}$, two possibilities arise. In the first possibility, (I_k, F_r, L_s) forms a blocking triplet, in which case, the corresponding triplet present in μ needs to be rejected as stated in Line 14, and then replaced by (I_k, F_r, L_s) in μ. Alternatively, if (I_k, F_r, L_s) does not form a blocking triplet to any other triplet in μ, it is just rejected by MBS. The proposed algorithm terminates when all the IoT devices made requests to some FAP-SAP pair, i.e., either the IoT device is matched with appropriate FAP-SAP pair to be included in μ, or it has been rejected by all FAP-SAP pairs.

5 ANALYSIS OF PROPOSED ALGORITHM

As the traditional three-sided matching is NP-complete problem, there is possibility that it would not converge to stable matching

---

Algorithm 1 Three-Sided Matching based Resource Allocation Algorithm

Input: Set of IoT devices $\mathbb{I}$, set of FAPs $\mathbb{F}$ with respective computational power i.e., M and c and set of SAPs $\mathbb{L}$ with respective available PRBs i.e., N.
Output: A stable three-dimension matching μ.

1: **Phase 1: Preference List Estimation**
2: Estimate $\Gamma_{k,r}^s$ based on Equation (1), for $I_k \in \mathbb{I}$, $F_r \in \mathbb{F}$ and $L_s \in \mathbb{L}$.
3: Each IoT device I_k, prepares the preference list over FAP-SAP agents based on Equation (10), and inform to MBS.
4: Each FAP, SAP prepare the preference list of IoT-SAP, FAP-IoT based on Equations (11) and (12), respectively and inform to MBS.
5: MBS prepares the preference lists $\mathbb{I}_{PrefList} = \{I_k\}_{k=1}^K$ for IoT devices, $\mathbb{F}_{PrefList} = \{F_r\}_{r=1}^R$ for FAPs, and $\mathbb{L}_{PrefList} = \{L_s\}_{s=1}^S$ for SAPs based on above lines 5-6.

6: **Phase 2: Matching**
7: **for each** $I_k \in \mathbb{I}$ **do**
8:   Send request to most preferred FAP-SAP agent such as $\arg\min_{(F_r, L_s)} \Gamma_{k,r}^s$
9:   **if** $F_r \in \mathbb{F}_{PrefList}$ and $L_s \in \mathbb{L}_{PrefList}$ **then**
10:     Define $\mu \leftarrow (I_k, F_r, L_s)$
11:     Update $\mathbb{I}_{PrefList} = \mathbb{I}_{PrefList} - I_k$, $\mathbb{F}_{PrefList} = \mathbb{F}_{PrefList} - F_r$, $\mathbb{L}_{PrefList} = \mathbb{L}_{PrefList} - L_s$;
12:   **else if** triplet (I_k, F_r, L_s) form blocking pair **then**
13:     $\mathbb{I}_{PrefList} = \mathbb{I}_{PrefList} - I_k$,
14:     FAP-SAP pair in μ reject their current match.
15:     Update match $\mu \leftarrow (I_k, F_r, L_s)$;
16:   **else**
17:     FAP-SAP pair (F_r, L_s) reject IoT I_k.

---

[28]. However, our proposed algorithm differs from the traditional three-sided matching problem in the sense that in our case agents are mutual, i.e., if computational time at FAP is less and data rate assigned by SAP between IoT-FAP is high, then the overall service latency of any IoT device will be low. In the other word, if computational and transmission latency of tasks are less then corresponding overall service latency will also be less. Thus, the preference lists of different agents in our proposed algorithm are mutual.

THEOREM 1. *The proposed algorithm terminates after a finite number of iterations.*

PROOF. The proposed Algorithm 1 will terminate after a fixed number of iterations. We can prove as follows: (a) an IoT device sends a request to a FAP-SAP pair only once, (b) the total number of FAP-SAP pairs are fixed, i.e., $R \times S$. In each iteration an IoT device sends a request to FAP-SAP pair which has not rejected to this IoT device earlier. Thus, as the number of iterations increases, the remaining choices over FAP-SAP get reduced. An IoT device has $R \times S$ number of choices and the maximum number of trial can not go more than $R \times S$ in the worst case. In the other words, either IoT device matched to FAP-SAP pair and no other pair will make

Description	Symbol	Value
Task data size (*MB*)	D	{100, 200, . . . , 1000}
Number of IoTs	K	{10, 20, 30, . . . , 300}
Number of CPUs at FAP	M	{2, 4, 8}
CPU frequency (*GHz*) of FAP	c	{1.5, 3, 6, 12, 14}
Number of PRBs	N_s	{2, 4, 6, 8, 10}

Table 2: Simulation Environment.

benefit in the service latency or IoT device not matched and all the FAP-SAP pairs have rejected it. Thus, the proposed algorithm will terminate after a finite number of iterations. □

THEOREM 2. *The proposed algorithm converges to a stable match.*

PROOF. Based on above Theorem 1 we conclude that the proposed algorithm terminates after a fixed number of iterations. However, to prove that the outcome of the proposed algorithm is stable, we need to show that the final matching μ will not have any blocking pair. Based on Phase 1 of the proposed algorithm we can guarantee that there will not be any blocking pair in the matching μ. Let's say a blocking triplet $\zeta_B = (I_k, F_r, L_s)$ exist in the final matching μ. According to line 12 of our algorithm, we say whenever there is a blocking pair in the temporary matching, either the FAP-SAP pair will reject all their previous matched triplets or they reject the current IoT device request because of which blocking arises (lines 12-18). Thus, the outcome of the proposed algorithm will never have a blocking pair and this contradicts. Hence, the proposed algorithm converges to stable matching. □

THEOREM 3. *The time complexity of proposed algorithm is O(KRS $log_2(RS)$)*

PROOF. Each IoT device prepares a preference ordering of FAP-SAP pairs in Phase 1. Using heap sort algorithm an IoT device can sort the preference list in O(RS $log_2(RS)$) time complexity. As we have K IoT devices thus, total complexity results as O($KRS log_2$(RS)). However, in Phase 2, each IoT device proposes at most $R \times S$ agents and there are K IoT devices, consequently time complexity results at O(KRS). Thus, the total time complexity of proposed algorithm is concluded at O(KRS $log_2(RS)$) + O(KRS), i.e., O(KRS $log_2(RS)$). □

6 PERFORMANCE STUDY

We validate our proposed algorithm using both virtual and real-world experiments. In the first case, we test our algorithm on simulated environments based on JAVA, which are then plotted using MATLAB. Later, we test our algorithm on a laboratory prototype using a smart watch as an IoT device, the hotspot in a smart phone as SAP and a laptop as a FAP. Details of all the experiments are given below.

6.1 Simulation Analysis

In order to evaluate the performance of the proposed algorithm, we have simulated a network model that consists of a random number of FAPs and SAPs ranging between 1 to 300, which are distributed uniformly over a geographical area. Each FAP is randomly assigned the number of processors, CPU frequency, and a non-zero number

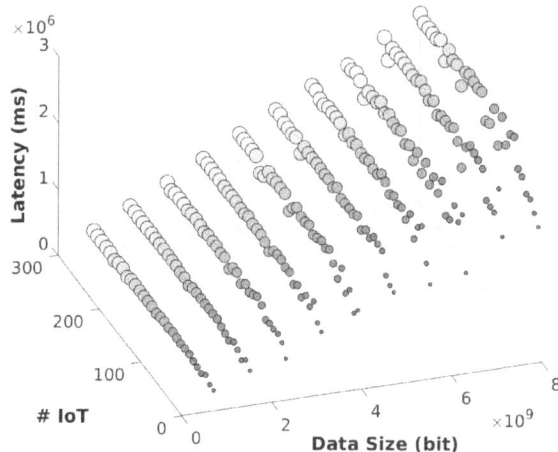

Figure 4: Latency of the system by varying the number of IoTs and the data size.

of SAP links. The number of available PRBs at each SAP is assigned randomly between 1 to 10. In addition, we assumed that the number of IoT devices can vary from 10 to 300 and that each of them can generate tasks with data sizes ranging from 100 MB to 1000 MB. Parameters used in the simulation are summarized in Table 2.

Service latency analysis: Fig. 4 represents the pattern of the average service latency while varying the number of IoT devices and data size. From the results we can conclude that with increase of data size service latency increases and with increase of number of IoT devices, there is a very slight variation in average latency. The reason is like, with increase of data size, transmission and computational latency increase, and consequently total service latency increases in the system.

Satisfaction analysis: In Fig. 5, we have shown a comparison between number of IoT devices, satisfaction and data size. Satisfaction of an IoT device under matching μ is defined as the rank (position) of the matched agents $\mu(I_k)$ in I_k's preference list as defined in the following:

$$Satisfaction(\%) = 100 \times \frac{size - rank}{size} \qquad (13)$$

where, *size* is the maximum size of preference list of any IoT device and *rank* is the position of matched agents. From the result, we can see that when number of IoT devices is less satisfaction is high, whereas with increase of number of devices on different data size, satisfaction becomes almost constant.

Execution time analysis: We examined the behavior of the algorithm execution time when the number of IoTs increases and the size of the data differs. From the result (Fig. 6), we can conclude that the total execution time grows with the number of IoT devices. This is because larger number of IoT devices result in longer preference lists, which in turn increases the time to compute a *stable match* among the three agents. However, the data size does not seem to have any effect on the execution time of different task sizes.

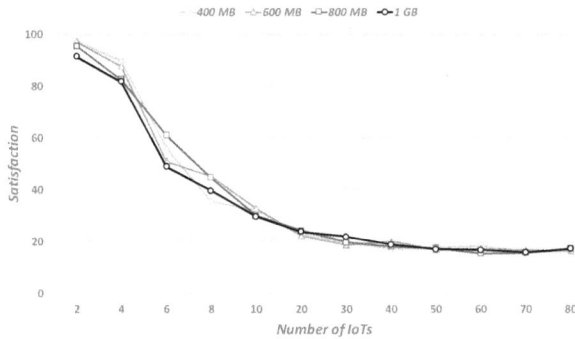

Figure 5: Comparison between number of IoT devices and satisfaction over different data sizes.

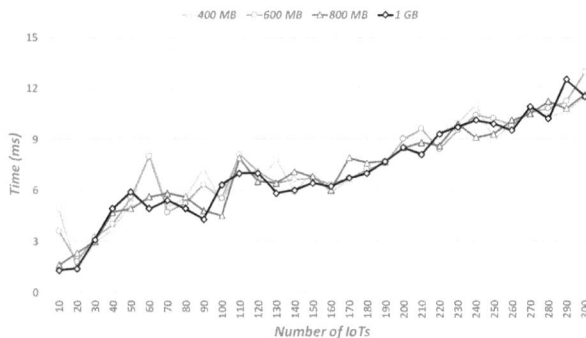

Figure 6: Comparison between number of IoT devices and execution time over different data sizes.

6.2 Laboratory Experiments

The next set of experiments aimed to test the performance of the proposed approach compared to real prototype data. Specifically, we consider a *Human Activity Recognition* (HAR) scenario, where data captured by motion sensors (e.g. accelerometer and gyroscope) within the IoT devices can be analyzed to infer user's current physical activity. In particular, personal smart devices are exploited to collect and send the sensors' raw data to the FAP for classification. In such a scenario, the IoT task submitted to the FAP is to infer the user's current physical activity via extracting feature vectors from a fixed time-window periodically, and classify the activity based on a machine learning algorithm.

The prototype of the proposed environment is depicted in Fig. 7, where a *2013 MacBook Pro Retina*, a *Samsung Gear S3 Frontier* smartwatch, and *Samsung Galaxy S7 Edge* smartphone are used as FAP, IoT and hotspot, respectively. The first is characterized by a 2.4 GHz dual-core Intel Core i5 processor, 4 GB of RAM, 128 GB of memory, and several communication capabilities, like WiFi and Bluetooth 4.0 wireless technology. The latter has an Exynos dual-core processor that works at the frequency of 1 GHz, 768 MB of RAM, Wi-Fi, and Bluetooth 4.2 communication capabilities.

The Human Activity Recognition system follows the guidelines described as in [7]. The smartwatch collects raw data with a sampling frequency of 100 Hz and forwards them to the FAP, over the

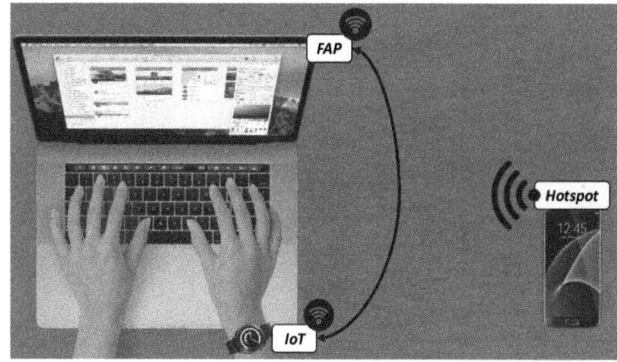

Figure 7: Test bed for the Human Activity Recognition task.

hotspot of a cellular smartphone. The FAP receives data and extract (i) max value, (ii) min value, (iii) mean, (iv) standard deviation, and (v) root mean square over the three accelerometer and gyroscope axes, within fixed-width windows of 3 seconds. Finally, the activity is classified by means of *K-Nearest Neighbors* (K-NN) algorithm and the result is sent back to the IoT device.

Fig. 8 shows that with the increase of data size total service latency increases. However, the service latency obtained in the real and numerical result is almost the same with increasing data sizes. The reason for the slight difference between real data and numerical result is due to the fact that, smart-phone and laptop used in the model are not dedicated as SAP and FAP respectively, and they were running other applications in the background at the time of data execution.

Comparison with existing work: We compared our algorithm with a state-of-art approach described in [13]. Here, authors propose a matching model based on Student Project Allocation (SPA) problem, where IoTs are considered as students who are assigned several projects under the assistance of the lecturers, i.e., service providers. The results obtained in Fig. 9 show that our algorithm reduces the average latency of the entire system by about a factor of 10 on average. This outperformance is justified by two key elements. First, in our case, the search for the best match is distributed by means that it is driven by each IoT, while in [13] it is entirely conducted by the service provider. Second, the authors propose a latency service model that tends to distribute resources equally among all IoT devices regardless of heterogeneous deadlines, limiting average service latency performance. However, sharing equal resources among different IoT's task is not a well motivating factor in the scenario where different tasks will have heterogeneous deadlines to be completed. Unlike the existing work, our model prepares the preference list of individual IoT's task and priorities the task having less required latency to be executed first. Thus, our model is more suitable for real applications where tasks will have heterogeneous deadlines to be completed.

7 CONCLUSION

In this paper, we address the problem of resource provisioning in the IoT environment exploiting fog computing and 5G cellular network

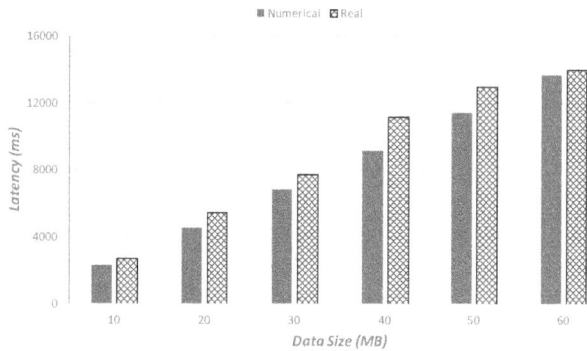

Figure 8: Comparison of service latency and data size on developed prototype and numerical result.

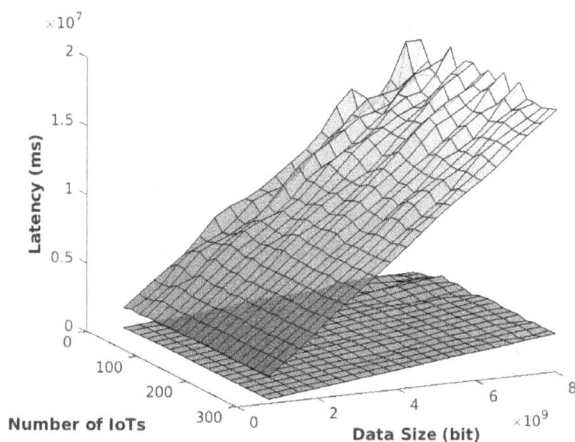

Figure 9: Comparison between proposed matching algorithm (green curve) with a state-of-art approach presented in [13] (orange curve).

model altogether. To this aim, we have formulated average service latency minimization as an optimization problem and proposed a three-sided stable matching algorithm to solve it. The extensive theoretical and experimental analysis showed the validity of the proposed scheme in terms of latency, users' satisfaction and execution time. Moreover, a comparison between our implementation and state-of-the-art techniques have been presented, to prove the effectiveness of our approach in a real scenario.

Acknowledgments: This work is partially supported by the NSF grants under award numbers CNS-1818942, CCF-1725755, CNS-1545037, CNS-1545050.

REFERENCES

[1] Vangelis Angelakis et al. 2016. Allocation of heterogeneous resources of an IoT device to flexible services. *IEEE Internet of Things Journal* 3, 5 (2016), 691–700.

[2] Eduardo M Azevedo et al. 2016. A supply and demand framework for two-sided matching markets. *Journal of Political Economy* 124, 5 (2016), 1235–1268.

[3] Flavio Bonomi et al. 2012. Fog Computing and Its Role in the Internet of Things. In *Proceedings of the First Ed. of the MCC Work. on Mobile Cloud Computing (MCC '12)*. ACM, New York, NY, USA, 13–16. https://doi.org/10.1145/2342509.2342513

[4] Min Chen et al. 2018. Data-driven computing and caching in 5G networks: Architecture and delay analysis. *IEEE Wir. Comm.* 25, 1 (2018), 70–75.

[5] Francesco Chiti et al. 2018. A Matching Theory Framework for Tasks Offloading in Fog Computing for IoT Systems. *IEEE Int. of Things Jour.* 5, 6 (2018), 5089–5096.

[6] S. Choy et al. 2012. The brewing storm in cloud gaming: A measurement study on cloud to end-user latency. In *2012 11th Annual Workshop on Network and Systems Support for Games (NetGames)*. IEEE, Piscataway, NJ, USA, 1–6. https://doi.org/10.1109/NetGames.2012.6404024

[7] Federico Concone et al. 2017. Smartphone Data Analysis for Human Activity Recognition. In *AI*IA 2017 Advances in Artificial Intelligence*. Springer International Publishing, Cham, 58–71.

[8] Yongsheng Ding et al. 2013. An intelligent self-organization scheme for the internet of things. *IEEE Computational Intelligence Magazine* 8, 3 (2013), 41–53.

[9] ETSI. 2017-08. LTE; Evolved Universal Terrestrial Radio Access (E-UTRA); Physical channels and modulation (3GPP TS 36.211 version 14.3.0 Release 14).

[10] LTE ETSI. 3rd Generation Partnership Project, Sophia-Antipolis, France, 3GPP Tech. Spec. TS 36.300 ver. 10.5.0, Oct. 2011. Evolved Universal Terrestrial Radio Access (E-UTRA) and Evolved Universal Terrestrial Radio Access Network (E-UTRAN); Overall Description; Stage 2.

[11] David Gale and Lloyd S Shapley. 1962. College admissions and the stability of marriage. *The American Mathematical Monthly* 69, 1 (1962), 9–15.

[12] Sanjeevini Devi Ganni, Ajay Pratap, and Rajiv Misra. 2017. Distributed Algorithm for Resource Allocation in Downlink Heterogeneous Small Cell Networks. In *Proceedings of the 7th ACM International Workshop on Mobility, Interference, and MiddleWare Management in HetNets (MobiMWareHN'17)*. ACM, New York, NY, USA, Article 5, 6 pages. https://doi.org/10.1145/3083201.3083203

[13] Yunan Gu et al. 2018. Joint radio and computational resource allocation in IoT fog computing. *IEEE Trans. on Veh. Techn.* 67, 8 (2018), 7475–7484.

[14] Nadeem Javaid et al. 2018. Intelligence in IoT-Based 5G Networks: Opportunities and Challenges. *IEEE Communications Magazine* 56, 10 (2018), 94–100.

[15] Boqi Jia et al. 2018. Double-matching resource allocation strategy in fog computing networks based on cost efficiency. *Journal of Communications and Networks* 20, 3 (2018), 237–246.

[16] Song Li et al. 2018. Energy-efficient resource allocation for industrial cyber-physical IoT systems in 5G era. *IEEE Transactions on Industrial Informatics* 14, 6 (2018), 2618–2628.

[17] Adusumalli Sai Manoj et al. 2019. Patient Health Monitoring Using IoT. In *Mobile Health Applications for Quality Healthcare Delivery*. IGI Global, Hershey, PA, USA, 30–45.

[18] Cheng Ng et al. 1991. Three-dimensional stable matching problems. *SIAM Journal on Discrete Mathematics* 4, 2 (1991), 245–252.

[19] Ajay Pratap et al. 2016. Randomized graph coloring algorithm for physical cell ID assignment in LTE-a femtocellular networks. *Wireless Personal Communications* 91, 3 (2016), 1213–1235.

[20] Ajay Pratap et al. 2018. Distributed Randomized k-Clustering Based PCID Assignment for Ultra-Dense Femtocellular Networks. *IEEE Transactions on Parallel and Distributed Systems* 29, 6 (2018), 1247–1260.

[21] Ajay Pratap et al. 2018. Random Graph Coloring-Based Resource Allocation for Achieving User Level Fairness in Femtocellular LTE-A Networks. *Wireless Personal Communications* 98, 2 (2018), 1975–1995.

[22] Ajay Pratap et al. 2018. Resource Allocation to Maximize Fairness and Minimize Interference for Maximum Spectrum Reuse in 5G Cellular Networks. In *2018 IEEE 19th International Symposium on" A World of Wireless, Mobile and Multimedia Networks"(WoWMoM)*. IEEE, Piscataway, NJ, USA, 1–9.

[23] Ajay Pratap et al. 2019. Maximizing Joint Data Rate and Resource Efficiency in D2D-IoT Enabled Multi-Tier Networks. In *to appear in 44th IEEE LCN*. IEEE, Piscataway, NJ, USA, 1–8.

[24] Ajay Pratap et al. 2019. On Maximizing Task Throughput in IoT-Enabled 5G Networks Under Latency and Bandwidth Constraints. In *2019 IEEE SMARTCOMP*. IEEE, Piscataway, NJ, USA, 217–224. https://doi.org/10.1109/SMARTCOMP.2019.00056

[25] Alvin E Roth. 2008. Deferred acceptance algorithms: History, theory, practice, and open questions. *international Journal of game Theory* 36, 3-4 (2008), 537–569.

[26] Surbhi Saraswa et al. 2019. Energy Efficient Data Forwarding Scheme in FogBased Ubiquitous System with Deadline Constraints. *IEEE Tranactions on Network and Service Management* 0, 0 (2019), 1–14.

[27] Stefania Sardellitti et al. 2015. Joint optimization of radio and computational resources for multicell mobile-edge computing. *IEEE Transactions on Signal and Information Processing over Networks* 1, 2 (2015), 89–103.

[28] Ashok Subramanian. 1994. A new approach to stable matching problems. *SIAM J. Comput.* 23, 4 (1994), 671–700.

[29] Huaqing Zhang et al. 2017. Computing resource allocation in three-tier IoT fog networks: A joint optimization approach combining Stackelberg game and matching. *IEEE Internet of Things Journal* 4, 5 (2017), 1204–1215.

[30] W. Zirwas, R. SivaSiva Ganesan, and B. Panzner. 2018. Sub Tiling - a flexible CSI Reference Signal Concept for 5G New Radio Systems. In *WSA 2018; 22nd International ITG Workshop on Smart Antennas*. IEEE, Piscataway, NJ, USA, 1–5.

DCTP-A and DCTP-I: Collection Tree Protocols for Dual Radio Platforms

Gabriel S. Luz
Universidade Federal de Minas Gerais
Belo Horizonte, Minas Gerais, Brazil
gabrielluz@dcc.ufmg.br

Luiz F. M. Vieira
Universidade Federal de Minas Gerais
Belo Horizonte, Minas Gerais, Brazil
lfvieira@dcc.ufmg.br

Marcos A. M. Vieira
Universidade Federal de Minas Gerais
Belo Horizonte, Minas Gerais, Brazil
mmvieira@dcc.ufmg.br

Omprakash Gnawali
University of Houston
Houston, Texas, USA
gnawali@cs.uh.edu

ABSTRACT

The use of two radios per node increases the energy efficiency of wireless sensor networks. Given that data collection is one of the most important functions in wireless sensor networks, this paper presents and compares two new data collection protocols for wireless sensor networks with two radios, DCTP-A and DCTP-I. DCTP-A builds the collection tree alternating the radio band each node while DCTP-I builds two independent collection trees. The protocols were implemented in TinyOS and evaluated experimentally in a testbed in the physical world using the 900MHz and 2.4GHz radio bands, compared to the state of the art (CTP and CTP-Multi) and to each other, considering the metrics delivery rate, latency, throughput in a saturated network scenario, total number of messages and the cost of maintaining routes. The results show the gain of the protocols for wireless sensor networks with two radios. DCTP-A achieved almost 100% of delivery rate, while DCTP-I achieved up to 90% delivery rate with less number of beacons messages.

CCS CONCEPTS

• **Computer systems organization** → **Sensor networks**; • **Networks** → **Network protocol design**; Network layer protocols.

KEYWORDS

wireless sensors networks, routing, dual radio, ctp, throughput

ACM Reference Format:
Gabriel S. Luz, Luiz F. M. Vieira, Marcos A. M. Vieira, and Omprakash Gnawali. 2019. DCTP-A and DCTP-I: Collection Tree Protocols for Dual Radio Platforms. In *22nd Int'l ACM Conference on Modeling, Analysis and Simulation of Wireless and Mobile Systems (MSWiM '19), November 25–29, 2019, Miami Beach, FL, USA.* ACM, New York, NY, USA, 8 pages. https://doi.org/10.1145/3345768.3355912

1 INTRODUCTION

A wireless sensors network (WSN) is a network composed of distributed sensor nodes. Each sensor node is equipped with a variety of application specific sensors, a microprocessor and a radio transceiver, allowing the direct communication between the network elements. Each node can act as a collector and forwarder of data [15]. With these characteristics, WSNs are easy to deploy, have great capacity for distributed sensing and are widely used in a variety of applications.

A large part of the WSNs applications involve sending data from the other nodes to specific nodes that are in charge of centralizing the collected information, this important process is called data collection. Several data collection protocols have been proposed in the literature, among them the Collection Tree Protocol (CTP) [3] gained recognition for its efficiency and reliability. CTP is briefly explained in the Related Work Section.

Recently, aiming to increase throughput and maintain a low power consumption per transmitted byte, WSN platforms were equipped with two radios transceivers in each sensor node. The cost of adding a second radio to a sensor node is small and can greatly improve network performance and power consumption. As an example we can cite the Opal platform [5], whose sensor node, shown in Figure 1, has a SAM3U Cortex-M3 MCU Atmel processor and two radios, a AT86FR212 that operates in the 900 MHz band (which has 10 channels) and a AT86RF231 that operates in the 2.4 GHz (which has 16 channels). As each radio operates in different radio bands, it is possible to prevent interference between the radios.

The use of multiple radios allows simultaneous transmissions between the nodes, which increases network throughput, stability, delivery rate and decreases power consumption per transmitted byte. As an illustration, the Opal mote radios consume 0.669 and 0.659 pj/bit/m^2, while the TelosB CC2420 consumes 11.89 pj/bit/m^2 [6]. The gains in energy consumption in the Opal platform have been shown with depth in [5]. In addition, Yin et al. [16] demonstrated that the 900 MHz ISM band has better connectivity than the 2.4 GHz ISM band. Consequently, using two radios also has benefits to link connectivity and quality. It is important to highlight that using multiple radios is different from using multiple channels. The latter approach does not enable a mote to transmit and receive simultaneously as in the first one. Furthermore, it is possible to use multiple channels when using multiple radios.

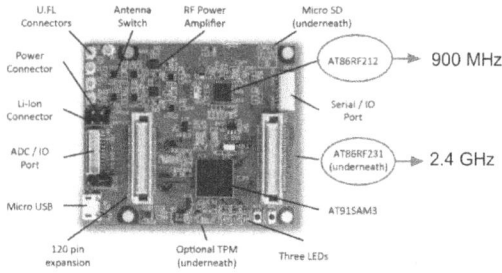

Figure 1: The Opal mote and its components. Source: [5]

The main contributions of this paper can be summarized as follows. We present DCTP-A and DCTP-I, two novel collection tree protocols for dual-radio networks. DCTP-A builds the collection trees alternating the radio bands while DCTP-I builds two independent collection trees. The protocols have low memory footprint and were implemented in the *TinyOS* platform. We compared the protocols with each other and with the state-of-art protocols, the original CTP and Multi-CTP. We present real world results, evaluating the protocols in a testbed composed of 100 Opal motes. We show that both protocols present gains in the delivery rate, throughput and latency.

The two new protocols aim to explore the effects of dual radio in data collection performance. CTP-Multi is a modification of CTP to use two radio bands, proposed in [6]. DCTP-A and DCTP-I are different from CTP-Multi in the way the radios are used, the new ones use the modification to improve throughput, reliability, latency and performance in general, while the other only uses it to find a better link for a single hop transmission. The novel protocols advantages were tested and evaluated in a real world testbed.

This paper is organized as follows. The next section 2 presents the related work and 3 describes the problem tackled by the protocols. The following two sections 4 and 5 present the new protocols, Dual Radio Collection Tree Protocol with Independent Trees (DCTP-I) and Dual Radio Collection Tree Protocol with Radio Alternation (DCTP-A). Section 6 discusses the experiments and results obtained. Finally, Section 7 concludes the paper.

2 RELATED WORK

2.1 Collection Tree Protocol (CTP)

The CTP was presented in the paper [3], along with two principles for routing protocols: *Datapath Validation* and *Adaptative Beaconing*. The protocol was implemented for the *TinyOS* platform and its description can be found in the document TEP 123 in the *TinyOS* documentation.

CTP is a data collection protocol based on tree routing. Each tree is rooted in a collection node, which is in charge of receiving and storing data collected by the nodes of its tree. A sensor node belongs to only one tree. A collection node announces itself as a root node, informing CTP, which takes on the role of creating a tree for the new root. A node does not know to which tree it belongs, it only knows which node is its father in the tree. A node sends all the collected data and forwards the packets it receives to its father. To build the routes (trees), the CTP estimates link quality using

the Expected Transmission Count (ETX) metric. To each direct transmission between two nodes it is associated with an ETX value, representing the quality of this link (the higher is the ETX, the worst is the link). To the nodes an ETX value is also associated, it is the sum of the ETX values of all the links that compose the path from this node to the root, as a result a root's ETX is zero. Figure 2 shows the tree generated by CTP for a 7 nodes network, the first node is the root.

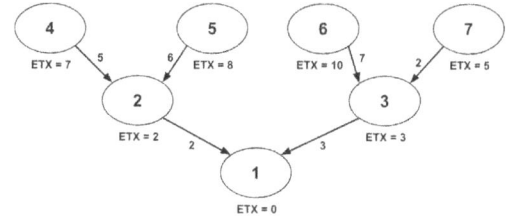

Figure 2: Example of a tree built by the CTP, with the nodes and links ETX values.

The operation of CTP can be divided into three main components: Link estimator, Routing and Forwarding.

The role of the Link Estimator is to estimate the transmission ETX value of a link between two neighbor nodes. To calculate the ETX, the estimator uses data packets sent by the forwarding component and the beacons sent by the routing. The beacons are sent as broadcast periodically according to a timer that increases exponentially to a max value and can be reduced to a minimum value if certain events occur. The longer the period of the timer, the fewer beacons are sent, and when it is set to the minimum value the send rate of beacons is the highest so that the network can adapt to changes in the topology. A change in a node or link is announced by setting some bits in the beacon header. This mechanism is called *Adaptative Beaconing* and was inspired by the *Trickle* [7] algorithm. A beacon contains the identifier and the ETX of the node that sent it, when a node receives a beacon it updates its routing table with the new ETX informed. The Link Estimator monitors whether the data packets reach or not the next hop, and use the aggregated information each time five data packets are sent to calculate the link ETX. The beacons are also used to estimate link quality, using a sequence number that is incremented at each transmission, the missing numbers indicate the number of lost beacons. Therefore, node u can estimate route quality to the root passing through node v, adding the ETX value of v, which was sent by a beacon from v to u, with the ETX of the link $u \rightarrow v$ that was obtained by monitoring data packets and beacons.

The Routing is responsible for choosing the next hop for a data packet transmission and for controlling the sending of beacons. The next hop, which is the father of the node in the tree, is the node that if chosen will provide the route with the smallest ETX to the root. The sending of beacons is done in the way explained in the Link Estimator.

The Forwarding controls the sending and forwarding of data packets. This component consults the Routing to get the next hop address, chooses when to send a packet, passes information to the Link Estimator and implements the principle of *Datapath Validation*.

A problem in WSN routing is the presence of loops in a route, which will confine the packets sent through this route preventing them from reaching the root. To deal with this problem, the packets contain the ETX value of the last node that transmitted it, as the ETX must decrease in direction to the root, then if a node receives a data packet carrying an ETX value lower than its value, then it detects a loop and sets the beacon timer to the minimum to correct this inconsistency. As a result, it is possible to validate the route using data packets. Another problem is the duplication of packets, which occurs when a node re-transmit a packet that had successfully arrived on the next hop, generating two equal packets in the network. This problem might grow exponentially and must be treated, CTP does it using a message cache in each node. If the message received is already in the node's cache then it discards it and does not forward it.

2.2 Protocols Similar to CTP

Many modifications to CTP have been proposed in the literature. The XCTP [12] provides in addition to the communication from nodes to root, the communication from root to nodes, extending the features of CTP. Another examples are *Matrix* [9] and *Mobile Matrix* [11] which uses data collection tree routing protocol, as CTP, as a base for a routing protocol with the hierarchical allocation of IPv6 addresses for mobile networks. Funneling Wider Bandwidth (FWB) [13] uses wider bandwidth channels to improve data collection and reduce the overall number of time slots. FlushMF [14] uses multiple frequencies as transport protocol. Other protocols use multiple channels to create better routes and reduce interference, an example is the protocol *Multi-channel CTP* [10].

However there is very little in the literature about using multiple paths to improve data collection. One example of work in this area is *MMCR* [1] that uses multiple radio interfaces and multiple channels. The main protocol found in the literature that adapts the CTP to use multiple radio interfaces and multiple channels is the CTP-Multi [6], which is a dual radio protocol that modifies the Link Estimator to choose the best radio band for a link and modifies the Routing to send beacons by multiple radios. It was implemented using a separate table for each radio band in the Link Estimator, obtaining different estimations for the link quality using different radio bands. The Routing only uses one routing table filled with the ETX values of the neighbor nodes obtained from the beacons received. At the moment of updating the route the neighbor with the best link and ETX and the respective radio are chosen for the next transmissions.

In this paper we explored two approaches that allow improving network performance not by choosing the best radio for a link as done by CTP-Multi, but by building two independent trees or alternating the radio band used at each transmission.

3 PROBLEM DEFINITION

The main goals that CTP [3] aims to achieve are:

- Reliability : A data collection protocol must be able to obtain a delivery rate higher than 90%.
- Robustness: A protocol must be able to operate without settings or configurations in a variety of topology, conditions and environments.

- Efficiency: The number of transmissions and states required to transmit a packet must be minimized..
- Hardware Independence: It should not assume specific hardware or radio chip characteristics.

Other factors are also important in data collection, specially latency and throughput. Low latency is very important for real time monitoring and applications that require a fast response to certain events. In [8] the researchers developed solutions for radio selection and data partitioning in one hop transmissions in multiple radio platforms, the aim was to fulfill real-time data transfer constraints and maximize energy efficiency. In the paper they used the example of medical applications that require real-time constraints to justify the importance of real-time protocols. Many others applications also require fast and efficient data transfer and to achieve this, data collection must have low latency and high throughput.

The problem this work aims to solve is creating new protocols using two radio bands that improve CTP in regard to reliability, robustness and efficiency, and also improve the end to end throughput and delay.

4 DUAL RADIO COLLECTION TREE PROTOCOL WITH INDEPENDENT TREES (DCTP-I)

DCTP-I expands the CTP concept from one to two trees rooted on the same root node. In this protocol each node belongs to two independent trees, the first is only used by radio 1 and the second is used only by radio 2. To create the trees, the Routing and Link Estimator were duplicated.

When a packet is created it has a bit that indicates which radio must be used to transmit it. A packet with the radio bit set to one can only be transmitted by radio 1, as a result this packet will remain in the same tree from the moment it was created until it reaches the root. The trees are designated to each packet in an alternate way, the first packet is assigned to the tree 1, the second to tree 2, the third to tree 1 , the fourth to tree 2 and so on. Consequently each tree receives half of the packets.

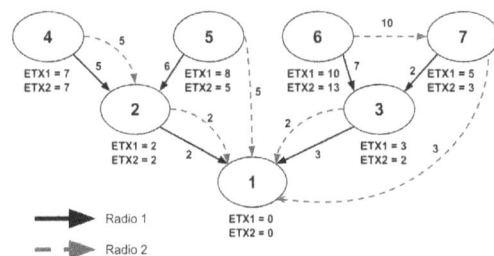

Figure 3: Example of the two trees formed by DCTP-I, with the ETX values of the nodes and links for each radio band.

As the Routing and Link Estimator components were duplicated, the trees are created independent of each other, but with the same root node. The two routing tables and the sending of beacons are independent for each radio. As a result, each node belongs to two trees and has two fathers, which can be different or not. As the radios operate at different bandwidth, their reach is also different.

89

Figure 3 shows the two trees created by DCTP-I for the same network of Figure 2. It shows that the nodes share the same root and each node has two fathers and two ETX values. The Forwarding sends packets according to the radio bit. Before sending, it verifies the bit radio and consults the respective Routing component to know which father to send the packet to.

5 DUAL RADIO COLLECTION TREE PROTOCOL WITH RADIO ALTERNATION (DCTP-A)

DCTP-A uses a different approach from DCTP-I. Instead of always using both radio bands to send and receive packets, this protocol makes a node always receives by one radio and sends by another. Figure 4 shows the tree formed by DCTP-A in the same network used in the last figures. Alternating radios follow the principle used by the routing protocols [2] and [4], which improved the throughput by enabling that a node sends and receives packets simultaneously.

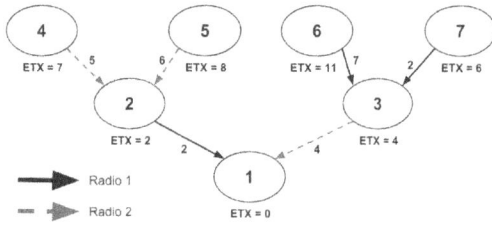

Figure 4: Example of the tree formed by DCTP-A, with the ETX values of nodes and links.

To implement DCTP-A the main components of CTP were modified. It uses two Link Estimators, one for each radio, which inform the link ETX values to the Routing component. The Routing stores a variable that indicates which radio band should be used to send packets and creates a routing table for each radio. Routing table X contains the ETX values of the neighbors to which radio X is used for the transmission. The Forwarding is similar to the CTP one, but it connects to both Link Estimators and before sending a packet it consults the Routing to know which radio to use. Therefore, the tree is formed so that a node only receives packets by one radio and only sends data packets and beacons by the other. However, it is possible that the tree is not perfect and a node may receive and send using the same radio band. A node always receives beacons by both radios.

To understand how the radios are alternated it is necessary to understand how the Routing behaves when a beacon is received and how the route is altered in each node. When a beacon is received by radio 2 containing the ETX value of a neighbor, we know that this ETX value is associated to radio 2, since a node only sends beacons and data packets with the same radio. To alternate the radio bands used, this ETX value and the neighbor identifier are placed into the radio 1 routing table. When a node updates its route (father node and ETX) it scans the two routing tables and picks the best neighbor from each one, to the table 1 neighbor's ETX we add the ETX value of the link using radio 1, to the table 2 neighbor's ETX

we add the ETX value of the link using radio 2. We choose the best neighbor from them, if the best neighbor ETX is better than the current ETX value subtracted from a certain threshold value, which indicates how much better the new ETX must be, it becomes the new father and the ETX value is updated. If the radio used to reach the new father is different from the last radio, then the radio used to transmit is updated and the beacon timer period is set to the minimum value, increasing the beacon sending rate to warn the neighbors about the change. Altering the radio band results in the node receiving and sending by the same band, creating a bottleneck in the path, in order to fix this all the nodes in the sub-tree of that node must change the radios they use to transmit, making this an expensive operation with a higher amount of beacons. Algorithm 1 shows the procedure that updates the father node and the ETX of a node. When a node needs to update its route, it executes this algorithm using its own routing tables.

Algorithm 1 Update Route

1: ▷ Procedure used by a node u to update its father node and its ETX value
2: Scans routing table 1 and picks the neighbor $v1$ with the smallest ETX
3: SmallestETX1 = $v1$ ETX + link ETX $u \rightarrow v1$
4: Scans routing table 2 and picks the neighbor $v2$ with the smallest ETX
5: SmallestETX2 = $v2$ ETX + link ETX $u \rightarrow v2$
6: **if** ($SmallestETX1 \geq SmallestETX2$) **then**
7:     SmallestETX = SmallestETX2
8: **else**
9:     SmallestETX = SmallestETX1
10: **if** ($SmallestETX < (CurrentETX - Father\ changing\ threshold)$) **then**{
11:     Father = Best Neighbor
12:     CurrentETX = SmallestETX
13:     Timer = Minimum Value} ▷ Increases the beacon sending rate

---

6 EXPERIMENTS AND RESULTS

6.1 General Experiments

In order to test and compare the protocols CTP, CTP-Multi, DCTP-I and DCTP-A, two types of experiments were made. Longer ones with a duration of 45 minutes with a moderate packet generation rate and shorter ones with a duration of 5 minutes in which the packet generation rate was altered from experiment to experiment. Experiments measured throughput, latency, number of data packets sent in the network, number of beacons sent and delivery rate.

The experiments were made in the Twonet *testbed*, which is placed in a building of the University of Houston. It contains 100 Opal motes and is subjected to interference, specially with *Wi-Fi*. The 5 minutes interval was chosen because it is the shortest duration possible in the *testbed*, it allows the formation of the trees and the sending of a considerable amount of data packets. The 45 minutes interval was chosen to compare the protocols with a moderate packet generation rate and for a longer duration, in which

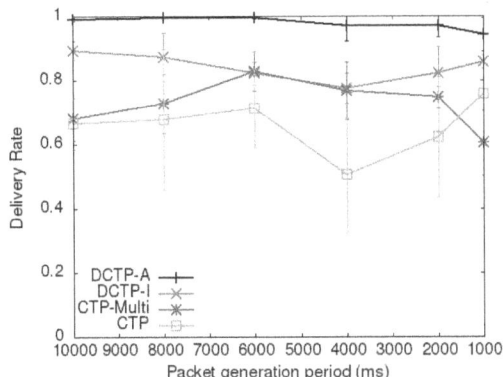

Figure 5: Delivery rate for packet generation period of 10,000 to 1,000 ms.

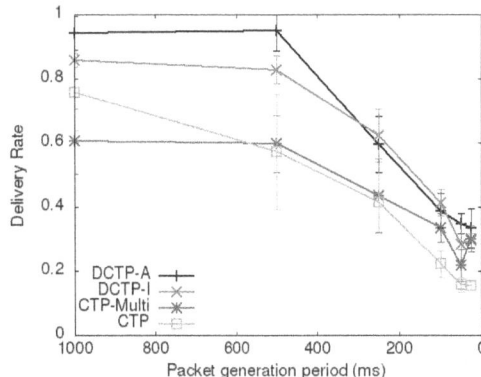

Figure 6: Delivery rate for packet generation period of 1,000 to 25 ms.

the network might suffer more changes than a shorter duration and be able to repair from them.

The 5 minutes experiments generate data packets at a constant rate defined by the packet generation period. This period varied from 10,000 milliseconds to 25 milliseconds, the shorter the period the higher the generation rate of packets. All of the 100 nodes of the *testbed* were used, but only half of them was in charge of generating data packets.

The short duration experiments were repeated 6 times and a confidence interval of 95%. The charts that show these results were divided into two, the first one shows from 10,000 milliseconds to 1,000 milliseconds and the second one shows from 1,000 milliseconds to 25 milliseconds, which is a more extreme situation for the protocols and with shorter intervals between the measurements. The protocols source code and the programs used to make experiments are available in a public repository in *GitHub*[1]. The delivery rate was calculated dividing the number of packets that arrived at the root by the number of data packets generated in the other nodes. When a node generates a packet it tries to send it, if it fails it tries again. Consequently the number of generated packets is not always the same. Duplicated packets are a problem, to minimize it every node was equipped with a packet cache.

All the protocols support multiple roots, which means that they can have more than one collection node. Using only one root makes the data collection harder, makes the trees deeper and, as a result, allows us to analyze the protocols in a harsher environment, in which the differences between them become more exposed than in a multiple roots environment. The use of more than one root is very advantageous, specially if the collection nodes are chosen in a way that almost the entire network is reached by a few multi-hop transmissions.

Figures 5 and 6 show the delivery rate of each protocol, which represents the reliability of each one. We can notice that DCTP-A is superior, achieving a delivery rate of almost a 100% until the 5,000 period and maintaining more than 90% until the 500 period (two packets generated per second in each node). It is followed by DCTP-I, which maintained rates between 80% and 90% until

[1]https://github.com/gabrielsluz/CTP-ALL

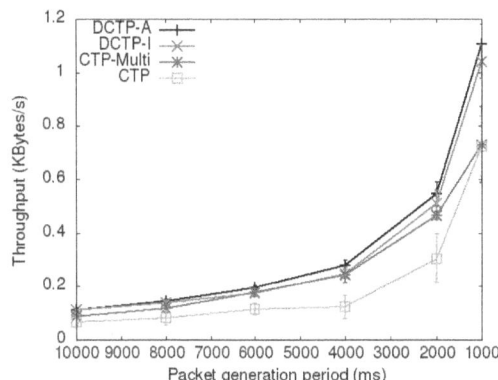

Figure 7: Throughput for packet generation period of 10,000 to 1,000 ms.

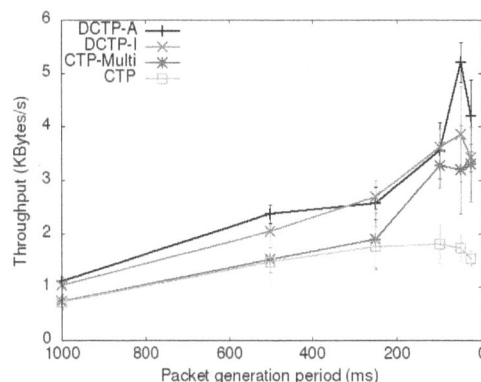

Figure 8: Throughput for packet generation period of 1,000 to 25 ms.

the 500 period. The protocols CTP and CTP-Multi started with a lower delivery rate, but CTP-Multi performed better. This can be explained by the fact that CTP-Multi has more possibilities to pick from and to avoid interference. After the 500 period, the delivery

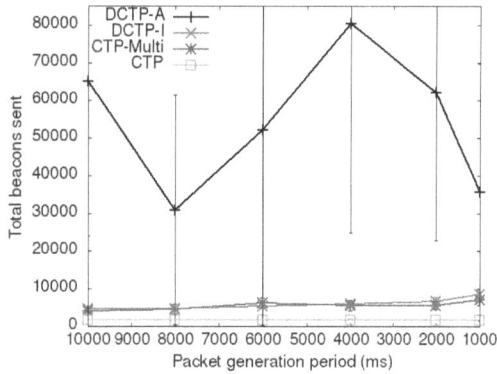

Figure 9: Total beacon sent for packet generation period of 10,000 to 1,000 ms.

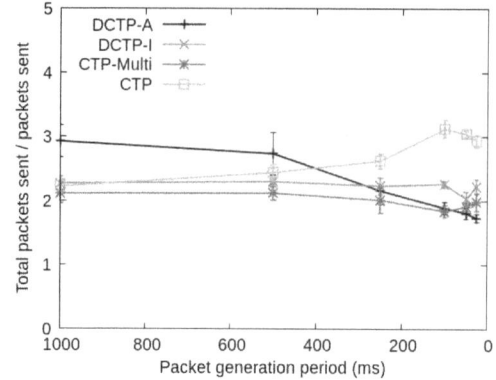

Figure 10: Total beacon sent for packet generation period of 1,000 to 25 ms.

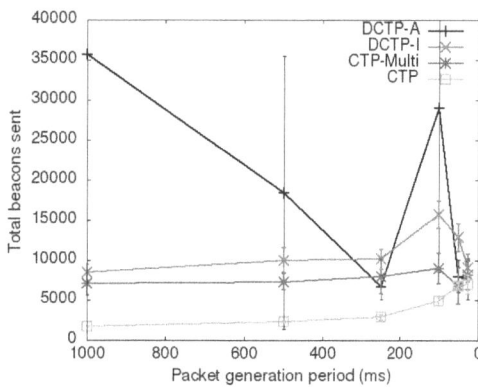

Figure 11: Total packets sent per packet generated for packet generation period of 10,000 to 1,000 ms.

rate in all protocols fall sharply as the network saturates, but the ones that were better remained superior.

Figures 7 and 8 show the throughput obtained by each protocol. The throughput corresponds to the number of data packets that

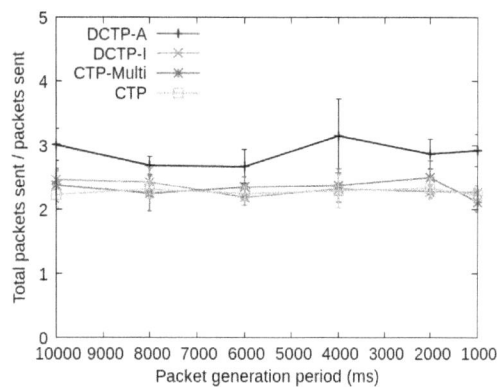

Figure 12: Total packets sent per packet generated for packet generation period of 1,000 to 25 ms.

reached the root divided by the time interval between the first and the last packet to arrive. It is important to point out that the graphics are on different scales, the throughput in the Figure 8 is much higher than the other. At the beginning (10,000) the throughput depends more on the packet generation rate than in the protocols, but shortly after the differences start to appear. The difference between DCTP-A and DCTP-I in relation to delivery rate is larger than in relation to throughput. The reason is that DCTP-A uses two radio bands to transmit, whereas the other only uses one, allowing DCTP-A to initiate a transmission through a radio while the other radio is still transmitting. CTP-Multi achieved a higher throughput than CTP, as expected due to the higher reliability of the dual radio protocol. The throughput of all protocols is improved til the mark of 50 milliseconds is reached, when it drops in all protocols.

The number of beacons sent is shown in Figures 9 and 10. This metric indicates the cost of maintaining the trees. The graphics reveal that DCTP-A sends, on average, much more beacons than the others. The higher cost of that protocol can be explained by the necessity of updating the entire sub-tree of a node when it changes its radio in order to avoid bottlenecks. A change in the radio used by a node closer to the root will cause that node to send beacons at a much higher rate and in order to propagate the change through the sub-tree all the nodes from it will change their radios and will send beacons at a higher rate. Consequently a change in the network caused by interference or by other reasons can cause a momentary but drastic increase in the beacon send rate, this explains the large variance of the results obtained. In some experiments the protocol operated on a low cost but in others the cost was much higher. DCTP-A minimum beacon send period was lower than the one used in the other protocols. The lowest cost protocol is CTP, followed by CTP-Multi. As DCTP-I uses two Routing components, it was expected to have a higher cost, but the difference between DCTP-I and CTP-Multi was small. For packet generation periods smaller than 1,000 milliseconds, DCTP-A number of beacons send lowered, while the other protocols kept on a similar rate to the other graphic.

Figures 11 and 12 are related to the protocols' efficiency, because it shows the number of data packets sent in the entire network divided by the number of data packets generated, which means that re-transmissions, packets forwarded and duplicated packets were counted, obtaining how many packets, in average, were necessary to send one generated packet to the root. For a period of more than 1,000 milliseconds, DCTP-A is the least efficient, while the others are very similar. However, due to the previous results, we know that DCTP-A performs better in relation to throughput and delivery rate. When the packet generation rate is increased, DCTP-A becomes more efficient.

The 45 minutes experiments were performed in the same way as the shorter ones, but with a packet generation rate fixed of 1,500 milliseconds and with a longer duration. The experiments were repeated 28 times for each protocol and used a 95% confidence interval. Table 1 shows the results for each protocol.

In relation to delivery rate, the results were similar to the 5 minutes experiments, DCTP-A maintained its superiority and, on average, CTP-Multi had a worse delivery rate than CTP, even though it was able to achieve a better throughput than the single radio protocol. We expected that CTP-Multi would obtain better reliability than CTP, but as it sent a larger volume of packets, obtaining a better throughput, it compensated the gains of radio diversity lowering its delivery rate. In relation to throughput, alternating radios and using two radios to send and receive achieved the best results.

The number of beacons also confirmed the results of the shorter experiments and shows the large variance of DCTP-A. The metric cost of each packet indicates the average number of packets necessary to send one generated data packet to the root, it counts packets forwarded, re-transmissions, duplicates and beacons, and is related to the protocols cost. We can notice that DCTP-A is the most costly protocol, due to the larger number of beacons and to the result obtained from the Figure 11. The cost of CTP-Multi is close to the cost of CTP, because the number of re-transmissions in CTP is bigger than the dual radio one.

Protocol / Metric	DCTP-A	DCTP-I	CTP-MULTI	CTP
Delivery rate (%)	93.27 ± 3.57	82.89 ± 4.16	74.25 ± 4.32	74.53 ± 2.92
Throughput(KBytes/s)	0.673 ± 0.027	0.648 ± 0.037	0.565 ± 0.035	0.440 ± 0.020
Number of Beacons	63,051 ± 48,044	51,045 ± 5,153	36,293 ± 4,126	3,082 ± 241
Cost of each packet	4.286 ± 0.954	3.386 ± 0.155	2.844 ± 0.177	2.753 ± 0.157

Table 1: Results of the 45 minutes experiments. The confidence interval is of 95%

6.2 Latency Results

In a single experiment of 45 minutes the arrival times of the first 2,000 packets to reach the root were measured. To show these results we constructed a cumulative distribution function (CDF) for each protocol, exposed in Figure 13. The more vertical is the function curve, the more packets were received in less time, which means that the protocol with the most vertical function curve is the protocol with the lowest latency. Consequently, DCTP-A and DCTP-I achieved a very similar latency and were better than the others. CTP-Multi achieved a lower latency than CTP.

6.3 Robustness to Failure

We tested the robustness to failure of each protocol using 10 minutes experiments in which 9 nodes, of the 100 nodes, were turned

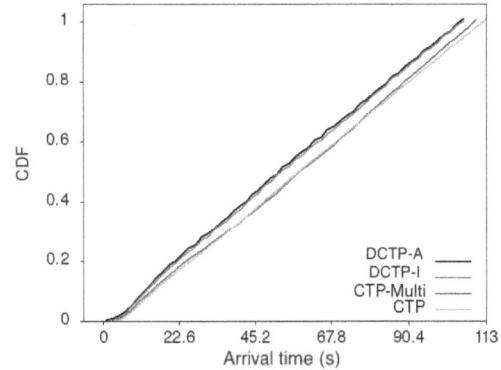

Figure 13: Cumulative distribution functions of the arrival times of the first 2,000 packets.

off at the fifth minute. We used a packet generation period of 1.000 ms and only half of the nodes were in charge of generating packets. The experiments were repeated 12 times for each protocol. At each minute all the packets generated in the network and all the packets received at the root were counted, we obtained the delivery rate of that minute in the experiment by dividing the number of packets generated by the number of packets received at the root. We calculated the average delivery of each minute and used a confidence interval of 95%, the results are exposed in figure 14.

The protocols DCTP-A and DCTP-I obtained better delivery rates than the other ones and, together with CTP, were not affected by the removal of the 9 nodes at minute 5. The only protocol that suffered heavily from the failure was CTP-Multi.

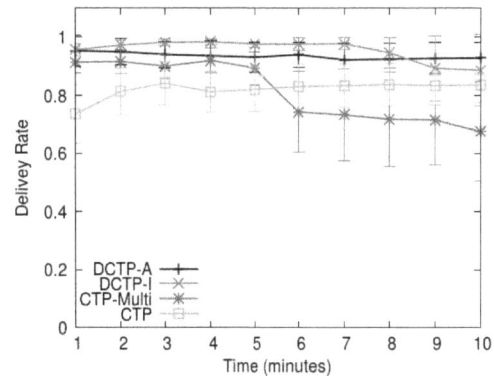

Figure 14: Delivery rate measured at each minute. Nodes fail at 5 minutes.

6.4 DCTP-I with Load Balancing

In an attempt to improve DCTP-I, we modified the Forwarding component of the protocol to use the best suited available radio to send a packet. In the original version DCTP-I a packet generated is sent by the same radio until it reaches the root, but in the modified version DCTP-I LB (Load balancing) a node can choose to send via another radio if the preferred one is busy. We compared DCTP-I

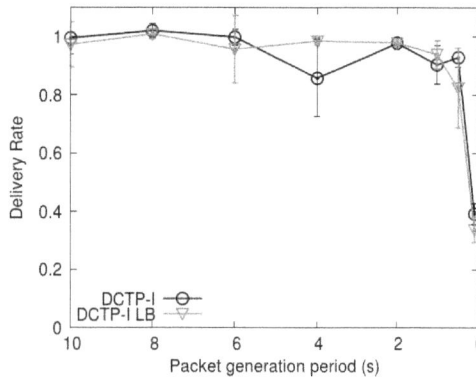

Figure 15: Delivery rate of DCTP-I with load balancing and DCTP-I for packet generation periods of 10 to 0.1 seconds.

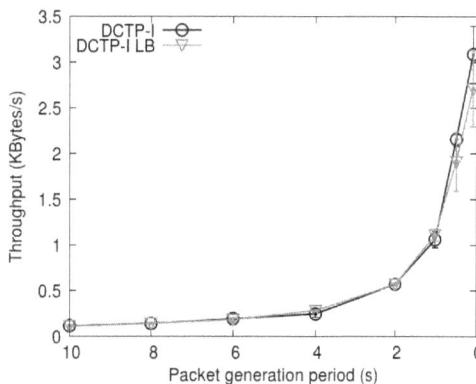

Figure 16: Throughput of DCTP-I with load balancing and DCTP-I for packet generation periods of 10 to 0.1 seconds.

LB with the original version using 5 minutes experiments, varying the packet generation period from 10 seconds to 0.1 second. We executed each protocol 10 times for each generation period and used a confidence interval of 95%. We evaluated the delivery rate (Figure 15), throughput (Figure 16) and number of beacons sent, in which the protocols had the same cost, and concluded that the modification did not improve the original version.

7 CONCLUSION AND FUTURE WORK

Based on the results from the experiments we can conclude that the new data collection protocols, DCTP-A and DCTP-I, were able to outperform, in delivery rate, throughput and latency, CTP and CTP-Multi, which are the current state-of-the-art in data collection. DCTP-A had the best performance, obtaining the best delivery rate and obtaining better but close results do DCTP-I in throughput and latency.

DCTP-I revealed to be a good alternative to DCTP-A, since it achieved good performance and does not have a cost too elevated. CTP-Multi obtained better routes than CTP, but its performance was exceeded by the new protocols, and the lower cost in relation to DCTP-I might not overshadow the benefits of the novel protocol. As

a result, the new protocols were able to better explore the benefits of using two radio bands in data collection.

As future work we can investigate ways to maintain the performance and reduce the number of beacons. Another possible future work is to explore the use of multiple channels, which in addition to the use of two radio bands can have a great impact in reducing interference and, consequently, improving data collection.

ACKNOWLEDGEMENTS

The authors would like to thank the research agencies CAPES, CNPq and FAPEMIG for their financial support.

REFERENCES

[1] R. Anguswamy, M. Zawodniok, and S. Jagannathan. 2009. A Multi-Interface Multi-Channel Routing (MMCR) Protocol for Wireless Ad Hoc Networks. In *2009 IEEE Wireless Communications and Networking Conference*. 1–6. https://doi.org/10.1109/WCNC.2009.4917512

[2] G. Ekbatanifard, P. Sommer, B. Kusy, V. Iyer, and K. Langendoen. 2013. Fast-Forward: High-Throughput Dual-Radio Streaming. In *2013 IEEE 10th International Conference on Mobile Ad-Hoc and Sensor Systems*. 209–213. https://doi.org/10.1109/MASS.2013.41

[3] Omprakash Gnawali, Rodrigo Fonseca, Kyle Jamieson, David Moss, and Philip Levis. 2009. Collection Tree Protocol. In *Proceedings of the 7th ACM Conference on Embedded Networked Sensor Systems (SenSys'09)*.

[4] Nildo Santos Ribeiro Júnior, Luiz Filipe Menezes Vieira, and Marcos Augusto Menezes Vieira. 2017. Maximizando a Vazão Através de Múltiplos Caminhos em Plataformas de Dois Rádios. In *Simpósio Brasileiro de Redes de Computadores e Sistemas Distribuídos (SBRC)*. SBRC.

[5] Raja Jurdak, Kevin Klues, Brano Kusy, Christian Richter, Koen Langendoen, and Michael Brünig. 2011. Opal: A multiradio platform for high throughput wireless sensor networks. *Embedded Systems Letters, IEEE* 3, 4 (2011), 121–124.

[6] B. Kusy, C. Richter, W. Hu, M. Afanasyev, R. Jurdak, M. BrÃijnig, D. Abbott, C. Huynh, and D. Ostry. 2011. Radio diversity for reliable communication in wsns.. In *Information Processing in Sensor Networks (IPSN),2011 10th International Conference*. IEEE, 270–281.

[7] P Levis, N Patel, David Culler, and S Shenker. 2004. Trickle: A selfregulating algorithm for code propagation and maintenance in wireless sensor networks. *In Proceedings of the first USENIX/ACM symposium on networked systems design and implementation (NSDI)* (01 2004), 15–28.

[8] Di Mu, Mo Sha, Kyoung-Don Kang, and Hyungdae Yi. 2019. Energy-Efficient Radio Selection and Data Partitioning for Real-Time Data Transfer.

[9] Bruna Peres, Bruno P. Santos, Otavio A. de O. Souza, Olga Goussevskaia, Marcos A. M. Vieira, Luiz F. M. Vieira, and Antonio A. F. Loureiro. 2018. Matrix: Multihop Address allocation and dynamic any-To-any Routing for 6LoWPAN. *Computer Networks* 140 (2018), 28 – 40. https://doi.org/10.1016/j.comnet.2018.04.017

[10] A. Phokaew, C. Tanwongvarl, and S. Chantaraskul. 2014. Adaptive multi-channel CTP for Wireless Sensor Networks. In *2014 International Electrical Engineering Congress (iEECON)*. 1–4. https://doi.org/10.1109/iEECON.2014.6925917

[11] Bruno P. Santos, Olga Goussevskaia, Luiz F.M. Vieira, Marcos A.M. Vieira, and Antonio A.F. Loureiro. 2018. Mobile Matrix: Routing under mobility in IoT, IoMT, and Social IoT. *Ad Hoc Networks* 78 (2018), 84 – 98. https://doi.org/10.1016/j.adhoc.2018.05.012

[12] B. P. Santos, M. A. M. Vieira, and L. F. M. Vieira. 2015. eXtend collection tree protocol. In *2015 IEEE Wireless Communications and Networking Conference (WCNC)*. 1512–1517. https://doi.org/10.1109/WCNC.2015.7127692

[13] Rodrigo C. Tavares, Marcos Carvalho, Marcos A. M. Vieira, Luiz F. M. Vieira, and Bhaskar Krishnamachari. 2018. FWB: Funneling Wider Bandwidth Algorithm for High Performance Data Collection in Wireless Sensor Networks. In *Proceedings of the 21st ACM International Conference on Modeling, Analysis and Simulation of Wireless and Mobile Systems (MSWIM '18)*. ACM, New York, NY, USA, 9–16. https://doi.org/10.1145/3242102.3242112

[14] R. C. Tavares, M. A. M. Vieira, and L. F. M. Vieira. 2016. FlushMF: A Transport Protocol Using Multiple Frequencies for Wireless Sensor Network. In *2016 IEEE 13th International Conference on Mobile Ad Hoc and Sensor Systems (MASS)*. 192–200. https://doi.org/10.1109/MASS.2016.033

[15] Marcos Augusto M. Vieira, Claudionor N Coelho Jr., Diógenes Cecilio da Silva Jr., and José M da Mata. 2003. Survey on wireless sensor network devices. In *Emerging Technologies and Factory Automation, 2003. Proceedings. ETFA'03. IEEE Conference*, Vol. 1. 537–544.

[16] S. Yin, O. Gnawali, P. Sommer, and B. Kusy. 2014. Multi channel performance of dual band low power wireless network. In *2014 IEEE 11th International Conference on Mobile Ad Hoc and Sensor Systems*. 345–353. https://doi.org/10.1109/MASS.2014.120

Toward Accurate Clock Drift Modeling in Wireless Sensor Networks Simulation

David Hauweele
University of Mons (UMONS)
Mons, Belgium
david.hauweele@umons.ac.be

Bruno Quoitin
University of Mons (UMONS)
Mons, Belgium
bruno.quoitin@umons.ac.be

ABSTRACT

The protocols used in Wireless Sensor Networks are subject to very strict temporal synchronization constraints. Radio Duty Cycle (RDC) protocols in particular are characterized by their very high synchronization accuracy requirements. In these protocols, synchronization errors are primarily caused by the natural clock drift observed in real nodes. The impact of the clock drift on the desynchronization issues can be investigated by the use of low-level node simulators.

In this paper, we show the limitation of the COOJA simulator to evaluate the impact of the clock drift. We show that its current mote execution model does not faithfully reproduce the requested clock drift. We identify the root cause of these inaccuracies and present a new algorithm that is able to precisely reproduce any requested clock drifts in simulation.

To demonstrate the new algorithm, we consider a well-documented RDC protocol issue where the clock drift would cause periodic communication blackouts. This phenomenon was observed on real nodes, but was previously impossible to reproduce by simulation. Our new algorithm not only allows to reproduce the blackouts but also provides additional insights that help to confirm the initial analysis of the phenomenon.

CCS CONCEPTS

• **Networks** → **Network simulations**; *Network experimentation*; • **Computer systems organization** → **Sensor networks**; • **Computing methodologies** → *Simulation evaluation*.

KEYWORDS

clock drift; wsn; simulation

ACM Reference Format:
David Hauweele and Bruno Quoitin. 2019. Toward Accurate Clock Drift Modeling in Wireless Sensor Networks Simulation. In *22nd Int'l ACM Conf. on Modeling, Analysis and Simulation of Wireless and Mobile Systems (MSWiM'19), Nov. 25–29, 2019, Miami Beach, FL, USA.* ACM, New York, NY, USA, 8 pages. https://doi.org/10.1145/3345768.3355911

1 INTRODUCTION

The nodes used in Wireless Sensor Networks (WSNs) have limited power resources. They must however stay autonomous for extended periods of time. In order to achieve their low power requirements, the Medium Access Control (MAC) protocols used often rely on time synchronization mechanisms to allow the radio to alternate between active and sleep periods. This process, known as Radio Duty Cycling (RDC), greatly reduces the power consumption of the nodes, allowing the radio to remain off most of the time.

A wide variety of such protocols have been proposed in the literature using variants of the Radio Duty Cycling mechanism to save energy [21]. The main difficulty is to ensure that the motes wake-up at the appropriate time to ensure successful communication while still limiting idle listening, overhearing, and collisions while doing so with a minimal overhead. The proposed solutions can generally be divided into two categories. Synchronous solutions such as TSCH [1] organize the wake-up time of the motes so that they are ready to transmit and receive messages on a known schedule. On the other hand, asynchronous solutions such as ContikiMAC [6] do not organize the wake-up time and let all motes run on their own schedule except for protocol constraints. In both cases the precision of those protocols is dependent on the precision of the clock used on the mote. Hence better clock synchronization usually translates to lower power consumption and reduced packet loss.

The impact of the clock drift on those protocols can be studied with real nodes [7]. However this type of experiment is difficult for several reasons. First injecting a precise frequency to emulate the clock drift per node requires dedicated hardware. Second if the experiment highlights a statistical behavior, the actual clock drift per node must be precisely measured. Even so the real clock drift can still evolve by a great margin with time and temperature. Lastly due to hardware cost and the difficulty of setting up, these experiments are generally limited to a handful of nodes and in duration.

The use of discrete event simulation allows to overcome much of this complexity along with complete control of the environment parameters within the limits of the models provided in the simulator. In this paper, we evaluate the limited support for clock drift modeling in one of the prominent simulators, COOJA and its companion node emulator, MSPSim. We first present inaccuracies observed in simulation and quantify to what extent this affects the results of experiments. We then propose and implement an alternative model that provides more accurate clock drift modeling. To demonstrate its usefulness, we use it to reproduce a well-documented RDC protocol synchronization issue [5].

Our paper is organized as follows. Section 2 presents an overview of the clock drift problem. Related work is discussed in Section 3.

Then we describe in Section 4, the execution model used in COOJA to emulate motes, as well as the existing clock drift model. In Section 5 we present an experiment to validate the simulation of the clock drift in COOJA and the inaccuracies we detected. We present and evaluate, in Section 6, a new implementation for accurate modeling of the clock drift in WSN simulation. Using this new model, we reproduce a synchronization issue that affects ContikiMAC in Section 7. Finally, in Section 8, we draw concluding remarks and suggest further work.

2 CLOCK DRIFT

The problem of clock source stability and its characterization has been regularly studied since the early-1960's [3, 4]. Ideally a noise-free non-drifting oscillator would generate a pure periodic signal at its output. However oscillators are influenced to some extent by their environment and manufacturing process tolerances. As a result, ambient temperature, supply voltages, magnetic fields or physical vibrations, to mention a few, can change the observed frequency.

This deviation is generally considered to be a combination of first a systematic, deterministic trend whose parameters can be predicted and second a random noise, characterized as a nondeterministic function of time. In [3], the authors model these two contributions

$$x(t) = \underbrace{x_0 + y_0 t + 1/2\, D t^2}_{\text{systematic trend}} + \underbrace{\varepsilon_x(t)}_{\text{random noise}} \qquad (1)$$

where $x(t)$ is the time deviation of the clock, x_0 the time offset, y_0 the frequency offset and D the frequency drift. In the context of this paper we are interested in the y_0 frequency offset parameter, a dimensionless ratio of deviation from the nominal frequency of the oscillator, which we denote here as the *clock drift*.

3 RELATED WORK

Numerous simulators dedicated to the study of Wireless Sensor Networks are available [14]. Among those, instruction-level simulators combine a mote emulator which allows executing the firmware as it would be on a real device and a network wide simulator which handles the coordination of events such as radio transmission between multiple motes. However, to our knowledge only a few instruction-level simulators provide a mechanism to configure the clock drift.

In this paper, we focus on the COOJA [15] simulator along with its companion mote emulator, MSPSim. COOJA is one of the most used simulators as is attested by a recent survey [11] which shows that 63 % of the papers on RPL routing protocol studies relied on COOJA to run their simulations. Although TI MSP430 based motes are quite old compared to modern solutions available for use in WSN, they are still frequently used along with COOJA for experiments and prototyping purposes [2, 10, 12, 17, 18]. COOJA specifies a clock deviation parameter which can be individually configured for each mote in the simulation. As an example, COOJA was used in [16] to induce a clock error in the nodes and assess the performance of a proposed optimisation of TSCH.

Renode [13], a more recent mote emulator, supports more modern platforms but is not widely used at this time. It does not seem to provide support for clock deviation. However, its simulation model

is similar to that of COOJA/MSPSim, meaning that it could be applied the same approach as in this paper. WSim and WSNet from the Worldsens environment [9] allow to configure the drift individually on each clock of the motes by using a nanosecond simulation step. However this simulator is seldom used and is unmaintained since 2011. The OpenWSN [20] framework provides support for mote-specific clock drift in its dedicated simulator, OpenSim. It is unclear however how the drift is modeled in OpenSim. OMNeT++ and the Castalia extension support modeling the clock drift [8]. OpenSim and OMNeT++ are not instruction-level simulators. That is, they are unable to run the firmware of motes unmodified.

4 COOJA/MSPSIM EXECUTION MODEL

In this section we present the model for concurrent execution of nodes in the COOJA simulator and MSPSim MSP430 mote emulator. Later, in Section 4.2, we present the current implementation of the deviation parameter, the model component responsible for the simulation of the clock drift.

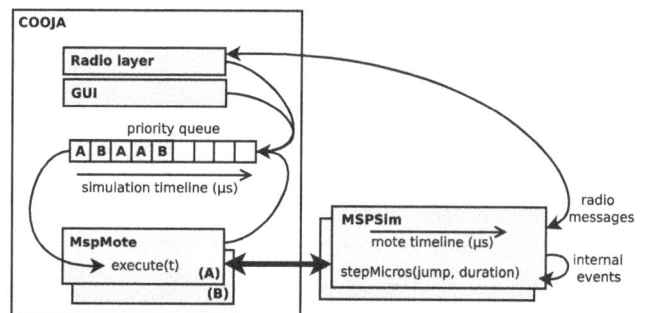

Figure 1: The COOJA/MSPSim simulator.

Figure 1 presents a high-level overview of the interactions between COOJA and MSPSim. Two timelines are involved during the simulation, a *simulation timeline* for the set of all motes and a *mote timeline* for each mote emulator. Both timelines have a microsecond precision and are discrete for performance reasons.

In COOJA, a priority queue schedules the executions of the motes along the simulator-specific timeline. Further execution on this queue are scheduled either by the motes own internal events, for instance timers, or scheduled by external events such as physical interactions from the GUI, peripherals and exchanged radio messages.

Each MSP mote in the simulation is coupled with an instance of the MSPSim mote emulator with its own distinct timeline. Normally both the mote and simulation timelines stay synchronized throughout the simulation and on each execution step the simulator advances the mote timeline proportionally to simulation time.

The same coupling also exists for the Avrora AVR motes emulator albeit with a different timeline precision. Contiki motes on their part run native versions of the Contiki OS. Hence their internal timelines are related to the host running the simulator. This distinction between simulation and emulation facilitates the integration of third-party emulators. It also enables the implementation of clock drift, described in Section 4.2, when not directly supported by the emulator as it is the case with MSPSim and Avrora.

4.1 Execution without deviation

We first detail the execution model of COOJA and the mote emulator MSPSim when no clock deviation is requested. Figure 2 illustrates the COOJA execution model for two simulation steps. The top timeline belongs to COOJA while the bottom timelines belong to a single emulated mote. The *cycles* timeline represents the internal mote time in term of CPU cycles.

At time t_0, the mote is scheduled for execution in the simulator. This triggers a period Δ, fixed in COOJA to 1 μs, for the emulator to evaluate instructions. To this end, MSPSim fixes itself a deadline Δ μs in the future during which it executes instructions and registers the elapsed cycles until the deadline is exceeded. At the end of this period, MSPSim reports the resulting possible advance on its own timeline to the simulator which accordingly schedules the next mote execution.

When MSPSim cycles count reaches the deadline c_1, it does not change its mote timeline yet. Hence the internal mote timeline is still at t_0. Instead it returns and waits for COOJA to provide it on the next execution step with the jump value necessary to keep track of the time advance. So at the next execution step t_1, COOJA reports to MSPSim that Δ μs has elapsed since its last execution. Accordingly MSPSim advances its mote timeline of Δ μs allowing both simulation and mote timelines to resynchronize.

At t_1 simulation time, COOJA again executes the mote and the same instruction evaluation process is reiterated. Now however one instruction switches the CPU off, triggering a long sleep period. From programmed timers, the emulator knows the exact cycles count c_3 at which the next internal event should be triggered and reports this duration to the simulator. Hence the simulator only schedules the next mote execution until t_2, taking the reported sleep period into account. This allows both simulator and emulator to avoid execution during sleep periods resulting in a substantial speedup.

This also explains why the responsability for the mote timeline advance is left to the simulator. Should an external interrupt occur during the sleep period, the simulator must be able to prematurely wake-up the mote, providing it with a jump value shorter than the initially intended sleep period.

Listing 1 and 2 present a simplified version of the execution model as it is currently implemented in COOJA and MSPSim. The grayed parts are only specific to the deviation parameter presented in the next section and can be ignored for this section.

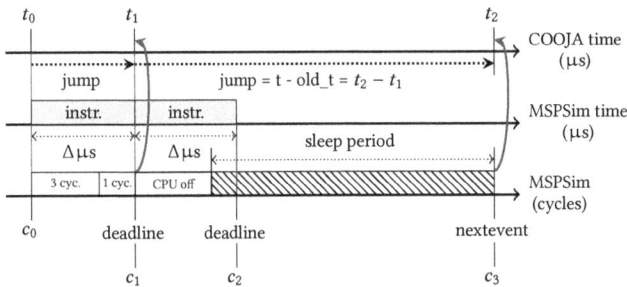

Figure 2: Two execution steps in COOJA and MSPSim.

```
1  MOTE_PARAMETER(deviation)
2  skipped = 0                                    deviation
3  total   = 0
4
5  old_t = 0
6  Δ = 1 # μs
7
8  def execute(t):
9    jump = t - old_t
10
11   if (1 - deviation) * total > skipped:
12     skipped += 1
13     jump    -= 1                                deviation
14     scheduleNextExecution(t + 1)
15   total += 1
16
17   step_duration  = MSPSim.stepMicros(jump, Δ)
18   step_duration += Δ
19
20   scheduleNextExecution(t + step_duration)
21
22   old_t = t
```

Listing 1: Execution of a mote in COOJA.

```
1  cycles = 0
2  micros = 0
3
4  def stepMicros(jump, duration):
5    micros    += jump
6    deadline  = ((micros + duration) * mcuFrqMHz)
7
8    while (cycles < deadline):
9      if cpuoff:
10       cycles  = MIN(deadline, nextevent)
11     else:
12       cycles += emulateOP()
13
14   if cpuoff:
15     sleep_cycles = nextevent - cycles
16     return sleep_cycles / mcuFrqMHz
17   else:
18     return 0
```

Listing 2: Execution of a mote in MSPSim.

The execution model for COOJA presented in Listing 1 is very simple. The simulator retains the last mote execution in the global variable `old_t`. Line 9 uses this variable to calculate the duration since the last execution, which we call the *jump* value. Line 17 triggers an execution step of Δ μs and provides MSPSim with the jump value previously calculated. MSPSim then reports the resulting possible advance on its mote timeline which the simulator uses to schedule the next mote execution on line 20.

Listing 2 presents the emulator side of the execution model. Line 5 uses the jump value provided by COOJA to resynchronize the mote timeline. Line 6 fixes a deadline for a Δ μs instruction evaluation period. Those instructions are evaluated in the loop at lines 8-12. Then the emulator reports the possible advance on its own timeline at lines 14-18.

4.2 Execution with deviation

In the simple execution model presented in Section 4.1, the simulation and the motes timelines were constantly synchronized. When clock drift is involved however, the simulator deliberately desynchronizes the mote-specific timeline from the simulation timeline to emulate a deviation of the mote clock from its base frequency. This can be configured in COOJA with the *deviation* parameter which this section describes.

The goal of this parameter is to run each mote on its own timescale, hence simulating a parametrable clock drift per mote. The resulting clock drift would be observable on all clock sources used in the microcontroller. The mote emulator supports two different clock sources, the main one driving the execution of instructions and a real-time clock. Both clocks are equally influenced by the deviation. Using the same notation as Section 2, it is expressed $d = 1 - y_0$ considering the other parameters of the model $x_0 = D = \varepsilon_x(t) = 0$. Its value cannot be greater than one. As a result it is only possible to run motes clocks slower than their base frequency.

The implementation of the deviation is a challenging task. The simulation can run at a microsecond granularity for multiple motes. Hence the complexity of the implementation would greatly impact the running time of the simulation as a whole. Thus, to limit the complexity, the simulation and motes timelines are all discretes. The deviation parameter, however, is a floating number and rounding errors accumulate for each execution step. Also the duration for each execution step is not constant when sleep is enabled. Still the implementation must maintain the microsecond precision for all other motes in the simulation.

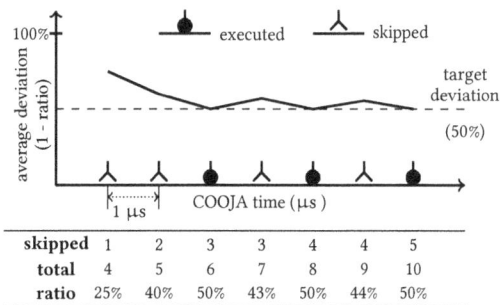

Figure 3: Convergence of the average deviation ratio.

The gray parts in Listing 1 present the current mechanism handling the deviation parameter in COOJA. In the implementation the execution speed of the mote is adjusted by skipping the execution until the requested deviation ratio is reached. Two counters, `skipped` and `total`, retain the number of skipped and the total number of execution steps which are the COOJA equivalent of the mote Δ µs evaluation period presented in Figure 2. These values are then used to compute the average deviation ratio at the beginning of each execution and decide whether to skip the current execution step or not.

This mechanism is illustrated on Figure 3. Steps are skipped as long as the two counters verify the inequation

$$\frac{\text{skipped}}{\text{total}} < 1 - \text{deviation} \qquad (2)$$

Thus the average deviation ratio, $1 - \frac{\text{skipped}}{\text{total}}$, quickly converges to the target deviation of 50%. Once the target deviation is reached, it is easy to observe that the error to the target deviation stays less or equal to $\frac{1}{\text{total}}$.

There are multiple remarks worth noting concerning this implementation. Since the implementation can only increment the number of skipped execution step, it only works for deviation values below the base frequency. Secondly it assumes that the timeline advances with a constant step, in this case Δ µs. This is not the case when low power modes are enabled and the mote can enter into a sleeping state for long durations. This is the origin of the effective clock drift inaccuracies which we explain in the next section.

5 MODEL INACCURACIES

In this section, we present an experiment to assess the validity of the current implementation for the simulation of the clock drift in COOJA. We observe inaccuracies and pinpoint their origin.

5.1 Experimental validation of clock drift

The goal of our experiment is to measure the actual clock drift observed in simulation by adjusting the deviation parameter. To do so, we measure at regular interval the number of CPU cycles elapsed since the mote started and we correlate this value on the simulation timeline in microseconds. We then use linear regression to infer the observed frequency for the simulated mote, thus the observed deviation from its base frequency.

For this experiment, we wrote a custom MSP430 firmware with a recurring parametrable sleep period. Our measurement of the number of CPU cycles happens at each node wake up. We also made sure that the firmware does not change the CPU clock speed after it has been configured. The CPU is configured to a frequency of 3.9 MHz and stays the same for all the simulations in our study.

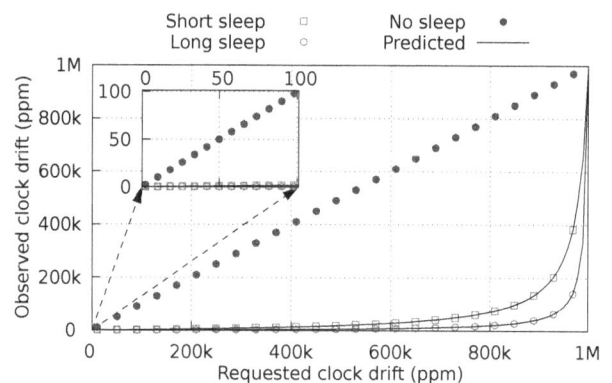

Figure 4: Comparison of observed to requested drift with a zoom on more realistic drift values from 0 to 100 ppm.

We ran this experiment for values of the drift y_0 from 0 to 99%. Recall that in COOJA the deviation d is expressed as $d = 1 - y_0$, hence this translates to deviation parameter values from 100% down to 1%. Each simulation was run for one hour simulation time. We then compared the observed deviation from the base frequency to the requested deviation. Figure 4 shows this comparison, expressed in parts per million (ppm) drift from the base frequency (bottom and left axes).

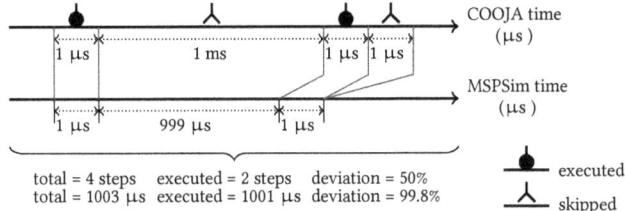

Figure 5: Origin of deviation parameter inaccuracies.

To reduce energy consumption, a firmware can switch the MCU to a sleep operating mode known as Low Power Mode (LPM). Contiki OS for example does this as soon as there is no event left on its scheduler. Figure 4 shows that when this LPM is disabled the observed clock drift exactly matches the value requested by the configured deviation parameter (see dataset "No sleep").

However when LPM is enabled, the observed clock drift lies far below its expected value. In our experiments, the firmware wakes up at a regular interval to toggle an LED and keeps the MCU in LPM for the remaining of the time. To assess the impact of sleep duration, we used two different wake-up intervals : 0.98 ms ("Short sleep") and 3.91 ms ("Long sleep") which correspond respectively to 32 and 128 ticks of the real-time clock running at 32768 Hz. We observe that with a requested deviation of 50% from the base frequency of 3.9 MHz and with a sleep interval of 0.98 ms, the observed frequency is 3.83 MHz instead of the expected 1.95 MHz. The longer sleep duration of 3.91 ms leads to an even larger error with an observed frequency of 3.88 MHz.

One can argue that deviations of 50% from the base frequency are seldom encountered in real clocks. For this reason, Figure 4 also zooms on smaller drift values ranging from 0 to 100 ppm. For those smaller deviations the error between observed and requested clock drift remains large and grows almost linearly.

Based on our understanding of the interaction between LPM and the clock drift model, we built a mathematical model that predicts the magnitude of the clock drift errors, from the requested deviation d and a variable α that summarizes the LPM behaviour, that is the average duration for the CPU sleep intervals in the firmware (see Eq. 3). The plain curves shown on Figure 4 and entitled "Predicted" perfectly match the observed values.

$$D(d, \alpha) = \frac{d(\alpha + 1)}{d\alpha + 1} \tag{3}$$

5.2 Inaccuracies origin

From the previous results, we know that the origin of the drift inaccuracies is bound to the sleep mechanism. Further experimentations have shown that the duration of the sleep periods also has an impact on the resulting clock drift.

To understand the origin of these inaccuracies, we take a look at the mote and simulation timelines when a sleep period occurs. This situation is presented in Figure 5 for a target deviation of 50%, although the reasoning also holds for other values of the deviation parameter. For simplicity, we consider that Δ is 1 µs long which is the case of the current implementation.

On this figure, we represent for each step on the COOJA timeline the duration to the last execution. That is the value of `jump` at line 9 in Listing 1. On the MSPSim timeline instead, we represent the value of `jump` passed to `stepMicros()` at line 17. That is after it has eventually been updated by the deviation condition at lines 11-14. If the condition is verified, the current step is considered as *skipped* and the value of `jump` decremented by 1 µs . Otherwise, the step is considered as *executed* and the value of `jump` left unchanged. It is this jump value which, passed to the emulator, dictates the advance of time on the mote timeline.

In the example, one of the step follows a sleep period resulting in a jump value of 1 ms. The other steps are normal execution resulting in jump values of 1 µs each. Counting the number of execution steps we have 2 *executed* over 4 steps in total, thus reaching a deviation of 50% from the point of view of the implementation. However, computing the ratio of time elapsed on both timelines, we have 1001 µs of executed mote time over 1003 µs of total simulation time, thus reaching an actual deviation of 99.8%. Thus, the origin of the inaccuracies lies in the discrepancies between the implementation assumption of execution steps with a constant duration of 1 µs , and sleep periods which are generally much larger than that.

6 ACCURATE DRIFT MODEL

In this section, we present a new algorithm to implement the deviation parameter. Then we evaluate its performance and show that it can accurately reproduce the requested clock drift for the same time complexity.

The implementation of the deviation parameter in COOJA has the particularity of being independent from the underlying mote emulators. We follow the same approach and implement the new algorithm in the COOJA execution model. Thus, it does not require modification in the motes emulators code, nor extensive changes inside COOJA. Also, since the usage of the deviation parameter does not change, it is possible to reuse the simulation setup of previous studies without any adaptation.

The current implementation uses step counters to compute the average deviation ratio and decide whether to skip or execute the current execution step. When sleep is involved, however, execution steps have a variable duration resulting in an incorrect deviation. Our solution uses a different approach and applies the deviation directly on the mote and simulation timelines carefully handling the resulting rounding errors.

This new algorithm continuously adjusts the advance in the mote timeline to reproduce the requested clock drift. Since the timelines are discrete, rounding errors need to be compensated to avoid their accumulation during the simulation. To do so, rounding errors are carried on the following execution steps.

Figure 6 illustrates a general working case for our new implementation starting with a mote execution scheduled at time t. At this point the simulator knows the duration since the last execution of the mote. Thus in the absence of clock deviation it must advance the mote timeline for a duration $j = t - \text{old\_t}$. When deviation exists this jump is corrected by multiplying j with the deviation parameter d and rounded down resulting in a jump error ε_j. It is important that the correction be rounded down instead of up so that the resulting advance in the mote timeline does not fall beyond

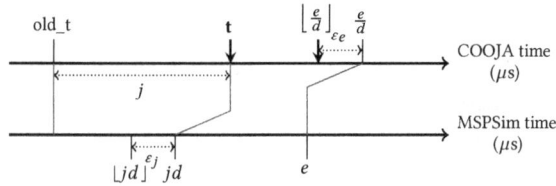

Figure 6: New implementation of the deviation parameter.

the emulator internal cycles limit. That is, that the value provided to the emulator does not jump beyond the next internal event or the current cycles count value. Doing so would result in an immediate abort of the simulation.

The executed instructions would eventually program an event e at some point in the future on the mote timeline and switch the CPU off until then. The emulator would return the duration to this event in term of its mote timeline to the simulator. Hence the simulator must anew correct this value taking into account the clock deviation by dividing e with the deviation parameter d, and schedule the next execution for this mote. Again this value must be rounded down to fit the discrete timeline resulting in an execution error ε_e.

With these double corrections alone, the rounding errors ε_j and ε_e would accumulate on each execution, quickly deviating from the requested clock drift. To counteract this effect for ε_j the algorithm keeps track of the accumulated error and carries a single timeline step when necessary. For ε_e the error would result in a mote scheduled earlier in the simulation than intended by the mote. Hence on the next mote execution, the advance on the mote timeline would end before the planned next mote event e. This gap would be reported by the emulator and carried on the next execution as a single step thus bounding the accumulated error ε_e similarly to ε_j.

With these two mechanisms the accumulated error for ε_e on the simulation timeline and ε_j on the mote timeline always stays

```
1  MOTE_PARAMETER(deviation)
2
3  old_t      = 0
4  jumpError  = 0.0
5  Δ = 1 # μs
6
7  def execute(t):
8      jump        = t - old_t
9      exactJump   = jump * deviation
10     jump        = floor(exactJump)
11
12     jumpError += exactJump - jump
13
14     if jumpError > 1.0:
15         jump += 1
16         jumpError -= 1.0
17
18     step_duration  = MSPSim.stepMicros(jump, Δ)
19     step_duration += Δ
20     step_duration  = floor(step_duration / deviation)
21
22     scheduleNextExecution(t + step_duration)
23     old_t = t
```

Listing 3: New implementation of the deviation parameter.

below 1 μs . The combination results in an error $\varepsilon_S = \varepsilon_e + \frac{\varepsilon_j}{d}$ on the simulation timeline. Thus at any point in the simulation, the instantaneous error for the execution of a particular mote on the simulation timeline is at worst $1 + \frac{1}{d}$ μs .

Listing 3 presents a simplified version of our new drift algorithm integrated in the COOJA execution model. Similarly to the previous implementation, the simulator retains the last mote execution in the global variable old_t. Lines 8-10 apply the deviation parameter to the advance on the mote timeline. Line 12 accumulates the jump error ε_j. Once the accumulated jump error exceeds 1 μs , lines 15-16 carry 1 μs on the current jump value, thus keeping the accumulated error below 1 μs . Again, line 16 triggers an execution step of Δ μs and provide MSPSim with the advance on its mote timeline. Line 20 converts the value returned by MSPSim from the mote back to the simulation timeline. Finally the simulator uses this value to schedule the next mote execution on line 22.

Again these changes only impact the mote execution model in COOJA and do not require any modification on the emulator side. Hence, they are non-intrusive and remain compatible with other supported emulators.

6.1 Achieved accuracy

We assessed the accuracy of the new implementation by conducting the same experiments presented in Section 5. In the results that follow we report the absolute clock drift error, that is the absolute difference in ppm between the clock drift value requested via the deviation parameter and the clock drift value observed at the end of a one hour simulation.

Figure 7 presents the clock drift error for very large values of the requested clock drift up to 1 million ppm. For all measurements the absolute clock drift error stays below 2.5×10^{-6} ppm. For requested clock drift values below 500000 ppm, the resulting clock drift error is even lower and stays below 1.5×10^{-10} ppm. Above this value, the drift gets so large that all the clocks run very slowly. Hence, not only are the time measurement from the firmware less precise, but only a very small subset of the measurements points are available to estimate the observed clock drift, resulting in a larger error.

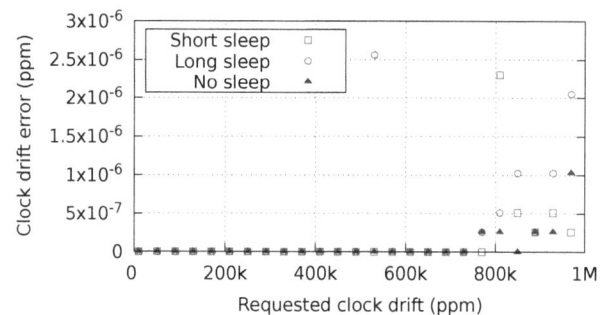

Figure 7: Clock drift error with the new drift algorithm.

For smaller, more realistic values of the clock drift in the range 0 to 100 ppm, the absolute clock drift error is 0 ppm. That is, we measure no error. At this point the absolute clock drift error is so small that it falls below the machine floating point precision.

6.2 Impact on simulation time

We also look at the time complexity of the new implementation. Figure 8 compares the duration of both the new and old implementation for 100 runs of a 600 s simulation and a sleep duration of 0.98 ms. This comparison is done for three values of the deviation parameter, 75 % of the base frequency, 10ppm from the base frequency and no clock drift at all with a deviation parameter of 100 %.

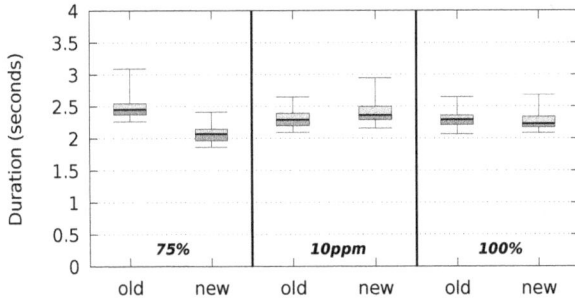

Figure 8: Duration of the execution of the legacy and new clock drift models for various values of the deviation. Minimum, 1st quartile, median, 3rd quartile and maximum are represented for each set of runs.

In all cases, the complexity of both algorithms stays in the same order of magnitude. However, with a deviation parameter of 75 % the new implementation is faster than the older version. In the old implementation the observed clock drift for a deviation of 75 % would be much lower than requested. As a result the node clock would run at a much higher frequency than initially intended. Hence, the additional execution steps contribute to the higher complexity of the simulation run.

With a smaller clock drift of 10 ppm instead, the new implementation is slightly slower. In this case, the complexity of the new algorithm outweighs the time benefit of a more accurate clock drift. However, since most simulations do not require clock deviation, the implementation bypasses all computations when no drift is requested. As a result the new implementation is also slightly faster in the common simulation scenario with the deviation parameter to its default value of 100 %, that is, when no clock drift is requested.

7 APPLICATION: CONTIKIMAC BLACKOUTS

In this section, we compare the new and legacy clock drift in a simulation experiment that aims to reproduce a behavior induced by the clock drift in real nodes. In particular we aim to show that the legacy clock drift cannot reproduce the behavior in simulation while our new implementation can.

In 2016, Uwaze et al. discovered PDR and latency inconsistencies for messages exchanged using the ContikiMAC RDC protocol [5, 19]. These inconsistencies appeared as periodic consecutive loss of packets called *blackouts* and were observed in a real testbed but not in simulation. Careful analysis of the radio traffic pinpointed the origin of these blackouts to recurring timing errors in the operation of ContikiMAC combined with the relative clock drift that happens

between real nodes. In this case, the drift causes the phase of the sender and receiver to become orthogonal hence preventing the reception of packets for a certain period.

With ContikiMAC, motes wake up asynchronously following a common duty cycle. When a mote has a frame to send, it transmits it repeatedly until an ACK frame is received and does so at most for the duration of a wake-up cycle. Since the phase difference between sender and receiver is arbitrary, a receiver may wake up at any time during the sender transmission. The receiver detects an incoming frame by performing two consecutive Clear Channel Assessments (CCA). If any of the two CCAs detects a signal, the receiver remains awaken to catch the incoming frame. Then, if the receiver is the destination, it sends an ACK frame.

In order for this scheme to work properly, some timing constraints must be satisfied, as illustrated on Figure 9. To ensure that a receiver has the opportunity to transmit an ACK frame, two consecutive DATA frames must be spaced by a time t_i which is longer than the ACK transmission time. The time between the receiver two CCAs is t_c. This time must be chosen so that two consecutive CCAs cannot fall between two DATA frames. The CCA length is t_r. Finally, we denote by t_s the transmission duration of a DATA frame.

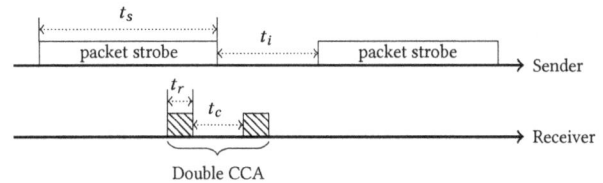

Figure 9: ContikiMAC timing parameters.

According to Uwaze et al. study of the problem, the blackout would last $(t_i \, t_c)/\delta f$ and repeat every $(t_s + t_i)/\delta f$ seconds, where δf is the relative clock drift. We tried to reproduce the same experiment in COOJA. To this end, we implemented a simple IPv6 UDP ping application in Contiki OS that sends each second a fixed packet of 65 Bytes from a sender to a receiver node. To ensure that the traffic never changes, we disabled RPL and IPv6 periodic neighbor discoveries and announcements. We also disabled CSMA to measure the behavior of ContikiMAC itself. Table 1 presents the measured values for t_s, t_i, t_c and t_r from our simulation.

Table 1: Measured value of the ContikiMAC parameters for the blackouts experiment in COOJA.

Parameter	Value (μs)
t_s	2082 ± 13
t_i	1367 ± 6
t_c	612 ± 0
t_r	333 ± 1

We use the COOJA deviation parameter to induce different clock drifts on the receiver node. Then we identify recurring loss of packets in the trace and measure their periodicity and duration.

Table 2 lists the characteristics of those blackouts for a clock drift parameter of 50 and 20 ppm with the new drift implementation. The simulation also allowed us to better refine the theoretical model from Uwaze et al. For the duration of the blackouts we now have $(t_i - t_c - t_r)/\delta f$.

Table 2: Periodicity and duration of the blackouts for the legacy and new implementation of the clock drift.

	New (s)	Theory (s)	Refined (s)
50 ppm			
Period	67.47 ± 10.01	68.98	68.98
Duration	6.64 ± 1.05	15.10	8.44
20 ppm			
Period	168.26 ± 21.82	172.44	172.44
Duration	17.93 ± 2.36	37.76	21.1

While the blackouts characteristics with the new drift implementation match the theoretical value observed on real nodes, the same cannot be said for the legacy drift implementation. Indeed, in the latter case, we did not observe regular loss of packets, hence resulting in a totally different outcome for the experiment.

8 CONCLUSION

Modeling clock drift is important to assess the validity of time-dependent algorithms and protocols such as for example Radio-Duty Cycling MAC protocols. To this end, some network simulators provide a means to make the clocks of nodes deviate from each other. This is the case with COOJA, one of the most frequently used simulator in the field of Wireless Sensor Networks. In this paper, we evaluate experimentally the clock drift model of COOJA. We show that in some cases, the observed clock deviation lies far from the requested one. Our results show errors as high as 90 % even for small requested deviations in the ppm range.

We identify the origin of these inaccuracies in an unsuspected interaction with modeling the low-power mode (LPM) of nodes. LPM is used extensively by most WSN firmwares to save on energy consumption. As a consequence, we suspect that a large fraction of simulations are affected by these inaccuracies. To understand the origin of clock deviation inaccuracies, we explain the inner workings of COOJA and its interaction with the MSPSim emulator. We also discuss the design decisions made by the authors of these tools to make the simulation of a large number of nodes scalable, such as using discrete timelines. We confirm our understanding by building an analytical model of the clock deviation error that we confront to our experimental data and show perfect match. In the end, we show that the clock deviation errors depend on the sleeping behaviour of the firmware, but in any case remain in the order of more than 89 % of the requested drift.

We then propose, implement and validate a modified algorithm to support accurate clock deviations within COOJA. We show that our algorithm keeps the error on the deviation no more than 2.5×10^{-6} ppm for all values of the requested clock drift. We also show that the improved algorithm only slightly affects the real-time

duration of simulations. In the future this could also be applied to other simulators such as the newcoming Renode or extended with a more complete drift model. Finally, to show the benefit of our new model, we apply it to reproduce a synchronization issue in a well-known RDC protocol, ContikiMAC, that causes periodic blackouts. To date, this issue was observed in a testbed but was previously impossible to reproduce through simulation.

ACKNOWLEDGMENTS

We thank Aris Koutsiamanis, Maximilien Charlier, Georgios Papadopoulos and Jacques Tiberghien for their comments on previous versions of this manuscript.

REFERENCES

[1] 2015. IEEE Standard for Local and metropolitan area networks - Part 15.4. *IEEE Std. 802.15.4-2015* (2015).

[2] S. Alharby, N. Harris, A. Weddell, and J. Reeve. 2018. Impact of duty cycle protocols on security cost of IoT. In *Information and Communication Systems (ICICS), 2018 9th International Conference on*. IEEE, 25–30.

[3] D. W. Allan et al. 1987. Time and frequency(time-domain) characterization, estimation, and prediction of precision clocks and oscillators. *IEEE transactions on ultrasonics, ferroelectrics, and frequency control* 34, 6 (1987), 647–654.

[4] J. A. Barnes et al. 1971. Characterization of frequency stability. *IEEE transactions on instrumentation and measurement* 1001, 2 (1971), 105–120.

[5] M. Bezunartea, B. Sartori, J. Tiberghien, and K. Steenhaut. 2017. Tackling Malfunctions Caused by Radio Duty Cycling Protocols That Do Not Appear in Simulation Studies. In *Proceedings of the First ACM FAILSAFE Workshop*. 10–15.

[6] A. Dunkels. 2011. *The ContikiMAC Radio Duty Cycling Protocol*. Technical Report. SICS.

[7] A. Elsts, S. Duquennoy, X. Fafoutis, G. Oikonomou, R. Piechocki, and I. Craddock. 2016. Microsecond-accuracy time synchronization using the IEEE 802.15.4 TSCH protocol. In *Proceedings of IEEE SenseApp*.

[8] F. Ferrari, A. Meier, and L. Thiele. 2010. Accurate Clock Models for Simulating Wireless Sensor Networks. In *Proceedings of the 3rd International ICST Conference on Simulation Tools and Techniques (SIMUTools '10)*. Article 21, 4 pages.

[9] A. Fraboulet, G. Chelius, and E. Fleury. 2007. Worldsens: development and prototyping tools for application specific wireless sensors networks. In *Proceedings of the 6th international conference on Information processing in sensor networks*.

[10] P. Ioulianou, V. Vasilakis, I. Moscholios, and M. Logothetis. 2018. A Signature-based Intrusion Detection System for the Internet of Things. *ICTF 2018* (2018).

[11] H.-s. Kim, J. Ko, D. Culler, and J. Paek. 2017. Challenging the IPv6 Routing Protocol for Low-Power and Lossy Networks (RPL): A Survey. *IEEE Communications Surveys and Tutorials* 19 (09 2017), 2502–2525.

[12] A. Kokkinis, A. Paphitis, L. Kanaris, C. Sergiou, and S. Stavrou. 2018. Physical and Network Layer Interconnection Module for Realistic Planning of IoT Sensor Networks. In *EWSN*.

[13] Antmicro Ltd. 2018. Renode - documentation. https://media.readthedocs.org/pdf/renode/latest/renode.pdf.

[14] I. Minakov, R. Passerone, A. Rizzardi, and S. Sicari. 2016. A Comparative Study of Recent Wireless Sensor Network Simulators. *ACM Transactions on Sensor Networks* 12, 3 (July 2016), 20:1–20:39.

[15] F. Osterlind, A. Dunkels, J. Eriksson, N. Finne, and Th. Voigt. 2006. Cross-level sensor network simulation with COOJA. In *Proceedings of the 31st IEEE conference on Local computer networks*.

[16] G. Z. Papadopoulos, A. Mavromatis, X. Fafoutis, N. Montavont, R. Piechocki, Th. Tryfonas, and G. Oikonomou. 2016. Guard time optimisation and adaptation for energy efficient multi-hop TSCH networks. In *Proceedings of IEEE WF-IoT*.

[17] A. P. Plageras, K. E. Psannis, Ch. Stergiou, H. Wang, and B. B. Gupta. 2018. Efficient IoT-based sensor BIG Data collection–processing and analysis in smart buildings. *Future Generation Computer Systems* 82 (2018), 349–357.

[18] N. Ramachandran, V. Perumal, S. Gopinath, and M. Jothi. 2018. Sensor Search Using Clustering Technique in a Massive IoT Environment. In *Industry Interactive Innovations in Science, Engineering and Technology*. Springer, 271–281.

[19] M.-P. Uwase, M. Bezunartea, J. Tiberghien, J.-M. Dricot, and K. Steenhaut. 2016. Poster: ContikiMAC, some critical issues with the CC2420 Radio.. In *EWSN*. 257–258.

[20] Th. Watteyne, X. Vilajosana, B. Kerkez, F. Chraim, K. Weekly, Q. Wang, S. Glaser, and K. Pister. 2012. OpenWSN: A Standards-Based Low-Power Wireless Development Environment. *ETT* 23 (08 2012), 480–493.

[21] W. Ye and J. Heidemann. 2004. Medium access control in wireless sensor networks. In *Wireless sensor networks*. Springer, 73–91.

HiPR: High-Precision UWB Ranging for Sensor Networks

Daniel Neuhold
University of Klagenfurt, Institute of
Networked and Embedded Systems,
Austria

Christian Bettstetter
University of Klagenfurt, Institute of
Networked and Embedded Systems,
Austria

Andreas F. Molisch
University of Southern California,
Viterbi School of Engineering, CA,
USA

ABSTRACT

We present a distance estimation technique based on ultra-wideband time-of-arrival measurements and assess it with IEEE 802.15.4-2011 devices by Decawave. Experiments show that our technique is about 30 times faster than Decawave's out-of-the-box solution, which can be exploited to improve the precision by one order of magnitude.

CCS CONCEPTS

• **Networks → Network experimentation; Network performance analysis; Network measurement; Mobile networks**.

KEYWORDS

ultra-wideband; UWB; ranging; localization

ACM Reference Format:
Daniel Neuhold, Christian Bettstetter, and Andreas F. Molisch. 2019. HiPR: High-Precision UWB Ranging for Sensor Networks. In *22nd Int'l ACM Conference on Modeling, Analysis and Simulation of Wireless and Mobile Systems (MSWiM '19), November 25–29, 2019, Miami Beach, FL, USA.* ACM, New York, NY, USA, 5 pages. https://doi.org/10.1145/3345768.3355931

1 INTRODUCTION

There is a growing demand for indoor localization in logistics, robotics, monitoring, and other areas [2, 15, 16]. Many localization techniques share the need for *distance estimation*—also called *ranging*—between two or more devices. The distance estimates should be accurate (near true value) and precise (have low statistical variability). Furthermore, the estimation process should be fast, which is especially crucial for real-time control tasks.

We propose a ranging technique based on ultra-wideband (UWB) technology, called HiPR. It is designed to be much faster than the native solution implemented in off-the-shelf UWB transceivers from Decawave, one of the leading companies in UWB-based localization. Specifically, experiments show that HiPR obtains an estimate in about 1/30th of the time required by Decawave's solution. This gain is achieved by reducing the delay from the moment when a timestamp is made to the moment when it is actually sent. Our approach utilizes hardware interrupts and short dummy beacons to acquire and share the points in time of the transmissions. The actual timestamp values are communicated subsequently in a standard message. The significantly reduced acquisition time along with the

short beacons enables HiPR to perform a *burst* of estimates for a given distance in the period required by the native solution to perform a single estimate. With this iterative approach, HiPR achieves a precision one order of magnitude better than the native solution.

The paper is organized as follows: Section II describes the hardware platform. Section III discusses ranging and introduces the HiPR protocol. Section IV presents the experimental results. Section V addresses related work before Section VI concludes.

2 SYSTEM

Our UWB testbed was developed for industrial and aerospace environments [24–26]. It uses Decawave EVK1000 boards and a self-developed communication protocol with automatic node discovery and scheduling based on time division multiple access (TDMA). HiPR runs on top of this protocol. The board features an IEEE 802.15.4-2011-compliant transceiver [1], enabling a data rate of 6.8 Mbps and a packet length of 1023 bytes. The nodes are tuned to operate at a center frequency of 4.5 GHz (channel 3) and a bandwidth of 500 MHz. The preamble length is set to 64 symbols with a pulse repetition frequency of 64 MHz. The non-standard start-frame-delimiter and an extended physical layer header are used.

The system operates in a centralized manner, where one UWB node acts as an access point (AP) to manage node discovery, TDMA scheduling, and ranging procedure, as well as forwarding measured data to a computer for evaluation.

3 RANGING

3.1 Definitions: Error, Accuracy, and Precision

A measurement $i \in \mathbb{N}$ yields a distance estimate $\hat{d}_i$ between two nodes. The *error* of this estimation is given by the difference between $\hat{d}_i$ and the true distance d, defined by $\epsilon_i(d) = \hat{d}_i - d$. This error can in general be positive or negative, although it is always positive in our setup due to the nature of the error involved.

Ideally, a ranging technique is both accurate and precise. It is accurate if the average distance estimate is close to the true distance. Along these lines, the *accuracy* of a ranging technique for a given distance can be defined as the average value of the distance errors, i.e., $\bar{\epsilon}(d) = \frac{1}{n} \sum_{i=1}^{n} \epsilon_i(d)$ with a sufficiently high number of estimates n. A ranging technique is precise if the distance estimates are close to each other. The *precision* can therefore be defined as the variance of the distance errors, i.e., $\sigma_\epsilon^2(d) = \frac{1}{n-1} \sum_{i=1}^{n} (\epsilon_i(d) - \bar{\epsilon}(d))^2$.

3.2 Sources of Ranging Errors

The distance d between two devices can be computed from the time that a signal needs to travel between the devices, whereby this time is often called the time of flight (ToF). Both the native and our ranging technique use timestamps to mark the moments at which a message is transmitted and received. The difference between these timestamps—denoted as propagation time T_{prop}—is in general not equal to the true ToF. Possible reasons causing this deviation are imprecise clocks, imprecise synchronization, and imprecise timestamps.

The clock in a device runs slightly faster or slower than the nominal clock frequency f; say, it runs at kf with k close to 1. The EVK1000 board employs a 20 ppm crystal oscillator, which means that $0.999980 \leq k \leq 1.000020$. The clock-induced error in a distance measurement between two devices is [8]

$$T_{\text{ClkErr}} = T_{\text{prop}}\left(1 - \frac{k_1 + k_2}{2}\right), \qquad (1)$$

which yields some picoseconds only [8]. For example, a range of $d = 100\,\text{m}$ yields $T_{\text{ClkErr}} \approx 7\,\text{ps}$, which relates to $\epsilon < 3\,\text{mm}$.

In order to avoid ranging errors caused by inaccurate synchronization, we employ a protocol that eliminates the need for synchronization, for instance, the double-sided two-way ranging (DS-TWR) protocol with three messages (MSGs) shown in Fig. 1 [7]. TS marks the moments when timestamps are created for the transmission (TX) or reception (RX) of a message, with T_{prop} defining their difference. The timestamp difference between the transmission and acknowledgment of a message is referred to as T_{round} and T_{reply}, respectively. For each distance measurement i, the ToF can be estimated from the timestamps as follows [7]:

$$\widehat{\text{ToF}} = \frac{T_{\text{round1}}\,T_{\text{round2}} - T_{\text{reply1}}\,T_{\text{reply2}}}{T_{\text{round1}} + T_{\text{round2}} + T_{\text{reply1}} + T_{\text{reply2}}} \,. \qquad (2)$$

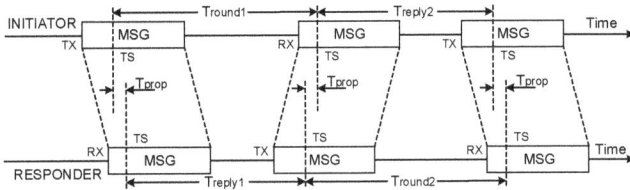

Figure 1: Double-sided two-way ranging protocol.

The limiting factor for precision is the time stamping process itself. A delay occurs between the timestamp generation and the actual moment when this message is physically sent or received. Whereas the antenna delay can be compensated by hardware calibration [9][1], HiPR reduces the additional nondeterministic error.

3.3 HiPR Protocol

We use beacons and hardware interrupts to capture the precise moment when a message is transmitted and received. Instead of adding a TX timestamp to the header of a message, we use hardware interrupts to trigger and timestamp the moment when a short beacon is emitted at the antenna. By reducing the delay between the message creation and the actual moment of transmission, we achieve more precise ToF estimations. HiPR embeds the timestamp of the beacon into a follow-up message of the DS-TWR protocol.

[1]The antenna delay is hardware-specific and therefore requires calibration of each individual sensor node. To reduce the calibration effort, reference values are provided by Decawave to account for this error [9].

Algorithm 1: HiPR Protocol with Error Handling

Data:
Number of distance measurements
Number re-iterations
Result:
Distance

```
/* Initiation */
Node Discovery;
Node Scheduling;
Establish Topology;
/* Start Ranging */
```
for *Number of Distance Measurements* **do**
    for *Number of Nodes* **do**
        `/* Execute the DS-TWR */`
        for *Three T_{prop} Measurements* **do**
            for *Number of Re-iterations* **do**
                `/* Error Handling */`
                if *Message Timeout Exceeded* **then**
                    Discard TX Timestamp;
                    Re-initiate the Message;
                else
                    Calculate T_{prop};
                    Collect Timestamps;
                end
            end
        `/* Calculate the Mean $T_{\text{prop}}$ */`
        $\bar{T}_{\text{prop}} = \text{Mean}(T_{\text{prop}})$;
    end
    `/* Use $T_{\text{round}}$ and $T_{\text{reply}}$ */`
    Calculate $\widehat{\text{ToF}}$;
    Return Distance;
end
`/* Optionally Broadcast Distance */`
Broadcast(Node IDs, Distances);
end

Furthermore, HiPR includes error handling, which detects and re-initiates lost messages. This enables us to repeat single measurements individually without the need to repeat the entire DS-TWR protocol. The re-initiation can further be used to quickly execute a larger number of consecutive measurements in each direction (e.g., initiator ⇆ responder). This avoids delays caused by frequent switches between transmission modes (e.g., transmission ⇆ reception) and consequently leads to a faster ToF acquisition.

The pseudocode shown in Alg. 1 states the logical sequence of HiPR. The protocol is flexibly designed to suit application-specific needs with the aim of supporting ranging tasks in a sensor network. In the initiation phase, sensor nodes are discovered and scheduled into a TDMA structure. The AP controls the scheduling of nodes and monitors the ranging progress.

Broadcasting of distance information in a ranging network permits 1) passively obtaining distances between pairs of nodes and 2) reducing the number of network-wide messages to populate distance information. A dedicated broadcast slot is therefore reserved in the TDMA structure to allow higher duty cycling and longer sleep periods of sensor nodes.

4 EXPERIMENTAL EVALUATION

This section presents an experimental assessment of HiPR and Decawave's ranging solution in terms of acquisition time, accuracy, and precision. The setup is a static office environment shown in Fig. 2. We operate one AP and one sensor node in a point-to-point manner and forward the acquired distance estimates to a computer. The AP remains fixed; the sensor node is placed at nine different distances from the AP. One thousand point-to-point measurements are made for each sensor location. The ground truth is established using a laser ranger with an accuracy of ± 2 mm (Bosch PLR 50 C). The antennas exhibit a deep notch on their vertical axis and a maximum gain on their perpendicular direction; we orient and tilt both antennas in a way that the main lobes of the AP and the sensor node face each other. All tests are performed under quasi-identical conditions.

In a first test series, we evaluate the acquisition time for a single location at $d = 2$ m. In a second test series, we assess the accuracy and precision for all distances.

4.1 Acquisition Time

In order to assess the time t_i required for a distance estimation i, we utilize the tick count to obtain the exact time from triggering to completion of a distance measurement at the microcontroller. In addition to the acquisition time for a single measurement, we are also interested in the value for multiple consecutive measurements, to assess the protocol overhead. The average acquisition time is $\bar{t} = \frac{1}{n} \sum_{i=1}^{n} t_i$ using $n = 1, 10, 100,$ or 1000 iterations. To obtain statistical validity, we perform 1000 estimates of $\bar{t}$ and compute

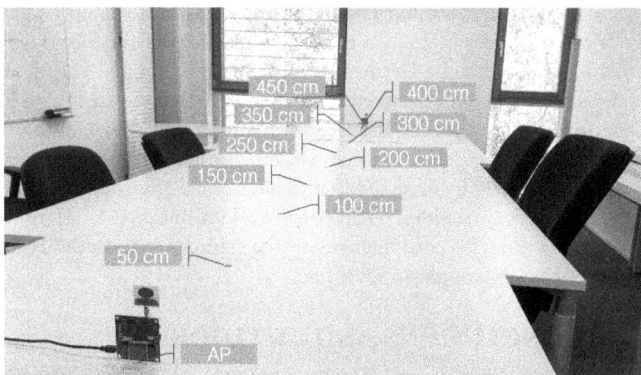

Figure 2: Static test environment with one access point and a single sensor node deployed at nine test locations between 50 cm and 450 cm marked as blue dots on the table.

Table 1: Average ranging acquisition times $\bar{T}$ in ms per iteration for Decawave's ranging application and HiPR.

	Number of iterations			
	1	10	100	1000
HiPR	25	14	12	11
Decawave out-of-the-box	881	564	508	506
Decawave time-optimized	761	426	389	387

its average $\bar{T}$. We expect $\bar{T}$ to decline with increasing n due to the overhead of initiating the DS-TWR protocol.

Decawave's ranging is operated in two variants: as the native, out-of-the-box version and as a modified, time-optimized version where we eliminate unnecessary peripheral interactions (e.g., LCD output, switching of LEDs).

Table 1 shows the acquisition times. A single measurement (first column) is expected to be completed in $\bar{T} = 25$ ms using HIPR, whereas it takes 881 ms (out-of-the-box) and 761 ms (time-optimized) with Decawave. This corresponds to a 30 times faster acquisition for HiPR compared with the time-optimized version of Decawave's ranging. The use of hardware interrupts outperforms the software-defined polling used by Decawave. Beyond this, the iterative approach for distance estimation distributes parts of the protocol overhead (e.g., ranging initiation) over many measurements. As expected, the average acquisition time declines with the number of iterations (other columns in Table 1). The gain of HiPR remains at a factor of several 10s. In the following, we use the time-optimized version of Decawave's ranging.

4.2 Accuracy and Precision

We now assess the accuracy and precision. Figure 3 shows histograms of the estimated distances at a true distance of $d = 200$ cm. Fitting a normal distribution shows that the mean values are similar for the two techniques (namely $\bar{\epsilon} = +29$ cm for HiPR and +27 cm for Decawave), although Decawave suffers from a higher variance (1.5 cm compared with 1.9 cm). Thus, in this particular setup, Decawave is slightly more accurate and HiPR is more precise. The histogram of HiPR appears to be symmetric around its mean.

This analysis is now extended to other distances. Due to its faster acquisition, HiPR is able to perform about 30 distance estimations when Decawave carries out one. Such multiple estimations can be exploited to either address multiple sensors or to perform multiple measurements with a single sensor to improve accuracy and precision. We focus on the second case. Each distance estimate by HiPR is the average value of 30 ToF estimates. The time required to collect and process the data equals the time required to obtain a single distance estimation with Decawave ranging.

Figure 4 shows the ranging error ϵ for different distances d. It can be observed that, in terms of accuracy, HiPR tends to have slightly lower ranging errors than Decawave for short distances but higher ones for longer distances. In terms of precision, HiPR always results in more precise ranging results. Its interquartile and interwhisker ranges are much smaller than those of Decawave ranging, for all

(a) HiPR

(b) Decawave ranging

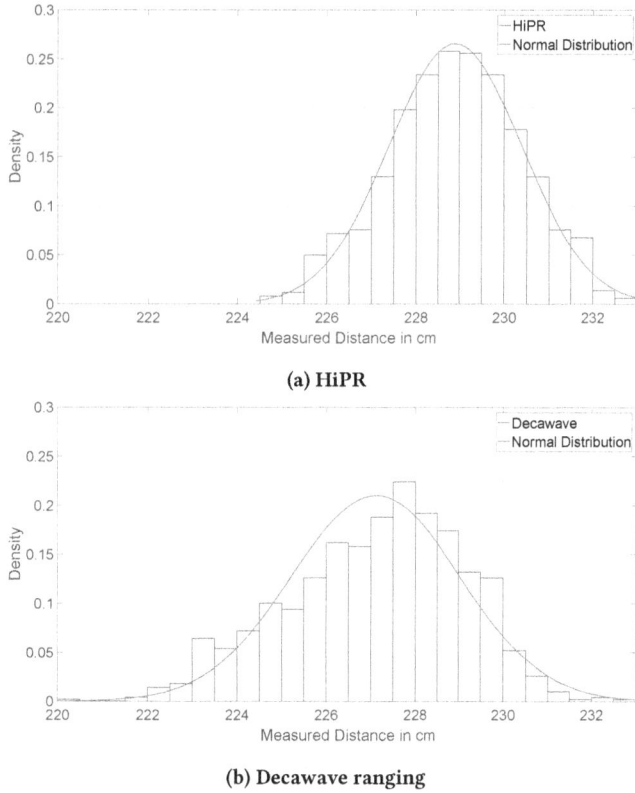

Figure 3: Histogram of measured distances for a true distance of two meters and distribution fitting.

(a) HiPR iterative

(b) Decawave ranging

Figure 4: Ranging accuracy over distance. The boxplots show the upper and lower quartiles (blue box), the median (horizontal red line in box), whiskers, and outliers (red +). The mean values are marked with a red dot and connected with a red line. A higher deviation of mean to median values indicates a larger skewness.

distances, and the number of outliers is much smaller. Its variance averaged over all distances is only 0.15 cm, compared with 6 cm, which is on average about 40 times more precise in this setup. The largest deviation occurred for a distance of one meter, where HiPR achieves an improvement by a factor of more than 100.

Overall, HiPR is superior if systematic errors can be compensated by a precise ranging technique.

5 RELATED WORK

Localization systems are categorized in many different ways, namely into technologies [6], parametric (e.g., position computed based on prior knowledge) and non-parametric localization techniques [5], and the type of sensors used [23]. Commonly-used positioning techniques consider radio signal strength (RSS), time of arrival (ToA), time difference of arrival (TDoA), angle of arrival (AoA) and hybrids therein [11, 13, 18, 20, 21, 27, 32, 36]. Indoor localization in particular is an emerging research field with various applications [2, 15, 16]. A comparison of different technologies [37] indicates that UWB is a potential candidate [3] for indoor localization with accurate ranging, a moderate power consumption and interference mitigating. We build upon the related work on localization [4] and tracking [19] and utilize Decawave's EVK1000 hardware platform with an ToA asymmetric two-way-ranging (TWR) approach [10, 14, 33]. The calibration, clock drift correction and time-of-flight error evaluation for the ToA TWR are addressed in

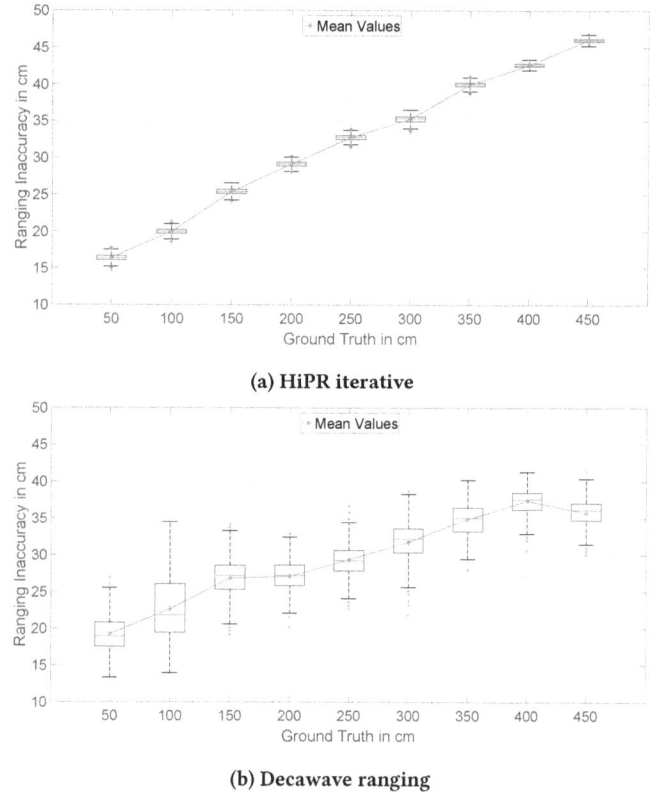

recent publications [29, 30, 35]. A performance comparison of three commercially available UWB platforms (Decawave, BeSpoon and Ubisense) in indoor and outdoor experiments are presented [17, 28]. The results indicate that Decawave performs best due to its advanced antenna system. A comparison of indoor and outdoor range estimations with the Decawave hardware is evaluated [22]. It is shown that the same transceiver configuration that we use for HiPR performs best and that distance estimations in the two environments are comparable. The standard noise and the ranging errors are experimentally assessed in a smaller office environment [12]. Additionally, two studies on precise UWB localization [31, 34] show variances around 5 cm, which reflect our findings with Decawave's out-of-the-box ranging application.

6 CONCLUSIONS AND OUTLOOK

We proposed, implemented, and tested the HiPR technique for distance estimation. It shows favorable properties in terms of precision and delay compared with Decawave's native ranging application. Additional measurement campaigns in other environments are necessary to draw firm conclusions on the factor of improvement.

We are currently working on accuracy compensation in dynamic environments and plan to deploy and further evaluate HiPR with small drones that require autonomous positioning. HiPR will be the basis for the lateration to reference points.

ACKNOWLEDGMENTS

A six-month research visit of D. Neuhold at the University of Southern California was partly funded by a mobility grant from the University of Klagenfurt, a scholarship from the Federation of Austrian Industries and the Carinthia Economic Chamber, and a scholarship from the Marshall Plan Foundation. C. Bettstetter is a core faculty member at the Karl Popper Kolleg on networked autonomous aerial vehicles at the University of Klagenfurt.

REFERENCES

[1] Standard for local and metropolitan area networks-Part 15.4: Low-Rate Wireless Personal Area Networks. IEEE Std 802.15.4, Sep. 2011.
[2] K. Al Nuaimi and H. Kamel. A survey of indoor positioning systems and algorithms. In *Proc. IEEE Int. Conf. on Innovations in Information Technology (IIT)*, pages 185–190, 2011.
[3] A. Alarifi, A. Al-Salman, M. Alsaleh, A. Alnafessah, S. Al-Hadhrami, M. Al-Ammar, and H. Al-Khalifa. Ultra wideband indoor positioning technologies: Analysis and recent advances. *Sensors*, 16(5):707, 2016.
[4] K. Balac, M. Akhmedov, M. Prevostini, and M. Malek. Topology optimization of wireless localization networks. In *Proc. European Wireless*, 2016.
[5] J. Chóliz, M. Eguizabal, Á. Hernández-Solana, and A. Valdovinos. Comparison of algorithms for UWB indoor location and tracking systems. In *Proc. IEEE Int. Conf. on Vehicular Technology Conference (VTC)*, pages 1–5, 2011.
[6] J. Collin, O. Mezentsev, G. Lachapelle, et al. Indoor positioning system using accelerometry and high accuracy heading sensors. In *Proc. ION GPS/GNSS Conf.*, pages 9–12, 2003.
[7] DecaWave. APS013 Application Note: The Implementation of Two-way Ranging with the DW1000, Version 2.2. Technical report, 2015.
[8] DecaWave. DW1000 User Manual: How to Use, Configure and Program the DW1000 UWB Transceiver, Version 2.05. Technical report, 2015.
[9] DecaWave. APS014 Application Note: Antenna Delay Calibration of DW1000 Based Products and Systems, Version 1.2. Technical report, 2018.
[10] A. Duru, E. Şehirli, and İ. Kabalcı. Ultra-wideband positioning system using TWR and lateration methods. In *Proc. ACM Int. Conf. Eng. & MIS*, page 58, 2018.
[11] W. Gerok, J. Peissig, and T. Kaiser. TDOA assisted RSSD localization in UWB. In *Proc. IEEE Workshop on Positioning, Navigation and Communication*, pages 196–200, 2012.
[12] F. Hartmann, C. Enders, and W. Stork. Ranging errors in uwb networks and their detectability. In *Proc. IEEE Int. Conf. on Telecommunications and Signal Processing (TSP)*, pages 194–198, 2016.
[13] M. Hedley and Q. Zhai. Wireless sensor network using hybrid tdoa/rss tracking of uncooperative targets. In *Proc. IEEE Int. Symp. on Wireless Personal Multimedia Communications (WPMC)*, pages 385–390, 2014.
[14] K. A. Horváth, G. Ill, and Á. Milánkovich. Passive extended double-sided two-way ranging algorithm for UWB positioning. In *Proc. IEEE Int. Conf. on Ubiquitous and Future Networks (ICUFN)*, pages 482–487. IEEE, 2017.
[15] F. Ijaz, H. K. Yang, A. W. Ahmad, and C. Lee. Indoor positioning: A review of indoor ultrasonic positioning systems. In *Proc. IEEE Int. Conf. on Advanced Communications Technology (ICACT)*, pages 1146–1150, 2013.
[16] G. Jekabsons, V. Kairish, and V. Zuravlyov. An analysis of Wi-Fi based indoor positioning accuracy. *Scientific Journal of Riga Technical University*, 44(1):131–137, 2011.

[17] A. R. Jiménez and F. Seco. Comparing decawave and bespoon uwb location systems: Indoor/outdoor performance analysis. In *Proc. IEEE Int. Conf. on Indoor Positioning and Indoor Navigation (IPIN)*, pages 1–8, 2016.
[18] Joon-Yong Lee and R. A. Scholtz. Ranging in a dense multipath environment using an uwb radio link. *IEEE Journal on Selected Areas in Communications*, 20(9):1677–1683, Dec 2002.
[19] J. Ko et al. Target tracking algorithms for UWB radar network. In *Proc. IEEE Int. Conf. Radioelektronika*, pages 319–324, 2016.
[20] M. Laaraiedh, S. Avrillon, and B. Uguen. Hybrid data fusion techniques for localization in UWB networks. In *Proc. IEEE Workshop on Positioning, Navigation and Communication*, pages 51–57, 2009.
[21] D. Macii, A. Colombo, P. Pivato, and D. Fontanelli. A data fusion technique for wireless ranging performance improvement. *IEEE Trans. Instrumentation and Measurement*, 62(1):27–37, 2013.
[22] M. Malajner, P. Planinšič, and D. Gleich. UWB ranging accuracy. In *Proc. IEEE Int. Conf. on Systems, Signals and Image Processing (IWSSIP)*, pages 61–64, 2015.
[23] R. Mautz. Indoor positioning technologies. Technical report, ETH Zurich, Department of Civil, Environmental and Geomatic Engineering, 2012.
[24] D. Neuhold, J. F. Schmidt, C. Bettstetter, J. Klaue, and D. Schupke. Experiments with UWB aircraft sensor networks. In *Proc. IEEE INFOCOM Workshops*, San Francisco, CA, Apr. 2016.
[25] D. Neuhold, J. F. Schmidt, C. Bettstetter, J. Sebald, and J. Klaue. UWB connectivity inside a space launch vehicle. In *Proc. European Wireless*, Aarhus, Denmark, May 2019.
[26] D. Neuhold, J. F. Schmidt, J. Klaue, D. Schupke, and C. Bettstetter. Experimental study of packet loss in a UWB sensor network for aircraft. In *Proc. ACM Intern. Conf. on Modeling, Analysis and Simulation of Wireless and Mobile Systems (MSWiM)*, pages 137–142, Miami Beach, FL, USA, Nov. 2017.
[27] L. Oliveira, C. Di Franco, T. E. Abrudan, and L. Almeida. Fusing time-of-flight and received signal strength for adaptive radio-frequency ranging. In *Proc. IEEE Int. Conf. on Advanced Robotics (ICAR)*, pages 1–6, 2013.
[28] A. R. J. Ruiz and F. S. Granja. Comparing ubisense, bespoon, and decawave uwb location systems: Indoor performance analysis. *IEEE Trans. Instrumentation and Measurement*, 66(8):2106–2117, 2017.
[29] C. L. Sang, M. Adams, T. Hörmann, M. Hesse, M. Porrmann, and U. Rückert. An analytical study of time of flight error estimation in two-way ranging methods. In *Proc. IEEE Int. Conf. Indoor Pos. and Indoor Navigation (IPIN)*, pages 1–8, 2018.
[30] J. Sidorenkoab, V. Schatza, N. Scherer-Negenborna, M. Arensa, and U. Hugentobler. Decawave UWB clock drift correction and powerself-calibration. *ArXiv preprint: 1902.11085*, 2019.
[31] B. Silva, Z. Pang, J. Åkerberg, J. Neander, and G. Hancke. Experimental study of uwb-based high precision localization for industrial applications. In *Proc. IEEE Int. Conf. on Ultra-WideBand (ICUWB)*, pages 280–285, 2014.
[32] Z. Song, G. Jiang, and C. Huang. A survey on indoor positioning technologies. In *Proc. Int. Conf. on Theoretical and Mathematical Foundations of Computer Science*, pages 198–206. Springer, 2011.
[33] S. Tewes, L. Schwoerer, and P. Bosselmann. Designing a basic IR-UWB-RTLS-raw-data position estimation utilizing TWR. In *Proc. Int. Conf. on European Conference on Smart Objects, Systems and Technologies (Smart SysTech)*, 2017.
[34] J. Wang, A. K. Raja, and Z. Pang. Prototyping and experimental comparison of IR-UWB based high precision localization technologies. In *Proc. IEEE Int. Conf. on on Ubiquitous Intelligence and Computing and IEEE Int. Conf. on Autonomic and Trusted Computing and Proc. IEEE Int. Conf. on Scalable Computing and Communications and Its Associated Workshops (UIC-ATC-ScalCom)*, pages 1187–1192, 2015.
[35] G. Xinzhe, S. Guo, Q. Chen, and L. Han. A new calibration method of UWB antenna delay based on the ADS-TWR. In *Proc. IEEE Chinese Control Conference (CCC)*, 2018.
[36] A. Yassin, Y. Nasser, M. Awad, A. Al-Dubai, R. Liu, C. Yuen, R. Raulefs, and E. Aboutanios. Recent advances in indoor localization: A survey on theoretical approaches and applications. *IEEE Communications Surveys & Tutorials*, 19(2):1327–1346, 2016.
[37] F. Zafari, A. Gkelias, and K. K. Leung. A survey of indoor localization systems and technologies. *IEEE Communications Surveys & Tutorials*, (1), 2019.

Maximum Gaps in Path Coverage

Simon Shamoun
City University of New York
New York, NY
srshamoun@yahoo.com

Tarek Abdelzaher
University of Illinois,
Urbana-Champaign
Urbana-Champaign, IL
zaher@illinois.edu

Amotz Bar-Noy
City University of New York
New York, NY
amotz@sci.brooklyn.cuny.edu

ABSTRACT

We study the maximum size of coverage gaps by sensors selected to cover a path. Gap sizes, and not just total coverage, are important because significant events can be missed during uncovered periods. The amount of knowledge about a path affects the ability to select sensors to cover it. We first study how coverage gaps are affected by increases in knowledge and improvements in selection strategies when sensors are selected to maximize path coverage. The gap size does not necessarily decrease in the same way that coverage increases with a better selection. We then show that even simple modifications to the algorithm can reduce the coverage gap, and show how this is affected about the level of knowledge.

KEYWORDS

sensor selection; path coverage; coverage gaps

ACM Reference Format:
Simon Shamoun, Tarek Abdelzaher, and Amotz Bar-Noy. 2019. Maximum Gaps in Path Coverage. In *22nd Int'l ACM Conf. on Modeling, Analysis and Simulation of Wireless and Mobile Systems (MSWiM'19), Nov. 25–29, 2019, Miami Beach, FL, USA.* ACM, New York, NY, USA, 4 pages. https://doi.org/10.1145/3345768.3355940

1 INTRODUCTION

One use of sensor networks is to monitor the paths of mobile objects. For example, numerous security cameras can monitor the paths of vehicles in a city. In cases like this, it is not feasible to use all the sensors to monitor each path because of the resources required to gather and process all the data. Instead, a select group of sensors should be used to monitor each path.

Sensors can only be selected to cover as much as is known about the path. For example, they can only be selected to cover steps near the starting point if only that is known. Previous studies showed the relationship between what is known about the path, the selection strategy, and the total fraction of the path covered [11, 12]. This paper complements them with a similar study of the maximum gap in coverage. This is important because significant events and waypoints may be missed during long uncovered periods of movement. A separate study is necessary because the amount of coverage does not necessarily correspond to the size of the gaps.

An obvious example is the difference between covering only the first half of a path and covering it at regular intervals. In the first case, there is a gap half the length of the path, while in the second case, the largest gap may only be a small fraction of the path length.

The remainder of the paper is organized as follows. Related research in this area is reviewed in Section 2, and the model of the problem studied here is described in Section 3. In Section 4, we evaluate the gaps when sensors are selected to maximize coverage. In Section 5, we highlight the challenge of minimizing the gaps and evaluate several heuristics for solving the problem. Section 6 concludes the paper.

2 RELATED WORK

The longest unsensed fragment of a path–the maximum gap as we call it–is listed as one of several measures of the *trackability* of a sensor network, which is the ability to estimate the trajectory of the target [9]. This measure is closely related to barrier coverage and intrusion detection, which is the ability to detect a target passing through the sensor field [2, 7, 10]. The goal there is somewhat different, in that the objective is to leave as little room as possible for the target to move without being detected.

Studies in these areas typically focus on the coverage properties of different deployment strategies or on the deployment strategies themselves. Ram, et al. [9], analyzed the stochastic properties of these measures for linear and curvilinear path in random networks, but not necessarily for the types of random paths we study. Megerian, et al., [7] show how to determine the maximum breach path, which is the path with the maximum distance from all sensors, for various arrangements using Voronoi diagrams. More related to our problem is the work of Sinha, et al. [13], which is to determine when to deploy sensors along a path to maintain connectivity. The idea is not to allow too large of a gap between sensors in order to minimize transmission costs, while not using too many sensors as well. In the case when the path is actually known, the problem can be closely related to vertex cover on dotted interval graphs, in which each sensor node covers various dots on a line, which segment the line into gaps, and two sensors are connected if they cover the same dot [5]. As the maximum allowable distance between dots increases, the runtime complexity increases.

3 PROBLEM MODEL

The purpose of this study is to understand how knowledge about a path affects the ability to select sensors that minimize the size of gaps in its coverage. We study *budgeted selection*, in which a fixed number of sensors, k, are selected, in order to compare knowledge levels when all other factors are equal. We distinguish between two types of selection strategies: static selection, in which all sensors

Table 1: Average number of steps and positions visited

q	path length	no. positions
0	71	71
0.3	101	86
0.6	181	119
0.9	874	357

are selected at the outset of the target's movement, and dynamic selection, in which the sensors are selected in stages as the target moves. Coverage under static selection highlights the fundamental difference knowledge makes. Dynamic selection shows how much those differences can be overcome. In order to understand the difference increased flexibility in the dynamic selection strategy makes, we also place a limit, t, on the number of selection rounds.

We model the sensor field as an $m \times n$ grid, limiting sensor and target locations to grid points, as has been done elsewhere [1, 3, 8]. This simplifies the simulations and their evaluation. Sensor coverage is modeled as a disk of radius r. Coverage of a point is defined by a binary value indicating whether or not it is in the coverage area of at least one selected sensor [4, 6, 9]. We assume that each sensor knows the position of an object it detects.

The target moves from start to destination according to the q-drunken mobility model [11, 12]. Each step, it moves to adjacent grid points in one of four directions: up, down, left, or right. With probability q, it moves in a random direction, and with probability $1 - q$, it takes the next step on one of the shortest paths to the destination, selected at random. When $q = 0$, the target moves strictly along one of the shortest paths from start to destination. When $q = 1$, its movement is entirely random until it reaches the destination. We previously showed that this model corresponds fairly well to real mobility patterns [12]. There, we studied six and eight directions of movement as well.

4 GAPS UNDER COVERAGE MAXIMIZATION

In this section, we study the size of coverage gaps when sensors are selected to maximize total coverage. This serves as a baseline since it is a natural starting point when choosing a strategy to minimize the gap sizes. We use the q-drunken mobility model as we did in the previous studies because it is easy to define distinct levels of knowledge with it, easily comparing the effect of knowledge on the selection. We defined the following five levels of knowledge, with the abbreviated form in boldface:

(1) **none** Nothing is known
(2) **s** Only the starting point is known
(3) **s+e** Both the start and end point are known
(4) **s+e+q** The start, end, and value of q are known
(5) **all** The whole path is known

The random factor q in the mobility model is significant because it creates a large gap in knowledge between knowing the start and end and knowing the whole path if q is not known. Table 1 shows the average path lenght and number of positions visited by the target for increasing values of q. The path length is different from the number of positions visited, since the target may visit the same point multiple times. The average was taken over five

hundred simulated walks from point $(20, 20)$ to $(60, 50)$ in an eighty-by-seventy unit field. It shows that there is approximately a double exponential growth in both, although significantly smaller for the number of positions visited. This means that no single assumption can be made about the path if q is not known.

We first study the gap sizes under static selection and then under dynamic selection.

4.1 Static Selection

We use a simple and intuitive method for static selection: The grid points are assigned weights according to what is known about the path, and then the sensors are greedily selected for maximal weighted coverage of the grid [12]. The idea is to assign weights according to where the target is expected to be and then maximize the expected coverage. For each level of knowledge, the weights are assigned as follows, where s and e indicate the start and end point, respectively, p the grid point being assigned a weight, and $d(a, b)$ the Euclidean distance between points a and b:

(1) **none** All grid points are assigned equal value.
(2) **s** $1/(1 + d(p, s))^m$, where m scales the weight, and one is added to the denominator to prevent division-by-zero.
(3) **s+e** $1/(1 + d(p, s) + d(p, e))^m$
(4) **sp** The probability of visiting p when the target follows the shortest path
(5) **s+e+q** The expected number of times the target visits p
(6) **all** The number of times the target actually visits p

The sp heuristic is an alternative to $s+e$ under the assumption that the target follows the shortest path, and is equivalent to $s+e+q$ when q equals zero. For the evaluations, m was set to one.

In the selection algorithm, all grid points are initially marked "uncovered". The sensors are selected one-by-one, each time selecting the one with the maximum total weight of uncovered points in its sensing area and marking them as covered. Although it does not necessarily select the sensors with maximum grid coverage, it guarantees the best approximation of the optimal solution, within a constant factor, of any known solution [14]. The pseudo-code appears below.

1: *Input:* sensor set S, grid points G, budget k
2: $L \leftarrow \{\}$ {selected sensors}
3: $U \leftarrow S$ {unselected sensors}
4: Mark all $p \in G$ as uncovered
5: **for** $i \leftarrow 1$ **to** k **do**
6:     $maxSensor \leftarrow \text{argmax}_s \sum_p weight_p$ such that p is uncovered and s covers p
7:     $L \leftarrow L \cup maxSensor$
8:     $U \leftarrow U \setminus maxSensor$
9:     Mark all points in $maxSensor$'s sensing area as covered
10: **end for**
11: **return** L

We generated five hundred paths from point $(20, 20)$ to $(60, 50)$ in an eighty-by-seventy unit field for values of q ranging from 0 to 0.9 in increments of 0.1. For each path, two hundred sensor locations were randomly selected, from which the sensors to cover the path were selected. The sensing radius was set to four. In this setting, fourteen sensors are enough for maximum coverage when the full path is known. Figure 1a shows the average exposure–which

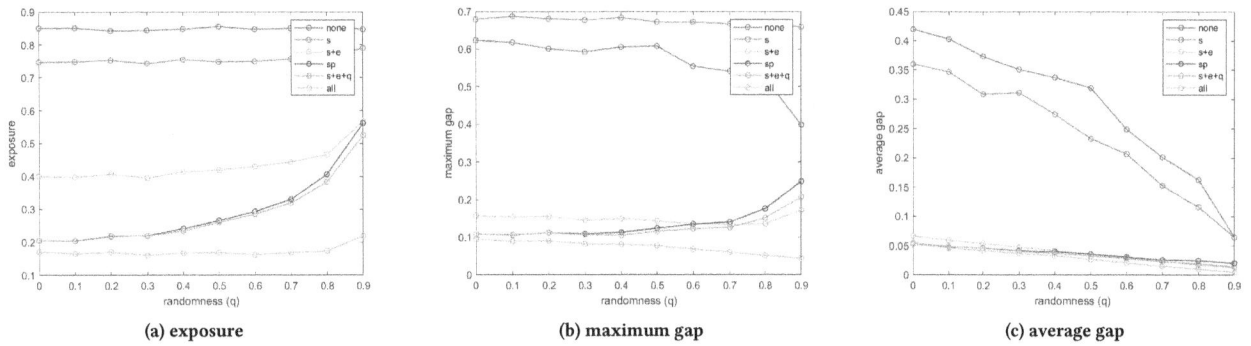

Figure 1: Change in total exposure, maximum gap size, and average gap size with q by static selection when $b = 14$

is the fraction of the path left uncovered–by fourteen selected sensors for increasing values of q, and Figure 1b shows the average length of the maximum gap as a fraction of the total path length. While the ranking of the heuristics by exposure corresponds to the knowledge hierarchy, the order between *none* and *s* is switched for the maximum gap. This is because *s* selects sensors clustered around the start, leaving a large gap towards the end, while *none* will divide the path further along the middle with high enough probability that the average is lower. The difference between the maximum gap of *s+e* and *s+e+q* is much less than the exposure. This is because sensors are selected at regular intervals between the start and end using *s+e*, while a higher concentration of sensors are selected near the start and end by *s+e+q* and *all*, which results in a relatively smaller gap by *s+e* with respect to the exposure.

The trends in change of exposure and maximum with q are very similar, except that the maximum gap decreases with q for *none* while the exposure changes very little. This is because the target moves in and out of the coverage zones of the selected sensors more frequently as q increases, breaking up the exposed path into many small segments. This is highlighted in Figure 1c, which shows that average size of all gaps decreases for all heuristics. Because *none* selects sensors with diverse locations, the maximum gap decreases as well.

4.2 Dynamic Selection

Dynamic selection is the same as static selection, but done in rounds as the target moves. In the strategies we study, there are either two, $k/2$, k rounds, with an equal number of sensors selected in each round, such that either $k/2$, two, or one sensors are selected each round, respectively. The first set of sensors are selected before the target begins to move. Each additional set is selected the first round the target moves out of coverage range of all sensors selected so far. Alternatively, there is a waiting period of one or two rounds before selecting more sensors in case the target moves back into coverage range of a selected sensor in order to conserve the budget for later steps along the path. We applied this strategy only to the case when the starting position alone is known. Each time new sensors are selected, the target's last known position is assumed to be the new starting position. More details about dynamic selection can be found in the original publication on the subject [11].

For all values of q, the exposure and maximum gap progressively decrease with the number of stages. However, the maximum gap relative to the uncovered portion of the path also decreases, meaning that while the maximum gap by static selection is about 0.9 times the total uncovered portion, it is less than 0.5 times the uncovered portion by k-stage selection. This shows that dynamic selection decreases the maximum gap not just by increasing coverage, but also by a better distribution of selected sensors along the path. This also applies to increasing the wait time from zero to one. Figure 2 shows the change in exposure with q when $k = 14$ for different wait times, and Figure 3 shows that of the maximum gap. Waiting reduces the gap in a more significant way than it reduces exposure. In particular, waiting two steps reduces the gap for all values of q, while it only reduces exposure when q is greater than 0.4.

5 COVERAGE GAP REDUCTION

In this section, we study the potential to reduce the maximum gap by the static selection strategy. We first study how much worse the maximum gap can be when the optimization goal is to maximize coverage rather than minimize the maximum gap when the full path is known. We generated two hundred paths and two hundred sensor locations for each as we did before. For each path, we used brute force to select all sets of k sensors with maximum coverage and to determine the maximum gap of each set of k sensors covering the path. We used the maximum gap from the first group and the minimum value from the second group to calculate the ratio of the maximum gap by the two optimization goals in the worst case. The ratio is 1.6 when $k = 1$ and decreases linearly with k until it is one for about fourteen sensors. Fourteen sensors is generally enough for maximum coverage in this scenario, which means that the coverage gaps will be minimal, too, so the ratio will be one. This shows that the coverage gaps can be reduced by a different selection strategy, even when the entire path is maximally covered.

Intuitively, one would select sensors evenly distributed throughout the expected area of the path in order to minimize the gap sizes with the idea that the target would regularly move into the coverage zone of a sensor. To approximate such a solution, we modified the static selection method in the previous section to select sensors according to different coverage models, even though the coverage model remained the same for evaluation purposes. The simplist

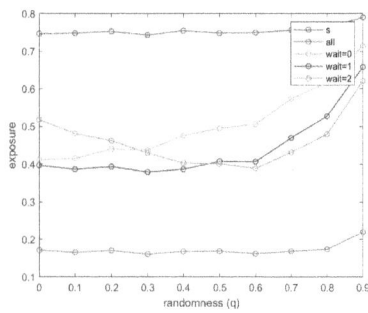

Figure 2: Exposure by k-round dynamic selection when knowing the start

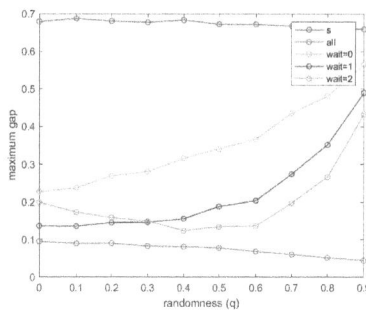

Figure 3: Maximum gap by k-round dynamic selection when knowing the start

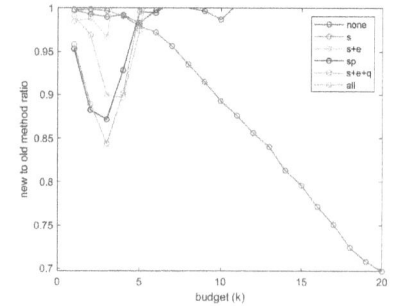

Figure 4: Ratio of maximum gap by static selection heuristic to the gap by standard static selection when $q = 0.4$

approach is to increase the sensing radius in order to select sensors with a little more distance between each other.

Figure 4 shows the average ratio of the maximum gap by the new method to the gap by the old method for the difference levels of knowledge when q is zero. It shows that there is up to a 15% reduction in the gap by $s+e+q$ for budget values under six, and that the ratio for s descreases as the budget gets larger, up to a 30% reduction. This shows that even a simple modification of the selection strategy can reduce the maximum gap, although this particularly strategy does not guarantee a reduction in the maximum gap length.

6   CONCLUSION

In any optimization problem, a maximum aggregate value may be the result of a widely disparate allocation of individual values, and sometimes with some reallocation and slight reduction in the aggregate value, a better distribution of values can be achieved. In our case, maximum coverage of a path may have large gaps that can be reduced by selecting sensors somewhat differently. In theory, this can be done optimally when the path is known. In practice, this is a hard problem to solve, which can be shown by the following reduction from set cover. Let the steps in the path be elements in a set, and the steps covered by each sensor the subsets to select from. A decision that a set of k sensors with no gap exists is equivalent to a decision that there are k sets that cover all the elements. Given the hardness of the problem, it is much more difficult to reduce gap sizes when less is known about the path. In general, an optimal solution would have some even distribution of selected sensors. We tried the heuristic of increasing the sensing radius for the sake of selection. Another possiblity would be to divide the budget according to likely regions of path segments. Future work would explore such heuristics, as well as heuristics and an analysis of the problem when the path is known.

ACKNOWLEDGMENT

Research was sponsored by the Army Research Laboratory and was accomplished under Cooperative Agreement Number W911NF-09-2-0053. The views and conclusions contained in this document are those of the authors and should not be interpreted as representing the official policies, either expressed or implied, of the Army Research Laboratory or the U.S. Government. The U.S. Government is authorized to reproduce and distribute reprints for Government purposes notwithstanding any copyright notation here on.

REFERENCES

[1] Edoardo Amaldi, Antonio Capone, Matteo Cesana, and Ilario Filippini. 2012. Design of Wireless Sensor Networks for Mobile Target Detection. *IEEE/ACM Trans. Netw.* 20, 3 (2012), 784–797. https://doi.org/10.1109/TNET.2011.2175746
[2] Paul Balister, Béla Bollobás, and Amites Sarkar. 2016. Barrier Coverage. *Random Struct. Algorithms* 49, 3 (2016), 429–478. https://doi.org/10.1002/rsa.20656
[3] Thomas Clouqueur, Veradej Phipatanasuphorn, Parameswaran Ramanathan, and Kewal K. Saluja. 2003. Sensor Deployment Strategy for Detection of Targets Traversing a Region. *MONET* 8, 4 (2003), 453–461. https://doi.org/10.1023/A:1024596016427
[4] Junko Harada, Shigeo Shioda, and Hiroshi Saito. 2009. Path coverage properties of randomly deployed sensors with finite data-transmission ranges. *Computer Networks* 53, 7 (2009), 1014–1026. https://doi.org/10.1016/j.comnet.2008.12.003
[5] Danny Hermelin, Julián Mestre, and Dror Rawitz. 2014. Optimization problems in dotted interval graphs. *Discrete Applied Mathematics* 174 (2014), 66–72. https://doi.org/10.1016/j.dam.2014.04.014
[6] Pallavi Manohar, S. Sundhar Ram, and D. Manjunath. 2009. Path coverage by a sensor field: The nonhomogeneous case. *TOSN* 5, 2 (2009), 17:1–17:26. https://doi.org/10.1145/1498915.1498923
[7] Seapahn Megerian, Farinaz Koushanfar, Miodrag Potkonjak, and Mani B. Srivastava. 2005. Worst and Best-Case Coverage in Sensor Networks. *IEEE Trans. Mob. Comput.* 4, 1 (2005), 84–92. https://doi.org/10.1109/TMC.2005.15
[8] Seapahn Megerian, Farinaz Koushanfar, Gang Qu, Giacomino Veltri, and Miodrag Potkonjak. 2002. Exposure in Wireless Sensor Networks: Theory and Practical Solutions. *Wireless Networks* 8, 5 (2002), 443–454. https://doi.org/10.1023/A:1016586011473
[9] S. Sundhar Ram, D. Manjunath, Srikanth K. Iyer, and D. Yogeshwaran. 2007. On the Path Coverage Properties of Random Sensor Networks. *IEEE Trans. Mob. Comput.* 6, 5 (2007), 494–506. https://doi.org/10.1109/TMC.2007.1000
[10] Anwar Saipulla, Cédric Westphal, Benyuan Liu, and Jie Wang. 2013. Barrier coverage with line-based deployed mobile sensors. *Ad Hoc Networks* 11, 4 (2013), 1381–1391. https://doi.org/10.1016/j.adhoc.2010.10.002
[11] Simon Shamoun, Tarek F. Abdelzaher, and Amotz Bar-Noy. 2019. Dynamic sensor selection for path coverage. In *Proceedings of the 20th International Conference on Distributed Computing and Networking, ICDCN 2019, Bangalore, India, January 04-07, 2019*, R. C. Hansdah, Dilip Krishnaswamy, and Nitin Vaidya (Eds.). ACM, 277–281. https://doi.org/10.1145/3288599.3288627
[12] Simon Shamoun, Jie Mei, Tarek F. Abdelzaher, and Amotz Bar-Noy. 2018. Leveraging Knowledge for Path Exposure. In *14th International Conference on Distributed Computing in Sensor Systems, DCOSS 2018, New York, NY, USA, June 18-20, 2018*. IEEE, 103–110. https://doi.org/10.1109/DCOSS.2018.00021
[13] Abhishek Sinha, Arpan Chattopadhyay, Kolar Purushothama Naveen, Prasenjit Mondal, Marceau Coupechoux, and Anurag Kumar. 2014. Optimal sequential wireless relay placement on a random lattice path. *Ad Hoc Networks* 21 (2014), 1–17. https://doi.org/10.1016/j.adhoc.2014.04.005
[14] Yong Yang, I-Hong Hou, Jennifer C. Hou, Mallikarjun Shankar, and Nageswara S. V. Rao. 2009. Sensor Placement for Detecting Propagative Sources in Populated Environments. In *INFOCOM*. IEEE, 1206–1214.

ns-3 meets OpenAI Gym: The Playground for Machine Learning in Networking Research

Piotr Gawłowicz
Technische Universität Berlin
Germany
gawlowicz@tu-berlin.de

Anatolij Zubow
Technische Universität Berlin
Germany
zubow@tu-berlin.de

ABSTRACT

Recently, we have seen a boom of attempts to improve the operation of networking protocols using machine learning techniques. The proposed reinforcement learning (RL) based control solutions very often overtake traditionally designed ones in terms of performance and efficiency. However, in order to reach such a superb level, an RL control agent requires a lot of interactions with an environment to learn the best policies. Similarly, the recent advancements in image recognition area were enabled by the rise of large labeled datasets (e.g. ImageNet [8]). This paper presents the ns3-gym — the first framework for RL research in networking. It is based on OpenAI Gym, a toolkit for RL research and ns-3 network simulator. Specifically, it allows representing an ns-3 simulation as an environment in Gym framework and exposing state and control knobs of entities from the simulation for the agent's learning purposes. Our framework is generic and can be used in various networking problems. Here, we present an illustrative example from the cognitive radio area, where a wireless node learns the channel access pattern of a periodic interferer in order to avoid collisions with it. The toolkit is provided to the community as open-source under a GPL license.

CCS CONCEPTS

• **Networks** → **Network simulations**; • **Computing methodologies** → **Reinforcement learning**; **Simulation tools**.

KEYWORDS

reinforcement learning; networking research; OpenAI Gym; network simulator; ns-3

ACM Reference Format:
Piotr Gawłowicz and Anatolij Zubow. 2019. ns-3 meets OpenAI Gym: The Playground for Machine Learning in Networking Research. In *22nd Int'l ACM Conference on Modeling, Analysis and Simulation of Wireless and Mobile Systems (MSWiM '19), November 25–29, 2019, Miami Beach, FL, USA*. ACM, New York, NY, USA, 8 pages. https://doi.org/10.1145/3345768.3355908

1 INTRODUCTION

Modern communication networks have evolved into extremely complex and dynamic systems. Although a network makes use of rather

simple to understand protocols, their composition makes network's behavior non-trivial with very often hidden (i.e. not directly explainable) dependencies between components' parameters and network performance metrics. For this reason, traditional approaches for the design of new solutions or the optimization of existing ones provide only limited gains as they are based on (over-)simplified models created according to people's understanding. Moreover, the approaches are mostly focused on a single component (e.g. protocol layer) neglecting the end-to-end network's nature (i.e. involving multiple layers across different nodes).

Furthermore, today's networks generate a large amount of monitoring data, that can help to improve the design and management of them. This, however, requires the processing of the raw data in order to find hidden dependencies. All this together makes machine learning (ML) techniques the perfect fit for modern networking [25]. ML can provide estimated models with tunable accuracy, that will help researchers to tackle intractable old problems, as well as encourage new applications in the networking domain potentially leading to breakthroughs [28]. We have already seen a boom in the usage of machine learning in general and reinforcement learning (RL) in particular for the optimization of communication and networking systems ranging from scheduling [2, 6], resource management [18], congestion control [14, 15, 29], routing [1] and adaptive video streaming [19]. Each proposed approach shows significant improvements compared to traditionally designed algorithms.

However, we believe that RL in networking (RLN) research is slowed down by the following factors:

- *The existence of a knowledge gap* — networking researchers lack ML related knowledge and experience while ML researchers lack knowledge in networking [28].
- *Lack of training environments* — RL requires a large number of interactions with an environment to properly train an agent. The best way is to use a real-world environment. However, it is time-consuming and researchers usually lack skills and/or hardware to setup a testbed, while an exploration (required in RL to learn) in real network deployments can be unsafe for their operation.
- *The need for reliable benchmarking* [4] — currently, researchers build and use their environments on a case-by-case basis. Some of them use network simulators, others real-world hardware, i.e. testbed. This issue makes the direct comparison of the performance of published algorithms difficult while tracking the RLN progress almost impossible.

Contribution: In this paper, we propose ns3-gym — a first attempt to tackle all the above problems. It is a benchmarking system for networking based on two well-known and acknowledged by research community frameworks, namely, ns-3 and OpenAI Gym.

It combines the advantages of these two, namely, the verified and tested models of ns-3 and the simplicity of prototyping RL-based algorithms in Python using numerical computation libraries (e.g. Tensorflow[1] and Keras[2]). Specifically, ns3-gym simplifies feeding the RL models with the data generated in the simulator.

The framework is generic and it can be easily extended and used in a wide range of networking problems. We provide the first set of problems along with baseline solutions that can be used by the community to directly compare the performance of different RL-based algorithms (i.e. agents) using the same virtual conditions of well-defined simulation scripts (i.e. environments). We believe that our work will help to motivate researchers from both networking and ML areas to collaborate in order to develop and share innovative algorithms and challenging environments, and hence speed up research and development in RLN area.

2 BACKGROUND

In this section, we provide an overview of reinforcement learning technique together with tools that simplify the development and training of RL models. Then, we briefly introduce the ns-3 simulator.

2.1 Reinforcement Learning

Reinforcement learning is being successfully used in robotics for years as it allows the design of sophisticated and hard to engineer behaviors [13]. The main advantage of RL is its ability to learn to interact with the surrounding environment based on its own experience. An RL agent interacts with an environment in the following way: i) it observes the current state of the environment, ii) based on the observation it selects an action and executes it in the environment, iii) which in turn returns a reward associated with this specific action in the particular state – Fig. 1. The way an environment transforms the agent's action taken in the current state into the next state and a reward is unknown. Hence, the agent's main goal is to approximate the environment's function and learn the best policy allowing it to select always the best action and maximize its cumulated reward.

2.2 RL Tools

OpenAI Gym [4] is a toolkit for developing and comparing reinforcement learning algorithms. It provides a simple API that unifies interactions between an RL-based agent and an environment. Specifically, any environment can be integrated into the Gym as long as all the observations, actions, and rewards can be represented as numerical values. Note, that Gym makes no assumptions about the structure of an agent (just provides input data and action knobs) and it is compatible with any numerical computation library. Based on the unified interface Gym provides access to a collection of standardized environments. The framework was already integrated with the variety of environments in areas ranging from video games (e.g. Ping-Pong) to robotics [4, 23, 24].

As mentioned in the previous section (§2.1), an RL agent attempts to approximate the environment's function. Usually, such functions are very complex and cannot be represented in closed-form. Fortunately, neural networks cope well in such cases. They are used to

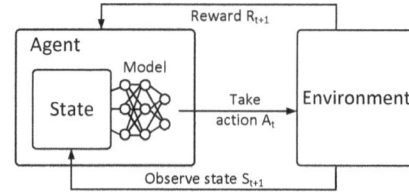

Figure 1: Reinforcement Learning.

approximate the function transforming inputs to outputs and during the learning process their parameters are tuned to find the best approximation. The learning is an iterative process during which a solver follows gradients that lead to smaller errors. In recent years, the task of developing and solving the neural networks was simplified by the emergence of numerical computation libraries. For instance, Keras provides a high-level API allowing to create and optimize even a very complex neural network in just a few lines of code. Keras runs on top of TensorFlow that allows representing numerical computation as a data flow graph, i.e. nodes represent mathematical operations, while edges represent the multidimensional data arrays that flow between them. Finally, with only minor changes, TensorFlow allows performing the computations on a single CPU and GPU as well as distributed clusters of them using the same code.

The replication of the published RL algorithms is a challenging task, especially for people entering the field of machine learning, as usually they are very complex and even a small difference (e.g. bug) in the implementation may affect their performance. Releasing a code repository along with the published paper is a good practice, however, still not the case for most of the publications. Fortunately, recently the high-quality reference implementations of RL algorithms become available [9, 10, 16]. Researchers can use them as a base and apply to the problems in their respective areas.

2.3 ns-3 Network Simulator

ns-3 is a discrete-event network simulator for networking systems, targeted primarily for research and educational use. It is an open-source project developed in C++ using object-oriented programming model [21, 22]. It became a standard in networking research as the results obtained are accepted by the community.

ns-3 tries to reflect the reality as close as possible, therefore it uses several core concepts and abstractions that map well to how computers and networks are built, i.e. a Node is a fundamental entity connected to the network. It is a container for Applications, Protocols and Network Devices. An application is a user program that generates packet flows. A protocol represents a logic of network and transport level protocols, e.g. TCP, OSRL routing. A Network Device is an entity connected to a Channel that is the basic communication sub-network abstraction. As in real-world, in order to build a network system, one has to perform set of task including installing network devices in nodes and connecting them to channels, allocating proper MAC addresses, configuring the protocol stacks of all nodes, etc. ns-3 provides a set of helpers that simplifies the tedious work behind easy to use API.

The introduced abstractions came with the unified interfaces between entities, what allowed the research community to work in parallel on different parts of the protocol stack without any

---

[1] https://www.tensorflow.org/
[2] https://keras.io/

problems during integration, e.g. any application can send packets over Ethernet or WiFi network devices. Based on the core concepts, the ns-3 community developed a vast set of networking protocols (e.g. IP, TCP, UDP) and communication technologies (e.g. Ethernet, WiFi, LTE, WiMAX) with detailed modeling of physical layer operations. Furthermore, ns-3 offers a variety of statistical models for wireless channels, mobility, and traffic generation. In addition, ns-3 can interact with external systems (e.g. real-time LTE testbed [11]), applications (e.g. using direct code execution technique [27]) and libraries (i.e. Click [26]).

Finally, ns-3 provides also generic *tracing* and *attribute configuration* subsystems, that signal state changes in a network model and allow monitoring the internal state and parameters of any entity (e.g. node, protocol, device) in a simulation; and control its parameters and attributes at run-time, respectively. Both subsystems serve as a basis for the ns3-gym framework.

3 MOTIVATION

The main goal of our work is to facilitate and shorten the time required for prototyping of novel RL-based networking solutions. We believe that developing control algorithms and training them with the data generated in a simulation is very often more practical (i.e. easier, faster and safer) in comparison to running experiments in the real world. Moreover, it gives an opportunity for everybody to test his/her ideas, without a need to buy and set up costly testbeds.

Furthermore, thanks to *transfer learning*, i.e. the ability to reuse previously acquired knowledge in a new (more complex) system or an environment, the agent trained in a simulation can directly interact or be retrained in the real world much faster than when starting from the scratch [7]. How well the agent copes with the real-world environment, depends on the accuracy of the simulations models that were used during training. Since ns-3 community strives to make its models reflect reality as close as possible, we believe the knowledge acquired in a simulation should remain reasonable also for the real world.

Finally, note that our framework is not constrained only to RL as one can use it to obtain observations from the simulation in order to generate data-sets and use them for the offline learning using a variety of ML algorithms (e.g. supervised learning).

4 SYSTEM ARCHITECTURE

The architecture of ns3-gym as depicted in Fig. 2 consists of the following major components, namely: ns-3 network simulator and OpenAI Gym framework. The former one is used to implement environments, while the latter one unifies their interface. The main contribution of this work is the design and implementation of a generic interface between OpenAI Gym and ns-3 that allows for seamless integration of those two frameworks. In the following, we describe our ns3-gym framework in detail.

4.1 Network Simulator

ns-3 is a core part of our framework since it is used to implement a *simulation scenario* serving as an environment for an RL agent. A simulation scenario contains a network model together with scheduled changes in simulation conditions. One can create even very complex network models and study them under various traffic and

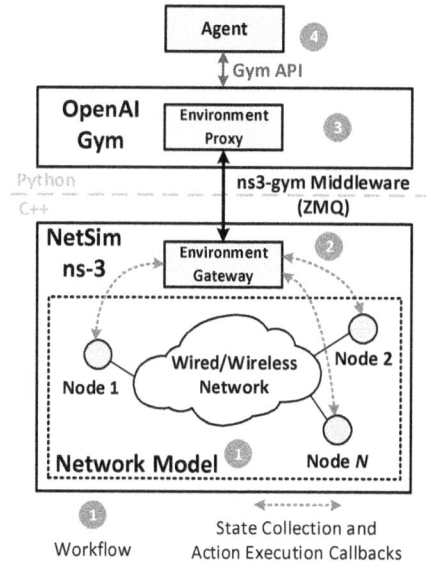

Figure 2: Architecture of ns3-gym framework.

mobility patterns by assembling the detailed models of communication components and channels provided in ns-3. An experimenter triggers changes in some conditions during the course of a simulation by scheduling proper events, e.g. start/stop traffic sources.

The state of the entire network model is a composition of states of its elements. The state representation of each entity depends on its implementation. For example, the state of a packet queue is a numerical value indicating the number of enqueued packets, while most of the protocols (e.g. TCP) are implemented as finite-state machines (FSM) jumping between predefined states. Note that in the latter case the state can be also encoded into numerical values. ns-3 provides proper interfaces allowing reading the internal state of each entity.

It is up to the designer to decide which part of the simulation state is going to be exposed to the agent for the learning purpose. In most cases, it will be sub-set of the network model state together with some statistics collected during the last step execution (e.g. number of TX/RX packets in a network device and mean inter-packet arrival interval). Usually, the observed state will be limited to a state of a single instance of the protocol that the RL-based agent is going to control. The rest entities of the network model implement and evolve the complex state of the environment the agent is going to interact with. Similarly, the possible actions are limited to changes of parameters of the observed entity. In other words, the agent is able to only partially observe the network model by interacting with it though taken actions and experiencing its response in changes of the local observations.

4.2 OpenAI Gym

The main purpose of the Gym framework is to provide a standardized interface allowing to access the state and execute actions in an environment. Note that the environment is defined entirely inside the simulation scenario making the Python code environment-independent, which allows to easily to exchange the agents' implementation while keeping the reproducibility of the environment's conditions.

4.3 ns3-gym Middleware

ns3-gym middleware interconnects ns-3 network simulator and OpenAI Gym framework. Specifically, it takes care of transferring state (i.e. observations) and control (i.e. actions) between the Gym agent and the simulation environment.

The middleware consists of two parts, namely Environment Gateway and Environment Proxy. The gateway resides inside the simulator and is responsible for gathering environment state into structured numerical data and translating the received actions, again encoded as numerical values, into corresponding function calls with proper arguments. The proxy receives environment state and expose it towards an agent through the *pythonic* Gym API. Note, that ns3-gym middleware transfers the state and actions as numerical values and it is up to the researcher to define their semantics.

5 IMPLEMENTATION

ns3-gym is a toolkit that consists of two software components (i.e. Environment Gateway written in C++ and the Environment Proxy in Python) being add-ons to the existing ns-3 and OpenAI Gym frameworks. The toolkit simplifies the tasks of development of the networking environments and training RL-based agents by taking care of the common tasks and hiding them behind easy to use API. Specifically, ns3-gym provides a way for the collection and exchange of information between frameworks (including connection initialization and data (de)serialization), takes care of the management of ns-3 simulation process life-cycle as well as freezing the execution of simulation during the interaction with an agent. The communication between components is realized with ZMQ[3] sockets using the Protocol Buffers[4] library for serialization of messages.

The software package together with clarifying examples is provided to the community as open-source under a GPL in our online repository: https://github.com/tkn-tub/ns3-gym. It is also available as a so-called ns-3 App, that can be integrated with any version of the simulator: https://apps.nsnam.org/app/ns3-gym

In the following subsections, we describe the ns3-gym components in details and explain how to use them with code examples.

5.1 Environment Gateway

In order to turn a ns-3 simulation scenario into a Gym environment, one need to *i)* instantiate OpenGymGateway and *ii)* implement its callbacks functions listed in Listing 1. Note, that the functions have to be registered in gateway object.

```
Ptr<OpenGymSpace> GetObservationSpace();
Ptr<OpenGymSpace> GetActionSpace();
Ptr<OpenGymDataContainer> GetObservation();
float GetReward();
bool GetGameOver();
std::string GetExtraInfo();
bool ExecuteActions(Ptr<OpenGymDataContainer> action);
```

Listing 1: ns3-gym C++ interface

The functions GetObservationSpace and GetActionSpace are used to define observation and action spaces (i.e. data structures

---

storing observations and actions encoded as numerical values), respectively. Both spaces descriptions are created during the initialization of the environment and send to the environment proxy object in the initialization message – Fig.3, where they are used to create corresponding spaces in Python domain. The following spaces defined in the OpenAI Gym framework are supported, namely:

(1) **Discrete** — a discrete number between 0 and N.
(2) **Box** — a vector or matrix of numbers of single type with values bounded between *low* and *high* limits.
(3) **Tuple** — a tuple of simpler spaces.
(4) **Dict** — a dictionary of simpler spaces.

Listing 2 shows an example definition of the observation space as C++ function. The space is going to be used to observe queue lengths of all the nodes available in the network. The maximal queue size was set to 100 packets, hence the values are integers and bounded between 0 and 100.

```
Ptr<OpenGymSpace> GetObservationSpace() {
  uint32_t nodeNum = NodeList::GetNNodes ();
  float low = 0.0;
  float high = 100.0;
  std::vector<uint32_t> shape = {nodeNum,};
  std::string type = TypeNameGet<uint32_t> ();
  Ptr<OpenGymBoxSpace> space =
    ↪CreateObject<OpenGymBoxSpace>(low,high,shape,type);
  return space; }
```

Listing 2: An example definition of the GetObservationSpace function

The step in ns3-gym framework can be executed *synchronously*, i.e. scheduled in predefined time-intervals (time-based step), e.g. every 100 ms, or *asynchronously*, i.e. fired by an occurrence of specific event (event-based step), e.g. packet loss. In both cases, one has to define a proper callback that triggers the Notify function of the OpenGymGateway object.

After being notified about the end of a step – Fig.4 – the gateway collects the current state of the environment by calling the following callback functions:

(1) GetObservation – collect values of observed variables and/or parameters in simulation;
(2) GetReward – get the reward achieved during last step;
(3) GetGameOver – check a predefined gameover condition;
(4) GetExtraInfo – (optional) get an extra information associated with current environment state.

The listing 3 shows example implementation of the GetObservation observation function. First, the box data container is created according to the observation space definition. Then the box is filled with the current size of the queue of WiFi interface of each node.

```
Ptr<OpenGymDataContainer> GetObservation() {
  uint32_t nodeNum = NodeList::GetNNodes ();
  std::vector<uint32_t> shape = {nodeNum,};
  Ptr<OpenGymBoxContainer<uint32_t>> box =
    ↪CreateObject<OpenGymBoxContainer<uint32_t>>(shape);

  for (uint32_t i=0; i<nodeNum; i++) {
    Ptr<Node> node = NodeList::GetNode (i);
    Ptr<WifiMacQueue> queue = GetQueue (node);
    uint32_t value = queue->GetNPackets();
    box->AddValue(value);
  }
  return box; }
```

Listing 3: An example definition of the GetObservation function

[3]http://zeromq.org/
[4]https://developers.google.com/protocol-buffers/

The ns3-gym middleware delivers the collected environment's state to an agent that in return sends the action to be executed. Note, that the execution of a simulation is stopped during this interaction. Similarly to the observation, the action is also encoded as numerical values in a container. The user is responsible to implement the ExecuteActions callback, that maps the numerical values to proper actions, e.g. setting minimum MAC contention window size for the 802.11 WiFi interface of each node – Listing 4.

```
bool ExecuteActions(Ptr<OpenGymDataContainer> action) {
  Ptr<OpenGymBoxContainer<uint32_t> > box =
      ↪DynamicCast<OpenGymBoxContainer<uint32_t> >(action);
  std::vector<uint32_t> actionVector = box->GetData();

  uint32_t nodeNum = NodeList::GetNNodes ();
  for (uint32_t i=0; i<nodeNum; i++) {
    Ptr<Node> node = NodeList::GetNode(i);
    uint32_t cwSize = actionVector.at(i);
    SetCwMin(node, cwSize);
  }
  return true;}
```

Listing 4: An example definition of the ExecuteActions function

5.2 Environment Proxy

The environment proxy is the northbound part of the middleware. It is wrapped by the Ns3GymEnv class that inherits from the generic Gym environment, which makes it accessible through OpenAI Gym API. Specifically, the proxy translates the Gym function calls into messages and sends them towards an environment gateway over ZMQ socket.

In the code listing 5, we present example Python script showing the usage of the ns3-gym framework. First, the ns-3 environment and agent are initialized — lines 5–7. Note, that the creation of ns3-v0 environment is achieved using the standard Gym API. Behind the scene, the ns3-gym engine starts an ns-3 simulation script located in the current working directory, establishes a ZMQ connection and waits for the environment initialization message — Fig.3. Optionally, the ns-3 environment can be adjusted by passing command line arguments during the start of the script (e.g. seed, simulation time, number of nodes, etc.). This, however, requires to use Ns3Env(args={arg=value,...}) constructor instead of standard Gym::make('ns-3-v0').

```
import gym
import ns3gym
import MyAgent

env = gym.make('ns-3-v0')
obs = env.reset()
agent = MyAgent.Agent()

while True:
  action = agent.get_action(obs)
  obs, reward, done, info = env.step(action)

  if done:
    break
```

Listing 5: Example Python script showing interaction between an agent and ns-3 environment

At each step, the agent takes the observation and returns, based on the implemented logic, the next action to be executed in the environment — lines 9–11. Note, that agent class is not provided in the framework and the developers are free to define them as they want. For example, the simplest agent performs random actions.

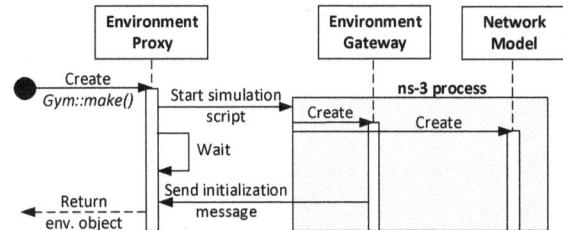

Figure 3: Implementation of the Gym::make() function.

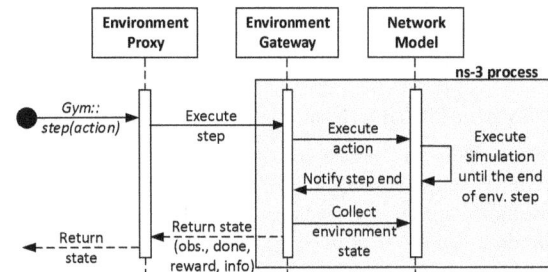

Figure 4: Implementation of the Gym::step(action) function.

The execution of the episode terminates (lines 13–14) when the environment returns done=true, that can be caused by the end of the simulation or meeting the predefined game-over condition.

In addition, a Gym environment exposes also a Gym::reset() function, that allows reverting the environment into the initial state. The ns3-gym implements the reset function by simply terminating the simulation process and starting a new one reusing mechanisms of the make function. Note, that the mapping of all the described functions between corresponding C++ and Python functions is done by the ns3-gym framework automatically hiding the entire complexity behind easy to use API.

5.3 Discussion

Although the ns-3 project supports Python bindings that would allow us to integrate it with OpenAI Gym directly in a single Python process, we have not taken this approach and decided to split ns3-gym into two communicating processes, ie. ns-3 (C++) and OpenAI Gym (Python). We believe that the split is essential due to the following reasons. First, during the learning process, an OpenAI Gym agent has to keep its state (i.e. gained knowledge) across multiple episodes (i.e. simulation runs). Having two separate processes makes this requirement easier to fulfill. Moreover, it allows running multiple ns-3 instances in parallel even in a distributed environment. Hence, the agent learning process can be executed on powerful machines with the support of GPUs, while ns-3 instances on ones equipped only with decent CPUs. This feature is especially important for techniques like A3C [20], that uses multiple agents interacting with their own copies of the environment for more efficient learning. Then, the independent, hence more diverse, experience of all agents is periodically fused to the global learning network. Second, the ns-3 project is developed in C++, while Python bindings are generated automatically as an add-on that allows only writing simulations scripts. Apparently, the development of scripts in C++ is easier for newcomers as there are much more code examples (while only a few in Python) and documentation as well as more support from the community. Finally, having the C++ implementation allows updating existing C++ simulation scripts and examples to be used as OpenAI Gym environments.

6 ENVIRONMENTS

In the following subsections, we present a typical workflow when using the ns3-gym framework. Then, we briefly describe the environments provided as examples. Finally, we discuss the feasibility of implementation of multi-agent environments and the direct usage of agents trained in a simulated environment in a real-world experiment using emulation technique.

6.1 Typical Workflow

A typical workflow of developing and training an RL-based agent is shown as numbers in Fig. 2: (1) Create a model of the network and configure scenario conditions (i.e. traffic, mobility, etc.) using standard functions of ns-3; (2) Instantiate ns3-gym environment gateway in the simulation, i.e. create `OpenGymGateway` object and implement callbacks functions that collect a state of the environment to be shared with the agent and execute actions received from it; (3) Create the ns3-gym environment proxy, i.e. create ns3-gym using the standard `Gym::make('ns3-gym')` function; (4) Develop an RL-based agent using available numerical Python libraries, that interacts with the environment using the standard `Gym::step(action)` function; (5*) Train the agent.

6.2 Example Environments

In addition to the generic ns3-gym interface where one can observe any variable in a simulation, we provide also custom environments for specific use-cases. For example, `TcpNs3Env` is an environment for controlling parameters of Transmission Control Protocol (TCP), where the observation state, action and reward function are predefined using the RL mapping proposed by [15]. This simplifies dramatically the development of own RL-based TCP solutions and can be further used as a benchmarking suite allowing to compare the performance of different RL approaches in the context of TCP.

`DashNs3Env` is another predefined environment for testing adaptive video streaming solutions using our framework. Again the RL mapping for observation state, action and reward is predefined, i.e. as proposed by [19].

6.3 Multi-Agent Environments

In multi-agent environments, a number of agents must collaborate or compete to achieve a predefined goal, e.g. maximize utilization of wireless resources. They belong to the most complex branch of RL research, as traditional RL approaches fail to learn in such environments, i.e. directly applying single-agent RL algorithms and assuming other agents to be a part of the environment is problematic as the environment is non-stationary from the view of any agent, what eventually violates Markov assumptions required for convergence and prevents learning [17].

As a communication network by nature is a multi-agent environment (e.g. wireless network), we believe that our ns3-gym framework may be a useful tool to advance research and knowledge in the multi-agent RLN area. Note that the implementation of

a multi-agent environment can be achieved using multiple (i.e. one for each agent) or a single instance of the `OpenGymGateway` in ns-3 simulation script. In the former case, the gateways communicate with corresponding agents in separate Python processes, while in the latter case all agents are being trained in a single Python process. This, however, requires to implement a switching mechanism steering observations and actions to the proper agents (e.g. based on node ID added to the observation vector).

6.4 Emulation

Since the ns-3 allows for usage of real Linux protocol stacks inside simulation [27] as well as can be run in the emulation mode for evaluating network protocols in real testbeds [5] (possibly interacting with real-world implementations), it can act as a bridge between an agent implemented in Gym and a real-world environment. Those capabilities give the researchers the possibility to train their RL agents in a simulated network (possibly very fast using parallel environments) and test them afterward in real testbed without having to change any single line of code. We believe that this intermediate step is of the great importance for the development of ML-based network control algorithms as it reduces the possible discontinuities when moving from simulation to real-world.

7 CASE-STUDY EXAMPLES

In this section, we present two examples of a Cognitive Radio (CR) transmitter, that learns the pattern of a periodic interferer in order to avoid collisions with it. In the first example, the transmitter is able to sense the entire bandwidth (i.e. $M = 4$ wireless channels) whereas in the second example it can only monitor its own channel.

Specifically, we consider the problem of radio channel selection in a wireless multi-channel environment, e.g. 802.11 networks with external interference. The objective of the agent is to select for the next time slot a channel free of interference. We consider a simple illustrative example where the external interference, e.g. a microwave oven, follows a periodic pattern, i.e. sweeping over all four channels in the same order as shown in Fig. 5.

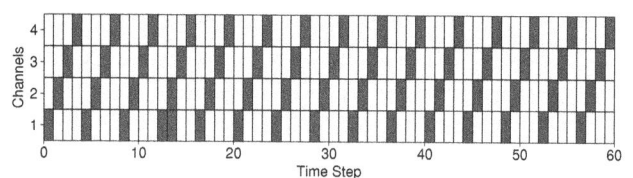

Figure 5: Channel access pattern of periodic interferer.

We created a simple simulation scenario using existing functionality from ns-3, i.e. interference created using `WaveformGenerator` class and sensing performed using `SpectrumAnalyzer` class. Our proposed RL mapping is:

- observation — occupation on each channel in the last time slot, i.e. a vector indicating whether a received signal power on each channel is below (-1) or above (+1) a predefined threshold, e.g. -82 dBm; in addition, we can combine observations from last N time-steps;
- action — set the channel to be used for the next time slot,
- reward — +1 if no collision with interferer; otherwise -1,

- gameover — if more than three collisions happened during the last ten time-slots

Our simple RL-based agent is based on deep Q-learning technique. It uses a small neural network with two fully connected layers, i.e. input and output. The $M \cdot N$ neurons in input layer use *ReLU* activation function, while the output layer uses *softmax* activation whose output $\mathbf{p} \in (0, 1)^M$ is a probability vector over the four possible channels. We use Adam solver [12] during training to tune the neural network parameters.

The source code of both examples (§7.1 and §7.2) is available in the online ns3-gym repository.

7.1 CR – Wideband Sensing

Fig. 6 shows the learning performance. We see that after around 25 episodes, using only its local (but wideband) observations, the agent has perfectly learned the behavior of the periodic interferer and was able to properly select the channel for the next time-slot avoiding any collision. Although it is not shown here, we observed that using observations of last N time-steps speeds up the learning process, i.e. with longer observation, the agent can learn more dependencies in a single step. In Fig. 6 we show the case when the agent was feed with the data containing the observations from the last four time-steps (i.e. history size $N = 4$).

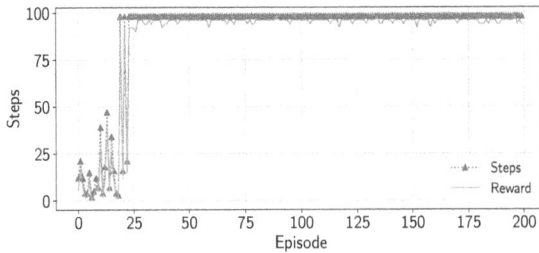

Figure 6: Learning performance of RL-based Cognitive Radio transmitter in case of wideband sensing.

7.2 CR – Narrowband Sensing

In contrast to the previous example, the CR transmitter has to learn to adapt to the interferer by performing narrowband sensing. Hence at a given point in time, the agent can only monitor the state of the channel it is operating on. The narrow-band observations of the CR transmitter are illustrated in Fig. 7. Note that in a single time-slot the TX can determine only whether the currently used channel is occupied by interfered (red, +1) or is free (blue, -1) and has no information about the other channels (white, 0). As shown in Fig. 8, we can observe that even narrowband sensing is sufficient to learn the behavior of the periodic interferer and to select an interference-free channel for the following time-slot. However, it requires a longer training process (i.e. around 75 episodes) comparing to the wideband sensing. Similar as in case of wideband sensing, we observe that longer observation history shortens the learning process. Again in Fig. 8 we show the agent's learning performance with the observation history size of $N = 4$.

8 RELATED WORK

Related work falls into three categories:

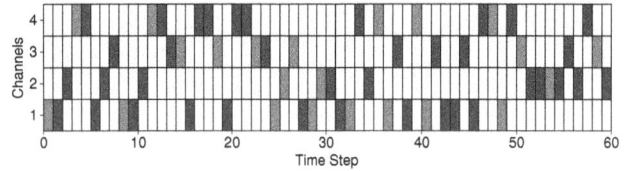

Figure 7: Narrow-band observations of cognitive radio transmitter: collision with interferer (red), no collision (blue), no information (white).

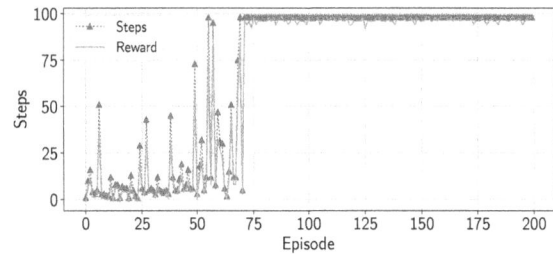

Figure 8: Learning performance of RL-based Cognitive Radio transmitter in case of narrowband sensing.

RL for networking applications: In the literature, a variety of works can be found proposing to use RL to solve networking related problems. We present two of those in more detail with emphasis on the proposed RL mapping.

Li et al. [15] proposed RL-based Transmission Control Protocol (TCP) where the objective is to learn to adjust the TCP's congestion window (CWND) to increase a utility function, which is computed based on the measurement of flow throughput and latency. The identified state space of the environment consists of exponentially weighted moving average (EWMA) of acknowledge (ACK) inter-arrival time, EWMA of packet inter-sending time, Round Trip Time (RTT) ratio, slow start threshold, and current CWND. The action space consists of increasing and decreasing the CWND respectively. Finally, the reward is specified by the value of a utility function, reflecting the desirability of the action picked.

Mao et al. proposed an RL-based adaptive video streaming [19] called Pensieve which learns the Adaptive Bitrate (ABR) algorithm automatically through experience. The observation state consists among other things of past chunk throughput, download time and current buffer size. The action space consists of the different bitrates which can be selected for the next video chunk. Finally, the reward signal is derived directly from the QoE metric, which considers the three factors: bitrate, rebuffering and smoothness.

Extension of OpenAI Gym: Zamora et al. [30] provided an extension of the OpenAI Gym for robotics using the Robot Operating System (ROS) and the Gazebo simulator with a focus on creating a benchmarking system for robotics allowing direct comparison of different techniques and algorithms using the same virtual conditions. Our work aims similar goals but targets the networking community. Chinchali et al. [6] build a custom network simulator for IoT using OpenAI's Gym environment in order to study the scheduling of cellular network traffic. With ns3-gym, it would be easier to perform such an analysis as the ns-3 contains lots of MAC schedulers which can serve as the baseline for comparison.

Custom RL solutions for networkings: Winstein et al. [29] implemented a RL-based TCP congestion control algorithm on the basis of the outdated ns-2 network simulator. Newer work on Q-learning for TCP can be found in [19]. In contrast to our work both proposed approaches are not generic as they provide only an API meant for reading and controlling TCP parameters. Moreover, custom RL libraries were used. Komondor[3] is a low-complexity wireless network simulator for the next-generation high-density WLANs including support for novel WLAN mechanisms like dynamic channel bonding (DCB) or spatial reuse. In addition, Komondor permits including intelligent ML-based agents in the wireless nodes to optimize their operation based on an implemented learning algorithm. In contrast to ns-3, Komondor is focused only on simulating WLAN operation and does not provide detailed models of other layers of the protocol stack nor different wireless technologies. This limits the potential of ML for cross-layer control/optimization or cross-technology cooperation.

9 CONCLUSIONS

In this paper, we presented the ns3-gym toolkit that simplifies the usage of reinforcement learning for solving problems in the area of networking. This is achieved by interconnecting the OpenAI Gym with the ns-3 network simulator. As the framework is generic, it can be used by the community in a variety of networking problems.

For the future, we plan to extend the set of available environments, which can be used to benchmark different RL techniques. Moreover, we are going to provide examples showing how it can be used with more advanced RL techniques, e.g. A3C [20]. We believe that ns3-gym will foster machine learning research in the networking area and research community will grow around it. Finally, we plan to set up a website – so-called leaderboard – allowing researchers to share their results and compare the performance of algorithms for various environments using the same virtual conditions.

ACKNOWLEDGMENTS

We are grateful to Georg Hoelger for helping us with the implementation of the CR examples.

This work was supported by the Central Innovation Programme of German Federal Ministry for Economic Affairs and Energy under grant agreement No. ZF4478901ED7 (HAFIES project).

REFERENCES

[1] Dafna Shahaf Aviv Tamar Asaf Valadarsky, Michael Schapira. 2017. Learning To Route with Deep RL. In *NIPS*.
[2] R. Atallah, C. Assi, and M. Khabbaz. 2017. Deep reinforcement learning-based scheduling for roadside communication networks. In *WiOpt*.
[3] Sergio Barrachina-Muñoz, Francesc Wilhelmi, Ioannis Selinis, and Boris Bellalta. 2018. Komondor: a Wireless Network Simulator for Next-Generation High-Density WLANs. *CoRR* abs/1811.12397 (2018). arXiv:1811.12397 http://arxiv.org/abs/1811.12397
[4] Greg Brockman, Vicki Cheung, Ludwig Pettersson, Jonas Schneider, John Schulman, Jie Tang, and Wojciech Zaremba. 2016. OpenAI Gym. *CoRR* (2016). http://arxiv.org/abs/1606.01540
[5] Gustavo Carneiro, Helder Fontes, and Manuel Ricardo. 2011. Fast prototyping of network protocols through ns-3 simulation model reuse. *Simulation modelling practice and theory, Elsevier* (2011).
[6] Sandeep Chinchali, Pan Hu, Tianshu Chu, Manu Sharma, Manu Bansal, Rakesh Misra, Marco Pavone, and Sachin Katti. 2018. Cellular Network Traffic Scheduling With Deep Reinforcement Learning. In *AAAI*.
[7] Paul F. Christiano, Zain Shah, Igor Mordatch, Jonas Schneider, Trevor Blackwell, Joshua Tobin, Pieter Abbeel, and Wojciech Zaremba. 2016. Transfer from Simulation to Real World through Learning Deep Inverse Dynamics Model. *CoRR* (2016). http://arxiv.org/abs/1610.03518
[8] J. Deng, W. Dong, R. Socher, L. Li, Kai Li, and Li Fei-Fei. 2009. ImageNet: A large-scale hierarchical image database. In *IEEE CVPR*.
[9] Prafulla Dhariwal, Christopher Hesse, Oleg Klimov, Alex Nichol, Matthias Plappert, Alec Radford, John Schulman, Szymon Sidor, Yuhuai Wu, and Peter Zhokhov. 2017. OpenAI Baselines. https://github.com/openai/baselines.
[10] Yan Duan, Xi Chen, Rein Houthooft, John Schulman, and Pieter Abbeel. 2016. Benchmarking Deep Reinforcement Learning for Continuous Control. *CoRR* abs/1604.06778 (2016). arXiv:1604.06778 http://arxiv.org/abs/1604.06778
[11] Rohit Gupta, Bjoern Bachmann, Russell Ford, Sundeep Rangan, Nikhil Kundargi, Amal Ekbal, Karamvir Rathi, Maria Isabel Sanchez, Antonio de la Oliva, and Arianna Morelli. 2015. Ns-3-based Real-time Emulation of LTE Testbed Using LabVIEW Platform for Software Defined Networking (SDN) in CROWD Project. In *Proceedings of the 2015 Workshop on Ns-3 (WNS3 '15)*.
[12] Diederik P. Kingma and Jimmy Ba. 2015. Adam: A Method for Stochastic Optimization. In *ICLR*. http://arxiv.org/abs/1412.6980
[13] Jens Kober, J Andrew Bagnell, and Jan Peters. 2013. Reinforcement learning in robotics: A survey. *The International Journal of Robotics Research* (2013).
[14] Yiming Kong, Hui Zang, and Xiaoli Ma. 2018. Improving TCP Congestion Control with Machine Intelligence. In *ACM NetAI*.
[15] Wei Li, Fan Zhou, Kaushik Roy Chowdhury, and Waleed M Meleis. 2018. QTCP: Adaptive Congestion Control with Reinforcement Learning. *IEEE Transactions on Network Science and Engineering* (2018).
[16] Eric Liang, Richard Liaw, Robert Nishihara, Philipp Moritz, Roy Fox, Ken Goldberg, Joseph E. Gonzalez, Michael I. Jordan, and Ion Stoica. 2018. RLlib: Abstractions for Distributed Reinforcement Learning. In *International Conference on Machine Learning (ICML)*.
[17] Ryan Lowe, Yi Wu, Aviv Tamar, Jean Harb, OpenAI Pieter Abbeel, and Igor Mordatch. 2017. Multi-agent actor-critic for mixed cooperative-competitive environments. In *Advances in Neural Information Processing Systems*.
[18] Hongzi Mao, Mohammad Alizadeh, Ishai Menache, and Srikanth Kandula. 2016. Resource Management with Deep Reinforcement Learning. In *ACM HotNets*.
[19] Hongzi Mao, Ravi Netravali, and Mohammad Alizadeh. 2017. Neural adaptive video streaming with pensieve. In *ACM SIGCOMM*.
[20] Volodymyr Mnih, Adrià Puigdomènech Badia, Mehdi Mirza, Alex Graves, Timothy P. Lillicrap, Tim Harley, David Silver, and Koray Kavukcuoglu. 2016. Asynchronous Methods for Deep Reinforcement Learning. *CoRR* (2016). http://arxiv.org/abs/1602.01783
[21] NS-3 Consortium. [n.d.]. ns-3 documentation. *https:www.nsnam.org*. Accessed: 2019-07-20.
[22] NS 3 Consortium. [n.d.]. ns-3 source code. *http:code.nsnam.org*. Accessed: 2019-07-20.
[23] OpenAI. [n.d.]. OpenAI Gym documentation. *https:gym.openai.com*. Accessed: 2019-07-20.
[24] OpenAI. [n.d.]. OpenAI Gym source code. *https:github.comopenaigym*. Accessed: 2019-07-20.
[25] Wojciech Samek, Slawomir Stanczak, and Thomas Wiegand. 2017. The Convergence of Machine Learning and Communications. *CoRR* (2017). http://arxiv.org/abs/1708.08299
[26] P. Lalith Suresh and Ruben Merz. 2011. Ns-3-click: Click Modular Router Integration for Ns-3. In *Proceedings of the 4th International ICST Conference on Simulation Tools and Techniques (SIMUTools '11)*. 8.
[27] Hajime Tazaki, Frédéric Uarbani, Emilio Mancini, Mathieu Lacage, Daniel Camara, Thierry Turletti, and Walid Dabbous. 2013. Direct Code Execution: Revisiting Library OS Architecture for Reproducible Network Experiments. In *ACM CoNEXT*.
[28] M. Wang, Y. Cui, X. Wang, S. Xiao, and J. Jiang. 2018. Machine Learning for Networking: Workflow, Advances and Opportunities. *IEEE Network* (2018).
[29] Keith Winstein and Hari Balakrishnan. 2013. TCP Ex Machina: Computer-generated Congestion Control. In *ACM SIGCOMM*.
[30] Iker Zamora, Nestor Gonzalez Lopez, Victor Mayoral Vilches, and Alejandro Hernandez Cordero. 2016. Extending the OpenAI Gym for robotics: a toolkit for reinforcement learning using ROS and Gazebo. *arXiv preprint arXiv:1608.05742* (2016).

A Simulation Execution Manager for ns-3

Encouraging reproducibility and simplifying statistical analysis of ns-3 simulations

Davide Magrin
University of Padova
Padova, Italy
magrinda@dei.unipd.it

Dizhi Zhou
Synopsys Inc.
Ottawa, Canada
dizhi.zhou@gmail.com

Michele Zorzi
University of Padova
Padova, Italy
zorzi@dei.unipd.it

ABSTRACT

The typical workflow for ns-3 users consists of coming up with an experiment, translating that idea to simulation code, running multiple simulations, analyzing the outcomes, and finally plotting results. So far, the ns-3 project has not been providing tools to cover the steps from running simulations to obtaining plots: research teams typically develop their own custom solutions, and often need to learn new tools in order to reproduce results found in the literature. In this work we propose a framework that allows ns-3 users to go from their simulation script to plots in as few lines of code as possible, hiding tedious details about simulation running and result management, and leveraging Python's widely established statistical analysis tools to quickly perform simulations, analyze their outcomes, and plot results. The code and its documentation, which have been in part developed under the Google Summer of Code 2018 program, are publicly available at [6, 7].

KEYWORDS

ns-3; simulation; result management; statistical analysis

ACM Reference Format:
Davide Magrin, Dizhi Zhou, and Michele Zorzi. 2019. **A Simulation Execution Manager for ns-3**: Encouraging reproducibility and simplifying statistical analysis of ns-3 simulations. In *22nd Int'l ACM Conference on Modeling, Analysis and Simulation of Wireless and Mobile Systems (MSWiM '19), November 25–29, 2019, Miami Beach, FL, USA.* ACM, New York, NY, USA, 5 pages. https://doi.org/10.1145/3345768.3355942

1 INTRODUCTION

Writing or modifying existing ns-3 [4] code to obtain a simulation script that correctly models the desired scenario is only the first step researchers need to take when using ns-3. Additional infrastructure is almost always needed to automatically explore a parameter space, perform enough repetitions for each configuration of the simulation scenario, manage the script's output files, process and format the results into appropriate data structures, and finally obtain the desired plots. This need for infrastructure has so far been answered through various approaches which vary widely

in flexibility, integration with the original simulator code, software design and offered features.

A possible approach consists in building the features mentioned above directly in the simulator code: this is a path that was followed by OMNET++ [12], which provides an integrated solution that can be accessed directly from its graphical interface and used for quick visualization of the results of some simulations. The documentation, however, also states that users should switch to custom Python systems for more advanced analysis.[1] Other ns-3 competitors, instead, choose not to integrate this kind of features directly in their codebase: this is the case of NetSim[2], which currently does not provide any way for the user to execute multiple runs of the same simulation script with different seeds from its primary interface, and instead relies on the users performing multiple simulations through bash or Python.

The creation of external frameworks is another possible solution to this issue. One of the first examples of such software is Akaroa2 [9], a multi-simulator framework that runs simulations in parallel, collects, and analyzes results to ensure acceptably low statistical errors. The framework can be interfaced with OMNET++, ns-2 and other simulators, but currently seems to be abandoned. SAFE [11] has so far been the main effort to create a simulation infrastructure expressly for ns-3. The framework was mainly focused on helping users obtain credible results, with some parallel efforts also going towards effective data visualization [8], and was based on previous work by the same authors [3]. Development of the framework was discontinued at the end of the project and the code was not merged into the official ns-3 release, meaning that the software is only compatible with version up to ns-3.13. In fact, one of the issues of approaches such as [9, 11] is their reliance on interfaces with the underlying simulation code in order to extract results: this coupling, which allows the introduction of useful features like dynamic termination of the simulation campaign once enough results are collected, also comes at the price of a tighter integration, which in turn demands changes to the simulator's API to be quickly reflected by changes to the framework, and ultimately results in less straightforward code maintenance.

Users who do not want to rely on an external framework, instead, are forced to adopt their own solutions, which typically fall into one of two categories. One possible solution involves adopting a pipeline of external tools, such as bash for the simulation execution and MATLAB or R as statistical analysis frameworks for plot generation. Multiple waf invocations may be performed through a shell script, and the results saved to a different folder for each invocation. After simulations have been run, results can be imported into a separate

---

[1] As explained at https://docs.omnetpp.org/tutorials
[2] https://www.tetcos.com/

component of the pipeline to be parsed and plotted. The main drawback of this solution is that simulation script execution and result analysis are performed in two distinct blocks: in case the experiment should change (e.g., requiring additional simulations or the exploration of a new parameter), each of these two blocks would need to be modified accordingly.

As an alternative approach, users might also consider performing simulation executions and data analysis directly from within their simulation script, using ns-3's Statistical Framework [10] to extract the relevant metrics and generate plots directly from within the C++ program. This approach, however, constrains the user to always perform simulation execution and result analysis together, foregoing the ability to change the analysis part without executing the simulations again, as can be desirable for larger simulation campaigns. It is also worth noting that this solution ties together the experiment script with its multiple executions and analysis logic, limiting the re-usability of the same simulation scenario for other kinds of analyses.

In this paper we propose a methodology for the execution and analysis of ns-3 simulations that does not incur the problems described above, and provide an implementation of this methodology consisting in a Python library that allows users to run and manage complex simulation campaigns. Additionally, the library provides smart scheduling of simulations, which can lead to significant time savings when compared to the random parallel execution currently employed in the state of the art and, likely, in custom solutions.

The rest of this paper is structured as follows: Section 2 provides a general introduction to our proposed solution, the Simulation Execution Manager, discussing the underlying software implementation by showing the creation of an example simulation campaign and motivating how this new framework will help the reproducibility issue. Section 3 shows how a simple scheduling expedient can significantly improve the performance, while Section 4 draws some conclusions and briefly discusses the proposed solution.

2 THE SIMULATION EXECUTION MANAGER

The Simulation Execution Manager (SEM) [7] is a Python library that enables users to run ns-3 simulations and plot results in a few lines of Python code. The software takes care of compiling ns-3, efficiently executing simulations, permanently saving results, parsing them to compute the desired metrics, and finally collecting them into easily accessible data structures. Installation of the library is straightforward: issuing the `pip3 install -u sem` command is enough to install SEM on the system for the current user. In order to use SEM, users can either write a Python script (also called the SEM script) in which they first import the library and then use it to perform their simulations and analysis, or use the provided command line tool to interactively run simulations and export results to data structures that can then be imported in other software packages such as MATLAB.

The SEM framework tries to strike a balance between the monolithic approach of performing both simulation execution and analysis directly from within the ns-3 script and the modular pipeline approach described in Section 1. The proposed solution respects the separation of scenario definition and experiment running (differently from the monolithic approach), since the ns-3 script only

has to build the topology, run a single simulation and generate results. When compared to the pipeline approach, instead, the proposed solution adds the advantage of having a single file specify both the simulation and the analysis: instead of running multiple tools sequentially to get to the plots, users only need to execute the SEM script once to get from a simple ns-3 installation to their plots. Finally, we want to remark that the simulation framework is as decoupled as possible from the simulator, in order to minimize the chance of changes in the ns-3 API breaking compatibility with SEM, and hopefully making both ns-3 and SEM easier to maintain in the future.

The library is built around three main components. A Simulation Runner is used to manage the ns-3 installation, from compilation to script execution; this class is the only component which will need to be adapted in case of changes to the build system in the ns-3 codebase. A Database Manager saves a simulation's output files in a database, keeping track of which simulations have already been run in order to avoid needlessly repeating experiments. Finally, a Campaign Manager connects and administers the previous two components, building new functionality on top of them and providing a cleaner interface for the user. The next few sections will illustrate the typical SEM workflow, further clarifying the role these components have and describing the features they provide.

2.1 The simulation campaign

The simulation campaign is the main abstraction used by SEM, and consists in a data structure containing various components that are needed to run simulations and save results (i.e., to interface with the ns-3 installation and with the database holding results). Campaigns can be either loaded from existing folders or created from scratch, using the `load()` and `new()` methods of the `CampaignManager` class. In the latter case, the user will only need a source-controlled installation of ns-3, the name of an ns-3 *script*, and a folder where to save results.

Behind the scenes, the SEM library will take care of creating a new database, registering the commit hash of the ns-3 installation, and querying the simulation script for the list of supported command line parameters, through which the library will then be able to run the ns-3 script testing different configurations in the simulated scenario. This information is then saved, and can be queried by printing out the campaign object, which is returned after loading or creation:

```
>>> print(campaign)
--- Campaign info ---
script: wifi-multi-tos
params: ['nWifi', 'distance', 'simulationTime',
        'useRts', 'mcs', 'channelWidth',
        'useShortGuardInterval']
HEAD: 9386dc7d106fd9241ff151195a0e6e5cb954d363
---------------------
```

After a campaign is created or loaded in the user script, the library is ready to run simulations. In order to do this, SEM requires the user to specify which values of the parameters should be used to perform the simulations.

2.2 Parameter spaces

In order to assess the impact of some design choices on the scenario under study, users are expected to work with parametric ns-3 scripts, which can be called with a set of command line arguments that influence the scenario and the protocols used in the simulation. In order to execute a single simulation, SEM needs a *parameter combination*, i.e., one value for each available command line parameter.

Users will typically want to use the SEM library to explore a *space* of the parameters exposed by their script. In order to facilitate this task, SEM uses the notion of parameter spaces, specifications which describe a set of parameter combinations. If a parameter space is passed to SEM instead of a simple parameter combination, all combinations contained in that space will be executed.

In SEM, parameter combinations are defined using Python dictionaries, mapping strings containing parameter names to the desired value for that parameter. In case the value for one or more parameters in the dictionary is set to an array of values, the dictionary represents a space, made up of all the possible combinations of the specified parameter values. In the case of the `wifi-multi-tos` campaign shown above, a parameter space might take the following form:

```
params = {'nWifi': 4,
          'distance': 10,
          'simulationTime': 10,
          'useRts': [False, True],
          'mcs': [1, 3, 5, 7],
          'channelWidth': 20,
          'useShortGuardInterval': False}
```

This specification means that we are interested in what happens when the employed MCS varies in the set $\{1, 3, 5, 7\}$ and when RTS is either enabled or disabled. When a SEM campaign is instructed to explore the `params` space, it will perform simulations using MCS 1 with RTS off, MCS 1 with RTS on, MCS 3 with RTS off, and so on. Note that, since the framework has no knowledge of the semantics of the parameters, it is the user's responsibility to either formulate simulation scenarios that support every possible parameter combination or to at least avoid performing simulations using meaningless or non-valid parameter combinations.

2.3 Running simulations

Once the user has defined its parameter space of interest, SEM provides facilities to cleanly and efficiently invoke the ns-3 campaign script multiple times, in order to cover the whole parameter space. If the parameter specification does not contain a value for RngRun, SEM's simulation running functions will accept as input an integer describing how many repetitions are wanted for each parameter combination, and the library will generate a unique RngRun value for each simulation. Alternatively, the user can also achieve finer control over the random number generation by directly setting the RngRun parameter in the parameter space, thus forcing some simulations to run with a certain and repeatable stream of pseudo-random numbers.

The simulation running component takes care of configuring and building the ns-3 code, and can run multiple simulations locally in parallel, leveraging Python's `multiprocessing` library. Additionally, simulations can be run on clusters supporting the DRMAA API [1], such as Sun Grid Engine, HTCondor, and SLURM, via the drmaa Python library[3]. The library makes the underlying architecture transparent to the user: the best choice is picked automatically, and the same simulation running API is used for the local and cluster use cases. This way, the same exact script can be employed in case it is decided to scale up the number of simulations by moving to a cluster architecture.

When simulation runs are requested to the library through the `run_missing_simulations()` method, re-executions of the same parameter combinations are skipped if already found in the database, preventing waste of computational resources. This feature makes running the same SEM script multiple times with a modified analysis part very fast, since the simulations are only performed once and are then cached in the database for future analysis.

Note that, since the commit hash is saved as part of the campaign, the library always verifies that the underlying ns-3 installation it is working on is at that commit hash, and that the repository is clean (i.e., it does not contain uncommitted changes). This prevents users from inadvertently mixing results obtained with different software versions, and ensures reproducibility and consistency of results obtained under the same campaign.

After the desired simulation runs are submitted and the library has verified that results for those parameter combinations are not available in the database already, execution of the simulations in parallel starts. The runner component will directly access the executable corresponding to the specified ns-3 script, without repeatedly passing through needless calls to `waf`, which is only used for configuration and compilation. The maximum number of parallel simulations can be set through a variable, to avoid overloading the system with simulations. During execution of the simulations the library keeps track of the current progress of the executions, and provides time estimates for the completion of the current batch of simulations:

```
>>> campaign.run_missing_simulations(params)
Running simulations: 50% 5/10 [00:40<00:38, 8s/sim]
```

Each ns-3 execution is performed in a dedicated folder, which is used to collect all output of the simulation script: besides any files generated by the C++ program, the library also redirects the standard output and the standard error streams to files, and treats them as a result of the simulation. After a simulation is completed, a *result* entry is inserted in a database, managed through the Python TinyDB library and consisting in a plaintext `json` file.

The entries describing the results of a simulation run consist of a unique id, the parameter combination used to obtain that result, and the amount of time elapsed to get the result. Output files are saved separately in a dedicated folder, marked with that result's id. Files generated by the simulations can thus be accessed either through facilities provided by the library or directly from the relevant subfolder. Once results are saved in the database, they can be either retrieved and exported for analysis in other frameworks, or directly processed and plotted from within the SEM script.

---

[3]github.com/pygridtools/drmaa-python

2.4 Parsing results and obtaining plots

When the simulations exploring a parameter space are completed, the user can move on to the analysis phase. At this point, the database will contain a collection of results in the form of files generated by the executions of the ns-3 script. These files can be read directly in Python through SEM's `get_complete_results()` function, which returns a dictionary mapping filenames to strings of file contents. These files now need to be converted into numerical results; in order to do so, users are asked to specify a parsing function: two approaches are possible at this point. For users who want to leave as much parsing to the library as possible, SEM provides a default parser, which will try and automatically read the contents of the result file specified by the user into a numerical matrix. For situations in which more sophisticated parsing is required (e.g., output files need to be processed before they can yield a clean and purely numerical data structure, or some computation on the resulting matrix is required), users are instead asked to define a function that determines what kind of numerical result they want to obtain from the files generated by the simulation. Once the parsing function is defined, it can be passed together with a parameter space to the library, which will fill data structures shaped like the specified parameter space with the matrix or metric of interest, and return these structures to the user. As an example, if the `param` space defined in Section 2.2 is specified, SEM will return a two-dimensional structure in which the first dimension has length 2 and represents the RTS parameter, while the second dimension represents the MCS parameter and has size 4. Examples about how Python libraries can be employed for easy computation of statistical quantities and for plotting are available at [6].

Figure 1 shows how the throughput of various Modulation Coding Scheme settings in a WiFi connection varies with the distance of the STA from the AP, and gives an example of how complex plots can be obtained with ease using SEM. The campaign used to plot the figure comprised a total of 960 simulations, testing 2 parameters with 16 and 3 values each and performing 20 independent runs for each combination. All the steps needed to create the figure, from compiling ns-3 to parsing the results and printing the plot as depicted here were performed using 9 lines of Python code, 4 of which were dedicated to plotting and axis labeling. The data underlying the plot can just as easily be saved to file through `numpy`'s `savetxt()` function, and directly employed to build a figure in a LaTeX document using the `Tikz` and `Pgfplots` libraries.

2.5 The Command Line Interface

For users who only wish to leverage SEM's parallel simulation running and result management capabilities, the library also offers a command line tool that can be used to create a campaign, run simulations, and export results without the need to interact with Python code. The command line interface is installed together with the library through pip, and shows a help message when invoked with the `sem --help` command. Differently from the Python API, for which the user needs to be aware of the interface by reading the documentation or working upon examples, the command line interface strives to be as easy to use and discoverable by the user as possible, at the price of slightly reduced functionality. Similarly to what is done by the `git` command line interface, the `sem` command

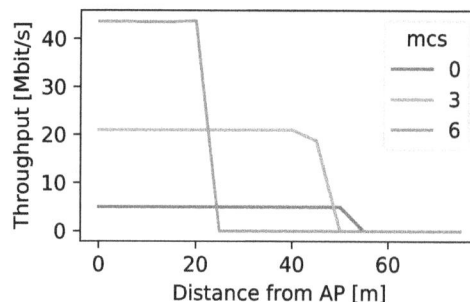

Figure 1: Example of a plot obtained using SEM and the Python `matplotlib` library.

expects a sub-command (e.g., `sem run` or `sem export`), to which the user can again pass the `--help` flag to obtain in-depth information about its usage. More details on the available commands for the SEM Command Line Interface are available in the online documentation [6].

2.6 Reproducibility

The library strives to make the analysis of simulation results both easy to share and easy to reproduce. Users willing to share their results will only need to make available the ns-3 code they employed and their SEM script: sharing the analysis would be as simple as sharing a git repository containing the SEM script, and in which ns-3 is installed as a git submodule pointing to the relevant branch in the researcher's public fork of ns-3. A person trying to reproduce the results, then, will only need a recursive clone of the git repository containing the analysis script followed by the execution of the SEM script to run the simulations and obtain the exact same plots that were published.

3 PARALLEL SIMULATION SCHEDULING

SEM's parallel simulation capabilities can be categorized as Multiple Replications In Parallel (MRIP), meaning that multiple randomized executions of a single simulation program are executed simultaneously. In general, simulations should be scheduled across processors in such a way that parallelism is fully exploited, avoiding cases in which few processors finish much later than the others, forcing them to wait in an idle state and thus wasting resources.

The makespan minimization problem with atomic jobs has been studied extensively in the field of operations research, and describes quite well the situation faced by SEM: given n tasks with required processing times j_i and m identical machines, the problem consists in finding the schedule that assigns a list of jobs to each machine, such that the makespan time (i.e., the time from the beginning of computation up to the time when the last job is completed) is minimized. While the problem is known to be NP-hard, approximations such as [5] can achieve an arbitrary error with respect to the optimum, and can be computed in polynomial time. A popular and even simpler approximation of the solution is given by the Longest Processing Time (LPT) algorithm, which assigns higher priority to tasks which have a longer processing time. This approach achieves

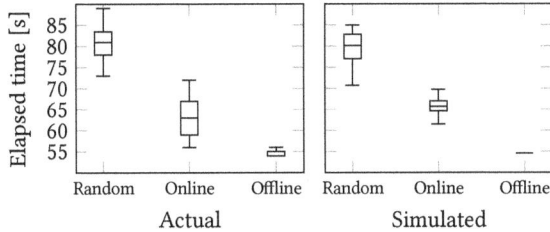

Figure 2: Makespan times when employing different parallel scheduling strategies.

an upper bound of $(4/3 - 1/3m)o$, where o is the optimum [2], and is quite easy to implement.

To assess the gain that can be expected using LPT we have written a simple multi-processor scheduling simulator that computes the makespan time for a set of tasks. The lengths of these simulated tasks were taken from actual ns-3 simulation campaigns, and consist in a single run for each parameter combination; each item is then used to spawn $r - 1$ tasks with identical running time, in order to simulate the r randomized simulations that will be performed using the RngRun parameter in SEM. Three simple approaches to scheduling were tested:

- *Random*: simulations are assigned to processors in no particular order, as soon as one of the workers becomes available. This is the approach that is followed in most state-of-the-art frameworks;
- *Online LPT*: after a first run for each parameter combination is performed, in order to measure processing times, the successive $r - 1$ runs are performed in decreasing order of length. This algorithm attempts to provide an approximation of a true LPT approach, in which all task lengths are known from the very beginning;
- *Offline LPT*: all runs for all parameter combinations are executed in decreasing order of length. It is assumed that this algorithm can access information about processing times that was collected during past simulations, and can thus schedule simulations exactly according to the LPT scheme.

Figure 2 shows the statistics of makespan time for the three policies, both simulated and applied to a real ns-3 simulation campaign. Firstly, we can observe that the simulator gave a good enough approximation of the actual results, which suffer from additional randomness due to the real system they are running on. It can be seen that the random scheduling policy is outperformed by both the Offline and the Online LPT policies, which in this specific case yield a mean time saving in the order of 15% and 25% respectively. Furthermore, the Offline LPT scheduler improves by 30% the worst case of the random scheduler; it should also be noted that, while the specific example shown here deals with makespan times in the order of seconds, the same gains would apply to simulations of any length, for instance bringing a simulation campaign normally lasting 4 hours down to 3 hours if the Offline LPT scheduler is employed.

4 CONCLUSIONS

In this paper we presented SEM, a framework for the management of ns-3 simulations. After identifying some issues with the methodologies that are currently employed to run multiple ns-3 simulations and analyze the results they produce, we described a new approach that hides in a Python library the infrastructure that is typically needed to efficiently run simulations, parse results, and obtain plots. This Python library, publicly available and easy to install, allows users to write a brief Python program, called the SEM script, which can produce plots directly from a simple ns-3 installation, and tries to be as decoupled as possible from the underlying simulation script in order to increase the maintainability of the project. Additionally, we showed that the scheduling approach used by SEM yields an improvement of around 20% with respect to the random scheduling typically used in the state of the art, potentially saving hours of simulation time. Besides aiding researchers and other ns-3 users with the task of managing complex simulation campaigns, we hope that this new tool will help promote reproducibility and further analysis of results found in the literature.

ACKNOWLEDGMENTS

This work was developed as part of the Google Summer of Code 2018 program.

REFERENCES

[1] Roger Brobst, Waiman Chan, Fritz Ferstl, Andreas Haas, Daniel Templeton, and John Tollefsrud. 2004. Distributed Resource Management Application API Specification 1.0. In *Grid Forum Document GFD*, Vol. 22.
[2] Ronald L. Graham. 1969. Bounds on multiprocessing timing anomalies. *SIAM J. Appl. Math.* 17, 2 (1969), 416–429.
[3] Andrew Hallagan, Bryan Ward, and L. Felipe Perrone. 2010. An experiment automation framework for ns-3. In *International ICST Conference on Simulation Tools and Techniques*.
[4] Thomas R Henderson, Mathieu Lacage, George F Riley, Craig Dowell, and Joseph Kopena. 2008. Network simulations with the ns-3 simulator. *SIGCOMM demonstration* 14, 14 (2008), 527.
[5] Dorit S. Hochbaum and David B. Shmoys. 1987. Using Dual Approximation Algorithms for Scheduling Problems: Theoretical and Practical Results. *J. ACM* 34, 1 (Jan. 1987), 144–162.
[6] Davide Magrin. 2018. A Simulation Execution Manager for ns-3 (Documentation). https://simulationexecutionmanager.readthedocs.io/en/develop/
[7] Davide Magrin. 2018. A Simulation Execution Manager for ns-3 (Github Repository). https://github.com/signetlabdei/sem
[8] Christopher S. Main, L. Felipe Perrone, and Greg L. Schrock. 2014. Data visualization for network simulations. In *Proceedings of the Winter Simulation Conference (WSC)*.
[9] D. McNickle, K. Pawlikowski, and G. Ewing. 2010. AKAROA2: A Controller of Discrete-Event Simulation which Exploits the Distributed Computing Resource. In *European Conference on Modelling and Simulation (ECMS)*.
[10] ns 3 Project. 2010. Statistical Framework. https://www.nsnam.org/docs/manual/html/statistics.html
[11] L. Felipe Perrone, Christopher S. Main, and Bryan C. Ward. 2012. SAFE: Simulation automation framework for experiments. In *Proceedings of the Winter Simulation Conference (WSC)*.
[12] András Varga and Rudolf Hornig. 2008. An Overview of the OMNeT++ Simulation Environment. In *Proceedings of the 1st International Conference on Simulation Tools and Techniques for Communications, Networks and Systems & Workshops (Simutools)*.

VuLCAN : A Low-cost, Low-power Embedded Visible Light Communication And Networking Platform

Artem Ageev, Emiliano Luci, Chiara Petrioli, Nupur Thakker*
Computer Science Department
University of Rome "La Sapienza"
Rome, Italy
[petrioli,thakker]@di.uniroma1.it

ABSTRACT

Visible Light Communication (VLC) offers a key alternative to the spectrum-challenged Radio Frequency (RF)-based forms of data transmission by tapping an unutilized and unregulated frequency band. Carefully designed low-cost VLC devices have the potential to enable the Internet of Things (IoT) at scale by reducing the current RF spectrum congestion, which is one of the major obstacles to the pervasiveness of the IoT. Wide adoption of VLC devices is however hindered by their current shortcomings, including low data rate, very short range and inability to communicate in noisy environment. In this paper we describe a new software-defined VLC prototype named VuLCAN for Visible Light Communication And Networking that overcomes these limitations. VuLCAN is based on an ARM Cortex M7 core microcontroller with fast sampling analog-to-digital converter along with power-optimized Digital Signal Processing (DSP) libraries. Using BFSK modulation, the prototype achieves a data rate of 65 Kbps over a communication range of 4.5 m. VuLCAN also provides robust and reliable communications in highly illuminated environments (up to 800 lux) using only a low power Light Emitting Diode (LED), largely exceeding the capabilities of current state-of-the-art prototypes.

CCS CONCEPTS

• **Hardware** → **Emerging optical and photonic technologies**;
• **Computer systems organization** → *Embedded hardware*; *Embedded software*.

KEYWORDS

Visible light communication; free-space optical; internet of things; embedded software

ACM Reference Format:
Artem Ageev, Emiliano Luci, Chiara Petrioli, Nupur Thakker. 2019. VuLCAN : A Low-cost, Low-power Embedded Visible Light Communication And Networking Platform. In *22nd Int'l ACM Conference on Modeling, Analysis and Simulation of Wireless and Mobile Systems (MSWiM '19), November 25–29, 2019, Miami Beach, FL, USA*. ACM, Miami, Florida, USA, 8 pages. https://doi.org/10.1145/3345768.3355919

---

* Author names are listed in alphabetical order, which is not indicative of contribution.

---

1 INTRODUCTION

The proliferation of networked wireless devices, especially those that populate the Internet of Things (IoT), demands novel approaches for their reliable and efficient interconnection. Relying on RF-based communication alone appears not to be a viable strategy anymore, as the usable RF bandwidth has become limited [3, 20]. In fact, most RF bands—especially those that are license-free—are already no longer efficiently usable due to their limited capacity and to the presence of strong sources of interference. The visible spectrum is a wide and unregulated band that could be effectively used for wireless *Visible Light-based Communication* (VLC). VLC systems could be used in conjunction with traditional RF-based devices to build networks with higher robustness, throughput and spectrum efficiency. Furthermore, as they can be seamlessly integrated with traditional illumination devices, VLC transmitters can be pervasively deployed. As a consequence, hybrid RF/VLC systems can provide an effective solution for the kind of ubiquitous networking required by IoT deployments [1].

Current VLC systems can be broadly categorized into high-end and low-end systems. High end VLC systems use Field Programmable Gate Array (FPGA) and costly, highly sensitive light sensors [26]. They utilize complex modulation techniques capable to achieve data rates up to Gbps. Most of the high-end systems are meant for infrastructure based deployment, e.g., lighting fixtures as network access points [10]. On the other hand, low-end VLC systems are based on low-cost embedded boards with limited range and data rates [7, 15, 23, 27]. Since these systems have very low bandwidth requirements and mostly operate in narrow, closed spaces, they are ideal to be used in IoT applications, including indoor localization and wireless sensor networking. Our work intends to make a contribution to low-end VLC systems.

In order to keep cost and complexity at bay, low-end VLC systems are based on the commercial-off-the-shelf (COTS) components and embedded boards (e.g., BeagleBone Black) [15, 22, 27]. Light modulation techniques are generally amplitude and pulse-based because of their simplicity. However, they are highly susceptible to ambient noise, i.e., light interference like that from conventional lamps or from sunlight from a window [11, 13, 15, 27]. In fact, one of the major challenges for developing a low-end VLC system is to adopt low-cost design choices that are robust to ambient noise, so that the performance of the system (including BER and data rate) are immune to device placement or illumination.

Several solutions have been proposed to alleviate the problem of ambient noise for low-end VLC systems [4, 6, 8, 28, 29, 31]. Hardware-based approaches focus on intensive analog circuit design, switching Light Emitting Diodes (LEDs) for photodiodes (PD) as receivers or gain control of receiver. Modulation-based approaches adopt frequency-based or other sophisticated modulation techniques. Unfortunately, these approaches suffer from link instability, complex hardware, and high-power consumption. The few prototypes that achieve acceptable robustness to ambient noise have to compromise on range (very short) and data rate (very low).

In this work we contribute to the research on ambient noise-resistant, low-cost, low-power, low-end VLC by designing, developing and testing the VuLCAN (for Visible Light Communication And Networking) system. VuLCAN takes advantage of frequency-based modulation paired with DSP techniques to obtain ambient noise cancellation while maintaining reasonable communication range, data rate and low power consumption. Particularly, VuLCAN employs FSK modulation and adopts the Chirp and Goertzel algorithm for signal detection and demodulation, respectively, thus following a software-defined approach [5, 21]. So far the implementation of such techniques was mainly confined to more high-end DSP boards, FPGA-based platform and costly USRPs. Recent advancements in low-cost high-performance embedded boards, like the ARM Cortex Series boards, afford us the opportunity of bridging the gap between low and high-end systems [19]. Particularly, VuLCAN is based on the ARM cortex-M ST32 F767ZI Nucleo board, which, besides its integrated high-speed Analog-to-Digital (ADC) and Digital-to-Analog Converter (DAC), features native support for operations that are common to DSP techniques.

The contributions of our work are summarized as follows:

- We design, build and test a low-cost and low-power embedded VLC prototype, named VuLCAN, following a software defined approach. VuLCAN achieves a data rate of 65 Kbps over a distance of 4.5 m with low BER (10^{-2}) under varying ambient light conditions (up to 800 lux). We implement the BFSK modulation with a sinusoid as the carrier wave.
- We provide a demodulation scheme based on the use of a Chirp algorithm for signal detection and on the Goertzel algorithm along with Sliding Discrete Fourier Transform (SDFT) for signal demodulation.
- We perform an experimental evaluation to demonstrate the robustness of the system under different indoor scenarios.

The rest of the paper is organized as follows. In Section 2 we describe system design considerations for VuLCAN. Sections 3 and 4 describe the hardware design and the software-defined physical layer of VuLCAN, respectively. Performance evaluation results of the proposed prototype are presented in Section 5. Related works are summarized in Section 6. Finally, Section 7 concludes the paper.

2 SYSTEM DESIGN CONSIDERATIONS

The main focus of our work is to design a system that is robust to ambient noise interference, which can be broadly divided into low frequency (50-60 Hz) and constant additive noise [13, 20]. The former is produced by lights running at the main grid frequency, while the latter mainly comes from natural lighting. This section discusses the system design choices considered for the prototype

implementation. It also provides background information on the modulation, signal detection, synchronization and demodulation techniques chosen.

2.1 Modulation

Binary Frequency Shift Keying (BFSK) is selected as the modulation technique using a sinusoid carrier wave [11]. BFSK, being a frequency modulation approach, offers resiliency to both types of noise identified above. The information transmitted is encoded in the variation of the intensity of the transmitted signal [13]. The instantaneous amplitude of the transmitted wave is proportional to:

$$A(t) \propto \sin(2\pi f(B(t))t + \phi)$$

$$f(s) = \begin{cases} f_0 & \text{if } s = 0 \\ f_1 & \text{if } s = 1, \end{cases}$$

where $f(s)$ is the frequency for symbol s and $B(t)$ is the symbol being modulated at time t and ϕ is the starting phase of the signal. The starting phase can be adjusted in order to have the transmitter power return to 0 after transmitting a symbol. Both symbols have a fixed, equal duration T_s. The bit encoding for our prototype[1] is shown in Figure 1. The duration of the symbol as well as the frequencies can be adapted depending on the ambient noise.

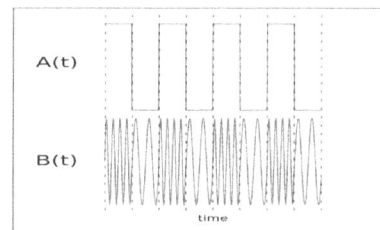

Figure 1: Bit Encoding.

2.2 Demodulation

The recovery of the digital signal from the modulated wave is comprised of two phases: signal detection and demodulation. The receiver produces a stream of values S by sampling the signal at a fixed rate. Standard DSP techniques are then used to identify and extract the frame from the stream.

2.2.1 Signal Detection. Signal detection is performed by pre-pending a chirp to the modulated data. A chirp is a linear sweep signal of finite duration between two frequencies that is represented as:

$$A(t) = A_{max} sin(2\pi(\frac{t}{2T}(f_1 - f_0) + f_0)t + \phi)$$

$$\text{with} \quad 0 \leq t \leq T \wedge f_1 \geq f_0 \geq 0,$$

where T is the duration of the chirp, f_0 and f_1 are the starting and final frequencies, A_{max} is the maximum amplitude of the wave and ϕ is the starting phase of the signal [2, 14]. The receiver precomputes the chirp by generating and sampling it at the same frequency as

---

[1]To ensure robust decoding, two periods per waveform are considered for each symbol.

the actual signal. This will constitute the template chirp c_k, the vector of the precomputed values of the chirp of length k. The chirp is detected by performing the correlation of c_k with the values of the stream. Given the stream S, let us call $S_i : S_{i+k}$ the vector of k values of S, starting from i, and also let s_c be the index of the first value of the chirp vector in S, then

$$f(i, k) := (S_i : S_{i+k}) \cdot c_k$$
$$\arg\max_i f(i, k) = s_c \quad \forall k,$$

that is since $f(i, k)$ is the dot product of a slice of the signal with the template chirp it will trivially have its maximum when the signal aligns with the template c_k.

2.2.2 Signal Demodulation. The demodulation is performed by repeated application of Goertzel algorithm to the signal values [21]. This algorithm calculates a single term of the Discrete Fourier Transform (DFT) in time $O(n)$. To recover an individual symbol the terms corresponding to f_0 and f_1 need to be computed and compared. Since the sampling rate of the receiver is R, then the window size, i.e., the number of samples per symbol will be $w_s = \lfloor \frac{T_s}{R} \rfloor$. This constitutes the length of the input that will be fed to Goertzel algorithm at each iteration. It follows that, in order to work, the demodulation window must be at every time aligned with a symbol in the stream. Let $s_d = (s_c + k)$ be the index of the first value of the data in S. If $\frac{T_s}{R} \in \mathbb{Z}$ then the decoding would be trivial since the start of each symbol would always be w_s samples away from the last. However most often $\frac{T_s}{R} \notin \mathbb{Z}$, thus a technique is needed in order to adjust for slight variations in the index of the first sample of the next symbol. This is achieved by using the Sliding Discrete Fourier Transform (SDFT) algorithm [9]. It follows from the definition of DFT that if the value of a term for a window $S_i : S_{i+k}$ of values is known, then the cost to compute the same term for the window $S_{i+1} : S_{i+1+k}$ is in $O(1)$. Consider a symbol with its first sample at index s_d, w.l.g. let it be the symbol for 0, call

$$m_0 = |G((S_{s_d} : S_{s_d+k}), bin(0))|$$
$$m_0' = |G((S_{s_d+1} : S_{s_d+k+1}), bin(0))|,$$

where $G(\text{values}, \text{bin})$ is the Goertzel function, $bin(s)$ is the bin corresponding to the symbol frequency, and m_0, m_0' are the magnitudes of the returned vectors. If $m_0 \geq m_0'$ then the window is synchronized with the symbols, otherwise it needs to be adjusted. In this case the next symbol will be decoded starting from $s_d + 1 + w_s$. This whole procedure is repeated L times for a frame of L symbols, thus the complexity of the decoding is linear w.r.t. the length of the frame.

3 HARDWARE DESIGN

The analog hardware design of the transceiver is fundamentally influenced by the chosen modulation technique. The transmission frequencies are constrained by the switching time of the LED, the response time of the PD and the overall bandwidth support of the analog circuitry. Furthermore, additional constraints are imposed by the receiver characteristics such as the ADC sampling rate as well as the processing power available for demodulation. A scheme

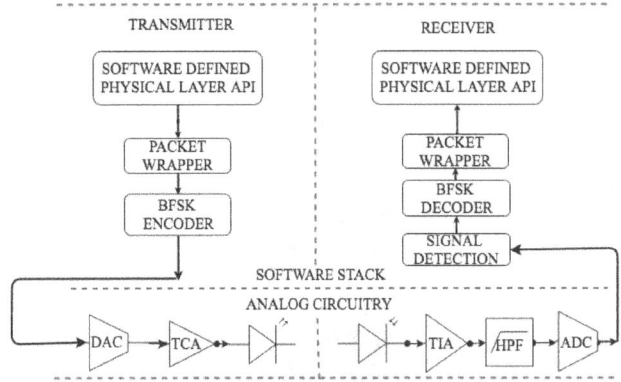

Figure 2: System Architecture.

of the system architecture is shown in Figure 2. The embedded board selected is a low cost STM32-F767ZI Nucleo with integrated high speed ADC and DAC [19]. It is powered by an ARM Cortex-M7 processor, which is especially designed for high performance energy efficient applications. This CPU has a dedicated Floating Point Unit (FPU) as well as a Direct Memory Access (DMA) controller. The DMA in particular completely offloads the CPU from moving the signal data from memory to DAC (for transmission) and from ADC to memory (for reception), as shown in Figure 3. This way it is possible to dedicate more computational power to the actual processing of the signal, which in turn translates into higher data rates. The analog part of the circuitry has been realized using low

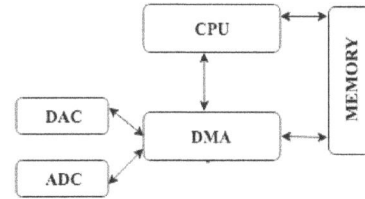

Figure 3: Input/Output Offloading.

cost COTS components. The approximate cost of our VLC prototype including the prototyping board and the analog circuitry is around 38 euros. The hardware prototype and the list of components are shown in Figure 4 and Table 1, respectively.

3.1 VLC Transmitter

The VLC transmitter (TX) consists of two parts: the Transconductance Amplifier (TCA) and the LED [13]. The TCA converts the voltage from the DAC to the current required to drive the LED, which in turn controls its intensity, and thus the instantaneous amplitude of the wave. The TCA has been selected based on its gain bandwidth product, slew rate, low noise and power consumption. The OPA2301AID has 150 MHz of unity-gain bandwidth and has an available shutdown function that reduces supply current to 5 μA when not in use is quite suitable for low-power applications. The LED has been selected based on its low power consumption, high directionality and fast switching time. The switching time of

Table 1: Electronic Components Used for the Prototype.

COMPONENT NAME	PURPOSE	PRICE (€)
STM32-F767ZI NUCLEO BOARD	Prototyping Board	€ 23
MTE7063NK2-UR	LED	€ 6
BPW34	Photodiode	€ 1
OPA380AID	Transimpedance amplifier (TIA)	€ 5
OPA2301AID	For Transconductance amplifier (TCA) and High pass filter (HPF)	€ 3

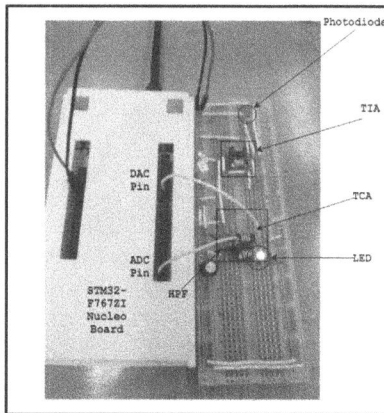

Figure 4: VuLCAN Prototype.

the LED determines the maximum transmission rate. The LED has a peak emission wavelength of 630 nm (red) and a field of view (FOV)[2] of 5°.

3.2 VLC Receiver

The VLC receiver (RX) consists of a Photodiode (PD), a Transimpedance Amplifier (TIA) and a High Pass Filter (HPF) as shown in Figure 2. The PD used for the prototype is BPW-34, which has been selected based on its fast response time, high surface area (7 mm^2) and good sensitivity in indoor applications. The PD is operated in photo-conductive mode, since it provides a better frequency response compared to the photo-voltaic mode. The current flowing through the PD is linearly dependent on the irradiance measured at the surface of the PD. A TIA is used to convert this current to voltage. OPA-380 is selected as the TIA as it provides high slew rate and 90 MHz Gain Bandwidth (GBW). It is ideally suited for high-speed photodiode applications. The gain of the TIA and hence in turn the feedback resistor value has to be accurately chosen which ultimately determines the saturation limit of the VLC receiver. A high gain will give high sensitivity and thus better range, but at the same time will lead to the saturation of the TIA in high ambient light conditions. Whereas a lower gain value is more resilient to external ambient noise but will impair the reception at longer ranges[3]. The HPF is the last stage of the analog circuit and thus

---

[2]Given that the PD has a wide FOV of 65°, by using multiple LEDs or wide FOV LEDs, the omnidirectional communication is possible and hence the prototype is not limited to point to point communication.

[3] A feedback resistor value of 150K ohms is chosen empirically which achieves best tradeoff in our current settings.

its output is fed to the ADC of the Nucleo STM32-F767ZI board. An active HPF is implemented using OPA2301AID. The choice of the cutoff frequency of the filter is influenced by the transmission and noise frequency. A high cutoff frequency will remove the ambient light noise from artificial luminaries and sunlight as shown in Figure 5. However, there must be a guard band between the cutoff and the transmission frequencies to ensure that the transmission frequencies will not get filtered out.

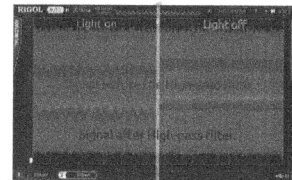

Figure 5: Effect of High Pass Filter on Ambient Light.

4 PHYSICAL SOFTWARE DEFINED LAYER

This section explains the software implementation for data encoding and modulation at the transmitter side, and signal detection and decoding at the receiver side. The firmware is implemented in C language using the HAL library provided by ST-Microelectronics and CMSIS library provided by ARM. These libraries in particular, have been optimized to make use of available FPUs to carry out common DSP operations in an efficient way.

4.1 Firmware for Transmitter

The Software Defined Physical Layer exposes an API to the upper layer of the network stack to queue data for transmission as shown in Figure 2. When a packet gets popped from the queue, it becomes the payload for a physical frame, whose format is shown in Figure 6. The packet wrapper builds the physical frame by pre-pending a preamble to the data. The preamble consists of a chirp followed by two bytes of synchronization (SYNC) bits. The transmitter pre-generates, samples and stores the waveform encoding of every possible byte. A frame to be transmitted is composed by copying the preamble and the byte waveforms onto a memory buffer. The DMA unit is initialized to transfer the values from this buffer to the

Chirp Encoding	Sync Bits	Payload
8 Symbol Periods	2 Bytes	1...64 Bytes

Figure 6: Packet Frame Format

DAC. The rate at which the DAC consumes the buffer determines the transmitting frequency of the signal. The pseudo code of the transmission firmware is shown in Figure 7.

```
def build_frame(packet):
    frame.preamble = fixed_preamble
    frame.payload = packet.data
    return frame

def modulate(frame):
    wave.chirp = generate_chirp()
    for bit in bin(frame):
        wave_symbol = modulate_bit(bit)
        wave.data.append(wave_symbol)
    return wave

def transmit(wave):
    # Start the transfer from memory
    # to DAC unit, returns immediately
    dma_unit.mem_to_dac(wave)

def transmission_done():
    transmitter_cond.signal()

while True:
    packet = packet_queue.pop()
    frame = build_frame(packet)
    wave = modulate(frame)

    transmitter_cond.wait()
    transmit(wave)
```

Figure 7: Pseudo Code of the Firmware for Transmission.

4.2 Firmware for Receiver

The receiver is always listening for incoming packets. The sampling of the signal is done through the combination of the onboard ADC and DMA. When the receiver is initialized, the ADC is started with a sufficiently high sampling rate and resolution (2.45 MSps and 8 bit, respectively) to ensure the best tradeoff between the conversion rate and the quantization error. The DMA is also started, to copy the values from the ADC to a memory location (logically a circular buffer). The raw data collected from the ADC is shown in Figure 8. This constitutes the stream of values on which the CPU operates to detect and decode the frames. Every time a frame arrives and is decoded, it is put on the outgoing queue from which the upper layer can read. The pseudo code for the receiver firmware is shown in Figure 9.

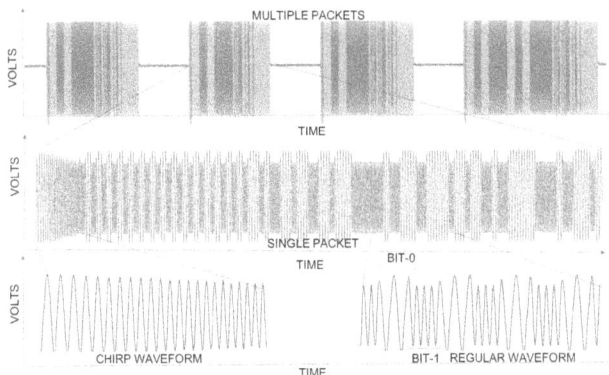

Figure 8: Raw Data Collected from ADC.

```
# Start the DMA unit to copy data
# from the ADC to the memory
dma_unit.adc_to_mem(circ_buffer)

while True:
    # Detect the signal start using the
    # chirp present in the preamble
    signal_start = detect_signal_start()

    # Use the preamble to correct sync
    # errors and find the start of data
    # symbols
    data_start = sync()

    while i < data_len :
        next_bit = decode_symbol(
            data_start + i)
        data.append(next_bit)
        i += symbol_len

    if(detect_desync()):
        resync()

    frame_queue.push(data)
```

Figure 9: Pseudo Code of the Firmware for Reception.

5 EXPERIMENTAL EVALUATION

We evaluate the performance of our prototype based on the following metrics : Bit Error Rate (BER) vs. Noise floor, BER vs. Distance, Estimated Signal-to-Noise-Ratio (SNR) vs. Distance, Power Consumption and Data Rate. We use a single TX-RX pair for the experiments. All results have been obtained by averaging the outcomes of 1536 packet transmission. This number of packets obtains a 95% confidence with 5% precision. The frame payloads are fixed to 8 and 16 Bytes for the experiments[4]. The experiments are repeated in various indoor scenarios covering different lighting conditions. The illuminance under each condition is measured using the ILM-01-RSPro light meter. The experimental setup is shown in Figure 10. The carrier wave frequencies used for the tests are 130 KHz and 260 KHz for the symbol 0 and 1, respectively. The sampling frequency of the ADC is set to 2.45 MSps which satisfies the Nyquist sampling criteria to ensure synchronization, correct decoding and minimal drifting with higher payloads, given the selected transmission frequencies. The cutoff frequency of the HPF is set to 80 KHz, providing an ample guard band of 50 KHz to the signal. The size of the chirp has been fixed to 114 samples per packet, which provides good signal detection performance while still being relatively fast to compute.

5.1 BER vs. Noise floor

To understand the impact of ambient light on BER, we fix the distance between TX and RX to 1 m[5] and the frame payload to 8 and 16 Bytes. We have attempted to cover the whole ambient light range possible in indoor scenarios (0-1000 lux). The experiments are performed in indoor scenarios ranging from dark room to room with bright artificial lights and with open and closed windows during daytime. The BER is calculated by comparing the transmitted sequence of bits to the received bits per packet and counting the number of errors. Figure 11a shows that the BER on an average is

---

[4]It was observed during experiments that the signal decoding algorithm is susceptible to misalignments in the decoding window for higher payloads (54 Bytes onward), leading to higher BER which can be improved by using a forward error correction (FEC) codes.

[5] We have performed this experiment keeping the distance fixed, well below the maximum range, while the noise floor varies. The distance must remain constant to rule out its impact on the bit error rate.

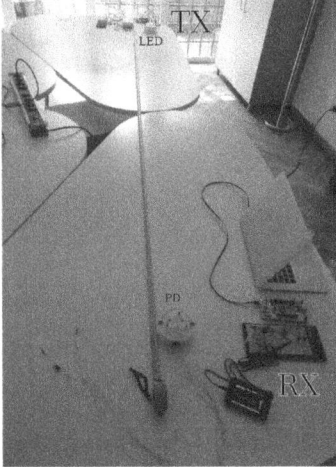

Figure 10: Experimental Setup.

less than 2.71% for the noise floor conditions until 700 lux. Then there is a slight increase in BER and reaches to 5.28% at 800 lux noise floor. Beyond 800 lux, the ambient light saturates the amplifier at the receiver side and hence make it difficult to detect and decode the signals. With our current setup, the VuLCAN works well until 800 lux which spans the entire indoor deployment. It is possible to upgrade the VuLCAN for outdoor deployments by adding highly sensitive light sensors.

5.2 BER vs. Distance

In this scenario, we fix the packet size to 8 and 16 Bytes. The tests are carried out in a noisy scenario of 490 lux (indoor office room with artificial lights on). The distance between TX and RX is then varied to evaluate the range performance. In Figure 11b, we observe that the BER on an average is in the order of 10^{-2} upto 4.5 m. Beyond 4.5 m, we consider the error rate to be unacceptable given the reliability requirements. The increase in BER is mainly due to extremely low signal strength at the receiver with large distances. Thus, the maximum operating range attained by VuLCAN is 4.5 m in an indoor environment. It is important to highlight that this long range is obtained with a low power single LED as the TX. It is mainly due to the effective signal detection algorithm (chirp algorithm) that the receiver is able to detect the signal even with low signal strength. Also, the prior knowledge of the receiver about the transmitted frequencies and the DFT based decoding make it possible to achieve reception at larger distances. In the current version, the working distance is 4.5 m, which is sufficient for indoor networking. Meanwhile, it is possible to improve the range and coverage of the VuLCAN by scaling the design with multiple LEDs or high power LEDs at the TX and with more stages of amplifier at the RX.

5.3 SNR evaluation

To understand the link quality of the signal on the VLC channel effectively, the estimated Signal-to-Noise-Ratio (SNR) evaluation has been conducted with an ambient illuminance at 490 lux. The standard definition of SNR is adopted for calculation.

$$SNR_{dB} = 20 \log_{10} \left(\frac{A_{signal}}{A_{noise}} \right),$$

where A_{signal} is the root mean square (RMS) voltage of signal and A_{noise} is the RMS voltage of the noise respectively. The estimate of the signal amplitude, A_{signal} is obtained from the recorded trace by fitting the already known transmitted signal waveform to the received values. The estimate of the noise, A_{noise} is calculated by subtracting the estimated signal from the recorded value. We observe from the Table 2 that with the frequency based modulation and demodulation technique, the prototype performs well even with extremely low SNR values.

Table 2: Estimated SNR.

Distance (m)	Estimated SNR (dB)
1.0	22.26
1.5	17.84
2.0	13.04
2.5	9.87
3.0	6.82
3.5	4.62
4.0	3.53
4.5	1.36

Table 3: Power Consumption of the Transceiver.

Components	Power Consumption (mW)
Nucleo Board (TX)	450
Nucleo Board (RX)	530 - 610
LED (MTE7063NK2-UR)	68.4
OPA 2301 (TCA and HPF)	59.5
OPA 380 (TIA)	26
Other components(resistor)	108

5.4 Power Consumption

The power consumption of the VuLCAN is measured as a combination of the TX and RX, as shown in Table 3. For each circuit component, we calculate its power by using the equation $P = VI$. The current flowing through the components is measured using a multimeter. The ARM based cortex-M STM32F7 nucleo board used in our prototype is a high performance device. Considering the aggregated power consumption of the TX and RX, the nucleo board consumes the biggest share ($\approx 67\%$). The LED (along with resistor) used in our prototype consumes 176.4 mW power which is nearly 4 times less the power consumption of high power LED (1-2 W) or multiple LEDs used as a transmitter antenna. The remaining analog circuit blocks including TCA, TIA and HPF consumes around 85.5 mW of power.

(a) BER vs. Noise Floor.

(b) BER vs. Distance.

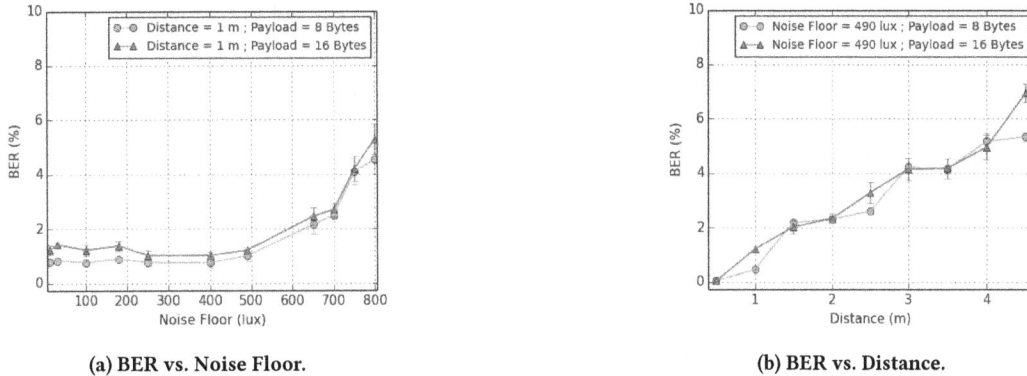

Figure 11: BER as a function of different parameters.

5.5 Data Rate

The data rate of the VLC prototype is mainly determined by the following factors: the ADC sampling frequency, the switching time of the LED circuitry, the slew rate of the OP-AMP, and the response time of the PD. The effective data rate attained by VuLCAN is 65 Kbps which is comparable with the current state of the art prototypes. Such a high data rate makes it suitable for a wide range of IoT scenarios.

6 RELATED WORK

This section aims at providing a brief review of the current state-of-the-art on low-end, embedded VLC prototypes with an emphasis on finding a balance between data rate, range, power and reliability in varied ambient noise conditions.

Schmid et al. present one of the first low-cost LED-to-LED communication system based on pulse position modulation (PPM) achieving a data rate of 800 bps at a distance of 2.5 m [23]. It is unclear if the prototype works in ambient light conditions. OpenVLC 1.0 is the first open source VLC prototype based on an embedded Linux platform (BBB) adopting OOK modulation. It achieves a UDP throughput of 12.5 Kbps at a distance up to 1 m [27]. Heydariaan et al. investigate the performance of the OpenVLC platform under different experimental settings. They report that the maximum ambient light conditions supported by the system is 300 lux [12]. A two-way VLC system with a low power single LED used as both TX and RX is presented in [17]. It achieves a data rate of 3 Kbps at a distance of a few tens of cm. The STM-32 microcontroller is used along with DC-DC booster and 9 W LED in the analog circuit to increase data rate and range performance [18].

Shine is the first low cost VLC platform that demonstrates multi-hop networking [15]. Another interesting work is the proof of concept describing how the Internet Protocol (IP) stack can operate on an LED-based VLC node [22]. However, these works do not report on tests to show resilience to ambient noise conditions. To realize effective VLC networking, robust and stable physical layer solutions are required that take into account the effect of realistic scenarios like ambient light interference.

Zhao et al. took a step forward and proposed a dedicated analog circuit to address the issue of noise cancellation in VLC receivers [31]. Similarly, Chang et al. present an attempt to remove

ambient noise from the VLC circuit [4]. Both works focus on circuit designs without details about data rate and range. Wang et al. present a holistic characterization of the OpenVLC board [28]. Although their approach make the system resilient to noise by utilizing the sensing property of the LED, it shows limited sensitivity and link stability due to switching between PD and LED as the receiver antenna. Schmid et al. present a software-defined adaptive VLC network that adapt the link sensitivity based on the strength of the input signal, obtaining a data rate and range up to 5.50 Kbps and 170 cm, respectively [23, 24]. However, the paper reports the increased uncertainty in the transmission duration and throughput with this approach. Costanzo et al. propose an adaptive VLC system with a fuzzy logic-based process that changes to LEDs of different colors depending on the interfering external lights [6]. The reported data rate was limited to 125 bps at a distance of around 8 m.

In the realm of prototypes addressing the issue of ambient noise cancellation, works worth citing include [8, 16, 25, 29, 30]. An adaptive ambient light cancellation receiver with BFSK modulation has been proposed that is based on OpenVLC platform [29]. The reported operating distance is limited to 50 cm with data rate up to 3 Kbps. *Epsilon* is a VLC prototype for indoor localization. It implements BFSK modulation with channel hopping to avoid collisions of light sources in a shared light medium [16]. Zhao et al. propose a modulation technique encoding data into ultra-short, imperceptible light pulses to sustain communication even when LEDs emit extremely low luminance [25]. The work by Yin et al. concerns a prototype named *Purple VLC* that uses the technique of polarization for bidirectional communication. The reported data rate is 50 Kbps, with a 6 m range in a single link [30]. OpenVLC 1.3 is the third version of the OpenVLC platform with a reported UDP throughput of 400 Kbps at a range of 4 m in noisy conditions [8]. However, a high power LED working at 2.8 W is used for transmission and the upper limit of the noise floor supported by the prototype is not clear.

Table 4 compares our prototype with current state-of-the-art embedded platforms based on their reported performance. When data was not available in the paper we list values based on our estimations based on the described system (items marked with "*"). This birds' eye comparison clearly shows the advantages of our

Table 4: Comparison of VuLCAN with state-of-the-art related VLC devices.

System Prototype	VuLCAN	Schmid et al. [23]	Klaver et al. [15]	Yin et al. [29]	Yin et al. [30]	Galisteo et al. [8]
Data Rate (Single Link)	65 Kbps	800 bps	1 Kbps	3 Kbps	50 Kbps	400 Kbps
Range	4.5 m	~2 m	~1 m	50 cm	6 m	4 m*
Modulation	BFSK	PPM	OOK	BFSK	OOK	OOK
Implementation	ARM-STM32	Atmel ATmega328P	Arduino	BBB	ARM + PRU	BBB and PRU
Ambient Noise-Floor Limit	800 lux	not reported*	not reported*	400 lux*	[Upper limit not reported]*	[Upper limit not reported]*
Antenna (TX-RX)	LED-to-PD	LED-to-LED	multiple LEDs-to-multiple PDs	LED-to-PD	multiple LEDs-to-PD*	High-Power LED-to-PD
Average Power Consumption	770 mW	~300 mW	4 W*	~315 mA (receiver circuitry)*	not reported*	not reported*

design, and its potential to enhance the RF-based IoT landscape with VLC-based low-cost devices.

7 CONCLUSIONS

We designed, build and tested VuLCAN, an embedded VLC platform for indoor applications that is robust to ambient noise. The prototype is built using the STM32-F767ZI nucleo board and uses low-cost and low-power COTS electronic components. We implemented DSP techniques making use of dedicated hardware and also used I/O offloading for increased efficiency. We evaluated our system under different ambient noise conditions. Results show that it can provide a reliable and robust communication link with low BER and a data rate of up to 65 Kbps over a distance of 4.5 m in the presence of ambient light ranging from 0 to 800 lux. The prototype pushes the envelope of existing low-end embedded VLC design, and expands the range of applications of VLC for IoT.

REFERENCES

[1] D. A. Basnayaka and H. Haas. 2015. Hybrid RF and VLC Systems: Improving User Data Rate Performance of VLC Systems. In *Proceedings of IEEE VTC.* IEEE, 1–5.

[2] J.V. Candy. 2016. *CHIRP-Like Signals: Estimation, Detection and Processing A Sequential Model-Based Approach.* Lawrence Livermore National Laboratory, Department of Energy, United States.

[3] N. Cen, J. Jagannath, S. Moretti, Z. Guan, and T. Melodia. 2019. LANET: Visible-light ad hoc networks. *Ad Hoc Networks* 84 (March 2019), 107–123.

[4] F. Chang, W. Hu, D. Lee, and C. Yu. 2017. Design and implementation of anti low-frequency noise in visible light communications. In *Proceedings of ICASI.* 1536–1538.

[5] Cw. Chow, Ch. Yeh, Y. Liu, and Yf. Liu. 2012. Digital signal processing for light emitting diode based visible light communication. *IEEE Photon. Soc. Newsletter* (October 2012), 9–13.

[6] A. Costanzo, V. Loscri', and S. Costanzo. 2018. Adaptive dual color visible light communication (VLC) system. *Trends and Advances in Information Systems and Technologies* 746 (May 2018), 1478–1487.

[7] A. Duque, R. Stanica, H. Rivano, and A. Desportes. 2016. Unleashing the power of LED-to-camera communications for IoT devices. In *Proceedings of ACM Workshop on Visible Light Communication Systems.* ACM, 55–60.

[8] A. Galisteo, D. Juara, and D. Giustiniano. 2019. Research in visible light communication systems with OpenVLC1.3. In *In Proceedings of IEEE WF-IOT.* IEEE.

[9] R. Garcia-Retegui, S. A. Gonzalez, M. A. Funes, and S. Maestri. 2007. Implementation of a novel synchronization method using Sliding Goertzel DFT. In *Proceedings of IEEE International Symposium on Intelligent Signal Processing.* IEEE, 1–5.

[10] H. Haas, L. Yin, Y. Wang, and C. Chen. 2016. What is LiFi? *Journal of Lightwave Technology* 34, 6 (March 2016), 1533–1544.

[11] S. Haykin. 2009. *Communication Systems.* Wiley Publishing.

[12] M. Heydariaan, S. Yin, O. Gnawali, D. Puccinelli, and D. Giustiniano. 2016. Embedded visible light communication: Link measurements and interpretation. In *Proceedings of EWSN.* Junction Publishing, 341–346.

[13] S. Hranilovic. 2009. *Wireless Optical Communication Systems.* Springer-Verlag.

[14] S.M. Kay. 1993. *Fundamentals of statistical signal processing.* Prentice Hall PTR.

[15] L. Klaver and M. Zuniga. 2015. Shine : A step towards distributed multi-hop visible light communication. In *Proceedings of IEEE MASS.* IEEE, 235–243.

[16] L. Li, P. Hu, C. Peng, G. Shen, and F. Zhao. 2014. Epsilon: A Visible Light Based Positioning System. In *USENIX Symposium on NSDI.* USENIX Association, 331–343.

[17] S. Li, A. Pandharipande, and F. M. J. Willems. 2017. Two-way visible light communication and illumination with LEDs. *IEEE Transactions on Communications* 65, 2 (Feb 2017), 740–750.

[18] C. Liu, X. Jin, W. Zhu, M. Jin, and Z. Xu. 2017. Demonstration of a low complexity ARM-based indoor VLC transceiver under strong interference. In *Proceedings of IWCMC.* IEEE, 622–627.

[19] ST Microelectronics. 2019. STM32, ARM Cortex- M 7 Nucleo-144 development board. https://www.st.com/en/evaluation-tools/nucleo-f767zi.html

[20] P. H. Pathak, X. Feng, P. Hu, and P. Mohapatra. 2015. Visible Light Communication, Networking, and Sensing: A Survey, Potential and Challenges. *IEEE Communications Surveys Tutorials* 17, 4 (2015), 2047–2077.

[21] John G. Proakis and Dimitris K. Manolakis. 2006. *Digital Signal Processing.* Prentice-Hall, Inc., NJ,USA.

[22] S. Schmid, T. Bourchas, S. Mangold, and T.R. Gross. 2015. Linux Light Bulbs: Enabling internet protocol connectivity for light bulb networks. In *Proceedings of the International Workshop on Visible Light Communications Systems.* ACM, 3–8.

[23] S. Schmid, G. Corbellini, S. Mangold, and T.R. Gross. 2013. LED-to-LED visible light communication networks. In *Proceedings of ACM MobiHoc.* ACM, 1–10.

[24] S. Schmid, B. von Deschwanden, S. Mangold, and T R. Gross. 2017. Adaptive software-defined visible light communication networks. In *Proceedings of IEEE/ACM IoTDI.* IEEE, 109–120.

[25] Z. Tian, K. Wright, and X. Zhou. 2016. The Darklight Rises: Visible light communication in the Dark: Demo. In *In Proceedings of ACM MobiCom.* ACM, New York City, New York, 495–496.

[26] D. Tsonev, S. Videv, and H. Haas. 2015. Towards a 100 Gb/s visible light wireless access network. *Optics Express* 23, 2 (Jan 2015), 1627–1637.

[27] Q. Wang, Giustiniano, and D. Puccinelli. 2015. An open source research platform for embedded visible light networking. *IEEE Wireless Communications* 22, 2 (April 2015), 94–100.

[28] Q. Wang, D. Giustiniano, and M. Zuniga. 2018. In light and in darkness, in motion and in stillness: A reliable and adaptive receiver for the internet of lights. *IEEE Journal on Selected Areas in Communications* 36, 1 (2018), 149–161.

[29] S. Yin and O. Gnawali. 2016. Towards embedded visible light communication robust to dynamic ambient light. In *Proceedings of IEEE GLOBECOM.* IEEE, 1–6.

[30] S. Yin, N. Smaoui, M. Heydariaan, and O. Gnawali. 2018. Purple VLC: Accelerating visible light communication in room-area through PRU offloading. In *Proceedings of ACM EWSN.* Madrid, Spain, Madrid, Spain, 67–78.

[31] Y. Zhao and J. Vongkulbhisal. 2013. Design of visible light communication receiver for on-off keying modulation by adaptive minimum-voltage cancelation. *Engineering Journal* 17, 4 (June 2013), 125–129.

Performance Evaluation of LED-to-Camera Communications

Alexis Duque
Adrien Desportes
Rtone
Lyon, France

Razvan Stanica
Hervé Rivano
Univ Lyon, INSA Lyon, Inria, CITI
Villeurbanne, France

ABSTRACT

The use of LED-to-camera communication opens the door to a wide range of use cases and applications, with diverse requirements in terms of quality of service. However, while analytical models and simulation tools exist for all the major radio communication technologies, the only way of currently evaluating the performance of a network mechanism over LED-to-camera is to implement and test it. Our work aims to fill this gap by proposing a Markov-modulated Bernoulli process to model the wireless channel in LED-to-camera communications, which is shown to closely match experimental results. Based on this model, we develop and validate *CamComSim*, the first network simulator for LED-to-camera communications.

KEYWORDS

visible light communications, optical camera communications, Markov-modulated Bernoulli process, simulation

ACM Reference Format:
Alexis Duque, Adrien Desportes, Razvan Stanica, and Hervé Rivano. 2019. Performance Evaluation of LED-to-Camera Communications. In *22nd Int'l ACM Conference on Modeling, Analysis and Simulation of Wireless and Mobile Systems (MSWiM '19), November 25–29, 2019, Miami Beach, FL, USA*. ACM, New York, NY, USA, 8 pages. https://doi.org/10.1145/3345768.3355922

1 INTRODUCTION

Visible-light communication (VLC) is an enabling technology that exploits illumination to provide a short-range wireless communication link. VLC systems take advantage of the license-free light spectrum and their immunity to radio frequency (RF) interference. In such systems, information is often relayed by modulating the output intensity of a light-emitting diode (LED). Any electronic device which can detect the presence or absence of visible light can be utilized as a VLC receiver. While most of the work in the field is focused towards using photo-diodes as receivers, because of their fast response and high bandwidth, some studies demonstrated that smartphone cameras can also be used to detect high-frequency light patterns [1].

Indeed, nowadays smartphone cameras widely use two types of image sensors, Charge Coupled Devices (CCD) or Complementary Metal Oxide Semiconductors (CMOS). These two technologies have some similarities, but one major distinction is the way each sensor exposes its pixels to light. CCD sensors use the Global Shutter readout mode, where all pixels are exposed simultaneously and then each pixel is read sequentially. This mechanism helps in capturing a still image of a moving object. On the other hand, CMOS sensors use the Rolling Shutter readout mode [2], where each row is exposed in a row-sequential way with fixed time delay. Due to this mechanism, there is a significant time difference between the beginning of the exposure of the first and the last row, making them no longer simultaneous. When an LED is modulated at a frequency higher than the rolling shutter speed, stripes of different light intensity are captured in the image. A row of pixels appears illuminated when the LED was ON during the row exposure time. On the other hand, a row appears dark when the LED was OFF during the exposure time. The intensity and width of the strip depend on the transmitter modulation frequency, allowing us to encode information in these illuminated and dark bands, similarly to the use of a bar code.

This LED-to-camera communication based on the Rolling Shutter effect opens the door to a wide range of use cases and applications, with diverse requirements in terms of quality of service [3]. To cite a few examples, both line-of-sight (LOS) [4, 5] and non-line-of-sight (NLOS) [6, 7] communications have been demonstrated in these settings, as well as ultra-reliable localization solutions [8, 9], sensing [10], or even scene protection against intrusive photographs [11]. However, while analytical models and simulation tools exist for all the major RF technologies, the only way of currently evaluating the performance of a network mechanism over LED-to-camera is to implement and test it. This results in heavy measurement and parameterisation campaigns that need to be repeated anytime a new VLC protocol or feature is imagined. Having access to standard performance evaluation tools in this type of network would certainly accelerate studies in the field, and nicely complement experimental field tests.

The work described in this paper aims to fill this gap by proposing models and tools that help in the assessment of LED-to-camera communication network mechanisms. Our contributions are threefold. First, we propose an analytical model for LED-to-camera communication systems in Sec. 3. Second, we design and implement *CamComSim*, a LED-to-camera communication simulator in Sec. 5. Finally, the model and the simulator allow us to benchmark several network redundancy mechanisms proposed in the literature. By checking against experimental results, we are able to confirm the correctness of our models in this context.

2 RELATED WORKS

LED-to-camera communication allows for low-throughput unidirectional message transmission, with a performance in range of a few kbit/s [4, 5]. Despite this limited throughput, LED-to-camera communication raises a lot of interest because it enables communication with no extra financial cost between any LED-equipped machine or instrument and any regular smartphone. This low cost also explains the fact that practically every study on this topic uses an experimental approach. While experiments are essential in evaluating new protocols and services, running an experimental campaign every time one wishes to evaluate a new idea can become cumbersome.

Designing analytical models and implementing them in simulation tools is standard practice in the wireless networking field in order to accelerate the evaluation of new protocols and mechanisms. Indeed, network simulation has been largely studied in the case of wireless communication [12]. Nonetheless, VLC performance evaluation remains poorly investigated and VLC simulation tools are still missing. The main efforts on simulating VLC systems have focused on indoor channel simulation [13], or on the 802.15.7 PHY [14, 15] and MAC [16] layers. These approaches rely on classical network simulation frameworks, such as those used for wireless and ad hoc networks, e.g. ns-2 [16], ns-3 [14], OMNET++ [15] or MATLAB [13]. All these works consider LED-to-Photodiode communication, hence LED-to-Camera communication is completely unexplored. Our work is the first effort in LED-to-Camera simulation reported in the literature, making CamComSim the first implementation of a LED-to-Camera VLC simulator.

3 MODELING LED-TO-CAMERA COMMUNICATION

In this section, we describe, for the first time in the literature from our knowledge, a LED-to-camera communication channel model. Based on the theory of Markov-modulated Bernoulli processes (MMBP) [17], discussed in Sec. 3.1, this model can be applied to all LED-to-camera communication systems, not only to the particular case of ours. The proposed model is not only generic, but also very accurate, as demonstrated by its validation with extensive experimental results in Sec. 3.4. As an example, we use the analytical model to compare two simple redundancy mechanisms, required to cope with the inherent losses of LED-to-camera communication and described in Sec. 3.2 and Sec. 3.3.

3.1 Model design

In a LED-to-camera system, data is received as a series of dark and illuminated stripes in a picture frame captured by the camera. In the following, we note by f_i the i-th frame captured by the camera and by δ_f the time between the beginning of two consecutive frames. Obviously, even at the highest frame rate allowed by the camera, data is not continuously received, as a minimum time δ_g exists between two frames. This is denoted as the inter-frame gap (IFG). Moreover, as depicted in Fig. 1, the distance between the LED and the camera also has an impact: when the camera is farther away, the LED transmission is captured for a shorter time, resulting in a smaller ROI.

3.1.1 Gilbert-Elliot model: A first idea to model LED-to-camera communication would be the Gilbert-Elliot model, which is widely used to model bursty losses [18]. This unique type of channel can intuitively be modeled by a two states Markov chain. In state S_1, the system is capturing a frame. The camera is receiving packets, and the reception probability is $1 - p_e$ where p_e is the packet decoding error probability. In state S_2, the camera is not capturing

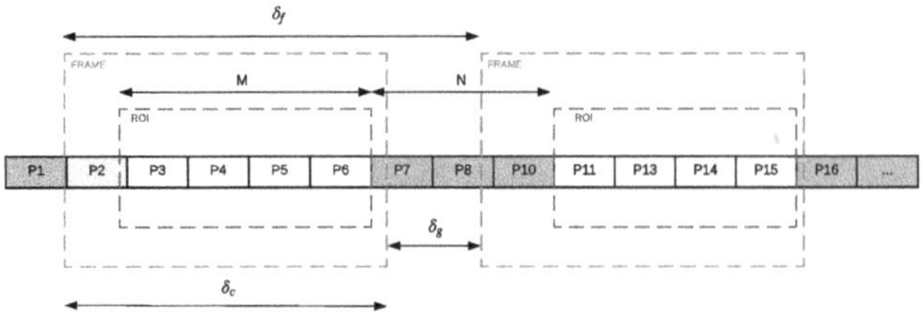

Figure 1: Frame capture time and inter-frame interval, and their relation with the MMBP parameters.

any pictures, therefore we consider the reception probability is 0. The transition probability between S_1 and S_2 (respectively S_2 and S_1) is denoted p (respectively q). The model assumes that p, q, p_e are independent and constant.

In this case, the probability of being in state S_1 under the steady-state regime can be easily computed as $p_{s_1} = \frac{p}{p+q}$. The probability of being in state S_2 is so $p_{s_2} = \frac{q}{p+q}$.

The values of p and q are function of the duration of the IFG, δ_g, the frame duration, δ_f, and the camera capture time δ_c, depicted in Fig. 1, and linked as the following:

$$p = 1 - q = \frac{\delta_f - \delta_g}{\delta_f} = \frac{\delta_c}{\delta_f} \quad (1)$$

3.1.2 MMBP model: If the model introduced just before is straightforward and widely used, it lacks realism in our case, where the transitions between ON and OFF states are almost deterministic. Practically, in our system, the transition probability from a state to another depends on the residence time in this state.

To improve this approach, we model the LED-to-camera channel using a Markov-modulated Bernoulli process (MMBP), represented in Fig. 2. In this figure, we depict a Markov chain with a total number of $M + N$ states. Each of these states represents a reception time slot, i.e. the time duration needed in order to receive one physical layer message (denoted as PHY-SDU in the following). The transition between two states representing successive time slots is automatic, i.e. it happens with a probability of 1.

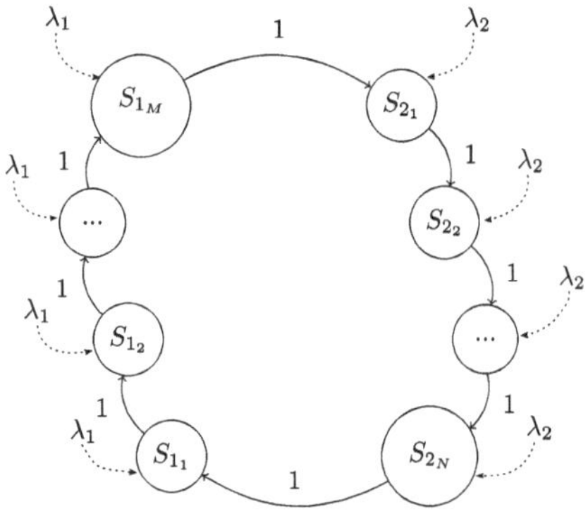

Figure 2: The MMBP model of the LED-to-camera channel.

Practically, the $M + N$ states in Fig. 2 represent a δ_f time interval, and they are divided in two groups: M states corresponding to the camera capture time δ_c (S_{ON} states), and N states corresponding to the inter-frame time δ_g (S_{OFF} states). A Bernoulli arrival process is associated with each of these $M + N$ states, representing the reception of a packet.

In S_{ON} states, the camera is receiving packets, and the arrival rate is $\lambda_1 = (1 - p_e)$, where p_e is the packet decoding error probability. In S_{OFF} states, the camera is not capturing any pictures, therefore we consider the arrival rate $\lambda_2 = 0$.

We denote as s a state in the Markov chain and we define state $s + j$ as the state reached after j transitions, starting from state s. The probability of being in state s under the steady-state regime can be easily computed as $\pi_s = \frac{1}{N+M}$. At the same time, the probability of noticing no arrivals (i.e. no packet reception) in state s is $p_0(s)$. This can be written as:

$$p_0(s) = \begin{cases} 1, & if \quad s \in N \\ p_e, & if \quad s \in M \end{cases} \tag{2}$$

As it can be seen from both models, the relatively high packet loss probability (compared with RF technologies) is an intrinsic property of the LED-to-camera communication channel. To overcome this problem, redundancy mechanisms are needed.

In the following, using classical redundancy mechanisms as an example, we show that the classical Gilbert-Elliot model is inaccurate, which highlights the need to rely on the MMBP theory. Then, we use the MMBP channel model to compare two simple, but widely used redundancy solutions: repeating a packet or repeating a sequence of packets.

3.2 Repeat Packet

The first strategy to cope with the inherent losses in the LED-to-camera communication system, used for example by *Ferrandiz-Lahuerta et al.* [7], is to send each packet twice in a row, to increase the probability that at least one of the transmissions will be fully captured by the smartphone camera. We generalize this approach in the Repeat Packet (RP) strategy, where each packet is repeated r times, one after the other. In this case, the r value needs to be chosen in order to attain a desired reception probability, its optimal value depending on the inter-frame time and on the packet size.

In the following, we study the probability of receiving a packet at least once when considering the RP strategy, for the two models introduced above.

3.2.1 Gilbert-Elliott Model:
If we consider the Gilbert-Elliott model, the probability of receiving a packet at least once can be written as $p_s^{RP} = 1 - p_0^{RP}$, where p_0^{RP} represents the probability of failing to receive a packet r times in a row, written as:

$$p_0^{RP} = \left(P_{S_1} \cdot p_e + P_{S_2} \right)^r = \left(\frac{p \cdot p_e + q}{q + p} \right)^r \tag{3}$$

3.2.2 MMBP Model:
If we consider the MMBP model, the probability of failing to receive a packet r times in a row p_0^{RP} can be written as:

$$p_0^{RP} = \frac{\sum_s \left(p_0(s) \cdot p_0(s+1) \cdot p_0(s+2) \cdot \ldots \cdot p_0(s+r-1) \right)}{N+M} \tag{4}$$

The value of p_0^{RP} will depend on m_s, defined as the number of S_{ON} states during the r retransmissions, when the first packet

transmission is in state s:

$$p_0^{RP} = \frac{1}{N+M} \cdot \sum_{s=1}^{M+N} (p_e)^{m_s} \tag{5}$$

Depending on the values of r, M and N, several cases can be distinguished. We present results for the two most current cases:

Case 1: $r < M, N$. This means that the number of retransmissions does not always cover the δ_g period (which counts N states). In this case, p_0^{RP} can be written a follows:

$$p_0^{RP} = P[s \in N \wedge (s+r) \in N] + P[s \in M \wedge (s+r) \in M]$$
$$+ P[s \in M \wedge (s+r) \in N) + P[s \in N \wedge (s+r) \in M]$$
$$= \frac{N-r+1}{M+N} + \frac{M-r+1}{M+N} \cdot p_e{}^r + \frac{1}{M+N}\sum_{i=1}^{r-1} p_e{}^i + \frac{1}{M+N}\sum_{i=1}^{r-1} p_e{}^{r-i}$$
$$= \frac{N-r+1}{M+N} + \frac{M-r+1}{M+N} \cdot p_e{}^r + \frac{2}{M+N} \cdot \frac{p_e - p_e{}^r}{1 - p_e} \tag{6}$$

Case 2: $N < r < M$. . This is the most common case, where the number of repetitions is chosen to cover the entire inter-frame period. However, a reception is still not certain in this case, because of the decoding error p_e. In this case:

$$p_0^{RP} = P[s \in M \wedge (s+r) \in M)] + P[s \in M \wedge (s+r) \in N]$$
$$+ P[s \in N \wedge (s+r) \in M]$$
$$= \frac{M-r+1}{M+N} \cdot p_e{}^r + \frac{1}{M+N}\sum_{i=1}^{r-1} p_e{}^i + \frac{1}{M+N}\sum_{i=1}^{N} p_e{}^{r-i}$$
$$= \frac{M-r+1}{M+N} \cdot p_e{}^r + \frac{1}{M+N} \cdot \frac{p_e - p_e{}^r}{1 - p_e} + \frac{1}{M+N}\sum_{i=1}^{N} p_e{}^{r-i}$$
$$= \frac{M-r+1}{M+N} \cdot p_e{}^r + \frac{1}{M+N} \cdot \frac{p_e - p_e{}^r}{1 - p_e} + \frac{1}{M+N} \cdot \frac{p_e{}^{r-N}(p_e - p_e{}^N)}{1 - p_e} \tag{7}$$

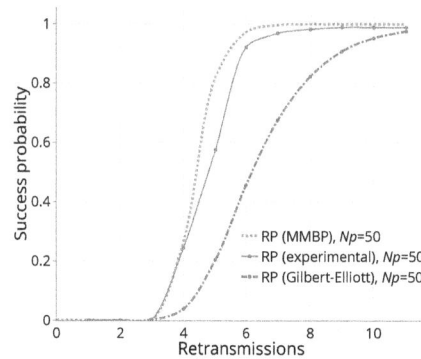

Figure 3: Probability to successfully receive N_p packets for the RP strategy. Dotted-lines show analytical results for the Gilbert-Elliott and MMBP models, while plain lines represent experimental results.

We compare the analytical results given by the two aforesaid models to experimentation results (obtained using our testbed described in [19]) in Fig. 3. This figure shows the success probability

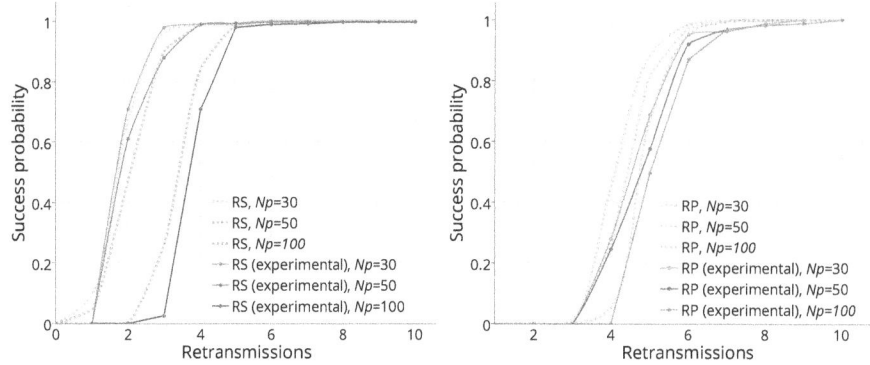

Figure 4: Probability to successfully receive N_p packets for the RS (left) and RP (right) strategies as a function of the number of retransmissions r. Dotted-lines show analytical results while plain lines represent experimental results.

of receiving a message of $N_p = 50$ packets of data, as a function of the number of retransmissions r.

The very different results between the Gilbert-Elliott model and the experimentation confirms that the stochastic transition assumptions of this model are quite far from reality. On the other hand, MMBP approximates quite well the experimental behavior, highlighting the need for this more complex, but finer grained model.

3.3 Repeat Sequence

A different approach to improve reliability is the Repeat Sequence (RS) strategy, consisting in the transmission of a sequence of N_p packets, repeated r times. In contrast with the previous mechanism, RS does not try to cover the inter frame time at the packet level, and it does not ensure that a packet is received before sending the next one. Instead, the reliability and presumed efficiency is based on the fact that the probability of losing the same packets over different transmitted sequences is low.

In the case of an RS strategy with a sequence of N_p packets retransmitted r times, the probability of receiving a packet at least once can be written as $p_s^{RS} = 1 - p_0^{RS}$. Using the MMBP model, the probability of failing to receive a packet r times in a row, p_0^{RS}, can be written as:

$$p_0^{RS} = \frac{1}{M+N} \cdot \sum_{s=1}^{M+N} \prod_{j=0}^{r-1} p_0(s + rN_p) \qquad (8)$$

3.4 Evaluation results

We use our MMBP analytical model to study the RP and RS strategies by focusing on the probability of delivering the entire quantity of information in a given number of transmissions. We provide both analytical and experimental results, allowing us to validate the proposed MMBP model.

Fig. 4 shows, for the two mechanisms, the probability of integrally receiving N_p packets of data as a function of the number of retransmissions r. In this figure, we set $M = 5$ and $N = 2$; these values are in line with the packet length, the transmitter frequency and the camera capture interval experimentally observed for a distance of 5 cm between LED and camera. The results show quite a

nice fit between the analytical and experimentation results, despite the assumptions required by our MMBP model.

To better understand the performance of the two retransmission strategies, we compare them in Fig. 5. This figure shows that, for the RS strategy, 3 retransmissions are needed to achieve a reception probability higher than 0.9, while this value raises to 6 for the RP strategy. On the right side of the figure, we show that the performance of the two strategies depends on the ratio between the number of S_{ON} and S_{OFF} states, $M : N$. When this ratio changes from $5 : 2$ to $2 : 5$, which practically corresponds to increasing the distance between the LED and the camera, RP gives better results than RS. Indeed, for the RS method, the success probability sharply decrease when $M < 3$ and stays below 0.6 even for 10 retransmission.

Practically, this means that RP is more suitable when the distance between the LED and the camera is higher, while RS is better for short communication distances. This phenomenon was previously unknown in the research community, but it is straightforward to study with our analytical model

4 ROI MODEL

An important phenomenon in LED-to-camera communications comes as a direct consequence of the distance between the LED and the camera. Indeed, as this distance increases, the size of the region of interest (ROI) in the picture reduces and, as a consequence, cuts down the number of messages that the camera can receive per frame, i.e. the M states in Fig. 1. To include this performance factor into our model, we propose an analytical function that gives the ratio between the ROI and the picture size. In the model discussed in Subsec. 3.1, this is the ratio of M states in the $M + N$ states.

We apply photogrammetry rules to give the ROI ratio as a function of the distance d, the LED size l, the camera CMOS sensor size ss, the image size on the sensor i and the camera focal distance fc. According to the optical system depicted in Fig 6, basic lens optic rules give the following Eq. 9:

$$\frac{i}{fc} = \frac{l}{d} \iff i = \frac{l \cdot fc}{d} \qquad (9)$$

To obtain the *ROI* as the ratio of the total number of pixels in the picture, we need as input the CMOS sensor size ss. We apply

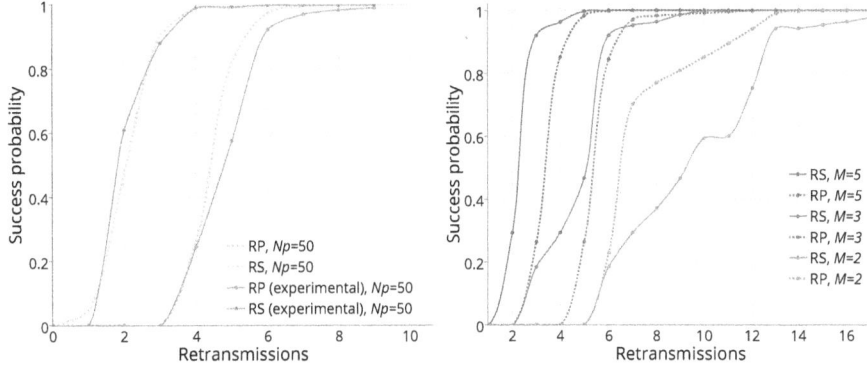

Figure 5: Comparison between RS and RP. On the left, analytical and experimental results for $M = 5$ and $N = 2$. On the right, analytical results when $M + N = 7$, but the $M : N$ ratio changes. In both cases, $N_p = 50$.

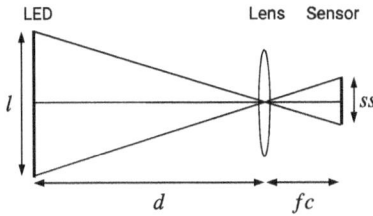

Figure 6: Formation of an image on a sensor by a converging lens.

the min function to normalise the $ROI \in [0, 1]$ even if the image size on the sensor, i, is larger than the sensor size, ss. The result is given in the following Eq. (10):

$$ROI = \min\left(1, \frac{l \cdot fc}{d \cdot ss}\right) \qquad (10)$$

To validate the results given by Eq. 10, we measure the ROI experimentally, using the testbed described in [19], for distances from 0 to 40 cm. Fig. 7 plots in orange the ROI ratio we observed during our experiments and in green the analytical results computed with a Nexus 5 sensor with the following characteristics: $fc = 35$, $ss = 5.7$ and $l = 10$. This shows that the analytical curve approximates quite well the experimental ROI ratio. However, we notice that the experimental results are better for a distance between 10 and 30 cm, and they become worse than the model at 35 cm. In fact, the light radiance on the camera lens, that our model does not take into account, artificially increases the LED size on the picture when the camera is close to the LED. The difference at larger distance is a consequence of the ambient light which was measured at 650 lux during the experiments, also neglected in Eq. (10).

The ROI model described in this section and the MMBP reception model validated in the previous section are the basis of the simulator implementation discussed in the following.

5 THE CAMCOMSIM SIMULATOR

As discusse in Sec. 2, the simulation of LED-to-camera communication remains completely unexplored in the field. Our work is the

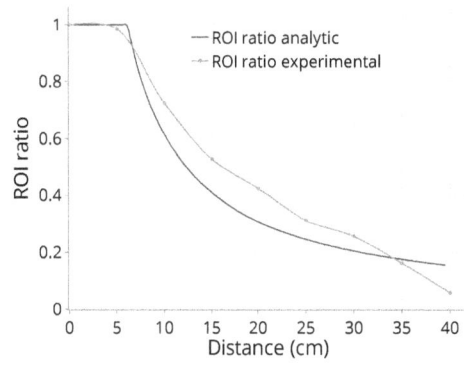

Figure 7: ROI as a function of distance. The orange line shows experimental results, while the green line represents analytical results given by Eq. 10.

first such effort reported in the literature, making *CamComSim* the first implementation of a LED-to-camera VLC simulator.

5.1 Simulator Implementation

5.1.1 Software architecture. *CamComSim* is an event-driven LED-to-camera simulator developed in Java, which makes it easy to maintain and distribute code, and it provides built-in multi-platform compatibility for systems with a Java Virtual Machine. Fig. 8 shows the *CamComSim* software architecture that consists of a simulator kernel class and four core packages. For interested readers, *CamComSim* is already available as an open-source software under Apache license at http://vlc.project.citi-lab.fr/camcomsim.

The `topology` package groups classes that describe the system components: `Led`, `Camera` and `Channel`. The classes in the `data` package implement the data encapsulation. For this, a `Message` is a set of PHY-SDU that encapsulates a `PhysduPayload`. A `Packet` is a `PhysduPayload` child class, with a sequence number as header and a payload that contains data. Before each simulation, a `Message` is created according to the user settings. The resulting set of `Physdu` is initialized with a `Packet` filled with

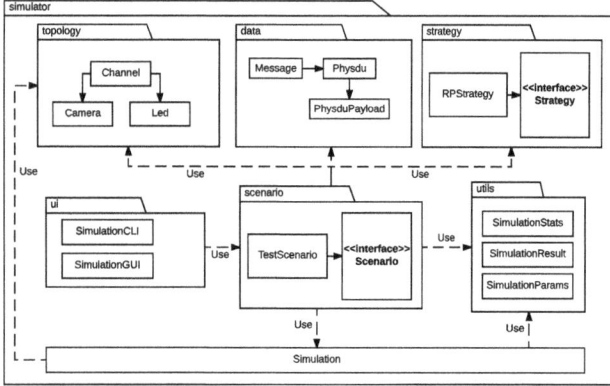

Figure 8: The *CamComSim* software architecture and packages dependency graph.

Param.	Description	Default Value
d	Distance between camera and LED (cm)	5
l	LED size (mm)	4
d_g	Camera inter-frame gap ratio	0.1
p_e	Decoder PHY-SDU Error Rate	0.001
f	Modulation frequency (Hz)	8000
P	PhysduPayload Header length (bit)	8
H	PhysduPayload Payload length (bit)	16
r	PHY-SDU repeat number	1
G	Message size (bytes)	50

Table 1: Simulator parameters and default values.

arbitrary data in the payload (real data could be used if available) and a unique sequence number in the header.

The broadcast strategy abstraction is given in the strategy package. Here, the Strategy interface lets the users implement their transmission strategy. This package also contains the straightforward ReapeatPhysduStrategy (RP) implementation that consists in repeating each PHY-SDU r times, one after the other, as described in Sec. 3.2. When the last PHY-SDU of the message is reached, the process is repeated from the beginning.

Finally, the scenario package proposes an interface to build a simulation, wiring together the Message, the Channel, the Led, the Camera and the Strategy with the Simulator kernel. Besides, the package utility provides helper classes used to compute the simulation results statistics, format and save the results as a JSON file and load or save the simulation parameters. The ui package contains a command-line interface (CLI) used to run a simulation scenario.

5.1.2 Simulator parameters. Our simulator exposes a set of finely grained parameters to describe the LED-to-camera communication system behavior. Table 1 shows the parameters we use in this work and expose through the *CamComSim* CLI. The performance of the LED-to-camera communication is significantly affected by the distance d, the IFG noted δ_g in Fig. 2, and the LED size l. The values of these parameters should therefore be carefully chosen, according to the available hardware and envisioned scenario.

Further parameters, introduced in Sec. 4, that refer to the CMOS sensor characteristics, are optional but can be considered to refine the channel model, as they impact the ROI. However, smartphone manufacturers rarely provide this information, e.g. regarding the sensor size ss and the focal distance fc.

The PER p_e is the consequence of the errors occurring in a M state when a PHY-SDU is well included in a picture but is wrongly decoded by the smartphone. These errors are bits substitutions induced by interference, low SNR, and artifacts on the picture. This value varies from a smartphone to another, but we did not observe major differences in our tests.

The PhysduPayload payload size P and the PhysduPayload header size H configure the data encapsulation mechanism. Given these two settings, the PHY-SDU size is computed as $P+H+SYNC+PB$, where $SYNC$ is the PHY-SDU delimiter symbol (4 bits in our tests), and PB is the number of parity bits (2 bits in our settings). This PHY-SDU size, along with d, l, δ_f and the modulation frequency f, determines the number of the M time slots in Fig. 2.

A transmission strategy among the Strategy interface implementations needs to be chosen as well. For now, we have implemented and considered only the RP strategy, for which the parameters are the size of the message to broadcast, G, and the number of consecutive PHY-SDU emissions, r.

5.1.3 Kernel Implementation. The *CamComSim* kernel is implemented in the Simulator class. Its role is to produce PHY-SDU emission events (TX) and manage their result. The number of events, i.e. the number of PHY-SDU sent, is noted c and is updated at run-time. At each clock tick, c is incremented, a TX event is created and processed as follow: (1) the next PHY-SDU in the transmission strategy queue is associated with this event; (2) considering p_e, f, P, H, c, the channel response function gives the event result. The result is one among: *reception success*, *reception with errors* or *loss during IFG*; (3) this result is stored in a list to further determine if all the PHY-SDU forming a message are received.

The simulator loops over (1), (2) and (3) until the stop condition is met, i.e. c has reached the maximum number of PHY-SDU emissions or the complete message is received. The simulation is repeated n_r times using the Java class for multi-threading purpose ThreadPoolExecutor. Finally, the simulations results and statistics are saved in a JSON file for further processing.

5.2 CamComSim validation

In this section, we present LED-to-camera simulation results given by *CamComSim*. To assess the correctness of our simulator, we conduct a series of experiments with the testbed presented in [19]. We set the emitter symbol rate to 8 kHz and place it in standard indoor illumination conditions, near a window and illuminated with neon lights. The illuminance has been measured with a luxmeter at around 650 lux. We compare the testbed performance with the results given by *CamComSim* for a set of key parameters: the message size G, the number of consecutive PHY-SDU emissions r, the distance d and the PHY-SDU payload length P.

5.2.1 PHY-SDU Retransmission. As discussed in Sec. 3.2, to face the IFG bits erasure and ensure that all the packets are well received, a possibility is to transmit consecutively each PHY-SDU r times in a row. The `ReapeatPhysduStrategy` class in *CamComSim* implements this retransmission strategy.

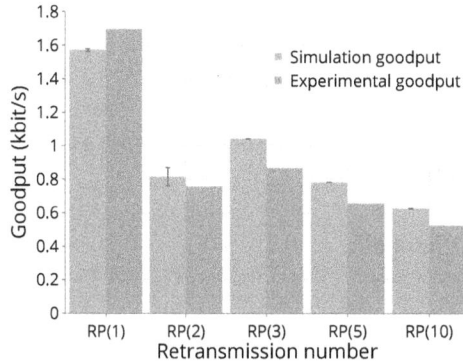

Figure 9: The experimental goodput (blue) compared with the simulation goodput (green) as a function of the number of consecutive PHY-SDU emissions. The bars on top are 95% confidence intervals.

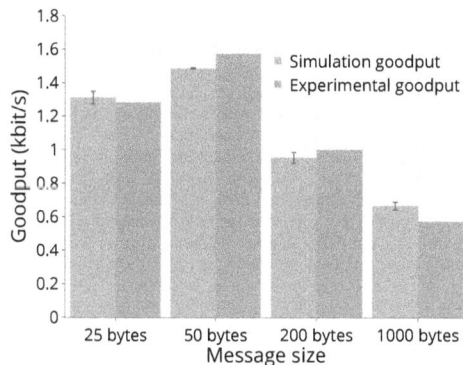

Figure 10: The experimental goodput (blue) compared with the simulation goodput (green) for different message size (G, bytes).

Fig. 9 shows the goodput at 5 cm for different values of PHY-SDU consecutive retransmissions r, with $G = 50$, $P = 19$, $H = 5$. When each PHY-SDU has been transmitted r times, the message transmission restarts, until the message is completely received. To avoid infinite loops, we stop the simulation when 50000 PHY-SDU are sent, even if the message is not received entirely. In such case, we consider the goodput is 0.

The results highlight that the simulation and testbed goodput follow the same tendency when r varies. The best case is when $r = 1$, for which the goodput is 1.6 kbit/s according to *CamComSim* and 1.7 kbit/s for the testbed, an estimation error of only 6%. Based

on these results, for all the simulations that follow we use the RP strategy implementation with $r = 1$.

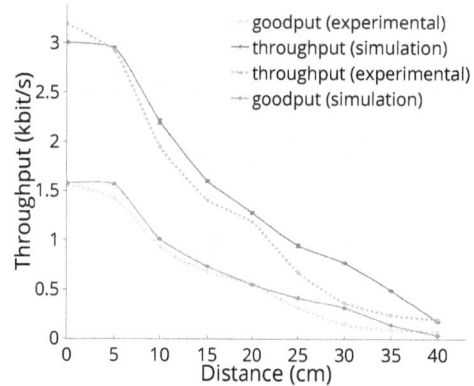

Figure 11: The throughput (red) as a function of the distance, compared with the goodput (green). Dotted-lines show experimental results while plain lines represent simulation results.

5.2.2 Message size. We now consider the impact of the message size G on the goodput at a 5 cm distance, with $r = 1$ and a 24 bits length PHY-SDU. Fig. 10 shows that *CamComSim* results are very close to those of the testbed, confirming that the simulator well considers the impact of the message size. The goodput reduces when the message size increases, as the RP strategy leads to a large number of useless transmissions: the simulator gives 1.6 kbit/s of goodput for $G = 50$ bytes, while this falls to 670 bit/s when $G = 1000$ bytes. These results differ from the testbed in no more than 7%.

5.2.3 Distance. Fig. 11 shows the goodput and the throughput as a function of the distance, when the LED broadcasts a 50 bytes message. The PHY-SDU payload is set to 24 bits, with $P = 19$ and $H = 5$. The results show a good match between the simulation and real life results. At 10 cm, *CamComSim* gives 2.2 kbit/s of throughput, against 1.94 kbit/s experimentally. The results are closer for the goodput: 0.94 and 1.0 kbit/s respectively for simulation and experimentation, that is only 6% of difference.

This section highlights that *CamComSim* gives results very close to the testbed for all the parameters we have studied. The difference is around 10% and often less. For all the cases we consider, *CamComSim* respects the behavior of the LED-to-camera communication system implemented by the testbed.

5.3 Use case

In this section, we detail a case study for *CamComSim*, applied to a real life scenario. A common issue with cheap consumer electronics is the lack of diagnostics when a dysfunction happens. Manufacturers often blink the state LED with a pattern and color that match with an error code. Such a mechanism is easy to implement but leads to inaccurate diagnostics. For these cases, we propose to benefit from this LED to perform LED-to-camera communication and broadcast a log file that would include helpful information to diagnose a dysfunction. We consider a worst case file size of 1 kbyte that is large enough for events history or debug traces.

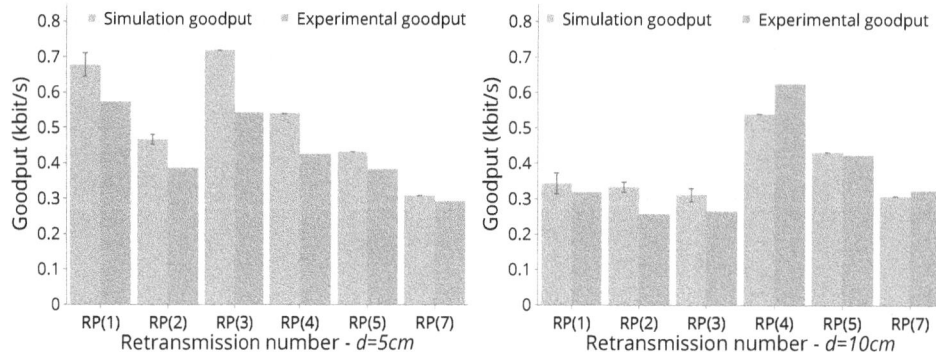

Figure 12: The experimental goodput (blue) compared with the simulation goodput (green) for the use case as a function of the number of consecutive PHY-SDU emission at 5 cm (left) and 10 cm (right).

Fig. 12 compares the goodput given by *CamComSim* with the goodput that our testbed achieved for the transfer of a 1 kbyte log file as a function of the number of PHY-SDU retransmissions r. Note that this is equivalent to $G = 1000$ bytes in Fig. 10. The transmission restarts until the message is received. The left side plot shows the results when the LED and the smartphone are 5 cm apart, while the distance is 10 cm on the right side figure. At 5 cm, the simulation brings out that, to obtain the higher goodput, the emitter should send each PHY-SDU one or three times consecutively, i.e. $r = 1$ or $r = 3$. The goodput is respectively 680 and 720 bit/s in these cases. This finding is similar to the testbed, where the goodput is 570 bit/s when $r = 1$ and 540 bit/s when $r = 3$.

Because the ROI decreases with the distance, the behavior is different when the smartphone is 10 cm far from the LED. In this situation, $r = 4$ stands out clearly to be the best choice both for the simulation and the experiments. The goodput then becomes 620 bit/s on the testbed and 540 bit/s with *CamComSim*.

Since the results are very close to the reality, using *CamComSim* highly reduces the search space for the experimental optimization of a system. As shown by these results, the best value for r can be decided using simulations only, removing the need for a lengthy experimental campaign.

6 CONCLUSION

In this paper, we introduced *CamComSim*, the first simulator for the design, the prototyping and the development of protocols and applications for LED-to-camera communication. Our event driven simulator is based on an MMBP channel model, and it relies on a standalone Java application that is easily extensible through a set of interfaces. We have validated *CamComSim* comparing simulation results with the performance reached by a real life testbed. Then, we illustrated with a practical use case the complete usage of *CamComSim* to tune a broadcast protocol that implements the transmission of a 1 kbyte log file. The results highlight that our simulator is very precise and can predict the performance of a LED-to-camera system with less than 10% of error in most cases. The availability of accurate performance evaluation tools offers a great ease of use and the opportunity to tune protocols without the burden of always realizing experiments on a testbed.

REFERENCES

[1] C. Danakis, M. Afgani, G. Povey, I. Underwood, H. Haas. "Using a CMOS Camera Sensor for Visible Light Communication". *Proc. IEEE OWC 2012*, Anaheim, CA, USA, Dec. 2012.

[2] T. Nguyen, Y.M. Jang. "High-speed Asynchronous Optical Camera Communication using LED and Rolling Shutter Camera". *Proc. ICUFN 2015*, Sapporo, Japan, Jul. 2015.

[3] P.H. Pathak, X. Feng, P. Hu, P. Mohapatra. "Visible Light Communication, Networking, and Sensing: A Survey, Potential and Challenges". *IEEE Communications Surveys & Tutorials*, vol. 17, no. 4, pp. 2047–2077, Oct. 2015.

[4] H.-Y. Lee, H.-M. Lin, Y.-L. Wei, H.-I. Wu, H.-M. Tsai, C.-J. Lin. "RollingLight: Enabling Line-of-Sight Light-to-Camera Communications". *Proc. ACM MobiSys 2015*, New York, NY, USA, May 2015.

[5] J. Hao, Y. Yang, J. Luo. "CeilingCast: Energy Efficient and Location-bound Broadcast through LED-camera Communication". *Proc. IEEE INFOCOM 2016*, San Francisco, CA, USA, Apr. 2016.

[6] H. Du, J. Han, X. Jian, T. Jung, C. Bo, Y. Wang, X.-Y. Li. "Martian: Message Broadcast via LED Lights to Heterogeneous Smartphones". *IEEE Journal on Selected Areas in Communications*, vol. 35, no. 5, pp. 1154â‚¬Ş-1162, May 2017.

[7] J. Ferrandiz-Lahuerta, D. Camps-Mur, J. Paradells-Aspas. "A Reliable Asynchronous Protocol for VLC Communications Based on the Rolling Shutter Effect". *Proc. IEEE GlobeCom 2015*, San Diego, CA, USA, Dec. 2015.

[8] C. Zhang, X. Zhang. "LiTell: Robust Indoor Localization using Unmodified Light Fixtures". *Proc. ACM MobiCom 2016*, New York, NY, USA, Oct. 2016.

[9] S. Zhu, X. Zhang. "Enabling High-Precision Visible Light Localization in TodayâŽs Buildings". *Proc. ACM MobiSys 2017*, Niagara Falls, NY, USA, Jun. 2017.

[10] T. Li, C. An, Z. Tian, A.T. Campbell, X. Zhou. "Human Sensing Using Visible Light Communication". *Proc. ACM MobiCom 2015*, Paris, France, Sep. 2015.

[11] S. Zhu, C. Zhang, X. Zhang. "Automating Visual Privacy Protection Using a Smart LED". *Proc. ACM MobiCom 2017*, Snowbird, UT, USA, Oct. 2017.

[12] M. Sharif, A. Sadeghi-Niaraki."Ubiquitous Sensor Network Simulation and Emulation Environments: A Survey". *Journal of Network and Computer Applications*, vol. 93, pp. 150â‚¬Ş181, Sep. 2017.

[13] D. Tagliaferri, C. Capsoni. "Development and Testing of an Indoor VLC Simulator". *Proc. IEEE IWOW 2015*, Istanbul, Turkey, Sep. 2015.

[14] A. Aldalbahi, M. Rahaim, A. Khreishah, M. Ayyash, R. Ackerman, J. Basuino, W. Berreta, T.D. Little. "Extending ns3 to Simulate Visible Light Communication at Network-level". *Proc. IEEE ICT 2016*, Thessaloniki, Greece, May 2016.

[15] C. Ley-Bosch, R. Medina-Sosa, I. Alonso-Gonzalez, D. Sanchez-Rodriguez. "Implementing an IEEE802.15.7 Physical Layer Simulation Model with OMNET++". *Proc. DCAI 2015*, Salamanca, Spain, Jun. 2015.

[16] A. Musa, M. D. Baba, H. M. Haji Mansor. "The Design and Implementation of IEEE 802.15.7 Module with ns-2 Simulator". *Proc. IEEE I4CT 2014*, Lisbon, Portugal, May 2014.

[17] S. Ozekici. "Markov Modulated Bernoulli Process". *Mathematical Methods of Operations Research*, vol. 45, no. 3, pp. 311â‚¬Ş-324, Mar. 1997.

[18] E.O. Elliott. "Estimates of Error Rates for Codes on Burst-Noise Channels". *Bell System Technical Journal*, vol. 42, no. 5, pp. 1977â‚¬Ş-1997, May 1963.

[19] A. Duque, R. Stanica, H. Rivano, A. Desportes. "Unleashing the Power of LED-to-Camera Communications for IoT Devices". *Proc. ACM VLCS 2016*, New York, NY, USA, Oct. 2016.

Joint Link-level and Network-level Reconfiguration for mmWave Backhaul Survivability in Urban Environments

Yuchen Liu, Qiang Hu and Douglas M. Blough

Georgia Institute of Technology, Atlanta, GA, 30332

ABSTRACT

mmWave communication has been recognized as a highly promising technology for 5G wireless backhaul, which is capable of providing multi-gigabit per second transmission rates. However, in urban wireless backhaul environments, unforeseen events can cause short-term blockages or node failures and, therefore, network survivability is extremely important. In this paper, we investigate a novel relay-assisted mmWave backhaul network architecture, where a number of small-cell BSs and relays are deployed, e.g. on the lampposts of urban streets. Relays are used to provide multi-hop line-of-sight paths between small-cell BSs, which form logical links of the network. In this scenario, the interconnected logical links make up a mesh network, which offers opportunities for both link-level and network-level reconfiguration. We propose two joint link-network level reconfiguration schemes for recovery after exceptional events. One prioritizes relay path (link-level) reconfiguration and uses alternate network-level paths only if necessary. The other splits traffic on both reconfigured links and backup paths to improve network throughput. Simulation results demonstrate that the proposed schemes significantly outperform purely link-level and purely network-level reconfiguration schemes. The proposed approaches are shown to not only maintain high network throughput but to also provide robust blockage/fault tolerance across a range of scenarios for urban mmWave backhaul networks.

CCS CONCEPTS

• Networks → Network reliability; Network protocol design; Network performance analysis.

KEYWORDS

Millimeter wave; wireless backhaul; relays; survivability; reconfiguration; robustness

ACM Reference Format:
Yuchen Liu, Qiang Hu and Douglas M. Blough. 2019. Joint Link-level and Network-level Reconfiguration for mmWave Backhaul Survivability in Urban Environments. In *22nd Int'l ACM Conference on Modeling, Analysis and Simulation of Wireless and Mobile Systems (MSWiM '19), November 25–29, 2019, Miami Beach, FL, USA.* ACM, New York, NY, USA, 9 pages.
https://doi.org/10.1145/3345768.3355913

1 INTRODUCTION

With the advent of 5G networks, it is expected that a large number of small-cell base stations (BSs) will be deployed in urban areas. Each small cell will cover a smaller area but will have much higher capacity and less interference. Millimeter wave (mmWave) communication is very well suited to this scenario, especially for self-backhauling [1–3], wherein a huge amount of data must be transmitted with high rates among the BSs.

Due to the trend for dense deployment that makes current wired backhaul costly and in some cases prohibitive, wireless backhaul becomes a very promising solution [4], [5]. With wireless backhaul, only a very small portion of BSs, referred to as anchored BSs (A-BS), will have fiber backhaul and the rest of the small-cell BSs (SBSs) backhaul to the fiber sites wirelessly. In order to fully realize mmWave wireless backhaul in urban environments, the poor propagation characteristics and higher penetration loss of mmWave communications are two challenges that must be overcome. With high-gain directional antennas and relaying techniques, a sequence of relatively short but very high rate mmWave links can be produced to compensate the high path loss.

Severe penetration loss makes blockage effects a serious problem in mmWave networks [6, 7], because the signal strength is degraded by about 30dB for non-line-of-sight (NLOS) paths when mmWave links are blocked by obstacles such as buildings, vehicles, or even humans [8]. For this reason, it is necessary to adopt an appropriate network topology with effective path reconfiguration mechanisms, which can be applied for maintenance of line-of-sight (LOS) mmWave paths with high rates in the presence of blockages.

There are primarily two kinds of network architecture for mmWave backhaul, which are the centralized and distributed architectures [9]. In a centralized architecture, a macrocell BS (M-BS) is situated in the center with a number of SBSs distributed around it, and these SBSs do not communicate with each other by direct links but rather they access the core network through the M-BS that is connected to the gateway by fiber links. This kind of system forms a star topology, which makes it hard to perform path reconfiguration for potential link failures since there exists only one route from each SBS to the M-BS. However, in a distributed architecture, backhaul data of each SBS are relayed to an A-BS instead of the M-BS, and these data are allowed to traverse mmWave links of adjacent SBSs and finally are collected by the A-BS to the core network through fiber links [10]. Therefore, a mesh-like backhaul network will be formed by the mmWave links. Compared with the centralized solution, the distributed architecture can achieve higher throughputs and be more reliable, mainly owing to sharing cooperative traffic among multiple wireless SBSs. In this architecture, when the communication of a path is blocked, the data can be transmitted to other adjacent SBSs and be routed on an alternate path to maintain the high-rate connectivity.

In this paper, we consider a relay-assisted mmWave backhaul network architecture in urban environments, where a number of SBSs and mmWave dedicated relays are deployed along the urban streets, which naturally produces a mesh network structure. The deployment of relays between each SBS pair provide multi-hop LOS relay paths between SBSs, which we refer to as logical links in the mesh network. These networks are susceptible to node failures[1] and/or obstacles in the form of large trucks or other objects that could block some of the primary LOS paths. An advantage of the use of multi-hop logical links is that they allow for link-level reconfiguration when an obstacle blocks an individual physical link. This provides opportunities for both link-level and network-level reconfiguration for network survivability in the presence of obstacles and/or node failures.

We propose two joint link-network level reconfiguration schemes to tolerate these exceptional events. The first approach is to prioritize link-level reconfiguration, and use a network-level backup path only when the performance of the reconfigured logical link drops below a threshold value. The second approach is designed to further improve the throughput performance, by using both reconfigured logical links and alternative backup paths for data transmission when blockage occurs. In this case, the traffic is split optimally and off-loaded to these multiple paths. Through simulation, we evaluate the performance of our proposed algorithms on backhaul networks under random obstacle scenarios. The results show that our proposed schemes substantially outperform purely link-level and purely network-level reconfiguration approaches. The results also demonstrate that our proposed approaches can provide near-optimal blockage tolerance while maintaining throughputs that can satisfy the rigorous data demands of wireless backhaul scenarios.

2 RELATED WORK

Prior work on path recovery in wireless networks can be broadly categorized into two main methods: network-level reconfiguration (NLR) and link-level reconfiguration (LLR).

2.1 Network-level reconfiguration schemes

In general, network-level reconfiguration includes the protection method and the restoration method [12]. The former method reserves backup resources before link failure occurs, whereas the restoration method finds a new path for the influenced traffic after failure occurs. Most related works focus on the protection method to prevent the link failure since it can achieve fast recovery [13–15]. The main idea in these approaches is to select a single disjoint backup path for each primary path based on the assumption that it is unlikely for a primary path and its backup path to fail simultaneously. [16] proposed a dynamic routing algorithm to select the best backup path with minimized total cost, which improves the utilization and reduces blocking in mesh networks. [17] introduced another method that is based on pre-finding a set of backup paths for each active path, and multiple survivable paths of a pair of nodes could be used to survive any single risk. In [18], the author

presented a predictive weather-assisted routing protocol that routes data around potential link failures ahead of time.

This kind of reconfiguration approach can also be applied in backhaul networks, where the central A-BS pre-computes several eligible backup paths for primary working paths, and once the blockage occurs between a pair of SBSs, the A-BS can efficiently switch to an alternate backup path as the new network-level path to maintain the high-rate backhaul data transmission. However, this approach is topology-dependent, and can only be applied in a mesh-like network, because if the network has a tree or star-like topology, there exists only one route between the A-BS any given SBS, and it is impossible to find any other network-level paths for blockage avoidance. In addition, backup paths might not always exist [17], because sometimes it is hard to find a candidate path that satisfies both rate and path length requirements of mmWave backhaul.

2.2 Link-level reconfiguration schemes

Another approach to blockage handling is based on link-level reconfiguration (LLR), which aims to reconfigure a new relay path within a single logical link between two wireless nodes when a physical link failure occurs. To the best of our knowledge, there are few works that considered multi-hop relay paths for blockage avoidance in outdoor environments [19], [20], and they are primarily concerned with finding a relay path with the highest probability of reaching the BS. In contrast, our work considers the maintenance of backhaul paths with very high rates in the presence of temporary blockages. In our previous work [21], the high-throughput path-level reconfiguration (HTPR) algorithm is proposed to reconfigure around temporary blockages in relay-assisted mmWave backhaul networks. In most situations, the HTPR scheme maintains high-rate connectivity for logical links between each SBS pair and, in this work, we use it as our comparison point for pure link-level reconfiguration schemes.

Here we note that LLR can be applied in all types of network topologies with relay assistance, and it can be conducted at the SBS level without the participation of the A-BS. However, the link quality will be degraded after reconfiguration since alternative physical links are always longer than the original link. On the other hand, while LLR may provide some network control benefits, it cannot handle some blockage cases where the logical link (relay path) is totally blocked.

3 SYSTEM OVERVIEW

In this section, we introduce the network topology, and channel and antenna models used in the remainder of the paper.

3.1 Network model in an urban area

For future 5G cellular networks, a large number of small-cell base stations will be deployed in urban areas to cooperatively provide a more reliable access experience for users. A number of works have proposed the use of mmWave wireless backhaul for 5G networks [22–24]. Here we consider a relay-assisted mmWave mesh network architecture for backhaul in urban areas [25], [26], where mmWave relay nodes are used to assist in connecting BSs of the wireless mesh network.

---

[1]The node-failure case is actually equivalent to a blockage case where an obstacle totally blocks the node. Thus, in the remainder of the paper, we mainly focus on blockage effects caused by random obstacles.

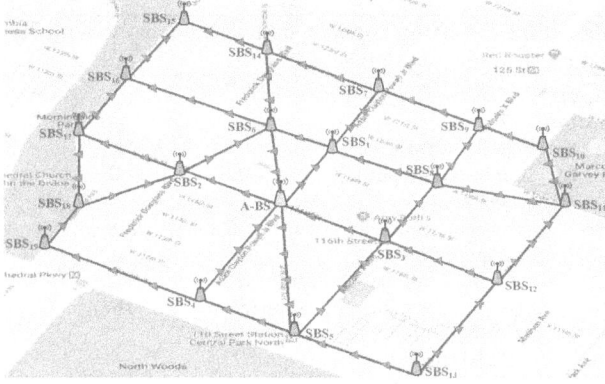

Figure 1: mmWave backhaul network model in a section of Manhattan.

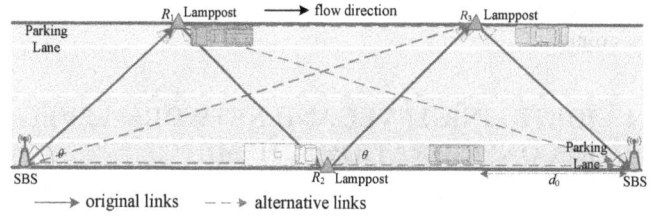

Figure 2: Original and alternative links in the triangular-wave topology.

An example relay-assisted mesh backhaul network is shown in Fig. 1. In this example, there are a single A-BS connected with a fiber to the core network, a number of SBSs deployed at street corners, and several mmWave relays along the roadside (shown with the green triangles). It is assumed that all these three entities can communicate in the mmWave band using directional antennas with steerable beams, which produce a number of interconnected mmWave links to form a wireless mesh network. There are three important entities in our mmWave backhaul network model:

- *Physical link*: An actual link between relay pairs or between a relay and its adjacent BS – the capacity of physical links is determined by Shannon's Theorem.
- *Logical Link (relay path)*: A path between BS pairs including SBS-to-SBS and A-BS-to-SBS, which consists of multiple physical links. The achievable capacity of each logical link is determined by the capacity of its bottleneck physical link pair [3].
- *Backhaul path*: A path between the A-BS and a SBS, which can consist of several logical links. For simplicity, we use $P_{0,i}$ to denote the backhaul path from the A-BS to SBS$_i$.

In this work, we adopt the "street canyon" model for relay paths forming logical links [25]. In the street canyon model, each logical link between BSs runs along a street and consists of a sequence of mmWave relays. As in [21], we assume that relays are deployed in a regular fashion on both sides of the road, e.g. by deploying them on equally-spaced lampposts. As shown in Fig. 2, these physical links within a given logical link form a triangular-wave topology, where the topology angle θ and horizontal distance between adjacent nodes d_0 are the same everywhere along the topology (as depicted by the blue links of Fig. 2). One advantage of this topology is that the mutual interference along the logical link can be eliminated if θ is made large enough relative to the beamwidth ϕ of the directional antennas (Theorem 1 in [11]), i.e. if $\theta - \arctan(\frac{\tan\theta}{3}) > \frac{\phi}{2}$. In this way, the logical link can support the high throughput of 10+ Gbps to meet the requirement of mmWave backhaul. On the other hand, this kind of topology is also capable of reconfiguring mmWave links to avoid obstacles (eg. parked large vehicles) that occur along the roadway. Through adaptive beam steering and dilation when one or more original links are blocked, alternative links can be used to restore the LOS connectivity of a logical link [27].

Note that the mmWave relay devices used in the network model are dedicated to a single logical link between a pair of BSs, because we assume relays are simple devices that cannot support the sharing between different logical links. In addition, we assume this kind of simple relay is subject to the primary interference constraint, which means a single relay cannot transmit and receive simultaneously. However, we assume that BSs (A-BS or SBSs) are not affected by these constraints since they are more complex devices with capability to use better antenna isolation and interference cancellation technologies.

From the view of the entire network model, the separation distances between each pair of BSs are around 350m, so the total modeled area in Fig. 1 is around 1200m × 1300m, which is a bit larger than the size of a typical 4G macrocell. By leveraging the geographical advantage with relaying technique in urban streets, this network architecture can not only eliminate mutual interference along logical links to achieve higher throughputs for backhaul, but it also naturally forms a mesh-like topology in an urban area, which makes it possible to jointly conduct the network-level and link-level reconfiguration for the improvement of network survivability.

3.2 Channel and antenna model

Here we make the standard assumption of additive white Gaussian noise channels. The rate of the directional unblocked physical link p follows Shannon's Theorem with an upper limitation, i.e.,

$$R_p \leq \beta \cdot B \cdot \log_2(1 + \min\{\frac{P_r(d)}{N_T}, T_{\max}\}) \qquad (1)$$

where B is channel bandwidth, N_T is the power of thermal noise, T_{max} is the upper bound of operating signal-noise ratio due to the limiting factors like linearity in the radio frequency front-end, and the link utility ratio $\beta \in (0, 1)$. Considering the primary interference of our simplified relays, $\beta \leq 0.5$, and a maximum end-to-end throughput of nearly 16 Gbps can theoretically be achieved in mmWave communications [3]. Here $P_r(d)$ is the received power of the intended transmitter's signal, and equals $k_0 P_t G_t G_r d^{-\alpha}$, where $k_0 \propto (\lambda_w/4\pi)^2$, λ_w is the signal's wavelength, d is the propagation distance, α is the path-loss exponent, and G_t and G_r are antenna gains at the transmitter and receiver, respectively.

In this work, a flat-top directional antenna model is adopted for each wireless node, which means that transceiver antennas have a high constant gain G_h within the beam, and a very low gain G_l that can be ignored outside the narrow beamwidth ϕ. For example, with the 61 element uniform hexagonal array antenna simulated by MATLAB software, the antenna gains G_h can be generated as

23.18 dBi and G_l is lower than 0 dBi when the antenna beamwidth is around $15°$.

4 JOINT LINK-LEVEL AND NETWORK-LEVEL RECONFIGURATION SCHEME

The ability to reconfigure logical links (relay paths) in the presence of obstacles provides multiple possible approaches to blockage tolerance for the mmWave backhaul network. Link-level blockage tolerance mainly adopts relay path reconfiguration schemes, i.e., finding an alternative physical link to substitute the original blocked link. As for network-level reconfiguration, it usually uses a new high-rate path between the source and destination nodes for blockage avoidance. In this section, we present joint link-network level reconfiguration schemes for fast recovery, which utilize relay path reconfiguration and alternate network-level paths in combination.

4.1 Prioritized Link-level Reconfiguration

In our considered relay-assisted network scenario, we first propose a prioritized link-level reconfiguration scheme (PLLR), which takes advantage of both link-level and network-level tolerance ability. The main idea is to prioritize relay path reconfiguration to avoid the use of alternate network-level paths whenever possible, so that the A-BS does not need to modify the routing table and inform the SBSs, which might complicate the network control. However, alternative network-level paths can be used if the performance of a reconfigured relay path drops so much that the throughput of that logical link is lower than a threshold value, which means that the original backhaul path $P_{0,i}$ cannot satisfy the data demand at SBS_i. In what follows, we introduce this novel approach in detail.

1) Backup path selection

To achieve fast recovery, we pre-calculate a set of backup paths for each primary backhaul path and store them in the survivable-path set (SS). Different from other related works that just find one totally disjoint backup path to recover from a single link failure, the SS is used to overcome multiple blockages since obstacles could block a primary path and some of its backup paths simultaneously in our considered scenario. On the other hand, there may not always exist a totally disjoint backup path which also satisfies the high-rate and few-hop constraints, but some partially disjoint paths that meet the requirements can avoid the blockage and could even have better performance than a totally disjoint backup path.

Therefore, our approach finds a SS that consists of a set of backup paths that may not be totally disjoint but can survive blockages, and this enables us to provide protection for a broader range of scenarios and increase the network survivability. Here the backup path selected into SS for potential path recovery should satisfy two requirements: 1) supporting high throughput for mmWave backhaul; 2) with fewer hops than a specified threshold, because too many hops will lead to an unacceptably high end-to-end latency between the A-BS and the associated SBS.

The approach of finding backup paths with higher rates and hop-count constraint is shown in Algorithm 1. Considering the hop counts of different logical links in the topology, we first find the minimum hop counts m among these logical links. Then, given a

---

Algorithm 1 Finding top-k widest backup paths with hop-count constraint

Input: $V, E, H, m, Hop, thrp, T$
Output: SS
1:    $maxHop \leftarrow \lceil H/m \rceil$;
2:    **for** each backhaul path $P_{s,i}$ btw A-BS and SBS_i **do**
3:       $ihop \leftarrow 0$;
4:       $SS[i] = searchBackupPath(s, i, V, E, maxHop, ihop)$;
5:       $SS[i].rmv(PrimPath)$;
6:       **for** each backup path BP_j in SS **do**
7:         **if** ($\sum_{l \in BP_j} Hop[l] > H \;||\; \min_{l \in BP_j} \{thrp_l\} < T$) **then**
8:           $SS[i].rmv(BP_j)$;
9:         $sort(BP_j, \min_{l \in BP_j} \{thrp_l\})$;
10:    **if** ($SS[i].size > k$) **then**
11:       $SS[i].rmv(last\ (SS[i].size - k)\ paths)$;
12:    **return** SS; // get survivable-path sets
     Function: searchBackupPath($s, i, V, E, maxHop, ihop$)
13:    $path.add(src)$;
14:    **if** ($i = src$) **then**
15:       $SS[i].add(path)$;
16:       $path.rmv(end\ node)$;
17:       **return**
18:    $id \leftarrow find(V.begin, V.end, src) - V.begin$;
19:    **for** each node j in V **do**
20:       **if** (j has been visited) **continue**;
21:       **if** ($E[id][j]! = Inf$ & $ihop + 1 <= maxHop$) **then**
22:         $searchBackupPath(j, i, V, E, maxHop, ihop + 1)$;
23:    $path.rmv(end\ node)$;

---

hop-count constraint H (including intermediate relays and relayed-SBSs), we compute a coarse allowable logical-level hops as the rounded-up H/m (Line 1). After conducting the depth-first search (DFS), we find all backup paths which have their logical-level hop counts $ihop$ no more than $maxHop$ (Line 13-23), and these paths can be further put into survivable path set $SS[i]$ only if they satisfy the following two conditions: 1) the total hop counts of this path are not larger than H, because $maxHop$ used in DFS steps actually relaxes the real hop-count constraint, and some searched backup paths with more than H hops need to be dropped; 2) the throughput of bottleneck logical link pair within this backup path should meet the high-rate backhaul requirement T (Lines 7-8).

Note that with an appropriate H in most network topologies, there are only a small number of backup paths in each SS. However, we also set an upper bound k on the number of backup paths in case the path length constraint is so weak that a large number of possible backup paths exist. In this scenario, we only put the k backup paths with highest rates into SS (Lines 10-12).

2) Combined link-level and network-level reconfiguration

Algorithm 2 shows the pseudocode for the proposed PLLR scheme, which jointly considers link-level and network-level reconfigurations. In the "Input" arguments, C is a vector that includes the achievable capacity of each logical link between BSs, and NP is a path set that contains each backhaul path $P_{0,k}$ between A-BS and SBS_k in the network. D and AD are the sets that include data-rate demand of each SBSs and the aggregated data-rate demand of each logical link, respectively, and the link much closer to the A-BS will have higher aggregated data-rate demand since it is required to carry more traffic to further SBSs. SS contains the survivable-path set SS_k of each $P_{0,k}$. When the logical link $\mathcal{L}$ between BS_i and BS_j is blocked, the high throughput link-level reconfiguration algorithm (HTPR) [21] is first executed for logical link recovery, and the achievable capacity of $\mathcal{L}$ will be degraded since one or more longer physical links would be selected for blockage avoidance, and then C is updated with the new capacity of $\mathcal{L}$ (Lines 1-3).

If the current throughput of the degraded link $\mathcal{L}$ drops lower than its aggregated data-rate demand (AD) (Line 3), all SBSs backhauled by the link $\mathcal{L}$ are found and put into $B_{\mathcal{L}}$ (Lines 4-5). Then the network-level reconfiguration will be activated to select alternate backup paths for some of affected SBSs.

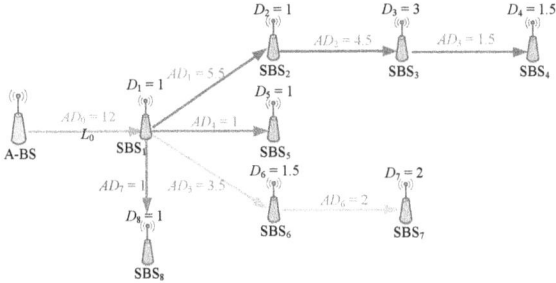

Figure 3: An example for minimizing rSBSs.

For example, Fig. 3 shows several primary backhaul paths, and every logical link has the achievable capacity of 12 Gbps and data-rate demand at each SBS_i is D_i. From further SBSs to A-BS, we can compute the AD of each logical link in turn (shown in Fig. 3). Now assuming the current capacity of link $\mathcal{L}_0$ (between ABS and SBS_1) drops to $C_{\mathcal{L}_0}$ ($C_{\mathcal{L}_0} < AD_0$), all backhauled SBSs ($SBS_1 \sim SBS_8$) are obtained. In order to avoid the use of more alternate network-level paths which might complicate the network control, we set an objective to minimize the number of SBSs that need to be reconfigured to use backup paths (referred to as rSBSs).

One direct method of minimizing rSBSs (MRS) is to formulate the following optimization problem:

$$\max_{S} \sum_{i \in B_l} s_i \qquad (2)$$

$$s.t. \sum_{i \in B_l} D_i \cdot s_i \leq C_{\mathcal{L}}, \; s_i \in \{0,1\} \qquad (3)$$

where s_i is the SBS backhauled by the logical link $\mathcal{L}$. The objective function in Eq. (2) aims to satisfy greatest number of SBSs affected by this link. Eq. (3) indicates the capacity constraint, where the aggregated data-rate demand on the link $\mathcal{L}$ cannot exceed its current capacity, and s_i will be set as 1 if SBS_i is chosen, otherwise it equals to 0. This optimization problem is similar to the *0/1 knapsack problem*, and in this case the optimal solution is to sort the SBSs in order of increasing data-rate demand and satisfy them in turn until there is not enough capacity of link $\mathcal{L}$ to backhaul any SBSs. As an example, in Fig. 3, when the capacity of the logical link between A-BS and SBS_1 (shown with green line) drops to 7, we need to reconfigure new bachaul paths for SBS_3 and SBS_7.

However, this MRS method does not take into account the primary working paths, so we introduce another method to minimize rSBSs with groups (MRG).

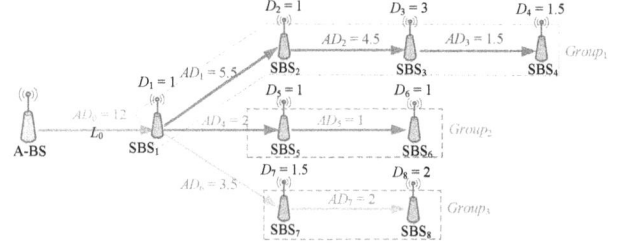

Figure 4: An example for minimizing rSBSs with groups.

In the MRG method, if the current capacity of link $\mathcal{L}$ drops below $AD_{\mathcal{L}}$, we first group all SBSs backhauled by link $\mathcal{L}$ according to their primary paths in set G. As an example, in Fig. 4, when $C_{\mathcal{L}_0} < AD_0$, all backhauled SBSs can be divided into three groups based on their primary paths. Then we start to minimize the number of groups that cannot be fully satisfied, i.e., maximize the number of satisfiable groups by solving the similar knapsack-like problem:

$$\max_{G} \sum_{g \in G_l} g_i \qquad (4)$$

$$s.t. \sum_{i \in G_l} AD_{g_i} \cdot g_i \leq C_{\mathcal{L}}, \; g_i \in \{0,1\} \qquad (5)$$

where each g_i includes the grouped SBSs backhauled by the logical link $\mathcal{L}$, and AD_{g_i} is the aggregated data-rate demand of each group. After obtaining the groups that can be fully satisfied, the remaining items in G are the groups g_r that need to be reconfigured. Starting from the g_r that comprises the maximum number of SBSs, we break g_r and repeat solving the problem in Eq. (2)-(3) with the remaining $C_{\mathcal{L}}$, so the minimum number of rSBSs in each group is obtained.

In this way, for each group g_r that is not fully satisfied, we only need to reconfigure the new backhaul path for the rSBS closest to the degraded link $\mathcal{L}$, i.e., the leader rSBS (L-SBS), because the paths from the L-SBS to other non-leader rSBSs (NL-SBS) can still be maintained within the group. Different from the MRS method that will alternate new backhaul paths for all rSBSs, here we try to force rSBSs in one group and then only take care of the leader rSBS, which can reduce the reconfiguration overhead.

Note that for those NL-SBSs in each group g_r, we also need to check whether or not each of them violates following constraints:

- *Hop-count constraint (HC)*: The total hop counts of the new reconfigured path and the maintained path for the NL-SBS should be less than the hop-count threshold H.
- *Data-demand constraint (DC)*: The available capacity of that new reconfigured path should be able to satisfy the data demand of the non-leader SBS.

If either HC or DC is violated, we need to select a backup path for that NL-SBS from its own SS. Note that the NL-SBS that has fewer backup paths should be checked first, because it has weaker network-level blockage tolerance and should be taken care of in the network first.

Here, the MRG method is adopted as an example shown in the Algorithm 2. As the procedure mentioned above, the reconfigured groups g_r and corresponding rSBSs can be obtained by solving a knapsack-like problem (Lines 6-14). Then, the network-level reconfiguration is activated to select a new network path for the leader SBS in g_r, and we always select the backup path that has the maximum achievable throughput from its SS (Line 16). Here the achievable throughput performance (Th) of each backup path BP_i can be evaluated as follow:

$$Th_i = \min_{\mathcal{L}_j \in BP_i} \{C_{\mathcal{L}_j} - AD_{\mathcal{L}_j}\} \qquad (6)$$

which is determined by the extra available capacity of the bottleneck logical link $\mathcal{L}_j$ within this path. Note that if no backup paths can meet its own data-rate demand, we have to give up selecting new paths for this SBS. For those NL-SBSs, if either HC or DC is violated, a new path will be selected in the same way (Lines 18-22). In the end, the aggregated data-rate demand set AD and the backhaul path set NP need to be updated (Line 23).

Algorithm 2 Prioritized Link-Level Reconfiguration

Input: C, NP, AD, SS, D
Output: updated NP
1: HTPR($\mathcal{L}$, Relay[i][j]); // link-level reconfiguration
2: C.update($C_{\mathcal{L}}$);
3: **if** ($C_{\mathcal{L}} < AD_{\mathcal{L}}$) **then**
4:    **for** each $P_{0,k}$ in NP contains $\mathcal{L}$ **do**
5:      $B_{\mathcal{L}}$.add(s_k);
6:      $G \leftarrow$ Group($s_k, P_{0,k}$);
7:      sort($g_k \in G, AD_k \uparrow$);
8:      **for** $k \leftarrow 0$ to size(G) **do**
9:        **if** ($AD_k \leq C_{\mathcal{L}}$) **then**
10:         G_s.add(s_k); // satisfied groups
11:         $C_{\mathcal{L}} \leftarrow C_{\mathcal{L}} - AD_k$;
12:       **else break**; // not enough capacity
13:     $G_r \leftarrow G \backslash G_s$; // get remaining groups from G
14:     solve(Eq.(2), from g_r with max SBSs);
15:     **for** each g_r in G_r **do**
16:       AltPath(L-SBS$_m$, when max(Th_i) $\geq D(m)$);
17:       max(Th_i)$\leftarrow$ max(Th_i) - $D(m)$;
18:       **for** each NL-SBS$_k$ with fewer backup path first **do**
19:         **if** (HC & DC) = false **then**
20:           AltPath(NL-SBS$_k$, when max(Th_j) $\geq D(k)$);
21:         **else**
22:           max(Th_i) $\leftarrow$ max(Th_i) - $D(k)$;
23:     AD.update; NP.update;
24: **return** NP; // get updated network-level paths

4.2 High-Throughput Multi-path Reconfiguration

To further improve throughput performance with blockages and better leverage the cooperation between the A-BS and SBSs, we introduce another reconfiguration approach based on the previous PLLR algorithm, which is referred to as high-throughput multi-path reconfiguration (HTMR) scheme. This approach is trying to use the primary path and backup paths in combination for data transmission when the blockage occurs, which will work well in networks that support multi-path routing. As a primary relay path's performance is degraded due to link-level reconfiguration around obstacles, some of its traffic can be off-loaded to backup paths so

that the reconfigured relay path and several alternative routes are used at the same time. Before adopting this algorithm instead of PLLR, we should pre-evaluate how much performance increase can be achieved compared to the PLLR scheme, since the benefit will depend on the overall network topology and the traffic flows, and HTMR scheme should be used for path recovery in the scenario where link outages occur infrequently and it can provide substantial benefits on throughput, and is therefore worth the added network control complexity for multi-path transmissions.

First, we need to solve a network flow problem in order to determine how to split traffic among the degraded primary path and backup paths which are totally disjoint. To split the traffic among multiple available paths, assuming there are n possible network paths between A-BS and SBS$_i$ with the data demand D, their respective achievable data rates R_i can be obtained according to Eq. (6). In this way, the required transmission time over each path is $t_i = d_i / R_i$ ($i \in P_s$), where d_i is the traffic assigned on path i. Assuming the data d_i over each path is transmitted from A-BS to SBS$_i$ at the same time, we can get the total required time T_r until all data D has been received as follow:

$$T_r = \max\{\frac{d_1}{R_1}, \frac{d_2}{R_2}, ..., \frac{d_n}{R_n}\} \qquad (7)$$

Thus the end-to-end throughput can be obtained as D/T_r. To maximize the throughput performance by splitting traffic over multiple paths, we formulate the optimization problem as follows:

$$\begin{aligned} \max_{\{d_i\}_{i \in P_s}} \quad & D \cdot \min\{\frac{R_1}{d_1}, \frac{R_2}{d_2}, ..., \frac{R_n}{d_n}\} \\ s.t. \quad & \sum_{i \in P_s} d_i = D, R_i \geq 0, d_i \geq 0. \end{aligned} \qquad (8)$$

Theorem 1. *To maximize the end-to-end throughput with given data demand D between A-BS and SBSs along n routes, the assigned traffic for each route is proportional to its achievable rate, i.e.,*

$$d_i = \frac{D \cdot R_i}{\sum\limits_{i \in P_s} R_i} \ (1 \leq i \leq n). \qquad (9)$$

PROOF. The objective function in Eq. (8) can be rewritten as $\max D\tau, R_i/d_i \leq \tau \ \forall i$. By making each R_i/d_i be equal, the Karush-Kuhn-Tucker condition will be satisfied and we can get the optimal solution as $\sum\limits_{i \in P_s} R_i$. Therefore, the optimal value d_i is obtained as $DR_i / \sum\limits_{i \in P_s} R_i$, which is proportional to R_i. If each R_i/d_i is not split equally, which means that $d_j = (D \cdot R_j / \sum\limits_{i \in P_s} R_i) - \epsilon$, and this would result in another split data $d_k = (D \cdot R_i / \sum\limits_{i \in P_s} R_i) + \epsilon$ since the total demand should be unchanged. Therefore, R_k/d_k becomes the bottleneck value and will reduce the original optimal solution. □

As an extension of the PLLR scheme, the basic logic of HTMR algorithm is similar to Algorithm 2, but the main difference is the method to select network-level paths for each rSBS (L-SBS or NL-SBS), which is shown in Algorithm 3. First, if the degraded logical link $\mathcal{L}$'s capacity is not used up (Line 2), both the primary path $P_{0,k}$ and backup paths can be possibly used for rSBS, otherwise only backup paths will be used for reconfiguration. In both of these cases, we first need to find the disjoint backup paths in SS (Line 4). Here, an approach referred to as *joint-weight selection* is designed to obtain the maximum number of disjoint backup paths in SS (shown in Eq. 10), where each selected path p_i does not have any overlapping logical links $\mathcal{L}$ with other paths.

$$\max_P \sum_{i \in SS} p_i$$
$$s.t. \mathcal{L}_{p_i} \cap \mathcal{L}_{p_j} = \emptyset, \; i \neq j, \; p_{i,j} = \{0,1\} \tag{10}$$

In the case where the primary path $P_{0,k}$ can still be used, we need to put $P_{0,k}$ in SS since it can also be viewed as one of backup paths (Line 3). Then, we start to find disjoint paths in SS_k (Lines 14-22). First, the joint weight W for each backup path BP_i is calculated, which represents the number of paths overlapping with BP_i in SS_k, and these joint paths are recorded in P (Lines 17-19). After that, we select the backup path BP_m with minimum weight W and put it into MP (Lines 20-21). Note that if there exist multiple paths with the same minimum W, the one which has higher throughput will be selected. Finally, we obtain the maximum number of disjoint backup paths of $P_{0,k}$ until SS_k is empty (Line 15). When the primary path cannot be used (i.e., $C_{\mathcal{L}} = 0$), we can find maximum number of disjoint backup paths in SS_k without $P_{0,k}$ in the same way.

After obtaining the multi-path set MP, the available backup paths are sorted in order of decreasing rate (Line 5), and the paths with highest rates will be iteratively selected until the data demand D_k at rSBS_k is satisfied (Lines 7-10). In the end, we split the data demand D_k according to Theorem 1, and assign the traffic to each selected path in MP' (Line 12).

Algorithm 3 Alternating Multiple Paths for Reconfiguration

Input: C, NP, AD, SS, D
Output: MP'
1: **for** each rSBS_k **do**
2:    **if** $(C_{\mathcal{L}} \neq 0)$ **then**
3:      SS_k.add($P_{0,k}$);
4:    MP = FindDjPath(SS_k);
5:    MP.sort($BP_i, R_i \downarrow$);
6:    $R_t \leftarrow 0$; // init R_t
7:    **for** $i \leftarrow 1$ to size(MP) **do**
8:      MP'.add($MP[i]$); // add the higher-rate path
9:      $R_t \leftarrow R_t + R_i$;
10:     **if** $(R_t \geq D_k)$ **then break**;
11:    **if** $(R_t < D_k)$ **then return** $\emptyset$; // do not alternate paths
12:    OptimalTS($path \in MP'$); // follow Theorem 1
13: **return** MP';
14: *Function*: FindDjPath(SS_k)
15: **while** $(SS_k \neq \emptyset)$ **do**
16:    **for** each backup paths $BP_i \in SS_k$ **do**
17:      **if** $(BP_i \cap BP_j \neq \emptyset, j \neq i)$ **then**
18:        $W_i \leftarrow W_i + 1$;
19:        $P[i]$.add(BP_j); // add BP_j in joint-path set
20:    FindPath(BP_m with min W);
21:    MP.add(BP_m);
22:    SS_k.rmv(BP_m & $path \in P[m]$);
23: **return** MP;

---

5 NUMERICAL SIMULATIONS AND RESULTS

In the face of obstacles that necessitate path recovery in mmWave backhaul networks, we evaluate the network performance including the throughput and blockage tolerance with different reconfiguration schemes. Here we conduct simulations where the mmWave backhaul network is deployed based on the Manhattan urban deployment shown in Fig. 1. With a single centralized A-BS, 19 SBSs at street corners and a number of relays along the roadside are selected. In this scenario, the established logical links between each pair of BSs, which consists of several physical links in a triangular-wave topology, form a mesh-like network that covers the area of over 1.2 km^2.

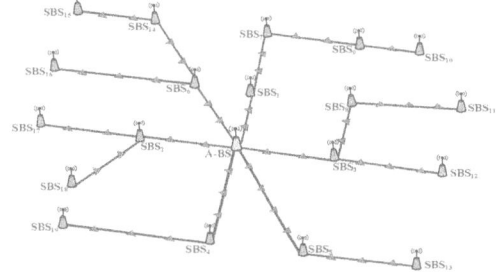

Figure 5: Primary backhaul paths in the mmWave backhaul network model.

In Fig. 5, without any link failures, we can compute that the network can support around 3 Gbps data demand for every SBS since each logical link (relay path) can achieve a throughput of around 13 Gbps. Considering potential blockages, we investigate the backhaul network survivability (BNS) [17] and satisfiable data demand for each SBS with our proposed reconfiguration schemes.

All evaluations are done at the mmWave frequency of 60 GHz with a 2.16 GHz bandwidth. The directional antenna gains G_t, G_r of each wireless node are 23.18 dBi and the transmit power is 1 watt. The attenuation from oxygen absorption is 17 dB/km, and a 15 dB link margin that covers rain attenuation and noise margin is included. Obstacles are generated randomly in the streets and modeled as rectangular vehicles, where their centers fall within the road and form a homogeneous Poisson point process (PPP) of density λ, the widths and lengths are assumed to be i.i.d. distributed and follow the normal distribution $\mathcal{N}(\mu_w=2.3m, \sigma_w=0.8)$ and $\mathcal{N}(\mu_l=8.0m, \sigma_l=2.5)$, and orientations are the same as the road's direction.

5.1 Network and Path Survivability

First, we evaluate the performance of the proposed PLLR scheme based on *minimize rSBS method* (MRS) and *minimize rSBS with groups method* (MRG), respectively. The aggregated user demand of each SBS is assumed to be around 1 Gbps, which follows the normal distribution $\mathcal{N}(D_\mu=1, D_\sigma=0.3)$. On hundreds of simulation runs with random-obstacle scenarios, Fig. 6 shows that MRS and MRG provide very similar BNS across a range of obstacle densities and the achieved BNS is relatively high (above 85% for all but the highest density). However, by adopting MRG method in reconfiguration schemes, the same high BNS can be achieved with fewer reconfigured network-level paths (see Fig. 7), especially when the obstacle density is not very high. This is because most of time we only reconfigure a new path for the leader rSBS instead of all rSBSs in the group, which substantially reduces the reconfiguration overhead. Based on this comparison, we adopt the MRG method in both PLLR and HTMR schemes in the remainder of the results.

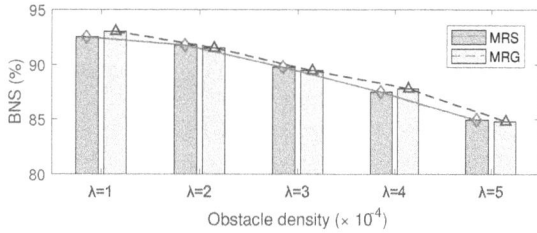

Figure 6: Survivability comparison between MRS and MRG.

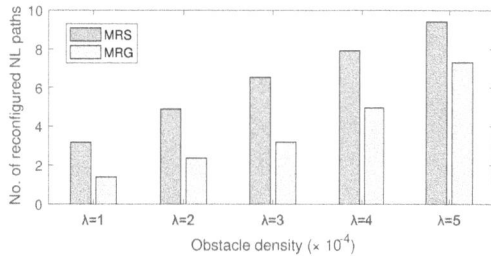

Figure 7: Number of reconfigured paths comparisons.

Second, we show the survivability performance with different reconfiguration schemes. As a comparison, an upper bound of BNS is also reported by solving the feasible-flow problem. By simulating a large number of random-obstacle cases, Fig. 8(a) shows the survivability performance of different reconfiguration schemes and the upper bound (labeled OPT). It is observed that the proposed PLLR and HTMR schemes provide significantly better robustness than purely link-level and purely network-level reconfiguration approaches, where BNS is obviously improved and still over 80% even with a high density of obstacles. Of particular note, the NLR scheme that is adopted by most previous work has worse performance than LLR, and has poor survivability with multiple blockages. On the other hand, we can see that the BNS of our proposed schemes is very close to the upper bound on BNS, and as the obstacle density increases, the performance gaps between the two proposed schemes and the upper bound BNS are 1.2%~4.8% and 3.5%~8.4%, respectively. Since the PLLR scheme only supports single-path routing and always reconfigures one path for each source-destination pair, the performance gap of PLLR scheme is a little larger than that of HTMR scheme, but it is still around 5% with a not very high obstacle density.

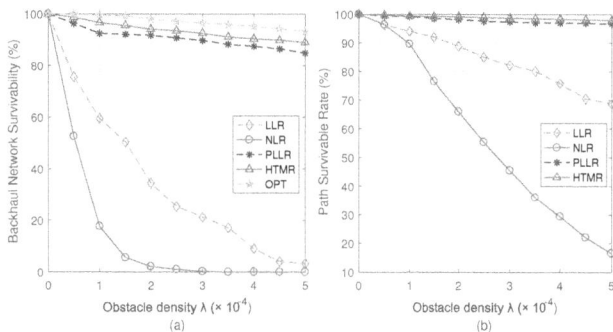

Figure 8: Network and path survivability comparisons.

Fig. 9 shows how the BNS of the proposed schemes and the upper bound vary with increasing data demand, for an obstacle density of $\lambda = 2 \cdot 10^{-4}$. As the demand increases, pure network level and pure link level reconfiguration fail to provide survivability in almost all cases. However, our proposed schemes maintain fairly high BNS and remain close to the upper bound over all simulated demands.

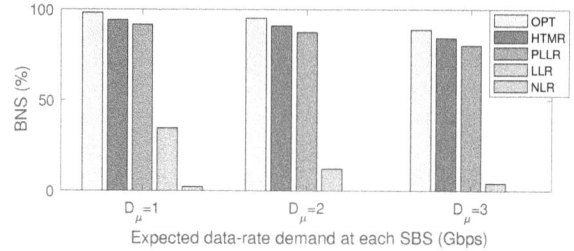

Figure 9: Network survivability comparisons with different expected data-rate demands.

To get more fine-grained results, we also evaluate the path survivable rate (PSR), which is defined as the fraction of total backhaul paths that remain connected with reconfiguration after blockages occur. Fig. 8(b) shows that PLLR and HTMR can provide over 97% PSR as the number of obstacles increases, which means that the communication from the A-BS to each SBS would be largely unaffected, even with multiple obstacles. Thus, with the proposed schemes, the blockage tolerance of the entire backhaul network is highly enhanced.

5.2 Throughput Performance

In this part, we evaluate whether or not the proposed reconfiguration algorithms can maintain high throughput with blockages, and the satisfied-BS percentage (SBP) is evaluated. SBP indicates the fraction of SBSs that have their respective data demands satisfied. Here, the aggregated user demand of each SBS is assumed to follow the normal distribution $\mathcal{N}(D_\mu=2, D_\sigma=0.3)$. From Fig. 10, we can see that HTMR scheme has the best SBP compared with other schemes, since it splits traffic for transmission on both the primary working path and backup paths, which compensates for degraded throughputs on the reconfigured relay paths.

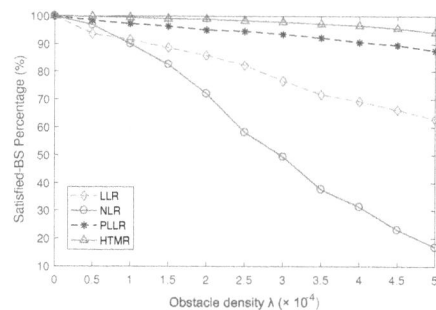

Figure 10: SBP comparisons among different schemes.

In addition, we vary the data demand D_μ of each SBS, and it is obvious to see that the SBP will decrease as D_μ increases with both PLLR and HTMR schemes (shown in Fig. 11 (a) and (b), respectively). By comparing the SBP based on the same D_μ between these two schemes, the HTMR scheme can satisfy more SBSs than the PLLR scheme with the same obstacle density, and the SBP is improved by more than 20% when $D_\mu = 3$ and the obstacle density is high. Because of such substantial benefits on throughput performance, it might be worth adopting HTMR despite its added complexity.

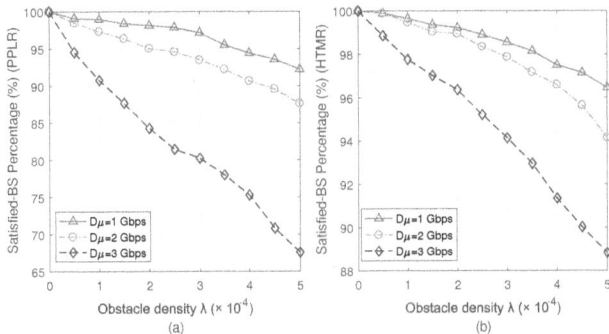

Figure 11: SBP for PLLR and HTMR with different D_μ.

5.3 Hop-constraint effects

Our problem formulation assumes that each eligible backup path selected for a specific backhaul path should satisfy a hop-number constraint, i.e., the total hops (including dedicated relays and relayed-SBSs) along this path must be fewer than a hop-number threshold H. Here we investigate how this H affects network survivability. With the obstacle density $\lambda = 1.2 \cdot 10^{-4}$ and data demand at each SBS of around 1 Gbps, Fig. 12 shows that the BNS will increase as H increases for all reconfiguration approaches except the LLR scheme. This is because with larger H, more backup paths for each backhaul path are put in the SS, which improves the network-level reconfiguration, but this has no effect on a purely link-level reconfiguration approach. In addition, by increasing H, PLLR and HTMR can even provide nearly 100% BNS, and NLR can also possibly provide better blockage tolerance than LLR. However, a larger H results in higher end-to-end latency and, therefore, this trade-off between latency and robustness in the network would need to be carefully considered with respect to application latency requirements.

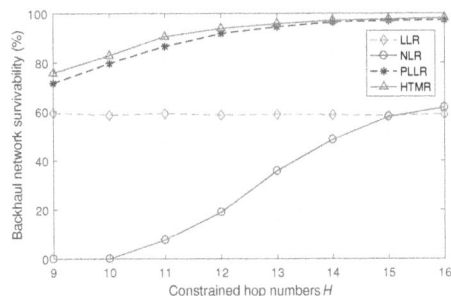

Figure 12: BNS comparisons with different schemes vs. constrained hop number H.

6 CONCLUSION

In this paper, we considered the problem of survivability in mmWave backhaul networks, where a single A-BS serves as a gateway for a number of SBSs and relays deployed along urban streets. In

such a scenario, joint link-level and network-level reconfiguration schemes are proposed to overcome blockage and failure effects. These schemes combine relay path reconfiguration with alternate backup paths for fast path recovery. Through simulation results, the performance of proposed schemes is shown to be always superior to purely link-level/network-level reconfiguration schemes. The approaches can provide a substantial improvement in backhaul network survivability, and also maintain backhaul throughputs, achieving the Gbps data demand for each SBS even in the presence of multiple blockages/failures. Future research will focus on path recovery in other network topologies of urban environments.

ACKNOWLEDGMENTS

This research was supported in part by the National Science Foundation through Award CNS–1813242.

REFERENCES

[1] F. Wei, Y. Li, D. Jin, L. Su, and S. Chen, "Millimetre-wave backhaul for 5G networks: Challenges and solutions"[J]. *Sensors*, 2016, 16(6): 892.
[2] M. Kulkarni, A. Ghosh and J. Andrews, "How Many Hops Can Self-Backhauled Millimeter Wave Cellular Networks Support?". arXiv:1805.01040, 2018.
[3] Q. Hu and D. Blough,"Relay Selection and Scheduling for Millimeter Wave Backhaul in Urban Environments", *IEEE MASS*, 2017.
[4] M. Jaber, et al., "Wireless Backhaul: Performance Modeling and Impact on User Association for 5G"[J], *IEEE Transactions on Wireless Communications*, 2018..
[5] B. Sahoo, C. Yao, H. Wei, "Millimeter-wave multi-hop wireless backhauling for 5G cellular networks". *IEEE Vehicular Technology Conference*, 2017.
[6] T. Bai, R. Heath, "Coverage and rate analysis for millimeter-wave cellular networks", *IEEE Transactions on Wireless Comm.*, 2015.
[7] Y. Liu and D. Blough, "Analysis of Blockage Effects on Roadside Relay-assisted mmWave Backhaul Networks", *IEEE ICC*, 2019.
[8] S. Sur, V. Venkateswaran, X. Zhang, et al., "60 ghz indoor networking through flexible beams: a link-level profiling", in *ACM SIGMETRICS*. ACM, 2015.
[9] X. Ge, H. Cheng, M. Guizani and T. Han, "5G wireless backhaul networks: challenges and research advances". *IEEE Network*, 2014.
[10] R. Rony, et al., "Joint access-backhaul perspective on mobility management in 5G networks", *IEEE Conf. on Standards for Comm. and Networking* (CSCN), 2017.
[11] Q. Hu and D. Blough, "Optimizing Millimeter-Wave Backhaul Networks in Roadside Environments," *IEEE International Communication Conference* (ICC), 2018.
[12] S. Ramamurthy, L. Sahasrabuddhe, B. Mukherjee, "Survivable WDM mesh networks". *Journal of Lightwave Technology* 21.4 (2003): 870.
[13] D. Xu, Y. Chen, Y. Xiong, C. Qiao, X. He, "On finding disjoint paths in single and dual link cost networks". *IEEE INFOCOM* 2004.
[14] S. Paira, M. Chatterjee, S. Khanam, et al., "GSWA: A Survivable Dynamic Multicast Efficient RWA Scheme in WDM Mesh Networks", *IEEE ICCCNT*, 2018.
[15] M. Elappila and S. Chinara. "Dynamic Survivable Path Routing for Fast Changing IoT Network Topologies". *IEEE TrustCom/BigDataSE*, 2018.
[16] A. Bigdeli, A. Tizghadam and A. Leon-Garcia, "Survivable routing using path criticality", *IEEE ICNC* 2012: 793-797.
[17] M. Parandehgheibi, H. Lee, et al., "Survivable path sets: A new approach to survivability in multilayer networks"[J]. *Journal of Lightwave Technology*, 2014.
[18] A. Jabbar, et al. "Survivable millimeter-wave mesh networks." Computer Communications 34.16 (2011): 1942-1955.
[19] Y. Niu, et al.. "Exploiting multi-hop relaying to overcome blockage in directional mmWave small cell", *Journal of Communications and Networks*, IEEE, 2016.
[20] S. Biswas, S. Vuppala, J. Xue, and T. Ratnarajah,"On the performance of relay aided millimeter wave networks", *IEEE J. Sel. Topics Signal Process.*, 2016.
[21] Y. Liu, Q. Hu, and D. Blough, "Blockage Avoidance in Relay Paths for Roadside mmWave Backhaul Networks", *IEEE PIMRC*, 2018.
[22] A. Nasr and Y. Fahmy, "Millimeter-wave wireless backhauling for 5G small cells: Scalability of mesh over star topologies", *IEEE WoWMoM*, 2017.
[23] Y. Liang, B. Li and M. Yang, et al., "MAC protocol framework for 5G mmWave backhaul network", *IEEE ICSPCC*, 2016: 1-6.
[24] R. Taori and A. Sridharan, "Point-to-multipoint in-band mmwave backhaul for 5G networks[J]", *IEEE Communications Magazine*, 2015, 53(1): 195-201.
[25] J. Du, E. Onaran, et al., "Gbps user rates using mmWave relayed backhaul with high gain antennas", *IEEE Journal on Selected Areas in Comm.*, 2017.
[26] B. Xie, Z. Zhang, and R. Hu, "Performance study on relay-assisted millimeter wave cellular networks", *IEEE Proc. Vehicular Technology Conference*, pp. 1-5, 2016.
[27] Y. Liu, Q. Hu and D. Blough, "Technical Report for Blockage Type Detection Process". (available at: http://blough.ece.gatech.edu/BTDTechReport.pdf)

Follow the Rays: Understanding the Interplay between Environment and System through In-Situ Wireless Modelling

Sascha Jungen
University of Duisburg-Essen
Germany
sascha.jungen@uni-due.de

Matteo Ceriotti
University of Duisburg-Essen
Germany
matteo.ceriotti@uni-due.de

Pedro José Marrón
University of Duisburg-Essen
Germany
pj.marron@uni-due.de

ABSTRACT

The Internet of Things and Cyber-Physical Systems rely on wireless interconnections. The importance of understanding the behaviour of wireless communication in practice has promoted many experimental studies, characterising signal propagation in specific environments. Despite the gathered knowledge, the perceived discrepancy between abstract models and actual network performance has supported the belief that system design and debugging can rely only on direct experience and trial-and-error. As a result, reasoning about wireless systems is nowadays a tedious, manual process.

This work walks the playground between model and reality to make wireless networks understand their own behaviour in the environment where they operate. First, we introduce a practical method able to efficiently and accurately characterise wireless signal propagation in 3D environments with obstacles. We then exploit the model to make systems autonomously derive the impact of obstacles such as doors and windows on the link conditions. With an outline of the operational scenario and measurements from deployed devices, it is possible to effortlessly generate a situated, dynamic wireless map. We demonstrate our approach in an indoor testbed, showing its practicability and effectiveness. Our evaluation shows that our approach attributes up to 91% of the measurements to the corresponding obstacles correctly. We also show that different modelling techniques have an impact on such detection accuracy, promoting the use of 3D environment descriptions.

KEYWORDS

3D Modelling; Ray Tracing; Wireless Propagation

ACM Reference Format:
Sascha Jungen, Matteo Ceriotti, and Pedro José Marrón. 2019. Follow the Rays: Understanding the Interplay between Environment and System through In-Situ Wireless Modelling. In *22nd Int'l ACM Conference on Modeling, Analysis and Simulation of Wireless and Mobile Systems (MSWiM '19), November 25–29, 2019, Miami Beach, FL, USA*. ACM, New York, NY, USA, 9 pages. https://doi.org/10.1145/3345768.3355904

1 INTRODUCTION

Wireless communication is becoming an integral part of our everyday life. Not only personal devices but also industrial equipment are embracing this vision with more and more integration of wireless elements. However, while for personal use an unreliable wireless connection is acceptable (even though admittedly annoying), industrial setups require known properties of the interconnection between the different components. An increasing number of interactions with domain experts highlights how reliability, timeliness and robustness are key requirements that cannot be traded off. Understanding wireless communication properties becomes, as a consequence, an essential challenge that needs to be undertaken.

This need was recognised since long time, motivating a plethora of experimental studies (Section 2). These studies have, over time, replaced modelling and simulation as the reference methodology to acquire knowledge about wireless communication. Arguably, such approach was justified by the experienced discrepancy between modelled environments and real ones, corresponding to a significant mismatch between expected behaviour analysed in simulation and measured performance of real systems. As a result, the design, deployment, validation and maintenance of systems nowadays rely mostly on factual, single knowledge and individual experience [24].

In this work, we resume modelling as a key methodology to reason about the behaviour of a deployed system situated in its operational environment. Our goal is to look at communication in indoor scenarios where obstacles impact wireless signals in unpredictable ways depending on their shapes and construction materials. Moreover, such unforeseeable effect on network performance can change over time depending on the different states and positions of such objects during the system lifetime. A dynamic model able to capture the cause-effect relationship between changes in the scenario and the resulting variations in the wireless signal propagation in the specific operational environment would allow to reason about the network behaviour, exposing new knowledge.

In our endeavour, we realise the tools able to generate accurate models of an environment with limited information (Section 3). We implement a ray tracing engine able to efficiently compute the propagation of the wireless signal in an indoor environment from a basic floor map. In addition to a traditional 2D approach based on computation performed by a CPU, we exploit current GPU computational power to obtain a faster 2D modelling as well as a complete 3D description. By doing this, our contribution lies in the exploration of the alternative modelling approaches and level of details, while realising an approach that can be used in practice.

Starting from this base, we devise a technique able to detect and localise events producing lasting changes to the interconnection between devices (Section 4). Through the observation of the actual link conditions and variations, we can exploit the computed model to derive which rays could have caused such changes and match them to the provided floor map, thus understanding the cause. This process then allows to make a match between a potential event in the environment and its actual fingerprint, localised in the specific deployment scenario. While alternative event detection approaches exist, we extend the state of the art by exploiting models to map the events and match the corresponding unique fingerprint.

We evaluate our approach in an indoor testbed consisting of 40 low-power wireless devices (Section 5). The analysis of the alternative models shows that we can increase the computation complexity and gain predictions closer to reality by adding the third dimension at no additional costs in time. The ability of our solution to detect events and correctly map them to their location is studied with respect to the number of devices active as well as the employed transmission power, thus exploring the impact of system properties on the detection accuracy. By increasing transmission power, we are able to attribute up to 91% of the measurements to the corresponding obstacles correctly. From this analysis, we identify further use cases where our approach could be exploited (Section 6). In conclusion (Section 7), we demonstrate that a system can automatically define an event-dependent dynamic model of its wireless communication properties mapped to in-situ gathered fingerprints.

2 RELATED WORK

Wireless communication and event detection have been studied along various directions. We discuss them to highlight our contributions and create the background our techniques base on.

2.1 Modelling Wireless Communication

It is possible to identify two alternative approaches to the problem of describing wireless communication properties. On one side, experimental studies have been largely used to characterise specific environments and technologies in details [7, 19], further highlighting the significant difference between distinct environments [16, 17] or distinct weather conditions [5]. While these studies provide invaluable insights on communication behaviour in real-world environments under specific conditions, they suggest the need of a manual experimentation in-situ before deployment. In this work, we explore how modelling techniques together with observations taken in an operational system can be used to understand the reasons for specific communication properties and variations.

On the other side, wireless communication bases on radio waves that propagate and interact with objects in the environment according to specific physics rules. However, reflection, refraction and diffraction are effects that are very hard to model due to impact of, e.g. object shapes and materials as well as of the exact location of senders and receivers [22]. While optimisations based on current GPU architectures [20] and efficient schemes to decrease the computation time for the modelling of, e.g. urban environments [11] have been proposed, they still require a significantly detailed description of the scenario. Our investigation, instead, highlights that also coarse information about the environment, e.g. a floor plan and the indication of big metallic objects like cupboards, are sufficient to make techniques like ray tracing practical and useful.

2.2 Modelling the Impact of Events on Wireless Signal and their Detection

A modelling aspect related to this work is the description of how specific events impact the propagation of the wireless signal. In literature, this has been predominantly studied in the context of indoor localisation. As the human body significantly attenuates wireless signals, modelling such impact allows to increase localisation accuracy [9] or enables new applications to detect human features [1, 15] through the appropriate analysis of RSSI measurements.

Even without the specific modelling of objects and their impact on the propagation of the wireless signal, the identification of deviations in the properties of links, e.g. RSSI, has been used in a variety of application scenarios. By monitoring RSSI variations over time, it is possible to localise people indoor [14] or outdoor [3]. In the case of queues, this information can be used to detect their state and length [6]. Advanced technology and specific classification algorithms can also expose human emotions [23].

To the best of our knowledge, however, specific models that describe how wireless waves exactly propagates in the case of typical objects that populate indoor environments, such as doors or windows in addition to humans, are lacking [2]. With this respect, this work provides a first step towards building a map of events happening in the environment against corresponding observed fingerprints, thus paving the way for further advancements in the modelling of environments that change over time.

3 MODELLING THE ENVIRONMENT

Modelling of actual wireless communication in real environments can be based, in practice, on statistical, experimental observations of signal properties between devices once deployed in a specific setup. This approach has the benefit of being fast to compute once measurements are available; no prior, detailed information is necessary about the scenario and, once a system is deployed, the obtained estimations adhere closely to the real existing environment and system structure. However, the measurements make it hard (if possible at all) to generalise the gathered description to other scenarios or even to other device positioning inside the same scenario. Similarly, it is impossible to reason about the causes of changes in the wireless signal as no description of the scenario is available.

On the other side, the physical properties of the environment and the rules of electromagnetic wave propagation offer the possibility, in theory, to exactly model the expected wireless features. This comes, however, at the cost of complexity in terms of both the degree of details that need to be provided in order to accurately describe the surroundings as well as the computation resources necessary to process the actual model features throughout the environment. In this section, we describe our specific contributions to make physical modelling practical both in 2D and 3D descriptions, in particular exploiting the use of GPU computational power.

3.1 Definition of a Map

The most important information for physical modelling is the map of the environment, including the objects present in it. While autonomous 3D mapping of environments is making significant progress [8], it is still challenging to perceive the specific features of relevance for techniques such as ray tracing. In particular, the

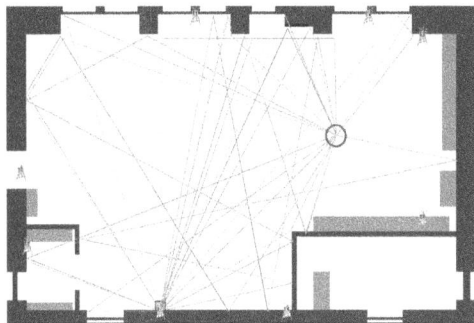

Figure 1: Example image of a 2D ray tracer showing different paths from the sender at the bottom to the destination (blue circle) located in the middle of the room.

understanding of the main involved materials is a tedious task that still relies on manual supervision. In our work, we make an effort in simplifying and reducing the information that needs to be gathered and provided as input to our various modelling engines.

For indoor environments, we need a two-dimensional representation of main elements such as inner and outer walls. Depending on the level of accuracy required, information about surrounding buildings that could reflect signals might also be provided. We additionally expect relevant objects like doors, windows and ceilings to be described with their height and, if applicable, tagged as objects that can change their state from closed to open and vice versa. The identification of the involved materials with their corresponding attenuation and reflection coefficients can be limited to coarse categories [21], e.g. thick, thin and exterior walls, as well as wooden, metallic and glass objects. While more details, e.g. chairs or tables could further increase the model accuracy, we refrain from including them and limit to big visible metallic furniture like cupboards. Finally, the position and height of wireless devices is required.

This information can easily be obtained through a floor map and a quick survey of the scenario, providing a machine-readable description that can be easily supported with computer-aided editing tools. Even though we restrict the amount of details to be provided, it must be clear that the accuracy of the supplied scenario descriptions is essential in defining the resulting model adherence to reality. In particular, centimetre accuracy is required in order to correctly compute con- and destructive interference from rays taking different paths to reach a destination. However, since providing such accuracy is impractical, we will introduce techniques to circumvent the necessity of highly detailed maps.

3.2 CPU Based 2D Ray Tracing Model

The first model that we introduce is a reference approach as depicted in the literature [13], from which we implement our own engine exploiting the same principles. In particular, our Java-based modelling tries to aim rays in order to reach the destination from the source directly (through line of sight in free space or through refraction) or indirectly (through diffraction or reflection) by identifying surrounding obstacles. An example of the computed ray paths from a source to a destination is given in Figure 1. In fact, a CPU-based approach offers limited parallelism, imposing the use of an aimed-approach in order to increase speed. Similarly, as rays depart from the source and encounter obstacles, the number of

possible paths to be computed grows exponentially, affecting the processing time. Simplifications are then necessary, in particular for the maximum number of effects to consider and their combinations (e.g. reflection and diffraction are not considered together).

For each ray, the angle at which obstacles are encountered is determined in order to identify the different components that either penetrate the object or are reflected from it. To decrease computation time, the paths of the signals and the visibility areas are precomputed and exploited to prune paths with minor contributions. Given the complexity of computing a full 3D model of the propagation with just the resources offered by a (even if multi-core) CPU, the computation remains in a "flat" 2D world. However, to provide better distance estimation and, as a consequence, more accurate description of the attenuation of the signal over distance, the modelling accounts for the heights of the wireless devices as well as of the obstacles. To increase fidelity, it is possible to consider the integration of the specific antenna radiation pattern of the deployed wireless devices. In fact, the notable impact that such details could have on network behaviour is known [25]. After some initial experimentation, we decided to discard this aspect and sacrifice accuracy in order to keep the approach practical.

3.3 GPU Based 2D/3D Ray Tracing Model

Generating an accurate wireless model is extremely computation intensive, with a complexity that drastically increases with the amount of obstacles present in the scenario. In general, it is possible to optimise this process by trying to either identify which rays might contribute more significantly to the received signal or testing which intersections with obstacles are relevant, discarding irrelevant ray paths. An alternative solution to handle the problem complexity is to exploit current GPU parallel architectures. Their intended usage, in fact, is to efficiently handle 3D environment with respect to light waves, which have similar properties to radio ones.

The computation of each individual ray departing from the source is, indeed, independent from the others until it reaches the destination. Therefore, it is conceivable to parallelise the computation of each ray path towards the destination and offload the processing to the thousands cores available in current GPUs. Not only this makes it much faster to compute the properties of the signal propagating from a source to a destination, but it allows to avoid prefiltering specific ray directions in favour of a full exploration of the space. Ultimately, the use of GPUs makes modelling wireless communication in 3D environments possible. In the remaining of this section, we introduce our own design for a GPU-based ray tracing engine, exploiting Aparapi [4] in order to compile Java code into more efficient OpenGL code able to run directly on GPUs.

3.3.1 Exploiting the Potential of GPUs. In order to exploit the characteristics of nowadays GPU architectures, the ray tracing engine introduced in Section 3.2 needs to be modified. We now discuss the design of a full 3D engine and then briefly discuss the downsized 2D version. First of all, the two dimensional environment description needs to be extended to include height information for all elements including doors and windows; walls can already be assumed to reach the ceiling; floor and ceiling need to be explicitly defined. The internal data representation needs to be modified as it is not possible to pass objects but only one-dimensional arrays containing maximum 2^{31} elements, which should be 32-bit integers or floats. Similarly, the necessary clear memory separation between the different processes makes splitting of rays and building path trees restrictive, limiting the possibilities for optimisation.

As a consequence, instead of directing rays in specific directions, GPU architectures favour the parallel analysis of rays "launched" by the sender in all different directions. Therefore, we distribute the rays according to the Fibonacci lattice [10], which spreads points on a sphere at equal distance. In order to counteract the loss of accuracy caused by both the gap between the rays launched from the sender and the distance between the devices, the receiver is represented by a sphere instead of a point. A small set of rays are additionally aimed at the receiver to further decrease the chances of missing the reception of a ray due to this discretisation procedure. In particular, the first rays starting from the sender or a diffraction edge are always directed exactly towards the destination. Indirect, single-reflected paths via floor and ceiling are also considered in this additional set of aimed rays. Even though other rays might reach the destination indirectly, via longer reflected paths, the use of image-method to identify the specific rays potentially reaching the destination would require post-processing, significantly increasing the complexity of the approach and its computation time.

The processing progresses in a sequence of steps. For each ray, the next collision with an obstacle (if existing) is computed by a single GPU core. If an obstacle is encountered, a split occurs between the refracted and the reflected part of the original ray, each of which is processed by a different GPU core in the next step. A special case is handled for diffractions. In fact, since each diffracted ray potentially produces a complete new wavefront, which would require a new computation process on its own, the procedure is simplified by only starting new rays in all directions of the diffraction edge basing on the strongest previous ray reaching this edge.

3.3.2 2D Model. To analyse the differences between the ray tracing engines independently of the added ability to handle full 3D descriptions of the environment, we created a downsized version of the GPU-based ray tracer handling only 2D scenario descriptions. In this case, the third dimension is fixed and the rays propagate on a plane. This allows to spread much more rays and increase their space density, thus increasing the space accuracy at higher distances at the cost of missing stronger signal paths possibly generated around obstacles detectable only through a third dimension. To make, however, the comparison between the two 2D models fair, we preserve the height information and use it a posteriori to compensate for incorrectness in the computed path length.

4 EVENT MATCHING

Now we focus on the possibility to understand the interplay between events happening in the environment with long lasting impact on communication and the wireless propagation properties between the devices. Pure statistical models based on measurements would only be able to passively observe changes in the communication properties as events happen in the environment but would not be able to trace back the actual cause of such changes. Only a model able to describe how wireless waves should be affected by a specific event can support this type of cause-effect reasoning.

A base measurement set is assumed available, which provides information about RSSI observations from all the links in an empty environment in its default state, e.g. with all doors and windows closed. Such measurements can be easily gathered at system deployment or at times in which the system is detected being in a quiet state. It is then necessary to gather individual traces for each possible event happening in the environment to complete the description of the links before and after an event. As discussed in Section 6, this procedure can be integrated in an online observation system to let systems calibrate themselves. The result is a mapping between localised events and corresponding fingerprints made of real-world wireless observations obtained by the deployed system. In this section, we describe our approach to build such a mapping.

4.1 Grouping of Links

Using the base measurements as reference, we create event fingerprints out of temporally and spatially correlated link changes, which manifest a significant variation above a given threshold. A fingerprint consists of RSSI average and variance values for all the affected and relevant links. In order to identify which links are relevant, a difference is computed with respect to the base measurements. Thereby, links that appeared or disappeared as a consequence of the event happening are recognised as well. Out of these links, the ones are preserved which are bidirectional, reliable with at least -90 dBm in both directions and where both directions change remarkably. In our experimentation, a threshold corresponding to the maximum between 2 dBm and twice the standard deviation of the link RSSI demonstrated to be sufficient to identify the relevant links.

Afterwards, the links are clustered based on the rooms in which they are located. In the given map, it is possible to identify rooms by searching for areas enclosed by walls. To each room, the position in the map can then be assigned as well as the nodes and obstacles contained. This offers the possibility to better localise events by tentatively assign them to one or more rooms. We first consult the map to identify the specific position and room of each node interconnected by links marked as significantly changed. A cluster is assigned to each room including the affected links that either have at least one end point in the room or simply traverse it. According to this scheme, the same link might be present in different clusters.

Subsequently, a phase starts with the goal of minimising the considered clusters. In order to achieve that, we keep pairs of clusters not sharing any link and remove complete subsets of others. In the case in which only a partial overlapping exists, if one cluster is smaller than another but the number of common links is sufficiently big, the two clusters are merged into one that is assigned to the room of the bigger. Finally, in the case in which both clusters have the same size and share enough links, the tie is resolved by finding the most occurring node in the links of both clusters and assigning the merge of the clusters to the room containing such a node. What remains are the clusters of spatially correlated changed links assigned to the most probable room of reference.

4.2 Measurements-to-Event Matching

The identification of links that changed over time and can be ascribed to the same event makes it possible to reason in more details about the actual cause for the observed link changes in addition to a first approximation of the possible event location. To make further inferences about potential causes, additional analysis is required. In this study, we focus our attention on obstacles able to change their status and influence the RSSI of links in a stable long-lasting manner with limited fluctuations. This type of events are in contrast to volatile ones, manifesting high variability and hindering the detection of stable events that are co-located.

If fingerprints observed in the specific scenario for all the possible events are available, it would be possible to match the actual observations against such database. We discuss this possibility in Section 6. Without such information, traces can only be analysed in comparison to the given map, through the lenses of the ray tracing models mentioned in Section 3. In order to study a specific obstacle as possible cause for an observed change, the theoretical influences of each obstacle on the network links have to be known.

By exploiting one of the introduced ray tracing models, it is possible to precompute, for each obstacle, its expected impact on communication links if its state or position is changed, e.g. in case of a door or window if it is opened or closed. An intuitive approach would be to check if any such event would cause changes matching the actual observations. In following this approach, however, we need to take into account that in most cases the scenario description does not provide centimetre accuracy for practical reasons (as in our case). Therefore, the model output cannot rely on the correct computation of interference effects, which however have been demonstrated to play a significant role in reality.

Without the possibility to account for the effect of interferences, the RSSI predictions computed by the model for a specific position become worthless when analysing the effect of small changes to the environment. In order to circumvent the consequences of a less accurate map on the model output as well as on the correctness of the event detection, we use an approach that depends less on the actual RSSI values. We exploit the ability of ray tracing to track each possible path of a radio signal between sender and receiver. For our needs, the relevant information corresponds to the existence of a possible path to a receiver at a sufficient signal strength that interacts with the investigated obstacle, e.g. via reflection, in at least one of its possible states, e.g. if a door is open or closed.

Once the sets of possibly influenced links for all the obstacles in the scenario have been generated, these can be compared against the clusters computed based on the gathered observations. As decision criterion, the Jaccard similarity coefficient [12] is used to measure the similarity between two sets. The size of the intersection of both link sets divided by the size of their union builds a target coefficient. The highest coefficient among all the set comparisons yields the decision regarding which obstacle is considered as the event cause.

5 EVALUATION

In this section, we experiment with our techniques in an indoor scenario. We analyse the performance of each modelling approach and the ability in matching wireless changes to their cause.

5.1 Scenario

Our evaluation bases on the experience in an indoor testbed made of 40 low-power 2.4 GHz wireless TelosB devices [18], a platform with well-known radio propagation irregularities that have a significant

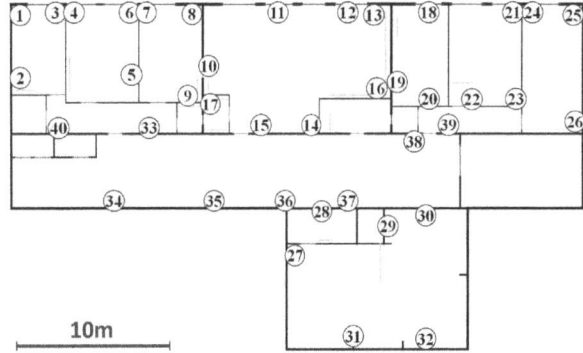

Figure 2: Map of the testbed including node positions.

impact on system behaviour [25]. Given that our models discard the description of such irregular patterns in order to keep the approach practical, this choice poses interesting challenges to our work. More current platforms or the use of omnidirectional external antennas should increase the accuracy of our approach. The devices are displaced in a university building over offices, big laboratories, small kitchens and long as well as short corridors, where also an elevator is present. The building is characterised by both thick walls significantly attenuating the signal as well as thin ones. The scenario and the location of the devices are shown in Figure 2.

Being the area completely under our control, we could experiment with different events in a systematic way without interference. In particular, we could analyse the impact of opening or closing doors and windows in an quiet environment without people. During the experiments, we scheduled the devices to perform RSSI measurements according to a transmission scheme avoiding collisions along different transmission powers. The computation of the ray tracing models was performed on a machine equipped with an Intel i7-7800X with 6 3.50GHz cores and a Geforce 1080 GTX Ti with 3584 cores. The CPU-only models were configured to account for 2 reflections, 1 diffraction and 5 refractions. For the GPU case, each computation cycle started with 50000 rays with a maximum of 5 reflections and/or refractions in arbitrary combinations, resulting in up to 1.6 million rays for each round. Given that each diffraction requires a complete new computation cycle, we limited them to a maximum of 2. The reception sphere was set to 0.1 meters.

5.2 Model Comparison

The first part of the evaluation analyses the behaviour of the models in a stationary environment. In particular, we focus on accuracy as well as computation time, a metric that we consider as an index of the possibility of using the approach in real-time. In analysing the accuracy of the models, we account for the fact that we disable the computation of constructive and destructive interference (even though available in our implementation) due to negative impact imposed by inaccuracies in the model description. Further, we refrain from integrating a description of the specific radiation patterns of the target wireless devices, whose integration in the required environment description would make the configuration of the ray tracing engines impractical, even more when the information needs to be provided in three dimensions. This affects our results by making our models more optimistic than reality.

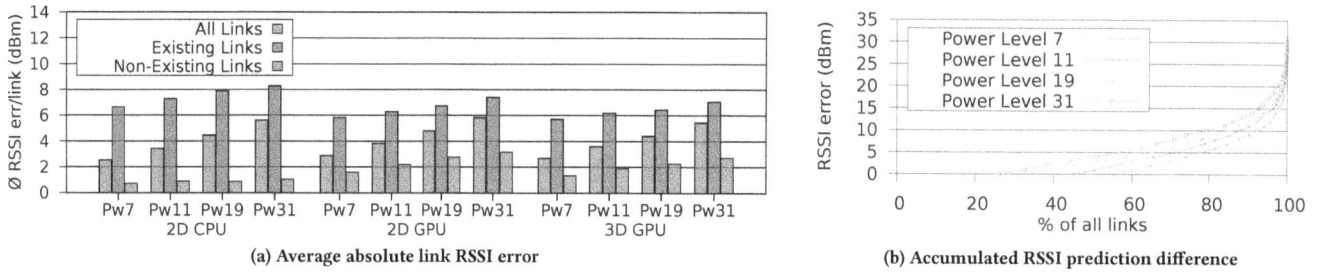

(a) Average absolute link RSSI error

(b) Accumulated RSSI prediction difference

Figure 3: (a) Average absolute error per link in the RSSI prediction performed by the different modelling techniques for various power levels. Values are based on three sets of links: the full set of possible links (1560), all measured existing links and all non-existing links in reality. (b) Percentage of links predicted by the 3D GPU model within a given RSSI threshold.

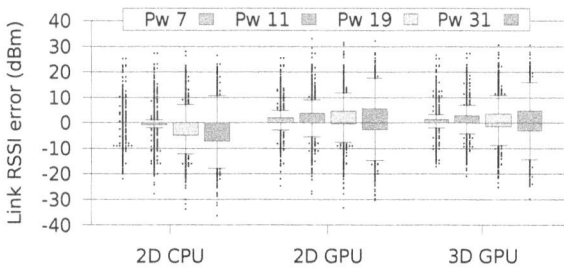

Figure 4: Error per link in the RSSI prediction performed by the different modelling techniques for various power levels. Due to the high number of correctly predicted, non-existing links, the median has a value of 0 in all cases.

Figure 3 shows the accuracy of our models for different transmission power levels. The average error depicted in Figure 3a is relatively low, even more if one considers that the map has imprecisions and various real effects are not modelled, like constructive and destructive interferences and radiation patterns. In particular, considering that we are analysing 2.4 GHz signals, the misplacement of objects and devices of few centimetres could lead to significant different behaviours. Interestingly enough, all the different models manifest similar overall behaviours when all links are considered. A further analysis shows that, however, a CPU approach makes bigger errors in predicting the links that exist while performing better for links that do not exist in reality. The opposite applies to the GPU case. We analyse this effect in more details later. Figure 3b shows a cumulative view of the error distribution for the 3D GPU computation, highlighting how higher errors are restricted to a small percentage of links. Furthermore, different power levels follow similar trends with a small shift due to increasing number of existing links for increasing transmission power.

In Figure 4, a further view on the accuracy is provided to display the variation inside the complete set of links. Indeed, the 2D CPU model underestimates the received signal strengths of most of the links whereas the predictions of both GPU models are more equally spread with a slight tendency to overestimate links. This behaviour will turn out to be beneficial during event matching as more possible ray paths with higher signal strength will be available. Table 1 reports the different number of links that each model predicts. All models foresee more links than what experienced in reality, an expected result caused by the anisotropic antenna of our devices

Table 1: Comparison of the number of predicted existing or non existing links for different power levels.

Used Model	2D CPU	2D GPU	3D GPU
Power Level 7			
Link$_{REAL}$		473	
Link$_{MODEL}$	590	792	758
False^{+}$_{(PRED<-90dbm)}$	182 (129)	348 (231)	311 (217)
False^{-}$_{(REAL<-90dbm)}$	65 (31)	29 (8)	26 (13)
Power Level 11			
Link$_{REAL}$		619	
Link$_{MODEL}$	714	914	907
False^{+}$_{(PRED<-90dbm)}$	178 (122)	338 (189)	326 (203)
False^{-}$_{(REAL<-90dbm)}$	83 (28)	43 (17)	38 (16)
Power Level 19			
Link$_{REAL}$		798	
Link$_{MODEL}$	847	1023	1012
False^{+}$_{(PRED<-90dbm)}$	160 (115)	285 (136)	269 (156)
False^{-}$_{(REAL<-90dbm)}$	111 (35)	60 (24)	55 (19)
Power Level 31			
Link$_{REAL}$		985	
Link$_{MODEL}$	1016	1088	1091
False^{+}$_{(PRED<-90dbm)}$	149 (104)	209 (88)	200 (92)
False^{-}$_{(REAL<-90dbm)}$	118 (41)	106 (36)	94 (35)

Table 2: Average computation times per link.

Used Model	2D CPU	2D GPU	3D GPU
⊘ CompTime / Link	12.70 ms	18.23 ms	12.29 ms
StdDeviation σ	0.40 ms	0.38 ms	0.10 ms

and the absence of a corresponding radiation pattern description in our models. This fact is clear when looking at the number of false positives, i.e. links predicted to exist but not present in reality, in comparison to the false negatives, i.e. links predicted not to exist but present in reality. To confirm our conjecture, the number of the former is significantly higher than the latter.

Table 2 describes the average time taken to compute the model of a wireless link. Indeed, the massive parallelisation capabilities of the graphics card help to complete the three-dimensional computation on a GPU slightly faster than the computation performed by a CPU in two dimensions only. To make the comparison fair, the two-dimensional model running on the GPU performs the same postprocessing to include the height information that is also computed in the CPU case. Given that such computations can be performed only once the GPU has processed all the rays and, therefore, are performed afterwards by the CPU, the time taken to describe a wireless link in the 2D GPU model is the highest.

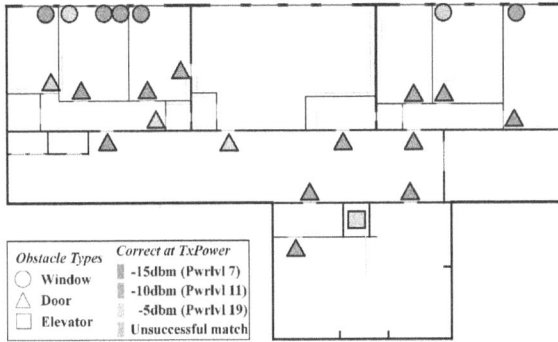

Figure 5: Map of the investigated obstacles (doors, windows and an elevator) and the minimum transmission power of correct assignment to the corresponding measurements using all 40 nodes on varying power levels, as computed through the use of the 3D GPU model. The colours denote successful assignments of obstacles beginning at a certain transmission power level as more links become available.

5.3 Matching Changing Wireless Properties

We now analyse to what extent the wireless communication descriptions are able to reveal information of real systems. This evaluation offers a specific usage scenario as an example of the more general applicability. We experimented with 23 different obstacles, whose state we could change, and measured different power levels as done in the previous analysis of the models. In particular, we considered various doors and windows and changed their state by opening and closing them. Similarly, we investigated the impact caused by the elevator when present or absent at the testbed floor. A map of our testbed including type, position and power level of the first successful matching is depicted in Figure 5. Most of the doors and windows have adjacent devices, allowing us to study if they are essential for the matching. Furthermore, in the upper left area, we chose a more fine grained set of windows to evaluate the ability of our solution to distinguish among close events sharing most links.

After taking a base RSSI measurement in an empty environment with all doors and windows closed and the elevator absent, we changed the state of the different obstacles one after the other while recording further RSSI samples. Afterwards, we processed the data as described in Section 4. Through the computation of the different models in the various possible object states, the sets of links that should be influenced by each object are determined. Then, the 23 complete measurement sets corresponding to the different changes are compared against the base measurement set to obtain the reference clusters of relevant links that have manifested a significant variation. These clusters serve as input for the matching algorithm to compare reality against the model predictions.

The results of the matching algorithm are listed in Table 3. The first evident result is that an increasing transmission power corresponds to a steady increase in the amount of correct matches. At the lowest transmission power only half of the changes find a correct match through the observations and two events are completely invisible as no variations have been observed on any link. This problem disappears for higher transmission powers, since the

Table 3: Number of events matched correctly against an obstacle for different models and power levels. On the weakest transmission power, 2 out of 23 events were reflected in no link change and resulted therefore invisible. In the corresponding matching percentages, these links were excluded.

Used Model	2D CPU	2D GPU	3D GPU
Power Level 7 (Only 21 Events Visible)			
Correct Matches	12	12	13
Percentage	57%	57%	62%
Power Level 11			
Correct Matches	15	14	17
Percentage	65%	61%	74%
Power Level 19			
Correct Matches	16	19	21
Percentage	70%	83%	91%
Power Level 31			
Correct Matches	20	20	21
Percentage	87%	87%	91%

number of links increases both in reality as well as in the models, effectively offering a richer set of information to exploit. With higher transmission powers, links increase their RSSI values and become stronger, better exposing changes in correspondence to environmental dynamics. In general, more connectivity is beneficial as it reduces the possible holes in the communication map caused by distant nodes in sparse regions. However, it must be taken into account that new links might disturb the matching, deviating the decision towards alternative obstacles. This can happen in particular if a ray to an obstacle should exist according to the model but it is not significantly affected in reality.

Before going into further details of the impact of specific nodes on the matching accuracy, we can observe that events with a high Jaccard similarity coefficient are more robust to the changes in the number of available links. At the centre of our environment, however, where more links are present, events happening are harder to match correctly. The Jaccard coefficient itself also presents limitations as a link match in a set with more links counts less for the coefficient. Finally, describing the correct communication frequency has a significant impact as well. In our study, moving the model from 2400 MHz to 2481 MHz (corresponding to the actual frequency of the measurements gathered from the testbed) made the 3D GPU model correctly match the changes caused by the elevator.

We now analyse the relevance of each individual node in matching the correct events happening in the environment. In Figure 6, we report the difference in the number of correct matching when one node is removed from the deployment. In general, it is possible to observe that the GPU-based modelling is more robust to the presence or absence of individual nodes. This behaviour can be justified by the fact that the CPU employs an aimed-approach where rays are targeted through obstacles towards a destination (the receiver), only through exclusive reflections or diffractions, without exploring their possible combinations. On the other side, instead, the GPU explores more possibilities by spreading rays equally in all directions and considering the combination of multiple effects together. From these results, it is also apparent, that specific nodes can contribute significantly to the matching, in particular node 4 and 33 in our case. We focus on these specific cases in the following.

Figure 7 depicts the specific events that node 4 and 33 contribute to detect when present or absent. Node 4 is a crucial node due to

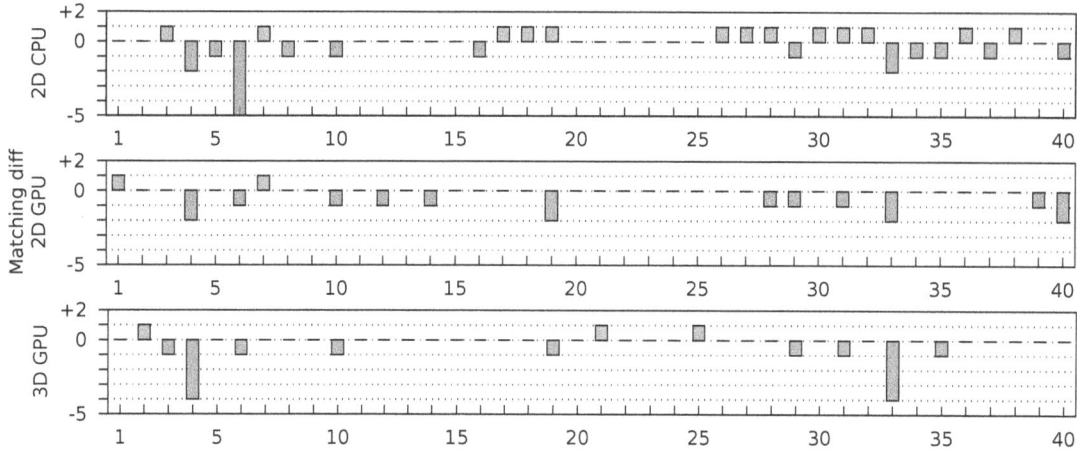

Figure 6: Consequences of removing a single node on the obstacle matching for the highest transmission power.

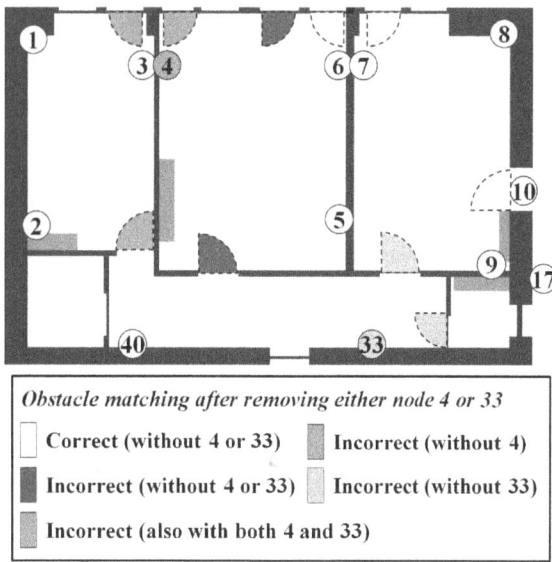

Figure 7: Consequences of removing either node 4 or 33 from the measurement on the matching using the 3D GPU model. For visual clarity, nodes 3,4,6 and 7 have been moved downwards from their original position next to the windows.

the high density of observable events in its surrounding with 5 windows and 2 doors close to it. Moreover, it lies on a line with many other nodes close to the set of windows and is essential to distinguish between different windows. Without node 4, in fact, the other links, e.g. between 3 and 6, would span at least 3 windows, making it harder to differentiate between them. Node 33 presents similar conditions since its links cross multiple adjacent doors. Without such node, indeed, these doors cannot be differentiated by the remaining links that would inevitable cross both.

6 DISCUSSION

After experimenting with our techniques, we discuss the limitations of our work in its current state as well as further possible scenarios in which we foresee the benefits of exploiting models of wireless communication through advancements of our approach.

6.1 Limitations

We first consider the complexity of the performed computations and their corresponding scalability. The first, most computationally intensive step in our solution involves the identification of the sets of links impacting each obstacle. At this stage, the ray tracing model is employed, whose computational complexity is affected by the details of the environment as these can increase the number of comparisons needed to evaluate the ray paths. Similarly, more nodes result in a quadratic grow of links that need to be investigated.

An appropriate filtering based on the environment properties can speed up these computation times. It is, however, worth noting that these factors affect the complexity of a first step that needs to be computed only at the very beginning. In the case of new or relocated nodes, exclusively the associated links and ray paths need to be recomputed, favouring scalability after the initial setup.

The second phase identifies correlated link changes among links as well as within rooms in comparison to the sets identified in the first stage. The corresponding computational effort increases linearly with each link, room, and comparison set, limiting its impact on scalability for bigger networks or more complex scenarios.

As we refrain from requiring centimetre accuracy, our approach is limited to reliably predict link changes, but not to quantify their actual change. For this reason, our approach is able to identify that an object has changed its status but not to distinguish between subtle changes in an obstacle state (e.g., the degree at which a door is open). This requires more accurate description of the environments and a supervised placement of nodes in an area. The same applies to the distinction among changes to objects spatially close to each other. Only the use of more detailed maps and a constrained positioning of devices would allow to address such limitations.

6.2 Online Detecting and Reasoning

The approach and analysis presented in this paper focus on individual events. However, multiple events can happen simultaneously making the matching of each event challenging due to the possible overlaps in the affected set of links. In addition, persons present in the environment affect links in a volatile manner while moving around. This produces complex fingerprints that need to be preprocessed in order to extract the different, individual components.

Even with a lower detection accuracy due to multiple events possibly happening in parallel, it is still possible to build a fingerprint that can be integrated in an overall library with a corresponding probability assigned to the possible causing events. By continuously observing the behaviour of the system, it is possible to refine such estimations to progressively increase the correctness of the acquired knowledge. Ultimately, this refinement cycle can allow systems to reason about their own behaviour. At the same time, the process can produce factual knowledge about fingerprints that our current models are not yet capable of perceiving, further systematically highlighting specific interesting cases worth investigating.

6.3　Exploiting Opportunistic Communication

The Internet of Things is made of devices with heterogeneous communication characteristics. Our modelling technique can seamlessly work with different radio frequencies, depending on the specific employed technologies. Considering that different frequencies correspond to different impacts of obstacles and materials on the signal propagation, it becomes interesting to explore how our approaches can exploit such richness of signals and observations. This would allow to better recognise events happening in the environment and identify the specific best radio technology to detect each of them.

In addition, it would offer the possibility to use the model in order to, e.g. position the devices in the environment if signals are not affected by walls and so on. Interestingly enough, this would allow any device visiting or settling in an environment to contribute with active measurements to the understanding of communication in the scenario, progressively refining their situated system and network knowledge. This could provide a significant step forward both in the ability of systems to self-configure and in the validation, diagnosis and debugging of operational systems over time.

6.4　Seeing Wireless Signals

To further support the deployment and design of the system with accessible interfaces, the employed ray tracing techniques could be used to guide, e.g. the placement of devices in an operational environment based on specific application requirements and utility functions. Considering the advancements in virtual and augmented reality, it is conceivable to let the user "see" actual wireless signals and navigate in an environment to explore the behaviour of a network and modify its configuration. In this respect, system reconfiguration and optimisations tasks could be integrated as well. With machine learning techniques it would be possible to explore the space of possibilities and learn about the impact of alternative configurations on the system performance and robustness against specific events. Considering, however, the complexity of exploring a 3D environment for optimal configurations, dedicated techniques need to be investigated in order to keep the problem tractable.

7　CONCLUSION

In this work, we turned our attention to modelling techniques in order to understand wireless communication in indoor environments. It turns out that computing 3D models of the environment in which the devices operate can be made practical and that its processing can be accelerated without sacrificing accuracy. Through this analysis, we identify the possibility to use the implemented models in

order to understand how events happening in the environment and causing stable changes to the wireless communication impact signal propagation. In particular, we can exploit the features of the employed models to localise such events and let networks reason about their own communication properties.

REFERENCES

[1] Fadel Adib et al. 2015. Capturing the Human Figure Through a Wall. *ACM Trans. Graph.* 34, 6, Article 219 (Oct. 2015), 13 pages.
[2] Alaa Alhamoud et al. 2014. Empirical investigation of the effect of the door's state on received signal strength in indoor environments at 2.4 GHz. In *Proceedings of the 39th Conference on Local Computer Networks Workshops (LCN Workshops)*. 652–657.
[3] Cesare Alippi et al. 2016. RTI Goes Wild: Radio Tomographic Imaging for Outdoor People Detection and Localization. *IEEE Transactions on Mobile Computing* 15, 10 (Oct 2016), 2585–2598.
[4] Aparapi. 2018. Open-source framework for executing native Java code on the GPU. http://aparapi.com
[5] Carlo Alberto Boano et al. 2013. Hot Packets: A Systematic Evaluation of the Effect of Temperature on Low Power Wireless Transceivers. In *Proceedings of the 5th Extreme Conference on Communication (ExtremeCom)*. 7–12.
[6] Falk Brockmann et al. 2018. RSSI Based Passive Detection of Persons for Waiting Lines Using Bluetooth Low Energy. In *Proceedings of the 2018 International Conference on Embedded Wireless Systems and Networks (EWSN'18)*. 102–113.
[7] Marco Cattani et al. 2017. An Experimental Evaluation of the Reliability of LoRa Long-Range Low-Power Wireless Communication. *Journal of Sensor and Actuator Networks* 6, 2 (2017).
[8] Matthias Faessler et al. 2016. Autonomous, Vision-based Flight and Live Dense 3D Mapping with a Quadrotor Micro Aerial Vehicle. *J. Field Robot.* 33, 4 (June 2016), 431–450.
[9] Ngewi Fet et al. 2013. A Model for WLAN Signal Attenuation of the Human Body. In *Proceedings of the 2013 ACM International Joint Conference on Pervasive and Ubiquitous Computing (UbiComp '13)*. 499–508.
[10] Álvaro González. 2009. Measurement of Areas on a Sphere Using Fibonacci and Latitude–Longitude Lattices. *Mathematical Geosciences* 42, 1 (28 Nov 2009), 49.
[11] Sajjad Hussain and Conor Brennan. 2017. An efficient ray tracing method for propagation prediction along a mobile route in urban environments. *Radio Science* 52, 7 (July 2017), 862–873.
[12] Paul Jaccard. 1902. Lois de distribution florale dans la zone alpine. *Bull Soc Vaudoise Sci Nat* 38 (1902), 69–130.
[13] Sascha Jungen et al. 2017. Situated Wireless Networks Optimisation Through Model-Based Relocation of Nodes. In *2017 IEEE 14th International Conference on Mobile Ad Hoc and Sensor Systems (MASS)*. 389–397.
[14] Ossi Kaltiokallio et al. 2012. Follow @grandma: Long-term device-free localization for residential monitoring. In *37th Annual IEEE Conference on Local Computer Networks - Workshops*. 991–998.
[15] Ossi Kaltiokallio et al. 2014. Non-invasive Respiration Rate Monitoring Using a Single COTS TX-RX Pair. In *Proceedings of the 13th International Symposium on Information Processing in Sensor Networks (IPSN '14)*. 59–70.
[16] Ramona Marfievici et al. 2013. How Environmental Factors Impact Outdoor Wireless Sensor Networks: A Case Study. In *2013 IEEE 10th International Conference on Mobile Ad-Hoc and Sensor Systems*. 565–573.
[17] Luca Mottola et al. 2010. Not All Wireless Sensor Networks Are Created Equal: A Comparative Study on Tunnels. *ACM Trans. Sen. Netw.* 7, 2, Article 15 (Sept. 2010), 33 pages.
[18] Joseph Polastre et al. 2005. Telos: Enabling Ultra-low Power Wireless Research. In *Proceedings of the 4th International Symposium on Information Processing in Sensor Networks (IPSN '05)*.
[19] Kannan Srinivasan et al. 2010. An Empirical Study of Low-power Wireless. *ACM Trans. Sen. Netw.* 6, 2, Article 16 (March 2010), 49 pages.
[20] Jundong Tan et al. 2015. A Full 3-D GPU-based Beam-Tracing Method for Complex Indoor Environments Propagation Modeling. *IEEE Transactions on Antennas and Propagation* 63, 6 (June 2015), 2705–2718.
[21] Robert Wilson. 2002. Propagation losses through common building materials 2.4 GHz vs 5 GHz. *E10589 Magis Networks, Inc* (2002).
[22] Zhengqing Yun and Magdy F. Iskander. 2015. Ray Tracing for Radio Propagation Modeling: Principles and Applications. *IEEE Access* 3 (2015), 1089–1100.
[23] Mingmin Zhao et al. 2016. Emotion Recognition Using Wireless Signals. In *Proceedings of the 22Nd Annual International Conference on Mobile Computing and Networking (MobiCom '16)*. 95–108.
[24] Xi Zheng et al. 2015. Perceptions on the State of the Art in Verification and Validation in Cyber-Physical Systems. *IEEE Systems Journal* 11, 4 (Dec 2015), 2614–2627.
[25] Gang Zhou et al. 2006. Models and Solutions for Radio Irregularity in Wireless Sensor Networks. *ACM Trans. Sen. Netw.* 2, 2 (May 2006), 221–262.

Analysis of Age of Information Threshold Violations

Antonio Franco
antonio.franco@eit.lth.se
Lund University
Department of Electrical and
Information Technology
Lund, Sweden

Björn Landfeldt
bjorn.landfeldt@eit.lth.se
Lund University
Department of Electrical and
Information Technology
Lund, Sweden

Ulf Körner
ulf.korner@eit.lth.se
Lund University
Department of Electrical and
Information Technology
Lund, Sweden

ABSTRACT

We study a scenario where a monitor is interested in the freshest possible update from a remote sensor. The monitor also seeks to minimize the number of updates that exceed a certain freshness threshold, beyond which, the information is deemed to be too old. Previous work has presented results for First Come First Served (FCFS) systems. However, it has been shown that Last Come First Served (LCFS) with preemption is more effective in terms of average Age of Information (AoI); we therefore study an M/G/1 LCFS system with preemption. The generality of the busy time distribution gives the advantage of applicability on any distribution inside the model. For example, one can use a deterministic distribution to study a TDMA system, a gamma distribution to model a routing network, or a more complicated distribution to study a CSMA access scheme. We find a general procedure to derive the exact expression of the outage update probability – i.e. the portion of time updates have information older than a certain threshold. We compare different busy time distributions to the ones already present in literature for equivalent FCFS systems, showing the benefit of using the former discipline. We further study how the variance of the busy time distribution affects the update outage probability. We compare the M/D/1 LCFS with preemption against the M/Γ/1 LCFS with preemption and let the variance of the busy time of the latter vary, while maintaining the same average busy time for both systems. We find that at low thresholds and low loads, higher variance gives an advantage in terms of update outage probability.

CCS CONCEPTS

• **Mathematics of computing** → **Queueing theory**; • **Computer systems organization** → *Sensor networks*; • **Networks** → Network performance analysis.

KEYWORDS

age of information; analytical; LCFS queues; preemption; status updates

ACM Reference Format:
Antonio Franco, Björn Landfeldt, and Ulf Körner. 2019. Analysis of Age of Information Threshold Violations. In *22nd Int'l ACM Conference on Modeling, Analysis and Simulation of Wireless and Mobile Systems (MSWiM '19), November 25–29, 2019, Miami Beach, FL, USA.* ACM, New York, NY, USA, 10 pages. https://doi.org/10.1145/3345768.3355909

1 INTRODUCTION

The Internet of Things (IoT), opens up new challenges in many ways and early studies of IoT systems have opened up new ways of thinking about networked systems. A new concept called Age of Information (AoI) [13], was put forward where information is considered as a combination of application specific parameters and network specific parameters. In the AoI view, the 'freshness' of data is considered, which may not follow network delay directly. In a sense, the cross layer nature of AoI, stemming from it being a characteristic of the end-to-end information flow, represents a broader view of information freshness than delay does. To illustrate the difference between network delay and AoI, consider a scenario with a single First Come First Served (FCFS) queueing system. If the data generation rate increases, the queueing delay increases which in turn increases the delay through the system. Decreasing the data generation rate leads to shorter delay through the system, but at the same time, the time between measurements increase, which leads to larger AoI.

In many IoT scenarios such as smart cities [4], a typical application might be sensor nodes continuously measuring and sending data, e.g. using an IEEE 802.11ah Wireless Local Area Network (WLAN) [1]. For example, sensor nodes might be interested in uploading the measured information to a remote unit, for storing or further processing. If the remote server is only interested in the freshest possible piece of the information sent by the sensor node, it is interested in the sensor node trying to minimize the AoI at the receiver.

Since the introduction of the concept of AoI, the performance of this metric has been studied in multiple queueing systems with different queueing disciplines. Last Come First Served (LCFS) has the advantage of not sending stale jobs to the receiver end, thus being preferable when the receiver is interested only in the freshest piece of information. LCFS systems with preemption have been studied for single queueing systems [14, 16, 17], resulting in a significant improvement in terms of average AoI compared to systems with a FIFO or LCFS discipline without preemption.

Some applications may be interested not only to keep the average AoI low, but also to ensure a statistical guarantee that the AoI will not be above a threshold for a certain percentage of the time. We call the percentage of time that the AoI is above a certain threshold update outage probability. In order to find the update outage probability, it is necessary to know the entire distribution of the AoI at the receiver end, being it the survival function of the AoI itself. The first work to address the complete stationary distribution in FCFS queueing systems is in [9], where the authors obtain a general expression for the stationary distribution of the AoI in a G/G/1 FCFS system and several close form expressions for said distribution in derived systems.

Two studies addressed statistical guarantees regarding updates. In [5] the authors proposed an optimization problem for computing an approximation on the bound on the tail of the AoI distribution in D/M/1 FCFS systems. In [7], on the other hand, the authors characterized the delay and peak Age of Information (pAoI) violation probabilities for packets generated according to a Bernoulli process, placed in an FCFS queue, and sent through an Additive White Gaussian Noise (AWGN) channel. This system has also an Automatic repeat request (ARQ) mechanism in place. They also found an optimal block-length that minimizes the aforementioned probabilities.

In this paper we study the update outage probability of an M/G/1 LCFS system with preemption, and compare systems with different busy time distributions to their equivalents using FCFS disciplines. We show that the former substantially outperforms the latter, especially at high loads (i.e. when the source generation rate λ jobs/s approaches the inverse of the average busy time). Also an LCFS system with preemption has the advantage of being stable for loads greater than one, thus making room for further reducing the update outage probability.

Of greater importance, we derive expressions for the deterministic, exponential and gamma distributions. The first models a TDMA system. The gamma distribution, or, more specifically, its special case the Erlang distribution, could be used to model an information stream traveling through multiple hops in a network where each node follows an LCFS discipline with preemption with exponentially distributed busy times. Additionally, we study how the variance of the busy time distribution affects the update outage probability by comparing the M/D/1 LCFS with preemption against the M/Γ/1 LCFS with preemption by varying the variance of the busy time of the latter while maintaining the same average busy time for both systems. We discover instances where having higher variances in the busy time is beneficial for reducing the probability of violating a threshold on the AoI. Finally, with the general service time distribution our work is applicable to general wireless networks where different standards lead to different access delay distributions [10, 18, 20, 22, 23].

The rest of this paper is subdivided as follows. In Section 2 the scenario is described in detail. In Section 3 a method to derive the expression of the update outage probability is derived for an M/G/1 LCFS system with preemption. In Section 4 the previous expressions are first tested against simulations, compared with the results in [9] and then we study the effect of the variance of the busy time distribution on the update outage probability. Finally in Section 5 conclusions are drawn.

2 MODEL DESCRIPTION

Our model consists of an LCFS M/G/1 queueing system with preemption, sending jobs to a sink. The source generates pieces of information according to an exponential inter-arrival distribution with average rate λ job per seconds, i.e.:

$$f_A(t) = \lambda e^{-\lambda t} \mathrm{H}(t),$$

where $\mathrm{H}(t)$ is the Heaviside step function defined as:

$$\mathrm{H}(t) = \begin{cases} 1 & , t \geq 0 \\ 0 & , t < 0 \end{cases}.$$

The source sends updates about a single information stream i.e. there is only one class of jobs. It is also worth mentioning that for the remainder of the paper the Probability Density Function (PDF) of a random variable X will be expressed as $f_X(x)$, its Cumulative Distribution Function (CDF) as $F_X(x) = \Pr\{X \leq x\}$, its Survival Function $G_X(x) = \Pr\{X > x\} = 1 - F_X(x)$ and its Moment Generating Function (MGF) $\Phi_X(s) = \mathrm{E}\left[e^{sX}\right]$. Also, we will indicate an M/G/1 LCFS system with preemption as M/G/1/1* —since, as we will see, there could be only one job in the system –, and an M/G/1 FCFS system without preemption will be shortened just as M/G/1.

Also, we will refer to the time generated when a job arrives to the server without finding any other job in service as **busy time**, while the time from the arrival of a job to the server and its departure from the system will be referred as **service time**. While in systems without preemption they are the same, in preemptive systems they are different, as we will see in the next paragraphs.

We consider a preemption in which each time a fresher piece of information is generated, the new job takes the place in the server of the previous one already in service. The service time experienced by the new job will be the residual service time of the preempted job. Substituting a job being served models, for example, substituting a frame containing staler information that was already in the transmission buffer, waiting to be sent; this could happen because of a duty cycle, or because there is a back-off mechanism in place (e.g. IEEE 802.11 is used), as in [8]. The substituted job is discarded. Since we consider only one information stream, there are no jobs in the queue; they can only be in service.

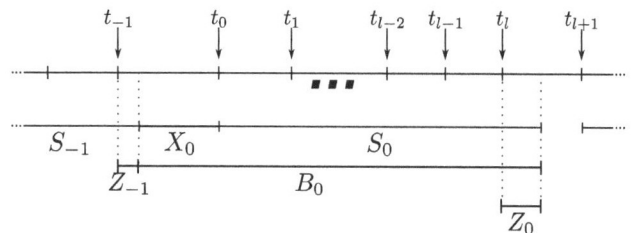

Figure 1: A typical busy/idle period.

In Figure 1 a typical busy/idle period is shown. The busy period S_{-1} ends before the arrival of job 0. Then, when job 0 is generated, a busy period starts again. A number of jobs gets preempted, until job l, because job $l+1$ happens to be generated after the busy period S_0 expires. The effective inter departure time for the two jobs that have survived (i.e. not preempted) is $B_0 = X_0 + S_0$, where X_0 is the idle period. Also, the successful job l will see a service time Z_0.

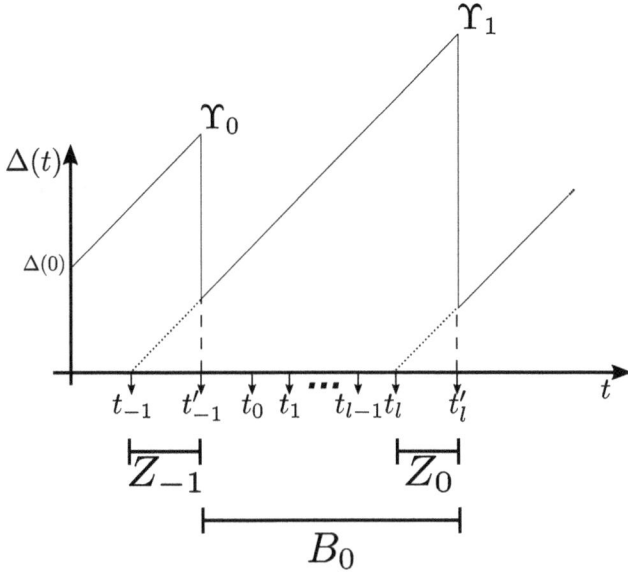

Figure 2: AoI over a typical busy/idle period. t_i is the i-th arrival time, while t_i' is the corresponding departure time.

The above timeline translates into the AoI function $\Delta(t)$ in Figure 2. When job -1 arrives at the sink, after a time Z_{-1}, the AoI will jump to the service time experienced by the latter. Then it will continue to grow with slope 1, until job l arrives, where it again jumps to its service time Z_0. The AoI just before the reception of a meaningful job is called peak AoI (pAoI) – marked as Υ_k, and it is, as seen in the figure, the sum of the effective inter-departure time for job k, B_k and the service time for the previous one, Z_{k-1}. Since the length of the inter-departure time B_k is independent from the the previous service time Z_{k-1}, at steady state:

$$\Phi_\Upsilon(s) = \Phi_B(s)\Phi_Z(s). \tag{1}$$

Also, since our system is ergodic, and we are considering the steady state distributions, we can calculate the CDF of the AoI (represented by the random variable Δ) by using [9, Lemma 1]:

$$F_\Delta(t) = \lambda_e \int_0^t F_Z(y) - F_\Upsilon(y)\mathrm{d}y, \tag{2}$$

where λ_e is the effective departure rate, expressed in jobs per second.

3 DISTRIBUTION OF THE AGE OF INFORMATION

In order to find the complete distribution of the AoI Δ (2), we need the effective departure rate λ_e, the CDF of the service time Z and of the pAoI Υ. In order to express the latter (1), we also need the MGF of the effective inter-departure time B.

We start by finding the distributions of B and Z, given that the busy time is a constant, i.e. t' seconds; our objective is to find an expression conditioned to the busy time being equal to a constant, in order to de-condition it; this in order to find the general form of the distribution of Δ. The busy time distribution will be t' seconds

with probability 1, i.e.:

$$f_{S|S=t'}(t) = \delta\left(t - t'\right). \tag{3}$$

where $\delta(t)$ is the Dirac delta function.

We now look at the distribution of the inter-departure time given that the busy time is t' seconds, i.e. $B|S = t'$. Looking at Figure 1 we notice that the inter-departure time B_k is the sum of the preceding idle time X_k and the busy time S_k. The idle time is the residual life of a point between two poissonian arrivals with rate λ jobs per second, so its distribution is also exponential with rate λ jobs per second (See the hippie paradox in [15]). Since there is no queueing delay, the effective departure rate λ_e will be:

$$\lambda_{e\,|(S=t')} = \frac{1}{\mathrm{E}\,[B]} = \frac{1}{\mathrm{E}\,[S] + \mathrm{E}\,[X]} = \frac{1}{t' + \frac{1}{\lambda}}. \tag{4}$$

Also, since the length of the busy time is independent from the preceding idle time, the steady state distribution of the inter-departure time $B|S = t'$ will be the convolution of (3) with an exponential distribution with rate λ jobs per second, i.e.:

$$f_{B|S=t'}(t) = \lambda e^{-\lambda(t-t')}\mathrm{H}\left(t - t'\right), \tag{5}$$

with CDF:

$$F_{B|S=t'}(t) = \left(1 - e^{-\lambda(t-t')}\right)\mathrm{H}\left(t - t'\right), \tag{6}$$

and associated MGF:

$$\Phi_{B|S=t'}(s) = \frac{\lambda}{\lambda - s}e^{st'}. \tag{7}$$

Looking at the conditioned service time $Z|S = t'$, we notice that, since the maximum length for a service time for a successful job is t' seconds, $Z|S = t'$ is less than t' with probability 1, i.e.:

$$\Pr\left\{Z|S = t' < t|t \geq t'\right\} = F_{Z|S=t'}\left(t : t \geq t'\right) = 1.$$

We also notice that $Z|S = t'$ is the age of a point between two poissonian arrivals with rate λ jobs per second, so its distribution is also exponential with rate λ jobs per second (Again, see the hippie paradox in [15]). By combining those two observations, we can write:

$$F_{Z|S=t'}(t) = \left(1 - e^{-\lambda t}\right)\mathrm{H}\left(t' - t\right) + \mathrm{H}\left(t - t'\right), \tag{8}$$

with associated PDF:

$$f_{Z|S=t'}(t) = \lambda e^{-\lambda t}\mathrm{H}\left(t' - t\right) + e^{-\lambda t'}\delta(t - t').$$

Finally we can calculate the MGF of $Z|S = t'$ as:

$$\begin{aligned}
\Phi_{Z|S=t'}(s) &= \lambda \int_0^\infty e^{-(\lambda-s)t}\mathrm{H}\left(t' - t\right)\mathrm{d}t + e^{-\lambda t'}e^{st'} \\
&= \lambda \int_0^{t'} e^{-(\lambda-s)t}\mathrm{d}t + e^{-\lambda t'}e^{st'} \\
&= \frac{\lambda}{\lambda - s} - \frac{\lambda}{\lambda - s}e^{-t'(\lambda-s)} + e^{-t'(\lambda-s)}. \tag{9}
\end{aligned}$$

At this point one could be tempted to use (7) and (9) in (1) in order to find $F_{\Upsilon|S=t'}(t)$, and then use it, along with (8) and (4) in (2) in order to find $F_{\Delta|S=t'}(t)$; then de-condition it for a particular distribution of t' in order to find the CDF of the AoI. This is not possible in general, since, although B and Z are independent, they are not conditionally independent with respect to S. In order to demonstrate it we will derive the CDF of the pAoI for an M/M/1/1* system and show that is not the same as de-conditioning $F_{\Upsilon|S=t'}(t)$ with:

$$f_S(t) = \mu e^{-\mu t} \mathrm{H}(t), \qquad (10)$$

where μ^{-1} is the average busy time, expressed in seconds. The proof will be presented in Lemma 3.1. Also notice that both Z and B are directly derived from the busy time S, so is always possible to de-condition them, being all the random variables from which they are derived conditionally independent with respect to S.

3.1 Update outage probability for an M/M/1 LCFS system with preemption

The effective departure rate will be:

$$\lambda_e^M = \frac{1}{\mathrm{E}[B]} = \frac{1}{\mathrm{E}[S] + \mathrm{E}[X]} = \frac{1}{\frac{1}{\mu} + \frac{1}{\lambda}} = \frac{\mu\lambda}{\lambda + \mu}. \qquad (11)$$

Also, the distribution of the inter-departure time B will be the sum of two exponential distributions with rates λ and μ respectively. The MGF will then be:

$$\Phi_B^M(s) = \frac{\lambda\mu}{(\lambda - s)(\mu - s)}. \qquad (12)$$

The effective service time will be the service time experienced by a successful job. It means is the service time of a job given that the next arrival comes after the remaining busy period, i.e:

$$
\begin{aligned}
F_Z^M(t) &= \Pr\{S < t | S < A\} = \frac{\Pr\{S < t, S < A\}}{\Pr\{S < A\}} \\
&= \frac{\int_0^\infty \Pr\{S < t, S < a\} f_A(a)\mathrm{d}a}{\int_0^\infty \Pr\{S < a\} f_A(a)\mathrm{d}a} \\
&= \frac{\left(\int_0^t F_S^M(a) f_A(a)\mathrm{d}a + F_S^M(t)\int_t^\infty f_A(a)\mathrm{d}a\right)}{\int_0^\infty F_S^M(a) f_A(a)\mathrm{d}a} \\
&= \frac{\lambda + \mu}{\mu}\left(\int_0^t F_S^M(a) f_A(a)\mathrm{d}a + F_S^M(t)\left[1 - F_A(t)\right]\right) \\
&= 1 - e^{-(\lambda+\mu)t}
\end{aligned}
\qquad (13)
$$

and its MGF:

$$\Phi_Z^M(s) = \frac{\lambda + \mu}{\lambda + \mu - s}. \qquad (14)$$

We now use (12) and (14) along with (1) in order to find $\Phi_\Upsilon(t)$:

$$
\begin{aligned}
\Phi_\Upsilon^M(s) &= \Phi_B^M(s)\Phi_Z^M(s) \\
&= \begin{cases} \frac{\lambda+\mu}{\lambda+\mu-s} - \frac{\lambda(\lambda+\mu)}{(\lambda-\mu)(\lambda-s)} + \frac{\mu(\lambda+\mu)}{(\lambda-\mu)(\mu-s)} & ,\lambda \neq \mu \\ \frac{2\lambda}{2\lambda-s} + \frac{2\lambda^2}{(\lambda-s)^2} - \frac{2\lambda}{\lambda-s} & ,\lambda = \mu \end{cases}
\end{aligned}
$$

with the associated CDF:

$$F_\Upsilon^M(t) = \begin{cases} 1 - e^{-(\lambda+\mu)t} + \frac{\lambda+\mu}{\lambda-\mu}\left(e^{-\lambda t} - e^{-\mu t}\right) & ,\lambda \neq \mu \\ 1 - 2\lambda t\, e^{-\lambda t} - e^{-2\lambda t} & ,\lambda = \mu \end{cases}. \qquad (15)$$

Finally, by using (11), (13) and (15) in (2) we find:

$$F_\Delta^M(t) = \begin{cases} 1 - \frac{\lambda}{\lambda-\mu}e^{-\mu t} + \frac{\mu}{\lambda-\mu}e^{-\lambda t} & ,\lambda \neq \mu \\ 1 - (\lambda t + 1)e^{-\lambda t} & ,\lambda = \mu \end{cases},$$

and its survival function:

$$G_\Delta^M(t) = 1 - F_\Delta^M(t) = \begin{cases} \frac{\lambda}{\lambda-\mu}e^{-\mu t} - \frac{\mu}{\lambda-\mu}e^{-\lambda t} & ,\lambda \neq \mu \\ (\lambda t + 1)e^{-\lambda t} & ,\lambda = \mu \end{cases}. \qquad (16)$$

3.2 A general method to find the update outage probability of an M/G/1 LCFS system with preemption

LEMMA 3.1. *The random variable B describing the inter-departure times and the random variable Z describing the service time are not, in general, conditionally independent with respect to the random variable describing the busy time S.*

PROOF. If B and Z were conditionally independent with respect to S, then, for every S it must hold:

$$\Upsilon|S = t' = (B + Z)|S = t' = B|S = t' + Z|S = t'.$$

This entails that for every S:

$$\Phi_{\Upsilon|S=t'}(s) = \Phi_{B|S=t'}(s)\Phi_{Z|S=t'}(s),$$

is the MGF of

$$f_{\Upsilon|S=t'}(t) = \mathcal{M}^{-1}\left\{\Phi_{\Upsilon|S=t'}(s)\right\}(t),$$

where $\mathcal{M}^{-1}\{\cdot\}$ is the inverse transform operator. The associated CDF is:

$$F_{\Upsilon|S=t'}(t) = \int_0^t f_{\Upsilon|S=t'}(\hat{t})\mathrm{d}\hat{t}.$$

Then it should be possible to obtain the CDF of Υ for any distribution of S, $f_S(t)$ as:

$$F_\Upsilon(t) = \int_0^\infty F_{\Upsilon|S=t'}(t)f_S(t')\mathrm{d}t'. \qquad (17)$$

We now choose $f_S(t)$ to be (10). By using Eq (7) and (9) in (1) we can then calculate the MGF of $\Upsilon|S = t'$:

$$\Phi_{\Upsilon|S=t'}(s) = \left(\frac{\lambda}{\lambda-s}\right)^2 e^{st'} - e^{-t'\lambda}\left(\frac{\lambda}{\lambda-s}\right)^2 e^{2st'} + e^{-t'\lambda}\frac{\lambda}{\lambda-s}e^{2st'},$$

associated with the CDF:

$$
\begin{aligned}
F_{\Upsilon|S=t'}(t) &= \gamma\left(\lambda(t-t'), 2\right)\mathrm{H}\left(t - t'\right) \\
&\quad + e^{-t'\lambda}\left[\left(1 - e^{-\lambda(t-2t')}\right) - \gamma\left(\lambda(t - 2t'), 2\right)\right]\mathrm{H}\left(t - 2t'\right) \\
&= \left[e^{-\lambda(t'-t)}\left(\lambda\left(t' - t\right) - 1\right) + 1\right]\mathrm{H}\left(t - t'\right) \\
&\quad - \lambda e^{-\lambda(t'-t)}\left(2t' - t\right)\mathrm{H}\left(t - 2t'\right), \qquad (18)
\end{aligned}
$$

where $\gamma(x, a)$ is the regularized lower incomplete gamma function defined as:

$$\gamma(x, a) = \frac{1}{\Gamma(a)}\int_0^x t^{a-1}e^{-t}\mathrm{d}t.$$

We now de-condition the previous using (10) (supposing $\lambda \neq \mu$) in (17), i.e.:

$$
\begin{aligned}
F_\Upsilon^M(t) &= \int_0^\infty F_{\Upsilon|S=t'}(t)\mu e^{-\mu t'}\mathrm{d}t' \\
&= \frac{e^{-\frac{3t(\lambda+\mu)}{2}}}{(\lambda-\mu)^2}\left(\lambda^2 e^{\frac{3t(\lambda+\mu)}{2}} + \mu^2 e^{\frac{3t(\lambda+\mu)}{2}} - \lambda^2 e^{\frac{t(3\lambda+\mu)}{2}}\right. \\
&\quad \left. - \mu^2 e^{\frac{t(\lambda+3\mu)}{2}} + 2\lambda\mu e^{t(\lambda+\mu)} - 2\lambda\mu e^{\frac{3t(\lambda+\mu)}{2}}\right),
\end{aligned}
$$

that is different from (15). So we conclude that, in general, B and Z are not conditionally independent with respect to S.   □

Also we can write some general expressions for a general PDF of the busy time $f_S(t)$. First if we write the de-conditioning of B using (5):

$$f_B(t) = \int_0^\infty \lambda e^{-\lambda(t-t')} H\left(t - t'\right) f_S(t') dt'$$

we notice that this is a convolution between an exponential distribution with rate λ and the busy time distribution, so we can write its MGF as:

$$\Phi_B(t) = \frac{\lambda}{\lambda - s} \Phi_S(s). \tag{19}$$

Now we write the CDF of the de-conditioning of Z using (8):

$$F_Z(t) = \int_t^\infty \left(1 - e^{-\lambda t}\right) f_S(t') dt' + \int_0^t f_S(t') dt'$$
$$= 1 - e^{-\lambda t} \left(1 - F_S(t)\right). \tag{20}$$

Similarly, for the PDF:

$$f_Z(t) = \lambda e^{-\lambda t} \int_t^\infty f_S(t') dt' + \int_0^\infty e^{-\lambda t'} f_S(t') \delta(t - t') dt'$$
$$= \lambda e^{-\lambda t} + e^{-\lambda t} f_S(t) - \lambda e^{-\lambda t} \int_0^t f_S(t') dt'.$$

By using the frequency translation and the time integral properties of the transform, we can finally write that the MGF of Z for a busy time S is:

$$\Phi_Z(s) = \frac{\lambda}{\lambda - s} + \Phi_S(s - \lambda) - \frac{\lambda}{\lambda - s} \Phi_S(s - \lambda). \tag{21}$$

We can now present a general method to find the update outage probability for an M/G/1 LCFS system with preemption. The method is the following:

(1) Given a particular PDF for S, $f_S(t)$, calculate the MGF of the pAoI as the product of (19) and (21)
(2) Anti-transform the previous in order to find its CDF
(3) Use (20), the effective departure rate and the CDF of Υ by substituting them in (2). Find the CDF of the AoI, and, finally, its survival function.

3.3 Update outage probability for some important systems

In this section we will derive the update outage probability for the M/D/1/1* and the M/Γ/1/1* systems. As we will see in the next sections, those two systems are linked by the fact that the gamma distribution approximates the deterministic distribution when letting one of its parameters to infinity.

3.3.1 Update outage probability for an M/D/1 LCFS system with preemption. Since the PDF of the busy time is (3), we can say that the CDF of the pAoI is (18) the CDF of the service time Z is (8) and the effective departure rate is (4). By using the previous in (2) we

find:

$$F_\Delta^D(t) = \frac{1}{t'\lambda + 1} \Bigg[\left(e^{-\lambda t} + \lambda t - 1\right) H\left(t' - t\right)$$
$$+ \left(e^{-t'\lambda} + t'\lambda - 1 + e^{-\lambda t} \left(t' e^{t'\lambda} - t e^{t'\lambda}\right)\right)$$
$$- \lambda e^{-\lambda t} \left(2 e^{t'\lambda} - 2 e^{\lambda t}\right) \Bigg) H\left(t - t'\right) + e^{-\lambda(t'+t)}$$
$$\times \left(e^{2t'\lambda} - e^{\lambda t} - 2 t'\lambda e^{2t'\lambda} + \lambda t e^{2t'\lambda}\right) H\left(t - 2t'\right) \Bigg],$$

and its survival function:

$$G_\Delta^D(t) = 1 - F_\Delta^D(t)$$
$$= 1 - \frac{1}{t'\lambda + 1} \Bigg[\left(e^{-\lambda t} + \lambda t - 1\right) H\left(t' - t\right)$$
$$+ \left(e^{-t'\lambda} + t'\lambda - 1 + e^{-\lambda t} \left(t' e^{t'\lambda} - t e^{t'\lambda}\right)\right)$$
$$- \lambda e^{-\lambda t} \left(2 e^{t'\lambda} - 2 e^{\lambda t}\right) \Bigg) H\left(t - t'\right) + e^{-\lambda(t'+t)}$$
$$\times \left(e^{2t'\lambda} - e^{\lambda t} - 2 t'\lambda e^{2t'\lambda} + \lambda t e^{2t'\lambda}\right) H\left(t - 2t'\right) \Bigg]. \tag{22}$$

3.3.2 Update outage probability for an M/Γ/1 LCFS system with preemption. The gamma distribution is an important distribution since it is possible to assign it a mean and let the variance be as little as we want, approximating the deterministic distribution. This property allows to study the effect of the variance to the update outage probability. The busy time distribution is:

$$f_S^\Gamma(t) = \frac{\beta^\alpha}{\Gamma(\alpha)} t^{\alpha-1} e^{-\beta t} H(t), \tag{23}$$

with mean $\mathrm{E}[S] = \frac{\alpha}{\beta}$ s and variance $\mathrm{Var}[S] = \frac{\alpha}{\beta^2}$ s^2. If we assign a mean $\mathrm{E}[S] = \frac{1}{\mu}$ s we can write:

$$\frac{\alpha}{\beta} = \frac{1}{\mu} \Rightarrow \mathrm{Var}[S] = \frac{\alpha}{\beta} \cdot \frac{1}{\beta} = \frac{1}{\mu} \cdot \frac{1}{\beta}$$

so when we take the limit for $\beta \to \infty$ and setting $\alpha = \frac{\beta}{\mu}$ in order to maintain the expected value constant:

$$\lim_{\alpha \to \infty} \mathrm{Var}[S] = \frac{1}{\mu} \lim_{\beta \to \infty} \frac{1}{\beta} = 0\, \mathrm{s}^2,$$

while the expected value remains $\mathrm{E}[S] = \frac{1}{\mu}$ s.

The effective departure rate is:

$$\lambda_e^\Gamma = \frac{1}{\frac{\alpha}{\beta} + \frac{1}{\lambda}} = \frac{\beta\lambda}{\alpha\lambda + \beta}. \tag{24}$$

We use (19) substituting the MGF of (23) in it in order to find the MGF of B:

$$\Phi_B^\Gamma(s) = \frac{\lambda}{\lambda - s} \left(\frac{\beta}{\beta - s}\right)^\alpha. \tag{25}$$

Similarly, using (21):

$$\Phi_Z^{\Gamma}(s) = \frac{\lambda}{\lambda - s} + \left(\frac{\beta}{\beta + \lambda - s}\right)^{\alpha} - \frac{\lambda}{\lambda - s}\left(\frac{\beta}{\beta + \lambda - s}\right)^{\alpha}. \quad (26)$$

We find its CDF using (20) i.e.:

$$F_Z^{\Gamma}(t) = 1 - e^{-\lambda t}\left(1 - \gamma(\beta t, \alpha)\right). \quad (27)$$

Next, the MGF of Υ will be, by multiplying (25) and (26):

$$\Phi_{\Upsilon}^{\Gamma}(s) = \left(\frac{\lambda}{\lambda - s}\right)^2 \left(\frac{\beta}{\beta - s}\right)^{\alpha} - \left(\frac{\lambda}{\lambda - s}\right)^2 \left(\frac{\beta}{\beta - s}\right)^{\alpha}\left(\frac{\beta}{\beta + \lambda - s}\right)^{\alpha}$$
$$+ \frac{\lambda}{\lambda - s}\left(\frac{\beta}{\beta - s}\right)^{\alpha}\left(\frac{\beta}{\beta + \lambda - s}\right)^{\alpha}$$
$$= \left(\frac{\lambda}{\lambda - s}\right)^2 \left(\frac{\beta}{\beta - s}\right)^{\alpha}$$
$$- \left(\frac{\beta}{\beta + \lambda}\right)^{\alpha}\left(\frac{\lambda}{\lambda - s}\right)^2 \left(\frac{\beta}{\beta - s}\right)^{\alpha}\left(\frac{\beta + \lambda}{\beta + \lambda - s}\right)^{\alpha}$$
$$+ \left(\frac{\beta}{\beta + \lambda}\right)^{\alpha}\frac{\lambda}{\lambda - s}\left(\frac{\beta}{\beta - s}\right)^{\alpha}\left(\frac{\beta + \lambda}{\beta + \lambda - s}\right)^{\alpha}.$$

The above is the sum of the distributions of three different sums of independent gamma variates (the exponential and Erlang distributions are particular cases of the gamma distribution). If we define Y_l with $l = 1 \ldots L$ a gamma variate with parameters (α_l, β_l), the CDF of $Y = \sum_{i=1}^{L} Y_l$ – i.e. the sum of L independent gamma random variables – is [2, Theorem 2]:

$$F_Y(t) = 1 + \left(\prod_{l=1}^{L}\beta_l^{\alpha}\right)\overline{H}_{L+1,L+1}^{0,L+1}\left[e^y \,\middle|\, \begin{matrix} \Xi_L^{(1)}, & (1,1,1) \\ \Xi_L^{(2)}, & (0,1,1) \end{matrix}\right],$$

where:

$$\Xi_k^{(1)} = (1 - \beta_1, 1, \alpha_1)(1 - \beta_2, 1, \alpha_2)\ldots(1 - \beta_k, 1, \alpha_k)$$
$$\Xi_k^{(2)} = (-\beta_1, 1, \alpha_1)(-\beta_2, 1, \alpha_2)\ldots(-\beta_k, 1, \alpha_k)$$

and $\overline{H}$ is the Fox's $\overline{H}$ function [19] defined as:

$$\overline{H}_{p,q}^{m,n}\left[z \,\middle|\, \begin{matrix} (a_j, A_j; \alpha_j)_{1,n} & (a_j, A_j)_{n+1,p} \\ (b_j, B_j)_{1,m} & (b_j, B_j; \beta_j)_{m+1,q} \end{matrix}\right]$$
$$= \frac{1}{2\pi i}\int_{\mathcal{V}}\chi(s)z^{-s}ds,$$

where:

$$\chi(s) = \frac{\left(\prod_{j=1}^{m}\Gamma(b_j + B_j s)\right)\left(\prod_{j=1}^{n}\Gamma(1 - a_j - A_j s)^{\alpha_j}\right)}{\left(\prod_{j=m+1}^{q}\Gamma(1 - b_j - B_j s)^{\beta_j}\right)\left(\prod_{j=n+1}^{p}\Gamma(a_j + A_j s)\right)}, \quad (28)$$

and $\mathcal{V}$ is a contour starting at the point $\tau - i\infty$ and terminating at the point $\tau + i\infty$ for some $\tau \in \mathbb{R}$. We notice that the Fox's $\overline{H}$ function could be also viewed as the inverse Mellin transform of (28). The CDF of Υ will then be:

$$F_{\Upsilon}^{\Gamma}(t) = 1 + \lambda^2\beta^{\alpha}\overline{H}_{3,3}^{0,3}\left[e^t \,\middle|\, \begin{matrix} \xi_1^{(1)} \\ \xi_1^{(2)} \end{matrix}\right] - \lambda^2\beta^{2\alpha}\overline{H}_{4,4}^{0,4}\left[e^t \,\middle|\, \begin{matrix} \xi_2^{(1)} \\ \xi_2^{(2)} \end{matrix}\right]$$
$$+ \lambda\beta^{2\alpha}\overline{H}_{4,4}^{0,4}\left[e^t \,\middle|\, \begin{matrix} \xi_3^{(1)} \\ \xi_3^{(2)} \end{matrix}\right], \quad (29)$$

where:

$$\xi_1^{(1)} = (1 - \lambda, 1, 2), (1 - \beta, 1, \alpha), (1,1,1)$$
$$\xi_1^{(2)} = (-\lambda, 1, 2), (-\beta, 1, \alpha), (0, 1, 1)$$
$$\xi_2^{(1)} = (1 - \lambda, 1, 2), (1 - \beta, 1, \alpha), (1 - \beta - \lambda, 1, \alpha), (1,1,1)$$
$$\xi_2^{(2)} = (-\lambda, 1, 2), (-\beta, 1, \alpha), (-\beta - \lambda, 1, \alpha), (0, 1, 1)$$
$$\xi_3^{(1)} = (1 - \lambda, 1, 1), (1 - \beta, 1, \alpha), (1 - \beta - \lambda, 1, \alpha), (1,1,1)$$
$$\xi_3^{(2)} = (-\lambda, 1, 1), (-\beta, 1, \alpha), (-\beta - \lambda, 1, \alpha), (0, 1, 1).$$

In order to find the CDF of Δ, we must combine (24), (27) and (29) in (2):

$$F_{\Delta}^{\Gamma}(t) = \frac{\beta\lambda}{\alpha\lambda + \beta}\left(\frac{e^{-\lambda t}}{\lambda} - \frac{1}{\lambda} + \int_0^t e^{-\lambda t'}\gamma(\beta t', \alpha)dt'\right.$$
$$- \lambda^2\beta^{\alpha}\int_0^t \overline{H}_{3,3}^{0,3}\left[e^{t'} \,\middle|\, \begin{matrix} \xi_1^{(1)} \\ \xi_1^{(2)} \end{matrix}\right]dt'$$
$$+ \lambda^2\beta^{2\alpha}\int_0^t \overline{H}_{4,4}^{0,4}\left[e^{t'} \,\middle|\, \begin{matrix} \xi_2^{(1)} \\ \xi_2^{(2)} \end{matrix}\right]dt'$$
$$\left. - \lambda\beta^{2\alpha}\int_0^t \overline{H}_{4,4}^{0,4}\left[e^{t'} \,\middle|\, \begin{matrix} \xi_3^{(1)} \\ \xi_3^{(2)} \end{matrix}\right]dt'\right) \quad (30)$$

We solve by parts:

$$\int_0^t e^{-\lambda t'}\gamma(\beta t', \alpha)dt'$$
$$= \frac{1 - e^{-\lambda t}}{\lambda}\gamma(\beta t, \alpha) - \frac{\beta^{\alpha}}{\Gamma(\alpha)}\int_0^t t'^{\alpha-1}e^{-\beta t'}\frac{1 - e^{-\lambda t}}{\lambda}dt'$$
$$= \lambda^{-1}\left(\frac{\beta}{(\beta + \lambda)}\right)^{\alpha}\gamma\left((\beta + \lambda)t, \alpha\right) - \lambda^{-1}e^{-\lambda t}\gamma(\beta t, \alpha). \quad (31)$$

Then we make use of the integration in time property of the Mellin transform, and that:

$$\frac{1}{s} = \frac{\Gamma(s)}{s\Gamma(s)} = \frac{\Gamma(s)}{\Gamma(1 + s)},$$

inserting the latter as an additional term in (28), using a reasoning similar to the proof of [2, Theorem 2], obtaining:

$$\prod_{l=1}^{L}\beta_l^{\alpha}\int_0^t \overline{H}_{L+1,L+1}^{0,L+1}\left[e^{t'} \,\middle|\, \begin{matrix} \Xi_L^{(1)}, & (1,1,1) \\ \Xi_L^{(2)}, & (0,1,1) \end{matrix}\right]dt'$$
$$= 1 + \prod_{l=1}^{L}\beta_l^{\alpha}\overline{H}_{L+2,L+2}^{0,L+2}\left[e^t \,\middle|\, \begin{matrix} \Xi_L^{(1)}, & (1,1,1), & (1,1,1) \\ \Xi_L^{(2)}, & (0,1,1), & (0,1,1) \end{matrix}\right]$$
$$= 1 + \prod_{l=1}^{L}\beta_l^{\alpha}\overline{H}_{L+1,L+1}^{0,L+1}\left[e^t \,\middle|\, \begin{matrix} \Xi_L^{(1)}, & (1,1,2) \\ \Xi_L^{(2)}, & (0,1,2) \end{matrix}\right].$$

We then use (31) and the above in (30) to finally obtain:

$$
\begin{aligned}
F_\Delta^\Gamma(t) = \frac{\beta\lambda}{\alpha\lambda+\beta}\Bigg(& \lambda^{-1}e^{-\lambda t} - \lambda^{-1} \\
& + \lambda^{-1}\left(\frac{\beta}{(\beta+\lambda)}\right)^\alpha \gamma\left((\beta+\lambda)t,\alpha\right) - \lambda^{-1}e^{-\lambda t}\gamma(\beta t,\alpha) \\
& - \lambda^2\beta^\alpha \overline{H}_{4,4}^{\,0,4}\left[e^t \middle| \begin{array}{cc} \xi_1^{(1)} & ,(1,1,1) \\ \xi_1^{(2)} & ,(0,1,1) \end{array}\right] \\
& + \lambda^2\beta^{2\alpha}\overline{H}_{5,5}^{\,0,5}\left[e^t \middle| \begin{array}{cc} \xi_2^{(1)} & ,(1,1,1) \\ \xi_2^{(2)} & ,(0,1,1) \end{array}\right] \\
& - \lambda\beta^{2\alpha}\overline{H}_{5,5}^{\,0,5}\left[e^t \middle| \begin{array}{cc} \xi_3^{(1)} & ,(1,1,1) \\ \xi_3^{(2)} & ,(0,1,1) \end{array}\right]\Bigg),
\end{aligned}
$$

from which we finally obtain the expression for the update outage probability:

$$
\begin{aligned}
G_\Delta^\Gamma(t) = 1 - \frac{\beta\lambda}{\alpha\lambda+\beta}\Bigg(& \lambda^{-1}e^{-\lambda t} - \lambda^{-1} \\
& + \lambda^{-1}\left(\frac{\beta}{(\beta+\lambda)}\right)^\alpha \gamma\left((\beta+\lambda)t,\alpha\right) - \lambda^{-1}e^{-\lambda t}\gamma(\beta t,\alpha) \\
& - \lambda^2\beta^\alpha \overline{H}_{4,4}^{\,0,4}\left[e^t \middle| \begin{array}{cc} \xi_1^{(1)} & ,(1,1,1) \\ \xi_1^{(2)} & ,(0,1,1) \end{array}\right] \\
& + \lambda^2\beta^{2\alpha}\overline{H}_{5,5}^{\,0,5}\left[e^t \middle| \begin{array}{cc} \xi_2^{(1)} & ,(1,1,1) \\ \xi_2^{(2)} & ,(0,1,1) \end{array}\right] \\
& - \lambda\beta^{2\alpha}H_{5,5}^{\,0,5}\left[e^t \middle| \begin{array}{cc} \xi_3^{(1)} & ,(1,1,1) \\ \xi_3^{(2)} & ,(0,1,1) \end{array}\right]\Bigg).
\end{aligned}
\tag{32}
$$

As a side note, by using the results in [2, Corollary 3], if we have an Erlang distribution instead of a gamma distribution (i.e. α is an integer), the update outage probability becomes:

$$
\begin{aligned}
G_\Delta^{\mathrm{Er}}(t) = 1 - \frac{\beta\lambda}{\alpha\lambda+\beta}\Bigg(& t + \lambda^{-1}e^{-\lambda t} - \lambda^{-1} \\
& + \lambda^{-1}\left(\frac{\beta}{(\beta+\lambda)}\right)^\alpha \gamma\left((\beta+\lambda)t,\alpha\right) - \lambda^{-1}e^{-\lambda t}\gamma(\beta t,\alpha) \\
& - \lambda^2\beta^\alpha \mathcal{G}_{4+\alpha,4+\alpha}^{\,0,4+\alpha}\left[e^{-t} \middle| \begin{array}{cc} \psi_1^{(1)} & ,1,1 \\ \psi_1^{(2)} & ,0,0 \end{array}\right] \\
& + \lambda^2\beta^{2\alpha}\mathcal{G}_{4+2\alpha,4+2\alpha}^{\,0,4+2\alpha}\left[e^{-t} \middle| \begin{array}{cc} \psi_2^{(1)} & ,1,1 \\ \psi_2^{(2)} & ,0,0 \end{array}\right] \\
& - \lambda\beta^{2\alpha}\mathcal{G}_{3+2\alpha,3+2\alpha}^{\,0,3+2\alpha}\left[e^{-t} \middle| \begin{array}{cc} \psi_3^{(1)} & ,1,1 \\ \psi_3^{(2)} & ,0,0 \end{array}\right]\Bigg),
\end{aligned}
$$

where $\mathcal{G}$ is the Meijer G function (for the definition see [3]), and:

$$
\psi_1^{(1)} = (1+\lambda),(1+\lambda),\overbrace{(1+\beta)\dots(1+\beta)}^{\alpha\ \text{times}}
$$

$$
\psi_1^{(2)} = (\lambda),(\lambda),\overbrace{(\beta)\dots(\beta)}^{\alpha\ \text{times}}
$$

$$
\psi_2^{(1)} = (1+\lambda),(1+\lambda),\overbrace{(1+\beta)\dots(1+\beta)}^{\alpha\ \text{times}},\overbrace{(1+\beta+\lambda)\dots(1+\beta+\lambda)}^{\alpha\ \text{times}}
$$

$$
\psi_2^{(2)} = (\lambda),(\lambda),\overbrace{(\beta)\dots(\beta)}^{\alpha\ \text{times}},\overbrace{(\beta+\lambda)\dots(\beta+\lambda)}^{\alpha\ \text{times}}
$$

$$
\psi_3^{(1)} = (1+\lambda),\overbrace{(1+\beta)\dots(1+\beta)}^{\alpha\ \text{times}},\overbrace{(1+\beta+\lambda)\dots(1+\beta+\lambda)}^{\alpha\ \text{times}}
$$

$$
\psi_3^{(2)} = (\lambda),\overbrace{(\beta)\dots(\beta)}^{\alpha\ \text{times}},\overbrace{(\beta+\lambda)\dots(\beta+\lambda)}^{\alpha\ \text{times}}.
$$

4 NUMERICAL RESULTS

We have conducted simulation studies using OMNeT++ [21]. We fixed the expected value of the busy time $\mathrm{E}[S] = 1$ s and let λ and the threshold vary. The expected value of the busy time is t' s for the M/D/1 systems, μ^{-1} s for the M/M/1 systems and $\frac{\alpha}{\beta}$ s for the M/Γ/1 systems. In the figures we plot against the threshold expressed in seconds, and system load $\rho = \lambda\mathrm{E}[S]$. All the plots involving simulations are presented with 95% confidence intervals, allowing for a sufficient warm-up period before taking measurements. All the plots make use of a black and white printer-friendly and accessible color scheme [6, 12]. Also, for the numerical inversion of the Laplace transforms we used the Python package mpmath [11]. First, we compared (22), (16) and (32) against the simulations (Figure 3, 4 and 5), in order to validate our expressions. The theoretical results are in agreement with the measured update outage probability.

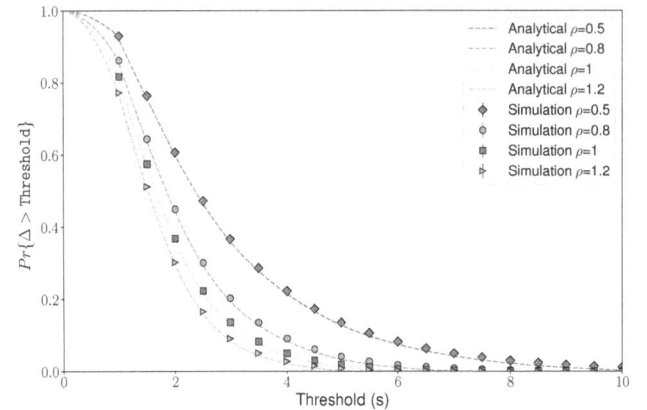

Figure 3: Update outage probability for an M/D/1/1* system (22); Simulation vs analytical.

The comparison of the outage probability for the M/D/1 LCFS with preemption system with the FCFS system is shown in Figure 6. We plot the outage probability when varying ρ between 0.1 and

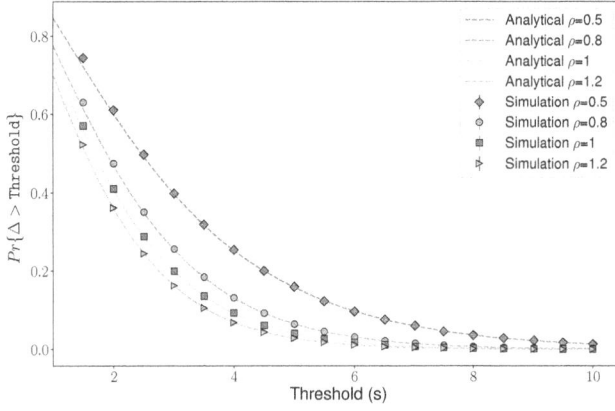

Figure 4: Update outage probability for an M/M/1/1* system (16); Simulation vs analytical.

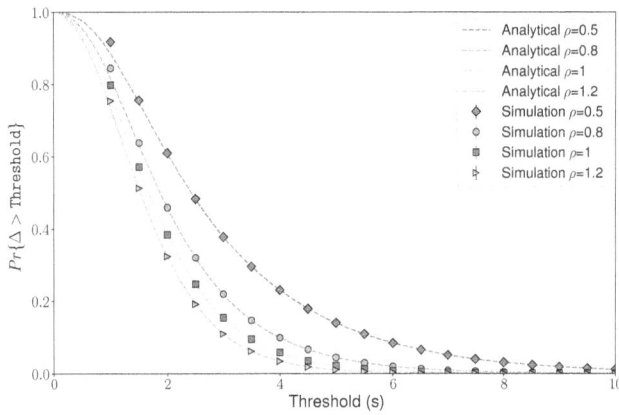

Figure 5: Update outage probability for an M/Γ/1/1* system (32); Simulation vs analytical.

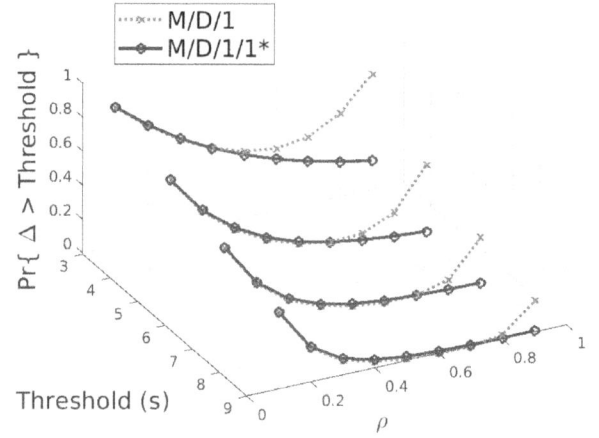

Figure 6: Update outage probability. M/D/1 LCFS with preemption (22) vs FCFS (33).

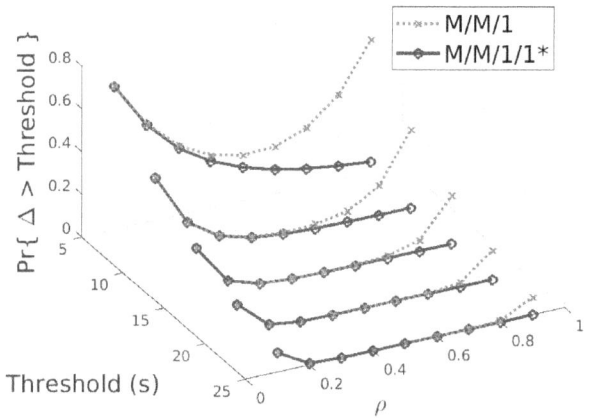

Figure 7: Update outage probability. M/M/1 LCFS with preemption (16) vs FCFS (34).

0.9 with different thresholds. We used [9, (20)] with a service time distributed as (3) to find the MGF of the AoI for an FCFS M/D/1 system:

$$\Phi^D_{\Delta_{FCFS}}(s) = \frac{s\,e^{t's}\,(t'\lambda - 1)}{s - \lambda\,e^{-t'(\lambda-s)}} - \frac{s\,e^{t's}\,(t'\lambda - 1)}{\lambda + s - \lambda\,e^{t's}},$$

then we numerically inverted it in order to find the associated CDF and, finally, its survival function, i.e.:

$$G^D_{\Delta_{FCFS}}(t) = 1 - F^D_{\Delta_{FCFS}}(t) = 1 - \mathcal{L}^{-1}\left\{\frac{1}{s}\Phi^D_{\Delta_{FCFS}}(-s)\right\}(t), \quad (33)$$

where $\mathcal{L}^{-1}\{\cdot\}$ is the inverse Laplace transform operator.

The comparison of the outage probability for the M/M/1 LCFS with preemption system with the FCFS system [9, Example 11] is shown in Figure 7. We plot the outage probability when varying ρ between 0.1 and 0.9 and the threshold between 5 and 25 seconds. Notice that the formula in the aforementioned paper for the CDF is

incorrect. The correct formula is:

$$F^M_{\Delta_{FCFS}}(t) = 1 - e^{-(\lambda-\mu)t} + \lambda t e^{-\mu t} - \frac{\mu}{\lambda - \mu}e^{-\mu t}$$
$$+ \frac{\mu}{\lambda - \mu}e^{-\lambda t}$$

where $\lambda < \mu$. The update outage probability then is:

$$G^M_{\Delta_{FCFS}}(t) = 1 - F^M_{\Delta_{FCFS}}(t) = e^{-(\lambda-\mu)t} - \lambda t e^{-\mu t} + \frac{\mu}{\lambda - \mu}e^{-\mu t}$$
$$- \frac{\mu}{\lambda - \mu}e^{-\lambda t}. \quad (34)$$

The comparison of the outage probability for the M/Γ/1 LCFS with preemption system with the FCFS system is shown in Figure 8. We plot the outage probability when varying ρ between 0.1 and 0.9 with different thresholds. We used [9, (20)] with a service time distributed as (23) to find the MGF of the AoI for an FCFS M/Γ/1

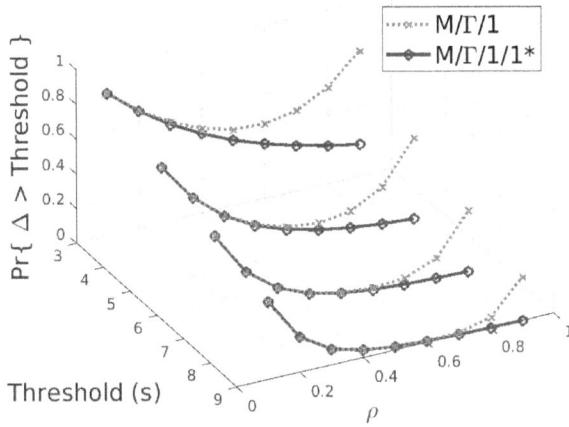

Figure 8: Update outage probability. M/Γ/1 LCFS with preemption (32) vs FCFS (35).

system:

$$\Phi^{\Gamma}_{\Delta_{FCFS}}(s) = \frac{\beta^{\alpha-1} s\,(\beta - \alpha\,\lambda)}{(\beta-s)^{\alpha}\left(\lambda+s-\frac{\beta^{\alpha}\lambda}{(\beta-s)^{\alpha}}\right)}$$
$$-\frac{\beta^{\alpha-1} s\,(\beta-\alpha\,\lambda)\,(\beta+\lambda-s)^{\alpha}}{(\beta-s)^{\alpha}\,(s\,(\beta+\lambda-s)^{\alpha}-\beta^{\alpha}\lambda)},$$

then we numerically inverted it in order to find the associated CDF and, finally, its survival function, i.e.:

$$G^{\Gamma}_{\Delta_{FCFS}}(t) = 1 - F^{\Gamma}_{\Delta_{FCFS}}(t) = 1 - \mathcal{L}^{-1}\left\{\frac{1}{s}\Phi^{\Gamma}_{\Delta_{FCFS}}(-s)\right\}(t). \quad (35)$$

The results show that the LCFS discipline with preemption significantly outperforms the FCFS discipline in all cases in terms of update outage probability, especially when the server is fully loaded i.e. $\rho \cong 1$, as the queueing delay becomes dominant in the FCFS system.

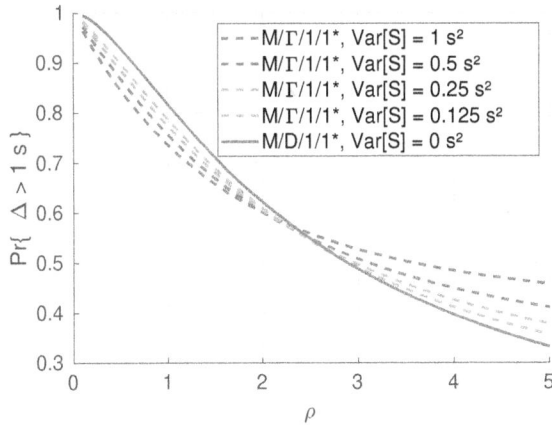

Figure 9: Effect of the variance of S on update outage probability.

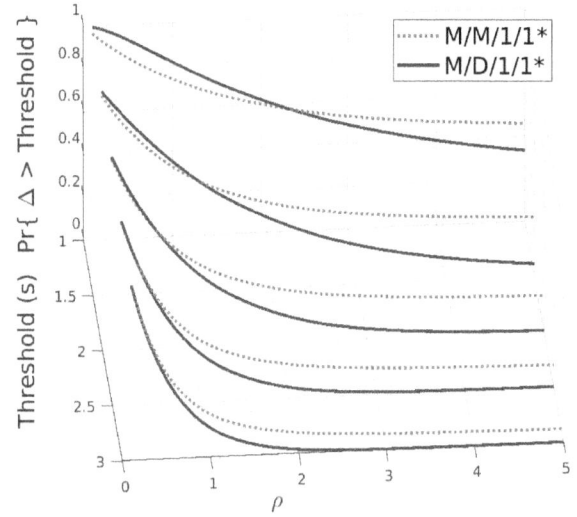

Figure 10: Update outage probability. M/D/1 LCFS with preemption (22) vs M/M/1 LCFS with preemption (16).

We now want to investigate the effects of the variance of S on the update outage probability. We already mentioned in Section 3.3.2 that the gamma distribution approximates a deterministic distribution as β approaches infinity, while maintaining the same expected value. As usual we fixed $E[S] = 1$ s, but we let α and β vary in order to obtain a different variance. In Figure 9 the update outage probability for a threshold of 1 s is presented. The M/D/1/1* system is the solid line, representing the limit when Var[S] is 0 s². Various M/Γ/1/1* with decreasing variances are presented as dashed lines. We notice that there is a break-point around a load of $\rho = 2.5$, where the M/D/1/1* system starts to have the lowest outage probability, while for lower loads the more variance seems to give lower outage. This means that, for example, instead of a TDMA system, which is modeled with a deterministic busy time distribution, given a load and a threshold, could be preferable to use a different access system with higher variance, such as a CSMA access system, in order to achieve a lower update outage probability.

In Figure 10, we plotted the outage probability for the M/D/1/1* versus the outage probability for the M/M/1/1* – that is simply the limiting case for a M/Γ/1/1* system with $\alpha = 1$ and $\beta = \mu$ jobs per second, where μ is the one defined in (10) – for different thresholds; we can see that the aforementioned behavior disappears for higher thresholds; this confirms that, when considering the update outage probability for different loads and thresholds, designers should be aware that higher variance does not necessarily mean worse performances.

Finally, as an example, we plotted the outage probability vs both the system load and the the threshold (Figure 11) for the M/D/1/1* system. It is a contour plot, where there are isolevel lines for the updated outage probability every 0.1. For very high loads, the outage update probability starts to fall under 50% only after a couple of inter-generation times. For lower inter-generation rates it becomes slightly worse. Figure 11 is an useful tool to design systems

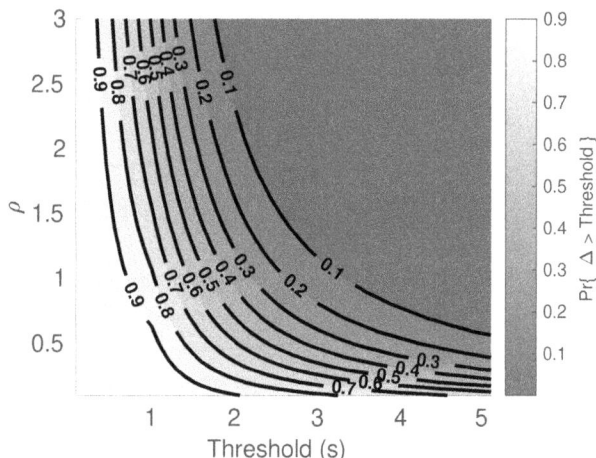

Figure 11: Update outage probability for an M/D/1 LCFS with preemption (22), contour plot.

by varying the system load in order to meet a statistical constraint on the update outage time.

5 CONCLUSIONS

In this paper we studied an M/G/1 LCFS system with preemption. We found a method to derive the closed expressions for the update outage probabilities for any distribution of the busy time and showed they are significantly lower than the ones in equivalent FCFS systems, especially at high loads. We also provided closed form expressions for the complete distribution of the AoI, pAoI and effective inter-generation times at the receiver end for various busy time distributions.

Of greater relevance, we discovered that using a busy time distribution with higher variance, for certain combinations of thresholds and loads, could bring benefits to the overall update outage probability. This means that, for example, for a TDMA system, which is modeled with a deterministic busy time distribution, given a load and a threshold, could, instead, be preferable to use a different access system with higher variance, such as a CSMA access system, in order to achieve a lower update outage probability.

Finally, the system we studied being an M/G/1 system, it is possible to plug in the busy time distribution of an access delay distribution already present in the literature, in order to study the update outage probability in different systems belonging to different wireless communication techniques and standards. This means that any aspect of the access process including channel loss, ARQ and access mechanism can be applied as long as the delay distribution is known.

ACKNOWLEDGMENTS

This work was supported by the "Excellence Center at Linköping-Lund in Information Technology (ELLIIT), Sweden".

REFERENCES

[1] T. Adame, A. Bel, B. Bellalta, J. Barcelo, and M. Oliver. 2014. IEEE 802.11ah: the WiFi approach for M2M communications. *IEEE Wireless Communications* 21, 6 (December 2014), 144–152. https://doi.org/10.1109/MWC.2014.7000982
[2] Imran Shafique Ansari, Ferkan Yilmaz, Mohamed-Slim Alouini, and Oğuz Kucur. 2017. New results on the sum of Gamma random variates with application to the performance of wireless communication systems over Nakagami-m fading channels. *Transactions on Emerging Telecommunications Technologies* 28, 1 (2017), e2912. https://doi.org/10.1002/ett.2912
[3] Harry Bateman. 1953. *Higher Transcendental Functions.* Vol. I. McGraw-Hill Book Company, Chapter: 5.3 - Definition of the G-function., 206 – 215.
[4] M. Batty, K. W. Axhausen, F. Giannotti, A. Pozdnoukhov, A. Bazzani, M. Wachowicz, G. Ouzounis, and Y. Portugali. 2012. Smart cities of the future. 214, 1 (December 2012), 481–518. https://doi.org/10.1140/epjst/e2012-01703-3
[5] J. P. Champati, H. Al-Zubaidy, and J. Gross. 2018. Statistical guarantee optimization for age of information for the D/G/1 queue. In *IEEE INFOCOM 2018 - IEEE Conference on Computer Communications Workshops (INFOCOM WKSHPS).* 130–135. https://doi.org/10.1109/INFCOMW.2018.8406909
[6] Cynthia Brewer, Mark Harrower and The Pennsylvania State University. 2013. *ColorBrewer.*
[7] R. Devassy, G. Durisi, G. C. Ferrante, O. Simeone, and E. Uysal-Biyikoglu. 2018. Delay and Peak-Age Violation Probability in Short-Packet Transmissions. In *2018 IEEE International Symposium on Information Theory (ISIT).* 2471–2475. https://doi.org/10.1109/ISIT.2018.8437671
[8] A. Franco, E. Fitzgerald, B. Landfeldt, N. Pappas, and V. Angelakis. 2016. LUPMAC: A cross-layer MAC technique to improve the age of information over dense WLANs. In *2016 23rd International Conference on Telecommunications (ICT).* 1–6. https://doi.org/10.1109/ICT.2016.7500469
[9] Y. Inoue, H. Masuyama, T. Takine, and T. Tanaka. 2017. The stationary distribution of the age of information in FCFS single-server queues. In *2017 IEEE International Symposium on Information Theory (ISIT).* 571–575. https://doi.org/10.1109/ISIT.2017.8006592
[10] F. Iradat and S. Ghani. 2010. Average end-to-end packet delay performance of IEEE 802.11 with Gamma distributed mean service time intervals. In *SoftCOM 2010, 18th International Conference on Software, Telecommunications and Computer Networks.* 27–34.
[11] Fredrik Johansson et al. 2018. *mpmath: a Python library for arbitrary-precision floating-point arithmetic (version 1.1.0).* http://mpmath.org/.
[12] Jonathan C. Lansey. 2015. *Beautiful and distinguishable line colors + colormap.*
[13] S. Kaul, R. Yates, and M. Gruteser. 2012. Real-time status: How often should one update?. In *2012 Proceedings IEEE INFOCOM.* 2731–2735. https://doi.org/10.1109/INFCOM.2012.6195689
[14] S. K. Kaul, R. D. Yates, and M. Gruteser. 2012. Status updates through queues. In *2012 46th Annual Conference on Information Sciences and Systems (CISS).* 1–6. https://doi.org/10.1109/CISS.2012.6310931
[15] Leonard Kleinrock. 1975. *Theory, Volume 1, Queueing Systems.* Wiley-Interscience, New York, NY, USA, Chapter: The queue M/G/1.
[16] E. Najm and R. Nasser. 2016. Age of information: The gamma awakening. In *2016 IEEE International Symposium on Information Theory (ISIT).* 2574–2578. https://doi.org/10.1109/ISIT.2016.7541764
[17] E. Najm and E. Telatar. 2018. Status updates in a multi-stream M/G/1/1 preemptive queue. In *IEEE INFOCOM 2018 - IEEE Conference on Computer Communications Workshops (INFOCOM WKSHPS).* 124–129. https://doi.org/10.1109/INFCOMW.2018.8406928
[18] T. Sakurai and H. L. Vu. 2007. MAC Access Delay of IEEE 802.11 DCF. *IEEE Transactions on Wireless Communications* 6, 5 (May 2007), 1702–1710. https://doi.org/10.1109/TWC.2007.360372
[19] RK Saxena. 1998. Functional relations involving generalized H-function. *Le Matematiche* 53, 1 (1998), 123–131.
[20] O. Tickoo and B. Sikdar. 2004. A queueing model for finite load IEEE 802.11 random access MAC. In *2004 IEEE International Conference on Communications (IEEE Cat. No.04CH37577),* Vol. 1. 175–179 Vol.1. https://doi.org/10.1109/ICC.2004.1312475
[21] András Varga. 2001. The OMNET++ discrete event simulation system. In *ESM'01.*
[22] H. L. Vu and T. Sakurai. 2006. Accurate delay distribution for IEEE 802.11 DCF. *IEEE Communications Letters* 10, 4 (April 2006), 317–319. https://doi.org/10.1109/LCOMM.2006.1613759
[23] Yang Yang and Tak-Shing Peter Yum. 2003. Delay distributions of slotted ALOHA and CSMA. *IEEE Transactions on Communications* 51, 11 (Nov 2003), 1846–1857. https://doi.org/10.1109/TCOMM.2003.819201

Stochastic Modeling and Simulation for Redundancy and Coexistence in Graphs Resulting from Log-Normal Shadowing

Steffen Böhmer, Daniel Schneider and Hannes Frey

{steffenboehmer,schneiderd,frey}@uni-koblenz.de

University of Koblenz-Landau, Germany

ABSTRACT

Recent studies have identified redundancy and coexistence as a supporting graph structure for building connected intersection free planar drawings in wireless network graphs. Empirical evidence suggests that under certain conditions these properties can be assumed to hold with high probability. In this paper we advance insight on these probabilities with a rigorous stochastic treatment studying randomly generated network graphs pertaining to the log-normal shadowing model. We derive nested integral expressions to compute probabilities of redundancy and coexistence numerically under the standard uncorrelated log-normal shadowing model. For a recent model extension including correlation among network links our findings provide a means for efficient stochastic simulation of these probabilities. We illustrate numerical and simulation application of the derived formulas with a comprehensive parameter study for redundancy and coexistence under correlated and uncorrelated log-normal shadowing modeled randomly generated graphs. We also demonstrate how far support for these properties can be improved by artificially cutting communication distance while keeping the network well connected in terms of percolation bounds.

CCS CONCEPTS

• **Networks** → **Ad hoc networks**; *Topology analysis and generation*; • **Mathematics of computing** → **Distribution functions**; • **Theory of computation** → **Random network models**.

KEYWORDS

redundancy, coexistence, log-normal shadowing, Poisson point process, percolation, stochastic analysis, stochastic simulation

ACM Reference Format:

Steffen Böhmer, Daniel Schneider and Hannes Frey. 2019. Stochastic Modeling and Simulation for Redundancy and Coexistence in Graphs Resulting from Log-Normal Shadowing. In *22nd Int'l ACM Conference on Modeling, Analysis and Simulation of Wireless and Mobile Systems (MSWiM '19), November 25–29, 2019, Miami Beach, FL, USA*. ACM, New York, NY, USA, 10 pages. https://doi.org/10.1145/3345768.3355933

1 INTRODUCTION

Construction of intersection free connected planar graph drawings is a fundamental building block for many algorithmic solutions for wireless multi-hop networks including sensor networks, sensor-actuator networks, and autonomous robots. Most prominent are localized geographic forwarding strategies for unicast [4, 11, 13], multicast [7, 25], geocast [27], anycast [21], mobicast [10], and broadcast [26, 28] (to mention a few out of many more publications which could be listed here). Other algorithmic solutions resorting to such intersection free drawings include void and boundary detection [6], distributed data storage [5, 24], tracking of mobile objects [30], localized address auto-configuration [14], and coordination of mobile sensors [29].

Many approaches for constructing intersection free drawings are based on removing edges from a given network graph and require that graph to be a unit disk graph (see for example [4, 9, 11, 15]). In such a graph two nodes are connected if and only if their euclidean distance is less or equal than a given unit disk radius. As this graph model hardly describes a realistic wireless network graph, the quasi unit disk graph model was introduced in [2] as a model extension. Here two nodes are connected if their euclidean distance is less or equal than a given minimum radius and not connected if their distance is more than a given maximum radius. In all other cases nodes may be connected or may be not connected. If the relation between maximum and minimum radius is less or equal than $\sqrt{2}$ and the graph is undirected, an intersection free subgraph can be found by edge removal and possible addition of virtual links. An algorithm on this was described in [2] and analyzed in [2, 12].

The concept of quasi unit disk graphs significantly reduces the gap between theoretical algorithmic research and practical applicability of such algorithms in real wireless networks. However, the model still requires a fixed minimum and maximum transmission range with a limited upper bounded relation. Moreover, virtual links are required in general to assure connectivity of the constructed intersection free graph. Constructing these virtual links requires message exchange with k hop neighbors, where k depends on the minimum distance between network nodes.

These limitations motivated the initial work published in [20, 23] asking for the underlying structural properties of unit disk graphs which actually assure that such a graph can be transformed into a intersection free subgraph by local rules. Two properties have been identified, the *redundancy property* as originally observed in [8] and defined in [23], and the *coexistence property* as observed and defined in [20]. From the same authors local algorithmic solutions for constructing intersection free subgraphs in networks satisfying redundancy and coexistence were introduced in [18–20, 23].

On the question how far intersection free subgraphs in real networks can be constructed – ideally based on local rules – the approaches described in [18–20] were in the same papers as well studied in network graphs resulting from the *log-normal shadowing* model. That model advances unit disk and quasi unit disk modeling by taking actual stochastic behaviour of wireless communication channels (here due to environmental clutter) into account.

Though log-normal shadowing generally does not assure redundancy and coexistence property to hold, surprisingly, the simulation studies so far suggest that these algorithms produce correct solutions (i.e. connected and intersection free subgraphs) in almost all cases; either directly [20] or by means of topological [18, 19] or geographic clustering [17].

These observations also motivated an algorithm independent simulation and empirical study [22] on the probability of redundancy and coexistence for networks pertaining to the log-normal shadowing model. On one hand the results reported there are promising and suggest that designing algorithms for graphs with redundancy and coexistence property is a promising link to narrow the gap between theoretic algorithmic research on constructing intersection free subgraphs and applicability of such algorithms in realistic wireless networks. On the other hand due to runtime and memory costs only a small set of parameters could be studied so far. This problem is aggravated if those properties are to be studied in large scale networks (and ideally in networks of arbitrary size) and even more aggravated when spatial correlations of communication links – considered here with *correlated log-normal shadowing* modeling as described in [1] – shall be taken into account.

Besides simulation, a pure formal stochastic analysis on redundancy and coexistence property is of particular interest. However, this quickly yields expressions which are hard to analyze just symbolically. For example, modeling links based on uncorrelated log-normal shadowing yields a "closed form" expression including the error function (tail distribution of a Gaussian random variable) [3]. Integrating over all possible node configurations and their link probabilities yields nested integral expressions over such error functions which can not be resolved further into a plain closed form. Moreover, when additionally taking spatial correlations among communication links into account, there is little hope to find a closed form expression which can be treated purely symbolic.

In this work we develop a hybrid approach between simulation and stochastic analysis. We analyze and describe a way to probabilistically characterize typical spatial node constellations for redundancy as well as coexistence property in arbitrary large network graphs. Then we exploit this result for an efficient way to sample node configurations (four sampled nodes involved in a constellation for redundancy and coexistence property, respectively) and to sample a network detail without the need to generate a large set of nodes to average over a whole randomly generated network graph. This allows for numerical evaluation in case of uncorrelated log-normal shadowing. For the correlated log-normal shadowing model it supports an efficient simulation method which significantly speeds up simulation time and reduces memory overhead while preserving the statistics of the whole network. It allows for an extensive parameter study – the second contribution of this paper – showing how far parameters of correlated and uncorrelated log-normal shadowing (path loss and log-normal variance) influence the probability that redundancy and coexistence are satisfied. In addition, by means of empirically determined percolation

bounds we study how far the communication range can artificially be cut to further improve the probability bounds on redundancy and coexistence while still keeping the network well connected.

The remainder of this paper is structured as follows. In the next section we define the notation, the mathematical graph model, and the properties to be studied here. We also provide a short overview on percolation which is used in connection with the simulation study. In section 3 we analyze typical spatial node constellations for redundancy and coexistence property when nodes are picked arbitrarily in randomly deployed networks. We then use that result in section 4 to describe an efficient way to simulate just the graph section of the nodes involved in the redundancy and coexistence property. We show then in section 5 results obtained from numerical evaluation of the derived integral expressions as well as results obtained from the described simulation method. We study in an extensive parameter range how far redundancy and coexistence can be assumed and at what point probability of these properties degrades. This is accompanied by a study on how far probability bounds of these properties can be improved by artificially cutting the transmission distance while still assuring percolation (a reasonable measure to characterize how far an arbitrary large stochastically behaving network keeps connectivity among many nodes). With section 6 we conclude our findings and point towards possible future research directions.

2 DEFINITIONS AND MODELS

2.1 Graph Properties

Let $G = (V, E)$ be an undirected graph consisting of node set V and edge set $E \subseteq V \times V$. We say two nodes u and v are *connected* if edge uv exists in E.

We consider the nodes of V to be located in $\mathbb{R}^2$ and edges uv to be drawn as line segments between u and v in $\mathbb{R}^2$. We say two edges intersect if they have one point in common which is different from their end points. We say three nodes u, v, w are forming a triangle $\nabla(u, v, w)$ in G if the edges uv, vw and wu exist in G.

We say two intersecting edges uv and wx in G satisfy the *redundancy property* if at least one edge end point in $S = \{u, v, w, x\}$ is connected to all the other nodes in S in G.

For any four nodes u, v, w, x in G with u, v, w forming a triangle $\nabla(u, v, w)$ in G and x lying inside of $\nabla(u, v, w)$ we say that these nodes satisfy the *coexistence property* if node x is connected to all triangle end points in G.

A sequence $v_1, v_2, \ldots, v_k$ of nodes in G where each subsequent nodes v_i and v_{i+1} are connected by an edge in E is a *path* between v_1 and v_k. We say a graph is *connected* if for each pair of nodes u and v in G there exists at least one path between u and v in G. We say a node is *isolated* if it is not connected to any other node in G. Obviously, a graph with at least one isolated node can not be connected.

2.2 Stochastic Network Graph Models

We consider networks with nodes randomly deployed in $\mathbb{R}^2$ according to a *homogeneous Poisson point process* Φ with *intensity* λ. The nodes are connected according to the *log-normal shadowing model* (LNS-model) as follows. We consider undirected communication links. The average received signal strength P_{RX}^{uv} in dBm of a transmission from node u to v (as well as from v to u) over euclidean distance $\|uv\|$ is given by

$$P_{RX}^{uv} = c - 10\alpha \log_{10}(\|uv\|/d_0) + X_\sigma^{uv} \qquad (1)$$

where $d_0 > 0$ is the reference distance, c the power received at reference distance, $\alpha > 1$ the path loss coefficient, and $X_\sigma^{uv} = X_\sigma^{vu}$ a Gaussian random variable with mean 0 and standard deviation $\sigma > 0$. Given a node configuration φ of Φ we sample a graph over φ either according to the *uncorrelated* or the *correlated* log-normal shadowing model.

In the uncorrelated model we consider each unordered node pair of nodes u and v from φ. We consider the euclidean distance $\|uv\|$ and sample the average received power (the local mean) according to the random variable P_{RX}^{uv} independently of all other nodes in φ. We say a link exists between u and v if $P_{RX}^{uv} \geq \theta$ for a fixed θ.

In the correlated model we take spatial correlations as derived in [1] into account. Given any finite set of nodes $\varphi = \{x_1, x_2, \ldots, x_n\}$ we consider for all possible pairs x_i and x_j with $i \neq j$ a multivariate Gaussian random variable consisting of the components $X_\sigma^{i,j}$ for $1 \leq i, j \leq n$ and $i \neq j$, where $X_\sigma^{i,j} = X_\sigma^{j,i}$ are Gaussian random variables with mean 0 and standard deviation $\sigma > 0$. Correlation among the variables $X_\sigma^{i,j}$ and $X_\sigma^{k,l}$ is given according the covariances (see equation (13) in [1])

$$\text{Cov}(X_\sigma^{i,j}, X_\sigma^{k,l}) = \frac{\sigma^2}{\delta\sqrt{\|x_i x_j\| \cdot \|x_k x_l\|}} \int_{L_{i,j}} \int_{L_{k,l}} e^{-\frac{\|uv\|}{\delta}} \, du \, dv$$

with a space constant $\delta > 0$ and $L_{i,j}$, $L_{k,l}$ representing the line segments between v_i to v_j and v_k to v_l, respectively. Basically, in that model the covariance depends on how close two links are located to each other (the mutual distances of the points visited by the two links). The closer the higher will be the correlation. Negative correlation does not exist here.

Existence of links between all possible unordered pairs of distinct nodes v_i and v_j from φ is determined by sampling all correlated $X_\sigma^{i,j}$ at once, computing the received signal strength $P_{RX}^{i,j} = P_{RX}^{v_i v_j}$ according to equation (1) and determining if $P_{RX}^{i,j} \geq \theta$ for θ fixed.

Let Ψ_c and Ψ_u denote the stochastic processes of the edges connecting the nodes in Φ according to the previously defined correlated and uncorrelated log-normal shadowing models. We use notation $\mathcal{G}_c = (\Phi, \Psi_c)$ and $\mathcal{G}_u = (\Phi, \Psi_u)$ accordingly to refer to the stochastic processes creating the graphs as defined. Note that we study graphs of arbitrary size. By definition $\mathcal{G}_c = (\Phi, \Psi_c)$ and $\mathcal{G}_u = (\Phi, \Psi_u)$ have a countably infinite node set with probability 1. We term randomly created graphs according to the log-normal shadowing model (uncorrelated and correlated) the LNS-model.

In addition we also consider distance restricted versions $\mathcal{G}_c^{(R)}$ and $\mathcal{G}_u^{(R)}$ of $\mathcal{G}_c$ and $\mathcal{G}_u$ defined by a maximum allowed communication distance R. Let $\mathcal{G} = (\Phi, \Psi)$ be any of both processes. The restricted version $\mathcal{G}^{(R)}$ is given by $(\Phi, \Psi^{(R)})$ with $\Psi^{(R)} = \{uv : uv \in \Psi \text{ and } \|uv\| \leq R\}$.

Finally, we also use as an auxiliary construct the graph $\mathcal{G}_{UDG}^{(R)}$ which consists of all nodes in Φ and all edges uv with $u, v \in \Phi$ and $\|uv\| \leq R$. We term randomly created graphs of that type the UDG model (unit disk graph model).

2.3 Percolation and Connectivity

Let $\mathcal{G}$ be any of the stochastic process $\mathcal{G}_c, \mathcal{G}_u \, \mathcal{G}_c^{(R)}, \mathcal{G}_u^{(R)}$ as defined before. It can be seen easily that for any given fixed parameter setting $\lambda > 0$, $d_0 > 0$, $\alpha > 1$, $\sigma > 0$, $\delta > 0$, c and θ the probability that a node may be isolated is greater than 0. Thus, with a countably infinite number of nodes, the probability to find a node in V which is isolated from all other nodes (and thus the graph being disconnected by definition) is 1. Thus, we need another measure to study how well the resulting graph instances are connected. Such measure is given by *percolation* bounds.

Given a graph G with a countably infinite node set V, we say $C \subseteq V$ is an *infinite connected component* if C is infinite and the induced subgraph on C is connected. The *percolation probability* is defined as the probability that the graph instances contain an infinite component.

Of interest in this work is an appropriate minimal setting of R such that the graph $\mathcal{G}^{(R)}$ percolates, i.e. the transition of $\mathcal{G}^{(R-\epsilon)}$ having percolation probability 0 to $\mathcal{G}^{(R)}$ having percolation probability 1.

3 ANALYSIS OF TYPICAL CONFIGURATIONS

3.1 Intersections in uncorrelated graphs

In this section we investigate the redundancy property in the randomly generated graphs $\mathcal{G}_u^{(R)}$ with a Poisson point process distributed node set. We are interested in the probability that an arbitrarily picked edge intersection is satisfying the redundancy property.

Since with probability 1 each intersection point is covered by at most (and hence exactly) two edges of the graph, each intersection is characterized by these two edges. Thus, sampling a random intersection is equivalent to sampling independently two random edges of the graph until we found a pair of intersecting edges. Of course the expected waiting time (i.e. the number of such sampling trials until we are successful) is infinite.

As we later on apply edge length distributions with sub exponential tail, we restrict our edge lengths to an arbitrary fixed R first. So the second edge can be assumed to be in an arbitrary large but finite neighbourhood Ω of the first edge and the expected waiting time gets finite. We will not find an intersection if the second edge would lie off Ω. By taking $\Omega \to \mathbb{R}^2$ we exploit the whole plane.

As we can move our observation window in a homogeneous Poisson point process wlog. to the first sampled edge, we furthermore can assume wlog. that the edge lies on the x axis. Let A be the random variable expressing the length of that edge.

Now the second edge is thrown uniformly at random into Ω. We first sample the edge length B i.i.d. to A. Since the length of the edge is fixed now, the edge is described by the position of one endpoint of the edge and the off-axis angle with respect to the x axis. Obviously the angle is uniformly distributed. The second edge is with probability 1 not parallel to the axis. So we can take the "lower" endpoint as our reference point and assume the angle Γ to be sampled uniformly from $(0, \pi)$. Now the reference endpoint is thrown uniformly at random into Ω.

Note that this could result in an edge, that leaves Ω. As Ω could be chosen large enough this edge would not intersect the first edge anyway, so we ignore this scenario, since we would discard this trial immediately.

Next we have to check if the two edges intersect (and discard otherwise). Obviously the two edges intersect iff the lower endpoint lies in the following parallelogram area (Fig. 1).

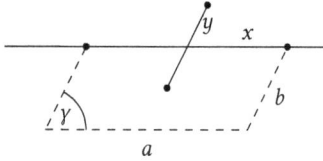

Figure 1: Parallelogram area required for an intersection.

Thus, the probability that the second edge intersects the first one is $\frac{AB \sin \Gamma}{|\Omega|}$ (i.e. the relation between parallelogram area and the whole area under consideration). Given any (restricted) edge length probability density $f_E^{(R)}(x)$ and using the probability above as thinning probability, we get the following density function for intersections:

$$\tilde{f}_X^{(R)}(a, b, \gamma) = \frac{1}{N_{\tilde{f}_X^{(R)}}} ab \sin(\gamma) f_E^{(R)}(a) f_E^{(R)}(b) \mathbb{1}_{\substack{a,b \in (0,R], \\ \gamma \in (0,\pi)}} \quad (2)$$

$N_{\tilde{f}_X^{(R)}}$ is the normalization as determined next. We will drop the indicator function from now on for notational simplicity. Note that the $1/|\Omega|$-factor is absorbed by the normalization constant:

$$N_{\tilde{f}_X^{(R)}} = \int_0^R \int_0^R \int_0^\pi ab \sin(\gamma) f_E(a) f_E(b) \mathrm{d}\gamma \, \mathrm{d}b \, \mathrm{d}a = 2\mathbb{E}[E^{(R)}]^2 \quad (3)$$

We can extend the calculations to the general (unrestricted) case if the limit $\lim_{R\to\infty} N_{\tilde{f}_X^{(R)}}$ exists, which is the case iff $\mathbb{E}[E^{(R)}] < \infty$.

Finally we have to introduce the exact position of the intersection on both edges. Since the position of the reference endpoint in the parallelogram is uniformly distributed it is joint uniformly distributed on both edges. Multiplying $\tilde{f}_X^{(R)}$ by the corresponding densities gives:

$$f_X^{(R)}(a, b, x, y, \gamma) = \frac{1}{N_{\tilde{f}_X^{(R)}}} \sin(\gamma) f_E^{(R)}(a) f_E^{(R)}(b) \mathbb{1}_{\substack{x \in (0,a), \\ y \in (0,b)}} \quad (4)$$

Again we will drop the notation of the indicator-functions but will apply them implicitly by appropriate integration bounds.

Note that integration over x and y results in $\tilde{f}_X^{(R)}$ and because of that the normalization factor remains the same.

By a, b, x, y, γ an intersection in the plane is entirely characterized. Let $p_{red}^{(R)}(a, b, x, y, \gamma)$ be the probability that a given intersection of that shape in a certain random graph model satisfies the redundancy-property. Thus, for the probability that a random intersection in a random graph model satisfies redundancy is

$$\int_0^R \int_0^R \int_0^\pi \int_0^a \int_0^b p_{red}^{(R)}(a, b, x, y, \gamma) f_X^{(R)}(a, b, x, y, \gamma) \mathrm{d}y \, \mathrm{d}x \, \mathrm{d}\gamma \, \mathrm{d}b \, \mathrm{d}a. \quad (5)$$

3.2 Distance to an arbitrary neighbor

The distribution of randomly picked intersections, randomly picked triangles as well as the derived probabilities on redundancy and co-existence all depend on the distribution of the length of a randomly picked edged.

We consider an arbitrary chosen node in a randomly generated graph (wlog. in the origin). For that node we select an arbitrary neighbor (provided one exists). We are interested in the distribution of the euclidean length of such arbitrary picked edge.

A homogeneous Poisson point process with density λ on a disk with radius R (centered at the origin) can be viewed as a two step process. At first we sample a Poisson-distributed number of nodes with mean $\lambda \pi R^2$. As a second step we position the nodes uniformly distributed into the disk. All at once or one by one. The probability that a randomly chosen node (say the first one) is thrown in a (smaller) disk centred at the origin with radius d is $\frac{\pi d^2}{\pi R^2}$. So the cumulative density function of the distance from a random point to the origin in a disk with radius R (and hence the distance between two points in a homogeneous Poisson point process with distance at most R) is $F_D^{(R)}(d) = \frac{d^2}{R^2}$. Differentiation yields the PDF (probability density function) $f_D^{(R)}(d) = \frac{2d}{R^2}$.

Assuming that the existence probability $p_E^{(R)}(d)$ of an edge (restricted on $(0, R]$) only depends on the distance d of its endpoints (which is the case in e.g. the restricted uncorrelated LNS-model), thinning yields the PDF of the distance E to a randomly selected neighbor in graph $\mathcal{G}_u^{(R)}$ and hence the probability density of the length of an arbitrary edge satisfies

$$f_E^{(R)}(d) = \frac{1}{N_E^{(R)}} d p_E^{(R)}(d). \quad (6)$$

Note again, the constant 2 and parameter R have been absorbed by the normalization constant $N_E^{(R)} = \int_0^R r p_E(r) \mathrm{d}r$. Furthermore, the distribution $f_E^{(R)}(d)$ can be extended to the entire plane if $\int_0^\infty r p_E(r) \mathrm{d}r < \infty$ (which is the case in the uncorrelated LNS-model). We have the following PDF $f_E(d)$ of the distance E to a randomly selected neighbor in $\mathcal{G}_u$

$$f_E(d) = \frac{1}{N_E} d p_E(d). \quad (7)$$

Note that as R tends to infinity, Ω has to be taken to the limit $\mathbb{R}^2$ as well. However, that is not of further interest as it immediately cancels out of our derivations in the first normalization step and hence the limiting process is independent of the choice of Ω.

Finally, with equation (4) we get

$$f_X^{(R)}(a, b, x, y, \gamma) = \frac{ab \sin(\gamma)}{2 {N_E^{(R)}}^2 \mathbb{E}[E^{(R)}]^2} p_E^{(R)}(a) p_E^{(R)}(b). \quad (8)$$

3.3 The redundancy probability

From now on we assume that all limiting distributions exist. So we will drop R from the notations to ease the presentation. All further steps hold for both the restricted and unrestricted case unless otherwise stated. After focusing on the f_X part of equation (5) in the previous part, we address $p_{red}(a, b, x, y, \gamma)$ now.

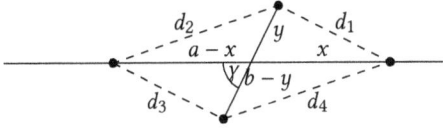

Figure 2: Tetragon to check for existence of edges

Assuming that our intersection exists, we now examine the probability that the edges $e_1, \ldots, e_4$ of the spanned tetragon exist (see Fig. 2). Since their existence probability only depends on the particular edge lengths d_i we need to derive them first. By the law of cosines and some basic angular transformations we get:

$$
\begin{pmatrix} d_1 \\ d_2 \\ d_3 \\ d_4 \end{pmatrix} = \begin{pmatrix} \sqrt{x^2 + y^2 - 2xy \cos \gamma} \\ \sqrt{(x-a)^2 + y^2 + 2(a-x)y \cos \gamma} \\ \sqrt{(x-a)^2 + (y-b)^2 - 2(a-x)(y-b) \cos \gamma} \\ \sqrt{x^2 + (y-b)^2 + 2x(y-b) \cos \gamma} \end{pmatrix} \quad (9)
$$

where d_i are functions of (a, b, x, y, γ).

Next we get the existence probabilities

$$
p_{E,i}(a, b, x, y, \gamma) = p_E(d_i(a, b, x, y, \gamma)).
$$

Since the redundancy property is satisfied iff from each pair of opposite edges one edge exists $((e_1 \vee e_3) \wedge (e_2 \vee e_4))$, and all of those existences are pairwise independent, we conclude:

$$
p_{red}(*) = (p_{E,1} + p_{E,3} - p_{E,1}p_{E,3})(p_{E,2} + p_{E,4} - p_{E,2}p_{E,4})(*) \quad (10)
$$

3.4 Triangles in uncorrelated graphs

For deriving the probability of coexistence property we have to characterize randomly picked triangles in our random graphs appropriately. Analogue to the redundancy derivation we now analyze the coexistence property. We will drop the (R)-index from the notation as we assume that all essential limits exist anyway but keep in mind that we do the calculations for the restricted case first and take the limit in the end.

We start once again by sampling one edge with length according to f_E. We sample immediately a second edge. Of course if we want to sample two edges sharing one endpoint their lengths are $A, B \sim E$ i.i.d. Furthermore, the angle Γ between those edges is uniformly distributed and independent of A and B. Because of symmetry we can once again wlog. restrict us to the case $\Gamma \sim unif((0, \pi))$.

Again we can assume wlog. that the first edge is part of the x axis and both edges' shared endpoint is the origin.

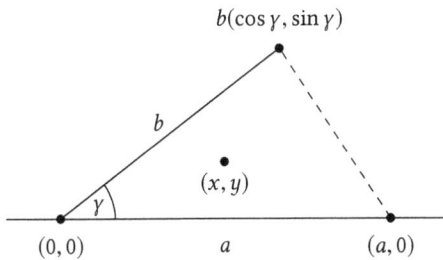

Figure 3: Construction of a randomly selected triangle

Of course we only get a triangle if the edge between $(A, 0)$ and $B(\cos \Gamma, \sin \Gamma)$ exists as well. We call its length $c(a, b, \gamma) = \sqrt{a^2 + b^2 - 2ab \cos \gamma}$. So the "two-incident-edges-distribution" is thinned by $p_E(c(a, b, \gamma))$.

Note that A, B and γ are now anything but distributed neither independently nor according to the original distributions. Obviously the third edge is not $\sim E$ distributed as well.

To get an instance for testing coexistence, we have to sample a fourth point. With probability $\frac{1/2AB \sin \Gamma}{|\Omega|}$ the node is located in the interior of the triangle and we get a proper instance. Note that only here the $R \to \infty$ process is necessary. So the total mass of coexistence instances is

$$
N_{\tilde{f}_\Delta} := \int_0^\infty \int_0^\infty \int_0^\pi \frac{1}{2} ab \sin(\gamma) f_E(a) f_E(b) p_E(c(a, b, \gamma)) d\gamma \, db \, da. \quad (11)
$$

Including the position of the interior point (x, y) we get the probability density function

$$
f_\Delta(a, b, x, y, \gamma) := \frac{1}{N_{\tilde{f}_\Delta}} f_E(a) f_E(b) p_E(c(a, b, \gamma)) \mathbb{1}(a, b, x, y, \gamma) \quad (12)
$$

with $\mathbb{1}(a, b, x, y, \gamma)$ being the indicator function on

$$
\left\{ \begin{aligned} & a > 0, b > 0, \gamma \in (0, \pi), y \in (0, b \sin \gamma), \\ & x \in \left(\frac{y}{\tan \gamma}, \frac{y}{\tan \gamma} + \left(1 - \frac{y}{b \sin \gamma} \right) a \right) \end{aligned} \right\}. \quad (13)
$$

Note that the surface $\frac{1}{2} ab \sin \gamma$ is absorbed by integrating over all possible interior points (whose total measure is obviously the surface of the triangle).

For the uncorrelated graph-model where the edge existence probability only depends on the distance we get

$$
f_\Delta(a, b, x, y, \gamma) = \frac{ab}{N_{\tilde{f}_\Delta}} p(\nabla) \mathbb{1}(a, b, x, y, \gamma) \quad (14)
$$

with $p(\nabla) = p_E(a) p_E(b) p_E(c(a, b, \gamma))$ being the existence probability of the triangle.

Let $p_{coex}(a, b, x, y, \gamma)$ be the probability that the respective instance of a triangle with a point in it satisfies the coexistence property. Thus, the probability that a random coexistence instance in a random graph model satisfies coexistence is

$$
\int_0^\infty \int_0^\infty \int_0^\pi \int_0^{b \sin \gamma} \int_{\frac{y}{\tan \gamma}}^{\frac{y}{\tan \gamma} + \left(1 - \frac{y}{b \sin \gamma} \right)} p_{coex}(a, b, x, y, \gamma)
$$

$$
\times f_\Delta(a, b, x, y, \gamma) dx \, dy \, d\gamma \, db \, da. \quad (15)
$$

3.5 The coexistence probability

Finally, we consider $p_{coex}(a, b, x, y, \gamma)$ assuming that the triangle exists and (x, y) is in the interior of it.

We get:

$$
\begin{pmatrix} d_5 \\ d_6 \\ d_7 \end{pmatrix} (a, b, x, y, \gamma) = \begin{pmatrix} \sqrt{x^2 + y^2} \\ \sqrt{(a-x)^2 + y^2} \\ \sqrt{(x - b \cos \gamma)^2 + (y - b \sin \gamma)^2} \end{pmatrix} \quad (16)
$$

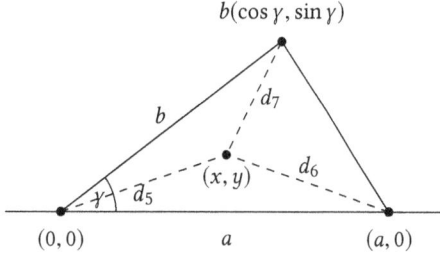

$b(\cos \gamma, \sin \gamma)$

Figure 4: Testing for coexistence property

We adopt the previous notation $p_{E,i}(*) = p_E(d_i(*))$. As all three interior edges have to exist to satisfy coexistence and their existence is independent, we conclude

$$p_{coex}(a,b,x,y,\gamma) = (p_{E,5}p_{E,6}p_{E,7})(a,b,x,y,\gamma) \quad (17)$$

3.6 The LNS-edge probability

Next we consider the probability of an edge with length d to exist in the LNS-model. We start with the unrestricted case $R = \infty$. By [3] we know that probability is (with reference distance $d_0 = 1m$)

$$p_E(d) = \frac{1}{2} - \frac{1}{2} \operatorname{erf}\left(\frac{10}{\sqrt{2}} \frac{\alpha}{\sigma} \log\left(\frac{d}{r_0}\right)\right) \quad (18)$$

with $r_0 = 10^{\frac{\theta-c}{10\alpha}}$. c and θ have been discussed in section 2.2. However, we will treat r_0 as arbitrary given. Note that the limiting case $\sigma \to 0$ yields the unit disk graph $\mathcal{G}_{UDG}^{(r_0)}$. As α, σ and r_0 are fixed for the moment, we get a fixed edge distribution and skip the index E to simplify the notation.

We substitute $d' = d/r_0$ and get

$$p(d) = p(d'r_0) = \frac{1}{2} - \frac{1}{2} \operatorname{erf}\left(\frac{10}{\sqrt{2}} \frac{\alpha}{\sigma} \log\left(\frac{d'r_0}{r_0}\right)\right) \quad (19)$$

$$= \frac{1}{2} - \frac{1}{2} \operatorname{erf}\left(\frac{10}{\sqrt{2}} \frac{\alpha}{\sigma} \log(d')\right) =: p'(d'). \quad (20)$$

Thus, the existence probability of an edge depends only on its relative length d'.

Note that for substitutions $a' = a/r_0$ and $b' = b/r_0$, all other possible edge lengths in the previous sections are scaled as well. For example for the length $c(a,b,\gamma)$ of the third triangle edge in 3.4 we get:

$$c(a'r_0, b'r_0, \gamma) = \sqrt{(a'r_0)^2 + (b'r_0)^2 - 2(a'r_0)(b'r_0)\cos\gamma} \quad (21)$$

$$= r_0\sqrt{a'^2 + b'^2 - 2a'b'\cos\gamma} = r_0 c(a', b', \gamma) \quad (22)$$

So for the existence probability of this edge we get

$$p(c(a,b,\gamma)) = p'(c(a',b',\gamma)). \quad (23)$$

Analogously the existence probabilities for all d_i's from sections 3.3 and 3.5 are transformed in the same way if we also substitute $x' = x/r$ and $y' = y/r$. So the probabilities p_{coex} and p_{red} are transformed in the same way. We get

$$p_{coex}(a,b,x,y,\gamma) = p'_{coex}(a',b',x',y',\gamma) \quad (24)$$

$$p_{red}(a,b,x,y,\gamma) = p'_{red}(a',b',x',y',\gamma). \quad (25)$$

By applying the substitutions to (5) one can derive:

$$\frac{\int_0^\infty \int_0^\infty \int_0^\pi \int_0^a \int_0^b p_{red}(a,b,x,y,\gamma) p(a)p(b)ab\sin\gamma\,dy\,dx\,d\gamma\,db\,da}{\int_0^\infty \int_0^\infty \int_0^\pi \int_0^a \int_0^b p(a)p(b)ab\sin\gamma\,dy\,dx\,d\gamma\,db\,da} \quad (26)$$

$$= \frac{\int_0^\infty \int_0^\infty \int_0^\pi \int_0^{a'} \int_0^{b'} p'_{red}(*')p'(a')p'(b')a'b'r_0^6\sin\gamma\,dy'\,dx'\,d\gamma\,db'\,da'}{\int_0^\infty \int_0^\infty \int_0^\pi \int_0^{a'} \int_0^{b'} p'(a')p'(b')a'b'r_0^6\sin\gamma\,dy'\,dx'\,d\gamma\,db'\,da'}. \quad (27)$$

As the r_0^6-factor cancels out, we get an expression that does not depend on r_0. Furthermore, edge existence and hence the redundancy probability depends only on the quotient $\frac{\sigma}{\alpha}$. The same transformation holds for coexistence.

3.7 The restricted LNS-model

Now we get back to the restricted LNS model that is induced by the edge existence probability $p_E^{(R)}(d) := p_E(d) \mathbb{1}_{d \le R}$. Executing the substitution steps from section 3.6 leads to similar expressions. We get $p_E^{(R)'}(d') = p'_E(d') \mathbb{1}_{d' \le R/r_0}$. So the coexistence and redundancy probabilities in the restricted model depend on both ratios, $\frac{\sigma}{\alpha}$ and $\frac{R}{r_0}$. Note that the limiting case $R \to \infty$ yields (27) and the respective coexistence expression again.

4 AN EFFICIENT SIMULATION METHOD

Based on the result of the analysis of the previous section an efficient way to simulate an arbitrary chosen four node configuration for testing relative frequency of redundancy and coexistence property statistically can be derived.

For the uncorrelated log-normal shadowing which allows for independent sampling of graph edges, the analytic result translates straight forward into the following simulation pseudo code.

Let $f_E^{(R)}(d)$ be the probability density of the edge length of an arbitrarily picked neighbor according to the uncorrelated log-normal shadowing model restricted to a maximum edge length R (see section 3.2 for the derivation of that density function). Set R to ∞ in case the simulation shall be executed without such restriction on R. With that we define the algorithms depicted in Alg. 1 and 2.

For the correlated log-normal shadowing we have to sample four randomly picked nodes similar as described by the previous described algorithms. We consider here the probability density $f_D^{(R)}(d)$ of the distance to an arbitrarily picked node in a Poisson point process having maximum distance $0 < R < \infty$ (see section 3.2 for the derivation of that density function).

For the generated nodes all potential links are then sampled at once according to the correlated log-normal shadowing model. The sample is discarded if it did not yield the configurations of two intersecting edges or three edges forming a triangle, respectively. The procedure is summarized in Alg. 3 and 4.

Note that for algorithms 3 and 4 the maximum radius R is a critical parameter which needs to be adjusted appropriately. If R

Algorithm 1 Sampling an arbitrarily picked intersection in the uncorrelated log-normal shadowing model

---

1: sample independently two edge lengths a and b according to $f_E^{(R)}(d)$.
2: sample angle γ uniformly distributed in $(0, \pi)$
3: sample uniformly distributed the intersection point $x \in (0, a)$ on edge of length a
4: sample uniformly distributed the intersection point $y \in (0, b)$ on edge of length b
5: Define with a, b, γ, x and y the edges $e_1 = u_1 v_1$ and $e_2 = u_2 v_2$ with end point positions as depicted in Fig. 1.
6: sample independently existence $\beta_1, \beta_2, \beta_3, \beta_4$ of edges $u_1 u_2$, $u_1 v_2$, $v_1 u_2$, $v_1 v_2$ according to the log-normal shadowing model (see eqn. (18))
7: $s \leftarrow ab \sin \gamma$ of the parallelogram defined by a, b and γ
8: **return** $(s, (\beta_1 \vee \beta_3) \wedge (\beta_2 \vee \beta_4))$

Algorithm 2 Sampling an arbitrarily picked triangle with interior point in the uncorrelated log-normal shadowing model

---

1: sample independently two edge lengths a and b according to $f_E^{(R)}(d)$.
2: **if** $a + b \leq R$ **then**
3:     sample angle γ uniformly distributed in $(0, \pi)$
4: **else**
5:     sample angle γ uniformly distributed in $(0, \arccos(\frac{1}{2}(\frac{a}{b} + \frac{b}{a} + \frac{R^2}{ab})))$
6: **end if**
7: Define with a, b, γ, the edges $e_1 = u_1 v_1$ and $e_2 = u_2 v_2$ with end point positions $u_1 = u_2 = (0,0)$ $v_1 = (a, 0)$ and $v_2 = b \cdot (\cos \gamma, \sin \gamma)$ as depicted in Fig. 4.
8: sample a point $p = (x, y)$ uniformly distributed in the triangle formed by e_1 and e_2
9: sample independently existence $\beta_1, \beta_2, \beta_3$ of edges pu_1, pv_1, pv_2 according to the log-normal shadowing model (see eqn. (18))
10: $s \leftarrow (\frac{1}{2} ab \sin \gamma)(p_E^{(R)}(\sqrt{a^2 + b^2 - 2ab \cos \gamma}))$
11: **return** $(s, \beta_1 \wedge \beta_2 \wedge \beta_3)$

Algorithm 3 Sampling an arbitrarily picked intersection in the correlated log-normal shadowing model

---

1: **repeat**
2:     create points u_1, v_1, u_2, v_2 as described in Alg. 1 but using the edge length distribution $f_D^{(R)}(d)$
3:     sample existence $\beta_1, \ldots, \beta_6$ of all six potential edges over u_1, v_1, u_2, v_2 according to the correlated log-normal shadowing model (as described in section 2.2)
4:     Let β_5 and β_6 represent potential existence of edges $u_1 v_1$ and $u_2 v_2$ (i.e. the intersection under consideration)
5: **until** $\beta_5 \wedge \beta_6$
6: $s \leftarrow ab \sin \gamma$ of the parallelogram defined by a, b and γ
7: **return** $(s, (\beta_1 \vee \beta_3) \wedge (\beta_2 \vee \beta_4))$

Algorithm 4 Sampling an arbitrarily picked triangle with interior point in the correlated log-normal shadowing model

---

1: **repeat**
2:     create points u_1, v_1, v_2, p as described in Alg. 2 but using the edge length distribution $f_D^{(R)}$
3:     sample existence $\beta_1, \ldots, \beta_6$ of all six potential edges over u_1, v_1, v_2, p according to the correlated log-normal shadowing model (as described in section 2.2)
4:     Let β_4, β_5 and β_6 represent potential existence of edges $u_1 v_1$ $u_1 v_2$ and $v_1 v_2$ (i.e. the triangle under consideration)
5: **until** $\beta_4 \wedge \beta_5 \wedge \beta_6$
6: $s \leftarrow (\frac{1}{2} ab \sin \gamma)(p_E^{(R)}(\sqrt{a^2 + b^2 - 2ab \cos \gamma}))$
7: **return** $(s, \beta_1 \wedge \beta_2 \wedge \beta_3)$

---

is chosen too large, sampling arbitrarily picked intersections or triangles may require many trials. If R is chosen very small, success rate of sampling a triangle will be high. However, then we will neglect the cases with very large edges which may have statistical relevance.

In the simulation study discussed in the next section we adjust R such that on average a certain high percentage (e.g. 95% here) of neighbor nodes in the uncorrelated log-normal shadowing model has distance less or equal to R.

For all four described sampling methods the relative frequency of redundancy and coexistence can then be determined by n independent simulation runs. In the following we describe an algorithm which covers generically all before mentioned sampling algorithms Alg. 1, 2, 3, and 4.

Algorithm 5 Determining the relative frequency of redundancy/coexistence in the uncorrelated/correlated log-normal shadowing model

---

1: $r \leftarrow 0$
2: $c \leftarrow 0$
3: **for** n times **do**
4:     $(s, \beta) \leftarrow$ sampling result of the considered algorithm Alg. 1, 2, 3, or 4
5:     $c \leftarrow c + s$ ▷ Note, $s \in \mathbb{R}^+$
6:     $r \leftarrow r + s\beta$ ▷ Note, $\beta \in \{0 = \text{false}, 1 = \text{true}\}$
7: **end for**
8: **return** r/c

---

5 EVALUATION

5.1 Numerical evaluation with σ / α

As we have seen in section 3.6 the probability of redundancy and coexistence in the uncorrelated log-normal model only depends on the quotient $\frac{\sigma}{\alpha}$. Figure 5 shows a numerical evaluation of expression (27) for redundancy and its counterpart for coexistence over σ / α. The evaluation is without any restriction on a maximum communication distance.

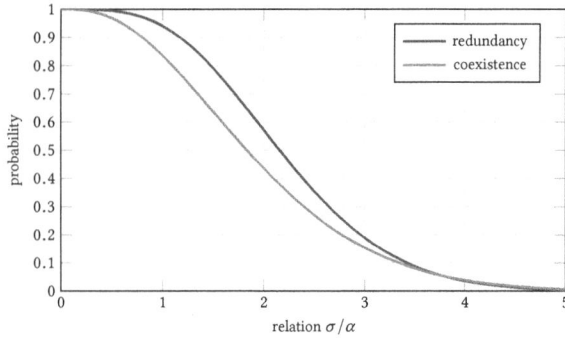

Figure 5: Probability of redundancy and coexistence over σ/α for $R = \infty$.

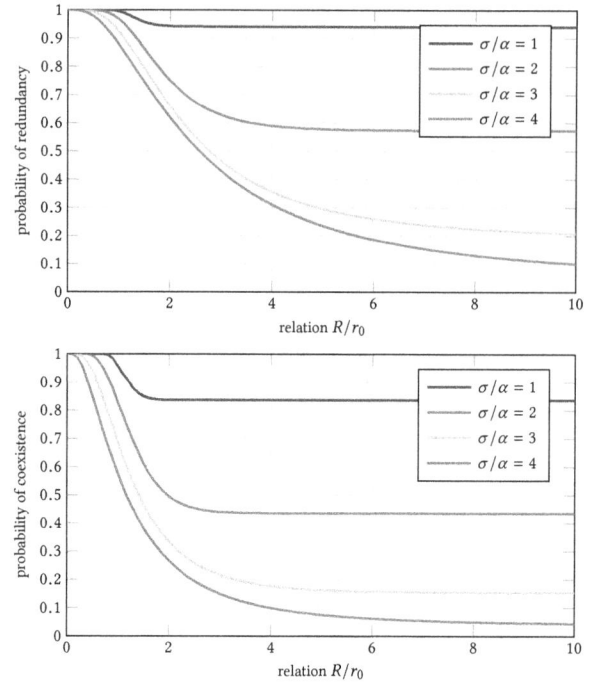

Figure 6: Probability of redundancy and coexistence for different σ/α over R/r_0.

As can be seen (resp. numerically derived), redundancy holds approximately between 97.11% to 100% for a relation $\sigma/\alpha \leq 1$. From there on probability begins to decrease significantly. For co-existence we observe that for $\sigma/\alpha \leq 1$ the probability ranges from approximately 87.55% to 100%.

The reason why coexistence performs worse than redundancy is due to the fact that this property requires exactly three potential edges to exists. For redundancy there is a choice of edges. Only one node has to be connected to all others (i.e. two additional edges from four possible edge pairs have to exists). The remaining potential edges may or may not exist.

In conclusion, given a target probability regarding redundancy and coexistence, higher path loss will support higher variation of log-normal shadowing.

5.2 Numerical evaluation with R/r_0

The numerical evaluation result suggests that higher probabilities for redundancy and coexistence can only be assumed for $\sigma/\alpha \leq 1$. The question arises what means are possible to improve probabilities when this relation can not be met by a given communication system. In the following we study the effect of artificially limiting a node's communication range up to a maximum communication distance R. Note, we are not reducing transmit power here. We just erase all communication links which are larger than a given R. This is for example possible if location information of the nodes is available.

Figure 6 shows the numeric results we obtain from plotting equation (27) for redundancy and its counterpart for coexistence when setting the relation σ/α fixed and plotting over the relation of R/r_0. Here R/r_0 is the factor of how far R is above or below the average maximum communication distance r_0 under the uncorrelated log-normal shadowing model (i.e. maximum communication distance in the area mean).

Depicted are plots for $\sigma/\alpha = 1, 2, 3, 4$ in the order from top to bottom. When R increases, the probabilities tend to the probabilities already discussed in the previous section 5.1. For example, the upper most curve (i.e. $\sigma/\alpha = 1$) tends to approximately 97.11% for redundancy and approximately 87.55% for coexistence as observed for $\sigma/\alpha = 1$ in the previous section.

Of particular interest is how far probabilities change if the artificially set maximum communication distance is reduced. For redundancy property we observe that for $\sigma/\alpha \leq 4$ the probability becomes more than 95% when setting R such that $R/r_0 = 1$ (i.e. setting R to the maximum communication distance in the area mean). For $\sigma/\alpha \leq 2$ it is even approximately 100% in this case.

Similar to the observation in section 5.1 we see that compared to redundancy the probability for coexistence drops faster.

Decreasing R further eventually yields probability 100% in all cases. With the smallest σ/α relation probability 100% is achieved the fastest when decreasing R.

5.3 Simulation with correlated LNS

The numerical evaluation based on our current findings requires the uncorrelated log-normal shadowing model. The properties we study here yield spatially collocated links. In practice, collocated links are typically correlated since they are subject to similar environmental clutter. The question thus arises how far the results are influenced by such correlation. We study the potential effect by means of simulation based on the correlated log-normal shadowing model introduced at the beginning (Sec. 2.2). We set the correlation space constant δ to 0.3 meter as it was empirically justified in [1].

We used Alg. 3 and 4 with different α and σ settings to generate the plots depicted in Fig. 7. Opposed to the numerical evaluation for the uncorrelated case in the previous section, for the correlated case the path loss coefficient α has an influence on the spatial correlation. Thus, simulations and plots are presented over σ for different fixed α settings. Since parameter settings for lower redundancy/coexistence

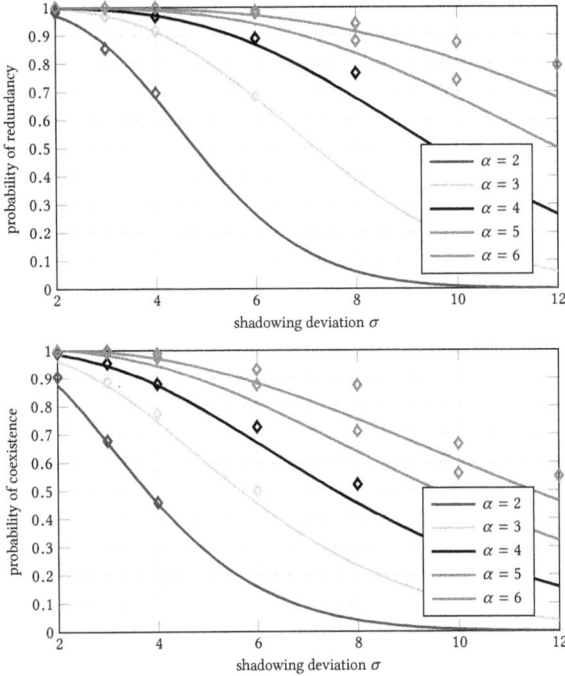

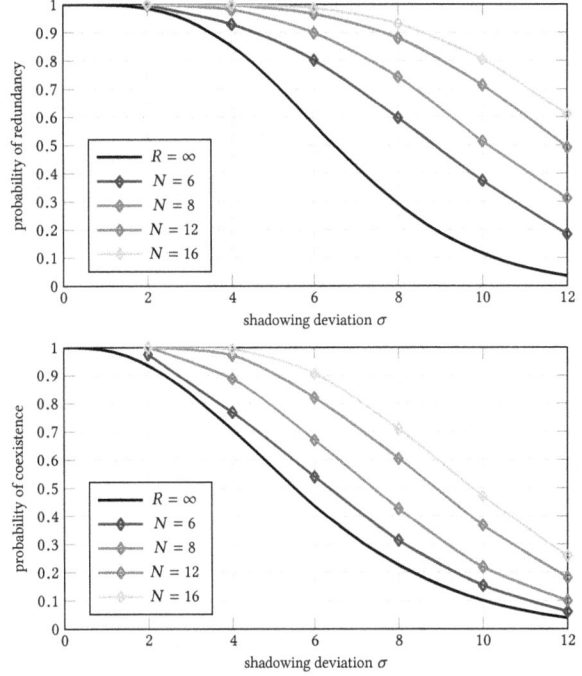

Figure 7: Probability of redundancy and coexistence over σ for fixed α. The uncorrelated values (the curves) are obtained numerically while the correlated ones (the dots above of the curves) by simulation.

Figure 8: Probability of redundancy and coexistence over σ at the empirical percolation radius $\bar{R}$ for fixed $\alpha = 3$ and varying average number N of neighbors.

probability yield many simulation trials for finding valid instances, we stopped simulations below success probability 0.65 / 0.45.

We observe a visible positive effect of correlation on redundancy and coexistence. What can be observed as well, the improvement due to correlation becomes more pronounced, when α is increased. This is due to the fact that increasing path loss will decrease the graphs edge lengths. Thus, for larger α intersecting edges are typically shorter as well as triangles will be smaller, i.e. there will be more spatial correlation among intersecting edges or edges forming a triangle. Correlation is positive which raises the probability that other edges required for redundancy/coexistence exist.

5.4 Exploiting percolation bounds

For any $\sigma/\alpha > 0$ reducing the relation $R/r_0 > 0$ eventually will reach probability of 100% both for redundancy and coexistence. Obviously, when R becomes 0 no links exist and thus any property is satisfied on the empty set. Thus, it is of particular interest how far the relation R/r_0 can be reduced while keeping the network well connected on one hand and on the other hand how far probability of redundancy and coexistence can be obtained then.

We determined a threshold value $\bar{R}$ for given σ, α and r_0 according to the simulation method described in [16]. For a given λ of the underlying homogeneous point process we determine a circle C such that on average 1000 nodes are located in C. We sample 100 point process instances. For each instance we generate the graph $G_u^{(R)}$ according to the uncorrelated log-normal shadowing model.

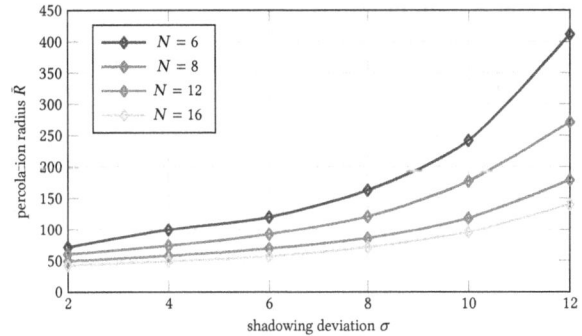

Figure 9: Empirical percolation radius $\bar{R}$ over σ for $\alpha = 3$ and different average number N of neighbors.

For that graph we determine R such that the number of nodes in the largest connected component of $G_u^{(R)}$ is 99% of the number of nodes in the largest component in the graph $G_u^{(\infty)}$. Averaging the measured values R over the 100 instances yields the average threshold value $\bar{R}$ we term percolation radius in the following.

Figure 9 shows the empirically determined values $\bar{R}$ for increasing σ and different densities of the underlying Poisson point process expressed as the expected number of neighbors in the uncorrelated log-normal shadowing model.

Figure 8 shows example numerical plots for fixed $\alpha = 3$ and varying σ. Here again, we plot over sigma and not σ/α since both path loss and shadowing variation have an influence on the empirical percolation radius $\bar{R}$.

As can be seen, by increasing intensity of the underlying Poisson point process (normalized to an average number of neighbors here) both redundancy and coexistence can visibly be improved. For example, for obtaining redundancy property with approximately 100%, σ can be increased from 2 to 6 when setting R to the approximate percolation radius for an average number of neighbors of 16. A similar trend can be observed for coexistence as σ can be increased from 1 to 4 for the same offset.

6   CONCLUSION AND FUTURE WORK

We studied the probability of the structural graph properties redundancy and coexistence in a random setting. In this study, nodes are placed according to a homogeneous Poisson process and nodes are connected according to an uncorrelated and correlated log-normal shadowing model. This model is reasonable for networks consisting of randomly and statically deployed nodes on a plane subject to signal attenuation due to random environmental clutter. We derived expressions for numerical evaluation under the uncorrelated model and an efficient simulation method for the correlated one. We illustrated with a comprehensive numerical and simulation study how far the properties can be assumed to hold with high probability and when randomness renders that assumption invalid.

The expressions and methods studied here can be extended in several future directions. Instead of a homogeneous Poisson point process other point processes can be considered. The analysis then will be more intricate. Additionally, of interest is further research on how far as well the correlated model from [1] can be treated analytically here. This requires extension of our analysis with respect to the Gaussian random field used in that model. Finally, we illustrated by simulation that percolation bounds can be exploited to improve the properties to hold. This and also other means of restructuring the graph for supporting redundancy and coexistence can be studied analytically in future work. Other means includes for example geographical clustering or k-hop clustering as it was already applied and studied empirically in [17, 19, 22].

ACKNOWLEDGMENTS

This work is funded in part by the DFG grants FR 2978/1-2 and FR 2978/2-1.

REFERENCES

[1] Piyush Agrawal and Neal Patwari. 2009. Correlated Link Shadow Fading in Multi-Hop Wireless Networks. *IEEE Transactions on Wireless Communications* 8, 8 (2009), 4024–4036.
[2] Lali Barrière, Pierre Fraigniaud, Lata Narayanan, and Jaroslav Opatrny. 2003. Robust position-based routing in wireless ad hoc networks with irregular transmission ranges. *Wireless Communications and Mobile Computing* 3, 2 (2003), 141–153.
[3] Christian Bettstetter and Christian Hartmann. 2005. Connectivity of wireless multihop networks in a shadow fading environment. *Wireless Networks* 11, 5 (2005), 571–579.
[4] Prosenjit Bose, Pat Morin, Ivan Stojmenović, and Jorge Urrutia. 2001. Routing with Guaranteed Delivery in Ad Hoc Wireless Networks. *Wireless Networks* 7, 6 (nov 2001), 609–616.
[5] Y. Deng and I. Stojmenovic. 2009. Partial Delaunay Triangulations Based Data-Centric Storage and Routing with Guaranteed Delivery in Wireless Ad Hoc and Sensor Networks. In *2009 Mexican International Conference on Computer Science.* 24–32.
[6] Qing Fang, Jie Gao, and L. J. Guibas. 2004. Locating and bypassing routing holes in sensor networks. In *IEEE INFOCOM 2004*, Vol. 4. 2458–2468 vol.4.
[7] H. Frey, F. Ingelrest, and D. Simplot-Ryl. 2008. Localized minimum spanning tree based multicast routing with energy-efficient guaranteed delivery in ad hoc and sensor networks. In *2008 International Symposium on a World of Wireless, Mobile and Multimedia Networks*. 1–8.
[8] Jie Gao, Leonidas J Guibas, John Hershberger, Li Zhang, and An Zhu. 2001. Geometric spanner for routing in mobile networks. In *Proceedings of the 2nd ACM international symposium on Mobile ad hoc networking & computing - MobiHoc '01*.
[9] Jie Gao, L. J. Guibas, J. Hershberger, Li Zhang, and An Zhu. 2005. Geometric spanners for routing in mobile networks. *IEEE Journal on Selected Areas in Communications* 23, 1 (Jan 2005), 174–185.
[10] Qingfeng Huang, Chenyang Lu, and G. C. Roman. 2004. Reliable mobicast via face-aware routing. In *IEEE INFOCOM 2004*, Vol. 3. 2108–2118 vol.3.
[11] Brad Karp and H. T. Kung. 2000. GPSR: Greedy Perimeter Stateless Routing for Wireless Networks. In *Proceedings of the 6th Annual International Conference on Mobile Computing and Networking*. 243–254.
[12] Fabian Kuhn, Roger Wattenhofer, and Aaron Zollinger. 2008. Ad hoc networks beyond unit disk graphs. *Wireless Networks* 14, 5 (oct 2008), 715–729.
[13] F. Kuhn, R. Wattenhofer, and A. Zollinger. 2008. An Algorithmic Approach to Geographic Routing in Ad Hoc and Sensor Networks. *IEEE/ACM Transactions on Networking* 16, 1 (Feb 2008), 51–62.
[14] X. Li, Y. Deng, V. Narasimhan, A. Nayak, and I. Stojmenovic. 2010. Localized address autoconfiguration in wireless ad hoc networks. In *2010 International Conference on Wireless Communications Signal Processing (WCSP)*. 1–6.
[15] Xiang-Yang Li, G. Calinescu, and Peng-Jun Wan. 2002. Distributed construction of a planar spanner and routing for ad hoc wireless networks. In *Proceedings.Twenty-First Annual Joint Conference of the IEEE Computer and Communications Societies*, Vol. 3. 1268–1277 vol.3.
[16] Yujun Li and Yaling Yang. 2010. Asymptotic connectivity of large-scale wireless networks with a log-normal shadowing model. In *IEEE Vehicular Technology Conference*. IEEE, 1–5.
[17] Emi Mathews. 2012. Planarization of Geographic Cluster-based Overlay Graphs in Realistic Wireless Networks. In *2012 Ninth International Conference on Information Technology - New Generations*. 95–101.
[18] Emi Mathews and Hannes Frey. 2010. Topological Cluster Based Geographic Routing in Multihop Ad Hoc Networks. In *Proceedings of the Fourth International Conference on Mobile Ubiquitous Computing, Systems, Services and Technologies (UBICOMM)*. Florence, Italy, 342–345.
[19] Emi Mathews and Hannes Frey. 2011. A Localized Planarization Algorithm for Realistic Wireless Networks. In *Proceedings of the 11th IEEE International Symposium on a World of Wireless, Mobile and Multimedia Networks (WoWMoM)*.
[20] Emi Mathews and Hannes Frey. 2012. A Localized Link Removal and Addition Based Planarization Algorithm. In *Proceedings of the 13th International Conference on Distributed Computing and Networking (ICDCN)*. 337–350.
[21] N. Mitton, D. Simplot-Ryl, and I. Stojmenovic. 2009. Guaranteed Delivery for Geographical Anycasting in Wireless Multi-Sink Sensor and Sensor-Actor Networks. In *IEEE INFOCOM 2009*. 2691–2695.
[22] Florentin Neumann, Daniel Vivas Estevao, Frank Ockenfeld, Jovan Radak, and Hannes Frey. 2016. Short Paper: Structural Network Properties for Local Planarization of Wireless Sensor Networks. In *Proceedings of the 15th International Conference on Ad-Hoc Networks and Wireless (ADHOC-NOW 2016)*, Vol. 9724. 229–233.
[23] Sumesh J Philip, Joy Ghosh, Hung Q Ngo, and Chunming Qiao. 2006. Routing on Overlay Graphs in Mobile Ad Hoc Networks. In *Proceedings of the IEEE Global Communications Conference, Exhibition & Industry Forum (GLOBECOM'06)*.
[24] Sylvia Rathnasamy, Brad Krap, Scott Shenker, Deborah Estrin, Ramesh Govindan, Li Yin, and Fang Yu. 2003. Data-Centric Storage in Sensornets with GHT, A Geographic Hash Table. *Mobile Networks and Applications* 8, 4 (Aug 2003), 427–442.
[25] Juan A. Sanchez, Pedro M. Ruiz, Jennifer Liu, and Ivan Stojmenovic. 2007. Bandwidth-Efficient Geographic Multicast Routing Protocol for Wireless Sensor Networks. *IEEE Sensors Journal* 7, 5 (may 2007), 627–636.
[26] Mahtab Seddigh, Julio Solano González, and Ivan Stojmenovic. 2001. RNG and Internal Node Based Broadcasting Algorithms for Wireless One-to-one Networks. *SIGMOBILE Mobile Computing and Communications Review* 5, 2 (April 2001), 37–44.
[27] I. Stojmenovic. 2004. Geocasting with guaranteed delivery in sensor networks. *IEEE Wireless Communications* 11, 6 (Dec 2004), 29–37.
[28] Ivan Stojmenovic, Mahtab Seddigh, and Jovisa Zunic. 2002. Dominating Sets and Neighbor Elimination-Based Broadcasting Algorithms in Wireless Networks. *IEEE Transactions on Parallel and Distributed Systems* 13, 1 (2002), 14–25.
[29] Jindong Tan. 2008. *A Scalable Graph Model and Coordination Algorithms for Mobile Sensor Networks*. Springer US, Boston, MA, 65–83.
[30] Hua-Wen Tsai, Chih-Ping Chu, and Tzung-Shi Chen. 2007. Mobile Object Tracking in Wireless Sensor Networks. *Computer Communications* 30, 8 (June 2007), 1811–1825.

Received Total Wideband Power Data Analysis

Multiscale wavelet analysis of RTWP data in a 3G network

John Garrigan
ARC-SYM Research Group
Dublin City University
Glasnevin, Dublin 9, Ireland
john.garrigan4@mail.dcu.ie

Martin Crane
ARC-SYM Research Group
Dublin City University
Glasnevin, Dublin 9, Ireland
martin.crane@dcu.ie

Marija Bezbradica
ARC-SYM Research Group
Dublin City University
Glasnevin, Dublin 9, Ireland
marija.bezbradica@dcu.ie

ABSTRACT

Received total wideband power (RTWP) data is a measurement of the wanted and unwanted power levels received by a 3G radio base station (RBS) and is a concise indicator of uplink network performance. Using a statistical physics approach, we aim to detect periods of unusual activity between cells by assessing a sample of RTWP measurement data from a live network. Using wavelet correlation and cross-correlation techniques we analyse multivariate non-stationary time series for statistical relationships at different time scales. We analyse the seasonal component of the dataset as well as examining the autocorrelation and partial autocorrelation methods. We then explore the Hurst exponent of the dataset and inspect the intraday correlations for patterns of events. Next, we examine the eigenvalue spectrum using different sized sliding windows. Finally, we compare approaches for assessing multiscale relationships among several variables using the wavelet multiple correlation and wavelet zero-lag cross-correlation on non-stationary RTWP time series data.

CCS CONCEPTS

• Networks~Wireless access points, base stations and infrastructure • Networks~Network performance analysis

KEYWORDS

3G; uplink; maximum overlap discrete wavelet transform; multiscale analysis; multivariate time series; non-stationary time series; received total wideband power

ACM Reference Format:

John Garrigan, Martin Crane and Marija Bezbradica. 2019. Received Total Wideband Power Data Analysis. In Proceedings of MSWiM '19, November 25–29, 2019, Miami Beach, FL, USA, 8 pages. DOI: 10.1145/3345768.3355905

MSWiM '19, November 25–29, 2019, Miami Beach, FL, USA
© 2019 Association for Computing Machinery
ACM ISBN 978-1-4503-6904-6/19/11...$15.00
https://doi.org/10.1145/3345768.3355905

1. Introduction

Wavelet techniques have been used extensively in a broad range of research areas e.g. engineering [1], medicine [2], fractals [3] and geophysics [4]. Robertson et al in [1], first used wavelets for power engineering to analyse electromagnetic transients from power system faults and switching. Since then there has been a significant increase in the application of wavelet transforms to power systems including power system protection, power quality and load forecasting. Biomedical engineering research has also used wavelet transforms, specifically in seizure prevention techniques and pre-surgical evaluations [2]. Identifying correlations between non-stationary signals is a common approach particularly in finance in measuring the relationship between two or more signals over time. In portfolio management, the maximum overlap discrete wavelet transform (MODWT) is used as part of an investment portfolio optimisation process [5]. The zero-lag cross-correlation matrix and the MODWT have also been used to analyse SenseCam images [6] to strengthen the wearers memory.

The typical observation of recorded RTWP levels in a 3G network is that levels vary during the day [7], with levels close to the noise floor in low traffic periods and levels rising during busy periods. Generally, noise levels for a cell in a network exhibit seasonality or periodic fluctuations every 24-hour cycle. 3G networks are noise limited systems, therefore increases to RTWP above normal operating levels could mean a loss of coverage for users at cell edge radio conditions and with an undesirable impact on network capacity.

When elevated RTWP levels are observed in a network, several factors can be responsible. Firstly, passive intermodulation (PIM)[1] within faulty hardware can result in intermodulation products in a cellular operator's uplink (UL) band; another possible cause is external interference; this can appear as spurious emissions from another party's transmitter; thirdly RTWP rises with user traffic; large volumes of high-speed packet access (HSPA) traffic correlate with increased RTWP levels. Correlations

---

[1] Passive Intermodulation occurs when two signals mix in a non-linear device such as a mechanical connector and generate a third frequency which falls within the operators own band resulting in interference.

and wavelet techniques have been used frequently in wired communication systems [8], [9], [10], [11] and have a rich history. In 3G networks, orthogonal spreading codes are combined with users' data packets to spread the data across the full 5MHz channel. At the radio base station receiver, the same spreading code sequence can extract the original data using signal correlation. This use of these orthogonal codes allows concurrent use of the RF physical channel by multiple users.

Using wavelets, RTWP data are decomposed into their component scales in short time windows, enabling us to study the correlation at various scales. This gives us a more convenient way to establish overall multiple relationships between cells and to minimise the time to fault find such issues. Using such techniques, it would allow a network optimisation engineer to quickly evaluate whether the interference patterns seen in the RTWP reports are correlated with the noise profiles of other neighbouring cells. This approach would also improve the turnaround time for fault detection as a large number of cells can be quantitively analysed together rather than a traditional approach of assessing each neighbouring cell individually. This paper is organised as follows: In Section 2 we review the methods used, Section 3 describes the RTWP dataset, meanwhile Section 4 details the results obtained and finally in Section 5 conclusions are provided.

2. Methods

While telecom networks have a rich store of data ready for interpretation, little research into RTWP datasets has taken place. In this section we introduce some aspects of the datasets using typical time series analysis techniques. We calculate the zero-lag cross-correlation matrices of the multivariate raw time series data to characterise dynamical changes. From this we look at the eigenspectrum for noise level patterns at different time scales. Finally, we measure the overall relationships at different scales among observations in a multivariate random variable with multiple wavelet correlation/cross-correlation approaches.

2.1 Correlation Dynamics

Using the zero-lag cross-correlation matrix (henceforth correlation matrix), dynamical changes in non-stationary multivariate time series can be characterised. To analyse the impact of abnormal noise rises in 3G networks, a cell with a known external interference source was included as per the analysis. To see how this source impacts on geographically neighboured cells and if any lead or lag pattern exists between such cells, we used a correlation matrix consisting of 10 geographically clustered cells. Of these, one has the source and we analyse its impact on the other 9. The correlation matrix is calculated using a sliding window of size less than the number of cells. Similar windowing techniques have been looked at in OLS hedging models [12].

Given a time-series of RTWP measurements $R_i(t), i = 1, ..., N$, the series within each window is normalised using $r_i(t) = [R_i(t) - \widehat{R_i(t)}]/\sigma_i$ where σ_i is the standard deviation of R_i and $\langle ... \rangle$ denotes a time average over the period and is given by $\sigma_i =$

$\sqrt{\langle R_i^2 \rangle - \langle R_i \rangle^2}$. The correlation matrix may be expressed in terms of $r_i(t)$ as follows: $C_{ij} = \langle r_i(t) r_j(t) \rangle$. C_{ij} has values $-1 \leq C_{ij} \leq 1$, where $C_{ij} = 1$ corresponds to perfect correlation, $C_{ij} = -1$ to perfect anti-correlation, and $C_{ij} = 0$, to uncorrelated pairs of cells. The correlation matrix can be expressed as $C = [RR^T]/T$ where T is the transpose of a matrix and R is an $N \times T$ matrix with elements r_{it} [13].

The eigenvalues λ_i and eigenvectors $\bar{v}_i$ of C come from the characteristic equation $C\bar{v}_i = \lambda_i\bar{v}_i$. The eigenvalues of C are ordered by size, such that $\lambda_1 \leq \lambda_2 \leq \cdots \leq \lambda_N$. Given that the sum of the matrix diagonal entries (the Trace, T_r)) remains constant under linear transformation [14], $\sum_i \lambda_i = T_r$ for C. Hence, if some eigenvalues increase then others must decrease, and vice versa, (Eigenvalue Repulsion) [15].

Two limiting cases [14],[16] exist for the distribution of the eigenvalues: (i) perfect correlation, $C_i \approx 1$, when the largest is maximised with value N, (all others being zero). (ii) when each time series compromises random numbers with average correlation $C_i \approx 0$ and the corresponding eigenvalues are distributed around 1, (where any deviation is due to spurious random correlations). For C_i between 0 and 1, the eigenvalues furthest away from λ_{max} can be much smaller. To investigate the dynamical changes in eigenvalue distribution we use sliding windows with eigenvalues normalised thus $\tilde{\lambda}_i(t) = [\lambda_i - \bar{\lambda}]/\sigma_\lambda$ where $\bar{\lambda}, \sigma_\lambda$ are mean, standard deviation of the eigenvalues from a subsection of the eigenspectrum of C. By normalising the eigenvalues, we can compare eigenvalues at both ends of the spectrum, though their magnitudes differ. To calculate $\bar{\lambda}$ and σ_λ, a low volatility part of the eigenspectrum is used to enhance the visibility of high periods (also the full time period can be used) [5].

2.1.1 Maximum Overlap Discrete Wavelet Transform.

The Maximum Overlap Discrete Wavelet Transform, (MODWT) [17], transforms a series into coefficients related to the variations over a set of scales. Like the DWT, the MODWT outputs a set of time-dependent wavelet and scaling coefficients with basis vectors associated with a location t and a unitless scale $\tau_j = 2^{j-1}$ for each decomposition level $j = 1, ..., J_0$ [13]. However, unlike the DWT, the MODWT, has a high level of redundancy. The advantages of the MODWT over DWT are its non-orthogonality and ability to handle any sample size $N \neq 2^j$ [13]. With MODWT, a signal can be broken into J levels by applying J pairs of filters. The coefficients at the Jth level are found by applying a rescaled *father* wavelet:

$$\widetilde{D}_{j,t} = \sum_{l=0}^{L_j-1} \tilde{\varphi}_{j,l} f_{t-l} \qquad (1)$$

for all $t = ..., -1, 0, 1,...$, where f is the function to be decomposed [13]. The rescaled *mother*, $\tilde{\varphi}_{j,t} = \frac{\varphi_{j,t}}{2^j}$, and father, $\tilde{\phi}_{j,t} = \frac{\varphi_{j,t}}{2^j}$, wavelets for the jth level are a set of scale-dependent localised differencing and averaging operators and can be seen as rescaled versions of the originals. The jth level equivalent filter coefficients have a width $L_j = (2^j - 1)(L - 1) + 1$, ($L$ is the width of the $j = 1$ base filter [13]). The filters for levels $j > 1$ are not explicitly constructed as the detail and scaling coefficients can be found, using an algorithm involving the $j = 1$ filters operating recurrently on the jth level scaling coefficients, to get the $j + 1$ level scaling and detail coefficients [13].

2.1.2 Wavelet Variance.

The wavelet variance $v_f^2(\tau_j)$ is defined as the expected value of $\widetilde{D}_{j,t}^2$ considering only non-boundary coefficients[2]. The unbiased estimator of the wavelet variance is achieved by omitting the coefficients impacted by boundary conditions and is calculated as follows:

$$v_f^2(\tau_j) = \frac{1}{M_j} \sum_{t=L_j-1}^{N-1} \widetilde{D}_{j,l}^2 \qquad (2)$$

where $M_j = N - L_j + 1$ is number of non-boundary coefficients at j^{th} level [13]. The series behaviour over different horizons on a scale-by-scale basis is shown by the wavelet variance.

2.1.3 Wavelet Covariance and Correlation

Like the wavelet variance above, the wavelet covariance between functions $f(t)$, $g(t)$ is defined as the covariance of wavelet coefficients at scale j. The unbiased estimator of the wavelet covariance at the jth scale is:

$$v_{fg}(\tau_j) = \frac{1}{M_j} \sum_{t=L_j-1}^{N-1} \widetilde{D}_{j,l}^{f(t)} \widetilde{D}_{j,l}^{g(t)} \qquad (3)$$

Again, all wavelet coefficients affected by the boundary are removed [13], and $M_j = N - L_j + 1$. The MODWT estimate of the wavelet correlation between functions $f(t)$ and $g(t)$ is found with the wavelet covariance and square root of the wavelet variance of the functions at each scale j [13]. The MODWT estimator, of the wavelet correlation is given by:

$$\rho_{fg}(\tau_j) = \frac{v_{fg}(\tau_j)}{v_f(\tau_j) v_g(\tau_j)} \qquad (4)$$

where, at scale j, $v_{fg}(\tau_j)$ is the covariance between $f(t)$ and $g(t)$, $v_f(\tau_j)$ is the variance of $f(t)$ and $v_g(\tau_j)$ is the variance of $g(t)$ [13].

2.1.4 Wavelet Multiple Correlation and Cross-Correlation

The wavelet multiple correlation and cross-correlation give the overall statistical relationship at different time scales among a set of multivariate random data. The wavelet multiple correlations (WMC) $\varphi_X(\lambda_j)$ are defined as one single set of multiscale correlations calculated from X_t where $X_t = (x_{1t}, x_{2t} \dots, x_{nt})$ is a multivariate stochastic process and $W_{jt} = w_{1jt}, w_{2jt}, \dots, w_{njt}$ the respective scale λ_j wavelet coefficients from application of the

maximum overlap discrete wavelet transform to each x_{it} process [18]. The wavelet multiple correlation is:

$$\varphi_X(\lambda_j) = Corr(w_{ijt}, \widehat{w}_{ijt}) = \frac{Cov(w_{ijt}, \widehat{w}_{ijt})}{\sqrt{Var(w_{ijt})Var(\widehat{w}_{ijt})}}, \qquad (5)$$

where w_{ij} is chosen to maximise $\varphi_X(\lambda_j)$ and $\widehat{w}_{ij}$ are the fitted values in the regression of w_{ij} on the rest of the wavelet coefficients as scale λ_j.

Allowing for a lag of τ between observed and fitted values of the variable selected [18] as the criterion variable at each scale λ_j the wavelet multiple cross-correlation (WMCC) is defined as:

$$Corr(w_{ijt}, \widehat{w}_{ijt+\tau}) = \frac{Cov(w_{ijt}, \widehat{w}_{ijt+\tau})}{\sqrt{Var(w_{ijt})Var(\widehat{w}_{ijt+\tau})}} \qquad (6)$$

3. The Dataset

The RTWP dataset (RNC20_30 data) has uplink receive level values at a radio base station (RBS) taken from a live 3G network. The dataset is extracted from the operations support system (OSS) database in CSV format and is post-processed in R. The analysis was performed offline due to the unavailability of dedicated hardware to perform real time analysis. In order to productionise this analysis a real time streaming engine would be configured to ingest the RTWP reports. From there an R or Python script would parse and manipulate the data before the wavelet algorithms analyse the data for correlations between cells to identify the presence or absence of external interference. RTWP data is available at granularities raw data (15 min), hourly and daily. The analysis here concentrates on a subsample of the RNC20_30 data dataset using the raw format for representation purposes. A site with a known external interference source was identified and its neighbouring cells analysed to see if a lead-lag relationship exists between these proximal sites.

3.1 Data Visualisation

In Fig. 1 we see RTWP levels in decibel-milliwatts (dBm) plotted against time for site LX0088. A Sector is the industry term for an antenna on a mast radiating a specific frequency, typically a site has 3 sectors, each covering a unique geographic area and so one expects different noise profiles based upon subscriber density and mobility in those areas.

In Fig. 1 below, Sector B (Sec B) shows a typical noise profile for a cell operating as normal. As usage decreases after midnight, the noise level is close to the noise floor of ≈-105dBm. Network activity increases into the day and again decreases at night. Sectors A and C show very different profiles to Sector B. Sudden bursts of noise such as on Sunday at ≈08:45am appear and vanish once again.

---

[2] The MODWT treats the time series as if they are periodic using "circular boundary conditions". There are L_j wavelet and scaling coefficients that are influenced by the extension, which are referred to as the boundary coefficients.

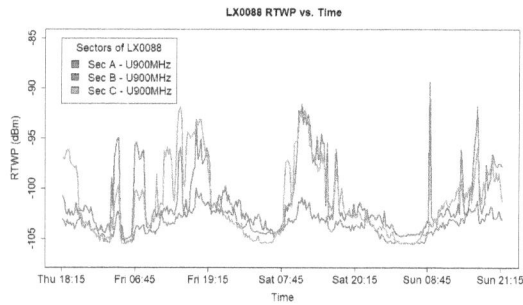

Figure 1: RTWP levels vs. Time showing the presence of external interference particularily on Sec A and C.

Early Friday morning there are two very obvious sudden bursts of noise in Sectors A and C and to a lesser extent in Sector B. From above, the chance of all three sectors exhibiting similar noise signatures such as that seen on Friday at 06:45 is very small as they cover different geographic areas, this strongly points to the presence of local external interference.

Table 1: Summary statistics for RNC20_30

Freq. Band	Mean (dBm)	Median (dBm)	S.D (dBm)	Max (dBm)	Min (dBm)	Count
U900 F0	-104.44	-105.10	1.14	-65	-110	1463
U21 F1	-104.98	-105.35	0.79	-73.63	-110	1527
U21 F2	-104.84	-105.24	0.87	-73.93	-110	1488
U21 F3	-105.04	-105.38	0.82	-75.03	-110	1509

Table 1 shows typical values for the 4 different frequencies in the network based on a sample of 5987 cells. The table shows that the U900MHz cells' mean exceeds that of the U2100MHz cells. Since the mean value for all the frequency bands is higher than the median, this is indicative of a right skewed distribution of values. The maximum values indicate the strength of interference sources which average 30dB of noise for U2100 and 40dB of noise for the U900 cells. Minimum values of -110dBm indicate that some "deaf" cells in the network should be investigated for physical build issues.

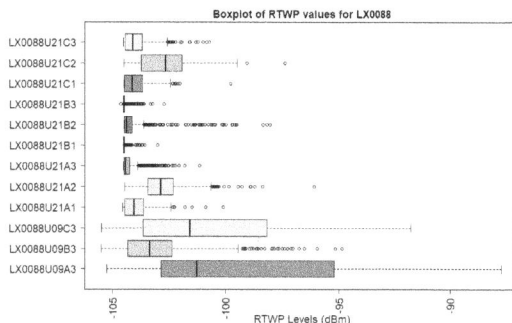

Figure 2: Boxplot of RTWP values for LX0088

The box plot in Fig. 2 shows RTWP values for all cells across all frequencies belonging to site LX0088. From this representation, the range of values for all three U900MHz cells is obviously much larger than that of the U2100MHz cells. The median values for U900MHz Sector A and C are higher than that of Sec B which is also evident on the U2100MHz cell particularly U21A2 and U21C2.

4. Results

4.1 Time Series Decomposition

Time series decomposition using Loess [19] splits the RTWP data into its four main components, the trend, cyclical, seasonal and irregular parts. Fig. 3 shows the seasonal decomposition for LX0088U09A3, the cell showing external interference as discussed in Fig. 1. Fig. 3 shows from top to bottom (a) the original time series, (b) the seasonal, (c) the trend and (d) the remainder components.

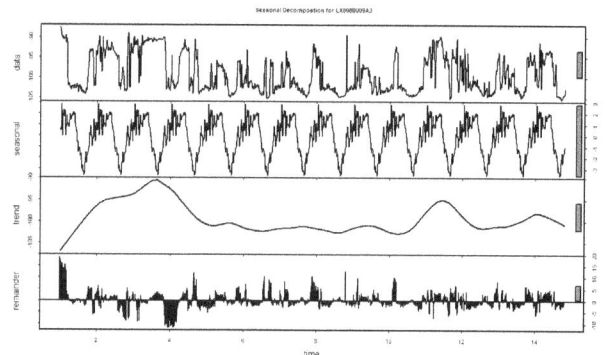

Figure 3: Seasonal decomposition for LX0099U09A3

The seasonal component indicates a daily periodicity and the vertical red bars on the right-hand side of the image show that the seasonal signal is large relative to the data *variation*. This component clearly shows the early morning and afternoon spike in noise levels typically associated with waking and lunch time heavy usage patterns. During the consistently high noise periods during day 2 and 3 in the original data, the trend also increases before falling with the noise after day 4.

4.2 Autocorrelation and Partial Autocorrelation Analysis

Other statistical properties of interest for patterns include the autocorrelation (ACF) and partial autocorrelation (PACF) functions. For a normal network cell, we should see a strong internal link between the signals at regular intervals given the strong seasonality from above. Before we assess the ACF and PACF, differencing was required in order to ensure data stationarity. First order differencing was used to stabilise the mean and ensured a constant variance around the mean.

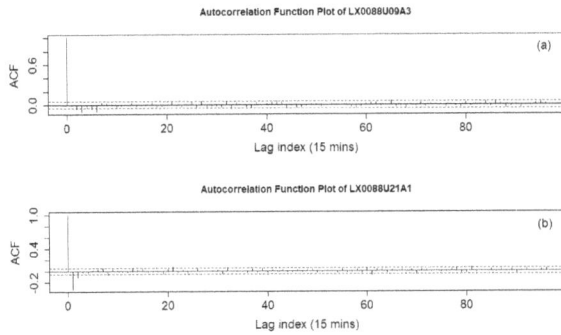

Figure 4: (a) Autocorrelation plot for LX0088U09A3, (b) autocorrelation for LX0088U21A1

Fig. 4(a) shows the ACF shut off immediately after lag 0 with a few significant negative lags at 2, 3 and 6. The corresponding PACF plot in Fig. 5(a) shows a slowly decaying negative PACF up to lag 7. These 2 plots, we use to reliably forecast future values for LX0088U09A3 an ARIMA(3,1,5) model [20]. Similarly, Fig. 4(b) and 6(b) show a comparable behaviour for LX0088U21A1 which covers the same geographic area.

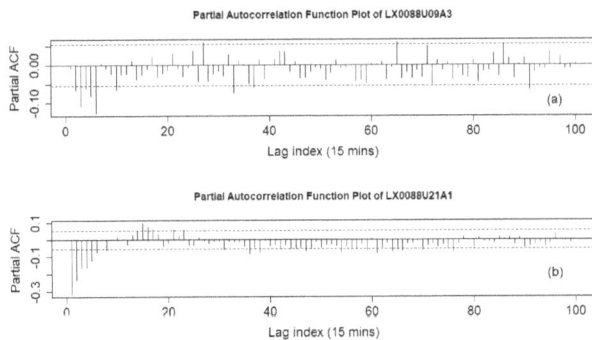

Figure 5: (a) Partial autocorrelation plot for LX0088U09A3, (b) partial autocorrelation plot for LX0088U21A1

In Fig. 4(b) we see a sudden shut off in ACF with large negative lags for values 1 & 2 while the corresponding PACF plot in Fig. 5(b) shows a gradual decrease in the PACF with significant lags for values up to 6. Again the process suggests an ARIMA(2,1,6) model. In Fig. 4(b) the first lag shows a negative autocorrelation at lag 1, implying that if a value is above average then subsequent values will be below average. The ACF plot for LX0088U09A3, the cell with a verified external interferer shows that the first significant value occurs at lag 2 and this is also negative. This implies that if an RTWP measurement is above average, the value is expected to remain above average until 2 lags have occurred which equates to 30 min. Comparing this to the equivalent ACF plot for LX0088U21A1, the U900MHz cell will remain above average for up to 30 min while the next value for the U2100MHz will be below average.

4.3 Hurst Exponent

The Hurst exponent is a statistical measure of the long-term memory of a time series and describes the rate of decrease of autocorrelations with lag. The Hurst quantifies the relative tendency of a time series either to regress strongly to the mean or to cluster in a certain direction [21]. It varies between 0 and 1: $H = 0.5$ implies a random walk or independent process; $0 \leq H < 0.5$ then the time series is *anti-persistent* meaning that a time series with decreasing trend is more likely to show an increasing trend next. If $0.5 < H \leq 1$ the process is persistent, (*i.e. if we have an increasing time series then it is more probable that it will continue to show an increasing trend* [22]).

The Hurst distribution for the RNC20_30 dataset was measured as $0.5 \leq H < 1$ and indicates long term positive autocorrelation such that high noise levels will likely be followed by other high values. Further, as the Hurst appeared normally distributed, we assume that the original data sampled from have similar properties.

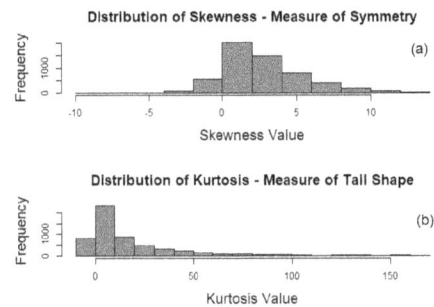

Figure 6: RNC20_30 Distribution of (a) Skewness and (b) Kurtosis

The skewness distribution in Fig. 6(a) indicates that many of the variables in the RNC20_30 dataset are clearly right skewed indicated by the positive values while the kurtosis distribution in Fig. 6(b) indicates that most of the variables in the same dataset have fat-tailed or *leptokurtic* distributions.

4.4 Intraday Correlations

The intraday correlations measure the co-movements of RTWP values between days for a small sample of cells and describe the intraday volatility for a cell with a known interference source and one without. The intraday correlations for both LX0088U21A1 and LX0088U09A3 were measured for a two-week period. LX0088U21A1 provides coverage to the same geographic area as LX0088U09A3 but uses a different frequency band which is less susceptible to *uplink* interference. The first noticeable observation from the correlation analysis was the strong positive correlation for cell LX0088U21A1 for all days with a minimum correlation of 0.4 between Day 7 and Day 8 while the strongest correlation occurred between Day 3 and Day 4 as well as between Day 3 and Day 11 with values of 0.9.

The intraday correlations for cell LX0088U09A3 which had a verified external interference source was also measured. LX0088U21A1 and LX0088U09A3 differ greatly: Comparing correlation values between these two cells we observed contrasting values between days. Between Day 7 and Day 10 the correlation for LX0088U21A1 is positive and strong, contrasting with strong negative correlations between Day 3 and Day 7 for LX0088U09A3. On average, the intraday correlations for LX0088U09A3 are typically weak with values between 0.2 and -0.2. Fig. 7 is a plot of RTWP for both cells over the 14 days. We see the contrast in RTWP values for both cells and the impact an external interference source has on LX0088U09A3.

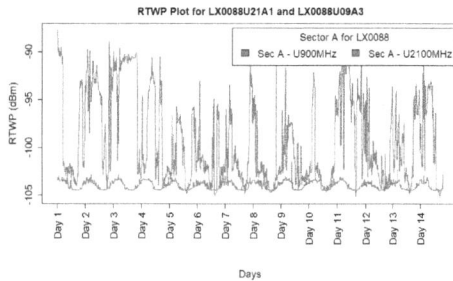

Figure 7: RTWP of LX0088U09A3 and LX0088U21A1

In Fig. 7, we see that on Day 3 the magnitude of the interference levels for LX0088U09A3 is consistently high throughout the entire day and rolls over into day 4 which explained the strong negative interday correlations between Day 3 and Day 7, Day 10, Day 12 and Day 13. Since the interference affected Day 4 also, we expect to see strong negative correlations for this day also.

4.5 Eigenvalue Dynamics

The first eigenvalue (λ_1) of a correlation matrix shows the maximal variance of the variables which can be accounted for with a linear model by a single underlying factor [23]. For all positive correlations, this first eigenvalue is roughly a linear function of the average correlation among the variables [24]. As per Fig. 3, the RTWP data has a seasonality of 24 hours, suggesting that the correlation between variables would also exhibit a periodicity across the same scale and likewise the eigenvalues of the correlation matrix.

With 10 cells from the RTWP dataset, one having a known interference source, we look at the eigenvalue dynamics for unusual patterns: Fig. 8 gives the largest eigenvalue for four different window sizes: (a) 90 mins, (b) 300 mins, (c) 750 mins and (d) 1500 mins. Using normalised eigenvalues as described above (1), the dynamics of (λ_{max}) should show the presence of unique events.

Obviously as the window size increases the high frequency information visible in Fig. 8(a) is lost due to the smoothing effect of the larger window size. The changes in magnitude of λ_1 for the different window sizes indicate substantial changes in the noise levels between cells at these time periods. In Fig. 8(c) we clearly

see 14 distinct double peaks, (some of these double peak events are identified by a red asterisks) a sudden rise followed by a small decline then a rise and then another drop. Each double peak represents a day's information. These troughs on the 14 peaks coincide with early afternoon noise levels and seem to signify low volatility periods as all cells are expected to have peak RTWP values at the busy times of day.

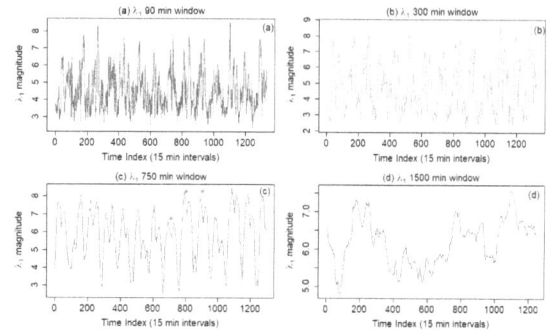

Figure 8: Largest Eigenvalue for (a) 90min (b) 300min (c) 750min (d) 1500min windows

In Fig. 8(d) we see a smoothly varying function with eigenvalue magnitudes varying between 5.0 and 7.0. This plot captures the daily noise variations between cells as a moving average and therefore any low frequency variations are smoothed out. As stated in Section 2.1 above, the sum of all eigenvalues must equal $Tr(C)$.

As C is a 10x10 matrix, from Fig. 8(d) we can say that λ_1 explains between 50-70% of the system noise and fluctuations between these values, evident between time index 400-700 are due to other sources of noise which cause variation in eigenvalue magnitudes at these times.

4.6 Wavelet Multiple Correlation

This section introduces the wavelet multiple correlation method to assess the overall statistical relationship between many variables. Macho [18] introduced this approach when studying the wavelet multiple correlation and cross-correlations between the Eurozone stock markets. The wavelet multiple correlation method produces a single statistical measure of the multivariate sample on a scale-by-scale basis. Using this approach, the wavelet correlation between pairs of variables can be assessed in a single visualisation rather than having to compare multiple wavelet statistics for all the variables under analysis.

We decomposed the RTWP dataset using the Daubechies least asymmetric (*LA8*) wavelet filter which has a filter of length *L*=8. This filter is used extensively in finance [12] [5] as it provides a reliable estimate of correlation between long memory time series [25]. Based on the findings in Section 4.3 this was an appropriate choice filter given an average *H* value of 0.7. The maximum level of decomposition using the LA8 filter is given by $log_2(T)$ where *T* is the time series length, in our case this is 1344 equating to a maximum decomposition level of 10. For this study, we use *J* = 7 resulting in 7 wavelet coefficients and one scaling coefficient for each interval in the RTWP dataset i.e. $\widetilde{\omega}_{i1}, ..., \widetilde{\omega}_{i8}$ and $\widetilde{v}_{i8}$ respectively. Since a MODWT approximates an ideal band-pass filter (with bandpass given by the frequency interval $[2^{-(j+1)}, 2^{-j}]$) for $J = 1, ..., J$. Inverting the frequency range, the corresponding periods are within $(2^j, 2^{j+1})$ time unit intervals [25].

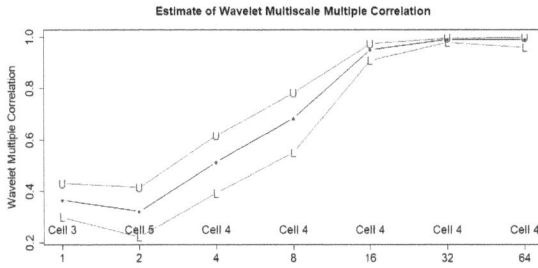

Figure 9: Estimate of wavelet multiscale correlation

Since the RTWP dataset is sampled at 15 min intervals, the wavelet coefficients represent the following intervals, 30-60 min, 1-2 hours, 2-4 hours, 4-8 hours, 8-16 hours, 16-32 hours (daily scale) and 32-64 hours (2-day scale).

Fig. 9 shows the wavelet multiple correlation for a sample of 10 cells from the RTWP dataset. It gives the strength of the wavelet correlations between the sample of 10 cells across the 7 wavelet scales. The straight blue lines represent the upper and lower bounds of the 95% confidence intervals. For each wavelet level, the variable which maximises the multiple correlation against a linear combination of the rest of the variables is also plotted. From the wavelet multiple correlation for a sample of 10 cells, we see that all the correlations are positive and indicate a strong positive relationship. The scale rises with the correlation between cells up to perfect cell correlation at the longest scale. It is also evident that as the scales increase the confidence interval narrows showing increasing certainty of the estimate. Since near perfect correlation exists at wavelet scales greater than 16, an exact linear relationship between the RTWP values of the 10 cells cannot be ruled out. The presence of such a relationship means that noise levels for any cell can be estimated by the overall noise levels of the other cells in the sample. Another interesting point is the brief decrease in correlation between scales 1 and 2 before the correlation almost linearly increases to perfect correlation at longer scales. This shows that, at smaller time scales, clear discrepancies exist between the RTWP levels but that over longer time periods the RTWP values follow the same overall trend.

4.7 Wavelet Multiple Cross-Correlation

Fig. 10 shows the wavelet multiple cross-correlation for different wavelet scales with leads and lags up to 25 hours. Like the wavelet multiple correlation above, the multiple cross-correlation decomposes the usual cross-correlation and produces patterns which show the relationship between multiple variables across various physical time scales [25]. Each wavelet scale plot shows in its upper left-hand corner the network cell maximising the multiple correlation against a linear combination of the other variables and, thus, signals a potential leader or follower for the whole system [18]. The wavelet multiple cross-correlation analysis was performed for several different lead/lag values and for brevity Fig. 10 shows the positive and negative lag up to 25 hours.

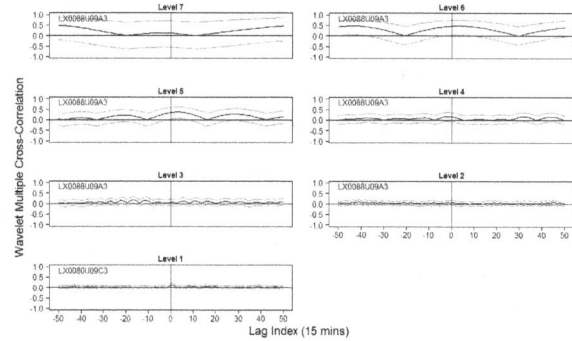

Figure 10: Wavelet multiple cross-correlation for a sample of 10 cells at different wavelet scales. The continuous red line corresponds to the upper and lower bounds of the 95% confidence interval.

Like Fig. 9, Fig. 10 also shows consistent positive correlations across all lags for all lead/lag values. Upper and lower bounds of the 95% confidence interval are shown as continuous red lines and again the variable maximising the multiple correlation against a linear combination of the rest of the variables is shown in the upper left-hand corner for each scale. When both confidence intervals are above the horizontal axis on the right-hand side of the graph, this indicates a positive statistically significant lagging wavelet cross-correlation and inversely, a positive confidence interval on the left-hand side of the chart indicates a positive statistically significant leading correlation. From the results in Fig. 10, we see that for the majority of lag values, the cross-correlation between the multivariates is statistically insignificant since neither of the confidence intervals are greater than zero. Clearly there are brief periods around the zero-lag mark across a number of wavelet scales indicating a statistically significant cross-correlation. Fig. 10 shows that there are statistically significant events in Levels 1, 5 & 6 for lags of 1, 4 and 4 respectively where levels 1, 5 & 6 represent 30-60 mins, 8-16 hours and 16-32 hours respectively. In Fig. 10, the Level 1 plot identifies the presence of a statistical lag relationship for LX0080U09C3 at lag 1 at the 30-60 min time scale. The Level 3 plot in Fig. 10 indicates that RTWP values for LX0088U09A3 tends to statistically lag the other cells for time scales of 4-8 hours. We see in the Level 3 (2-4 hours) plot statistically significant periods for LX0088U09A3 at lag values of -11 and -17 indicating possible RTWP levels for LX0088U09A3 leading the other cells in the analysis for time scales of 2-4 hours. The Level 6 plot also shows a statistically significant lag for LX0088U09A3 at lag values of 4 for time scales 16-32 hours.

5. Conclusion

High RTWP levels have serious consequences in modern wireless networks due to their adverse effect on coverage of a wireless transceiver site and negative impact on customer satisfaction. Quickly classifying the cause and identifying the source of the problem is key to resolving issues as efficiently as possible while at the same time minimising operational expenditure in the fault-finding process. With the explosion in usage of noisy packet switched data sessions, monitoring and protecting *uplink* noise levels is key for a wireless operator hence alternative data mining techniques are needed.

By examining the eigenvalue spectrum of the correlation matrix for a small sample of cells we looked at dynamical changes in the RTWP values using different window sizes which reflect large changes in the RTWP values of the sample. Using this approach an engineer could quickly identify major changes in RTWP values for a group of cells rather than assessing individual graphs of RTWP values and quickly quantify the magnitude of the change in noise levels for a group of cells rather than assessing the impact at an individual cell level.

The maximum overlap discrete wavelet transform enabled the multilevel decomposition of the raw RTWP time series into their respective coefficients for different time horizons. This technique enables RTWP measurements to be investigated for correlations and cross-correlations over several different time horizons. The multiscale wavelet correlation showed how it can be used to pinpoint short term deviations in RTWP values when assessed over numerous scales. Similarly, the multiscale wavelet cross-correlation identified a number of different lead and lag relationships not evident in standard approaches. These lead/lag relationships need further investigation to fully understand the complex interplay that exists between each network element.

Future work includes investigating the eigenvalue spectrum of the wavelet correlation matrix using a heatmap diagram for evidence of significant events across various wavelet scales. In this way, an engineer could easily identify periods of high RTWP values across different time horizons. To quantify the significance and meaning of the elements of the cross-correlation matrix C, it would be advantageous to quantify the correlations between such cells by comparing the statistics of the cross-correlation matrix to the null hypothesis of a random matrix using RMT as per [26], if the properties of C conform to those of a random correlation matrix, it signifies random correlations in C. Deviations of the properties of C from those of the random matrix convey information about genuine correlations requiring further investigation.

Another possible approach to be considered could involve time series clustering based on similarity or distance measurements, the discrete wavelet transform can be used as a metric of similarity. In doing so, time series that are similar are clustered together and may assist in identifying cells which exhibit similar patterns of interference. These clusters could then be further analysed to identify cells which are spatially grouped which may signal the presence of an external interference source.

References

[1] D. C. Robertson, O. I. Camps, J. S. Mayer and W. B. Gish, "Wavelets and electromagnetic power system transients," IEEE T Power Deliver, vol. 11, no. 2, pp. 1050-1058, 1996.
[2] T. Conlon, H. J. Ruskin and M. Crane, "Seizure characterisation using frequency-dependent multivariate dynamics," Comput. Biol. Med, vol. 39, no. 9, pp. 760-767, 2009.
[3] J. F. Muzy, E. Bacry and A. Arneodo, "Multifractal formalism for fractal signals: The structure-function approach versus the wavelet-transform modulus-maxima method," Phys Rev E, pp. 875-884, 1993.
[4] A. Grinsted, J. C. Moore and S. Jevrejeva, "Application of the cross wavelet transform and wavelet coherence to geophysical time series," Nonlinear Process. Geophys., vol. 11, no. 5/6, pp. 561-566, 2004.
[5] T. Conlon, H. J. Ruskin and M. Crane, "Multiscales cross-correlation dynamics in financal time-series," Advances in Complex Systems, vol. 12, no. 04n05, pp. 439-454, 2009.
[6] N. Li, M. Crane and H. J. Ruskin, "Automatically Detecting "Significant Events" on SenseCam," Int J Wavelets, Multi, vol. 11, no. 06, p. 1350050, 2013.
[7] H. Holma and A. Toskala, WCDMA for UMTS, Fifth Edition ed., Chichester: Wiley, 2005, p. 48.
[8] S. P. Girija and K. D. Rao, "Smoothing term based noise correlation matrix construction for MIMO-OFDM wireless networks for impulse noise mitigation," Macao, 2015.
[9] P. K. Gkonis, G. V. Tsoulos and D. I. Kaklamani, "Dual code Tx diversity with antenna selection for spatial multiplexing in MIMO-WCDMA networks," IEEE Commun Lett, pp. 570-572, 2009.
[10] B. A. Bjerke, Z. Zvonar and J. G. Proakis, "Antenna Diversity Combining Schemes for WCDMA Systems in Fading Multipath Channels," IEEE T Wirel Commun Le, pp. 97-106, 2004.
[11] M. Keskinoz, S. Olcer and H. Sadjadpour, "Advances in signal processing for wireless and wired communications [Guest Editorial]," IEEE Commun Mag, vol. 47, no. 1, pp. 30-31, 2009.
[12] T. Conlon and J. Cotter, "An empirical analysis of dynamic multiscale hedging using wavelet decomposition," J Futures Markets, vol. 32, no. 3, pp. 272-299, 2011.
[13] D. B. Percival and A. T. Walden, Wavelet methods for time series analysis, Cambridge, United Kingdom: Cambridge Univ. Press, 2008.
[14] K. Schindler, H. Leung, C. E. Elger and K. Lehnertz, "Assessing seizure dynamics by analysing the correlation structure of multichannel intracranial EEG," Brain, vol. 130, no. 1, pp. 65-77, 2006.
[15] G. Oas, "Universal cubic eigenvalue repulsion for random normal matrices," Phys Rev E, vol. 55, no. 1, pp. 205-211, 1997.
[16] M. Muller, G. Baier, A. Galka, U. Stephani and H. Muhle, "Algorithm for the Detection of Changes of the Correlation Structure in Multivariate Time Series," Electronics and Electrical Engineering, 2012.
[17] S. C. Burrus, R. A. Gopinath and H. Guo, An introduction to wavelets and wavelet transforms: A Primer, 1st ed., Prentice-Hall, 1995.
[18] J. Fernandez-Macho, "Wavelet multiple correlation and cross-correlation: A multiscale analysis of Eurozone stock markets," Physica A, vol. 391, no. 4, pp. 1097-1104, 2012.
[19] R. B. Cleveland, W. S. Cleveland, J. E. McRae and I. Terpenning, "STL: A seasonal-trend decomposition procedure based on loess.," J Off Stat, vol. 6, no. 1, p. 3, 1990.
[20] R. J. Hyndman and G. Athanasopoulos, "Forecasting: principles and practice," Otexts.org, [Online]. Available: https://www.otexts.org/fpp.
[21] T. Kleinow, "Testing continuous time models in financial markets," Doctoral dissertation, Humboldt-Universität zu Berlin, Wirtschaftswissenschaftliche Fakultät, 2002.
[22] M. Kale and F. Butar Butar, "Fractal analysis of time series and distribution properties of Hurst exponent. Diss," Sam Houston State University, 2005.
[23] G. H. Dunteman, Principal components analysis, Newbury Park [etc.]: Sage Publications, 2016.
[24] S. Friedman and H. F. Weisberg, "Interpreting the First Eigenvalue of a Correlation Matrix," Educ. Psychol. Meas, pp. 11-21, 1981.
[25] B. Whitcher, P. Guttorp and D. B. Percival, "Wavelet analysis of covariance with application to atmospheric time series.," J. Geophys. Res., vol. 105, no. D11, pp. 14941-14962, 2000.
[26] T. Conlon , H. J. Ruskin and M. Crane, "Random matrix theory and fund of funds portfolio optimisation," Physica A, vol. 382, no. 2, pp. 565-576, 2007.

Spatial Issues in Modeling LoRaWAN Capacity

Andrzej Duda
andrzej.duda@imag.fr
Univ. Grenoble Alpes, CNRS, Grenoble INP, LIG
Grenoble, France

Martin Heusse
martin.heusse@imag.fr
Univ. Grenoble Alpes, CNRS, Grenoble INP, LIG
Grenoble, France

ABSTRACT

All existing models for analyzing the performance of LoRaWAN assume a constant density of nodes within the gateway range. We claim that such a situation is highly unlikely for LoRaWAN cells whose range can attain several kilometers in real-world deployments. We thus propose to analyze the LoRa performance under a more realistic assumption: the density of nodes decreases with the inverse square of the distance to the gateway.

We use the LoRaWAN capacity model by Georgiou and Raza to find the Packet Delivery Ratio (PDR) for an inhomogeneous spatial distribution of devices around a gateway and obtain the number of devices that benefit from a given level of PDR. We analyze the LoRaWAN capacity in terms of PDR for various spatial configurations and Spreading Factor allocations.

CCS CONCEPTS

• **Networks** → **Network performance modeling**; *Very long-range networks*; *Sensor networks*.

KEYWORDS

LoRaWAN; Packet Delivery Ratio; capacity; modeling; inhomogeneous density

ACM Reference Format:
Andrzej Duda and Martin Heusse. 2019. Spatial Issues in Modeling Lo-RaWAN Capacity. In *22nd Int'l ACM Conference on Modeling, Analysis and Simulation of Wireless and Mobile Systems (MSWiM '19), November 25–29, 2019, Miami Beach, FL, USA.* ACM, New York, NY, USA, 8 pages. https://doi.org/10.1145/3345768.3355932

1 INTRODUCTION

LoRa [1] is a recent example of a Low Power Wide Area Network (LPWAN) that can provide wireless connectivity to a large number of IoT devices over long distances. It defines a physical layer based on the Chirp Spread Spectrum (CSS) modulation [2] and a simple channel access method similar to ALOHA called LoRaWAN [3]. The LoRa CSS modulation results in good sensitivity enabling transmissions over long distances: a range of several kilometers outdoors and hundreds of meters indoors.

A LoRa end device can vary several transmission parameters: channel bandwidth (BW), transmission power (TP), coding rate (CR), and spreading factor (SF). The achievable data rates depend on some of the parameters: a higher bit rate results from lower SF (at the cost of a shorter range), higher BW, and CR of 4/5. The bit rates range from 293 b/s to 11 kb/s, the low bit rate resulting in long transmission times: 2.466 s for sending 59 B at SF12.

In addition to the physical layer parameters, the LoRa performance in terms of the Packet Delivery Ratio (PDR) and scalability to a large number of devices strongly depend on the LoRaWAN access method similar to unslotted ALOHA: a device may wake up at any instant and start transmitting a packet without testing for on-going transmissions.

The previous analytical studies investigated LoRa performance for an increasing number of nodes around a gateway with an important assumption: the density of nodes within the gateway range is uniform [4–9]. However, such an assumption is not realistic for cells covering large areas of several square kilometers for two reasons.

First, measurement studies in cellular networks showed that spatial traffic distribution is highly non-uniform across different cells [10–14] with complex patterns that include hot spots with a high density and other less dense places. For instance, Lee et al. [11] demonstrated based on traffic measurements that the spatial distribution of the traffic density across different cells can be approximated by the log-normal or Weibull distributions depending on time and space. As cells in cellular networks can be smaller than LPWANs (target range of several kilometers), we expect that spatial traffic distribution in LoRa networks will also be highly non-uniform. We can also consider that the distribution of devices follows in fact the same pattern as we can usually observe for population and building densities in cities: apart from the saturated downtown, the density decreases with the distance from the center—it is much higher downtown than in suburbs. The deployment of gateways by LPWAN operators will probably also follow the same strategy as in cellular networks—place networks close to potential users and create hot spots near high density areas.

Second, there is a discouraging effect when placing a device far from the gateway in a LoRaWAN cell: the device needs to use large SF (e.g., SF11 or SF12) to get its transmissions through, which means long transmission times, so increased contention (more collisions) and higher energy consumption. For instance, a device using SF11 will roughly consume 10 times more energy for a transmission than when using SF7. Moreover, if we consider an equidistant distribution of spreading factors, which is the most popular spatial model adopted in the analyses with concentric annuli spaced at 1 km intervals, there are more devices with larger SF such as SF11 and SF12 than devices in the area of SF7. There are also no devices outside the zone of SF12, a kind of a disruptive irregularity difficult to observe in real world deployments.

We claim that uniform node density is highly unlikely for large cells so we propose to analyze LoRa performance under a more realistic assumption: the density of nodes decreases with the *inverse square of the distance* to the gateway. The *inverse-square law* is common in physics stating that a specified physical quantity or intensity is inversely proportional to the square of the distance from the source of that physical quantity. For instance, radio wave transmission in free space follows an inverse square law for power density. We consider that such a spatial model corresponds better to real-world LoRaWAN deployments than the models based on the constant density.

In this paper, we use the model by Georgiou and Raza [4] to find the Packet Delivery Ratio (PDR) for inhomogeneous spatial distributions of devices around a gateway and obtain the number of devices that benefit from a given level of PDR. Unlike Georgiou and Raza, we adopt a realistic assumption about generated traffic: nodes send packets at the smallest possible time interval determined by the largest duty cycle possible at SF12. Under this assumption, devices generate packets in a way defined by a sensing application unlike the model by Georgiou and Raza that assumes 1% duty cycle of all devices regardless of SF, which means that a device that changes from SF8 to SF7 starts sending packets twice more often. We also modify the model expression for traffic intensity so it correctly reflects the unslotted ALOHA behavior (instead if slotted ALOHA).

In the rest of the paper, we describe the basics of LoRa networks (Section 2) and present the PDR model (Section 3). In Section 4, we analyze LoRaWAN capacity in terms of PDR for different spatial configurations. Finally, we discuss related work (Section 5) and draw some conclusions (Section 6).

2 LORAWAN BASICS

We briefly recall the basic characteristics of LoRaWAN.

Devices can control the physical layer of LoRaWAN through the following parameters [15]:

- Bandwidth (BW): it is the range of transmission frequencies. We can configure the bandwidth between 7.8 kHz and 500 kHz. A larger bandwidth allows for a higher data rate, but results in lower sensitivity.
- Spreading Factor (SF) characterizes the number of bits carried by a chirp: SF bits are mapped to one of $N = 2^{SF}$ possible frequency shifts in a chirp. SF varies between 6 (7 in practice) and 12, with SF12 resulting in the best sensitivity and range, at the cost of achieving the lowest data rate and worst energy consumption. Decreasing the SF by 1 unit roughly doubles the transmission rate and divides by 2 the transmission duration as well as energy consumption.
- Coding Rate (CR): it corresponds to the rate of Forward Error Correction (FEC) applied to improve packet error rate in presence of noise and interference. A lower coding rate results in better robustness, but increases the transmission time and energy consumption. The possible values are: 4/5, 4/6, 4/7, and 4/8.
- Transmitted Power (TP): LoRaWAN defines the following values of TP for the EU 863-870 MHz band: 2 dBm, 5 dBm, 8 dBm, 11 dBm, and 14 dBm.

Table 1 presents SFj, data rate DRj, Signal-to-Noise Ratio (SNR) limit, airtime τ_j, and s_{max}, the maximum payload size. τ_j denotes

Table 1: LoRa parameters for BW of 125 kHz.

SFj	SNR limit q_j	Airtime τ_j	Bit rate DRj	s_{max}
7	-7.5 dB	102.7 ms	DR5: 5469 b/s	230 B
8	-10 dB	184.8 ms	DR4: 3125 b/s	230 B
9	-12.5 dB	328.7 ms	DR3: 1758 b/s	123 B
10	-15 dB	616.5 ms	DR2: 977 b/s	59 B
11	-17.5 dB	1315 ms	DR1: 537 b/s	59 B
12	-20 dB	2466 ms	DR0: 293 b/s	59 B

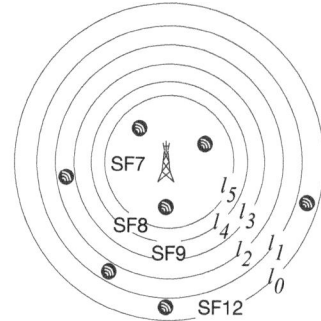

Figure 1: Annuli of SF configurations around a gateway

the transmission duration of the maximum size frame at data rate DRj.

LoRaWAN defines an access method similar to ALOHA: a device wakes up at any instant and sends a packet right away. It then wakes up after a delay to receive a downlink frame, if the transmitted frame was of the Confirmed Data type. Collisions occur when two devices transmit packets at the same time. However, unlike in the pure ALOHA scheme, a receiver can correctly receive a frame in presence of interfering signals, because the LoRa physical layer is robust enough to resist significant interference. The capture effect has important impact on LoRa performance. Taking into account the capture effect, Haxhibeqiri et al. [16] showed that when the number devices increases to 1000 per gateway, the packet loss rate only increases to 32%, which is low compared to 90% in pure ALOHA for the same load.

In the following sections, we assume LoRa modulations with 125 kHz bandwidth and spreading factors SF$\{12 - j\}$ that result in data rates DRj, with $j = 0, 1, \ldots 5$ (see Table 1).

3 MODEL FOR SUCCESSFUL PACKET DELIVERY

We consider a LoRaWAN cell in which devices choose SF (so the data rate) based on the distance to the gateway, which corresponds to the annuli view presented in Figure 1. l_j denotes the distance to the farthest device that uses SF$\{12 - j\}$ so its data rate is DRj. l_0 is the maximum transmission range.

We assume that devices are located at random in the annulus at l_j according to a Poisson Point Process (PPP) with intensity ρ_j. Inside the annulus, the spatial density is constant, so the number

Table 2: Equidistant SF boundaries [km], S_j/π [km^2]: value proportional to the number of devices (constant node density ρ in all annuli).

	SF7 l_5	SF8 l_4	SF9 l_3	SF10 l_2	SF11 l_1	SF12 l_0
l_j [km]	1	2	3	4	5	6
S_j/π [km^2]	1	3	5	7	9	11

Table 3: Notation

Traffic generation intensity	λ_t
Frame transmission duration at data rate DRj	τ_j
Distance of farthest node using DRj	l_j
Surface of annulus j	S_j
Spatial density of nodes in annulus j	ρ_j
Total number of nodes	n
Average number of nodes in annulus j	n_j
Traffic occupancy (in Erlang) at DRj	v_j
Average channel gain at distance d	$g(d)$
SNR threshold for DRj	q_j
Transmission power, in-band noise power	P, N
Success probability, due to attenuation, fading	H
Success probability, due to collisions	Q_1

of nodes using SF$\{12 - j\}$ and data rate DRj is proportional to ρ_j and the surface of the annulus between l_{j+1} and l_j.

Table 2 presents the values of l_j for the *equidistant* SF configuration with maximum range l_0 of 6 km and a *homogeneous* density (Mahmood et al. considered such boundaries [7] and Georgiou and Raza provided numerical examples for the double maximum range: l_0 of 12 km [4]). The number of devices in a disk or annulus is proportional to surface S_j so it increases with the distance. Note that energy consumption of a node in annulus j is proportional to airtime τ_j, which attains large values for high SF.

We give below the details of the model [4] to compute PDR based on the notation in Table 3.

Provided that there is no collision, a frame transmission succeeds as long as the SNR at the receiver for this transmission is above q_j, the minimum SNR for the corresponding spreading factor [17]. We consider a Rayleigh channel, so that the received signal power is affected by a multiplicative random variable with an exponential distribution of unit mean (and standard deviation). Recent measurements confirm the validity of the hypothesis for LoRa transmissions [18]. Thus, the signal power depends on the distance and the Rayleigh fading gain, whereas the noise power is the constant thermal noise for a 125 kHz-wide band: $N = -123$ dBm. We consider the maximum transmission power of $P = 14$ dBm.

Thus, the probability of successful transmission at distance l_j with data rate DRj is [4]:

$$H(l_j) = \exp\left(-\frac{Nq_j}{Pg(l_j)}\right), \qquad (1)$$

where $g(l_j)$ is the average channel gain at distance l_j. We use the Okumura-Hata model for path loss attenuation.

We use an approximate expression for the success probability in presence of concurrent traffic [4] reflecting the behavior of unslotted ALOHA with capture:

$$Q_1(l_j, v_j) = \frac{2\exp(-2v_j)l_j^\eta(\eta + 2)S_j}{\pi 2 v_j l_j^{\eta+2} + l_j^\eta(2(\eta + 2)S_j - 2\pi v_j l_j^2)}, \qquad (2)$$

where η is the path loss exponent (we assume $\eta = 4$ in the numerical examples below, which gives relative attenuation values that closely match those of the propagation model). Note that we double the traffic intensity in the expression by Georgiou and Raza to reflect correctly the behavior of unslotted ALOHA.

Finally, PDR of nodes in annulus j is the following:

$$PDR(l_j, v_j) = H(l_j) \times Q_1(l_j, v_j) \qquad (3)$$

To use these expressions, we need to define traffic intensity v_j. We consider that nodes generate traffic according to a Poisson process of intensity λ_t. For SF $= 12 - j$ and n_j, the number of contending nodes in annulus j, traffic occupancy is

$$v_j = n_j \tau_j \lambda_t \qquad (4)$$

in Erlang and the number of nodes in annulus j is:

$$n_j = \frac{S_j \rho_j n}{\sum_j S_j \rho_j} \qquad (5)$$

We set λ_t to the traffic intensity of nodes operating at DR0 and SF12 at their maximal duty cycle and using 59 B packets, the maximum size at this rate. The duty cycle depends on the frequency band: LoRa devices have to limit their occupation of each frequency band to 1% of time with 3 to 5 frequency channels in each band in Europe. The airtime of maximum size packets at DR0 corresponds to 2.47 s so they can be sent every 747 s to achieve 0.33% duty cycle per frequency channel. Thus,

$$\lambda_t = \frac{1}{747\,s}. \qquad (6)$$

4 PROBABILITY OF SUCCESSFUL PACKET DELIVERY FOR DIFFERENT SPATIAL CONFIGURATIONS

In this section, we analyze PDR for different spatial configurations.

4.1 SF Allocation Strategies

There are several ways of allocating SF to nodes, which means finding the annuli boundaries l_j (we restrict our analysis to non-overlapping allocations in which all nodes in a given annulus use the same value of SF) [5, 7, 19]:

(1) *Equidistant* SF allocation with $l_{j+1} - l_j = l_0/6$ (also called equal-interval-based [19]).
(2) *Equal-area-based* SF allocation with $l_j = l_0\sqrt{j/6}$ [19].
(3) *SNR-based* SF allocation with $l_j = \{d : H(d) \geq \theta\}$ (also called path loss based [7]).
(4) *PDR-based* SF allocation with $l_j = \{d : H(d) \times Q_1(d) \geq \theta\}$.

Mahmood et al. showed that equidistant and SNR-based SF allocations performed the best, nevertheless, they did not consider the PDR-based allocation [7]. Lim and Han analyzed the PDR-based

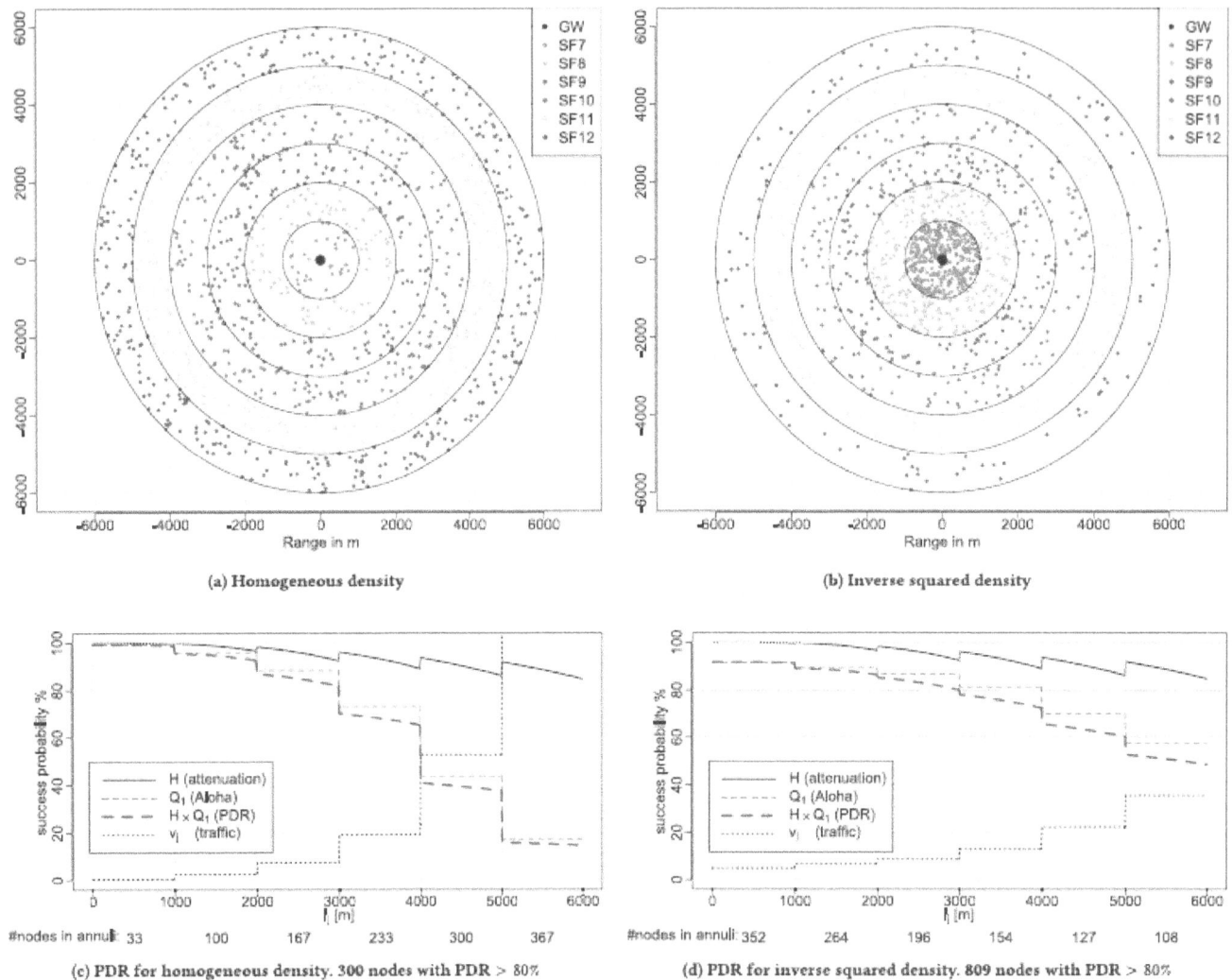

(a) Homogeneous density

(b) Inverse squared density

(c) PDR for homogeneous density. 300 nodes with PDR > 80%

(d) PDR for inverse squared density. 809 nodes with PDR > 80%

Figure 2: Comparison of spatial models, $n = 1200$.

SF allocation and showed that it performs the best with the equal-area-based SF allocation ranked second [19]. However, they did not take into account the capture effect important to evaluate the probability of success reception under the LoRaWAN access method. The analyses assumed a constant node density within the range.

Note that the complexity of computing SF allocations increases with the order of allocations presented above: equidistant and equal-area-based allocations only depend on the distance, the SNR-based allocation requires solving Eq. 1 numerically, and PDR-based allocations lead to a nonlinear optimization problem.

The SNR-based allocation resulting from solving Eq. 1 numerically for each j gives the values of l_j presented in Table 4 for three values of threshold θ: 90%, 95%, and 99%. We can observe that increasing the threshold results in smaller cells.

The SNR-based and PDR-based allocations can be implemented in a similar way to the Adaptive Data Rate (ADR) algorithm defined in LoRaWAN. In ADR, the gateway estimates the average SNR level for the last 20 packets of a node. It then chooses SF and TP suitable for the given level of SNR, while keeping a 5 dB margin, and sends the parameters in the LinkADRReq frame to the node. In a similar way, the gateway can estimate PDR and choose the right parameters for the node. Nevertheless, such allocations require sending downlink messages, whereas the gateways have very limited transmission capacity.

4.2 Inhomogeneous Node Density

We have already discussed the reasons for which assuming constant node density ρ for all annuli is not realistic. Moreover, the allocation of SF in LoRaWAN strongly impacts energy consumption so that far devices that need to use high values of SF will consume much

Table 4: SNR-based SF boundaries [km], $H(l_j)$ is the success probability due to attenuation, fading, thermal noise. S_j/π [km^2]: value proportional to the number of devices. Node density in an annulus based on the inverse-square law so $S_j/\pi \times \rho(l_j)$ is proportional to the number of devices.

	SF7 l_5	SF8 l_4	SF9 l_3	SF10 l_2	SF11 l_1	SF12 l_0
$l_j : H(l_j) \geq 90\%$	2.23	2.68	3.23	3.89	4.54	5.30
S_j/π [km^2]	4.96	2.23	3.24	4.69	5.49	7.47
ρ_j	1	0.69	0.48	0.33	0.24	0.18
$S_j/\pi \times \rho(l_j)$	4.96	1.54	1.54	1.54	1.32	1.32
$l_j : H(l_j) \geq 95\%$	1.84	2.21	2.66	3.20	3.74	4.37
S_j/π [km^2]	3.38	1.50	2.19	3.17	3.74	5.1
ρ_j	1	0.69	0.48	0.33	0.24	0.18
$S_j/\pi \times \rho(l_j)$	3.38	1.03	1.05	1.05	0.9	0.9
$l_j : H(l_j) \geq 99\%$	1.18	1.43	1.72	2.07	2.41	2.82
S_j/π [km^2]	1.40	0.63	0.91	1.33	1.55	2.11
ρ_j	1	0.69	0.48	0.33	0.24	0.18
$S_j/\pi \times \rho(l_j)$	1.40	0.44	0.44	0.44	0.37	0.37

more energy than devices with low SF, which will discourage the placement of nodes far from the gateway. There is also another adverse effect of using high values of SF: increased transmission times lead to more contention and collisions, thus affecting the probability of successful packet reception.

To take into account these considerations, we adopt a more realistic model for the spatial distribution of nodes based on the inverse-square law for node density:

$$\frac{\rho_j}{\rho_{j-1}} = \frac{l_{j-1}^2}{l_j^2} \qquad (7)$$

Table 4 also presents node density ρ_j for each annulus based on this relation and the value proportional to the number of devices. To see the effect of the decreasing node density, we can observe that such a distribution favors the annuli close to the gateway with a higher number of devices using SF7 and results in less devices with SF 11 and SF12.

Figure 2 compares the spatial models—Figures 2a and 2b visualize the distribution of nodes for homogeneous and inverse squared density (n = 1200 nodes generated with a Monte Carlo method, randomly placed in equidistant annuli). We can observe that the number of nodes in the SF12 annulus is much lower for inverse squared density: 108 vs. 367 (see Figures 2c and 2d).

4.3 LoRaWAN capacity for different spatial configurations

In this section, we present figures with PDR computed according to the model in Section 3. The total number of nodes (1200, 1700, and 2100) for the figures was chosen so that they give the maximal number of nodes that benefit from PDR > 80% for the respective SNR thresholds (we discuss this aspect at the end of this Section).

4.3.1 Equidistant SF frontiers. Figures 2a and 2c present the spatial distribution of nodes and PDR in equidistant SF annuli for a

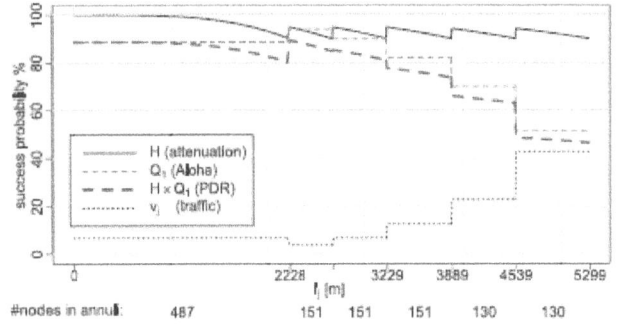

Figure 3: Inverse squared density and SNR SF annuli for $H(l_j) \geq 90\%$, n = 1200. 787 nodes with PDR > 80%.

homogeneous density and n = 1200 nodes. The existing studies use this distribution and equidistance frontiers of SF allocation to analyze the LoRa capacity. Figure 2c shows PDR and its components: channel attenuation H and Q_1, the success probability under ALOHA with capture. We can observe that Q_1 goes down at each frontier because of increased traffic v_j that comes from an increased number of nodes. As the annuli surface increases with the distance, the homogeneous node density results in the number of nodes in annuli growing with the distance and attaining 367 for SF12 with only 33 nodes using SF7. The estimated number of nodes that benefit from PDR > 80% is 300. The spatial model assumes that there are no nodes outside the last annuli.

Figures 2b and 2d present the distribution of nodes and PDR when the density of nodes is inversely proportional to the square of distance. PDR goes down with the distance much slowly than in Figure 2c because there are less nodes in higher SF annuli: 352 nodes using SF7 and 108 for SF12. The estimated number of nodes that benefit from PDR > 80% is 809. We can observe that the number of nodes in each annulus decreases with the distance.

This basic example shows the importance of the spatial model for evaluating LoRaWAN capacity: just changing the spatial distribution of nodes raises the number of nodes with good PDR from 300 to 809. So, the choice of the spatial model may result in misleading results on LoRaWAN capacity and scalability.

4.3.2 SNR-based SF frontiers. Figure 3 presents PDR in SNR-based SF allocation for the inverse squared density and n = 1200 nodes. For $H(l_j) \geq 90\%$ threshold, the range of the cell is relatively large with 5.3 km. 787 nodes benefit from PDR > 80% out of 1200.

Figure 4 and Figure 5 present the same data for $H(l_j) \geq 95\%$ and $H(l_j) \geq 99\%$ thresholds and the total number of nodes n = 1700 and n = 2100, respectively. The increased value of the threshold results in smaller cells (2.82 km for $H(l_j) \geq 99\%$) because of the dependance of funtion H on the distance. The number of nodes that benefit from PDR > 80% is 1115 and 1377, respectively.

We can observe that the assumption of the inhomogeneous density results in an interesting effect: smaller cells can provide good PDR for an increased number of nodes. It evokes "cell breathing" in cellular networks in which heavily loaded cells decrease in size.

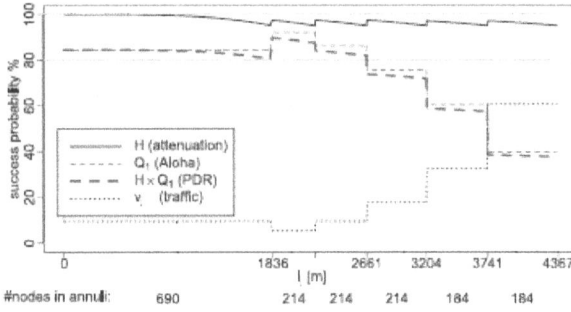

Figure 4: Inverse squared density and SNR SF annuli for $H(l_j) \geq 95\%$, $n = 1700$. **1115 nodes with PDR > 80%.**

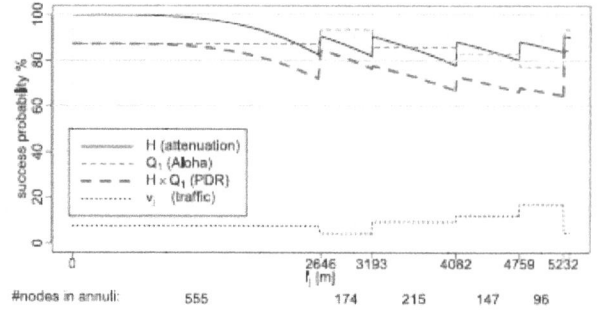

Figure 7: Inverse squared density and PDR SF annuli for $H(l_j) \geq 90\%$, $n = 1200$. **460 nodes with PDR > 80%.**

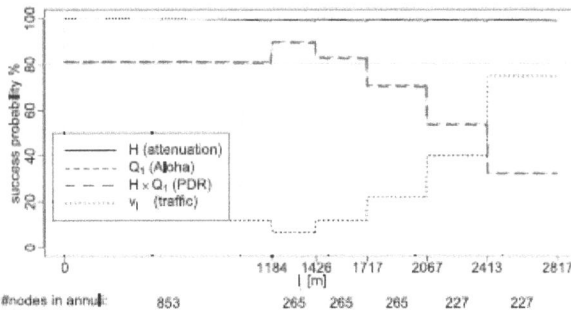

Figure 5: Inverse squared density and SNR SF annuli for $H(l_j) \geq 99\%$, $n = 2100$. **1377 nodes with PDR > 80%.**

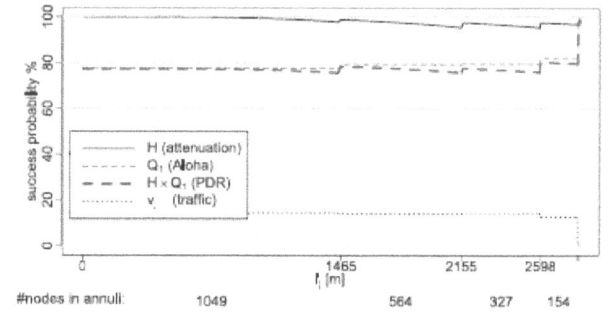

Figure 8: Inverse squared density and PDR SF annuli for $H(l_j) \geq 99\%$, $n = 2100$. **No nodes with PDR > 80%.**

4.3.3 PDR-based SF frontiers. For PDR-based SF allocations, we use the Nelder-Mead simplex [20] to find

$$\underset{l_0 .. l_5}{\arg\max} \, min(H \times Q_1). \qquad (8)$$

The optimization starts with the maximal range l_0 that we set to the thresholds for two extreme SNR-based allocations: 5.30 km for 90% and 2.82 km for 99% (we skip the intermediate threshold of 95%), and looks for more uniform distribution of PDR values across SF annuli with the maxmin objective. We still assume the density of nodes inversely proportional to the square of distance.

Figure 7 presents PDR in the first case of a large cell: $l_0 = 5.30$ km for 90% for the same total number of nodes as in Figure 3. Compared to Figure 3, the minimum value of PDR is higher (PDR > 60%), however, there are less nodes that benefit from good PDR > 80% (460 vs. 787).

Similarly, Figure 8 shows PDR for the small cell: 2.82 km for 99%. When comparing with Figure 5, we can see a similar effect—the minimal value of PDR is high (almost reaching 80%), but still the number of nodes that benefit from good PDR > 80% is low, which shows that the call has attained its capacity. If we lower the total number of nodes in the network to 1500, the maxmin PDR allocation gives very good results: Figure 9 shows that all nodes achieve PDR > 80%.

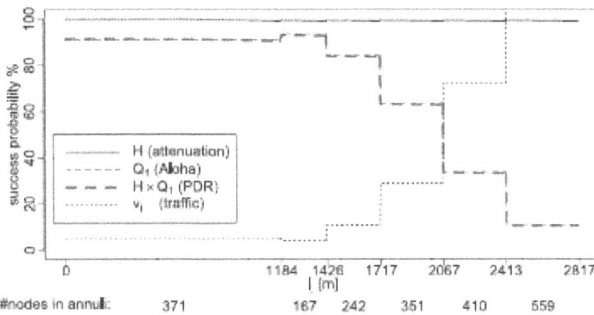

Figure 6: Homogeneous density and SNR SF annuli for $H(l_j) \geq 99\%$, $n = 2100$. **776 nodes with PDR > 80%.**

Note that the nodes benefiting from PDR > 80%, use low SF values: SF7, SF8, and SF9, which also means that their energy consumption stays low.

Figure 6 presents the results for a homogeneous density to compare with Figure 5: there are 776 nodes with PDR > 80%.

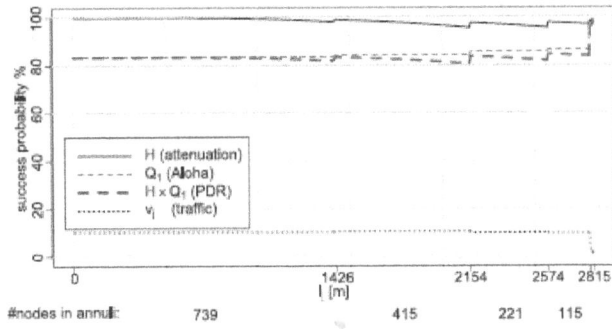

Figure 9: Inverse squared density and PDR SF annuli for $H(l_j) \geq 99\%$, $n = 1500$. All 1500 nodes with PDR > 80%.

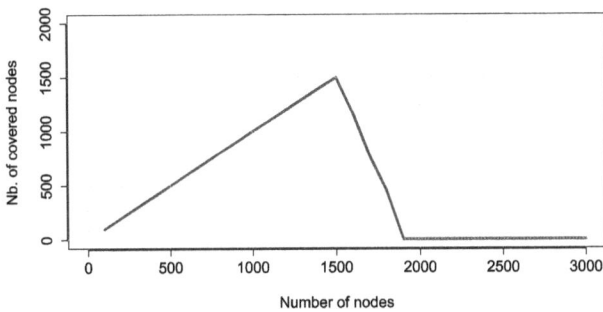

Figure 11: Number of nodes with PDR > 80% in function of the total number of nodes in the network. SNR allocation of annuli frontiers l_j.

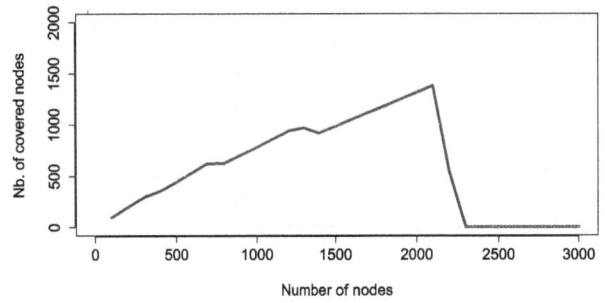

Figure 10: Number of nodes with PDR > 80% in function of the total number of nodes in the network. Optimal allocation of annuli frontiers l_j as in Figure 9.

Note that the allocation exhibits strong asymmetry—it favors lower SF over high SF: there are 739 nodes in the SF7 annuli compared to only 8 nodes with SF12. As H is as high as 99%, the most important factor for PDR is Q_1, which depends on the traffic load almost constant for all annuli with low SF (see Figure 9) in this allocation. Such an allocation has also an advantage of low overall energy consumption as only a few nodes use SF11 and SF12, expensive in terms of energy.

4.3.4 Scalability. Figure 10 shows the number of nodes that benefit from good PDR > 80% in function of the total number of nodes in the network for the small cell of the 2.82 km range. We fix the allocation of annuli frontiers l_j to the optimal allocation presented in Figure 9 and we vary the total number of nodes. At the beginning, the number of nodes with PDR > 80% increases and achieves the maximum for $n = 1500$. Then, the number of nodes with PDR > 80% decreases because PDR begins to drop below 80%, which means that the network has attained its capacity.

A question remains: how does the SNR allocation perform compared to the PDR based one? Figure 11 shows the corresponding data for the SNR allocation. It achieves a lower maximum number of nodes with PDR > 80% (1377 nodes for $n = 2100$, see also Figure 5), but it can handle a slightly larger total number of nodes.

5 RELATED WORK

We briefly review previous work on modeling LoRa capacity and inhomogeneous spatial models.

5.1 LoRa capacity models

Georgiou and Raza [4] provided a stochastic geometry framework for modeling the performance of a single gateway LoRa network. They showed that the coverage probability drops exponentially as the number of contending devices grows. Their model assumes that the airtime is filled up—nodes use the shortest interval between packet transmissions allowed at given SF, which means that switching to lower SF results in generating twice as much traffic. Moreover, the model of the access method corresponds to slotted ALOHA. In this paper, we have used the model with the modifications concerning the intensity of packet generation and the expression for the success probability reflecting the behavior of unslotted ALOHA.

Mahmood et al. [7] proposed an analytical model of a single-cell LoRa system that takes into account interference among transmissions over the same SF (co-SF) as well as different SFs (inter-SF). They derived the signal-to-interference ratio (SIR) distributions for several interference conditions. Due to imperfect orthogonality, inter-SF interference exposes the network for additional 15% coverage loss for a small number of concurrently transmitting end-devices.

Li et al. [5] analyzed interference in the time-frequency domain using a stochastic geometry model assuming transmissions as patterns on a two-dimensional plane to quantify the capture effect. They use the model to analyze LoRaWAN by characterizing the outage probability and throughput.

Based on a simple model for collisions and capture effect, Caillouet et al. [9] introduced a theoretical framework for maximizing the LoRaWAN capacity in terms of the number of end nodes.

All the presented models assumed a homogeneous node density around a gateway.

5.2 Inhomogeneous spatial models

Gotzner and Rathgeber [10] challenged the homogeneous assumption in spectrum frequency analysis and proposed to model the spatial inhomogeneity of real cellular traffic with log-normal distributions.

Lee et al. [11] observed that modeling and simulation of a cellular network typically assume the target area divided into regular hexagonal cells and a uniform distribution of mobile devices scattered in each cell. In reality, the spatial traffic distribution is highly non-uniform across different cells, which requires adequate spatial traffic models. They reported on traffic measurements collected from commercial cellular networks and demonstrated that the spatial distribution of the traffic density (the traffic load per unit area) can be approximated by the log-normal or Weibull distribution depending on time and space.

Mirahsan et al. [12] used maps of Paris, France to study the spatial traffic heterogeneity of outdoor users in dense areas of the city center. They found that the statistical distribution of spatial metrics is close to Weibull. Their results show that the building topology in a city imposes a significant degree of heterogeneity on the spatial distribution of the wireless traffic.

Taufique et al. [14] investigated the problem of planning future cellular networks. They noticed that the cell size increasingly adapts to the spatial traffic variation. Instead of having the same cell size throughout, areas with low traffic density can have larger cells compared to areas with high traffic density, resulting in energy and cost savings. As planning future cellular networks faces heterogeneous and ultra dense networks, the issue is to find the optimal base station placement jointly for macrocells and small cells in a non uniform user density scenario. They showed an example of such a deployment for a Gaussian spatial user distribution.

Wang et al. [13] characterized temporal and spatial dynamics in cellular traffic through a big cellular usage dataset covering 1.5 million users and 5,929 cell towers in a major city of China. Their results reveal highly non-uniform spatial distribution of the traffic density.

6 CONCLUSIONS

In this paper, we have shown that adopting inhomogeneous spatial node distribution leads to much different results on LoRaWAN capacity than that reported previously. The existing measurement studies of the traffic density in cellular networks showed high diversity of the node density in urban settings. We expect that LoRaWAN networks will follow the same deployment pattern with the placement of gateways close to high density areas.

We have used the model by Georgiou and Raza [4] to analyze the capacity of a LoRaWAN cell for various types of SF allocations: equidistant, SNR-based, and PDR-based. We can draw several conclusions from the numerical results presented in this paper:

- For a required PDR level and a target communication range, we can find an allocation of annuli l_j that results in the maximal number of nodes that benefit from the PDR level.
- There is a natural trend towards configurations composed of smaller cells that concentrate nodes close to the gateway.

In this way, nodes benefit from low SF, which also means lower energy consumption.

- To provide the required PDR level to more nodes, we need to consider multiple gateways that will increase the overall capacity while maintaining moderate energy consumption.

In future work, we plan to explore a model in which the density of nodes is a continuous distribution in function of the distance from the gateway, which may better reflect realistic deployment scenarios.

We also want to develop models for capacity prediction in case of multiple gateways.

ACKNOWLEDGMENTS

This work has been partially supported by the French Ministry of Research project PERSYVAL-Lab under contract ANR-11-LABX-0025-01.

REFERENCES

[1] LoRa^TM Alliance. A Technical Overview of LoRa and LoRaWAN.
[2] A. J. Berni and W. Gregg. On the Utility of Chirp Modulation for Digital Signaling. *IEEE Trans. Commun.*, 21, 1971.
[3] Nicolas Sornin. LoRaWAN 1.1 Specification. Technical report, LoRa Alliance, October 2017.
[4] Orestis Georgiou and Usman Raza. Low Power Wide Area Network Analysis: Can LoRa Scale? *IEEE Wireless Commun. Letters*, 6(2):162–165, 2017.
[5] Zhuocheng Li et al. 2D Time-Frequency Interference Modelling Using Stochastic Geometry for Performance Evaluation in Low-Power Wide-Area Networks. In *2017 ICC*, May 2017.
[6] Antoine Waret et al. LoRa Throughput Analysis with Imperfect Spreading Factor Orthogonality. *IEEE Wireless Communications Letters*, 2018.
[7] Aamir Mahmood et al. Scalability analysis of a lora network under imperfect orthogonality. *IEEE Trans. Industrial Informatics*, 15(3):1425–1436, 2019.
[8] Martin Heusse et al. How Many Sensor Nodes Fit in a LoRAWAN Cell? *submitted for publication*, 2019.
[9] Christelle Caillouet et al. Optimal SF Allocation in LoRaWAN Considering Physical Capture and Imperfect Orthogonality. In *2019 IEEE GLOBECOM Conference*, 2019.
[10] U. Gotzner and R. Rathgeber. Spatial Traffic Distribution in Cellular Networks. In *VTC '98. 48th IEEE Vehicular Technology Conference. Pathway to Global Wireless Revolution (Cat. No.98CH36151)*, volume 3, pages 1994–1998 vol.3, May 1998.
[11] Dongheon Lee et al. Spatial Modeling of the Traffic Density in Cellular Networks. *IEEE Wireless Commun.*, 21(1):80–88, 2014.
[12] Meisam Mirahsan et al. Measuring the Spatial Heterogeneity of Outdoor Users in Wireless Cellular Networks Based on Open Urban Maps. In *2015 ICC*, pages 2834–2838, 2015.
[13] Xu Wang et al. Spatio-Temporal Analysis and Prediction of Cellular Traffic in Metropolis. In *25th IEEE ICNP*, pages 1–10, 2017.
[14] Azar Taufique et al. Planning Wireless Cellular Networks of Future: Outlook, Challenges and Opportunities. *IEEE Access*, 5:4821–4845, 2017.
[15] Semtech. SX1272/73 - 860 MHz to 1020 MHz Low Power Long Range Transceiver, 2017. URL https://www.semtech.com/uploads/documents/sx1272.pdf.
[16] Jetmir Haxhibeqiri et al. LoRa Scalability: A Simulation Model Based on Interference Measurements. *Sensors*, 17(6):1193, 2017.
[17] Claire Goursaud and Jean-Marie Gorce. Dedicated networks for IoT : PHY / MAC state of the art and challenges. *EAI endorsed transactions on Internet of Things*, 2015.
[18] Takwa Attia et al. Experimental Characterization of LoRaWAN Link Quality. In *2019 IEEE GLOBECOM Conference*. IEEE, 2019.
[19] J. Lim and Y. Han. Spreading Factor Allocation for Massive Connectivity in LoRa Systems. *IEEE Communications Letters*, 22(4):800–803, April 2018.
[20] J. A. Nelder and R. Mead. A Simplex Method for Function Minimization. *The Computer Journal*, 7(4):308–313, 01 1965.

Evaluation of LoRaWAN Transmission Range for Wireless Sensor Networks in Riparian Forests

Pablo Avila-Campos
Fabian Astudillo-Salinas
Andres Vazquez-Rodas
Alcides Araujo
pablo.avila@ucuenca.edu.ec
fabian.astudillos@ucuenca.edu.ec
andres.vazquezr@ucuenca.edu.ec
alcides.araujo@ucuenca.edu.ec
University of Cuenca
Department of Electrical, Electronic and Telecommunications Engineering
Cuenca, Ecuador

ABSTRACT

Low power wide area networks (LPWAN) such as long range wide area networks (LoRaWAN), provide several advantages on monitoring systems development in forested environments due to its simple set-up, low cost, low power consumption, and wide coverage. Regarding the coverage area, the transmission in forested environments can be highly attenuated by foliage and must be defined to optimize the number of nodes. This paper discusses an empirical study of LoRa with LoRaWAN transmission range in riparian forests, based on path-loss modeling, using both received signal strength indicator (RSSI) and signal-to-noise-ratio (SNR). The measurements have been conducted in the riparian forest of three local rivers at urban, semi-urban, and rural environments located in the city of Cuenca, Ecuador. The measurement results found that there is a significant distribution difference among measurement places, a high correlation between two banks of the same river, a higher standard deviation in urban measurements and a larger coverage in rural areas.

KEYWORDS

LoRa; LoRaWAN; IoT; RSSI; SNR; path loss; forested; riverside; propagation; model; riparian

ACM Reference Format:
Pablo Avila-Campos, Fabian Astudillo-Salinas, Andres Vazquez-Rodas, and Alcides Araujo. 2019. Evaluation of LoRaWAN Transmission Range for Wireless Sensor Networks in Riparian Forests. In *22nd Int'l ACM Conf. on Modeling, Analysis and Simulation of Wireless and Mobile Systems (MSWiM'19), Nov. 25–29, 2019, Miami Beach, FL, USA.* ACM, New York, NY, USA, 8 pages. https://doi.org/10.1145/3345768.3355934

1 INTRODUCTION

Program for water and soil management (PROMAS for its acronym in Spanish) monitors a wealth of environmental information regarding wind, rain, temperature, humidity, barometric pressure, and water level of rivers. For this purpose, around 130 remote weather stations have been deployed in a large area of Azuay, Cañar, and Chimborazo. PROMAS has two projects related to limnigraphic sensors. The first one is the early flood warning and the other is the flow prediction using neural networks [6].

Our research team is working on the design and implementation of a wireless network to gather the sensors information and transmit it to the PROMAS data center. The goal is to take advantage of wireless technologies to reduce the displacement of people in charge of downloading the data. Consequently, this will maximize the availability of limnigraphic information in an hour-based transmissions, reduce the risk of losing information, and minimize mobilization expenses that can be used for maintenance purposes.

LPWANs represent a new trend in the evolution of wireless communication technologies. This communication technology is able to connect and monitor high number of sensors, covering wide areas at low energy cost [2]. One of the newest approaches to this technology is long range (LoRa) [18]. LoRa gives all the LPWAN advantages, adding low device cost and easy deployment. LoRa-based wireless sensor networks (WSNs) are able to collect real time information such as temperature, rain, humidity, flow, and other weather factors. A clear application scenario for LoRa is forest environments.

LoRaWAN is a medium access control layer created by the LoRa Alliance. It uses the advantages of LoRa modulation to create networks, and it is focused on the Internet of Things (IoT) paradigm [21]. LoRaWAN uses a star topology where the nodes, collect the sensor information and send it to the gateways (GW). The GWs convert the data to the internet protocol (IP) and forward it to a remote application server via Internet. This architecture is shown in Fig. 1.

When any wireless network is designed, the main question that must be answered is the maximum distance between two nodes that still ensures a reliable wireless connection. Environmental vegetation plays a significant role in the fading phenomena in wireless

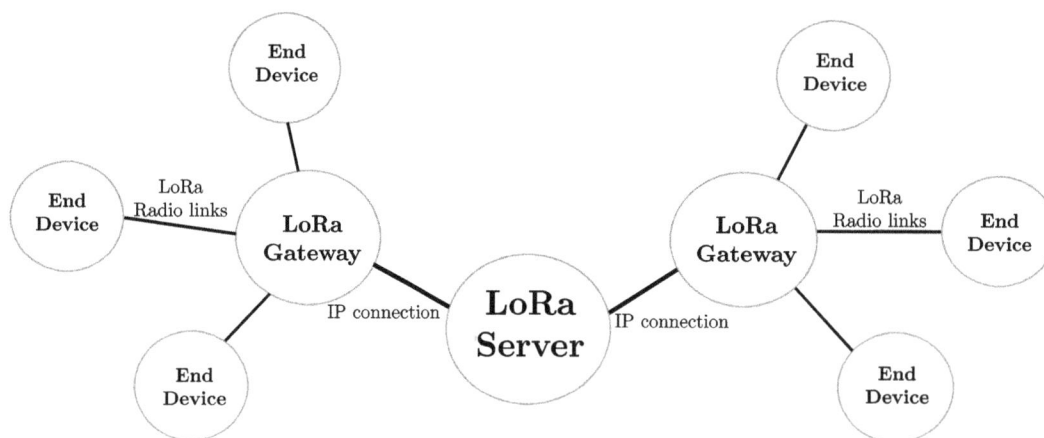

Figure 1: LoRaWAN Architecture [20]

communications [12]. The answer also depends on different technical parameters such as the transmitter power, receiver sensitivity, signal propagation and signal frequency [8]. Until now, there are studies reported in the literature about performance, scalability, indoor propagation, and range evaluation, but given that LoRa is a rather new technology, there are no reported measurements of propagation in riparian forest.

The contribution of this paper is to present the results of a 915 MHz ISM band, LoRa modulation riparian forest propagation measurement campaign. This is a typical limnigraphic measurement scenario. The main task is to capture channel statistics through received signal strength indicator (RSSI), signal-to-noise ratio (SNR), and packet error rate (PER) under different LoRaWAN available data rates (DR) at a height of under 2 m [19].

To the best of our knowledge, this is the first low antenna height LoRa measurement campaign conducted in a riparian forest. This collected data will be used to adjust a path loss model (P_L) to the specific measurement locations [14]. This study will help to a faster design and deployment of LoRa sensor networks, making it easier to calculate the useful coverage area of a LoRaWAN system.

2 BACKGROUND
2.1 LPWAN

The IoT ecosystem is broad, containing devices with data rates ranging from a few bps to Mbps. The coverage is also variable from a few centimeters to several kilometers. LPWAN is responsible for covering these needs in new applications that arise daily [3]. Although these networks must cover different needs, there are common requirements in the design of an LPWAN network. The main characteristics of an LPWAN network are:

- LPWAN requires a minimum energy consumption during operation. This because the limited capacity of batteries and its high cost.
- Cost is an important factor. Especially in the nodes, easy-to-install tools must be provided, and both the hardware and software should be low-cost.
- The level of activity depends on the specific application. However, the device must be able to wake up only when be

needed to send information. This point would support the idea of star type architectures against mesh architectures.
- The network infrastructure must be easy to assemble. The addition of devices or the transfer to other countries must comply with international standards.
- The transferred information between the node and the final user must be safe.
- Nodes are not in motion in most of these applications, thus the channel remais almost constant.

2.2 LoRa

LoRa is a proprietary modulation scheme derived from the Chirp Spread Spectrum modulation (CSS). Its main objective is to improve sensitivity at the cost of a reduction in the data rate for a given bandwidth (BW). LoRa implements variable data rates, using orthogonal Spreading Factors (SF). It allows a compromise between the data rate and coverage, as well as optimizing the performance of the network with a constant bandwidth.

LoRa is a physical layer implementation and does not depend on higher layers implementations. This allows it to coexist with different network architectures. Some basic concepts about LoRa modulation and the advantages to develop an LPWAN network are presented [18].

In information theory, Shannon's Theorem - Hartley, defines the maximum rate at which the information can be transmitted on a communication channel with a specific bandwidth in presence of noise. From this well-known equation, it can be concluded that if it increases bandwidth, it can compensate the degradation of the SNR of the radio channel.

In Direct Sequence Spread Spectrum (DSSS), the transmitter carrier phase changes according to a code sequence. This process is achieved by multiplying the desired data signal with a spreading code, known as chip sequence. This chip sequence has a higher rate than the data signal, so widens the bandwidth of the original signal.

As a result, a reduction in the amount of interference occurs due to a processing gain. DSSS is widely used in communication applications. However, there are challenges when it is necessary to reduce the cost and energy consumption of devices with this technology.

LoRa modulation solves the DSSS problems by providing an alternative of lower cost and lower energy consumption. In LoRa modulation, the spread spectrum is achieved by generating a chirp signal that continuously varies in the frequency domain. An advantage of this method is that the timing and frequency variations between the transmitter and the receiver are equivalent, reducing the receiver complexity.

This chirp bandwidth is equivalent to the spectral signal bandwidth. The desired signal is widened with a chip and modulated on a chirp. The relationship between the desired data rate, the symbol rate and the chip rate for LoRa, is expressed by the Eq. (1).

$$R_b = SF \frac{\text{CodeRate}}{\frac{2^{SF}}{BW}} \text{bits/sec} \qquad (1)$$

where:

- R_b = Bit rate of the modulation
- SF = Spreading factor $(7 - 12)$
- CR = Code rate $(1 - 4)$
- BW = Bandwidth (Hz)
- CodeRate = $4/(4 + CR)$

2.3 Transmission Parameters

LoRa devices can be configured using different Transmission Power (TP), Carrier Frequency (CF), Spreading Factor (SF), Bandwidth (BW) and Coding Rate (CR). This parameters are tuned to achieve the best connection performance and the lowest energy consumption.

The previous variables combination results in around 6720 possible configurations, which allows a user to completely adjust LoRa to the required application [4]. Next, a brief description of the mentioned parameters is presented [5]:

(1) **Transmission Power (TP)**: It can varies between −4 dBm and 20 dBm, but due to implementation limits, it can be adjusted from 2 dBm to 20 dBm. With transmission power of more than 17 dBm, only 1% of the duty cycle can be used.

(2) **Carrier Frequency (CF)**: It is the central frequency that can be varied in 61 Hz steps between 137 MHz and 1020 MHz, depending on the chip and the region of use.

(3) **Spreading Factor (SF)**: It is the ratio between the symbol rate and the chip rate. A higher SF not only increases the SNR, range and sensitivity, but also the air time of the packet. Each increase in the SF also reduces the transmission rate, doubling the duration of the transmission and the energy consumption. The SF can vary between 6 and 12, being useful for network separation since the SFs are orthogonal.

(4) **Bandwidth (BW)**: It is the frequency range in the transmission band. A higher BW gives a higher data rate (less airtime), but lower sensitivity for noise aggregation. A lower BW requires more precise crystals, that is, less parts per million (ppm). The data is sent at a chip rate equivalent to the BW. A BW of 125 kHz is equivalent to a chip rate of 125 kcps. A typical LoRa network operates at: 125 kHz, 250 kHz or 500 kHz.

(5) **Code Rate (CR)**: It is the Forward Error Correction rate (FEC) used by LoRa against interference. It can be configured with: 4/5, 4/6, 4/7 and 4/8. A larger CR offers more protection against noise, but increases the airtime. Transmitters with different CR can communicate since the CR is in the header of the packet that is always encoded at a 4/8 rate.

2.4 Key LoRa Modulation Properties

In the following we describe some key aspects that highlight LoRa and make it one of the best candidates for IoT applications [18]:

- **Scalable Bandwidth**: It can be used in narrow band frequency jumps and broadband direct sequence applications.
- **Low Energy Consumption**: Power output can be reduced compared to FSK, while keeping the same or better link budget.
- **High Robustness**: Due to its asynchronous nature, the LoRa signal is resistant to in-band and out-band interference.
- **Fade Resistant**: Thanks to the broadband chirp pulses, LoRa offers fading and multipath immunity, making it ideal for urban and suburban environments.
- **Doppler Resistant**: Doppler shift causes a small frequency shift in the LoRa pulse that introduces a non significant time axis shift of the baseband signal, making it immune to the Doppler effect.
- **Wide Coverage Capability**: Compared to FSK, maintaining the same transmission power, the link budget is higher in LoRa.
- **Enhanced Network Capability**: SemTech LoRa modulation employs orthogonal SFs that allow multiple propagation signals to be transmitted at the same time and on the same channel without substantial sensitivity degradation. The modulated signals with different SFs appear as noise to the target receiver and can be treated as such.

2.5 RSSI and SNR based Path Loss Model

In this section, we give a brief review of RSSI and SNR-based propagation models used in this study. Path Loss models are usually expressed in a logarithmic form as shown in Eq. (2) [9].

$$P_L(dB) = P_0(dBm) + 20 \ \log\left(\frac{d}{d_0}\right) + X_\theta \qquad (2)$$

where d and d_0 are the transmission distance and reference distance respectively. P_0 is the power strength at d_0. X_θ is a random variable normally distributed with standard deviation θ.

Another widely used model is the exponential decay model, shown in Eq. (3) [17]. This equation shows that path loss is an exponential function with frequency f and distance d. This equation was proposed for cases were the antennas are located near to trees and thus the signal propagates through the trees. Weissberger and COST-235 models are modifications of this model to different forested environments.

$$L(dB) = A \ f^B d^C \qquad (3)$$

These models can be simplified into Eq. (4), as is proposed in [9].

$$P_L(dB) = a + b \, \log(d) + X_\theta \qquad (4)$$

In this case, all the characteristics of Eq. (3) are expressed in Eq. (4). The exponential factor of distance is b, and the other components are expressed by a. As in Eq. (2), the randomness of the received signal is expressed in X_θ. It is assumed that the error of fitting in Eq. (4) follows a normal distribution with zero mean and standard deviation (θ). In this work, the standard deviation is calculated between the fitted curve and the mean values of every measurement point as shown in Eq. (5).

$$\theta = \text{std}(P_L - \text{FittedCurve}) \qquad (5)$$

To calculate the P_L values from RSSI and SNR, Eq. (6) is used according to [14].

$$P_L = |\text{RSSI}| + \text{SNR} + P_{\text{tx}} + G_{\text{rx}} \qquad (6)$$

3 RELATED WORK

In this section, we briefly discuss some of the most important works related to propagation and coverage measurements, made with LoRa.

In [14], the authors present a study of performance and coverage that uses LoRa transceivers and RSSI as the main measurement variable to develop a path loss model. This work differs from our research mainly in two relevant aspects. First, this study is conducted in water and a coast environment. Second, they use European 868 MHz ISM band while we use American 915 MHz ISM band. This is because our study is conducted in Latin America allowing us to use different channels, and transmission power.

Another outdoor measurement based study is presented in [1], where the authors use PER and RSSI to estimate the performance of the system under two different tests. Authors evaluate the system under different payload length, bandwidth (BW), spreading factor (SF), and modulation schemes. The principal differences with our study are the use of different payload length, transmission with the FSK modulation scheme, and that the Fresnel zone is taken into account.

Another work, [21], presents a general evaluation of LoRa using multiple gateways; RSSI and ACKs to estimate the connection rate. A main aspect of the study is the reliability that was measured using long transmission periods. The study detected mobile network interference during certain hours that are not considered in the current work.

Indoor measurements have been conducted in [7] and [16]. In [7], DR, SF, bandwidth and bit rate are fixed and RSSI is used to measure performance. In [16], the study is more specific, the authors evaluated the performance of LoRa in health and wellbeing applications. The main difference is that we take into account an outside riparian environment of three rivers for measurements.

4 MATERIALS AND METHODS

This section presents a detailed description of the device parameters, environmental conditions and statistical tests used in the current work.

4.1 Equipment and Configuration

Propagation measurements are made at 915 MHz utilizing Microchip's Evaluation kit - 900. The Evaluation kit consists of a gateway working with the LoRa Semtech chip SX1301, two nodes that include light and temperature sensors with the RN2903. Transmission power, spreading factor, code rate and bandwidth are controlled by the LoRaWAN MAC protocol included [19]. The operation Data Rates (DR) can vary from 0 to 3 and the maximum power index of 5 gives a transmission power of 18.5 dBm. Technical modulation parameters are shown in Table 1. LoRaWAN DRs parameters are shown in Table 2.

For this experiment, we used one node transmitting 10 numerated messages transmitted with DR0, and 10 messages with DR3. The gateway is connected to a virtual server in a laptop to register the RSSI, SNR and the number of received messages at every transmission. Transmitter and receiver were located two meters above ground level. Physical configuration scheme is presented in Fig. 2. The implementation is available in [15].

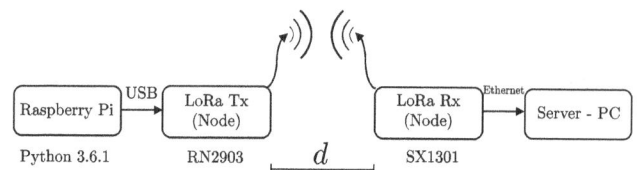

Figure 2: Equipment Physical Configuration

Table 1: Equipment and Parameters of Transmission [13]

Parameters/Equipment	Values/Description
Transmitter	RN2903
Receiver	SX1301
Antenna Gains	1.3 dBi
Modulation	LoRa
Spreading Factor	$7 - 10$
Bandwidth	125 kHz
Code Rate	4/5
Power Level	18.5 dBm

Table 2: Equipment Data Rates [19]

Data Rate	Configuration [SF/BW]	Bit Rate [bit/sec]
0	SF10/125 kHz	980
1	SF9/125 kHz	1760
2	SF8/125 kHz	3125
3	SF7/125 kHz	5470

4.2 Environment and Measurement Procedure

In this work, we carried out four measurements based on the previously mentioned PROMAS project using three different locations in the city of Cuenca, Ecuador. The first two measurements were made at the two riversides of Tomebamba river in an urban environment. This zone is characterized by different tree species of heights between 2 and 6 meters with irregular separations ranging from 4 to 6 meters. The ground is covered with short grass. The third measurement was done in one riverside of the Machángara river in a semi-urban zone of the same city. This place have mainly tree species of more than 5 meters in height, separations from 3 to 6 meters. The ground is covered by grass and rocks. The last measurement was done at a rural zone in the riverside of the Yanuncay River. In this zone, there are different trees species of heights between 1 to 6 meters with irregular separations from 1 to 4 meters. All rivers have a width of approximately 10 meters.

At each location, measurements were collected using a process called local average power, explained in [10]. According to this measurement procedure, one has to move a distance d of 20λ to 40λ in every measurement. Ten meters was selected in this study with the transmitter moving and the receiver (GW) fixed. As said before, at each point 20 packets were sent and registered by the receiver. Fig. 3 shows the sampling points represented by circles and the receiver location represented by the star at the upper left of the map.

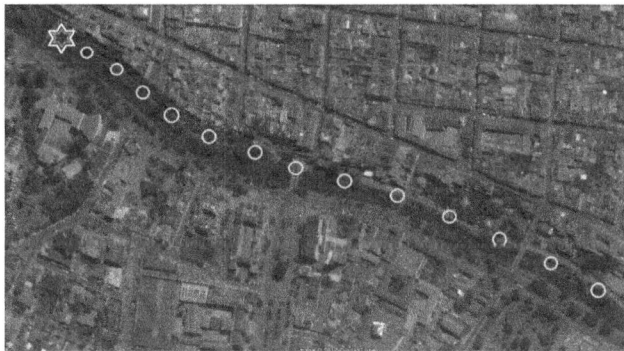

Figure 3: Sampling location map - Measurement 1

4.3 Statistical Analysis and Fitting

In the first place, a correlation analysis was done using the Measurements 1 and 2 to prove the relationship between the RSSI values of the same river. A statistical analysis is done to reject the hypothesis that the urban, semi-urban and rural RSSI measurements follow the same distribution. Kruskal-Wallis and Dunn tests are used to prove the hypothesis [11]. DR0 and DR3 RSSI means measurements follow a similar distribution as shown in Fig. 4, for this reason, the tests were performed only with DR0.

This study focuses on generating a path loss model based on RSSI and SNR values. Fig. 5 shows the fitting result of the urban environment with the minimum data rate. The empirical model generated is useful to determine the number of required nodes in a riparian forested environment, that uses LoRaWAN and similar technologies.

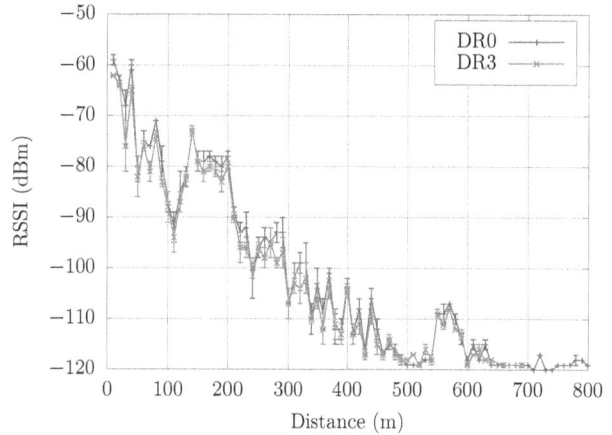

Figure 4: RSSI measurement 1 with DR0 and DR3

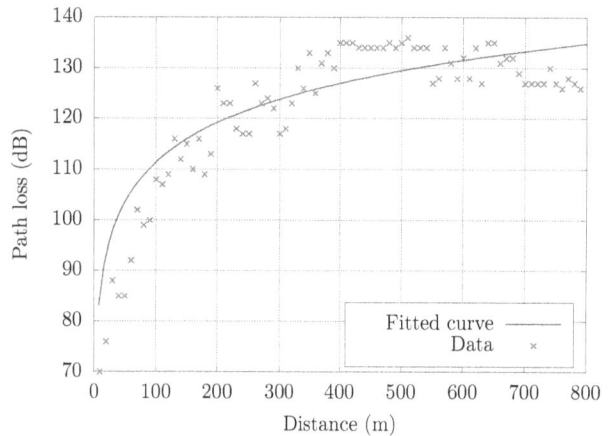

Figure 5: P_L fitting in urban environment with minimum data rate

5 RESULTS AND DISCUSSION

This section discusses and shows the measurement results of LoRa transmission on different riparian forested environments. In the first place, we show the correlation found between the riversides in the urban environment. Then the Kruskal-Wallis, Dunn tests and Path loss fitting results of DR0 and DR3 are presented. Finally, the variables of maximum coverage and standard deviation are compared between the different measurements.

5.1 Previous Measurements

To find the best number of messages to send at every sampling point, we did previous measurements of RSSI and SNR. Table 3 shows the standard deviations of RSSI for the different number of packets. Standard deviations show an expected tendency to decrease with the increase of sent messages. However, 10 packets were selected to send at every transmission point due to a low standard deviation variation of about 1 dBm.

Table 3: Standard deviation of RSSI with different number of packets

Test	Packets	RSSI Standard Deviation (dBm)
1	10	1.94
2	20	1.16
3	30	1.76
4	40	1.63
5	50	2.06
6	60	1.57
7	70	1.18
8	80	1.10
9	90	1.25
10	100	1.05

5.2 Statistical Analysis

In this section, we show the RSSI correlation analysis and Kruskal-Wallis and Dunn analysis results as described in Section 4.3.

- **Correlation Analysis:** It was carried out to know how correlated the RSSI measurements are between the two banks of the same river. In the case of measurements with the minimum data rate, a correlation value of 0.923 was obtained. Therefore, it is concluded that the correlation is high. This relationship is shown in Fig. 6.

  In the same way, in the case of RSSI measurements with the maximum data rate, a correlation coefficient of 0.922 was obtained, so it is concluded that there is a strong relationship between measurement 1 and measurement 2. This is shown in Fig. 7.

  The correlation value indicates that there is a strong relationship between the RSSI values. However, it does not mean that the LoRa coverage on the banks of the same river is the same, as it is shown in Section 5.4.

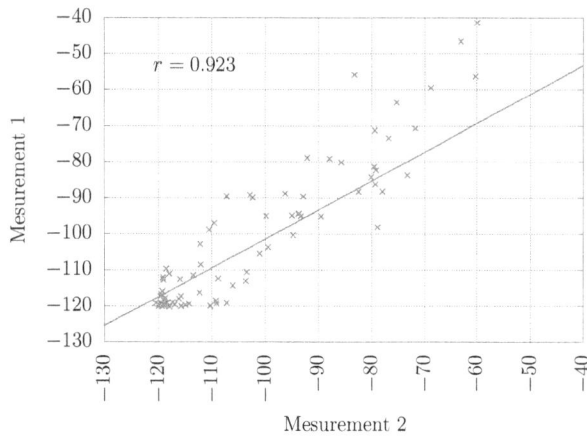

Figure 6: RSSI values at Tomebamba river with DR0

- **Distribution Comparison:** Two statistical tests were performed to determine the relationship between RSSI measurement distributions in the three selected environments. At

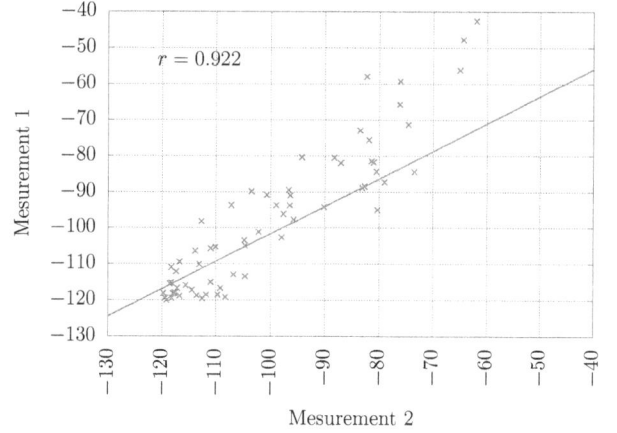

Figure 7: RSSI values at Tomebamba river with DR3

first, the null hypothesis that the three environments had equal distributions was rejected using the Kruskal-Wallis test that resulted in a p-value of 0.01 [11].

Then, the Dunn test was performed to compare the environment combinations. These tests are focused on proving a hypothesis of equality of distributions. Table 4 presents p-values of the test. P-values shows that there is not a distribution relationship between rural with semi-urban and urban with semi-urban environments.

Table 4: P-values of Dunn test

P-value	Rural	Semi-urban
Semi-urban	0.0010	
Urban	0.3788	0.0100

5.3 Path Loss Fitting

With RSSI and SNR mean values, Eq. (6) was used to calculate the path loss (P_L). The obtained values were fitted to Eq. (4). Finally, Eq. (5) was used to calculate the standard deviation.

(1) Propagation on Urban Environment (Measurement 1): Fig. 4 shows the RSSI measurements with DR0 and DR3. Using RSSI and SNR data, path loss is modeled and expressed in Eq. (7) and Eq. (8) for DR0 and DR3 respectively. Eq. (8) shows less standard deviation and greater range, as shown in Tables 5 and 6. The lowest standard deviation may be because DR3 has fewer samples to adjust by its lower SF.

$$P_{L,DR0}(dB) = 59.53 + 11.26\ \log(d) + X_\theta(\theta = 6.29) \quad (7)$$

$$P_{L,DR3}(dB) = 53.38 + 12.98\ \log(d) + X_\theta(\theta = 5.12) \quad (8)$$

(2) Propagation on Urban Environment (Measurement 2): Compared with measurement 1, lower standard deviations are observed in DR0 and DR3, in addition to greater coverage, this is due to the topographic characteristics of the place that

are similar to those of Measurement 1 but are not the same. The logarithmic fittings are observed in Eqs. (9) and (10).

$$P_{L,DR0}(dB) = 44.96 + 13.39 \log(d) + X_\theta(\theta = 5.83) \qquad (9)$$
$$P_{L,DR3}(dB) = 26.24 + 17.49 \log(d) + X_\theta(\theta = 3.72) \qquad (10)$$

(3) Propagation on Semi-Urban Environment (Measurement 3): The third measurement was performed in a semi-urban environment. Standard deviations are lower compared to the urban measurements due to the lower number of obstacles in the environment. This is shown in the Eqs. (11) and (12). The maximum coverage also improved to 1170 and 1100 meters for DR0 and DR3 respectively.

$$P_{L,DR0}(dB) = 61.55 + 10.7 \log(d) + X_\theta(\theta = 2.92) \qquad (11)$$
$$P_{L,DR3}(dB) = 62.74 + 10.67 \log(d) + X_\theta(\theta = 3.20) \qquad (12)$$

(4) Propagation on Rural Environment (Measurement 4): The last measurement was taken in a rural setting. In this case, the obstacles were mainly trees and shrubs beside the own topography of the place. The transmission range is the best since 1600 and 1500 meters were reached for DR0 and DR3 respectively. The logarithmic fittings are observed in Eqs. (13) and (14).

$$P_{L,DR0}(dB) = 55.36 + 11.27 \log(d) + X_\theta(\theta = 3.73) \qquad (13)$$
$$P_{L,DR3}(dB) = 61.13 + 10.55 \log(d) + X_\theta(\theta = 3.88) \qquad (14)$$

5.4 Comparison of Fittings

This section summarizes the comparison of the four measurements performed. The results show that the urban environment is the one that would need a greater number of nodes to build a network with LoRaWAN technology.

- **Measurements with the Minimum Data Rate:** Fig. 8 shows a comparison of the path losses for the measured environments. It can be observed that the rural environment has the largest range. In the same way, it also can be observed that the Measurement 1, corresponding to the urban environment decays faster, as expected.
  The Measurement 3, corresponding to the semi-urban environment has the lowest standard deviation. This indicates that it fits the best to the data and presents less shadowing as shown in Table 5.

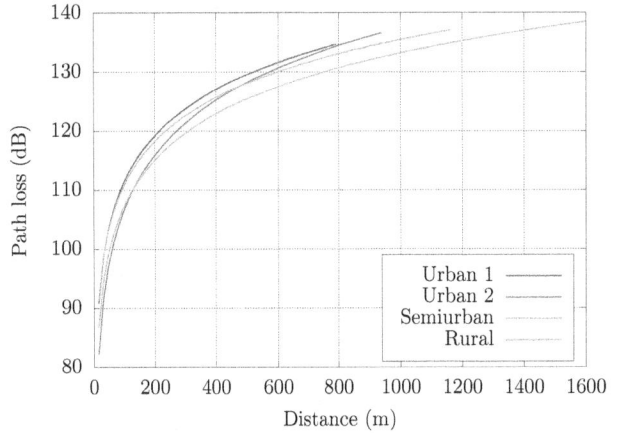

Figure 8: P_L fitted models with DR0

- **Measurements with Maximum Data Rate:** The results obtained in the measurements with DR3 are very similar to those obtained with DR0 with the difference that the coverage is lower in all the measurements. The results are shown in Fig. 9 and Table 6.

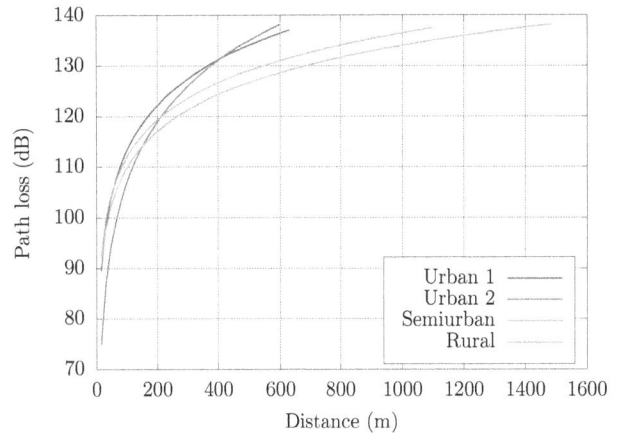

Figure 9: P_L fitted models with DR3

Table 5: Propagation characteristics comparison with DR0

Parameter	Measurement			
	Urban 1	Urban 2	Semiurban	Rural
Max. Distance (m)	800.00	950.00	1170.00	1600.00
Standard Deviation (dB)	6.29	5.83	2.92	3.73

Table 6: Propagation characteristics comparison with DR3

Parameter	Measurement			
	Urban 1	Urban 2	Semiurban	Rural
Max. Distance (m)	640.00	600.00	1100.00	1500.00
Standard Deviation (dB)	5.12	5.72	3.20	3.88

6 CONCLUSION AND FUTURE WORK

The transmission performance of LoRaWAN has been empirically evaluated by measuring RSSI and SNR in different riparian forested environments. The measurements found that the transmission range depends strongly on the environment. The high correlation between RSSI measurements between the two banks shows a strong relationship between them. DR0 and DR3 present the same attenuation but DR0 presents a larger range in all the measurements. Correlation Standard deviation decreases in semi-urban and rural environments due to fewer obstacles. For delivering the measurements results, the path loss characteristics have been expressed as logarithmic models.

Future work will vary the transmitter and receiver antennas height to improve transmission range. Scalability in forested environments have not been proved and could present challenges to the transmission with this technology.

ACKNOWLEDGMENT

We acknowledge the financing of *Dirección de Investigación de la Universidad de Cuenca* (DIUC) and *PROgrama para el Manejo del Agua y el Suelo* (PROMAS) of the University of Cuenca.

REFERENCES

[1] Mohamed Aref and Axel Sikora. 2014. Free space range measurements with Semtech LoRa technology, In Wireless Systems within the Conferences on Intelligent Data Acquisition and Advanced Computing Systems: Technology and Applications (IDAACS-SWS), 2014 2nd International Symposium on. *2014 2nd International Symposium on Wireless Systems within the Conferences on Intelligent Data Acquisition and Advanced Computing Systems, IDAACS-SWS 2014* September, 19–23. https://doi.org/10.1109/IDAACS-SWS.2014.6954616

[2] Aloÿs Augustin, Jiazi Yi, Thomas Clausen, and William Townsley. 2016. A Study of LoRa: Long Range & Low Power Networks for the Internet of Things. *Sensors* 16, 9 (2016), 1466. https://doi.org/10.3390/s16091466

[3] JP Bardyn, T Melly, and O Seller. 2016. IoT: The era of LPWAN is starting now. *European Solid-State* (2016). http://ieeexplore.ieee.org/abstract/document/7598235/

[4] M Bor and U Roedig. 2017. LoRa Transmission Parameter Selection. *Proceedings of the 13th IEEE International* (2017). http://www.research.lancs.ac.uk/portal/services/downloadRegister/164374357/lora{_}tps{_}r1342.pdf

[5] Martin Bor, John Vidler, and Utz Roedig. 2016. LoRa for the Internet of Things. *Proceedings of the 2016 International Conference on Embedded Wireless Systems and Networks* (2016), 361–366.

[6] Cisneros Felipe, Veintimilla Jaime, Vanegas Pablo, and Cuenca Ecuador PROMAS. 2013. Artificial neural networks applied to flow prediction scenarios in Tomebamba River-Paute watershed, for flood and water quality control and management at City of Cuenca Ecuador. In *EGU General Assembly Conference Abstracts*.

[7] Lukas Gregora, Lukas Vojtech, and Marek Neruda. 2016. Indoor Signal Propagation of LoRa Technology. *2016 17th International Conference on Mechatronics - Mechatronika (ME)* (2016), 13–16.

[8] Valeria Harvanova and Tibor Krajcovic. 2011. Implementing ZigBee network in forest regions - Considerations, modeling and evaluations. *2011 International Conference on Applied Electronics* (2011), 1–4.

[9] Iswandi, Herlina Tri Nastiti, Ina Eprilia Praditya, and I. Wayan Mustika. 2017. Evaluation of XBee-Pro transmission range for Wireless Sensor Network's node under forested environments based on Received Signal Strength Indicator (RSSI). *Proceedings - 2016 2nd International Conference on Science and Technology-Computer, ICST 2016* (2017), 56–60. https://doi.org/10.1109/ICSTC.2016.7877347

[10] WCY Lee. 1985. Estimate of local average power of a mobile radio signal. *IEEE Transactions on Vehicular Technology* (1985). http://ieeexplore.ieee.org/abstract/document/1623289/

[11] William Mendenhall, Robert Beaver, and Barbara Beaver. 2010. *Introducción a la probabilidad y estadística.* 780 pages. http://investigadores.cide.edu/aparicio/data/refs/Mendenhall_Prob_Estadistica_13.pdf

[12] Yu Song Meng, Yee Hui Lee, and Boon Chong Ng. 2008. Investigation of rainfall effect on forested radio wave propagation. *IEEE Antennas and Wireless Propagation Letters* 7 (2008), 159–162. https://doi.org/10.1109/LAWP.2008.922052

[13] Microchip. 2016. *LoRa Technology Evaluation Suite User's Guide.*

[14] Konstantin Mikhaylov. 2016. On the Coverage of LPWANs: Range Evaluation and Channel Attenuation Model for LoRa Technology. In *ITS Telecommunications (ITST), 2015 14th International Conference on.* 55–59.

[15] Avila Pablo, Astudillo-Salinas Fabian, Vazquez-Rodas Andres, and Araujo Alcides. 2017. Lora. https://github.com/pavilac/lora.

[16] J Petäjäjärvi and K Mikhaylov. 2016. Evaluation of LoRa LPWAN technology for remote health and wellbeing monitoring. *(ISMICT), 2016 10th ...* (2016). http://ieeexplore.ieee.org/abstract/document/7498898/

[17] T. Rama Rao, D. Balachander, A. Nanda Kiran, and S. Oscar. 2012. RF propagation measurements in forest & plantation environments for Wireless Sensor Networks. *International Conference on Recent Trends in Information Technology, ICRTIT 2012* (2012), 308–313. https://doi.org/10.1109/ICRTIT.2012.6206765

[18] Semtech. 2015. *LoRa Modulation Basics.* Technical Report May. Semtech. 1–26 pages. http://www.semtech.com/images/datasheet/an1200.22.pdf

[19] N (Semtech) Sornin, M (Semtech) Luis, T (IBM) Eirich, T (IBM) Kramp, and O (Actility) Hersent. 2015. *LoRaWAN ™ Specification.* Technical Report. LoRa Alliance.

[20] Lorenzo Vangelista, Andrea Zanella, and Michele Zorzi. 2015. Long-range IoT technologies: The dawn of LoRaTM. *Lecture Notes of the Institute for Computer Sciences, Social-Informatics and Telecommunications Engineering, LNICST* 159, Fabulous (2015), 51–58. https://doi.org/10.1007/978-3-319-27072-2_7

[21] Andrew J. Wixted, Peter Kinnaird, Hadi Larijani, Alan Tait, Ali Ahmadinia, and Niall Strachan. 2017. Evaluation of LoRa and LoRaWAN for wireless sensor networks. *Proceedings of IEEE Sensors* 0 (2017), 5–7. https://doi.org/10.1109/ICSENS.2016.7808712

Performance of a Cell-Free MIMO Under RF Mismatch

Rafael M. Duarte
Federal University of Campina
Grande
Campina Grande, PB, Brazil
rafael.duarte@ee.ufcg.edu.br

Danilo B. Almeida
Federal University of Campina
Grande
Campina Grande, PB, Brazil
danilo.brito@ee.ufcg.edu.br

Marcelo S. Alencar
Federal University of Campina
Grande
Campina Grande, PB, Brazil
malencar@dee.ufcg.edu.br

Fabrício B. S. Carvalho
Federal University of Paraíba
João Pessoa, PB, Brazil
fabricio@cear.ufpb.br

Waslon T. A. Lopes
University of Toronto
Toronto, ON, Canada
waslon.lopes@utoronto.ca

ABSTRACT

Cell-free wireless communications systems are characterized by the absence of base stations responsible for covering a specifically region and, then, all access points ideally can communicate with all user equipments. In this work, the performance analysis of cell-free systems subject to gain mismatches of the transceiver radio frequency circuits is presented at the access points, when they operate in the downlink mode. We also adapt a LMMSE channel estimation for this scenario. The analyses consider scenarios with two levels of mismatch, as well as the presence of pilot interference. The results have shown that the average system transmission rates are reduced when there is RF mismatch at the access points operating in transmission mode. It also demonstrated that increasing of mismatch level reduces system's achievable rates. The comparison between curves which consider or not RF mismatch during precoding have shown that the precoder which considers the mismatch gives achievable rates slightly higher.

CCS CONCEPTS

• **Mathematics of computing** → **Coding theory;** • **Networks** → **Wireless personal area networks.**

KEYWORDS

RF mismatch, Channel Estimation, Pilot Interference, Cell-free systems, Achievable Rates.

ACM Reference Format:
Rafael M. Duarte, Danilo B. Almeida, Marcelo S. Alencar, Fabrício B. S. Carvalho, and Waslon T. A. Lopes. 2019. Performance of a Cell-Free MIMO Under RF Mismatch. In *22nd Int'l ACM Conference on Modeling, Analysis and Simulation of Wireless and Mobile Systems (MSWiM '19), November 25–29, 2019, Miami Beach, FL, USA.* ACM, New York, NY, USA, 4 pages. https://doi.org/10.1145/3345768.3355943

1 INTRODUCTION

Communications systems with concentrated base station arrays and multicellular spatial division have been extensively studied. Recently, the distributed systems, in which the base station antennas are scattered across the cell at access points (APs) or remote antenna units (RAUs), attracted the interest of researchers [4] [15]. Specifically, cell-free systems [10], in which the radio base stations are not responsible for the control of specific geographic regions, have been the subject of many publications. In these systems, as in regularly distributed systems, the access points are distributed along the whole space. However, all access points can serve all users of the system. Since not all access points would receive signals that are strong enough to be useful, some authors have suggested a user-based access point selection method [2].

With the decrease in the size of cells, and with the popularization of the concept of systems without cells, there is a need to compare the performance of this new type of system with small cell systems. Considering a channel model composed of small and large-scale fading [5], it has been shown that cell-free systems enable the increase in transmission rates on the uplink and downlink links [13]. In particular, when the shading coefficients are spatially correlated, the performances of both systems are affected. However, cell-free systems seem to be more robust.

One of the topics studied in this new system is the criterion of downlink power control. In order to allow more uniform system transmission rates, Ngo *et al* [12] obtained a closed expression for the achievable rate of downlink, and used it in conjunction with the max-min power control criterion. The performance of this system was compared to the one composed of small cells, and resulted in a higher concentration of rates around specific values. In addition, the authors demonstrated that the use of special criteria for the distribution of pilot sequences are advantageous when some sequence is reused.

The improvement of the optimization of the power control coefficients in the downlink link was also studied in the work of Bashar *et al* [1]. In this case, the optimization takes place in uplink transmissions. This improvement leads to an increase in the complexity of the methods, and the authors presented a solution to this problem. In addition to solving this problem, the authors obtained a closed expression for the achievable rate, and developed an iterative algorithm capable of solving the optimization problem. Using this method, the reception coefficients are defined, and a better power allocation is found.

In this paper, the performance of cell-free systems with imperfect Channel State Information (CSI) and radio frequency RF mismatch is discussed. Although the influence of imperfect CSI and RF mismatch on cellular systems have been studied, their impact on cell-free systems has yet to be explored. In particular, the variance of the distributions that characterize the radio frequency mismatch is obtained, a minimum mean square error based expression to estimate channel coefficients is found. Cell-free system performance under radio frequency mismatch is also analyzed, using achievable rates.

2 SYSTEM MODEL

The cell-free system used in this work consists of K single-antenna [6] user equipments (UE) and M access points (AP) uniformly distributed in a region with area $d \times d$. In this model, each access point has a single antenna and it is connected to the central processing unity (CPU) through the backhaul. As shown in Figure 1, in these systems, the coverage area of the system is not divided into cells. All access points serve all user equipment. It was also assumed the use of Time Division Duplexing (TDD).

In this model, the channel coefficient g_{mk} between the k-th user equipment and the m-th access point is modeled using small-scale and large-scale fading. It is given by [16]

$$g_{mk} = h_{mk}\sqrt{\beta_{mk}}, \qquad (1)$$

in which the small scale fading coefficient h_{mk} is a complex Gaussian random variable with mean zero and unitary variance. The large scale fading coefficient β_{mk} is modeled using two factors: geometric loss and shadowing. In this work, it is assumed that large-scale fading coefficients change every 40 intervals of coherence of small-scale fading.

Geometric losses are modeled using the Hata-COST231 model [12], in which there are three geometric loss curves, that are separated by two breakpoints [14]: d_0 and d_1. The first breakpoint occurs at 10 m from the base station, and the second is at 50 m from the station. In this path-loss model, frequency f is given in MHz, and transmitter and receiver heights, h_{AP} and h_{UE}, are given in meters. Geometric losses, in decibels (dB), are given by

$$PL = \begin{cases} -L - 15\log_{10}(d_1) - 20\log_{10}(d), & \text{if } d_0 < d_{mk} \le d_1 \\ -L - 35\log_{10}(d), & \text{if } d_{mk} > d_1 \\ -L - 15\log_{10}(d_1) - 20\log_{10}(d_0), & \text{if } d_{mk} \le d_0, \end{cases} \qquad (2)$$

where

$$\begin{aligned} L = &46.3 + 33.9\log_{10}(f) - 13.82\log_{10}(h_{AP}) \\ &- 0.8 - [1.11\log_{10}(f) - 0.7]h_{UE} + 1.56\log_{10}(f), \end{aligned} \qquad (3)$$

In this model, shadowing is include by using the coefficient z_{mk}, modeled by a log-normal r.v. with zero mean and unitary variance. Since the shadowing standard deviation is σ_{sh}, the large-scale fading β_{mk} is given by $10^{PL/10} 10^{\sigma_{sh}z_{mk}/10}$ and, as considered by Hien et al [13], σ_{sh} =8 dB, h_{AP} =15 m, h_{UE}=1.65 m and f = 1900 MHz.

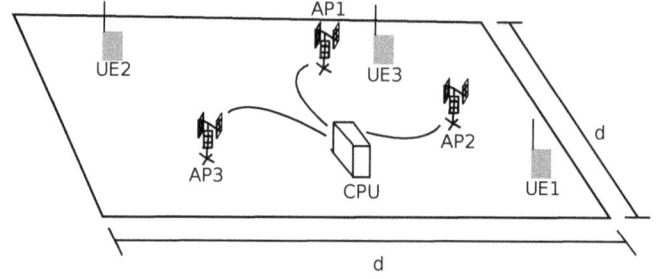

Figure 1: Cell-free system.

3 RF MISMATCH AND CHANNEL ESTIMATION

The radio frequency mismatch effect consists of channel asymmetries (non-reciprocity) between downlink and uplink due to gain mismatches in RF circuits. One way to model this effect is to use truncated normal random variables [9] to model phase and amplitude of the mismatch coefficients. These truncated Normal can be defined by its associated Normal distribution mean (a_0) and variance (σ_a^2), and by its truncation limits (a_a e a_b). These parameters can be combined into one quadruple notation, given by $(a_0, \sigma_a^2, [a_a; a_b])$. In this work, moderate and high level of mismatch were used. In these cases, phase (in degrees) and gain (in dB) are, respectively, $(0, 0.5, [-20; +20])$ and $(0, 1, [-50; +50])$ and $(0, 0.5, [-1; 1])$ and $(0, 1, [-4; +4])$ [9].

Considering the occurrence of mismatch only in the access points, in the transmission ($h_{bt,m}$) and in the reception ($h_{br,m}$), the uplink channel, which influences the estimation, is $g_{mk}^{UL} = h_{br,m}g_{mk}$, and downlink channel is given by $g_{mk}^{DL} = h_{bt,m}g_{mk}$.

In cell-free systems, estimation occurs in a decentralized manner, which means that each AP performs channel estimates independently [12]. With RF mismatch, the vector of signals received by the m-th AP over the τ estimation periods is given by

$$\mathbf{y}_{P,m} = \sqrt{\tau P_p}\sum_{k'=1}^{K} g_{mk'}^{UL}\phi_{k'} + \mathbf{w}_{P,m}, \qquad (4)$$

in which $\mathbf{w}_{P,m}$ is the receiver noise vector along τ estimation periods. When pilot sequences are reused, non-orthogonality between them causes an effect called pilot interference, which results in larger estimation errors [7, 8].

Considering the absence of sequence reuse, pilot-matched method can provide a good channel estimate [2]. Otherwise, Minimum Mean Square Error (LMMSE) is the most appropriate method [13]. The first method consists of project $\mathbf{y}_{P,m}$ onto ϕ_k^H, which results in

$$\tilde{\mathbf{y}}_{P,m} = \sqrt{\tau P_p}g_{mk}^{UL} + \sqrt{\tau P_p}\sum_{k'=1}^{K} g_{mk'}^{UL}\phi_k^H\phi_{k'} + \phi_k^H\mathbf{w}_{P,m}. \qquad (5)$$

In order to obtain the estimation of the uplink channel by LMMSE with radio frequency mismatch,

$$c_{mk}^{rf} = \frac{E\{\hat{y}_{P,mk}^* g_{mk}^{UL}\}}{E\{|\hat{y}_{P,mk}|^2\}}. \qquad (6)$$

which leads to

$$c_{mk}^{rf} = \frac{\sqrt{\tau P_p}|h_{br,m}|^2 \beta_{mk}}{\tau P_p \sum_{k'=1}^{K} \beta_{mk'}|h_{br,m}|^2 |\phi_k^H \phi_{k'}|^2 + 1}. \tag{7}$$

In this scenario, multiplying c_{mk}^{rf} by the signal $\tilde{\mathbf{y}}_{P,mk}$, one obtains $\hat{g}_{mk}^{UL} = h_{br,m}g_{mk} + \check{g}_{mk}^{UL}$. The estimation by LMMSE requires that the large scale fading coefficients and the RF mismatch coefficients of the access points operating in the receive mode are known previously. According to Chen et al [3], the mismatch coefficients vary slowly, so it is plausible to assume that they are known. In this case, the variance of the estimated channel is given by $\gamma_{mk}^{rf} = E\{|\hat{g}_{mk}^{UL}|^2\}$. Therefore,

$$\gamma_{mk}^{rf} = \frac{\tau P_p \beta_{mk}^2 |h_{br,m}|^4}{\tau P_p \sum_{k'=1}^{K} |h_{br,m}|^2 \beta_{mk'}|\phi_k^H \phi_{k'}|^2 + 1}. \tag{8}$$

Since $\check{g}_{mk}^{UL} = g_{mk}^{UL} - \hat{g}_{mk}^{UL}$ [11], $\check{g}_{mk}^{UL}$ variance, α_{mk}^{UL}, is given by

$$E\{|g_{mk}^{UL}|\} - \gamma_{mk}^{rf}, \tag{9}$$

which leads to

$$\beta_{mk}|h_{br,m}|^2 - \gamma_{mk}^{rf}. \tag{10}$$

In practice, it is desired to extract g_{mk} from g_{mk}^{UL}, by dividing the second by $h_{br,m}$, to correct the mismatch. Thus, the downlink signal is given by

$$r_{d,k} = \sqrt{P_d} \sum_{m=1}^{M} \eta_{mk}^{1/2} h_{bt,m} g_{mk} \left(\frac{\hat{g}_{mk}^{UL}}{h_{br,m}}\right)^* q_k + w_{d,k}$$
$$+ \sqrt{P_d} \sum_{m=1}^{M} \sum_{k' \neq k}^{K} h_{bt,m} \eta_{mk'}^{1/2} g_{mk} \left(\frac{\hat{g}_{mk'}^{UL}}{h_{br,m}}\right)^* q_{k'}, \tag{11}$$

in which η_{mk} is the power control coefficient calculated without taking into account the RF mismatch and P_d is the normalized downlink transmission power. Since P_d^{cf} is the downlink transmitted power, this normalized power can be obtained by dividing P_d^{cf}/P_n, where P_n is the noise power, and it is given by $BW\,F\,k_B\,T_0\,F$. In this equation, BW is the bandwidth, F is the noise factor, T_0 is the absolute temperature, and k_B is the Boltzmann constant. In this work, as considered by Hien et al [13], a noise figure (NF) of 9 dB is used, $T_0 = 290$ K and $k_B = 1.381 \times 10^{23}$ and $BW = 20$ MHz.

Based on the received signal in downlink mode in the presence of the RF mismatch, the Signal-to-Interference-plus-Noise Ratio (SINR) is given by

$$\varsigma_k = \frac{P_d |\sum_{m=1}^{M} \eta_{mk}^{1/2} h_{bt,m} g_{mk} \hat{g}_{mk}^*|^2}{P_d \sum_{k' \neq k}^{K} |\sum_{m=1}^{M} \eta_{mk}^{1/2} h_{bt,m} g_{mk} \hat{g}_{mk'}^*|^2 + 1}. \tag{12}$$

In the presence of the RF mismatch, and using uniform distribution of power properly, one must recalculate η_{mk} from downlink coefficients that take into account transmission RF mismatch coefficients of all access points. In this case, since $\mathbf{W}_{m,MRT} = (h_{bt,m}/h_{br,m})^* [\hat{g}_{11}^{UL}, ..., \hat{g}_{1K}^{UL}]^*$, the new power allocation coefficient of the m-th access point is given by

$$\eta_{mk,rf} = \frac{1}{E\{\mathbf{W}_{m,MRT} \mathbf{W}_{m,MRT}^H\}}, \tag{13}$$

which leads to,

$$\eta_{mk,rf} = \frac{1}{\sum_{k'=1}^{K} E\{|\hat{g}_{m,k'}^{UL}|^2\}|h_{bt,m}/h_{br,m}|^2}, \tag{14}$$

in which $E\{|\hat{g}_{m,k'}^{UL}|^2\} = \gamma_{m,k'}^{rf}$. Finally,

$$\eta_{mk,rf} = \frac{1}{\sum_{k'=1}^{K} \gamma_{m,k'}^{rf}(|h_{bt,m}/h_{br,m}|)^2}. \tag{15}$$

In this case, downlink signal is given by

$$r_{d,k} = \sqrt{P_d} \sum_{m=1}^{M} \eta_{mk,rf}^{1/2} h_{bt,m} g_{mk} \left(\frac{h_{bt,m}\hat{g}_{mk}^{UL}}{h_{br,m}}\right)^* q_k + w_{d,k}$$
$$+ \sqrt{P_d} \sum_{m=1}^{M} \sum_{k' \neq k}^{K} h_{bt,m} \eta_{mk',rf}^{1/2} g_{mk} \left(\frac{h_{bt,m}\hat{g}_{mk'}^{UL}}{h_{br,m}}\right)^* q_{k'}, \tag{16}$$

and the SINR$_k$ is given by

$$\varsigma_k^{rf} = \frac{P_d |\sum_{m=1}^{M} \eta_{mk,rf}^{1/2} |h_{bt,m}|^2 g_{mk} \hat{g}_{mk}^{UL}/h_{br,m}^*|^2}{P_d \sum_{k' \neq k}^{K} |\sum_{m=1}^{M} \eta_{mk',rf}^{1/2} |h_{bt,m}|^2 g_{mk} \hat{g}_{mk'}^{UL}/h_{br,m}^*|^2 + 1}. \tag{17}$$

4 RESULTS

In this work, for the channel estimation and downlink modes, as suggested by Hien et al. [13], the transmission powers are, respectively, $p_p^{cf} = 100$ mW and $p_d^{cf} = 200$ mW. For channel estimation, $\tau = 20$ is considered, and the region has an area of 500×500 m^2. In each simulation, $25 \cdot 10^4$ iterations were used.

Figure 2 shows the CDF curves of the system average achievable with ($K = 30$) and without ($K = 15$) pilot interference. In these curves, it is observed that the CDF curves with and without severe RF mismatch in the absence of the pilot interference are distanced. The curves corresponding to $K = 30$, with and without RF mismatch are closer.

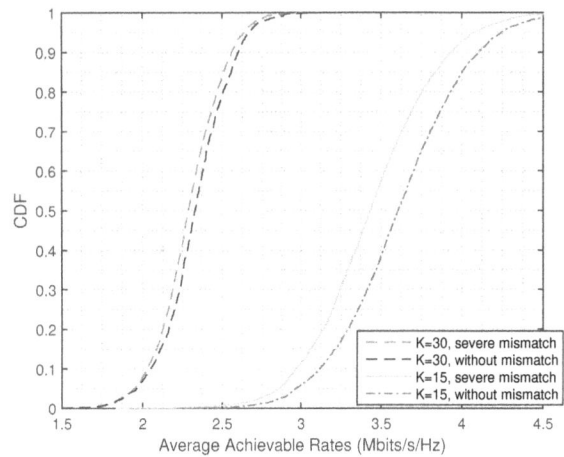

Figure 2: CDF curves of the average achievable rates of a cell-free system operating in downlink mode, with and without RF mismatch, considering $K = 15$ and $K = 30$.

Figure 3 shows the CDF curves of the system average achievable rates obtained with moderate and severe levels of RF mismatch in the access points. From these curves, it can be seen that the average system rates decrease with an increasing level of mismatch. Finally, also in 3, is shown the curve the CDF curve of the system average achievable rates obtained with MRT precoding with adjustment. The results revealed that the performance of the adjusted MRT operating system is slightly superior to those in which the existence of the mismatch is not taken into account. The improvement is probably due to the fact that, with this adjustment, the term referring to mismatch coefficient only contributes constructively. As expected from MRT, the contribution of the signal of interest is greater than the interference contribution.

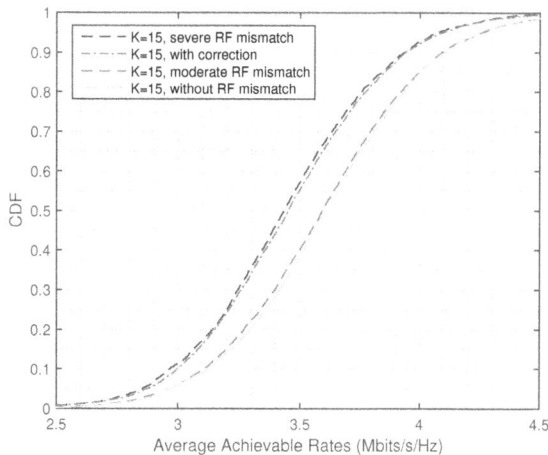

Figure 3: CDF curves of the average achievable rates of a cell-free system operating in downlink mode, with moderate and severe moderate RF mismatch and with corrections in MRT.

5 CONCLUSION

The results obtained from this research show the influence of the pilot interference on the systems without cells operating in downlink mode, with precoding MRT. That is why LMMSE channel estimator was adapted for this scenario.

The cumulative probability distribution curves show that the average system transmission rates are reduced when there is RF mismatch at the access points operating in transmission mode. That is why the RF mismatch eliminates channel non-reciprocities, and the SINR is reduced. When the level of mismatch is reduced from severe to moderate values, the average achievable rates approached those observed in the system without mismatch. Finally, when the MRT precoding is corrected to take into account the mismatch, the average achievable rates of the system increases slightly.

As a future work, a performance analysis of the cell-free system operating with multiple antennas in the access points could be done. A performance analysis of zero-forcing pre-encoding could also be done.

ACKNOWLEDGMENTS

The authors of this paper thank the Coordination for the Improvement of Higher Education Personnel (Capes) and the Institute of Advanced Studies in Communications (Iecom) for financing and providing the means to carry out this work.

REFERENCES

[1] Manijeh Bashar, Kanapathippillai Cumanan, Alister G. Burr, Mérouane Debbah, and Hien Quoc Ngo. 2018. Enhanced Max-Min SINR for Uplink Cell-Free Massive MIMO Systems. In *2018 IEEE International Conference on Communications (ICC)*. Kansas City, USA.

[2] Stefano Buzzi and Carmen D'Andrea. 2017. Cell-Free Massive MIMO: User-Centric Approach. *IEEE Wireless Communications Letters* 6, 6 (December 2017), 706 – 709.

[3] Yan Chen, Xiqi Gao, Xiang-Gen Xia, and Li You. 2018. A Robust Precoding for RF Mismatched Massive MIMO Transmission. In *IEEE ICC 2017 Signal Processing for Communications Symposium*. Paris, France.

[4] Jiamin Li, , Dongming Wang, Pengcheng Zhu, Jiangzhou Wang, and Xiaohu You. 2018. Downlink Spectral Efficiency of Distributed Massive MIMO Systems with Linear Beamforming Under Pilot Contamination. *IEEE Transactions on Vehicular Technology* 67, 2 (February 2018), 1130 – 1145.

[5] Waslon Terllizzie Araújo Lopes and Marcelo Sampaio Alencar. 2002. QPSK Detection Schemes for Rayleigh Fading Channels. In *Proceedings of the IEEE International Telecommunications Symposium (ITS'02)*. Natal, RN, Brazil.

[6] Waslon Terllizzie Araújo Lopes, Giuseppe Glionna, and Marcelo Sampaio Alencar. 2002. Generation of 3D Radiation Patterns: A Geometrical Approach. In *Proceedings of The IEEE 55th Semiannual Vehicular Technology Conference (VTC'2002-Spring)*, Vol. 2. Birmingham, Alabama, USA, 741–744.

[7] Waslon Terllizzie Araújo Lopes, Francisco Madeiro, Juraci Ferreira Galdino, and Marcelo Sampaio Alencar. 2006. Impact of the Estimation Errors and Doppler Effect on the Modulation Diversity Technique. In *Proceedings of the 64th IEEE Vehicular Technology Conference 2006 Fall (VTC'2006Fall)*. Montréal, Canada, 1–5.

[8] Thomas L. Marzetta. 2010. Noncooperative Cellular Wireless with Unlimited Numbers of Base Station Antennas. *IEEE Transactions on Wireless Communications* 9, 11 (November 2010), 3590 – 3600.

[9] De Mi, Mehrdad Dianati, Lei Zhang, Sami Muhaidat, and Rahim Tafazolli. 2017. Massive MIMO Performance with Imperfect Channel Reciprocity and Channel Estimation Error. *IEEE Transactions on Communications* 65, 9 (September 2017), 3734 – 3748.

[10] Elina Nayebi, Alexei Ashikhmin, Thomas L. Marzetta, and Hong Yang. 2015. Cell-Free Massive MIMO Systems. In *2015 49th Asilomar Conference on Signals, Systems and Computers*. Pacific Grove, California, EUA, 695 – 699.

[11] Elina Nayebi, Alexei Ashikhmin, Thomas L. Marzetta, Hong Yang, and Bhaskar D. Rao. 2017. Precoding and Power Optimization in Cell-Free Massive MIMO Systems. *IEEE Transactions on Wireless Communications* 16, 7 (July 2017), 4445 – 4459.

[12] Hien Quoc Ngo, Alexei Ashikhmin, Hong Yang, Erik G. Larsson, and Thomas L. Marzetta. 2015. Cell-Free Massive MIMO: Uniformly great service for everyone. In *2015 IEEE 16th International Workshop on Signal Processing Advances in Wireless Communications (SPAWC)*. Stockolm, Sweden.

[13] Hien Quoc Ngo, Alexei Ashikhmin, Hong Yang, Erik G. Larsson, and Thomas L. Marzetta. 2017. Cell-Free Massive MIMO Versus Small Cells. *IEEE Transactions on Wireless Communications* 16, 3 (March 2017), 1834 – 1850.

[14] Ao Tang, JiXian Sun, and Ke Gong. 2001. Mobile Propagation Loss with a Low Base Station Antenna for NLOS Street. In *IEEE VTS 53rd Vehicular Technology Conference, Spring 2001*. Rhodes, Greece, 333 – 336.

[15] Dongming Wang, Jiangzhou Wang, Xiaohu You, Yan Wang, Ming Chen, and Xiaohu You. 2013. Spectral Efficiency of Distributed MIMO Systems. *IEEE Journal on Selected Areas in Communications* 31, 10 (October 2013), 2112 – 2127.

[16] Kan Zheng, Suling Ou, and Xuefeng Yin. 2014. Massive MIMO Channel Models: A Survey. *International Journal of Antennas and Propagation* 2014 (2014), 1 – 10.

Experimental Evaluation of Antenna Polarization and Elevation Effects on Drone Communications

Mahmoud Badi, John Wensowitch, Dinesh Rajan, and Joseph Camp

Southern Methodist University

{mbadi,jwensowitch,rajand,camp}@smu.edu

ABSTRACT

In the next wave of swarm-based applications, unmanned aerial vehicles (UAVs) need to communicate with peer drones in any direction of a three-dimensional (3D) space. On a given drone and across drones, various antenna positions and orientations are possible. We know that, in free space, high levels of signal loss are expected if the transmitting and receiving antennas are cross polarized. However, increasing the reflective and scattering objects in the channel between a transmitter and receiver can cause the received polarization to become completely independent from the transmitted polarization, making the cross-polarization of antennas insignificant. Usually, these effects are studied in the context of cellular and terrestrial networks and have not been analyzed when those objects are the actual bodies of the communicating drones that can take different relative directions or move at various elevations. In this work, we show that the body of the drone can affect the received power across various antenna orientations and positions and act as a local scatterer that increases channel depolarization, reducing the cross-polarization discrimination (XPD). To investigate these effects, we perform experimentation that is staged in terms of complexity from a controlled environment of an anechoic chamber with and without drone bodies to in-field environments where drone-mounted antennas are in-flight with various orientations and relative positions with the following outcomes: (*i.*) drone relative direction can significantly impact the XPD values, (*ii.*) elevation angle is a critical factor in 3D link performance, (*iii.*) antenna spacing requirements are altered for co-located cross-polarized antennas, and (*iv.*) cross-polarized antenna setups more than double spectral efficiency. Our results can serve as a guide for accurately simulating and modeling UAV networks and drone swarms.

1 INTRODUCTION

The commercial use of UAVs, in addition to military applications, has been exponentially increasing. In 2017, the number of commercial drones increased by 58% in North America compared to 2016 with a projected global market of $11.61 billion by 2022 [1]. With the new advancements in UAVs such as the ability to hover and rapidly change locations and respond to control commands, UAVs are becoming more attractive to many organizations in a diversified array of applications (*e.g.*, inspection, mapping, monitoring). The next wave of these and other applications will be coordination of drone swarms to achieve automated tasks, leading researchers to extensively study UAV-based communications. The majority of literature, however, focuses on simulations ([2] and references within) or optimization models that target the optimal placement of a UAV [3–6] in various applications. These methods are important research tools and give valuable insight but may be misleading if these tools are not grounded in reality. Recently, measurement-based studies have been conducted with the majority of them focusing on air-to-ground (AtG) communications [7–13]. Experiments that investigate air-to-air (AtA) links mainly focus on received signal variations with distance and finding path-loss exponents with little emphasis on the body effects, antenna radiation pattern, polarization, and their joint effects. For example, authors in [14] measure the received signal strength (RSS) over various altitudes and empirically model the ground effects on multipath propagation. Furthermore, authors in [15] investigate network performance of AtA and AtG links in different network topologies and measure throughput at various distances and find the path-loss exponent. More elaborate details on related work are presented in §5.

As drones are expected to communicate in swarms, carry 5G traffic, and be integrated in IoT applications [6, 9], drone-based MIMO systems that offer higher throughput and more robust airborne links are becoming more attractive than ever [11–13]. However, it is well known that the capacity of these MIMO systems can be significantly reduced due to high spatial correlation of its channels [26, 33]. The MIMO spatial correlation is known to largely depend on antenna spacing, radiation pattern and polarization; factors that are found to be crucial when modeling polarized MIMO [25–28] channels in 3D. These factors are of particular interest to us because of the unique form factor and the potential effects of the body on the radiation pattern and polarization, the ability to move freely in 3D space (*i.e.*, in elevation and azimuth planes), and the limited space on UAVs, which might pose a challenge on antenna spacing and correlation in MIMO applications.

Cross-polarization discrimination (XPD) has a significant impact on the spatial correlation of the MIMO channel [26, 33] and according to the geometrical theory of channel depolarization [24] and measurement campaigns [25], depends largely on the environment and local scatterers around a receiving body. However, none of the current works that model 3D UAV channels [30, 31] investigate and quantify the impact of the drone body on XPD. In this paper, we experimentally measure how the drone body can affect the received power and XPD in different blocking scenarios. Furthermore, as elevation between drones can cause polarization mismatch and consequent power losses, we measure the RSS in a UAV-to-UAV link at different elevation angles for six different antenna orientation combinations to determine which antenna orientations are best to cover movement in 3D space. Based on our results, we accurately model drone networks with an awareness of antenna spacing and orientations and relative elevations for use in simulation or real-world deployments. Our contributions in this paper are as follows.

- We build a UAV-based 1×2 diversity system using Software Defined Radio (SDR) to explore the effects of the UAV body, elevation and antenna orientation on the performance of UAV-to-UAV links.
- In an anechoic chamber, we experimentally characterize the effects of the designed UAV platform and show that the drone body significantly impacts channel depolarization and reduce XPD by an average of 14.5 dB over all azimuth directions compared to an isolated antenna scenario.
- We perform in-field measurements and characterize the body-induced losses on RSS when two drones move in different azimuth directions at the same altitude. We show that the relative direction of one drone to another can reduce RSS by up to 16 dB compared to when the two drones are exactly facing each other. Based on this finding, we propose a range of body excess loss that should be added to the conventional log-distance path-loss model for more accurate predictions of UAV-to-UAV links. This model is shown to achieve a lower absolute error in prediction by 89% compared to the conventional model.
- We perform in-field measurements on the impact of the elevation angle on RSS and SNR improvements due to diversity for six different antenna orientation combinations. We find that when the two drones are facing each other, performance of UAV-to-UAV links in 3D space is mainly driven by the elevation angle. We show that the average RSS can change by more than 30 dB, even when the polarization is matched.
- We provide recommendations on antenna placement and orientations based on our measurement results. We find that, in general, a $\frac{2}{3}\lambda$ is enough spacing to achieve a correlation coefficient that is less than 0.7. Furthermore, in order to achieve the best performance in UAV-to-UAV links in 3D space, we show that horizontal antennas perform better than vertical antennas when near locations that are above or below the transmit drone while other locations are best covered by vertical antennas.

This paper is organized as follows. We present a baseline understanding of the effects of the drone body on co-polarized and cross-polarized channels and XPD degradation in §2. In §3, we report results from in-field experiments that demonstrate the impact of the drone body and relative direction on RSS and cross-polarized channels and propose an initial model that takes body-induced losses into account to provide more accurate large-scale fading predictions. Then, in §4, we discuss correlation, antenna placement, and the impact of elevation angle on RSS and diversity. Related work is discussed in §5, and we conclude in §6.

2 BASELINE UNDERSTANDING OF DRONE BODY EFFECTS USING ANECHOIC CHAMBER MEASUREMENTS

To begin our experimentation, we first characterize the body-induced effects of the drone on the radiation pattern in the elevation and azimuth planes for co-polarized (co-pol) and cross-polarized (x-pol) channels. Understanding the body-induced effects on radiation pattern and XPD can be crucial for researchers in establishing and analyzing models for polarized MIMO channels [25–31] that take radiation pattern, XPD, and correlation coefficients into consideration. These factors can affect drone-based design decisions such as antenna placement, orientation, and optimal location of a drone in 3D space. Therefore, in this section, we aim to address these issues. The experiments are carried out in an anechoic chamber, and the results are presented for two main scenarios: (*i*) Isolated, and (*ii*) Drone-mounted. In the isolated scenario, the radiation pattern of the dipole antenna is characterized with the antenna being mounted without the drone. In the drone-mounted scenario, the antenna is mounted on the drone and the same procedure for determining the radiation pattern is repeated. For a fair comparison between the two scenarios, the same dipole antenna is used and the same measurement rules [23] are followed with the drone configuration matching that of the in-field experimentation in the following section. The setup for the drone-based scenario is shown in Fig. 2.

2.1 Body Effects on Co-Polarized Channels

Since polarization mixing between the horizontal and vertical components of an electromagnetic wave can occur because of antenna imperfections or due to the propagation environment (channel depolarization) [24, 25], it is useful to show the radiation pattern of the two scenarios (isolated and drone mounted) so that the channel-induced effects, which are caused by the body of the drone, can be quantified. We start by analyzing the drone-body effects on the co-polarized channel, and then move to the cross-polarized channel and present the measured XPD, analyzing how it can be significantly reduced by the drone body.

Here, we study the effects of the drone body on the co-polarized azimuth and elevation radiation patterns. The azimuth radiation pattern is obtained by rotating the platform over the ϕ direction (azimuth rotation) and capturing the received power in the P_{VV} channel. The elevation radiation pattern is obtained by the same procedure for the P_{HH} channel; VV indicates that the transmitting and receiving antennas are both vertically polarized, and HH means they are both horizontally polarized. Note that it is widely accepted in literature [24, 26, 27] (and verified by our measurements, but omitted due to limited space) that $P_{VV} = P_{HH}$ and $P_{VH} = P_{HV}$. This reduces the complexity in getting the elevation pattern when the antenna is mounted on the drone. The automatic rotation in the chamber is in $1.8°$ increments from $0°$ to $360°$ and the received power level is captured for every $1.8°$. The received power levels are then normalized to the maximum power level and the results are plotted. The radiation patterns for the two scenarios (isolated and drone-mounted) are compared against each other in the VV and HH channels. Figs. 1(a) and 1(b) show the results.

It can be clearly seen that both the elevation and azimuth patterns are affected by the drone body, at some angles more significantly

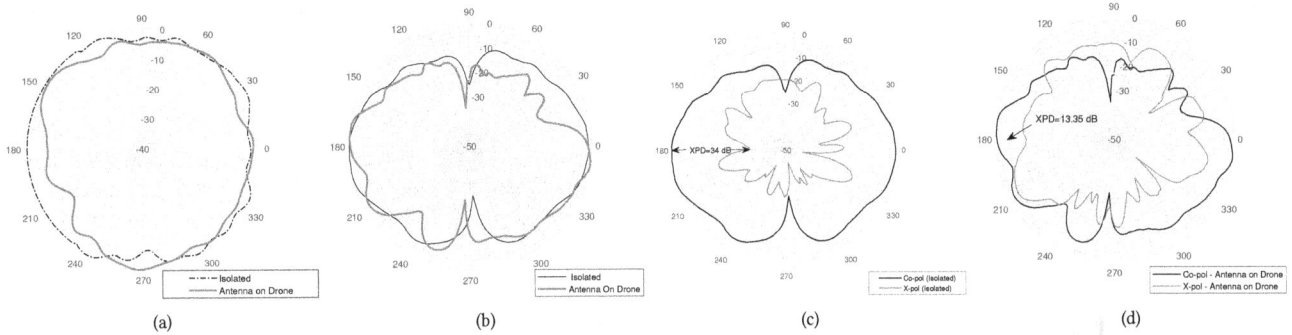

Figure 1: Effects of the drone body on co-polarized azimuth (a) and elevation (b) radiation patterns for two scenarios: isolated (no drone), and drone-mounted. Effects of the drone body on cross-polarized power levels and XPD when the receiving antenna is isolated (c) and drone-mounted (d).

Figure 2: Anechoic chamber characterization of the radiation pattern when the antenna is mounted on the drone (Drone-mounted scenario) for the P_{VV} channel.

than others. *In the azimuth plane*, we can see that the drone body can reduce the received power by a maximum of 11 dB approximately when the drone is facing away (around $\phi = 210°$). This result agrees with many other findings in literature [9–11, 14]. *In the elevation plane*, we can see that the effect of the body is more significant and less symmetrical when compared to the isolated case. We can see that the received power when the antenna is mounted on the drone can be reduced by up to (max difference) 18 dB compared to the isolated case. It is worth mentioning that the same experiments were conducted for another antenna position on the drone (right position in Fig. 2) and, albeit a different radiation pattern was obtained, similar differences in values (average and standard deviations) were found.

The min, max, average, and standard deviation of the difference in power levels between the isolated and the drone-mounted case in the azimuth and elevation planes are denoted by $Ł_{azimuth}$ and $Ł_{elevation}$ and defined as $P_{VV,isolated} - P_{VV,drone-mounted}$ and $P_{HH,isolated} - P_{HH,drone-mounted}$ for the azimuth and elevation planes, respectively. The results are summarized in Table 1.

Table 1: Body-Induced Losses on co-polarized azimuth and elevation power levels

Plane	Min.	Max.	Avg.	SD
$Ł_{azimuth}(dB)$	0.016	10.96	3.03	2.53
$Ł_{elevation}(dB)$	0.02	18.72	4.13	4.06

2.2 Body Effects on Cross-Polarized Channels

In this section, we analyze the impact of the drone body on the cross-polarization discrimination (XPD), which describes how well the two orthogonal polarization components can be separated. XPD is calculated as the ratio of the amount of power received in the co-polarized versus cross-polarized directions [28]:

$$XPD = P_{copol}/P_{xpol} \qquad (1)$$

Here, we present results of the P_{HH} (black solid lines in Figs. 1(c) and 1(d)) and P_{VH} (red lines in the same figures) and calculate the difference between the two as the angle-specific XPD value. It is well known that channel induced XPD can vary depending on the distance, environment (LOS or NLOS), and the angle between transmitters and receivers[25]. This is because of the variations in the number and nature of scatterers along the path between the transmit and receive antennas. In scenarios where multipath does not exist, and for identical antennas at the same orientation angle, the XPD is found to be approximately constant and independent of distance [32]. Therefore, it is expected that a higher amount of polarization mixing might occur due to reflections from the drone body surrounding the antenna, and, as a result, lower XPD values are expected in the drone-mounted scenario. From Fig. 1(d) we can see a clear impact of the drone body on the cross-polarized power measured by the receiving antenna when it is mounted on the drone. Even when the receiving antenna (when drone-mounted) is directly facing the transmitter ($\phi = 0°$), the drone body can reduce the the XPD by approx. 9 dB (from 24 dB in the isolated scenario to 15 dB when drone-mounted). More significant reduction appears when the drone is facing-away with an XPD reduction by 20.6 dB. We find that, on average over all angles, the XPD is reduced from 19.2 dB in the isolated case to 4.6 dB when drone-mounted. In addition, the maximum XPD in the isolated case is found to be 41.15 dB as opposed to 28.02 dB in the drone-mounted case. Results are summarized in Table 2. These are significant findings due to the impact that XPD can have on correlation and achieved capacity in MIMO [33] or diversity applications [34] that leverage differently-polarized channels. For example, an average XPD value of 0 dB means that the rank of the MIMO channel is 1. Hence, spatial multiplexing is not possible [33]. On the other hand, the same 0 dB value can indicate a richness of scatterers in the multipath environment, which leads to a low correlation coefficient and high diversity gains [29]. Surprisingly, and to the best of our knowledge, there is no prior work that characterizes polarization mixing and XPD degradation due to the sole effects of the drone body.

Table 2: XPD in The Isolated and Drone-mounted Scenarios

Setup	Min.	Max.	Avg.	SD
$XPD_{isolated}(dB)$	-10.14	41.15	19.22	8.17
$XPD_{drone-mounted}(dB)$	-19.23	28.02	4.61	8.41

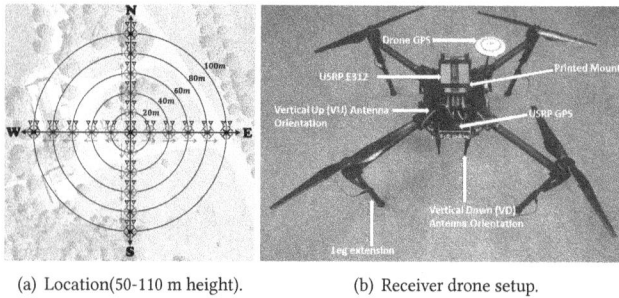

(a) Location(50-110 m height).

(b) Receiver drone setup.

Figure 3: In-field experiment location with receiver in center and transmitter in pictured locations along four cardinal directions (a). UAV-based SDR platform for the receiver drone with two (VU and VD) of the three antenna orientations(b).

After understanding the effect of the drone body on the received power in polarized channels, it is now possible to experimentally analyze (in-field) UAV-to-UAV links with different antenna orientations and at different elevation angles to understand the impact of the drone body and its location in space on performance.

3 IN-FIELD EXPERIMENTS: BODY-INDUCED EFFECTS ON POLARIZED AIR-TO-AIR CHANNELS

In this section, we investigate the body-induced effects on the received signal strength when the transmitting drone moves in four relative directions (North, South, East, and West) to the receiving drone; this means that it can be in front of (North), on the side (East or West), or behind (South) the receiving drone. Thus, the RSS may be affected differently depending on the transmitter's relative location. First, we explain the experimental setup and procedure. Then, we discuss measurement results and show how a prediction that is based only on a log-distance path loss model can significantly differ from the measured values because of the drone body-induced effects. Finally, we quantify these effects and give a range of values of excess loss that might be added to the conventional path-loss model to obtain more accurate predictions of the RSS in UAV-to-UAV links. The results presented here can be integrated in simulated or in-field environments where multiple different connections (*e.g.*, in swarms) are needed on different sides of the drone and relative direction becomes an important aspect in decisions made by drones that aim to optimize their links [19].

3.1 Hardware and Software Setup

We use the Universal Software Radio Peripheral (USRP) Ettus E312, which is a battery-operated 2×2 MIMO software defined radio platform with an operational frequency range of 70 MHz – 6 GHz and up to 56 MHz of instantaneous bandwidth. The transmission power of the USRP at 2.5 GHz was calibrated by connecting the USRP to a Rohde and Schwarz FSH8 Spectrum Analyzer using an SMA connector and a 50Ω cable, and a measured value of 6.2 dBm was recorded. Then, using GNU Radio blocks and through a Python script, we configure the transmitter to send a constant envelope sinusoid at a sampling rate of 32k samples/second and build a receiver that can simultaneously record the received signal on two

receiving RF chains through two antennas mounted at a distance of $\frac{2}{3}\lambda$ where λ is the wavelength of the transmitted carrier. We develop shell scripts that perform GPS logging and capture velocity, altitude, and IMU data while the drones are hovering. These sensor measurements are then used in splicing the data sets for analysis.

Using a ROBO 3D printer and MatterControl (printing software), we design and 3D print mounts for the USRP and antennas to be installed on a DJI Matrice 100 drone. Three different antenna mounts are built: vertical up (VU), horizontal (H), and vertical down (VD). In this set of experiments, the VU and H orientations are implemented at the receiver while the transmitting drone has a VU antenna orientation. The VD mount is used for the next set of experiments where we explore elevation effects. These antenna mounts are securely fastened to the central frame on the front of the Matrice 100. The placement decision was based on the measured stability against vibrations while maintaining the load of the USRP at the center of the drone body. Furthermore, it is often desired to focus electromagnetic energy at some directions more than others, which might dictate the placement decisions of the antennas on a drone [9, 10, 12] to be on a certain side. The in-phase (r_I) and quadrature (r_Q) components of the received signal of both RF chains are stored in a *.dat* file. Then, the signal envelope $|r|$ is obtained as $|r| = \sqrt{r_I^2 + r_Q^2}$. The received power is calculated and a per-location analysis is carried out according to sensor measurements.

3.2 Experiment Procedure

Throughout this set of experiments, the heading direction (which corresponds to the locations of the antennas in our experiments) for both UAVs is North. We fly the receiving UAV and let it continuously hover at a 60-m altitude in the same location (fixed) throughout all experiments while the transmitting UAV moves in the same plane. The transmitting drone starts at 20 m away in each cardinal direction (North, South, East, and West) and then flies in 20-m increments away from the receiving drone until it reaches 100 m of separation distance, creating 5 distinct hovering locations per direction, each at a height of 60 m (*i.e.*, these hovering locations are all at the same altitude). We define each experiment by its corresponding relative transmit drone direction. For example, an East experiment means that, with both UAVs facing North, the transmitting UAV moves linearly, 20 m away from the receiving drone in the East direction (see Fig. 3(a)).

3.3 Relative Direction and Body Effects on RSS

Given that no obstacles exist in the path between the two UAVs with negligible ground effects on multipath at 60 m altitude [14], one would expect that the relative direction of one drone to the other would not result in significant variations in received signal levels. Interestingly, our results show that the relative direction of the drone and its body placement with respect to its receiving antennas can result in a different RSS of up to 16 dB. If we look at the results of the least squares fitting of the average RSS values in Fig. 4, we see how signal reception can significantly vary according to the relative direction of the transmitting drone. For example, at 40 m distance, when the transmit drone is in the relative North direction, the average received signal is 12 dB higher than when it is in the South direction. This additional loss due to the drone body

Figure 4: Comparing the measured average RSS to the predicted values using the conventional PL model

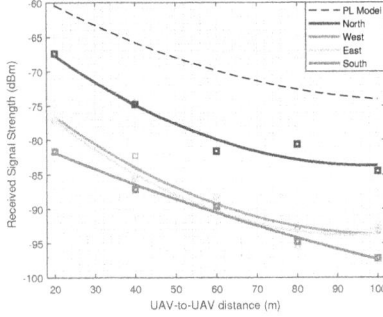

orientation agrees well with our expectations from the anechoic chamber measurements in Fig. 1(a), which indicates that a 10 dB loss in received power is expected when facing away ($\phi = 180°$) from the transmitter. A slight difference from anechoic measurements is reasonable and expected because of flight vibrations and real environment conditions. Furthermore, we analyze this reduction in RSS on estimated throughput and find that, with an average noise floor level of -110 dBm measured at the same altitude and location, the average estimated spectral efficiency can be reduced from 11.62 bps/Hz to 7.64 bps/Hz, a reduction that can be significant when throughput is a concern in drone swarms.

Furthermore, the East and West directions are found to result in approximately the same average values of the RSS at all hovering locations. The range of these average values lies below the North direction and slightly above the South direction, implying less obstruction compared to South but more compared to North. The average of the RSS standard deviations over all hovering location for the North, South, East, and West are 3.32 dB, 4.29 dB, 2.29 dB, and 1.86 dB, respectively. From these results, we conclude that when two drones have their transmit/receive antennas mounted on the same side and facing the same direction, the relative direction of the transmitter to the receiver, and, consequently, the receiver's body placement with respect to its antennas can result in two distinct cases where the average RSS can change by up to 15 dB. This finding can be crucial when drones autonomously attempt to optimize their spatial location in terms of estimated channel parameters [19].

3.4 UAV Body Effects on Cross-Polarized Channels

Interestingly, the relative direction of one drone to another is found to affect also the cross-polarized components. Here, we investigate the extent to which relative direction and body blockage can affect channel depolarization in an in-flight scenario as opposed to in an anechoic chamber (Fig. 1(d)), which showed that at 0° elevation, the horizontally-oriented antenna (same antenna at exactly the same position) is expected to receive 13 dB to 15 dB less power compared to the vertically-oriented antenna. However, even though the two antennas (V and H) are identical, the spacing between them makes it difficult to distinguish the depolarization due to radiation pattern differences from the depolarization that occurred due to actual channel scatterers. Therefore, we do not claim that

the following analysis provide exact XPD values but rather show an interesting trend where the difference in received power between the co-polarized and cross-polarized links can greatly differ based on the relative direction of the transmitter and the resulting body blockage at the receiver. We follow [32] in determining the polarization decoupling between the two orthogonal components as follows. We calculate the path loss for the two links as $PL_{VV}(d)(dB) = P_{t,v} - P_{r,v}$ and $PL_{VH}(d)(dB) = P_{t,v} - P_{r,h}$, where d is the distance between the two drones for each of the four relative directions of the transmit UAV, $P_{t,v}$ is the transmit power (in dBm) of the vertically-oriented antenna at the transmit drone, $P_{r,v}$ and $P_{r,h}$ are the received power levels of the vertical and horizontal receiving antennas, respectively. Now, the difference between the cross-polarized (H) and co-polarized (V) components is denoted here as Δ_{HV} and is calculated as:

$$\Delta_{HV}(dB) = PL_{VH}(d)(dB) - PL_{VV}(d)(dB) \qquad (2)$$

This difference quantifies how much greater power the vertically-oriented (co-pol) antenna receives as compared to the horizontally-oriented antenna. For example, when the transmitting drone is in the South direction at d = 20 m separation distance, $PL_{VV} = 88.16$ dB and $PL_{VH} = 93.84$ dB. As a result, Δ_{HV} is 5.68 dB. This means that the vertically-oriented antenna can receive 5.68 dB higher RSS compared to the horizontally-oriented antenna at that location. In other words, *despite matching the same polarization settings as the anechoic chamber, we record 7.5 dB less (Fig. 1(d) when mounted on a drone at $\phi = 180°$), which indicates that flight mechanics and/or relative drone headings can increase polarization mixing by more than 7 dB compared to the anechoic chamber measurements, where the drone body is fixed and does not move.* Furthermore, we report that all values of Δ_{HV} here (in the four experiments) are within the NLOS condition of the XPD values reported in [35]. This might be due to the fact that the two drones do not exactly face each other in any of these four directions. The average Δ_{HV} value over all hovering locations when the transmitting drone is North is 2.24 dB, while it is 8.55 dB and 5.34 dB when it is East and South, respectively. It is interesting to see that the lowest Δ_{HV} values were recorded for the North (which resulted previously in highest RSS). This means that *when the transmitting drone is facing away, the transmitted polarization becomes almost independent of the received polarization, as the body of the transmitting drone completely changes the transmitted wave's polarization.* These results indicate that higher average RSS values do not necessarily mean a higher decoupling of orthogonal polarizations (XPD) will be exhibited in air-to-air links that implement polarization diversity schemes as XPD becomes highly dependent (by more than 6 dB) on the relative azimuth location of the transmitter.

To further give a better understanding of the statement made above, we compare the previous findings to a reference Δ_{HV}, which we measure when the two drones are exactly facing each other and the antennas are mounted exactly at the same positions with the same separation distance of 20 m. In this scenario, where no body blockage exists at neither the transmit nor the receiver drone, we find that $\Delta_{HV} = 16$ dB, which is significantly greater than the values obtained from previous experiments in which the drone body resided along the path between the antennas. Also, this greater received power agrees with our results from the anechoic chamber measurements (Fig. 1(d)), *signaling the loss is more due to the drone body than the in-flight vibrations.* Furthermore, this value agrees with the LOS XPD values range found in [25, 35]. With these experimental findings, we conclude that: (*i.*) the relative direction of a transmitter drone to another can affect both the average RSS in a co-polarized channel by 16 dB and the decoupling between orthogonally-polarized waves represented by XPD by more than 14 dB, (*ii.*) unless the two drones are facing each other Δ_{HV}, which represents XPD in our field experiments, is reported to fall in the NLOS range of the XPD values reported in [35], and (*iii.*) when the two drones are facing each other, we find that $\Delta_{HV} = 16$ dB, which is the highest value compared to the different relative direction scenarios and agrees well with the LOS XPD measurements reported in [25, 35]. These findings would be valuable to researchers when modeling and deploying UAV swarms that incorporate various antenna orientations and move freely in any direction.

Table 3: Additional Drone Body Losses Per Hovering Location When Tx Drone is in The North and South Directions

Avg.loss \ Distance	20m	40m	60m	80m	100m
$\Gamma_{0°}(dB)$	6.92	8.97	10.05	10.26	9.66
$\Gamma_{180°}(dB)$	21.16	20.66	20.7	21.58	23.15

3.5 Body-Induced Effects on Predicting Large-Scale Fading

In this section, we discuss how predicting the performance of UAV-to-UAV links can give erroneous results if the blockage created by the different relative directions is not taken into consideration. We use the path-loss model given by [12, 14]:

$$P_r = P_t - P_{L(d_o)} - 10\alpha log(d/d_o) + \xi_s \qquad (3)$$

Here, P_r and P_t are the received and transmitted power (in dBm), respectively. $P_L(d_o)$ is the path loss at a reference distance (d_o) and is given by $P_L(d_o) = 20log(4\pi d o/\lambda)$, and d is the distance between the transmitter and receiver. The shadowing parameter ξ_s is normally distributed with zero mean, and a standard deviation σ in dB. Finally, α is the path loss exponent, which is known to depend largely on the surrounding environment of the transmitter and receiver and found to be close to 2 in many drone-to-drone links [7]. In this model, the transmit power is 6.2 dBm, and the standard deviation of the shadowing parameter is chosen to be $\sigma = 2$ dB. The measured reference path loss ($P_L(d_o)$ at $d_o = 20$ m) with both UAVs facing each other (PL = 67.7 dB) is found to be very close to the free-space path-loss at this distance (PL = 66.41 dB), which indicates that when UAVs are facing each other. No additional drone body losses need to be included and the log-distance path-loss model can accurately describe such links [15].

However, this is not the case when drones move in different directions from each other. According to our measurements, and as we saw in Fig. 4, when the transmit drone moves in various relative directions with respect to the receiving drone, the body of the transmitting and receiving drones become an obstacle in the received signal's path causing significant reductions in the average RSS level (up to 16 dB). We quantify the difference between the measured PL in the four directions and the PL predicted using the

Figure 5: Absolute error in prediction using our model and the conventional PL model.

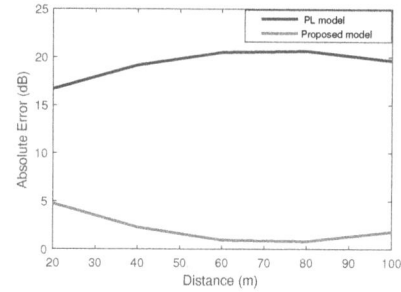

conventional model (which gave accurate predictions of the case when the two drones are facing each other) and propose a range of additional losses that should be added to the conventional model for improved prediction accuracy.

Based on the results of Fig. 4, we choose the North and South cases to cover the range of values of the additional loss that should be added to the model. This additional loss, denoted by Γ_ϕ, is defined here as the difference between the average RSS of the case when both drones are facing each other (which is accurately predicted by the conventional PL model) and the average RSS when the transmit drone is at a certain ϕ direction. For example, in our case, the North and South directions of the Tx drone correspond to $\phi = 0°$ and $\phi = 180°$, respectively, with regards to the Rx drone location (see Fig. 3(a)). The values of Γ_ϕ at each hovering location for both directions are summarized in Table 3. From the values given in the table, we can clearly see how the additional loss can be a function of the relative azimuth direction (ϕ) between the two drones. For example, when the Tx drone is North, the additional loss does not exceed 10.26 dB. When it is South, however, it can reach up to 23 dB. The minimum value of the additional loss is $\Gamma_{0°} = 6.92$ dB and the maximum value is $\Gamma_{180°} = 23.15$ dB. Therefore, the modified path loss equation when the Tx drone takes different relative directions can be expressed as:

$$PL_{UAV} = PL_{log-distance} + \Gamma_\phi \qquad (4)$$

Here, $PL_{log-distance}$ is the log-distance path loss model when the two drones are facing each other (no different relative directions). To demonstrate the applicability of this approach, the measured mean RSS values in the East direction are taken as an example. The measured values at the hovering locations can be found in Fig. 4. The predicted values (using the reference path loss when the drones are facing each other) are: -60.5 dBm, -65.79 dBm, -69.85 dBm, -72.59 dBm, and -74.02 dBm. On average, the absolute difference (absolute error) between the prediction made by the conventional model (that is very accurate and within 1 dB of accuracy when the two drones are facing each other) and the measured values when the Tx drone is East is 19.32 dB. However, *if we implement (4) using the average value of* $\Gamma_{180°}$, *which is equal to 21.45 dB, the absolute error is reduced to 2.12 dB (a 89% decrease in error).* The results are shown in Fig. 5. These findings may be generalized to other UAV-to-UAV scenarios where links are established at the same altitudes with negligible reflections from the ground [14] and the relative direction of one drone to the other is changing.

4 IMPACT OF ELEVATION ANGLE ON RSS AND DIVERSITY WITH DIFFERENT ANTENNA ORIENTATIONS

It is well established in literature that the performance of MIMO systems highly depends on the spatial correlation of the channel matrix. This spatial correlation is found to vary according to changes in the channel induced by different antenna radiation patterns, spacing, orientation, polarization, and elevation and azimuth angle of arrivals [26, 27, 33, 34]. In addition, recent studies, such as [36], found that, in drone swarm applications, if all ground station antennas are identically oriented and a UAV is moving at different elevation angles, the received signal can be effectively lost due to polarization mismatch. This motivates us to experimentally investigate the effects of elevation angle on the RSS with various antenna orientations at the receiver drone in a 1×2 receive diversity system. First, we discuss the experiment procedure. Then, the effect of the elevation angle on RSS for different antenna orientations is analyzed. After that, we discuss antenna spacing and correlation and conclude the section with SNR gains due to diversity and their dependence on antenna orientation and elevation.

4.1 Experiment Procedure

In this set of experiments, the transmitting UAV is hovering at an altitude of 80 m with its transmitting antenna oriented vertically upward (VU), facing the receiving drone which moves around the transmitting UAV in a predefined sequence of hovering locations, creating a 3D shape (Fig. 6). Diversity is implemented at the receiving UAV which flies in an automated, repeatable fashion using waypoints and resulting in four distinct (negative) angles below the transmitter and four (positive) angles above the transmitter. The below and above points are separated by an elevation angle of $\theta_{elev.} = 0°$. The horizontal distance (d_h) between the Tx and Rx drones is 20 m at $\theta_{elev.} = 0°$ and the angle-specific distance is $d_{\theta_{elev.}} = \sqrt{d_h^2 + d_v^2}$, where d_v is the vertical distance, which varies from -30 m (i.e., 50 m above ground) to +30 m (i.e., 110 m above ground) in 10-m increments. The different elevation angles made (in sequence) are: $-90°, -56.3°, -45°, -26.5°, 0°, +26.5°, +45°, +56.3°$ and $+90°$ and can be calculated as $\theta_{elev.} = \arctan(d_v/d_h)$.

Experiments are carried out for six different antenna orientation combinations (VU-VU, VU-VD, VU-H, VD-VD, H-H and H-VD) where VU, VD, and H represents vertical-up, vertical-down, and horizontal antenna orientations, respectively. See Fig. 6. The RSS is recorded at each hovering location for 30 s at a sampling rate of 32k samples/s and averaged over 10 seconds. The two UAVs are in a perfect LOS condition at a carrier frequency of 2.5 GHz 5 and a measured average noise floor of -110 dBm. The average RSS values are fitted using a second-order polynomial in the range $\theta_{elev.} = -56°$ to $+56°$, and the results are plotted and analyzed.

4.2 Effect of Elevation Angle on RSS

In this section, we study the dependence of RSS on the elevation angle between two drones for different antenna orientations. In general, if we look at Figs. 7(a) and 7(b), we observe an expected trend where the average RSS follows an arch-like shape in all vertically-oriented antennas in the range $\theta_{elev.} = -56°$ to $+56°$, with the

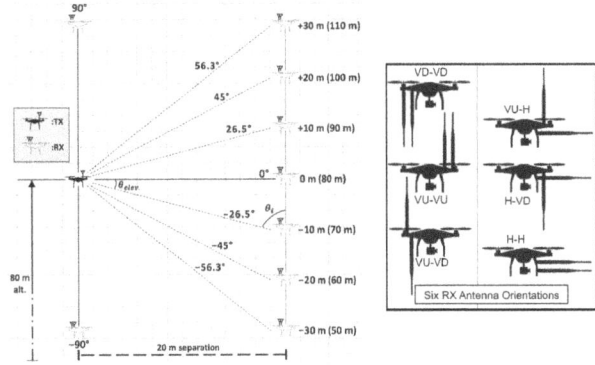

Figure 6: 3D experiment setup with 6 Rx antenna orientation combinations in the 1×2 diversity system.

strongest average RSS recorded at an elevation angle of $\theta_{elev.} = 0°$; this is where the two drones exhibit perfect LOS at the same altitude. As the receiving drone starts moving up (to 110 m) or down (to 50 m), reductions in the signal level start to appear. These reductions are mainly caused by polarization mismatch and the elevation profile of the radiation pattern [18], which we characterized in the anechoic chamber (see Fig. 1(b)) for isolated (no drone, antenna only) and drone-mounted scenarios.

We first analyze results from the vertically-oriented receivers (VD-VD) (Fig. 7(b)) to understand the effect of elevation on RSS between two UAVs when the antennas used are identical with matched orientations (vertical). We can see that the two receiving antennas undergo the same behavior versus the elevation angle. The received signal level increases from around -87 dBm to -67 dBm (20 dB increase) when the receiving drone moves from -56.3° to 0° elevation angle. Then, as the drone moves higher (from 0° to +56° elevation), the received signal level decreases from -67 dBm to -85 dBm (18 dB decrease), until it reaches around -91 dBm as it reaches exactly above the transmitting drone (+90°). When this receiving drone moves to the -90° elevation location (right below the Tx drone), an average RSS level of -97 dBm is reported. This trend is observed for all vertically-oriented receivers.

We conclude here that in an air-to-air links where two drones have the same antenna types and orientation, *movement of the receiving drone at different elevation angles can reduce the signal level by up to 30 dB*. This 30 dB difference in RSS can be crucial when designing algorithms for optimal drone placement [19]. Similar findings in cellular to UAV and air-to-ground scenarios were reported in [18], and [10]. However, in addition to not covering air-to-air links, the proximity of the receiver or transmitter to the ground in both studies makes it difficult to isolate the elevation factor from multipath and the surrounding environment.

Furthermore, the nature of drone movement in 3D space and the low RSS levels measured by vertical antennas at $\theta_{elev.} = |90|°$ motivate us to employ polarization diversity [21] that is represented by using two co-located orthogonally-oriented antennas. If we look at Fig. 7(a), where we implement a horizontally-oriented (H) receive antenna in addition to a vertically-oriented (VD) antenna, we can see that although VD results in higher RSS values throughout most elevation angles, around +56° the RSS for the H receiver starts to increase, where lower RSS values for the VD receiver are measured.

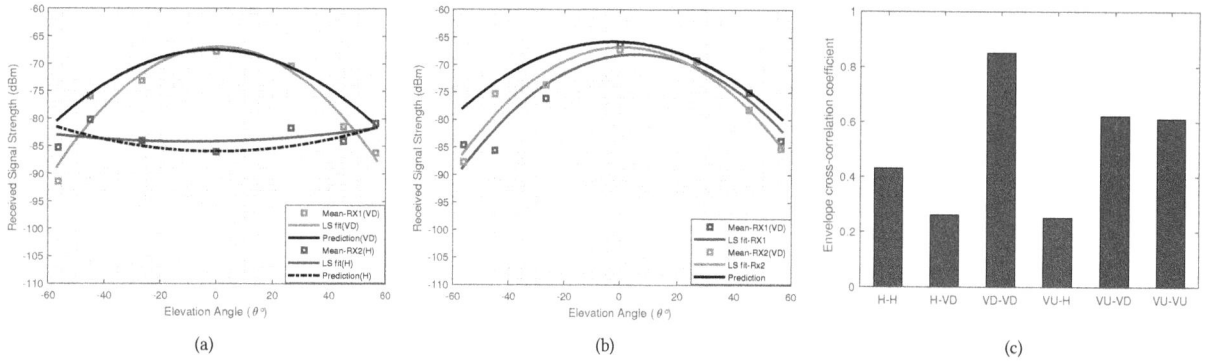

(a)   (b)   (c)

Figure 7: Average RSS vs. elevation angle for two different antenna orientation combinations: H-VD (a) and VD-VD (b). Correlation coefficient for the received signal envelope in the 1×2 drone-based system with different antenna orientations (c).

For example, at exactly $+90°$, H is reported to measure an average RSS value of -85.8 dBm, where VD results in an average RSS of -98 dBm (approx. 12 dB higher RSS at H). In another example (VU-H experiment) the H antenna captures 20 dB higher average RSS compared to the VU antenna. These results also agree with our anechoic chamber measurements (Fig. 1(d)) that show a measured received power of 16 dB higher for the H orientation.

To predict the average RSS and compare against the measured values, we add a polarization-mismatch loss [36] to the model in (3). Polarization-mismatch loss, also known as polarization loss factor (PLF), between a linearly-polarized (LP) incoming wave and LP antennas is a function of δ, which is the difference between the antenna tilt angle (θ_{tilt}) and the incident angle of the incoming wave (θ_i) [17]. This PLF is given by $PLF(dB) = 20\log(\cos(\delta))$. The reference received power is taken at 20 m when both drones are facing each other with vertical antennas. It is assumed that the location of the drone is known to the model; that is, for the same $d_{\theta_{elev.}}$, it is known whether the drone is at a positive or a negative $\theta_{elev.}$. This is important because of the different direction-specific gain values of the antenna (see Fig. 1(b)). We include these radiation pattern gain values at the elevation angles as G_t and G_r for the transmit and receive antennas, respectively. A shadowing of $\sigma = 1.5$ dB is used, and the prediction results are plotted in the same figures.

4.3 Antenna Placement, Orientation and Correlation

Since the orientation and spacing of two co-located receiving antennas can greatly affect the correlation and consequently the capacity of a MIMO system [29], we analyze the cross-correlation coefficient of the received signal at the two receiving branches in all of our six experiments. In doing so, we see how our antenna spacing decision of $\frac{2}{3}\lambda$ compares against what has been studied in literature and provide recommendations on antenna placement and polarization decisions. The correlation coefficient between the two received signal envelopes is calculated according to [34]:

$$\rho_{i,j} = \frac{\sum_{n=1}^{N}(r_i - \overline{r_i})(r_j - \overline{r_j})}{\sqrt{\sum_{n=1}^{N}(r_i - \overline{r_i})^2}\sqrt{\sum_{n=1}^{N}(r_j - \overline{r_j})^2}} \quad (5)$$

Here, N is the total number of samples, and $\overline{r_i}$ is the mean value of the fast-fading signal envelope r_i, which corresponds to the first antenna orientation. The term r_j corresponds to the second receiver's antenna orientation. For example, $\rho_{h,vd}$ is the correlation coefficient between the signal envelopes of the H and VD antennas in the H-VD experiment. We calculate this correlation coefficient for the signal envelopes received throughout the flight path mentioned above and find that, except for one antenna orientation combination (VD-VD), the correlation coefficient is found to always be less than 0.7. For example, the VU-VU and VU-VD experiments result in $\rho_{vu,vu} = 0.61$ and $\rho_{vu,vd} = 0.62$. Furthermore, the orthogonal antenna orientations (H-VD and VU-H) result in the lowest correlation coefficients (around 0.2) among all experiments, which can offer greater diversity gains. The obtained values from our $\frac{2}{3}\lambda$ antenna spacing and orientations are similar to the values found by [29] of 0.6λ in which a correlation coefficient of 0.7 and 0.3 were found for the VU-VU and VU-H orientations, respectively. The correlation coefficient for the six antenna orientation combinations are shown in Fig. 7(c). *Using these results and based on the objective (diversity or multiplexing gains), researchers can make informed decisions when selecting antenna orientation and spacing for drone communications.*

4.4 Elevation Impact on SNR Improvements for Different Antenna Orientations

We now analyze the effect of elevation on the SNR improvements that can be achieved by selection diversity in all of the six experiments. The SNR improvement over a reference branch i at an elevation angle θ is defined here (in dB) as the expected value of the difference between the selected (maximum) SNR in the 1×2 setup over the reference branch. It is given by:

$$\gamma_i^\theta = \mathbb{E}[SNR_{1\times2}^\theta - SNR_i^\theta] \quad (6)$$

For example, in the VU-VD experiment, γ_1 and γ_2 indicate the SNR improvement over the VU and VD antenna orientations, respectively. Refer to Fig. 6 for the antenna orientations. As we saw earlier, different antenna polarizations can perform differently at different elevation angles due to the elevation radiation pattern and polarization mismatch. For example, the SNR improvement in the VU-H setup over H as the reference branch (*i.e.*, γ_2) at $0°$ elevation would be significantly different from the improvement at 45° elevation. This is due to the fact that the highest SNR at 0° angle was measured by the VU antenna, which matches the transmitter's antenna orientation and outperforms the SNR achieved by the horizontally-oriented antenna that receives a lower signal level. In contrast, at $|90|°$ elevation, the H antenna, as mentioned above, records significantly higher SNR levels compared to the VU antenna, and the SNR improvement in this case (γ_1) is significantly higher than (γ_2). In Fig. 8, γ_H and γ_{VU} are the SNR improvements over the H and VU antenna orientations, respectively. We can see clearly that a higher SNR of 20 dB can be achieved around 0° elevation due to the VU antenna orientation (γ_H is higher). Additionally, around 18.5 dB SNR improvement can be achieved around +90° elevation due to the H orientation (γ_{VU} is higher). These results agree with our expectations from the anechoic chamber that showed a 16 dB higher received power in H compared to VU at 90° elevation. Furthermore, at $\theta_{elev.} = 56°$, γ_{VU} becomes greater, indicating SNR improvements due to the H orientation over VU. This is due to the polarization mismatch mentioned in the previous sections. Namely, a vertically-oriented antenna ($\theta_{tilt}=0°$) at $\theta_{elev.} = 56°$ would exhibit a PLF of -5.04 dB. However, at the same angle, a horizontally-oriented antenna ($\theta_{tilt}=90°$) would exhibit a PLF of -1.6 dB, resulting in higher received power level. At 45°, the improvements are the lowest due to equal polarization mismatch between the two orientations, and improvements are strictly due to spatial diversity. Finally, to give an intuition for what these SNR improvements mean to the performance of 3D UAV-to-UAV links, let us take the 18.5 dB improvement at $\theta_{elev.} = +90°$ as an example. With an average measured noise floor of -110 dBm, this improvement could *enable a doubling (96% increase) in the spectral efficiency from 6.29 bps/Hz to 12.35 bps/Hz, a significant improvement that could be crucial in applications that require high throughput.*

The SNR improvement over the first and second branch in each experiment are summarized in Table 4. We can clearly see that SNR improvements vary according to the different antenna orientations with the maximum not exceeding 10 dB in all co-polarized setups (first four columns). Also, we notice that in co-polarized setups, one antenna placement can dominate the other in terms of achieved SNR improvements. For example, in the VU-VU experiment, the improvement over the first branch is only 2.1 dB at one elevation angle. However, the improvement over the second branch can be up to 9.6 dB. In the VU-VD setup, more than double the maximum improvement can be achieved due to the first branch (8.7 dB) compared to the second branch (4 dB). This shows how *antenna placement decisions can affect SNR diversity improvements by more than 4 dB.* On average, cross-polarized receiving antennas achieve higher SNR gains than all co-polarized setups. Note that this is the case when the two drones are facing each other, and the average XPD value is 16 dB. It is interesting to explore SNR diversity improvements when the two drones do not face each other. We expect for all improvements to be within the same range since all gains would be strictly due to spatial diversity because of low XPD values.

From these results, we conclude that having cross-polarized antennas when drones move in three dimensions is important, especially at angles above/below 45° because of polarization mismatch losses. *Measured improvements in SNR values of 20 dB can be achieved using cross-polarized receiving antennas, which can lead to an increase in throughput of 6 bps/Hz. On the other hand, SNR*

Figure 8: SNR improvement due to diversity in VU-H setup.

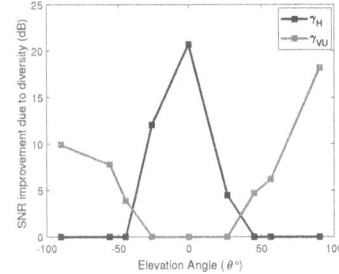

Table 4: SNR improvement (in dB) due to diversity: improvement is with respect to branch 1 (γ_1) and branch 2 (γ_2)

γ_i(dB)	VU-VU	VD-VD	VU-VD	H-H	H-VD	VU-H
$\gamma_1(max)$	2.1	6.3	4.0	8.8	16.1	18.2
$\gamma_1(avg)$	2.1	1.1	1.7	4.3	4.5	5.6
$\gamma_2(max)$	9.6	8.5	8.7	0.3	11.5	20.7
$\gamma_2(avg)$	5.5	1.90	2.4	0.3	2.8	4.13

improvements do not exceed 10 dB when using co-polarized receiving antennas, and the throughput increase does not exceed 2.5 bps/Hz.

5 RELATED WORK

A few measurement-based studies have been recently conducted to understand drone-based communications. For example, an ultra-low altitude drone to deliver 5G connectivity was implemented with different positions of a user on the ground [9]. Furthermore, in [7], air-to-ground experiments were performed with vertical and horizontal mobility of the transmit UAV with little emphasis on air-to-air links. In their work, the RSS was recorded at different elevations from the ground and for various rotations of the drone with two antenna orientation setups. Other work focused on the effect of having different antenna orientations with a fixed-wing UAV on IEEE 802.11a air-to-ground wireless link performance [8]. The work conducted by Niklas *et al.* helps in understanding the ground effects on multipath at a receiving UAV through measurements of an air-to-air link and the proposal of an empirical model that captures the variations of the Rician K factor versus flight altitude [14]. Others focused on the network performance of three different network topologies and studies throughput versus distance [15]. Akram *et al.* modeled the cellular-to-UAV (CtU) channel through measurements conducted in a suburban environment [18]. The OpenAirInterface Software Alliance (OSA) deployed a UAV-based LTE relay that passes UDP packets to a moving target on the ground with a placement algorithm that is based on a predefined set of channel parameters [19]. Qualcomm reported results from experiments demonstrating connectivity and base station detection capability for a drone UE at different altitudes and carrier frequencies [20]. These studies, though relevant, do not investigate the impact of drone body on the radiation pattern in the elevation and azimuth spectrum and on XPD. Furthermore, none of the existing works experimentally characterize the elevation impact on AtA links with different antenna orientations and discuss antenna placement on drones. In this work, we cover these aspects in great detail and provided valuable insight that can help simulating, modeling, and deploying drone-based networks.

6 CONCLUSION

In this work, we presented results from experiments that mainly investigate the effects of the drone body and elevation on the performance of polarized UAV-to-UAV links. First, we analyzed the impact of relative direction and body obstruction on the RSS when two drones are in the same plane and showed that the average RSS can be reduced by up to 16 dB depending on the relative direction of the transmitter. Then, we investigated the impact of the drone body on polarization mixing and XPD and found that the body of the drone can manipulate the polarization of the incoming waves and reduce XPD by more than 20 dB compared to when the antenna is isolated and not mounted on a drone; a result that can be crucial when modeling polarized UAV-based MIMO channels. Second, we proposed a model that includes these additional body-induced losses for more accurate results when predicting the large-scale fading behavior of air-to-air links with different relative movements and directions in the azimuth plane. Third, we analyzed the impact of elevation angle on the RSS and the improvements due to diversity in a LOS UAV-to-UAV link for six different antenna orientation setups. In doing so, we found that the overall performance in three dimensions with various antenna orientations is mainly driven by the elevation angle. The RSS for the same antenna orientation can change dramatically (by up to 30 dB) depending on the elevation angle of the receiving drone with respect to the transmitting drone. We also showed that a correlation coefficient less than 0.7 and reasonable diversity gains can be achieved with an antenna spacing of $\frac{2}{3}\lambda$ for both co-polarized and cross-polarized channels. We believe that these results can affect drone-based antenna placement and selection algorithms, optimization models that target drone placement, and future UAV-based channel models that currently fall short in capturing the discussed effects.

7 ACKNOWLEDGEMENTS

This work has been supported by the U.S. Department of Homeland Security (DHS), Countering Weapons of Mass Destruction (CWMD) Office, under a competitively awarded grant No. 18DNARI00029-01-00. This support does not constitute an express or implied endorsement on the part of the Government. This work was also supported in part by the National Science Foundation under grants CNS-1526269 and CNS-1823304.

REFERENCES

[1] "Global Commercial Drones Market 2018-2022," in *Business Wire*, August 2018.
[2] S. Baidya, Z. Shaikh, and M. Levorato, "FlyNetSim: An Open Source Synchronized UAV Network Simulator based on ns-3 and Ardupilot," in *Proc.of the 21st ACM Intern. Conference on Modeling, Analysis and Simulation of Wireless and Mobile Systems (ACM MSWiM)*, 2018.
[3] A. Al-Hourani, S. Kandeepan, and S. Lardner, "Optimal LAP Altitude For Maximum Coverage," in *Proc. of IEEE Letters on Wireless Communications*, December 2014.
[4] E. Kalantari, M. Shakir, H. Yanikomeroglu, and A. Yongacoglu, "Backhaul-aware Robust 3D Drone Placement in 5G+ Wireless Networks," in *Proc. IEEE Intern. Conference on Communications Workshops (ICC Workshops)*, July, 2017
[5] R. Ghanavi, E. Kalantari, M. Sabbaghian, H. Yanikomeroglu, and A. Yongacoglu "Efficient 3D aerial base station placement considering users mobility by reinforcement learning," in *Proc. of IEEE WCNC*, 2018.
[6] M. Mozaffari, W. Saad, M. Bennis, and M. Debbah, "Mobile Internet of Things: Can UAVs Provide an Energy-Efficient Mobile Architecture?," *Proc. of IEEE Global Communications Conference (GLOBECOM)*, 2016.
[7] E. Yanmaz, R. Kuschnig, and C. Bettstetter, "Achieving air-ground communications in 802.11 networks with three-dimensional aerial mobility," in *Proc. of IEEE Intern. Conf. Comp. Commun. (INFOCOM), Mini conference,*, April 2013.
[8] C.-M. Cheng, P.-H. Hsiao, H. Kung, and D. Vlah, "Performance measurement of 802.11a wireless links from UAV to ground nodes with various antenna orientations," in *Proc. of Intl. Conf. Computer Comm. and Networks*, October 2006.
[9] Philip A. Catherwood, Brendan Black, Ebrahim Bedeer, Adnan Ahmad Cheema, Joseph Rafferty, James A. D. McLaughlin,"Radio Channel Characterization of Mid-Band 5G Service Delivery for Ultra-Low Altitude Aerial Base Stations," IEEE Access 7: 8283-8299, Jan. 2019.
[10] E. Yanmaz, R. Kuschnig, and C. Bettstetter, "Channel measurements over 802.11a-based UAV-to-ground links," in Proc. Intern. Workshop on Wireless Networking for Unmanned Autonomous Vehicles, 2011.
[11] T. Willink, C. Squires, G. Colman, and M. Muccio, "Measurement and characterization of low altitude air-to-ground MIMO channels," IEEE Trans. Veh. Technol., vol. 65, no. 4, Apr. 2016
[12] Y. Shi, R. Enami, J. Wensowitch, and J. Camp, "UABeam: UAV-Based Beamforming System Analysis with In-Field Air-to-Ground Channels," *Proc. of 15th Annual IEEE Intern. Conference on Sensing, Communication, and Networking (SECON)*, 2018.
[13] J. Chen, B. Daneshrad, and W. Zhu, "MIMO performance evaluation for airborne wireless communication systems," in Proc. IEEE MILCOM, 2011.
[14] N. Goddemeier and C. Wietfeld, "Investigation of Air-to-Air Channel Characteristics and a UAV Specific Extension to the Rice Model," *Proc. of IEEE Globecom Workshops (GC Wkshps)*, 2015.
[15] E. Yanmaz, S. Hayat, J. Scherer, and C. Bettstetter, "Experimental Performance Analysis of Two-Hop Aerial 802.11 Networks," in *Proc. of IEEE WCNC*, 2014.
[16] D. Tse and P. Viswanath, "Fundamentals of Wireless Communication," *Cambridge University Press*, 2005.
[17] W. Stutzman and G. Thiele, "Antenna Theory and Design," *3rd Ed. Wiley*, 2013.
[18] A. Al-Hourani and K. Gomez, "Modeling Cellular-to-UAV Path-Loss for Suburban Environments," in *IEEE Wireless Communications Letters*, vol. 7, no.1, Feb. 2018.
[19] R. Gangula, O. Esrafilian, D. Gesbert, C. Roux, F. Kaltenberger, and R. Knopp, "Flying Rebots: First Results on an Autonomous UAV-Based LTE Relay Using Open Airinterface," *Proc. of IEEE 19th International Workshop on Signal Processing Advances in Wireless Communications (SPAWC)*, June 2018.
[20] "LTE Unmanned Aircraft Systems: Trial Report," *Qualcomm*, May 2017.
[21] R. Vaughan, "Polarization Diversity in Mobile Communications," IEEE Transactions on Vehicular Technology, Vol. 39, No. 3, August 1990, pp. 177-186
[22] R. G. Vaughan and J. B. Andersen, "Antenna diversity in mobile communications," IEEE Trans. Veh. Technol., vol. VT-36, Nov. 1987.
[23] V. Rodriguez, "Basic Rules for Indoor Anechoic Chamber Design [Measurements Corner]," IEEE Antennas Propagat. Mag., Vol. 58, No. 6, Dec. 2016
[24] S.-C. Kwon and G. L. St Áluber, "Geometrical theory of channel depolarization," IEEE Trans. Veh. Technol., vol. 60, Oct. 2011
[25] M. Shafi, M. Zhang, A. Moustakas, P. Smith, A. Molisch, F. Tufvesson, and S. Simon, "Polarized MIMO channels in 3-D: models, measurements and mutual information," IEEE J. Select. Areas Commun., vol. 24, no. 3, Mar. 2006
[26] "Spatial channel model for multiple input multiple output MIMO simulations," 3GPP, vol. TR 25.996, v6.1.0, Sep. 2003
[27] J. Wang, J. Zhao, and X. Gao, "Modeling and analysis of polarized MIMO channels in 3D propagation environment," in PIMRC, 2010.
[28] X. Su, D. Choi, X. Liu, and B Peng, "Channel Model for Polarized MIMO Systems With Power Radiation Pattern Concern," IEEE Access, vol. 4, Mar. 2016
[29] M.-T. Dao, V.-A. Nguyen, Y.-T. Im, S.-O. Park, and G. Yoon, "3D polarized channel modeling and performance comparison of MIMO antenna configurations with different polarizations," IEEE Trans. Antennas Propag., vol. 59, no. 7, 2011.
[30] L. Zeng, X. Cheng, C.-X. Wang, and X. Yin, "A 3D geometry-based stochastic channel model for UAV-MIMO channels," in Proc. IEEE WCNC, Mar. 2017.
[31] H. Jiang, Z. Zhang, L. Wu, and J. Dang, "Three-dimensional geometry based UAV-MIMO channel modeling for A2G communication environments," IEEE Commun. Lett., vol. 22, no. 7, Jul. 2018.
[32] Y. Xing, O. Kanhere, S. Ju, T. S. Rappaport, and G. R. MacCartney Jr., "Verification and calibration of antenna cross-polarization discrimination and penetration loss for millimeter wave communications," 2018 IEEE 88th Vehicular Technology Conference (VTC2018-Fall), Chicago, USA, Aug. 2018.
[33] Y.-G. Lim, Y. J. Cho, T. Oh, Y. Lee, and C.-B. Chae, "Relationship between cross-polarization discrimination (XPD) and spatial correlation in indoor small-cell MIMO systems," IEEE Wireless Commun. Lett., vol. 7, no. 4, Aug. 2018
[34] Y. Yao, J. Zheng, and Z. Feng,"Diversity measurements for on-body channels using a tri-polarization antenna at 2.45 GHz," IEEE Antennas Wirel. Propag. Lett., 2012.
[35] T. Neubauer and P. C. F. Eggers, "Simultaneous characterization of polarization matrix components in pico cells," in Proc. Veh. Technol. Conf., 1999.
[36] P. Chandhar, D. Danev, and E. G. Larsson, "Massive MIMO for communications with drone swarms," IEEE Transactions on Wireless Communications, vol. 17, no. 3, March 2018.

Simulation of ISO/IEEE 11073 Personal Health Devices in WBANs

Robson A. Lima
robsonal@midiacom.uff.br
MídiaCom Lab, Institute of
Computing
Niterói, Rio de Janeiro

Vinicius C. Ferreira
vinicius@midiacom.uff.br
MídiaCom Lab, Institute of
Computing
Niterói, Rio de Janeiro

Egberto Caballero
egbertocr@midiacom.uff.br
MídiaCom Lab, Institute of
Computing
Niterói, Rio de Janeiro

Célio V. N. Albuquerque
celio@midiacom.uff.br
MídiaCom Lab, Institute of
Computing
Niterói, Rio de Janeiro

Débora C. Muchaluat Saade
debora@midiacom.uff.br
MídiaCom Lab, Institute of
Computing
Niterói, Rio de Janeiro

ABSTRACT

Simulating new protocols for e-health systems is very important, as it allows an initial evaluation before a real implementation is made. On the other hand, network simulators do not offer proper support to represent medical applications or components to facilitate running simulations modeling e-health applications. The lack of simulators that specify the sensor type and its communication requirements make real experiments harder. Aiming at fulfilling this gap, this paper proposes the use of ISO/IEEE 11073 standard for Personal Health Devices (X73-PHD) in e-health network simulations, representing realistic medical applications and investigating the behavior of medical devices (sensors or actuators) in Wireless Body Area Network (WBAN) scenarios. We developed a free and open-source implementation of X73-PHD for Castalia Simulator, providing five different PHD types to act like real ISO/IEEE 11073 devices in WBAN simulations. Our implementation supports Agent-initiated mode, where PHDs take the initiative to send measurements to the hub. Our implementation also supports the unconfirmed communication mode and the confirmed communication mode, where the receiver sends an acknowledgment to the sender every time it receives a packet. Simulation results showed that the confirmed communication mode did not perform well in WBANs when the interval between transmissions is too small, due to the long period of timeout proposed in the X73-PHD standard. Therefore, we propose a new extension to the confirmed mode standard that decreases the overhead of control packets over the network, using smaller timeouts and delivering more packets.

CCS CONCEPTS

• **Networks** → **Application layer protocols; Network simulations.**

KEYWORDS

WBAN, personal health devices, ISO/IEEE 11073, Castalia, Antidote

ACM Reference Format:
Robson A. Lima, Vinicius C. Ferreira, Egberto Caballero, Célio V. N. Albuquerque, and Débora C. Muchaluat Saade. 2019. Simulation of ISO/IEEE 11073 Personal Health Devices in WBANs. In *22nd Int'l ACM Conference on Modeling, Analysis and Simulation of Wireless and Mobile Systems (MSWiM '19), November 25–29, 2019, Miami Beach, FL, USA*. ACM, New York, NY, USA, 4 pages. https://doi.org/10.1145/3345768.3355939

1 INTRODUCTION

Wireless Sensor Networks (WSNs) can be applied to different scenarios, such as Internet of Things, Smart Cities, Medical Systems, etc. Due to increasing research efforts in WSN and telemedicine areas, a new type of network emerged: Wireless Body Area Networks (WBANs) or Body Area Networks (BANs) [8]. A WBAN consists of intelligent devices, attached to the skin or implanted in the body, capable of exchanging data over a wireless network [3].

The lack of commercial devices and health hazards make real experiments with WBANs rare [9]. Therefore, simulation is an important tool to allow feasible tests with less cost and time. Castalia [2] is a widely-used free and open source simulator for wireless sensor networks and wireless body area networks.

In Castalia, a body sensor is represented by a node that performs network functions, but the applications available in the simulator are generic, and do not specify the sensor type and its communication requirements. Castalia was chosen over others simulators because it has the WBAN MAC layer already implemented.

In order to represent a more realistic simulation scenario, the use of a real standardized medical application is vital. The ISO/IEEE 11073 standard for Personal Health Devices describes data exchange, data representation, and terminology for communication between Personal Health Devices. Thus, this standard can be used as a role model for medical applications in WBAN scenarios.

The X73-PHD standard defines two types of devices: Agents and Managers. Agents are typically low power sensors or actuators, with limited processing power, whereas managers are devices with a greater processing power, which could be connected to an energy source.

The goal of this work is to propose the use of X73-PHD standard in e-health network simulations, representing realistic medical applications and investigating the behavior of medical devices (sensors or actuators) in WBAN scenarios. Examples of personal health devices are oximeters, thermometers, ECGs (electrocardiographs), glucose meters, blood pressure monitors, etc.

We implemented five different PHDs to act like real X73-PHD devices in WBAN simulations using the Antidote Library [10] as a basis. Antidote Stack or Antidote Library is an implementation of the Optimized Exchange Protocol (IEEE 11073-20601) developed by Signove as part of the SigHealth Platform [1]. Our implementation also supports a confirmed communication mode, where the receiver sends an acknowledgement to the sender every time it receives a packet. The X73-PHD standard was created as an application layer relying on reliable transport layer services. However, in many WSNs and WBAN scenarios, the transport layer is absent. Therefore, the protocol's reliable data transfer mechanism had to be adjusted to the dynamics of a faulty wireless channel, and the lack of transport layer services. Thus, we propose an extension to the standard that decreases the overhead of control packets over the network.

The rest of the paper is organized as follows: In Section 2, an overview of our proposal is given. In Section 3, we discuss the operations modes used in our simulation. The scenario and simulations parameters are discussed in Section 4. Results are given in Section 5 and, finally, conclusions in Section 6.

2 SYSTEM ARCHITECTURE

Antidote has a plug-in based architecture. So, a Castalia plugin was developed to support communication between Antidote Stack and Castalia Modules. As Antidote is developed to work with real devices, modifications had to be made to the library to work in Castalia Simulator. Communication, encoders, agent and manager are some of the Antidote's modules modified.

Antidote itself is portable and uses ANSI C language to create a standard and clean library [5]. To provide a communication between Antidote and other systems, like Castalia, we must adapt and develop the necessary communication plug-ins.

The proposed plug-in allows Castalia and Antidote to talk with each other through Castalia plug-in module. There is a set of callback functions in Castalia plug-in module that are passed to Antidote during the initialization process of each agent. These callback functions are passed to communication module of Antidote as pointers to functions. This way, whenever the communication module needs to retrieve or send a message, it just triggers the correspondent callback function.

The Communication module is one of the most important modules in the Antidote Library. The start, the end, transmissions, machine state phases of all nodes are controlled by this module. In a real scenario, each device has its own communication module, running its own copy of the code. But in a single-machine simulation, it is a bit different. Only one communication module has to handle all nodes, since the Antidote Library is installed in the operating system as a dynamic library.

3 CASTALIA APPLICATION LAYER

We have created an application for the Castalia Application Layer. This application is agent and manager-initiated, that is, the agent takes the initiative to send readings to the manager or the manager may request measurements to an agent. To stop a transmission in agent-initiated mode, agents can send an *Association Release* message when there is no more measurements to be sent. In the manager-initiated mode, a *Stop Request* message is sent to an agent requesting to stop data transmission.

We provide five different X73-PHD agent types in our implementation: pulse oximeter, glucose meter, thermometer, blood pressure monitor and a basic ECG. The pulse oximeter transmits the pulse rate in beats per second and the percentage of arterial hemoglobin oxygen saturation (SpO$_2$). The glucose meter sends the glucose level, that is, the concentration of glucose in the blood in milligrams per deciliter (mg/dL). The thermometer measures temperature in Celsius (°C). The blood pressure sends a data compound of systolic, diastolic and the mean arterial pressure in millimeters of mercury (mmHg). The basic ECG sends eighty samples of the heart's electric potential in millivolt (mV) per packet. All these agent samples are randomly produced during a simulation, except the basic ECG agent that transmits real values obtained from the data base found in [4].

The X73-PHD standard defines **confirmed** and **unconfirmed events**. The confirmed events expect the reception of an acknowledgement from the manager and the unconfirmed events do not. Control messages, like *Association request* and *Association release*, are always sent in confirmed mode, but measurements can be configured to use confirmed or unconfirmed mode.

In Unconfirmed Measurement Events, when an agent intends to associate with the manager for the first time, it sends an *Association request*. When the manager receives the *Association request*, it checks if the agent was previously associated. If it is the agent's first association, the manager sends a *Get attributes* message along with the *Association response*. So, the agent sends its configuration and starts to send the measurements to the manager. When there are no more readings to transmit, the agent sends an *Association release* and the manager responds with an *Association release response*.

The initial procedure of a Confirmed Measurement Event is the same as explained above, the difference is that the manager sends an acknowledgment for every measurement received. After sending a measurement data, the agent must wait three seconds for an ACK. If an ACK is not received in this period, the agent sends an *Association abort* to the manager, and transits to the unassociated state. If the agent still has readings to send, a new association must be made.

3.1 Proposed modification in confirmed measurement events

The X73-PHD standard assumes that there will be a reliable transport layer on real devices. In the Castalia simulator, as in usual wireless sensor networks, a transport layer can not be used. So we propose a stop-and-wait system as a sub-application-layer to retransmit agent packets whose ACKs have not been received. It reduces the unnecessary exchange of several control packets made in association procedures. Rather than making a new association when an ACK is lost, we just retransmit the packet *n* times or until

---

[1]SigHealth is a platform for remote patient monitoring and data management using personal wireless devices for health.

an ACK is received. The user may define a number n of retransmissions, and the agent will retransmit that message up to n times until a corresponding ACK is received. If the manager receives a duplicated message, it will retransmit immediately another ACK to the agent. We call our proposal **Retransmission Mode**.

4 USE CASE AND SIMULATION PARAMETERS

All results presented in this section are relative to the application layer. We run simulations on a computer with 8GB RAM memory, CPU Intel Core i5-7200U and Ubuntu 18.04 LTS operating system. All runs last 43201s seconds (12 hours) with the first second used just for network setup (e.g., nodes requesting connections). The simulation was executed 15 times with 95% of confidence interval.

This simulation is used to represent Remote Monitoring and Independent living for elderly care, which is one of the use cases of the X73-PHD standard. The sensors and actuators proposed for this use case are: blood pressure monitor, thermometer, glucose meter, pulse oximeter and basic ECG [6]. In this work, we have used an hypothetical elderly patient who has cardiac problems, diabetes and hypertension, and needs to be monitored in his home.

Figure 1 shows the topology setup used in our simulation. We used this set to test our proposed features. These nodes' positions have the advantage of experimental measurements of path loss, made for every pair of nodes, as discussed in [1].

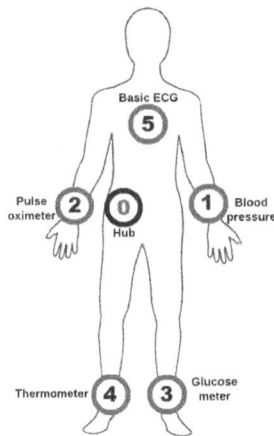

Figure 1: The simulated network topology.

In this work we simulate three agent-initiated scenarios. The scenarios are: i) Unconfirmed Mode, where the agents take the initiative to send measurements to the manager without confirmation. ii) Confirmed Mode, agents wait for three seconds the ACK from the manager. If an ACK is not received, the agent has to try to establish a new association to finalize the transmission of the measurement packets. iii) Retransmission Mode, agents expect an ACK from the manager during the time period defined by the user in *timeOutToRetransmitPacket* and in case it is not received, the packet is retransmitted up to *maxNumOfRetransmition* also defined by the user. If all retries are made and a confirmation is not received, a new association is made.

The MAC layer used is the IEEE 802.15.6 (WBAN) [7] with path loss map and temporal model for wireless channel supplied by Castalia. The radio used meets with the IEEE 802.15.6 radio proposal [7] with −15dBm as transmission power.

The configuration of the nodes is set as follows: the total simulation time is 43201 seconds (12 hours). Node 0 uses the *Manager* application and is the hub. The blood pressure monitor transmits one measurement every 15 minutes, totaling 48 measurements to be sent in our simulation. The thermometer sends one read every 3 minutes, then, 240 measurements should be sent. The glucose meter transmits one measurement every 5 minutes, that is, 144 measurements in 43201 seconds. Thermometer sends the temperature every 3 minutes then 240 in total. In this work, we assume the basic ECG as a device that receives signals of all electrodes deployed in the body, and transmits these signals to the manager. So, it will transmit 80 milivolt samples per 0.8 seconds, which gives 54000 measurement packets in 43201s of simulation.

5 RESULTS

The first result discussed is the total of successful measurements delivered to the manager using the agent-initiated mode.

We can see in Figure 2 that the percentage of delivered packets is improved for all agents when the proposed retransmission mode is used. For some agents, such as the oximeter, the unconfirmed mode delivered almost all packets, although it provides no reliability. As expected the confirmed mode improves reliability but pays the penalty of frequent reassociations. The retransmission mode improved the results in all scenarios, delivering nearly 100% of all messages, by avoiding the waiting time of an new association handshake, and by retransmitting the messages sooner.

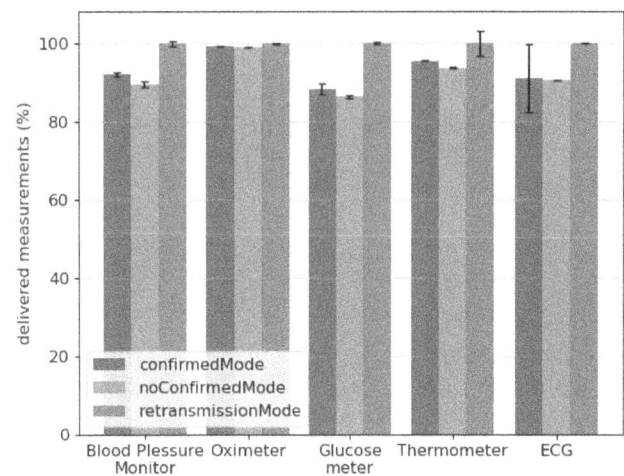

Figure 2: Measurement packets successfully delivered per node using Agent-initiated mode

The overhead of control packets exchanged between a node and the manager is crucial in this scenario, as in the case of a new association due to a non-received ACK. The association procedure involves a maximum of four packets for a new node, and a minimum of two packets, when the agent's attributes are previously known.

The average total number of control packets exchanged between each node and the manager per operation mode is depicted in Figure 3. Notice that nodes transmit different number of packets in the same simulation. While the blood pressure monitor conveys 48 measurements in 12 hours, the ECG has to transmit 54000 measurements in the same time period. It is expected to have less control packets in retransmission mode when compared to confirmed mode. Although, for the ECG in Figure 3, the retransmission mode has used more control packets than the confirmed mode does, because the retransmission mode delivered more measurement packets than the confirmed mode, as it was already seen in Figure 2.

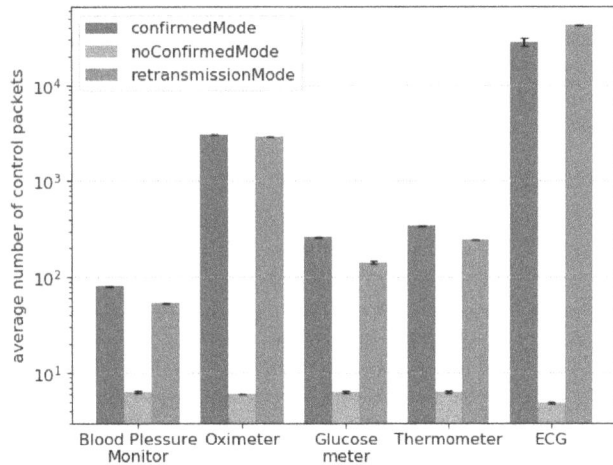

Figure 3: The average number of control packets exchanged of all nodes in Agent-initiated mode.

The number of associations made per node is extremely high with the confirmed mode, since it tries a new association after every lost packet. Figure 4 shows the average number of associations that each node made in Agent-initiated modes. As expected, the confirmed mode has the highest average of association attempts, while the unconfirmed mode made just one association. The retransmission mode tries a new association after all the attempts to resend a message, or if the agent receives an abort message from the manager. This is the reason for the low average of associations in this mode. The ECG, which has the worst wireless link, requires almost 2000 new associations to finalize the transmission of 54000 measurements in confirmed mode. Glucose meter failed to establish an association in one simulation, that's why the average less than one association.

6 CONCLUSION

In this paper, we have presented a proposal to simulate personal health devices in Castalia Simulator. Our application layer follows the X73-PHD standard with the aid of the Antidote Library. Five agents were implemented, and they simulate real personal health devices. In addition, a new reliable data transfer mode was proposed, the retransmission mode, to adjust the X73-PHD protocol to WBAN scenarios, where a reliable transport layer is usually not available. The retransmission mode aimed at reducing the number

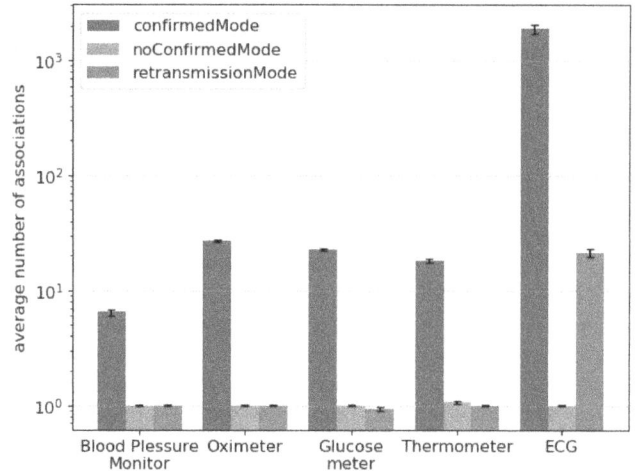

Figure 4: The average number of associations made per node

of disassociation/reassociations that take place after a message or acknowledgement is lost.

As future work, we intend to calculate the *timeOutToRetransmitPacket* dynamically based on the current latency of a packet. Thus, the user does not need to set this values in the simulation file. The codes for Castalia Application and for Antidote Modified Library can be found respectively at https://github.com/conqlima/Antidote and https://github.com/conqlima/11073PhdApplication. [2]

REFERENCES

[1] Athanassios Boulis and Yuri Tselishchev. 2010. Contention vs. polling: a study in body area networks MAC design. In *Proceedings of the fifth international conference on body area networks*. ACM, 98–104.
[2] Boulis, Athanassios. 2013. Castalia: A simulator for Wireless Sensor Networks and Body Area Networks (User's manual). https://github.com/boulis/Castalia. Online; accessed 7 January 2019.
[3] Vinicius Ferreira, Helga Balbi, Flavio Seixas, Celio Albuquerque, and Debora Muchaluat-Saade. 2017. Wireless Body Area Networks: An Overview. *XXXV Brazilian Communications and Signal Processing Symposium* (September 2017).
[4] Ary Goldberger, Luís Amaral, L Glass, Shlomo Havlin, J M. Hausdorg, Plamen Ivanov, R G. Mark, J E. Mietus, G B. Moody, Chung-Kang Peng, H Stanley, and Physiotoolkit Physiobank. 2000. Components of a new research resource for complex physiologic signals. *PhysioNet* 101 (01 2000).
[5] Yuri F Gomes, Danilo FS Santos, Hyggo O Almeida, and Angelo Perkusich. 2015. Integrating MQTT and ISO/IEEE 11073 for health information sharing in the Internet of Things. In *Consumer Electronics (ICCE), 2015 IEEE International Conference on*. IEEE, 200–201.
[6] ISO/IEEE. 2012. Health informatics - Personal health device communication Part 00103: Overview. *IEEE Std 11073-00103-2012* (Aug 2012), 1–80.
[7] ISO/IEEE. 2012. IEEE Standard for Local and metropolitan area networks - Part 15.6: Wireless Body Area Networks. *IEEE Std 802.15.6-2012* (Feb 2012), 1–271.
[8] S. Movassaghi, M. Abolhasan, J. Lipman, D. Smith, and A. Jamalipour. 2014. Wireless Body Area Networks: A Survey. *IEEE Communications Surveys Tutorials* 16, 3 (Third 2014), 1658–1686.
[9] Egberto Caballero Célio Albuquerque Débora Muchaluat-Saade Robson Lima, Vinicius Ferreira. 2019. Uma Proposta de Camada de Aplicação baseada no Padrão IEEE 11073 para Simulação de Aplicações de Saúde Digital em Redes Corporais sem Fio. *19 Simpósio Brasileiro de Computação Aplicada à Saúde* (jun 2019), 234–245.
[10] Signove. 2011. Antidote: Program Guide, documentation for developers of applications based on Antidote IEEE 11073 library. http://oss.signove.com/images/c/c7/AntidoteProgramGuide.pdf. Online; accessed 7 January 2019.

[2]This work is partially supported by INCT-MACC, CNPq, CAPES, FAPERJ and FAPESP.

A Byzantine-Tolerant Distributed Consensus Algorithm for Connected Vehicles Using Proof-of-Eligibility

Huiye Liu
huiyeliu@gatech.edu
Georgia Institute of Technology

Chung-Wei Lin
cwlin@csie.ntu.edu.tw
National Taiwan University

Eunsuk Kang
eskang@cmu.edu
Carnegie Mellon University

Shinichi Shiraishi
shinichi.shiraishi@tri-ad.global
Toyota Research Institute - Advanced
Development, Inc.

Douglas M. Blough
doug.blough@ece.gatech.edu
Georgia Institute of Technology

ABSTRACT

Emerging applications in connected vehicles have tremendous potential for advances in safety, navigation, traffic management and fuel efficiency, while also posing new security challenges such as false information attacks. This paper targets the problem of securing critical information that is disseminated among nearby vehicles for safety and traffic efficiency purposes through distributed consensus. We present a consensus algorithm, which uses a "proof of eligibility" test to establish that a group of vehicles are actually within the vicinity of the information source. With the presence of a limited number of compromised (Byzantine faulty) participants, our algorithm provides correct consensus among healthy vehicles in real time. The algorithm provides fast and reliable consensus group formation and private key distribution without privileged members, trusted setup, or leader election. In addition to proving a safety property of our consensus algorithm, we have implemented it on top of a widely-used vehicle simulation environment (SUMO, OMNeT++ and Veins) and evaluated its performance on a model of the streets in a real midtown area. Simulation results demonstrate that the algorithm can reach consensus very efficiently (within 9.5s) and with up to 30% of compromised vehicles in a given area. The simulations also demonstrate the ability of our algorithm to more quickly disseminate information about a traffic accident and more efficiently route traffic around the accident site, as compared to previous robust information dissemination approaches.

CCS CONCEPTS

• **Networks** → **Application layer protocols**; • **Computing methodologies** → **Distributed algorithms**; • **Security and privacy** → *Mobile and wireless security*.

KEYWORDS

connected vehicles, distributed system, security

ACM Reference Format:
Huiye Liu, Chung-Wei Lin, Eunsuk Kang, Shinichi Shiraishi, and Douglas M. Blough. 2019. A Byzantine-Tolerant Distributed Consensus Algorithm for Connected Vehicles Using Proof-of-Eligibility. In *22nd Int'l ACM Conference on Modeling, Analysis and Simulation of Wireless and Mobile Systems (MSWiM '19), November 25–29, 2019, Miami Beach, FL, USA*. ACM, New York, NY, USA, 10 pages. https://doi.org/10.1145/3345768.3355910

1 INTRODUCTION

Connected vehicle technologies are changing the ways we commute and communicate. The automotive industry is being completely reshaped by emerging communication technologies (V2V, V2X, V2I, etc.), mobility apps, electric vehicles, and vehicle automation. This provides an opportunity to reorganize our transportation infrastructure, improving safety, security, traffic efficiency, human comfort, and energy efficiency. For example, a connected vehicle can be informed if an emergency vehicle is approaching far away or a smart intersection can consider the estimated arrival times of connected vehicles to schedule those vehicles and increase the intersection throughput.

However, security becomes a paramount concern for connected vehicles, as they inevitably make control decisions based on information from other vehicles and external sources. In this scenario, the vehicular network is especially vulnerable to false information attacks. Fake messages can create problems like longer time required to reach destination, more gas consumption than needed, traffic jams, and even collisions. For instance, taking advantage of the connectivity, an attacker may compromise vehicles to lie about its own vehicle's position and speed, to make false warnings about a non-existent accident thus leaving an empty street for itself to freely pass through, or to report fake arriving time to a traffic signal control system causing congestion/traffic jams or even to ease criminals' getaways from crime scenes [28].

To date, research in automotive security has addressed many different perspectives. The goals include secure communication protocols integrated with existing standards and protocols at the external network layer, Intrusion Detection Systems (IDSs) and firewalls at the gateway layer, lightweight message authentication and encryption at the in-vehicular network layer, and Hardware Security Modules (HSMs), secure boot, and secret key control at the component layer.

Nevertheless, even with good security mechanisms at each of those layers, it is necessary to address security at the application layer, especially for application information. In this paper, we address this issue through Byzantine-tolerant distributed consensus on application information. Several example use cases include:

Dynamic maps: weather condition, parking availability, EV charging station availability, etc. are all important information comprising a powerful dynamic map. Information reported by a single device/vehicle is not complete and reliable.

Traffic alerts: to provide trust in traffic condition warnings such as collision, congestion, and emergency vehicle(s) approaching, and to avoid inappropriate reactions, distributed consensus can be used to provide trusted alert dissemination.

Intersection management: the next-generation transportation system such as Intelligent Traffic Signal System (I-SIG) relies on vehicles' reported speed and location information to estimate the queuing line, and assigns green/red light time as needed. However, attacks [8] have been found to potentially cause serious problems.

Despite the conceptual appeal of this approach, realizing distributed consensus poses many challenges in connected vehicle systems. One challenge is *safety-critical operation* in the face of *real-time constraint*. For example, if an emergency vehicle needs to take priority at an intersection, this information is only important when it is approaching the intersection. After the vehicle passes, the information is no longer useful. However, forcing consensus within a short period of time could lead to incorrect decisions that may make the situation worse than without connected vehicle system. The second challenge is the *high mobility* and *communication loss/delay*, which could significantly affect the ability to reach consensus among devices. The third major challenge is the *lack of trust* in connected vehicle systems. Compromised vehicles with valid credentials will appear as trusted entities [1], which is a difficult situation to handle. Moreover, it is not necessary for compromised vehicles to always behave incorrectly. They may behave as healthy devices at one time and act incorrectly at another time, thus making it hard to rely on reputational trust. To address these challenges, we introduce a distributed consensus algorithm based on *Proof-of-Eligibility (PoE)*. To the best of our knowledge, this is the first work addressing distributed consensus in the face of the challenges listed above. Contributions of the paper include the following:

- We introduce the concept of Proof-of-Eligibility Challenge, which limits the impact of compromised vehicles from outside of an event area by preventing them from participating in the consensus process.
- We present the Byzantine-fault-tolerant consensus algorithm for connected vehicles (BFCV) to ensure information security among vehicles, without requiring privileged members, leader election, nor trusted shared key distribution. The algorithm also provides dynamic consensus group formation in an environment without a known pre-defined set of consensus participants.
- We report on the implementation of a BFCV prototype and simulation of it in a realistic environment built on top of Veins, SUMO and OMNet++. Evaluation results show that BFCV provides fast consensus satisfying both safety and liveness requirements.

The remainder of the paper is organized as follows. Section 2 discusses a motivating example, elaborating how the BFCV algorithm can be applied to a real-world problem. Problem formulation,

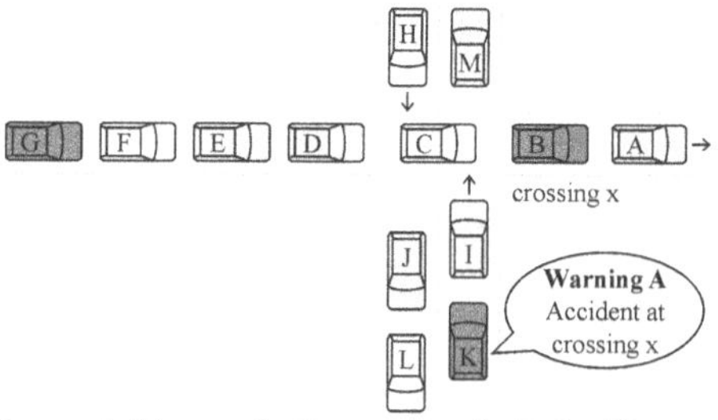

Figure 1: Example Scenario of a Fake Report

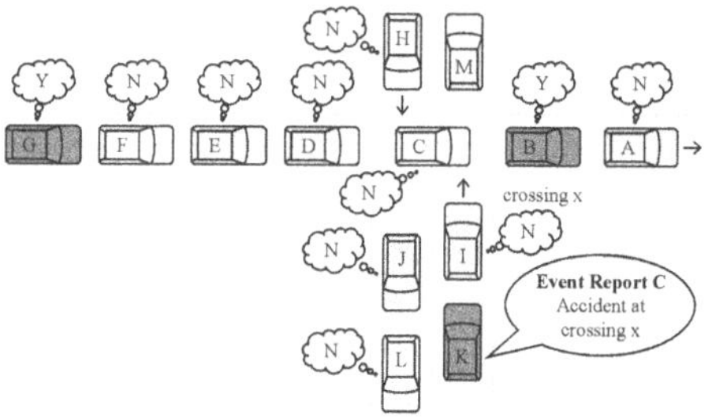

Figure 2: Example Scenario of a Fake Report with BFCV (where vehicles B, G, and K are compromised)

assumptions, threat model, and system model are provided in Section 3. We present the BFCV Algorithm in Section 4 and provide a proof sketch of its safety property. In Section 5, we present a concrete implementation of BFCV with details of environment set up, design of the experiments, and simulation results. Related work is discussed in Section 6 and we conclude in Section 7.

2 MOTIVATING EXAMPLE

In this section, we use dissemination of an accident alert as an example to illustrate how our proposed PoE-based consensus algorithm tackles the information security problem in connected vehicle systems. Figure 1 demonstrates a fake warning reported by compromised vehicle K. Each vehicle is labeled with letters as its name. Vehicles in green and yellow, representing different brands of vehicles, are honest nodes following the protocol and vehicles in red representing compromised nodes are trying to attack. Without a cooperative evaluation approach, a vehicle can only rely on its received data and local plausibility check as discussed in [15, 22, 31, 32] to make local decisions. Vehicles that are not able to "see" the crossing, may believe the false alert and could potentially reroute and transmit false information to further vehicles, if K is a compromised vehicle with valid credentials.

Our algorithm approaches this problem by using the concept of event reports, whose content could be an unconditional lane shift, slowing speed/congestion, observation of emergency vehicles, crashed vehicles, abnormal behaviors of neighboring vehicles, etc. In order for a created event report to be accepted by other vehicles in the network, a consensus group is formed with a group of eligible vehicles, who can solve a Proof-of-Eligibility (PoE) puzzle, to cooperatively evaluate the report content and reach consensus on whether or not the report is true. Only after that, the true report will be broadcast with group members' signatures. Upon receiving the signed report, other vehicles will react accordingly after verifying the attached signatures.

As depicted in Figure 2, after vehicle K broadcasts an event report about an accident at crossing x, all vehicles within communication range (A-L) are able to receive the report. They try to solve a PoE puzzle attached in the event report to obtain a shared secret key. PoE is a set of consistency checks, which aims to prove that a vehicle is authentically relevant and eligible to participate in the cooperative evaluation of a reported event. The PoE puzzle is based on the local environment and can, therefore, only be solved by vehicles that are within close range of the event. PoE lessens the difficulties and shortens the delay of distributing shared keys among a temporarily formed group of moving vehicles. Let us consider a worst case scenario that both compromised vehicles B and G are able to solve the PoE puzzle and join the consensus group. During the consensus stage, compromised vehicles send false opinions agreeing with the fake report that there is an accident at crossing x while the honest vehicles dispute the report. Compromised vehicles B and G may also drop the consensus message received from other members to affect the group evaluation. However, as we will see later, with a minority of compromised vehicles participating, false consensus can never be reached with the BFCV Algorithm. In most cases, the group of honest vehicles will reach agreement that the report is false and disseminate a signed message repudiating the report.

In the above, the BFCV Algorithm description has been simplified to briefly introduce the general concept. A detailed algorithm description is provided in Section 4.

3 PROBLEM FORMULATION

3.1 Assumptions

In this paper, we assume active (engine-on) vehicles communicating with each other wirelessly. Vehicles routinely exchange information and monitor the environment, following these four steps: *Detection* – a vehicle detects new events (traffic condition, abnormal behavior, etc.) by receiving data from on-board sensors and surrounding vehicles. *Dissemination* – if a detected event is critical, a vehicle creates and broadcasts an event report to other nearby vehicles. *Decision* – upon receiving an event report, a vehicle evaluates the content of the report and makes a decision to accept it or not. *Reaction* – if an event report is accepted, a vehicle takes the corresponding action(s) such as to brake, accelerate, switch lanes, change routes, disseminate the event report, etc.

We mainly focus on dissemination and decision stages, which are the cornerstones of achieving reliable final reactions. Our goal is to identify potential security violations when attackers have the ability to tamper with information in messages and to mitigate the impact in a timely way. Before describing the threat and system models, we first state some assumptions: (1) The distributed system is asynchronous (unbounded communication delays) and we ensure the safety of our consensus protocol. However, liveness is not guaranteed unless enough messages are received within a time upper bound. (2) An attacker may exhibit compromised behavior at any point in time and remain benign at another time i.e., any vehicle in the network at time period $[t_i, t_{i+1}]$ can be compromised, even if it is behaving normally at time period $[0, t_i]$. (3) We assume that adversaries have limited computing power so that they cannot

break the encryption and digital signatures. In other words, the cryptographic algorithms adopted are computationally secure. (4) Vehicles have public key certificates signed by trusted entities such as NHTSA [23] and/or vehicle manufacturers. (5) Private keys cannot be obtained by an attacker without a physical attack. However, by compromising a vehicle through software, an attacker can use an API to sign fake messages but does not know the actual key. This prevents remote attackers from stealing a valid private key from one vehicle and using it within a different vehicle or device.

3.2 System Model

We consider a set of vehicles that communicate by sending messages. We assume an unreliable communication medium where messages can be lost or delayed. A vehicle cannot receive other vehicles' messages if they are outside of the communication range (e.g., 200–300 meters for DSRC). Each vehicle can identify the sender of every message it receives by the sender's unique public key.

We assume that consensus begins with a vehicle generating an event report about conditions it observes on the road. The challenge, as expressed earlier, is for a set of vehicles nearby the event, that were previously unknown to each other, to form a group and reach consensus on whether the event report is accurate in a timely fashion despite the presence of compromised vehicles in the event area. Each vehicle that is nearby the reported event can form an opinion about whether the event report is accurate. We assume that non-compromised vehicles can correctly determine the accuracy of a report most of the time but occasionally a non-compromised vehicle might produce a wrong evaluation due to inaccurate or ambiguous sensing. We refer to vehicles that are not compromised but produce a wrong evaluation of an event report as *incorrect*. In this situation, it is useful for vehicles to learn a group opinion of the report accuracy to verify that their local sensor values are correct.

3.3 Threat and Fault Models

We are primarily concerned with attackers who compromise vehicles with valid credentials, and exploit improper/incomplete authorization checks. We adopt a very general threat model, where a compromised vehicle behaves arbitrarily (known as the Byzantine fault model), i.e. it may arbitrarily deviate from the protocol execution and can influence the data sent to communication channel. Through compromised software running on a vehicle, an attacker can broadcast any random or customized false data to the network, but cannot modify others' signed messages or otherwise interfere with others' message creation. In the most basic form, after successfully compromising a vehicle, typical exploits include withholding messages and sending out false data or irregular messages to others. Such attacks are successful when attackers can obtain compromised vehicles' valid certificates and credentials. Otherwise, the sent information cannot pass the authentication checks.

We assume that the number of compromised or incorrect vehicles within a small area is limited. To be specific, we assume that $f < u_{\min}/3$, where f is the number of vehicles in an area that are compromised or incorrect and $u_{\min}$ is a configurable parameter. Later, we will discuss how PoE puzzles can be used to limit participation in the consensus procedure to only those vehicles that are within the vicinity of the reported event area. This helps to limit the number of compromised vehicles that can influence the consensus, allowing f and $u_{\min}$ to remain fairly small. This, in turn, improves the overall efficiency of the consensus operation and allows consensus to be completed faster, as compared to larger consensus groups that would be required for higher values of f. This also allows the total number of compromised vehicles in the network, beyond the vicinity of the reported event area, to be much larger than f.

Sybil attacks, first introduced in [11], are also a critical problem. An attacker launches a Sybil attack by creating multiple non-existent vehicles with valid identities spreading false information in the network. Various Sybil detection methods have been studied in the past, for example based on: directional antennas [29], received signal strength indicator (RSSI), fingerprinting [35], and interference-aware RSSI-based localization [12]. We assume that Sybil attacks are prevented by existing methods and so we do not consider them herein.

We also assume that there is no large-scale prearranged collusion between compromised vehicles to share answers to PoE puzzles. So, for example, a compromised vehicle does not predetermine PoE puzzles and distribute the answers to large numbers of other compromised vehicles. However, within a consensus group, compromised vehicles can collude arbitrarily (the Byzantine fault model, including collusion, applies within a consensus group).

3.4 Consensus Properties

Let Π represent a set of vehicles running a consensus algorithm on some event report R and let v_i be some vehicle in Π. Let x denote the correct evaluation result of R and $\bar{x}$ denote the opposite (incorrect) evaluation result. Finally, let $S_{ix} = \{v_j : v_i \text{ has heard } x \text{ from } v_j\}$, let $S_{i\bar{x}} = \{v_j : v_i \text{ has heard } \bar{x} \text{ from } v_j\}$, and let $S_i = S_{ix} \cup S_{i\bar{x}}$. S_{ix} contains the vehicles from which v_i has an evaluation result of x, $S_{i\bar{x}}$ contains the vehicles from which v_i has an evaluation result of $\bar{x}$, and S_i contains the vehicles that v_i knows about.

(1) *False Consensus* occurs when the following condition holds:

FC: $\exists Q \subseteq \Pi$ such that $|Q| > \frac{2u_{\min}}{3}$ and $\forall v_i \in Q, |S_{i\bar{x}}| > \frac{2|S_i|}{3}$ and $|S_i| \geq u_{\min}$ and $\forall v_i, v_j \in Q, i \neq j, S_i = S_j$.

Condition FC occurs when there is a group of vehicles of size greater than $\frac{2u_{\min}}{3}$ that all have heard the wrong evaluation result from more than 2/3 of the vehicles they have heard from and that also agree on the group membership at the end of algorithm execution. If this situation occurs with our BFCV algorithm presented later, a false event report will be disseminated. It is important to prevent this outcome.

(2) *Correct Consensus* occurs when Condition FC does not hold *and* the following condition holds:

CC: $\exists Q \subseteq \Pi$ such that $|Q| > \frac{2u_{\min}}{3}$ and $\forall v_i \in Q, |S_{ix}| > \frac{2|S_i|}{3}$ and $|S_i| \geq u_{\min}$ and $\forall v_i, v_j \in Q, i \neq j, S_i = S_j$.

Condition CC occurs when Condition FC does not occur and there is a group of vehicles of size greater than $\frac{2u_{\min}}{3}$ that all have heard the wrong evaluation result from more than 2/3 of the vehicles they have heard from and that also agree on the group membership at the end of algorithm execution. Note that

if there are two large enough groups formed where one group agrees on the incorrect result and the other group agrees on the correct result, we still consider this to be false consensus. So, correct consensus is a large enough group agreeing on the correct result and the membership while no other large enough group agrees on the incorrect result. This is the ideal outcome for a protocol.

(3) *No Consensus* occurs when $\nexists Q \subseteq \Pi$, satisfying Condition CC or Condition FC.

This describes the situation where there is no consensus reached on either the evaluation result or the group membership or both at the end of algorithm execution. This situation would apply to algorithms that need a result within a certain time bound and terminate algorithm execution if it takes too long without reaching consensus. No consensus is preferable to false consensus but is still an outcome we would like to minimize. If the rate of no consensus is too high, valid event reports will not reach vehicles in a timely way, and this could potentially cause systemic problems.

4 BFCV ALGORITHM

4.1 Design Overview

BFCV has three features that differ from existing consensus algorithms that are targeted at connected vehicle systems.

First, it provides fast, reliable consensus group formation and shared key distribution without privileged members. The algorithm does not require trusted set up or leader election and only relies on very basic cryptographic assumptions. Each vehicle running on streets is considered as an untrusted entity equipped with valid credentials and some shares of knowledge describing the environment (traffic, weather, pedestrian, road-signs, etc.). Based on the assumption that at run time, the system does not know which entity is trustworthy and which is not, we do not follow the leader-election paradigm to construct evaluation groups. Instead, we use a set of challenge problems to perform plausibility checks, only allowing entities with sufficient proof of related knowledge and presence nearby the event location to join the cooperative evaluation.

Second, in most cases, BFCV guarantees all participating healthy vehicles reach agreement on the information being disseminated. In cases where the number of healthy vehicles is small or there is a very high rate of message loss, no consensus will be reached but false consensus will not occur (see Section 4.6 for a proof sketch).

Third, BFCV is agnostic to wireless communication technology as long as it supports inter-vehicle communication and underlying applications. No additional functionality such as remote cloud for computing, secure channel for message exchange, or trusted entities is required – it is fully distributed and self-maintained.

We next present the BFCV algorithm, which is divided into four phases: Report Generation, Proof-of-Eligibility, Evaluation Group Consensus and Report Verification. Notations used in the following sections are defined in Table 1.

4.2 Event Report Generation

An event report $R_E = (RID, E, EType, Cert_i, Q, \mathcal{H}(A), t_R, T_q)$, is generated and broadcast when a vehicle detects an unreported new

Table 1: Notation Table

v_i	Vehicle i
K_i^+, K_i^-	Public and private key of v_i
$Cert_i$	Certificate of v_i
D_i	Perception data of v_i
S_i	Hash table that records consensus status of v_i for different types of event reports
P_i	Event look-up table of v_i
F_i	Set of PoE challenge problem functions of v_i
E	An event
EID	An event's ID
$EType$	An event's type (collision, congestion, etc.)
R	An event report
RID	An event report's ID
Q	PoE challenge problems
A	Event Reporters' Answers to Q
$\mathcal{H}(A)$	Hash of A
t_R	Time stamp of report creation time
X	Signature
T_c	Time bound for reaching consensus
T_q	Time bound for solving Q, $T_q < T_c$
u_{min}	Minimum consensus group size
u_i	Membership list of v_i

event, where RID is the report ID, E is the event content, including location and estimated event life time based on criticalness, $EType$ is the event type, $Cert_i$ is the vehicle's certificate, Q is the PoE challenge problem, $\mathcal{H}(A)$ is the hash of computed answers to Q generated by the reporting vehicle, t_R is the event report time, and T_q is the time bound allowed for solving puzzle Q.

In real life scenarios, it is rare that within 200-300 meters, multiple critical events of the same type (such as rear-end collision, vehicle roll-over, etc.) exist. To improve the system efficiency and discourage compromised vehicles from flooding the network with fake reports, we allow only one event report for one $EType$ of event to be created and broadcast at a time. Once a report is broadcast, the reporter can neither join a different consensus group of the same event type, nor create another event report of the same type until the time bound of the consensus protocol for its current report is reached. If a vehicle does not follow the protocol and broadcasts a new event report before finishing the consensus time period, the inconsistency can be easily caught by other honest vehicles when they are solving the PoE challenge.

4.3 Proof-of-Eligibility

Before an event report can be accepted by other vehicles, it needs a valid group of vehicles to approve it. How vehicles are selected to form a valid evaluation group is the key to our proposed algorithm. We introduce the the concept of Proof-of-Eligibility to address this.

PoE challenge is powerful, but very application specific. In general, there is a large challenge problem pool pre-installed in vehicles. Let Φ denote the pool stored in vehicles, Q denote a selected challenge problem set from Φ, and function f denote a single problem in Q. Every time an event report is created, a Q will be automatically selected from Φ based on the event type, the event reporter's sensor

data, the event time, and a randomly generated nonce. Each set Q must consist of problems of the following types:

View - this type of problem proves the vehicle's proximity to the target position and whether it has a potential view of the event. For instance, even if two vehicles are geographically close in distance, the two vehicles might be on two sides of a big building. Then if an accident happens on one side A, the vehicle on the other side is very unlikely to detect it. Thus, we consider that the vehicle on the other side has a close enough position but does not have a qualified view. Problems in this category use features such as position, speed, acceleration, speed limit, moving direction, colors of a nearby building, number of stop signs, etc.

Knowledge - this type of problem proves whether the vehicle has a certain amount of knowledge about the event of interest. For example, if the vehicle itself is at street S_a and the event is about whether the green vehicle moving on street S_a is compromised. If the vehicle does not even observe a green vehicle on S_a, it definitely has no knowledge of the event. Problems in this category include true or false questions such as whether the vehicle received a BSM (basic safety message) from location A or whether the vehicle's current speed is below 60 mph.

Consistency - this proves the consistency of a vehicle. Even if a vehicle gets all problems from category 1 and category 2 correct, its answers could have been lucky guesses. This type of problem aims to ask a sequence of true or false questions to further check whether the answers have inconsistencies. For example, questions in category 1 may ask the color of a building and a moving direction. Then question in this category may ask whether the vehicle can see another building of another color. However, the vehicle cannot see this color unless it moves in the opposite direction. If the vehicle's answer is true, then it fails the consistency test.

Algorithm 1: Proof-of-Eligibility Challenge

1   vehicle v_j receives $R_E = (RID, E, Cert_i, Q, \mathcal{H}(A), t_R, X)$ from v_i;
2   **while** $(v_j$ is operating$) \wedge (s_j[EType] = idle)$ **do**
3   **if** $(t - t_R) < T_q$ and X is correct **then**
4       $A' = RID$;
5   **for** $f \in Q$ **do** $A' = concatenateBits(A', f(D_j))$;
6   **if** $(\mathcal{H}(A') = \mathcal{H}(A)) \wedge (t < T_q)$ **then**
7   obtain shared key $K_R^- = KeyGen(A')$;
8   set $S_j[EType]$ to busy until $(t - t_R) > T_c$ or consensus is reached;
9   **else** drop R_E;

In the proposed algorithm, once an event report is received by a vehicle, it tries to solve the puzzle Q within time bound T_q; in the end, qualified vehicles are able to obtain a seed to feed into their local key generation function thus obtaining a shared secret key K_R^-. Vehicles then use the obtained K_R^- to initiate a *Hello* message to other group members. By using the PoE puzzle, evaluation groups are able to form at run time without a selected leader, which saves the time spent on leader election and avoids the risk of granting privileges to a compromised leader. In our proposed model, all group members have the same privilege. The procedure of proof-of-eligibility is presented in Algorithm 1.

In practice, not all of the above problem types can be easily implemented, due to limitations of current vehicles. In our prototype, we only implemented category 1 and 2 problems, excluding problems that require a camera and image processing. In our prototype, only problems that can be answered from existing sensors such as speed, acceleration, GPS location, etc., are implemented. Better PoE challenge design is the subject of future research. Emerging technologies will likely help with this. For example some newly emerged light flashing techniques [33] produce light not visible to drivers but allow vehicles equipped with cameras to capture it, and these techniques will work very well for PoE applications.

4.4 Evaluation Group Consensus

Reaching consensus in dynamic vehicular networks in a timely fashion is the key feature of our proposed algorithm. As described in the last subsection, a vehicle that successfully solves the PoE challenge broadcasts an encrypted hello message, M_H, with below format, to establish connections with other members:

$$M_H = Enc(K_R^-, Cert_i, R_E, x_i, Sign(K_i^-, R_E, x_i)), \quad (1)$$

where x_i is v_i's local opinion of the event report value.

Once some connections among group members are established, encrypted consensus messages, M_C, with below format are sent to initiate voting consensus among members:

$$M_C = Enc(K_R^-, Cert_i, R_E, u_i, x_i,$$
$$Sign(K_i^-, R_E, x_i), Sign(K_i^-, u_i)), \quad (2)$$

where u_i is the known-member list by v_i. Each member in u_i is represented by its public key. The signature of $Sign(K_i^-, x_i)$ denotes attesting of the opinion by the sender, and $Sign(K_i^-, u_i)$ denotes attesting of the sender's recognized group member list.

Traditional consensus algorithms require fixed and known membership. However this is extremely hard to obtain in a highly dynamic vehicular network. We perform consensus on the group membership list G and the opinion list O simultaneously, instead of first agreeing on group membership and then initiating opinion consensus among agreed-upon members. Each element in G and O is uniquely linked to a group member which had its hello message received. For example, if a vehicle v_k receives a hello message from vehicle v_j, v_j is added to v_k's membership list, then $G_k[j]$ is initialized to 0 indicating that v_j is now a known member of v_k. O_k gets updated with $O_k[j] = 1$ if v_j agrees with v_k, otherwise, $O_k[j] = 0$. Moreover, $G_k[j]$ is set to 1 if the membership list of v_j is the same as that of v_k. This is realized by comparing the membership list obtained from M_H with v_k's local membership list. A consensus is reached when more than 2/3 of the vehicles in one vehicle's membership list agree both on the membership and the report value (opinion). The more than 2/3 requirement satisfies the well-known bound for Byzantine agreement. At this point, if the group membership size is at least as large as the minimum group size, then a decision message is broadcast to the network.

A time bound for consensus T_c is set to ensure the effectiveness of the algorithm in vehicular networks. If consensus is reached before T_c, the consensus process terminates with a decision message being broadcast. If consensus is not reached before T_c, the consensus process terminates and the related event report is dropped.

Additionally, we introduce a time variable t_{step} such that for every t_{step}, the vehicle broadcasts a message M_C even when there are no consensus messages or hello messages received. This is important when the vehicle's previously sent messages suffer from packet loss and the vehicle becomes disconnected from the other members. The detailed procedure is presented in Algorithm 2.

Finally, in order to tolerate packet loss, delay, and Byzantine behavior, we allow a vehicle to add another vehicle to its group list when it observes the vehicle in enough other vehicles' group lists even if it did not receive a hello message from the vehicle. The threshold we set for this is more than $\frac{1}{3}$ of the minimum group size to ensure that at least one healthy vehicle has heard a hello message from the new vehicle. In order to keep the code description fairly simple, we do not show this aspect in the pseudocode.

Algorithm 2: Evaluation Group Consensus

---

10   v_k obtained K_R^- by solving PoE challenges;

11   v_k receives a message M from v_j ($j \neq k$), set $t' = t$;

12   **while** $(t - t_R) < T_c \wedge$ (consensus is not reached) **do**

13   **if** $t \geq (t' + t_{step})$ **then** set $t' = t$, create and broadcast M_C;

14   **if** M can be decoded using K_R^- and verified **then**

15   **if** M is a hello message $\wedge$ $v_j \notin u_k \wedge !\Pi_{sync}$ **then**

16   add v_j to u_k;

17   **if** $x_j \neq x_k$, then $O_k[j] = 0$, otherwise $O_k[j] = 1$;

18              $t' = t$, create and broadcast M_C;

19   **else if** M is a consensus message $\wedge$ $v_j \in u_k$ **then**

20   **if** $! \Pi_{sync}$ **then**

21   **if** $v_k \notin u_j$ **then** send hello message M_H;

22   **if** $x_j \neq x_k$ **then** $O_k[j] = 0$;

23   **else** $O_k[j] = 1$;

24   **if** $u_j \neq u_k$ **then** $G_k[j] = 0$;

25   **else** $G_k[j] = 1$;

26   **if** $|\{l \mid G_k[l] = 1, O_k[l] = 1, l \in u_k\}| > \frac{2|u_k|}{3}$ $\wedge |u_k| \geq u_{min} \wedge (t - t_R) > T_q$ **then**

27   Π_{sync} = true and set consensus flag to true;

28   create and broadcast decision message;

29   **else** Π_{sync} = false;

4.5 Event Report Verification

A decision message is created if more than 2/3 of the vehicles agree on the same value and on the group membership. A decision message is denoted by:

$$M_D = (R_E, \alpha, CERTs, SIGs), \quad (3)$$

where α is the decision result, $CERTs$ is a set of certificates of the group members, and $SIGs$ is a set of signed opinions of the members in u such that for each v_i, $Sig_i = Sign(K_i, x_i)$.

When a vehicle receives a decision message and either it is not part of the consensus group or it is part of the consensus group but has not yet reached a decision, it examines the attached signatures. If the group size is at least u_{min}, all signatures are valid, and more than 2/3 of the signed values agree with the decision value, the vehicle accepts the decision. In this way, vehicles that are not compromised but have the incorrect value will accept the group decision about the event's status. Any message with one or more invalid signatures or a group size less than u_{min} will be discarded. If multiple different decision messages regarding the same event report are received by a vehicle, it accepts the valid decision message with the longest signature chain and rejects the others.

4.6 Proof Sketch of Protocol Correctness

As is typical for distributed consensus protocols in challenging environments, the PoE protocol guarantees safety but not liveness. However, liveness is demonstrated through our simulation experiments described in Section 5.

Our main safety property is that false consensus does not occur as long as less than 1/3 of the vehicles in the vicinity of the event are compromised or incorrect. Thus, the only possible outcomes of the protocol are correct consensus and no consensus. This is detailed in the following claim and proof sketch.

Claim: Let the minimum consensus group size be u_{min}. As long as the number of compromised vehicles and incorrect vehicles in the area of an event report $R_E(t)$ between the time of the report t and the time $t + T_c$ is less than $u_{min}/3$, then false consensus cannot occur.

Proof Sketch:

The proof of eligibility challenge plays a fundamental role in ensuring safety. Only vehicles that can observe the area of the event report are capable of passing the challenge. This prevents compromised vehicles from *outside* of the event area from participating in the consensus. Thus, only compromised vehicles within the area of the report during the time that the consensus protocol is executed need be considered.

Additionally, we assume that the number of healthy vehicles in the event area that do not correctly verify the status of an event report is very small so that the total of compromised and incorrect vehicles in the vicinity of the report is less than $u_{min}/3$.

False consensus requires agreement on the wrong value of an event report (e.g. "no accident" when an accident has actually occurred) and agreement on group membership. This could possibly occur in two situations: 1) when a vehicle correctly reports an event but enough compromised and incorrect vehicles within the formed consensus group conclude the event did not occur, or 2) when a compromised or incorrect vehicle falsely reports an event and enough other vehicles support the false report during the consensus procedure.

In either situation, there are two possibilities; either a consensus group of size at least u_{min} is formed for the event report or no large enough group is formed. If no large enough group is formed before time $t + T_C$, then no healthy node can broadcast a decision (see Lines 29–32 of Alg. 2 pseudocode) and the event report is dropped (this is a no consensus outcome).

If a large enough consensus group is formed, this means there are fewer than $u_{min}/3$ compromised or incorrect nodes within the group that support the wrong event status. Thus, there are simply not enough nodes to broadcast the false evaluation value for any healthy node to accept it, since that would require more than $2u_{min}/3$ false evaluations to be broadcast by distinct nodes. In this situation. If enough nodes that receive more than $2u_{min}/3$ correct evaluation results also agree on membership of the consensus group, the result is correct consensus but if there are not enough nodes that agree on the membership, the result is no consensus. However, in neither case, can false consensus occur.

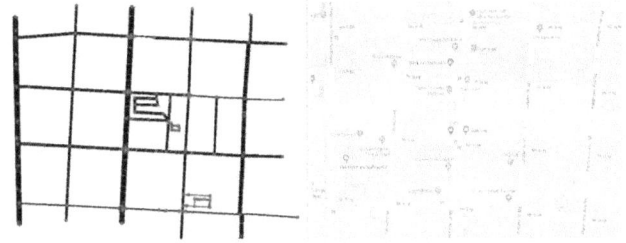

Figure 3: Evaluation Scenario - Urban

5 EVALUATION

5.1 Implementation

We implemented a prototype of BFCV in C++, which can simulate different scenarios by changing the map and system parameters. It is build on top of Veins [30] which provides a comprehensive suite of models of IEEE 802.11p, IEEE 1609.4 DSRC/WAVE and obstacle shadowing. We add additional layers to simulate packet loss/delay, cypto schemes supporting 128, 192, and 256 bit ECDSA keys for encryption, signing and verification, SHA-256 as the hash function. Our prototype consists of approximately 3500 lines of written code. Experimental maps are obtained from OpenStreetMap (OSM) [26] with manual corrections of speed limit, traffic lights, number of lanes on the road, etc. to improve the accuracy. Vehicle mobility and routes are computed based on demand definition and shortest path algorithm using SUMO [17].

Different from previous works, the prototype includes realistic aspects of the vehicle dynamics (safe distance, mass, dimensions, vehicle types, braking distance, traffic lights, etc.), detailed modeling of the communication network, and real-life street maps with varying scales.

5.2 Simulation Results

Experiment Scenario: Our evaluation is conducted in a simulated midtown area of a major city in the U.S. with a capacity of around 700 moving vehicles (see Figure 3). We simulate a worst-case scenario where compromised vehicles behave honestly when there is no event to be reported. Thus, it is very hard for honest vehicles to catch bad behaviors prior to an event report. In the simulation scenario, a collision happens at a random time, and honest vehicles that detect the event create and broadcast "collision occurred" event reports leaving others to evaluate them. We also have compromised vehicles broadcast conflicting event reports saying "collision cleared" at the same time. Thus, there can be several consensus executions happening at the same time among different groups of vehicles to try to reach agreement to accept one of these conflicting reports. We also have compromised vehicles drop, delay or not send messages, and submit wrong opinions for evaluation.

BFCV Evaluation Results: Unless otherwise noted, the following parameters were used in all experiments: $T_q = 5s$, $T_c = 14s$, $u_{min} = 7$, vehicle density = 250 and beacon message frequency = 10Hz. Natural packet loss and delay (not including compromised vehicles' behavior) were simulated such that messages were randomly dropped at receiving vehicles with a drop rate of 15% and packets were randomly delayed within a range of 100ms - 1500ms. The communication range among vehicles was set to 300m based on NHTSA's proposed rule [24]. We use the following two metrics to evaluate the latency of BFCV:

- *Consensus Time:* the time spent on reaching consensus on a single event report. This starts from the event report creation time and ends when there is a decision message received by every member of the group contained in the message.
- *Decision Time:* the time spent on ultimately reaching consensus. This starts from the first event report creation time and ends when there is a decision message received by every member of the group contained in the consensus message. Note that this could involve multiple consensus attempts if the first attempt does not produce a consensus.

We first evaluated how BFCV's performance varies with minimum group size and vehicle density. We ran simulations with 10% of vehicles compromised, varied u_{min} from 4 to 10 with an increment of 1, and varied vehicle density from 50 to 450 vehicles with an increment of 100. 50 simulation runs were done for each parameter combination, where a single consensus period was simulated in each run. The possible results of each run are: Correct Consensus (CC), False Consensus (FC) and No Consensus (NC). Note that, as described above, there can be multiple consensus executions happening concurrently for "collision occurred" and "collision cleared" event reports. In case multiple large enough consensus groups succeed in reaching consensus, we record the result as FC as long as at least one of the groups agreed on "collision cleared". The results are shown in Figure 4.

Figure 4(a) shows the average consensus time in seconds vs. minimum group size and vehicle density. Note that NC outcomes are not included in the average, because there is no definite termination of the consensus in those cases. Not surprisingly, consensus time increases with both minimum group size and vehicle density since an increase in either parameter will cause the number of messages exchanged by the algorithm to increase. Figure 4(b)(c)(d) shows the different consensus outcomes vs. the two parameters. Note that, if the minimum group size is too small, compromised vehicles can form a group and reach false consensus. Also, if the vehicle density is too low, there are not enough vehicles in the event area to form a consensus group, and this leads to a high rate of NC outcomes. However, for a fairly wide range of group sizes and vehicle densities, there are zero FC results and a very low rate of NC outcomes. These results demonstrate that the choice of u_{min} should be based on both adversarial assumptions and expected vehicle density.

We also evaluated BFCV's performance versus the percentage of compromised vehicles with $u_{min} = 7$ and a vehicle density of 250. For percentages from 5% to 40% with 5% increments, we repeated the simulation 50 times. The results are shown in Table 2. From the table, we can see that as the percentage of compromised vehicles increases, the percentage of CC decreases from 100% to 79%. However, even with 40% of the vehicles in the network being compromised, the BFCV Algorithm did not experience a single false consensus outcome.

We also evaluated how well BFCV handles failure to reach consensus (NC outcomes). Instead of stopping the simulation immediately after the single-round consensus timeout, T_c, occurred, we

Table 2: Performance vs % of Compromised Vehicles

Mal_V	CC	FC	NC	AvgConsensusTime
5%	100%	0%	0%	5.228s
10%	99%	0%	1%	5.701s
15%	99%	0%	1%	6.206s
20%	99%	0%	1%	6.718s
25%	97%	0%	3%	8.542s
30%	93%	0%	7%	9.325s
35%	88%	0%	12%	10.446s
40%	79%	0%	21%	13.118s

extended the simulation if consensus was not reached the first time. If a report evaluation fails to reach consensus within time T_c, then our algorithm drops the report. However, if this occurs in the simulation, another honest vehicle nearby will submit a new event report for consensus. By extending the simulation time, we examined whether the BFCV algorithm can recover from NC outcomes. In this case, we recorded the final decisions, i.e. whether there was ultimately a correct decision made after an event happened, possibly after more than one consensus attempt.

Figure 5 shows the average decision time for different compromised vehicle percentages and different vehicle densities with $u_{min} = 7$. When the percentage of compromised vehicles was low, the decision was made very quickly with an average that is well below the single-round consensus time bound T_c. However, as the percentage of compromised vehicles was increased, the time spent on evaluation rose. Note that, in some cases, the average decision time was close to or exceeded $T_c = 14s$, implying that more than one round of consensus was some times needed for those cases.

Comparison Results: We also simulated two related protocols, DC [27] and PoR [5], and evaluated them under the same experiment conditions. These protocols both use threshold-based voting, which is the most widely-used prior approach. Two metrics are introduced to compare the results:

- *Percentage of Vehicles Taking Action:* the percentage of vehicles in the network that reach a correct decision about the event report and take action to avoid the accident location
- *Average Commute Time:* the average simulation time that vehicles take to reach their destinations (vehicles not taking action to avoid the accident location experience a longer commute time due to backups around the accident site)

There was no explicit method described in [5] to set the threshold for the PoR algorithm. However, it should be based on the report criticality and the network status, which is similar to the minimum group size in our proposed algorithm. Therefore, we set both of these parameters to 7 in these simulations. The DC algorithm provides an explicit method for dynamically adjusting its threshold value, which we adhered to in our DC implementation. Other parameters of BFCV were the same as in the previous experiments.

Figure 6 depicts the percentage of vehicles taking action as the simulations progressed when 5% and 15% of vehicles were compromised, respectively. There are two main reasons why BFCV performed better than DC and PoR. First, with BFCV, vehicles make a group decision and act accordingly. For DC and PoR, each vehicle

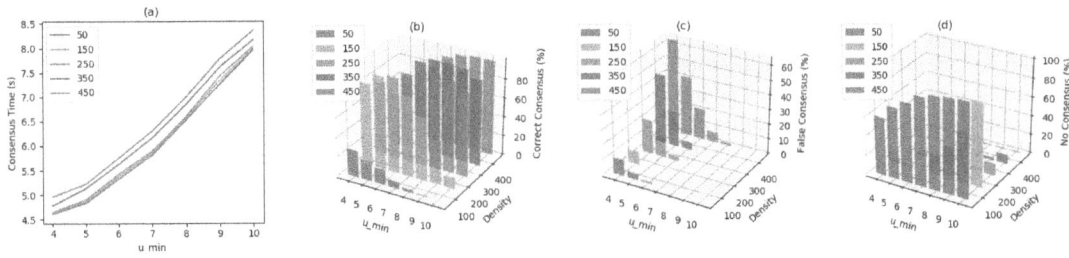

Figure 4: Consensus Time and Consensus Result vs. Minimum Group Size and Vehicle Density

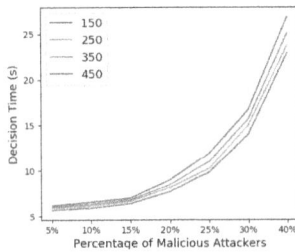

Figure 5: Decision Time vs % Compromised Vehicles

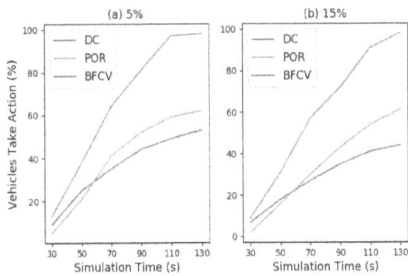

Figure 6: Vehicles Taking Action (%) vs Simulation Time

makes its own decision when enough endorsements from other vehicles are collected and, thus, not all vehicles make the same decision. In particular, since there are both "collision occurred" and "collision cleared" reports being circulated at the same time, some vehicles collect enough votes for "collision cleared" and reach the wrong decision even though most vehicles reach the correct decision. Second, BFCV uses PoE, which prevents compromised vehicles from outside the event area from participating. Since DC and PoR cannot verify location information of vehicles, they cannot filter out fake reports from compromised vehicles anywhere in the network that falsely report their location as being near the event, which increases the chances that enough votes can be collected to accept a fake report.

Table 3 depicts average commute time versus percentage of compromised vehicles ranging from 5% to 20%. For vehicles that were stuck in the simulation area at the end of the simulation, for the purposes of computing an average, we assigned them a commute time of 300 sec. From the table, we see that BFCV produced 15-22% lower commute times than PoR and 10-40% lower times than DC. As the percentage of compromised vehicles increased, most of the

Table 3: Avg. Commute Time vs. % of Compromised Vehicles

Mal_V	DC(s)	PoR(s)	BFCV(s)
5%	171	179	155
10%	194	197	162
15%	244	223	183
20%	286	248	203

vehicles actually ended up being stuck for the DC Algorithm (avg. commute time approached 300 sec.), and a significant number were also stuck with PoR, while most of the vehicles actually reached their destinations during the simulated interval with BFCV.

6 RELATED WORK

In this section, we first review the existing approaches proposed for information security in connected vehicles. Node centric methods such as reputation systems [9, 10, 21, 31] inspect the past and present behavior of nodes and use this to predict the future misbehavior, which assumes that the nodes who behave well in the past are more likely to behave well in the future. However, smart adversaries may only initiate attacks at critical times, which is a fundamental problem that reputation systems cannot handle.

Data centric methods focus on analyzing transmitted data among nodes and information verification. Vehicles that use local methods, e.g. [13, 20, 31], verify information locally without relying on other vehicles' cooperation. Though these methods are light-weight, easy to scale and can tolerate intermittent communication, they heavily rely on location information and have a limited view of what is happening on the road, which reduces their accuracy. Cooperative schemes, as surveyed in [2], are more accurate than local methods with lower false positive and false negative rates. Nevertheless, they are more vulnerable to packet loss/delay and the ratio of compromised to honest vehicles. Threshold-based voting has been adopted in PoR [5], DC [27] to filter false data that honest vehicles only accept a report when they receive more than X signatures attesting to it. PoR improves the efficiency of communication by using growth codes, but the performance is sensitive to a preset threshold, while the DC method in [27] dynamically sets the threshold based on the criticality and the density of the network. However, [27] assumes 1-D communication, detection, and reaction, primarily limiting its use to highway scenarios. Moreover, threshold voting does not provide true consensus, because each vehicle decides independently and, therefore, different honest vehicles can reach different decisions.

True consensus algorithms satisfying *termination, agreement, and validity* properties have been well studied in other contexts. Paxos[18] and Raft [25] are well known algorithms to achieve consensus among unreliable nodes, but they do not address Byzantine faults [19]. Traditional Byzantine agreement protocols, e.g. [3, 6, 16] do not handle highly dynamic network connectivity such as occurs in vehicular networks. In general, traditional consensus algorithms require heavy computation, frequent message exchanges, and/or a fixed wired network, making them hard to be adapted to vehicular networks. While efforts have been made to adapt traditional consensus algorithms for dynamic and intermittent topologies in MANETs, e.g. [4, 7, 14, 34], none of these efforts address both unreliable links and Byzantine faults.

Although information security in vehicular networks has been previously studied, efficient collaborative methods that guarantee all healthy nodes make the same decision have not been developed to date. Our work presented herein provides an algorithm that provides timely and efficient consensus while supporting vehicles' high mobility as well as intermittent connections. In addition to achieving true consensus, our algorithm makes use of a novel proof of eligibility concept that prevents compromised vehicles from outside of an event report area from participating in decisions about the event. Prior approaches could not limit the participation of compromised vehicles in this way and were thus much more susceptible to intentional manipulation. As demonstrated in Section 5, our BFCV algorithm is the first to achieve true consensus with low latency in realistic vehicular scenarios with $\frac{1}{3}$ or more of the vehicles in the entire simulated area acting in a Byzantine faulty manner.

7 CONCLUSION

We presented BFCV, a distributed consensus algorithm based on "proof-of-eligibility", which achieves Byzantine agreement with unknown group membership and unreliable communication channels and is targeted at vehicular network environments. BFCV leverages the unique characteristics of moving vehicles and cryptographic primitives to prevent a large number of compromised and unrelated vehicles from joining the consensus group. This significantly speeds up the consensus procedure, providing a new paradigm of Byzantine-tolerant fast consensus for connected vehicles.

8 ACKNOWLEDGEMENT

This work is partially supported by Ministry of Education (MOE) in Taiwan under Grant Numbers NTU-107V0901 and NTU-108V0901 and Ministry of Science and Technology (MOST) in Taiwan under Grant Number MOST-108-2636-E-002-011.

REFERENCES

[1] M. Al-Kahtani. 2012. Survey on security attacks in Vehicular Ad hoc Networks (VANETs). In *Signal Processing and Communication Systems (ICSPCS), 2012 6th International Conference on*. IEEE.
[2] M. Arshad, Z. Ullah, N. Ahmad, M. Khalid, H. Criuckshank, and Y. Cao. 2018. A survey of local/cooperative-based malicious information detection techniques in VANETs. *EURASIP Journal on Wireless Communications and Networking* 1 (2018).
[3] J. Augustine, G. Pandurangan, and P. Robinson. 2013. Fast byzantine agreement in dynamic networks. In *Proceedings of the 2013 ACM symposium on Principles of distributed computing*. ACM.
[4] Abdulkader B., Pascale L., and Frédéric G. 2015. Solving Consensus in Opportunistic Networks. In *ICDCN*.
[5] Z. Cao, J. Kong, U. Lee, M. Gerla, and Z. Chen. 2008. Proof-of-relevance: Filtering false data via authentic consensus in vehicle ad-hoc networks. In *INFOCOM Workshops 2008, IEEE*. IEEE.
[6] M. Castro, B. Liskov, et al. 1999. Practical Byzantine fault tolerance. In *OSDI*, Vol. 99.
[7] D. Cavin, Y. Sasson, and A. Schiper. 2004. Consensus with unknown participants or fundamental self-organization. In *International Conference on Ad-Hoc Networks and Wireless*. Springer.
[8] Q. Chen, Y. Yin, Y. Feng, Z M. Mao, and H. Liu. [n. d.]. Exposing Congestion Attack on Emerging Connected Vehicle based Traffic Signal Control. ([n. d.]).
[9] Q. Ding, X. Li, M. Jiang, and X. Zhou. 2010. Reputation management in vehicular ad hoc networks. In *Int'l Conf. on Multimedia Technology*. IEEE.
[10] F. Dotzer, L. Fischer, and P. Magiera. 2005. Vars: A vehicle ad-hoc network reputation system. In *World of Wireless Mobile and Multimedia Networks, 2005. WoWMoM 2005. Sixth IEEE International Symposium on a*. IEEE.
[11] J. Douceur. 2002. The sybil attack. In *International workshop on peer-to-peer systems*. Springer.
[12] T. Garip, H. Kim, P. Reiher, and M. Gerla. 2017. INTERLOC: An interference-aware RSSI-based localization and Sybil attack detection mechanism for vehicular ad hoc networks. In *14th Annual Consumer Comm. & Networking Conf*. IEEE.
[13] M. Ghosh, A. Varghese, A. Gupta, A. A Kherani, and S. Muthaiah. 2010. Detecting misbehaviors in VANET with integrated root-cause analysis. *Ad Hoc Networks* 8, 7 (2010), 778–790.
[14] F. Greve and S. Tixeuil. 2007. Knowledge connectivity vs. synchrony requirements for fault-tolerant agreement in unknown networks. In *Dependable Systems and Networks, 2007. DSN'07. 37th Annual IEEE/IFIP International Conference on*. IEEE.
[15] J. Grover, Nitesh. Prajapati, V. Laxmi, and Manoj. Gaur. 2011. Machine learning approach for multiple misbehavior detection in VANET. In *International Conference on Advances in Computing and Communications*. Springer.
[16] R. Guerraoui, F. Huc, and A. Kermarrec. 2013. Highly dynamic distributed computing with byzantine failures. In *Proceedings of the 2013 ACM symposium on Principles of distributed computing*. ACM.
[17] D. Krajzewicz, J. Erdmann, M. Behrisch, and L. Bieker. 2012. Recent Development and Applications of SUMO - Simulation of Urban Mobility. *International Journal On Advances in Systems and Measurements* 5, 3&4 (December 2012).
[18] L. Lamport et al. 2001. Paxos made simple. *ACM Sigact News* 32, 4 (2001).
[19] L. Lamport, R. Shostak, and M. Pease. 1982. The Byzantine generals problem. *ACM Transactions on Programming Languages and Systems (TOPLAS)* 4, 3 (1982).
[20] T. Leinmüller, E. Schoch, F. Kargl, and C. Maihöfer. 2010. Decentralized position verification in geographic ad hoc routing. *Security and communication networks* 3, 4 (2010).
[21] Z. Li and C. Chigan. 2014. On joint privacy and reputation assurance for vehicular ad hoc networks. *IEEE Transactions on Mobile Computing* 13, 10 (2014).
[22] N. Lo and H. Tsai. 2007. Illusion attack on vanet applications-a message plausibility problem. In *Globecom Workshops, 2007 IEEE*. IEEE.
[23] NHTSA. [n. d.]. Federal Motor Vehicle Safety Standards; V2V Communications. https://www.federalregister.gov/documents/2017/01/12/2016-31059/federal-motor-vehicle-safety-standards-v2v-communications#h-1
[24] NHTSA. 2017. Federal Motor Vehicle Safety Standards; V2V Communications. Retrieved May 20, 2019 from https://www.federalregister.gov/documents/2017/01/12/2016-31059/federal-motor-vehicle-safety-standards-v2v-communications
[25] D. Ongaro and J. Ousterhout. 2014. In search of an understandable consensus algorithm.. In *USENIX Annual Technical Conference*.
[26] OpenStreetMap contributors. 2017. Planet dump retrieved from https://planet.osm.org . https://www.openstreetmap.org.
[27] J. Petit and Z. Mammeri. 2011. Dynamic consensus for secured vehicular ad hoc networks. In *Wireless and Mobile Computing, Networking and Communications (WiMob), 2011 IEEE 7th International Conference on*. IEEE.
[28] C. Qi and M. Z. Morley. [n. d.]. Connected cars can lie, posing a new threat to smart cities. https://theconversation.com/connected-cars-can-lie-posing-a-new-threat-to-smart-cities-95339
[29] K. Rabieh, M. Mahmoud, T. N Guo, and M. Younis. 2015. Cross-layer scheme for detecting large-scale colluding Sybil attack in VANETs. In *2015 IEEE International Conference on Communications (ICC)*. IEEE.
[30] C. Sommer, R. German, and F. Dressler. 2011. Bidirectionally Coupled Network and Road Traffic Simulation for Improved IVC Analysis. *IEEE Transactions on Mobile Computing* 10, 1 (January 2011). https://doi.org/10.1109/TMC.2010.133
[31] R. van der Heijden, S. Dietzel, and F. Kargl. 2013. Misbehavior detection in vehicular ad-hoc networks. *1st GI/ITG KuVS Fachgespräch Inter-Vehicle Communication. University of Innsbruck* (2013).
[32] R. van der Heijden, S. Dietzel, T. Leinmüller, and F. Kargl. 2016. Survey on misbehavior detection in cooperative intelligent transportation systems. *arXiv preprint arXiv:1610.06810* (2016).
[33] L. Wu and H. Tsai. 2013. Modeling vehicle-to-vehicle visible light communication link duration with empirical data. In *Globecom Workshops, 2013*. IEEE.
[34] W. Wu, J. Cao, and M. Raynal. 2008. Eventual clusterer: A modular approach to designing hierarchical consensus protocols in manets. *IEEE Transactions on Parallel & Distributed Systems* 6 (2008).
[35] Y. Yao, B. Xiao, G. Wu, X. Liu, Z. Yu, K. Zhang, and X. Zhou. 2019. Multi-channel based Sybil attack detection in vehicular ad hoc networks using RSSI. *IEEE Transactions on Mobile Computing* 18, 2 (2019).

Towards Data VSN Offloading in VANETs Integrated into the Cellular Network

Douglas L. L. Moura
Department of Computer Science,
Federal University of Minas Gerais,
Brazil
douglas.moura@dcc.ufmg.br

Andre L. L. Aquino
Computer Institute, Federal
University of Alagoas, Brazil
alla@laccan.ufal.br

Antonio A. F. Loureiro
Department of Computer Science,
Federal University of Minas Gerais,
Brazil
loureiro@dcc.ufmg.br

ABSTRACT

Vehicular sensing network consists of a promising remote sensing paradigm, in which a variety of new applications will be possible through the processing of data periodically collected by vehicles. However, the acquisition of a large amount of sensing data and the increasing demand for traffic cellular requires mechanisms to decongest the cellular network infrastructure. Thus, this work uses a centrality measure to propose an offloading scheme in which certain vehicles will collect data from their neighbors and transmit it in the cellular uplink. The presented article models the problem as a *minimum d-hop dominating set* and create a greedy algorithm to solve it. The evaluation considers a realistic dataset to evaluate the proposed approach. When compared with the non-offloading scheme, it shows a cost reduction of up to 82.09% in the best-case and 13.45% in the worst-case.

CCS CONCEPTS

• **Networks** → **Mobile ad hoc networks**.

KEYWORDS

Offloading, VANETs, cellular networks

ACM Reference Format:
Douglas L. L. Moura, Andre L. L. Aquino, and Antonio A. F. Loureiro. 2019. Towards Data VSN Offloading in VANETs Integrated into the Cellular Network. In *22nd Int'l ACM Conference on Modeling, Analysis and Simulation of Wireless and Mobile Systems (MSWiM '19), November 25–29, 2019, Miami Beach, FL, USA.* ACM, New York, NY, USA, 5 pages. https://doi.org/10.1145/3345768.3355937

1 INTRODUCTION

Nowadays, the vehicular industry has been increased its interest in automotive sensors and its importance for Intelligent Transportation System (ITS) applications. Each vehicle had about 60 to 100 sensors onboard at the end of 2017 [12]. Specialists estimate that this number will reach 200 sensors by the year 2020 [8]. The increase in the number of sensors is due to its proven benefits, such as the reduction in the number of traffic accidents, improved vehicle performance and steering, vehicle diagnostic services, and environmental monitoring [1]. Vehicles in a vehicular ad hoc network (VANET) can act as mobile sensors [13] and perform monitoring of the urban environment, providing information applications, efficient traffic management and long-term urban planning. Therefore, the VANET provides data for remote sensing paradigm, known as Vehicular Sensor Networks (VSN) [17]. The VSN is an intersection between VANET and Wireless Sensor Network (WSN), but unlike a traditional WSN, power constraints do not affect the vehicles, and they have powerful processing units, wireless communication, GPS receivers and different sensing devices, such as chemical detectors, video cameras, and vibration/acoustic sensors [9]. A variety of new applications will be possible through the processing of data periodically collected by vehicles, e.g., improving road safety, traffic management, intelligent navigation, pollution monitoring, urban surveillance and forensic investigations [4].

Many continuous monitoring applications require periodic uploading of the data, generating significant traffic in the uplink channel. According to Cisco [6], the total monthly mobile data traffic is forecast to be 77 exabytes by 2022, in which 20% of IP traffic will be from mobile devices. The 5G network is a fundamental step for the so-called Internet of Things (IoT), which aims to connect different types of wireless devices. Although this scenario favors the emergence of new VANETs based on cellular communication, the rapid growth in traffic demand requires a means of reducing the overhead in the cellular network. This work focus on periodic upload of VSN data for remote processing, in which the sensing application originates a massive amount of data and transmitted in the cellular network. Therefore, some strategies try to save bandwidth and prevent cell network overload.

Previous studies tried to solve this problem through the mobile data offloading, the central theme of this manuscript. The system offloaded the data transmitted in the cellular uplink, into a complementary and low-cost network, such as Wi-Fi, 802.11p, and device-to-device (D2D) [10]. Some studies focus on downlink transfers in which the stations transmit the content to one vehicle, and this vehicle disseminates the content to the others from broadcast transmissions [5, 11, 14]. Other studies proposed data offloading in the uplink direction, when a large amount of information must be transmitted on the Internet and received by a remote server for processing and analysis. Bazzi et al. [4] proposed a solution based on vehicle-to-infrastructure (V2I) communication. The results obtained showed a complete reduction in cellular network access in high vehicle density scenarios. However, the high cost of deploy roadsides units (RSUs) would become impractical to implantation an infrastructure capable of covering all vehicles in the scenario.

Stanica et al. [15] considered the vehicle-to-vehicle (V2V) communication rather than V2I and propose the Reservation-Based (RB) algorithm. In this work, techniques for combining data from different sources are used to reduce the number of transmissions. As a result, the cellular network access decrease by more than 80%. The RB algorithm requires synchronization, thus a possible real application of the RB may be difficult.

This article explores V2V communication to select vehicles to collect and aggregate VSN data from neighboring vehicles and upload this data to the Base Station (BS), which will transmit the data for analysis and remote processing. Therefore, the problem is how to determine a subset of selected vehicles to offload the VSN data via V2V communication? We want to use the minimal number of vehicles to transmit in the cellular network and reduce the upload cost. This article models the problem as a *minimum d-hop dominating set* [2] and present a decentralized solution to perform the offloading of the VSN data. The proposed approach is a greedy algorithm based a centrality measure, known as *closeness centrality* [7], to find a subset of uploaders vehicles.

The experiments use a highly realistic scenario, and the results, when compared with the traditional upload, show an upload cost reduction of up to 82.09%, in which it was possible to reduce by up to 83.14% the number of vehicles transmitting in the cellular upload channel. When compared with the RB approach, achieve a cost reduction of around 32% in best-case.

We organize the remainder of this paper as follows: Section 2 discusses about the problem formulation. Section 3 shows our proposed solution for the VSN offloading problem. Section 4 presents the scenarios applied and results achieved. Finally, Section 5 concludes the work and shows possible future work.

2 FORMULATION PROBLEM

The domination problem in graphs has been widely studied in literature and has application in communication networks. These applications led to the emergence of variants of the original problem. The *d-hop dominating set problem* was introduced in the literature in the context of wireless networks, in which it was possible to explore the multi-hop communication to form an backbone infrastructure.

Let $G = (V, E)$ be an undirected graph, where $V = \{v_1, v_2, ..., v_n\}$ is the set of vehicles in the scenario and $E = \{e_1, e_2, ..., e_m\}$ denotes the set of edges. The neighborhood $N_G^d(v_i)$ consists of all neighbors of v_i separated by at most d-hops:

$$N_G^d(v_i) = \{v_j \mid dist(v_i, v_j) \leq d\} \qquad (1)$$

The distance $dist(v_i, v_j)$ between a vehicle v_i and v_j is given by the length of the shortest path between v_i and v_j. We calculate the length of the path between two vertices by taking the number of hops, i.e., the number of edges separating the two vertices.

The interest of this work is to find a subset of nodes to collect data from its neighbors, aggregate this data, and transmit it in the cellular uplink. Thus, the decision problem can be defined as:

Definition 2.1. (Problem) Given a graph $G = (V, E)$ and the positive integers $d \geq 1$ and $K \leq |V|$. Is there a d-hop dominating set of size less than or equal K? In other words, there exists a subset $S \subseteq V$ of vertices with $|S| \leq K$, such that for all $v_i \in (V - S)$ there is at least one vertex $v_j \in S$ in which $dist(v_i, v_j) \leq d$?

In this work, we aim to minimize the size of the *d-hop dominating set*, i.e., find the *minimum d-hop dominating set*. Its counterpart as an optimization problem is a NP-Hard problem:

$$Min \quad \sum_{i=1}^{N} y_i \qquad (2)$$

Subject to

$$\sum_{v_j \in N_G^d(v_i)} y_j + y_i \geq 1 \qquad i = 1, 2, ..., N; \forall y \qquad (3)$$

$$y_i \in \{0, 1\} \qquad (4)$$

Consider $Y = \{y_1, y_2, ..., y_n\}$ as a set of variables associated with the set of vehicles V, if the element $y_i \in Y$ assume the value 1, then $v_i \in V$ will be contained in S. The Equation 3 requires that for all vehicle v_i, at least one vehicle in $\{v_i\} \cup N_G^d(v_i)$ should be contained in S. In this way, it is ensured that S will be a dominating set of a minimum size in which each node in V will be distant at most d-hops from at least one vertex in S.

3 MULTI-HOP BASED ON CLOSENESS CENTRALITY

Networks derived from real data have structures and characteristics that can be studied through models and metrics. The measure of centrality defined for a vehicle is a metric that aims to classify it according to its position in the network. Thus, it is possible to use the measure of centrality to find out which vehicles play the highest topological importance within that structure.

The shortest path between two vertices in an unweighted graph G is defined as the smallest sequence of edges connecting them. Thus, the *closeness centrality* (C) of a node v_i in the network is a measure of centrality defined in Equation 5:

$$C(v_i) = \frac{1}{\sum_{v_i \neq v_j} dist(v_i, v_j)} \qquad (5)$$

Find the shortest paths can be performed in linear time in the size of the adjacency list with a **breadth-first search** and a complexity $O(V + E)$. The step is repeated for each vertex of the network. Thus the cost of closeness centrality in a connected graph can be expressed as $O(V^2 + VE)$. However, our main interest is the relative importance of the node and not in the numerical value of centrality. Thus, there is still a cost $O(V \log V)$ necessary to sort the vertices according to their centrality measures, resulting in a final cost $O(V^2 + VE + V \log V)$ in connected graphs with uniform cost paths.

Although the algorithm can be easily parallelized by running the processing of each vertex on different threads, it is highly costly to run on large-scale networks, i.e., networks formed by thousands or millions of nodes. Therefore, the estimate closeness centrality is very useful. In the estimate closeness centrality (C_k) only paths with distances less than $k \geq 1$ are considered:

$$C_k(v_i) = \frac{1}{\sum_{v_i \neq v_j} dist(v_i, v_j)}; \quad \forall dist(v_i, v_j) \leq k \qquad (6)$$

The cutoff parameter k sets a threshold depth for the search, which will stop after reaching the k-th level. In this way, only the vertices separated by at most k-hops will be considered in the calculation of centrality of the vertex v_i. In addition to reducing the execution cost of the algorithm, whose complexity will now be limited to the vertices within the threshold depth, the network overhead will also be reduced, since fewer messages will be disseminated for the discovery of the nodes.

The **multi-hop based closeness centrality (MHC)** starts from the local communications established by each vehicle to model the network and extract structural information from the graph. Through this information, it is possible to explore vehicular mobility to determine the centrality of the vehicles and select those that will access the cellular network.

The following steps describe the MHC:

(1) **Awareness** - Some neighbor discovery service will be used to establish the proximity relationship between the vehicles;

(2) **Modeling** - Each base station will model the network topology from the discovery service information;

(3) **Selection** - The station will use closeness centrality in a greedy approach (see Algorithm 1) to select which vehicles will access the cellular uplink;

(4) **Upload** - Finally, a vehicle selected to access the cellular uplink will receive a message from the base station requesting the upload. The vehicle can then transmit the collected data.

Each cellular base station will model the V2V communication graph of its associated vehicles and resolve an instance of the *minimum d-hop dominating set* problem. Algorithm 1 shows our greedy algorithm (MHC) to solve this problem. MHC receives as input: the graph (G) that models the V2V communication, number of hops for multi-hop communication (d) and the maximum path length (k) for centrality estimation.

Algorithm 1 Multi-hop based on closeness centrality (MHC)

Input G, d, k
Output S
1: $S \leftarrow \emptyset$
2: $C_k \leftarrow$ Compute $C_k(v_i), \forall v_i \in V$
3: **while** $V \neq \emptyset$ **do**
4:     Select $v_i \in V$ that maximizes C_k
5:     $S \leftarrow S \cup v_i$
6:     **for** each $v_j \in N_G^d(v_i)$ **do**
7:         **if** $v_j \notin S$ **then**
8:             $V \leftarrow V \setminus v_j$
9:     $V \leftarrow V \setminus v_i$

Initially, MHC will compute the closeness centrality for each vehicle in G according to the cutoff k (Line 2). While there are vehicles in G, the vertex with the most considerable centrality measure will be removed from G and added in the solution set S (Lines 3-5). The next step is to remove from the graph G each vertex that is neighbor of the selected vehicle in Line 4, and that is not in the set S (Lines 6-8). This step ensures that vehicles selected for cellular communication will be separated from each other by at least d-hops. Finally, when the MHC achieves the stop condition, it returns S with the set of vehicles that access the cellular uplink. In cases where the graph network is not connected, each isolated vehicle will be added in S and will transmit its VSN data.

4 COMPUTATIONAL EXPERIMENTS

We used a scenario created from the trace mobility of Cologne. The dataset is available by project TAPASCologne [16], an initiative of the Institute of Transportation Systems (ITS-DLR) at the German Aerospace Center. The dataset covers an area of $400 \ km^2$ for 24 hours and granularity of 1 second; more than 700.000 individual car trips were used. We use the mobility traces to model V2V communication (e.g., based on the 802.11p standard or D2D communication), in which the connections between vehicles follow the unit disk model. We assume that each vehicle has a transmission range equal to 100 meters.

We consider two local aggregation models [3]:

(1) **Best-case:** Each vehicle $v_i \in S$ will compress data received from their neighbors and upload a single packet to the BS. The BS will receive only a summary of the reported measurements, such as the average value. We consider packets transmitted with a payload $p = 100$ bytes and TCP/IP headers with a size $h = 20$ bytes. Resulting in packets of constant size $m = h + p$ and an upload cost:

$$cost_1(t) = \sum_{v_i \in S} m = m \times |S| \qquad (7)$$

The total cost at the instant of time t will be directly proportional to the size of the subset S.

(2) **Worst-case:** The individual data of each vehicle need to be transmitted in the cellular network. The payload from different vehicles can be transmitted in the same packet, so that its size does not exceed the maximum size of an IP packet $m_{max} = 1,440$ bytes. Thus, it is still possible to reduce the TCP/IP headers overhead. We also consider packets with payload $p = 100$ bytes and TCP/IP headers $h = 20$ bytes. The resulting cost at time t is:

$$cost_2(t) = \sum_{v_i \in S} (R_i \times h + N_i \times p) \qquad (8)$$

$$R_i = \left\lceil \frac{N_i \times p}{m_{max} - h} \right\rceil \qquad (9)$$

where R_i is the number of packets transmitted by vehicle v_i and N_i is the number of neighbors of v_i.

The next sections report the experiments performed to evaluate the MHC in the best and worst-case with an upload period of 10 seconds. The results of the MHC was compared with the RB algorithm proposed in Stanica et al. [15] and the optimal solution by means IBM ILOG CPLEX Optimization Studio 12.9[1]. The number of slots in the RB was fixed as 256 (value previously defined by the authors), and the results are the average cost of 10 runs.

4.1 Best-case aggregation

The first part of the experiments showed that the MHC could significantly reduce the upload cost in the best-case aggregation. For this purpose, we considered different values of $d = \{1, 2, 3\}$ and $k = \{1, 2, 3, 4\}$. The results suggest the MHC achieved a better solution when $k > d + 1$. This occurs because the offloading reached d-hop neighbors, then $k < d$ did not provide enough topological

---
[1] Available at https://www.ibm.com/br-pt/products/ilog-cplex-optimization-studio/

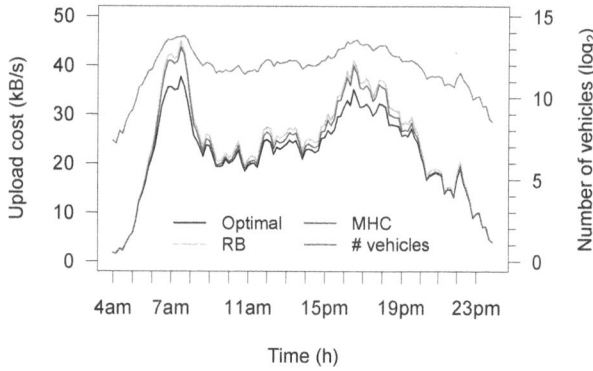

(a) Upload cost in the best-case local aggregation.

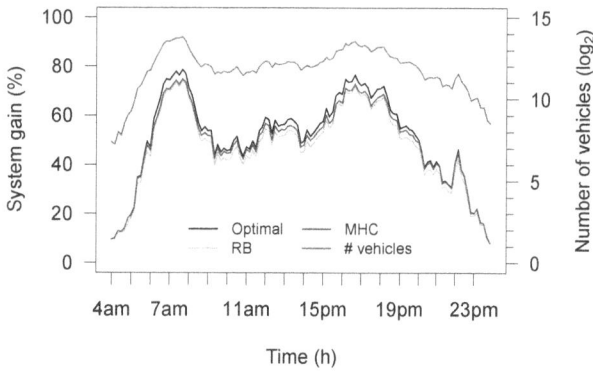

(b) System gain obtained by algorithms.

Figure 1: Single-hop communication.

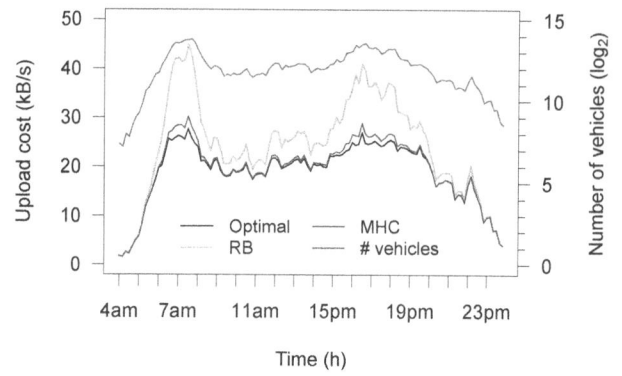

(a) Upload cost in the best-case local aggregation.

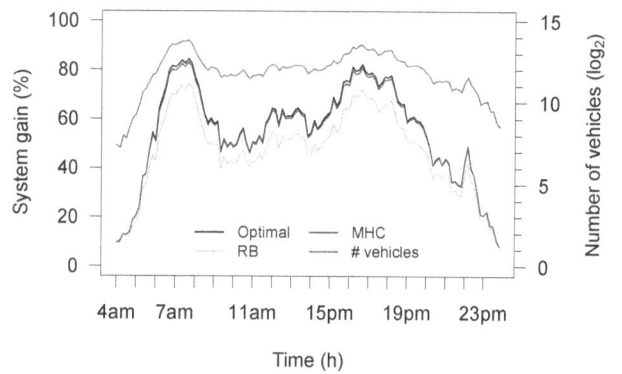

(b) System gain obtained by algorithms.

Figure 2: Multi-hop communication.

information to calculate the centrality measure for that neighborhood. For each d, the MHC achieved the better upload costs when the closeness centrality was estimated by $k = 4$. Therefore, we fixed the MHC with $k = 4$ and compared the results with those obtained by the RB approach, and the optimal solution by CPLEX.

Figure 1 presents the upload cost and system gain for single-hop communication, i.e., when d is equals to 1. The MHC algorithm, compared with the RB approach, decreased up to 1.86 kB/s of the upload cost. There are some instances where the MHC result is the optimal solution, this approximation decreases during peak hours, in which the difference was 6.26 kB/s.

Increasing the value of d allows for exploring ever-increasing neighborhoods. However, the benefit of multi-hop communication is limited by the network diameter. Figure 2 presents the upload cost and system gain for multi-hop communication, i.e., when d is equals to 3. In this case, the upload cost of MHC decreased from 43.66 kB/s to 30.16 kB/s during peak hours and has nearly optimal performance. The optimal solution is a *minimum 3-hop dominating set*. We keep the RB upload cost in this figure, in which MHC compared with the RB solution achieve a cost reduction up to 14.76 kB/s.

We evaluate the system gain to understand the results in terms of the number of users connected in the cellular network. This measure gives us information about the size of the subset S, the smaller the number of vehicles accessing the cellular uplink, the higher the system gain. The main difference in the system gains is due to the model problem. The RB aims to solve instances of the Minimum Dominating Set (MDS) problem. However, the algorithm does not guarantee an optimal solution. Besides, a vehicle may have more than one dominant, resulting in redundancy in transmissions. On the other hand, the MHC modeled the problem as a *minimum d-hop dominating set*. The MHC also does not guarantee the optimal solution, but the multi-hop communication can significantly reduce the size of the dominating set, in which domination was not restricted to the immediate neighbors.

4.2 Worst-case aggregation

In the traditional approach, the upload cost reached 167.50 kB/s during peak hours. In contrast, the upload cost in the MHC exceeded 213 kB/s. As mentioned earlier, a vehicle may have more than one dominator, resulting in an excessive cost because of redundant transmissions. Ancona et al. [3] solved this problem by introducing a confirmation mechanism, in which each non-dominator vehicle will share its data with a single dominator.

Figure 3 presents the upload cost after adding a confirmation mechanism. In addition, we also presents the upload cost of the RB and non-offloading (i.e., the traditional upload) approaches. Again, $k = 4$ is the best result for all values of d. In this case, we hide the results of the optimal solution because it does not guarantee the minimum upload cost. When $d = 1$, the MHC is close to RB solution. However, when $d = 3$ our solution, compared with the RB approach, decreased up to 2.19 kB/s of the upload cost. The results are close, but this means a reduction of about 112 headers per second. The MHC with 3-hops reduces the cost by 22.49 kB/s at peak hours compared to a non-offloading scheme, that is a reduction up to 13.45%.

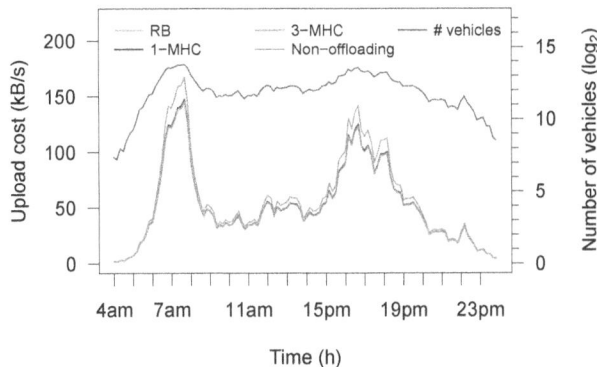

Figure 3: Upload cost in the worst-case local aggregation.

In the best-case scenario, the MHC decreased up to 82.09% compared with the non-offloading approach. In the both cases, the upload cost is higher at peak hours, where the results show the highest system gain and cost reduction. These results occur because the V2V communication benefits the massive data offloading, which is higher when the network is little fragmented. The network becomes fragmented as the number of vehicles decreases, then more isolated vehicles will individually upload their data. This behavior is not a critical problem because fewer clients will be connected in the cellular network.

Increasing the transmission range may decrease the fragmentation of the network, but a densely connected network requires more time to determine the uploaders. This behavior can affect the restrictions of the application, which in certain conditions may require an upload in a short period. The MHC delimits the diameter of the computation by adjusting the parameters d and k. For example, in the Cologne scenario, with a transmission range equals to 400 meters, the CPLEX took about 112 minutes to compute the *2-hop dominating set*. The MHC with $k = 1$, running centrally, found an approximate solution in 4 minutes.

5 CONCLUSION

This work presented a decentralized solution to perform the offloading of massive VSN data in vehicular networks. The proposed algorithm is based on a greedy approach and uses a measure of centrality in order to capture the closeness relation between vehicles and use it as information to guide the construction of the solution. The results, when compared with the non-offloading scheme, show a cost reduction of up to 82.09% in the best-case and 13.45% in the worst-case.

Some challenges still have to be faced because this is a topic that includes emerging technologies. The primary challenge is the highly dynamic mobility pattern of the vehicular network, which makes it difficult to disseminate messages on the network and to maintain the cluster formed by vehicles. The adoption of the D2D communication of the fifth generation of cellular telephony will increase the sensing capacity of the network, in which several devices with sensing capacity can contribute to new information. However, the heterogeneity of sources of information is a challenge to be faced. Moreover, although a large amount of data provides a better sampling of the sensed environment, the need for real-time sensing requires means that provide scalability to the network.

ACKNOWLEDGMENTS

We would like to thank the research agencies, CAPES, CNPq, FAPEMIG, FAPEAL, and grant 15/24494-8, São Paulo Research Foundation (FAPESP).

REFERENCES

[1] Sherin Abdelhamid, Hossam S. Hassanein, and Glen Takahara. 2014. Vehicle as a mobile sensor. *Procedia Computer Science* 34 (2014), 286–295.

[2] A. D. Amis, R. Prakash, T. H. P. Vuong, and D. T. Huynh. 2000. Max-min d-cluster formation in wireless ad hoc networks. In *Proceedings IEEE INFOCOM 2000*, Vol. 1. IEEE, Tel Aviv, Israel, Israel, 32–41 vol.1.

[3] S. Ancona, R. Stanica, and M. Fiore. 2014. Performance boundaries of massive Floating Car Data offloading. In *Conference on Wireless On-demand Network Systems and Services*. IEEE, Obergurgl, Austria, 89–96.

[4] Alessandro Bazzi, Barbara M Masini, Alberto Zanella, and Gianni Pasolini. 2015. IEEE 802.11p for cellular offloading in vehicular sensor networks. *Computer Communications* 60 (2015), 97–108.

[5] Amit Dua, Neeraj Kumar, and Seema Bawa. 2017. Game theoretic approach for real-time data dissemination and offloading in vehicular ad hoc networks. *Journal of Real-Time Image Processing* 13, 3 (01 Sep 2017), 627–644.

[6] Cisco VNI Forecast. 2019. Global Mobile Data Traffic Forecast Update, 2017-2022. https://www.cisco.com/c/en/us/solutions/collateral/service-provider/visual-networking-index-vni/white-paper-c11-738429.html. [Accessed: 2019-08-26].

[7] Linton C. Freeman. 1978. Centrality in social networks conceptual clarification. *Social Networks* 1, 3 (1978), 215 – 239.

[8] MEMS Journal. 2017. Automotive Sensors and Electronics Expo 2017. http://www.automotivesensors2017.com/. [Accessed: 2019-04-05].

[9] Uichin Lee, Eugenio Magistretti, Mario Gerla, Paolo Bellavista, Pietro Liò, and Kang-Won Lee. 2008. Bio-Inspired Multi-agent Collaboration for Urban Monitoring Applications. In *Bio-Inspired Computing and Communication*. Springer Berlin Heidelberg, Berlin, Heidelberg, 204–216.

[10] Guoqiang Mao, Zijie Zhang, and Brian D O Anderson. 2016. Cooperative Content Dissemination and Offloading in Heterogeneous Mobile Networks. *IEEE Transactions on Vehicular Technology* 65, 8 (2016), 6573–6587.

[11] Farouk Mezghani, Riadh Dhaou, Michele Nogueira, and Andre-Luc Beylot. 2016. Offloading Cellular Networks Through V2V Communications - How to Select the Seed-Vehicles?. In *IEEE International Conference on Communications*. IEEE, Kuala Lumpur, Malaysia, 1–6.

[12] Paulo H. Rettore, Guilherme Maia, Leandro A. Villas, and Antonio A. F. Loureiro. 2019. Vehicular Data Space: The Data Point of View. *IEEE Communications Surveys & Tutorials* 21, 3 (2019), 2392–2418.

[13] Paulo H. L. Rettore, André B. Campolina, Artur Souza, Guilherme Maia, Leandro A. Villas, and Antonio A. F. Loureiro. 2018. Driver Authentication in VANETs based on Intra-Vehicular Sensor Data. In *Proceedings of the 23rd IEEE International Symposium on Computers and Communications (ISCC '18)*. 1–6.

[14] P. Salvo, I. Turcanu, F. Cuomo, A. Baiocchi, and I. Rubin. 2016. LTE floating car data application off-loading via VANET driven clustering formation. In *Wireless On-demand Network Systems and Services*. IEEE, Cortina d'Ampezzo, Italy, 1–8.

[15] R. Stanica, M. Fiore, and F. Malandrino. 2013. Offloading Floating Car Data. In *IEEE WoWMoM*. IEEE, Madrid, Spain, 1–9.

[16] Sandesh Uppoor, Oscar Trullols-Cruces, Marco Fiore, and Jose M. Barcelo-Ordinas. 2014. Generation and analysis of a large-scale urban vehicular mobility dataset. *IEEE Transactions on Mobile Computing* 13, 5 (2014), 1061–1075.

[17] J. Wang, C. Jiang, K. Zhang, T. Q. S. Quek, Y. Ren, and L. Hanzo. 2018. Vehicular Sensing Networks in a Smart City: Principles, Technologies and Applications. *IEEE Wireless Communications* 25, 1 (February 2018), 122–132.

Characterizing Car Trips Through Information Theory Metrics

André Campolina
acampoli@uottawa.ca
University of Ottawa
Universidade Federal de Minas Gerais

Azzedine Boukerche
boukerch@site.uottawa.ca
University of Ottawa

Antonio A. F. Loureiro
loureiro@dcc.ufmg.br
Universidade Federal de Minas Gerais

ABSTRACT

In this work, we apply information theory metrics to car trips logged by volunteers around the world and use quantifiers such as location entropy to reveal aspects of users' mobility, like the context in which trips happened. The dataset used in this work was collected from the enviroCar project and contains not only location logs but also sensor readings associated with each location. Information theory measurements can also reveal relationships between sensor measurements in order to reveal rare occurrences and reduce uncertainty. This work shows that it is possible to differentiate driving contexts and capture relationships among sensors using location entropy and mutual information, respectively. These contributions pave the way for developing new features that may ultimately improve traffic context classification results.

CCS CONCEPTS

• **Information systems** → **Spatial-temporal systems**; • **Human-centered computing** → **Ubiquitous and mobile computing systems and tools.**

KEYWORDS

information theory, vehicular sensor data

ACM Reference Format:
André Campolina, Azzedine Boukerche, and Antonio A. F. Loureiro. 2019. Characterizing Car Trips Through Information Theory Metrics. In *22nd Int'l ACM Conference on Modeling, Analysis and Simulation of Wireless and Mobile Systems (MSWiM '19), November 25–29, 2019, Miami Beach, FL, USA.* ACM, New York, NY, USA, 5 pages. https://doi.org/10.1145/3345768.3355938

1 INTRODUCTION

Vehicular data can reveal valuable knowledge in the design of new protocols, services and applications for Vehicular Ad-Hod Networks (VANETs). The location and operational state of multiple vehicles observed for a period of time make it possible to simulate artificial environments inspired by real situations in which vehicles are able to communicate with each other and with the roadside infrastructure. To gain better insights about data used in simulations or design better services, it is necessary to understand certain characteristics of the trajectory data [7], a complex task given the heterogeneity and size of these datasets.

MSWiM '19, November 25–29, 2019, Miami Beach, FL, USA
© 2019 Association for Computing Machinery.
ACM ISBN 978-1-4503-6904-6/19/11...$15.00
https://doi.org/10.1145/3345768.3355938

There are statistical and theoretical tools and techniques that allow to summarize large volumes of data according to certain aspects of them [5, 14]. For instance, complex network theory provides two concepts that analyze human mobility: radius of gyration and stay points. The first metric measures the average distance subjects move away from a determined base point, while stay points are places or regions within a certain distance of which subjects stay for at least a certain amount of time. On the other hand, there are tools defined by information theory [4, 15], which also investigate aspects like compression, uncertainty and shared information in data. In this work, we show that an information theory metric, entropy, is affected by the same phenomena as other metrics, such as radius of gyration. We also point that conditional entropy, and, consequently, mutual information is a way to capture physical relationships between sensor data present in datasets such as the enviroCar dataset, which was used in this study.

The goal of this work is to present metrics and tools based on information theory and complex network theory concepts, as well as their applications and meanings when applied to vehicular trajectory data. In order to do so, we use such measurements to provide a characterization of a real dataset of vehicular trajectories. With such characterization, we not only shed light on the meanings of the evaluated metrics' results but also reveal relationships between them that may help complex tasks to identify, for instance, contexts in trips, among other issues.

The remainder of this work is organized as follows: Section 2 presents the related work that deals with characterization and application of information theory and complex network theory metrics to vehicular data; Section 3 describes the experimental setup used in this work and presents the results obtained by applying the selected metrics to a vehicular trajectory dataset; finally, Section 4 presents our final remarks and discusses some possible future directions.

2 RELATED WORK

Human mobility is an active and important research topic, as it impacts other areas, such as mobile networks [1]. Understanding human mobility and its patterns is an important task in this area [14]. Moreover, by exploring logs of human movement it is possible to conduct a variety of studies [17, 19, 26], such as to reveal spatial and temporal dependencies between properties of taxi trips [21]. Using the same type of data, it is possible to identify popular destination areas through time and paths linking these destinations [10, 16, 18, 22]. Mobility data can also be used to extract road usage information from raw location data, and with that improving travel times [24].

Vehicle position data also serves the purpose of modeling human mobility at scale [12]. Papallardo et al. [20] derived road mobility patterns from trip data, and compared them to expected generic human mobility models. Barbosa et al. [8] presented a comprehensive review of mobility models, as well as metrics and techniques used in the process of modelling. Souza et al. [5] characterized different mobility models based on a set of metrics related to time, space and social aspects.

Complex networks measure relationships among their members regarding their structure, and social and spatial features. Gao et al. [13] provided a review of applications of such techniques to time series. Tang et al. [23] used traffic flow data and complex network techniques to extract information such as the defining characteristics of nodes, communities. Tang et al. [9] also used this data to measure dynamics and periodicity in traffic. Finally, Yan et al. [25] characterized traffic flow states in a city transit network.

Concepts related to information theory are also used to enable valuable insights based on raw vehicular data. Aquino et al. [2] presented a study that uses the concept of statistical complexity to differentiate driving situations such as free flow and congestion. Silva et al. [11] also proposed using statistical complexity, an information theory measure, to extract information about the time aspect of the driver's behavior and traffic conditions.

The present work differs from others found in the literature as it takes an approach based on classic information theory metrics. Aquino et al. [2] aimed at differentiating between traffic conditions using metrics such as statistical complexity and permutation entropy, while we chose to use simpler metrics such as location entropy to derive traffic context information. Furthermore, we use metrics from complex network theory, like Tang et al. [9], but as a way of supporting the results yielded by information theory quantifiers.

3 PERFORMANCE EVALUATION

We used data collected from the enviroCar project [3, 6], which is a public project that encourages users to collect, share and analyze data generated by sensors embedded on vehicles or on smartphones used to run the project's application. The enviroCar dataset contains more than 16,000 trips collected around the world by volunteer drivers. Each trip is comprised of multiple observations that depict vehicles' states at collection time with sensor readings. These observations can have measurements from up to 24 sensors, however, not every vehicle provides readings for all of these sensors. In total, there are more than 5.5 million observations in the dataset.

Using the enviroCar dataset, we investigate the measurements of information theory and complex network theory metrics to sensor data collected in real scenarios. With this, we hope to show the potential of such quantifiers in summarizing large data collections and revealing abnormal events and trips in the dataset. We will show applications of the metrics and will also provide discussions on the meaning of their results, specifically in a dataset of vehicular data.

3.1 Information Content

Information content serves as a basis for other measurements, such as Shannon entropy and mutual information. According to its definition [4], the higher the probability associated with an outcome, the lower its information content will be, so that uncommon events are emphasized by their higher information contents. Applying this metric to a set of sensor readings in this dataset may reveal and

direct attention to specific observations that are related to abnormal situations and behaviors.

An important aspect to observe when calculating information content is its scope, as it can consider only values from a single trip or the entire dataset. Dealing with values from an individual trip, information content will highlight abnormal points within that restricted universe of observations, while using the observed probability distribution of the entire dataset reveals unusual observations within all recorded trips. These rare points in the global context may even be common within certain trips, which may be valuable when selecting logs with unique behavior or properties.

Figure 1 shows an example of such differences in scope. In particular, it shows raw speed sensor data and the information content associated with each observation in blue and red, respectively. Despite being different trips, the two graphs demonstrate the differences between using local and global probability in calculating information content, local referring to a single trip, and global to the entire dataset.

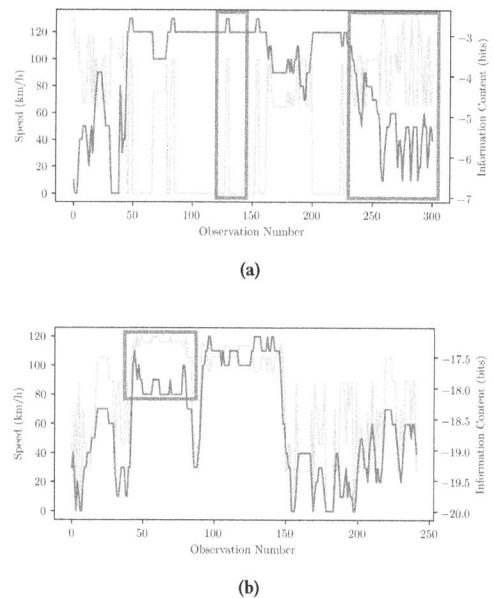

(a)

(b)

Figure 1: Sensor Readings and Information Content

The first trip in Figure 1a has most of its readings with high speeds compatible with highways, and some observations in lower speeds typical of urban environments. These two scenarios, and their frequency on this trip make the information content of high speeds lower than that of slower moments, as highlighted by the two rectangles. The left rectangle evidences that although high speeds are common, there are values that hold high information content, while the right rectangle shows that in the context of this trip, slow speeds are abnormal, and thus present higher information content.

Figure 1b shows a second trip, which also contains observations in different ranges of speeds, but the information content was calculated using the global probability. The information content, in this case, shows how rare observations are inside the entire dataset, and, thus, we should advocate for the diversity of observations in this trip. The rectangle in this figure draws attention to a range of values that yield the most information content and their rarity is a reflex of an aspect of the dataset.

3.2 Entropy

When dealing with location data, it is also desirable to gain information about the context in which this data was acquired, which adds more value to it. A basic piece of context that is not directly contained in position data is whether a trip was recorded in a urban environment or not, that is, if the vehicle providing the data was riding on a regular street or on a highway. Shannon entropy provides a way to differentiate these two contexts by leveraging their nature and the way data is produced in these scenarios.

Figure 2 illustrates the differences in entropy caused by urban and highway environments. We manually selected two trips that happened in these environments: one was registered inside a urban area, and the other in a trip between two cities. Both trips have similar traveled distances, 25.3 km for the urban one and 29.8 km for the highway trip, however, uncertainty about their locations is different, as demonstrated by the entropy values on top of each log. This difference in entropy value for trips in different contexts may lead to new features that improve the classification of these types of trips.

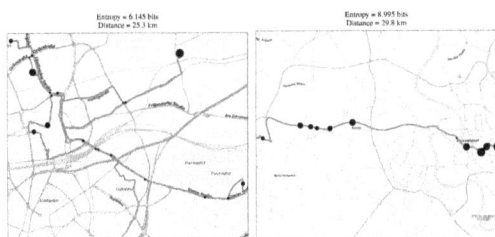

Figure 2: Entropy as a tool to differentiate urban and highway trips

In Figure 2, the leftmost trajectory was recorded in a trip in a urban setting, while the right one in a highway. It is important to note that there are points in both tracks that indicate places where more than one observation was logged. These points also vary in size, which indicates the amount of time spent at each of these locations. It is also interesting to notice that the urban trip has more stay points, which could indicate stop signs or stop lights, both common in such context. On the other hand, the highway trip has fewer stop points, which are also quicker, and could indicate tollbooths or even light traffic jams.

Entropy also has a relationship with traveled distance, which is closely related to the chances of passing through unique locations. As a vehicle travels longer distances, the chances of it passing through repeated locations at different times reduce, since most vehicles often do not travel in circuits. As a consequence of this, longer trips tend to be comprised of more unique locations, resulting in an observed distribution close to a uniform probability

distribution. We depict the relationship between entropy and distance in Figure 3. In the figure, points are separated into two groups, both of which present an exponential relationship between the two variables.

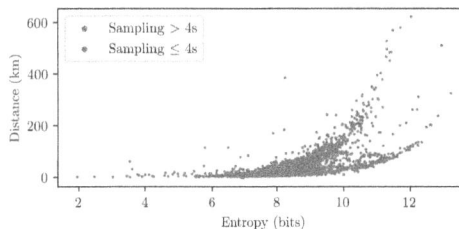

Figure 3: Entropy and traveled distance relationship

That picture contains a point for each trip in our dataset, and entropy and distances were measured using their raw location data. Since the dataset contains data from multiple contributors, there are multiple collection setups, and one of those differences shows the collection frequency, which varies from 1 to 10 seconds. Different collection interval values affect the relationship between distance and entropy, as seen by the different groups in Figure 3. Trips with higher sampling frequencies also have the property of having lower chances of observing the same location two or more times as the traveled distance increases, but at a different rate, due to points being recorded more frequently. In fact, if two trips have sampling frequencies f_1 and f_2, $f_1 = 2.f_2$, and distances d_1 and d_2, $d_1 = \frac{1}{2}.d_2$, both trips would have the same number of points recorded if both vehicles travel at the same constant speed. Granted that there are no repeated points in both logs, their entropies would also be the same.

Another information theory concept that may be applied to this dataset is conditional entropy. Vehicles use a transmission system composed of different gears to deliver power generated by their engines to the wheels, and each of these gears delivers power at a different rate. It is possible to measure these different ratios by observing two variables: the engine's revolutions per minute (RPM) and vehicle speed. Since these two variables are physically related to the transmission gears, there is shared information between the data of these sensors. Specifically, we will show that it is possible to reduce uncertainty about RPM values by having previous knowledge about speed readings.

Figure 4 illustrates the reduction in the uncertainty of RPM values given that a single speed reading is known. The figure takes the entire dataset into account, and the individual values respect the property that uncertainty about an ensemble will never increase given that information about the other ensemble is taken into account. In fact, regarding the observed distributions in the dataset, there is a decrease in RPM entropy for every speed value, as comparing the blue points in the figure to the red line. Conditional entropy may also be calculated using an entire ensemble, that is, all the speed readings in the dataset and this value is shown by the green line.

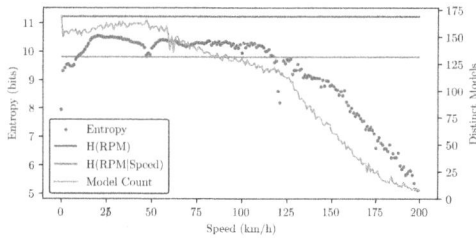

Figure 4: Conditional entropy of RPM given speed values

It is possible to note in Figure 4 that entropy values have a significant drop, especially at higher speeds, and this may be assigned to the nature of the dataset, which is comprised of readings from numerous vehicle models and manufacturers. It is expected that different models and manufacturers use different transmission systems in their projects, which result in different relationships between speed and RPM. In fact, the reduction in entropy values happens in speeds over 125 km/h, at which point there is a reduced number of vehicles, and, consequently, gear relations that recorded trips, as shown by the orange line in the figure.

3.3 Radius of Gyration

Another concept related to trajectories is radius of gyration, which measures different aspects of a logged trip. Instead of measuring uncertainty about a vehicle's position, or the distance it traveled in a trip, radius of gyration measures a radius from a central point within which an entity is expected to circulate. Similar to entropy, higher radii of gyration indicate that entities travel longer distances from their central points, but there are cases in which long traveled distances may not translate to a high entropy or radius of gyration values. These cases are typical of urban environments, where multiple roads cross a single region. Vehicles that travel through these roads multiple and repetitive times in a single trip will register increasing distances, but, as long as they are contained to such region, radius of gyration will be limited. In this type of situation, as roads are recorded multiple times, precise locations are also expected to be repeated, thus, decreasing the entropy values for such trips.

The relationship between entropy and traveled distance has already been shown in Figure 3. Now, we discuss the relationship between radius of gyration and traveled distance for the trips in the dataset. Figure 5 shows that points have an exponential relationship, with the exception of a group indicated by the red rectangle. We investigated such abnormal relationships to describe the type of trips belonging to the exponential relationship, and those that do not follow it, contained in the rectangle.

Trip 1, depicted in Figure 5, is an example of urban scenario. Although it may be viewed as a linear trip, with no branching roads, it goes through the same path two times, in different directions, similar to a bus route. On the other hand, Trip 2 refers to a highway trip between two urban areas, and does not contain many different roads. As a result of these characteristics, Trip 1 has a smaller radius of gyration than Trip 2, as the first one travels more than one time through the same locations, while the second only passes once, and in a straighter line.

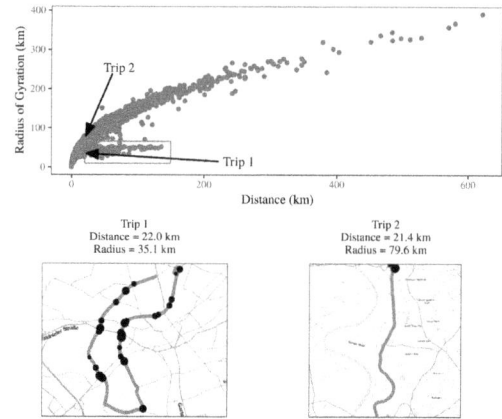

Figure 5: Radius of gyration and traveled distance relationship

3.4 Stay Points

Stay points are regions in which an entity stays within a certain distance and for a minimum time interval. These points are important in detecting points of interest in a city, detecting and differentiating traffic lights and stop signs, and even detecting traffic jams. Stay points also have an impact on trajectories' entropy values, since as entities stay close to the same points, chances of observing duplicate locations increase, thus reducing uncertainty about these entities' position. Moreover, the longer entities stay within a stay point, the higher impact on entropy these events will have, due to the potentially higher number of repeated points contained in a trajectory.

To investigate the relationship between stay points and entropy in trajectories, we applied a simple stay point detection strategy. We considered that an observation belongs to a stay point if the distance to it is zero, that is, if two or more points have the same exact coordinates. Additionally, we established the minimum number of three observations at the same location at any time of the trip to identify a stay point.

Figure 6 depicts the relationship between entropy and the ratio of stay points in all trips of the enviroCar dataset. Although there is no clear exponential or linear relationships between the two variables, it is possible to note that the more frequent and numerous stay points are in a trip, the higher the stay point ratio will be, and the less uncertainty there will be about this trip's location, thus, reducing entropy.

That figure highlights two trips and presents their trajectories in detail in its lower part. These trips have similar entropy values, although their traveled distances are significantly different, 25.1 km and 41.9 km, which can be assigned to the number of points in each trip considered as stay points. While entropy grows exponentially with the traveled distance, the number and duration of stay points in Trip 2 contribute to reducing their uncertainty about the location.

4 CONCLUSION

This work investigated the use of information theory and complex network theory metrics to describe human mobility as per observed

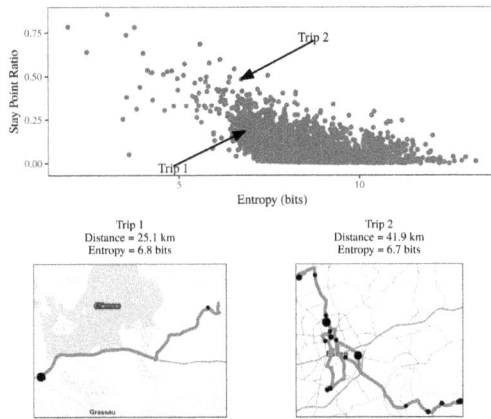

Figure 6: Effects of stay point ratio on location entropy

by vehicle trips. We showed that such techniques are not only fit to solve communication problems, as originally proposed, but also to summarize and extract valuable information from large datasets like the one created by the enviroCar project. In fact, using metrics such as location entropy and radius of gyration we were able to summarize aspects of vehicular mobility that would require other multiple metrics to draw similar conclusions.

Given that the dataset is comprised of voluntarily collected data, there are numerous trip recording settings. In this work, we observed that the exponential relationship between traveled distance and location entropy has two main modes, determined by the collection frequency, which also impacts the entropy. Additionally, we also observed characteristics of the data contained in the dataset through the information content metric, which showed that trips in speed ranges compatible with urban and highway environments are numerous, but few trips recorded transitions between these two contexts.

We analyzed other metrics used to describe and model human mobility derived from complex networks theory. By analyzing radius of gyration and traveled distance we were able to observe how urban and highway environments affect these two measurements, We also observed the correlation between the ratio of stay points in a trip and its entropy. By registering duplicate locations, uncertainty about the entire trip's location distribution is reduced, and we showed this difference by comparing two trip logs.

As future work, we plan to expand the applications of information theory beyond the description of datasets of vehicular sensor readings. One way to do so is to develop new features and feature spaces to improve classification and model driver's behavior.

ACKNOWLEDGMENTS

This work was partially supported by NSERC, Canada Research Chairs Program, NSERC CREATE - TRANSIT Program, CNPq, CAPES, grant #15/24494-8, São Paulo Research Foundation (FAPESP).

REFERENCES

[1] Mimonah Al Qathrady and Ahmed Helmy. 2018. Toward Advanced Indoor Mobility Models Through Location-Centric Analysis: Spatio-Temporal Density Dynamics. In *Proceedings of the 21st ACM International Conference on Modeling,* *Analysis and Simulation of Wireless and Mobile Systems (MSWiM '18)*. ACM, New York, NY, USA, 347–350.
[2] Andre L.L. Aquino, Tamer S.G. Cavalcante, Eliana S. Almeida, Alejandro C. Frery, and Osvaldo A. Rosso. 2015. Characterization of vehicle behavior with information theory. *The European Physical Journal B* 88, 10 (2015), 257.
[3] André B. Campolina, Azzedine Boukerche, Max do V. Machado, and Antonio A. F. Loureiro. 2018. Fuel Efficient Routes Using Vehicular Sensor Data. In *Proceedings of the 16th ACM International Symposium on Mobility Management and Wireless Access (MobiWac'18)*. ACM, New York, NY, USA, 29–36.
[4] Thomas M. Cover and Joy A. Thomas. 2005. *Elements of Information Theory*. John Wiley & Sons, Inc., Hoboken, NJ, USA. 1–12 pages.
[5] Fabrício R. de Souza, Augusto C.S.A. Domingues, Pedro O.S. Vaz de Melo, and Antonio A F Loureiro. 2018. MOCHA: A Tool for Mobility Characterization. In *Proceedings of the 21st ACM International Conference on Modeling, Analysis and Simulation of Wireless and Mobile Systems - MSWIM '18*. ACM Press, New York, New York, USA, 281–288.
[6] Arne Bröring et al. 2015. enviroCar: A Citizen Science Platform for Analyzing and Mapping Crowd-Sourced Car Sensor Data. *Transactions in GIS* (2015).
[7] Fabrício A. Silva et al. 2015. Filling the Gaps of Vehicular Mobility Traces. In *Proceedings of the 18th ACM International Conference on Modeling, Analysis and Simulation of Wireless and Mobile Systems (MSWiM '15)*. ACM, New York, NY, USA, 47–54.
[8] Hugo Barbosa et al. 2018. Human mobility: Models and applications. *Physics Reports* 734 (2018), 1–74.
[9] Jinjun Tang et al. 2014. Dynamic analysis of traffic time series at different temporal scales: A complex networks approach. *Physica A: Statistical Mechanics and its Applications* (2014).
[10] Linjiang Zheng et al. 2018. Spatial-temporal travel pattern mining using massive taxi trajectory data. *Physica A: Statistical Mechanics and its Applications* 501 (2018), 24–41.
[11] Mauricio J. Silva et al. 2019. Study about vehicles velocities using time causal Information Theory quantifiers. *Ad Hoc Networks* 89 (2019), 22–34.
[12] Anna Förster, Anas Bin Muslim, and Asanga Udugama. 2018. TRAILS - A Trace-Based Probabilistic Mobility Model. In *Proceedings of the 21st ACM International Conference on Modeling, Analysis and Simulation of Wireless and Mobile Systems (Mswim '18)*. ACM, New York, NY, USA, 295–302.
[13] Zhong-Ke Gao, Michael Small, and Jürgen Kurths. 2016. Complex network analysis of time series. *EPL (Europhysics Letters)* 116, 5 (2016), 50001.
[14] Marta C. González, César A. Hidalgo, and Albert-László Barabási. 2008. Understanding individual human mobility patterns. *Nature* 453, 7196 (2008), 779–782.
[15] Bartosz Kowalik and Marcin Szpyrka. 2019. An Entropy-Based Car Failure Detection Method Based on Data Acquisition Pipeline. *Entropy* 21, 4 (2019), 426.
[16] Kassio Machado, Azzedine Boukerche, Eduardo Cerqueira, and Antonio A. F. Loureiro. 2017. A Socially-Aware In-Network Caching Framework for the Next Generation of Wireless Networks. *IEEE Communications Magazine* 55 (2017), 38–43.
[17] Kassio L. S. Machado, Azzedine Boukercheb, Eduardo C. Cerqueira, and Antonio A. F. Loureiro. 2019. A Data-Centric Approach for Social and Spatiotemporal Sensing in Smart Cities. *IEEE Internet Computing* 23, 1 (2019), 9–18.
[18] Willi Mueller, Thiago H. Silva, Jussara M. Almeida, and Antonio A. F. Loureiro. 6. Gender Matters! Analyzing Global Cultural Gender Preferences for Venues Using Social Sensing. *EPJ Data Science* 5 (6), 1–21.
[19] Shamma Nikhat and Mustafa Mehmet-Ali. 2018. An Analysis of User Mobility in Cellular Networks. In *Proceedings of the 16th ACM International Symposium on Mobility Management and Wireless Access (MobiWac'18)*. ACM, New York, NY, USA, 74–81.
[20] Luca Pappalardo, Salvatore Rinzivillo, Zehui Qu, Dino Pedreschi, and Fosca Giannotti. 2013. Understanding the patterns of car travel. *The European Physical Journal Special Topics* 215, 1 (2013), 61–73.
[21] Diego O. Rodrigues, Azzedine Boukerche, Thiago H. Silva, Antonio A. F. Loureiro, and Leandro A.Villas. 2018. Combining Taxi and Social Media Data to Explore Urban Mobility Issues. *Computer Communications* 132 (2018), 111–125.
[22] Thiago H. Silva, Aline Carneiro Viana, Fabrício Benevenuto, Leandro Villas, Juliana Salles, Antonio Loureiro, and Daniele Quercia. 2019. Urban Computing Leveraging Location-Based Social Network Data: A Survey. *Comput. Surveys* 52, 1 (2019), 17:1–17:39.
[23] Jinjun Tang, Yinhai Wang, and Fang Liu. 2013. Characterizing traffic time series based on complex network theory. *Physica A: Statistical Mechanics and its Applications* 392, 18 (2013), 4192–4201.
[24] Pu Wang, Timothy Hunter, Alexandre M. Bayen, Katja Schechtner, and Marta C. González. 2012. Understanding Road Usage Patterns in Urban Areas. *Scientific Reports* 2, 1 (2012), 1001.
[25] Ying Yan, Shen Zhang, Jinjun Tang, and Xiaofei Wang. 2017. Understanding characteristics in multivariate traffic flow time series from complex network structure. *Physica A: Statistical Mechanics and its Applications* (2017).
[26] Shen Zhang, Jinjun Tang, Haixiao Wang, Yinhai Wang, and Shi An. 2017. Revealing intra-urban travel patterns and service ranges from taxi trajectories. *Journal of Transport Geography* 61, April (2017), 72–86.

COLiDeR: A Cross-Layer Protocol for Two-Path Relaying

Raphaël Naves
Thales SIX GTS France
raphael.naves@thalesgroup.com

Gentian Jakllari
IRIT-INPT/ENSEEIHT - France
gentian.jakllari@enseeiht.fr

Hicham Khalifé
Thales SIX GTS France
hicham.khalife@thalesgroup.com

Vania Conan
Thales SIX GTS France
vania.conan@thalesgroup.com

André-Luc Beylot
IRIT-INPT/ENSEEIHT - France
andre-luc.beylot@enseeiht.fr

ABSTRACT

In this work, we present COLiDeR, the first practical system for two-path relaying using off-the-shelf half-duplex radios. While two-path relaying has been mostly studied from a theoretical perspective in the literature, our solution addresses the challenges of making it practical by introducing two key contributions. First, using a measurement-driven approach, we identify the best approach for a radio to handle two overlapping signals. Just as important, we carefully quantify its limits and introduce the concept of the decoding areas. Second, we introduce a cross-layer protocol that seamlessly navigates the decoding areas with the objective of maximizing throughput while minimizing decoding failures. Experiments on a 4-USRP testbed show that COLiDeR delivers between 80-95% of the relaying performance of an ideal full-duplex radio while incurring negligible decoding failures.

ACM Reference Format:
Raphaël Naves, Gentian Jakllari, Hicham Khalifé, Vania Conan, and André-Luc Beylot. 2019. COLiDeR: A Cross-Layer Protocol for Two-Path Relaying. In *22nd Int'l ACM Conference on Modeling, Analysis and Simulation of Wireless and Mobile Systems (MSWiM '19), November 25–29, 2019, Miami Beach, FL, USA.* ACM, New York, NY, USA, 5 pages. https://doi.org/10.1145/3345768.3355941

1 INTRODUCTION

Two-path relaying was introduced as a solution to increase the throughput in the 4-node scenario depicted in Fig. 1. In this scenario, the source node, S, wants to send a batch of packets to the destination, D, which is too far to receive the packets via direct transmissions. Assuming a TDMA (Time-Division Multiple Access) channel access protocol for ease of presentation, a single-path relaying strategy can not deliver a end-to-end throughput higher than 0.5 frame per slot because of half-duplex hardware limitation. However, with a two-path relaying approach, the source, S, can transmit on every slot, alternating between two relays. As depicted in Fig. 1, in slot k, S transmits a packet to R_1. In slot $k + 1$, R_1 forwards the packet to the destination, D, while S transmits a second packet, this time to R_2. If R_2 can successfully decode the packet

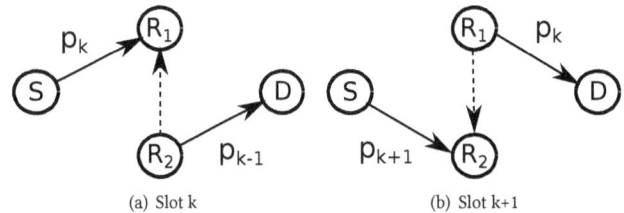

(a) Slot k   (b) Slot k+1

Figure 1: Two-path relaying illustration

from S, despite the interference from R_1, it will forward it to D in the following slot, while S will transmit a third packet to R_1. Thus, as long as one relay can decode a packet from the source while the other is transmitting a packet to the destination, two-path relaying can eliminate the multiplexing loss.

While two-path relaying has been studied theoretically [1, 2], realizing it in practice faces several challenges. First and foremost, two-path relaying requires a relay to successfully decode a transmission from the source when the other relay is transmitting. To this end, many theoretical works [1–3] rely on the well-known concept of Successive Interference Cancellation (SIC). Indeed, it is assumed that the inter-relay channel is very strong, allowing the interference to be decoded first and then eliminated from the received signal. However, in a practical system, there is no guarantee as to the inter-relay channel, especially if the nodes are mobile. In parallel, other works employ sophisticated amplify-and-forward coding techniques [4] while recent studies [5] propose to simply alternate between two-path relaying and a traditional one-path relaying depending on the packet decoding success rate at relays. The question, however, of how the stations would know which particular relaying approach to use was left open. More generally, to the best of our knowledge, there is no thorough comparative study, particularly using real-hardware implementations, on what is the best approach to be adopted by the relays.

In this work, we present COLiDeR, a novel PHY/MAC CrOss-Layer protocol for practical decode-and-forward Diamond[1] Relaying. Based on a testbed-driven evaluation and analysis of the best approach for a relay to decode a packet from the source node while the other relay is transmitting a packet to the destination, COLiDeR is capable of identifying the relaying strategy that maximizes throughput while minimizing packet losses due to decoding failures.

---

[1]Due to the geometrical shape of the Fig. 1 topology, two-path relaying is also known as a diamond relay network.

Figure 2: USRP testbed used for implementing and evaluating diamond-based relaying.

We implement COLiDeR on a 4-node USRP radio testbed with the GNU Radio framework [6], and evaluate its performance using over-the-air transmissions exclusively. The experimental results show that COLiDeR delivers between 80-95% of the relaying performance of an ideal full-duplex radio while incurring negligible decoding failures.

2 SIMULTANEOUS RECEPTION OF MULTIPLE PACKETS: A MEASUREMENT-DRIVEN ANALYSIS

Since the feasibility of two-path relaying closely depends on the ability of relays to decode the packet sent by the source while the other relay is also transmitting, we carry out in this section an experimental study to identify the best strategy for the relays to handle the simultaneous reception of two signals.

2.1 Problem formulation

To simplify the presentation, we consider one part of two-path relaying as depicted in Fig. 1(a). S transmits a packet, p_S, to R_1 while R_2 transmits a packet, p_{R_2}, to the destination, with R_1 facing the challenge of decoding p_S. All the results shown apply to the second part, taking place in the subsequent slot, as depicted in Fig. 1(b).

We consider that packets are sent using an OFDM coding structure with a QPSK (Quadrature Phase-Shift Keying) symbol modulation on each subcarrier. Denoting with $x_S^{m,k}$ and $x_{R_2}^{m,k}$ the symbol transmitted simultaneously on the m-th OFDM symbol and the k-th subcarrier by nodes S and R_2, respectively, the symbol $y^{m,k}$ received by R_1 can be expressed as follows:

$$y^{m,k} = h_{SR_1}^{m,k} x_S^{m,k} + h_{R_2R_1}^{m,k} x_{R_2}^{m,k} + n \qquad (1)$$

where, $h_{XY}^{m,k}$ is the channel coefficient of the m-th OFDM symbol on the k-th subcarrier between X and Y nodes and n is the ambient noise.

Obviously, the symbol $x_S^{m,k}$ is the signal of interest for R_1.

2.2 The decoding candidates

We consider three decoding techniques that could potentially be applied at R_1.

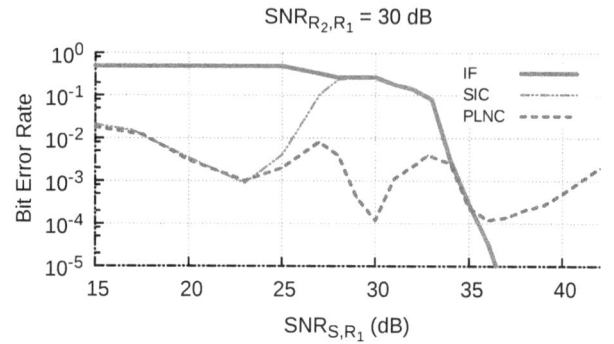

Figure 3: Error Rate at R_1 with different values of SNR_{S,R_1}

1) Interference-Free (IF) equalization [3][5]: R_1 decodes directly the packet p_S considering the part $h_{R_2R_1}^{m,k} x_{R_2}^{m,k} + n$ of Eq. (1) as Gaussian noise. In particular, R_1 estimates the symbol $\hat{s}_S^{m,k}$ sent by S on the k-th subcarrier of the m-th OFDM symbol using the minimum distance criteria.

2) Successive Interference Cancellation (SIC) [3][5][2]: This decoding technique is used to decode many packets received simultaneously with different power levels. The principle is to decode the strongest one with an IF equalization and then to cancel its contribution in equation (1), repeating the operation until the signal of interest is decoded [7].

When $SNR_{R_2,R_1} > SNR_{S,R_1}$[2], SIC equalization becomes a two-step decoding process. R_1 estimates the symbol $\hat{s}_{R_2}^{m,k}$ sent by R_2, removes its contribution from the the received signal and finally it estimates $\hat{s}_S^{m,k}$ with second IF equalization.

3) Physical-Layer Network Coding (PLNC): Never before associated with two-path relaying, we make it the third candidate because it is designed to benefit from two interfering signals. In its simplest form, PLNC [8] consists of decoding a linear combination (typically a XOR combination) of two interfering packets rather than the two individual packets. In the considered scenario for instance, R_1 aims to decode a linear combination of p_S and p_{R_2} rather than p_S only. To do so, we apply the optimal decoding technique in the sense of the minimum distance criteria introduced in [9]. Note that, with PLNC, R_1 decodes a linear combination of p_S and p_{R_2} rather than the individual packet p_S. The destination, using previously received packets (the very first is a single native packet) can perform the PLNC decoding.

2.3 IF vs. SIC vs. PLNC

Experimental platform: To compare the performance of the three decoding techniques, we use the testbed depicted in Fig. 2. It consists of 4 Ettus Research Universal Software Radio Peripherals (USRPs) N210 equipped with an SBX daughterboard and GPS antennas. Communications take place over the 1.8 GHz frequency band with a sampling rate of 400kB/s and the signal/MAC processing is done

---

[2]$SNR_{X,Y}$ denotes the Signal-To-Noise Ratio of a signal sent by node X measured at node Y.

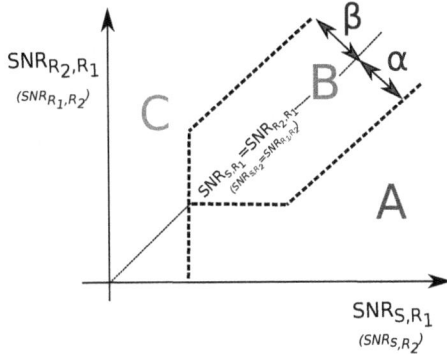

Figure 4: Three decoding strategies at R_1 depending on the intra-diamond channel (IDC)

in C++ and Python within the GnuRadio framework [6]. A slotted TDMA channel access is built thanks to the GPS synchronization.

Implementation details: Packets are 1280 bit-long and each OFDM symbol includes 64 subcarriers: 40 subcarriers for data symbols, 12 guard subcarriers and 12 pilot subcarriers. To estimate the channel coefficients $\hat{h}_{R_2 R_1}^{m,k}$ and $\hat{h}_{S R_1}^{m,k}$ each interfering payload transmission is preceded by two interference-free preambles sent by S and R_2 successively [10].

Experiment description: To evaluate R_1's capability to decode the signal from the source under diverse intra-diamond channel conditions, we keep the inter-relay link stable and vary the source transmission power. Specifically, we start by modulating the transmission power of R_2 so as to obtain $SNR_{R_2,R_1} = 30\ dB$. Leaving R_2's transmission power unchanged for the rest of the experiment, we vary the transmission power of node S and evaluate the Bit Error Rate (BER) at R_1. When PLNC decoding is applied, the BER is obtained by comparing the decoded packet to $p_S \oplus p_{R_2}$ or $p_S \oplus Rot(p_{R_2})$, depending on the θ value obtained at R_1.

Results: Figure 3 delivers two main lessons. First and probably most surprisingly, contrary to what is recommended by almost all literature on the subject [2, 3, 5], SIC is a poor enabler of two-path relaying. Instead, the data shows that on off-the-shelf hardware, using PLNC yields an acceptable BER ($< 10^{-2}$)) for far more intra-diamond channel values.

The second lesson is that depending on the intra-diamond channel state, there are three distinct areas relevant to two-path relaying. When $SNR_{S,R_1} > SNR_{R_2,R_1}$ by more than 5dB (right part of the curve), R_1 can easily decode p_S by using IF, as expected. Second, when the difference in SNR between the two signals is between $(5dB, -15dB)$ – a wide region – using PLNC enables R_1 to decode with a reasonable BER. Finally, when the desired signal becomes too weak ($< 15dB$), the BER starts reaching unacceptable levels.

Then, from a higher perspective, the empirical study showed that the performance of two-path relaying will highly depend on the intra-diamond channel (IDC). Thus, we identify three IDC-level decoding areas, depicted in Fig. 4, which could lead, as shown in § 3, to different decoding strategies at relays:

- **Area A** – the desired signal is stronger than the interfering signal. Using interference-free equalization (IF), the relay, say R_1 (resp. R_2), can decode the packet from the source while the other

relay, R_2 (resp. R_1), is transmitting a packet to the destination. Therefore, the source and R_2 (resp. R_1) can transmit simultaneously.

- **Area B** – the desired signal is similar in strength to the interfering signal. Using PLNC-based decoding, the relay, say R_1 (resp. R_2), can decode the xor-ed packet containing the packet from the source while the other relay, R_2 (resp. R_1), is transmitting a packet to the destination. Therefore, the source and R_2 (resp. R_1) can transmit simultaneously.

- **Area C** – the desired signal is significantly weaker than the interfering signal. In this case, there is no known approach for one of the relays, say R_1 (resp. R_2), to decode the desired signal coming from the source, if the other relay, R_2 (resp. R_1) transmits to the destination at the same time. These transmissions have to be orthogonalized.

3 COLIDER

In this section, we introduce COLiDeR, a CrOss-Layer Diamond Relaying protocol, whose design is driven by the measurement study presented in § 2. The goal is to achieve two complementary objectives: maximizing the received throughput at the destination while minimizing the number of packet losses due to decoding failures.

3.1 IDC-aware states and scheduling

As our measurement study in Sec. 2 demonstrated, the performance of two-path relaying depends on the intra-diamond channel (IDC). To successfully navigate the state of the diamond, COLiDeR identifies 5 states: for three of them scheduling is trivial while for the other two a new scheduling approach is introduced. Each state is defined by the the ability of R_1 and R_2 to handle interfering signals.

3.1.1 States 0 and 0'. None of the relays can decode a packet transmitted from the source, S, while the other relay is transmitting – area C in Fig. 4 for the two relays. In this case, COLiDeR relays packets through R_1 only (state 0) or R_2 only (state 0'), following the traditional one-path relaying approach. As a result, the source can send at most 1 packet every 2 time slots, for a 0.5 frames/slot maximum throughput.

3.1.2 States 1 and 1'. R_1 can handle the reception of two signals while R_2 cannot (state 1) or R_2 can handle the reception of two signals while R_1 cannot (state 1') – areas A or B in Fig. 4 for one of the relays and area C for the other. In this situation, COLiDeR introduces the concept of 2/3-capacity two-path relaying. To illustrate it, let us consider the case in which R_1 can handle the reception of two signals while R_2 cannot (State 1), as depicted in Fig. 5(b). In slot 1, the source, S, transmits an interference-free packet to R_2. In slot 2, R_2 relays the packet to the destination while at the same time S transmits a second packet to R_1. Finally, in slot 3, R_1 transmits the second packet, interference-free, to the destination, which ends up receiving two packets over 3 time slots (0.66 packets/slot) – a 2/3-capacity relaying.

3.1.3 State 2. Both relays can decode packets transmitted by the source while the other is transmitting – areas A or B in Fig. 4 for the two relays. In this case, COLiDeR switches to full-capacity two-path relaying, as depicted in Fig. 5(c). The source transmits 1 packet

(a) State 0 (half-capacity relaying)

(b) State 1 (2/3-capacity relaying)

(c) State 2 (full-capacity relaying)

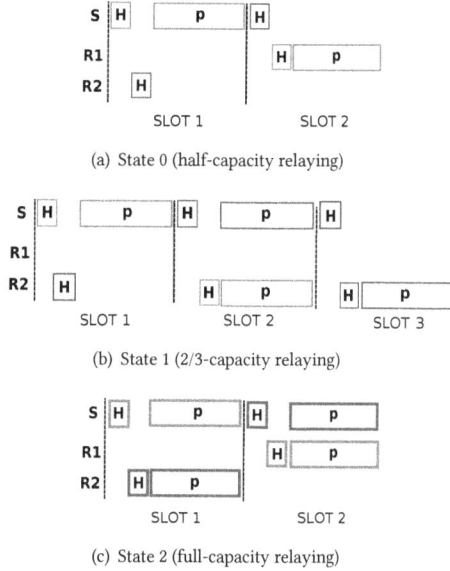

Figure 5: COLiDeR introduces 3 scheduling policies: the traditional half-capacity one-path relaying (5(a)); 2/3-capacity two-path relaying (5(b)); and full-capacity two-path relaying (5(c)).

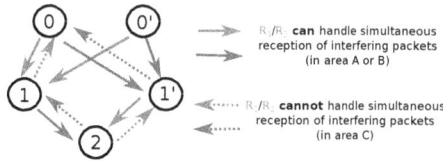

Figure 6: Source rate adaptive protocol state machine

per slot while either R_1 or R_2 relays a packet to the destination, which receives 1 packet/slot.

3.2 Distributed state transition

In this section, we describe how COLiDeR addresses the challenge of identifying the proper two-path relaying state out of the 5 possible introduced in § 3.1. What makes this task challenging is that the state depends on the intra-diamond state. Not only this information is not known in advance by any of the stations, but it can be subject to change due to the dynamic nature of the wireless channel.

At the high level, COLiDeR's approach is to have the source drive the transitions, with input from relays which are in the best position to estimate the best decoding strategy. The information necessary for the coordination is shared via the transmission of orthogonal control packets (H packets in Fig. 5). We use the finite-state machine, depicted in Fig. 6, to model the selection of the two-path relaying state. The initial state, as well as the conditions for each transition, are as follows:

Initial state: To bootstrap, COLiDeR uses the traditional single-relay, half-capacity forwarding of packets. Either R_1 (state 0) or R_2 (state 0') exclusively forwards the packets from the source to the destination.

Transitioning to a higher state: The source and two relays periodically transmit control packets, as depicted in Fig. 5. Leveraging the reception of these packets, R_1 (resp. R_2) can estimate SNR_{S,R_1} and SNR_{R_2,R_1} (resp. SNR_{S,R_2} and SNR_{R_1,R_2}), necessary for deciding in which decoding area of Fig. 4 it most likely is. If R_1 estimates that decoding two signals is possible, i.e. area A or B, it notifies the source in the next control packet it transmits. The source, based on the the control packets it receives, decides whether to transition to a higher state. To avoid overreacting to what could be a momentary change, the source only moves to a higher state if it receives a given number of consecutive packets notifying that a relay is in area A or B. Before transitioning, the source notifies the relays to immediately update their adopted state. This information is included within source's control packets.

Transitioning to a lower state: The source will decide to shift to a lower state if one of the two events occur: a) it receives a given number of control packets from a relay notifying that it is in area C (the relay can not receive two simultaneous packets), or b) it receives no control packets that pass the CRC check for a given number of cycles. Should that happen, the source executes a state change by modifying the adopted state field in the control packets it sends out, similarly to the transition to higher state.

To account for the fact that packet losses are inevitable, the relays will transition by themselves to the initial state if they receive no control packets from the source passing the CRC check for a given number of cycles.

4 GENERAL EVALUATION

To evaluate the reactivity and the overall performance of COLiDeR in different channel conditions, we implement a scenario incorporating four representative configurations. Initially, configuration I, the 4 USRP radios depicted in Fig. 2 are placed in the classic diamond topology and the transmission power levels are selected such that only one relay can handle two simultaneous transmissions with a reasonable bit error rate. At time $t_0 = 100$ slots, relay R_2 is switched off, creating configuration t_0 aimed at emulating a relay loss due to mobility. At $t_1 = 200$ slots, relay R_2 is switched back on, emulating the selection of a new relay. In the final configuration, at $t_2 = 300$ slots, the source transmission power is increased, emulating a scenario in which the source moves closer to the relays.

Comparison: Our goal is to evaluate how COLiDeR navigates the trade-off between reliability and throughput, its principle design consideration. Note that COLiDeR could optimize reliability by permanently staying in state 0, the equivalent of traditional one-path relaying. Thus, this approach is included in the study. On the opposite side, having COLiDeR permanently in state 2 may maximize throughput although it causes severe packet losses. To see why this is true, consider the case in which R_1 and R_2 can not handle the reception of two interfering signals. While R_1 is transmitting a packet to the destination, the source has two choices. It can transmit to R_2, the maximalist approach, leading to a packet loss. Or it does not transmit, which is what COLiDeR would have done since it would have transitioned to state 0. In terms of throughput, assuming layer two will retransmit the same packet in the following slot, the maximalist approach did no worse than COLiDeR even though it transmitted unnecessarily, wasting energy and augmenting interference. COLiDeR, however, may sometimes do worse than the maximalist approach in terms of throughput, either because it is designed to wait for a few rounds before it transitions to the next best state, or because it chooses to be in a lower state to avoid packet losses. Thus, we also compare COLiDeR to this maximalist approach, when used with a static PLNC decoding at relays.

Results: Figure 7 plots the end-to-end throughput (Fig. 7(a)) and percentage of lost packets (Fig. 7(b)) against time. Each value is obtained by computing the throughput and loss ratio over the 30 previous slots.

In the initial configuration, I, R_1 can handle the reception of two signals with a reasonable bit error rate whereas R_2 cannot. COLiDeR adopts scheduling state 1 (§ 3.1), resulting in 0.66 packets/slot throughput and no packet losses – the best joint throughput-reliability performance. When the source adopts the maximalist approach and transmits a packet every slot, a slightly higher (around 8%) throughput is achieved, because occasionally, R_2 successfully decodes the interfering packets. It comes, however, with a high penalty in terms of packet losses, around 25%. Furthermore, COLiDeR performs just as well as one-path relaying in terms of packet losses while outperforming it by 25% in terms of throughput.

At $t_0 = 100$ slots R_2 is switched off, leaving a single path to the destination. Obviously, as Fig. 7(a) shows, the maximum throughput in this case, realized by all schemes, is 0.5 packet/slot. Having the source sending 1 packet/slot when only R_1 is active, however, leads to an inevitable 50% rate loss. As described in § 3.2, COLiDeR, after receiving no control packets from R_2, transitions from state 1 to state 0, limiting the packet losses.

At $t_1 = 200$ slots, relay R_2 is switched back on and is eventually integrated back to two-path relaying, enabling the two-path relaying schemes to realize the performance observed in the period 0-100 slots. Finally, at $t_2 = 300$ slots the source transmission power is increased, enabling R_2 to handle the reception of two simultaneous signals with a reasonable bit error rate. COLiDeR takes advantage of the newly created opportunity and transitions to state 2, achieving close to channel-capacity performance in terms of throughput with almost zero packet losses. The maximalist approach, while also transmitting 1 packet/slot, only includes one decoding technique (PLNC), explaining its inferior performance when compared to COLiDeR.

5 CONCLUSION AND FUTURE WORK

We have presented COLiDeR a PHY/MAC cross-layer solution for adaptive two-path relaying. Experimentally driven, our approach combines interference-free equalization and Physical-Layer Network Coding (PLNC) for decoding at relays, and relies on a source rate adaptation mechanism to respond to channel state and topology changes. Experimental results have shown that COLiDeR ensures smooth and efficient sailing between the defined protocol states, achieving between 80-95% of the relaying performance of the ideal full-duplex radio while incurring negligible decoding failures.

While this work was focused on minimizing the relaying multiplexing loss, as future work we aim to integrate and evaluate COLiDeR in large-scale wireless networks. Therefore, two complementary questions are of major interest. First, how to identify

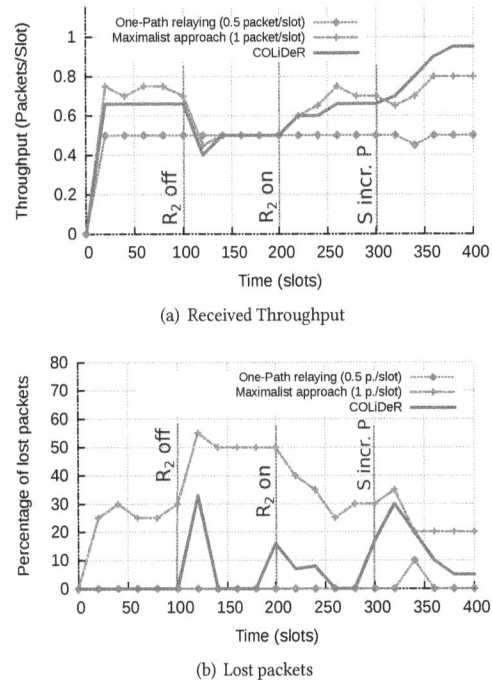

(a) Received Throughput

(b) Lost packets

Figure 7: COLiDeR performance in a general evaluation scenario

diamonds in a network with multiple flows? Then, how should we adapt the TDMA framework to fit most of current ad-hoc networks relying on CSMA-based channel reservation methods?

ACKNOWLEDGMENTS

This work was supported in part by the Agence Nationale de la Recherche under the ANR JCJC CiTADEL grant.

REFERENCES

[1] C. Zhai, W. Zhang, and P. C. Ching, "Cooperative spectrum sharing based on two-path successive relaying," *IEEE Transactions on Communications, Vol. 61, No. 6, 2013.*

[2] R. Simoni, V. Jamali, N. Zlatanov, R. Schober, L. Pierucci, and R. Fantacci, "Buffer-aided diamond relay network with block fading and inter-relay interference," *IEEE Transactions on Wireless Communications, Vol. 15, No. 11, 2016.*

[3] Y. Fan, C. Wang, J. Thompson, and H. V. Poor, "Recovering multiplexing loss through successive relaying using repetition coding," *IEEE Transactions on Wireless Communications, Vol. 6, No. 12, 2007.*

[4] H. Wicaksana, S. H. Ting, C. K. Ho, W. H. Chin, and Y. L. Guan, "Af two-path half duplex relaying with inter-relay self interference cancellation: diversity analysis and its improvement," *IEEE Transactions on Wireless Communications, vol. 8, no. 9, pp. 4720–4729, September 2009.*

[5] F. Tian, W. Zhang, W.-K. Ma, P. Ching, and H. V. Poor, "An effective distributed space-time code for two-path successive relay network," *IEEE Transactions on Communications, Vol. 59, No. 8, 2016.*

[6] "Gnuradio overview available at http://www.gnuradio.org/."

[7] D. Halperin, T. Anderson, and D. Wetherall, "Taking the sting out of carrier sense: Interference cancellation for wireless lans," in *Proc. IEEE MOBICOM Conference*, 2008.

[8] S. Zhang, S. Liew, and P. Lam, "Hot topic: physical-layer network coding," in *Proc. ACM MobiCom Conference*, 2006.

[9] V. N. V. T. Muralidharan and B. Rajan, "Wireless network-coded bidirectional relaying using latin squares for m-psk modulation," *IEEE Transactions On Information Theory, Vol. 59, No. 10, 2013.*

[10] L. You, S. Liew, and L. Lu, "Network-coded multiple access ii: Toward real-time operation with improved performance," *IEEE Journal On Selected Areas in Communications, Vol. 33, No. 2, 2015.*

LAMA: Location-Assisted Medium Access for Position-Beaconing Applications

Holger Döbler
Humboldt-Universität zu Berlin
Berlin, Germany
holger.doebler@informatik.hu-berlin.de

Björn Scheuermann
Humboldt-Universität zu Berlin
Berlin, Germany
scheuermann@informatik.hu-berlin.de

ABSTRACT

It is nowadays common in all kinds of traffic—maritime, air, road—that vehicles use beaconing systems to broadcast their position and other navigational data to nearby vehicles to improve situational awareness. MAC protocols for the beaconing use case face special challenges: protocol overhead has a significant performance impact due to small packet size, fair and frequent access to the channel is required, and the broadcast nature limits the applicability of hand shakes. We propose LAMA, a MAC protocol for position awareness beaconing that is based on the locally shared position information. Our contention-free approach uses neither handshakes nor forwarding of state, thereby requiring only small constant protocol overhead per beacon and scaling well with large neighbor counts. Yet, it successfully suppresses interference, including hidden-terminal-type, while maximizing channel utilization through coordinated spatial reuse. In a quantitative evaluation using the ns-3 discrete event simulator we compare LAMA against SO-TDMA, the MAC protocol used in the maritime automatic identification system. We find that LAMA outperforms SO-TDMA with respect to several metrics in synthetic random topologies as well as in scenarios based on real vessel traffic traces.

CCS CONCEPTS

• **Networks** → **Network protocol design**; **Location based services**; *Network resources allocation, Physical topologies, Network mobility*;

KEYWORDS

medium access control, cooperative awareness, maritime wireless networks

ACM Reference Format:
Holger Döbler and Björn Scheuermann. 2019. LAMA: Location-Assisted Medium Access for Position-Beaconing Applications. In *22nd Int'l ACM Conference on Modeling, Analysis and Simulation of Wireless and Mobile Systems (MSWiM '19), November 25–29, 2019, Miami Beach, FL, USA*. ACM, New York, NY, USA, 8 pages. https://doi.org/10.1145/3345768.3355925

1 INTRODUCTION

Many of today's transportation systems achieve cooperative awareness by means of wireless beaconing. This includes ETSI ITS/WAVE for road traffic [4, 9], Automatic dependent surveillance—broadcast (ADS–B) for air traffic [5], and the automatic identification system (AIS) for maritime traffic [14].

All of these systems share the common feature that every vehicle periodically broadcasts small wireless beacons containing its geographical position, along with identification data and other navigational information. On the one hand these use cases share a set of challenging requirements for their wireless Medium Access Control (MAC) protocol: the number of participating nodes is potentially large and distributed over a large area; nodes move, thereby constantly changing the network topology; all transmissions are link-local broadcasts, limiting the use of handshakes; successful, collision-free transmissions are safety-critical. On the other hand the use cases imply that nodes know not only their own position but also their neighbors' locations.

We propose to explicitly utilize the locally shared knowledge of node positions to resiliently avoid collisions while requiring only a small constant overhead per beacon. Our protocol *LAMA*, a Location-Assisted Medium Access control protocol for beaconing applications, is especially suited to *large-scale* cooperative awareness applications. LAMA's basic idea is simple: in a slotted time, a distinct random *fire position* in the plane is assigned to each slot by means of a hash of the slot number. For a specific slot, the node whose real position is closest to the fire position is allowed to use the slot for transmission while all other nodes must remain silent. Some extensions to this idea that allow for spatial reuse and improve channel access fairness are also discussed.

LAMA's advantage lies in the utilization of information that is locally shared between nodes anyway, as it is required by the primary use case itself. To the best of our knowledge, LAMA is the first MAC protocol for pure link-local-broadcast communication in dynamic topologies that achieves two-hop desynchronization, i.e., avoiding collisions also over longer distance and resolving the hidden terminal problem (HTP), without any neighbor state forwarding.

We have identified the maritime AIS as a well-fitting use case for the following three reasons: first, AIS is operated in the VHF band with high transmission power on the high seas, enabling typical communication ranges over 30 km. This leads to potentially high neighbor counts. Second, AIS messages carry a payload of only 152 bit, so they are relatively small. Therefore, the impact of MAC protocol overhead is particularly strong in AIS, which may prohibit the use of more complex collision avoidance approaches. Third, due to the absence of large obstacles in the maritime environment, the channel's radio propagation properties are well predictable and homogeneous across different regions. LAMA can likewise constitute an interesting basis in other application areas, where cooperative awareness and tracking based on beacons is used. This includes, for instance, Intelligent Transportation Systems (ITS) or air traffic.

In our evaluation, we use large-scale maritime cooperative awareness as the use case and compared the implementation of our protocol to self-organizing time division multiple access (SO-TDMA), the MAC protocol used by AIS and therefore the state of the art in that field. In a comparative evaluation performed using the ns-3 discrete event simulator we show that LAMA outperforms SO-TDMA. The benefits are clear over a wide range of node densities, both in synthetic random topologies as well as for real marine vessel trajectory traces.

The remainder of this article is structured as follows. Sec. 2 gives an overview of the related work, especially discussing various medium access approaches. Our own approach is explained in detail in Sec. 3. In Sec. 4 we present a detailed performance evaluation of LAMA in comparison to SO-TDMA. Finally, a conclusion and a discussion of possible extensions of the LAMA approach is given in Sec. 5.

2 RELATED WORK

MAC protocols for wireless networks have been studied extensively. According to [13], MAC protocols for wireless networks can be either contention based, like CSMA, or contention free, like time division multiple access (TDMA). In some cases, a mixture of both is used. The LAMA protocol proposed here is a distributed single-channel pure TDMA protocol. As LAMA is mainly a slot-allocation mechanism, it can be extended to multiple (sub-)channels and combined with orthogonal codes; such extensions are beyond the scope of this article, though.

Since beaconing for the purpose of position awareness is an inherently distributed use case, we skip the discussion of centralized protocols that are based on a base station, access point or head node that coordinates medium access of all nodes in range.

Distributed contention-based protocols either require significant additional resources like DBTMA [8] or suffer from a significant overhead due to control packets [3, 13, 18]. The same holds for distributed hybrid MAC protocols such as HyMAC [16], which in addition assumes one or more base station (BS) nodes, acting as a data sink. Static contention-free MAC protocols that allocate fixed fractions of the resources available to each node are not applicable to networks of changing topology and unbound size.

Dynamic distributed contention-free MAC protocols typically map the MAC problem to a dynamic TDMA slot-allocation problem. Some of these protocols have *multi-channel* capabilities, i. e., they further divide each time slot in the frequency (frequency division multiple access, FDMA) or code (code division multiple access, CDMA) domain. In Unifying Dynamic Distributed Multichannel TDMA Slot Assignment protocol (USAP) [20] nodes select unused TDMA slots and once in a while communicate their local slot allocation view to one-hop neighbors using special *control packets* in order to achieve two-hop desynchronization. In PTMAC [10] a similar approach is presented to resolve two-hop collisions in

TDMA in the context of vehicular ad-hoc networks. This comes at the cost of MAC protocol overhead that scales with the number of neighbors.

Recent efforts to make the two-hop broadcasting of node states more efficient in the domain of vehicular ad-hoc network use Bloom filters [11]. They still require more overhead to broadcast Bloom filters than LAMA imposes. The Five Phase Reservation Protocol (FPRP) [21], as well as Evolutionary-TDMA [22], which uses FPRP for broadcast scheduling, use a five-way handshake in order to (re-)negotiate a broadcast slot assignment every time the topology changes. Thereby FPRP is applicable to dynamic, but slowly changing topologies. Despite the necessity for a significant amount of overhead, the FPRP mechanism relies on the nodes' capability to tell apart packet collisions from the absence of transmissions. This is a strong assumption, especially in a distributed setting. In SO-TDMA [14], on the other hand, no forwarding of neighbors' slot reservations is performed, thereby scaling well for large neighbor counts but suffering from the hidden terminal problem. LAMA requires neither handshakes nor other kind of control packets or state forwarding to achieve two-hop desynchronization, thereby generating less overhead.

Many existing approaches for cooperative awareness beaconing for road traffic in the absence of cellular network infrastructure are based on IEEE 802.11p or LTE-V2V sidelink mode 4 [1]. The former uses CSMA/CA and hence suffers severe performance degradation [2] in high node density settings. LTE-V2V (sidelink mode 4) on the other hand uses contention-free single carrier FDMA; nodes use Sidelink Control Information messages for reservation of resources similar to slot reservation in SO-TDMA. In favor of dedicated control messages SO-TDMA, used by AIS, includes reservation information in every beacon header. In our performance evaluation, we compare LAMA against SO-TDMA as this protocol was designed specifically for small beacon sizes and data rates.

Our proposed MAC protocol LAMA is a distributed dynamic contention-free TDMA slot-allocation protocol that makes use of the nodes' locations to negotiate medium access without need for explicit slot reservations. LAMA has a considerably small overhead of $O(\log_2(\text{\# of neighbors}))$ bits per packet and uses no control/request/confirmation packets at all. It does, however, require the nodes to know each other's locations approximately. In case of a transponder system whose primary goal is to broadcast location information, this is no overhead at all.

Medium access based on node locations has been used in geographic opportunistic routing, e. g., Füßler et al. [6]. In contrast to LAMA, however, this work targets unicast routing; relative position information is used for (implicit) forwarder selection, whereas we use absolute positions for broadcast medium access coordination.

3 LOCATION-ASSISTED MEDIUM ACCESS
3.1 Problem Statement

We propose a MAC protocol that is particularly suitable for large-scale cooperative awareness beaconing. Each of a large number of nodes distributed over a wide geographical area repeatedly broadcasts beacons containing its own navigational data. Each node is equipped with a radionavigation satellite receiver providing it with the position information to be broadcast. This typically at the same time provides clock synchronization, the other key ingredient for TDMA slot alignment.

In order to provide high quality positional awareness, nodes need to send beacons frequently, providing low-latency position information to their neighbors. At the same time interference on the wireless channel must be avoided.

3.2 The Basic LAMA Protocol

The basic idea of LAMA is to use the nodes' locations to mediate access to the wireless medium. This location information is particularly suitable for cooperative position awareness beaconing applications because up-to-date knowledge about neighbors' locations is inherent in this use case. LAMA is a single-channel TDMA protocol. Let us for the moment assume that at all times each node exactly knows all nodes' positions within a sufficiently large bounding box.[1] For each slot, let there be a so-called *fire position*: a 2D position, sampled uniformly from the bounding box, known by all nodes. For a certain slot, each node draws the same fire position; this can, e. g., be realized by using the same pseudorandom number generator (PRNG) for sampling the fire positions, or by hashing the time slot ID to a position. Fire positions for different slots are assumed to be statistically independent; using a good PRNG or a good hash function serves the purpose.

Using this mechanism, a simple medium access scheme—and the starting point for LAMA—is the following: *A node uses a slot for transmission iff it is closer to the fire position than all other nodes.* If nodes have perfect knowledge about all nodes' positions, this completely prevents collisions, because in every slot exactly one node sends. Perfect knowledge about all other nodes will of course not be given in practice. However, we will see that the performance degradation caused by typical position inaccuracies is very limited.

A remaining problem with this naïve first protocol is that it prohibits any spatial reuse, which results in poor channel utilization for networks covering larger areas. Let the length L be a parameter that describes the desired distance scale of spatial reuse. Instead of a single *fire position*, we assign a set of many fire positions to each slot that are mutually L or further apart. To maximize the number of fire positions in each slot, a hexagonal lattice of edge-length L can be used.

A node then selects the lattice point closest to its own position as the slot's *nearest fire position* (np) and uses the slot for transmission if no other node is even closer to np. Apart from enabling spatial reuse, this gets rid of the necessity for a bounding box: the fire positions can now simply be drawn uniform at random from the lattice's unit cell in order to achieve a spatially homogeneous fire-position probability density across the entire plane. This mechanism can, however, lead to simultaneous transmissions of arbitrarily close nodes: two nodes aware of each other can correctly get different nps in the same slot, thereby each being closer to its np than the other one and hence both transmit. To prevent this, we define a *base send region* around each node's position and let a node transmit only if the np lies within this region (in addition to being the nearest node).

The protocol described so far can suppresses most interference while enabling spatial reuse, once a steady state is reached where

[1]We will soon drop this assumption.

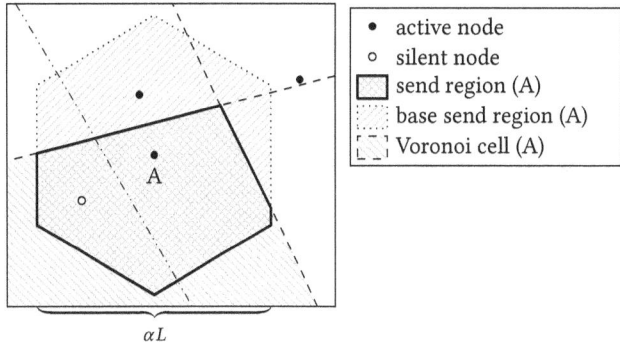

Figure 1: Schematic of the LAMA protocol mechanism. A node uses a slot for transmission only if a fire position lies within the node's send region.

each node knows at least its direct neighbors. To improve bootstrapping and situations where new nodes join the network, nodes skip a constant fraction of their assigned slots probabilistically. When a node is about to transmit in a certain slot, it does so with probability $P^a \in (0, 1]$ and listens for unknown nodes otherwise. New nodes know their own position and therefore do not need any specific behavior in order to join: they transmit just like any other node when they are closest to the fire position. This comes with a (small) probability of collisions, but as we will see is perfectly bearable. Throughout our evaluation we used a value of $P^a = 0.95$, which is sufficient to allow joining of new nodes while at the same not affecting channel utilization too much.

Exact definition of the (basic) LAMA protocol. A node A at position $\mathbf{x}_A$ performs the following steps to decide if it transmits a packet in slot i:

- It deterministically draws a *base* fire position $\mathbf{p}_i$ from the lattice's unit cell uniformly at pseudo-random. All nodes compute the same $\mathbf{p}_i$ for the same slot i.
- $\mathbf{p}_i$ defines a hexagonal lattice $\mathbf{P}_i$ of fire positions.

$$\mathbf{P}_i = \{\, \mathbf{p}_i + jL \cdot (1,0) + kL \cdot (\tfrac{1}{2}, \tfrac{\sqrt{3}}{2}) \mid j, k \in \mathbb{Z} \,\}$$

- From that, it computes its *nearest fire position* (np):

$$\mathbf{np}_i(\mathbf{x}_A) := \text{argmin}_{\mathbf{p} \in \mathbf{P}_i} \|\mathbf{p} - \mathbf{x}_A\|_2$$

- Node A sends in slot i if all of conditions (1)–(3) hold:

$$\|\mathbf{np}_i(\mathbf{x}_A) - \mathbf{x}_A\|_2 < \|\mathbf{np}_i(\mathbf{x}_A) - \mathbf{x}_B\|_2 \ \forall B \in \{\text{other nodes}\} \quad (1)$$

$$\left| (\mathbf{np}_i(\mathbf{x}_A) - \mathbf{x}_A) \cdot (\cos\theta, \sin\theta) \right| < \frac{\alpha L}{2} \ \forall \theta \in \{0, \tfrac{\pi}{3}, \tfrac{2\pi}{3}\} \quad (2)$$

$$X_{[0,1)} < P^a \quad (3)$$

where $\alpha \in (0, 1]$ and $P^a \in (0, 1]$ are parameters of the protocol and $X_{[0,1)}$ is a uniform pseudo-random variable with range $[0, 1)$. For a visualization see Fig. 1. The first condition is fulfilled iff $\mathbf{np}_i(\mathbf{x}_A)$ is within the node's Voronoi cell. The second condition is fulfilled iff $\mathbf{np}_i(\mathbf{x}_A)$ is within the node's base send region, which we chose to be a regular hexagon with a minimal diameter of αL, centered at the node's position. For $\alpha = 1$ the base send region is the lattice's Wigner-Seitz cell shifted to the node's position and thus Condition (2) is always true. For $\alpha < 1$, Condition (2) assures

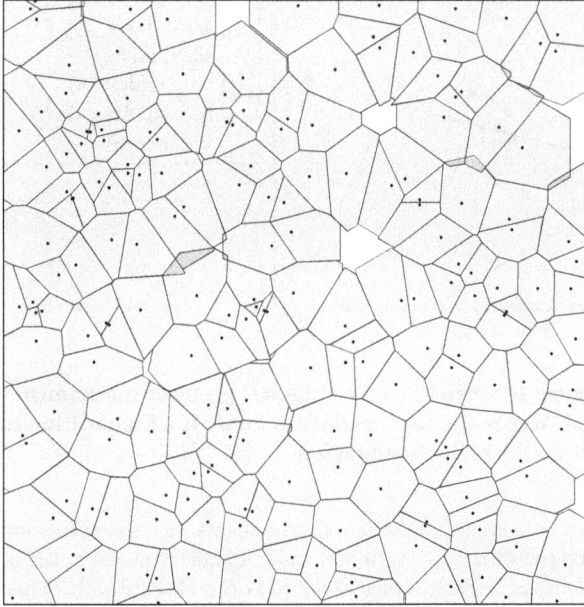

Figure 2: Node positions and send regions in basic LAMA. The send regions (light gray) nearly form a Voronoi diagram of nodes. Only few regions show uncovered gaps (white) and small overlaps (dark gray).

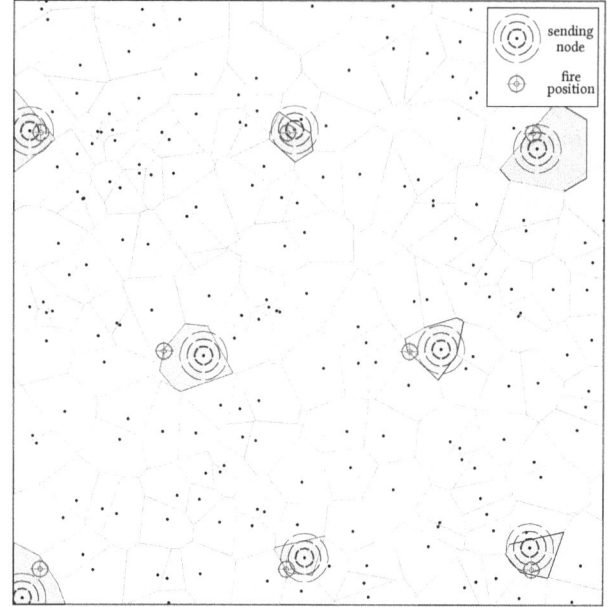

Figure 3: Sample lattice of fire positions and the resulting senders in the situation depicted in Fig. 2. The positions of sending nodes approximately replicate the hexagonal lattice structure.

that two nodes referring to distinct NFPs can only send in the same time slot if they are at least $(1 - \alpha)L$ apart. Condition (3) manifests probabilistic skipping of slots. We emphasize that in contrast to the globally chosen fire position $\mathbf{p}_i$, the $X_{[0,1)}$ of different nodes shall be statistically independent. In Fig. 2 we show a snapshot of an example simulation run of this simple variant of our protocol we call *basic LAMA*. This already yields good effective channel utilization and robustness as shown in Sec. 4.

3.3 De-Allocation of Slots

Basic LAMA is a zero-overhead collision-avoiding slot allocation mechanism. No information needs to be communicated beyond the node positions, which are the targeted applications' primary payload and are therefore exchanged anyway. Despite its efficiency, basic LAMA can lead to unfair, counterproductive allocation: first, it under-represents nodes that are surrounded by very close neighbors. Second, each node's transmissions schedule resembles a discrete Bernoulli process. If the gap between successive beacons of a node is too short, the second beacon carries only little additional information. If that gap is too long, the position awareness accuracy suffers.

We therefore introduce a simple mechanism that allows nodes to de-allocate future slots: each beacon's header contains a positive integer v that encodes a vow of silence that the source node will be silent in the following v slots. In this extended version of our protocol, that we call just LAMA, each node keeps track of its neighbors' silence state and only non-silent neighbors are considered when evaluating Condition (1). As a heuristic which value of v a node chooses to send, we use $v = v(k - \alpha^{-2})$, where k is the number of

entries in the node's neighbor table and v is a real-valued protocol parameter. In scenarios of homogeneous node density, a node with k neighbors in range should transmit every $k + 1$ slots on average. Using $v = k$, however, a node would remain silent for k slots after each transmission. Afterwards it would still need to wait at least until the **np** hits into its base send region, which is why we subtract α^{-2}. A natural choice for v is 1, but we will investigate the effects of this parameter in our evaluation. This mechanism induces a small amount of protocol overhead as $\log_2 k^{\max}$ bits are needed to encode v in each beacon's header, where $k^{\max}$ is an upper bound of the number of neighbors a node is anticipated to observe at once.

Moving nodes. So far we have not explicitly considered node movement, even though the main purpose of a beaconing application is to create up-to-date knowledge of *moving* nodes' positions. Every time a node sends a beacon, it includes its current position and saves this position. When evaluating Eq. (1), however, it uses the position it had sent in its most recent beacon instead of its current position, because its neighbors' state tables cannot contain more recent position information.

Non-planar geometry. We assumed nodes to be in a flat plane but vessels are located on the Earth's near-spherical surface. A spherical generalization of LAMA is straightforward, but requires to replace the hexagonal lattice with a maximal set of fire positions, pseudo-randomly drawn for every slot, with pairwise great-circle distance of at least L. The somewhat convoluted mathematics needed to that end would have increased this article's complexity without contributing much to the original idea, so we constrain ourselves to a flat-plane approximation here.

Forgetting nodes. The protocol relies on each node's neighbor state table and its size. To prevent the table from growing indefinitely, nodes should delete neighbors from their table if no beacon was received for a certain amount of time. In our evaluation based on real-world vessel movement traces, we experimented with neighbor expiration timeout values between 1 and 25 minutes, and found no significant impact on the protocol's performance.

4 EVALUATION

We evaluate LAMA in the setting of AIS and compare it against SO-TDMA, the latter being the MAC protocol defined in [14] and designed particularly for that use-case.

4.1 Simulation Setup

We implemented both LAMA and SO-TDMA for the AIS use-case in ns-3 [15]. AIS uses VHF channels modulated in binary GMSK with 9600 bit/s. For TDMA slots of $\frac{2}{75}$ s $\hat{=}$ 256 bit are used. Each position report uses one slot and consists of roughly two bytes of slot reservation information and 19 bytes for the node's navigational state, including the sender ID. The remaining 11 bytes are used for header, trailer, and buffer time. SO-TDMA nodes explicitly reserve slots 1–7 minutes ahead of time, avoiding slots reserved by other nodes. For further details of AIS and SO-TDMA we refer to the standard [14]. In our AIS implementation, we consider only position reports in continuous self-organizing mode of so-called "Class A" nodes[2] a single channel, and a fixed reporting rate of 30 messages per minute, to avoid unnecessary protocol complexity that is hardly relevant for a MAC performance comparison. Our LAMA implementation uses exactly the same payload size and slot/frame structure; instead of the slot reservation data, the vow-of-silence value v is transmitted.

Packet loss was simulated using the signal-to-interference-plus-noise mechanism of *YansErrorRateModel* of ns-3, adapted to the characteristics of the maritime VHF channel: a SINR of 10 dB results in a packet error rate (PER) of 20% [14]. For path loss and fading produced by Earth curvature and sea roughness, a two-log-distance model [12] was used with first path loss exponent $n_0 = 2.6$ according to [17] (with 3.75 m antenna height, 1.5 m sea surface height, $f_{carrier} = 162$ MHz) and second path loss exponent $n_1 = 4.69$ [12] with transition distance $d_1 = 6.22$ km yielding a PER of 20% at 20 NM (nautical miles) distance. Following [17] a normal random propagation log with $\sigma = 0.65$ dB was added.

To study the effect of different average node densities, we use the *random walk with reflection* mobility model, where nodes are confined to a 222 km square box. This is approximately six times the typical reception range in AIS. Inter-transition times and node speeds are drawn uniformly from $[0, 600\,s]$ and $[0, 30\,m/s]$ respectively. In the steady state node positions are distributed uniformly and the node speed distribution equals the speed distribution at transitions [7].

We also use real AIS traces of vessels [23], that contain a set of position reports. Based on the trace of Jun 1st, 2017, 1:00–3:00 pm UTC, we applied a UTM transform to obtain Cartesian coordinates and cropped it to a 200 km × 300 km rectangle to reduce the number of nodes to $\approx$ 550. Between resulting waypoints, constant velocities were simulated. To increase the real traces' node density, we took a

cropped 400 km × 400 km rectangle of traces with 904 nodes, and scaled time and space coordinates by a factor of 1/2 to increase node density without reducing movement velocity.

Each measurement was performed with ten ns-3 simulator runs with independently seeded random number sequences. To shorten the time required for protocol bootstrapping, we did not start all nodes at the same time, but applied a staggered startup procedure where one node is added every 4 seconds. After all nodes joined the simulation, plus an additional initial equilibration period, data was measured for 30 simulated minutes in each run.

4.2 LAMA's Parameters

LAMA has three parameters that may systematically affect its performance: the lattice spacing L, the relative size of the base send region α, and the vow-of-silence scaling parameter v. In the following, we explore their effects.

A simple robust performance metric is what we call the effective channel utilization (ECU): for a node, it is defined as the number of messages that a node received divided by the number of slots which the node itself did not use for transmission. Fig. 4a shows the channel utilization of LAMA for different values of α and different topologies. For $\alpha \in \{.3, .5, .7\}$, the channel utilization varies between 30% and 45% across all topologies considered. For the best value $\alpha = 0.7$, which we use for the rest of our evaluation, LAMA outperforms SO-TDMA by a factor of 1.6–4.4 in terms of ECU.

We also measured the effective channel utilization of LAMA for values of $L \in \{20, 30, 40, 50, 60\}$ nautical miles (NM). The results are given in Fig. 4b. The effective channel utilization of LAMA is maximized for $L \approx 40$ NM which is twice the maximum transmission range of the simulated model. However, the performance depends only weakly on the choice of L. The robustness of LAMA with respect to L is a beneficial trait of the protocol. In maritime scenarios the transmission range may depend on environmental factors such as weather and could vary over time or over different regions on earth. Our results indicate that LAMA performs well in terms of effective channel utilization for a wide range of L.

In Sec. 3.3 we introduced the vow-of-silence mechanism in order to improve the transmission rate fairness between nodes, as well as homogenization of inter-transmission times for each node. In order to quantify these effects, we varied v in $[0, 1]$ for an 800-nodes random walk topology and measured the resulting effective channel utilization and the distribution of transmission rates. The effective channel utilization (see Fig. 4c) shows no significant dependency on v, including $v = 0$ which corresponds to basic LAMA. The distribution of transmission rates however (see Fig. 5) exposes that, as intended, higher values of v reduce the width of the transmission rate distribution by effectively reducing the occurrence of both, very high and very low transmission rates. This indicates that $v = 1$ is appropriate if transmission fairness is desired. This distribution was measured as follows: for a single simulation run, for every consecutive full minute (after the start-up phase) we measured every node's average transmission rate during that minute. Fig. 5 shows the cumulative distribution of these atomic measurements, combined from ten simulation runs.

---

[2]Class A AIS transceivers are required for large vessels on international voyages.

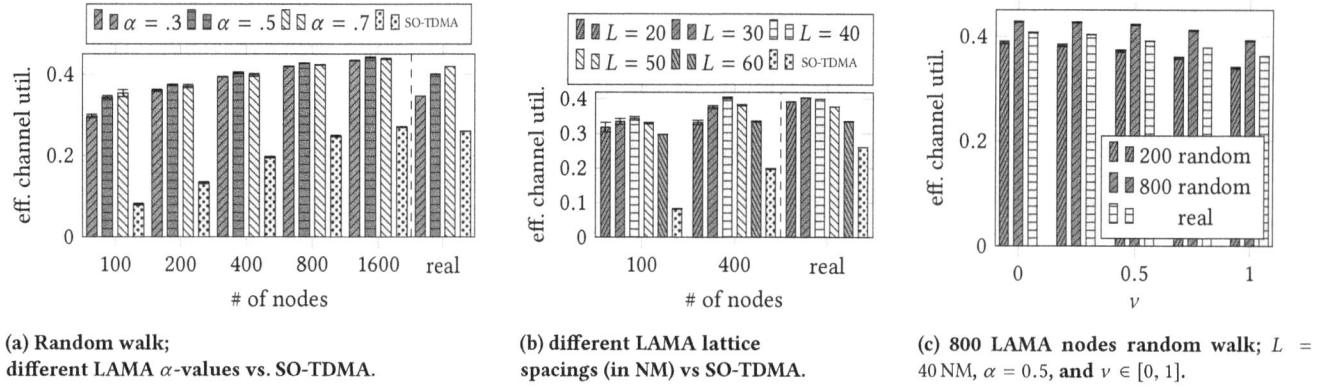

(a) Random walk; different LAMA α-values vs. SO-TDMA.

(b) different LAMA lattice spacings (in NM) vs SO-TDMA.

(c) 800 LAMA nodes random walk; $L = 40$ NM, $\alpha = 0.5$, and $v \in [0, 1]$.

Figure 4: Effective channel utilization for different parameter sets. Error bars depict 95% confidence intervals.

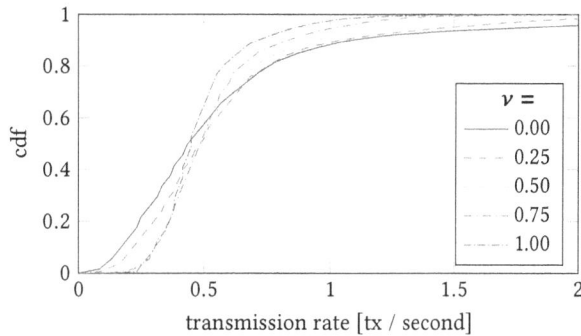

Figure 5: Distribution of nodes' transmission rates in messages/second for 800 nodes random walk topology and different values of v.

4.3 Location-Prediction (In-)Accuracy

The goal of cooperative position awareness is to optimize the nodes' knowledge about each other's navigational state. Typically, low-latency mutual knowledge of navigational state is more important the closer nodes are. Therefore, as an application-oriented performance metric, we measured the nodes' position prediction errors as a function of the distance between two nodes: at a given time t, we recorded the sequence of tuples

$$\left(\overbrace{\|\mathbf{x}_A - \mathbf{x}_B\|_2}^{d(A,B)}, \overbrace{\|\mathbf{x}_A - \mathbf{y}_A(B)\|_2}^{\Delta_{\text{predict}}(A,B)} \mid \forall A \in \{\text{nodes}\} \ \forall B \in \{\text{nodes}\} \setminus \{A\} \right)$$

where $\mathbf{x}_A$ is the true position of node A at time t and $\mathbf{y}_A(B)$ is the position of A predicted by node B based on the last received message, containing A's position and velocity vector, using linear dead reckoning. We define $\Delta_{\text{predict}}(A, B) := \infty$ if B has never received a message from A. For a simulation run, we collected these samples for every ordered pair of nodes once every 7 s. The samples were then binned by $d(A, B)$ in consecutive bins of 1 km and for every bin we determined the 50% percentile of $\Delta_{\text{predict}}(A, B)$. A comparison of LAMA @($L = 50$ NM, $\alpha = 0.75$, $v = 1.0$) and SO-TDMA is given for a 1600-node random walk topology (Fig. 6a) as well as for the real and scaled real topology (Fig. 6b, 6c). In all scenarios and both

methods, the median prediction error appears to be monotonic in the nodes' distance. It starts with a plateau ranging from 0 to 10 NM–18 NM, depending on scenario and protocol, where the prediction error is < 2 m. Each plateau is followed by a steep increase and error medians < 100 m are never observed for distances greater than 20 NM which is the maximum transmission range of channel model. In case of the original real topology both protocols achieve a small prediction error for distances up to approximately 19 NM which we explain with a small overall node density that does not challenge the MAC protocol. In the other scenarios, however, we observe that the steep increase of the prediction error of SO-TDMA occurs at ≈ 4 NM shorter distances compared with LAMA. The beginning of SO-TDMA's increase at 10 NM–12 NM matches the fact that two nodes further apart than 20 NM are likely unable to desynchronize their transmissions. Thus nodes in the middle between them suffer from HTP-type interference. A comparison for LAMA at different topologies (Fig. 7) shows that an increased node density mainly results in a prediction error curve shifted towards lower node distances.

4.4 Distance of Senders and Interferers

To visualize the effectiveness in avoiding collisions we measured the geographical distance of the sender to nearest simultaneously transmitting node for each transmission. Small distances to the next transmitting node are an indication for packet collisions while large distances indicate poor spatial reuse and therefore a waste of channel capacity. The cumulative distributions for LAMA @ $L = \{50, 60\}$ NM as well as SO-TDMA in a 400 nodes random topology are given in Fig. 8. The measurements where recorded over a time of ≈ 14 min and a total of $2.4 \cdot 10^5$ (LAMA, $L = 50$ NM) / $1.9 \cdot 10^5$ (LAMA, $L = 60$ NM) / $1.7 \cdot 10^5$ (SO-TDMA) transmissions have occurred in total. The corresponding distributions in case of LAMA are narrower than in case of SO-TDMA; 95% of the distance samples fall in 28 NM–55 NM ($L = 50$ NM) and 28 NM–64 NM ($L = 60$ NM) respectively. 55% of SO-TDMA's transmissions on the other hand where closer than 28 NM to the next sender producing both primary and HTP-type secondary interference, whereas either variant of LAMA scheduled only 2.5% of the transmissions within that distance range. This shows that even though LAMA was able to schedule more transmissions in total in the same time,

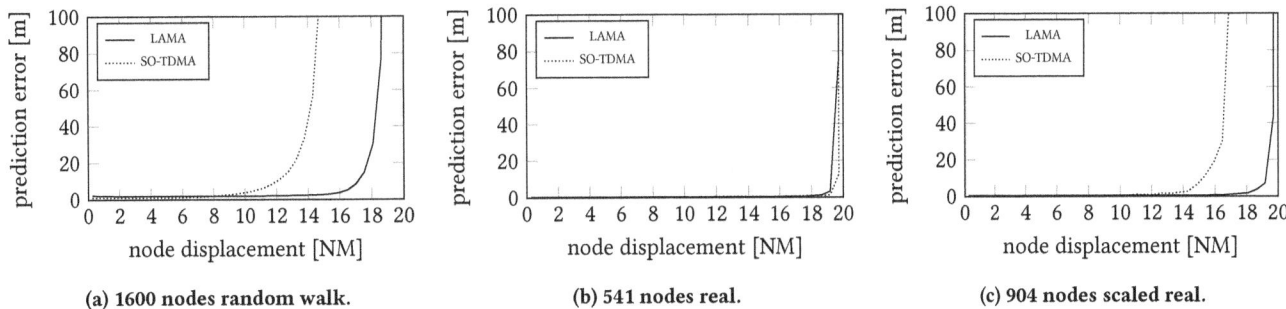

(a) 1600 nodes random walk.

(b) 541 nodes real.

(c) 904 nodes scaled real.

Figure 6: Prediction error median as a function of node distance for LAMA and SO-TDMA in (a) a 1600 nodes random walk topology, (b) a real topology and (c) a scaled real topology. Error bars are omitted to avoid visual clutter.

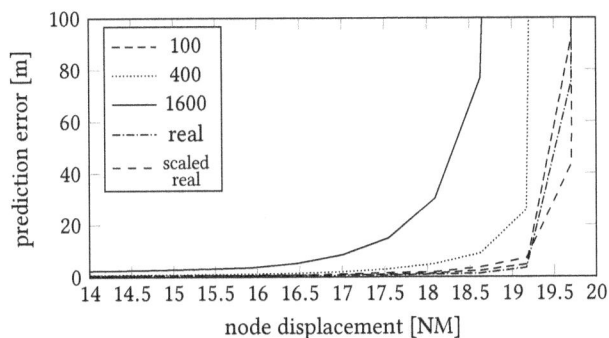

Figure 7: Prediction error median as a function of node distance for LAMA in different random walk topologies as well as real and scaled real topology.

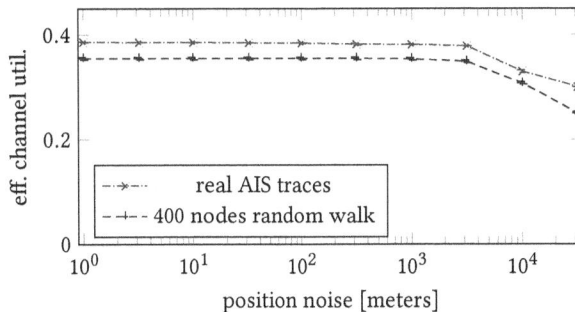

Figure 9: Average ECU achieved by LAMA with $L = 40\,\mathrm{NM}$ depending on emulated node localization error. Error bars depict standard error measured in 10 runs.

4.5 Effect of Erroneous (self-)Localization

So far we assumed perfect knowledge of each node's own position by means of a radionavigation device even though, e. g., for GPS positional errors of 1 m–20 m are not uncommon [19]. To quantify the effect of this self-localization error we carried out a series of simulations with noisy position information: each time a LAMA device queries its node's position, it obtains the true position shifted by a pseudorandom noise vector. The noise vector's direction is drawn uniformly at random; the magnitude is the absolute value of a normally distributed variable with mean 0 and standard deviation A. The resulting average ECU for noise amplitudes $A \in [1\,\mathrm{m}, 32\,\mathrm{km}]$ for $L = 40\,\mathrm{NM} \approx 74\,\mathrm{km}$ is show in Fig. 9. No significant effect is observable for realistic localization errors smaller than 1 km.

5 CONCLUSION

In this publication we proposed the idea of LAMA, a radically new approach for a contention-free TDMA MAC protocol that efficiently achieves two-hop collision avoidance with only a small constant overhead per packet. LAMA is specifically well suited to the use case of transponder systems which require both short message sizes and high robustness with respect to topology changes. By combining a deterministic pseudo-random location-based slot assignment that is hard-coded into the protocol with a highly robust local arbitration mechanism we completely circumvent the necessity for two-hop state broadcasting. This distinguishes our approach from

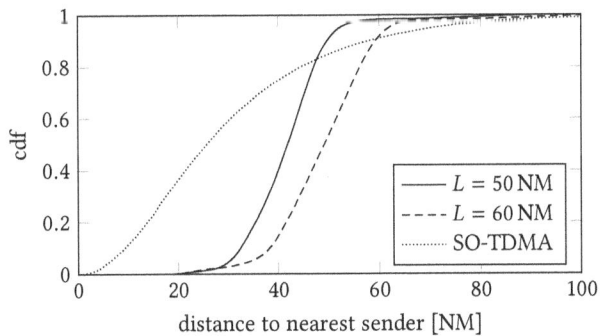

Figure 8: Cumulative distribution of the distance of each transmitting node to the nearest simultaneously transmitting node in a 400 nodes random topology.

it performed dramatically better in avoiding simultaneous transmissions of nearby nodes. As L represents the scale of spatial reuse, a distance slightly greater than twice the achievable or desired maximum transmission range seems appropriate.

contention-based or contention-free MAC protocols known so far. The pledge of any state-forwarding makes our protocol inherently scalable with respect to the number of neighbor nodes as well as with respect to the total network size and diameter.

In our evaluation, we demonstrated LAMA's effectiveness to achieve high channel utilization and effective collision avoidance in synthetic random scenarios as well as for real-world vessel movement trajectories. Compared to SO-TDMA which is the MAC protocol of the AIS, our protocol has shown to be superior in terms of position prediction accuracy as well as all other metrics considered.

ACKNOWLEDGMENTS

This work was supported by the German Research Foundation (DFG) under grant number SCHE 1649/7-1.

REFERENCES

[1] A. Bazzi, B. Masini, A. Zanella, and I. Thibault. On the performance of IEEE 802.11p and LTE-v2v for the cooperative awareness of connected vehicles. *IEEE Trans. Veh. Technol.*, 66(11), Nov. 2017.

[2] K. Bilstrup, E. Uhlemann, E. Strom, and U. Bilstrup. Evaluation of the IEEE 802.11p MAC method for vehicle-to-vehicle communication. In *VTC '08-Fall*, Sept. 2008.

[3] F. De Rango, A. Perrotta, and S. Ombres. A energy evaluation of E-TDMA vs IEEE 802.11 in wireless ad hoc networks. In *SPECTS '10*, July 2010.

[4] European Telecommunications Standards Institute. Intelligent Transport Systems (ITS); Vehicular Communications; Basic Set of Applications; Part 2: Specification of Cooperative Awareness Basic Service, Apr. 2010.

[5] Federal Aviation Administration. Automatic dependent surveillance—broadcast (ADS–B) out performance requirements to support air traffic control (ATC) service; final rule, May 28, 2010. 14 CFR Part 91.

[6] H. Füßler, J. Widmer, M. Käsemann, M. Mauve, and H. Hartenstein. Contention-based forwarding for mobile ad hoc networks. *Ad Hoc Networks*, 1(4), Nov. 1, 2003.

[7] S. Gowrishankar, T. Basavaraju, and S. Sarkar. Effect of random mobility models pattern in mobile ad hoc networks. *IJCSNS*, 7(6), 2007.

[8] Z. Haas and J. Deng. Dual busy tone multiple access (DBTMA)-a multiple access control scheme for ad hoc networks. *IEEE Trans. Commun.*, 50(6), June 2002.

[9] IEEE P1609.4 standard for wireless access in vehicular environments (WAVE)-multi-channel operation. draft standard ed. 2006.

[10] X. Jiang and D. Du. PTMAC: a prediction-based TDMA MAC protocol for reducing packet collisions in VANET. *IEEE Trans. Veh. Technol.*, 65(11), Nov. 2016.

[11] F. Klingler, R. Cohen, C. Sommer, and F. Dressler. Bloom hopping: bloom filter based 2-hop neighbor management in VANETs. *IEEE Trans. Mobile Comput.*, 18(3), Mar. 2019.

[12] J. Pathmasuntharam, J. Jurianto, P.-Y. Kong, Y. Ge, M. Zhou, and R. Miura. High speed maritime ship-to-ship/shore mesh networks. In *ITST '07*, June 2007.

[13] A. Rajandekar and B. Sikdar. A survey of MAC layer issues and protocols for machine-to-machine communications. *IEEE Internet Things J.*, 2(2), Apr. 2015.

[14] Recommendation ITU-R M.1371-5: Technical characteristics for an automatic identification system using time division multiple access in the VHF maritime mobile frequency band. Technical report, Feb. 2014.

[15] G. Riley and T. Henderson. The ns-3 Network Simulator. In *Modeling and tools for network simulation*. Springer, 2010.

[16] M. Salajegheh, H. Soroush, and A. Kalis. HYMAC: hybrid TDMA/FDMA medium access control protocol for wireless sensor networks. In *PIMRC '07*, Sept. 2007.

[17] I. Timmins and S. O'Young. Marine communications channel modeling using the finite-difference time domain method. *IEEE Trans. Veh. Technol.*, 58(6), July 2009.

[18] V. Toldov, L. Clavier, and N. Mitton. Multi-channel distributed MAC protocol for WSN-based wildlife monitoring. In *WiMob '18*, Oct. 2018.

[19] M. Wing, A. Eklund, and L. Kellogg. Consumer-grade global positioning system (GPS) accuracy and reliability. *Journal of Forestry*, 103(4), June 1, 2005.

[20] C. Young. USAP: a unifying dynamic distributed multichannel TDMA slot assignment protocol. In *MILCOM '96*, Oct. 1996.

[21] C. Zhu and M. Corson. A five-phase reservation protocol (FPRP) for mobile ad hoc networks. *Wireless Networks*, 7(4), July 1, 2001.

[22] C. Zhu and M. Corson. An evolutionary-TDMA scheduling protocol (E-TDMA) for mobile ad hoc networks, University of Maryland, 1998.

[23] URL: ftp://ftp.ais.dk/ais_data/dk_csv_jun2017.rar (visited on 12/02/2018).

Multi-Access Spreading over Time: MAST

Sami Akın

sami.akin@ikt.uni-hannover.de

Institute of Communications Technology

Leibniz Universität Hannover

Hannover, Germany

Markus Fidler

markus.fidler@ikt.uni-hannover.de

Institute of Communications Technology

Leibniz Universität Hannover

Hannover, Germany

ABSTRACT

In this paper, we consider a multi-access communication channel with many transmitters that randomly enter a channel and send their data to a receiver. The transmitters are not synchronized and the receiver does not send any feedback to the transmitters. We propose a Medium Access Control (MAC) protocol, which we call Multi-Access Spreading over Time (MAST). In this protocol, in order to mitigate the effects of user interference, each transmitter spreads its access over a time frame that is much larger than its encoded and modulated packet size. In order to perform this operation, the transmitters choose a spreading matrix from a set, which is known by all the transmitters and the receiver. We obtain the packet decoding probability analytically under user interference conditions, and substantiate our results with simulations. We finally compare the symbol-error probability performance of our protocol with the one of the Zig-zag protocol, and show that MAST outperforms the Zig-zag protocol under the same spreading conditions in both low and high signal-to-noise ratio regimes.

CCS CONCEPTS

• **Networks** → **Network performance modeling**; • **Computing methodologies** → *Modeling methodologies*.

KEYWORDS

multi-access communication, medium access control, feedback-less communication, access spreading, zig-zag decoding, Aloha

1 INTRODUCTION

Since the proposal of the ALOHA protocol more than four decades ago, data transmission in random multiple access communication settings became one of the research objectives in communication studies. One of the investigation targets is the minimization of user interference on other users. Nevertheless, with changing conditions and advances in emerging technologies, there is still a need for better medium access control (MAC) protocols and transmission methodologies. For instance, increasing network density, steadily growing demand for higher data rates, spectrum scarcity and hidden-node problems may lead to imminent packet collisions

[23]. Likewise, the rise of machine-type communications brings up the necessity to support a massive number of transceivers that become active in an uncoordinated manner, and hence requires the use of coding theory and its tools for designing efficient random access protocols [15]. Moreover, the transmission of data packets without error, or with error as small as possible, is another challenge in device-to-device communications because of the constraint of no-feedback messages [21].

In this paper, we focus on a multi-access channel scenario where many transmitters randomly enter a wireless medium to send their data to a common receiver. One can consider *Internet of things* or *cyber-physical systems* where certain units (transmitters) make certain measurements within certain time periods, and send the collected data to a sink (receiver). We assume that collisions of data packets are inevitable and that the receiver cannot send any feedback to many transmitters. Since there is no information flow from the receiver to the transmitters, the transmitters are non-synchronized, which makes the transmission of data packets with error as small as possible very crucial. In order to mitigate the effects of user interference on decoding performance at the receiver, we introduce a MAC protocol, where each transmitter spreads its access over a time frame longer than its encoded and modulated packet size. Particularly, each transmitter converts its data packets into larger transmission packets by multiplying them with a spreading matrix. We call our protocol Multi-Access Spreading over Time (MAST). MAST is easy to implement at the transmitters and the receiver, and it can support the receiver to decode data in case of collisions involving many packets. Moreover, unlike the Zig-zag decoding protocol, which was introduced by Gollakota *et al.* [7] and studied by many others, the receiver is required to detect only one packet rather than many copies of one packet. Given a desired packet error probability constraint, MAST also supports more transmitters than ALOHA does.

In the sequel, we continue with the related work in Section 1.1. Then, we describe our transmission protocol in Section 2. Specifically, we start with simple examples for a smooth introduction of the protocol in Section 2.1, and then define the spreading matrix in Section 2.2. Subsequently, we achieve analytical performance measures when a single spreading matrix is employed, and substantiate them with numerical demonstrations in Sections 2.3 and 2.4, respectively. We further improve the protocol by employing a set of spreading matrices instead of using a single spreading matrix in Section 3. Subsequently, we compare the performance of MAST with the Zig-zag protocol in Section 4. Finally, we conclude the paper in Section 5.

MSWiM '19, November 25–29, 2019, Miami Beach, FL, USA

© 2019 Association for Computing Machinery.

ACM ISBN 978-1-4503-6904-6/19/11...$15.00

https://doi.org/10.1145/3345768.3355927

1.1 Related Work

There is a growing body of literature about the Zig-zag decoding protocol, which has been introduced in [7] as a solution to combat user interference in asynchronous multi-access channels. The authors showed that the Zig-zag decoding can attain the same throughput as if the colliding packets were a priori scheduled in separate time slots, while causing no change to the 802.11 protocol and introducing no extra overhead when there are no collisions. Considering the Zig-zag decoding as hard-decision belief propagation, the authors in [25] built a soft-decoding technique on top of the existing Zig-zag protocol, which maintains likelihoods and runs in a loopy manner on the factor graph created by the linear equations formed by collided packets. Moreover, taking into account the possible effects of propagation delays on the performance of the Zig-zag protocol, the authors in [27] proposed a distributed random access MAC protocol named Asynchronous Flipped Diversity ALOHA, which combines a flipped diversity transmission scheme and the Zig-zag protocol.

Regarding the performance, the authors in [19] analyzed the performance of the Zig-zag protocol for the case of two receiving nodes with two simultaneous transmitters in an additive white Gaussian noise (AWGN) channel and showed that the expected length of the error burst is less than two symbols. The authors in [20] proposed an iterative Zig-zag decoding protocol to mitigate the error aggregation, and showed that their approach can effectively defeat the error aggregation. Furthermore, the authors in [12] analyzed and simulated the Zig-zag decoding in idealized multi-access channel models, and showed that the Zig-zag decoding can significantly increase the performance levels when compared to ALOHA and Carrier-sense multiple access protocols. More recently, the authors in [24] proved that the Zig-zag protocol introduces lower encoding and decoding complexities than the other existing techniques at the expense of a slight transmission rate loss.

At the same time, there are techniques proposed as an alternative to the Zig-zag decoding. For instance, the authors in [17, 18] introduced static and dynamic assignment schemes to select transmission slots out of available ones in a frame using group divisible (combinatorial) designs. Moreover, the authors in [2] and the ones in [5] proposed the differential overlap decoding and the iterative collision recovery, respectively. Another approach to deal with the adverse results of random access is based on graph codes. The authors in [11] viewed the iterative collision resolution process as message-passing decoding on an appropriately defined Tanner graph, and showed that the well-known solution distribution is optimal and that the resulting throughput efficiency can be arbitrarily close to one. The authors in [14, 16] exploited a bipartite graph representation of the successive interference cancellation process, resembling iterative decoding of generalized low-density parity-check codes over the erasure channel, to optimize the selection probabilities of the component erasure correcting codes through a density evolution analysis. They derived the component codes that approach the capacity bounds. More recently, the authors in [22] developed a multiple access scheme for machine-to-machine communications based on the capacity-approaching analog fountain code to efficiently minimize the access delay.

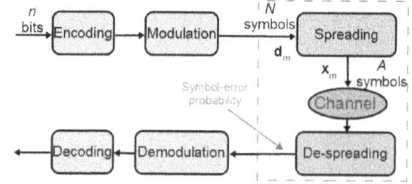

Figure 1: Transmitter block diagram for transmitter m.

2 TRANSMISSION PROTOCOL

We consider a communication scenario, in which many transmitters send data to a receiver. The transmitters are non-synchronized; each transmitter randomly enters the channel and sends its data regardless of the activities of the other transmitters. We assume that, following the reception of each packet, the receiver does not send any acknowledgment to the corresponding transmitter to inform about the status of its packet. Therefore, the transmitters send their packets only once. All the transmitters encode and modulate the same number of bits, n, into one data packet, where a packet is composed of N symbols. Moreover, all the transmitters use the same encoding and modulation techniques. After the composition of each packet, the transmitters spread their packets over time so that the receiver can take advantage of this spreading to decode the data in case of a packet collision. In other words, each transmitter converts an encoded and modulated packet of N symbols into a super packet of A symbols, where $A > N$. The relevant transmitter block diagram is displayed in Figure 1. Specifically, given that $\mathbf{d}_m = [d_{m1}^*, \cdots, d_{mN}^*]^*$ and $\mathbf{x}_m = [x_{m1}^*, \cdots, x_{mA}^*]^*$ are the data packet and the super packet sent by transmitter m, respectively, the spreading process is expressed as follows: $\mathbf{x}_m = \mathbf{G}\mathbf{d}_m$, where $\mathbf{G}$ is the $A \times N$ spreading matrix. Above, $\{*\}$ is the conjugate transpose operator. Notice that when a transmitter enters the channel without spreading its access, its packet takes a space of N symbols in the channel over time. On the other hand, after the spreading process, its packet takes a space of A symbols over time. Therefore, we define the entire process as Multi-Access Spreading over Time and use the term *MAST*. Here, our objective is to decrease the symbol-error probability before the demodulation process as much as possible.

In order to better understand the aforementioned transmission protocol, we first provide a simple example, and then provide a general model definition and substantiate our results with numerical results in the following sub-sections.

2.1 3-Transmitter and 4-Transmitter Collisions

Let us consider the collision cases given in Figure 2 and Figure 3, where transmitter m has $\mathbf{d}_m = [d_{m1}^* \ d_{m2}^* \ d_{m3}^*]^*$ as the 3×1 input vector (data packet) to the spreading process and $\mathbf{x}_m = [x_{m1}^* \cdots x_{m9}^*]^*$ as the 9×1 channel input vector (super packet) for $m \in \{1, 2, 3\}$. As one can see, the channel input vector, $\mathbf{x}_m$, is composed of symbols formed by re-ordering and adding the symbols of the input vector, $\mathbf{d}_m$, in a specified pattern. For instance, the first two symbols sent by transmitter m over the channel are

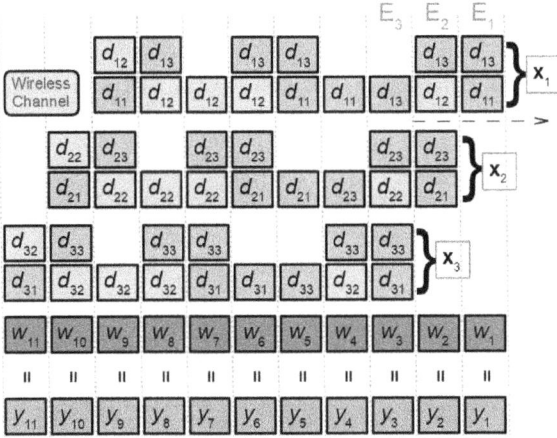

Figure 2: Three packets collide in three entries. E_i: i^{th} entry for $i \in \{1, 2, 3\}$. The dashed arrow indicates the direction.

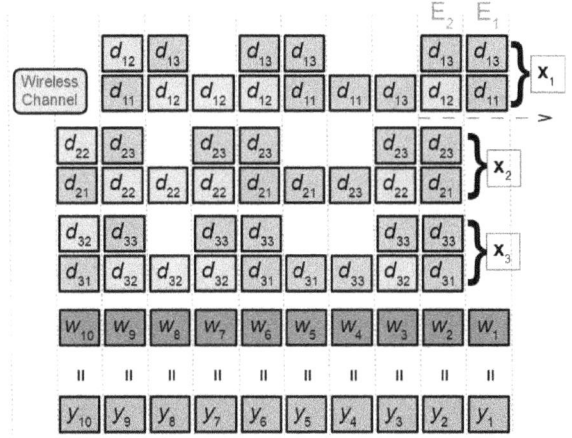

Figure 3: Three packets collide in two entries. E_i: i^{th} entry for $i \in \{1, 2\}$.

$x_{m1} = d_{m1} + d_{m3}$ and $x_{m2} = d_{m2} + d_{m3}$, respectively. The transmitters enter the channel in different time slots[1] and their packets collide partially with each other in Figure 2, while transmitter 2 and transmitter 3 enter the channel in the same time slot and transmitter 1 enters in a different time slot in Figure 3. Here, if one or more transmitters enter the channel in one time slot, we call it an *entry*. Therefore, we have three entries in Figure 2 and two entries in Figure 3. Furthermore, we have y_i as the channel output in the ith time slot, which contains the noise component, w_i, as well.

The channel input-output relation in Figure 2 is written as

$$y = \begin{bmatrix} Gd_1 \\ 0_{2\times 1} \end{bmatrix} + \begin{bmatrix} 0_{1\times 1} \\ Gd_2 \\ 0_{1\times 1} \end{bmatrix} + \begin{bmatrix} 0_{2\times 1} \\ Gd_3 \end{bmatrix} + w = Hd + w, \quad (1)$$

where $\mathbf{d} = [\mathbf{d}_1^* \, \mathbf{d}_2^* \, \mathbf{d}_3^*]^*$ is the 9×1 input vector, $\mathbf{y} = [y_1^* \, \cdots \, y_{11}^*]^*$ is the 11×1 received vector, and

$$H = \begin{bmatrix} 0_{0\times 3} & 0_{1\times 3} & 0_{2\times 3} \\ G & G & G \\ 0_{2\times 3} & 0_{1\times 3} & 0_{0\times 3} \end{bmatrix} \quad (2)$$

is the 11×9 channel matrix. Above, $0_{a\times b}$ is the $a \times b$ zero matrix, and the spreading matrix for this specific example is

$$G = \begin{bmatrix} 1 & 1 & 1 & 0 & 1 & 1 & 0 & 1 & 0 \\ 0 & 1 & 0 & 0 & 0 & 1 & 1 & 1 & 1 \\ 1 & 0 & 0 & 1 & 1 & 0 & 0 & 0 & 1 \end{bmatrix}^\dagger, \quad (3)$$

where $\{\dagger\}$ is the transpose operator. Furthermore, $\mathbf{w} = [w_1^* \, \cdots \, w_R^*]^*$ is the noise vector with zero-mean, and independent and identically distributed samples. While $\mathbf{G}$ is a fixed matrix throughout the entire data transmission process, the channel matrix $\mathbf{H}$ is random and changes element-wise and in size depending on the time slots in which the transmitters enter the channel. Now, re-ordering (1) as

$$(H^*H)^{-1}H^*y = d + (H^*H)^{-1}H^*w, \quad (4)$$

we can state that if the rank of $\mathbf{H}$ is 9 and $\mathbf{H}^*\mathbf{H}$ is invertible, and if the transmission power is relatively large with respect to the noise power, the receiver can possibly decode[2,3] all the data. Principally, given $\mathbf{G}$ in (3), the receiver can decode all the data in case of a collision of 3 packets or less with any form of $\mathbf{H}$ as long as the transmitters enter the channel in different time slots.

As for the case in Figure 3, one can see that forming the channel input as $\mathbf{d} = [\mathbf{d}_1^* \, \mathbf{d}_2^* \, \mathbf{d}_3^*]^*$ will not help the receiver obtain the messages, because the channel matrix will be

$$H = \begin{bmatrix} G & 0_{1\times 3} & 0_{1\times 3} \\ 0_{1\times 3} & G & G \end{bmatrix}, \quad (5)$$

which has rank less than 9. On the other hand, we can re-define the input as $\mathbf{d} = [\mathbf{d}_1^*, \mathbf{d}_2^* + \mathbf{d}_3^*]^*$, which is a 6×1 vector, and the channel matrix as

$$H = \begin{bmatrix} G & 0_{1\times 3} \\ 0_{1\times 3} & G \end{bmatrix}, \quad (6)$$

where $\mathbf{H}$ is a 10×6 matrix with rank 6. Hence, after a successful decoding, the receiver obtains $\mathbf{d}_1$ and $\mathbf{d}_2 + \mathbf{d}_3$. However, the $\mathbf{d}_2$-$\mathbf{d}_3$ pair has more than one solution. Basically, in case more than one user enters the channel in the same time slot, the receiver, being able to detect these simultaneous entries, can treat them as one packet during the decoding process and discard them after the decoding process. Similarly, let us consider the case given in Figure 4, where 4 packets from four different users collide, and two of them enter the channel in the same time slot. In this case, the receiver can obtain packets $\mathbf{d}_1$ and $\mathbf{d}_4$, but not $\mathbf{d}_2$ and $\mathbf{d}_3$. Here, we define the channel input as $\mathbf{d} = [\mathbf{d}_1^*, \mathbf{d}_2^* + \mathbf{d}_3^*, \mathbf{d}_4^*]^*$, which is a 9×1 vector, and the channel matrix as given in (2). Specifically, the receiver obtains $\mathbf{d}_1$, $\mathbf{d}_2 + \mathbf{d}_3$ and $\mathbf{d}_4$, and discards $\mathbf{d}_2 + \mathbf{d}_3$ because there is no

---

[1]One time *slot* is equal to one signal sampling or symbol period. We assume that relative delay and phase offsets of each user in one time slot are estimated at the receiver by employing pilot symbols [19].

[2]Since we focus on interference management in the MAC layer rather than the effects of packet detection and noise on system performance in the physical layer, we assume that the receiver can detect all the collisions correctly, and we keep the noise parameter out of our analysis unless otherwise needed, and assume that the signal-to-noise ratio is high enough to consider the noise negligible. However, we employ the noise parameter in our simulations in low signal-to-noise ratio regimes. As for the detection, we refer interested readers to [1, 6, 8, 26] and references therein.

[3]One can consider (4) as least squares-based zero forcing.

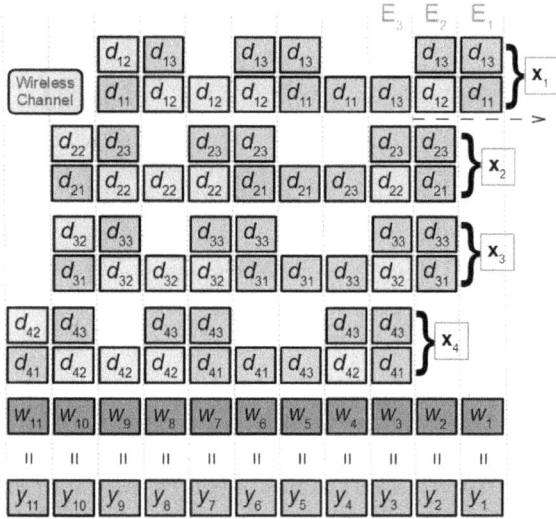

Figure 4: Four packets collide in three entries. E_i: i^{th} **entry for** $i \in \{1, 2, 3\}$.

single solution for the $\mathbf{d}_2$-$\mathbf{d}_3$ pair. This limitation will be resolved in Section 3.

2.2 Spreading Matrix

Given $\mathbf{G}$ in (3), as long as the number of entries is less than or equal to 3 in any collision case with any $\mathbf{H}$, the receiver can decode all the packets that do not enter the channel in the same time slot because the rank of any random $\mathbf{H}$ is 9, 6 and 3 in the case of 3, 2 entries and 1 entry, respectively, and the inverse of any random $\mathbf{H}^*\mathbf{H}$ exists. Herein, apart from the matrix in (3), we can find any other spreading matrix with rank 3 and size A-by-3 for $A \geq 7$, which will provide the receiver the flexibility to decode at most three packets in case of a collision of three or more packets with maximum three different entries. In more detail, the receiver in the aforementioned example can decode a packet from a user, if the packet enters the channel in a collision with three or less entries and shares its entry with no other user.

REMARK 1. *When there is a collision of three entries, the size of $\mathbf{H}$, i.e., the number of rows, randomly changes between $A + 2$ and $3A - 2$. Because the number of rows in $\mathbf{H}$ should be minimum 9 in the given example, we have $A \geq 7$.*

Generalizing the aforementioned scenario, given that we want to establish a multi-access communication protocol, in which the receiver can decode up to Q transmitted packets in a collision case of maximum Q entries, what should the spreading matrix, $\mathbf{G}$, be? In the following, we provide a definition for the spreading matrix that we consider in MAST.

Definition 2.1 (Spreading Matrix). Let $\mathbf{G}$ be an $A \times N$ complex matrix, i.e., $\mathbf{G} \in \mathbb{C}^{A \times N}$, where $A \geq (N - 1)Q + 1$ and $0 < Q \in \mathbb{N}^+$. Then, if any random channel (collision) matrix $\mathbf{H}$ has rank qN in the case of q entries for $q \leq Q$ and $q \in \mathbb{N}^+$, and if the inverse of any $\mathbf{H}^*\mathbf{H}$ exists, we call $\mathbf{G}$ a *spreading matrix*.

REMARK 2. *The Asynchronous Flipped Diversity ALOHA protocol provided in [27] is a special case of MAST as it can be expressed with a spreading matrix; $\mathbf{G} = \left[\mathbf{I}_N \ \widetilde{\mathbf{I}}_N \right]^\dagger$, where $\mathbf{I}_N$ and $\widetilde{\mathbf{I}}_N$ are the $N \times N$ identity and anti-diagonal identity matrices, respectively. $\mathbf{G}$ supports decoding up-to 2 entries.*

2.3 Performance Analysis

We conduct a performance analysis from the perspective of one transmitter entering the channel along with many other transmitters, given a multi-access communication scenario, where every transmitter employs the same encoding and modulation techniques, and the same spreading matrix, $\mathbf{G}$, which is defined in Definition 2.1. We assume that transmitter m enters the channel in the slot at time t_0. Notice that transmitter m spreads its data packet over a frame of A time slots from t_0 to $t_0 + A - 1$. Moreover, we denote the number of transmitters entering the channel in one time slot by random variable K with probability mass function $\Pr(K = k)$. Particularly, the probability that k transmitters enter the channel in the same time slot is $\Pr(K = k)$. We also consider infinitely many transmitters that can possibly become active at any time.

The receiver will fail decoding the packet of transmitter m, when one or more other transmitters enter the channel in time slot t_0 alongside transmitter m, or when transmitter m enters the channel in a collision with more than Q entries. Hence, we have the following proposition regarding the decoding success probability.

PROPOSITION 2.2. *In the aforementioned multi-access scenario, where each transmitter employs the spreading matrix given in Definition 2.1, the decoding success probability is*

$$\Pr \left\{ \begin{array}{c} \text{Successful decoding} \\ \text{probability of a packet} \\ \text{of transmitter } m \\ \text{at the receiver} \end{array} \right\} = \sum_{q=1}^{Q} q\rho^{2A-1} \left(1 - \rho^{A-1} \right)^{q-1}, \quad (7)$$

where $\rho = \Pr(K = 0)$ is the probability that there are zero transmitters entering the channel in one time slot.

Proof: See Appendix A. □

2.4 Numerical Results

We substantiate our analytical results with numerical demonstrations and simulations. Throughout the rest of the paper, unless otherwise stated, we consider the following settings. We assume that the number of transmitters entering the channel in one time slot, K, is Poisson-distributed, i.e., $\Pr(K = k) = \exp(-\lambda)\frac{\lambda^k}{k!}$, where λ is the average number of transmitters that enter the channel in one time slot. We further consider that the symbol rate is $W = 10^6$ *symbols per second.* Hence, the average number of transmitters that enter the channel in one second is $10^6\lambda$, which can be considered as the average number of packets in the channel in one second.

In Figure 5, we plot the average number of transmitters entering the channel in one second as a function of the packet decoding failure probability, i.e., the complement of the probability in (7), for different maximum number of entries to be supported in one collision case, Q. Given any Q, we employ $\mathbf{G}$ with size $A \times N$, and set $A = (N - 1)Q + 1$. Notice that $Q = 1$ refers to the ALOHA protocol. We have the packet size 50 and 100 in the upper and lower figures, respectively, i.e., $N = 50$ and $N = 100$. We compare the simulation results with the analytical results. There is a performance increase with increasing Q; the system can support more transmitters in the channel for a desired packet decoding failure probability. Moreover, the performance gap increases with the decreasing packet decoding failure probability. The reason behind this increase is the fact that the probability of collisions with more entries than the entries that the spreading matrix can support decreases with the increasing spreading size.

We further plot the decoding success probability as a function of the maximum number of entries to be supported, Q, in Figure 6 for different packet sizes, i.e., $N = 50, 75$ and 100. We set the average number of transmitters per second to 1000 and 2000 in the upper and lower figures, respectively. The decoding success probability is high when the packet size is smaller. This is because we have a smaller super packet size when the packet size is smaller, which leads to collisions with fewer entries. Therefore, the probability of decoding failure decreases with the decreasing packet size. However, the average number of bits transmitted reliably without error, i.e., the packet size times the decoding success probability, shows a different tendency. As seen in Figure 7, the reliable transmission performance is better with higher N in certain Q ranges. We display the results in Figure 7 because the transmitters may have to transmit as much data as possible in certain circumstances.

3 TRANSMISSION PROTOCOL WITH A SET OF SPREADING MATRICES

In Section 2, we consider MAST with a fixed spreading matrix, $\mathbf{G}$, i.e., all the transmitters employ the same spreading matrix. Although there is an increase in the performance with the increasing spreading matrix size, i.e., increasing Q, as seen in Figure 5, the receiver is not able to decode the packets of the transmitters that enter the channel in the same time slot even if the number of entries in one collision case is less than the maximum number of entries to be supported. On the other hand, if two or more transmitters send their data packets after spreading their access over time by employing different spreading matrices, the receiver will possibly be able to decode the packets of the transmitters even if they enter the channel in the same time slot. For instance, let us consider the example given in Figure 3, and assume that the transmitters choose a spreading matrix from a defined set, $\mathcal{G}$:

$$\mathcal{G} = \left\{ \underbrace{\begin{bmatrix} 1 & 0 & 1 \\ 1 & 1 & 0 \\ 1 & 0 & 0 \\ 0 & 0 & 1 \\ 1 & 0 & 1 \\ 1 & 1 & 0 \\ 0 & 1 & 0 \\ 1 & 1 & 0 \\ 0 & 1 & 1 \end{bmatrix}}_{\mathbf{G}_1}, \underbrace{\begin{bmatrix} 0 & 1 & 1 \\ 0 & 0 & 1 \\ 1 & 1 & 1 \\ 1 & 0 & 1 \\ 1 & 0 & 1 \\ 0 & 1 & 0 \\ 0 & 0 & 1 \\ 1 & 0 & 1 \\ 1 & 1 & 0 \end{bmatrix}}_{\mathbf{G}_2}, \underbrace{\begin{bmatrix} 0 & 1 & 0 \\ 1 & 1 & 1 \\ 0 & 1 & 0 \\ 1 & 0 & 0 \\ 1 & 0 & 1 \\ 0 & 0 & 0 \\ 0 & 1 & 1 \\ 1 & 1 & 1 \\ 0 & 1 & 1 \end{bmatrix}}_{\mathbf{G}_3} \right\}. \tag{8}$$

Recall that $\mathbf{G}_1$ is given also in (3). Now, let us take into account the example that each transmitter picks one of the three matrices separately, i.e., the transmitters do not choose the same matrix. Particularly, let us assume that transmitter m chooses $\mathbf{G}_m$ for $m \in$

$\{1, 2, 3\}$. Then, we can re-write the channel matrix given in (5) as $\mathbf{H} = \begin{bmatrix} \mathbf{G}_1 & \mathbf{0}_{1\times3} & \mathbf{0}_{1\times3} \\ \mathbf{0}_{1\times3} & \mathbf{G}_2 & \mathbf{G}_3 \end{bmatrix}$, which is 10×9 matrix with rank 9. Now, one can easily see that the inverse of $\mathbf{H}^*\mathbf{H}$ exists and that (1) has one solution. Even if all the transmitters in the same example enter the channel in the same time slot, the receiver will be able to obtain the transmitted symbols correctly as long as the transmitters employ different spreading matrices.

Regarding a scenario with more transmitters than the cardinality of the spreading matrix set, which is 3 in the example, one can design a system in which the transmitters randomly choose a spreading matrix from the set[4]. Now, for instance, given that two transmitters enter the channel in the same time slot, the probability that the transmitters choose the same spreading matrix is $\frac{1}{3}$. Notice that with the increasing cardinality of the given set, the probability that two or more transmitters entering the channel in the same time slot choose the same spreading matrix decreases. We note that we display only three spreading matrices as examples in $\mathcal{G}$; however, one can easily extend the set into a set with more than three matrices by finding the matrices that guarantee that the inverse of $\mathbf{H}^*\mathbf{H}$ exists in any collision case of up-to 3 entries.

As for the packet decoding probability, it is not straightforward to obtain an analytical expression given a set of spreading matrices since we have to consider all of the possible collision cases and take the expectation over all the available spreading matrices in the defined set. Therefore, we rather take advantage of simulation tools and compare the performance levels of the aforementioned protocols, i.e., the protocol with the single spreading matrix given in (3), $\mathbf{G}$, and the protocol with the set of spreading matrices given in (8), $\mathcal{G}$. Regarding high signal-to-noise ratio and considering that the binary-phase shift keying (BPSK) modulation is employed, we plot the symbol-error probability as a function of the average number of transmitters per time slot in Figure 8. The blue solid line is the performance obtained when the transmitters employ only $\mathbf{G}$, and the red dotted line indicates the performance levels obtained after employing $\mathcal{G}$. Clearly, we observe a significant increase in the decoding performance.

Moreover, we employ larger sets, $\mathcal{G}$, and calculate the symbol-error probability when the packet size is 50 and 100. We have composed three different sets for each packet size setting. Specifically, we have employed the following sets:

(1) Set 1 has $M = 20$ matrices with size 1000×50,
(2) Set 2 has $M = 30$ matrices with size 1500×50,
(3) Set 3 has $M = 40$ matrices with size 2000×50,

when $N = 50$, and

(1) Set 1 has $M = 20$ matrices with size 2000×100,
(2) Set 2 has $M = 30$ matrices with size 3000×100,
(3) Set 3 has $M = 40$ matrices with size 4000×100,

when $N = 100$. In order to obtain the aforementioned sets, we find matrices by running exhaustive search methods, with which we can obtain the inverse of $\mathbf{H}^*\mathbf{H}$ in any collision case of up-to M entries[5].

---

[4]In a system where there is no information flow from the receiver to the transmitters, one can embed the spreading matrix set to the transmitters and the receiver during the system initialization process.

[5]In some cases, especially when the data packets are larger, even if the inverse of $\mathbf{H}^*\mathbf{H}$ exists, $\mathbf{H}^*\mathbf{H}$ may be ill-conditioned, and hence amplifies the noise. Here, several regularization techniques, e.g., ridge regression, can be considered at the receiver.

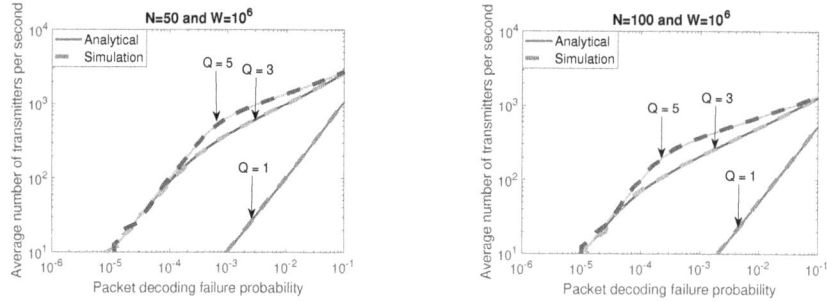

Figure 5: Average number of transmitters per second vs. packet decoding failure probability. The solid and dashed lines indicate the analytical and simulation results, respectively.

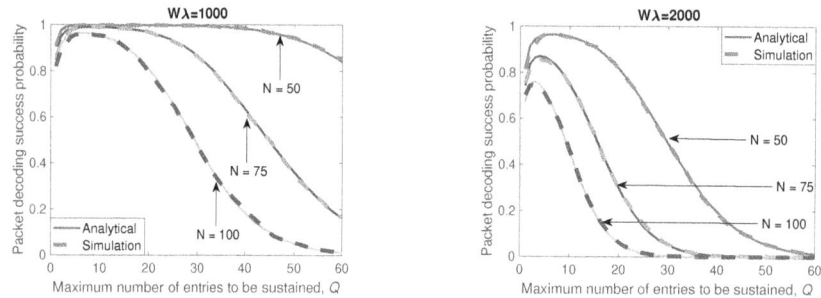

Figure 6: Decoding success probability vs. number of entries to be supported.

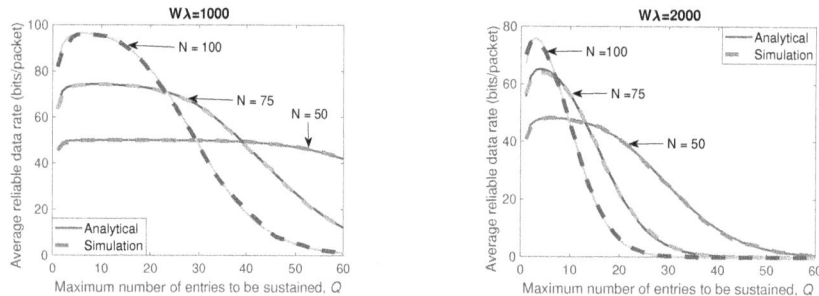

Figure 7: Average reliable data rate vs. number of entries to be supported.

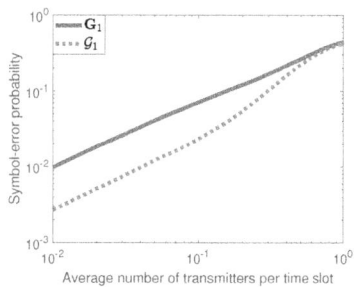

Figure 8: Symbol-error probability vs. average number of transmitters per time slot.

We set the maximum number of entries to be supported to $Q = M$.

We assume that there are infinitely many potential transmitters and that the number of transmitters entering the channel in one time slot is Poisson-distributed. We set the sampling rate to $W = 10^6$ symbols per second. Hence, the average number of transmitters entering the channel in one second is $W\lambda$. We further note that because we employ the BPSK modulation, the symbol-error probability is equal to the uncoded bit error probability after the demodulation process. However, our analysis can easily be extended to scenarios with other modulation techniques.

In Figure 9, we plot the symbol-error probability as a function of the average number of transmitters entering the channel per second. We consider a high signal-to-noise ratio regime; therefore, the noise is negligible. The reason behind this assumption is to understand the effects of user interference on performance levels. We can observe that the decoding performance gets better with the

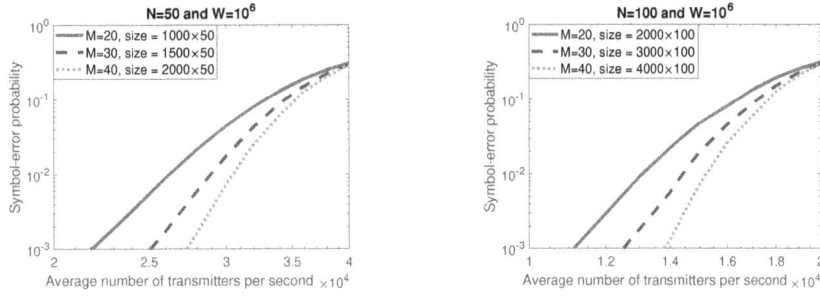

Figure 9: Symbol-error probability vs. average number of transmitters per time second. M is the cardinality of a given set.

increasing cardinality of the sets, and the increasing access spreading (i.e., the increasing spreading matrix size). We also emphasize that, as seen in Figure 9, the symbol-error probability decreases to 10^{-3} when the average number of transmitters is around 2.5×10^4 and 1.25×10^4 given that the packet size is 50 and 100 symbols, respectively, in a channel sampled with rate 10^6 symbols per second. This means that one can easily reach a complete channel utilization with the choice of appropriate error-control coding techniques.

Moving on now to understand the decoding performance in low signal-to-noise ratio regimes, we set the average number of transmitters per second to 3×10^4 and 1.5×10^4 when the packet size is 50 and 100, respectively. Then, we plot the symbol-error probability as a function of the signal-to-noise ratio in Figure 10. We define the signal-to-noise ratio at transmitter m as

$$\text{SNR}_m^{\text{MAST}} = \frac{\mathbb{E}\{||\mathbf{x}_m||^2\}}{N\sigma_w^2} = \frac{\mathbb{E}\{||\mathbf{G}\mathbf{d}_m||^2\}}{N\sigma_w^2}, \qquad (9)$$

where σ_w^2 is the noise variance and $\mathbb{E}\{\cdot\}$ is the expectation operator. Notice in Figure 9 that the symbol-error probability is 0.0445, 0.0178, and 0.0074, when the cardinality of the spreading matrix set is 20, 30, and 40, respectively, given that the packet size is 50 and the average number of transmitters is 3×10^4. Likewise, the symbol-error probability is 0.0479, 0.0194, and 0.0072, when the cardinality of the spreading matrix set is 20, 30, and 40, respectively, given that the packet size is 100 and the average number of transmitters is 1.5×10^4. Specifically as seen in Figure 10, we can observe that with the increasing signal-to-noise ratio, the symbol-error probability decreases to the values that are obtained in Figure 9. Finally, the decoding performance gets better in low signal-to-noise ratio regimes with the increasing cardinality and spreading size.

4 COMPARISON WITH THE ZIG-ZAG PROTOCOL

As far as asynchronous multi-access protocols are concerned, the Zig-zag protocol is one leading technique in the literature that can mitigate the effects of user interference. However, there is an implementation cost following the deployment of the Zig-zag protocol. Specifically, receivers have to detect all the copies of the transmitted packets, or they have to detect as many copies as possible to alleviate user interference. In addition, each copy of a packet necessitates the use of a header and preambles in order to be detected over a channel. On the contrary, MAST spreads a data packet over a larger time frame and sends one copy only;

hence, receivers have to detect only once. Since there is only one big packet, the cost of headers and preambles is decreased as well. Hence, in order to compare MAST with the Zig-zag protocol, we translate the Zig-zag protocol into our framework.

REMARK 3. *In the Zig-zag protocol, we can express the channel input with a spreading matrix. Particularly, we can formulate the spreading matrix as follows:* $\mathbf{G} = \left[\mathbf{I}_N \ \mathbf{0}_{N \times \alpha_1} \ \mathbf{I}_N \ldots \mathbf{0}_{N \times \alpha_{Z-1}} \ \mathbf{I}_N \right]^\dagger$, *where Z is the number of packet repetitions, and α_z for $z \in \{1, \cdots, Z-1\}$ is a random variable, which indicates the time gap between the zth and $(z+1)^{th}$ copies of a packet. The matrix, $\mathbf{G}$, is composed of Z identity matrices and $Z-1$ zero matrices. In addition, the size of $\mathbf{G}$ varies randomly. For more information on the Zig-zag protocol and other repetition-based packet transmissions, we refer interested readers to [3, 4, 7, 9, 10, 13]. We also note that one can easily compose a set in MAST, which has spreading matrices with varying column size although we have sets with fixed-size matrices in our example in Figure 9 and Figure 10.*

We compare the performance levels of MAST and the Zig-zag protocol under the conditions of spreading range and packet size. With spreading range, we refer to the period that the copies of a packet spans over time in the Zig-zag protocol and the access spreading in MAST that we describe in Section 2. As for the Zig-zag protocol, we have two implementations, namely Zig-zag 10 and Zig-zag 20, which refer to the Zig-zag protocol with 10 and 20 packet repetitions, respectively. Each transmitter waits for a random amount of time between the copies of a packet, where the waiting duration is uniformly distributed over a range between one time slot and three times the packet size, i.e., between one time slot and $3 \times N$ time slots. Notice that when a packet of 50 symbols is transmitted in Zig-zag 10 and Zig-zag 20, its copies span a range up-to 1850 and 3850 time slots, respectively, and that when a packet of 100 symbols is transmitted in Zig-zag 10 and Zig-zag 20, its copies span a range up-to 3700 and 7700 time slots, respectively. In the aforementioned MAST protocols, a message spans 1000, 1500 and 2000 time slots when the packet size is 50, and 2000, 3000 and 4000 time slots when the packet size is 100.

In both MAST and the Zig-zag protocol, since we are interested in understanding the system performance associated with asynchronous user interference management, we do not focus on the detection of transmitted packets by the receiver; therefore, we assume that the start and end of data packets in terms of time slots are detected correctly and available at the receiver. We refer interested

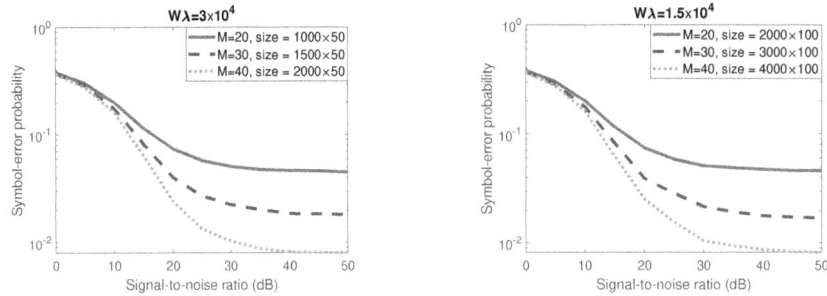

Figure 10: Symbol-error probability vs. signal-to-noise ratio.

readers to [7, Sec. 5] for more information on packet collisions and detections. Moreover, we define the signal-to-noise ratio in the Zig-zag protocol as

$$\text{SNR}_m^{\text{Zig-zag}} = \frac{10\mathbb{E}\{||\mathbf{d}_m||^2\}}{N\sigma_w^2} \text{ and } \text{SNR}_m^{\text{Zig-zag}} = \frac{20\mathbb{E}\{||\mathbf{d}_m||^2\}}{N\sigma_w^2},$$

when the packet repetition is 10 and 20, respectively. Particularly, when we have $\text{SNR}_m^{\text{Zig-zag}} = \text{SNR}_m^{\text{MAST}}$, the amount of energy spent for the transmission of one data packet is same in all the protocols. This is an important constraint in low signal-to-noise ratio regimes in order to perform a fair comparison.

As seen in Figure 11 and Figure 12, the red solid and light blue dashed lines with plus ('+') marker indicate the performance levels when Zig-zag 10 and Zig-zag 20 are employed, respectively. As seen in the figures, the performance of MAST with spreading size 1500 and 2000 outperforms Zig-zag 10 with spreading size 1850 when $N = 50$, and similarly, the performance of MAST with spreading size 3000 and 4000 outperforms Zig-zag 20 with spreading size 3700 when $N = 100$. The performance of Zig-zag 20 is better, but it takes an effort of 20 copies of a packet with a span over a range up-to 3850 and 7700 time slots given $N = 50$ and $N = 100$, respectively. Particularly, the Zig-zag protocol needs to span a packet on a time frame more than MAST needs in order to catch the performance of MAST. Considering that we do not have the preambles, which increase the size of transmitted packets, and the detection errors in these simulations, we expect that the performance of MAST will be better than the performance of the Zig-zag protocol in practice. Note that the transmitters send preambles only once in MAST, while they have to send a group of preambles for each copy in the Zig-zag protocol. Moreover, the receiver has to detect one packet in MAST, whereas it has to detect more than one packet in the Zig-zag protocol.

5 CONCLUSION

We have proposed a MAC protocol in multi-access communication scenarios that we named MAST. Our proposed technique is simple to implement at the transmitter and receiver. We have introduced MAST with simple examples, and then formulated the performance measures. We have performed simulations to substantiate our results. We have shown that MAST can serve more transmitters than ALOHA does for a desired minimum packet decoding failure probability. Our results also indicate that one can easily reach a complete

channel utilization using MAST because the symbol-error probability can be decreased to 10^{-3}. Finally, we have compared the performance of MAST with the Zig-zag protocol, and showed that our protocol outperforms the Zig-zag protocol when we consider the spreading of a message over time in both protocols.

ACKNOWLEDGMENTS

This work was supported by the German Research Foundation (DFG) – FeelMaTyc (FI 1236/6-1).

REFERENCES

[1] Yihenew Dagne Beyene, Riku Jäntti, and Kalle Ruttik. 2017. Random access scheme for sporadic users in 5G. *IEEE Transactions on Wireless Communications* 16, 3 (2017), 1823–1833.
[2] Jingye Cao, Feng Yang, Lianghui Ding, Liang Qian, and Cheng Zhi. 2013. Differential Overlap Decoding: Combating hidden terminals in OFDM systems. In *Wireless Communications and Networking Conference (WCNC)*. IEEE, Shanghai, China, 3732–3736.
[3] Enrico Casini, Riccardo De Gaudenzi, and Oscar Del Rio Herrero. 2007. Contention resolution diversity slotted ALOHA (CRDSA): An enhanced random access schemefor satellite access packet networks. *IEEE Transactions on Wireless Communications* 6, 4 (2007), 1408 – 1419.
[4] Federico Clazzer and Mario Marchese. 2014. Layer 3 throughput analysis for advanced ALOHA protocols. In *IEEE International Communications Conference (ICC)*. IEEE, Sydney, NSW, Australia, 533–538.
[5] Yan Du, Liang Qian, Lianghui Ding, Cheng Zhi, and Feng Yang. 2013. Iterative Collision Recovery for OFDM based WLAN. In *International Conference on Wireless Communications and Signal Processing (WCSP)*. IEEE, Hangzhou, China, 1–6.
[6] Alyson K Fletcher, Sundeep Rangan, and Vivek K Goyal. 2009. A sparsity detection framework for on-off random access channels. In *IEEE International Symposium on Information Theory (ISIT)*. IEEE, Seoul, Korea, 169–173.
[7] Shyamnath Gollakota and Dina Katabi. 2008. Zigzag Decoding: Combating Hidden Terminals in Wireless Networks. In *Proceedings of the ACM SIGCOMM 2008 Conference on Data Communication*. ACM, Seattle, WA, USA, 159–170.
[8] Gabor Hannak, Martin Mayer, Gerald Matz, and Norbert Goertz. 2016. Bayesian QAM demodulation and activity detection for multiuser communication systems. In *IEEE International Communications Conference (ICC)*. IEEE, Kuala Lumpur, Malaysia, 596–601.
[9] Christian Kissling. 2011. Performance enhancements for asynchronous random access protocols over satellite. In *IEEE International Communications Conference (ICC)*. IEEE, Kyoto, Japan, 1–6.
[10] Gianluigi Liva. 2011. Graph-based analysis and optimization of contention resolution diversity slotted ALOHA. *IEEE Transactions on Communications* 59, 2 (2011), 477–487.
[11] Krishna R Narayanan and Henry D Pfister. 2012. Iterative collision resolution for slotted ALOHA: An optimal uncoordinated transmission policy. In *International Symposium on Turbo Codes and Iterative Information Processing (ISTC)*. IEEE, Gothenburg, Sweden, 136–139.
[12] Jeongyeup Paek and Michael J Neely. 2011. Mathematical analysis of throughput bounds in random access with ZIGZAG decoding. *Mobile Networks and Applications* 16, 2 (2011), 255–266.
[13] Enrico Paolini, Gianluigi Liva, and Marco Chiani. 2011. High throughput random access via codes on graphs: Coded slotted ALOHA. In *IEEE International Communications Conference (ICC)*. IEEE, Kyoto, Japan, 1–6.

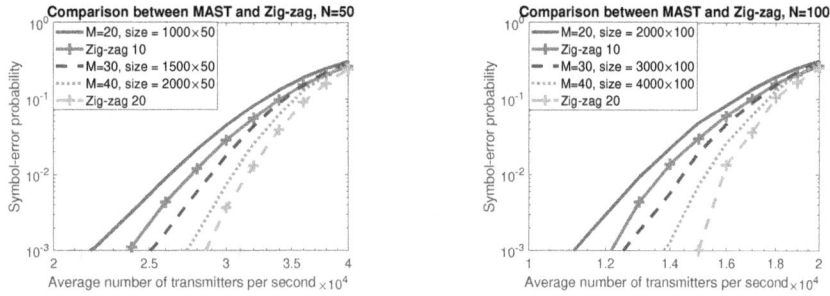

Figure 11: Symbol-error probability vs. average number of transmitters per second.

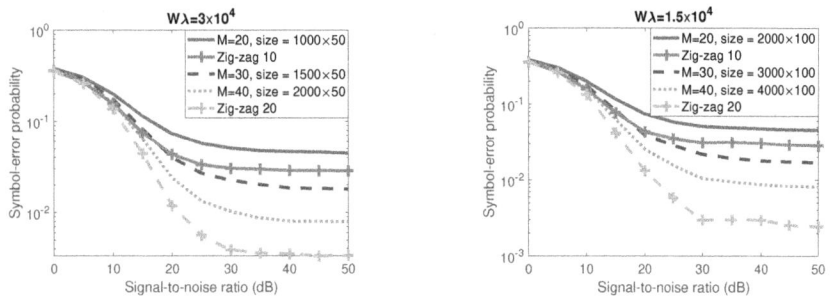

Figure 12: Symbol-error probability vs. signal-to-noise ratio.

[14] Enrico Paolini, Gianluigi Liva, and Marco Chiani. 2015. Coded slotted ALOHA: A graph-based method for uncoordinated multiple access. *IEEE Transactions on Information Theory* 61, 12 (2015), 6815–6832.

[15] Enrico Paolini, Cedomir Stefanovic, Gianluigi Liva, and Petar Popovski. 2015. Coded random access: applying codes on graphs to design random access protocols. *IEEE Communications Magazine* 53, 6 (2015), 144–150.

[16] Enrico Paolini, Cedomir Stefanovic, Gianluigi Liva, and Petar Popovski. 2015. Coded random access: applying codes on graphs to design random access protocols. *IEEE Communications Magazine* 53, 6 (2015), 144–150.

[17] Gino T Peeters, R Bocklandt, and Benny Van Houdt. 2009. Multiple access algorithms without feedback using combinatorial designs. *IEEE Transactions on Communications* 57, 9 (2009), 2724–2733.

[18] Gino T Peeters and Benny Van Houdt. 2010. Design and analysis of multi-carrier multiple access systems without feedback. In *2010 22nd International Teletraffic Congress (ITC 22)*. IEEE, Amsterdam, Netherlands, 1–8.

[19] David Qiu, Frederick J Block, and Everest W Huang. 2010. Analysis and extension of zigzag multiuser detection. In *IEEE Military Communications Conference (MILCOM)*. IEEE, Shanghai, China, 1771–1776.

[20] Md Shahriar Rahman, Yonghui Li, and Branka Vucetic. 2010. An iterative ZigZag decoding for combating collisions in wireless networks. *IEEE Communications Letters* 14, 3 (2010), 242–244.

[21] Mei-Ju Shih, Guan-Yu Lin, and Hung-Yu Wei. 2015. A distributed multi-channel feedbackless MAC protocol for D2D broadcast communications. *IEEE Wireless Communications Letters* 4, 1 (2015), 102–105.

[22] Mahyar Shirvanimoghaddam, Yonghui Li, Mischa Dohler, Branka Vucetic, and Shulan Feng. 2015. Probabilistic rateless multiple access for machine-to-machine communication. *IEEE Transactions on Wireless Communications* 14, 12 (2015), 6815–6826.

[23] Hossein Shokri-Ghadikolaei, Carlo Fischione, Petar Popovski, and Michele Zorzi. 2016. Design aspects of short-range millimeter-wave networks: A MAC layer perspective. *IEEE Network* 30, 3 (2016), 88–96.

[24] Chi Wan Sung and Xueqing Gong. 2014. Combination network coding: Alphabet size and zigzag decoding. In *International Symposium on Information Theory and its Applications (ISITA)*. IEEE, Melbourne, VIC, Australia, 699–703.

[25] Arash Saber Tehrani, Alexandros G Dimakis, and Michael J Neely. 2011. Sigsag: Iterative detection through soft message-passing. *IEEE Journal of Selected Topics in Signal Processing* 5, 8 (2011), 1512–1523.

[26] Qiwei Wang, Guangliang Ren, and Jueying Wu. 2015. A multiuser detection algorithm for random access procedure with the presence of carrier frequency offsets in LTE systems. *IEEE Transactions on Communications* 63, 9 (2015), 3299–3312.

[27] Lei Zheng and Lin Cai. 2015. AFDA: Asynchronous flipped diversity ALOHA for emerging wireless networks with long and heterogeneous delay. *IEEE Transactions on Emerging Topics in Computing* 3, 1 (2015), 64–73.

A PROOF OF PROPOSITION 2.2

We can easily calculate the decoding failure of the packet of transmitter m due to the entries of others at t_0 as

$$\text{Pr}\left\{\begin{array}{l}\text{One or more transmitters other than}\\\text{transmitter } m \text{ enter the channel at } t_0\\\text{given that transmitter } m \text{ is in the channel}\end{array}\right\} = 1 - \underbrace{\text{Pr}(K = 0)}_{\rho}. \quad (10)$$

Notice that when there is another transmitter entering the channel at the time transmitter m enters, it is not important for transmitter m if there are other transmitters entering the channel within the same collision or not. As for the probability that there are q number of entries in the same collision around t_0 but there are zero transmitters entering the channel at time t_0, we have

$$\text{Pr}\left\{\begin{array}{l}q \text{ number of entries in one}\\\text{collision case but zero other}\\\text{transmitters at } t_0\\\text{given that transmitter } m \text{ is}\\\text{in the channel at } t_0\end{array}\right\} = q\rho^{2A-1}\left(1 - \rho^{A-1}\right)^{q-1}. \quad (11)$$

Note that one of the entries in (11) is the entry of transmitter m at t_0, and transmitter m is the only transmitter entering the channel at t_0. In order to obtain (11), we first remark that given a collision case, we know that there are no entries in the first $A - 1$ time slots after the last entry in the collision, and in the last $A - 1$ time slots before the first entry in the collision. As seen in Figure 13, where we have $A = 5$ as an example, there are no entries in the first 4 time slots after the last entry and in the last 4 time slots before the first entry in all three cases. Now, let us follow an induction approach, calculate the probability that there is only one entry, which is the

(a) Transmitter m only

(b) Transmitter m plus one entry (one or more transmitters entering at the same time)

(c) Transmitter m plus two entries (one or more transmitters in each entry)

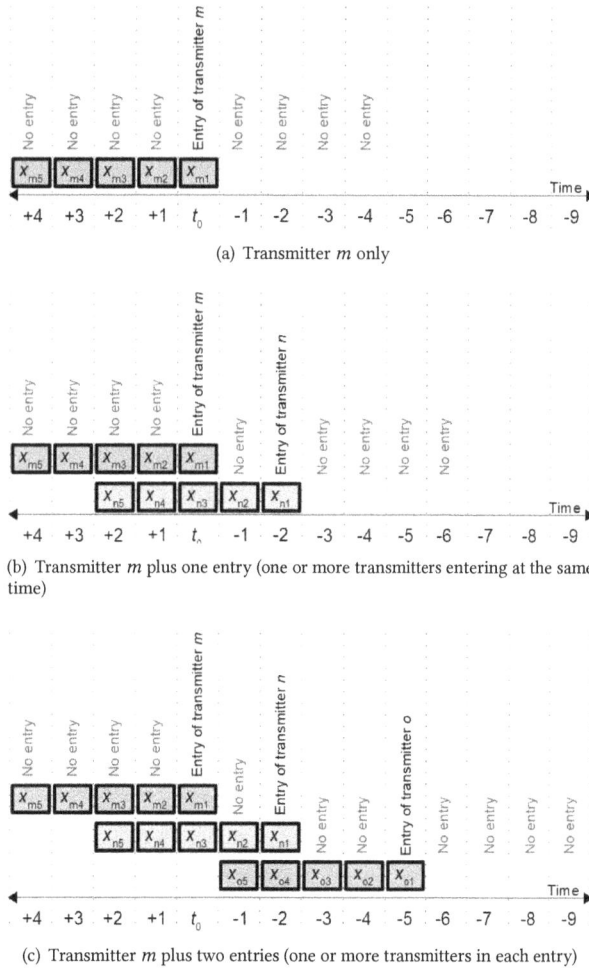

Figure 13: No collision case, i.e., transmitter m is not interfered, and two collision cases with two entries and three entries, respectively.

entry of transmitter m, given that transmitter m enters the channel at t_0, as seen in Figure 13(a). It is easily seen that the probability that transmitter m is the only transmitter in the channel between time instants $t_0 - 4$ and $t_0 + 4$ is equal to the probability that there are no transmitters entering the channel between time instants $t_0 - 4$ and $t_0 + 4$, which is expressed as $\rho^9 = \rho^{2A-1}$. As for the case in Figure 13(b) with two entries, we initially note that transmitter(s) n can enter the channel[6] either before or after transmitter m. However, we can consider the case transmitter n enters the channel before transmitter m, and multiply the probability by two. We also note that we do not consider the case, when both transmitter m and transmitter n enter the channel at t_0 because this case is already included in (10). Now, noting that transmitter n may enter the channel in time slots between $t_0 - 1$ and $t_0 - 4$ (i.e., $t_0 - 1$ and

$t_0 - A + 1$), we can easily calculate the probability that there are two number of entries in one collision case but zero other transmitters at t_0 given that transmitter m enters the channel at t_0 as

$$2\rho^9 \left[(1 - \rho) + (1 - \rho)\rho + (1 - \rho)\rho^2 + (1 - \rho)\rho^3 \right]$$
$$= 2\rho^9 (1 - \rho) \left[1 + \rho + \rho^2 + \rho^3 \right]$$
$$= 2\rho^{2A-1}(1 - \rho) \left[1 + \rho + \rho^2 + \rho^{A-2} \right] = 2\rho^{2A-1}(1 - \rho^{A-1}),$$

where 2 in front of the equation comes from the fact that transmitter n may enter the channel before or after transmitter m. Furthermore, $(1 - \rho)$ refers to the probability that one or more transmitters enter the channel at the same time, and ρ^9 comes from the fact that there are no other transmitters entering the channel at t_0 and that there are no transmitters in the first $A - 1$ time slots after t_0 and the last $A - 1$ time slots before the collision starts. Now, considering Figure 13(c), we can again see that transmitter m may enter the channel first, second or last. Therefore, because all cases are equally likely and have the same probability, we will only consider the case transmitter m enters the channel last. Initially, let us consider that the second transmitter or group of transmitters (i.e., transmitter n) enter the channel at time instant $t_0 - 2$ is given, and then write the probability as

$$\rho^9 \rho (1 - \rho) \left[(1 - \rho) + (1 - \rho)\rho + (1 - \rho)\rho^2 + (1 - \rho)\rho^3 \right]$$
$$= \rho^9 \rho (1 - \rho)(1 - \rho^4),$$

where ρ^9 comes again due to that there are no entries at t_0 other than transmitter m and that there are no transmitters in the first $A - 1$ time slots after t_0 and the last $A - 1$ time slots before the collision starts. Furthermore, $\rho(1 - \rho)$ is due to the position of transmitter n, and the rest is the sum of the probabilities of all the possible positions of transmitter o. Furthermore, considering all the possible positions of transmitter n and generalizing the result, we obtain the probability that there are three number of entries in one collision case but zero other transmitters at t_0 given that transmitter m enters the channel at t_0 as

$$3\rho^9 \left[(1 - \rho) + (1 - \rho)\rho + (1 - \rho)\rho^2 + (1 - \rho)\rho^3 \right] (1 - \rho^4)$$
$$= 3\rho^9 (1 - \rho) \left[1 + \rho + \rho^2 + \rho^3 \right] (1 - \rho^4)$$
$$= 3\rho^9 (1 - \rho^4)^2 = 3\rho^{2A-1}(1 - \rho^{A-1})^2,$$

where 3 in front of the equation comes from the fact that transmitter m may enter the channel first, second or last. Now, generalizing the aforementioned probabilities for q number of entries in one collision case, we obtain the result in (11). Hence, noting the cases the receiver succeeds the decoding of a packet, we reach the result in Proposition 2.2.

---

[6]With transmitter(s) n, we refer to one entry, i.e., one or more transmitters entering the channel in the same time slot. However, we show only one transmitter in the examples in Figure 13.

Benchmarking the Physical Layer of Wireless Cards using Software-Defined Radios

Liangxiao Xin
xlx@bu.edu
Boston University
Boston, MA

Johannes K Becker
jkbecker@bu.edu
Boston University
Boston, MA

Stefan Gvozdenovic
tesla@bu.edu
Boston University
Boston, MA

David Starobinski
staro@bu.edu
Boston University
Boston, MA

ABSTRACT

Many performance characteristics of wireless devices are fundamentally influenced by their vendor-specific physical layer implementation. Yet, characterizing the physical layer behavior of wireless devices usually requires complex testbeds with expensive equipment, making such behavior inaccessible and opaque to the end user. In this work, we propose and implement a new testbed architecture for software-defined radio-based wireless device performance benchmarking. The testbed is capable of accessing and measuring physical layer protocol features of real wireless devices. The testbed further allows tight control of timing events, at a microsecond time granularity. Using the testbed, we measure the receiver sensitivity and signal capture behavior of Wi-Fi devices from different vendors. We identify marked differences in their performance, including a variation of as much as 20 dB in their receiver sensitivity. We further assess the response of the devices to truncated packets and show that this procedure can be employed to fingerprint the devices.

CCS CONCEPTS

• **Networks** → **Network performance analysis**; Mobile and wireless security; *Wireless local area networks*; • **Hardware** → *Analog, mixed-signal and radio frequency test*.

KEYWORDS

Testbed, Wi-Fi, device fingerprinting, signal synthesis, interference, capture effect.

ACM Reference Format:
Liangxiao Xin, Johannes K Becker, Stefan Gvozdenovic, and David Starobinski. 2019. Benchmarking the Physical Layer of Wireless Cards using Software-Defined Radios. In *22nd Int'l ACM Conference on Modeling, Analysis and Simulation of Wireless and Mobile Systems (MSWiM '19), November 25–29, 2019, Miami Beach, FL, USA*. ACM, New York, NY, USA, 8 pages. https://doi.org/10.1145/3345768.3355907

1 INTRODUCTION

With the explosion of wireless device adoption, the problems of Wi-Fi channel congestion and resilience to interference are becoming more acute than ever, especially in densely populated areas. New Wi-Fi specifications such as 802.11ax (Wi-Fi 6) aim to mitigate this problem by supporting existing as well as anticipated additional unlicensed spectra (such as the new 3.5 GHz spectrum [25] and the expanded 6 GHz spectrum [9]) to avoid congestion. However, the large and growing number of legacy Wi-Fi devices means that performance bottlenecks on the given spectrum cannot be avoided. Hence, ensuring high performance despite channel congestion and interference is essential.

Wi-Fi devices are commodity hardware on a product level. Yet, subtle manufacturer-specific physical layer implementations can result in substantial performance differences that are opaque to end users. Benchmarking Wi-Fi performance and investigating behavior resulting from complex real-world situations, such as hidden nodes, currently require expensive physical setups in anechoic chambers under high time synchronization constraints. Specialized test equipment vendors offer wireless device testing equipment consisting of specialized hardware and software modules [15, 17, 23], which have to be integrated by trained specialists to perform as intended, and require considerable capital investment to procure.

To address this problem, we propose in this work a novel testbed architecture for physical layer benchmarking that consists of a simple setup made from cost-effective components. The key novelty of this architecture resides in emulating parts of the channel environment (including interference from other users) within a Software-Defined Radio (SDR)-based toolchain. The testbed reduces the complexity and expense required to conduct high-precision physical layer performance benchmarking, while leveraging the precise time synchronization and parameter control within the SDR to enable consistent and reproducible testing results.

We demonstrate the testbed capabilities by comparing the behavior and performance of Wi-Fi cards from four different manufacturers under precisely controlled physical layer testing conditions. First, we show that the cards exhibit noticeable differences in their receiver sensitivity (i.e., the lowest power level at which they can detect and demodulate RF signals). Next, we subject the devices to precisely time- and power-controlled collisions to assess their response to perturbed signals, thus demonstrating their different signal capture behavior. Finally, we show how device types can be fingerprinted based on chipset-specific implementations. In particular, our results indicate distinct device responses to truncated (non-standard) packets that the testbed allows us to craft.

In summary, this paper makes the following contributions:

(1) We propose an experimental testbed architecture for generating precisely timed traffic on the physical layer, subjecting real network devices to reproducible test conditions. The testbed can generate one or multiple packets at different power levels, emulate wireless interference and signal collisions on SDR hardware, and transmit the resulting composite signal to the device under test (DUT).

(2) We demonstrate key features of the experimental testbed by measuring the devices' sensitivity and packet loss rate under different signal gains, and subjecting real Wi-Fi devices to packet collisions with high-fidelity control of timing and signal-to-interference ratio (SIR) parameters.

(3) We show that it is possible to fingerprint different Wi-Fi devices based on their distinct sensitivity curves and different response to the capture effect and truncated packets.

The rest of this paper is organized as follows. In Section 2, we discuss related work. In Section 3, we describe our testbed architecture and our experimental setup. In Section 4, we discuss the experimental results. Finally, we conclude the paper and discuss future work in Section 5.

2 RELATED WORK

In this section, we provide an overview of previous work related to wireless testbeds and benchmarking, as well as theoretical and experimental analysis of the capture effect in Wi-Fi.

2.1 Benchmarking and Testbeds

Nychis et al. [16] propose an SDR-based platform that achieves precise packet timing by pre-loading a packet from the host to the FPGA and triggering its transmission based on the FPGA main clock on the USRP instead of the host clock (general purpose processor). Subsequent works aiming to satisfy the real-time requirements of wireless protocols follow this "split functionality" approach as well [2, 6], delegating the most real-time constrained functions within the protocol to customized FPGA modules. These workarounds are required to overcome processing, queuing, and bus transfer delays, which can add up to hundreds of microseconds [24]. Our testbed is significantly simpler, since it requires no FPGA modifications. Moreover, overlapping frames are added in software so that their offset is not affected by the host-radio hardware latency.

Park et al. [20] propose a wired testbed where signal of interest and interferers are generated on separate USRPs which are combined with a power combiner. While that testbed uses a sync cable to synchronize the two USRPs, our testbed generates both signals on the same device and therefore the same clock, precluding any frequency offset/drift errors.

In [11], Khorov et al. present a Wi-Fi testbed for investigating the capture effect. The testbed generates two data streams on the application layer, and processes them in parallel USRP transmission chains before sending them out over two antennas, generating a packet collision over-the-air. The offset between the frames is set by assigning each frame a different number and duration of backoff

slots. The two transmitters are synchronized with a common local oscillator. However, our testbed only requires a single transmission chain for multiple colliding packets, and does not require additional synchronization mechanisms.

Our work differs from the related works in the following aspects. First, we provide a cost effective (single USRP) experimental testbed that allows fine control of transmission frame parameters such as power, delay offset between frames, modulation, and frequency channel. As such, we are able to intentionally generate precise collision scenarios of interest instead of relying on a large volume of collision-producing traffic and subsequent filtering of suitable collisions in post-processing [20]. Furthermore, our testbed can easily compare multiple Wi-Fi devices directly, and without requiring calibration. This allows us to reveal differences in manufacturer implementation of the physical layer. Although we showcase the testbed with Wi-Fi devices, this methodology can be applied to devices implementing other protocols. This opens the door for device co-existence testing with multiple protocol stacks easily implemented in GNU Radio, similar to Liu et al. [13].

2.2 Capture Effect

The *capture effect* describes a scenario in which a Wi-Fi receiver receives multiple transmissions at once, and can properly decode the stronger frame despite the signals overlapping. This effect is highly time dependent. The physical layer (PHY) state machine in 802.11 starts by detecting a signal preamble, and – after successfully receiving metadata on the demodulation type and decoding rate of the signal – subsequently decoding the contained symbols into received data. If a stronger signal arrives at just the right time, it may supersede the existing signal on the receiver. Note that overlapping signals can occur in several practical situations, for instance if two nodes transmit (or re-transmit) packets at the same back-off slot time [1] or in a hidden node scenario [21, 31, 32] when two transmitting nodes cannot sense each other.

Traditional analytical models for IEEE 802.11 performance analysis do not take the capture effect into consideration. For instance, Bianchi's Markov chain model [1] and its refined models [10, 14, 22, 28] simply regard a packet collision as a packet loss. The work in [7] analyzes the performance of multi-hop 802.11 networks, under a full capture model (i.e., the stronger signal always captures the channel) and a limited capture model (i.e., the stronger signal captures the channel only if it comes first). In our paper, we show that none of the tested Wi-Fi devices behaves in full accordance with either one of these models.

Other work, such as Chatzimisios et al. [4] and Daneshgaran et al. [5], propose analytical models to calculate packet loss based on the bit error rate (BER). However, those analytical results are only verified in simulation environments and do not consider the additional complexities arising from physical layer implementation in real hardware.

Experimental studies on IEEE 802.11 networks consider the physical layer behavior of Wi-Fi devices. Ware et al. [29] demonstrate that the channel is always captured by the packet having the strongest SIR in hidden node scenarios. This capture behavior can cause unfairness issues within Wi-Fi networks, despite the use of request to send/ clear to send (RTS/CTS). However, the SIR is

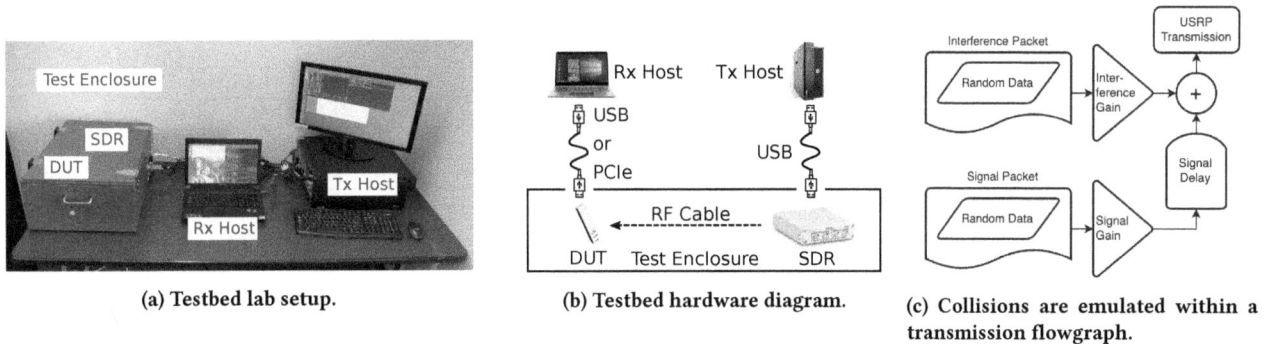

(a) Testbed lab setup.

(b) Testbed hardware diagram.

(c) Collisions are emulated within a transmission flowgraph.

Figure 1: Testbed architecture. The SDR and the device under test (DUT) are placed in a shielded test enclosure and controlled from dedicated hosts on the outside.

the only parameter studied in that work. In this paper, we consider additional parameter such as packet arrival time and different chipsets.

The work by Ganu et al. [8] evaluates the capture effect using the ORBIT indoor wireless testbed [19] in a scenario with no hidden nodes. Their experimental results show that the capture effect significantly reduces throughput fairness: When two stations transmit packets to the same receiver, the transmitter with weaker received signal strength indication (RSSI) has higher packet loss probability and longer backoff delays, resulting in negative impact on its throughput. However, they do not test the capture effect in a hidden node scenario. In this paper, we evaluate the capture effect in situations when the transmitters could be hidden nodes with respect to each other (i.e., there is a significant delay between the starts of overlapping frames). Furthermore, we do not require an expensive and complex setup to generate precisely timed signal collisions.

Lee et al. [12] design a testbed based on Atheros Wi-Fi cards and carry out a measurement study on the capture effect with hidden node scenario in IEEE 802.11a networks. They reveal the conditions under which the capture effect takes place, such as packet arrival timing, signal-to-interference ratio (SIR), and bit rate. Furthermore, they show that the the packet preamble is more vulnerable to interference than the payload. However, this testbed consists of several independent Wi-Fi nodes, acting as sender, interferer, receiver, and sniffers. As a result, time synchronization between the nodes drifts over time, and other parameters like SIR cannot be precisely controlled. Our testbed allows for full control over all relevant parameters while requiring fewer devices and no complex topology and device manipulation in order to obtain precise results.

Finally, all aforementioned papers except [11] focus on evaluating the behavior of a single type of Wi-Fi card (chipset). In contrast, we compare the behaviors of multiple cards and show that they vary significantly.

3 TESTBED AND EXPERIMENTAL SET-UP

3.1 Testbed

The proposed testbed emulates one or multiple transmission signals on a single host and sends the resulting signal with a USRP to real wireless devices, where reception statistics are collected. Thus, the testbed allows us to emulate physical layer signal collisions and

allows fine-grained control of the parameters of the transmitting frames and of the channel, such as gain (attenuation), offset between frames, modulation, and channel frequency.

3.1.1 Hardware. The hardware setup of the testbed involves a transmitting host and a receiving host, and can be set up on a simple lab desk (see Figure 1(a)), whereas other wireless testbeds such as the ORBIT require extremely complex hardware configurations [18].

As shown in Figure 1(b), the transmitter consists of an Ettus USRP B200 SDR board connected to a host PC[1] via USB, and the receiver consists of a separate host PC configured with the appropriate USB- or PCIe-based network card (i.e., the device under test (DUT)). We use a RF cable to connect the USRP to the DUT. The cable has configurable attenuation to emulate signal loss on the transmission path. The SDR and the DUT are placed in a shielded enclosure to eliminate other interference sources.

3.1.2 Software. The software stack of our testbed consists of GNU Radio for signal generation, and the packet analyzer tcpdump [26] for collecting receiver data. On the transmitter side, we periodically generate Wi-Fi packets, using the gr-ieee802-11 library [3]. We emulate channel environment characteristics, such as relative signal strength, packet collision, and interference, directly on the transmitting host.

As shown in Figure 1(c), complex samples of signal and interference packets are summed up before transmission. Their transmission power gain as well as their delay relative to each other can be precisely controlled since they are both generated and added together on a symbol-level in software on the host (i.e., in GNU Radio) and transmitted with a single USRP. This setup ensures time synchronization in a much more straightforward way compared to setups with multiple physical transmitters. The two competing packets (signal of interest and interferer) are sent out with different MAC addresses to allow for easy packet statistics collection on the receiver side.

On the receiver side, a Wi-Fi card under test is connected to a separate host PC to receive Wi-Fi packets from the USRP. The card is set to monitor mode and data is collected via tcpdump. We then

---

[1]Dell Precision Tower 5810 XCTO Base (CPU: Intel Xeon Processor E5-1607 v3 3.10 GHz × 4, RAM: 15.6 GB).

Table 1: Tested Wi-Fi cards.

Make	Model	Interface	Protocols	Chipset
Atheros	AR5B22	Mini PCIe	a/b/g/n	Atheros AR9462
TP-Link	TL-WN722N N150	USB	b/g/n	Atheros AR9271
Panda Wireless	PAU06 300Mbps N	USB	b/g/n	Ralink RT5372
AmazonBasics	Wi-Fi 11N USB Adapter - 300 Mbps	USB	b/g/n	Realtek RTL8192EU

count the number of received signal packets and compare it to the number of packets transmitted to obtain the packet loss statistics under each configuration.

3.2 Experimental Setup

We next describe the experiments performed using the testbed, including experimental setup, parameters, and performance metrics.

3.2.1 Devices under Test (DUTs). Our objective is to benchmark Wi-Fi cards with USB and PCIe-based interfaces, as shown in Table 1. All tested devices are popular, commodity devices using different Wi-Fi chipsets.

3.2.2 Parameters. The experiments take advantage of the high degree of parameter control that the testbed offers. In particular, we control the following parameters:

Delay offset (Δt), defined as the difference between the start time of the signal packet and the start time of the interference packet. Note that if the signal packet starts before the interference packet, the delay offset is negative. In the experiments, the delay offset is varied in steps of 1 μs.

Signal and interference gains, which can be controlled directly within the transmission flowgraph.

Signal-to-interference ratio (SIR), which is the ratio of the strength of the signal packet to the strength of the interference packet in dB. Precise control of the SIR allows for reproducibility in experiments related to packet collisions.

3.2.3 Signal Gain and SIR. In order to achieve desired signal and interference gains and SIR, we adjust the amplitudes of the signal and interferer samples before they are summed up in GNU Radio.

Specifically, a wireless signal s can be represented as a sequence of discrete complex samples, with the nth sample denoted by $s[n]$. We denote the transmission power gain of signal s by G_s. The (normalized) power of signal s is

$$P_s(G_s) = \frac{1}{N} \sum_{n=0}^{N-1} |G_s s[n]|^2. \qquad (1)$$

The parameter G_s allows us to control the gain of the signal. Therefore, converting to dB units, we have

$$P_s(G_s)\,(\text{dB}) = 20 \log_{10}(G_s) + P_{\text{USRP}}, \qquad (2)$$

with the first term in the right hand side representing the *signal gain* (in dB), and the second term representing the transmission power offset of the USRP. We stress that the signal gain G_s is a relative quantity that is not calibrated to a specific output transmission power (i.e., one needs to estimate P_{USRP} if one wishes to know the actual transmission power P_s).

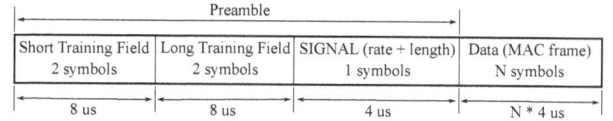

Figure 2: IEEE 802.11a/g packet format.

Note that Equation (2) is only applicable in the linear region of the transmitter's RF power amplifier. A too large value for G_s will eventually saturate the output power P_s to its maximum rated output power. Conversely, a too low value for G_s will flatten the output power at the noise floor.

Next, if we consider a desired signal s and interference signal i, we can express the signal-to-interference ratio (SIR) as

$$\text{SIR} = P_s - P_i = 20 \log_{10}(\frac{G_s}{G_i}), \qquad (3)$$

where P_i is the interference power and G_i is the interference gain. In this paper, we use Equation (3) to calculate the SIR (e.g., setting $G_s = 1.0$ and $G_i = 0.1$ results in a SIR of -20 dB). G_s and G_i are chosen within the linear region of the transmitter's RF power amplifier where Equation (2) holds.

3.2.4 Experiments. In the experiments conducted in this paper, the signal packets consist of 200 byte-long IEEE 802.11g packets transmitted at 6 Mbit/s. The generated packets have payload containing random contents. The results are averaged over a larger number of packets (e.g., 100 or 1000).

Each packet contains both a preamble and a data payload (see Figure 2). Therefore, the duration of each packet is 328 μs, whereby the duration of the preamble is always 20 μs and the duration of the data is 308 μs. The preamble consists of a 2-symbol (or 8 μs) short training field. The following long training field (of the same length) is used for channel estimation, fine frequency offset estimation, and fine symbol timing offset estimation [27]. Finally, the third part of the packet preamble (the SIGNAL field) lasts 4 μs and encodes the packet length and bit rate.

Using this configuration, we conduct the following experiments and measure the corresponding packet loss statistics:

(1) **Receiver sensitivity** experiments measure and compare how devices react to different transmission power levels. We increase the signal gain G_s from -80 dB to 0 dB in steps of 4 dB. At each step, we transmit 1000 packets and record packet loss statistics. The RF cable has a 60 dB attenuation to protect the DUT. In this experiment, no interference packet is added.

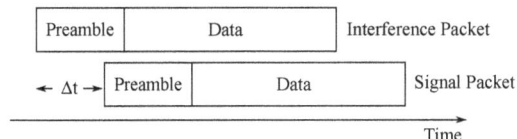

Figure 3: Packet transmissions for the capture effect.

(2) **Capture effect** experiments investigate packet loss during packet transmissions, as illustrated in Figure 3. Each experiment generates two packets: one packet defined as the *signal packet* and another packet defined as the *interference packet*. We craft precisely-timed packet collisions and measure whether the DUT experiences the capture effect, i.e., captures the signal packet despite the presence of an interference packet. We subject the DUTs to a range of colliding transmissions, varying Δt in increments of 1 µs. We transmit 1000 packets for each setting and record packet loss statistics. We further distinguish between the following three cases:

(a) *Preamble capture effect:* The signal packet starts before or during the preamble of the interference packet.

(b) *Body capture effect:* The signal packet starts during the frame (body) of the interference packet.

(c) *Trailer capture effect:* The signal packet starts near the end of the interference packet.

Note that all the packet reception statistics reported in this paper pertain to signal packets. Interference packets are only used for emulating collisions.

(3) **Truncated Packet Fingerprinting** experiments aim to characterize different devices based on their behavior in the presence of a specially crafted collision. We create an interference packet that contains a preamble, but no data afterwards. This truncated packet collides with a regular signal packet. We investigate how long it takes for a device to recover from such a bogus packet, i.e., at what time after the end of bogus packet can a valid packet be received again. We vary the delay offset from −5 µs to 335 µs to capture packet loss statistics across the full length of a signal packet.

4 EXPERIMENTAL RESULTS

In this section, we detail the results of our of experiments for each of the four DUTs listed in Table 1.

4.1 Receiver Sensitivity

In our first experiment, we evaluate DUT performance in terms of their receiver sensitivity. Specifically, we measure the packet loss ratio as a function of the transmission power gain G_s.

Subjecting all DUTs to test packets with varying signal gain G_s, we obtain the results shown in Figure 4. We can clearly identify and distinguish the receiver sensitivity of different devices with great precision (the 95% confidence interval based on 1000 samples is tight (±0.47% around the mean), as indicated by the barely visible colored bands around the chart lines.

Interestingly, the devices exhibit markedly different sensitivity. In particular, the Atheros and TP-Link cards first start picking up packets at −60 dB and −56 dB, respectively, whereas the Panda card

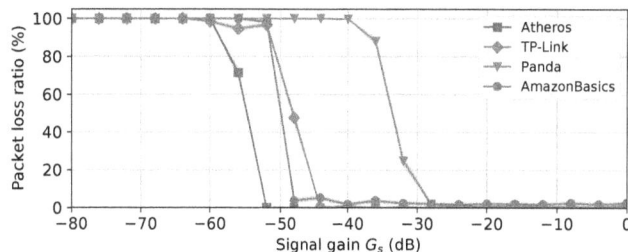

Figure 4: Receiver sensitivity of different Wi-Fi cards depending on the transmission power gain G_s.

only starts picking up packets at −36 dB. Being able to distinguish these differences in receiver sensitivity allows us to compare devices regarding their performance in weak signal scenarios, such as strong attenuation occurring in densely developed areas.

We also note that in the range between −28 dB and 0 dB, packets are reliably picked up by all of the devices. In subsequent experiments involving packet collision, we use signal gains in this range, as we need to ensure that packets would have been received correctly if they were transmitted without overlap.

4.2 Capture Effect

We then apply our testbed to investigate the capture effect occurrence in different Wi-Fi devices. Successful capture in the presence of interference depends on different parameters, such as the SIR, and the delay offset Δt.

4.2.1 SIR. We first determine the power and delay conditions under which the capture effect occurs. We vary the SIR from 0 dB to 36 dB by fixing $G_s = 0$ dB and varying the interfering signal gain from 0 dB to −36 dB in steps of 4 dB. We also vary the delay offset from −1 µs ≤ Δt ≤ 10 µs. For each configuration, we generate 100 packets and measure the packet loss of signal packets. Note that we reduce the number of packets for this experiment due to the high number of different SIR and delay offset combinations examined, this after confirming that the confidence intervals remain acceptable: We indeed observe an average 95%-confidence interval of ±1.3% around the mean across all measurements.

Figure 5 shows the packet loss of signal packets at different SIRs and Δt. This graph shows bright spots for all parameter configurations with reliable reception (low packet loss) of the signal packet and darker spots wherever the packet loss is high.

In Figure 5, we observe that the devices behave quite differently, i.e., they experience the capture effect within different boundary conditions. For example, the TP-Link manages to receive the signal packet only if the SIR is above 4 dB, but, independently of the SIR, only up to a delay of 3 µs. In contrast, the Panda Wireless device requires a higher SIR for successful reception, but is capable of receiving the signal up to 8 µs after the interference packet, while showing a greater variance in its behavior overall.

In general, the data shows that the capture effect requires a certain minimum SIR and gives reason to assume that after a certain Δt, the capture effect does not occur any more – independent of the

(a) Atheros AR5B22   (b) TP-Link TL-WN722N   (c) Panda Wireless PAU06   (d) AmazonBasics Wi-Fi 11N

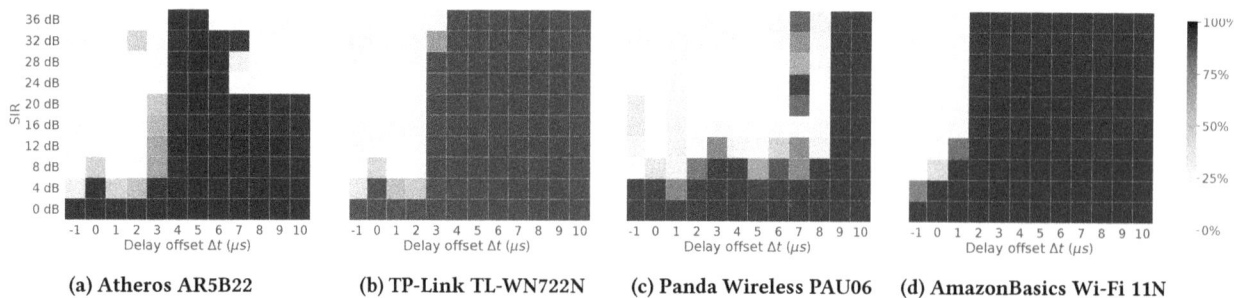

Figure 5: Impact of SIR and packet delay on the capture effect in different Wi-Fi cards. Darker shade means higher packet loss.

SIR. This may be due to the receiver already locking on to a signal during the preamble, based in individual vendor implementation.

The Atheros AR5B22 card is an exception to this observation. In Figure 5(a), we observe that the Atheros card stops capturing new packets – independent of the chosen SIR – at 4 μs, but then resumes capture above a certain SIR threshold. To confirm this finding, we conduct further related experiments in Section 4.2.2.

4.2.2 Delay Offset.
The previous experiments showed that after a certain delay offset, the capture effect does no longer occur in several of the devices. We investigate whether this result remains consistent throughout the whole range of possible delay offsets, i.e., for all possible overlaps between interference and signal packets.

In the following, we fix the signal gain $G_s = 1.0$ and $G_i = 0.1$, such that SIR = 20 dB. At these settings, both packets would be reliably received if they were sent without overlap. We vary the delay offset Δt and transmit 1000 packets for each configuration, collecting packet loss statistics at the receiver. This time, the range of Δt values considered exceeds the length of a single packet transmission (328us). The goal is to find out whether signal capture behavior occurs when a signal packet starts right after an interference packet.

Figure 6(a) shows the capture effect of different cards for low Δt. We observe that each tested device has a characteristic capture behavior, and transitions to 100% packet loss after a certain delay offset. This result indicates that the capture effect occurs only if the delay offset is small, and implies that the receiver locks on to the packet after it receives the first few bits of a packet. Then, receivers typically cannot detect another packet until the packet transmission

ends. This result shows that the delay offset plays a critical role in the packet loss of the signal packets.

Indeed, this behavior remains consistent until the end of the interference packet. However, as shown in Figure 6(b), we can observe that devices again behave differently after receiving an incoming packet. Some devices exhibit the capture effect shortly before the interference packet ends (at 328 μs), while others cannot immediately switch to receive the signal packet after the end of the interference packet. We believe this is again due to different physical layer implementations of the standard in the various chipsets.

Coming back to the Atheros AR9642 chipset, we run additional tests on the Atheros AR5B22 card only, varying the SIR from between 16, 24, and 32 dB SIR, and testing the whole range of Δt from the beginning of the interferer preamble at $\Delta t = 0$ μs until the end of the packet (at $\Delta t = 328$ μs) in steps of 5 μs. Indeed, as shown in Figure 7, capture is possible not only during the whole length of the preamble, but along the full length of the interference packet, if the SIR is strong enough. In other words, the Atheros AR9462 chipset seems to implement body capture above a certain SIR[2]. We note that this behavior can be found in the Atheros AR9462 chipset, but not in the AR9271 chipset of the TP-Link device that we tested.

4.3 Truncated Packet Fingerprinting

Wi-Fi devices implement the physical layer as a state machine, i.e., the receiver has one state to detect the packet preamble and another

---

[2]This confirms a recent finding by Khorov et al. [11], who identified the body capture effect in the similar, but not identical, AR9485.

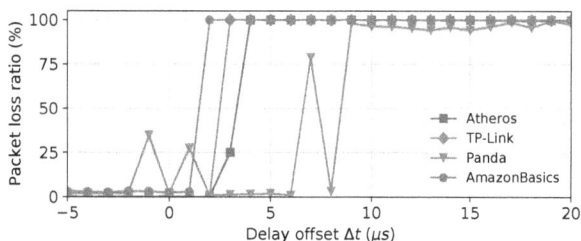

(a) Packet loss ratio at the beginning of an interference packet.

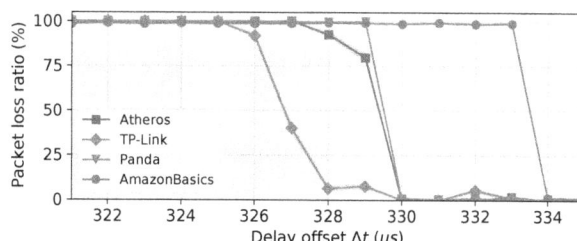

(b) Packet loss ratio at the end of an interference packet.

Figure 6: Packet loss depending on the signal delay offset Δt relative to the beginning of an interference packet at 20 dB SIR. Figure (a) shows packet loss at low Δt, and Figure (b) around the end of the interference packet. Yellow and orange background indicates collision with the preamble and payload of the interference packet, respectively.

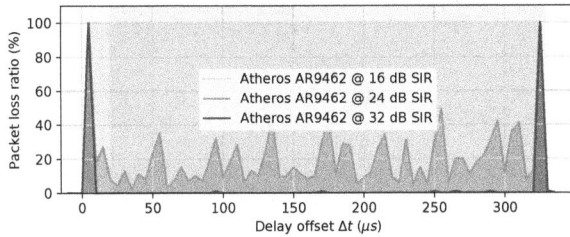

Figure 7: The Atheros AR9462 chipset captures new packets even while it is already receiving a packet body, if the SIR is sufficiently high. The graph shows packet loss for different packet delay offsets and SIR.

state to receive the packet frame [30]. We next investigate whether different devices implement such state machines in different ways by examining their response to certain crafted signals.

The experiment setup is the same as in Section 4.2.2, except that the interference is not a valid Wi-Fi packet this time. Instead, we only transmit a preamble and truncate the packet data (MAC frame). Generally, if the signal packet arrives after the end of the interference preamble (without a frame) and experiences loss, such packet loss is not caused by a collision (as there is no data to collide with). Instead, the reason for the packet loss is that the receiver is in a state that does not allow it to capture a new packet.

Figure 8 depicts the results of this experiment. When $\Delta t \leq 20$ µs, the interference packet collides with the preamble of the truncated packet. The packet loss ratio jumps to 100% after a few microseconds delay offset, in the same chipset-specific way that we observed in the capture effect experiment. This shows that the truncated packet colliding with the preamble of the signal packet results in the same capture behavior as described in the previous section.

Once Δt exceeds 20 µs, the delay offset is such that the signal preamble would collide with the data field of the interference packet. However, since the truncated interference packets have no data field, there is no data to collide with. Interestingly, the behavior of the DUTs in this scenario varies considerably: Whereas after 30 to 50 microseconds the TP-Link and AmazonBasics cards recover to a state in which they can capture new packets, the Atheros card experiences about 50% packet loss for the whole duration of the non-existent interference packet's data, and the Panda card experiences near total packet loss until the nominal end of the expected packet duration. This demonstrates that the tested cards have widely different state machine implementations, especially regarding the transition from the state of packet preamble detection to the state of packet reception and back.

Probing devices with such specially crafted signals allows for physical layer fingerprinting of the devices based on their chipset implementation. Such way of fingerprinting could be used, for instance, as an additional factor in authentication scenarios in which the physical device identity is critical, confirming or rejecting that communication is coming from the desired device without alerting the application layer.

5 CONCLUSION

In this paper, we present an SDR-based testbed that achieves precise parameter control suitable for wireless device testing. We use the testbed to evaluate a range of Wi-Fi cards regarding different performance aspects. In particular, the receiver sensitivity of the cards varies by as much as 20 dB. We also investigate the capture effect on IEEE 802.11 networks by designing experiments that allow us to capture differences emerging on the scale of microseconds. Thanks to the precise parameter control made possible by the testbed, we provide quantitative analysis on the impact of packet arrival time, SIR and manufacturer-specific implementation on the occurrence of the capture effect. Notably, among the four different Wi-Fi cards tested, capture of the preamble varies by as much as 7 µs in terms of the delay offset. The experiments further show that some Wi-Fi cards exhibit body capture effects while others do not, thus cross-validating findings from [11].

Our work shows that it is valuable to compare multiple cards at high temporal resolution, because manufacturers differently implement physical layer features that are not precisely defined in the standard. Thus, one should not assume that implementation characteristics of a specific Wi-Fi card are generally applicable to all Wi-Fi cards. This finding is especially important when developing analytical and simulation models of Wi-Fi networks.

Another interesting finding is that two of the tested Wi-Fi chipsets appear to return to the preamble detection state earlier than the standard defines. This specific feature may potentially have performance benefits in congested networks, allowing them to detect PHY preambles more aggressively.

The experimental results of this paper can further serve to fingerprint the tested devices, especially based on their physical layer responses to truncated interference packets. Since these responses are hardwired into the chipset, the fingerprints may be of interest both as an additional authentication factor, as well as for covert device tracking devices (circumventing higher layer anonymization).

Much additional work can be performed based on the testbed proposed in this paper, as it provides a flexible platform for any kind of wireless experimentation and is not limited to a specific communication protocol. For instance, one could investigate fingerprinting groups of similar devices as compared to fingerprinting individual devices from separate vendors, as done in this work. Aside from further expansion on performance characterization of Wi-Fi cards (including different 802.11 variants), one could expand the scope of this work to investigate low-layer performance, privacy, and security characteristics of other popular wireless protocols, such as Bluetooth. Future work could also involve expanding the testbed to bidirectional communication testing, which opens up a new range of methods, e.g., fingerprinting based on response delays.

ACKNOWLEDGMENTS

This work is funded in part by NSF under grant CNS-1409053.

REFERENCES

[1] Giuseppe Bianchi. 2000. Performance analysis of the IEEE 802.11 distributed coordination function. *IEEE Journal on Selected Areas in Communications* 18, 3 (3 2000), 535–547. https://doi.org/10.1109/49.840210
[2] Bastian Bloessl, Andre Puschmann, Christoph Sommer, and Falko Dressler. 2014. Timings matter. In *Proceedings of the 9th ACM international workshop on Wireless network testbeds, experimental evaluation and characterization - WiNTECH '14.*

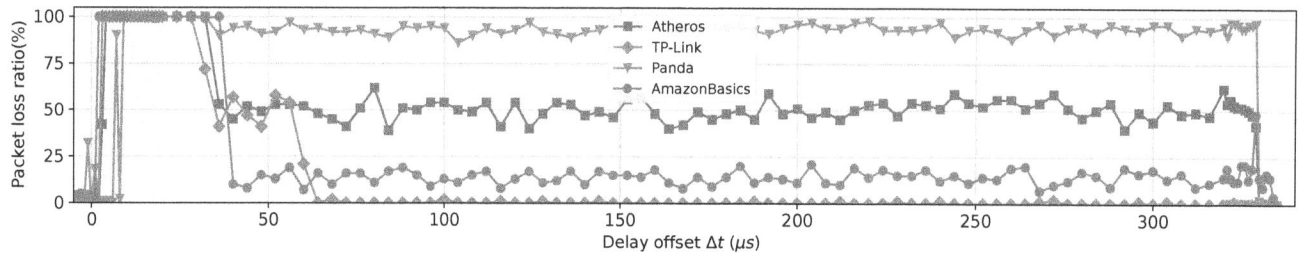

Figure 8: To fingerprint Wi-Fi chipsets, we generate collisions between signal packets and specially crafted truncated packets containing only a preamble, and measure the DUT's packet loss. Note that no actual signal collision occurs after the end of the preamble, i.e., packet loss at $\Delta t \geq 20$ μs is only a result of the receiver's physical layer state machine implementation.

ACM Press, New York, New York, USA, 57–64. https://doi.org/10.1145/2643230.2643240

[3] Bastian Bloessl, Michele Segata, Christoph Sommer, and Falko Dressler. 2013. An IEEE 802.11 a/g/p OFDM Receiver for GNU Radio. In *Proceedings of the second workshop on Software radio implementation forum*. ACM, 9–16.

[4] Periklis Chatzimisios, A.C. Boucouvalas, and Vasileios Vitsas. 2004. Performance analysis of IEEE 802.11 DCF in presence of transmission errors. In *2004 IEEE International Conference on Communications (IEEE Cat. No.04CH37577)*, Vol. 7. IEEE, IEEE, 3854–3858. https://doi.org/10.1109/ICC.2004.1313274

[5] Fred Daneshgaran, Massimiliano Laddomada, Fabio Mesiti, Marina Mondin, and Massimiliano Zanolo. 2008. Saturation throughput analysis of IEEE 802.11 in the presence of non ideal transmission channel and capture effects. *IEEE Transactions on Communications* 56, 7 (7 2008), 1178–1188. https://doi.org/10.1109/TCOMM.2008.060397

[6] Paolo Di Francesco, Seamas McGettrick, Uchenna K Anyanwu, James C. O'Sullivan, Allen B MacKenzie, and Luiz A DaSilva. 2015. A Split MAC Approach for SDR Platforms. *IEEE Trans. Comput.* 64, 4 (4 2015), 912–924. https://doi.org/10.1109/TC.2014.2308197

[7] M. Durvy, O. Dousse, and P. Thiran. 2007. Modeling the 802.11 Protocol Under Different Capture and Sensing Capabilities. In *IEEE INFOCOM 2007 - 26th IEEE International Conference on Computer Communications*. IEEE, 2356–2360. https://doi.org/10.1109/INFCOM.2007.280

[8] Sachin Ganu, Kishore Ramachandran, Marco Gruteser, Ivan Seskar, and Jing Deng. 2006. Methods for restoring MAC layer fairness in IEEE 802.11 networks with physical layer capture. In *Proceedings of the second international workshop on Multi-hop ad hoc networks: from theory to reality - REALMAN '06*. ACM, ACM Press, New York, New York, USA, 7. https://doi.org/10.1145/1132983.1132986

[9] Neil Grace. 2018. FCC Proposes More Spectrum For Unlicensed Use. https://www.fcc.gov/document/fcc-proposes-more-spectrum-unlicensed-use

[10] Zoran Hadzi-Velkov and Boris Spasenovski. 2003. Saturation throughput - delay analysis of IEEE 802.11 DCF in fading channel. In *IEEE International Conference on Communications, 2003. ICC '03.*, Vol. 1. IEEE, IEEE, 121–126. https://doi.org/10.1109/ICC.2003.1204154

[11] Evgeny Khorov, Aleksey Kureev, Ilya Levitsky, and Andrey Lyakhov. 2018. Testbed to Study the Capture Effect: Can We Rely on this Effect in Modern Wi-Fi Networks. In *2018 IEEE International Black Sea Conference on Communications and Networking (BlackSeaCom)*. IEEE, 1–5. https://doi.org/10.1109/BlackSeaCom.2018.8433688

[12] Jeongkeun Lee, Wonho Kim, Sung-Ju Lee, Daehyung Jo, Jiho Ryu, Taekyoung Kwon, and Yanghee Choi. 2007. An experimental study on the capture effect in 802.11a networks. In *Proceedings of the the second ACM international workshop on Wireless network testbeds, experimental evaluation and characterization - WinTECH '07*. ACM, ACM Press, New York, New York, USA, 19. https://doi.org/10.1145/1287767.1287772

[13] Wei Liu, Eli De Poorter, Jeroen Hoebeke, Emmeric Tanghe, Wout Joseph, Pieter Willemen, Michael Mehari, Xianjun Jiao, and Ingrid Moerman. 2017. Assesing the Coexistence of Heterogeneous Wireless Technologies With an SDR-Based Signal Emulator: A Case Study of Wi-Fi and Bluetooth. *IEEE Transactions on Wireless Communications* 16, 3 (2017), 1755–1766. https://doi.org/10.1109/TWC.2017.2654256

[14] David Malone, Ken Duffy, and Doug Leith. 2007. Modeling the 802.11 Distributed Coordination Function in Nonsaturated Heterogeneous Conditions. *IEEE/ACM Transactions on Networking* 15, 1 (2 2007), 159–172. https://doi.org/10.1109/TNET.2006.890136

[15] National Instruments. 2019. Simple Solutions to Complex Problems. http://www.ni.com/en-us/shop.html

[16] George Nychis, Thibaud Hottelier, Zhuocheng Yang, Srinivasan Seshan, and Peter Steenkiste. 2009. Enabling MAC Protocol Implementations on Software-de ned Radios. *NSDI'09 Proceedings of the 6th USENIX symposium on Networked systems design and implementation* (2009), 91–105.

[17] octoScope Inc. 2019. Wireless Personal Testbeds. http://octoscope.com/English/Products/Ordering/index.html

[18] ORBIT Lab. 2016. Hardware. https://www.orbit-lab.org/wiki/Hardware

[19] ORBIT Lab. 2019. Open-Access Research Testbed for Next-Generation Wirless Networks (ORBIT). https://www.orbit-lab.org/

[20] Jin Soo Park, Hyungoo Yoon, and Byung Jun Jang. 2016. SDR-based frequency interference analysis test-bed considering time domain characteristics of inter-ferer. *International Conference on Advanced Communication Technology, ICACT* 2016-March (2016), 517–521. https://doi.org/10.1109/ICACT.2016.7423454

[21] Saikat Ray, David Starobinski, and Jeffrey B. Carruthers. 2005. Performance of wireless networks with hidden nodes: a queuing-theoretic analysis. *Computer Communications* 28, 10 (6 2005), 1179–1192. https://doi.org/10.1016/j.comcom.2004.07.024

[22] J.W. Robinson and T.S. Randhawa. 2004. Saturation Throughput Analysis of IEEE 802.11e Enhanced Distributed Coordination Function. *IEEE Journal on Selected Areas in Communications* 22, 5 (6 2004), 917–928. https://doi.org/10.1109/JSAC.2004.826929

[23] Rohde & Schwarz GmbH. 2019. Test Systems & Accessories. https://www.rohde-schwarz.com/us/products/test-and-measurement/wireless-communications-testers-systems/wireless-communication-testers-systems/test-systems-accessories_86246.html

[24] Thomas Schmid, Oussama Sekkat, and Mani B. Srivastava. 2007. An experimental study of network performance impact of increased latency in software defined radios. (2007), 59. https://doi.org/10.1145/1287767.1287779

[25] Cecilia Sulhoff. 2018. FCC Takes Action To Encourage Increased Investment And Deployment In The 3.5 GHz Band. https://www.fcc.gov/document/fcc-acts-increase-investment-and-deployment-35-ghz-band

[26] TCPDUMP & LIBPCAP. 2019. TCPDUMP & LIBPCAP. https://www.tcpdump.org/

[27] The Mathworks Inc. 2019. WLAN Packet Structure. https://www.mathworks.com/help/wlan/ug/wlan-packet-structure.html#buytqq7-12

[28] Ilenia Tinnirello, Giuseppe Bianchi, and Yang Xiao. 2010. Refinements on IEEE 802.11 Distributed Coordination Function Modeling Approaches. *IEEE Transactions on Vehicular Technology* 59, 3 (3 2010), 1055–1067. https://doi.org/10.1109/TVT.2009.2029118

[29] Christopher Ware, John Judge, Joe Chicharo, and Eryk Dutkiewicz. 2000. Unfairness and capture behaviour in 802.11 adhoc networks. In *2000 IEEE International Conference on Communications. ICC 2000. Global Convergence Through Communications. Conference Record*, Vol. 1. IEEE, IEEE, 159–163. https://doi.org/10.1109/ICC.2000.853084

[30] Liangxiao Xin and David Starobinski. 2018. Cascading Attacks on Wi-Fi Networks with Weak Interferers. In *Proceedings of the 21st ACM International Conference on Modeling, Analysis and Simulation of Wireless and Mobile Systems - MSWIM '18*. ACM Press, New York, New York, USA, 255–258. https://doi.org/10.1145/3242102.3242142

[31] Liangxiao Xin and David Starobinski. 2018. Mitigation of Cascading Denial of Service Attacks on Wi-Fi Networks. In *2018 IEEE Conference on Communications and Network Security (CNS)*. IEEE, Beijing, China, 1–9. https://doi.org/10.1109/CNS.2018.8433124

[32] Liangxiao Xin, David Starobinski, and Guevara Noubir. 2016. Cascading denial of service attacks on Wi-Fi networks. In *2016 IEEE Conference on Communications and Network Security (CNS)*. IEEE, 91–99. https://doi.org/10.1109/CNS.2016.7860474

SEE: Scheduling Early Exit for Mobile DNN Inference during Service Outage

Zizhao Wang
School of Computer Science,
University of Sydney
zwan5430@uni.sydney.edu.au

Wei Bao
School of Computer Science,
University of Sydney
wei.bao@sydney.edu.au

Dong Yuan
School of Electrical and Information
Engineering,
University of Sydney
dong.yuan@sydney.edu.au

Liming Ge
School of Computer Science,
University of Sydney
lige0519@uni.sydney.edu.au

Nguyen H. Tran
School of Computer Science,
University of Sydney
nguyen.tran@sydney.edu.au

Albert Y. Zomaya
School of Computer Science,
University of Sydney
albert.zomaya@sydney.edu.au

ABSTRACT

In recent years, the rapid development of edge computing enables us to process a wide variety of intelligent applications at the edge, such as real-time video analytics. However, edge computing could suffer from service outage caused by the fluctuated wireless connection or congested computing resource. During the service outage, the only choice is to process the deep neural network (DNN) inference at the local mobile devices. The obstacle is that due to the limited resource, it may not be possible to complete inference tasks on time. Inspired by the recently developed *early exit* of DNNs, where we can exit DNN at earlier layers to shorten the inference delay by sacrificing an acceptable level of accuracy, we propose to adopt such mechanism to process inference tasks during the service outage. The challenge is how to obtain the optimal schedule with diverse early exit choices. To this end, we formulate an optimal scheduling problem with the objective to maximize a general overall utility. However, the problem is in the form of integer programming, which cannot be solved by a standard approach. We therefore prove the Ordered Scheduling structure, indicating that a frame arrived earlier must be scheduled earlier. Such structure greatly decreases the searching space for an optimal solution. Then, we propose the Scheduling Early Exit (SEE) algorithm based on dynamic programming, to solve the problem optimally with polynomial computational complexity. Finally, we conduct trace-driven simulations and compare SEE with two benchmarks. The result shows that SEE can outperform the benchmarks by 50.9%.

CCS CONCEPTS

• Networks → **Network performance modeling**.

KEYWORDS

Edge computing; DNN inference; computation offloading; early exit

ACM Reference Format:
Zizhao Wang, Wei Bao, Dong Yuan, Liming Ge, Nguyen H. Tran, and Albert Y. Zomaya. 2019. SEE: Scheduling Early Exit for Mobile DNN Inference during Service Outage. In *22nd Int'l ACM Conference on Modeling, Analysis and Simulation of Wireless and Mobile Systems (MSWiM '19), November 25–29, 2019, Miami Beach, FL, USA*. ACM, New York, NY, USA, 10 pages. https://doi.org/10.1145/3345768.3355917

1 INTRODUCTION

In recent years, we have experienced rapid advances in deep neural networks (DNNs) and DNN-based video applications. Due to the improvement in both the processing capability of smart devices and the accuracy of DNN models, these advances have accelerated a wide range of smart applications. For example, by using well trained DNN models, a pair of augmented reality (AR) glasses can recognize surrounding objects promptly to display contextual labels overlaying actual scenery.

DNN-based applications require strong computing capacity at the mobile devices, which is often unavailable due to limited hardware and energy. An alternative solution is to resort to edge/cloud computing by offloading the inference tasks to the edge/cloud. This solution heavily depends on the reliability of wireless connection and the availability of computing resource. However, it is challenging to maintain a high-speed communication channel and guarantee computing resource anytime and anywhere. Many factors may significantly impact the service and lead to service outage. A list of typical factors is shown in Table 1. For example, in a WiFi network, a handover will take at least 1 second [25] to reconnect to the new access point, which will impact at least 25 frames of a video recognition application with 25 frames per second (fps). A self-driving car with 60 km/h entering a 1 km tunnel will be disconnected for 60 seconds, impacting 1500 frames. The uplink data rate of a 4G cellular network may be as low as 1.2 Mbps [1], which is insufficient to transmit a compressed 480p (around 2.5 Mbps [2]) video.

In the presence of service outage, the only solution is to resort to processing DNN inference tasks at the local mobile device. However, since the computing capability is limited, it may not be able to complete the tasks on time. In order to handle this issue, a question

Factor	Impact
Complicated Wireless Environment	Low data rate or intermittent connection.
No Coverage (e.g., Tunnel)	Disconnection.
Handover	Disconnection.
Congestion at Edge/Cloud Server	No available computing resource.

Table 1: A list of factors causing service outage.

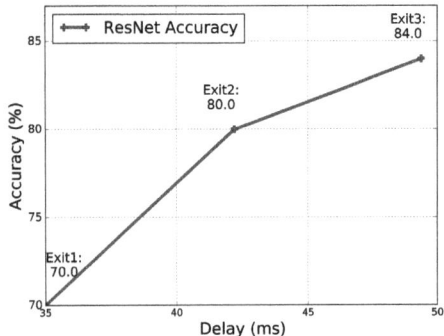

Figure 1: Inference Delay and Accuracy of ResNet.

naturally arises: Can we reduce the processing delay by sacrificing an acceptable degree of accuracy? Thanks to the recently developed DNN variants with *early exits* (e.g., BranchyNet [29]), we can exit a DNN earlier (to save time) with a lower inference accuracy. There are multiple available exit points, providing us a bunch of choices with different accuracy and delay levels.

The decision on *where to exit* for each inference task depends on a variety of factors. One important factor is the frame inter-arrival time in comparison to delays at different exit points. Fig. 1 shows the inference delay vs. accuracy of ResNet [13]. If the frame inter-arrival time is 40 ms (25 fps), then the Exit 1 will lead to a sub-40 ms delay, which is satisfactory if every frame is processed in this way. However, Exit 2 and Exit 3 will introduce delays more than 40 ms, which are not affordable for every frame. From Fig. 1, we observe that we may choose Exit 1 twice and Exit 3 once for every three frames (sub-40ms per frame on average), which is better than choosing Exit 1 only.

In this work, we are motivated to investigate the optimal scheduling of DNN inference with early exits, to maximize the overall utility.[1] We decide *whether* or not to process each frame; If so, we further decide *when* to start and *where* to exit. It is hard to directly solve this optimization problem, as it is in the form of integer programming, with a huge searching space. Instead, we explore one important structure in solving the problem: Referred as the Ordered Scheduling structure, we prove that a frame arrived earlier should also be scheduled earlier. Based on this important structure, we propose a computationally efficient Scheduling Early Exit (SEE) approach to solve the problem optimally, through a dynamic programming approach.

Finally, trace-driven simulation is conducted to demonstrate the effectiveness of SEE. The trace-driven simulation results show that SEE can significantly improve the overall utility. SEE can achieve a

[1] The utility of a frame can be an arbitrary function of its inference accuracy. If we just aim to maximize the average accuracy, it is straightforward to set the utility equal to inference accuracy.

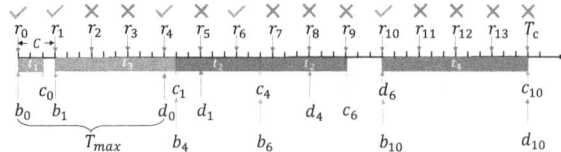

Figure 2: The example of system model. Frames arrive every 3 time units. There are four exit points. $\checkmark$ indicates the frame is processed; $\times$ indicates the frame is not processed.

performance gain of 50.9% and 36.1% compared with two benchmark schemes.

The rest of the paper is organized as follows. In Section 2, we describe the problem formulation. In Section 3, we present the Ordered Scheduling structure. In Sections 4–5, we present our design of SEE and demonstrate its optimality. In Section 6, we present trace-driven simulation to demonstrate the effectiveness of SEE. In Section 7, we discuss the relation between our work and prior works. Finally, conclusions are given in Section 8.

2 PROBLEM FORMULATION

2.1 System Model

We consider a video analytic application, where a sequence of video frames arrive at a mobile device to be processed. As shown in Fig. 2, each frame will be processed by a DNN model to generate the outcome of the inference (e.g., recognition of the video frame). There are multiple exit points that can be employed for the inference, but different exit points lead to different processing delays and quality levels (e.g., recognition accuracy). Our aim is to design an optimal scheduling of frame inference jobs to maximize the overall utility.

We assume that the system is operated in **integer** units of time. Without otherwise specified, all parameters defined in this paper are integers. A single machine will be used to process a sequence of frames (non-preemptive jobs) to maximize the overall utility. Each frame can be processed by a range of exit points with different quality levels. Higher quality will lead to higher utility but also cause longer delay.

We define a sequence of frames, denoted as $\{0, 1, 2, \ldots\}$. The frames arrive with a constant time interval. Let C denote the inter-arrival time. r_j is the arriving time instant of frame j. We have $r_j = j \cdot C$ for the jth frame. Please note that the frame arrives at 0 is referred to as the 0th frame.

Each frame must be completed by its deadline. We define $T_{\max}$ as the maximum tolerated delay of each frame since it arrives. Let $d_j = r_j + T_{\max}$, where d_j is the deadline for frame j.

Each frame can be processed with different exit points that have different delay and utility. We assume that there are L exit points. u_l and t_l, $l = 1, 2, \ldots, L$, denote the utility and delay of the lth exit point. We also assume that if a frame is completed before its deadline, it will bring a full utility u_l. If a frame is not processed or it missed its deadline, it brings zero utility. Without loss of generality, we assume that $t_1 < t_2 < \ldots < t_L$ and $u_1 < u_2 < \ldots < u_L$, i.e., a longer processing effort will lead to a higher utility. In addition, we assume $t_L \leq T_{\max}$. Otherwise, if the processing delay at an exit point is already greater than $T_{\max}$, we can simply ignore this exit point. We further define $\mathcal{L} \triangleq \{1, 2, \ldots, L\}$, $\mathcal{U} \triangleq \{u_1, u_2, \ldots, u_L\}$, and $\mathcal{T} \triangleq \{t_1, t_2, \ldots, t_L\}$. Let $t_{\min} = \min_{l=1,2,\ldots,L}\{t_l\}$ denote the minimum possible inference delay of a frame.

The system is operated from time 0 to time T_c. We aim to maximize the accumulated system utility at T_c. Let $\mathcal{J} = \{0, 1, 2, \ldots, \lfloor\frac{T_c}{C}\rfloor\}$ denote the frames arriving before T_c. We allow frames arriving after T_c but only frames in $\mathcal{J}$ may generate positive utility. If a frame is not completed by T_c, it will not generate utility either.

2.2 Frame Scheduling and Optimization Problem Formulation

Let x_{lj} be a 0-1 variable, indicating whether or not we process the jth frame using exit point l. We have $\sum_{l\in\mathcal{L}} x_{lj} \leq 1$ as we only can choose at most one exit point for the jth frame. We also allow not to process the jth frame. In this case, we have $\sum_{l\in\mathcal{L}} x_{lj} = 0$. For each frame j, we also need to choose a start time of it, which is defined as b_j. Then, its complete time is $c_j = b_j + \sum_{l\in\mathcal{L}} t_l x_{lj}$. Please note that if we do not process it, $\sum_{l\in\mathcal{L}} t_{lj} x_{lj} = 0$ so that the frame is equivalently not processed.

Therefore, we reach the following optimization problem, which will be referred to as OPT

$$\max_{x_{lj}, \forall l\in\mathcal{L}, j\in\mathcal{J}; b_j, \forall j\in\mathcal{J}} \sum_{l\in\mathcal{L}, j\in\mathcal{J}} u_l x_{lj}, \tag{1a}$$

$$\text{s. t. } b_j \geq r_j, \forall j \in \mathcal{J}, \tag{1b}$$

$$b_j + \sum_{l\in\mathcal{L}} t_l x_{lj} \leq \min(d_j, T_c), \tag{1c}$$

$$\sum_{l\in\mathcal{L}} x_{lj} \leq 1, \forall j \in \mathcal{J}, \tag{1d}$$

$$x_{lj} \in \{0, 1\}, \forall l \in \mathcal{L}, j \in \mathcal{J}, \tag{1e}$$

$$b_k \geq b_j + \sum_{l\in\mathcal{L}} t_l x_{lj} \text{ OR} \tag{1f}$$

$$b_k \leq b_j - \sum_{l\in\mathcal{L}} t_l x_{lk}, \forall k, j \in \mathcal{J}, k \neq j.$$

where (1a) is the sum utility; (1b) indicates that the jth frame must be started after its arrival; (1c) indicates that the jth frame must be completed no later than its deadline and T_c; (1d) indicates that the jth frame can be processed by choosing at most one exit point; (1f) indicates that the processing durations of the jth frame and the kth frame are not overlapping.

Problem OPT is in the form of integer programming, which cannot be solved directly using standard methods. In what follows, we first introduce the Ordered Scheduling structure, proving that a frame arrived earlier must be scheduled earlier. Based on the structure, we are able to obtain the optimal structure through a dynamic programming approach.

3 ORDERED SCHEDULING STRUCTURE

THEOREM 1. *An optimal solution to the OPT problem satisfies the following structure: if $j < j'$, $x_{lj} = 1$ for some $l \in \mathcal{L}$, and $x_{l'j'} = 1$ for some $l' \in \mathcal{L}$, then $b_j < b_{j'}$. In other words, if frame j arrives earlier than frame j', and we decide to process both of them, then we should process frame j before frame j'.*

PROOF. As shown in Fig. 3, suppose there is an optimal solution satisfies: $\exists j < j'$, $x_{lj} = 1$ for some $l \in \mathcal{L}$ and $x_{l'j'} = 1$ for some

$l' \in \mathcal{L}$, we have $b_j > b_{j'}$.[2] Then, we aim to find another solution with $b_j < b_{j'}$ leading to an equal utility.

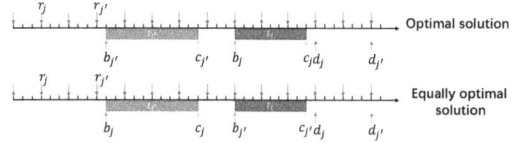

Figure 3: An example to prove Theorem 1.

Because only one frame can be processed at one time and each frame is non-preemptive, we have $b_{j'} < c_{j'} \leq b_j < c_j$, $c_{j'} \leq d_{j'}$, $c_j \leq d_j$, and $d_j < d_{j'}$, as shown in Fig. 3. c_j denotes the completion time of frame j. Frame j is processed by the exit point l and frame j' is processed by the exit point l'. Then, consider an alternative solution to swap the order of frame j and frame j', as well as their exit points. In other words, we process frame j in $[b_{j'}, c_{j'}]$ by the exit point l' and frame j' in $[b_j, c_j]$ by the exit point l but to keep the scheduling of all other frames unchanged. It is straightforward to show that this alternative solution is a feasible solution because $r_j \leq b_{j'} < c_{j'} \leq d_j$ and $r_{j'} \leq b_j < c_j \leq d_{j'}$. In this case, the overall utility is not changed.

Therefore, we reach an equivalent optimal solution that satisfies the condition in Theorem 1. □

The Ordered Scheduling structure plays a significant role to find an optimal solution. If we have already scheduled frame j, all frames before j will not be considered any more. Note that there may still be other optimal solutions that do not follow the Ordered Scheduling structure. However, our objective is to find one optimal solution (following the Ordered Scheduling structure) rather than all optimal solutions.

4 DYNAMIC PROGRAMMING SOLUTION

In this section, we first define an (x, y) tuple to characterize the system state. Then we define possible actions at the state (x, y), the utility of each action on the state, and state transitions. Then, we construct the Bellman formula based on the defined state and action.

4.1 System State

4.1.1 Definition of System State. Let $\mathbf{s} = (x, y)$ denote the system state where x is the current time instant to make a decision and y indicates the *time gap of the next available frame*, which can be defined as follows.

Given that we are at time instant x, *past available frames* are defined as non-processed frames arriving in $[x + t_{\min} - T_{\max}, x]$. In other words, if we start to process a past available frame at x, it could be completed before its deadline. Completed frames are not counted as they do not need to be considered any more.

Given that we are at time instant x, *future available frames* are defined as frames arriving after x.

The joint of *past available frames* and *future available frames* are called *available frames*, and the *earliest available frame* is defined as the earliest arriving frame of available frames. Please note that

---

[2]It is not possible to schedule frame j and j' at the same time, so that $b_j = b_{j'}$ is not possible.

(a) The example of $y \geq 0$ at time x.

(b) The example of $y < 0$ at time x.

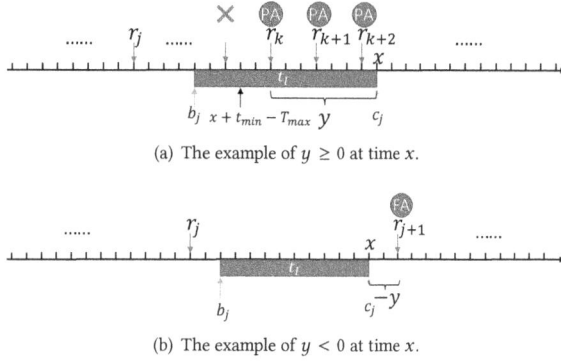

Figure 4: Fig. 4(a) gives an example of *past available frames* **which are the labeled by 'PA' in the figure. In this case, the frame labeled by $\times$ cannot be processed as it will miss its deadline. The time gap between the arriving time of earliest** *past available frame* **and x is labeled as y, where $y \geq 0$. In Fig. 4(b), there exists no available frames between the arriving time of frame j and time x, then frame $j+1$ is the earliest available frame in the future (labeled by 'FA'). Then we have $y = x - r_{j+1}$, which represents the time gap between time x and arriving time of** *earliest future available frame*. **In this case, y is negative.**

there may be no past available frames so that the earliest available frame is equivalent to the next arriving frame.

We define *time gap of the next available frame y* as x minus the arrival time of earliest available frame. If y is non-negative, there exists a frame arrived on or before x, which can be processed at x. If y is negative, all available frames are in the future so that the system has to wait. An example of the aforementioned definitions is shown in Fig. 4.

4.1.2 Insights of System State. We take (x, y) as the state of the system. The reason is as follows. x indicates the time instant that we can make a decision (either a frame is just completed or the system is idle). Each frame is non-preemptive. Whenever a frame is being processed, we have to wait until the frame is completed to make our next decision. y memorizes which frame we can process at x. We can process any frame on or after $x - y$ and we ignore any frames before $x - y$. This is because of the Ordered Scheduling structure (Theorem 1): we can find an optimal scheduling by ignoring unordered schedules. If a frame is processed, we can ignore all frames arriving before it. A single y value is enough to indicate which frames can be processed and which frames can be ignored.

Without the Ordered Scheduling structure, it is not possible to just use a single value to characterize the system state. For example, whenever we want to make a decision at time x, if a frame j has been processed, frame $j-1$ has not been processed, and frame $j-1$ can meet its deadline if we start to process it at x, we cannot exclude the possibility to process frame $j-1$. In this case, we have to memorize whether each previous frame has been processed or not, leading to a much larger state space and much higher computational complexity.

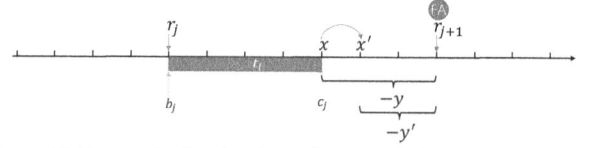

Figure 5: Example for (x, y) evolution under $y < 0$. The system completes frame j at time x, but there is no available frame at time x. Then we should wait for one time unit and the next state is $(x', y') = (x + 1, y + 1)$.

4.2 Evolution of System State

In this subsection, we characterize the possible actions that can be taken given the state is at (x, y). Such characterization will be essential to formulate the Bellman formula to realize a dynamic programming solution.

Let an action $\mathbf{a} = (k, l)$, $k \in \mathcal{J}, l \in \mathcal{L}$ indicate that we take the action to process the kth frame at exit point l. Such an action is defined as an *active action*. We also allow a do-nothing action (i.e., wait), which is denoted as $(0, 0)$. It is referred to as an *inactive action*.

In state $\mathbf{s} = (x, y)$, only a set of actions are allowed, which is defined as the *feasible action set* of $\mathbf{s}$ denoted by $\mathcal{A}(\mathbf{s})$. Let $\mathcal{A}_1(\mathbf{s}) \subset \mathcal{A}(\mathbf{s})$ denote feasible active action set.

Given a system state (x, y) and an action (k, l) taken in this state, let $r((x, y), (k, l))$ denote the resultant system state, and $u((x, y), (k, l))$ denote the utility gained by such action. In what follows, we analyze the state transitions in different cases. By definition, $x \in [0, T_c)$.

4.2.1 $y < 0$ Case. For a state (x, y) where $y < 0$, it means that the next available frame is in the future so that the only possible action is to wait. Therefore, the feasible active action set $\mathcal{A}_1(\mathbf{s}) = \emptyset$ and the feasible action set $\mathcal{A}(\mathbf{s}) = \{(0, 0)\}$. By taking the action $(0, 0)$, the system waits for one unit of time and the state is transited to $(x', y') = (x + 1, y + 1)$, i.e., $r((x, y), (0, 0)) = (x + 1, y + 1)$. Through this action, the utility gained is 0, i.e., $u((x, y), (0, 0)) = 0$. An example is shown in Fig. 5.

4.2.2 $y \geq 0$ Case with an Active Action. If $y \geq 0$, we would have at least one available frames that have already arrived. The earliest past available frame arrived at $x - y$ by definition. In $[x - y, x]$, there may be other past available frame k at time instant $k \cdot C$ where k is any integer in the range of $[\frac{x-y}{C}, \lfloor \frac{x}{C} \rfloor]$, as shown in Fig. 6(a).

Therefore, at (x, y), we can select one of the past available frames to process at a feasible exit point (as long as it can satisfy the deadline).

Suppose that we select the k_0th frame, $k_0 \in [\frac{x-y}{C}, \lfloor \frac{x}{C} \rfloor]$, we have the following three observations.

- Any frame before k_0 will not be processed. This is because of Theorem 1.
- For the k_0th frame, we have to satisfy its deadline requirement. In other words, we can only choose exit point l such that $x + t_l - k_0 C \leq T_{\max}$.
- For the k_0th frame, we need to complete it by T_c, i.e., $x + t_l \leq T_c$. Otherwise, it is not necessary to process this frame.

Therefore, as shown in Fig. 6(b), the active action set under (x, y) satisfies the following condition

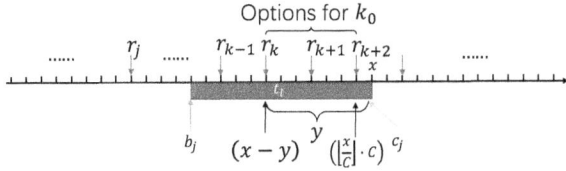

(a) Example for frame k_0 that can be processed at state (x, y) when $y \geq 0$.

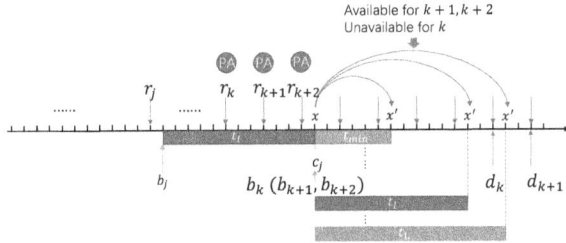

(b) Example of feasible actions at (x, y). At state (x, y), we may process one of the available frames from the past $\{k, k+1, k+2\}$, as marked in the figure. For each available frame, we may process at different exit points. Any actions that will breach the deadline should not be considered. Frame k cannot be processed with t_L in our example since it will breach the deadline. Frame $k+1$, $k+2$ can be processed with t_L.

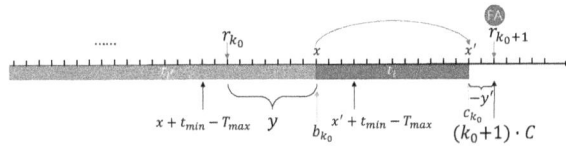

(c) When $y \geq 0$, (x, y) takes an active action then it only has *future available frames* arrived at time $(k_0 + 1) \cdot C$. Then the y' value for the new resultant state (x', y') will be negative.

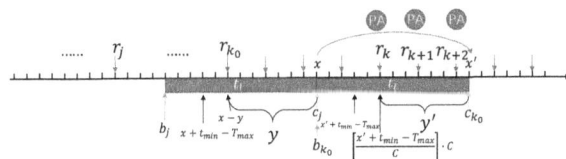

(d) When $y \geq 0$, (x, y) takes an active action to go to state (x', y'). This resultant state (x', y') has *past available frames* which are arrived after $\lceil \frac{x' + t_{min} - T_{max}}{C} \rceil \cdot C$ and before x'.

Figure 6: Examples for (x, y) evolution under $y > 0$.

$$\mathcal{A}_1((x,y)) = \left\{ (k_0, l) \mid k_0 \in \left[\frac{x-y}{C}, \left\lfloor \frac{x}{C} \right\rfloor \right] \text{ and} \right.$$
$$\left. x + t_l - k_0 C \leq T_{max} \text{ and } x + t_l \leq T_c \right\}. \tag{2}$$

Please note that we also allow the inactive action $(0, 0)$ so that $\mathcal{A}((x, y)) = \mathcal{A}_1((x, y)) \cup \{(0, 0)\}$, which will be discussed shortly.

Given that we process frame k_0 with exit point l and (k_0, l) is in the action set, we then need to characterize the state transition as follows.

First, $x' = x + t_l$ as it takes t_l to process the frame. Second, y' involves as follows: (1) The next available frame should be at least $k_0 + 1$, as in Fig. 6(c). (2) If we start to process the next available frame, it is possible to be completed by its deadline. In other words,

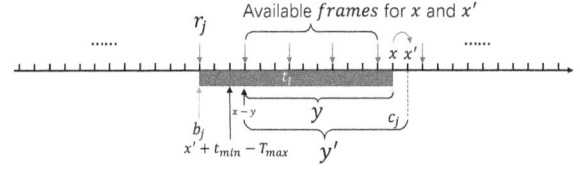

(a) If (x, y) take an inactive action and the earliest *available frame* is still available. Then y' will become $y + 1$.

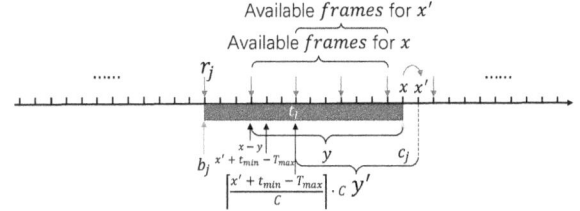

(b) If (x, y) take an inactive action and the earliest *available frame* is no longer available. Then, for the resultant state (x', y') has $y' = x' - \lceil \frac{x' + t_{min} - T_{max}}{C} \rceil \cdot C$.

Figure 7: At state (x, y), we can take an inactive action and the evolution of y' will have the two possible outcomes.

the frame should arrive no early than $\lceil \frac{x' + t_{min} - T_{max}}{C} \rceil \cdot C$, as shown in Fig. 6(d). (Otherwise, it is not possible to meet the deadline even if we use the earliest exit point.)

Therefore, we have

$$(x', y') = r((x, y), (k_0, l)) \tag{3}$$

$$\begin{cases} x' = x + t_l, \\ y' = x + t_l - \max \left\{ \lceil \frac{x + t_l + t_{min} - T_{max}}{C} \rceil \cdot C, (k_0 + 1) \cdot C \right\}. \end{cases} \tag{4}$$

Since we employ exit point l, the gained utility is as follows.

$$u((x, y), (k_0, l)) = u_l. \tag{5}$$

4.2.3 $y \geq 0$ Case with an Inactive Action. In the state (x, y), we also allow to take the inactive action $(0, 0)$. Let $(x', y') = r((x, y), (0, 0))$. We have $x' = x + 1$. For y' since we wait for one unit time, we need to update the y' state. Still, the frame starting at x' should be possibly completed before its deadline. As shown in Fig. 7, $y' = \min \left\{ x' - \lceil \frac{x' + t_{min} - T_{max}}{C} \rceil \cdot C, y + 1 \right\}$. Therefore,

$$(x', y') = r((x, y), (0, 0)) \tag{6}$$

$$\begin{cases} x' = x + 1, \\ y' = \min \left\{ x + 1 - \lceil \frac{x + 1 + t_{min} - T_{max}}{C} \rceil \cdot C, y + 1 \right\}. \end{cases} \tag{7}$$

The utility gained in this case is 0 so that

$$u((x, y), (0, 0)) = 0. \tag{8}$$

4.3 Bellman Formula

In this subsection, we investigate the accumulated utility to formulate its optimal evolution. We define $f(x, y)$ as the accumulated utility at state (x, y), i.e., the sum utility of processed frames. Then, given (x, y) and we take an action (k, l) where $(k, l) \in \mathcal{A}((x, y))$, the accumulated utility at $(x', y') = r((x, y), (k, l))$ is

$$f(x', y') = f(x, y) + u((x, y), (k, l)). \tag{9}$$

Let $f^*(x, y)$ denote the optimal accumulated utility at (x, y), then we have

$$f^*(x', y') = \max_{\substack{\forall (x,y),(k,l), \\ \text{s.t., } r((x,y),(k,l))=(x',y')}} \left\{ f^*(x, y) + u((x, y), (k, l)) \right\}. \tag{10}$$

Through this Bellman formula, we can employ a dynamic programming approach to derive an optimal solution to the original problem OPT.

The system is initiated at state $(0, 0)$ with optimal accumulated utility $f^*(0, 0) = 0$. The system stops at state (T_c, y) for some y value. Please note that the x value of the system state will never exceed T_c. The feasible action set expression (2) blocks actions that lead to $x > T_c$. Therefore, the optimal solution to the original problem OPT is $\max_y f^*(T_c, y)$.

4.4 Interpretation by Graph

The aforementioned analysis can also be interpreted as a directed acyclic graph (DAG). For each state (x, y), we construct a vertex, denoted by $v(x, y)$. For each action $(k, l) \in \mathcal{A}((x, y))$, which leads to state $(x', y') = r((x, y), (k, l))$ we construct an edge starting from $v(x, y)$ to $v(x', y')$ with a weight of $u((x, y), (k, l))$. The accumulated utility $f(x, y)$ is equivalent to the accumulated weights of the path from $v(0, 0)$ to $v(x, y)$ and the optimal accumulated utility is equivalent to the longest path from $v(0, 0)$ to $v(x, y)$.

5 SEE ALGORITHM

5.1 SEE Algorithm Design

Following the analysis in Section 4, we now formally propose the SEE algorithm as in Algorithm 1.

One remaining challenge of SEE is that we do not know if an arbitrary state (x, y) can be reached at the beginning. Therefore, we maintain a dictionary $StateY(x)$ to memorize all possible y such that (x, y) exists, which is constructed gradually throughout the algorithm. Given that we are at state (x, y), by taking an action $(k, l) \in \mathcal{A}((x, y))$, we reach state (x', y'), then it means that (x', y') exists and we add y' to the $StateY(x')$.[3] Please also note that the state transition from (x, y) to (x', y') must satisfy $x' > x$, i.e., a successor state must have a larger x value. Therefore, we can confirm whether a state (x', y') exists if all states with $x \le x' - 1$ are visited. As a consequence, in the algorithm, we visit the states from $x = 0$ to $x = T_c - 1$ with an increment of 1 to ensure that all states are visited.

Lines 1–6 shows the initialization of the SEE Algorithm. Then, for each x (Line 7) and each existing y (Line 8), we traverse all possible actions of (x, y) to explore the next state (Line 10) and utility (Line 11). If we reach a new state (x', y'), the state is reachable and we add y' to $StateY(x')$. Then we calculate the accumulated utility according to equation (9). If the new accumulated utility is greater than a previously found accumulated utility, we update it and record predecessor as $FatherState$ (Line 15–17). When we reach T_c, we judge if we reach the optimal solution in Lines 19–21.

In Lines 22–24 we traverse the optimal predecessor to show the optimal path.

---

[3]At the beginning, $StateY(0) = \{0\}$ as $(0, 0)$ is the initial state.

Algorithm 1: Scheduling Early Exit (SEE)

1 $Start\ State\ s = (0, 0)$
2 $Initialise\ StateY,\ FatherState,\ OptimalPath$
3 $StateY(0) = \{0\}$
4 $FatherState((0, 0)) = \emptyset$
5 $Optimal = -\infty$
6 $FinalState=()$
7 **for** $x \in [0, T_c]$ **do**
8   **for** $y \in StateY(x)$ **do**
9   **for** $(k, l) \in \mathcal{A}((x, y))$ **do**
10       $(x', y') = r((x, y), (k, l))$
11       $u = u((x, y), (k, l))$
12   **if** $y' \notin StateY(x')$ **then**
13   Append y' to $StateY(x')$
14         $f(x', y') = -\infty$
15   **if** $f(x', y') < f(x, y) + u((x, y), (k, l))$ **then**
16         $f(x', y') = f(x, y) + u((x, y), (k, l))$
17         $FatherState((x', y')) = (x, y)$
18   **if** $x' == T_c$ **then**
19   **if** $Optimal < f(x', y')$ **then**
20           $Optimal = f(x', y')$
21           $FinalState = (x', y')$
22 **while** $FatherState(FinalState) \neq \emptyset$ **do**
23   Append $FinalState$ to $OptimalPath$
24   $FinalState = FatherState(FinalState)$
25 **return** $Optimal, OptimalPath$

5.2 Complexity Analysis

In this subsection, we analyze the computational complexity of SEE. SEE includes three levels of loops. First, the outer loop in Line 7 leads to a computational complexity of T_c.

Second, in the intermediate loop in Line 8, we visit all $StateY(x)$ given x. The size of $StateY(x)$ can be analyzed as follows. As shown in Fig. 4(a) the past available frames can only be located at $[x + t_{\min} - T_{\max}, x]$, and must be a multiple of C. This leads to at most $\lceil \frac{T_{\max}-t_{\min}}{C} \rceil$ possibilities. The future available frame has only one possibility. Therefore, the size of $StateY(x)$ is at most $\lceil \frac{T_{\max}-t_{\min}}{C} \rceil + 1$.

Third, in the inner loop, we visit all possible actions. For active actions, we can process one of the frames located at $[x + t_{\min} - T_{\max}, x]$, leading to at most $\lceil \frac{T_{\max}-t_{\min}}{C} \rceil$ possibilities. For each frame, we can select one of the L exit points. We can also take the inactive action. In summary, there are at most $\lceil \frac{T_{\max}-t_{\min}}{C} \rceil \cdot L + 1$ actions.

As a consequence, the overall complexity of the algorithm is

$$O\left(T_c \cdot \left(\lceil \tfrac{T_{\max}-t_{\min}}{C} \rceil \right)^2 \cdot L \right).$$

6 TRACE-DRIVEN EVALUATION

In this section, we will evaluate the performance of our proposed SEE algorithm by trace-driven simulation and demonstrate its advantages compared with benchmarks schemes.

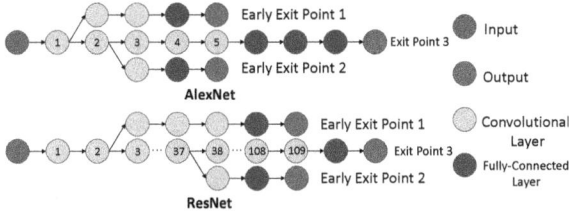

Figure 8: The topology structure of AlexNet and ResNet.

6.1 Trace Employed for Simulation

We implement two sample DNN models with early exits and test their delay and accuracy at different exit points. The DNN models we adopted are AlexNet [17] and ResNet [13] with multiple exit points. First, we follow the model described in [29], where each DNN model has only three exit points. The topologies of the two DNNs are shown in Fig. 8.

We test the delay of inference at different exit points, using a laptop computer (Apple MacBook Pro A1708, Core i5-7360U CPU, and 8GB memory). We test 500 samples and obtain the average delay performance at each exit point. The outcome is shown in the following Table 2, where 1, 2, and 3 indicate the three exit points of the two models. This is referred to as the 3-exit case.[4]

In order to evaluate the performance of our SEE with even more choices of exit points, we also consider two additional exit points by interpolation. We add $1p$ and $2p$ by Piecewise Cubic Hermite Interpolating Polynomial [24]. The delay of $1p$ is in the midpoint of 1 and 2. The delay of $2p$ is in the midpoint of 2 and 3. The accuracy values of $1p$ and $2p$ are the outcomes of the interpolation. This is referred to as the (virtual) 5-exit case.

Exit Point		1	1p	2	2p	3
AlexNet	Delay (ms)	18.9	28.0	37.1	48.8	60.5
	Accuracy	70.0	71.2	76.0	77.7	78.0
ResNet	Delay(ms)	35.0	38.6	42.2	45.8	49.4
	Accuracy	70.0	70.7	80.0	83.1	84.0

Table 2: Trace of AlexNet and ResNet.

6.2 Benchmark Schemes

We consider two benchmarks which are called the *Simple Greedy* algorithm and the *Advanced Greedy* algorithm.

The *Simple Greedy* algorithm chooses the best exit point with a delay smaller than C. It can simply complete all frames by using this exit point. (A few frames right before T_c are regarded as lost if they cannot be completed by T_c.)

The *Advance Greedy* algorithm will make decisions dynamically as follows. Whenever the system becomes idle, it chooses the best exit point that can meet the deadline. If there are multiple frames satisfying this condition, it will choose the earliest one. If no frame can meet its deadline, the system will wait until the arrival of next frame.

6.3 System Parameters

The utility of each exit point is considered as follows. If a frame is processed without an error, it will obtain a utility of 1. If a frame

---

[4]Data of 1, 2, and 3 of ResNet is the same as Fig. 1 at the beginning of this paper.

is processed with an error, it will obtain a negative utility of α. Therefore, if the accuracy at an exit point is η, the mean utility is calculated as $\eta - \alpha(1 - \eta)$.

We also consider the performance under different $T_{\max}$, C, and T_c values. By default, we assume $T_{\max} = 80$ ms, $T_c = 10$ s, and $\alpha = 2$. $C = 20$ ms for AlexNet and $C = 40$ ms for ResNet (as ResNet is a more complicated DNN with larger processing delay). We will change the parameters to evaluate the performance of SEE and benchmark schemes. The unit time is 0.1 ms. (The system evolves in multiples of 0.1 ms.) These values are referred to as the default setting.

The utility vs. delay curves of AlexNet/ResNet in 3-exit/5 exit cases are shown in Fig. 9(a) and Fig. 9(c). For reference, we also show the utility per unit time in Fig. 9(b) and Fig. 9(d).

6.4 Performance Evaluation

6.4.1 Performance under Different T_c. First, we evaluate the performance of different schemes under different T_c values. Other values follow their default setting. T_c is the overall time, which indicates the duration of outage. We set $T_c = \{0.1, 1, 10, 100\}$ s. Fig.10(a), Fig. 10(b), Fig. 10(e), and Fig. 10(f) show the average utility per frame (overall utility over number of arriving frames) of different models, and Fig.10(c), Fig. 10(d), Fig. 10(g), and Fig. 10(h) show the percentage of frames choosing different exit points.

For the 3-exit case (Fig. 10(a) and Fig. 10(b)), SEE leads to the best utility compared with benchmark schemes in all cases. In the AlexNet (resp. RestNet) case, Simple Greedy simply chooses exit point 1 (resp. 1) for all frames. This leads to 18.9 ms (resp. 35 ms) ms delay for all frame, which is just smaller than the inter-arrival time 20 ms (resp. 40 ms). Since the processing time is smaller than the inter-arrival time, the system is idle for a portion of time, leading to wastage of time. The Advanced Greedy chooses multiple exit points alternatively, so that the time will be fully utilized to process frames, achieving a higher utility. The optimal solution derived by SEE is to choose exit point 2 for most frames but to give up a small portion of frames, this is because exit point 2 gives significantly higher utility but only increases a little delay (high utility per unit time in Fig. 9(b)). In summary, SEE achieves a performance gain up to 50.9% compared with Simple Greedy, and 36.1% compared with Advanced Greedy.

For the 5-exit case (Fig. 10(e) and Fig. 10(f)), still, SEE leads to the best utility compared with benchmark schemes in all cases. However, an interesting observation is that the performance of the Advanced Greedy of ResNet is worse (compared with the 3-exit case), even if we have more feasible exit points. This is mainly because the greedy algorithm cannot optimally handle the non-linearity of the utility curve. Choosing a smaller portion of 1 and a larger portion of 2 is better than choosing a larger portion of $1p$ and a smaller portion of 2 (as 2 has a much higher utility per time unit compared with 1 and $1p$). However, the Advanced Greedy prefers $1p$ and 2 if $1p$ is additionally available. In contrast, SEE gives better optimal performance, if $1p$ and $2p$ are additional choices.

6.4.2 Performance under Different $T_{\max}$. We then evaluate the performance of different schemes under different $T_{\max}$ values. $T_{\max}$ ranges from 20 ms to 90 ms for AlexNet and from 40 ms to 180 ms for ResNet. Other values follow their default setting. For all

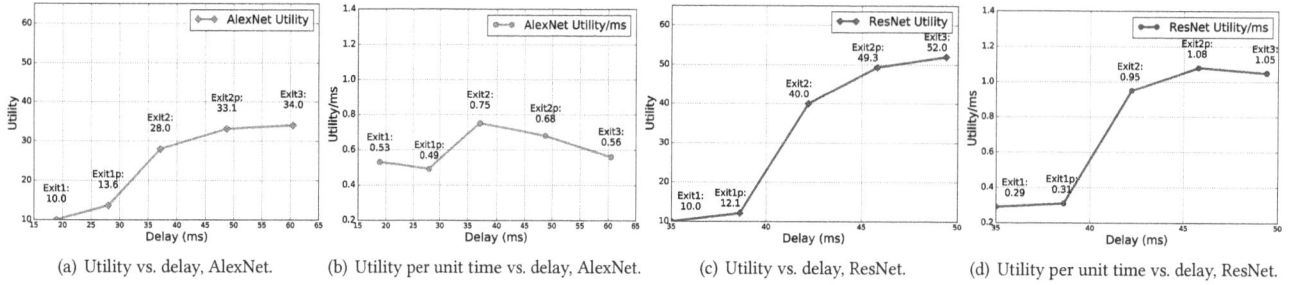

(a) Utility vs. delay, AlexNet. (b) Utility per unit time vs. delay, AlexNet. (c) Utility vs. delay, ResNet. (d) Utility per unit time vs. delay, ResNet.

Figure 9: Utility of different DNN models.

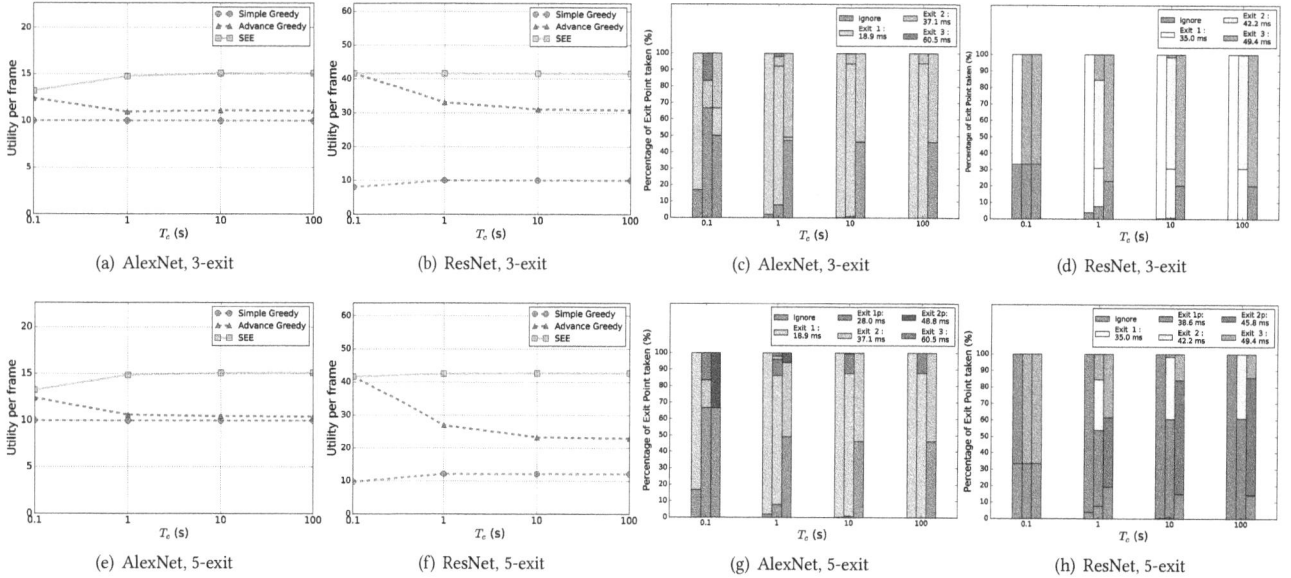

(a) AlexNet, 3-exit. (b) ResNet, 3-exit. (c) AlexNet, 3-exit. (d) ResNet, 3-exit.

(e) AlexNet, 5-exit. (f) ResNet, 5-exit. (g) AlexNet, 5-exit. (h) ResNet, 5-exit.

Figure 10: Evaluation of different T_c. Each group of three bars, Left: Simple Greedy; Middle: Advanced Greedy; Right: SEE.

cases (AlexNet, ResNet, 3-exit, 5-exit), SEE outperforms benchmark schemes, especially when T_{max} is large enough. This is mainly because if T_{max} is small, some of the exit points become infeasible (i.e., T_{max} is smaller than the processing time). Therefore, there are fewer choices and the greedy algorithms are already good enough. For example, as shown in Fig. 11(b) and Fig. 11(d), if $T_{max} = 40$ ms for ResNet in the 3-exit case, exit point 1 is the only choice and thus all algorithms choose 1, leading to the same performance.

6.4.3 Performance under Different C. We finally evaluate the performance of different schemes under different C values. Other values follow their default setting. For all cases, as shown in Fig. 12, SEE outperforms benchmark schemes. By increasing C, the performance of SEE increases as we can tolerate longer processing time for each frame so that the optimal utility per frame will be improved. However, the performance of Simple Greedy and Advanced Greedy may not increase due to the non-linearity of the utility curve. They cannot guarantee optimality as greedily choosing exit points may happen to choose exit points with low utility per unit time. For the Advanced Greedy, there is a drop from 32 to 38 for ResNet. It happens that $C = 38$ will force the algorithm to choose a large portion of exit point 1 in the 3-exit case (a very large portion of exit points 1 and 1p in the 5-exit case), which will generate low utility. The

utilities per unit time of 1 and 1p are lower so that choosing them will give even lower performance. When C is large, all algorithms agree to choose the best exit point 3 as there is enough time to process every frame with the highest accuracy.

7 RELATED WORK

7.1 Computation Offloading and Service Outage

In recent years, due to the fast evolution of cloud and edge computing, computation offloading from the device to more powerful cloud or edge servers received much attention and has been investigated intensively [3, 22, 23]. Computation offloading addresses a key issue that mobile and IoT devices have limited resources. It has shown a great potential to reduce the computation time [9] as well as the energy usage [18].

One obstacle of computation offloading is the possibility of service outage: Caused by wireless disconnection or congestion at server, the computational jobs may not be successfully uploaded or processed. In order to handle unstable wireless connection, [34] proposed a Markov decision process (MDP) model to obtain an optimal policy for mobile offloading with intermittent connectivity. Handover is another reason to interrupt on-going job offloading. Quite

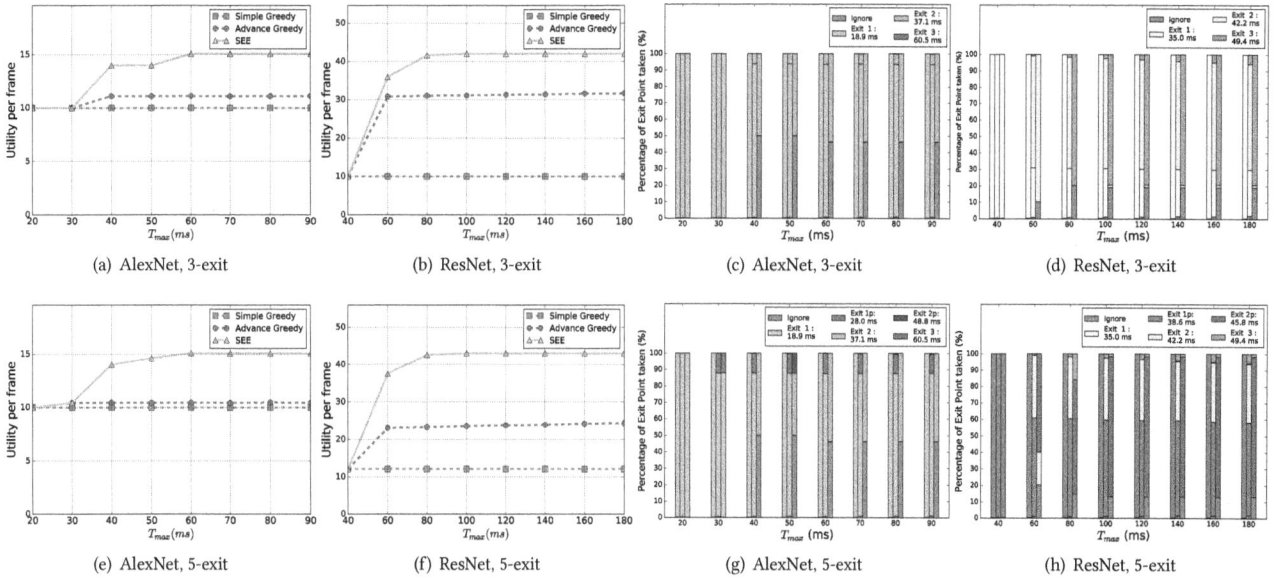

(a) AlexNet, 3-exit
(b) ResNet, 3-exit
(c) AlexNet, 3-exit
(d) ResNet, 3-exit

(e) AlexNet, 5-exit
(f) ResNet, 5-exit
(g) AlexNet, 5-exit
(h) ResNet, 5-exit

Figure 11: Evaluation of different T_{max}. Each group of 3 bars, Left: Simple Greedy; Middle: Advanced Greedy; Right: SEE.

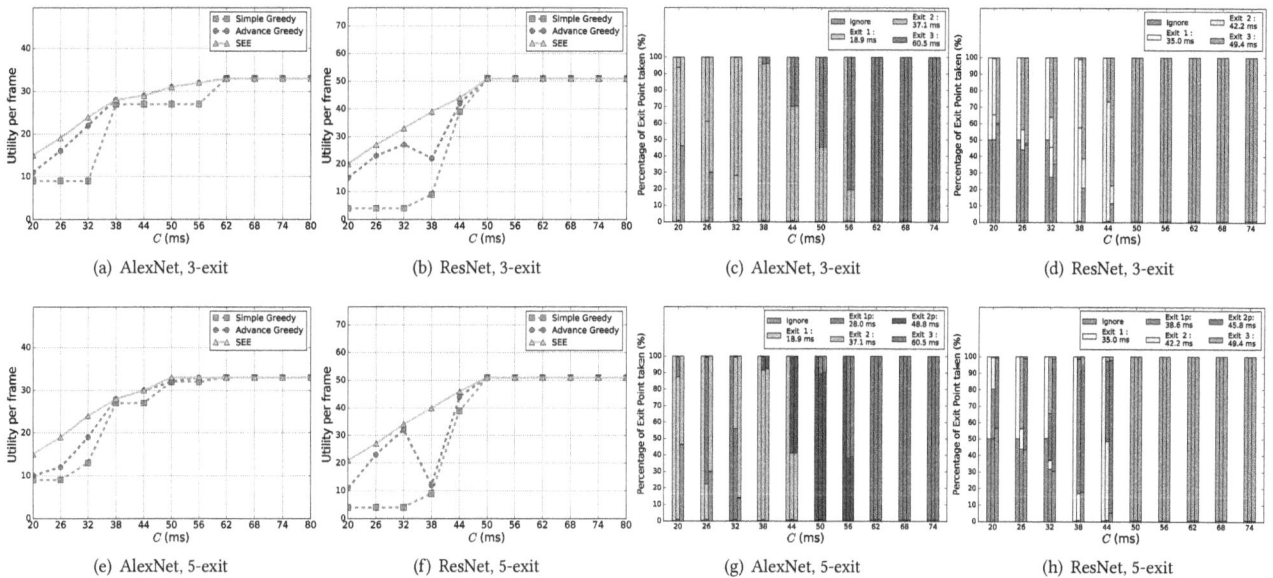

(a) AlexNet, 3-exit
(b) ResNet, 3-exit
(c) AlexNet, 3-exit
(d) ResNet, 3-exit

(e) AlexNet, 5-exit
(f) ResNet, 5-exit
(g) AlexNet, 5-exit
(h) ResNet, 5-exit

Figure 12: Evaluation of different C. Each group of 3 bars, Left: Simple Greedy; Middle: Advanced Greedy; Right: SEE.

a few mechanisms are proposed to tackle this problem, such as pre-migration [5], VM migration [12], and container migration [21]. Edge computing may also experience relatively long-term wireless disconnection, which can be handled by adding ad-hoc relay nodes [26]. The service outage may also be caused by limited resource at the edge/cloud server [4, 32], and admission control strategies are proposed. Due to the limited resource at the edge/cloud server, in a game-theoretical perspective, a set of mobile users have to give up offloading but to compute its task locally [10]. However, the aforementioned studies did not consider the special characteristics of DNN models: a delay-accuracy tradeoff can be realized by early exit.

7.2 DNN Inference at the Edge

As a growing number of smart applications are directly handled at the device and edge, another category of papers study how to effectively carry out DNN inference at the device and edge [8, 35]. As device-only solutions, DNN inference can be accelerated at local devices in two ways: One is to compact DNN models to adapt to resource limitations [20, 27, 28]. The other approach is to optimize the DNN execution at local devices (e.g., optimized resource allocation and runtime acceleration) [6, 16]. However, there are still scenarios where the devices themselves are inadequate to carry out DNN inference. Thus, a range of systems are implemented to offload the inference tasks to the edge servers [11, 19]. Another type of studies adopted DNN partition to balance the communication and computation, where the first part of DNN is processed at the device and the second part is processed at the edge [14, 15, 33]. However, these previous papers did not consider connection or service outage.

The concept of early exit of DNN was firstly proposed in [29], which allows faster inference by using the same DNN (but exit early). A range of variants of early exit are developed in [30], [7], [31] which further improved the adaptability and flexibility. The concept of early exit is an ideal solution to handle service outage. It can provide more choices for mobile devices to process DNN inference with a compromised accuracy (rather than a complete failure). To the best of our knowledge, this is the first work optimally scheduling DNN inference tasks during service outage by employing early exit.

8 CONCLUSION

In this paper, we propose SEE, a device-based scheduling algorithm to find the optimal schedule for the inference tasks during the service outage. Initially, we formulate an optimal scheduling problem with the goal to maximize the overall utility. We further prove the Ordered Scheduling structure to narrow down the searching space for this problem. Based on this structure, we propose SEE, a dynamic programming approach to solve the problem optimally with a polynomial computational complexity. Finally, we present trace-driven simulation for SEE. This evaluation focuses on two typical DNNs (AlexNet and ResNet) with the different exit choices (i.e.,3−exits and 5−exits). The outcome shows that SEE significantly outperforms both the benchmarks under a variety of system settings.

REFERENCES

[1] 2017. LTE upload speed super slow everywhere. Retrieved May 31, 2019 from https://community.verizonwireless.com/t5/iPhone-X-Xr-Xs/LTE-upload-speed-super-slow-everywhere/td-p/1026178
[2] 2019. Recommended upload encoding settings - YouTube Help. Retrieved May 31, 2019 from https://support.google.com/youtube/answer/1722171?hl=en
[3] N. Abbas, Y. Zhang, A. Taherkordi, and T. Skeie. 2018. Mobile Edge Computing: A Survey. IEEE Internet of Things Journal 5, 1 (Feb. 2018), pp. 450–465.
[4] J. Almeida, V. Almeida, D. Ardagna, Í. Cunha, C. Francalanci, and M. Trubian. 2010. Joint admission control and resource allocation in virtualized servers. J. Parallel and Distrib. Comput. 70, 4 (2010), 344 – 362.
[5] W. Bao, D. Yuan, Z. Yang, S. Wang, B. Zhou, S. Adams, and A. Zomaya. Oct. 2018. sFog: Seamless Fog Computing Environment for Mobile IoT Applications. In Proceedings of ACM International Conference on Modeling, Analysis and Simulation of Wireless and Mobile Systems (MSWiM). Montreal, Canada.
[6] S. Bhattacharya and Nicholas D. Lane. Nov. 2016. Sparsification and Separation of Deep Learning Layers for Constrained Resource Inference on Wearables. In Proceedings of ACM Conference on Embedded Network Sensor Systems (SenSys). Stanford, CA, USA.
[7] T. Bolukbasi, J. Wang, O. Dekel, and V. Saligrama. Aug. 2017. Adaptive Neural Networks for Efficient Inference. In Proceedings of International Conference on Machine Learning (ICML). Sydney, NSW, Australia.
[8] J. Chen and X. Ran. 2019. Deep Learning With Edge Computing: A Review. Proc. IEEE 107, 8 (Aug 2019), 1655–1674.
[9] M. Chen and Y. Hao. 2018. Task Offloading for Mobile Edge Computing in Software Defined Ultra-Dense Network. IEEE Journal on Selected Areas in Communications 36, 3 (Mar. 2018), pp. 587–597.
[10] X. Chen, L. Jiao, W. Li, and X. Fu. 2016. Efficient Multi-User Computation Offloading for Mobile-Edge Cloud Computing. IEEE/ACM Transactions on Networking 24, 5 (Oct. 2016), pp. 2795–2808.
[11] Z. Fang, D. Hong, and R. K. Gupta. Jun. 2019. Serving Deep Neural Networks at the Cloud Edge for Vision Applications on Mobile Platforms (MMSys). Amherst, MA, USA.

[12] K. Ha, Y. Abe, T. Eiszler, Z. Chen, W. Hu, B. Amos, R. Upadhyaya, P. Pillai, and M. Satyanarayanan. April. 2017. You Can Teach Elephants to Dance: Agile VM Handoff for Edge Computing. In Proceedings of ACM/IEEE Symposium on Edge Computing (SEC). San Jose/Fremont, CA, USA.
[13] K. He, X. Zhang, S. Ren, and J. Sun. Jun. 2016. Deep residual learning for image recognition. In Proceedings of the IEEE conference on computer vision and pattern recognition (CVPR). Las Vegas, USA.
[14] C. Hu, W. Bao, D. Wang, and F. Liu. Apr.-May. 2019. Dynamic Adaptive DNN Surgery for Inference Acceleration on the Edge. In Proceedings of IEEE International Conference on Computer Communications (INFOCOM). Paris, France.
[15] Y. Kang, J. Hauswald, C Gao, A. Rovinski, T. Mudge, J. Mars, and L. Tang. Apr. 2017. Neurosurgeon: Collaborative intelligence between the cloud and mobile edge. In Proceedings of ACM International Conference on Architectural Support for Programming Languages and Operating Systems (ASPLOS). Xi'an, China.
[16] Y. Kim, J. Kim, D. Chae, D. Kim, and J. Kim. Mar. 2019. μLayer: Low Latency On-Device Inference Using Cooperative Single-Layer Acceleration and Processor-Friendly Quantization. In Proceedings of European Conference on Computer Systems (EuroSys). Dresden, Germany.
[17] Alex Krizhevsky, I. Sutskever, and G. E. Hinton. 2012. ImageNet Classification with Deep Convolutional Neural Networks. In Advances in Neural Information Processing Systems 25, F. Pereira, C. J. C. Burges, L. Bottou, and K. Q. Weinberger (Eds.). Curran Associates, Inc.
[18] K. Kumar and Y. Lu. 2010. Cloud Computing for Mobile Users: Can Offloading Computation Save Energy? Computer 43, 4 (Apr. 2010), pp. 51–56.
[19] L. Liu, H. Li, and M. Gruteser. Oct. 2019. Edge assisted real-time object detection for mobile augmented reality. In Proceedings of Annual International Conference on Mobile Computing and Networking (MobiCom). Los Cabos, Mexico.
[20] J. Luo, J. Wu, and W. Lin. Oct. 2017. ThiNet: A Filter Level Pruning Method for Deep Neural Network Compression. In Proceedings of IEEE International Conference on Computer Vision (ICCV). Venice, Italy.
[21] L. Ma, S. Yi, and Q. Li. 2017. Efficient Service Handoff Across Edge Servers via Docker Container Migration. In Proceedings of ACM/IEEE Symposium on Edge Computing (SEC). San Jose/Fremont, CA, USA.
[22] P. Mach and Z. Becvar. 2017. Mobile Edge Computing: A Survey on Architecture and Computation Offloading. IEEE Communications Surveys Tutorials 19, 3 (Mar. 2017), pp. 1628–1656.
[23] Y. Mao, C. You, J. Zhang, K. Huang, and K. B. Letaief. 2017. A Survey on Mobile Edge Computing: The Communication Perspective. IEEE Communications Surveys Tutorials 19, 4 (Aug. 2017), pp. 2322–2358.
[24] MATLAB. [n. d.]. Piecewise Cubic Hermite Interpolating Polynomial (PCHIP). Retrieved May 31, 2019 from https://au.mathworks.com/help/matlab/ref/pchip.html#References
[25] C. Pei, Z. Wang, Y. Zhao, Z. Wang, Y. Meng, D. Pei, Y. Peng, W. Tang, and X. Qu. May. 2017. Why it takes so long to connect to a WiFi access point. In Proceedings of IEEE International Conference on Computer Communications (INFOCOM). Atlanta, GA, USA.
[26] D. Satria, D. Park, and M. Jo. 2017. Recovery for overloaded mobile edge computing. Future Generation Computer Systems 70 (May. 2017), pp. 138 – 147.
[27] V. Sindhwani, T. N. Sainath, and S. Kumar. 2015. Structured Transforms for Small-Footprint Deep Learning. In Advances in Neural Information Processing Systems 28. Curran Associates, Inc.
[28] M. Sun, D. Snyder, Y. Gao, V. Nagaraja, M. Rodehorst, S. Panchapagesan, N. Strom, S. Matsoukas, and S. Vitaladevuni. Aug. 2017. Compressed Time Delay Neural Network for Small-Footprint Keyword Spotting. In Proceedings of Annual Conference of the International Speech Communication Association (INTERSPEECH). Stockholm, Sweden.
[29] S. Teerapittayanon, B. McDanel, and HT. Kung. Dec. 2016. Branchynet: Fast inference via early exiting from deep neural networks. In Proceedings of International Conference on Pattern Recognition (ICPR). Cancun, Mexifco.
[30] S. Teerapittayanon, B. McDanel, and H. T. Kung. Jun. 2017. Distributed Deep Neural Networks Over the Cloud, the Edge and End Devices. In Proceedings of IEEE International Conference on Distributed Computing Systems (ICDCS). Atlanta, GA, USA.
[31] X. Wang, F. Yu, Z.Y. Dou, T. Darrell, and J. E. Gonzalez. Sep. 2018. SkipNet: Learning Dynamic Routing in Convolutional Networks. In Proceedings of the European Conference on Computer Vision (ECCV). Munich, Germany.
[32] Q. Xia, W. Liang, and W. Xu. Oct. 2013. Throughput maximization for online request admissions in mobile cloudlets. In Proceedings of Annual IEEE Conference on Local Computer Networks. Sydney, NSW, Australia.
[33] M. Xu, F. Qian, M. Zhu, F. Huang, S. Pushp, and X. Liu. 2019. DeepWear: Adaptive Local Offloading for On-Wearable Deep Learning. IEEE Transactions on Mobile Computing (2019).
[34] Y. Zhang, D. Niyato, and P. Wang. 2015. Offloading in Mobile Cloudlet Systems with Intermittent Connectivity. IEEE Transactions on Mobile Computing 14, 12 (Dec. 2015), pp. 2516–2529.
[35] Z. Zhou, X. Chen, E. Li, L. Zeng, K. Luo, and J. Zhang. 2019. Edge Intelligence: Paving the Last Mile of Artificial Intelligence with Edge Computing. CoRR abs/1905.10083 (2019). arXiv:1905.10083

CrowdSenSim 2.0: a Stateful Simulation Platform for Mobile Crowdsensing in Smart Cities

Federico Montori
federico.montori2@unibo.it
Department of Computer Science and
Engineering, University of Bologna
Bologna, Italy

Emanuele Cortesi
emanuele.cortesi2@studio.unibo.it
Department of Computer Science and
Engineering, University of Bologna
Bologna, Italy

Luca Bedogni
luca.bedogni4@unibo.it
Department of Computer Science and
Engineering, University of Bologna
Bologna, Italy

Andrea Capponi
andrea.capponi@uni.lu
FSTC-CSC, University of Luxembourg
Esch-sur-Alzette, Luxembourg

Claudio Fiandrino
claudio.fiandrino@imdea.org
IMDEA Networks Institute
Madrid, Spain

Luciano Bononi
luciano.bononi@unibo.it
Department of Computer Science and
Engineering, University of Bologna
Bologna, Italy

ABSTRACT

Mobile crowdsensing (MCS) has become a popular paradigm for data collection in urban environments. In MCS systems, a crowd supplies sensing information for monitoring phenomena through mobile devices. Typically, a large number of participants is required to make a sensing campaign successful. For such a reason, it is often not practical for researchers to build and deploy large testbeds to assess the performance of frameworks and algorithms for data collection, user recruitment, and evaluating the quality of information. Simulations offer a valid alternative. In this paper, we present CrowdSenSim 2.0, a significant extension of the popular Crowd-SenSim simulation platform. CrowdSenSim 2.0 features a stateful approach to support algorithms where the chronological order of events matters, extensions of the architectural modules, including an additional system to model urban environments, code refactoring, and parallel execution of algorithms. All these improvements boost the performances of the simulator and make the runtime execution and memory utilization significantly lower, also enabling the support for larger simulation scenarios. We demonstrate retro-compatibility with the older platform and evaluate as a case study a stateful data collection algorithm.

CCS CONCEPTS

• **Human-centered computing** → **Mobile computing**; • **Software and its engineering** → **Simulator / interpreter**; *Publish-subscribe / event-based architectures*; • **General and reference** → *Validation*; • **Networks** → *Network simulations*.

KEYWORDS

mobile crowdsensing, simulation, modeling, distributed algorithms

ACM Reference Format:
Federico Montori, Emanuele Cortesi, Luca Bedogni, Andrea Capponi, Claudio Fiandrino, and Luciano Bononi. 2019. CrowdSenSim 2.0: a Stateful Simulation Platform for Mobile Crowdsensing in Smart Cities. In *22nd Int'l ACM Conf. on Modeling, Analysis and Simulation of Wireless and Mobile Systems (MSWiM'19), Nov. 25–29, 2019, Miami Beach, FL, USA.* ACM, New York, NY, USA, 8 pages. https://doi.org/10.1145/3345768.3355929

1 INTRODUCTION

Mobile crowdsensing (MCS) gained exponential interest in the last years and has become one of the most promising paradigms for data collection in urban environments within the scope of smart cities [3]. MCS systems gather data from sensors typically embedded in citizens' mobile devices, such as smartphones, tablets, and wearables. The number of worldwide smartphones sales is still increasing according to Gartner statistics, reaching 1.55 billion units in 2018 [7]. The crowd analytics market is projected to reach USD 1 142.5 million by 2021, raising from USD 385.1 million of 2016 at a compound annual growth rate of 24.3% [11].

The success of a MCS campaign typically relies on large participation of users [14]. Unfortunately, often it is not feasible to develop testbeds and platforms that involve a multitude of citizens[1]. On the one hand, the cost of recruitment scales with the number of users involved and the amount of data collected. On the other hand, the required time for setting up a large-scale sensing campaign is prohibitively long. To this end, simulators offer a valid alternative to assess the performance of MCS systems in city-wide scenarios with large user participation in a reasonable time. Specifically, simulators are well-suited to assess and compare the performance of specific aspects of MCS systems (e.g., the decision process to sense and report data).

In this work, we present CrowdSenSim 2.0, a stateful simulation platform for developing MCS systems in urban environments for Smart Cities applications. The simulator has been developed in order to be general-purpose, i.e., to cover many use cases and architectures as well as implementing several MCS aspects such as energy, coverage, realistic user mobility, real urban environments, communication infrastructures, recruitment, and data collection

---

[1]In the rest of the paper, we will use the terms users, citizens, and participants interchangeably

algorithms. CrowdSenSim 2.0 is based on the architecture of Crowd-SenSim [5]. From the original version, we kept its core architecture and re-implemented almost integrally the simulator engine, besides several other improvements. As a matter of fact, the legacy version of CrowdSenSim can simulate with a high level of detail MCS systems in urban scenarios and assess the energy consumption of mobile devices. However, it lacks adaptation to several MCS applications that require features such as statefulness and flexible event triggering. Indeed, as it will be explained in § 3, the original CrowdSenSim featured only stateless use cases and was oriented to model network and energy consumption characteristics rather than algorithmic ones.

With respect to the original CrowdSenSim [5], we make the following contributions:

(1) We significantly improve the original platform by implementing a set of crucial features tailored to embrace a larger class of MCS algorithms and frameworks. In a nutshell, CrowdSenSim 2.0 supports stateful simulations (i.e., where the simulation events are chronologically dependent and the algorithm operation relies on such dependence), MGRS spatial encoding, a flexible time interval for event generation, and the integration of a new algorithm to determine user trajectories.

(2) We optimize the computational performance by means of a full code refactoring and the introduction of algorithm-level parallelism, which enables researchers to run several MCS algorithms simultaneously or several runs of the same algorithm at the same time.

Furthermore, besides the above contributions directly inherent to the simulation platform, the paper makes these additional contributions:

- We validate the benefits CrowdSenSim 2.0 brings in terms of runtime execution and memory utilization.
- We present as use case an analysis of a stateful distributed data collection algorithm implemented in CrowdSenSim 2.0.

In conclusion, the paper has the following structure: Section 2 outlines the main research efforts in the area, Section 3 describes the simulator with particular focus on the improvements, Section 4 validates its computational performance in comparison to Crowd-SenSim, Section 5 describes the distributed data collection algorithm that we integrated, implementation details of such algorithm, and its results. Finally, Section 6 concludes the work.

2 RELATED WORKS

After having scanned the state-of-the-art thoroughly, it has become evident that it does not exist a simulation tool that covers all the components of MCS. This is because MCS is a general paradigm which groups highly heterogeneous components. For example, data collection can be opportunistic or participatory according to the degree of user involvement. Users might contribute freely to a sensing campaign or can be recruited through specific policies. The objective of MCS research spans over a number of areas, including quality and coverage of information over an area of interest, user recruitment, and incentive mechanisms [3, 17]. Thus, such research areas typically propose optimization frameworks or algorithms

that are evaluated standalone and often leave apart important components that impact on the correct modeling. These components include realistic user mobility [16] and modeling of urban environments [1] as well as modeling of the network that transfers sensing readings from end-users to the cloud where it is typically processed.

For the above reasons, a number of proposed simulation platforms are not suitable to properly evaluate MCS systems because they typically focus on one component at a time [9]. For example, in [19] the authors propose to leverage the capabilities of Network Simulator 3 (NS-3) to simulate ad-hoc scenarios for reporting incidents. NS-3 is a highly detailed simulation tool for networking purposes and models network protocols down to the granularity of the single packet across all the layers of the network stack. This strongly limits scalability, as the level of detail in such simulations is too high and modeling typical MCS sensing campaigns with thousands of users overall contributing during hours/days timescale becomes prohibitive. The same applies to similar simulation tools such as OMNeT++, used in [18]. CupCarbon, proposed in [12], is a WSN-based simulator in which the researcher can individually deploy both sensors and base stations on realistic urban environments obtained from OpenStreetMap (OSM)[2]. Sensors can be mobile and can have dedicated paths along the roads, which makes it suitable for MCS scenarios. However, CupCarbon limits the size of the scenario, which precludes scalability to thousands of nodes. The most notable effort in the last years is given by CrowdSenSim [5], a simulator for MCS scenario capable of supporting a high number of users (order of hundreds of thousands) and their motion along the roads of cities imported by OSM without modeling in full the network stack, yet providing a sufficient level of detail on battery consumption statistics and number of tasks executed. The focus of the simulator is heavily energy-driven, implementing a number of algorithms, both in participatory and opportunistic scenarios, aiming to reduce the energy consumption per device. Being primarily implemented for energy consumption oriented scenarios, CrowdSenSim lacks adaptability to many MCS use cases as it does not support a number of features, such as statefulness, that are required by the majority of MCS systems.

3 THE CROWDSENSIM 2.0 ARCHITECTURE

This section presents the architecture of CrowdSenSim 2.0 by highlighting its novelties over the original CrowdSenSim. In particular, we detail the architecture of the simulator outlining the role of each module and we expose the new features and improvements.

3.1 General Architecture

Figure 1 shows the architecture of CrowdSenSim 2.0, which includes major modifications and added features to the previous version of CrowdSenSim. Main novel contributions include a stateful approach that is fundamental for specific classes of MCS applications, support for a more flexible generation of events in terms of temporal granularity and other configurable parameters, MGRS spatial encoding, and generation of highly-precise user trajectories. These features will be explained in detail throughout the section.

The simulator generates a set of participants moving within a street network, contributing data through the sensors of their

---

[2]https://www.openstreetmap.org/

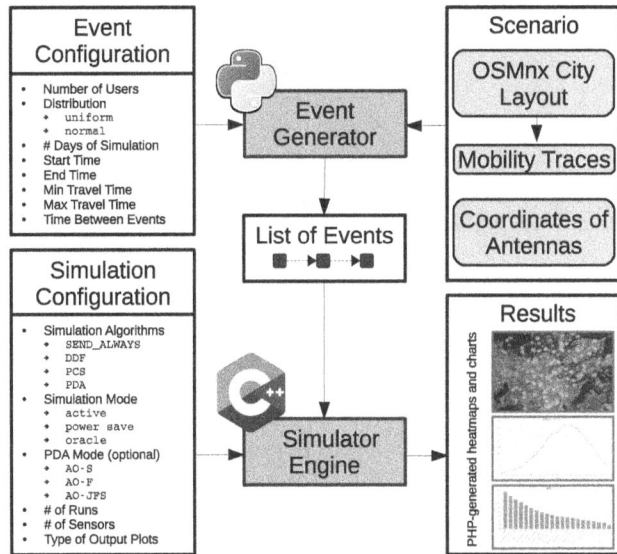

Figure 1: Simulator modular architecture, including original features of CrowdSenSim and novelties of CrowdSenSim 2.0.

mobile devices, and reporting it through the closest cellular base station or WiFi access point, according to the design of the MCS campaign. The Event Generator module consists of creating events, defined as "the arrival of a participant in a given location at a defined time". To this end, it takes in input the City Layout, the User Mobility, the Coordinates of the Antennas, and a set of parameters from the Event Configuration file. After such a macro step has been performed, the list of events is passed to the Simulator Engine, which defines the behavior of each participant upon each event. Both the Simulator Engine and the Event Generator have been integrally rewritten to make possible the integration of a set of necessary functionalities, which are explained thereafter. Additionally, significantly more code cleanliness was enforced.

3.2 City Layout
The City Layout module allows researchers to define the urban street network of a city-wide scenario over which the participants move. The street network is defined as a set of coordinates where pedestrians can be located, including *latitude*, *longitude*, and *altitude*.

3.2.1 High-precision street network design. While CrowdSenSim received as input a *.txt* file with a list of all coordinates to generate the city layout, CrowdSenSim 2.0 automatically gets the coordinates by exploiting OSMnx, an open-source Python package to download and simplify street networks from OSM [2]. Furthermore, CrowdSenSim 2.0 implements the AOP algorithm [21] to augment the precision of the graph describing the street network, with a granularity chosen according to the needs and the objectives of the MCS campaign under study. Fig. 2(a) shows the map of the city layout and the street network where users can walk. Pedestrian movement is generated over the points, which correspond to the set of downloaded coordinates.

3.2.2 MGRS Support. CrowdSenSim 2.0, in addition, supports Military Grid Reference System (MGRS) spatial encoding [8], which allows the developer to design data collection algorithms on top of such hierarchical spatial encoding. As a matter of fact, the usage of MGRS is crucial in data collection algorithms for MCS and several applications are built on top of it [6, 10, 15]. In particular, each event is generated along with its MGRS coordinates with the finest possible granularity and such data is then passed to the Simulator Engine module for processing.

3.3 User Mobility and Event Generation
The User Mobility module defines the initial user placement, at what time they "spawn" in the urban environment and how they move. Users are generated using a spatial distribution function and move according to different possible models. For instance, mobility can be uniformly or randomly distributed, based on real traces, or built upon different weights according to the point of interests and time of the day (e.g., following the distribution of Google Popular Times[3]). Each participant has a certain travel time (e.g., 20 min walk) and its trajectory is generated consequentially as a sequence of events, defined in § 3.1, equally spaced in time. After an event is generated, the participant jumps to a location over the urban network topology reachable in a certain time given its walking speed, which is generated uniformly within the interval 1 - 1.5 m/s.

3.3.1 User Trajectories. User mobility is generated as pedestrian trajectories with a random start and end point according to the walking period of each citizen over the street network of the chosen city. This feature allows highlighting the periods of active contribution of users along their paths according to the data collection framework (DCF) under analysis. For instance, Fig. 2(b) illustrates the trajectories of 5 participants walking in Luxembourg City and contributing with a Deterministic Distributed Framework (DDF) [4] in which users stop the sensing process after a certain amount of collected data. The circle represents the starting walking point and the star the ending point. The green path indicates when users contribute data, the purple one when they do not sense data. Each user sends data to the closest cellular base station (BS) or WiFi access point (AP) according to the chosen communication technology. For instance, Fig. 2(c) shows the concentration of users connected to each BS in Luxembourg City at a given instance of time of the simulation runtime.

3.3.2 Event Configuration. In CrowdSenSim 2.0 many options in the generation of events have been made configurable (see the block "Event Configuration" in Figure 1). The distribution function for generating users can be selected when configuring the simulation, e.g., a normal or uniform distribution, whereas in the old version users were generated only uniformly. By selecting among various generation functions, it is now possible to simulate different density of the users throughout the simulation runtime. The amount of time each user moves in the urban environment can be configured like in the original CrowdSenSim. The time interval Δt between two events has been made configurable as well, while in CrowdSenSim was fixed to 60s. This enables to simulate possibly more complex scenarios, in which the time between updates is not decided at

---

[3]https://support.google.com/business/answer/2721884

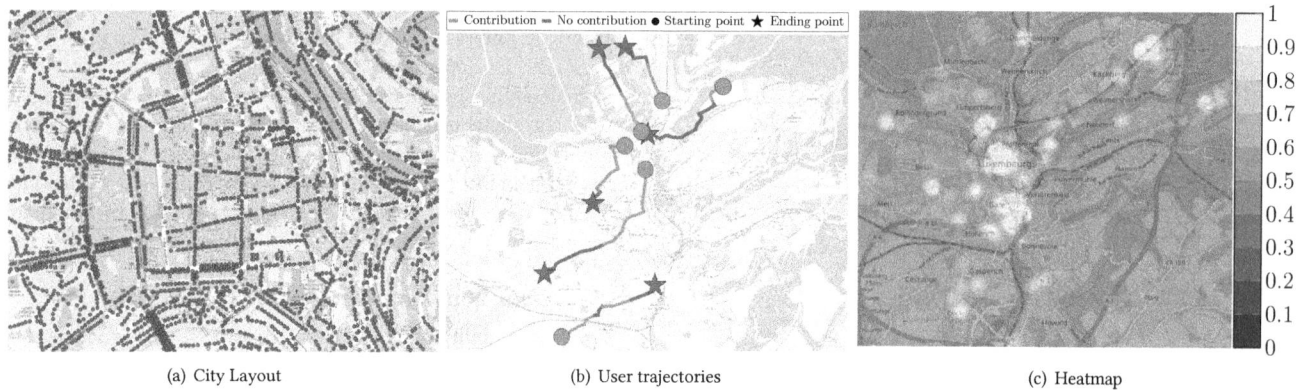

(a) City Layout

(b) User trajectories

(c) Heatmap

Figure 2: City layout, user trajectories and distribution of users connected to BSs in Luxembourg City

design time, but can change through configuration. This makes the number of supported applications significantly higher.

3.4 Simulator Engine

The simulator engine is written in C++ and, as shown in Fig. 1, it takes in input a list of events, corresponding to the time in which users perform an action. In turn, each event triggers the sampling of each sensor as well as the communication module of each device because the Simulator Engine implements an apposite callback function. In practice, the Simulator Engine defines the behavior of each participant by implementing the action performed upon each event.

3.4.1 Global Statefulness. CrowdSenSim 2.0 executes the events in absolute chronological order. To make the present CrowdSenSim 2.0 simulator more oriented to the algorithmic side rather than energy consumption of MCS systems, we implemented the Simulator Engine in a way in which events are ordered chronologically, whereas, in the previous version, events were executed per-participant – i.e., all the events of the first participant were executed before all the events of the second, and so on – making the implementations of certain algorithms unfeasible. In fact, the original CrowdSenSim could implement any stateless algorithms as well as any algorithm requiring only local statefulness, i.e., a state maintained only internally by each participant and does not interact with other participants in any case. With the novel version of the simulator presented in this paper, CrowdSenSim 2.0, we can implement any algorithm with global statefulness, i.e., the state is maintained by each participant as well as a central entity, and each event can be influenced by the past ones. Note that this increases the expressiveness of the simulator without preventing data collection algorithms that were implementable in the past version to be also implemented in CrowdSenSim 2.0.

3.4.2 Algorithm-level Data Collection Parallelism. Comparing the performance of multiple algorithms (e.g., for data collection) at a time is often a desirable feature in simulation platforms. Crowd-SenSim 2.0 makes it possible to run different algorithms within the same run, simply by defining more than one callback function relative to each event. More in detail, any time the Simulator Engine

is triggered upon the occurrence of an event, it is possible to specify more than one function to be called separately. In this way, it is possible to define a number of algorithms to run at the same time, that will output their results separately just as if they were separate runs. Obviously, one can also run the same algorithm several times in parallel with a different random seed. Such advance boosts the performance of the simulator significantly, as in a single run several algorithms can be tested at the same time. We show performance evaluation of this aspect in § 4. As shown in Figure 1, parameters such as the algorithms used as well as the number of runs can be specified in the Simulation Configuration file. The simulator implements DDF, PCS, and PDA algorithms as in [20], in particular, PDA has been re-designed in its global stateful version [13] (§ 5).

3.4.3 Participant Awareness. To enable applications and algorithms that require privacy or fine-grained energy savings mechanisms, CrowdSenSim 2.0 allows the simulated users to be aware of certain information detained by the central entity organizing the sensing campaign. For example, instructions about the amount of yet to be delivered information in a certain area. Therefore, users can be in:

- **Power-save mode**, thus eligible to receive such information when it is piggybacked on another communication (e.g., when they are pushing data).
- **Active mode**, thus eligible to receive such information upon each of their events occur.
- **Oracle mode**, thus aware of such information at any time.

When looking at such division from a privacy perspective, users in power-save mode are those with limited access to global information because they are not trustworthy, whereas users in oracle mode have higher privileges. Clearly, the additional state may be implemented in case the simulated scenario requires it.

4 PERFORMANCE EVALUATION

The newly developed CrowdSenSim 2.0 has undergone a complete code refactoring procedure as detailed in Section 3. Such operation has been extremely delicate as we needed to assure that every feature of the original CrowdSenSim was left intact. In other words, the novel simulator should be retro compatible with the previous implementation, to achieve results reproducibility regardless of the simulator version used. In this section, we show that both CrowdSenSim and CrowdSenSim 2.0 exhibit the same behavior on common use cases and we highlight the benefits in terms of RAM utilization that the new version brings.

4.1 Validation of CrowdSenSim 2.0 over CrowdSenSim

Both the instances of CrowdSenSim and CrowdSenSim 2.0 that we used throughout the paper have been launched on a virtual machine using 1 core of the host machine with 4 GB of dedicated RAM and running Ubuntu 16.04.6 LTS. The host machine is an AMD Ryzen 5 1600 at 3.2 GHz (6 core, 12 thread) with 16 GB RAM and running Windows 10 Pro 1809.

In order to efficiently validate CrowdSenSim 2.0, we referred to an energy consumption analysis of the DDF data collection algorithm originally proposed in [4] that was implemented and practically evaluated in [20]. DDF is a locally stateful data collection algorithm in which participants keep on generating data up to a certain threshold of energy consumption depending on their battery capacity. For the sake of energy-related analysis, we left the energy calculation of the original CrowdSenSim untouched. In detail, we equipped each participant with a mobile device carrying an accelerometer, a pressure sensor, and a temperature sensor. As in [5], the sensors generate readings with the same sampling frequency. For all the simulations, we resort to 10 000 participants in the center of Luxembourg City, which covers an area of 51.73 km^2 with a perimeter of 52.5 km and a population of 119 214 inhabitants as of the end of 2018. The simulation has a duration of 12-hours (starting at 12:00 PM and ending at 11:59 PM) and paths are generated with a duration uniformly distributed between 20min and 40min.

We fed both CrowdSenSim and CrowdSenSim 2.0 with the same set of events, which are sampled per-participant with a frequency of 60s. We ran extensive simulations and measured the current drain of the device of each participant in relation to the sensing and reporting activity, and we plot the results in Fig. 3. Devices use the WiFi technology for communication as in [5]: a number of WiFi hotspots are deployed in the area of interest, and every time a participant needs to transmit it sends data through the closest AP in the map. We observed that both CrowdSenSim and CrowdSenSim 2.0 generate the exact same values, which proves their equivalence in terms of results output.

In order to further strengthen our claim, we also compared the transmission consumption between the two simulators. As we did for the sensors, we did not modify the way in which participants transmit data. Again the values produced by the two simulators match perfectly, validating their equivalence.

4.2 Performance Analysis of Runtime Execution and Memory Utilization

The code refactoring and the parallel processing feature brought a significant boost in the simulation performance in terms of the time of execution and memory consumption.

Fig. 4 shows the simulator runtime in seconds on top of the number of algorithms run. Even in one single run, CrowdSenSim 2.0 achieves a lower run time than CrowdSenSim (7s in average

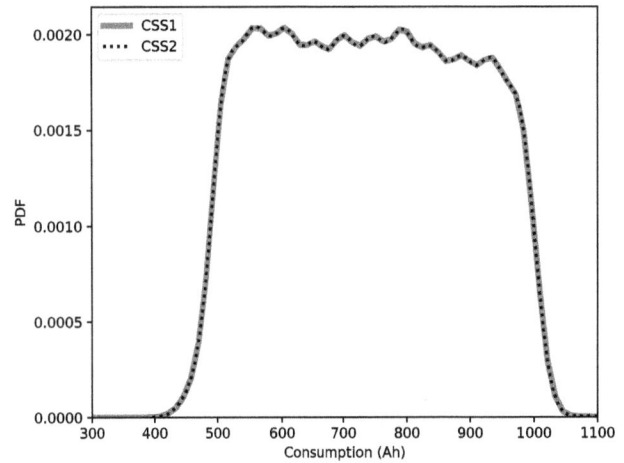

Figure 3: Density of the energy consumed by participants with CrowdSenSim and CrowdSenSim 2.0.

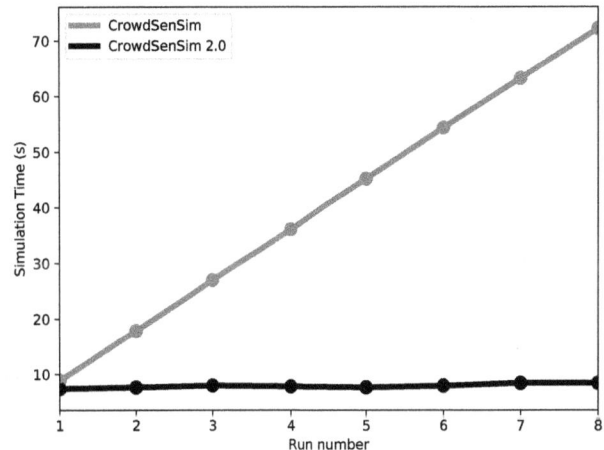

Figure 4: Runtime execution of DDF with multiple runs.

against 8s). Furthermore, as CrowdSenSim 2.0 allows for multiple algorithms to run in parallel – or multiple runs of the same algorithm, – the time execution remains almost constant whereas in the original CrowdSenSim it scales linearly. Indeed, to perform multiple runs, the original CrowdSenSim needs to be launched several times sequentially.

Fig. 5 shows in boxplot form the performance of CrowdSenSim and CrowdSenSim 2.0 in terms of RAM consumption. For a fair comparison, we used only one algorithm at a time. CrowdSenSim 2.0 outperforms CrowdSenSim significantly. This is due to several code optimizations, such as the use of integers as identifiers instead of strings.

5 CASE STUDY: A STATEFUL DISTRIBUTED OPPORTUNISTIC ALGORITHM

In this section, we outline our Asymptotic Opportunistic algorithm for Joint Fairness and Satisfaction index (AO-JFS) that was initially

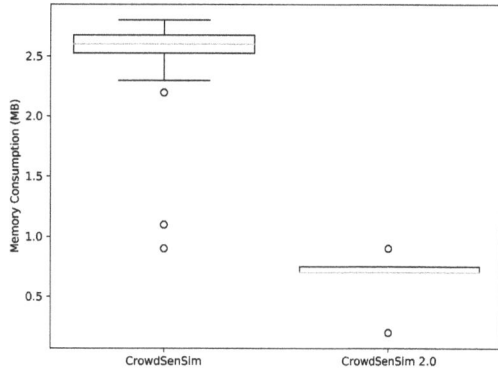

Figure 5: Performance of CrowdSenSim and CrowdSenSim 2.0 in terms of RAM consumption.

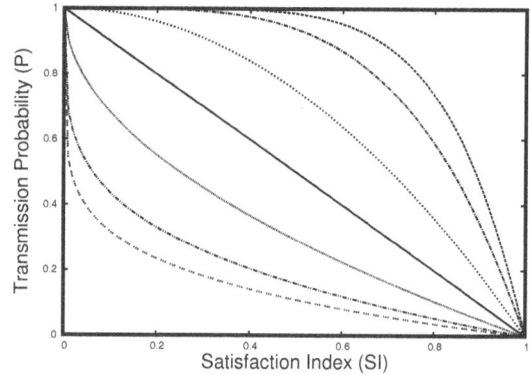

Figure 6: Base probability plus different booster values

proposed in [13] along with its simplified versions AO-F and AO-S, both implemented in CrowdsSenSim 2.0 as members of a family of algorithms called Probabilistic Distributed Algorithms (PDA). Originally, performance evaluation was conducted using an ad-hoc simulator. The algorithm has been designed for data collection control, that is, preventing the whole scenario from generating too much or excessively less data. Too less data would result in a poor mapping of a phenomenon on an urban (or rural) environment, whereas too much data may result in too much noise to get rid of as well as an unbearable amount of users to reward for data that is much more than required and, consequently, an unnecessary energy consumption. We model such scenario in a push-based and totally anonymous distributed algorithm in which the central entity has no direct control over the single users – i.e., it cannot specifically query users about certain resources – neither it has knowledge of where the users are and how many of them are contributing. Participants can contribute pushing their data at a defined frequency to the central entity, which will only reply with a Satisfaction Index (SI), a number that resembles how much the server is "satisfied" about the number of observations received in a defined time window about a resource. Consequentially, participants decide with a probabilistic distribution whether to contribute or not at the following time slot on top of the received SI: if the satisfaction is low, they are pushed to contribute more, if it is high, their contribution is discouraged.

A similar version of such algorithm was implemented in the original CrowdSenSim [20] and called PDA, although CrowdSenSim 2.0 for its stateful approach would have been required to assess AO-JFS properly. Indeed, AO-JFS requires the central entity to be aware of all data delivered by the participants at each instant of time in order to correctly calculate the SI. With the original CrowdSenSim, each participant executes all its events completely before the events of another participant can take place. Hence, the chronological order of the events is violated. Therefore, CrowdSenSim 2.0 with its stateful approach is necessary for any MCS algorithm that heavily depends on the chronological sequence of the events. In the rest of the section, we will outline in detail the behavior of AO-JFS.

5.1 AO-JFS Core Idea

We can model the problem as N different stations (we use the terms stations, users, and participants interchangeably) that adhere

to the MCS campaign and perform observations against a given phenomenon. Such number N can vary over time due to mobility, in particular, participants may leave the interested area, whereas new ones may join it. We assume to split our timeline in time slices Δt_i, that represent the atomic units during which a station cannot transmit more than once due to internal clocks. We also assume that the stations will send observations relative to v certain resources $\Psi_0, \ldots, \Psi_v$ periodically. The central entity's goal is to obtain exactly M_j observations about Ψ_j for $j \in [0, v]$ within every time window T_i, the length of which is given by $|T| = w$. We follow the approach of the sliding window, thus $T_i = \{\Delta t_{i-w}, \ldots, \Delta t_i\}$, this means that T_i and T_{i-1} are overlapping by $w - 1$ time slots. The central entity displays the performances of the data collection process through the above-cited SI. Such value is calculated upon each time window T_i and it is defined as $SI_{i,j} = \frac{m_{i,j}}{M_j}$, where $m_{i,j}$ is the actual number of observations received by the central entity within T_i for the resource Ψ_j. The aim of the central entity is to obtain a SI equal to 1 for each resource.

We assume that each participant knows the SI values at all times (i.e., the central entity broadcasts the SI constantly) and, for each atomic time slot, performs a decision of whether to send or not the local measurement of the sensor (for each resource). In detail, at the time Δt_{i+1}, each participant calculates a probability of sending the measurement relative to the sensor Ψ_j that is basically the inverse of the received $SI_{i,j}$, therefore $P_{i,j} = 1 - CSI_{i-1,j}$ with $CSI_{i,j}$ being the Constrained Satisfaction Index:

$$CSI_{i,j} = \begin{cases} \epsilon & \text{if } SI_{i,j} < \epsilon, \\ 1 - \epsilon & \text{if } SI_{i,j} > 1 - \epsilon, \\ SI_{i,j} & \text{otherwise}, \end{cases} \tag{1}$$

with ϵ being a very small number (in our case 0.001). This forces the SI to range from a very small number close to 0 to a number close to 1 for the purpose of probability calculation.

5.2 Boosting Runtime Execution

To prevent contributions to stabilize at a too low or too high SI, we introduced boosters for the probability calculation. We define a booster as an exponent E to which we elevate the CSI in the probability calculation: $P_{i,j} = 1 - CSI_{i-1,j}^E$. Fig. 6 shows the probability curve for different values of E (the central straight line is obviously for $E = 1$). Specifically, we introduce an overall booster value b_j and an individual value k_j per sensor.

Suppose the aim is to maintain SI in the range $SI \in [\sqcap_{SI}; \sqcup_{SI}]$, where the bounds are, for example, set as 0.95 and 1.15. Then $\forall i, j$, if $SI_{i,j} > \sqcap_{SI}$ then $b_j = dec(b_j)$, whereas if $SI_{i,j} < \sqcup_{SI}$ then $b_j = inc(b_j)$ with:

$$inc(b) = \begin{cases} \frac{1}{(1/b)-1} & \text{if } b < 1, \\ b + 1 & \text{otherwise.} \end{cases} \quad (2)$$

$$dec(b) = \begin{cases} b - 1 & \text{if } b > 1, \\ \frac{1}{(1/b)+1} & \text{otherwise.} \end{cases} \quad (3)$$

k is the attempting factor, calculated individually by each station on top of the received b as

$$k_j = \begin{cases} \lfloor \log_2(\eta) \rfloor & \text{if } b_j < 1, \\ \eta \cdot b_j & \text{if } b_j \geq 1, \end{cases} \quad (4)$$

where $\eta > 0$ is the number of Δt_i slots elapsed since the last transmission. In the end, the probability is calculated as

$$P_{i,j} = 1 - CSI_{i-1,j}^{inc^k(b)}. \quad (5)$$

Note that the term $f^n(x)$ indicates the iterative composition as $f^n(x) = f \circ f^{n-1}(x)$.

5.3 Implementation and Testing of AO-JFS

We outline how to integrate the AO-JFS algorithm (§ 5) with CrowdSenSim 2.0. AO-JFS is a distributed algorithm where the active part is given by the participants and the central entity is only "reactive". In more details, each event generated by the event generator on the map triggers an action by a participant. Since events are processed in chronological order, each of them depends on the sequence of events previously occurred. Thus CrowdSenSim 2.0 can be employed for its analysis. We implemented AO-JFS only in Active Mode, which means that each participant receives information about the status of the SI once every time slot Δt. Upon the occurrence of an event, each participant at time slot t_i (for each sensor j, with $j \in [0, v]$):

(1) Retrieves the known value of the $SI_{i,j}$ and transform it to a $CSI_{i,j}$ for the purpose of the probability calculation using Equation 1.
(2) Retrieves the known value of the global booster b.
(3) Sets the local attempting factor k using Equation 4.
(4) Calculates the actual probability $P_{i,j}$ to send the observation for the resource Ψ_j using Equation 5.

Therefore, events for an AO-JFS simulation are merely the instants in which a participant decides whether to send observations or not. When all the events for t_i occurred, then the values of the SI are updated before taking into account the next time slot.

Our implementation of AO-JFS is evaluated for 2 hours long simulations in the center of Luxembourg City. Parallelism is used to test 50 runs of AO-JFS at the same time, each of them using a different random seed. Δt is set to 10s and $w = 30$, therefore the time window T is 5min. We set $v = 3$, in particular, we used the three sensors mentioned in § 4 as our resources, and fixed the desired amount of observations as $M_1 = 7500, M_2 = 5000, M_3 = 2500$. We generated users using a uniform distribution and set the total number G as 2500, 5000 and 10000. Fig. 7 shows the number of

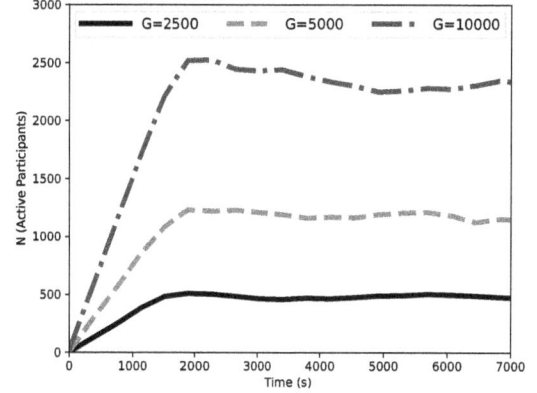

Figure 7: Number of active users N over time for 3 different values of generated users G (G=2500, G=5000, G=10000).

active users N over time. As the distribution is uniform, N tends to reach a steady state after an initial transient.

Fig. 8 shows the results of the simulations. In particular, the values of the SI for the three sensors Ψ_1, Ψ_2, and Ψ_3 are shown for each configuration in the form of a Probability Distribution Function (PDF) in which the data points are the value of the SI sampled each Δt. For each sensor, the SI value stabilizes around 1, which is the goal of AO-JFS. In more details, Fig. 8(b) shows the behavior of the SI at $G = 5000$, with the number of active users over time N floating around 1200. This number is in a good balance with the number of required observations, in fact the SI value for all the sensors tends to cluster almost regularly around 1. Fig. 8(c) shows the behavior of the SI with $G = 10000$, with N settling around 2300. This number is very high in comparison to the number of required measurements. Therefore the effort of AO-JFS is in limiting the number of contributions by the participants. This is even more evident for Ψ_3, the resource for which the fewer contributions are needed, as the respective SI values tend to cluster at a slightly higher value (i.e., around 1.1). On the other hand, Fig. 8(a) shows the SI for $G = 2500$ and, consequently, N floating around 500, which is a low number in comparison to the contribution required. Although the behavior of the SI is quite similar to the other plots, we can appreciate a slight difference for Ψ_3, as its values are more spread. This is due to b being quite high: as the participants are pushed to contribute more, the probability curve gets very high for most of the CSI values in input and causes more likely peaks and troughs in the contribution over time.

6 CONCLUSIONS

This paper presents CrowdSenSim 2.0[4], which extends with major advances the existing CrowdSenSim platform for simulations of MCS activities in realistic urban environments. CrowdSenSim 2.0 exhibits two main novel aspects. First, the simulator features a stateful approach that enforces all events to be executed in chronological order with a higher fine-grained temporal resolution. Second, it features two models to generate the city layouts over realistic street networks where users move, based on the popular OSM and the

---

[4]We make publicly available all the source files and scripts of CrowdSenSim 2.0 under https://crowdsensim.gforge.uni.lu/download.html.

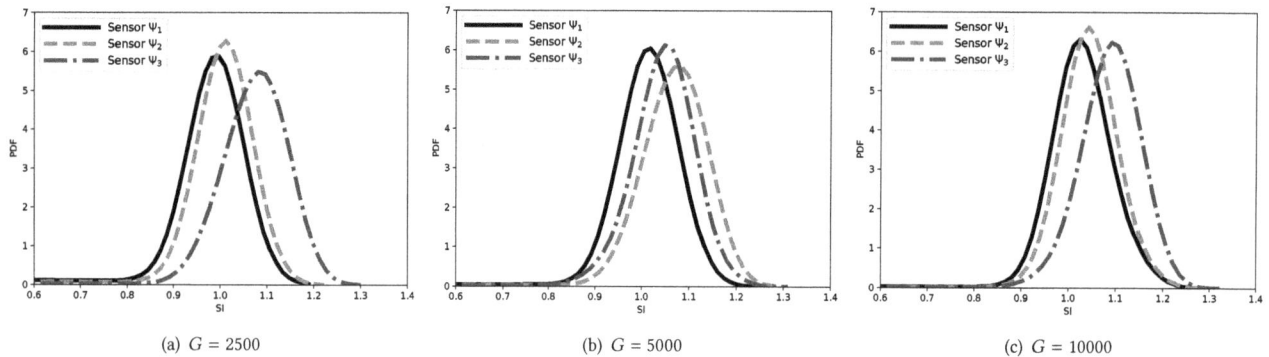

(a) $G = 2500$ (b) $G = 5000$ (c) $G = 10000$

Figure 8: PDF of the SI for the three sensors for different values of G.

Military Grid Reference System. In a nutshell, other advances include extensions of the architectural modules, code refactoring, and algorithms' parallel execution that boost performance by making significantly lower the runtime execution and memory utilization. This clearly enables the simulation of larger scale scenarios, which is of paramount importance for research in MCS. We demonstrate that when feeding CrowdSenSim 2.0 and the original CrowdSenSim with the same list of events, they perform identically in terms of mobile device energy consumed for sensing and reporting, thus making CrowdSenSim 2.0 compatible with previous studies. As an example of use case, we showcase the performance evaluation of a distributed opportunistic algorithm for data collection that shows how the stateful approach is fundamental for specific applications.

ACKNOWLEDGMENT

Dr. Fiandrino's work is supported by the Juan de la Cierva grant from the Spanish Ministry of Economy and Competitiveness (FJCI-2017-32309).

REFERENCES

[1] Luca Bedogni, Marco Fiore, and Christian Glacet. 2018. Temporal Reachability in Vehicular Networks. In *Proc. of IEEE Conference on Computer Communications (INFOCOM)*. 81–89. https://doi.org/10.1109/INFOCOM.2018.8486393
[2] Geoff Boeing. 2017. OSMnx: New methods for acquiring, constructing, analyzing, and visualizing complex street networks. *Computers, Environment and Urban Systems* 65 (2017), 126–139. https://doi.org/10.1016/j.compenvurbsys.2017.05.004
[3] Andrea Capponi, Claudio Fiandrino, Burak Kantarci, Luca Foschini, Dzmitry Kliazovich, and Pascal Bouvry. 2019. A Survey on Mobile Crowdsensing Systems: Challenges, Solutions and Opportunities. *IEEE Communications Surveys Tutorials* (May 2019), 1–49. https://doi.org/10.1109/COMST.2019.2914030
[4] Andrea Capponi, Claudio Fiandrino, Dzmitry Kliazovich, Pascal Bouvry, and Stefano Giordano. 2017. A Cost-Effective Distributed Framework for Data Collection in Cloud-Based Mobile Crowd Sensing Architectures. *IEEE Transactions on Sustainable Computing* 2, 1 (Jan 2017), 3–16. https://doi.org/10.1109/TSUSC.2017.2666043
[5] Claudio Fiandrino, Andrea Capponi, Giuseppe Cacciatore, Dzmitry Kliazovich, Ulrich Sorger, Pascal Bouvry, Burak Kantarci, Fabrizio Granelli, and Stefano Giordano. 2017. Crowdsensim: a simulation platform for mobile crowdsensing in realistic urban environments. *IEEE Access* 5 (Feb 2017), 3490–3503. https://doi.org/10.1109/ACCESS.2017.2671678
[6] Yali Gao, Xiaoyong Li, Jirui Li, and Yunquan Gao. 2017. A dynamic-trust-based recruitment framework for mobile crowd sensing. In *Proc. of IEEE International Conference on Communications (ICC)*. 1–6. https://doi.org/10.1109/ICC.2017.7997420
[7] Gartner. 2019. Gartner Says Global Smartphone Sales Stalled in the Fourth Quarter of 2018. https://www.gartner.com/en/newsroom/press-releases/2019-02-21-gartner-says-global-smartphone-sales-stalled-in-the-fourth-quart
[8] Raino Lampinen. 2001. Universal transverse mercator (UTM) and military grid reference system (MGRS).

[9] Imre Lendák and Károly Farkas. 2015. Evaluation of simulation engines for crowdsensing activities. (2015).
[10] Martina Marjanović, Lea Skorin-Kapov, Krešimir Pripužić, Aleksandar Antonić, and Ivana Podnar Žarko. 2016. Energy-aware and quality-driven sensor management for green mobile crowd sensing. *Journal of Network and Computer Applications* 59 (Jan 2016), 95–108. https://doi.org/10.1016/j.jnca.2015.06.023
[11] MarketsandMarkets. 2018. Crowd analytics market worth $1,142.5 million by 2021. https://www.marketsandmarkets.com/PressReleases/crowd-analytics.asp
[12] Kamal Mehdi, Massinissa Lounis, Ahcène Bounceur, and Tahar Kechadi. 2014. Cupcarbon: A multi-agent and discrete event wireless sensor network design and simulation tool. In *Proc. of 7th International ICST Conference on Simulation Tools and Techniques*. 126–131. https://doi.org/10.4108/icst.simutools.2014.254811
[13] Federico Montori, Luca Bedogni, and Luciano Bononi. 2017. Distributed data collection control in opportunistic mobile crowdsensing. In *Proc. of ACM SMARTOBJECTS*. 19–24. https://doi.org/10.1145/3127502.3127509
[14] Federico Montori, Luca Bedogni, and Luciano Bononi. 2018. A Collaborative Internet of Things Architecture for Smart Cities and Environmental Monitoring. *IEEE Internet of Things Journal* 5, 2 (Apr 2018), 592–605. https://doi.org/10.1109/JIOT.2017.2720855
[15] Federico Montori, Luca Bedogni, Alain Di Chiappari, and Luciano Bononi. 2016. SenSquare: A mobile crowdsensing architecture for smart cities. In *Proc. of IEEE 3rd World Forum on Internet of Things (WF-IoT)*. 536–541. https://doi.org/10.1109/WF-IoT.2016.7845471
[16] Federico Montori, Marco Gramaglia, Luca Bedogni, Marco Fiore, Farid Sheikh, Luciano Bononi, and Andrea Vesco. 2017. Automotive Communications in LTE: A Simulation-Based Performance Study. In *Proc. of IEEE 86th Vehicular Technology Conference (VTC-Fall)*. 1–6. https://doi.org/10.1109/VTCFall.2017.8288297
[17] Federico Montori, Prem Prakash Jayaraman, Ali Yavari, Alireza Hassani, and Dimitrios Georgakopoulos. 2018. The Curse of Sensing: Survey of techniques and challenges to cope with sparse and dense data in mobile crowd sensing for Internet of Things. *Pervasive and Mobile Computing* 49 (Jul 2018), 111–125. https://doi.org/10.1016/j.pmcj.2018.06.009
[18] Riccardo Pinciroli and Salvatore Distefano. 2017. Characterization and evaluation of mobile crowdsensing performance and energy indicators. *ACM SIGMETRICS Performance Evaluation Review* 44, 4 (2017), 80–90. https://doi.org/10.1145/3092819.3092829
[19] Cristian Tanas and Jordi Herrera-Joancomartí. 2013. Crowdsensing simulation using ns-3. In *International Workshop on Citizen in Sensor Networks*. Springer, 47–58. https://doi.org/10.1007/978-3-319-04178-0_5
[20] Mattia Tomasoni, Andrea Capponi, Claudio Fiandrino, Dzmitry Kliazovich, Fabrizio Granelli, and Pascal Bouvry. 2018. Why energy matters? Profiling energy consumption of mobile crowdsensing data collection frameworks. *Pervasive and Mobile Computing* 51 (2018), 193–208. https://doi.org/10.1016/j.pmcj.2018.10.002
[21] Piergiorgio Vitello, Andrea Capponi, Claudio Fiandrino, Paolo Giaccone, Dzmitry Kliazovich, and Pascal Bouvry. 2018. High-precision design of pedestrian mobility for smart city simulators. In *Proc. of IEEE International Conference on Communications (ICC)*. 1–6. https://doi.org/10.1109/ICC.2018.8422599

An In-depth Analysis of the Impact of Battery Usage Patterns on Performance of Task Allocation Algorithms in Sparse Mobile Crowdsensing

Garvita Bajaj & Pushpendra Singh
IIIT-Delhi, India

ABSTRACT

Mobile Crowdsensing leverages the sensing capabilities of multiple mobile devices to execute large-scale sensing tasks by breaking them into smaller tasks for execution on individual mobile devices. Task allocation algorithms are used to efficiently distribute these smaller sensing tasks to a subset of participants while optimizing system-level goals (such as location accuracy or data quality) for participant selection. The sensing tasks, e.g., collecting GPS tagged data, are often energy-intensive and battery consumption during sensing task execution remains a major concern for participants. So far no in-depth study exists that evaluates the impact of battery consumption on allocation algorithms.

In this work, we conducted an in-depth study on the effects of battery consumption patterns of smartphone users. We studied the impact of battery consumption patterns extracted from a real-world data-set on standard as well as state-of-the-art algorithms to show how different battery usage patterns affect the performance of allocation algorithms. Our work provides an important insight into factors affecting the performance of allocation algorithms and advocates incorporating battery usage patterns for the future development of these algorithms.

ACM Reference format:
Garvita Bajaj & Pushpendra Singh IIIT-Delhi, India. 2019. An In-depth Analysis of the Impact of Battery Usage Patterns on Performance of Task Allocation Algorithms in Sparse Mobile Crowdsensing. In *Proceedings of 22nd Int'l ACM Conference on Modeling, Analysis and Simulation of Wireless and Mobile Systems, Miami Beach, FL, USA, November 25–29, 2019 (MSWiM '19)*, 10 pages.
https://doi.org/10.1145/3345768.3355930

1 INTRODUCTION

Smartphones equipped with sensing technologies are now ubiquitously available. This ubiquity enables the domain of Mobile CrowdSensing (MCS)—a paradigm where volunteering individuals with sensor-enabled mobile devices contribute to large-scale sensing. The initial research in this domain was primarily focused on high-level goals such as facilitating the development of large-scale

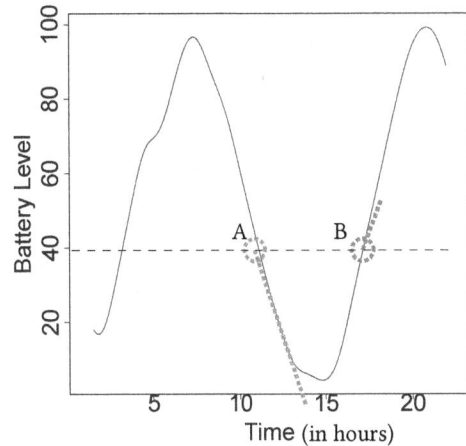

Figure 1: A smartphone battery consumption pattern

sensing applications [10, 14, 21, 47, 52] and proposing novel applications [6, 17, 22, 30, 38, 48, 53, 55, 57, 58, 71]. Lately, researchers have started delving into fine-grained problems associated with inefficient energy consumption on devices that impact user participation [23, 37, 69].

To provide efficient sensor data collection, *Sparse Mobile Crowd sensing* [63] has been proposed. Sparse MCS advocates sensor data collection from only a subset of participants instead of *all* participants to improve energy efficiency for all available participants. To allow this subset selection, several *task allocation algorithms* have been proposed in the literature [15].

However, task execution on selected participants is still energy-intensive and consumes the battery available on mobile devices, which remains a major concern for participants. Existing task allocation algorithms and frameworks [10, 14, 42, 47] either completely overlook the battery available on mobile devices during task allocation or only consider the residual battery level [1], which provides partial information. The residual battery level only indicates an instantaneous state that varies continuously, depending on the characteristics of the user and/or device [20, 31]. For example, with a real battery consumption pattern of a mobile device is at 40% level, as shown in Figure 1, the device may last for two to five hours, depending on the battery age, battery type, and device usage. Moreover, this device can either be in a discharging state or plugged into a power source, but this information is not conveyed at the instantaneous residual battery level.

Our research shows that the *performance of allocation algorithms is greatly affected by the battery consumption pattern of a device.* We have studied the impact of different real-world battery consumption patterns, obtained from real datasets, on the performance of allocation algorithms. We have evaluated four task allocation algorithms, namely: *(a)* two state-of-the-art algorithms, MinAST [76] and NVGreedy [7], which propose fair and balanced allocation schemes respectively; and *(b)* two standard scheduling algorithms, Round-Robin and Random, which are used in the absence of any defined algorithm [2, 5, 27]. Based on our analysis, we comment on the relevant factors affecting the efficiency of allocation algorithms. We also provide insights into incorporating battery usage patterns for future use and the development of algorithms. To summarize, the main contributions of our work are:

(1) To the best of our knowledge, this is the first work that provides a detailed, in-depth study about the impact of real-world battery consumption patterns on the performance of task allocation algorithms in sparse MCS systems.

(2) To identify real-world battery consumption patterns reflecting real-world device usage, we use a data-driven approach (Section 3) to identify similarities (shape- and feature-based) in battery consumption across 411 patterns identified in the Livelab battery dataset[1]. We also show the use of different time-series clustering techniques (hierarchical and partitional) to identify representative battery consumption patterns empirically.

(3) We identify critical battery consumption patterns (Section 4) and analyze their impact on the performance of task allocation algorithms (Section 5).

Our work provides a foundation to explore and include the impact of device battery consumption patterns on task allocation algorithms. Since batteries continue to remain the most precious resource of mobile devices and with the increasing need for efficient MCS algorithms, we provide an important insight into how future MCS algorithms should be developed.

2 RELATED WORK

We review two main aspects of task allocation algorithms proposed in the literature. First, we broadly categorize the approaches proposed so far. Next, we compare works that directly or indirectly consider battery usage of devices for energy efficiency that impacts the performance of allocation algorithms.

2.1 Task Allocation in MCS

There are two types of task allocation models used in MCS [56]: (i) *Worker Selected Tasks* (WST) where participants manually decide which tasks to execute based on their preferences; (ii) *Server Allocated Tasks* (SAT) where a central server having a global view of participants allocates tasks to achieve a system-level optimization goal. WST is a simpler but sub-optimal approach as manual selection of tasks by participants does not offer any guarantee of timely task execution. This approach has been used by frameworks and applications [11, 13, 14] to provide flexibility and privacy to users. On the other hand, the SAT provides a more optimal approach where a central server, with a global view of participants, is

responsible for allocating tasks to participants based on application-specific optimization goals. These optimization goals, prevalent in the literature, can be broadly categorized into four buckets: (i) *minimize travel distance/makespan time* [8, 28, 40, 61, 65, 75]: to allocate tasks to participants that are closest to task locations or require the least amount of time to provide sensor data in return for user incentives or privacy guarantees; (ii) *maximize location coverage* [24, 34, 66, 68]: to select a subset of participants that provide large geographical coverage based on their historic/predicted locations while minimizing user incentives or travel distances; (iii) *maximize sensor data quality* [39, 54, 59, 60, 62]: to ensure high data quality or QoI (Quality of Information) for better accuracy either within budget constraints, or while considering user reputations or contexts such as location; and (iv) *ensure energy efficiency* [7, 76]: to efficiently utilize resources available on mobile participants. The efficient utilization of resources is required to maintain a fair or balanced distribution of tasks among participants so that participants don't feel overburdened by task requests and can use their limited resources to perform regular tasks with their devices (e.g., making phone calls and sending SMSs). We now discuss some of these energy-efficient approaches proposed for task allocation for improved performance.

2.2 Performance Improvements

Network bandwidth and limited battery life remain the primary concerns for mobile users. In this section, we discuss works that either aim to improve network bandwidth utilization or consider device battery levels and their impact on the performance of task allocation algorithms. *Piggybacking* has been shown to reduce network costs by up to 50% [64], but their impact on battery consumption has not been studied in detail. Piggybacking also offers opportunities to minimize user incentives [68] while satisfying probabilistic coverage [74] and *k*-depth coverage [67] constraints. Although piggybacking can ensure an expected number of participants returning the sensed results [69] and is well-suited for systems with dynamic tasks [34], the timeliness of task execution still relies solely on a user's interactions with smartphones, which also impacts the battery usage of devices. *Compressive CrowdSensing* (CCS) has been proposed to minimize the number of users required for task execution while ensuring sufficient data quality [62] or providing overall system accuracy [70]. However, CCS only ensures that selected users are not over-burdened with task execution *after* tasks have been allocated to them. There is no way of ensuring that the participants selected for task execution have sufficient resources available and are not burdened by task allocation. Further, the impact of CCS on battery consumption has also not been considered in detail by the existing works. Some works have proposed task allocation in a *fair and balanced manner* to overcome the problem associated with overburdening participants based on different parameters, such as overall sensing time of a system [76], available device resources [7], and social relationships of participants [19], but their effect on limited battery of participants has not been validated extensively.

Unlike processing capabilities and network technologies, the *battery capacity* of mobile devices has failed to keep up with the rapid rate of smartphone evolution [18]. The effects of task allocation algorithms on the limited battery capacity of smartphones

---

[1]http://livelab.recg.rice.edu/traces.html

have not yet been studied in detail. Only some algorithms have incorporated battery levels of participants [1, 25, 37]. Some of them propose to use the contextual parameters of the participants, such as sociability [1] and activity [25], while accounting for residual battery levels of participants and discouraging device participation below a certain battery threshold.

While a fixed threshold makes it convenient for allocation algorithms to filter out "inefficient" participants, it becomes irrelevant when both the participants and the tasks are heterogeneous in nature. Liu et al. [37] propose a behavioral battery model to identify this threshold. Their model considers the battery levels of participants upon entering a sensing region and upon being allocated certain sensing tasks. Their model relies only on the initial battery level and not on the battery consumption pattern, once the tasks are assigned. This research gap was identified, and a detailed approach to studying the impact of the battery consumption pattern on the performance of task allocation algorithms is presented.

3 IDENTIFYING REPRESENTATIVE BATTERY PATTERNS

Studying battery usage patterns is different from using traditional battery models [29, 32]. Battery models are used to describe the effects of device power consumption on the instantaneous state of the battery. This needs to be updated, as the battery ages over time [33]. In this research, real-life battery usage patterns, provided by the Livelab dataset[1], have been used to identify long-term battery usage patterns. As a first step, the representative patterns from the dataset must be identified. This is challenging because, like any other real-world dataset, the battery usage patterns available in the dataset are noisy and irregular in nature. In order to identify a representative set of real-world battery usage patterns, we propose a methodological approach for processing and clustering the noisy, real-world battery usage data on the basis of their charging/discharging trends. In the following sections, we describe the details of the Livelab dataset, our approach for data-cleaning, and the clustering technique used to identify representative patterns.

3.1 Preprocessing the Dataset

The Livelab dataset [49] consists of time series data with anonymized battery readings (in %) collected from 34 smartphones. The data is collected at a frequency of 20 seconds over a period of 6–12 months. Each entry in the dataset contains an anonymized user id, UNIX timestamp, battery level, charging state, amount of charge remaining, and the hour of the day. For this work, we have used the UNIX timestamps and battery levels. To identify representative battery usage patterns and study their impact on the performance of task allocation algorithms, we identify similarities in (dis)charging characteristics for battery traces available in the dataset. A small timeslice of a random user's battery pattern from the Livelab dataset is shown in Figure 2a. From the figure, we identify two major problems with the data: (i) *Absence of regular patterns*: the (dis)charging rates in battery traces vary with time in an irregular manner. (ii) *Missing values*: battery levels are not recorded for all time intervals. These problems are persistent across the entire dataset. We preprocess the data (as described below) to solve these issues and extract useful traces.

We use time-series data analysis, as battery data is time-dependent and univariate. Figure 2 highlights the preprocessing steps. We first extract long patterns of battery usage from the available battery traces of anonymized users (Figure 2b). We then convert these extracted patterns (with missing values and noise) to time-series objects using R libraries (Figure 2c). This allows the interpolation of missing values. To further eliminate noise from the extracted patterns (Figure 2d), we decompose the time series patterns using standard *R* libraries—stlplus and lubridate—to extract actual battery usage trends [50].

We restrict ourselves to studying only long battery traces to identify trends prevailing over a period of time. To define the length of traces, we set a threshold of 24 hours (86400 seconds) and consider all traces in the SQL dataset with at least 2500 battery readings during this duration (50% of the total 4320 readings possible in the 24-hour duration at a frequency of 20 seconds). This eliminates time windows with no battery data available over long durations and provides a total of 411 long battery traces from the Livelab dataset. Once this data is available, we convert it to time-series format using the standard ts() function in R. Figure 2b shows a sample trace extracted with this technique. We use linear interpolation offered by the zoo library on these time series objects to extract missing values. This defines their dependence on time, which helps in processing the noisy data further. Figure 2c shows an example of a generated time-series. Next, we use standard libraries for time-series decomposition to eliminate noise components from the extracted traces (Figure 2d). We decompose the 411 extracted time series objects to extract data trends using the stl() function of the stlplus library. Figure 3, which is a zoomed-in version of Figure 2d, shows the components extracted from a sample battery trace. The decomposed battery traces have a negligible seasonality component (±2), indicating that battery patterns do not repeat over time. The noise component in the available data is also small (±5.0); we, therefore, eliminate it from battery patterns to extract battery usage trends. For the rest of this work, without any loss of generality, we use the terms 'trend', 'trace', and 'pattern' interchangeably to denote the trend components of extracted battery traces.

3.2 Clustering the battery trends

We use clustering techniques to group similar battery usage patterns together and use corresponding cluster centroids as representative traces. This is done to identify similarities in phases of battery charge/discharge across all identified traces as battery usage patterns are largely affected by users' contexts. For example, all users in a corporate desk-job, having access to charging points, can have frequent and regular charging patterns, while users in a field job might have more disruptive charging cycles. We use cluster analysis or clustering techniques to identify such similarities in battery usage/charging cycles among all 411 identified trace.

Clustering allows grouping data into clusters such that data in the same cluster are more similar (intra-cluster distance is low) than data in different clusters (inter-cluster distance is high). Several clustering algorithms have been proposed in the literature [36]. To identify the best method for our data, we concentrate on appropriate similarity measures, clustering algorithms, and cluster quality.

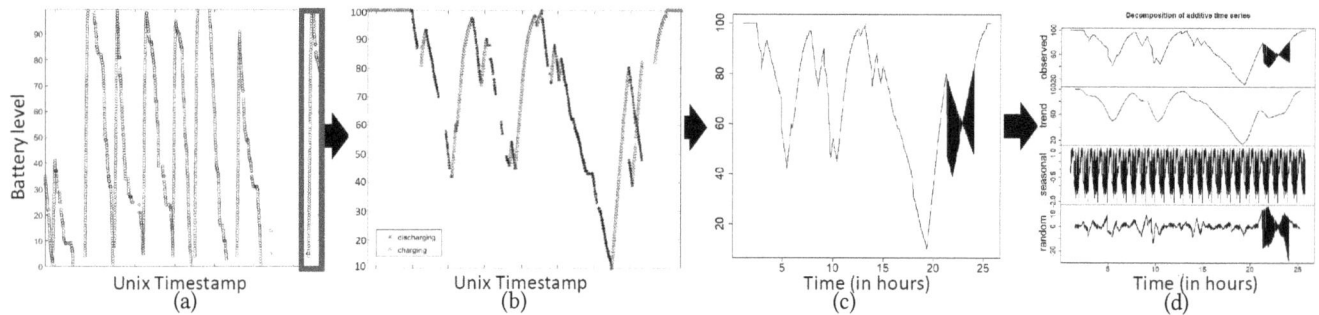

Figure 2: [Best viewed in color] Steps involved in cleaning and processing the battery data: (a) Extracting raw SQL dumps comprising timestamped battery levels from Livelab dataset, (b) Extracting continuous battery traces available over a long period of time. The trace highlighted within the blue box in Figure 2a is shown. (c) Converting the extracted traces (incomplete and noisy) to time-series objects for further processing, (d) Decomposing time series objects to extract usage trend and eliminate noise and seasonality components (please refer Figure 3 for a zoomed-in image).

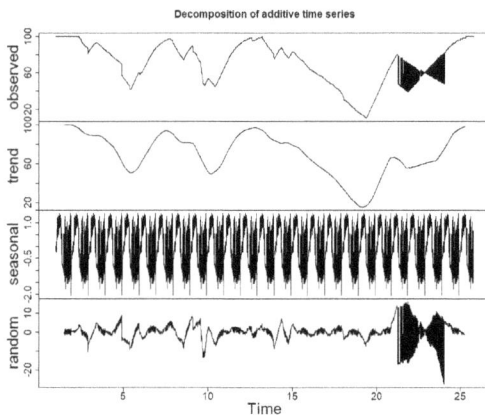

Figure 3: Decomposition of time series data into trend, seasonality, and noise components. The observed data is the raw time series data, trend reflects the pattern, seasonal component indicates frequency of repetition, and noise indicates random component of data.

Similarity Measure: Several similarity measures have been used for time-series data [44]. For this work, based on the inherent properties of battery data, we use two similarity measures *(i)* **Elastic shape-based**: The choice of elastic shape-based measure is motivated by the fact that we want to extract similar shapes/trends of battery usage (charging/discharging patterns). We, therefore, use DTW [35] and SBD [45] measures that allow one-to-many points and one-to-none point mapping, i.e., a point on one shape (pattern in our case) may be mapped to zero or more points on other shapes. This also allows a comparison of battery trends of unequal lengths. *(ii)* **Feature-based**: The reason behind using feature-based measures is that the battery dataset exhibits high correlation (autocorrelation and partial auto-correlation), i.e., battery level at one timestamp is highly related to the battery levels before and after

that timestamp. We, therefore, use ACF and PACF distance measures [43] that aim to identify hidden features (correlations) in data.

Clustering Algorithm: For clustering the data based on these similarity measures, we opt for clustering algorithms based on **connectivity models and centroid models**. Connectivity-based models include hierarchical clustering algorithms where data objects are grouped based on the distance between them. The connectivity between clusters is defined using one of the several cluster amalgamation methods available: single, average, complete, and minimum variance (ward.D2) [26]. For detailed explanations about these linkage methods, we refer the readers to work by Punj et al. [46].

For the centroid model, we consider Partitioning Around Medoids (PAM) clustering algorithm. PAM is robust to noise and outliers in data as it selects actual data points as cluster centers. For our dataset, we use these two clustering algorithms (hierarchical and PAM) while considering all possible cluster amalgamation techniques, with all distance measures identified (DTW, SBD, ACF, and PACF). This generates 20 combinations (4 distance measures with 5 algorithms each—hierarchical clustering with 4 different linkages and partitional clustering). Using empirical analysis, we identify the best combination of distance measure and clustering algorithm for our data. The results are presented in Section 3.3.

Cluster Quality: To determine the quality (goodness) of clusters generated with different combinations of similarity measures and clustering algorithms, we use **internal cluster validation** as there is no external information available about the data (ground truth or data labels). Internal validation helps in testing two statistical properties of clusters—compactness and separation. Compactness is related to intra-cluster distance (how close the cluster members are) and separation is associated with inter-cluster distance (are the clusters well separated). We use Silhouette Width (SW) as the measure of internal validation as it provides a non-linear combination of both these properties. Silhouette Width "validates the clustering performance based on the pairwise difference of between and within-cluster distances" [41].

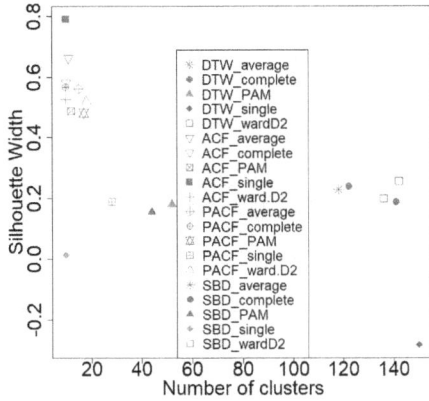

Figure 4: [Best viewed in color] Empirical analysis of cluster quality (Silhouette Width) obtained using different clustering algorithms and similarity measures.

3.3 Results

We calculated the average SW for different cluster structures identified using the 20 combinations of distance measures and clustering algorithms. The average SW obtained for different cluster sizes (represented using x-axis) are shown in Figure 4. From the figure, we observe that clusters identified based on ACF distance have good or strong structures (average SW > 0.5). This is because most of the battery patterns have similar correlations. The highest average SW (0.78) is obtained for 10 clusters obtained with ACF distance for hierarchical clustering with the single linkage method. For these 10 clusters obtained, we extract their centroids to represent all cluster members. Figure 5 shows the 10 cluster centroids ({$B1, B2, ...B10$}) identified. Although centroids B6–B9 appear similar and in 100% charged state, the deviations in their peaks are different. To study the impact of these variations, we also include these centroids in our analysis.

4 PERFORMANCE IMPACT ANALYSIS

In this section, we focus on evaluating the impact of representative battery patterns (identified in Section 3) on the performance of task allocation algorithms in sparse MCS. To focus exclusively on resource utilization, we consider a spatially-blind sparse MCS system that services location-independent tasks using M available participants. For each task issued to the system, a task allocation algorithm is required to select N devices for task execution from the M devices available (where $N \subset M^2$ and $N \geq 1$).

We consider two state-of-the-art algorithms, MinAST [76] and NVGreedy [7], that aim to provide fair and balanced allocation of tasks to participants. ***MinAST*** aims to be fair in an energy-efficient manner and allocates tasks such that the maximum aggregate sensing time of participants is minimized. Two versions of the algorithm have been proposed - offline and online. We only consider the online version of MinAST, that uses a greedy allocation approach and is meant for systems where tasks arrive dynamically. The second

algorithm—***NVGreedy***—aims to allocate dynamic tasks to participants in a balanced way such that the system can service more tasks. It is based on a model of "richness" of participants based on their dynamic resource levels. We also consider standard approaches of ***Round-Robin*** and ***Random*** allocation schemes for task allocation.

Evaluation Metrics: We define two metrics to capture the state of participants with the ability to participate in sensing tasks:

DEFINITION 4.1. *Service Lifetime (SVL) The total number of tasks for which at least N participants stay alive with the system (in the absence of any external intervention) and service tasks.*

DEFINITION 4.2. *System Lifetime (SL): The total number of tasks for which all M participants remain alive with the system (in the absence of any external intervention).*

Figure 6 shows a visual representation of these lifetimes. We conduct MATLAB simulations to calculate these lifetimes achieved by different task allocation algorithms for different battery patterns.

4.1 Simulation Setup

Our goal is to identify the battery patterns that result in high lifetimes (SL and SVL) for task allocation algorithms. We consider a MCS system with 100 available participants (M), where tasks arrive dynamically. Each task requests a subset of these available participants (N). Different task allocation algorithms select different subsets of participants, and each selected participant spends some energy (consumes battery) for task execution in addition to their normal battery charge/discharge rate. The battery decay (β) incurred by participants in task execution can be homogeneous (equal decay for all) or heterogeneous (variable decay depending on device characteristics). To assess the impact of battery patterns on the performance of task allocation algorithms using simulations, we initialized all participants with a similar battery usage pattern. Please note that in the real-world, participants may have different battery usage patterns; however, for simulations, we limited all participants to have the same battery patterns in order to analyze their performances independent of battery patterns. To further analyze the individual effect of each participant, we assumed non-overlapping and sequential homogeneous tasks, i.e., at a given instance of time, the selected participants served at most one task and spent equal amounts of battery on the task execution. The results obtained can then be applied to the real-world for better performance.

For simulations, we varied the number of participants and the amount of battery spent by them on sensing task execution. The number of participants varied from 20% to 80% of available participants ($N = \{20, 40, 60, 80\}$). Each participant spends the same amount of energy (β) for task execution, which varies from 2% to 6%. Thus, if in non-sensing time duration, a participant spends x% of battery, then for the same time duration, if a sensing task is allocated to this participant, it would end up spending $(x + \beta)$% of battery. Since the sensing tasks have a well-defined time frame, this allows us to model the battery level of the participants even after the sensing task execution is finished. Table 1 summarizes the simulation settings used. For each combination of N and β, we

---

[2]Please note that if all available devices are required for task execution, then all the performance of all task allocation algorithms with all battery patterns will be identical. Hence, we consider $N \subset M$.

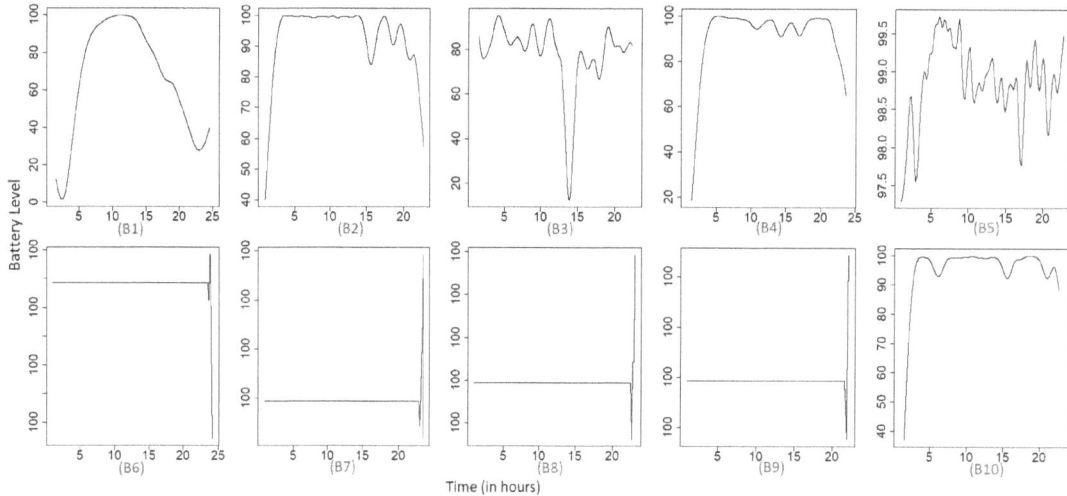

Figure 5: Representative battery patterns ($B1, B2, ...B10$) identified as cluster centroids.

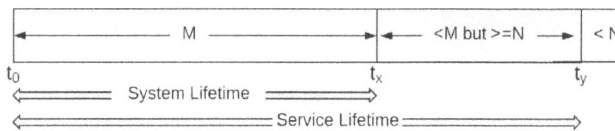

Figure 6: Performance of algorithms is measured in terms of lifetimes. The numbers in blocks represent the number of participants alive for different tasks ($t_0, .., t_x, ...t_y$).

Table 1: Simulation Settings

PARAMETER	VALUE
Number of participants (M)	100
Required participants (N)	{20,40,60,80}
Task duration	5 units each
Tasks issued	500
Battery decay for a task (β)	{2%,4%,6%}
Number of battery patterns used	10
Number of iterations	100

perform 100 iterations to evaluate the performance of task allocation algorithms with representative battery patterns. The lifetime values considered for each algorithm are the average of lifetimes calculated over 100 iterations.

4.2 Experiment 1: Initial Hypothesis Validation

Our initial hypothesis is that solely using the residual battery level is insufficient to decide whether task allocation to participants will be energy efficient or not.

We conduct simulations to allocate tasks to 40 out of 100 available participants ($N = 40$, $M = 100$), where each selected participant experiences a uniform battery decay of 2% for task execution[3] ($\beta =$

[3]Please note that similar results are achieved for other values of N and β.

2). We randomly select 140 battery usage patterns (approximately one-third of identified 411 patterns). At the start of every simulation, we initialize all 100 participants with one of the selected battery traces and issue sequential tasks until the devices die out. For 140 patterns selected, we conduct 140 simulations (100 iterations each) and calculate the average SLs and SVLs achieved with each battery pattern using different task allocation algorithms.

Results: We plot the average lifetimes (SLs and SVLs) achieved with different task allocation algorithms against two features of the battery patterns considered—the initial residual battery level and charging state at the start of simulations. Figure 7 shows that multiple battery patterns initially at the same residual level (represented on the x-axis) and charging state (represented using colors) lead to varying lifetimes. Some instances of this behavior are highlighted in Figures 7a and 7b using boxes. As an example, two battery patterns at initial levels of 82% and in different charging states lead to different SLs (17, 47, and 49) with the MinAST algorithm. Further, it is to be noted that although lifetimes obtained are higher when participants are in the charging state (upper triangular halves of Figure 7), the lifetimes obtained are still variable.

This proves our initial hypothesis that **the performance of algorithms varies with battery usage patterns of participants and does not depend on the residual battery level or even their charging state**. Therefore, relying on a threshold battery level is insufficient for defining efficient allocation in a sparse MCS.

4.3 Experiment 2: Varying Performance with Battery Patterns

The goal of this experiment is to identify which representative battery patterns largely affect the performance of task allocation algorithms. These patterns are referred to as 'critical battery patterns' that cause drastic variations in the performance of task allocation algorithms. In order to identify critical patterns, 120 simulations (with 100 iterations each) are conducted for all the possible combinations of N and β for 10 representative battery traces ($|N| * |\beta| * 10 = 120$). At the start of each simulation, all the available participants are

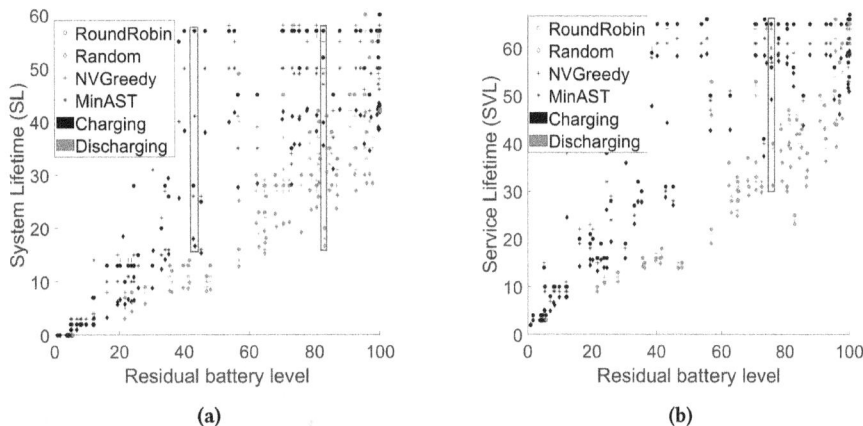

(a) (b)

Figure 7: [Best viewed in color] Multiple patterns with same initial battery levels and charging states result in varying system and service lifetimes (SL and SVL respectively) for task allocation algorithms. For all points marked in rectangular boxes, task allocation algorithms achieve different lifetimes for patterns starting at same initial battery level and charging state.

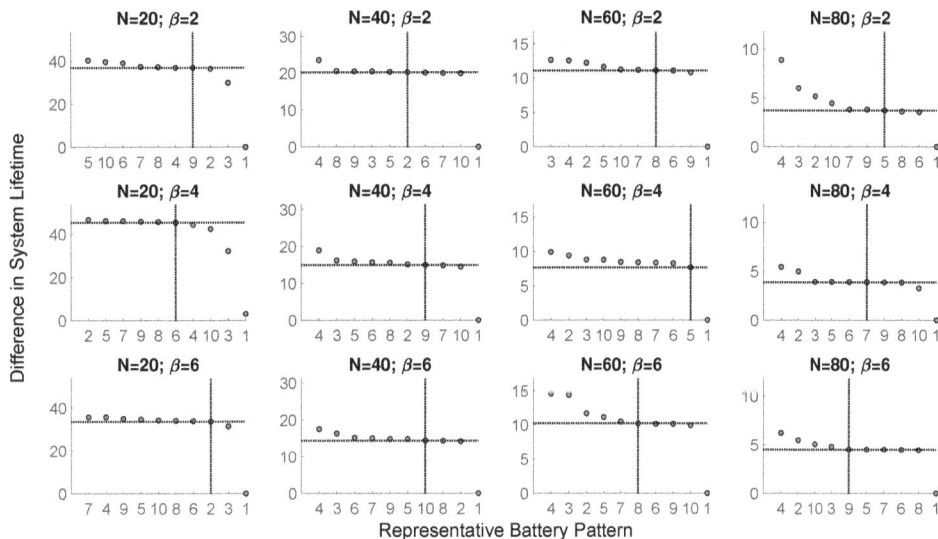

Figure 8: Difference in the maximum and minimum SLs (arranged in descending order) attained with representative battery patterns for different task allocation algorithms for varying N and β. All patterns lying on or to the left of dotted line (knee-point) are critical points that cause large differences in lifetimes of task allocation algorithms.

initialized with one representative battery trace, and they are issued with sequential, homogeneous tasks to the system. The lifetimes (SL and SVL) achieved are monitored by using different task allocation algorithms for each representative battery pattern. Similar to the results of the previous experiment, task allocation algorithms achieve varying lifetimes for the different battery patterns that are considered. To further quantify the extent of these variations, the difference in the possible maximum and minimum lifetimes for a battery pattern with different task allocation algorithms is calculated. For example, if a battery trace achieves lifetimes of t_1, t_2, and

t_3 tasks with three different algorithms, then the difference in lifetimes is $max(t_1, t_2, t_3) - min(t_1, t_2, t_3)$. Figure 8 shows the difference in SLs (arranged in descending order) achieved with representative battery traces (x-axis) for the four task allocation algorithms considered (for varying values of N and β)[4].

To identify the critical patterns based on variations in lifetimes achieved with task allocation algorithms, we follow a three-step approach. In the first step, we filter out patterns that do not cause "large" differences in lifetimes by empirically defining "large" for

---

[4]The corresponding differences obtained in SVL are similar.

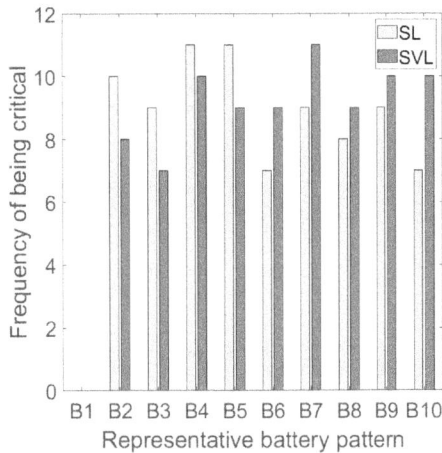

Figure 9: Frequency distribution chart showing the number of times a representative trace serves as a critical pattern

each experiment, i.e., we eliminate patterns that result in similar lifetimes for all task allocation algorithms. In the second step, we identify critical patterns specific to each parameter setting (each simulation). In the final step, we identify common critical patterns that mostly affect the performance of task allocation algorithms across different parameter settings.

For the first step, the difference in maximum and minimum lifetimes (SL and SVL) for a pattern provides information about the extent of performance variation of task allocation algorithms in sparse MCS. For some patterns, the difference in lifetimes is unpretentious ($\leq$ 20%), while for others, the difference is exceptional ($\geq$ 90%). For the difference in lifetimes shown in Figure 8, we observe that for all parameter settings, there are relatively large differences in lifetimes ($\geq$ 50% of the max) for at least half the representative patterns. To empirically define the value of "large" differences for each experiment, we identify knee-points of lifetime difference curves that define a sudden change in performance of task allocation algorithms across battery patterns. The knee-points, indicated with dotted lines in Figure 8 therefore, define a boundary between patterns that cause exceptional changes in lifetimes and those that lead to unpretentious differences. The patterns lying on and to the left of this boundary are critical that cause large performance variations, while the patterns on the right seem to have no effect on the performance of task allocation algorithms.

Since the critical battery patterns identified for each parameter setting are different, we focus on identifying critical patterns that are common across parameter settings causing large variations in SL and SVL for task allocation algorithms. Figure 9 shows the frequency distribution chart for the number of times a pattern behaves critically (leads to large variations in SL and SVL). From the figure, we observe that some patterns are more sensitive to SL (e.g., B2 and B3) while others are more sensitive to SVL (e.g., B7 and B10). We also observe that patterns B6–B9 that appeared to have similar trends also behave differently. Pattern B1, however, does not have any effect on the performance of task allocation algorithms. We investigate the factors responsible in the following section.

5 FINDINGS & CONCLUSION

We now reflect upon the results of our experiments. Each plot in Figure 8 corresponds to the difference in SLs for representative battery patterns. We observe that along with battery patterns, this difference also varies with task requirements—the difference gradually decreases as the value of N (varying for columns) and/or β (varying for rows) increases. This shows that as the number of participants required for task execution increases, the variations in the performance of task allocation algorithms becomes less obscure with varying battery patterns. In other words, **battery usage patterns drastically affect the performance of task allocation systems when $N \ll M$. This highlights the need for careful selection of task allocation algorithms for works that emphasize selecting a smaller number of participants for efficient task execution** [23]. An intuitive interpretation for the large variations in lifetime difference is that as the required number of participants increases, task allocation algorithms start broadcasting tasks to a large set of participants, forcing them to exhibit similar behavior and therefore, lesser variations. Another important observation from Figure 8 is that as the difference in lifetimes decreases with N and β, the knee-points, representing the threshold of large differences, also keep decreasing. Since the number of required participants for a task increases, the system is able to service fewer tasks and hence, smaller lifetimes are achieved across algorithms, which also reduces the overall difference in lifetimes.

For the result shown in Figure 9, we observe that apart from B1, all other representative patterns (B2 to B10) serve as critical patterns that cause large variations in lifetimes. The reason for the exceptional behavior of B1 is the initial discharging state with a very low residual battery at the start of simulations (when tasks are issued). At this time, the residual battery available with B1 is sufficient to service at most one task after which participants die out irrespective of the allocation algorithm. This highlights that SL depends on the initial residual battery level (b_0) of participants and the amount of battery required for task execution (β). This indicates that for task allocation algorithms, deciding a threshold battery level ($b_0 > \beta$) can help achieve higher SL. However, by comparing B1 and B4, we find that even though both patterns are at similar residual levels at the start of simulations, the performance of task allocation algorithms with B4 is much better than that of B1. Since the two patterns vary in their charging states, this highlights that the charging state of patterns is equally important while deciding a threshold for residual battery levels to improve the performance of task allocation algorithms. This highlights **that for real-world scenarios, algorithms can rely on a threshold battery level (b_0) based on the energy consumption of tasks (β) and their charging state to improve higher SLs.**

We further delve into the characteristics of different task allocation algorithms and their performance with respect to the representative patterns considered. For all identified critical patterns, we observe that **the worst performance with all critical patterns is associated with random task allocation** for all parameter settings. The reason behind this is that random allocation assigns tasks to participants in a probabilistic manner—with a high probability of participants getting selected for task allocation in a uniform manner. However, unlike RoundRobin which maintains an order while selecting participants leading to higher SLs (and all values of N and β), there is no order of participant selection in random allocation. This leads to participants being selected multiple times, which results in participants dying out early, and thus, lower SLs and SVLs. **For improved performance, MCS systems should, therefore, refrain from using random task allocation schemes**, and **systems that rely on random task allocation [13] can achieve better performance by even switching to other scheduling techniques such as RoundRobin to achieve better resource utilization of participants.** We also found that the balanced allocation of tasks with NVGreedy leads to highest lifetimes (lifetimes achieved with RoundRobin are comparable). Unlike other algorithms that rely on optimization goals (such as minimizing sensing times using MinAST), NVGreedy relies on dynamic battery levels of participants and the rate of change of battery to identify the "richest" participants for task allocation. This validates our hypothesis that **algorithms should consider the trends of battery usage patterns of participants for better resource utilization**.

To summarize, we observed that battery usage patterns drastically affect the performance of task allocation algorithms in sparse MCS settings where the required number of participants for task execution is relatively smaller than the number of available participants. With the increasing use of mobile phoens in every sphere of life [3, 4, 9, 12, 16, 51, 72, 73], developers should carefully design algorithms to account for mobile users with varying battery usage characteristics in MCS settings. In addition, we also found that the performance of algorithms is affected by the charging state of participants and the energy consumed by them during task execution. Based on our analysis, we find that a random algorithm, although easy to implement, generally leads to poor performance (lowest lifetimes).

REFERENCES

[1] Fazel Anjomshoa and Burak Kantarci. Sober-mcs: Sociability-oriented and battery efficient recruitment for mobile crowd-sensing. *Sensors*, 18(5):1593, 2018.

[2] Aleksandar Antonić, Martina Marjanović, Krešimir Pripužić, and Ivana Podnar Žarko. A mobile crowd sensing ecosystem enabled by cupus: Cloud-based publish/subscribe middleware for the internet of things. *Future Generation Computer Systems*, 2016.

[3] Siddhartha Asthana and Pushpendra Singh. Mvoice: a mobile based generic ict tool. In *Proceedings of the Sixth International Conference on Information and Communications Technologies and Development: Notes-Volume 2*, pages 5–8. ACM, 2013.

[4] Garvita Bajaj, Georgios Bouloukakis, Animesh Pathak, Pushpendra Singh, Nikolaos Georgantas, and Valérie Issarny. Toward enabling convenient urban transit through mobile crowdsensing. In *2015 IEEE 18th International Conference on Intelligent Transportation Systems*, pages 290–295. IEEE, 2015.

[5] Garvita Bajaj and Pushpendra Singh. Sahyog: A middleware for mobile collaborative applications. In *New Technologies, Mobility and Security (NTMS), 2015 7th International Conference on*, pages 1–5. IEEE, 2015.

[6] Garvita Bajaj and Pushpendra Singh. Sensing human activity for assessing participation in evacuation drills. In *Adjunct Proceedings of the 2015 ACM International Joint Conference on Pervasive and Ubiquitous Computing and Proceedings of the 2015 ACM International Symposium on Wearable Computers*, UbiComp/ISWC'15 Adjunct, New York, NY, USA, 2015. ACM.

[7] Garvita Bajaj and Pushpendra Singh. Load-balanced task allocation for improved system lifetime in mobile crowdsensing. In *2018 19th IEEE International Conference on Mobile Data Management (MDM)*, June 2018.

[8] Rim Ben Messaoud, Yacine Ghamri-Doudane, and Dmitri Botvich. Preference and mobility-aware task assignment in participatory sensing. In *Proceedings of the 19th ACM International Conference on Modeling, Analysis and Simulation of Wireless and Mobile Systems*, pages 93–101. ACM, 2016.

[9] Abhishek Bhardwaj, Pandarasamy Arjunan, Amarjeet Singh, Vinayak Naik, and Pushpendra Singh. Melos: a low-cost and low-energy generic sensing attachment for mobile phones. In *Proceedings of the 5th ACM workshop on Networked systems for developing regions*, pages 27–32. ACM, 2011.

[10] Niels Brouwers and Koen Langendoen. Pogo, a middleware for mobile phone sensing. In *Proceedings of the 13th International Middleware Conference*. Springer-Verlag New York, Inc., 2012.

[11] Iacopo Carreras, Daniele Miorandi, Andrei Tamilin, Emmanuel R Ssebaggala, and Nicola Conci. Matador: Mobile task detector for context-aware crowd-sensing campaigns. In *Pervasive Computing and Communications Workshops (PERCOM Workshops), 2013 IEEE International Conference on*, pages 212–217. IEEE, 2013.

[12] Prabha S Chandra, Soumya Parameshwaran, Veena A Satyanarayana, Meiya Varghese, Lauren Liberti, Mona Duggal, Pushpendra Singh, Sangchoon Jeon, and Nancy R Reynolds. I have no peace of mind—psychosocial distress expressed by rural women living with hiv in india as part of a mobile health intervention—a qualitative study. *Archives of women's mental health*, 21(5):525–531, 2018.

[13] Zhuo Chen, Wenlu Hu, Kiryong Ha, Jan Harkes, Benjamin Gilbert, Jason Hong, Asim Smailagic, Dan Siewiorek, and Mahadev Satyanarayanan. Quiltview: a crowd-sourced video response system. In *Proceedings of the 15th ACM HotMobile*, 2014.

[14] Cory Cornelius, Apu Kapadia, David Kotz, Dan Peebles, Minho Shin, and Nikos Triandopoulos. Anonysense: privacy-aware people-centric sensing. In *Proceedings of the 6th international conference on Mobile systems, applications, and services*, pages 211–224. ACM, 2008.

[15] Milad Davari and Haleh Amintoosi. A survey on participant recruitment in crowdsensing systems. In *Computer and Knowledge Engineering (ICCKE), 2016 6th International Conference on*. IEEE, 2016.

[16] Koushik Sinha Deb, Anupriya Tuli, Mamta Sood, Rakesh Chadda, Rohit Verma, Saurabh Kumar, Ragul Ganesh, and Pushpendra Singh. Is india ready for mental health apps (mhapps)? a quantitative-qualitative exploration of caregivers' perspective on smartphone-based solutions for managing severe mental illnesses in low resource settings. *PloS one*, 13(9):e0203353, 2018.

[17] Yi Fei Dong, Salil Kanhere, Chun Tung Chou, and Ren Ping Liu. Automatic image capturing and processing for petrolwatch. In *Networks (ICON), 2011 17th IEEE International Conference on*, pages 236–240. IEEE, 2011.

[18] J Elliott, A Kor, and Oluwafemi Ashola Omotosho. Energy consumption in smartphones: An investigation of battery and energy consumption of media related applications on android smartphones. 2017.

[19] Xiaochen Fan, Panlong Yang, and Qingyu Li. Fairness counts: Simple task allocation scheme for balanced crowdsourcing networks. In *Mobile Ad-hoc and Sensor Networks (MSN), 2015 11th International Conference on*, pages 258–263. IEEE, 2015.

[20] Denzil Ferreira, Anind K Dey, and Vassilis Kostakos. Understanding human-smartphone concerns: a study of battery life. In *International Conference on Pervasive Computing*, pages 19–33. Springer, 2011.

[21] Shilpa Garg, Pushpendra Singh, Parameswaran Ramanathan, and Rijurekha Sen. Vividhavahana: Smartphone based vehicle classification and its applications in developing region. In *Proceedings of the 11th International Conference on Mobile and Ubiquitous Systems: Computing, Networking and Services*, 2014.

[22] Abhishek Gupta, Jatin Thapar, Amarjeet Singh, Pushpendra Singh, Vivek Srinivasan, and Vibhore Vardhan. Simplifying and improving mobile based data collection. In *Proceedings of the Sixth International Conference on Information and Communications Technologies and Development: Notes-Volume 2*, pages 45–48. ACM, 2013.

[23] Sara Hachem, Animesh Pathak, and Valérie Issarny. Probabilistic registration for large-scale mobile participatory sensing. In *2013 IEEE PerCom*.

[24] Guangjie Han, Li Liu, Sammy Chan, Ruiyun Yu, and Yu Yang. Hysense: A hybrid mobile crowdsensing framework for sensing opportunities compensation under dynamic coverage constraint. *IEEE Communications Magazine*, 55(3):93–99, 2017.

[25] Alireza Hassani, Pari Delir Haghighi, and Prem Prakash Jayaraman. Context-aware recruitment scheme for opportunistic mobile crowdsensing. In *Parallel and Distributed Systems (ICPADS), 2015 IEEE 21st International Conference on*, pages 266–273. IEEE, 2015.

[26] Sabine Schulte Im Walde. Experiments on the automatic induction of german semantic verb classes. *Computational Linguistics*, 32(2):159–194, 2006.

[27] Valerie Issarny, Vivien Mallet, Kinh Nguyen, Pierre-Guillaume Raverdy, Fadwa Rebhi, and Raphael Ventura. Dos and don'ts in mobile phone sensing middleware: Learning from a large-scale experiment. In *Proceedings of the 17th International Middleware Conference*. ACM, 2016.

[28] Shenggong Ji, Yu Zheng, and Tianrui Li. Urban sensing based on human mobility. In *Proceedings of the 2016 ACM International Joint Conference on Pervasive and Ubiquitous Computing*, pages 1040–1051. ACM, 2016.

[29] Marijn R Jongerden and Boudewijn R Haverkort. Which battery model to use? *IET Software*, 3(6):445–457, 2009.

[30] Konstantinos Kazakos, Siddharth Asthana, Madeline Balaam, Mona Duggal, Amey Holden, Limalemla Jamir, Nanda Kishore Kannuri, Saurabh Kumar, Amarendar Reddy Manindla, Subhashini Arcot Manikam, et al. A real-time ivr platform for community radio. In *Proceedings of the 2016 CHI Conference on Human Factors in Computing Systems*, pages 343–354. ACM, 2016.

[31] Dongwon Kim, Yohan Chon, Wonwoo Jung, Yungeun Kim, and Hojung Cha. Accurate prediction of available battery time for mobile applications. *ACM Trans. Embed. Comput. Syst.*, 15(3):48:1–48:17, May 2016.

[32] Rafael J Lajara, Juan J Perez-Solano, and Jose Pelegri-Sebastia. A method for modeling the battery state of charge in wireless sensor networks. *IEEE Sensors Journal*, 15(2):1186–1197, 2015.

[33] Jaeseong Lee, Yohan Chon, and Hojung Cha. Evaluating battery aging on mobile devices. In *Proceedings of the 52nd Annual Design Automation Conference*, page 135. ACM, 2015.

[34] Hanshang Li, Ting Li, and Yu Wang. Dynamic participant recruitment of mobile crowd sensing for heterogeneous sensing tasks. In *IEEE 12th International Conference on Mobile Ad Hoc and Sensor Systems (MASS)*, 2015.

[35] Yingmin Li, Huiguo Chen, and Zheqian Wu. Dynamic time warping distance method for similarity test of multipoint ground motion field. *Mathematical Problems in Engineering*, 2010, 2010.

[36] T Warren Liao. Clustering of time series data—a survey. *Pattern recognition*, 38(11):1857–1874, 2005.

[37] Chi Harold Liu, Bo Zhang, Xin Su, Jian Ma, Wendong Wang, and Kin K Leung. Energy-aware participant selection for smartphone-enabled mobile crowd sensing. *IEEE Systems Journal*, 11(3):1435–1446, 2017.

[38] Jingwei Liu, Huijuan Cao, Qingqing Li, Fanghui Cai, Xiaojiang Du, and Mohsen Guizani. A large-scale concurrent data anonymous batch verification scheme for mobile healthcare crowd sensing. *IEEE Internet of Things Journal*, 2018.

[39] Shengzhong Liu, Zhenzhe Zheng, Fan Wu, Shaojie Tang, and Guihai Chen. Context-aware data quality estimation in mobile crowdsensing. In *INFOCOM 2017-IEEE Conference on Computer Communications, IEEE*, pages 1–9. IEEE, 2017.

[40] Yan Liu, Bin Guo, Yang Wang, Wenle Wu, Zhiwen Yu, and Daqing Zhang. Taskme: multi-task allocation in mobile crowd sensing. In *Proceedings of the 2016 ACM International Joint Conference on Pervasive and Ubiquitous Computing*, pages 403–414. ACM, 2016.

[41] Yanchi Liu, Zhongmou Li, Hui Xiong, Xuedong Gao, and Junjie Wu. Understanding of internal clustering validation measures. In *Data Mining (ICDM), 2010 IEEE 10th International Conference on*, pages 911–916. IEEE, 2010.

[42] Rim Ben Messaoud and Yacine Ghamri-Doudane. Fair QoI and energy-aware task allocation in participatory sensing. In *WCNC 2016 IEEE*.

[43] Pablo Montero and José Vilar. TSclust: An R package for time series clustering. *Journal of Statistical Software, Articles*, 62(1):1–43, 2014.

[44] Usue Mori, Alexander Mendiburu, and Jose A Lozano. Distance measures for time series in r: The tsdist package. *R Journal*, 8(2):451–459, 2016.

[45] John Paparrizos and Luis Gravano. k-shape: Efficient and accurate clustering of time series. In *Proceedings of the 2015 ACM SIGMOD International Conference on Management of Data*, pages 1855–1870. ACM, 2015.

[46] Girish Punj and David W Stewart. Cluster analysis in marketing research: Review and suggestions for application. *Journal of marketing research*, pages 134–148, 1983.

[47] Moo-Ryong Ra, Bin Liu, Tom F. La Porta, and Ramesh Govindan. Medusa: A programming framework for crowd-sensing applications. In *Proceedings of the 10th International Conference on Mobile Systems, Applications, and Services, MobiSys '12*. ACM, 2012.

[48] Nancy R. Reynolds, Veena Satyanarayana, Mona Duggal, Meiya Varghese, Lauren Liberti, Pushpendra Singh, Mohini Ranganathan, Sangchoon Jeon, and Prabha S. Chandra. Mahila: a protocol for evaluating a nurse-delivered mhealth intervention for women with hiv and psychosocial risk factors in india. *BMC Health Services Research*, 16(1):352, 2016.

[49] Clayton Shepard, Ahmad Rahmati, Chad Tossell, Lin Zhong, and Phillip Kortum. Livelab: measuring wireless networks and smartphone users in the field. *ACM SIGMETRICS Performance Evaluation Review*, 38(3):15–20, 2011.

[50] Galit Shmueli and Kenneth C Lichtendahl. *Practical Time Series Forecasting with R: A Hands-On Guide*. Axelrod Schnall Publishers, 2016.

[51] Amarjeet Singh, Vinayak Naik, Sangeeta Lal, Raja Sengupta, Deepak Saxena, Pushpendra Singh, and Ankur Puri. Improving the efficiency of healthcare delivery system in underdeveloped rural areas. In *2011 Third International Conference on Communication Systems and Networks (COMSNETS 2011)*, pages 1–6. IEEE, 2011.

[52] Pushpendra Singh, Nikita Juneja, and Shruti Kapoor. Using mobile phone sensors to detect driving behavior. In *Proceedings of the 3rd ACM Symposium on Computing for Development*, page 53. ACM, 2013.

[53] Pushpendra Singh, Amarjeet Singh, Vinayak Naik, and Sangeeta Lal. Cvdmagic: a mobile based study for cvd risk detection in rural india. In *Proceedings of the fifth international conference on Information and Communication Technologies and Development*, pages 359–366. ACM, 2012.

[54] Zheng Song, Chi Harold Liu, Jie Wu, Jian Ma, and Wendong Wang. Qoi-aware multitask-oriented dynamic participant selection with budget constraints. *IEEE Transactions on Vehicular Technology*, 63(9):4618–4632, 2014.

[55] Vivek Srinivasan, Vibhore Vardhan, Snigdha Kar, Siddhartha Asthana, Rajendran Narayanan, Pushpendra Singh, Dipanjan Chakraborty, Amarjeet Singh, and Aaditeshwar Seth. Airavat: An automated system to increase transparency and accountability in social welfare schemes in india. In *Proceedings of the Sixth International Conference on Information and Communications Technologies and Development: Notes-Volume 2*, pages 151–154. ACM, 2013.

[56] Hien To, Gabriel Ghinita, and Cyrus Shahabi. A framework for protecting worker location privacy in spatial crowdsourcing. *Proceedings of the VLDB Endowment*, 7(10):919–930, 2014.

[57] Maria Uther, James Uther, Panos Athanasopoulos, Pushpendra Singh, and Reiko Akahane-Yamada. Mobile adaptive call (mac): A lightweight speech-based intervention for mobile language learners. In *Eighth Annual Conference of the International Speech Communication Association*, 2007.

[58] Maria Uther, Iraide Zipitria, James Uther, and Pushpendra Singh. Mobile adaptive call (mac): A case-study in developing a mobile learning application for speech/audio language training. In *IEEE International Workshop on Wireless and Mobile Technologies in Education (WMTE'05)*, pages 5–pp. IEEE, 2005.

[59] Jiangtao Wang, Yasha Wang, Daqing Zhang, Feng Wang, Haoyi Xiong, Chao Chen, Qin Lv, and Zhaopeng Qiu. Multi-task allocation in mobile crowd sensing with individual task quality assurance. *IEEE Transactions on Mobile Computing*, 2018.

[60] Jiangtao Wang, Yasha Wang, Daqing Zhang, Leye Wang, Haoyi Xiong, Abdelsalam Helal, Yuanduo He, and Feng Wang. Fine-grained multitask allocation for participatory sensing with a shared budget. *IEEE Internet of Things Journal*, 3(6):1395–1405, 2016.

[61] Leye Wang, Dingqi Yang, Xiao Han, Tianben Wang, Daqing Zhang, and Xiaojuan Ma. Location privacy-preserving task allocation for mobile crowdsensing with differential geo-obfuscation. In *Proceedings of the 26th International Conference on World Wide Web*, pages 627–636. International World Wide Web Conferences Steering Committee, 2017.

[62] Leye Wang, Daqing Zhang, Animesh Pathak, Chao Chen, Haoyi Xiong, Dingqi Yang, and Yasha Wang. Ccs-ta: quality-guaranteed online task allocation in compressive crowdsensing. In *Proceedings of the 2015 ACM International Joint Conference on Pervasive and Ubiquitous Computing*, pages 683–694. ACM, 2015.

[63] Leye Wang, Daqing Zhang, Yasha Wang, Chao Chen, Xiao Han, and Abdallah M'hamed. Sparse mobile crowdsensing: challenges and opportunities. *IEEE Communications Magazine*, 54(7):161–167, 2016.

[64] Leye Wang, Daqing Zhang, Haoyi Xiong, John Paul Gibson, Chao Chen, and Bing Xie. ecosense: Minimize participants' total 3g data cost in mobile crowdsensing using opportunistic relays. *IEEE Transactions on Systems, Man, and Cybernetics: Systems*, 47(6):965–978, 2017.

[65] Mingjun Xiao, Jie Wu, Liusheng Huang, Ruhong Cheng, and Yunsheng Wang. Online task assignment for crowdsensing in predictable mobile social networks. *IEEE Transactions on Mobile Computing*, (1):1–1, 2017.

[66] Haoyi Xiong, Daqing Zhang, Guanling Chen, Leye Wang, and Vincent Gauthier. Crowdtasker: Maximizing coverage quality in piggyback crowdsensing under budget constraint. In *Pervasive Computing and Communications (PerCom), 2015 IEEE International Conference on*, pages 55–62. IEEE, 2015.

[67] Haoyi Xiong, Daqing Zhang, Guanling Chen, Leye Wang, Vincent Gauthier, and Laura E Barnes. icrowd: Near-optimal task allocation for piggyback crowdsensing. *IEEE Transactions on Mobile Computing*, 15(8):2010–2022, 2016.

[68] Haoyi Xiong, Daqing Zhang, Zhishan Guo, Guanling Chen, and Laura E Barnes. Near-optimal incentive allocation for piggyback crowdsensing. *IEEE Communications Magazine*, 55(6):120–125, 2017.

[69] Haoyi Xiong, Daqing Zhang, Leye Wang, and Hakima Chaouchi. Emc 3: Energy-efficient data transfer in mobile crowdsensing under full coverage constraint. *IEEE Transactions on Mobile Computing*, 14(7):1355–1368, 2015.

[70] Liwen Xu, Xiaohong Hao, Nicholas D Lane, Xin Liu, and Thomas Moscibroda. More with less: Lowering user burden in mobile crowdsourcing through compressive sensing. In *Proceedings of the 2015 ACM International Joint Conference on Pervasive and Ubiquitous Computing*, pages 659–670. ACM, 2015.

[71] Deepika Yadav, Pushpendra Singh, Kyle Montague, Vijay Kumar, Deepak Sood, Madeline Balaam, Drishti Sharma, Mona Duggal, Tom Bartindale, Delvin Varghese, et al. Sangoshthi: Empowering community health workers through peer learning in rural india. In *In Proceedings of the 26th International Conference on World Wide Web (WWW '17). International World Wide Web Conferences Steering Committee, Republic and Canton of Geneva, Switzerland*, pages 499–508, 2017.

[72] Kuldeep Yadav, Vinayak Naik, Amarjeet Singh, Pushpendra Singh, Ponnurangam Kumaraguru, and Umesh Chandra. Challenges and novelties while using mobile phones as ict devices for indian masses: short paper. In *Proceedings of the 4th ACM Workshop on Networked Systems for Developing Regions*, page 10. ACM, 2010.

[73] Kuldeep Yadav, Vinayak Naik, Pushpendra Singh, and Amarjeet Singh. Alternative localization approach for mobile phones without gps. In *Middleware'10 Posters and Demos Track*, page 1. ACM, 2010.

[74] Daqing Zhang, Haoyi Xiong, Leye Wang, and Guanling Chen. CrowdRecruiter: selecting participants for piggyback crowdsensing under probabilistic coverage constraint. In *Proceedings of the 2014 ACM International Joint Conference on Pervasive and Ubiquitous Computing*. ACM, 2014.

[75] Xinglin Zhang, Zheng Yang, Yue-Jiao Gong, Yunhao Liu, and Shaohua Tang. SpatialRecruiter: maximizing sensing coverage in selecting workers for spatial crowdsourcing. *IEEE Transactions on Vehicular Technology*, 2017.

[76] Qingwen Zhao, Yanmin Zhu, Hongzi Zhu, Jian Cao, Guangtao Xue, and Bo Li. Fair energy-efficient sensing task allocation in participatory sensing with smartphones. In *INFOCOM, 2014 Proceedings IEEE*. IEEE, 2014.

Elastic Offloading of Multitasking Applications to Mobile Edge Computing

Houssemeddine Mazouzi, Nadjib Achir, Khaled Boussetta
L2TI, Institut galilée, Université Paris 13
Villetaneuse, France

ABSTRACT

This paper focuses on offloading multitasking applications to a Mobile Edge Computing (MEC) environment. We address this issue through a mobile user's perspective that is seeking to obtain the execution result of a resource-hungry multitasking application, possibly through offloading some tasks to a mobile multiple edge servers' environment. The completion time of the application is constrained by a predefined strict deadline and the offloading decision aims to minimize the terminal's energy consumption. Moreover, the multitasking application is modeled by a weighted Directed Acyclic Graph (DAG) which characterizes the dependencies between tasks. To tackle this issue, we first model the multitasking offloading problem in a mobile multiple edge servers' environment as a Zero-one Integer Programming problem. Then, we propose an efficient adaptive offloading algorithm, named eTOMEC (Elastic Tasks graph Offloading for MEC), which decides which task must be offloaded and accordingly selects the edge server that will perform the task execution. Compared to many state-of-the-art offloading approaches, our proposal allows parallel offloading of tasks to several edge servers. Assessment results show that our proposal achieves better performances in terms of completion time for the application and energy consumption of the user's terminal.

CCS CONCEPTS

• Networks → Cloud computing;

KEYWORDS

Computation offloading, Mobile Edge Computing, Tasks graph.

ACM Reference Format:
Houssemeddine Mazouzi, Nadjib Achir, Khaled Boussetta. 2019. Elastic Offloading of Multitasking Applications to Mobile Edge Computing. In *22nd Int'l ACM Conf. on Modeling, Analysis and Simulation of Wireless and Mobile Systems (MSWiM'19), Nov. 25–29, 2019, Miami Beach, FL, USA.* ACM, New York, NY, USA, 8 pages. https://doi.org/10.1145/3345768.3355926

1 INTRODUCTION

Novel mobile services, such as Augmented Reality or face/speech recognition, are often computationally intensive and consequently, the users quality of experience is highly dependent on the terminal's

processing capabilities. A possible approach to circumvent the limit of portable terminals resources is to partially or completely offload the computation of resource-hungry applications to the cloud [2]. However, the geographical distance to the remote cloud server might induces significant delays that are not tolerated by many time-sensitive applications, such as online mobile gaming. To cope with the above issue, Mobile Edge Computing (MEC) [19] paradigm has recently emerged as a credible solution to support resource-hungry and time-sensitive mobile services.

Computation offloading to MEC is a hot research topicSeveral recent works in the literature addressed the offloading decision problem, which primary aims to determine whether the application execution should be completely or partially offloaded to the MEC. The decision covers also the choice of the corresponding execution location, including either the terminal or an established set of edge or cloud servers. A fundamental criterion for such decision is the completion time of the application. Other performance metrics such as the amount of consumed resources on the terminal (processing capacity or battery), on the network (bandwidth) and on the remote servers (processing capacity and energy) are often considered [9, 13, 14]. Another important aspect regarding offloading decision is related to the single-task or to the multitasking architecture type of the application.

This work addresses computation offloading of a mobile multitasking application, characterized by a task-dependency graph, to a multiple edge servers MEC environment. Our objective is to design an offloading policy that is able to scale the number of concurrent offloaded tasks accordingly with the number of available edge servers, while taking into consideration tasks dependencies. The offloading decision aims to minimize the terminal's energy consumption, while satisfying the hard deadline of the application's completion time. The design of such offloading policy is quite challenging, since offloading decisions must integrate on one side, tasks dependencies and their resource requirements (processing and communication capacities) and on the other side, available resources on different servers and communication aspects (available bandwidth, delay and energy costs) at access and at backbone links.

The first contribution of this paper is the formalization of the above optimal offloading policy as a Zero-one Integer Programming problem. Given that the resulting problem is NP-hard, we then propose a heuristic solution, named eTOMEC.

The rest of paper is organized as follows: Section 2 presents related work, and section 3 describes the studied system. Multitasking offloading problem is formulated in Section 4. Our proposed solution is then developed in section 5. Performance evaluation is discussed in section 6. Finally, a conclusion is drawn in Section 7.

2 RELATED WORK

Computation offloading has attracted considerable attention over the past several years. Many works investigate the importance of computation offloading to improve the performance of the application. Most of the existing works focus on the offloading over mono-task application scenario such as [13, 14, 17]. In [17], Tuyen X. et al. consider a multi-edge server multi-user MEC. Every user has one computation task. The main objective is to decide which users should offload and to which edge server. In our previous work [14], we introduced an efficient offloading policy for multi-edge server MEC. The main objective of the proposed approach is to determine whether a user offloads its task and to which edge server. This work was extended in [13] to consider two-tier MEC.

Other works explore the multitasking application. Meng-Hsi Chen et al. [4] present an offloading approach in order to minimize the energy consumption of the user terminal. It decides which tasks should be performed locally and which ones should be offloaded to the remote cloud. Similarly, Thinh Quang Dinh et al. [6] propose a joint multitasking offloading and bandwidth allocation in MEC, with the objective the minimization of the energy consumption of the user terminal. Finally, Weiwei Chen et al. [5] study the device to device computation offloading, where user terminals can offload their computation to each other. The objective is to offload some tasks from overloaded terminals to underloaded ones in order to reduce the total energy consumption. However, all these works assume that the tasks are independent and can be executed without any constraint between them. Unfortunately, this is not the case for most of the applications.

To address this issue, some works consider more realistic multitasking application and includes the precedence constraints between tasks. One of the most general model to define dependent multitasking application is to use a Directed Acyclic Graph (DAG) model. Using this model, we can represent the application as a set of tasks under precedence constraints and dependencies between tasks. Considering this model, both Dong Huang et al. [10] and Songtao Guo et al. [9] have proposed a new offloading method that takes into account the dependencies between the application's tasks. In addition, of selecting the tasks to be offloaded, Songtao Guo et al. [9] compute the bandwidth that should be allocated to the task. Finally, Lei Yang et al. [19] focus only on applications with linear tasks graph and select the tasks to offload in order to minimize the terminal's energy consumption. The main drawback of the last approaches is related to the fact that a user can offload its tasks to only one edge server. As a result, it is difficult to maximize the parallelization of tasks to reduce the completion time.

In addition to the works referred above, the literature is also rich of works on graph-based tasks scheduling on multiprocessing systems. Works such as Yusuf Özkaya et al. [15] and Guan Wang et al. [11] focus on the scheduling of multitasking applications on homogeneous and heterogeneous multiprocessor systems. The main objective is to minimize the completion time of the application. Unfortunately, even though these algorithms can be very efficient in a multiprocessor system, they can not be directly considered in MEC. The processor access delay on multiprocessor systems can be neglected compared to the time required to offload a task to the edge server. Indeed, the bandwidth constraints between the mobile terminal and the edge servers have a great impact on the decision and the location of the offloading. Peng Sun et al. [16] investigate parallel offloading of multitasking application to MEC in order to minimize completion time. They use a leveling heuristic that partitions the graph onto several levels. Tasks in same level are then offloaded to different edge servers. However, this heuristic is not well adopted for highly dependents tasks. Moreover, energy consumption is not considered in [16].

3 SYSTEM DESCRIPTION

3.1 Mobile Edge Computing Infrastructure

As illustrated in Figure 1, we consider a multi-tier mobile edge computing environment, which is composed of several physical or virtual machines offering computing resources at the edge and at the cloud. We study this system through a single user's perspective, which is connected to this environment through an Access Point (AP) and that is seeking to execute a computationally intensive application. This application is composed of a set of inter-dependent tasks. Each task can be performed locally by the user terminal, offloaded to edge servers or offloaded further to the remote cloud.

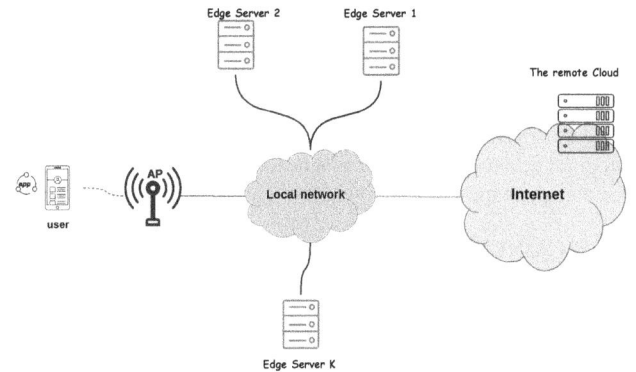

Figure 1: Illustration of MEC infrastructure environment.

Let $\mathcal{K} = \{0, 1, 2, ..., K, K + 1\}$ denotes the set of all possible processing locations of tasks, where 0 refers to user's terminal, the edge servers are represented by 1 to K and $K + 1$ represents the remote cloud. In the remainder, each element of $\mathcal{K}$ is referred as *server*. Each server offers a computational resource capacity, denoted f^k, expressed as a CPU-cycles per second. Similarly, to [9, 19], we assume that user's terminal has a limited computing capabilities compared to the edge/cloud. Formally, $\forall k \in \mathcal{K} \setminus \{0\}, f^0 \ll f^k$.

3.2 Multitasking Application Modelling

We consider a mobile user that is seeking to obtain the execution result of a resource-hungry multitasking application by offloading some tasks to a MEC environment. The offloading decision aims to minimize the terminal's energy consumption while ensuring that the completion time of the application is constrained by a predefined strict deadline.

The multitasking application is composed of a set of fine granularity atomic non-preemptive tasks. The dependencies between tasks is modeled using a weighted Directed Acyclic Graph (DAG), noted $G = (V, E)$, where the vertices in V represent tasks and the edges in E represent dependencies. In the following, we will refer to the number of tasks composing the application as $n = |V|$.

The construction of such multitasking DAG depends on how the developers model their applications [9, 14]. Hence, several DAG could be associated to different implementations of a given multitasking application. For instance, figure 3 illustrates four DAG that correspond to different implementations on Android terminals of a video navigation application [12]. In this figure, each edge illustrates the precedence dependencies between tasks. Concretely, any edge $(i, j) \in E$ means that task i must be performed before task j. In the following, we will use $pred(i) = \{j | (j, i) \in E\}$ to refer to the immediate predecessors of a vertex $i \in V$ and $succ(i) = \{j | (i, j) \in E\}$ to represent the immediate successors of i in G.

We can also distinguish in figure 3, two type of vertexes: blue and red ones. The latters are either (a) a vertex without any predecessors, called *entry task* (task 1), from which the application execution begins or (b) a vertex without any successors called *exit task* (task 14), which is the latest task executed by the application. Since these tasks are usually related to users interactions (e.g, user inputs and results rendering), we assume that both *entry* and *exit* tasks must be performed on the user's terminal. Such local execution requirement can be extended to other tasks, which cannot been performed remotely due to some hardware or software constraints [4, 13]. To identify those tasks we introduce an *non-offloadability indicator*, denoted y_i, which is set to 0 if task i can be offloaded on a remote server, and 1 if it must be processed on the mobile's terminal. In particular, we have $y_1 = 1$ and $y_n = 1$.

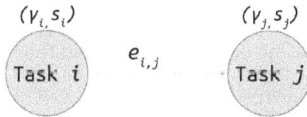

Figure 2: Example of dependent tasks

In addition to the precedence order expressed by each edge, we associate to any edge $(i, j) \in E$ a weight, denoted $e_{i,j}$. Concretely, this weight expressed in bytes, indicates the amount of task i resulting data that will serve as input data to process task j. A generic example of this weighted graph is illustrated in figure 2. As shown in this figure, a weight (γ_i, s_i) is also associated to each vertex $i \in V$. Here, γ_i denotes the computation capacity, in CPU-cycles, which is required to process task i. The second parameter, s_i, is the source code size, in bytes, which needs to be transferred to a remote server when task i is offloaded. Hence, the weights on a vertex i and on its entering edges characterize the resources (processing capacity and data quantity) needed to process task i.

4 MULTITASKING OFFLOADING PROBLEM

4.1 Problem Statement

The purpose of this paper is to design an offloading policy that decides 1) which tasks should be offloaded and 2) determines which server will process each offloaded task. The objective of this policy is to minimize the energy consumed by the user terminal, denoted $\mathcal{Z}$. Moreover, the offloading decisions must fulfill the following requirements: First of all, each task needs to be scheduled onto exactly one server with respect to the precedence constraints, which is given by the weighted Directed Acyclic Graph associated to the multitasking application. Second, the offloading policy must ensure that the maximum completion time of the application, denoted $\mathcal{T}$, does not exceed a given threshold, denoted t_{max}. This hard constraint is introduced with the aim to enforce Quality of Services requirements of time-sensitive applications. Finally, non-offloadable tasks must be performed locally by the user terminal.

Formally, the optimal offloading policy is the solution of the following Zero-one Integer Programming problem:

Minimize $\mathcal{Z}$

Subject to:

$C1 : \mathcal{T} \leq t_{max}$

$C2 : \sum_{k \in \mathcal{K}} x_i^k = 1, \forall i \in V$

$C3 : 1 - x_i^0 \leq y_i, \forall i \in V$

$C4 : x_i^k \in \{0, 1\}$

Here, x_i^k as a binary variable that indicates if task $i \in V$ is offloaded to server k. The first constraint ($C1$) guarantees that the application's completion-time, $\mathcal{T}$, is below the given deadline t_{max}. Constraint $C2$ indicates that each task must be performed by exactly one server. Constraint $C3$ is relative to the fact that the non-offloadable tasks must be performed at the user's terminal. Finally, constraint $C4$ ensures that every decision variable is binary.

In the following, we will detail the expressions of the objective function $\mathcal{Z}$ and the constrained application's completion-time $\mathcal{T}$. To this purpose, we will first describe the network communication model. Then we will develop different time-related metrics that will be used to model the application's completion time and to derive the expression of energy consumption.

4.2 Completion Time

Clearly, the completion of the application is obtained when the *exit* task is processed. Thus, the expression of $\mathcal{T}$ is composed of the processing duration of all application's tasks, plus different transmission times. Indeed, communications occur at different steps of the offloading process. Precisely, whenever a task is offloaded to the MEC environment, its source code is transmitted from the user terminal to the remote server. Moreover, dependencies among tasks lead to data exchanges among different locations processing the tasks. Hence, to derive the expression of $\mathcal{T}$ we will first characterize the bandwidth at access and at backhaul networks and then express different transmission times quantities.

4.2.1 Bandwidth capacity. Let first focus on the allocated wireless bandwidth at access network. To this purpose, we suppose that the AP uses an orthogonal frequency division multiple-access (OFDMA) technology. Without loss of generality and in a seek of presentation simplicity, we assume that the bandwidth allocated on the uplink (i.e. from the user to the AP) is the same to the bandwidth allocated on the downlink (i.e. from the AP to the user terminal). In

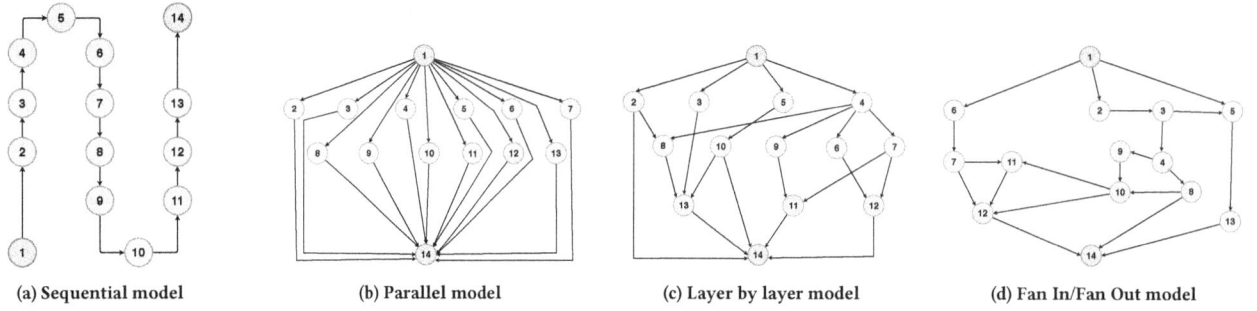

(a) Sequential model   (b) Parallel model   (c) Layer by layer model   (d) Fan In/Fan Out model

Figure 3: The DAG associated to video navigation application [12].

addition, we admit that the channel from the user to the AP follows quasi-static Rayleigh fading. In other words, the channel state is stationary during the offloading period of the application.

Let B denote the available wireless bandwidth in the AP. This quantity is expressed in Hertz (Hz). Since we are considering OFDMA, B is divided into C subcarriers. We define p^{tx} as the user's transmission power, and h^{tx} as the power gain. We consider both path loss and shadowing attenuation as in [8]. We model the noise as *Additive White Gaussian Noise (AWGN)* [8] random variable with zero mean and variance σ^2. Thus, the maximum achievable rate (in bps) for the uplink can be expressed as follows:

$$w^{tx} = c \cdot \frac{B}{C} \cdot log_2(1 + \frac{p^{tx} \cdot (h^{tx})^2}{\Gamma(b^{tx}) \cdot \sigma^2}) \qquad (1)$$

where $\Gamma(BER)$ represents the SNR margin introduced to meet the desired target bit error rate (BER) with a QAM constellation, b^{tx} is the BER, and c the number of subcarriers allocated to the user. $\Gamma(BER)$ can be expressed as follows:

$$\Gamma(x) = -2 \cdot \frac{log(5x)}{3} \qquad (2)$$

Similarly, the maximum achievable bitrate (in bps) for downlink can be derived by the following equation:

$$w^{rx} = c \cdot \frac{B}{C} \cdot log_2(1 + \frac{p_{ap} \cdot (h^{rx})^2}{\Gamma(b^{rx}) \cdot \sigma^2}) \qquad (3)$$

where p_{ap} denotes the transmission power of the AP. h^{rx} indicates the power gain from the user to the AP when user receives data due to path loss and shadowing attenuation [8].

Finally, regarding the backhaul network, the bandwidth capacity between any server $m \in \mathcal{K}$ and any server $k \in \mathcal{K}$, denoted $W^{m,k}$, is supposed to be symmetric and fixed during the application execution period. Notice that when $m = 0$ then $W^{0,k}$ refers to the bandwidth between the access point and a server $k \in \mathcal{K} - 0$.

4.2.2 Transmission time of source code. Using equation 1, we can derive the time required to transmit the source code of task i from user terminal to server k. This time, denoted sr_i^k, can be expressed as the ratio between the amount of source code (s_i) and the available uplink bandwidth between user i and server k. Formally:

$$sr_i^k = \begin{cases} 0 & \text{if } k=0 \\ \dfrac{s_i}{w^{tx}} + \dfrac{s_i}{W^{0,k}} & \text{otherwise} \end{cases} \qquad (4)$$

4.2.3 Transmission time of input data from predecessor tasks. As mentioned previously, the input data of task i is the amount of all data communicated from its predecessor tasks. Let $j \in pred(i)$ be a predecessor of task i and suppose that task j has been performed by server m, then the time required to transmit the depending on data between tasks j and i from server m to server k, denoted by $\mathcal{D}_{j,i}^{m,k}$, must be expressed as a function of the amount of data, $e_{j,i}$, the location of the servers m and k, and the available network bandwidth between server m and k. We can distinguish four cases:

(1) When task j is performed locally ($m = 0$) and i is performed remotely ($k > 0$) then $\mathcal{D}_{j,i}^{m,k}$ is the upload time of data dependency between user terminal and server k.

(2) When task j is performed remotely and task i is going to be performed locally, i.e: $k = 0, m > 0$ then $\mathcal{D}_{j,i}^{m,k}$ is the download time of the data dependency.

(3) When both tasks i and j will be performed by remote servers, i.e: $m > 0, k > 0$ then $\mathcal{D}_{j,i}^{m,k}$ corresponds to the backhaul transmission time between servers m and k.

(4) Finally, if both tasks j and i are executed by the same server then there is no communication and thus $\mathcal{D}_{j,i}^{m,k} = 0$.

Therefore, using equations 1 and 3, we can obtain:

$$\mathcal{D}_{j,i}^{m,k} = \begin{cases} \dfrac{e_{j,i}}{w^{tx}} + \dfrac{e_{j,i}}{W^{m,k}} & \text{if } m = 0 \text{ and } k \neq 0 \\ \dfrac{e_{j,i}}{w^{rx}} + \dfrac{e_{j,i}}{W^{m,k}} & \text{if } m \neq 0 \text{ and } k = 0 \\ \dfrac{e_{j,i}}{W^{m,k}} & \text{if } (m \neq k) \\ 0 & \text{otherwise} \end{cases} \qquad (5)$$

4.2.4 Task Processing Time. A task $i \in V$ can be processed by a server $k \in \mathcal{K}$ if enough processing resources are available at server k and when both input data and source code of the task have been received by server k. Let st_i^k denote the time at which the processing of the task i in server k can start. Formally:

$$st_i^k = max(com_i^k, av^k, sr_i^k) \qquad (6)$$

where com_i^k is the time required to receive all the input data of task i. av^k refers to the time at which to server k is ready to perform task i, and time to transmit the source code of task i to server k, sr_i^k, is given by equation 4. Following [9], com_i^k can be defined as the last arrived data dependency from the predecessors tasks:

$$com_i^k = \max_{m \in \mathcal{K}} (\max_{j \in pred(i)} [x_j^m \cdot (ft_j^m + \mathcal{D}_{j,i}^{m,k})]) \tag{7}$$

where ft_j^m is the finish time of the task j in the server m. The time to transmit dependency data, $\mathcal{D}_{j,i}^{m,k}$, is given by equation 5. It is worth noting here the presence of the binary offloading decision variable, x_j^m in the expression com_i^k. Similarly,

$$av^k = \max_{i \in V} (x_i^k \cdot ft_i^k) \tag{8}$$

The processing time of task i in serve k, denoted by T_i^k, can be estimated as the ratio between the required and the allocated computing resource in the server [5, 14]:

$$T_i^k = \frac{\gamma_i}{f^k}, \forall k \in \mathcal{K} \tag{9}$$

The finish time of a task $i \in V$ in server k, denoted ft_i^k, is defined as the summation of the start time and the processing time:

$$ft_i^k = st_i^k + T_i^k \tag{10}$$

Finally, since application's completion corresponds to the finish time of *exit* task and given that the later is non-offloadable, then:

$$\mathcal{T} = ft_n^0 \tag{11}$$

4.3 Consumed Energy

Let now express on the objective function that we seek to minimize. Namely, energy consumption of the user's terminal. This quantity is composed of four parts:

(1) The energy consumed by the local CPU due to local processing of tasks.
(2) The energy consumed by the wireless network interface when uploading to remote servers code source and data of offloaded tasks.
(3) The energy consumed by the wireless network interface when downloading tasks execution results from remote servers.
(4) The energy consumed by the wireless network interface when it is in idle mode. This mode is enabled when user terminal is waiting for the execution of those offloaded tasks.

Using the model presented in [14, 17] and according to the last considerations, we can compute the total energy consumption, noted $\mathcal{Z}$, as follows:

$$\mathcal{Z} = \sum_{i \in V} (\mathcal{E}_i^l + \mathcal{E}_i^{tx} + \mathcal{E}_i^{rx}) + \mathcal{E}^{idle} \tag{12}$$

where $\mathcal{E}_i^l$ is the energy consumed by the user's terminal to process task i locally. Following [3], this energy is related to the local CPU frequency and the execution duration of the task. Formally:

$$\mathcal{E}_i^l = \kappa \cdot (f^0)^3 \cdot T_i^0 \cdot x_i^0 \tag{13}$$

Here κ is the effective switched capacitance, which depends on the chip architecture, and is used to adjust the processor frequency. As in [3], we set $\kappa = 10^{-9}$.

$\mathcal{E}_i^{tx}$ represents the energy consumed by the terminal to transmit the data dependency between task i and all its predecessors, plus the energy consumed to upload the source code corresponding to that task. This energy can be expressed as:

$$\mathcal{E}_i^{tx} = \sum_{k \in \mathcal{K}} x_i^k \cdot p^{tx} (sr_i^k + \sum_{j \in pred(i)} (x_j^0 \cdot \mathcal{D}_{j,i}^{0,k})) \tag{14}$$

where p^{tx} is the radio transmission power [9, 13].

Similarly, $\mathcal{E}_i^{rx}$ is the energy consumed by the terminal to receive the data from remote servers that have processed predecessors tasks of i. Given that task i is executed locally, then:

$$\mathcal{E}_i^{rx} = \sum_{k \in \mathcal{K}} \sum_{j \in pred(i)} x_j^k \cdot x_i^0 \cdot p^{rx} \cdot \mathcal{D}_{j,i}^{k,0} \tag{15}$$

where p^{rx} is the power consumed when receiving data [9, 14].

Finally, $\mathcal{E}^{idle}$ represents the amount of energy consumed by the network interface when it is in idle mode. This energy consumption depends on the offloading solution and the start times of each offloaded tasks. However, its accurate expression is quite challenging to obtain. To tackle this problem, we consider a pessimistic estimation of $\mathcal{E}^{idle}$, by supposing that all the tasks are transmitted sequentially. Formally:

$$\mathcal{E}^{idle} = \max_{k \in \mathcal{K}} \mathcal{E}_k^{idle} \tag{16}$$

Here, $\mathcal{E}_k^{idle}$ is the upper bound of the idle energy consumption for the tasks that are performed by the server k. This quantity, can be computed as follows:

$$\mathcal{E}_k^{idle} = \sum_{i \in V} p^{idle} \cdot x_i^k \cdot T_i^k + \sum_{i \in V} \sum_{j \in pred(i)} \sum_{m \in \mathcal{K}} p^{idle} \cdot x_i^k \cdot x_j^m \cdot \mathcal{D}_{j,i}^{m,k} \tag{17}$$

where p^{idle} is the power consumption when the network interface of the terminal is in idle mode.

5 PROPOSED MULTITASKING OFFLOADING POLICY

As introduced earlier, our objective is to decide which task must be offloaded and to which server, in order to minimize the energy consumption of the user terminal. Formally, considering the optimization problem presented in section 4.1, we need to determine the best values of $x_i^k, \forall i \in V, k \in \mathcal{K}$. Unfortunately, this optimization problem is NP-complete, since it can be easily reduced to a classical scheduling problem by putting the idle energy consumption to zero and removing the constraint C1, which is considered as NP-complete [7]. Considering the NP-hardness of the problem, it is difficult to achieve an optimal solution. In order to solve the problem 4.1 and get a feasible solution in a reasonable amount of time, we resort to heuristic based solution. We propose a new offloading heuristic, named eTOMEC for *Elastic Task graph Offloading in Mobile Edge Computing* environment, which consists of two steps.

The first step of eTOMEC is built on top of the well-known tasks scheduling approach Bottom Level Early Start Time (BL-EST) [18]. The main objective of BL-EST is to map a graph of tasks onto a set of processors, in order to reduce the completion time of the application. It uses an ordered list of tasks to decide with task to schedule first. To that purpose a priority is assigned to each task. This priority is defined as the largest weight path from the current task to the exit task, including the processing time and communication time. Unfortunately, unlike BL-EST, our communication time depends on where the task is scheduled (i.e. offloading server), which includes the necessary delay to send both source code and data to that server. Consequently, we propose to assign to each task a new priority that corresponds to the worst case offloading decision. Formally, the priority assigned to each task is expressed as:

$$bl(i) = \max_{k \in \mathcal{K}} (T_i^k + sr_i^k) + \begin{cases} 0 & \text{if } succ(i) = \emptyset \\ \max_{\substack{j \in succ(i) \\ k,m \in \mathcal{K}}} (bl(j) + \mathcal{D}_{i,j}^{k,m}) & \text{otherwise} \end{cases}$$

(18)

As we can see, from equation 18, that the priority assigned to each task is defines as the sum of: (i.) the maximum time necessary to transmit the source code and to schedule the task i, among all possible servers $k \in \mathcal{K}$, plus (ii.) the maximum, among all the successors of the task i, of the priority assigned to that successor plus the time required to send the data dependency between i and that successor in the case where the choice of offloading servers is the most unfavorable. This function guarantees an upper-bound of the bottom level function.

Once we assign to each task its priority, we define two sets noted as S_{ready} and S_{exec}. S_{ready} is an ordered set according to the priority assigned to each task i, i.e. $bl(i)$. At any moment, S_{ready} contains only tasks that have no predecessor or have all their predecessors already been scheduled. Initially, this list contains only the first task of the DAG, since it has no predecessor. Once scheduled, a task i will be removed and inserted onto the second set S_{exec}. Thus, S_{exec} contains only tasks that have been already scheduled. Finally, as in [18], we use heap data structure as implementation for S_{ready} in order to make the priority-based insertion of tasks more efficient. As illustrated in Algorithm 1, at each iteration, the task i with the highest priority in S_{ready} is selected to be offloaded on the server that would result to the lowest energy consumption for the mobile terminal. In order to select the best offloading server, we choose the server that minimize the following optimization **problem 2**:

$$\text{Minimize}_{k \in \mathcal{K}} (\mathcal{E}_i^l + \mathcal{E}_i^{tx} + \mathcal{E}_i^{rx} + p^{idle} \cdot x_i^k \cdot T_i^k$$
$$+ \sum_{j \in pred(i)} \sum_{\substack{m \in \mathcal{K} \\ m \neq 0}} p^{idle} \cdot x_i^k \cdot x_j^m \cdot \mathcal{D}_{j,i}^{m,k})$$

Subject to: C3

where $\mathcal{E}_i^l$, $\mathcal{E}_i^{tx}$ and $\mathcal{E}_i^{rx}$ are defined in 13, 14 and 15, respectively. The fourth term is an upper-bound of the energy consumed in the idle mode, when all the predecessor of the task i have to send their dependency data to the server k. The last term correspond the energy consumed in the idle mode when the task i is executed by the server k. The basic idea of this objective function is to select the server that minimize the extra amount of energy that could be consumed by the user terminal when scheduling the task i on the server k. Finally, the only constraint that we consider in this problem is the $C3$, which guarantees that the non-offloadable tasks must be performed at the user's terminal.

After selecting the optimal offloading server k^*, we move the task i from the S_{ready} to S_{exec} and we update the decision variable

x_i^k. We also check if there are new tasks that can be inserted in S_{ready}. Finally, we select the next task with the highest priority, and we iterate again until S_{ready} becomes empty.

Once we affect all the tasks, the second step is to ensure that the obtained solution is feasible, which means that it must respect the completion time constraint $C1$. In this case, we propose to merges some tasks in order to reduce the completion time of the application. Basically, we select from the DAG the adjacent tasks (i, j) that are offloaded to different servers and have the highest edge weight. More precisely, the tasks with the most important dependency data transfer time. Thereafter, among the two possible locations, we decide to merge the two tasks to the server that reduce the most the application competition time. This step is repeated until we obtain a feasible solution.

Algorithm 1 *eTOMEC approach*

Output: The offloading decisions $\mathcal{X}$, energy consumption $\mathcal{Z}$;
Input: Tasks graph G = (V,E), servers and bandwidth allocation;
1: ***Step 1:***
2: bl ← computePriority(G);
3: S_{ready} ← ∅ ;
4: insert task 1, entry task , in S_{ready} with key bl(1);
5: av^k ← 0, S_{exec} ← ∅;
6: **while** (S_{ready} ≠ ∅) **do**
7:    i ← extractMax(S_{ready});
8:    compute ft_i^k using equation 10, $\forall k \in \mathcal{K}$;
9:    k^* ← solution of **problem 2**;
10:    $x_i^{k^*}$ ← 1, av^{k^*} ← $ft_i^{k^*}$;
11:    Insert next ready tasks into S_{ready} using bl as key;
12:    Add task i to S_{exec}
13: **end while**
14: ***Step 2:***
15: S_{merge} ← All edges in G with key as the edge weight;
16: **while** ($ft_n^0 > t_{max}$ and S_{merge} ≠ ∅) **do**
17:    ft ← ft_n^0, (i,j) ← extractMax(S_{merge});
18:    k, m ← servers that performs tasks i and j;
19:    **if** (k ≠ m) **then**
20:      x_i^k = 0, x_i^m = 1, ft1 ← compute new ft_n^0;
21:      x_i^k = 1, x_i^m = 0, x_j^m = 0, x_j^k = 1; ft2 ← compute new ft_n^0;
22:      **if** (ft1 > ft2 and ft2 < ft) **then**
23:        merge task i with j;
24:      **else if** ft1 < ft **then**
25:        merge task j with j;
26:      **end if**
27:    **end if**
28: **end while**

---

6 PERFORMANCE EVALUATION

6.1 Complexity Analysis

In the worst case eTOMEC iterates $n \cdot (K + 1)^2$ for the function computePriority using 18 to compute priority of tasks. In addition to $n(log(n) + 2(K + 1))$ iterations for the step 1, n times in the first while loop. For each iteration, it delete and insert tasks in the heap which has a complexity of log(n). In addition to 2*(K+1) operations to select the best server for each task, Similarly, it iterates $|E|(log(|E|) + 4(K + 1))$ in the second wile loop, merge phase.In conclusion, the total complexity of eTOMEC approach is $O(n \cdot K^2 + n \cdot log(n) + n \cdot K + |E| \cdot log(|E|) + |E| \cdot K)$. That makes eTOMEC a quick algorithm to solve the problem formulated in section 4.1.

6.2 Results Analysis

In this section, we discuss the simulation results of eTOMEC. We consider a MEC environment with a wireless access network composed of one AP and 4 edge servers and one remote cloud. In addition, we consider that the edge servers have the same computing capability to perform the tasks. As in [13, 14], we assume that both the cloud and edge servers has a computing capability of 5 *Giga cycles/s*. Moreover, we suppose that user terminal has a local computing capacity of 1 *Giga cycles/s*.

Table 1: The parameter setting of the network interface

Parameter	Value	Parameter	Value
B	5 Mhz	c	50
C	256	$b^{rx} = b^{tx}$	10^{-3}
σ^2	5×10^{-5}	p^{tx}	1.28 Watts
p^{rx}	1.18 Watts	p^{idle}	0.1 Watts
p_{ap}	10 Watts	$h^{tx} = h^{rx}$	0.1

Table 1 shows the wireless network parameter settings as presented in [5, 6, 17]. For the backhaul network, we use the parameters presented in [13, 14]. Finally, the user wants to perform one application composed of 14 tasks as shown in Figure 3. To understand the application graph effect, we assume that all the tasks require the same computing resource and transmit the same amount of data. Every task requires 30 *Giga cycles* [9, 14]. The dependencies between tasks is set to 300*KB* and the source code data to 2*MB*. The results of eTOMEC are compared with the following approaches:

- **WFM** [1]: A list-based scheduling approach. First, it determines the level of the tasks in a breadth-first-search traversal of the DAG. Then, the tasks in each level are assigned to different servers using a round robin algorithm.

- **HEM** [1]: A clustering-based approach. Initially, it assigns the (K+2) heaviest tasks to the servers. Then, it sorts the edges in decreasing order of their weight. The endpoints, tasks, of each edge are clustered if the completion time does not increase.

- **MCOP** [9]: A DAG-based offloading algorithm with one single edge server.

Figure 4 investigates the offloading performance for different DAG-based applications. We notice that eTOMEC outperforms WFM, HEM and MCOP in terms of total energy consumption and completion time. The only exception is for the sequential graph, this is because of the consideration of offloading to multi-edge servers by eTOMEC, in the sequential graph all the offloaded tasks are assigned to the same edge server in order to reduce the communication cost between those tasks. In addition, the figure shows that depending on the application graph eTOMEC achieves better performance than the classical tasks scheduling approaches WFM and HEM.

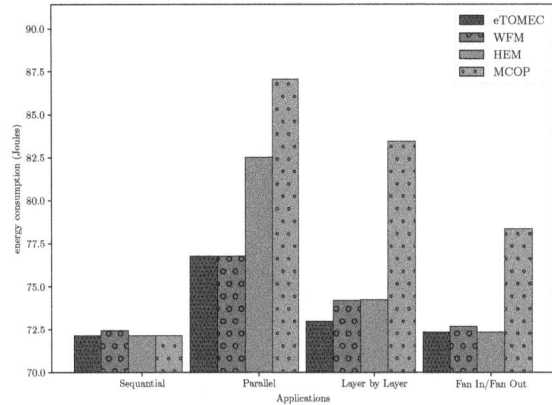

(a) Energy consumption

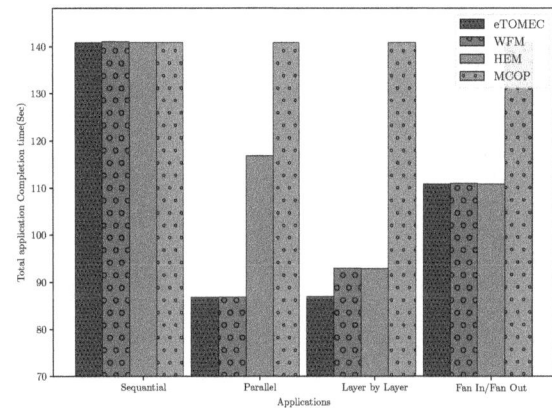

(b) Completion Time

Figure 4: Performance comparison for different application graphs

For example, eTOMEC and WFM are 6.94% better than HEM in energy consumption and 25.67% in completion time with parallel graph. However, eTOMEC and HEM have the same performance for Fan In/Fan Out. Furthermore, the energy consumption of the application depends highly on the graph.

We also observe that energy consumption is highly related to the degree of tasks that are executed in the terminal, which is the case of tasks 1 and 14. For instance, in the case of sequential graph the user terminal uploads the data related to the dependency between tasks 1 and 2 and download the data between tasks 13 to the task 14. On the other hand, in the case of parallel graph the user terminal have to send and receive data from several tasks. Hence, the additional energy consumption is due to upload and the download of data from remote and local tasks.

In order to evaluate the effect of the application graph on the performance of the computation offloading, we study in Figure 5, the completion time and energy consumption when varying the number of available edge servers, when using our approach (eTOMEC).

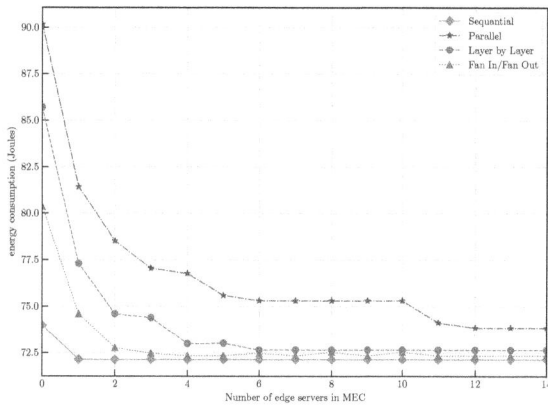

(a) Energy consumption

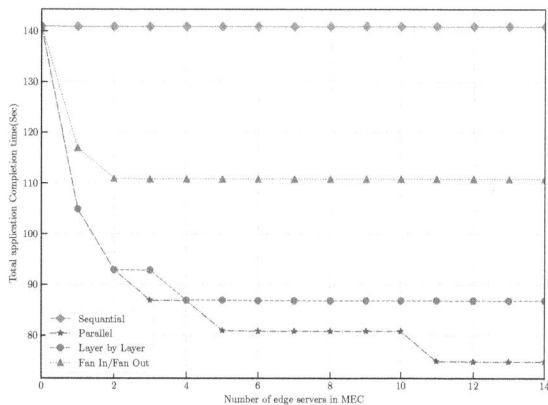

(b) Completion Time

Figure 5: Performance of eTOMEC for different application graphs

We note that completion time decreases when we increase the number of available edge servers, except for sequential graph. We can also observe that the completion time reaches a constant value after a given number of available edge servers. This number depends on the graph, for example, for sequential graph it is 1, but it is equal to 12, 4 and 2 for parallel, Layour by Layour and Fan In/Fan Out graphs, respectively. This is due to the maximum number of tasks that we can perform in parallel. In Figure 5a depicts also the same behavior for the total energy consumption. As conclusion, the application graph affects strongly the performance of offloading.

7 CONCLUSION

In this paper, we present a new computation offloading approach for multitasking mobile application in Multi-edge server MEC. The proposed offloading approach decides which tasks should be offload and to which server. We formalize this offloading problem as a Zero-one Integer Programming problem. Thereafter, and due to the NP-hardness of the problem, we propose a heuristic approach named

eTOMEC. Using our efficient offloading algorithm, we where able to scale the number of concurrent offloaded tasks accordingly with the number of available edge servers, while taking into consideration tasks dependencies. Finally, we assessed the performances of the proposed approach in relation to several literature approaches. The obtained results show that eTOMEC results in better performances in terms of completion time and energy consumption. We also studied the effect of several application's graph on the performance of the computation offloading. The results show that performance relies strongly on the application's DAG pattern.

REFERENCES

[1] Nancy M Amato and Ping An. 2000. Task scheduling and parallel mesh-sweeps in transport computations. *TR00-009, Department of Computer Science, Texas A&M University* (2000).

[2] Rajesh Krishna Balan, Mahadev Satyanarayanan, So Young Park, and Tadashi Okoshi. 2003. Tactics-based remote execution for mobile computing. In *Proceedings of the 1st international conference on Mobile systems, applications and services*. ACM, 273–286.

[3] Aaron Carroll, Gernot Heiser, et al. 2010. An Analysis of Power Consumption in a Smartphone.. In *USENIX annual technical conference*, Vol. 14. Boston, MA, 21–21.

[4] Meng-Hsi Chen, Ben Liang, and Min Dong. 2016. Joint offloading decision and resource allocation for multi-user multi-task mobile cloud. In *2016 IEEE International Conference on Communications (ICC)*. IEEE, 1–6.

[5] Weiwei Chen, Dong Wang, and Keqin Li. 2018. Multi-user multi-task computation offloading in green mobile edge cloud computing. *IEEE Transactions on Services Computing* (2018).

[6] Thinh Quang Dinh, Jianhua Tang, Quang Duy La, and Tony QS Quek. 2017. Offloading in mobile edge computing: Task allocation and computational frequency scaling. *IEEE Transactions on Communications* 65, 8 (2017), 3571–3584.

[7] Michael R. Garey and David S. Johnson. 1990. *Computers and Intractability; A Guide to the Theory of NP-Completeness*. W. H. Freeman & Co., New York, NY, USA.

[8] Andrea Goldsmith. 2005. *Wireless Communications*. Cambridge University Press. https://doi.org/10.1017/CBO9780511841224

[9] Songtao Guo, Bin Xiao, Yuanyuan Yang, and Yang Yang. 2016. Energy-efficient dynamic offloading and resource scheduling in mobile cloud computing. In *IEEE INFOCOM 2016-The 35th Annual IEEE International Conference on Computer Communications*. IEEE, 1–9.

[10] Dong Huang, Ping Wang, and Dusit Niyato. 2012. A dynamic offloading algorithm for mobile computing. *IEEE Transactions on Wireless Communications* 11, 6 (2012), 1991–1995.

[11] Vinay Kumar, CP Katti, and PC Saxena. 2014. A Novel Task Scheduling Algorithm for Heterogeneous Computing. *International Journal of Computer Applications* 85, 18 (2014).

[12] S. Eman Mahmoodi, R.N. Uma, and K.P. Subbalakshmi. 2016. Optimal Joint Scheduling and Cloud Offloading for Mobile Applications. *IEEE Transactions on Cloud Computing* 7161, c (2016), 1–1.

[13] Houssemeddine Mazouzi, Nadjib Achir, and Khaled Boussetta. 2018. Maximizing Mobiles Energy Saving Through Tasks Optimal Offloading Placement in two-tier Cloud. In *Proceedings of the 21st ACM International Conference on Modeling, Analysis and Simulation of Wireless and Mobile Systems*. ACM, 137–145.

[14] Houssemeddine Mazouzi, Nadjib Achir, and Khaled Boussetta. 2019. Dm2-ecop: An efficient computation offloading policy for multi-user multi-cloudlet mobile edge computing environment. *ACM Transactions on Internet Technology (TOIT)* 19, 2 (2019), 24.

[15] M Yusuf Özkaya, Anne Benoit, Bora Uçar, Julien Herrmann, and Umit Catalyurek. 2019. A scalable clustering-based task scheduler for homogeneous processors using DAG partitioning. In *IPDPS 2019-33rd IEEE International Parallel & Distributed Processing Symposium*. IEEE, 1–11.

[16] Peng Sun, Heli Zhang, Hong Ji, and Xi Li. 2018. Task Allocation for Multi-APs with Mobile Edge Computing. In *2018 IEEE/CIC International Conference on Communications in China (ICCC Workshops)*. IEEE, 314–318.

[17] Tuyen X Tran and Dario Pompili. 2019. Joint task offloading and resource allocation for multi-server mobile-edge computing networks. *IEEE Transactions on Vehicular Technology* 68, 1 (2019), 856–868.

[18] H. Wang and O. Sinnen. 2018. List-Scheduling versus Cluster-Scheduling. *IEEE Transactions on Parallel and Distributed Systems* 29, 8 (Aug 2018), 1736–1749.

[19] Lei Yang, Bo Liu, Jiannong Cao, Yuvraj Sahni, and Zhenyu Wang. 2019. Joint computation partitioning and resource allocation for latency sensitive applications in mobile edge clouds. *IEEE Transactions on Services Computing* (2019).

Modeling Realistic Bit Rates of D2D Communications between Android Devices

Clément Bertier[*,◇], Marcelo Dias de Amorim[*], Farid Benbadis[◇], and Vania Conan[◇]

[*]LIP6/CNRS – Sorbonne Université   [◇]Thales SIX GTS France

ABSTRACT

Although D2D communications have been extensively investigated in the literature, relatively few works have focused on understanding the capacity of direct links in a real setup. In this paper, we propose an empirical characterization of the currently available high-speed D2D technologies in Android, namely *Wi-Fi P2P* and *Google Nearby*. To this end, we developed a custom Android application called *Ocat* which interacts with the available D2D APIs and measures the link's goodput. From the experimental campaign, we derive several useful observations. Concerning communication capacity, the goodput between Android devices ranges between 320 Mbits/s when nodes are within 20 meters of each other and 0.1 Mbits/s when the distance grows to 300 meters. Based on the experimental measurements, we propose a model of the upper-bound goodput as a function of the distance between two devices. Using the wireless signal strength as a link measurement, we combine it with the two-ray ground-reflection model to infer the goodput and obtain a good fit for the characterization of D2D links between Android devices. Our findings provide a reality check in regards to actual direct data-exchange capabilities of Android devices and can help assess system performance of D2D applications.

CCS CONCEPTS

• **Networks** → **Network performance modeling**; **Network performance analysis**.

KEYWORDS

D2D, model, experimentation, Android, measurements, RSSI.

ACM Reference Format:
Clément Bertier[*,◇], Marcelo Dias de Amorim[*], Farid Benbadis[◇], and Vania Conan[◇]. 2019. Modeling Realistic Bit Rates of D2D Communications between Android Devices. In *22nd Int'l ACM Conference on Modeling, Analysis and Simulation of Wireless andMobile Systems (MSWiM '19), November 25–29, 2019, Miami Beach, FL, USA.* ACM, New York, NY, USA, 8 pages. https://doi.org/10.1145/3345768.3355918

1 INTRODUCTION

Albeit significant advances in the design of protocols and algorithms for device-to-device (D2D) communications, the research community still lacks experimental works that focus on finely understanding D2D links *in real setups*. Several fundamental questions concerning the expected performance of direct links remain open: "*what is the expected transfer rate between two smartphones if they are 25m apart?*" or "*how far can these two smartphones communicate reliably?*". As a result, there are gaps in the state of the art when it comes to modeling D2D exchanges. For example, when simulating D2D communications in the *The ONE* simulator, the user has to select a maximum communication range as well as a constant throughput between the devices. Due to the scarcity of studies quantifying these parameters, authors often adopt rough estimates for the physical layer bit rate used by the wireless medium [24].

In this paper, we characterize the link quality of device-to-device communications based on empirical measurements of Wi-Fi Direct. We model the upper-bound of D2D bit rate as a function of the distance, thus shedding light on the applicability of D2D solutions. We expect to help protocol and algorithm designers better select their parameters in their simulations.

Studies tackling the performance of Wi-Fi links in infrastructure mode exist [20]; however, these studies differ from ours in several ways. Firstly, D2D links differ from traditional infrastructured communications because of hardware differences. By considering off-the-shelf smartphones using the latest OS updates (Android 8+ at the time of the writing of this paper), we provide up-to-date results. Secondly, to the best of our knowledge, this is the first characterization of a D2D link based on Google's Nearby Connections API. Thirdly, our results bring a number of new insightful observations for smartphone-based direct communications which notably differ from previous works in the literature. In a nutshell, we explore the state of current tools which enable high-speed D2D communications in Android and establish a model of the upper-bound bit rate using off-the-shelf devices.

As a summary, our contributions are:

- We explore the currently available high-speed D2D APIs in stock Android. As some APIs are proprietary, their inner-workings are not always disclosed, which requires indirect analysis to assess their behaviors.
- We design Ocat, a measurement application that stores data transfer information for post-processing. We detail our experimental procedure to collect data by using Ocat on Android smartphones considering both Google Nearby and Wi-Fi P2P APIs. We vary the distance between the devices up to the distance beyond which the devices lose connectivity (around 300 m in our experiments).
- We propose a model, after a thorough analysis of the collected data, to estimate the upper-bound of the goodput between two devices as a function of the distance.

This work aims to be a stepping-stone on how to accurately model D2D communications between Android devices in real-life.

While there are still limited efforts to leverage D2D communications as an applicable data-exchange solution [7], we are hopeful results provided in this work entice the community to do so.

The rest of this paper is organized as follows. In Section 2, we explain the different available APIs, while in Section 3 we introduce Ocat, our measurement application for Android devices. We detail the experimental work in Section 4; in particular, we provide a thorough analysis of the RSSI measurements in D2D links and how to model them accurately. In Section 5, we give a reality-check based on our goodput analysis and how we perform the goodput-to-distance modeling. We postpone the related work to Section 6, so that the reader has enough material to best capture our contributions. Finally, we conclude the paper and identify ideas for future work in Section 7.

2 STOCK ANDROID HIGH-SPEED D2D APIS

To establish the upper-bound of D2D bit rate according to distance, we carry out field measurements. To this end, we first take a look at currently available D2D APIs in Android. As of now, there are two supported APIs for high-speed D2D in stock Android, namely Wi-Fi P2P [11] and Google Nearby Connections [10]. The former is an implementation of the Wi-Fi Direct standard [3], while the latter is a closed-source framework to send files, strings (e.g., URLs), or even data streams (e.g., VoIP) to surrounding devices.

2.1 Wi-Fi P2P

Wi-Fi P2P is the Android implementation of Wi-Fi Alliance's Wi-Fi Direct standard. In short, peer-to-peer (P2P) devices communicate through *P2P Groups*, which are dynamically formed by electing a device as the P2P Group Owner, which embodies the role of the access point. A P2P device can concurrently act as a P2P Group Owner and as a P2P Client of another group.

While the standard's inner-workings have been thoroughly reviewed in the literature [3], the Android implementation reveals technical restrictions. For instance, while the standard does not state any limitations in the number of clients in a P2P group, we were not able to maintain more than one Wi-Fi P2P connection using this API. Once two P2P devices have detected each other, one (or both) can initiate a Wi-Fi P2P connection, as shown in Figure 1. This connection needs to be approved by the user(s) via a pop-up notification. The Wi-Fi Direct standard imposes the connection to be set-up through the Wi-Fi Protected Setup protocol, and IP addresses are then configured through DHCP. After the assignment of IP addresses to both devices, a socket has to be opened to establish a two-way communication link between the two devices. In our implementation (see Section 3), we use TCP.

2.2 Nearby

Google Nearby Connections appeared in 2017 as a framework meant to completely abstract network-related complexities of D2D data exchange so that developers can focus on application features rather than communications technicalities. For the rest of this paper, we refer to this API as *Nearby*. Other than the application level functions and callbacks available to developers, technical specification of the inner-workings of Nearby are close to none.

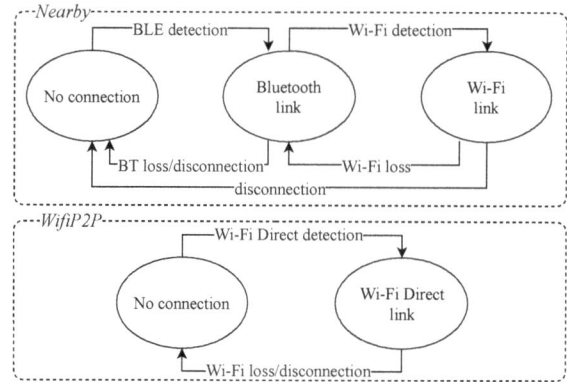

Figure 1: Summary of the connection process of both APIs.

The framework supports two types of topology: cluster and star. Cluster topology acts in a completely decentralized fashion, where any device can accept/start a connection from/with any other device. A star topology is more restrictive, as a clear client/server design has to be made prior to the connection. In a star, servers can accept all incoming connections but cannot initiate a connection, and a client can only be connected to a single server.

Nearby uses the commonly available wireless technologies found in off-the-shelf smartphones, namely Bluetooth Low Energy (BLE), Bluetooth, and Wi-Fi. In this paper, we consider the star topology as it is the only one to use Wi-Fi (the cluster topology uses Bluetooth), and because we aim to establish the upper-bound of D2D bit rates.

Using the adb software [9] and a spectrum analyzer, we unveil that the connection process is actually three-fold, as summarized in Figure 1. First, a BLE beacon is sent to notify all users within communication range that a server is available (*advertiser*) or a client is looking for a server to connect to (*discoverer*). Once two devices have detected each other, they first establish a Bluetooth connection in order to begin the data transfer as soon as possible. During this Bluetooth data transfer, the two devices attempt to establish a Wi-Fi connection; if they succeed, they automatically switch the data transfer over to the Wi-Fi link. If the Wi-Fi link drops due to poor signal, they fall back to the Bluetooth connection. The choices of the Wi-Fi standard and of the carrier frequency are always set by the server (advertiser) which acts as an AP.

After the establishment of the D2D link, the file transfer can start. Nearby triggers regular callbacks to notify the user-space of internal events, such as a status update on the transfer of the file.

2.3 Goodput measurement

We focus on Wi-Fi P2P and Nearby because they both enable higher transfer speeds than BLE and Bluetooth. Unfortunately, there is no integrated way in neither Wi-Fi P2P nor Nearby APIs to obtain the throughput of the D2D wireless link (i.e., the data exchange rate between the two Wi-Fi interfaces). Thus, instead of obtaining the throughput, we consider the *goodput* in the remainder of this paper, defined as the bit rate at the application level.

To obtain the goodput, we look at the behavior of the APIs. Nearby triggers a callback every time a *chunk* is received. A chunk is a application-level data block of $\leq 2^{16}$ bytes (the Nearby API

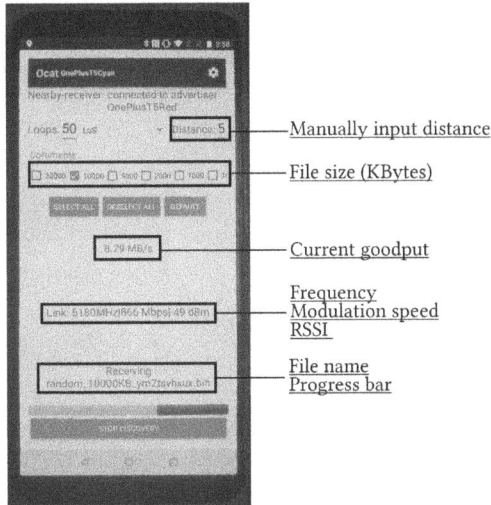

Figure 2: Ocat user interface.

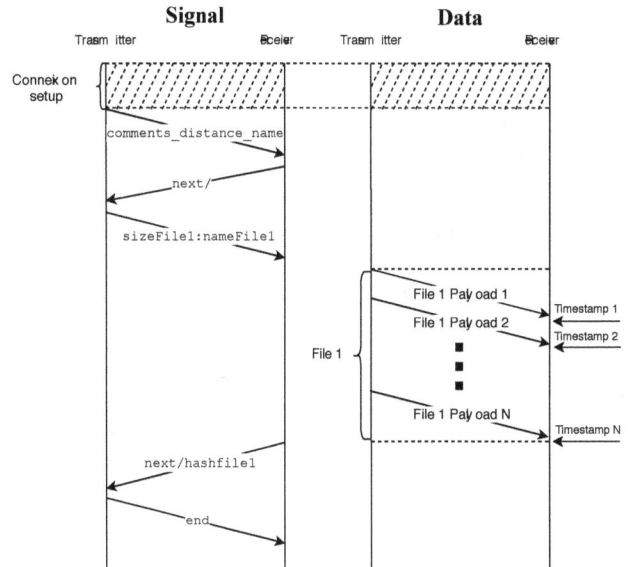

Figure 3: Representation of the synchronization protocol implemented in Ocat.

enforces this size). To obtain the mean goodput after the file has been sent, we collect timestamps at the arrival of each chunk. For both Nearby and Wi-Fi P2P APIs, we define the mean goodput as:

$$\text{Mean Goodput} = \frac{\sum_{n=2}^{N} \text{sizeChunk}(n)}{\text{Timestamp N} - \text{Timestamp 1}}. \qquad (1)$$

We start at $n = 2$ because we cannot obtain the timestamp before the arrival of the first chunk.

2.4 Network-related data collection

To better understand D2D characteristics, we intend to collect any accessible network-related information or statistics, when using either APIs. As we have not found any straightforward means to obtain extra information using Nearby and Wi-Fi P2P APIs, we require the use of a third API supported in stock Android that solves the issue at least for the Nearby case. This API, called Wifi-Manager [12], is built to handle regular client Wi-Fi connections in Android. We exploit the fact that once Nearby establishes a D2D link through Wi-Fi, this link acts as a standard Wi-Fi connection; thus, it becomes possible to use WifiManager to query the Wi-Fi interface to obtain extra information. Thanks to this workaround, we obtain the received signal strength indication (RSSI, in dBm), the link speed (in Mbit/s), and the used frequency (in MHz). Unfortunately, this technique exclusively works on the client side of the connection, due to the AP-side information being inaccessible in Android for privacy issues. While there arguably could be complex software solutions such as installing a custom Android firmware on the device, this falls outside of the scope of this paper since we focus on stock Android. We used in our experiments OnePlus 5T smartphones, which uses Wi-Fi 5 (802.11ac) in both Nearby and Wi-Fi P2P (contrarily to other brands that use Wi-Fi 4 for Nearby).

3 EXPERIMENTAL PROCEDURE

We designed and implemented Ocat (Opportunistic communications assessment tool), a mobile application whose purpose is to measure the connectivity characteristics between two or more devices using (so far) either Nearby or Wi-Fi P2P.

3.1 Ocat

In Figure 2, we show the user interface of the application. The process consists of generating random files of 10 MBytes, transmitting them between the devices, and storing the gathered information in a log file for post-processing. Recall that we only collect information once the data reaches the application level at the receiver side, as we cannot access network-related information at the OS level.

We unfortunately noticed that Nearby prematurely notified the transmitter user-space of transfer completion, even though significant part of the file was still being transferred. In Figure 3, we show the protocol exchanges implemented in Ocat. The purpose of the control plane is mainly to keep the synchronization between the transmitter and the receiver. This synchronization scheme allowed us to enforce strict transmission rules so that two files are never sent concurrently, which is paramount to fine-grained measurement of file transfer rates, thus solving the premature file transmission notification issue.

To ensure that files arrive correctly, the receiver sends a hash of the file to the transmitter along with the next command in order to request the next file in the queue. If the hash is correct, the transmitter sends the next file; otherwise, it sends the same file again (up to 5 times in our experiments).

3.2 Empirical goodput as a function of distance

For our experimental methodology, we laid on the ground a measuring tape which we used as a mean to measure the exact distance d between the transmitter and receiver devices. We put the smartphones on tripods, both of them set at the height of 1.3 m. We start by putting them 1 m apart, as seen in Figure 4, and then we

Figure 4: Photography of the experimental procedure. Both smartphones run the Ocat application, and we move one of the tripods according to a chosen stepping along the measuring tape (white line on the ground).

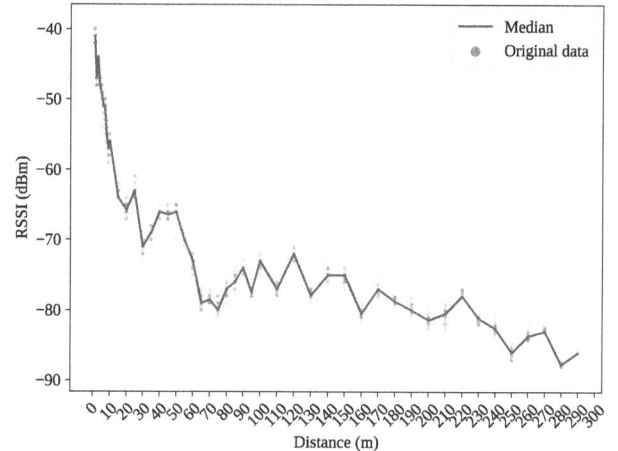

Figure 5: RSSI to distance measurements using the One-Plus 5T devices.

gradually increase the distance. Using Ocat, we connect two devices using either Wi-Fi P2P or Nearby (implemented as an option in the app). With an active D2D connection, the transmitter sends 100 randomly generated files to the receiver. Once all files have been sent, we move the receiver to the next mark and start the next round of transmissions. We repeat the process until the devices are too far to establish a connection.

In practice, a plethora of parameters related to the wireless medium has to be considered, such as shadowing, refraction, or fading. To limit as much as we could the influence of these parameters, we conducted our experiments in a rural environment with little to no external interference (Figure 4). This is compliant with our goal of measuring the maximum reachable transfer speeds. We checked for interference using a spectrum analyzer by verifying that no signal above noise-level (-100dBm in our case) was detected on the 2.4 GHz and 5 GHz bands.

4 RSSI FOR GOODPUT ESTIMATION

As previously explained, we can only access the RSSI, as Android does not give access to the transmission power. The RSSI, in dBm, is calculated as:

$$\text{RSSI}(d) = P_t + G_t + G_r - L - PL(d), \qquad (2)$$

where d is the distance between the transmitter and the receiver, P_t is the transmission power, G_t is the transmitter's antenna gain, G_r is the receiver's antenna gain, L is the loss of the system, and $PL(d)$ is the path loss according to distance d. For the off-the-shelf smartphones that we use in our experiments, most of these parameters are not disclosed.

We first assume that smartphones transmit at constant power, meaning that P_t is fixed. We simplify the equation by letting $A = P_t + G_t + G_r - L$. This is done since we can only measure the RSSI, hence making it impossible to differentiate the terms. We have then:

$$\text{RSSI}(d) = A - PL(d). \qquad (3)$$

4.1 Modeling the RSSI

We present in Figure 5 the RSSI measurements between two One-Plus 5T following the measurement methodology presented in Section 3. While at short distances (1 m to 20 m), the strength of the signal seems to be monotonically decreasing, it is not the case throughout the entire experiment. For instance, from 30 m to 50 m there is an apparent increase in the signal strength even though we increased the distance between the devices. While counter-intuitive, this increase of signal in spite of the growth of distance is a behavior typically found in the rural environment [21].

We consider three different models, namely the free-space path loss propagation model [2], the log-distance path loss model [2], and the accurate version of the two-ray ground-reflection model (as opposed to the approximation often found in the literature) [19, 21]. As the model yielding the best results is the accurate version of the two-ray ground-reflection model, as we will see below, we present further details of this model in the Appendix.

We estimate the parameters for each model through a best-fit approach. As we only have the RSSI at each receiver, we need to estimate the global gain of the system A (see Equation 3) for all models. To find which path loss model leads to the best fit, we perform a least-square curve fitting using *lmfit* [16]. We remind the reader that, depending on the *PL* model used, several parameters are used to find the best fit. These parameters are listed in Table 1, where η is the attenuation exponent of the log-distance model and ϵ is a parameter that depends on the material of the reflection surface and h_r/h_t the height of the receiver/transmitter.

We show in Figure 6 how the different models fit our measures. The free-space model leads to a pretty good fitting by using a global gain $A \approx 10.46$. The log-distance model seems to exhibit the same behavior, however, the best-fit yields a gain of $A \approx 8.3$ and the attenuation exponent is set to $\eta \approx 1.8$; the problem is that η is under

Table 1: Summary of the models and their parameters.

RSSI/PL Model	Param 1	Param 2	Param 3
Freespace	A	-	-
Log-Distance	A	η	-
Two-Ray ground-reflection	A	ϵ	h_r/h_t

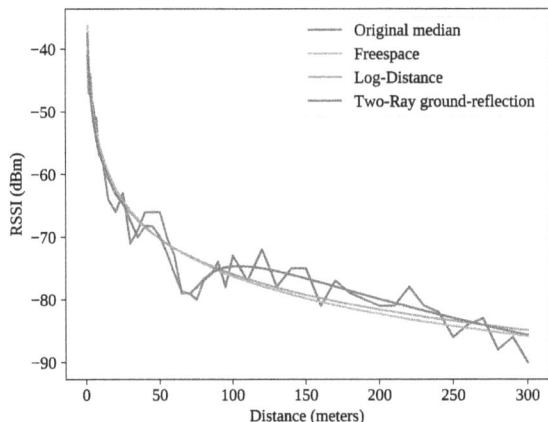

Figure 6: RSSI Models after least-square fitting. The two-ray ground ground-reflection model is the only model capturing the signal increase while augmenting the distance.

the minimum value of 2 which corresponds to the propagation of a signal in free-space. Thus, we consider this fit to be invalid and ignore it since fixing this parameter to a minimum of 2 is equivalent to calculating the free-space model.

The two-ray ground-reflection model gives the best results. It can capture specific phenomena such as the signal increase observed between 30 m and 50 m (which is the consequence of constructive interference due to the ground reflection). The algorithm fixes the parameters $A \approx 9.19$ dB and $\epsilon = 1.009$. It is not a surprise that the algorithm gave $h_r = h_s \approx 1.38m$, which corresponds to the height of the phones on top of the tripods.

4.2 RSSI and Goodput

To derive a distance-to-goodput model, we need to establish if a clear correlation between a given RSSI value and a goodput exists. We know from the Wi-Fi 5 standard that, for each value of RSSI, a particular modulation is chosen in order to achieve the best trade-off between throughput and error resilience [6]. Typically, modulations reaching the highest throughputs are quite sensitive to noise and are unsuitable for long-distance communications. If we were in a noisy environment, the RSSI measurements should be correlated to a throughput through a rate-adaptation algorithm, but since this is not the case, the sole RSSI is enough for our upper-bound model.

Recall that, in Android, the modulation used by the Wi-Fi interface is not disclosed; still, it can be inferred from the link speed if the number of MIMO antennas is known. We compiled Table 2 from the Wi-Fi 5 standard to better understand the behavior of the

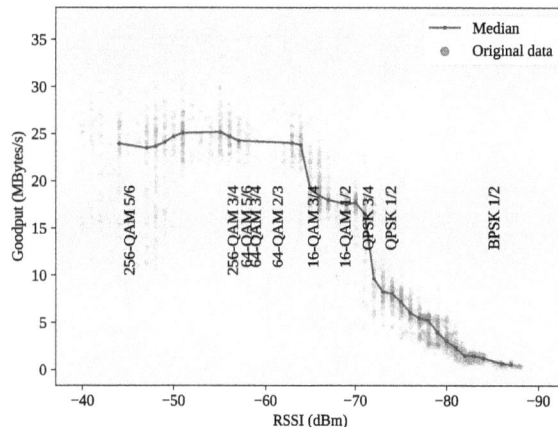

Figure 7: Empirical RSSI-to-goodput relationship with the indication of the modulation used.

MCS	Bit rate	Modulation	Redundancy	Max RSSI	Min RSSI
9	866	256-QAM	5/6	-	-55
8	780	256-QAM	3/4	-56	-57
7	650	64-QAM	5/6	-58	-58
6	585	64-QAM	3/4	-59	-59
5	520	64-QAM	2/3	-60	-63
4	390	16-QAM	3/4	-64	-67
3	260	16-QAM	1/2	-68	-70
2	195	QPSK	3/4	-71	-72
1	130	QPSK	1/2	-73	-75
0	65	BPSK	1/2	-76	-

Table 2: Android Wi-Fi 5 theoretical maximum throughput using 80MHz bandwidth & 2*2 MIMO, 400ns GI

throughput. The BPSK modulation does not have a minimum RSSI in the tested devices as it continues to operate until the signal is lost, and the same logic applies to the 256-QAM which operates no matter how high the RSSI is.

The units we consider are dBm for the RSSI and MBytes/s for the goodput. In Section 2.3, we calculated a mean goodput per file, and we now apply the same idea to the RSSI. The RSSI given by WifiManager is not guaranteed to be up-to-date. We mitigate this issue by weighting the RSSI of each chunk using the transmission time of the chunk to establish the mean RSSI of the file.

As the choice of a specific RSSI value is not left to the user, we cannot guarantee that all possible values of RSSI are covered. However, by moving the tripods back and forth several times, we were able to cover a wide range of possible values, from -40 dBm to -87 dBm. In Figure 7, we present plot the mean goodput per file sent, as a function of the mean RSSI during the file transmission. Each red dot on the figure represents a sample (a file transmitted), and we additionally superimposed the RSSI range of all modulations to give a physical layer perspective to the reader. The blue line represents the median values of all values of RSSI, given that at least 50 samples over the same RSSI are available.

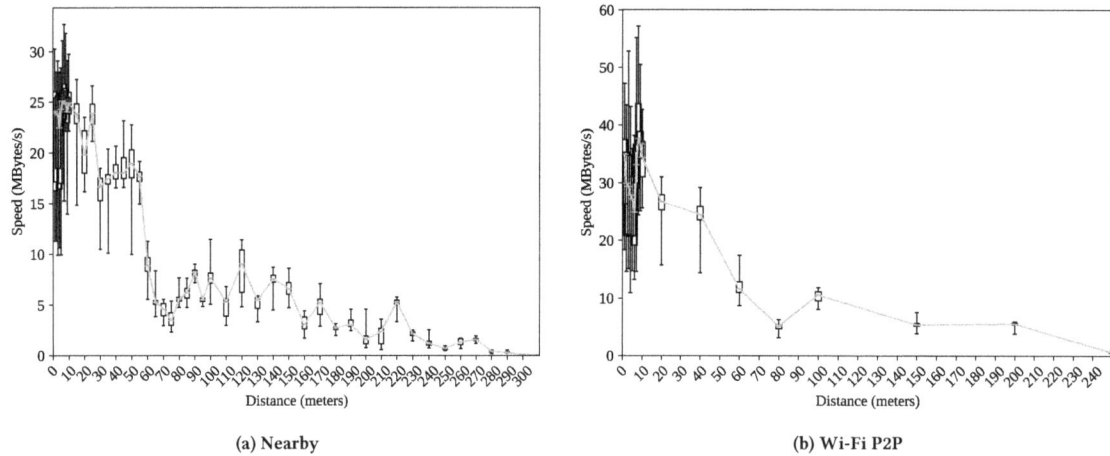

(a) Nearby

(b) Wi-Fi P2P

Figure 8: Goodput measurements from OnePlus 5T to OnePlus 5T connections with both APIs. The box-plots' whiskers include 95% of the data.

We note that the median does not significantly change in the range -40 dBm to -62 dBm despite five different modulations. Since prior works have found a clear correlation between modulation and energy consumption in smartphones [23], this reveals a potential energy consumption issue. As the goodput using the modulations between 256-QAM 5/6 and 64-QAM 2/3 are unequivocally equivalent, it seems that using the 64-QAM 2/3 modulation from -40 dBm to -62 dBm could be a better alternative as we know that it consumes less energy. Also, there are two significant drops in the measured median goodput, at precisely -63 dBm and -72 dBm. While it would seem intuitive to think that they correspond to a modulation change, they are not correlated to a particular modulation.

We can also observe a large spread around the median goodput from -40 to -50dBm. For instance, the goodput varies from 7 MBytes/s to 35 MBytes/s with a median around 24.5 MBytes/s.

The goodput as a function of RSSI, i.e. the results presented in Figure 7 can be easily approximated by a linear piecewise function $\overline{goodput}(x)$, where x is the RSSI:

$$\overline{goodput}(x) = \begin{cases} 24.26 & x \geq -64, \\ -0.36x + 42.35 & -64 < x \leq -71, \\ -0.79x + 66.44 & -71 < x \leq -82, \\ -0.24x + 21.13 & -82 < x. \end{cases} \tag{4}$$

Now that we defined our model of the goodput as a function of the RSSI, we need to extend it to become as a function of the distance. This is the topic of the next section.

5 GOODPUT VS. DISTANCE

5.1 Analysis of empirical observations

We were able to maintain a D2D connection up to 280 m distance using Wi-Fi P2P and up to 310 m using Nearby. This difference is explained by the fact that Wi-Fi P2P is solely based on Wi-Fi 5 (5 GHz band) while Nearby may fall back to Bluetooth (2.4 GHz

band), as explained in Section 2.2. Nonetheless, when Nearby we enforced Nearby to remain in the 5 GHz band, the distance limit is around 280 m, exactly like Wi-Fi P2P. To the best of our knowledge, there is no reference in the literature reporting D2D experiments that achieve such distances using off-the-shelf Android devices.

In Figure 8, we show the goodput results when the devices communicate using both Nearby and Wi-Fi P2P. When we observe the results for Nearby (Figure 8a), several patterns emerge. On short distances (1 m to 20 m), the throughput seems relatively constant ranging from 23 MBytes/s to 25 MBytes/s. The dispersion around the median is however quite large, with values as high as 33 MBytes/s and as low as 10 MBytes/s – but this is consistent with our observations in the RSSI analysis in Section 4.2, where a close-range communication generated more spread around the median. We also observe an increase in the goodput in the range 30 m to 50 m. We were expecting this behavior as it corresponds to the constructive interference due to ground reflection (see Section 4.2). This enables the devices to maintain a high goodput, ranging from 13 MBytes/s to 17 MBytes/s; it is notable that such a high goodput is achieved within medium-range distances.

As for the Wi-Fi P2P API (Figure 8b), we see that the large variance is also found within short distances (1 m to 20 m). The median ranges from 35 MBytes/s to 39 MBytes/s, which is significantly higher than the speed reached with Nearby. We believe that this difference is due to a software bottleneck. Another hint is the RSSI-to-goodput relationship (Section 4.2) that showed no increase of throughput, albeit modulations with higher theoretical speeds. Hence, we can deduce that Nearby's maximum goodput is, in fact, software-related more than hardware-related.

The next pattern, which we labeled as the sawtooth behavior, can be observed in the range 60 m to approximately 270 m. This is a consequence of the low RSSI over long-range communications, where any obstacle may increase or decrease the signal (e.g., leaves on the ground and nearby trees). Regardless, the goodput ranges from 1 MByte/s to 7 MBytes/s, which is still a significant value.

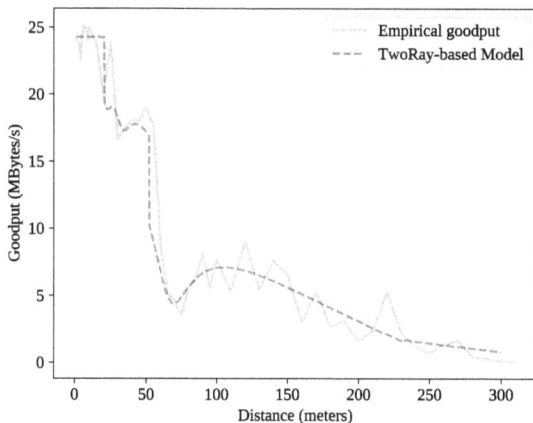

Figure 9: Comparison between the empirical data and our model for Nearby.

Over even longer distances, between 280 m and 310 m, the goodput measurements are less accurate due to Nearby's behavior. When the Wi-Fi connection drops between two devices, which can happen when the RSSI is around -85 to -90 dBm, Nearby automatically falls back to the Bluetooth connection. Nearby still allows devices to exchange data, but this time with a significantly lower bit-rate between 10 KBytes/s to 100 KBytes/s.

5.2 Model of the goodput in function of the distance

We now propose a model to estimate the goodput based on the distance between two Android devices. We use the $PL_{\text{tworay}}(d)$ model (see Appendix 7) to estimate the path loss and fix the inner parameters from the least-square estimation, where $A \approx 9.19$ (see Section 4.1). From Equation 3, we derive:

$$\widehat{\text{RSSI}}(d) = 9.19 - PL_{\text{tworay}}(d). \tag{5}$$

To obtain the goodput as a function of the distance, we combine Equations 4 and 3:

$$\text{goodput}(d) = \widehat{\text{goodput}}(\widehat{\text{RSSI}}(d)). \tag{6}$$

In Figure 9, we show how this model fits the dataset. The original data is the same as the one presented in Figure 8a, but in Figure 9 we only show the median for the sake of readability. Our model presents the expected characteristics that we observed in practice, notably the sudden surge in goodput in the range 30 m to 50 m along with the significant drop after 70 m.

Our proposed model, which is the upper-bound of D2D communication in off-the-shelf Android smartphones, now allows the research community to estimate the bit rate based on the distance between two devices.

6 RELATED WORK

Given the ubiquitous nature of Wi-Fi in modern devices, there are several studies that evaluate the performance of the different Wi-Fi

standards. Zeng *et al.* explore the relationship between overlapping Wi-Fi standards (e.g., 802.11n/ac using the same frequency) and power consumption [23]. Saha et al. extend this idea by focusing on the characterization of the relationship between Wi-Fi throughput of smartphones and battery consumption using several popular models [20]. Chowdhury *et al.* [5] have previously proposed to use the estimation of the RSSI as a mean to obtain the throughput between a base station and a mobile client, based on the distance between the two. Contrary to our empirical approach, they took the physical speed of the Wi-Fi 4 as a reference model. Certain domains commonly infer the distance between two devices from the received signal strength. This is notably done in wireless sensor networks [13, 22], vehicular networks [4, 21], and in mobility detection of smartphones [17].

Qayyum *et al.* [18] take an empirical measurement of the throughput according to distance using a mobile Android application. Interestingly, while they admittedly use dated hardware and software compared to ours, they report significantly shorter range of ≈ 10 m and undeniably slower throughput as they used Bluetooth.

Several authors have implemented D2D-based frameworks using Android devices Android. For instance, Keller et al. propose a cooperative streaming system named Microcast [14]. Other examples of full-fledged D2D data sharing solutions exist, but they all assume the devices communicate within a short range [1, 15]. Another issue is the assumption that devices can maintain several simultaneous D2D connections, while in reality this is not guaranteed and switching from one Wi-Fi Direct connection to the next may create a latency of several seconds [8]. On top of this, while these frameworks may be functional, they are not found in stock Android and are therefore not always available to developers nor have guaranteed support.

While all these works are substantial to their domains, they often ignore the importance of distance as a parameter for the throughput estimation in a D2D context or were outdated in regards to hardware and software. Hopefully, our work is an appreciated contribution to this goal.

7 CONCLUSION AND FUTURE WORK

In this paper, we explored the current state of D2D communications in stock Android devices. To this end, we first designed and implemented Ocat, an Android application that eases the measurement process of D2D communications through both Google Nearby and Wi-Fi P2P. As a result, we were able to establish a model for the upper-bound goodput of D2D communications as a function of the distance between the communicating devices.

We showed that the Nearby API can maintain a goodput of 25 MBytes/s in the 1 m to 20 m range. Within the same range, Wi-Fi P2P can reach up to 39 MBytes/s, showing that Nearby possibly lacks software optimization to achieve similar speeds. In our findings, we note that the ground reflection has a significant impact on goodput performance, which can be positive within medium distances between 30 m to 50 m, enabling a steady goodput rate between 13 MBytes/s to 17 MBytes/s. To our surprise, devices were able to communicate at fairly long distances (280 m to 310 m), which was undocumented so far.

In our future work, to better assess D2D data sharing capabilities, we intend to exchange data between several devices at the same time and at different distances. We also want to model the asymmetrical relationship between emitter and transmitter devices, since our tests showed that devices may perform differently when they transmit or receive signals. Ultimately, this work enables a new sort of characterization for D2D communications by establishing how much data can be exchanged between devices through a spatiotemporal contact. We believe that our work will significantly help researchers and application designers understand the possibilities and limits of D2D communications using Android devices.

REFERENCES

[1] Xuan Bao, Yin Lin, Uichin Lee, Ivica Rimac, and Romit Roy Choudhury. 2013. DataSpotting: Exploiting naturally clustered mobile devices to offload cellular traffic. In *2013 Proceedings IEEE INFOCOM*. IEEE, 420–424. https://doi.org/10.1109/INFCOM.2013.6566807
[2] K. Benkic, M. Malajner, P. Planinsic, and Z. Cucej. 2008. Using RSSI value for distance estimation in wireless sensor networks based on ZigBee. *Proceedings of the 15th International Conference on Systems, Signals and Image Processing* (2008), 303–306. https://doi.org/10.1109/IWSSIP.2008.4604427
[3] D. Camps-Mur, A. Garcia-Saavedra, and P. Serrano. 2013. Device-to-device communications with Wi-Fi Direct: overview and experimentation. *IEEE Wireless Communications* 20, 3 (jun 2013), 96–104. https://doi.org/10.1109/MWC.2013.6549288
[4] Chien-Ming Chou, Chen-Yuan Li, Wei-Min Chien, and Kun-chan Lan. 2009. A Feasibility Study on Vehicle-to-Infrastructure Communication: WiFi vs. WiMAX. In *2009 Tenth International Conference on Mobile Data Management: Systems, Services and Middleware*. IEEE, 397–398. https://doi.org/10.1109/MDM.2009.127
[5] Helal Chowdhury, Janne Lehtomäki, Juha-Pekka Mäkelä, and Sastri Kota. 2010. Data Downloading on the Sparse Coverage-Based Wireless Networks. *Journal of Electrical and Computer Engineering* 2010 (2010), 1–7. https://doi.org/10.1155/2010/843272
[6] Cisco. 2014. *802.11ac: The Fifth Generation of Wi-Fi*. Technical Report March. 1–4 pages. https://www.cisco.com/c/dam/en/us/products/collateral/wireless/aironet-3600-series/white-paper-c11-713103.pdf
[7] Marco Conti and Silvia Giordano. 2014. Mobile ad hoc networking: milestones, challenges, and new research directions. *IEEE Communications Magazine* 52, 1 (jan 2014), 85–96. https://doi.org/10.1109/MCOM.2014.6710069
[8] Colin Funai, Cristiano Tapparello, and Wendi Heinzelman. 2017. Enabling multi-hop ad hoc networks through WiFi Direct multi-group networking. In *2017 International Conference on Computing, Networking and Communications (ICNC)*. IEEE, 491–497. https://doi.org/10.1109/ICCNC.2017.7876178 arXiv:1601.00028
[9] Google. [n.d.]. ADB. https://developer.android.com/studio/command-line/adb
[10] Google. [n.d.]. Nearby - Connections API Overview. https://developers.google.com/nearby/connections/overview
[11] Google. [n.d.]. Wi-Fi peer-to-peer overview. https://developer.android.com/guide/topics/connectivity/wifip2p
[12] Google. [n.d.]. WifiManager. https://developer.android.com/reference/android/net/wifi/WifiManager
[13] Lei Guan, Xing Zhang, Zongchao Liu, Yu Huang, Ruoqian Lan, and Wenbo Wang. 2013. Spatial modeling and analysis of traffic distribution based on real data from current mobile cellular networks. *Proc. of ICCP'13 - 2013 IEEE International Conference on Computational Problem-Solving* (2013), 135–138. https://doi.org/10.1109/ICCPS.2013.6893524
[14] Lorenzo Keller, Anh Le, Blerim Cici, Hulya Seferoglu, Christina Fragouli, and Athina Markopoulou. 2012. MicroCast: Cooperative Video Streaming on Smartphones. In *Proceedings of the 10th international conference on Mobile systems, applications, and services - MobiSys '12*, Vol. 68. ACM Press, New York, New York, USA, 57. https://doi.org/10.1145/2307636.2307643
[15] Kyunghan Lee, Injong Rhee, Joohyun Lee, Song Chong, and Yung Yi. 2010. Mobile data offloading. In *Proceedings of the 6th International COnference on - Co-NEXT '10*, Vol. 21. ACM Press, New York, New York, USA, 1. https://doi.org/10.1145/1921168.1921203
[16] Matthew Newville and Till Stensitzki. 2017. Non-Linear Least-Squares Minimization and Curve-Fitting for Python Matthew Newville, Till Stensitzki, and others. (2017).
[17] Pavan Kumar Pedapolu, Pradeep Kumar, Vaidya Harish, Satvik Venturi, Sushil K Bharti, Vinay Kumar, and Sudhir Kumar. 2017. Mobile Phone User's Speed Estimation using WiFi Signal-to-Noise Ratio. In *Proceedings of the 18th ACM International Symposium on Mobile Ad Hoc Networking and Computing - Mobihoc '17*. ACM Press, New York, New York, USA, 1–2. https://doi.org/10.1145/3084041.3084072
[18] Shiraz Qayyum, Mehrab Shahriar, Mohan Kumar, and Sajal K. Das. 2013. PCV: Predicting contact volume for reliable and efficient data transfers in opportunistic networks. *Proceedings - Conference on Local Computer Networks, LCN* (2013), 801–809. https://doi.org/10.1109/LCN.2013.6761335
[19] Theodore Rappaport. 2001. Wireless Communications: Principles and Practice. (2001).
[20] Swetank Kumar Saha, Pratik Deshpande, Pranav P Inamdar, Ramanujan K Sheshadri, and Dimitrios Koutsonikolas. 2015. Power-throughput tradeoffs of 802.11n/ac in smartphones. In *2015 IEEE Conference on Computer Communications (INFOCOM)*, Vol. 26. IEEE, 100–108. https://doi.org/10.1109/INFOCOM.2015.7218372
[21] Christoph Sommer, Stefan Joerer, and Falko Dressler. 2012. On the applicability of Two-Ray path loss models for vehicular network simulation. In *2012 IEEE Vehicular Networking Conference (VNC)*. IEEE, 64–69. https://doi.org/10.1109/VNC.2012.6407446
[22] Jiuqiang Xu, Wei Liu, Fenggao Lang, Yuanyuan Zhang, and Chenglong Wang. 2010. Distance Measurement Model Based on RSSI in WSN. *Wireless Sensor Network* 02, 08 (2010), 606–611. https://doi.org/10.4236/wsn.2010.28072
[23] Yunze Zeng, Parth H. Pathak, and Prasant Mohapatra. 2014. A first look at 802.11ac in action: Energy efficiency and interference characterization. In *2014 IFIP Networking Conference*, Vol. 20. IEEE, 1–9. https://doi.org/10.1109/IFIPNetworking.2014.6857103
[24] Xiangming Zhu, Yong Li, Depeng Jin, and Jianhua Lu. 2017. Contact-Aware Optimal Resource Allocation for Mobile Data Offloading in Opportunistic Vehicular Networks. *IEEE Transactions on Vehicular Technology* 66, 8 (aug 2017), 7384–7399. https://doi.org/10.1109/TVT.2017.2668396

TWO RAY GROUND REFLECTION MODEL

The idea behind this model is that the receiver obtains two copies of the same signal, the original one and a copy reflected from the ground. The principle is to calculate the phase difference between the two copies of the signal to verify whether the interference is constructive or destructive, based on the heights of the transmitter and the receiver. In our case, these heights are equal, which guarantees that the line of sight distance between the two devices is $d_{los} = d$. The distance of the reflected signal is $d_{reflect} = \sqrt{d^2 + (h_r + h_t)^2}$, where h_r and h_t are the heights of the transmitter and receiver devices, respectively (again, equal in our setup). The phase difference as $\varphi = 2\pi \frac{d_{los} - d_{reflect}}{\lambda}$.

To obtain the final model, we also need the reflection coefficient, which gives the capacity of the ground to reflect an electromagnetic wave. It is given by $\Gamma_\perp = \frac{\sin\theta - \sqrt{\epsilon - \cos^2\theta}}{\sin\theta + \sqrt{\epsilon - \cos^2\theta}}$, where θ is the angle of incidence of the reflected signal based on the heights of the transmitter and receiver, and ϵ is a fixed parameter based on the material.

The two-ray ground reflection model is then written as [21]:

$$PL_{\text{tworay}}(d) = 20\log_{10}\left[4\pi\frac{d}{\lambda}|1 + \Gamma_\perp e^{i\varphi}|^{-1}\right]. \quad (7)$$

Using Euler's formula, we replace the complex exponential in the equation as:

$$PL_{\text{tworay}}(d) = 20\log_{10}\left[4\pi\frac{d}{\lambda}|1 + \Gamma_\perp \cos\varphi + \Gamma_\perp i \sin\varphi|^{-1}\right]. \quad (8)$$

As the modulus of a complex number yields a real number, we use this final equation:

$$PL_{\text{tworay}}(d) = 20\log_{10}\left[4\pi\frac{d}{\lambda}\sqrt{(1 + \Gamma_\perp \cos\varphi)^2 + \Gamma_\perp^2 \sin^2\varphi}^{-1}\right]. \quad (9)$$

Secure Routing in Multi-hop IoT-based Cognitive Radio Networks under Jamming Attacks

Haythem Bany Salameh and
Rawan Derbas
Yarmouk University
Irbid, Jordan
{rderbas;haythem}@yu.edu.jo

Moayad Aloqaily
Al Ain University
Al Ain, UAE
maloqaily@ieee.org

Azzedine Boukerche
University of Ottawa
Ottawa, ON, Canada
aboukerc@uottawa.ca

ABSTRACT

Integrating Cognitive Radio (CR) technology in Internet-of-Things (IoT) devices allows efficient large-scale deployment of IoT systems. Recently, research efforts are shifted toward adopting CR in IoT as a response for the spectrum scarcity problem. Unfortunately, CR Networks (CRNs) share the same security weaknesses with traditional wireless networks. CR communication is also vulnerable to jamming attacks which can significantly affect network performance, consume network resources and results in delays, that make it less suitable for IoT time-critical systems. Routing in CR-based IoT networks, in general, considered as a challenging issue. Under the jamming attack, routing becomes even more challenging. In this paper, we introduce a new jamming-aware routing and channel assignment protocol that deals with proactive jamming attacks in CR-based IoT networks without requiring extra resources. The proposed protocol attempts at improving the overall packet delivery ratio in the network while considering the primary user's activities, multi-channel fading and jamming behavior. The proposed protocol consists of three phases: route discovery, channel assignment, and path selection. The channel assignment problem along each path is formulated as an optimization problem with the objective of maximizing the end-to-end probability of success. This problem is shown to be an uni-modular problem, which can be solved in polynomial-time using linear programming techniques. Compared to reference protocols, simulation results reveal that the proposed protocol significantly improves network performance in terms of packet delivery ratio.

KEYWORDS

Jamming Attacks; Cognitive Radio Networks; Secure Routing; IoT

ACM Reference Format:
Haythem Bany Salameh and Rawan Derbas, Moayad Aloqaily, and Azzedine Boukerche. 2019. Secure Routing in Multi-hop IoT-based Cognitive Radio Networks under Jamming Attacks. In *22nd Int'l ACM Conf. on Modeling, Analysis and Simulation of Wireless and Mobile Systems (MSWiM'19), Nov. 25–29, 2019, Miami Beach, FL, USA.* ACM, New York, NY, USA, 5 pages. https://doi.org/10.1145/3345768.3355944

1 INTRODUCTION

Recently, the IoT has acquired the researchers' attention in academic as well as industrial sectors. This concern is because of the capabilities that IoT can offer for daily human life. It is expected to enable a world with smart objects that communicate and cooperate with each other with minimal human involvement [1, 2]. IoT objects and devices are envisioned to be interconnected with each other using wireless transmission technologies. However, a large number of IoT devices will introduce huge pressure on the limited RF spectrum. To deal with this issue, the IoT objects can be equipped with cognitive capabilities. Thus, the research efforts are shifted toward integrating CR technology into IoT [3]. The idea of CR is proposed because of the high demand and the inefficient utilization of the RF spectrum where the statistical measurements indicate that the real utilization of the spectrum varies from 15% to 85%. CR technology allows the unlicensed users (secondary users (SUs)) to share the same spectrum with the legitimate Primary Radio (PR) users without interfering their activities. CR users can dynamically access the idle portions of the licensed spectrum. CR technology can enable IoT objects (operating as SUs) to be intelligent in taking decisions with the objective of achieving interference-free and enabling on-demand services [4].

Many security threats and attacks can affect the performance of CRNs such as spoofing, DoS, Primary User Emulation (PUE), Prob and jamming attacks [5]. The jamming attack is considered as one of the most dangerous and common security issues in CRNs. It aims to interrupt the ongoing CR transmissions by sending an RF signal over idle PR channels. In the presence of jammers, it is hard to guarantee network availability, reliability or the delay limit of the sent packets [6]. The attackers equipped with intelligent jamming hardware (they may also have CR capabilities) so they can easily jam the CR transmission resulting in failure of data transmission [7]. Because of the nature of CR (i.e, dynamic availability of spectrum and the need to vacating channels when PRs are detected), jammers can significantly affect network performance. They consume resources and results in delays which make it not suitable for IoT time-sensitive applications. Communication delays resulting from jamming attacks in critical applications can result in services unavailability [8]. These issues make the existing communication protocols designed for CRNs are not suitable for delay-sensitive IoT applications [9]. Therefore, there is a need to design a new security-aware communication protocols that deal with jamming attacks in IoT-based multi-hop CRNs without incurring extra resources.

In this paper, we introduce a new security-aware routing algorithm that deals with proactive jamming attacks which target

IoT-based multi-hop CRNs, namely, *security-aware probability of success (SA-PoS)*. SA-PoS considers both PR activities and CR link quality conditions along with jamming attacks without the need for any extra resources. For each CR IoT source-destination pair, SA-PoS algorithm assigns the most secure channel for each hop based on solving optimization problems, which are derived in Section 4. Then, it selects the best path among the possible paths. The proposed algorithm aims at enhancing network performance by considering jamming attacks in the selecting process. It has been noted that the most related work to the proposed algorithm is the MaxPoS routing protocol [8], where both channel condition and PR activities are considered in assigning channels and choosing the path between communicating CR IoT pair. Simulations are conducted over a multi-hop IoT CRN. The results indicate that our SA-PoS protocol can remarkably enhance network performance with regards to PDR compared to the MaxPoS.

The rest of the paper is structured as follows. Section 2 overview the related work. Section 3 introduces the network model. We present the new SA-PoS routing protocol and formulation in Section 4. Section 5 evaluates the performance of the proposed routing protocol. We conclude 2the paper in Section 6

2 RELATED WORK

Several routing algorithms have been designed for CRNs. The authors in [10] have surveyed the security opportunistic routing at the wireless network addressing communication reliability and security. CRNs performance enhancements has been studied in [11] and a routing metric that enhances the performance of the CRNs considering the interference to PRs have have proposed. Route determination has been also investigated. The authors of [12] proposed a probabilistic routing metric aimed at determining the appropriate route in terms of available capacity. In addition, resource allocation was looked at to minimize the end-end delay by designing a cross-layer protocol that jointly considers the routing and resource allocation [13].

When it comes to CR based IoT networks, a routing algorithm for CR based-IoT was proposed in [14]. The optimal route was found using two metrics: one is aimed at decreasing the rerouting delivery success probability by considering only one re-transmission, while in the second metric by average transmission delay over all channels. Moreover, In [15], the authors proposed a routing protocol for mobile CRs called SEARCH. SEARCH protocol optimizes the available paths between a CR source-destination as well as channel assignment to reduce the end-to-end latency taking into consideration the spectrum availability. Yet another routing protocol is presented in [16]. In this protocol, the authors considered both energy efficient and the spectrum status. As a result, they decreased energy consumption and delivery latency.

To the best of our knowledge, most of these studies have not take into consideration the jamming attack, which is considered the most popular and dangerous type of attacks. on the contrary, other researches have started exploring the jamming attacks. Those researchers presented methods for detection, prevention, and countermeasuring. Many systems were proposed for detecting the jamming attacks using Intrusion Detection Systems (IDSs) [5, 17, 18, 19, 20].

IDS mainly depends on the behavior of the attack which is either anomaly-based or signature-based. Many researches were also studying the effect of jamming attack (e.g., [21]). They aimed at mitigating the jamming effect by introducing a random data/control channel assignment. However, most of these studies are frequency hopping-based and not suitable for the problem described in this research. In [22], the authors provided a time-based hopping technique for sensor CRNs, where a channel is assigned to each user for a certain time. They considered mobile sensor CR users and assumed that there is no channel-switching when the channel is jammed. Although these schemes can deal with jamming attacks effectively, they require involving many nodes in monitoring and data collection process, which is waste to network resources and consume more energy.

IoT paradigm requires awareness in using nodes energy and resources which involve many nodes or duplicate resources. Mobile nodes in large-scale networks considers another challenge for such networks [23, 24]. Therefore, prevention techniques are not a suitable solutions for IoT-based Networks jamming attacks due to the dynamic availability of spectrum,

3 NETWORK MODEL

We consider a CSMA/CA-based multi-hop IoT network, where each node has a CR capability. Thus, it can sense any PR channel and dynamically access idle ones. The CR IoT network geographically coexists with a number of different PR networks (PRNs). The set of all PR channels is denoted as M, each with bandwidth (BW). We suppose the accessibility to channel $i in M$ for CR IoT transmissions follows an ON/OFF state model. The ON state means that channel i is busy (occupied by a PR user) with average busy time T_{on}. The CR IoT cannot transmit over this channel during this period. The OFF state means that channel i is idle with average available time T_{off}, hence it can be used by CRs. Note that T_{off} and T_{on} are random variables with pdf distributions $f_{T_{on}}(t)$ and $f_{T_{off}}(t)$, respectively. We assume that a CR source can cooperate with neighboring CR IoT devices to obtain PR spectrum occupancy pattern. For a given hop h along a given path p, there is a set of available channels $M_{p,h} \in \mathcal{M}$. Each channel has a received SINR less than a certain threshold (μ_*) will be excluded. Hence the remaining channels will be denoted as $M^*_{p,h} \in M_{p,h}$. The Shannon capacity formula is used to reckon the CR achievable rate over each idle channel i for hop h in path p ($R^{(i)}_{p,h}$).

The required transmission time can be found as $t^{(i)}_{x_{p,h}} = \frac{L}{R^{(i)}_{p,h}}$, where L is the data packet length. The CR IoT devices uses the maximum permissible power set by the FCC over each channel i. A Rayleigh fading channel model is used to describe the channel quality between any neighboring CR IoT devices. We consider the maximum likelihood estimation MLE-technique that proposed in [25] for identifying the proactive jamming strategy $g\left(T^{(i)}_{jam}\right)$, where $T^{(i)}_{jam}$ is the jamming period between two adjacent jamming signals. In [8], the authors derived the successful probability under proactive jamming, where the packet is successfully received if both the jamming time T_j and channel idle time T_{off} are greater than the packet transmission time t_x over a given channel. The success probability was derived as [8]:

$$p_{succ} = Pr(\min\{T_{off}, T_{jam}\} \geq t_x) = e^{-t_x \frac{T_{off}+T_{jam}}{T_{off} T_{jam}}} \quad (1)$$

4 SECURITY-AWARE CHANNEL ASSIGNMENT AND PATH SELECTION

4.1 Problem Statement and Design Constraints

Our routing problem can be stated as follows: Given a CR IoT source-destination pair (C_S and C_D), the set of possible paths between them $\mathcal{P}$, the number of hops for each path $p \in \mathcal{P}$ (denoted by N_p), the set of available channels $M_{h,p} \in \mathcal{M}$ for each hop $h \in N_p$ and for all $p \in \mathcal{P}$, the average availability time $\bar{T}_{off}^{(i)}$ and average jamming interval $\bar{T}_{jam}^{(i)}$, $\forall i$, our goal is to find the most secure path p^* between C_S and C_D along with the appropriate channel assignment Φ_p^* such that the maximum PoS is achieved for the end-to-end transmission subject to:

- **C1. Single-transceiver constraint:** Each IoT device is provided with one CR transceiver.
- **C2. Half-duplex feasibility constraints:** For a given path p with N_p hops, a selected channel i for the transmission of hop h can be scheduled (time-shared) to be used for the transmission of another hop $k > h$ if-and-only-if the transmitter of hop k is outsider hop h's receiver reception range and the transmitter of hop h is outside the reception range of the receiver of hop k (i.e., at least 3 hop-away).
- **C3: The SINR Constraint** The received SINR should be greater than a given threshold μ^*.

4.2 Route Selection and Channel assignment

The main purpose of the proposed protocol is to choose the most secure path long the channel assignment between a given source C_S and destination C_D while considering the link-quality conditions, PR activities and jamming levels over each available channel over each hop for all possible paths. This can be achieved by performing three phases: (1) route discovery, (2) channel assignment and (3) route selection.

4.2.1 Route Discovery Phase. To establish a route between a given C_S and C_D, C_S sends a flooding Route REQuest (RREQ) message in the network until reaching the destination. When the destination C_D receives the first RREQ, it starts a time-out period to collect an adequate number of RREQ packets and identify the set of possible paths $\mathcal{P}$. After the timeout period, the PoS of over channel for each hop along each path ($p_{succ}{}_{p,h}^{(i)}$) is computed using (1).

4.2.2 Channel Assignment Phase. Given the set of paths $\mathcal{P}$ and the computed $p_{succ}{}_{p,h}^{(i)}$, our channel assignment aims at selecting the most secure channel for each hop over each path such that the maximum possible PoS is achieved over each path. To proceed in our analysis, we define the following binary variable for each path p as:

$$X_{p,h}^{(i)} = \begin{cases} 1, & \text{if channel } i \text{ is given to hop } h \text{ in path } p \\ 0, & \text{otherwise.} \end{cases} \quad (2)$$

Given $M_{h,p}$, μ_*, $p_{succ}{}_{\{p,h\}}^{(i)}$, $\text{SINR}_{p,h}^{(i)}$, $\forall i \in M_{h,p}$, $\forall h \in N_p$, and noting that the success probabilities over the different hops are independent, the assignment problem that maximizes the PoS over each hop along p can be formulated as:

$$\max_{X_{p,h}^{(i)} \in \{0,1\}} \sum_{h=1}^{N_p} \sum_{i=1}^{M_{h,p}} p_{succ}{}_{\{p,h\}}^{(i)} X_{p,h}^{(i)}$$

$$\text{s.t. } \sum_{i=1}^{M_{h,p}} X_{p,h}^{(i)} \leq 1, \forall h \in N_p$$

$$X_{p,h}^{(i)} + X_{p,h+1}^{(i)} + X_{p,h+2}^{(i)} \leq 1, \forall i \in M_{h,p}, h = \{1...N_p - 2\}$$

$$\text{SINR}_{p,h}^{(i)} \geq \mu_* \quad (3)$$

Note that the last constraint can be guaranteed by setting $X_{p,h}^{(i)} = 0$, $\forall i$ with $\text{SINR}_{p,h}^{(i)} \leq \mu_*$. The formulation in (3) indicates that our channel assignment problem is a BLP problem, which can be expressed in standard matrix form as:

$$\max_x \{\mathbf{c}^T \mathbf{x} \text{ s.t } \mathbf{A}\mathbf{x} \leq \mathbf{b}, \mathbf{x} \in \{0,1\}\} \quad (4)$$

where $\mathbf{x}$ is the victor of the decision variables $X_{p,h}^{(i)}$'s, $\mathbf{c} = \left[p_{succ\{p,1\}}^{(1)}, \ldots, p_{succ\{p,1\}}^{(M)}, \ldots, p_{succ\{p,N_p\}}^{(1)}, \ldots, p_{succ\{p,N_p\}}^{(M)}\right]$ represents the objective function, $\mathbf{A} = \begin{bmatrix} \mathbf{A}_1{}_{N_p \times N_p M} \\ \mathbf{A}_2{}_{M(N_p-2) \times N_p M} \end{bmatrix}$ is the linear-constrain matrix and $\mathbf{b} = \overbrace{[1\,1\,1\,1\,\ldots\,1]}^{(N_p + M(N_p-2))}{}^T$ represents the right-hand-side of our optimization.

The matrices $\mathbf{A}_1$ and $\mathbf{A}_2$ can be expressed as:

$$\mathbf{A}_1 = \begin{bmatrix} \overbrace{1\ldots1}^{M} & \overbrace{0\ldots0}^{M} & \ldots & \ldots & 0\ldots0 \\ 0\ldots0 & 1\ldots1 & 0\ldots0 & \ldots & 0\ldots0 \\ \vdots & \ddots & \ddots & \ddots & \vdots \\ 0\ldots0 & 0\ldots0 & 1\ldots1 & \ldots & 0\ldots0 \\ \vdots & & \ddots & \ddots & \\ 0\ldots0 & \ldots & \ldots & \ldots & 1\ldots1 \end{bmatrix},$$

$$\mathbf{A}_2 = \begin{bmatrix} \overbrace{10\ldots0}^{M} & \overbrace{10\ldots0}^{M} & \overbrace{10\ldots0}^{M} & 0\ldots0 & \ldots & \overbrace{0\ldots0}^{M} \\ 01\ldots0 & 01\ldots0 & 01\ldots0 & 0\ldots0 & \ldots & 0\ldots0 \\ \vdots & \vdots & \ddots & \vdots & & \vdots \\ 0\ldots01 & 0\ldots01 & 0\ldots01 & 0\ldots0 & \ldots & 0\ldots0 \\ \vdots & \vdots & \vdots & \vdots & & \vdots \\ \vdots & \vdots & \ddots & \vdots & & \vdots \\ 0\ldots0 & \ldots & 0\ldots0 & 10\ldots0 & 10\ldots0 & 10\ldots0 \\ 0\ldots0 & \ldots & 0\ldots0 & 01\ldots0 & 01\ldots0 & 10\ldots0 \\ \vdots & \vdots & \vdots & \vdots & \vdots & \vdots \\ 0\ldots0 & \ldots & 0\ldots0 & 10\ldots0 & 10\ldots0 & 10\ldots0 \end{bmatrix}.$$

The formulation satisfies the unimoduler properties. Thus, the optimal solution for our optimization problem can be found in polynomial-time using standard linear programming (LP) methods [26]. Note that our formulation satisfies the uni-modular properties as the objective function (i.e., c) is linear, the right-hand-side of the constraints (b) is integer, and the constraint matrix ($\mathbf{A}$) is uni-modular matrix that meets the uni-modularity conditions (i.e., All components of matrix $\mathbf{A}$ is either 0 or 1, every column of $\mathbf{A}$ contains at most two 1's and every column in $\mathbf{A}$ contains at least one non-zero entry). Thus, our channel assignment that provides the most secure channel for each hop h along path $p \in \mathcal{P}$ can be calculated in polynomial-time using standard LP techniques. Let $\Phi_p^* = \{i_1^*, i_2^*, \ldots, i_h^*, \ldots, i_{N_p}^*\}$ be the optimal channel assignment provided by solving our assignment problem, where i_h^* is the optimal channel assignment for hop h along path p. Given Φ_p^*, the PoS over each $h \in N_p$ along the path p is given by:

$$p_{succ\{p,h\}}^* = p_{succ\{p,h\}}^{\left(i_h^*\right)}, \forall h \in N_p \qquad (5)$$

Given $p_{succ_{p,h}}^*$, the PoS of path p with the optimal channel assignment can be calculated as follows:

$$p_{succ\{p\}}^* = \min\left\{p_{succ\{p,1\}}^*, p_{succ\{p,2\}}^*, \cdots p_{succ\{p,N_p\}}^*\right\}. \qquad (6)$$

4.2.3 The Proposed Route Selection Solution. After assigning the most secured channels along all discovered paths, our algorithm chooses the path with highest success probability:

$$p^* = \arg\max_{p \in \mathcal{P}} p_{succ}^*\{p\}. \qquad (7)$$

5 PERFORMANCE EVALUATION

MATLAB has been used to simulate and examine the performance of the proposed SA-PoS routing protocol.

5.1 Simulation Setup

We consider an IoT-based CRN with 100 CR IoT devices that co-exist with ten PRNs in a field of 500×500 m. The PRNs are licensed to operate over the 900 MHz bands with 10 orthogonal frequency channels, each with a bandwidth of 5 MHz. As mentioned in Section II, the status of each channel follows the ON/OFF channel-availability model. The average availability times for the ten channels are 5, 100, 30, 5, 45, 50, 100, 5, 45, 30 ms, respectively. We use the Rayleigh fading channel model with $n = 4$ to describe the link-quality between any two CR IoT users over each channel.

The thermal noise power density, the control packet size, the data-packet size, the maximum power and the SINR threshold are set to 0.5×10^{-12} W/Hz, 120 bits, 2-KByte, $P_{max}^{(i)} = 1$ W, $\forall i$ and $\mu_* = 5$ dB, $\forall i$, respectively. In order to calculate the transmission rate over each idle channel, the Shannon capacity formula is used. The locations of the communicating CR IoT devices are randomly distributed within the simulation area. To simulate the jamming attacks, we consider a proactive jammer with a memory-less jamming strategy. The average jamming intervals over the different channels are 5, 0.7, 5, 2, 10, 5, 1, 2.9, 20, 0.3 $\times \xi$ ms, over each channel respectively. Note that the parameter ξ indicates the jamming attack level (as ξ increases the jamming become less severe).

5.2 Simulation Results

To evaluate the effectiveness of our protocol, we compare its performance with that of MaxPoS [14] and Minimum Hop (MH) protocols. For the MH, we consider both security-aware (SA) and security-unaware (SUA) variants. For SA-MH, we use our proposed channel assignment while in SUA-MH, the MaxPoS's channel assignment algorithm is used.

First, we investigate the impact of PRs activity on network performance (i.e., PDR) under different levels of jamming attacks. The PRs activity varies from low to high (i.e., from 0.1 to 0.9). Fig. 1(a)-(b) show that our proposed SA-PoS and SA-MH protocols outperform

both the MaxPoS and SUA-MH algorithms under high ($\xi = 0.1$) and moderate ($\xi = 1.5$) jamming levels, respectively. Fig. 1(c) reveals that under low ($\xi = 8$) jamming attack the performance of Max-PoS outperforms MH variants, while our proposed protocol still outperforms the other protocols. Fig. 1 discloses that our protocol enhances the PDR performance compared with MaxPoS algorithm. This enhancement is due to the jamming-awareness in our channel assignment and route selection on the contrary of MaxPoS and SUA-MH routing protocols. Fig. 1 shows that as the channels availability decreases (P_B increases), network performance decreases for all protocols and the improvement gain decreases as P_B increases. We also investigate the impact of jamming attack level under different values of PR activities (i.e., low ($P_B = 0.1$), moderate ($P_B = 0.5$) and high ($P_B = 0.9$) PR activity).

The jamming activities varies from high to low (i.e., the jamming parameter ξ increases from low-to-high values). Fig. 2(a) shows that at high PR activity, the network performance is severely degraded especially for MH-variants. Fig. 2(b)-(c) show that at high jamming attacks levels, our SA protocols outperform the SUA protocols. When the jamming attacks become less sever, the performance of the SA protocols degrade to that of the SUA protocols. In general, Fig. 2 reveals that as the attack level decreases, the PDR performance is improved for all protocols. This because of the jamming period between two jamming signals becomes longer, which allows for the packets to be successfully delivered. It also shows that as the PR activities increase, the chance to select the proper channels decreases which result in decreasing the PDR.

6 CONCLUSIONS AND FUTURE WORK

In this paper, a new jamming-aware channel assignment and routing protocol for CR-based IoT, namely, SA-PoS has been proposed. The proposed protocol represents a solution for alleviating jamming attacks in multi-hop CRNs, where it takes into consideration the jamming attack as well as PRs availability and channel quality. The proposed channel assignment and route selection mechanism provides the source-destination communicating pair with the most secured channel and path with maximum PoS, which leads to improve network performance (measured by PDR). The performance of the proposed routing protocol and the performance of MaxPoS and MH protocols have been compared. The behavior of SA-PoS protocol has been studied under different network scenarios such as impact of PR activity and impact of data packet size, impact of transmission power, impact of channel bandwidth and impact of CR transmission range. Simulations results showed that the proposed routing protocol can remarkably improves network performance against proactive jamming attacks. It also showed that as the PR activity or jamming attacks increases, the proposed SA-PoS outperforms the other protocols.

The future work of this paper is to include intelligent and learning AI to automatically predict and detect the jamming attack.

REFERENCES

[1] Al Ridhawi, Ismaeel, et al. "A Profitable and Energy-Efficient Cooperative Fog Solution for IoT Services." IEEE Transactions on Industrial Informatics (2019).

[2] V. Balasubramanian, F. Zaman, M. Aloqaily, I. A. Ridhawi, Y. Jararweh and H. B. Salameh, "A Mobility Management Architecture for Seamless Delivery of 5G-IoT Services," ICC 2019 - 2019 IEEE International Conference on Communications (ICC), Shanghai, China, 2019, pp. 1-7.

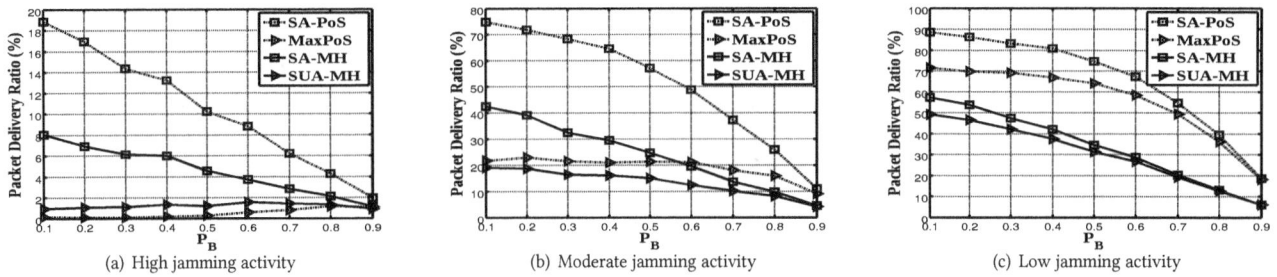

Figure 1: PDR performance vs. PR activity under different value of PR activities levels.

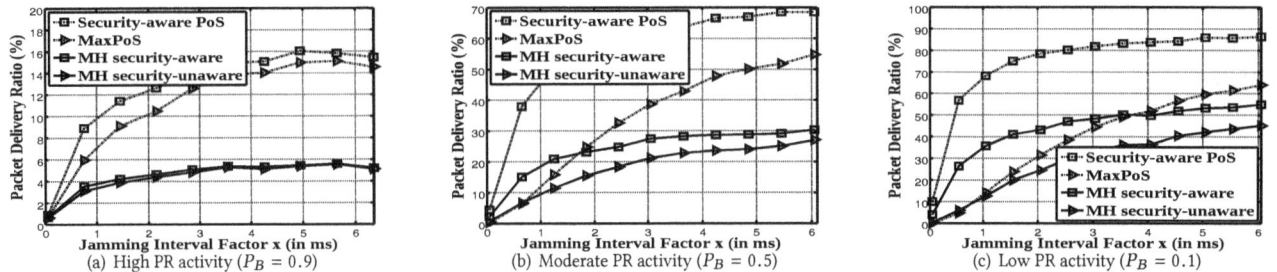

Figure 2: PDR performance vs. jamming activity under different levels of PR activities.

[3] D. Singh, G. Tripathi, and A. J. Jara, "A survey of Internet-of-Things: Future vision, architecture, challenges and services,"s in Proc. IEEE World Forum Internet Things, Mar. 2014, pp. 287-292.

[4] A. A. Khan, M. H. Rehmani, and A. Rachedi, "When Cognitive Radio Meets the Internet of Things?," IEEE 12th IntâĂŹl. Wireless Commun. & Mobile Computing Conf., Paphos, Cyprus, Sept. 5-9 2016.

[5] Aloqaily, Moayad, et al. "An intrusion detection system for connected vehicles in smart cities." Ad Hoc Networks 90 (2019): 101842.

[6] Z. Lu, W. Wang, and C. Wang, "Modeling, evaluation and detection of jamming attacks in time-critical wireless applications," IEEE Transactions on Mobile Computing, Vol. 13, No. 8, pp. 1746-1759, 2014.

[7] K. Mourougayane and S. Srikanth, "Intelligent jamming threats to cognitive radio based strategic communication networks - a survey," in 2015 3rd International Conference on Signal Processing, Communication and Networking (ICSCN), March 2015, pp. 1-6.

[8] H. Bany Salameh, S. Almajali, M. Ayyash and H. Elgala, "Spectrum assignment in cognitive radio networks for internet-of-things delaysensitive applications under jamming attacks," IEEE Internet of Things Journal, vol. 5, no. 3, pp. 1903-1913, June 2018.

[9] Otoum, Safa, Burak Kantarci, and Hussein T. Mouftah. "Detection of known and unknown intrusive sensor behavior in critical applications." IEEE Sensors Letters 1.5 (2017): 1-4.

[10] Salehi, M., Boukerche, A. (2019). Secure opportunistic routing protocols: methods, models, and classification. Wireless Networks, 25(2), 559-571.

[11] H. Rawi and K. Yau, "Route selection for minimizing interference to primary users in cognitive radio networks: A reinforcement learning approach," in Proc. IEEE Symp. Comput. Intell. Commun. Syst. Netw., Singapore, 2013, pp. 24-30.

[12] H. Khalife, S. Ahuja, N. Malouch, and M. Krunz, "Probabilistic path selection in opportunistic cognitive radio networks" , in Proc. IEEE GlobeCom , 2008, pp. 1-5.

[13] A. El-Sherif and A. Mohamed, "Joint routing and resource allocation for delay minimization in cognitive radio based mesh networks," IEEE Trans. Wireless Commun., vol. 13, no. 1, pp. 186-197, Jan. 2014.

[14] M. Kaushik, Y. Yoganandam i S.K. Sahoo, "Quality and Availability of spectrum based routing for Cognitive radio enabled IoT networks" , Journal of Communications Software and Systems, vol.14, br. 3, str. 239-48, 2018.

[15] K. Chowdhury and M. Di Felice, "Search: A routing protocol for mobile cognitive radio ad-hoc networks," in Sarnoff Symposium, 2009. SARNOFF âĂŹ09. IEEE, 2009, pp. 1-6.

[16] S. Ji, M. Yan, R. Beyah and Z. Cai, "Semi-Structure Routing and Analytical Frameworks for Cognitive Radio Networks," in IEEE Transactions on Mobile Computing, vol. 15, no. 4, pp. 996-1008, 1.

[17] S. Otoum, B. Kantarci and H. Mouftah, "Empowering Reinforcement Learning on Big Sensed Data for Intrusion Detection," ICC 2019 - 2019 IEEE International Conference on Communications (ICC), Shanghai, China, 2019, pp. 1-7.

[18] S. Otoum, B. Kantarci and H. Mouftah, "Empowering Reinforcement Learning on Big Sensed Data for Intrusion Detection," ICC 2019 - 2019 IEEE International Conference on Communications (ICC), Shanghai, China, 2019, pp. 1-7.

[19] Otoum, Safa, Burak Kantarci, and Hussein T. Mouftah. "On the feasibility of deep learning in sensor network intrusion detection." IEEE Networking Letters 1.2 (2019): 68-71.

[20] C. Manogna and K. Naik, "Detection of Jamming Attack in Cognitive Radio Networks" , International Journal of Recent Advances in Engineering & Technology (IJRAET), Vol. 2, Issue 6, pp. 69-72, 2014.

[21] L. Xiao, T. Chen, J. Liu, and H. Dai, "Anti-jamming transmission stackelberg game with observation errors," Communications Letters, IEEE, vol. 19, no. 6, pp. 949-952, June 2015.

[22] N. Adem and B. Hamdaoui, "Jamming resiliency and mobility management in cognitive communication networks" , in Proc. of the IEEE International Conference on Communications (ICC), May 2017

[23] Khamayseh, Yaser, et al. "Dynamic framework to mining Internet of Things for multimedia services." Expert Systems (2019): e12404.

[24] Aloqaily, Moayad, et al. "Data and service management in densely crowded environments: Challenges, opportunities, and recent developments." IEEE Communications Magazine 57.4 (2019): 81-87.

[25] Y. Wu, B. Wang, and K. Liu, "Optimal defense against jamming attacks in cognitive radio networks using the Markov decision process approach" , in Proc. of the IEEE Globecom Conference, 2010

[26] H. Bany Salameh, " Rate-Maximization Channel Assignment Scheme for Cognitive Radio Networks," in IEEE Global Telecommunications Conference GLOBE-COMâĂŹ10, Miami, FL, 2010, pp. 1-5.

Author Index

www.ingramcontent.com/pod-product-compliance
Lightning Source LLC
Chambersburg PA
CBHW080918220326
41598CB00034B/5605